W9-BII-050

Marketing Management

TWELFTH EDITION

Welcome Kevin Lane Keller.

I'm thrilled to introduce Professor Kevin Lane Keller as my co-author on the twelfth edition of *Marketing Management.* Kevin is acknowledged as one of the top academics of his generation. Currently the E.B. Osborn Professor of Marketing at the Tuck School of Business at Dartmouth, he received his Ph.D. from Duke University's Fuqua School of Business. His path-breaking research and writings on brands, branding, and brand equity have been widely cited and received numerous awards. He is also actively involved with industry as a popular speaker and marketing confidant to such top companies as Accenture, American Express, Disney, Ford, Intel, Levi-Strauss, Procter & Gamble, and Starbucks. Thanks to his tireless efforts, I am confident we've crafted the best edition yet.

We hope you enjoy reading the twelfth edition as much as we enjoyed writing it, and that it serves as a practical resource during your education and career.

Marketing Management

TWELFTH EDITION

Marketing Management

TWELFTH EDITION

PHILIP KOTLER
Northwestern University

KEVIN LANE KELLER
Dartmouth College

Pearson Education International

Acquisitions Editor: Katie Stevens
Associate Editor: Wil Mara
VP/Editorial Director: Jeff Shelstad
Assistant Editor: Melissa Pellerano
Editorial Assistant: Rebecca Lembo
Developmental Editor: Jeannine Ciliotta
Media Project Manager: Peter Snell
Marketing Manager: Michelle O'Brien
Marketing Assistant: Joanna Sabella
Senior Managing Editor (Production): Judy Leale
Production Editor: Theresa Festa
Permissions Supervisor: Charles Morris
Manufacturing Buyer: Diane Peirano
Design Manager: Maria Lange
Art Director: Janet Slowik
Interior Design: Amanda Kavanagh
Cover Design: Amanda Kavanagh
Art Studio: ElectraGraphics, Inc.
Director, Image Resource Center: Melinda Reo
Manager, Rights and Permissions: Zina Arabia
Manager, Visual Research: Beth Brenzel
Manager, Cover Visual Research & Permissions: Karen Sanatar
Image Permission Coordinator: Debbie Latronica
Photo Researcher: Debra Hershkowitz and Elaine Soares
Manager, Print Production: Christy Mahon
Composition/Full-Service Project Management: Carlisle Communications, Ltd.
Printer/Binder: Courier-Kendallville / Lehigh Press

Credits and acknowledgments borrowed from other sources and reproduced, with permission, in this textbook appear on appropriate page within text and on page C1.

Pearson Education LTD.
Pearson Education Singapore, Pte. Ltd
Pearson Education, Canada, Ltd
Pearson Education–Japan
Pearson Education Australia PTY, Limited
Pearson Education North Asia Ltd
Pearson Educación de Mexico, S.A. de C.V.
Pearson Education Malaysia, Pte. Ltd
Pearson Education, Upper Saddle River, New Jersey

10 9 8 7 6 5 4 3 2 1
ISBN 0-13-196853-X

DEDICATION

This book is dedicated to my wife and best friend, Nancy, with love.

This book is dedicated to my wife, Punam, and my two daughters, Carolyn and Allison, with much love and thanks.

ABOUT THE AUTHORS

Philip Kotler *is one of the world's leading authorities on marketing. He is the S. C. Johnson & Son Distinguished Professor of International Marketing at the Kellogg School of Management, Northwestern University. He received his master's degree at the University of Chicago and his Ph.D. at MIT, both in economics. He did post-doctoral work in mathematics at Harvard University and in behavioral science at the University of Chicago.*

Dr. Kotler is the co-author of Principles of Marketing *and* Marketing: An Introduction. *His* Strategic Marketing for Nonprofit Organizations, *now in its sixth edition, is the best seller in that specialized area. Dr. Kotler's other books include* Marketing Models; The New Competition; Marketing Professional Services; Strategic Marketing for Educational Institutions; Marketing for Health Care Organizations; Marketing Congregations; High Visibility; Social Marketing; Marketing Places; The Marketing of Nations; Marketing for Hospitality and Tourism; Standing Room Only—Strategies for Marketing the Performing Arts; Museum Strategy and Marketing; Marketing Moves; Kotler on Marketing; Lateral Marketing: Ten Deadly Marketing Sins; *and* Corporate Social Responsibility.

In addition, he has published more than one hundred articles in leading journals, including the Harvard Business Review, Sloan Management Review, Business Horizons, California Management Review, *the* Journal of Marketing, *the* Journal of Marketing Research, Management Science, *the* Journal of Business Strategy, *and* Futurist. *He is the only three-time winner of the coveted Alpha Kappa Psi award for the best annual article published in the* Journal of Marketing.

Professor Kotler was the first recipient of the American Marketing Association's (AMA) Distinguished Marketing Educator Award (1985). The European Association of Marketing Consultants and Sales Trainers awarded him their Prize for Marketing Excellence. He was chosen as the Leader in Marketing Thought by the Academic Members of the AMA in a 1975 survey. He also received the 1978 Paul Converse Award of the AMA, honoring his original contribution to marketing. In 1995, the Sales and Marketing Executives International (SMEI) named him Marketer of the Year. In 2002, Professor Kotler received the Distinguished Educator Award from The Academy of Marketing Science. He has received honorary doctoral degrees from Stockholm University, the University of Zurich, Athens University of Economics and Business, DePaul University, the Cracow School of Business and Economics, Groupe H.E.C. in Paris, the Budapest School of Economic Science and Public Administration, and the University of Economics and Business Administration in Vienna.

Professor Kotler has been a consultant to many major U.S. and foreign companies, including IBM, General Electric, AT&T, Honeywell, Bank of America, Merck, SAS Airlines, Michelin, and others in the areas of marketing strategy and planning, marketing organization, and international marketing.

He has been Chairman of the College of Marketing of the Institute of Management Sciences, a Director of the American Marketing Association, a Trustee of the Marketing Science Institute, a Director of the MAC Group, a member of the Yankelovich Advisory Board, and a member of the Copernicus Advisory Board. He was a member of the Board of Governors of the School of the Art Institute of

ABOUT THE AUTHORS

Chicago and a member of the Advisory Board of the Drucker Foundation. He has traveled extensively throughout Europe, Asia, and South America, advising and lecturing to many companies about global marketing opportunities.

Kevin Lane Keller *is the E. B. Osborn Professor of Marketing at the Tuck School of Business at Dartmouth College. Professor Keller has degrees from Cornell, Carnegie-Mellon, and Duke universities. At Dartmouth, he teaches an MBA elective on strategic brand management and lectures in executive programs on that topic. Previously, Professor Keller was on the faculty of the Graduate School of Business at Stanford University, where he also served as the head of the marketing group. Additionally, he has been on the marketing faculty at the University of California at Berkeley and the University of North Carolina at Chapel Hill, been a visiting professor at Duke University and the Australian Graduate School of Management, and has two years of industry experience as Marketing Consultant for Bank of America.*

Professor Keller's general area of expertise is in consumer marketing. His specific research interest is in how understanding theories and concepts related to consumer behavior can improve marketing strategies. The research has been published in over fifty papers in three of the major marketing journals—the Journal of Marketing, *the* Journal of Marketing Research, *and the* Journal of Consumer Research. *He also has served on the Editorial Review Boards of those journals. His research has been widely cited and has received numerous awards.*

Professor Keller is acknowledged as one of the international leaders in the study of brands, branding, and strategic brand management. Actively involved with industry, he has worked on a host of different types of marketing projects. He has served as brand confidant to marketers for some of the world's most successful brands, including Accenture, American Express, Disney, Ford, Intel, Levi Strauss, Miller Brewing, Procter & Gamble, and Starbucks. He has done additional brand consulting with other top companies such as Allstate, Beiersdorf (Nivea), Blue Cross Blue Shield, Campbell Soup, General Mills, Goodyear, Kodak, The Mayo Clinic, Nordstrom, Shell Oil, Unilever, and Young & Rubicam. He is also an academic trustee for the Marketing Science Institute. A popular speaker, he has conducted marketing seminars and workshops with top executives in a variety of forums.

Professor Keller is currently conducting studies that address marketing strategies and tactics to build, measure, and manage brand equity. His textbook on those subjects, Strategic Brand Management, *the second edition of which was published September 2002 by Prentice-Hall, has been heralded as the "bible of branding."*

An avid sports, music, and film enthusiast, in his spare time, he helps to manage and market one of Australia's great rock and roll treasures, The Church. *Professor Keller lives in New Hampshire with his wife, Punam (also a Tuck marketing professor), and his two daughters, Carolyn and* Allison.

BRIEF CONTENTS

CONTENTS

CONTENTS

CONTENTS

CONTENTS

CONTENTS

CONTENTS

CONTENTS

CONTENTS

CONTENTS

CONTENTS

CONTENTS

CONTENTS

CONTENTS

CONTENTS

CONTENTS

CONTENTS

CONTENTS

CONTENTS

PREFACE

Marketing Management is the leading marketing text because its content and organization consistently reflect changes in marketing theory and practice. The very first edition of *Marketing Management*, published in 1967, introduced the concept that companies must be customer-and-market driven. But there was little mention of what have now become fundamental topics such as segmentation, targeting, and positioning. Concepts such as brand equity, customer value analysis, database marketing, e-commerce, value networks, hybrid channels, supply chain management, and integrated marketing communications were not even part of the marketing vocabulary then. Firms now sell goods and services through a variety of direct and indirect channels. Mass advertising is not nearly as effective as it was. Companies are exploring new forms of communication, such as experiential, entertainment, and viral marketing. Customers are increasingly telling companies what types of product or services they want and when, where, and how they want to buy them.

In response, companies have shifted gears from managing product portfolios to managing customer portfolios, compiling databases on individual customers so they can understand them better, and construct individualized offerings and messages. They are doing less product and service standardization and more niching and customization. They are replacing monologues with customer dialogues. They are improving their methods of measuring customer profitability and customer lifetime value. They are intent on measuring the return on their marketing investment and its impact on shareholder value. They are also concerned with the ethical and social implications of their marketing decisions.

As companies change, so does their marketing organization. Marketing is no longer a company department charged with a limited number of tasks—it is a company-wide undertaking. It drives the company's vision, mission, and strategic planning. Marketing includes decisions like who the company wants as its customers; which needs to satisfy; what products and services to offer; what prices to set; what communications to send and receive; what channels of distribution to use; and what partnerships to develop. Marketing succeeds only when all departments work together to achieve goals: when engineering designs the right products, finance furnishes the required funds, purchasing buys quality materials, production makes quality products on time, and accounting measures the profitability of different customers, products, and areas.

And as marketing techniques and organization have changed, so has this text. The biggest change is the addition of a co-author. Kevin Lane Keller is one of the top marketing academics of his generation. He has conducted ground-breaking research and written a highly successful text, *Strategic Brand Management.* He has also worked with marketing executives from companies around the globe to help them become better marketers. He brings fresh thinking and new perspectives to *Marketing Management.*

The twelfth edition reflects a collaborative effort between the two authors with a goal of creating the best edition of *Marketing Management* ever. Extensive focus groups were conducted to fully understand the course and classroom needs of the instructor. Based on this input, the twelfth edition is designed to preserve the strengths of previous editions while introducing new material and organization to further enhance learning. It is dedicated to helping companies, groups, and individuals adapt their marketing strategies and management to the marketplace realities of the twenty-first century.

::: Revision Strategy for the Twelfth Edition

Marketing is of interest to everyone, whether they are marketing goods, services, properties, persons, places, events, information, ideas, or organizations. As the "ultimate authority" for students and educators, *Marketing Management* must be kept up-to-date and contemporary. Students (and instructors) should feel that the book is talking directly to them in terms of both content and delivery.

PREFACE

The success of *Marketing Management* can be attributed to its ability to maximize three dimensions that characterize the best marketing texts—depth, breadth, and relevance—as reflected by the following questions.

- **Depth.** Does the book have solid academic grounding? Does it contain important theoretical concepts, models, and frameworks? Does it provide conceptual guidance to solve practical problems?
- **Breadth.** Does the book cover all the right topics? Does it provide the proper amount of emphasis on those topics?
- **Relevance.** Does the book engage the reader? Is the book interesting to read? Does it have lots of compelling examples?

The twelfth edition builds on the fundamental strengths of past editions:

- **Managerial Orientation.** The book focuses on the major decisions that marketing managers and top management face in their efforts to harmonize the organization's objectives, capabilities, and resources with marketplace needs and opportunities.
- **Analytical Approach.** This book presents conceptual tools and frameworks for analyzing recurrent problems in marketing management. Cases and examples illustrate effective marketing principles, strategies, and practices.
- **Multidisciplinary Perspective.** This book draws on the rich findings of various scientific disciplines—economics, behavioral science, management theory, and mathematics—for fundamental concepts and tools.
- **Universal Applications.** This book applies strategic thinking to the complete spectrum of marketing: products and services, consumer and business markets, profit and nonprofit organizations, domestic and foreign companies, small and large firms, manufacturing and intermediary businesses, and low- and high-tech industries.
- **Comprehensive and Balanced Coverage.** This book covers all the topics an informed marketing manager needs to understand to execute strategic, tactical, and administrative marketing.

New Themes: Holistic Marketing

One major new theme in this edition is holistic marketing. *Holistic marketing* can be seen as the development, design, and implementation of marketing programs, processes, and activities that recognize the breadth and interdependencies involved today's marketing environment. Holistic marketing recognizes that "everything matters" with marketing and that a broad, integrated perspective is often necessary. Holistic marketing has four key dimensions:

1. **Internal marketing**–ensuring everyone in the organization embraces appropriate marketing principles, especially senior management.
2. **Integrated marketing**–ensuring that multiple means of creating, delivering and communicating value are employed and combined in the optimal manner.
3. **Relationship marketing**–having rich, multi-faceted relationships with customers, channel members and other marketing partners.
4. **Socially responsible marketing**-understanding the ethical, environmental, legal, and social effects of marketing.

These four dimensions are woven throughout the book and at times spelled out explicitly. Two additional themes of this text are *marketing personalization* and *marketing accountability.* The former reflects all the attempts to make marketing more individually relevant; the latter reflects the need to understand and justify the return on marketing investments within organizations.

Organization

The twelfth edition preserves the major topics of the eleventh edition, but reorganizes them into a new modular structure. There are now eight parts as compared to five to allow for greater flexibility in the classroom.

Part 1	Understanding Marketing Management
Part 2	Capturing Marketing Insights
Part 3	Connecting with Customers
Part 4	Building Strong Brands
Part 5	Shaping the Market Offerings
Part 6	Delivering Value
Part 7	Communicating Value
Part 8	Creating Successful Long-Term Growth

The most significant organizational changes are:

- A new part on capturing marketing insights that includes the two research-oriented chapters, placed even earlier in the book (Chapters 3 and 4).
- A new section on creating long-term growth that brings together chapters on new products and new markets (global) as well as a revised concluding chapter, placed at the end of the book (Chapters 20–22)
- Chapters 16 and 17 are now aligned more definitely in terms of mass and personal communications.
- The marketing plan material has been upgraded and moved into Chapter 2 to help students gain concrete marketing skills. We have also created an appendix to Chapter 2 with an illustrative example of an actual company marketing plan and another appendix to the book itself with a series of marketing plan exercises.
- The new Marketing Plan appendix, at the end of the book, provides detailed information on how to develop a marketing plan and includes a series of exercises to help students develop a formal marketing plan using the hypothetical example of Sonic PDA.
- A Glossary containing all the key terms and definitions has been added at the end of the book.

Chapter by Chapter Changes

This edition has been both streamlined and expanded to bring essentials and classic examples into sharper focus, while covering new concepts and ideas in depth. Some chapters received more extensive revisions than others. Here is an overview of the chapter changes:

Chapter 1, *Defining Marketing for the 21st Century,* now consolidates the "big picture" material from the first two chapters of the eleventh edition to introduce key marketing topics, how they have changed and are likely to change in the future.

Chapter 2, *Developing Marketing Strategies and Plans,* provides more discussion on holistic marketing and more detail on marketing plans, including a sample marketing plan.

Chapter 3, *Gathering Information and Scanning the Environment,* is now couched in terms of macro approaches to marketing research.

Chapter 4, *Conducting Marketing Research and Forecasting Demand* , is framed in terms of micro approaches and includes a new section on Marketing Productivity.

Chapter 5, *Creating Customer Value, Satisfaction, and Loyalty,* consolidates material from several chapters related to customers and introduces new material on Customer Equity.

Chapter 6, *Analyzing Consumer Markets,* introduces a new section on Other Theories of Consumer Decision-Making.

Chapter 7, *Analyzing Business Markets,* contains a section on Managing Business-to-Business Customer Relationships.

Chapter 8, *Identifying Market Segments and Targets,* adds new material on local marketing, conversion marketing, experiential marketing and marketing to Generation Y.

Chapter 9, *Creating Brand Equity,* has been completely reworked and expanded to capture more of the important concepts in building, measuring, and managing brand equity.

Chapter 10, *Crafting the Brand Positioning,* introduces a contemporary approach to positioning based on the concepts of points-of-parity and points-of-difference.

Chapter 11, *Dealing with Competition,* includes fresh material on how to increase product consumption.

Chapter 12, *Setting Product Strategy,* has been reorganized to cover material on sources of differentiation.

Chapter 13, *Designing and Managing Services,* introduces a new section on Managing Service Brands.

Chapter 14, *Developing Pricing Strategies and Programs,* contains a new section on understanding pricing with material on consumer psychology and pricing.

Chapter 15, *Designing and Managing Value Networks and Channels,* includes material on e-commerce marketing practices and new material on channel power, conflict and cooperation.

Chapter 16, *Managing Retailing, Wholesaling, and Logistics,* includes relevant material on store activities and experiences and has been reorganized to include private labels.

Chapter 17, *Designing and Managing Integrated Marketing Communications,* introduces a section on the Role of Marketing Communications and information on coordinating media.

Chapter 18, *Managing Mass Communications: Advertising, Sales Promotions, Events, and Public Relations,* includes a new section on Events and Experiences Marketing.

Chapter 19, *Managing Personal Communications: Direct Marketing and Personal Selling,* introduces new material on interactive marketing.

Chapter 20, *Introducing New Market Offerings,* includes new material on idea generation.

Chapter 21, *Tapping into Global Markets,* covers new material on country-of-origin effects.

Chapter 22, *Managing a Holistic Marketing Organization,* contains new sections on social marketing and the future of marketing.

Additional concepts that have been added or explored in greater detail include: brand management principles, cause-related marketing, consumer decision heuristics, consumer involvement, consumer memory models, events and experiences, innovation and creativity, qualitative research techniques, marketing metrics, mental accounting, reference prices, and sponsorships.

::: Chapter Pedagogy

Each chapter includes:

Chapter Introduction, which includes brief commentary and a short vignette that set the stage for the chapter material to follow. By covering topical brands or companies, the vignettes serve as great discussion starters.

Marketing Insight boxes that delve into important marketing topics, often highlighting current research findings. New and updated Marketing Insight boxes include such topics as "Views on Marketing from Chief Executive Officers," "Progress and Priorities in Customer Equity Management," "Consumer Trends for the Future," and "Small Business, Big Sales: The Burgeoning Small-Midsize Business Market."

Marketing Memo boxes that offer practical advice and directions in dealing with various decisions at all stages of the marketing management process. New and updated Marketing Memo boxes include "Managing Customer Knowledge," "Decision Traps," "Average American Consumer Quiz," and "Guidelines for Selling to Small Businesses."

Text Examples Each chapter also includes 10–15 in-text examples that provide vivid illustrations of chapter concepts using actual companies and situations. Virtually all these examples of good and bad company marketing practices are new to the twelfth edition and cover a variety of products, services, and markets. Many have accompanying illustrations in the form of ads or product shots.

End-of-Chapter Exercises These include Marketing Applications and the Marketing Spotlight.

- The *Marketing Applications* section has two practical exercises to challenge students: *Marketing Debate* suggests opposing points-of-view on an important marketing topic from the chapter and asks student to take a side. *Marketing Discussion* identifies provocative marketing issues and allows for a personal point-of-view.
- The *Marketing Spotlight*, an in-depth examination of one of the world's most successful marketing companies, includes questions for class discussion or student assignments.

::: The Teaching and Learning Package

Marketing Management is an entire package of materials available to students and instructors. This edition includes a number of ancillaries designed to make the marketing management course an exciting, dynamic, interactive experience.

Marketing Management Cases

Prentice Hall Custom Business Resources can provide instructors and students with all of the cases and articles needed to enhance and maximize learning in a marketing course. Instructors can create Custom CoursePacks or Custom CaseBooks. Resources include top-tier cases from Darden, Harvard, Ivey, NACRA, and Thunderbird, plus full access to a database of articles. For details on how to order these value-priced packages, contact your local rep or visit the Prentice Hall Custom Business Resources Web site at www.prenhall.com/custombusiness.

Instructor's Resource Manual

Prepared by Ronald N. Borrieci, the Instructor's Resource Manual includes chapter/summary overviews, key teaching objectives, answers to end-of-chapter materials, Harvard Business School case suggestions, exercises, projects, and detailed lecture outlines. A new feature, "Professors on the Go!", was created with the busy professor in mind. It brings key material upfront, where an instructor who is short on time can find key points and assignments that can be incorporated into the lecture, without having to page through all the material provided for each chapter.

Instructor's Resource Center (IRC)

- **IRC—CD-ROM:** One source for all of your supplement needs. New interface and searchable database makes sorting through and locating specific resources easier than ever before. Includes all the same supplements hosted at our IRC Online; however, the PowerPoint Media Rich set is provided only on this CD-ROM due to its larger file size and embedded video clips. The CD-ROM also contains many images from the textbook, which you may incorporate into your lectures.

- **IRC—ONLINE:** One destination for all of your supplement needs. The Prentice Hall catalog at www.prenhall.com/marketing is where instructors can access our complete array of teaching materials. Simply go to the catalog page for this text and click on the Instructor link to download the Instructor's Manual, Video Guide, Test Item File, TestGen EQ, PowerPoint slides (Basic only), and more.

NOTE: Prentice Hall manually checks *every* password request and verifies each individual's instructor status before issuing a password.

Test Item File

Prepared by John R. Brooks, Jr. of Houston Baptist University, the Test Item File contains more than 3,000 multiple-choice, true-false, short-answer, and essay questions, with page reference and difficulty level provided for each question. *A new feature is an entire section dedicated to application questions.* These real-life situations take students beyond basic chapter concepts and vocabulary and ask them to apply marketing skills. Prentice Hall's **TestGen EQ** test-generating software is new for this edition. This supplement is available in two places: Download from the *IRC Online* (www.prenhall.com/kotler) or from the *IRC on CD-ROM.*

- PC/Mac compatible and preloaded with all of the Test Item File questions.
- Manually or randomly view test bank questions and drag-and-drop to create a test.
- Add or modify test bank questions using the built-in Question Editor.
- Print up to 25 variations of a single test and deliver the test on a local area network using the built-in QuizMaster feature.
- Free customer support is available at media.support@pearsoned.com or 1-800-6-PROFESSOR between 8:00 A.M. or 5:00 P.M. CST.

PowerPoints

When it comes to PowerPoints, Prentice Hall knows one size does not fit all. That's why *Marketing Management 12e* offers instructors more than one option.

- **PowerPoint BASIC:** This simple presentation includes only basic outlines and key points from each chapter. No animation or forms of rich media are integrated, which makes the total file size manageable and easier to share online or via email. BASIC was also designed for instructors who prefer to customize PowerPoints or want to avoid having to strip out animation, embedded files, or other media rich features.
- **PowerPoint MEDIA RICH:** This media rich alternative includes basic outlines and key points from each chapter, plus advertisements and art from the text, images from outside the text, discussion questions, Web links, and embedded video snippets from the accompanying video library. The best option if you want a complete presentation solution. Instructors can further customize this presentation using the image library featured on the IRC on CD-ROM. Both the BASIC and MEDIA RICH version of slides were authored by Tracy Tuten Ryan.

Aside from these three PowerPoint options, a select number of slides, based on the MEDIA RICH version, are also available as overhead transparencies.

Marketing Management Video Gallery 2006

Make your classroom "newsworthy." PH has updated the Marketing Management video library for the 12th Edition. Using today's popular newsmagazine format, students are taken on location and behind closed doors. Each news story profiles a well-known or up-and-coming company leading the way in its industry. Eighteen new video segments accompany this edition, covering key topics using leading companies such as American Express, Song Airlines, the NFL, Eaton, and Wild Planet. Issue-focused footage includes interviews with top executives, objective reporting by real news anchors, industry research analysts and marketing and advertising campaign experts. A full video guide, including synopses, discussion questions, and teaching suggestions, is available to accompany the video library.

Companion Web Site

Available at www.prenhall.com/kotler. This FREE site offers students valuable resources. Two quizzes are offered per chapter. The Concept Check Quiz is to be administered prior to reviewing the chapter, in order to assess students' initial understanding. The Concept Challenge Quiz is to be administered after reviewing the chapter. Also featured is the text glossary, plus a link to the new Instructor's Resource Center.

Marketing Plan: A Handbook, 2nd edition with MarketingPlan Pro 6.0

Marketing PlanPro is a highly rated commercial software program that guides students through the entire marketing plan process. The software is totally interactive and features ten sample marketing plans, step-by-step guides, and customizable charts. Customize your marketing plan to fit your marketing needs by following easy-to-use plan wizards. Follow the clearly outlined steps from strategy to implementation. Click to print, and your text, spreadsheet, and charts come together to create a powerful marketing plan. The new *Marketing Plan: A Handbook*, by Marian Burk Wood, supplements the in-text marketing plan material with an in-depth guide to what student marketers really need to know. A structured learning process leads to a complete and actionable marketing plan. Also included are timely, real-world examples that illustrate key points, sample marketing plans, and Internet resources. The Handbook and Marketing PlanPro software are available as value-pack items at a discounted price. Contact your local Prentice Hall representative for more information.

ACKNOWLEDGMENTS

The twelfth edition bears the imprint of many people.

From Phil Kotler: My colleagues and associates at the Kellogg Graduate School of Management at Northwestern University continue to have an important impact on my thinking: James C. Anderson, Robert C. Blattberg, Bobby J. Calder, Gregory S. Carpenter, Alex Chernev, Anne T. Coughlan, Dawn Iacobucci, Dipak C. Jain, Robert Kozinets, Lakshman Krishnamurti, Angela Lee, Vincent Nijs, Christie Nordhielm, Mohanbir S. Sawhney, John F. Sherry Jr., Louis W. Stern, Brian Sternthal, Alice M. Tybout, and Andris A. Zoltners. I also want to thank the S. C. Johnson Family for the generous support of my chair at the Kellogg School. Completing the Northwestern team is my former dean, Donald P. Jacobs, and my current dean, Dipak Jain, both of whom have provided generous support for my research and writing.

Several former faculty members of the marketing department had a great influence on my thinking when I first joined the Kellogg marketing faculty, specifically Richard M. Clewett, Ralph Westfall, Harper W. Boyd, and Sidney J. Levy. I also want to acknowledge Gary Armstrong for our work on *Principles of Marketing.*

I am indebted to the following coauthors of international editions of Marketing Management and Principles of Marketing who have taught me a great deal as we worked together to adapt marketing management thinking to the problems of different nations:

- Swee-Hoon Ang and Siew-Meng Leong: National University of Singapore
- Chin-Tiong Tan: Singapore Management University
- Friedhelm W. Bliemel: Universitat Kaiserslautern (Germany)
- Peter Chandler, Linden Brown, and Stewart Adam: Monash and RMIT University (Australia)
- Bernard Dubois: Groupe HEC School of Management (France) and Delphine Manceau: ESCP-EAP European School of Management
- John Saunders (Loughborough University) and Veronica Wong (Warwick University, United Kingdom)
- Jacob Hornick: Tel Aviv Univesity (Israel)
- Walter Giorgio Scott: Universita Cattolica del Sacro Cuore (Italy)
- Ronald E. Turner and Peggy Cunningham: Queen's University (Canada)

I also want to acknowledge how much I have learned from working with coauthors on more specialized marketing subjects: Alan Andreasen, Christer Asplund, Paul N. Bloom, John Bowen, Roberta C. Clarke, Karen Fox, Michael Hamlin, Thomas Hayes, Dipak Jain, Somkid Jatusripitak, Hermawan Kartajaya, Neil Kotler, Nancy Lee, Suvit Maesincee, James Maken, Gustave Rath, Irving Rein, Eduardo Roberto, Joanne Scheff, Norman Shawchuck, Martin Stoller, and Bruce Wrenn.

My overriding debt continues to be to my lovely wife, Nancy, who provided me with the time, support, and inspiration needed to prepare this edition. It is truly our book.

From Kevin Lane Keller: I continually benefit from the wisdom of my colleagues at Tuck—Scott Neslin, Punam Keller, Kusum Ailawadi, Praveen Kopalle, Koen Pauwels, Yiorgos Bakamitsos, Fred Webster, Gert Assmus, and John Farley—as well as the leadership of Dean Paul Danos. I also gratefully acknowledge the invaluable research and teaching contributions from my faculty colleagues and collaborators through the years. I owe a considerable debt of gratitude to Duke University's Jim Bettman and Rick Staelin for helping to get my academic career started and serving as positive role models. I am also appreciative of all that I have learned from working with industry executives who have generously shared their insights and experiences. Finally, I give special thanks to Punam, my wife, and Carolyn and Allison, my daughters, who make it all happen and make it all worthwhile.

We owe a debt of thanks to the colleagues who joined us for three focus-group sessions that were extremely helpful in planning the revision:

ACKNOWLEDGMENTS

In Boston: Neeraj Baharadwaj, Babson College; Piotr Chelminski, Providence University; Al Della Bitta, University of Rhode Island; Dan Dunn, Northeastern University; Michael McGinty, Providence University; Nada Nasr, Bentley College; Alphonso Ogbuehi, Bryant College; John Teopaco, Northeastern University; Elizabeth Wilson, Boston College; Fred Wright, Babson College.

In Chicago: Tim Aurant, Northern Illinois University; Roger Baran, DePaul University; Janelle Barcelona, North Central College; Sanjay Dhar, University of Chicago; Lori Feldman, Purdue/Calamet; Stephen Goodwin, Illinois State University; Michael LaRocco, St. Francis College; Laura Leli-Carmine, Lewis University; Lawrence Hamer, DePaul University; Chem Narayana, University of Illinois/Chicago; James Oakley, Purdue University; Richard Slovacek, North Central College; Paul Wellen, Roosevelt University.

In New York: Sandy Becker, Rutgers University; Frank Fish, St. Thomas Aquinas College; Jack Lee, Baruch College, and his students; Gary Lynn, Stevens Institute.

We are indebted to the following colleagues at other universities who reviewed this new edition:

- Alan Au, University of Hong Kong
- Sandy Becker, Rutgers University
- Frederic Brunel, Boston University
- Lisa Cain, University of California at Berkeley and Mills College
- Bob Cline, University of Iowa
- Alton Erdem, University of Houston at Clear Lake
- Elizabeth Evans, Concordia University
- Betsy Gelb, University of Houston at Clear Lake
- Barbara Gross, California State University at Northridge
- Eric Langer, Johns Hopkins University
- Bart Macchiette, Plymouth University
- Paul McDevitt, University of Illinois at Springfield
- Francis Mulhern, Northwestern University
- Zhou Nan, University of Hong Kong
- Lisa Klein Pearo, Cornell University
- Abe Qastin, Lakeland University
- Lopo Rego, University of Iowa
- Richard Rexeisen, University of St.Thomas
- Anusorn Singhapakdi, Old Dominion University
- Mark Spriggs, University of St. Thomas
- Sean Valentine, University of Wyoming
- Ann Veeck, West Michigan University
- Kevin Zeng Zhou, University of Hong Kong

We would also like to thank colleagues who have reviewed previous editions of *Marketing Management*:

Hiram Barksdale, University of Georgia
Boris Becker, Oregon State University
Sunil Bhatla, Case Western Reserve University
John Burnett, University of Denver
Surjit Chhabra, DePaul University
Dennis Clayson, University of Northern Iowa
Brent Cunningham, Ph.D.: Jacksonville State University

John Deighton, University of Chicago
Ralph Gaedeke, California State University, Sacramento
Dennis Gensch, University of Wisconsin, Milwaukee
David Georgoff, Florida Atlantic University
Bill Gray, Keller Graduate School of Management
Arun Jain, State University of New York, Buffalo
Ron Lennon, Barry University
H. Lee Matthews, Ohio State University
Paul McDevitt, University of Illinois, Springfield
Kenneth P. Mead: Central Connecticut State University
Mary Ann McGrath, Loyola University, Chicago
Henry Metzner, University of Missouri, Rolla
Pat Murphy, University of Notre Dame
Jim Murrow, Drury College
Nicholas Nugent, Boston College
Donald Outland, University of Texas, Austin
Albert Page, University of Illinois, Chicago
Hank Pruden, Golden Gate University
Christopher Puto, Arizona State University
Scott D. Roberts, Northern Arizona University
Robert Roe, University of Wyoming
Alex Sharland, Hofstra University
Dean Siewers, Rochester Institute of Technology
Michael Swenso, Brigham Young University, Marriott School
Dr. R. Venkatesh, University of Pittsburgh—Katz Graduate School of Business
Greg Wood, Canisius College

The talented staff at Prentice Hall deserves praise for their role in shaping the twelfth edition. Our editors, Wendy Craven and Katie Stevens, offered excellent advice and direction for this new edition. We benefited greatly from the superb editorial help of Jeannine Ciliotta, who again lent her considerable talents as a development editor to this edition. We thank Nancy Brandwein, who researched and updated the examples, as well as Debra Hershkowitz, who found the wonderful new ads, photos, and product illustrations. We also want to acknowledge the fine production work of Theresa Festa, the creative design work of Janet Slowik, and the editorial assistance of Rebecca Lembo. We thank Melissa Pellerano, William Mara, and Peter Snell for their work on the supplements and media packages. We also thank our marketing manager, Michelle O'Brien. And finally, thanks to Andrea Meyer for providing the new Marketing Spotlights feature.

Philip Kotler
S. C. Johnson Distinguished Professor of International Marketing
Kellogg School of Management
Northwestern University
Evanston, Illinois

Kevin Lane Keller
E. B. Osborn Professor of Marketing
Tuck School of Business
Dartmouth College
Hanover, New Hampshire

PART

1

UNDERSTANDING MARKETING MANAGEMENT

IN THIS CHAPTER, WE WILL ADDRESS THE FOLLOWING QUESTIONS:

1. Why is marketing important?
2. What is the scope of marketing?
3. What are some fundamental marketing concepts?
4. How has marketing management changed?
5. What are the tasks necessary for successful marketing management?

CHAPTER 1 ::: DEFINING MARKETING FOR THE 21ST CENTURY

one

Marketing is everywhere. Formally or informally, people and organizations engage in a vast number of activities that could be called marketing. Good marketing has become an increasingly vital ingredient for business success. And marketing profoundly affects our day-to-day lives. It is embedded in everything we do—from the clothes we wear, to the Web sites we click on, to the ads we see:

Two teenage girls walk into their local Starbucks. One goes to the counter and hands the barista cards for two free peppermint lattes and purchases some pastries. The other sits at a table and opens her Apple PowerBook. Within a few seconds, she connects to the Internet courtesy of Starbucks' deal with T-mobile to create wireless HotSpots at over a thousand Starbucks stores. Once on the Net, the girl "Googles" the name of the band that played the soundtrack of the movie she saw last night. A number of Web sites come up along with two ads—one for tickets to the band's concert tour and another for the soundtrack CD and movie DVD at Amazon.com. When she clicks through to the Amazon ad, search engine giant Google rings up some money. (Through its adwords program, it gets paid whenever someone clicks on an advertiser's ad.) Now her friend has returned with lattes in hand. Teen #2 is eager to show off her parents' Sweet Sixteen gift to her—a ruby-red A220 Samsung cell phone created by a team of young Korean designers after months of market research and >>>

New York's Time Square: a live demonstration of the many faces of marketing today.

focus groups. The phone resembles a cosmetic compact and dispenses dieting tips as well as advice on how to dress for the weather. The two girls are oohing and aahing over the tiny display that doubles as a mirror when they see the reflection of a city bus sporting a giant banner ad for the newest HBO comedy series. . . .

Good marketing is no accident, but a result of careful planning and execution. Marketing practices are continually being refined and reformed in virtually all industries to increase the chances of success. But marketing excellence is rare and difficult to achieve. Marketing is both an "art" and a "science"—there is constant tension between the formulated side of marketing and the creative side. It is easier to learn the formulated side, which will occupy most of our attention in this book; but we will also describe how real creativity and passion operate in many companies. This book will help to improve your understanding of marketing and your ability to make the right marketing decisions. In this chapter, we lay the foundation for our study by reviewing a number of important marketing concepts, tools, frameworks, and issues.

::: The Importance of Marketing

Financial success often depends on marketing ability. Finance, operations, accounting, and other business functions will not really matter if there is not sufficient demand for products and services so the company can make a profit. There must be a top line for there to be a bottom line. Many companies have now created a Chief Marketing Officer, or CMO, position to put marketing on a more equal footing with other C-level executives such as the Chief Executive Officer (CEO) and Chief Financial Officer (CFO). Press releases from organizations of all kinds—from consumer goods makers to health care insurers and from non-profit organizations to industrial product manufacturers—trumpet their latest marketing achievements and can be found on their Web sites. In the business press, countless articles are devoted to marketing strategies and tactics.

Marketing is tricky, however, and it has been the Achilles' heel of many formerly prosperous companies. Large, well-known businesses such as Sears, Levi's, General Motors, Kodak, and Xerox have confronted newly empowered customers and new competitors, and have had to rethink their business models. Even market leaders such as Microsoft, Wal-Mart, Intel, and Nike recognize that they cannot afford to relax. Jack Welch, GE's brilliant former CEO, repeatedly warned his company: "Change or die."

But making the right decisions is not always easy. Marketing managers must make major decisions such as what features to design into a new product, what prices to offer customers, where to sell products, and how much to spend on advertising or sales. They must also make more detailed decisions such as the exact wording or color for new packaging. (The "Marketing Memo: Marketers' Frequently Asked Questions" is a good checklist for the questions marketing managers ask, all of which we examine in this book.) The companies at greatest risk are those that fail to carefully monitor their customers and competitors and to continuously improve their value offerings. They take a short-term, sales-driven view of their business and ultimately, they fail to satisfy their stockholders, their employees, their suppliers, and their channel partners. Skillful marketing is a never-ending pursuit.

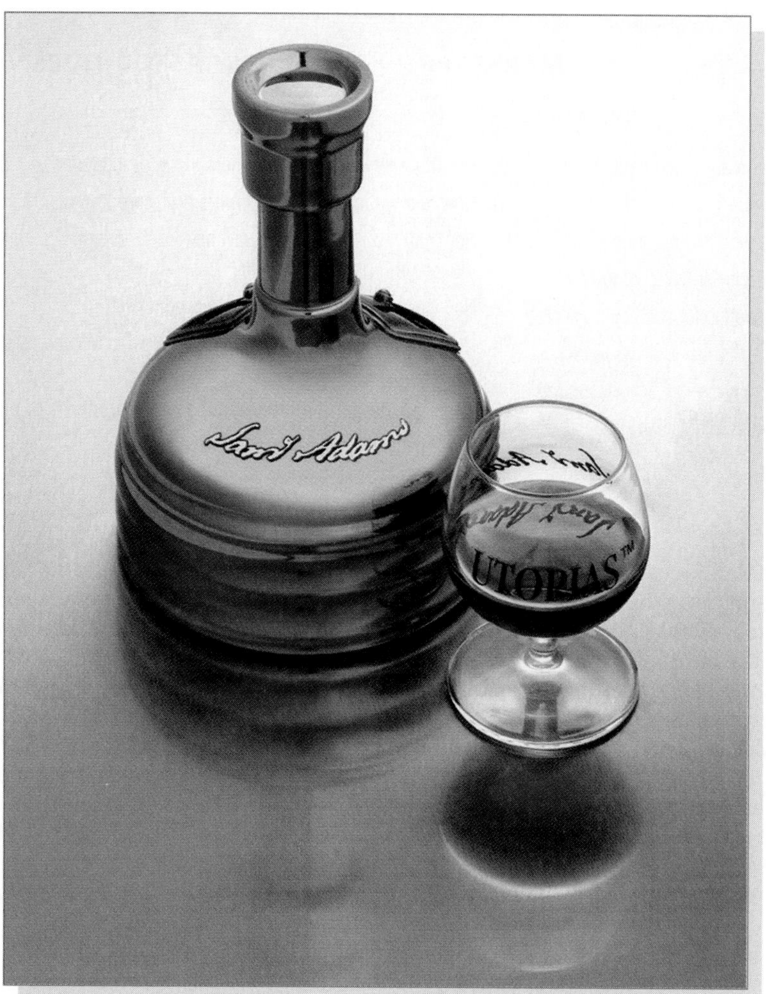

A bottle of Utopias, Boston Beer's unique, limited edition "extreme" brew. At 50-proof, it warrants the label "The Strongest Beer in the World."

BOSTON BEER COMPANY

Jim Koch, founder of Boston Beer Company, whose Samuel Adams beer has become a top-selling "craft" or "micro" beer, started out in 1984 carrying bottles of Samuel Adams from bar to bar to persuade bartenders to carry it. For 10 years he couldn't afford an advertising budget; he sold his beer through direct sales and grassroots public relations. His hard work paid off. Boston Beer found its sales passing the $200 million mark as it became the leader in the craft beer market. As a consequence, it began to spend millions of dollars on TV advertising, employ dozens of salespeople, and carry on sophisticated marketing research. It discovered that continued success required setting up and managing a capable marketing department. But the original passion and desire to move forward remains. In 2002, Boston Beer introduced a unique, limited edition "extreme" brew, Samuel Adams Utopias. The potent 50-proof, $100-a-bottle Utopias claimed the official record as "The Strongest Beer in the World." "At Samuel Adams, we are constantly innovating and creating new ideas that will push the envelope and revolutionize beer drinkers' expectations for beer," said founder Koch.[1]

::: The Scope of Marketing

To prepare to be a marketer, you need to understand what marketing is, how it works, what is marketed, and who does the marketing.

What Is Marketing?

Marketing deals with identifying and meeting human and social needs. One of the shortest definitions of marketing is "meeting needs profitably." When eBay recognized that people

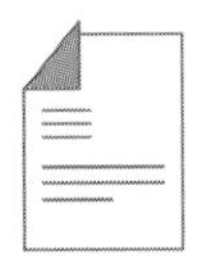

MARKETING **MEMO** | **MARKETERS' FREQUENTLY ASKED QUESTIONS**

1. How can we spot and choose the right market segment(s)?
2. How can we differentiate our offerings?
3. How should we respond to customers who buy on price?
4. How can we compete against lower-cost, lower-price competitors?
5. How far can we go in customizing our offering for each customer?
6. How can we grow our business?
7. How can we build stronger brands?
8. How can we reduce the cost of customer acquisition?
9. How can we keep our customers loyal for longer?
10. How can we tell which customers are more important?
11. How can we measure the payback from advertising, sales promotion, and public relations?
12. How can we improve sales force productivity?
13. How can we establish multiple channels and yet manage channel conflict?
14. How can we get the other company departments to be more customer-oriented?

were unable to locate some of the items they desired most and created an online auction clearinghouse or when IKEA noticed that people wanted good furniture at a substantially lower price and created knock-down furniture, they demonstrated marketing savvy and turned a private or social need into a profitable business opportunity.

The American Marketing Association offers the following formal definition: *Marketing is an organizational function and a set of processes for creating, communicating, and delivering value to customers and for managing customer relationships in ways that benefit the organization and its stake holders.*[2] Coping with exchange processes calls for a considerable amount of work and skill. Marketing management takes place when at least one party to a potential exchange thinks about the means of achieving desired responses from other parties. We see **marketing management** as *the art and science of choosing target markets and getting, keeping, and growing customers through creating, delivering, and communicating superior customer value.*

We can distinguish between a social and a managerial definition of marketing. A social definition shows the role marketing plays in society. One marketer said that marketing's role is to "deliver a higher standard of living." Here is a social definition that serves our purpose: *Marketing is a societal process by which individuals and groups obtain what they need and want through creating, offering, and freely exchanging products and services of value with others.* For a managerial definition, marketing has often been described as "the art of selling products," but people are surprised when they hear that the most important part of marketing is not selling! Selling is only the tip of the marketing iceberg. Peter Drucker, a leading management theorist, puts it this way:

> There will always, one can assume, be need for some selling. But the aim of marketing is to make selling superfluous. The aim of marketing is to know and understand the customer so well that the product or service fits him and sells itself. Ideally, marketing should result in a customer who is ready to buy. All that should be needed then is to make the product or service available.[3]

When Sony designed its Play Station, when Gillette launched its Mach III razor, and when Toyota introduced its Lexus automobile, these manufacturers were swamped with orders because they had designed the "right" product based on careful marketing homework.

Exchange and Transactions

A person can obtain a product in one of four ways. One can self-produce the product or service, as when one hunts, fishes, or gathers fruit. One can use force to get a product, as in a holdup or burglary. One can beg, as happens when a homeless person asks for food; or one can offer a product, a service, or money in exchange for something he or she desires.

Exchange, which is the core concept of marketing, is the process of obtaining a desired product from someone by offering something in return. For exchange potential to exist, five conditions must be satisfied:

1. There are at least two parties.
2. Each party has something that might be of value to the other party.

WE COULD HAVE LEFT WELL ENOUGH ALONE.
BUT THAT WOULD HARDLY BE VERY CHARACTERISTIC.
NOW WOULD IT?
LEXUS

"We could have left well enough alone. But that would hardly be very characteristic. Now would it?" Lexus ads, and its campaign slogan, "The Passionate Pursuit of Perfection," express the company's marketing philosophy: only the best is good enough for its customers.

3. Each party is capable of communication and delivery.
4. Each party is free to accept or reject the exchange offer.
5. Each party believes it is appropriate or desirable to deal with the other party.

Whether exchange actually takes place depends on whether the two parties can agree on terms that will leave them both better off (or at least not worse off) than before. Exchange is a value-creating process because it normally leaves both parties better off.

Two parties are engaged in exchange if they are negotiating—trying to arrive at mutually agreeable terms. When an agreement is reached, we say that a transaction takes place. A **transaction** is a trade of values between two or more parties: A gives X to B and receives Y in return. Smith sells Jones a television set and Jones pays $400 to Smith. This is a classic monetary transaction; but transactions do not require money as one of the traded values. A barter transaction involves trading goods or services for other goods or services, as when lawyer Jones writes a will for physician Smith in return for a medical examination.

A transaction involves several dimensions: at least two things of value, agreed-upon conditions, a time of agreement, and a place of agreement. A legal system supports and enforces compliance on the part of the transactors. Without a law of contracts, people would approach transactions with some distrust, and everyone would lose.

A transaction differs from a transfer. In a **transfer**, A gives X to B but does not receive anything tangible in return. Gifts, subsidies, and charitable contributions are all transfers. Transfer behavior can also be understood through the concept of exchange. Typically, the transferer expects to receive something in exchange for his or her gift—for example, gratitude or seeing changed behavior in the recipient. Professional fund-raisers provide benefits to donors, such as thank-you notes, donor magazines, and invitations to events. Marketers have broadened the concept of marketing to include the study of transfer behavior as well as transaction behavior.

In the most generic sense, marketers seek to elicit a behavioral response from another party. A business firm wants a purchase, a political candidate wants a vote, a church wants an active member, and a social-action group wants the passionate adoption of some cause. Marketing consists of actions undertaken to elicit desired responses from a target audience.

To make successful exchanges, marketers analyze what each party expects from the transaction. Simple exchange situations can be mapped by showing the two actors and the wants and offerings flowing between them. Suppose John Deere, a worldwide leader in agricultural equipment, researches the benefits that a typical large-scale farm enterprise wants when it buys tractors, combines, planters, and sprayers. These benefits include high-quality equipment, a fair price, on-time delivery, good financing terms, and good parts and service. The items on this want list are not equally important and may vary from buyer to buyer. One of John Deere's tasks is to discover the relative importance of these different wants to the buyer.

John Deere also has a want list. It wants a good price for the equipment, on-time payment, and good word of mouth. If there is a sufficient match or overlap in the want lists, a basis for a transaction exists. John Deere's task is to formulate an offer that motivates the farm enterprise to buy John Deere equipment. The farm enterprise might in turn make a counteroffer. This process of negotiation leads to mutually acceptable terms or a decision not to transact.

What Is Marketed?

Marketing people are involved in marketing 10 types of entities: goods, services, experiences, events, persons, places, properties, organizations, information, and ideas.

GOODS Physical goods constitute the bulk of most countries' production and marketing effort. Each year, U.S. companies alone market billions of fresh, canned, bagged, and frozen food products and millions of cars, refrigerators, television sets, machines, and various other mainstays of a modern economy. Not only do companies market their goods, but thanks in part to the Internet, even individuals can effectively market goods.

SERVICES As economies advance, a growing proportion of their activities is focused on the production of services. The U.S. economy today consists of a 70–30 services-to-goods mix. Services include the work of airlines, hotels, car rental firms, barbers and beauticians, maintenance and repair people, as well as professionals working within or for companies, such as accountants, bankers, lawyers, engineers, doctors, software programmers, and management consultants. Many market offerings consist of a variable mix of goods and services. At a fast-food restaurant, for example, the customer consumes both a product and a service.

EVENTS Marketers promote time-based events, such as major trade shows, artistic performances, and company anniversaries. Global sporting events such as the Olympics or World Cup are promoted aggressively to both companies and fans. There is a whole profession of meeting planners who work out the details of an event and make sure it comes off perfectly.

EXPERIENCES By orchestrating several services and goods, a firm can create, stage, and market experiences. Walt Disney World's Magic Kingdom represents experiential marketing: Customers visit a fairy kingdom, a pirate ship, or a haunted house. So does the Hard Rock Café, where customers can enjoy a meal or see a band in a live concert. There is also a market for customized experiences, such as spending a week at a baseball camp playing with some retired baseball greats, paying to conduct the Chicago Symphony Orchestra for five minutes, or climbing Mount Everest.[4]

PERSONS Celebrity marketing is a major business. Today, every major film star has an agent, a personal manager, and ties to a public relations agency. Artists, musicians, CEOs, physicians, high-profile lawyers and financiers, and other professionals are also getting help from celebrity marketers.[5] Some people have done a masterful job of marketing themselves—think of Madonna, Oprah Winfrey, the Rolling Stones, Aerosmith, and Michael Jordan. Management consultant Tom Peters, himself a master at self-branding, has advised each person to become a "brand."

PLACES Cities, states, regions, and whole nations compete actively to attract tourists, factories, company headquarters, and new residents.[6] Place marketers include economic development specialists, real estate agents, commercial banks, local business associations, and advertising and public relations agencies. To fuel their high-tech industries and spawn entrepreneurship, cities such as Indianapolis, Charlotte, and Raleigh-Durham are actively wooing 20- to 29-year-olds through ads, PR, and other communications. Louisville, Kentucky, spends $1 million annually on e-mails, events, and networking approaches to convince 20-somethings of the city's quality of life and other advantages.

PROPERTIES Properties are intangible rights of ownership of either real property (real estate) or financial property (stocks and bonds). Properties are bought and sold, and this requires marketing. Real estate agents work for property owners or sellers or buy residential or commercial real estate. Investment companies and banks are involved in marketing securities to both institutional and individual investors.

ORGANIZATIONS Organizations actively work to build a strong, favorable, and unique image in the minds of their target publics. Companies spend money on corporate identity ads. Philips, the Dutch electronics company, puts out ads with the tag line "Let's Make Things Better." In the United Kingdom, Tesco's "Every Little Bit Helps" marketing program has vaulted it to the top of the supermarket chains in that country. Universities, museums, performing arts organizations, and non-profits all use marketing to boost their public images and to compete for audiences and funds.

INFORMATION Information can be produced and marketed as a product. This is essentially what schools and universities produce and distribute at a price to parents, students, and communities. Encyclopedias and most nonfiction books market information. Magazines such as *Road and Track* and *Byte* supply information about the car and computer worlds, respectively. The production, packaging, and distribution of information is one of our society's major industries.[7] Even companies that sell physical products attempt to add value through the use of information. For example, the CEO of Siemens Medical Systems, Tom McCausland, says, "[our product] is not necessarily an X-ray or an MRI, but information. Our business is really health-care information technology, and our end product is really an electronic patient record: information on lab tests, pathology, and drugs as well as voice dictation."[8]

IDEAS Every market offering includes a basic idea. Charles Revson of Revlon observed: "In the factory, we make cosmetics; in the store we sell hope." Products and services are platforms for delivering some idea or benefit. Social marketers are busy promoting such ideas as "Friends Don't Let Friends Drive Drunk" and "A Mind Is a Terrible Thing to Waste."

This is the watch Stephen Hollingshead Jr., was wearing when he encountered a drunk driver. Time of death 6:55 P.M. Friends Don't Let Friends Drive Drunk. An ad from the "Friends Don't Let Friends Drive Drunk" campaign promotes an idea, not a product.

Who Markets?

MARKETERS AND PROSPECTS A **marketer** is someone who seeks a response (attention, a purchase, a vote, a donation) from another party, called the **prospect**. If two parties are seeking to sell something to each other, we call them both marketers.

Marketers are skilled in stimulating demand for a company's products, but this is too limited a view of the tasks they perform. Just as production and logistics professionals are responsible for supply management, marketers are responsible for demand management. Marketing managers seek to influence the level, timing, and composition of demand to meet the organization's objectives. Eight demand states are possible:

1. ***Negative demand*** – Consumers dislike the product and may even pay a price to avoid it.
2. ***Nonexistent demand*** – Consumers may be unaware or uninterested in the product.
3. ***Latent demand*** – Consumers may share a strong need that cannot be satisfied by an existing product.
4. ***Declining demand*** – Consumers begin to buy the product less frequently or not at all.
5. ***Irregular demand*** – Consumer purchases vary on a seasonal, monthly, weekly, daily, or even hourly basis.
6. ***Full demand*** – Consumers are adequately buying all products put into the marketplace.
7. ***Overfull demand*** – More consumers would like to buy the product than can be satisfied.
8. ***Unwholesome demand*** – Consumers may be attracted to products that have undesirable social consequences.

In each case, marketers must identify the underlying cause(s) of the demand state and then determine a plan for action to shift the demand to a more desired state.

MARKETS Traditionally, a "market" was a physical place where buyers and sellers gathered to buy and sell goods. Economists describe a market as a collection of buyers and sellers who transact over a particular product or product class (e.g., the housing market or grain market). Modern economies abound in such markets. Five basic markets and their connecting flows are shown in Figure 1.1. Manufacturers go to resource markets (raw material markets, labor markets, money markets), buy resources and turn them into goods and services, and then sell finished products to intermediaries, who sell them to consumers. Consumers sell their labor and receive money with which they pay for goods and services. The government collects tax revenues to buy goods from resource, manufacturer, and intermediary markets and uses these goods and services to provide public services. Each nation's economy and the global economy consist of complex interacting sets of markets linked through exchange processes.

On the other hand, marketers often use the term *market* to cover various groupings of customers. They view the sellers as constituting the industry and the buyers as constituting the market. They talk about need markets (the diet-seeking market), product markets (the shoe market), demographic markets (the youth market), and geographic markets (the French market); or they extend the concept to cover other markets, such as voter markets,

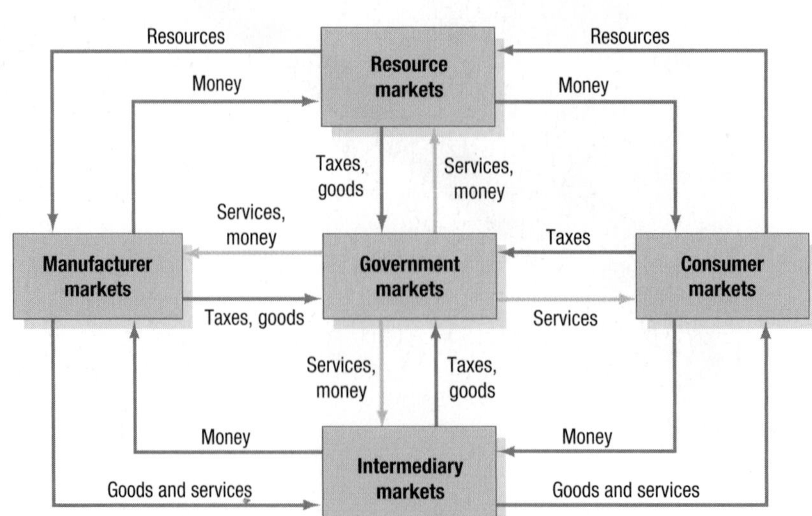

FIG. 1.1

Structure of Flows in a Modern Exchange Economy

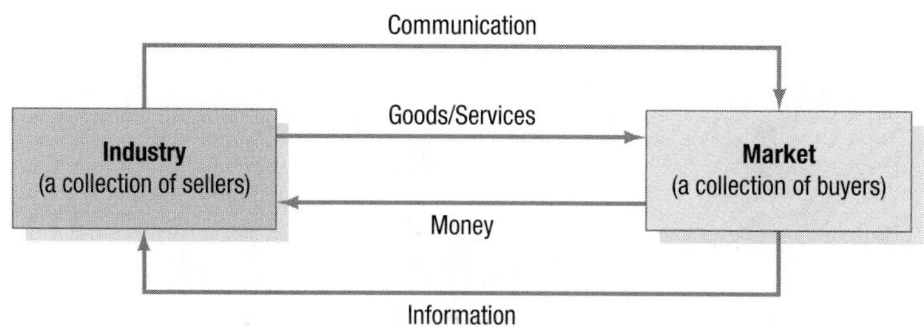

FIG. 1.2

A Simple Marketing System

labor markets, and donor markets. Figure 1.2 shows the relationship between the industry and the market. Sellers and buyers are connected by four flows. The sellers send goods and services and communications (ads, direct mail) to the market; in return they receive money and information (attitudes, sales data). The inner loop shows an exchange of money for goods and services; the outer loop shows an exchange of information.

KEY CUSTOMER MARKETS Consider the following key customer markets: consumer, business, global, and nonprofit.

Consumer Markets Companies selling mass consumer goods and services such as soft drinks, cosmetics, air travel, and athletic shoes and equipment spend a great deal of time trying to establish a superior brand image. Much of a brand's strength depends on developing a superior product and packaging, ensuring its availability, and backing it with engaging communications and reliable service. Complicating this task is the always changing consumer market (see "Marketing Insight: New Consumer Capabilities").

Business Markets Companies selling business goods and services often face well-trained and well-informed professional buyers who are skilled in evaluating competitive offerings. Business buyers buy goods in order to make or resell a product to others at a profit. Business marketers must demonstrate how their products will help these buyers achieve higher revenue or lower costs. Advertising can play a role, but a stronger role may be played by the sales force, price, and the company's reputation for reliability and quality.

Global Markets Companies selling goods and services in the global marketplace face additional decisions and challenges. They must decide which countries to enter; how to

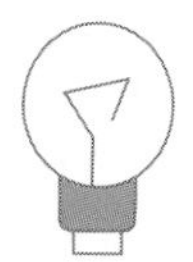

MARKETING INSIGHT | NEW CONSUMER CAPABILITIES

The digital revolution has placed a whole new set of capabilities in the hands of consumers and businesses. Consider what consumers have today that they didn't have yesterday:

- ***A substantial increase in buying power.*** Buyers today are only a click away from comparing competitor prices and product attributes. They can get answers on the Internet in a matter of seconds. They don't need to drive to stores, park, wait on line, and hold discussions with salespeople. Consumers can even name the price they want to pay for a hotel room, airline ticket, or mortgage, and see if there are any willing suppliers. Business buyers can run a reverse auction where sellers compete to capture the buyer's business. Buyers can join with others to aggregate their purchases to achieve deeper volume discounts.
- ***A greater variety of available goods and services.*** Today a person can order almost anything over the Internet: furniture (Ethan Allen), washing machines (Sears), management consulting ("Ernie"), medical advice (WebMD). Amazon.com advertises itself as the world's largest bookstore, with over 3 million books; no physical bookstore can match this. Furthermore, buyers can order these goods from anywhere in the world, which helps people living in countries with very limited local offerings to achieve great savings. It also means that buyers in countries with high prices can reduce their costs by ordering in countries with lower prices.
- ***A great amount of information about practically anything.*** People can read almost any newspaper in any language from anywhere in the world. They can access online encyclopedias, dictionaries, medical information, movie ratings, consumer reports, and countless other information sources.
- ***A greater ease in interacting and placing and receiving orders.*** Today's buyers can place orders from home, office, or mobile phone 24 hours a day, 7 days a week, and the orders will be delivered to their home or office quickly.
- ***An ability to compare notes on products and services.*** Today's customers can enter a chat room centered on some area of common interest and exchange information and opinions.

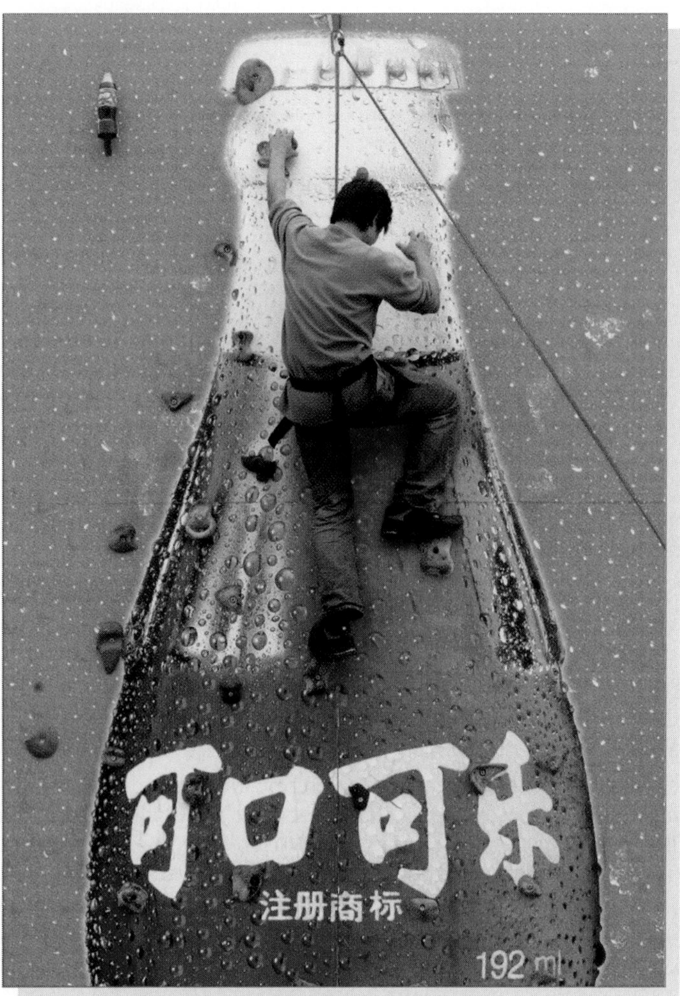

Global marketing: Wall climbing on a Coke ad to attract attention (and customers) at the first China International Beverage Festival in Beijing in 2003.

enter each country (as an exporter, licenser, joint venture partner, contract manufacturer, or solo manufacturer); how to adapt their product and service features to each country; how to price their products in different countries; and how to adapt their communications to fit different cultures. These decisions must be made in the face of different requirements for buying, negotiating, owning, and disposing of property; different culture, language, and legal and political systems; and a currency that might fluctuate in value.

Nonprofit and Governmental Markets Companies selling their goods to nonprofit organizations such as churches, universities, charitable organizations, or government agencies need to price carefully because these organizations have limited purchasing power. Lower prices affect the features and quality that the seller can build into the offering. Much government purchasing calls for bids, with the lowest bid being favored, in the absence of extenuating factors.

MARKETPLACES, MARKETSPACES, AND METAMARKETS Today we can distinguish between a *marketplace* and *marketspace.* The marketplace is physical, as when you shop in a store; marketspace is digital, as when you shop on the Internet.[9]

Mohan Sawhney has proposed the concept of a *metamarket* to describe a cluster of complementary products and services that are closely related in the minds of consumers but are spread across a diverse set of industries. The automobile metamarket consists of automobile manufacturers, new car and used car dealers, financing companies, insurance companies, mechanics, spare parts dealers, service shops, auto magazines, classified auto ads in newspapers, and auto sites on the Internet. In purchasing a car, a buyer will get involved in many parts of this metamarket, and this has created an opportunity for metamediaries to assist buyers to move seamlessly through these groups, although they are disconnected in physical space. One example is Edmund's (www.edmunds.com), a Web site where a car buyer can find the stated features and prices of different automobiles and easily click to other sites to search for the lowest-price dealer, for financing, for car accessories, and for used cars at bargain prices. Metamediaries can also serve other metamarkets such as the home ownership market, the parenting and baby care market, and the wedding market.[10]

How Business and Marketing Are Changing

A recent book entitled *Beyond Disruption* praises companies such as Apple, Sony, and TAG Heuer for achieving exponential sales growth despite being in established, but stagnant, markets.[11] The explanation offered for these success stories was that these companies adopted a clear vision of the proper direction in which to take their brands and challenged marketing convention through product innovation, advertising, or some other aspect of marketing. Another recent book entitled *Radical Marketing* spotlights companies such as Harley-Davidson, Virgin Atlantic Airways, and Boston Beer for adopting a different approach to marketing that focuses on stretching limited resources, staying in close contact with customers, and creating more satisfying solutions to customer needs. (See "Marketing Memo: The Ten Rules of Radical Marketing.")

We can say with some confidence that "the marketplace isn't what it used to be." It is radically different as a result of major, sometimes interlinking societal forces that have created new behaviors, new opportunities, and new challenges:

- ***Changing technology.*** The digital revolution has created an Information Age. The Industrial Age was characterized by mass production and mass consumption, stores stuffed with inventory, ads everywhere, and rampant discounting. The Information Age promises to lead to more accurate levels of production, more targeted communications, and more relevant pricing. Moreover, much of today's business is carried on over electronic networks: intranet, extranets, and the Internet.
- ***Globalization.*** Technological advances in transportation, shipping, and communication have made it easier for companies to market in other countries and easier for consumers to buy products and services from marketers in other countries.
- ***Deregulation.*** Many countries have deregulated industries to create greater competition and growth opportunities. In the United States, long-distance telephone companies can now compete in local markets and local phone companies can now offer long distance. Similarly, electrical utilities can now enter other local markets.

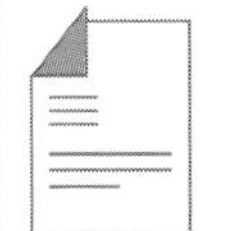

MARKETING MEMO | THE TEN RULES OF RADICAL MARKETING

In their book *Radical Marketing,* Sam Hill and Glenn Rifkin lay out a set of guidelines that can help other companies emulate the radical marketers.

1. ***The CEO must own the marketing function.*** CEOs of radical marketers never delegate marketing responsibility.
2. ***The marketing department must start small and flat and stay small and flat.*** CEOs of radical marketers must not allow layers of management to grow between them and the market.
3. ***Get face-to-face with the people who matter most—the customers.*** Radical marketers know the advantages of direct interaction with customers.
4. ***Use market research cautiously.*** Radical marketers prefer grassroots techniques.
5. ***Hire only passionate missionaries, not marketers.*** Radical marketers "don't have marketers, they have missionaries."
6. ***Love and respect customers as individuals, not as numbers on a spreadsheet.*** Radical marketers recognize that the core customers are responsible for the bulk of their companies' successes.
7. ***Create a community of consumers.*** Radical marketers "encourage their customers to think of themselves as a community, and of the brand as a unifier of that community."
8. ***Rethink the marketing mix.*** For example, radical marketers use "surgical strike advertising" characterized by short, targeted ad campaigns.
9. ***Celebrate common sense and compete with larger competitors through fresh and different marketing ideas.*** Radical marketers, for example, limit distribution in order to create loyalty and commitment among distributors and customers.
10. ***Be true to the brand.*** Radical marketers "are obsessive about brand integrity, and they are fixated on quality."

Source: Sam Hill and Glenn Rifkin, *Radical Marketing* (New York: HarperCollins, 1999), pp. 19–31.

- ***Privatization.*** Many countries have converted public companies to private ownership and management to increase their efficiency, such as British Airways and British Telecom in the United Kingdom.
- ***Customer empowerment.*** Customers increasingly expect higher quality and service and some customization. They are more and more time-starved and want more convenience. They perceive fewer real product differences and show less brand loyalty. They can obtain extensive product information from the Internet and other sources, which permits them to shop more intelligently. They are showing greater price sensitivity in their search for value.
- ***Customization.*** The company is able to produce individually differentiated goods whether ordered in person, on the phone, or online. By going online, companies essentially enable consumers to design their own goods. The company also has the capacity to interact with each customer personally, to *personalize* messages, services, and the relationship. Using smart software and new manufacturing equipment, catalog house Lands' End put customized chinos up for sale in 2001 and is now expanding its number of customized products. Because items are cut to order, the company doesn't have to keep as much inventory around.[12]
- ***Heightened competition.*** Brand manufacturers are facing intense competition from domestic and foreign brands, which is resulting in rising promotion costs and shrinking profit margins. They are being further buffeted by powerful retailers who command limited shelf space and are putting out their own store brands in competition with national brands.
- ***Industry convergence.*** Industry boundaries are blurring at an incredible rate as companies are recognizing that new opportunities lie at the intersection of two or more industries. Pharmaceutical companies, at one time essentially chemical companies, are now adding biogenetic research capacities in order to formulate new drugs, new cosmetics (cosmoneu-

Cosmoneuticals: An ad for dermatology drugs marketed by Shiseido, the Japanese cosmetics firm. The WH/SIS product line targets spots and freckles, and includes cleanser, lotion, emulsion, day/night whitening beauty essence, and medication to be taken orally. It is sold only in Japan, mainly in drugstores.

ticals), and new foods (nutriceuticals). Shiseido, the Japanese cosmetics firm, now markets a portfolio of dermatology drugs. Christmas 2003 saw the convergence of the computing and consumer electronics industries as the giants of the computer world such as Dell, Gateway, and Hewlett-Packard released a stream of entertainment devices—from MP3 players to plasma TVs and camcorders. The shift to digital technology, in which devices needed to play entertainment content are more and more like PCs, is fueling this massive convergence.[13]

- ***Retail transformation.*** Small retailers are succumbing to the growing power of giant retailers and "category killers." Store-based retailers are facing growing competition from catalog houses; direct-mail firms; newspaper, magazine, and TV direct-to-customer ads; home shopping TV; and e-commerce on the Internet. In response, entrepreneurial retailers are building entertainment into stores with coffee bars, lectures, demonstrations, and performances. They are marketing an "experience" rather than a product assortment.
- ***Disintermediation.*** The amazing success of early online dot-coms such as AOL, Amazon, Yahoo, eBay, E'TRADE, and dozens of others who created *disintermediation* in the delivery of products and services, struck terror in the hearts of many established manufacturers and retailers. In response to disintermediation, many traditional companies engaged in *reintermediation* and became "brick-and-click," adding online services to their existing offerings. Many brick-and-click competitors became stronger contenders than the pure-click firms, since they had a larger pool of resources to work with and well-established brand names.

::: Company Orientations Toward the Marketplace

What philosophy should guide a company's marketing efforts? What relative weights should be given to the interests of the organization, the customers, and society? Very often these interests conflict. The competing concepts under which organizations have conducted marketing activities include: the production concept, product concept, selling concept, marketing concept, and holistic marketing concept.

The Production Concept

The production concept is one of the oldest concepts in business. It holds that consumers will prefer products that are widely available and inexpensive. Managers of production-oriented businesses concentrate on achieving high production efficiency, low costs, and mass distribution. This orientation makes sense in developing countries such as China where the largest PC manufacturer, Legend, and domestic appliances giant Haier take advantage of the country's huge inexpensive labor pool to dominate the market. It is also used when a company wants to expand the market.[14]

The Product Concept

The product concept holds that consumers will favor those products that offer the most quality, performance, or innovative features. Managers in these organizations focus on making superior products and improving them over time. However, these managers are sometimes caught up in a love affair with their products. They might commit the "better-mousetrap" fallacy, believing that a better mousetrap will lead people to beat a path to their door. A new or improved product will not necessarily be successful unless the product is priced, distributed, advertised, and sold properly.

The Selling Concept

The selling concept holds that consumers and businesses, if left alone, will ordinarily not buy enough of the organization's products. The organization must, therefore, undertake an aggressive selling and promotion effort. The selling concept is epitomized in the thinking of Sergio Zyman, Coca-Cola's former vice president of marketing: The purpose of marketing is to sell more stuff to more people more often for more money in order to make more profit.[15]

The selling concept is practiced most aggressively with unsought goods, goods that buyers normally do not think of buying, such as insurance, encyclopedias, and funeral plots. Most firms practice the selling concept when they have overcapacity. Their aim is to sell what they make rather than make what the market wants. However, marketing based on hard selling carries high risks. It assumes that customers who are coaxed into buying a product will like it; and that if they do not, they will not return it or bad-mouth it or complain to consumer organizations, or might even buy it again.

The Marketing Concept

The marketing concept emerged in the mid-1950s.[16] Instead of a product-centered, "make-and-sell" philosophy, business shifted to a customer-centered, "sense-and-respond" philosophy. Instead of "hunting," marketing is "gardening." The job is not to find the right customers for your products, but the right products for your customers. The marketing concept holds that the key to achieving organizational goals consists of the company being more effective than competitors in creating, delivering, and communicating superior customer value to its chosen target markets.

> Theodore Levitt of Harvard drew a perceptive contrast between the selling and marketing concepts: Selling focuses on the needs of the seller; marketing on the needs of the buyer. Selling is preoccupied with the seller's need to convert his product into cash; marketing with the idea of satisfying the needs of the customer by means of the product and the whole cluster of things associated with creating, delivering and finally consuming it.[17]

Several scholars have found that companies who embrace the marketing concept achieve superior performance.[18] This was first demonstrated by companies practicing a *reactive market orientation*—understanding and meeting customers' expressed needs. Some critics say this means companies develop only low-level innovations. Narver and his colleagues argue that high-level innovation is possible if the focus is on customers' latent needs. He calls this a *proactive marketing orientation.*[19] Companies such as 3M, HP, and Motorola have made a practice of researching or imagining latent needs through a "probe-and-learn" process. Companies that practice both a reactive and proactive marketing orientation are implementing a *total market orientation* and are likely to be the most successful.

DIEBOLD

The $1.9 billion automated teller machine (ATM) maker Diebold is not only focused on what its customers want, but looks ahead to what its customers' customers want. For instance, the North Canton, Ohio, company not only develops ATMs that have brighter screens or are easy to install, but embeds advanced end-user capabilities into the ATMs. These include on-demand banking statements, automatic bill payment and instant crediting of deposits—with or without a deposit envelope. With advances like these, Diebold's customers, mainly financial institutions and retailers, can offer more services to their customers after banking hours.[20]

In the course of converting to a marketing orientation, a company faces three hurdles: organized resistance, slow learning, and fast forgetting. Some company departments (often manufacturing, finance, and R&D) believe a stronger marketing function threatens their power in the organization. Initially, the marketing function is seen as one of several equally important functions in a check-and-balance relationship. Marketers argue that their function is more important. A few enthusiasts go further and say marketing is the major function of the enterprise, for without customers there is no company. Enlightened marketers clarify the issue by putting the customer at the center of the company. They argue for a customer orientation in which all functions work together to respond to, serve, and satisfy the customer.[21]

The Holistic Marketing Concept

A whole set of forces that appeared in the last decade call for new marketing and business practices. Companies have new capabilities that can transform the way they have been doing marketing (see "Marketing Insight: The Internet Advantage"). Companies need fresh thinking about how to operate and compete in a new marketing environment. Marketers in the twenty-first century are increasingly recognizing the need to have a more complete, cohesive approach that goes beyond traditional applications of the marketing concept. Look at Puma.

PUMA

German athletic footwear company Puma has used holistic marketing to bring its product back from being a sentimental mainstay of the 1970s to one of the trendiest athletic shoes around. Puma uses multiple marketing approaches that work synergistically to set Puma apart as an edgy, trend-setting brand. Puma designs products with distinct customer groups in mind—such as snowboarders, car racing fans, and yoga enthusiasts—using market research generated by its retailer partners. Puma also targets the armchair athlete—its two most popular models are the Mostro, a walking shoe with a nubbed wraparound sole, and the Speed Cat, a flat $65 sneaker modeled on shoes worn by Formula One race car drivers. It generates word of mouth or "viral marketing" by clever promotions—from partnering with BMW/Mini, Terence Conran Design Shop, and the Jamaican Olympic team—or holding promotional events at sushi restaurants during the 2002 World Cup to outfitting Serena Williams and showcasing products in well-chosen TV shows and movies. The approach is working: Puma's sales have increased for 10 straight years from 1994 to 2004, tripling in total.[22]

The **holistic marketing** concept is based on the development, design, and implementation of marketing programs, processes, and activities that recognizes their breadth and interdependencies. Holistic marketing recognizes that "everything matters" with marketing—and that a broad, integrated perspective is often necessary. Four components of holistic marketing are relationship marketing, integrated marketing, internal marketing, and social responsibility marketing.

Holistic marketing is thus an approach to marketing that attempts to recognize and reconcile the scope and complexities of marketing activities. Figure 1.3 provides a schematic overview of four broad themes characterizing holistic marketing.

RELATIONSHIP MARKETING Increasingly, a key goal of marketing is to develop deep, enduring relationships with all people or organizations that could directly or indirectly affect the success of the firm's marketing activities. **Relationship marketing** has the aim of building mutually satisfying long-term relationships with key parties—customers, suppliers, distributors, and

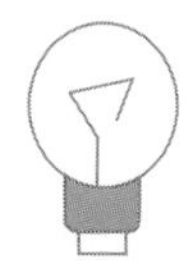

MARKETING INSIGHT | THE INTERNET ADVANTAGE

The Internet gives today's companies a new set of capabilities:

- Companies can operate a powerful new information and sales channel, the Internet, with augmented geographical reach to inform and promote their businesses and products worldwide. By establishing one or more Web sites, a company can list its products and services, its history, its business philosophy, its job opportunities, and other information of interest to visitors. Unlike the ads and brochures of the past, the Internet permits a company to transmit an almost unlimited amount of information.
- Companies can collect fuller and richer information about markets, customers, prospects, and competitors. They can also conduct fresh marketing research using the Internet to arrange for focus groups, send out questionnaires, and gather primary data in several other ways.
- Companies can facilitate and speed up internal communication among their employees by using the Internet as a private intranet. Employees can query one another, seek advice, and download or upload needed information from and to the company's main computer.
- Companies can have two-way communications with customers and prospects, and more efficient transactions. The Internet makes it easy for individuals to e-mail companies and receive replies, and more companies today are developing extranets with suppliers and distributors for sending and receiving information, placing orders, and making payments more efficiently.
- Companies are now able to send ads, coupons, samples, and information to customers who have requested these items or have given the company permission to send them.
- Companies can customize offerings and services by using database information on the number of visitors to their Web sites and visit frequency.
- Companies can improve purchasing, recruiting, training, and internal and external communications.
- Companies can achieve substantial savings by using the Internet to compare sellers' prices, and to purchase materials at auction or by posting their own terms. Companies can recruit new employees. Many are also preparing Internet training products that can be downloaded to employees, dealers, and agents.
- Companies can improve logistics and operations for substantial cost savings while improving accuracy and service quality. The Internet provides a more accurate and faster way to send and receive information, orders, transactions, and payments between companies, their business partners, and their customers.

FIG. 1.3

Holistic Marketing Dimensions

other marketing partners—in order to earn and retain their business.[23] Relationship marketing builds strong economic, technical, and social ties among the parties.

Relationship marketing involves cultivating the right kind of relationships with the right constituent groups. Marketing must not only do customer relationship management (CRM), but also partner relationship management (PRM) as well. Four key constituents for marketing are customers, employees, marketing partners (channels, suppliers, distributors, dealers, agencies), and members of the financial community (shareholders, investors, analysts).

The ultimate outcome of relationship marketing is the building of a unique company asset called a marketing network. A **marketing network** consists of the company and its supporting stakeholders (customers, employees, suppliers, distributors, retailers, ad agencies, university scientists, and others) with whom it has built mutually profitable business relationships. Increasingly, competition is not between companies but between marketing networks, with the prize going to the company that has built the better network. The operating principle is simple: Build an effective network of relationships with key stakeholders, and profits will follow.[24]

The development of strong relationships requires an understanding of the capabilities and resources of different groups, as well as their needs, goals, and desires. A growing number of today's companies are now shaping separate offers, services, and messages to individual customers. These companies collect information on each customer's past transactions, demographics, psychographics, and media and distribution preferences. They hope to achieve profitable growth through capturing a larger share of each customer's expenditures by building high customer loyalty and focusing on customer lifetime value.

The ability of a company to deal with customers one at a time has become practical as a result of advances in factory customization, computers, the Internet, and database marketing software. BMW's technology now allows buyers to design their own models from 350 variations, 500 options, 90 exterior colors, and 170 trims. The company claims that 80 percent of the cars bought by individuals in Europe and up to 30 percent of those in the United States are built to order. British supermarket giant Tesco is outpacing its rival store, Sainsbury, by using its Clubcard data to personalize offers according to individual customer attributes.[25]

Yet the practice of one-to-one marketing is not for every company: The required investment in information collection, hardware, and software may exceed the payout. It works best for companies that normally collect a great deal of individual customer information, carry a lot of products that can be cross-sold, carry products that need periodic replacement or upgrading, and sell products of high value.

Rich, multifaceted relationships with key constituents create the foundation for a mutually beneficial arrangement for both parties. For example, tired of having its big rigs return empty after making a delivery as often as 15 percent of the time, General Mills entered a program with Fort James and a dozen other companies to combine one-way shipping routes into a cross-country loop via a tag-team of contracted trucks. As a result, General Mills reduced its empty truck time to 6 percent, saving 7 percent on shipping costs in the process.[26]

FIG. 1.4

The Four P Components of the Marketing Mix

INTEGRATED MARKETING The marketer's task is to devise marketing activities and assemble fully integrated marketing programs to create, communicate, and deliver value for consumers. The marketing program consists of numerous decisions on value-enhancing marketing activities to use. Marketing activities come in all forms. One traditional depiction of marketing activities is in terms of the marketing mix, which has been defined as the set of marketing tools the firm uses to pursue its marketing objectives.[27] McCarthy classified these tools into four broad groups, which he called *the four Ps* of marketing: product, price, place, and promotion.[28]

The particular marketing variables under each P are shown in Figure 1.4. Marketing-mix decisions must be made for influencing the trade channels as well as the final consumers. Figure 1.5 shows the company preparing an offering mix of products, services, and prices, and utilizing a communications mix of advertising, sales promotion, events and experiences, public relations, direct marketing, and personal selling to reach the trade channels and the target customers.

The firm can change its price, sales force size, and advertising expenditures in the short run. It can develop new products and modify its distribution channels only in the long run. Thus the firm typically makes fewer period-to-period marketing-mix changes in the short run than the number of marketing-mix decision variables might suggest.

The four Ps represent the sellers' view of the marketing tools available for influencing buyers. From a buyer's point of view, each marketing tool is designed to deliver a customer

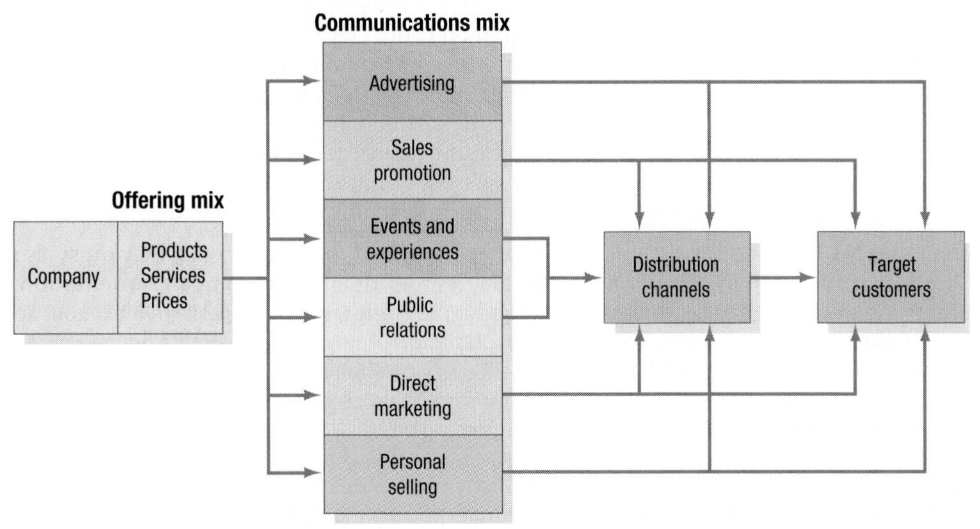

FIG. 1.5

Marketing-Mix Strategy

benefit. Robert Lauterborn suggested that the sellers' four Ps correspond to the customers' four Cs.[29]

Four Ps	Four Cs
Product	Customer solution
Price	Customer cost
Place	Convenience
Promotion	Communication

Winning companies will be those that can meet customer needs economically and conveniently and with effective communication.

Two key themes of integrated marketing are that (1) many different marketing activities are employed to communicate and deliver value and (2) all marketing activities are coordinated to maximize their joint effects. In other words, the design and implementation of any one marketing activity is done with all other activities in mind. Businesses must integrate their systems for demand management, resource management, and network management.

For example, an integrated communication strategy involves choosing communication options that reinforce and complement each other. A marketer might selectively employ television, radio, and print advertising, public relations and events, and PR and Web site communications so that each contributes on its own as well as improves the effectiveness of others. Because there was already a buzz for its remake of the cult 1974 film *The Texas Chainsaw Massacre,* New Line Cinema relied on a combination of both traditional TV ads and trailers, as well as interactive marketing via AOL's Instant Messenger and "bots"—robot agents—to help spread the word and get teens talking about the film. Their goal was to create a peer-to-peer communication, that is, getting teens to do the marketing for them![30] Integrated channel strategy involves ensuring that direct (e.g., online sales) and indirect channels (e.g., retail sales) work together to maximize sales and brand equity.

INTERNAL MARKETING Holistic marketing incorporates *internal marketing,* ensuring that everyone in the organization embraces appropriate marketing principles, especially senior management. Internal marketing is the task of hiring, training, and motivating able employees who want to serve customers well. Smart marketers recognize that marketing activities within the company can be as important as, or even more so than, marketing activities directed outside the company. It makes no sense to promise excellent service before the company's staff is ready to provide it.

Internal marketing must take place on two levels. At one level, the various marketing functions—sales force, advertising, customer service, product management, marketing research—must work together. Too often, the sales force thinks product managers set prices or sale quotas "too high"; or the advertising director and a brand manager cannot agree on an advertising campaign. All these marketing functions must be coordinated from the customer's point of view. The following example highlights the coordination problem:

> The marketing vice president of a major European airline wants to increase the airline's traffic share. His strategy is to build up customer satisfaction through providing better food, cleaner cabins, better-trained cabin crews, and lower fares; yet he has no authority in these matters. The catering department chooses food that keeps food costs down; the maintenance department uses cleaning services that keep down cleaning costs; the human resources department hires people without regard to whether they are naturally friendly; the finance department sets the fares. Because these departments generally take a cost or production point of view, the vice president of marketing is stymied in creating an integrated marketing mix.

At another level, marketing must be embraced by the other departments; they must also "think customer." Marketing is not a department so much as a company orientation. Marketing thinking must be pervasive throughout the company (see Table 1.1). Xerox goes so far as to include in every job description an explanation of how that job affects the customer. Xerox factory managers know that visits to the factory can help sell a potential customer if the factory is clean and efficient. Xerox accountants know that customer attitudes are affected by Xerox's billing accuracy and promptness in returning calls.

SOCIAL RESPONSIBILITY MARKETING Holistic marketing incorporates *social responsibility marketing* and understanding broader concerns and the ethical, environmental, legal, and social context of marketing activities and programs. The cause and effects of marketing

TABLE 1.1

Assessing Which Company Departments Are Customer-Minded

R&D

- They spend time meeting customers and listening to their problems.
- They welcome the involvement of marketing, manufacturing, and other departments to each new project.
- They benchmark competitors' products and seek "best of class" solutions.
- They solicit customer reactions and suggestions as the project progresses.
- They continuously improve and refine the product on the basis of market feedback.

Purchasing

- They proactively search for the best suppliers.
- They build long-term relationships with fewer but more reliable, high-quality suppliers.
- They don't compromise quality for price savings.

Manufacturing

- They invite customers to visit and tour their plants.
- They visit customer plants.
- They willingly work overtime to meet promised delivery schedules.
- They continuously search for ways to produce goods faster and/or at lower cost.
- They continuously improve product quality, aiming for zero defects.
- They meet customer requirements for "customization" where possible.

Marketing

- They study customer needs and wants in well-defined market segments.
- They allocate marketing effort in relation to the long-run profit potential of the targeted segments.
- They develop winning offers for each target segment.
- They measure company image and customer satisfaction on a continuous basis.
- They continuously gather and evaluate ideas for new products, product improvements, and services.
- They urge all company departments and employees to be customer-centered.

Sales

- They have specialized knowledge of the customer's industry.
- They strive to give the customer "the best solution."
- They only make promises that they can keep.
- They feed back customers' needs and ideas to those in charge of product development.
- They serve the same customers for a long period of time.

Logistics

- They set a high standard for service delivery time and meet this standard consistently.
- They operate a knowledgeable and friendly customer service department that can answer questions, handle complaints, and resolve problems in a satisfactory and timely manner.

Accounting

- They prepare periodic "profitability" reports by product, market segment, geographic areas (regions, sales territories), order sizes, channels, and individual customers.
- They prepare invoices tailored to customer needs and answer customer queries courteously and quickly.

Finance

- They understand and support marketing expenditures (e.g., image advertising) that produce long-term customer preference and loyalty.
- They tailor the financial package to the customer's financial requirements.
- They make quick decisions on customer creditworthiness.

Public Relations

- They send out favorable news about the company and "damage control" unfavorable news.
- They act as an internal customer and public advocate for better company policies and practices.

Source: Philip Kotler, *Kotler on Marketing,* 1999, New York: The Free Press, pp. 21–22.

clearly extend beyond the company and the consumer to society as a whole. Social responsibility also requires that marketers carefully consider the role that they are playing and could play in terms of social welfare.

Are companies that do an excellent job of satisfying consumer wants necessarily acting in the best long-run interests of consumers and society? Consider the following criticism:

> The fast-food hamburger industry offers tasty but unhealthy food. The hamburgers have a high fat content, and the restaurants promote fries and pies, two products high in starch and fat. The products are wrapped in convenient packaging, which leads to much waste. In satisfying consumer wants, these restaurants may be hurting consumer health and causing environmental problems.

Recognizing these criticisms, companies like McDonald's have added healthier items to their menus (e.g., salads) and introduced environmental initiatives (e.g., replacing polystyrene foam sandwich clamshells with paper wraps and lightweight recycled boxes). Recently, McDonald's announced its largest environmental initiative to date. McDonald's Corp., which buys 2.5 billion pounds of poultry, beef, and pork a year for its 30,000 restaurants worldwide, ordered its suppliers to eliminate the use of antibiotics that are also given to humans, specifically when those drugs are used to make chickens, pigs and, less often, cattle, grow faster. "We saw lots of evidence that showed the declining rate of effectiveness of antibiotics in human medicine," said Bob Langert, McDonald's senior director of social responsibility. "We started to look at what we could do."[31]

Situations like this one call for a new term that enlarges the marketing concept. Among those suggested are "humanistic marketing" and "ecological marketing." We propose calling it the "societal marketing concept." The *societal marketing concept* holds that the organization's task is to determine the needs, wants, and interests of target markets and to deliver the desired satisfactions more effectively and efficiently than competitors in a way that preserves or enhances the consumer's and the society's well-being.

The societal marketing concept calls upon marketers to build social and ethical considerations into their marketing practices. They must balance and juggle the often conflicting criteria of company profits, consumer want satisfaction, and public interest. Table 1.2 displays some different types of corporate social initiatives, as illustrated with McDonald's.

Yet a number of companies—including the Body Shop, Ben & Jerry's, and Patagonia—have achieved notable sales and profit gains by adopting and practicing a form of the societal marketing concept called *cause-related marketing.* Pringle and Thompson define this as

TABLE 1.2 | Corporate Social Initiatives

Type	Description	Example
Corporate social marketing	Supporting behavior change campaigns	McDonald's promotion of a statewide childhood immunization campaign in Oklahoma
Cause marketing	Promoting social issues through efforts such as sponsorships, licensing agreements, and advertising	McDonald's sponsorship of Forest (a gorilla) at Sydney's Zoo—a 10-year sponsorship commitment, aimed at preserving this endangered species
Cause-related marketing	Donating a percentage of revenues to a specific cause based on the revenue occurring during the announced period of support	McDonald's earmarking of $1 for Ronald McDonald Children's Charities from the sale of every Big Mac and pizza sold on McHappy Day
Corporate philanthropy	Making gifts of money, goods, or time to help nonprofit organizations, groups, or individuals	McDonald's contributions to Ronald McDonald House Charities
Corporate community involvement	Providing in-kind or volunteer services in the community	McDonald's catering meals for firefighters in the December 1997 bushfires in Australia
Socially responsible business practices	Adapting and conducting business practices that protect the environment, and human and animal rights	McDonald's requirement that suppliers increase the amount of living space for laying hens on factory farms

Source: Philip Kotler and Nancy Lee, *Corporate Social Responsibility: Doing the Most Good for Your Company and Your Cause* (Wiley, December 2004).

activity by which a company with an image, product, or service to market builds a relationship or partnership with a "cause," or a number of "causes," for mutual benefit."[32]

Companies see cause-related marketing as an opportunity to enhance their corporate reputation, raise brand awareness, increase customer loyalty, build sales, and increase press coverage. They believe that customers will increasingly look for signs of good corporate citizenship that go beyond supplying rational and emotional benefits. Avon has been one of the most successful cause marketers.

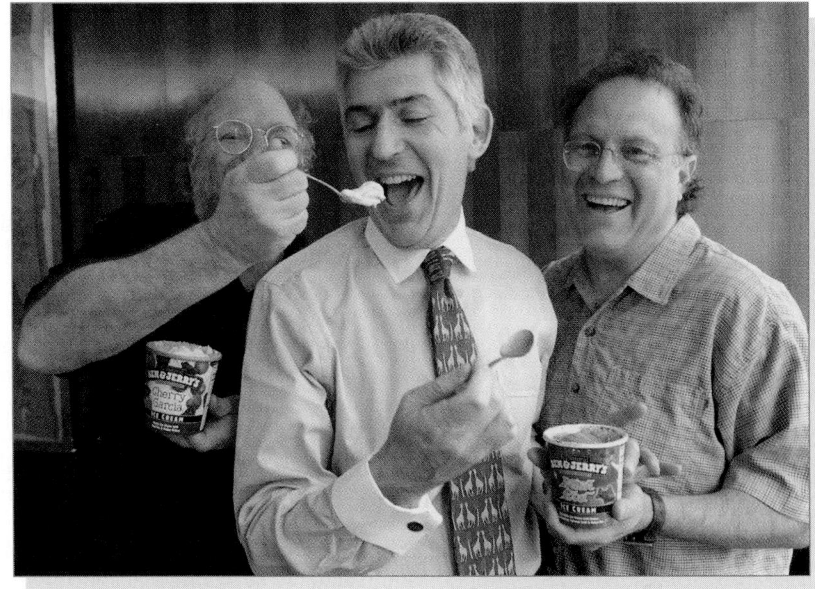

Ben & Jerry's co-founders Ben Cohen (left) and Jerry Greenfield (right) feed Unilever US CEO Richard Goldstein in May 2000, when Ben & Jerry's was bought by Unilever. Cohen and Greenfield agreed to the deal after months of negotiations to ensure that the company's high standards and corporate social consciousness would be maintained.

THE AVON WALK FOR BREAST CANCER

The Avon Walk for Breast Cancer is one of many projects of the Avon Foundation Breast Cancer Crusade, a global initiative of Avon Products, Inc., that was launched in the United States in 1993. Its mission has been to support access to care and finding a cure for breast cancer, with a focus on those who are medically underserved, by funding education, screening and diagnosis, treatment, support services, and scientific research. Worldwide, Avon is the largest corporate supporter of the breast cancer cause, with more than $250 million generated since the first program in 1992. The Avon Breast Cancer Crusade raises funds to accomplish this mission through many programs: sales of special Crusade "pink ribbon" products by Avon's nearly 600,000 U.S. independent sales representatives; concerts, walks, races, and other special events around the world; direct online fund-raising; and the Avon Walk for Breast Cancer series of weekend events in the United States (avonfoundation.org, avonwalk.org).

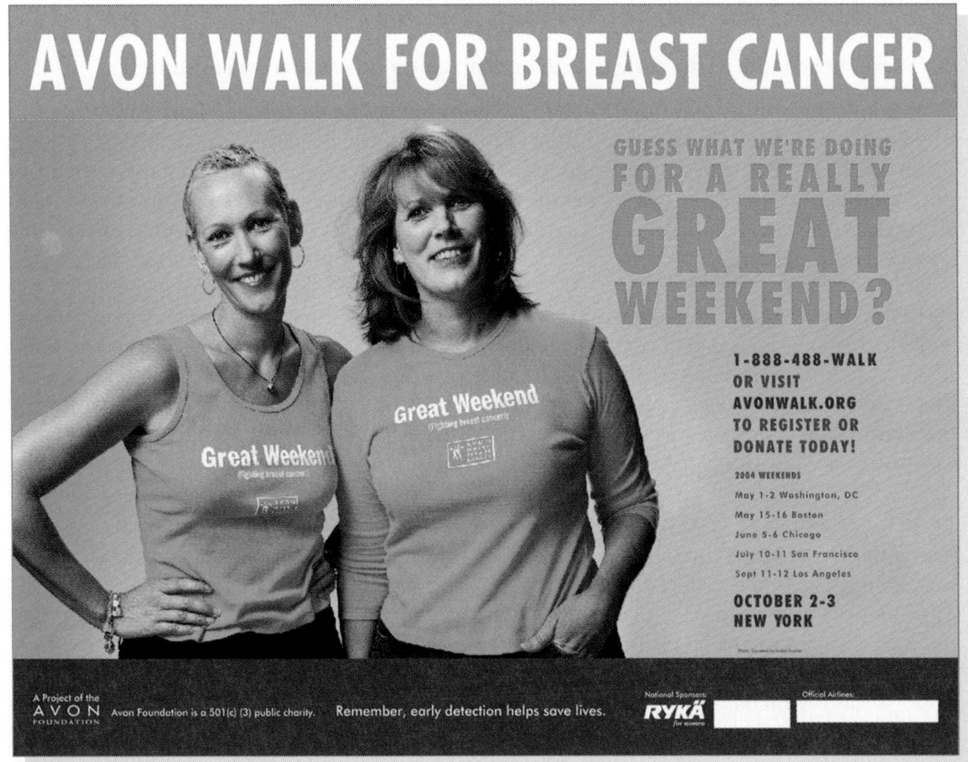

Print ad for an Avon Walk for Breast Cancer series of weekend events.

::: Fundamental Marketing Concepts, Trends, and Tasks

To understand the marketing function, we need to understand certain fundamental concepts and tasks, along with current trends.

Core Concepts

A core set of concepts creates a foundation for marketing management and a holistic marketing orientation.

NEEDS, WANTS, AND DEMANDS The marketer must try to understand the target market's needs, wants, and demands. *Needs* are the basic human requirements. People need food, air, water, clothing, and shelter to survive. People also have strong needs for recreation, education, and entertainment. These needs become *wants* when they are directed to specific objects that might satisfy the need. An American needs food but may want a hamburger, French fries, and a soft drink. A person in Mauritius needs food but may want a mango, rice, lentils, and beans. Wants are shaped by one's society. *Demands* are wants for specific products backed by an ability to pay. Many people want a Mercedes; only a few are willing and able to buy one. Companies must measure not only how many people want their product but also how many would actually be willing and able to buy it.

These distinctions shed light on the frequent criticism that "marketers create needs" or "marketers get people to buy things they don't want." Marketers do not create needs: Needs preexist marketers. Marketers, along with other societal factors, influence wants. Marketers might promote the idea that a Mercedes would satisfy a person's need for social status. They do not, however, create the need for social status.

Understanding customer needs and wants is not always simple. Some customers have needs of which they are not fully conscious, or they cannot articulate these needs, or they use words that require some interpretation. What does it mean when the customer asks for a "powerful" lawnmower, a "fast" lathe, an "attractive" bathing suit, or a "restful" hotel? Consider the customer who says he wants an "inexpensive car." The marketer must probe further. We can distinguish among five types of needs:

1. Stated needs (the customer wants an inexpensive car).
2. Real needs (the customer wants a car whose operating cost, not its initial price, is low).
3. Unstated needs (the customer expects good service from the dealer).
4. Delight needs (the customer would like the dealer to include an onboard navigation system).
5. Secret needs (the customer wants to be seen by friends as a savvy consumer).

Responding only to the stated need may shortchange the customer. Many consumers do not know what they want in a product. Consumers did not know much about cellular phones when they were first introduced. Nokia and Ericsson fought to shape consumer perceptions of cellular phones. Consumers were in a learning mode and companies forged strategies to shape their wants. As stated by Carpenter, "Simply giving customers what they want isn't enough any more—to gain an edge companies must help customers learn what they want."[33]

In the past, "responding to customer needs" meant studying customer needs and making a product that fit these needs on the average, but some of today's companies instead respond to each customer's individual needs. Dell Computer does not prepare a perfect computer for its target market. Rather, it provides product platforms on which each person customizes the features he or she desires in the computer. This is a change from a "make-and-sell" philosophy to a philosophy of "sense and respond."

TARGET MARKETS, POSITIONING, AND SEGMENTATION A marketer can rarely satisfy everyone in a market. Not everyone likes the same cereal, hotel room, restaurant, automobile, college, or movie. Therefore, marketers start by dividing up the market into segments. They identify and profile distinct groups of buyers who might prefer or require varying product and services mixes by examining demographic, psychographic, and behavioral differences among buyers. The marketer then decides which segments present the greatest opportunity—which are its *target markets.* For each chosen target market, the firm develops a *market offering.* The offering is *positioned* in the minds of the target buyers as delivering some central benefit(s). For example, Volvo develops its cars for buyers to whom automobile

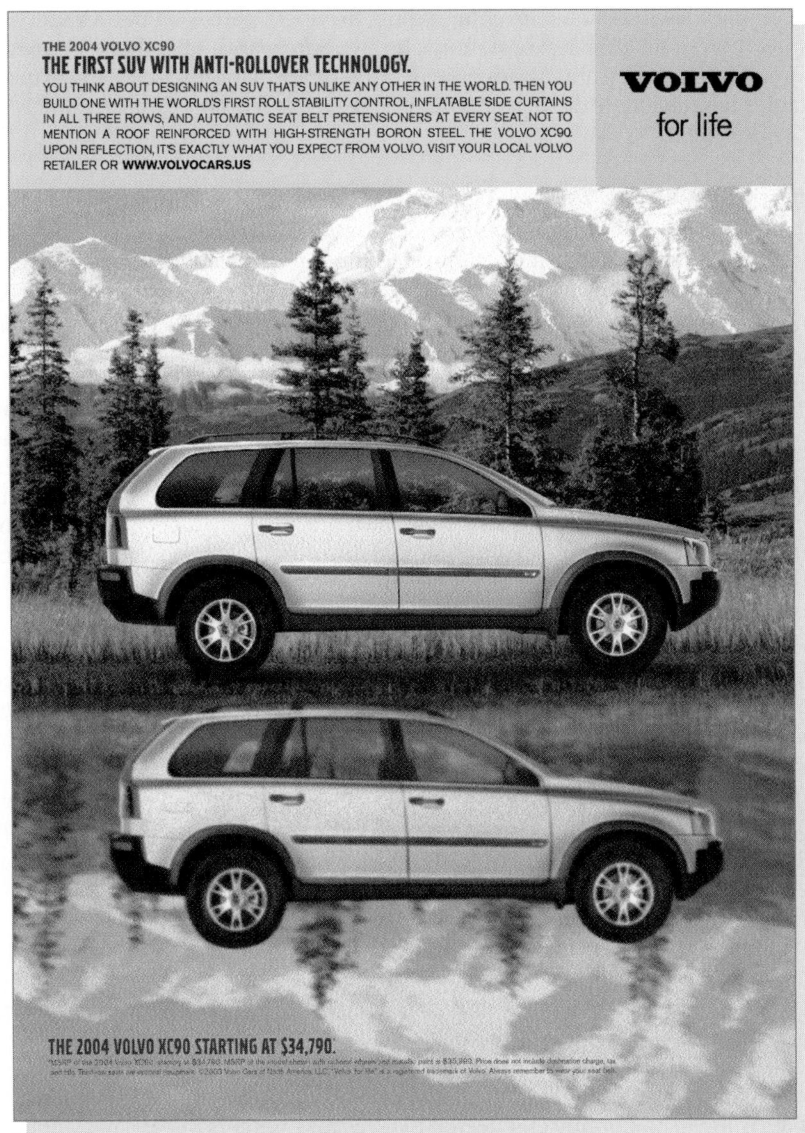

Positioning: "The First SUV with Anti-Rollover Technology." A Volvo ad focuses on the company's central benefit, safety.

safety is a major concern. Volvo, therefore, positions its car as the safest a customer can buy. Companies do best when they choose their target market(s) carefully and prepare tailored marketing programs.

OFFERINGS AND BRANDS Companies address needs by putting forth a value proposition, a set of benefits they offer to customers to satisfy their needs. The intangible value proposition is made physical by an *offering,* which can be a combination of products, services, information, and experiences.

A *brand* is an offering from a known source. A brand name such as McDonald's carries many associations in the minds of people: hamburgers, fun, children, fast food, convenience, and golden arches. These associations make up the brand image. All companies strive to build brand strength—that is, a strong, favorable, and unique brand image.

VALUE AND SATISFACTION The offering will be successful if it delivers value and satisfaction to the target buyer. The buyer chooses between different offerings on the basis of which is perceived to deliver the most value. *Value* reflects the perceived tangible and intangible benefits and costs to customers. Value can be seen as primarily a combination of quality, service, and price (qsp), called the "customer value triad." Value increases with quality and service and decreases with price, although other factors can also play an important role.

Value is a central marketing concept. Marketing can be seen as the identification, creation, communication, delivery, and monitoring of customer value. *Satisfaction* reflects a person's comparative judgments resulting from a product's perceived performance (or outcome) in relation to his or her expectations. If the performance falls short of expectations, the customer is dissatisfied and disappointed. If the performance matches the expectations, the customer is satisfied. If the performance exceeds expectations, the customer is highly satisfied or delighted.

MARKETING CHANNELS To reach a target market, the marketer uses three kinds of marketing channels. *Communication channels* deliver and receive messages from target buyers, and include newspapers, magazines, radio, television, mail, telephone, billboards, posters, fliers, CDs, audiotapes, and the Internet. Beyond these, communications are conveyed by facial expressions and clothing, the look of retail stores, and many other media. Marketers are increasingly adding dialogue channels (e-mail and toll-free numbers) to counterbalance the more normal monologue channels (such as ads).

The marketer uses *distribution channels* to display, sell, or deliver the physical product or service(s) to the buyer or user. They include distributors, wholesalers, retailers, and agents.

The marketer also uses *service channels* to carry out transactions with potential buyers. Service channels include warehouses, transportation companies, banks, and insurance companies that facilitate transactions. Marketers clearly face a design problem in choosing the best mix of communication, distribution, and service channels for their offerings.

SUPPLY CHAIN Whereas marketing channels connect the marketer to the target buyers, the supply chain describes a longer channel stretching from raw materials to components to final products that are carried to final buyers. The supply chain for women's purses starts with hides, and moves through tanning operations, cutting operations, manufacturing, and the marketing channels bringing products to customers. The supply chain represents a value delivery system. Each company captures only a certain percentage of the total value generated by the supply chain. When a company acquires competitors or moves upstream or downstream, its aim is to capture a higher percentage of supply chain value.

COMPETITION Competition includes all the actual and potential rival offerings and substitutes that a buyer might consider. Suppose an automobile company is planning to buy steel for its cars. There are several possible levels of competitors. The car manufacturer can buy steel from U.S. Steel or other integrated steel mills in the United States (e.g., from Bethlehem) or abroad (e.g., from Japan or Korea); or buy steel from a mini-mill such as Nucor at a cost savings; or buy aluminum for certain parts of the car to lighten the car's weight (e.g., from Alcoa); or buy engineered plastics for bumpers instead of steel (e.g., from GE Plastics). Clearly, U.S. Steel would be thinking too narrowly of competition if it thought only of other integrated steel companies. In fact, U.S. Steel is more likely to be hurt in the long run by substitute products than by its immediate steel company rivals. It must also consider whether to make substitute materials or stick only to those applications where steel offers superior performance.

MARKETING ENVIRONMENT Competition represents only one force in the environment in which the marketer operates. The marketing environment consists of the task environment and the broad environment.

The *task environment* includes the immediate actors involved in producing, distributing, and promoting the offering. The main actors are the company, suppliers, distributors, dealers, and the target customers. Included in the supplier group are material suppliers and service suppliers such as marketing research agencies, advertising agencies, banking and insurance companies, transportation companies, and telecommunications companies. Included with distributors and dealers are agents, brokers, manufacturer representatives, and others who facilitate finding and selling to customers.

The *broad environment* consists of six components: demographic environment, economic environment, physical environment, technological environment, political-legal environment, and social-cultural environment. These environments contain forces that can have a major impact on the actors in the task environment. Market actors must pay close attention to the trends and developments in these environments and make timely adjustments to their marketing strategies.

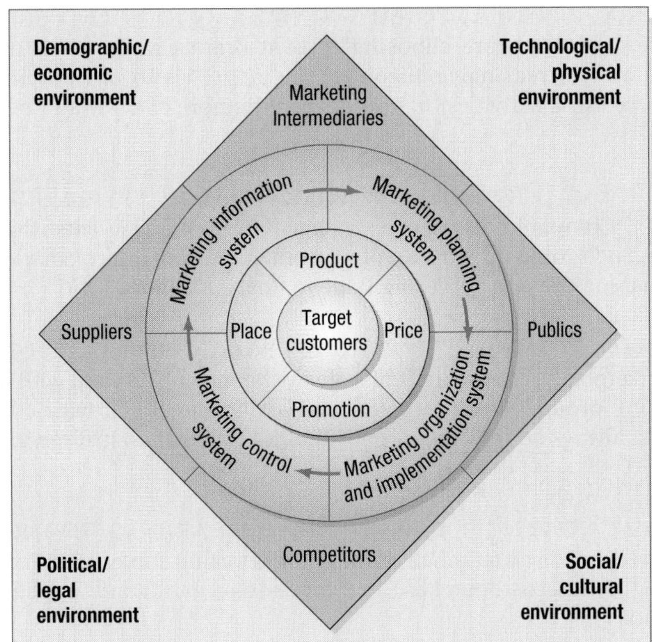

FIG. 1.6

Factors Influencing Company Marketing Strategy

MARKETING PLANNING In practice, there is a logical process that marketing follows. The marketing planning process consists of analyzing marketing opportunities; selecting target markets; designing marketing strategies; developing marketing programs; and managing the marketing effort. Figure 1.6 presents a grand summary of the marketing process and the forces shaping the company's marketing strategy.

Shifts in Marketing Management

A number of important trends and forces are eliciting a new set of beliefs and practices on the part of business firms. Marketers are fundamentally rethinking their philosophies, concepts, and tools. Here are 14 major shifts in marketing management that smart companies have been making in the twenty-first century. These major themes will be examined throughout this book to help marketers and companies sail safely through the rough but promising waters ahead. Successful companies will be those who can keep their marketing changing with the changes in their marketplace—and marketspace.

FROM MARKETING DOES THE MARKETING TO EVERYONE DOES THE MARKETING Companies generally establish a marketing department to be responsible for creating and delivering customer value. But as the late David Packard of Hewlett-Packard observed, "Marketing is far too important to leave to the marketing department." Companies now know that marketing is not done only by marketing, sales, and customer support personnel; every employee has an impact on the customer and must see the customer as the source of the company's prosperity. Consequently, companies are beginning to emphasize interdepartmental teamwork to manage key processes. More emphasis is also being placed on the smooth management of core business processes, such as new-product realization, customer acquisition and retention, and order fulfillment.

FROM ORGANIZING BY PRODUCT UNITS TO ORGANIZING BY CUSTOMER SEGMENTS Some companies are now switching from being solely product-centered with product managers and product divisions to manage them to being more customer-segment-centered. In late 1999, Royal Bank of Canada reorganized itself around customer segments, not products or territories. By studying these segments carefully, Royal Bank developed a number of new profit-generating products and services such as first mortgages and estate settlements. As a result, revenues increased by $1 billion over the next three years and the stock price rose 100 percent in the midst of a stagnant bear market.[34]

FROM MAKING EVERYTHING TO BUYING MORE GOODS AND SERVICES FROM OUTSIDE More companies are choosing to own brands rather than physical assets. Companies are also increasingly subcontracting activities to outsourcing firms. Their maxim: Outsource those activities that others can do more cheaply and better, but retain core activities.

FROM USING MANY SUPPLIERS TO WORKING WITH FEWER SUPPLIERS IN A "PARTNERSHIP" Companies are deepening partnering arrangements with key suppliers and distributors. Such companies have shifted from thinking of intermediaries as customers to treating them as partners in delivering value to final customers.

FROM RELYING ON OLD MARKET POSITIONS TO UNCOVERING NEW ONES In highly competitive marketplaces, companies must always be moving forward with marketing programs, innovating products and services, and staying in touch with customer needs. Companies must always be seeking new advantages rather than just relying on their past strengths.

FROM EMPHASIZING TANGIBLE ASSETS TO EMPHASIZING INTANGIBLE ASSETS Companies are recognizing that much of their market value comes from intangible assets, particularly their brands, customer base, employees, distributor and supplier relations, and intellectual capital.

FROM BUILDING BRANDS THROUGH ADVERTISING TO BUILDING BRANDS THROUGH PERFORMANCE AND INTEGRATED COMMUNICATIONS Marketers are moving from an overreliance on one communication tool such as advertising or sales force to blending several tools to deliver a consistent brand image to customers at every brand contact.

FROM ATTRACTING CUSTOMERS THROUGH STORES AND SALESPEOPLE TO MAKING PRODUCTS AVAILABLE ONLINE Consumers can access pictures of products, read the specs, shop among online vendors for the best prices and terms, and click to order and pay. Business-to-business purchasing is growing fast on the Internet. Personal selling can increasingly be conducted electronically, with buyer and seller seeing each other on their computer screens in real time.

FROM SELLING TO EVERYONE TO TRYING TO BE THE BEST FIRM SERVING WELL-DEFINED TARGET MARKETS Target marketing is being facilitated by the proliferation of special-interest magazines, TV channels, and Internet newsgroups. Companies are also making substantial investments in information systems as the key to lowering costs and gaining a competitive edge. They are assembling information about individual customers' purchases, preferences, demographics, and profitability.

FROM FOCUSING ON PROFITABLE TRANSACTIONS TO FOCUSING ON CUSTOMER LIFETIME VALUE Companies normally would aim to make a profit on each transaction. Now companies are focusing on their most profitable customers, products, and channels. They estimate individual customer lifetime value and design market offerings and prices to make a profit over the customer's lifetime. Companies now are placing much more emphasis on customer retention. Attracting a new customer may cost five times as much as doing a good job to retain existing customers.

FROM A FOCUS ON GAINING MARKET SHARE TO A FOCUS ON BUILDING CUSTOMER SHARE A bank aims to increase its share of the customer's wallet; the supermarket aims to capture a larger share of the customer's "stomach." Companies build customer share by offering a larger variety of goods to existing customers. They train their employees in cross-selling and up-selling.

FROM BEING LOCAL TO BEING "GLOCAL"—BOTH GLOBAL AND LOCAL Firms are adopting a combination of centralization and decentralization to better balance local adaptation and global standardization. The goal is to encourage more initiative and "intrepreneurship" at the local level, while preserving the necessary global guidelines and standards.[35]

FROM FOCUSING ON THE FINANCIAL SCORECARD TO FOCUSING ON THE MARKETING SCORECARD Top management is going beyond sales revenue alone to examine the marketing scorecard to interpret what is happening to market share, customer loss rate, customer satisfaction, product quality, and other measures. They know that changes in marketing indicators predict changes in financial results.

FROM FOCUSING ON SHAREHOLDERS TO FOCUSING ON STAKEHOLDERS Top management respects the importance of creating co-prosperity among all business partners and customers. These managers develop policies and strategies to balance the returns to all the key stakeholders.

Marketing Management Tasks

These core concepts and others provide the input for a set of tasks that make up successful marketing management. We'll use the following situation to illustrate these tasks in the context of the plan of the book.

> Zeus, Inc. (name disguised), operates in several industries, including chemicals, cameras, and film. The company is organized into SBUs. Corporate management is considering what to do with its Atlas camera division. At present, Atlas produces a range of 35 mm and digital cameras. The market for cameras is intensely competitive. Although Zeus has a sizable market share and is producing much revenue for the company, the 35 mm market itself is growing very slowly and its market share is slipping. In the faster-growing digital camera segment, Zeus is facing strong competition and has been slow to gain sales. Zeus's corporate management wants Atlas's marketing group to produce a strong turnaround plan for the division. Marketing management has to come up with a convincing marketing plan, sell corporate management on the plan, and then implement and control it.

DEVELOPING MARKETING STRATEGIES AND PLANS The first task facing Atlas is to identify its potential long-run opportunities given its market experience and core competencies (see Chapter 2). Atlas can design its cameras with better features. It can also consider making a line of video cameras, or it can use its core competency in optics to design a line of binoculars and telescopes. Whichever direction it chooses, it must develop concrete marketing plans that specify the marketing strategy and tactics going forward.

CAPTURING MARKETING INSIGHTS To understand what is happening inside and outside the company, Atlas needs a reliable marketing information system; it will want to closely monitor its marketing environment. Atlas's microenvironment consists of all the players who affect the company's ability to produce and sell cameras—suppliers, marketing intermediaries, customers, and competitors. Its macroenvironment consists of demographic, economic, physical, technological, political-legal, and social-cultural forces that affect sales and profits (see Chapter 3).

Atlas also needs a dependable marketing research system. Marketing research is an indispensable tool for assessing buyer wants and behavior and actual and potential market size. An important part of gathering environmental information includes measuring market potential and forecasting future demand. To transform marketing strategy into marketing programs, marketing managers must make basic decisions on marketing expenditures, marketing activities, and marketing allocation.[36] How many dollars should support Atlas's two or three camera lines? Direct versus distributor sales? Direct-mail advertising versus trade-magazine advertising? East Coast markets versus West Coast markets? To make these allocations, marketing managers may use sales-response functions that show how sales and profits would be affected by the amount of money spent in each application (see Chapter 4).

CONNECTING WITH CUSTOMERS Atlas must consider how to best create value for its chosen target markets and develop strong, profitable, long-term relationships with customers (see Chapter 5). To do so, Atlas needs to understand consumer markets (see Chapter 6). How many households plan to buy cameras? Who buys and why do they buy? What are they looking for in the way of features and prices? Where do they shop? What are their images of different brands? How does the digital segment differ from the 35 mm segment? Atlas also sells cameras to business markets, including large corporations, professional firms, retailers, and government agencies (see Chapter 7). Purchasing agents or buying committees make the decisions. Atlas needs to gain a full understanding of how organizational buyers buy. It needs a sales force that is well trained in presenting product benefits.

Atlas will not want to market to all possible customers. Modern marketing practice calls for dividing the market into major market segments, evaluating each segment, and targeting those market segments that the company can best serve (see Chapter 8).

BUILDING STRONG BRANDS Atlas must understand the strengths and weaknesses of the Zeus brand with customers (see Chapter 9). Is it so strongly associated with certain technologies that it could not be used to brand new products in related categories? Is its 35 mm film heritage a detriment in the digital camera market? Suppose Atlas decides to focus on the consumer market and develop a positioning strategy (see Chapter 10). Should Atlas position its cameras as the "Cadillac" brand, offering superior cameras at a premium price with excellent service and strong advertising? Should it build a simple, low-priced camera aimed at more price-conscious consumers? Should it develop a medium-quality, medium-priced camera? After launch the product's strategy will need modification at the different stages in the product life cycle: introduction, growth, maturity, and decline. Furthermore, strategy choice will depend on whether the firm is a market leader, challenger, follower, or nicher. Atlas must also pay close attention to competitors (see Chapter 11), anticipating its competitors' moves and knowing how to react quickly and decisively. It may want to initiate some surprise moves, in which case it needs to anticipate how its competitors will respond.

SHAPING THE MARKET OFFERINGS At the heart of the marketing program is the product—the firm's tangible offering to the market, which includes the product quality, design, features, and packaging (see Chapter 12). As part of its product offering, Atlas may provide various services, such as leasing, delivery, repair, and training (see Chapter 13). Such support services can provide a competitive advantage in the global marketplace.

A critical marketing decision relates to price (see Chapter 14). Atlas has to decide on wholesale and retail prices, discounts, allowances, and credit terms. Its price should be commensurate with the offer's perceived value; otherwise, buyers will turn to competitors' products.

DELIVERING VALUE Atlas must also determine how to properly deliver the value embodied by these products and services to the target market. Channel activities include the various activities the company undertakes to make the product accessible and available to target customers (see Chapter 15). Atlas must identify, recruit, and link various marketing facilitators to supply its products and services efficiently to the target market. It must understand the various types of retailers, wholesalers, and physical-distribution firms and how they make their decisions (see Chapter 16).

COMMUNICATING VALUE Atlas must also adequately communicate the value embodied by its products and services to the target market. Marketing communications activities are the means by which firms attempt to inform, persuade, and remind consumers—directly or indirectly—about the brands they sell. Atlas has to develop an integrated marketing communication program that maximizes the individual and collective contribution of all communication activities (see Chapter 17). Atlas has to set up mass communication programs consisting of advertising, sales promotion, events, and public relations (see Chapter 18). It also has to set up more personal communications in the form of direct and interactive marketing and must also hire, train, and motivate salespeople (see Chapter 19).

CREATING LONG-TERM GROWTH Atlas must also take a long-term view of its products and brands and how its profits should be grown. Based on its product positioning, it must initiate new-product development, testing, and launching (see Chapter 20). The strategy also will have to take into account changing global opportunities and challenges (see Chapter 21).

Finally, Atlas must organize its marketing resources and implement and control the marketing plan. The company must build a marketing organization that is capable of implementing the marketing plan (see Chapter 22). Because of surprises and disappointments that can occur as marketing plans are implemented, Atlas will need feedback and control.[37] Marketing evaluation and control processes are necessary to understand the efficiency and effectiveness of marketing activities and how both could be improved.

SUMMARY :::

1. From a managerial point of view, marketing is the process of planning and executing the conception, pricing, promotion, and distribution of ideas, goods, and services to create exchanges that satisfy individual and organizational goals. Marketing management is the art and science of choosing target markets and getting, keeping, and growing customers through creating, delivering, and communicating superior customer value.
2. Marketers are skilled at managing demand: They seek to influence the level, timing, and composition of demand. Marketers are involved in marketing many types of entities: goods, services, events, experiences, persons, places, properties, organizations, information, and ideas. They also operate in four different marketplaces: consumer, business, global, and nonprofit.
3. Businesses today face a number of challenges and opportunities, including globalization, the effects of advances in technology, and deregulation. They have responded by changing the way they conduct marketing in very fundamental ways.
4. There are five competing concepts under which organizations can choose to conduct their business: the production concept, the product concept, the selling concept, the marketing concept, and the holistic marketing concept. The first three are of limited use today.
5. The holistic marketing concept is based on the development, design, and implementation of marketing programs, processes, and activities that recognize their breadth and interdependencies. Holistic marketing recognizes that "everything matters" with marketing and that a broad, integrated perspective is often necessary. Four components of holistic marketing are relationship marketing, integrated marketing, internal marketing, and socially responsible marketing.
6. Marketing management has experienced a number of shifts in recent years as companies seek marketing excellence.
7. The set of tasks necessary for successful marketing management includes developing marketing strategies and plans, connecting with customers, building strong brands, shaping the market offerings, delivering and communicating value, capturing marketing insights and performance, and creating successful long-term growth.

APPLICATIONS :::

Marketing Debate Does Marketing Create or Satisfy Needs?

Marketing has often been defined in terms of satisfying customers' needs and wants. Critics, however, maintain that marketing goes beyond that and creates needs and wants that did not exist before. According to these critics, marketers encourage consumers to spend more money than they should on goods and services they really do not need.

Take a position: Marketing shapes consumer needs and wants versus Marketing merely reflects the needs and wants of consumers.

Marketing Discussion

Consider the broad shifts in marketing. Are there any themes that emerge in these shifts? Can they be related to the major societal forces? Which force has contributed to which shift?

IN THIS CHAPTER, WE WILL ADDRESS THE FOLLOWING QUESTIONS:

1. How does marketing affect customer value?
2. How is strategic planning carried out at different levels of the organization?
3. What does a marketing plan include?

CHAPTER 2 ::: DEVELOPING MARKETING STRATEGIES AND PLANS

two

A key ingredient of the marketing management process is insightful, creative marketing strategies and plans that can guide marketing activities. Developing the right marketing strategy over time requires a blend of discipline and flexibility. Firms must stick to a strategy but must also find new ways to constantly improve it.[1] Marketing strategy also requires a clear understanding of how marketing works.[2]

Walk into a trendy Soho boutique in New York City and you might see high-fashion T-shirts selling for $250. Go into an H&M clothing store and you can see a version of the same style for $25. Founded 55 years ago as a provincial Swedish clothing company, H&M (Hennes and Mauritz) has morphed into a clothing colossus with 950 stores in 19 countries and an ambitious plan to expand by 100 stores a year. The reason H&M has reached this point while so many other stores—such as once-hot Italian retailer Benetton—have floundered is that the company has a clear mission and the creative marketing strategies and concrete plans with which to carry it out. "Our business concept is to give the customer unbeatable value by offering fashion and quality at the best price," is the H&M mission as expressed on the company's Web site. Nothing could sound simpler. Yet, fulfilling that mission requires a well-coordinated set of marketing activities. For instance, it takes H&M an average of three months to go from a designer's idea to a product on a store shelf, and that "time to market" falls >>>

An H&M store in Brussels, Belgium.

to three weeks for "high-fashion" products. H&M is able to put products out quickly and inexpensively by:

- *having few middlemen and owning no factories*
- *buying large volumes*
- *having extensive experience in the clothing industry*
- *having a great knowledge of which goods should be bought from which markets*
- *having efficient distribution systems*
- *being cost-conscious at every stage*

This chapter begins by examining some of the strategic marketing implications involved in creating customer value. It then provides several perspectives on planning and describes how to draw up a formal marketing plan.

::: Marketing and Customer Value

Marketing involves satisfying consumers' needs and wants. The task of any business is to deliver customer value at a profit. In a hypercompetitive economy with increasingly rational buyers faced with abundant choices, a company can win only by fine-tuning the value delivery process and choosing, providing, and communicating superior value.

The Value Delivery Process

The traditional view of marketing is that the firm makes something and then sells it (Figure 2.1[a]). In this view, marketing takes place in the second half of the process. The company knows what to make and the market will buy enough units to produce profits. Companies that subscribe to this view have the best chance of succeeding in economies marked by

(a) Traditional Physical Process Sequence

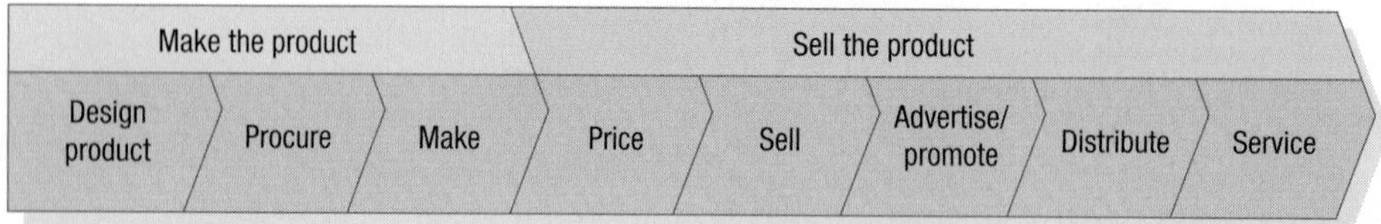

(b) Value Creation and Delivery Sequence

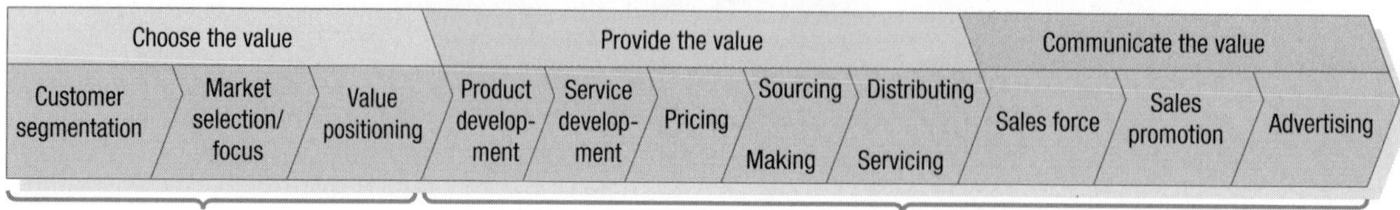

FIG. 2.1 | Two Views of the Value Delivery Process

Source: Michael J. Lanning and Edward G. Michaels, "A Business Is a Value Delivery System," McKinsey Staff Paper no. 41, June 1988. Copyright © McKinsey & Co., Inc.

goods shortages where consumers are not fussy about quality, features, or style—for example, with basic staple goods in developing markets.

The traditional view of the business process, however, will not work in economies where people face abundant choices. There, the "mass market" is actually splintering into numerous micromarkets, each with its own wants, perceptions, preferences, and buying criteria. The smart competitor must design and deliver offerings for well-defined target markets. This belief is at the core of the new view of business processes, which places marketing at the beginning of planning. You can see this in action at your local mall. In the struggle to grow, retail chains are creating spinoffs that appeal to ever-smaller micromarkets:

SPINOFFS

Gymboree, a 530-store chain, sells children's clothing to upscale parents. Since there are not enough parents making more than $65,000 per year to support even more stores, Gymboree has created Janie and Jack, a chain selling upscale baby gifts. Hot Topic, a chain that sells rock-band-inspired clothes for teens, recently launched Torrid to give plus-size teens the same fashion options. Women's clothing store Ann Taylor spawned Ann Taylor Loft, with lower-priced fashions, and Chico's, a chain aimed at women in their forties and fifties, begat Pazo, for slightly younger working women.[3]

Instead of emphasizing making and selling, these companies see themselves as part of a value delivery process.

Figure 2.1(b) illustrates the value creation and delivery sequence. The process consists of three parts. The first phase, *choosing the value,* represents the "homework" marketing must do before any product exists. The marketing staff must segment the market, select the appropriate market target, and develop the offering's value positioning. The formula "segmentation, targeting, positioning (STP)" is the essence of strategic marketing. Once the business unit has chosen the value, the second phase is *providing the value.* Marketing must determine specific product features, prices, and distribution. The task in the third phase is *communicating the value* by utilizing the sales force, sales promotion, advertising, and other communication tools to announce and promote the product. Each of these value phases has cost implications.

NIKE

Critics of Nike often complain that its shoes cost almost nothing to make yet cost the consumer so much. True, the raw materials and manufacturing costs involved in the making of a sneaker are relatively cheap, but marketing the product to the consumer is expensive. Materials, labor, shipping, equipment, import duties, and suppliers' costs generally total less than $25 a pair. Compensating its sales team, its distributors, its administration, and its endorsers, as well as paying for advertising and R&D, adds $15 or so to the total. Nike sells its product to retailers to make a profit of $7. The retailer therefore pays roughly $47 to put a pair of Nikes on the shelf. When the retailer's overhead (typically $30 covering personnel, lease, and equipment) is factored in along with a $10 profit, the shoe costs the consumer over $80.

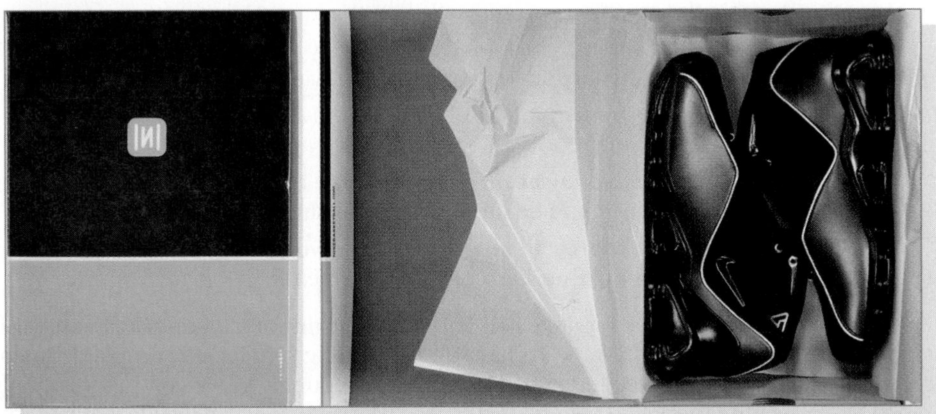

A pair of Nike shoes.

As Figure 2.1(b) shows, the value delivery process begins before there is a product and continues while it is being developed and after it becomes available. The Japanese have further refined this view with the following concepts:

- ***Zero customer feedback time.*** Customer feedback should be collected continuously after purchase to learn how to improve the product and its marketing.
- ***Zero product improvement time.*** The company should evaluate all improvement ideas and introduce the most valued and feasible improvements as soon as possible.
- ***Zero purchasing time.*** The company should receive the required parts and supplies continuously through just-in-time arrangements with suppliers. By lowering its inventories, the company can reduce its costs.
- ***Zero setup time.*** The company should be able to manufacture any of its products as soon as they are ordered, without facing high setup time or costs.
- ***Zero defects.*** The products should be of high quality and free of flaws.

Nirmalya Kumar has put forth a "3 Vs" approach to marketing: (1) define the *value segment* or customers (and his/her needs); (2) define the *value proposition;* and (3) define the *value network* that will deliver the promised service.[4] Dartmouth's Frederick Webster views marketing in terms of: (1) *value defining processes* (e.g., market research and company self-analysis), (2) *value developing processes* (e.g., new-product development, sourcing strategy, and vendor selection), and (3) *value delivering processes* (e.g., advertising and managing distribution).[5]

The Value Chain

Michael Porter of Harvard has proposed the **value chain** as a tool for identifying ways to create more customer value (see Figure 2.2).[6] According to this model, every firm is a synthesis of activities performed to design, produce, market, deliver, and support its product. The value chain identifies nine strategically relevant activities that create value and cost in a specific business. These nine value-creating activities consist of five primary activities and four support activities.

The *primary activities* cover the sequence of bringing materials into the business inbound logistics), converting them into final products (operations), shipping out final products (outbound logistics), marketing them (marketing and sales), and servicing them (service). The *support activities*—procurement, technology development, human resource management, and firm infrastructure—are handled in certain specialized departments, as well as elsewhere. Several departments, for example, may do procurement and hiring. The firm's infrastructure covers the costs of general management, planning, finance, accounting, legal, and government affairs.

The firm's task is to examine its costs and performance in each value-creating activity and to look for ways to improve it. The firm should estimate its competitors' costs and performances as *benchmarks* against which to compare its own costs and performance. It should go further and study the "best of class" practices of the world's best companies.[7]

The firm's success depends not only on how well each department performs its work, but also on how well the various departmental activities are coordinated to conduct *core business processes.*[8] These core business processes include:

- ***The market sensing process.*** All the activities involved in gathering market intelligence, disseminating it within the organization, and acting on the information.
- ***The new offering realization process.*** All the activities involved in researching, developing, and launching new high-quality offerings quickly and within budget.
- ***The customer acquisition process.*** All the activities involved in defining target markets and prospecting for new customers.
- ***The customer relationship management process.*** All the activities involved in building deeper understanding, relationships, and offerings to individual customers.
- ***The fulfillment management process.*** All the activities involved in receiving and approving orders, shipping the goods on time, and collecting payment.

Strong companies develop superior capabilities in managing and linking their core business processes. For example, Wal-Mart has superior strength in its stock replenishment process. As Wal-Mart stores sell their goods, sales information flows via computer not only to Wal-Mart's headquarters, but also to Wal-Mart's suppliers, who ship replacement mer-

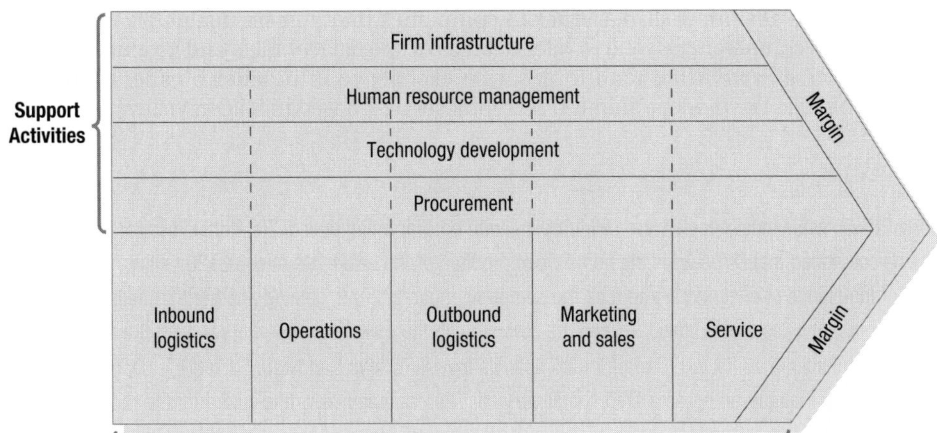

FIG. 2.2

The Generic Value Chain

Source: Reprinted with the permission of The Free Press, an imprint of Simon & Schuster, from Michael E. Porter, *Competitive Advantage. Creating and Sustaining Superior Performance.* Copyright 1985 by Michael E. Porter.

chandise to the stores almost at the rate it moves off the shelf.[9] The idea is to manage flows of goods, not stocks of goods. Wal-Mart has turned over this responsibility to its leading vendors in a system known as vendor-managed inventories VMI).

Strong companies are also reengineering the work flows and building cross-functional teams responsible for each process.[10] At Xerox, a Customer Operations Group links sales, shipping, installation, service, and billing so that these activities flow smoothly into one another. Winning companies are those that excel at managing core business processes through cross-functional teams. AT&T, Polaroid, and Motorola have reorganized their employees into cross-functional teams; cross-functional teams are also found in nonprofit and government organizations as well. Drug store chain Rite Aid is using cross-functional teams to try to push its store from third to first place in the drug store hierarchy. The company has created teams to focus on sales and margin growth, operational excellence, market optimization, continued supply chain improvements, and continued cost control.[11]

To be successful, a firm also needs to look for competitive advantages beyond its own operations, into the value chains of suppliers, distributors, and customers. Many companies today have partnered with specific suppliers and distributors to create a superior **value delivery network** also called a **supply chain**.[12]

BAILEY CONTROLS

An Ohio-headquartered, $300-million-a-year manufacturer of control systems for big factories, Bailey Controls treats some of its suppliers as if they were departments within Bailey. The company recently plugged two of its suppliers directly into its inventory management system. Every week Bailey electronically sends Montreal-based Future Electronics its latest forecasts of the materials it will need for the next six months. Whenever a bin of parts falls below a designated level, a Bailey employee passes a laser scanner over the bin's bar code, alerting Future to send the parts at once. Although arrangements like this shift inventory costs to the suppliers, the suppliers expect those costs to be more than offset by the gain in volume. It is a win–win partnership.

Core Competencies

To carry out its core business processes, a company needs resources—labor power, materials, machines, information, and energy. Traditionally, companies owned and controlled most of the resources that entered their businesses, but this situation is changing. Many companies today outsource less critical resources if they can be obtained at better quality or lower cost. Frequently, outsourced resources include cleaning services, landscaping, and auto fleet management. Kodak even turned over the management of its data processing department to IBM.

The key, then, is to own and nurture the resources and competencies that make up the essence of the business. Nike, for example, does not manufacture its own shoes, because certain Asian manufacturers are more competent in this task; Nike nurtures its superiority in shoe design and shoe merchandising, its two core competencies. We can say that a **core competency** has three characteristics: (1) It is a source of competitive advantage in that it makes a significant contribution to perceived customer benefits, (2) it has applications in a wide variety of markets, and (3) it is difficult for competitors to imitate.[13]

Competitive advantage also accrues to companies that possess distinctive capabilities. Whereas core competencies tend to refer to areas of special technical and production expertise, *distinctive capabilities* tend to describe excellence in broader business processes. Consider Netflix, the pioneer online DVD rental service, based in Silicon Valley.[14]

NETFLIX

Back in 1997, while most people were still fumbling with programming their VCRs, Netflix founder Reed Hastings became convinced that DVDs were the home video medium of the future. He raised $120 million, attracted hundreds of thousands of customers, and took the company public in 2002, gaining another $90 million. Netflix has distinctive capabilities that promise to keep the company on top even as competitors like Blockbuster and Wal-Mart try to muscle in on its turf. One of the company's investors says that Netflix is really a sophisticated software company masquerading as a DVD rental service. The company has fine-tuned its file recommendation software, merchandising, and inventory control system to such a degree that new orders are automatically generated even as the old orders are returned. In addition, all 12 of the company's DVD distribution centers can be polled before a customer is told that the movie he or she wants next is out of stock.

George Day sees market-driven organizations as excelling in three distinctive capabilities: market sensing, customer linking, and channel bonding.[15]

Competitive advantage ultimately derives from how well the company has fitted its core competencies and distinctive capabilities into tightly interlocking "activity systems." Competitors find it hard to imitate companies such as Southwest Airlines, Dell, or IKEA because they are unable to copy their activity systems.

A Holistic Marketing Orientation and Customer Value

A holistic marketing orientation can also provide insight into the process of capturing customer value. One conception of holistic marketing views it as "integrating the value exploration, value creation, and value delivery activities with the purpose of building long-term, mutually satisfying relationships and co-prosperity among key stakeholders."[16] According to this view, holistic marketers succeed by managing a superior value chain that delivers a high level of product quality, service, and speed. Holistic marketers achieve profitable growth by expanding customer share, building customer loyalty, and capturing customer lifetime value. Figure 2.3, a holistic marketing framework, shows how the interaction between relevant actors (customers, company, and collaborators) and value-based activities (value exploration, value creation, and value delivery) helps to create, maintain, and renew customer value.

FIG. 2.3

A Holistic Marketing Framework

Source: P. Kotler, D. C. Jain, and S. Maesincee, "Formulating a Market Renewal Strategy," in *Marketing Moves* (Part 1), Fig. 1-1 (Boston: Harvard Business School Press, 2002), p. 29.

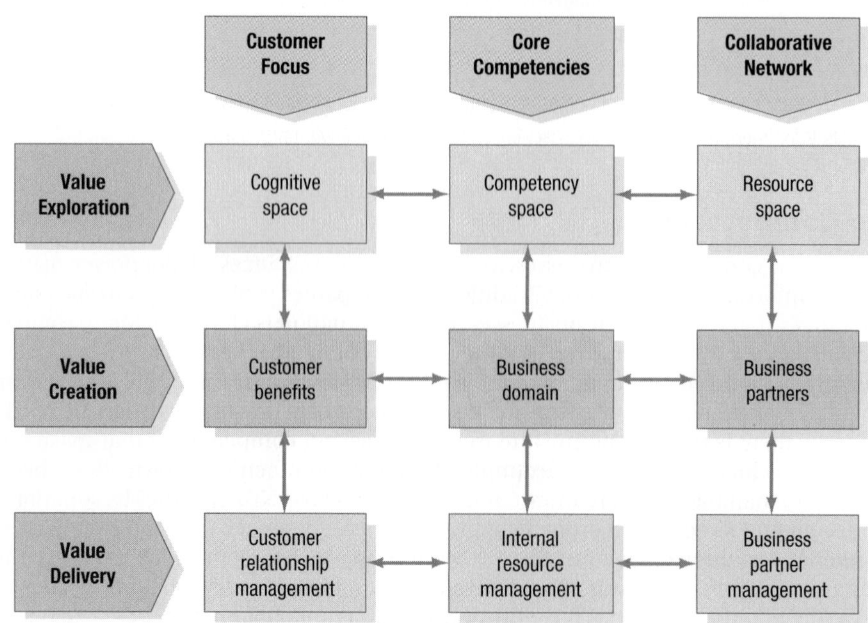

The holistic marketing framework is designed to address three key management questions:

1. ***Value exploration*** – How can a company identify new value opportunities?
2. ***Value creation*** – How can a company efficiently create more promising new value offerings?
3. ***Value delivery*** – How can a company use its capabilities and infrastructure to deliver the new value offerings more efficiently?

VALUE EXPLORATION Because value flows within and across markets that are themselves dynamic and competitive, companies need a well-defined strategy for value exploration. Developing such a strategy requires an understanding of the relationships and interactions among three spaces: (1) the customer's cognitive space; (2) the company's competence space; and (3) the collaborator's resource space. The customer's *cognitive space* reflects existing and latent needs and includes dimensions such as the need for participation, stability, freedom, and change.[17] The company's *competency space* can be described in terms of breadth—broad versus focused scope of business; and depth—physical versus knowledge-based capabilities. The collaborator's *resource space* involves horizontal partnerships, where companies choose partners based on their ability to exploit related market opportunities, and vertical partnerships, where companies choose partners based on their ability to serve their value creation.

VALUE CREATION To exploit a value opportunity, the company needs value-creation skills. Marketers need to: identify new customer benefits from the customer's view; utilize core competencies from its business domain; and select and manage business partners from its collaborative networks. To craft new customer benefits, marketers must understand what the customer thinks about, wants, does, and worries about. Marketers must also observe who customers admire, who they interact with, and who influences them.

Business realignment may be necessary to maximize core competencies. It involves three steps: (1) (re)defining the business concept (the "big idea"); (2) (re)shaping the business scope (the lines of business); and (3) (re)positioning the company's brand identity (how customers should see the company). This is what Kodak is doing as sales from its traditional core businesses of film, camera, paper, and photo development have sagged, and consumers have abandoned film cameras for increasingly cheaper digital equipment, products, and services. On September 25, 2003, Chairman and Chief Executive Daniel A. Carp stood in front of shareholders and unveiled the company's new strategy. He announced that Kodak was "determined to win in these new digital markets." In order to do that the company plans to expand its line of digital cameras, printers, and other equipment for consumers, who are now using the Internet to transmit and display their digital images. Kodak also is stepping up efforts to deliver on-demand, color printing products for business and wants to increase its market share of the lucrative medical images and information services businesses.[18]

VALUE DELIVERY Delivering value often means substantial investment in infrastructure and capabilities. The company must become proficient at customer relationship management, internal resource management, and business partnership management. *Customer relationship management* allows the company to discover who its customers are, how they behave, and what they need or want. It also enables the company to respond appropriately, coherently, and quickly to different customer opportunities. To respond effectively, the company requires *internal resource management* to integrate major business processes (e.g., order processing, general ledger, payroll, and production) within a single family of software modules. Finally, *business partnership management* allows the company to handle complex relationships with its trading partners to source, process, and deliver products.

The Central Role of Strategic Planning

Successful marketing thus requires companies to have capabilities such as understanding customer value, creating customer value, delivering customer value, capturing customer value, and sustaining customer value. "Marketing Insight: Views on Marketing from Chief Executive Officers" addresses some important senior management priorities in improving marketing. Only a handful of companies stand out as master marketers: Procter & Gamble, Southwest Airlines, Nike, Disney, Nordstrom, Wal-Mart, McDonald's, Marriott Hotels, and several Japanese (Sony, Toyota, Canon) and European (IKEA, Club Med, Bang & Olufsen,

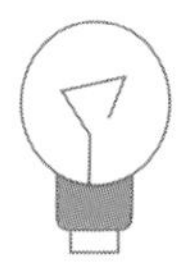

MARKETING INSIGHT | VIEWS ON MARKETING FROM CHIEF EXECUTIVE OFFICERS

Marketing faces a number of challenges in the twenty-first century. Based on an extensive 2002 research study, McKinsey identified three main challenges as reflected by differences in opinion between chief executive officers (CEOs) and their most senior marketing executives or chief marketing officers (CMOs).

- ***Doing more with less.*** CEOs need and expect all areas of their organizations to be more efficient; CMOs indicate that they anticipate that their budgets will grow.
- ***Driving new business development.*** CEOs want marketing to play a more active role in driving new business development—not just new products but also new markets, channels, lines of business; CMOs cited new-product development as their primary concern.
- ***Becoming a full business partner.*** CEOs look for marketing to become a more central business partner that helps to drive profits; CMOs are unsure that their groups have the skills to do so.

McKinsey suggests that bridging these gaps will require changes in spending, organization skills, and culture for many marketers. To accommodate the pressure to simultaneously grow revenues while also reducing marketing costs as a percentage of sales, they offer three recommendations:

1. Link spending priorities to profit potential, for example, as measured by size and anticipated growth rate of current customers—not historical performance;
2. Focus spending on brand drivers (features and benefits truly important to customers), not antes (features and benefits that a brand needs to stay in the game); and
3. Deepen insights on how customers get product information and make buying decisions.

Based on research on companies that successfully develop big ideas, McKinsey identifies three characteristics that help to position marketers as business development leaders:

1. Force the widest view when defining their business, assets, and competencies;
2. Combine multiple perspectives, for example, using attitudinal and need profiles as well as behavior-based segments—to identify market opportunities or sweet spots; and
3. Focus idea generation through a combination of marketing insight and business analysis—but identify profitable unmet needs before they brainstorm creative solutions.

Finally, McKinsey offers two recommendations to overcome CEOs' concerns about the role and performance of marketing.

1. Marketers must test and develop programs more quickly as they enhance planning processes and research approaches; and
2. Marketers must more effectively evaluate the performance and profit impact of investments in the expanding marketing arena (e.g., CRM technology, sponsorships, Internet marketing, and word of mouth).

Source: David Court, Tom French, and Gary Singer, "How the CEO Sees Marketing," *Advertising Age,* March 3, 2003, p. 28.

Electrolux, Nokia, Lego, Tesco) companies. These companies focus on the customer and are organized to respond effectively to changing customer needs. They all have well-staffed marketing departments, and all their other departments—manufacturing, finance, research and development, personnel, purchasing—also accept the concept that the customer is king. (See "Marketing Insight: Keys to Long-Term Market Leadership.")

Creating, providing, and communicating value requires many different marketing activities. To ensure that the proper activities are selected and executed, strategic planning is paramount. Strategic planning calls for action in three key areas: The first is managing a company's businesses as an investment portfolio. The second involves assessing each business's strength by considering the market's growth rate and the company's position and fit in that market. The third is establishing a strategy. For each business, the company must develop a game plan for achieving its long-run objectives.

Marketing plays a critical role in this process. At Samsung Electronics America, strategic marketing could be considered a religion. When Samsung executives, engineers, marketers, and designers consider new products, they must answer one central question: "Is it wow?" If "wow" is the company mantra, then the high priest of "wow" is Peter Weedfald, the company's vice president of strategic marketing. His realm includes marketing, advertising, customer and partner relations, research, the consumer information center, and B2B and B2C commerce. He is responsible for crafting marketing strategies that reach across five different divisions: consumer electronics, information technology, telecom, semiconductors, and home appliances. Unlike many other companies, such as Sony, in which each division has its own marketing strategy, Samsung unifies strategy for all five divisions. "In most companies," says Weedfald, "there is a vice president of CRM [customer relationship management]

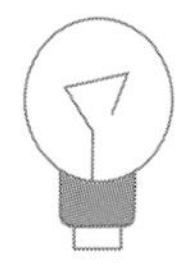

MARKETING INSIGHT | KEYS TO LONG-TERM MARKET LEADERSHIP

The question of what accounts for the success of long-lasting, successful companies was addressed in a six-year study by Collins and Porras called *Built to Last.* The Stanford researchers identified two companies in each of 18 industries, one that they called a "visionary company" and one that they called a "comparison company." The visionary companies were acknowledged as the industry leaders and widely admired; they set ambitious goals, communicated them to their employees, and embraced a high purpose beyond making money. They also outperformed the comparison companies by a wide margin. The visionary companies included General Electric, Hewlett-Packard, and Boeing; the corresponding comparison companies were Westinghouse, Texas Instruments, and McDonnell Douglas.

The authors found three commonalities among the 18 market leaders. First, the visionary companies each held a distinctive set of values from which they did not deviate. Thus, IBM has held to the principles of respect for the individual, customer satisfaction, and continuous quality improvement throughout its history; and Johnson & Johnson holds to the principle that its first responsibility is to its customers, its second to its employees, its third to its community, and its fourth to its stockholders. The second commonality is that visionary companies express their purpose in enlightened terms. Xerox wants to improve "office productivity" and Monsanto wants to "help end hunger in the world." According to Collins and Porras, a company's core purpose should not be confused with specific business goals or strategies and should not be simply a description of a company's product line. The third commonality is that visionary companies have developed a vision of their future and act to implement it. IBM worked at establishing leadership as a "network-centric" company and not simply as a computer manufacturer.

In his next book, *Good to Great,* Collins provided additional insight into enduring leadership. He defined a "good-to-great" transition as a 10-year fallow period followed by 15 years of increased profits. Examining every company that ever made the *Fortune* 500—approximately 1,400—he found 11 that met the criteria: Abbott, Circuit City, Fannie Mae, Gillette, Kimberly-Clark, Kroger, Nucor, Philip Morris, Pitney Bowes, Walgreen's, and Wells Fargo. Contrasting these 11 to the appropriate comparison companies again led to some clear conclusions. While the companies that achieved greatness were all in different industries, he found that making the transition from good to great didn't require a high-profile outside CEO, cutting-edge technology, or even a fine-tuned business strategy per se. Rather, what was found to be the key was a corporate culture that identified and promoted disciplined people to think and act in a disciplined manner. Leaders with a blend of personal humility and professional integrity were the most effective, and good-to-great companies were driven by core values and purpose that went beyond simply making money.

Sources: James C. Collins and Jerry I. Porras, *Built to Last: Successful Habits of Visionary Companies* (New York: HarperBusiness, 1994); F. G. Rodgers and Robert L. Shook, *The IBM Way: Insights into the World's Most Successful Marketing Organization* (New York: Harper and Row, 1986); James C. Collins, *Good to Great: Why Some Companies Make the Leap . . . and Others Don't* (New York: HarperCollins, 2001).

that doesn't even talk to the person in charge of TV advertising. . . . We're threaded holistically from global marketing in Korea to the last three feet of the sale." That last three feet is where the "wow" needs to kick in—when the consumer is still an arm's length away from the product, either literally, in the store, or online.[19]

To understand marketing management, we must understand strategic planning. Most large companies consist of four organizational levels: the corporate level, the division level, the business unit level, and the product level. Corporate headquarters is responsible for designing a corporate strategic plan to guide the whole enterprise; it makes decisions on the amount of resources to allocate to each division, as well as on which businesses to start or eliminate. Each division establishes a plan covering the allocation of funds to each business unit within the division. Each business unit develops a strategic plan to carry that business unit into a profitable future. Finally, each product level (product line, brand) within a business unit develops a marketing plan for achieving its objectives in its product market.

The **marketing plan** is the central instrument for directing and coordinating the marketing effort. The marketing plan operates at two levels: strategic and tactical. The **strategic marketing plan** lays out the target markets and the value proposition that will be offered, based on an analysis of the best market opportunities. The **tactical marketing plan** specifies the marketing tactics, including product features, promotion, merchandising, pricing, sales channels, and service.

Today, teams develop the marketing plan with inputs and sign-offs from every important function. These plans are then implemented at the appropriate levels of the organization. Results are monitored, and necessary corrective action taken. The complete planning, implementation, and control cycle is shown in Figure 2.4. We next consider planning at each of these four levels of the organization.

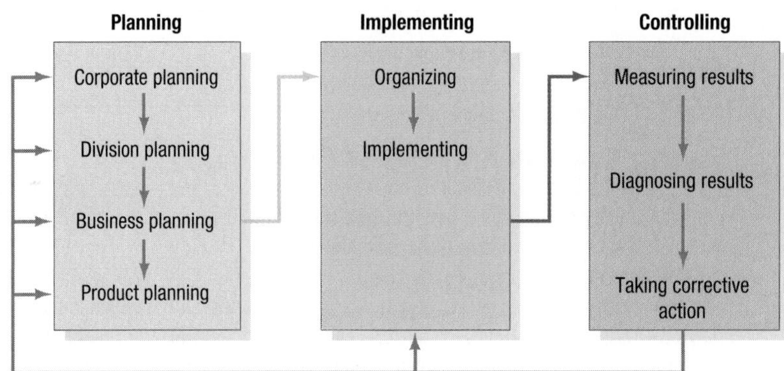

FIG. 2.4

The Strategic Planning, Implementation, and Control Processes

::: Corporate and Division Strategic Planning

By preparing statements of mission, policy, strategy, and goals, headquarters establishes the framework within which the divisions and business units prepare their plans. Some corporations give their business units a lot of freedom to set their own sales and profit goals and strategies. Others set goals for their business units but let them develop their own strategies. Still others set the goals and participate in developing individual business unit strategies.[20]

All corporate headquarters undertake four planning activities:

1. Defining the corporate mission
2. Establishing strategic business units
3. Assigning resources to each SBU
4. Assessing growth opportunities

Defining the Corporate Mission

An organization exists to accomplish something: to make cars, lend money, provide a night's lodging, and so on. Its specific mission or purpose is usually clear when the business starts. Over time the mission may change, to take advantage of new opportunities or respond to new market conditions. Amazon.com changed its mission from being the world's largest online bookstore to aspiring to become the world's largest online store. eBay changed its mission from running online auctions for collectors to running online auctions covering all kinds of goods.

To define its mission, a company should address Peter Drucker's classic questions:[21] What is our business? Who is the customer? What is of value to the customer? What will our business be? What should our business be? These simple-sounding questions are among the most difficult a company will ever have to answer. Successful companies continuously raise these questions and answer them thoughtfully and thoroughly. A company must redefine its mission if that mission has lost credibility or no longer defines an optimal course for growth.[22]

Organizations develop **mission statements** to share with managers, employees, and (in many cases) customers. A clear, thoughtful mission statement provides employees with a shared sense of purpose, direction, and opportunity. The statement guides geographically dispersed employees to work independently and yet collectively toward realizing the organization's goals.

Mission statements are at their best when they reflect a vision, an almost "impossible dream" that provides a direction for the company for the next 10 to 20 years. Sony's former president, Akio Morita, wanted everyone to have access to "personal portable sound," so his company created the Walkman and portable CD player. Fred Smith wanted to deliver mail anywhere in the United States before 10:30 A.M. the next day, so he created FedEx. Table 2.1 gives examples of three mission statements.

Good mission statements have three major characteristics. First, they focus on a limited number of goals. The statement, "We want to produce the highest-quality products, offer the most service, achieve the widest distribution, and sell at the lowest prices" claims too much. Second, mission statements stress the company's major policies and values. They narrow the range of individual discretion so that employees act consistently on

TABLE 2.1

Sample Mission Statements

Rubbermaid Commercial Products, Inc.

"Our Vision is to be the Global Market Share Leader in each of the markets we serve. We will earn this leadership position by providing to our distributor and end-user customers innovative, high-quality, cost-effective and environmentally responsible products. We will add value to these products by providing legendary customer service through our Uncompromising Commitment to Customer Satisfaction."

Motorola

"The purpose of Motorola is to honorably serve the needs of the community by providing products and services of superior quality at a fair price to our customers; to do this so as to earn an adequate profit which is required for the total enterprise to grow; and by so doing provide the opportunity for our employees and shareholders to achieve their reasonable personal objectives."

eBay

"We help people trade practically anything on earth. We will continue to enhance the online trading experiences of all—collectors, dealers, small businesses, unique item seekers, bargain hunters, opportunity sellers, and browsers."

important issues. Third, they define the major competitive spheres within which the company will operate:

- ***Industry.*** The range of industries in which a company will operate. Some companies will operate in only one industry; some only in a set of related industries; some only in industrial goods, consumer goods, or services; and some in any industry. For example, DuPont prefers to operate in the industrial market, whereas Dow is willing to operate in the industrial and consumer markets. 3M will get into almost any industry where it can make money.
- ***Products and applications.*** The range of products and applications a company will supply. St. Jude Medical aims to "serve physicians worldwide with high-quality products for cardiovascular care."
- ***Competence.*** The range of technological and other core competencies that a company will master and leverage. Japan's NEC has built its core competencies in computing, communications, and components to support production of laptop computers, television receivers, and handheld telephones.
- ***Market segment.*** The type of market or customers a company will serve. For example, Porsche makes only expensive cars. Gerber serves primarily the baby market.
- ***Vertical.*** The number of channel levels from raw material to final product and distribution in which a company will participate. At one extreme are companies with a large vertical scope; at one time Ford owned its own rubber plantations, sheep farms, glass manufacturing plants, and steel foundries. At the other extreme are "hollow corporations" or "pure marketing companies" consisting of a person with a phone, fax, computer, and desk who contracts out for every service, including design, manufacture, marketing, and physical distribution.[23]
- ***Geographical.*** The range of regions, countries, or country groups in which a company will operate. At one extreme are companies that operate in a specific city or state. At the other are multinationals such as Unilever and Caterpillar, which operate in almost every country in the world.

Defining the Business

Companies often define their businesses in terms of products: They are in the "auto business" or the "clothing business." But Levitt argues that market definitions of a business are superior to product definitions.[24] A business must be viewed as a customer-satisfying process, not a goods-producing process. Products are transient; basic needs and customer groups endure forever. Transportation is a need: the horse and carriage, the automobile, the railroad, the airline, and the truck are products that meet that need.

Levitt encouraged companies to redefine their businesses in terms of needs, not products. Pitney-Bowes Inc., an old-line manufacturer of postage meters, is in the process of doing just that. With old-fashioned paper mail under siege, Pitney-Bowes can no longer

A Caterpillar ad in French, with the focus on users' confidence in CAT products: "Pascal knows very well that his clients won't accept any excuses. He Has been in the business long enough to know that what's important is to do the work well, without delays and within budget. People say he's a perfectionist. He answers that he is simply a good professional and that's why clients depend on him. . . . Pascal uses CAT." Multinationals such as Caterpillar operate in almost every country in the world.

afford to be defined by its main product, even though it currently holds 80 percent of the domestic market and 62 percent of the global market. The company is redefining itself as a leading service provider in the much larger mail and document management industry. With its wealth of engineers, cryptographers, and even workplace anthropologists, as well as 2,300 patents and several labs, Pitney-Bowes is well positioned to help companies organize their communications. In a new series of ads in business publications such as *Fortune*, Pitney-Bowes is spreading the word about its new mission. For instance, one ad boasts that "we can generate remarkable changes across your entire business, including a sizeable increase in profits. A good example: BP. Our document solution helped them shorten billing cycles and enabled rapid receipt of payments, freeing millions in working capital." The tagline: "Pitney-Bowes: Engineering the flow of communication."[25]

IBM redefined itself from a hardware and software manufacturer to a "builder of networks." Table 2.2 gives several examples of companies that have moved from a product to a market definition of their business. It highlights the difference between a target market definition and a strategic market definition. A *target market definition* tends to focus on selling a product or service. Pepsi could define its target market as everyone who drinks a cola beverage and competitors would therefore be other cola companies. A *strategic market definition* could be everyone who might drink something to quench his or her thirst. Suddenly, Pepsi's competition would then include non-cola soft drinks, bottled water, fruit juices, tea,

TABLE 2.2

Product-Oriented Versus Market-Oriented Definitions of a Business

Company	Product Definition	Market Definition
Missouri-Pacific Railroad	We run a railroad.	We are a people-and-goods mover.
Xerox	We make copying equipment.	We help improve office productivity.
Standard Oil	We sell gasoline.	We supply energy.
Columbia Pictures	We make movies.	We market entertainment.
Encyclopaedia Britannica	We sell encyclopedias.	We distribute information.
Carrier	We make air conditioners and furnaces.	We provide climate control in the home.

and coffee. To better compete, Pepsi might decide to sell additional beverages whose growth rate appears to be promising.

A business can be defined in terms of three dimensions: customer groups, customer needs, and technology.[26] Consider a small company that defines its business as designing incandescent lighting systems for television studios. Its customer group is television studios; the customer need is lighting; and the technology is incandescent lighting. The company might want to expand. It could make lighting for other customer groups, such as homes, factories, and offices; or it could supply other services needed by television studios, such as heating, ventilation, or air conditioning. It could design other lighting technologies for television studios, such as infrared or ultraviolet lighting.

Large companies normally manage quite different businesses, each requiring its own strategy. General Electric classified its businesses into 49 **strategic business units (SBUs)**. An SBU has three characteristics:

1. It is a single business or collection of related businesses that can be planned separately from the rest of the company.
2. It has its own set of competitors.
3. It has a manager who is responsible for strategic planning and profit performance and who controls most of the factors affecting profit.

The purpose of identifying the company's strategic business units is to develop separate strategies and assign appropriate funding. Senior management knows that its portfolio of businesses usually includes a number of "yesterday's has-beens" as well as "tomorrow's breadwinners." Yet it cannot rely on impressions; it needs analytical tools to classify its businesses by profit potential.[27]

Assessing Growth Opportunities

Assessing growth opportunities involves planning new businesses, downsizing, or terminating older businesses. The company's plans for existing businesses allow it to project total sales and profits. If there is a gap between future desired sales and projected sales, corporate management will have to develop or acquire new businesses to fill it.

Figure 2.5 illustrates this strategic-planning gap for a major manufacturer of blank compact disks called Musicale (name disguised). The lowest curve projects the expected sales over the next five years from the current business portfolio. The highest curve describes desired sales over the same period. Evidently, the company wants to grow much faster than its current businesses will permit. How can it fill the strategic-planning gap?

The first option is to identify opportunities to achieve further growth within current businesses (intensive opportunities). The second is to identify opportunities to build or acquire businesses that are related to current businesses integrative opportunities). The third is to identify opportunities to add attractive businesses that are unrelated to current businesses (diversification opportunities).

INTENSIVE GROWTH Corporate management's first course of action should be a review of opportunities for improving existing businesses. Ansoff proposed a useful framework for detecting new intensive growth opportunities called a "product–market expansion grid" (Figure 2.6).[28]

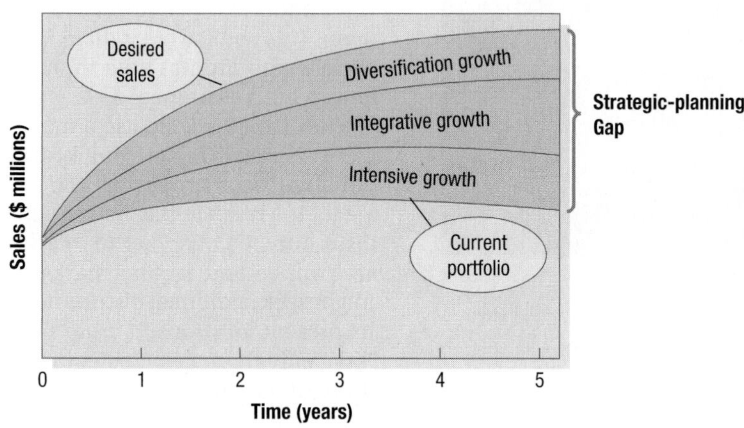

FIG. 2.5

The Strategic Planning Gap

FIG. 2.6

Three Intensive Growth Strategies: Ansoff's Product–Market Expansion Grid

	Current Products	New Products
Current Markets	1. Market-penetration strategy	3. Product-development strategy
New Markets	2. Market-development strategy	(Diversification strategy)

Source: Adapted and reprinted by permission, *Harvard Business Review.* From "Strategies for Diversification," by Igor Ansoff, September–October 1957.

The company first considers whether it could gain more market share with its current products in their current markets (market-penetration strategy). Next it considers whether it can find or develop new markets for its current products (market-development strategy). Then it considers whether it can develop new products of potential interest to its current markets (product-development strategy). Later it will also review opportunities to develop new products for new markets (diversification strategy).

STARBUCKS

Starbucks is a company that has achieved growth in many different ways. When Howard Schultz, Starbucks' CEO until 2000, came to the company in 1982, he recognized an unfilled niche for cafés serving gourmet coffee directly to customers. This became Starbucks' market-penetration strategy, and helped the company attain a loyal customer base in Seattle. The market-development strategy marked the next phase in Starbucks' growth: It applied the same successful formula that had worked wonders in Seattle, first to other cities in the Pacific Northwest, then throughout North America, and finally, across the globe. Once the company established itself as a presence in thousands of cities internationally, Starbucks sought to increase the number of purchases by existing customers with a product-development strategy that led to new in-store merchandise, including compilation CDs, a Starbucks Duetto Visa card that allows customers to receive points toward Starbucks purchases whenever they use it, and high-speed wireless Internet access at thousands of Starbucks "HotSpots" through a deal with T-Mobile. Finally, Starbucks pursued diversification into grocery store aisles with Frappuccino® bottled drinks, Starbucks brand ice cream, and the purchase of tea retailer Tazo® Tea.[29]

Howard Schultz of Starbucks waves after cutting the ribbon to inaugurate Starbucks' first store outside North America, in the Ginza in Tokyo, August 1996. Today Starbucks has stores across the globe.

How might Musicale use these three major intensive growth strategies to increase its sales? Musicale could try to encourage its current customers to buy more. This could work if its customers could be shown the benefits of using more compact disks for recording music or for data storage. Musicale could try to attract competitors' customers. This could work if Musicale noticed major weaknesses in competitors' products or marketing programs. Finally, Musicale could try to convince nonusers of compact disks to start using them. This could work if there are still enough people who are not able to or do not know how to burn a compact disk.

How can Musicale use a market-development strategy? First, it might try to identify potential user groups in the current sales areas. If Musicale has been selling compact disks only to consumer markets, it might go after office and factory markets. Second, it might seek additional distribution channels in its present locations. If it has been selling its disks only through stereo equipment dealers, it might add mass-merchandising channels.

Third, the company might consider selling in new locations in its home country or abroad. If Musicale sold only in the United States, it could consider entering the European market.

Management should also consider new-product possibilities. Musicale could develop new features, such as additional data storage capabilities or greater durability. It could offer the CD at two or more quality levels, or it could research an alternative technology such as digital audiotape.

By examining these intensive growth strategies, management may discover several ways to grow. Still, that growth may not be enough. In that case, management must also look for integrative growth opportunities.

INTEGRATIVE GROWTH A business's sales and profits may be increased through backward, forward, or horizontal integration within its industry. For example, drug company giant Merck has gone beyond just developing and selling ethical pharmaceuticals. It purchased Medco, a mail-order pharmaceutical distributor in 1993, formed a joint venture with DuPont to establish more basic research, and another joint venture with Johnson & Johnson to bring some of its ethical products into the over-the-counter market.

Media companies have long reaped the benefits of integrative growth. Here is how one business writer explains the potential that NBC could reap from its merger with Vivendi Universal Entertainment to become NBC Universal. Admittedly a far-fetched example, it gets across the possibilities inherent in this growth strategy:[30]

> [When] the hit movie *Seabiscuit* (produced by Universal Pictures) comes to television, it would air on Bravo (owned by NBC) or USA Network (owned by Universal), followed by the inevitable bid to make the movie into a TV series (by Universal Television Group), with the pilot being picked up by NBC, which passes on the show, but it's then revived in the "Brilliant But Canceled" series on cable channel Trio (owned by Universal) where its cult status leads to a Spanish version shown on Telemundo (owned by NBC) and the creation of a popular amusement-park attraction at Universal Studios.

How might Musicale achieve integrative growth? The company might acquire one or more of its suppliers (such as plastic material producers) to gain more control or generate more profit (backward integration). It might acquire some wholesalers or retailers, especially if they are highly profitable (forward integration). Finally, Musicale might acquire one or more competitors, provided that the government does not bar this move (horizontal integration). However, these new sources may still not deliver the desired sales volume. In that case, the company must consider diversification.

DIVERSIFICATION GROWTH Diversification growth makes sense when good opportunities can be found outside the present businesses. A good opportunity is one in which the industry is highly attractive and the company has the right mix of business strengths to be successful. For example, from its origins as an animated film producer, Walt Disney Company has moved into licensing characters for merchandised goods, entering the broadcast industry with its own Disney Channel as well as ABC and ESPN acquisitions, and developed theme parks and vacation and resort properties.

Several types of diversification are possible. First, the company could seek new products that have technological or marketing synergies with existing product lines, even though the new products themselves may appeal to a different group of customers (concentric strategy). It might start a laser disk manufacturing operation because it knows how to manufacture compact disks. Second, the company might search for new products that could appeal to current customers even though the new products are technologically unrelated to its current product line (horizontal strategy). Musicale might produce compact disk cases, even though producing them requires a different manufacturing process. Finally, the company might seek new businesses that have no relationship to its current technology, products, or markets (conglomerate strategy). Musicale might want to consider such new businesses as making application software or personal organizers.

DOWNSIZING AND DIVESTING OLDER BUSINESSES Companies must not only develop new businesses; they must also carefully prune, harvest, or divest tired old businesses in order to release needed resources and reduce costs. Weak businesses require a disproportionate amount of managerial attention. Managers should focus on growth opportunities, and not fritter away energy and resources trying to salvage hemorrhaging businesses. Heinz sold its 9-Lives and Kibbles 'n Bits pet food, StarKist tuna, College Inn broth, and All-in-One baby formulas to Del Monte in 2002 after years of stagnant sales, to allow it to focus on its core brands in ketchup, sauces, and frozen foods.

BLUE CROSS/BLUE SHIELD

William Van Faasen, CEO of Blue Cross/Blue Shield of Massachusetts, offers this advice: "If it's not core to your business, if it's not adding value to your customer's experience, if it's not bolstering the bottom line, get out of it." Van Faasen learned this lesson in 1996, when Blue Cross/Blue Shield was engaged in a number of peripheral activities that were draining its balance sheet—from owning and operating health centers to funding biotechnology ventures. At the same time, managed care came along and caused havoc with prices. At first the company priced services too low and then became aggressive and lost market share. The result was a $100 million loss in 1995 that served as a "two-by-four over the head" for Blue Cross/Blue Shield to create a clear, focused agenda. The company quickly got out of activities that were a drain on resources or not aligned with its core business.[31]

Organization and Organizational Culture

Strategic planning is done within the context of the organization. A company's **organization** consists of its structures, policies, and corporate culture, all of which can become dysfunctional in a rapidly changing business environment. Whereas structures and policies can be changed (with difficulty), the company's culture is very hard to change. Yet changing a corporate culture is often the key to successfully implementing a new strategy.

What exactly is a **corporate culture**? Most businesspeople would be hard-pressed to find words to describe this elusive concept, which some define as "the shared experiences, stories, beliefs, and norms that characterize an organization." Yet, walk into any company and the first thing that strikes you is the corporate culture—the way people are dressed, how they talk to one another, the way they greet customers.

Sometimes corporate culture develops organically and is transmitted directly from the CEO's personality and habits to the company employees. Such is the case with computer giant Microsoft, which began as an entrepreneurial upstart. Even as it grew to a $32 billion company in 2003, Microsoft did not lose the hard-driving culture established by founder Bill Gates. In fact, most feel that Microsoft's ultracompetitive culture is the biggest key to its success and to its much-criticized dominance in the computing industry.[32]

What happens when entrepreneurial companies grow and need to create a tighter structure? This was the case with Yahoo! Inc. When the Internet icon was floundering in 2001, new CEO Terry Semel imposed a more conservative, buttoned-down culture on the freewheeling Internet start-up. At the new Yahoo!, spontaneity is out and order is in. Whereas new initiatives used to roll ahead following free-form brainstorming sessions and a gut check, now they wind their way through tests and formal analysis. Ideas either rise or fall at near-weekly meetings of a group called the Product Council. The group sizes up business plans to make sure all new projects bring benefits to Yahoo!'s existing businesses.[33]

What happens when companies with clashing cultures enter a joint venture or merger? In a study by Coopers & Lybrand of 100 companies with failed or troubled mergers, 855 of executives polled said that differences in management style and practices were the major problem.[34] Conflict was certainly the case when Germany's Daimler merged with Chrysler in 1998.

DAIMLERCHRYSLER

Daimler-Benz AG and Chrysler Corp. merged in 1998 to form DaimlerChrysler. Executives from both companies thought a host of synergies would enable DaimlerChrysler to swiftly build a global automotive empire. Fundamental differences in the way the two corporations did business, however, contributed to early departures by executives, a stock price slide, management restructuring, and even considerable losses by the American manufacturer. The two companies had contrasting management styles, Daimler preferring to operate a classic bureaucracy and Chrysler traditionally giving decision-making ability to managers lower in the ranks.[35]

Successful companies may need to adopt a new view of how to craft their strategies. The traditional view is that senior management hammers out the strategy and hands it down. Gary Hamel offers the contrasting view that imaginative ideas on strategy exist in many places within a company.[36] Senior management should identify and encourage fresh ideas from three groups who tend to be underrepresented in strategy making: employees with youthful perspectives; employees who are far removed from company headquarters; and employees who are new to the industry. Each group is capable of challenging company orthodoxy and stimulating new ideas.

NOKIA

Finnish mobile-phone giant Nokia has managed to remain the frontrunner in the mobile-phone industry, with annual sales of $30.8 billion across 130 countries and a global market share of 38 percent, by installing a culture of innovation at all levels, using small, nimble, creative units to let new ideas bubble up through the ranks. Innovations are as likely to come from a junior application designer as from a seasoned engineer. One example of how the company creates its culture can be seen in the company cafeteria where employees view a slide show as they eat. It's not just any slide show, but one of pictures taken with camera phones by some of Nokia's 1,500 employees—part of an internal corporate competition that rewards staff creativity. Nokia even has a watchword for its culture of continuous innovation: "renewal."[37]

Strategy must be developed by identifying and selecting among different views of the future. The Royal Dutch/Shell Group has pioneered scenario analysis. A **scenario analysis** consists of developing plausible representations of a firm's possible future that make different assumptions about forces driving the market and include different uncertainties. Managers need to think through each scenario with the question: "What will we do if it happens?" They need to adopt one scenario as the most probable and watch for signposts that might confirm or disconfirm that scenario.[38]

::: Business Unit Strategic Planning

The business unit strategic-planning process consists of the steps shown in Figure 2.7. We examine each step in the sections that follow.

The Business Mission

Each business unit needs to define its specific mission within the broader company mission. Thus, a television studio-lighting-equipment company might define its mission as, "The company aims to target major television studios and become their vendor of choice for lighting technologies that represent the most advanced and reliable studio lighting arrangements." Notice that this mission does not attempt to win business from smaller television studios, win business by being lowest in price, or venture into nonlighting products.

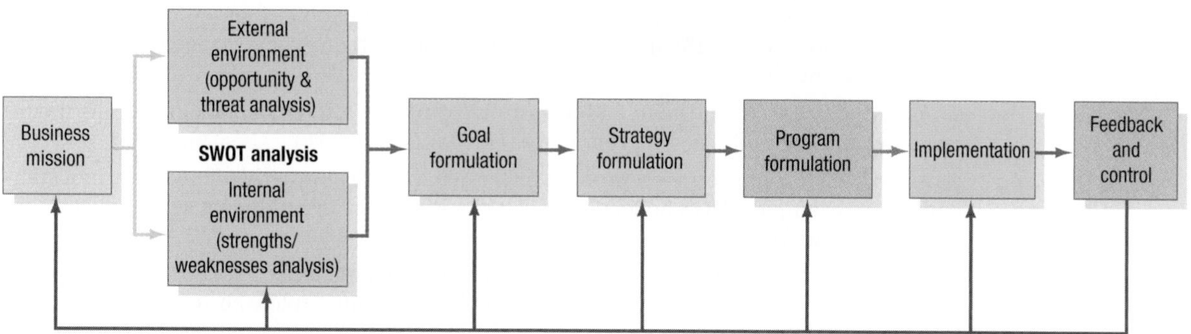

FIG. 2.7 The Business Unit Strategic-Planning Process

SWOT Analysis

The overall evaluation of a company's strengths, weaknesses, opportunities, and threats is called SWOT analysis. It involves monitoring the external and internal marketing environment.

EXTERNAL ENVIRONMENT (OPPORTUNITY AND THREAT) ANALYSIS A business unit has to monitor key *macroenvironment forces* (demographic-economic, natural, technological, political-legal, and social-cultural) and significant *microenvironment actors* (customers, competitors, suppliers, distributors, dealers) that affect its ability to earn profits. The business unit should set up a marketing intelligence system to track trends and important developments. For each trend or development, management needs to identify the associated opportunities and threats.

A major purpose of environmental scanning is to discern new opportunities. In many ways, good marketing is the art of finding, developing, and profiting from opportunities.[39] A **marketing opportunity** is an area of buyer need and interest in which there is a high probability that a company can profitably satisfy that need. There are three main sources of market opportunities.[40] The first is to supply something that is in short supply. This requires little marketing talent, as the need is fairly obvious. The second is to supply an existing product or service in a new or superior way. There are several ways to uncover possible product or service improvements: by asking consumers for their suggestions (*problem detection method*); by asking consumers to imagine an ideal version of the product or service (*ideal method*); and by asking consumers to chart their steps in acquiring, using, and disposing of a product (*consumption chain method*). The third source often leads to a totally new product or service.

SEGWAY

Meeting a need with a new product or service is perhaps the most rewarding way—when you get it right—but it is the riskiest as well, as Segway LLC found out. When Dean Kamen created the Segway Human Transporter, a $5,000 electric scooter, he had high hopes that it would be a popular, nonpolluting alternative to walking. Yet, so far the high-priced scooter has not found its market, in part because it flies in the face of a powerful *macroenvironment force* —the current concern with obesity and interest in the health benefits of walking. The company may have more success in looking at how *microenvironment actors*—such as local government agencies and the military—can benefit from the product. Early reports indicate that Segway is well received in some government agencies; Seattle water meter readers have been testing Segways, and in Los Angeles, the police of the Metropolitan Transportation Authority have found the Segway useful.[41]

Opportunities can take many forms, and marketers have to be good at spotting them. Consider the following:

- A company may benefit from converging industry trends and introduce hybrid products or services that are new to the market. Example: At least five major cell phone manufacturers released phones with digital photo capabilities.
- A company may make a buying process more convenient or efficient. Example: Consumers can now use the Internet to find more books than ever and search for the lowest price with a few clicks.
- A company can meet the need for more information and advice. Example: Guru.com facilitates finding professional experts in a wide range of fields.
- A company can customize a product or service that was formerly offered only in a standard form. Example: P&G's Reflect.com Web site is capable of producing a customized skin care or hair care product to meet a customer's need.
- A company can introduce a new capability. Example: Consumers can now create and edit digital "iMovies" with the new iMac and upload them to an Apple Web server to share with friends around the world.
- A company may be able to deliver a product or a service faster. Example: FedEx discovered a way to deliver mail and packages much more quickly than the U.S. Post Office.

- A company may be able to offer a product at a much lower price. Example: Pharmaceutical firms have created generic versions of brand-name drugs.

To evaluate opportunities, companies can use **Market Opportunity Analysis (MOA)** to determine the attractiveness and probability of success:

1. Can the benefits involved in the opportunity be articulated convincingly to a defined target market(s)?
2. Can the target market(s) be located and reached with cost-effective media and trade channels?
3. Does the company possess or have access to the critical capabilities and resources needed to deliver the customer benefits?
4. Can the company deliver the benefits better than any actual or potential competitors?
5. Will the financial rate of return meet or exceed the company's required threshold for investment?

In the opportunity matrix in Figure 2.8(a), the best marketing opportunities facing the TV-lighting-equipment company are listed in the upper-left cell (#1). The opportunities in the lower-right cell (#4) are too minor to consider. The opportunities in the upper-right cell (#2) and lower-left cell (#3) should be monitored in the event that any improve in attractiveness and success probability.

Some developments in the external environment represent threats. An **environmental threat** is a challenge posed by an unfavorable trend or development that would lead, in the absence of defensive marketing action, to lower sales or profit. Threats should be classified according to seriousness and probability of occurrence. Figure 2.8(b) illustrates the threat matrix facing the TV-lighting-equipment company. The threats in the upper-left cell are major, because they can seriously hurt the company and they have a high probability of occurrence. To deal with them, the company needs contingency plans that spell out changes it can make before or during the threat. The threats in the lower-right cell are very minor and can be ignored. The threats in the upper-right and lower-left cells need to be monitored carefully in the event that they grow more serious.

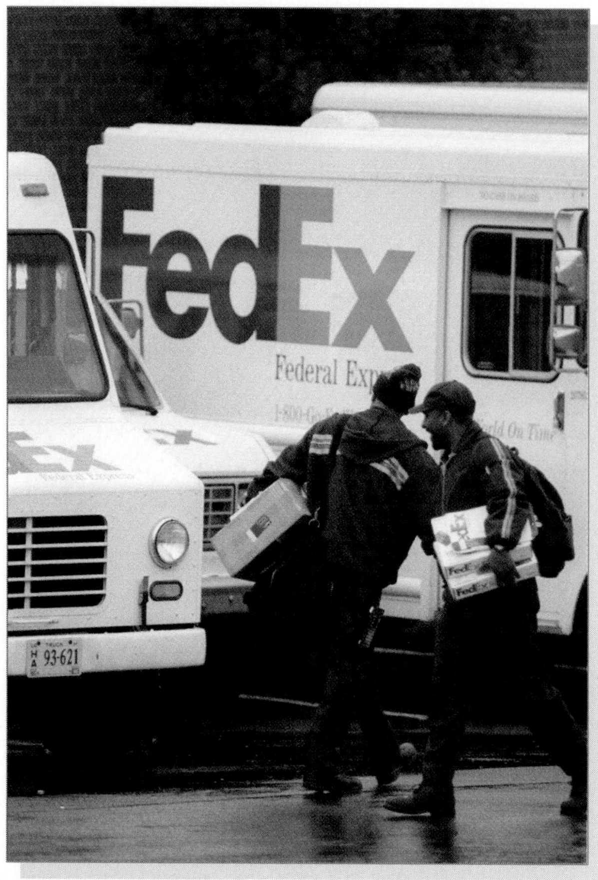

FedEx employees walk to their trucks on the first Sunday delivery at the company's suburban Washington center. The new service was introduced based on customer request and market demand.

Once management has identified the major threats and opportunities facing a specific business unit; it can characterize that business's overall attractiveness.

INTERNAL ENVIRONMENT (STRENGTHS/WEAKNESSES) ANALYSIS It is one thing to find attractive opportunities and another to be able to take advantage of them. Each business needs to evaluate its internal strengths and weaknesses. It can do so by using a form like the one shown in "Marketing Memo: Checklist for Performing Strengths/Weaknesses Analysis."

Clearly, the business does not have to correct all its weaknesses, nor should it gloat about all its strengths. The big question is whether the business should limit itself to those opportunities where it possesses the required strengths or whether it should consider opportunities that mean it might have to acquire or develop certain strengths. For example, managers at Texas Instruments (TI) were split between those who wanted TI to stick to industrial electronics (where it has clear strength) and those who wanted the company to continue introducing consumer products (where it lacks some required marketing strengths).

Sometimes a business does poorly not because its people lack the required strengths, but because they do not work together as a team. In one major electronics company, the engineers look down on the salespeople as "engineers who couldn't make it," and the salespeople look down on the service people as "salespeople who couldn't make it." It is therefore critical to assess interdepartmental working relationships as part of the internal environmental audit. Honeywell does exactly this.

FIG. 2.8

Opportunity and Threat Matrices

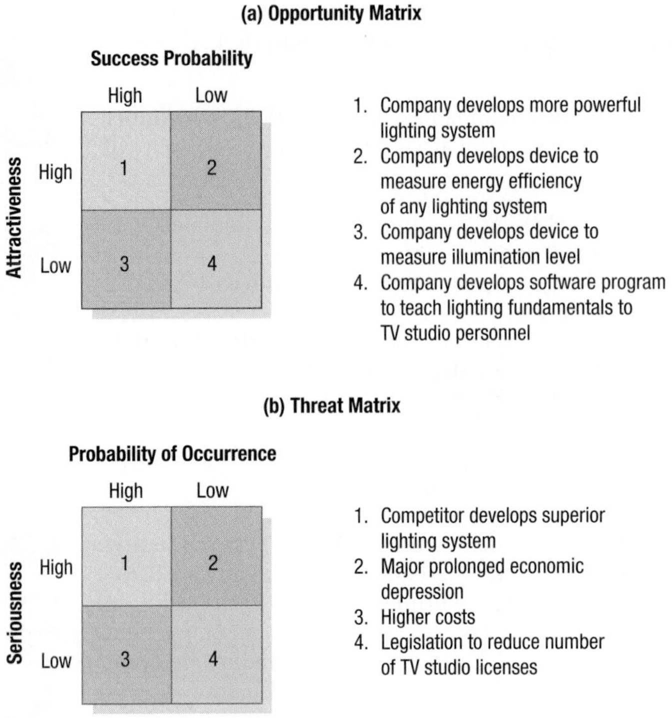

(a) Opportunity Matrix

Attractiveness \ Success Probability	High	Low
High	1	2
Low	3	4

1. Company develops more powerful lighting system
2. Company develops device to measure energy efficiency of any lighting system
3. Company develops device to measure illumination level
4. Company develops software program to teach lighting fundamentals to TV studio personnel

(b) Threat Matrix

Seriousness \ Probability of Occurrence	High	Low
High	1	2
Low	3	4

1. Competitor develops superior lighting system
2. Major prolonged economic depression
3. Higher costs
4. Legislation to reduce number of TV studio licenses

HONEYWELL

Each year, Honeywell asks each department to rate its own strengths and weaknesses and those of the other departments with which it interacts. The notion is that each department is a supplier to some departments and a customer of other departments. If Honeywell engineers frequently underestimate the cost and completion time of new products, for example, their "internal customers" (manufacturing, finance, and sales) will be hurt.

George Stalk, a leading management consultant, suggests that winning companies are those that have achieved superior in-company capabilities, not just core competencies.[42] Every company must manage some basic processes, such as new-product development, sales generation, and order fulfillment. Each process creates value and requires interdepartmental teamwork. Although each department may possess specific core competencies, the challenge is to develop superior competitive capability in managing the company's key processes. Stalk calls this *capabilities-based competition.*

Goal Formulation

Once the company has performed a SWOT analysis, it can proceed to develop specific goals for the planning period. This stage of the process is called **goal formulation.** Managers use the term *goals* to describe objectives that are specific with respect to magnitude and time.

Most business units pursue a mix of objectives including profitability, sales growth, market share improvement, risk containment, innovation, and reputation. The business unit sets these objectives and then manages by objectives (MBO). For an MBO system to work, the unit's objectives must meet four criteria:

1. ***They must be arranged hierarchically, from the most to the least important*** – For example, the business unit's key objective for the period may be to increase the rate of return on investment. This can be accomplished by increasing the profit level and reducing the amount of invested capital. Profit itself can be increased by increasing revenue and reducing expenses. Revenue can be increased by increasing market share and prices. By

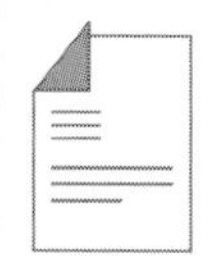

MARKETING **MEMO**

CHECKLIST FOR PERFORMING STRENGTHS/WEAKNESSES ANALYSIS

	Performance					Importance		
	Major Strength	**Minor Strength**	**Neutral**	**Minor Weakness**	**Major Weakness**	**Hi**	**Med**	**Low**
Marketing								
1. Company reputation	____	____	____	____	____	____	____	____
2. Market share	____	____	____	____	____	____	____	____
3. Customer satisfaction	____	____	____	____	____	____	____	____
4. Customer retention	____	____	____	____	____	____	____	____
5. Product quality	____	____	____	____	____	____	____	____
6. Service quality	____	____	____	____	____	____	____	____
7. Pricing effectiveness	____	____	____	____	____	____	____	____
8. Distribution effectiveness	____	____	____	____	____	____	____	____
9. Promotion effectiveness	____	____	____	____	____	____	____	____
10. Sales force effectiveness	____	____	____	____	____	____	____	____
11. Innovation effectiveness	____	____	____	____	____	____	____	____
12. Geographical coverage	____	____	____	____	____	____	____	____
Finance								
13. Cost or availability of capital	____	____	____	____	____	____	____	____
14. Cash flow	____	____	____	____	____	____	____	____
15. Financial stability	____	____	____	____	____	____	____	____
Manufacturing								
16. Facilities	____	____	____	____	____	____	____	____
17. Economies of scale	____	____	____	____	____	____	____	____
18. Capacity	____	____	____	____	____	____	____	____
19. Able, dedicated workforce	____	____	____	____	____	____	____	____
20. Ability to produce on time	____	____	____	____	____	____	____	____
21. Technical manufacturing skill	____	____	____	____	____	____	____	____
Organization								
22. Visionary, capable leadership	____	____	____	____	____	____	____	____
23. Dedicated employees	____	____	____	____	____	____	____	____
24. Entrepreneurial orientation	____	____	____	____	____	____	____	____
25. Flexible or responsive	____	____	____	____	____	____	____	____

proceeding this way, the business can move from broad to specific objectives for specific departments and individuals.

2. ***Objectives should be stated quantitatively whenever possible*** – The objective "increase the return on investment (ROI)" is better stated as the goal "increase ROI to 15 percent within two years."
3. ***Goals should be realistic*** – They should arise from an analysis of the business unit's opportunities and strengths, not from wishful thinking.
4. ***Objectives must be consistent*** – It is not possible to maximize sales and profits simultaneously.

Other important trade-offs include short-term profit versus long-term growth, deep penetration of existing markets versus developing new markets, profit goals versus nonprofit goals, and high growth versus low risk. Each choice in this set of trade-offs calls for a different marketing strategy.

Many believe that adopting the goal of strong market share growth may mean having to forego strong short-term profits. For years, Compaq priced aggressively in order to build its market share in the computer market. Subsequently, Compaq decided to pursue profitability at the expense of growth. Yet Charan and Tichy believe that most businesses can be a growth business and can grow profitably.[43] They cite success stories such as GE Medical, Allied Signal, Citibank, and GE Capital, all enjoying profitable growth. Some so-called trade-offs may not be trade-offs at all.

Strategic Formulation

Goals indicate what a business unit wants to achieve; **strategy** is a game plan for getting there. Every business must design a strategy for achieving its goals, consisting of a *marketing strategy*, and a compatible *technology strategy* and *sourcing strategy*.

PORTER'S GENERIC STRATEGIES Michael Porter has proposed three generic strategies that provide a good starting point for strategic thinking: overall cost leadership, differentiation, and focus.[44]

- ***Overall cost leadership.*** The business works hard to achieve the lowest production and distribution costs so that it can price lower than its competitors and win a large market share. Firms pursuing this strategy must be good at engineering, purchasing, manufacturing, and physical distribution. They need less skill in marketing. The problem with this strategy is that other firms will usually compete with still lower costs and hurt the firm that rested its whole future on cost.
- ***Differentiation.*** The business concentrates on achieving superior performance in an important customer benefit area valued by a large part of the market. The firm cultivates those strengths that will contribute to the intended differentiation. Thus the firm seeking quality leadership, for example, must make products with the best components, put them together expertly, inspect them carefully, and effectively communicate their quality.
- ***Focus.*** The business focuses on one or more narrow market segments. The firm gets to know these segments intimately and pursues either cost leadership or differentiation within the target segment.

The online air travel industry provides a good example of these three strategies: Travelocity is pursuing a differentiation strategy by offering the most comprehensive range of services to the traveler. Lowestfare is pursuing a lowest-cost strategy; and Last Minute is pursuing a niche strategy in focusing on travelers who have the flexibility to travel on very short notice.

According to Porter, firms pursuing the same strategy directed to the same target market constitute a **strategic group**. The firm that carries out that strategy best will make the most profits. Firms that do not pursue a clear strategy and try to be good on all strategic dimensions do the worst. International Harvester went out of the farm equipment business because it did not stand out in its industry as lowest in cost, highest in perceived value, or best in serving some market segment. Porter drew a distinction between operational effectiveness and strategy.[45]

Many companies believe they can win by performing the same activities more effectively than their competitors; but competitors can quickly copy the operationally effective company using benchmarking and other tools, thus diminishing the advantage of operational effectiveness. Porter defines strategy as "the creation of a unique and valuable position involving a different set of activities." A company can claim that it has a strategy when it "performs different activities from rivals or performs similar activities in different ways." Companies such as IKEA, Southwest Airlines, Dell Computer, Saturn, and Home Depot run their businesses much differently from their competitors; and these competitors would find it hard to copy and synchronize all the different activities that a strategically differentiated company carries out.

STRATEGIC ALLIANCES Companies are also discovering that they need strategic partners if they hope to be effective. Even giant companies—AT&T, IBM, Philips, Siemens—

A celebration at a Star Alliance inaugural. The Star Alliance brings together 16 airlines that cover most of the globe.

often cannot achieve leadership, either nationally or globally, without forming alliances with domestic or multinational companies that complement or leverage their capabilities and resources.

Just doing business in another country may require the firm to license its product, form a joint venture with a local firm, or buy from local suppliers to meet "domestic content" requirements. As a result, many firms are rapidly developing global strategic networks, and victory is going to those who build the better global network. The Star Alliance, for example, brings together 16 airlines—Lufthansa, United Airlines, Mexicana, Air Canada, ANA, Austrian Airlines, British Midland, Singapore Airlines, Tyrolean, Lauda, SAS, Thai Airways, Varig, Air New Zealand, Asiana Airlines, and Spanair—into a huge global partnership that allows travelers to make nearly seamless connections to about 700 destinations.

Many strategic alliances take the form of marketing alliances. These fall into four major categories.

1. ***Product or service alliances*** – One company licenses another to produce its product, or two companies jointly market their complementary products or a new product. For instance, H&R Block and Hyatt Legal Services—two service businesses—have also joined together in a marketing alliance.
2. ***Promotional alliances*** – One company agrees to carry a promotion for another company's product or service. McDonald's, for example, has often teamed up with Disney to offer products related to current Disney films as part of its meals for children.
3. ***Logistics alliances*** – One company offers logistical services for another company's product. For example, Abbott Laboratories warehouses and delivers all of 3M's medical and surgical products to hospitals across the United States.
4. ***Pricing collaborations*** – One or more companies join in a special pricing collaboration. Hotel and rental car companies often offer mutual price discounts.

Companies need to give creative thought to finding partners that might complement their strengths and offset their weaknesses. Well-managed alliances allow companies to obtain a greater sales impact at less cost. To keep their strategic alliances thriving, corporations have begun to develop organizational structures to support them and have come to view the ability to form and manage partnerships as core skills (called **Partner Relationship Management, PRM**).[46]

Both pharmaceutical and biotech companies are starting to make partnership a core competency. In the 1980s and 1990s pharmaceutical and biotech firms were vertically integrated, doing all the research, development, and marketing and sales themselves. Now they are joining forces and leveraging their respective strengths. For example, Erbitux, a new drug to aid treatment of colorectal cancer, is the result of just such a partnership. The drug was originally discovered in biotech company ImClone Systems' clinical labs, but will be marketed via ImClone's partnership with pharmaceutical giant Bristol-Meyers Squibb.[47]

Program Formulation and Implementation

Once the business unit has developed its principal strategies, it must work out detailed support programs. A great marketing strategy can be sabotaged by poor implementation. If the unit has decided to attain technological leadership, it must plan programs to strengthen its R&D department, gather technological intelligence, develop leading-edge products, train the technical sales force, and develop ads to communicate its technological leadership.

Once the marketing programs are formulated, the marketing people must estimate their costs. Questions arise: Is participating in a particular trade show worth it? Will a specific sales contest pay for itself? Will hiring another salesperson contribute to the bottom line? Activity-based cost (ABC) accounting should be applied to each marketing program to determine whether it is likely to produce sufficient results to justify the cost.[48]

In implementing strategy, companies also must not lose sight of their multiple stakeholders and their needs. Traditionally, most businesses focused on stockholders. Today's businesses are increasingly recognizing that unless they nurture other stakeholders—customers, employees, suppliers, distributors—the business may never earn sufficient profits for the stockholders. A company can aim to deliver satisfaction levels above the minimum for different stakeholders. For example, it might aim to delight its customers, perform well for its employees, and deliver a threshold level of satisfaction to its suppliers. In setting these levels, a company must be careful not to violate the various stakeholder groups' sense of fairness about the relative treatment they are receiving.[49]

There is a dynamic relationship connecting the stakeholder groups. A smart company creates a high level of employee satisfaction, which leads to higher effort, which leads to higher-quality products and services, which creates higher customer satisfaction, which leads to more repeat business, which leads to higher growth and profits, which leads to high stockholder satisfaction, which leads to more investment, and so on. This is the virtuous circle that spells profits and growth. "Marketing Insight: Marketing's Contribution to Shareholder Value" highlights the increasing importance of the proper bottom-line view to marketing expenditures.

According to McKinsey & Company, strategy is only one of seven elements in successful business practice.[50] The first three elements—strategy, structure, and systems—are considered the "hardware" of success. The next four—style, skills, staff, and shared values—are the "software."

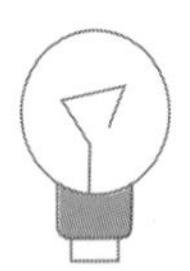

MARKETING INSIGHT | MARKETING'S CONTRIBUTION TO SHAREHOLDER VALUE

Companies normally focus on profit maximization rather than on shareholder value maximization. Doyle, in his *Value-Based Marketing,* charges that profit maximization leads to short-term planning and underinvestment in marketing. It leads to a focus on building sales, market share, and current profits. It leads to cost cutting and shedding assets to produce quick improvements in earnings, and erodes a company's long-term competitiveness by neglecting to invest in new market opportunities.

Companies normally measure their profit performance using ROI (return on investment, calculated by dividing profits by investment). This has two problems:

1. Profits are arbitrarily measured and subject to manipulation. Cash flow is more important. As someone observed: "Profits are a matter of opinion; cash is a fact."
2. Investment ignores the real value of the firm. More of a company's value resides in its intangible marketing assets—brands, market knowledge, customer relationships, and partner relationships—than in its balance sheet. These assets are the drivers of long-term profits.

Doyle argues that marketing will not mature as a profession until it can demonstrate the impact of marketing on shareholder value, the market value of a company minus its debt. The market value is the share price times the number of shares outstanding. The share price reflects what investors estimate is the present value of the future lifetime earnings of a company. When management is choosing a marketing strategy, Doyle wants it to apply shareholder value analysis (SVA) to see which alternative course of action will maximize shareholder value.

If Doyle's arguments are accepted, marketing will finally get the attention it deserves in the boardroom. Instead of seeing marketing as a specific function concerned only with increasing sales or market share, senior management will see it as an integral part of the whole management process. It will judge marketing by how much it contributes to shareholder value.

Source: Peter Doyle, *Value-Based Marketing: Marketing Strategies for Corporate Growth and Shareholder Value* (Chichester, England: John Wiley & Sons, 2000).

The first "soft" element, *style,* means that company employees share a common way of thinking and behaving. McDonald's employees smile at the customer, and IBM employees are very professional in their customer dealings. The second, *skills,* means that the employees have the skills needed to carry out the company's strategy. The third, *staffing,* means that the company has hired able people, trained them well, and assigned them to the right jobs. The fourth, *shared values,* means that the employees share the same guiding values. When these elements are present, companies are usually more successful at strategy implementation.[51]

Another study of management practices found that superior performance over time depended on flawless execution, a company culture based on aiming high, a structure that is flexible and responsive, and a strategy that is clear and focused.[52]

Feedback and Control

As it implements its strategy, a firm needs to track the results and monitor new developments. Some environments are fairly stable from year to year. Other environments evolve slowly in a fairly predictable way. Still other environments change rapidly in major and unpredictable ways. Nonetheless, a company can count on one thing: The marketplace will change; and when it does, the company will need to review and revise its implementation, programs, strategies, or even objectives.

A company's strategic fit with the environment will inevitably erode because the market environment changes faster than the company's 7 Ss. Thus, a company might remain efficient while it loses effectiveness. Peter Drucker pointed out that it is more important to "do the right thing" (effectiveness) than "to do things right" (efficiency). The most successful companies excel at both.

Once an organization fails to respond to a changed environment, it becomes increasingly hard to recapture its lost position. Consider what happened to Lotus Development Corporation. Its Lotus 1-2-3 software was once the world's leading software program, and now its market share in desktop software has slipped so low that analysts do not even bother to track it.

LOTUS

Sales of the original IBM-PC were driven by Lotus 1-2-3, which combined an accounting spreadsheet with a program that could turn rows of numbers into charts and graphs. Yet Lotus ultimately did not keep pace as the PC evolved, and missed opportunities with Apple Macintosh, Microsoft Windows, and suite applications. Following IBM's acquisition of the company in 1995, Lotus capitalized on the growing popularity of corporate e-mail systems with its Notes software, but Microsoft's ability to tie applications to operating systems gave it an unbeatable advantage. The company now works in concert with Microsoft to make sure its latest Smart Suite software takes full advantage of Windows software.[53]

Organizations, especially large ones, are subject to inertia. Inertia has been affecting giant Kraft Foods, Inc., a company renowned for its expertise in creating brand extensions.

KRAFT

While the company was busy rolling out products like Jell-O gel cups, Mini Oreos, and Ooey Gooey Warm N' Chewy Chips Ahoy!, it missed some important trends in supermarket food. As supermarkets' own private labels put out deeply discounted cheeses and cookies and other processed foods, Kraft has become increasingly perceived as too high-priced. More important, Kraft neglected the trend toward healthier products with organic ingredients and less fat. Alongside brands like Stonyfield Farm, Starbucks, or SilkSoy products, Kraft has begun looking more like a producer of expensive processed food.[54]

Organizations are set up as efficient machines, and it is difficult to change one part without adjusting everything else. Yet organizations can be changed through strong leadership, preferably in advance of a crisis. The key to organizational health is willingness to examine the changing environment and to adopt new goals and behaviors.

::: Product Planning: The Nature and Contents of a Marketing Plan

To carry out their responsibilities, marketing managers follow a marketing process. Working within the plans set by the levels above them, product managers come up with a marketing plan for individual products, lines, brands, channels, or customer groups. Each product level (product line, brand) must develop a marketing plan for achieving its goals. A **marketing plan** is a written document that summarizes what the marketer has learned about the marketplace and indicates how the firm plans to reach its marketing objectives.[55] It contains tactical guidelines for the marketing programs and financial allocations over the planning period.[56] It is one of the most important outputs of the marketing process.

Marketing plans are becoming more customer- and competitor-oriented and better reasoned and more realistic than in the past. The plans draw more inputs from all the functions and are team-developed. Marketing executives increasingly see themselves as professional managers first, and specialists second. Planning is becoming a continuous process to respond to rapidly changing market conditions.

SONY

Sony originally planned to sell 10 million PlayStation 2 units worldwide within the first year of introduction. The marketing plan called for an aggressive presale promotional campaign to build demand and overshadow competitive game units from Nintendo and other rivals. Sony initially launched the new product in Japan, where the planned hype caused a buying frenzy in which almost 1 million units were sold within the first three days. However, unexpected components shortages kept the company from building enough units to stay on schedule. As a result, Sony was forced to revise its marketing plan by delaying the European launch and reducing the number of PlayStation 2 units shipped to stores in Europe and the United States; this delay, in turn, prevented Sony from reaching its corporate sales and profit objectives for the year.[57]

At the same time, marketing planning procedures and content vary considerably among companies. The plan is variously called a "business plan," a "marketing plan," and sometimes a "battle plan." Most marketing plans cover one year. The plans vary in length from under 5 to over 50 pages. Some companies take their plans very seriously, whereas others see them only as a rough guide to action. Eisenhower once observed: "In preparing for battle I have always found that plans are useless but planning is indispensable." The most frequently cited shortcomings of current marketing plans, according to marketing executives, are lack of realism, insufficient competitive analysis, and a short-run focus. (See "Marketing Memo: Marketing Plan Criteria" for some guideline questions to ask in developing marketing plans.)

What, then, does a marketing plan look like? What does it contain?

Contents of the Marketing Plan

- ***Executive summary and table of contents.*** The marketing plan should open with a brief summary of the main goals and recommendations. The executive summary permits senior management to grasp the plan's major thrust. A table of contents that outlines the rest of the plan and all the supporting rationale and operational detail should follow the executive summary.
- ***Situation analysis.*** This section presents relevant background data on sales, costs, the market, competitors, and the various forces in the macroenvironment. How is the market defined, how big is it, and how fast is it growing? What are the relevant trends affecting the market? What is the product offering and what are the critical issues facing the company? Pertinent historical information can be included to provide context. All this information is used to carry out a SWOT (strengths, weaknesses, opportunities, threats) analysis.
- ***Marketing strategy.*** Here the product manager defines the mission and marketing and financial objectives. The manager also defines those groups and needs that the market offerings are intended to satisfy. The manager then establishes the product line's competitive positioning, which will inform the "game plan" to accomplish the plan's objectives. All this is done with inputs from other organizational areas, such as purchasing, manufacturing, sales,

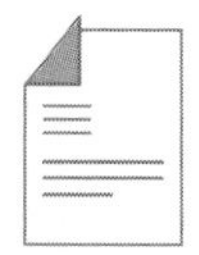

MARKETING MEMO | MARKETING PLAN CRITERIA

Here are some questions to ask in evaluating a marketing plan.

1. ***Is the plan simple?*** Is it easy to understand and act on? Does it communicate its content easily and practically?
2. ***Is the plan specific?*** Are its objectives concrete and measurable? Does it include specific actions and activities, each with specific dates of completion, specific persons responsible, and specific budgets?
3. ***Is the plan realistic?*** Are the sales goals, expense budgets, and milestone dates realistic? Has a frank and honest self-critique been conducted to raise possible concerns and objections?
4. ***Is the plan complete?*** Does it include all the necessary elements?

Source: Tim Berry and Doug Wilson, *On Target: The Book on Marketing Plans* (Eugene, OR: Palo Alto Software, 2000).

finance, and human resources, to ensure that the company can provide proper support for effective implementation. The marketing strategy should be specific about the branding strategy and customer strategy that will be employed.

- ***Financial projections.*** Financial projections include a sales forecast, an expense forecast, and a break-even analysis. On the revenue side, the projections show the forecasted sales volume by month and product category. On the expense side, the projections show the expected costs of marketing, broken down into finer categories. The break-even analysis shows how many units must be sold monthly to offset the monthly fixed costs and average per-unit variable costs.
- ***Implementation controls.*** The last section of the marketing plan outlines the controls for monitoring and adjusting implementation of the plan. Typically, the goals and budget are spelled out for each month or quarter so management can review each period's results and take corrective action as needed. A number of different internal and external measures must be taken to assess progress and suggest possible modifications. Some organizations include contingency plans outlining the steps management would take in response to specific environmental developments, such as price wars or strikes.

Sample Marketing Plan: Pegasus Sports International*

1.0 Executive Summary

Pegasus Sports International is a start-up aftermarket inline skating accessory manufacturer. In addition to the aftermarket products, Pegasus is developing SkateTours, a service that takes clients out, in conjunction with a local skate shop, and provides them with an afternoon of skating using inline skates and some of Pegasus' other accessories such as SkateSails. The aftermarket skate accessory market has been largely ignored. Although there are several major manufacturers of the skates themselves, the accessory market has not been addressed. This provides Pegasus with an extraordinary opportunity for market growth. Skating is a booming sport. Currently, most of the skating is recreational. There are, however, a growing number of skating competitions, including team-oriented competitions such as skate hockey as well as individual competitions such as speed skate racing. Pegasus will work to grow these markets and develop the skate transportation market, a more utilitarian use of skating. Several of Pegasus' currently developed products have patents pending, and local market research indicates that there is great demand for these products. Pegasus will achieve fast, significant market penetration through a solid business model, long-range planning, and a strong management team that is able to execute this exciting opportunity. The three principals on the management team have over 30 years of combined personal and industry experience. This extensive experience provides Pegasus with the empirical information as well as the passion to provide the skating market with much-needed aftermarket products. Pegasus will sell its products initially through its Web site. This "Dell" direct-to-the-consumer approach will allow Pegasus to achieve higher margins and maintain a close relationship with the customers, which is essential for producing products that have a true market demand. By the end of the year, Pegasus will have also developed relationships with different skate shops and will begin to sell some of its products through retailers.

TABLE 1.0 | Sales Forecast

Sales Forecast			
Sales	**2003**	**2004**	**2005**
Recreational	$455,740	$598,877	$687,765
Competitive	$72,918	$95,820	$110,042
Total Sales	$528,658	$694,697	$797,807
Direct Cost of Sales	**2003**	**2004**	**2005**
Recreational	$82,033	$107,798	$123,798
Competitive	$13,125	$17,248	$19,808
Subtotal Cost of Sales	$95,159	$125,046	$143,605

2.0 Situation Analysis

Pegasus is entering its first year of operation. Its products have been well received, and marketing will be key to the development of brand and product awareness as well as the growth of the customer base. Pegasus International offers several different aftermarket skating accessories, serving the growing inline skating industry.

2.1 Market Summary

Pegasus possesses good information about the market and knows a great deal about the common attributes of the most prized customer. This information will be leveraged to better understand who is served, what their specific needs are, and how Pegasus can better communicate with them.

Target Markets

Recreational
Fitness
Speed
Hockey
Extreme

2.1.1 Market Demographics

The profile for the typical Pegasus customer consists of the following geographic, demographic, and behavior factors:

Geographics

- Pegasus has no set geographic target area. By leveraging the expansive reach of the Internet and multiple delivery services, Pegasus can serve both domestic and international customers.
- The total targeted population is 31 million users.

Demographics

- There is an almost equal ratio between male and female users.
- Ages 13–46, with 48 percent clustering around ages 23–34. The recreational users tend to cover the widest age range, including young users through active adults. The fitness users tend to be ages 20–40. The speed users tend to be in their late twenties and early thirties. The hockey players are

TABLE 2.1 | Target Market Forecast

Target Market Forecast							
Potential Customers	**Growth**	**2003**	**2004**	**2005**	**2006**	**2007**	**CAGR**
Recreational	10%	19,142,500	21,056,750	23,162,425	25,478,668	28,026,535	10.00%
Fitness	15%	6,820,000	7,843,000	9,019,450	10,372,368	11,928,223	15.00%
Speed	10%	387,500	426,250	468,875	515,763	567,339	10.00%
Hockey	6%	2,480,000	2,628,800	2,786,528	2,953,720	3,130,943	6.00%
Extreme	4%	2,170,000	2,256,800	2,347,072	2,440,955	2,538,593	4.00%
Total	10.48%	31,000,000	34,211,600	37,784,350	41,761,474	46,191,633	10.48%

generally in their teens through their early twenties. The extreme segment is of similar age to the hockey players.

- Of the users who are over 20, 65 percent have an undergraduate degree or substantial undergraduate coursework.
- The adult users have a median personal income of $47,000.

Behavior Factors

- Users enjoy fitness activities not as a means for a healthy life, but as an intrinsically enjoyable activity in itself.
- Users spend money on gear, typically sports equipment.
- Users have active lifestyles that include some sort of recreation at least 2–3 times a week.

2.1.2 Market Needs

Pegasus is providing the skating community with a wide range of accessories for all variations of skating. The company seeks to fulfill the following benefits that are important to its customers:

- ***Quality craftsmanship.*** The customers work hard for their money and do not enjoy spending it on disposable products that only work for a year or two.
- ***Well-thought-out designs.*** The skating market has not been addressed by well-thought-out products that serve skaters' needs. Pegasus' industry experience and personal dedication to the sport will provide it with the needed information to produce insightfully designed products.
- ***Customer Service.*** Exemplary service is required to build a sustainable business that has a loyal customer base.

2.1.3 Market Trends

Pegasus will distinguish itself by marketing products not previously available to skaters. The emphasis in the past has been to sell skates and very few replacement parts. The number of skaters is not restricted to any one single country, continent, or age group, so there is a world market. Pegasus has products for virtually every group of skaters. The fastest-growing segment of this sport is the fitness skater. Therefore, the marketing is being directed toward this group. BladeBoots will enable users to enter establishments without having to remove their skates. BladeBoots will be aimed at the recreational skater, the largest segment. SkateAids, on the other hand, are great for everyone.

The sport of skating will also grow through SkateSailing. This sport is primarily for the medium-to-advanced skater, and its growth potential is tremendous. The sails that Pegasus has manufactured have been sold in Europe, following a pattern similar to windsurfing. Windsailing originated in Santa Monica but did not take off until it had already grown big in Europe.

Another trend is group skating. More and more groups are getting together on skating excursions in cities all over the world. For example, San Francisco has night group skating that attracts hundreds of people. The market trends are showing continued growth in all directions of skating.

2.1.4 Market Growth

With the price of skates going down due to competition by so many skate companies, the market has had steady growth throughout the world, with 22.5 million units sold in 1999 to over 31 million in 2002. The growth statistics for 2003 were estimated to be over 35 million units. More and more people are discovering—and in many cases rediscovering—the health benefits and fun of skating.

2.2 SWOT Analysis

The following SWOT analysis captures the key strengths and weaknesses within the company, and describes the opportunities and threats facing Pegasus.

2.2.1 Strengths

- In-depth industry experience and insight.
- Creative, yet practical product designers.
- The use of a highly efficient, flexible business model utilizing direct customer sales and distribution.

2.2.2 Weaknesses

- The reliance on outside capital necessary to grow the business.
- A lack of retailers who can work face-to-face with the customer to generate brand and product awareness.
- The difficulty of developing brand awareness as a start-up company.

2.2.3 Opportunities

- Participation within a growing industry.
- Decreased product costs through economy of scale.
- The ability to leverage other industry participants' marketing efforts to help grow the general market.

2.2.4 Threats

- Future/potential competition from an already established market participant.
- A slump in the economy that could have a negative effect on people's spending of discretionary income on fitness/recreational products.
- The release of a study that calls into question the safety of skating or the inability to prevent major skating-induced traumas.

2.3 Competition

Pegasus Sports International is forming its own market. Although there are a few companies that do make sails and foils that a few skaters are using, Pegasus is the only brand that is truly designed for and by skaters. The few competitors' sails on the market are not designed for skating, but for windsurfing or for skateboards. In the case of foils, storage and carrying are not practical. There are different indirect competitors who are manufacturers of the actual skates. After many years in the market, these companies have yet to become direct competitors by manufacturing accessories for the skates that they make.

2.4 Product Offering

Pegasus Sports International now offers several products:

- The first product that has been developed is BladeBoots, a cover for the wheels and frame of inline skates, which allows skaters to enter places that normally would not allow them in with skates on. BladeBoots come with a small pouch and belt which converts to a well-designed skate carrier.
- The second product is SkateSails. These sails are specifically designed for use while skating. Feedback that Pegasus has received from skaters indicates skatesailing could become a very popular sport. Trademarking this product is currently in progress.
- The third product, SkateAid, will be in production by the end of the year. Other ideas for products are under development, but will not be disclosed until Pegasus can protect them through pending patent applications.

2.5 Keys to Success

The keys to success are designing and producing products that meet market demand. In addition, Pegasus must ensure total customer satisfaction. If these keys to success are achieved, it will become a profitable, sustainable company.

2.6 Critical Issues

As a start-up business, Pegasus is still in the early stages. The critical issues are for Pegasus to:

- Establish itself as the premier skating accessory company.
- Pursue controlled growth that dictates that payroll expenses will never exceed the revenue base. This will help protect against recessions.
- Constantly monitor customer satisfaction, ensuring that the growth strategy will never compromise service and satisfaction levels.

3.0 Marketing Strategy

The key to the marketing strategy is focusing on the speed, health and fitness, and recreational skaters. Pegasus can cover about 80 percent of the skating market because it produce products geared toward each segment. Pegasus is able to address all of the different segments within the market because, although each segment is distinct in terms of its users and equipment, its products are useful to all of the different segments.

3.1 Mission

Pegasus Sports International's mission is to provide the customer with the finest skating accessories available. "We exist to attract and maintain customers. With a strict adherence to this maxim, success will be ensured. Our services and products will exceed the expectations of the customers."

3.2 Marketing Objectives

- Maintain positive, strong growth each quarter (notwithstanding seasonal sales patterns).
- Achieve a steady increase in market penetration.
- Decrease customer acquisition costs by 1.5 percent per quarter.

3.3 Financial Objectives

- Increase the profit margin by 1 percent per quarter through efficiency and economy-of-scale gains.
- Maintain a significant research and development budget (as a percentage relative to sales) to spur future product developments.
- A double- to triple-digit growth rate for the first three years.

3.4 Target Markets

With a world skating market of over 31 million that is steadily growing (statistics released by the Sporting Goods Manufacturers Association), the niche has been created. Pegasus' aim is to expand this market by promoting SkateSailing, a new sport which is popular in both Santa Monica and Venice Beach in California. The Sporting Goods Manufacturers Association survey indicates that skating now has more participation than football, softball, skiing, and snowboarding combined. The breakdown of participation in skating is as follows: 1+% speed (growing), 8% hockey (declining), 7% extreme/aggressive (declining), 22% fitness (nearly 7 million—the fastest growing), and 61% recreational (first-timers). Pegasus' products are targeting the fitness and recreational groups, because they are the fastest growing. These groups are gearing themselves toward health and fitness, and combined, they can easily grow to 85 percent (or 26 million) of the market in the next five years.

3.5 Positioning

Pegasus will position itself as the premier aftermarket skating accessory company. This positioning will be achieved by leveraging Pegasus' competitive edge: industry experience and passion. Pegasus is a skating company formed by skaters for skaters. Its management is able to use its vast experience and personal passion for the sport to develop innovative, useful accessories for a broad range of skaters.

3.6 Strategies

The single objective is to position Pegasus as the premier skating accessory manufacturer, serving the domestic market as well as the international market. The marketing strategy will seek to first create customer awareness concerning the offered products and services and then develop the customer base. The message that Pegasus will seek to communicate is that it offers the best-designed, most useful skating accessories. This message will be communicated through a variety of methods. The first will be the Pegasus Web site, which will provide a rich source of product information and offer consumers the opportunity to purchase. A lot of time and money will be invested in the site to provide the customer with the perception of total professionalism and utility for Pegasus' products and services.

The second marketing method will be advertisements placed in numerous industry magazines. The skating industry is supported by several different glossy magazines designed to promote the industry as a whole. In addition, a number of smaller periodicals serve the smaller market segments within the skating industry. The last method of communication is the use of printed sales literature. The two previously mentioned marketing methods will create demand for the sales literature, which will be sent out to customers. The cost of the sales literature will be fairly minimal, because it will use the already compiled information from the Web site.

3.7 Marketing Mix

Pegasus' marketing mix is comprised of the following approaches to pricing, distribution, advertising and promotion, and customer service.

- ***Pricing.*** This will be based on a per-product retail price.
- ***Distribution.*** Initially, Pegasus will use a direct-to-consumer distribution model. Over time, it will use retailers as well.
- ***Advertising and Promotion.*** Several different methods will be used for the advertising effort.
- ***Customer Service.*** Pegasus will strive to achieve benchmarked levels of customer care.

3.8 Marketing Research

Pegasus is blessed with the good fortune of being located in the center of the skating world: Venice, California. It will be able to leverage this opportune location by working with many of the different skaters that live in the area. Pegasus was able to test all of its products not only with its principals, who are accomplished skaters, but also with the many other dedicated and "newbie" users located in Venice. The extensive product testing by a wide variety of users provided Pegasus with valuable product feedback and has led to several design improvements.

4.0 Financials

This section will offer the financial overview of Pegasus related to marketing activities. Pegasus will address break-even analysis, sales forecasts, expense forecast, and indicate how these activities link to the marketing strategy.

4.1 Break-even Analysis

The break-even analysis indicates that $7,760 will be required in monthly sales revenue to reach the break-even point.

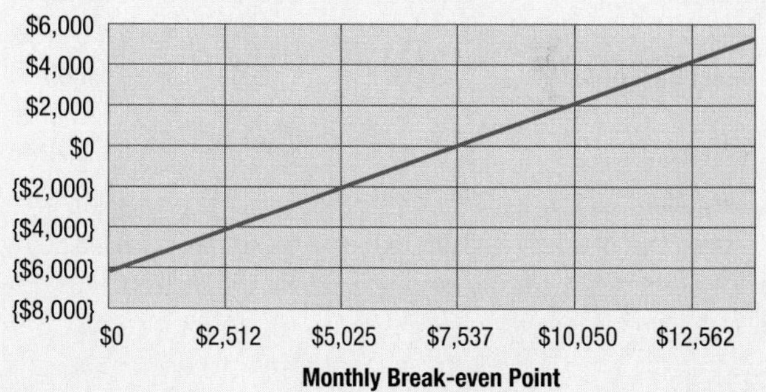

Break-even Analysis

Break-even point = where line intersects with 0

TABLE 4.1 | Break-even Analysis

Break-even Analysis:	
Monthly Units Break-even	62
Monthly Sales Break-even	$ 7,760
Assumptions:	
Average Per-Unit Revenue	$125.62
Average Per-Unit Variable Cost	$ 22.61
Estimated Monthly Fixed Cost	$ 6,363

4.2 Sales Forecast

Pegasus feels that the sales forecast figures are conservative. It will steadily increase sales as the advertising budget allows. Although the target market forecast (Table 2.1) listed all of the potential customers divided into separate groups, the sales forecast groups customers into two categories: Recreational and Competitive. Reducing the number of categories allows the reader to quickly discern information, making the chart more functional.

Monthly Sales Forecast

TABLE 4.2 | Sales Forecast

Sales Forecast			
Sales	**2003**	**2004**	**2005**
Recreational	$455,740	$598,877	$687,765
Competitive	$ 72,918	$ 95,820	$110,042
Total Sales	$528,658	$694,697	$797,807
Direct Cost of Sales	**2003**	**2004**	**2005**
Recreational	$ 82,033	$107,798	$123,798
Competitive	$ 13,125	$ 17,248	$ 19,808
Subtotal Cost of Sales	$ 95,159	$125,046	$143,605

4.3 Expense Forecast

The expense forecast will be used as a tool to keep the department on target and provide indicators when corrections/modifications are needed for the proper implementation of the marketing plan.

Monthly Expense Budget

TABLE 4.3 | Marketing Expense Budget

Marketing Expense Budget	2003	2004	2005
Web site	$25,000	$8,000	$10,000
Advertisements	$8,050	$15,000	$20,000
Printed Material	$1,725	$2,000	$3,000
Total Sales and Marketing Expenses	$34,775	$25,000	$33,000
Percent of Sales	6.58%	3.60%	4.14%
Contribution Margin	$398,725	$544,652	$621,202
Contribution Margin/Sales	75.42%	78.40%	77.86%

5.0 Controls

The purpose of Pegasus' marketing plan is to serve as a guide for the organization. The following areas will be monitored to gauge performance:

- Revenue: monthly and annual
- Expenses: monthly and annual
- Customer satisfaction
- New product development

5.1 Implementation

The following milestones identify the key marketing programs. It is important to accomplish each one on time and on budget.

Milestones

TABLE 5.1 | Milestones

Milestones			Plan		
Milestone	**Start Date**	**End Date**	**Budget**	**Manager**	**Department**
Marketing plan completion	1/1/03	2/1/03	$0	Stan	Marketing
Web site completion	1/1/03	3/15/03	$20,400	outside firm	Marketing
Advertising campaign #1	1/1/03	6/30/03	$3,500	Stan	Marketing
Advertising campaign #2	3/1/99	12/30/03	$4,550	Stan	Marketing
Development of the retail channel	1/1/03	11/30/03	$0	Stan	Marketing
Totals			$28,450		

5.2 Marketing Organization

Stan Blade will be responsible for the marketing activities.

5.3 Contingency Planning

Difficulties and Risks

- Problems generating visibility, a function of being an Internet-based start-up organization.
- An entry into the market by an already established market competitor.

Worst Case Risks Include

- Determining that the business cannot support itself on an ongoing basis.
- Having to liquidate equipment or intellectual capital to cover liabilities.

SUMMARY :::

1. The value delivery process involves choosing (or identifying), providing (or delivering), and communicating superior value. The value chain is a tool for identifying key activities that create value and costs in a specific business.
2. Strong companies develop superior capabilities in managing core business processes such as new-product realization, inventory management, and customer acquisition and retention. Managing these core processes effectively means creating a marketing network in which the company works closely with all parties in the production and distribution chain, from suppliers of raw materials to retail distributors. Companies no longer compete—marketing networks do.
3. According to one view, holistic marketing maximizes value exploration by understanding the relationships between the customer's cognitive space, the company's competence space, and the collaborator's resource space; maximizes value creation by identifying new customer benefits from the customer's cognitive space, utilizing core competencies from its business domain, and selecting and managing business partners from its collaborative networks; and maximizes value delivery by becoming proficient at customer relationship management, internal resource management, and business partnership management.
4. Market-oriented strategic planning is the managerial process of developing and maintaining a viable fit between the organization's objectives, skills, and resources and its changing market opportunities. The aim of strategic planning is to shape the company's businesses and products so that they yield target profits and growth. Strategic planning takes place at four levels: corporate, division, business unit, and product.
5. The corporate strategy establishes the framework within which the divisions and business units prepare their strategic plans. Setting a corporate strategy entails four activities: defining the corporate mission, establishing strategic business units (SBUs), assigning resources to each SBU based on its market attractiveness and business strength, and planning new businesses and downsizing older businesses.
6. Strategic planning for individual businesses entails the following activities: defining the business mission, analyzing external opportunities and threats, analyzing internal strengths and weaknesses, formulating goals, formulating strategy, formulating supporting programs, implementing the programs, and gathering feedback and exercising control.
7. Each product level within a business unit must develop a marketing plan for achieving its goals. The marketing plan is one of the most important outputs of the marketing process.

APPLICATIONS :::

Marketing Debate What Good is a Mission Statement?

Virtually all firms have mission statements to help guide and inspire employees as well as signal what is important to the firm to those outside the firm. Mission statements are often the product of much deliberation and discussion. At the same time, some critics claim that mission statements sometimes lack "teeth" and specificity. Moreover, critics also maintain that in many cases, mission statements do not vary much from firm to firm, and make the same empty promises.

Take a position: Mission statements are critical to a successful marketing organization, *or* Mission statements rarely provide useful marketing value.

Marketing Discussion

Consider Porter's value chain and the holistic marketing orientation model. What implications do they have for marketing planning? How would you structure a marketing plan to incorporate some of their concepts?

PART

2 CAPTURING MARKETING INSIGHTS

IN THIS CHAPTER, WE WILL ADDRESS THE FOLLOWING QUESTIONS:

1. What are the components of a modern marketing information system?
2. What are useful internal records?
3. What is involved in a marketing intelligence system?
4. What are the key methods for tracking and identifying opportunities in the macroenvironment?
5. What are some important macroenvironment developments?

CHAPTER 3 ::: GATHERING INFORMATION AND SCANNING THE ENVIRONMENT

three

Developing and implementing marketing plans involves a number of decisions. Making those decisions is both an art and a science. To provide insight into and inspiration for marketing decision making, companies must possess comprehensive, up-to-date information on macro trends as well as more micro effects particular to their business. Holistic marketers recognize that the marketing environment is constantly presenting new opportunities and threats, and they understand the importance of continuously monitoring and adapting to that environment.

Obesity has officially been called an epidemic by the Centers for Disease Control (CDC): 30 percent of U.S adults are considered obese and its prevalence among kids age 6 to 11 has quadrupled since the 1970s. Obesity is caused by several factors—poor eating habits, a lack of exercise, and sedentary lifestyles—but there has been increased scrutiny of the $200 billion packaged-foods industry. Company responses have taken all forms. Frito-Lay reformulated its entire line of chips and pretzels so that they had zero grams of trans fat. Nestlé has been looking for growth with nutritionally enhanced products that cross food and pharmaceuticals, dubbed "phood." The company sells a breakfast bar called Nesvital containing carbohydrates that are absorbed quickly and make people feel full more quickly. The low-carbohydrate craze drove the sales of products like

>>>

An ad for Atkins Nutritionals breakfast products.

Michelob Ultra and Miller Lite beer (which happily proclaimed it contained half the carbs of category leader Bud Light) and a whole line of products from Atkins Nutritionals.[1]

The food industry isn't alone in having to make adjustments. The sales slump in the apparel sector has been attributed in part to a failure to properly design and size clothing to reflect a wider variety of American shapes, sizes, and cultures.[2] In this chapter, we consider how firms can develop processes to track trends. We also identify a number of important macroenvironment trends. Chapter 4 reviews how marketers can conduct more customized research that addresses specific marketing problems or issues.

::: Components of a Modern Marketing Information System

The major responsibility for identifying significant marketplace changes falls to the company's marketers. More than any other group in the company, they must be the trend trackers and opportunity seekers. Although every manager in an organization needs to observe the outside environment, marketers have two advantages: They have disciplined methods for collecting information and they also spend more time interacting with customers and observing competition.

Some firms have developed marketing information systems that provide management with rich detail about buyer wants, preferences, and behavior.

DUPONT

DuPont commissioned marketing studies to uncover personal pillow behavior for its Dacron Polyester unit, which supplies filling to pillow makers and sells its own Comforel brand. One challenge is that people don't give up their old pillows: 37 percent of one sample described their relationship with their pillow as being like "an old married couple," and an additional 13 percent characterized it as being like a "childhood friend." They found that people fell into distinct groups in terms of pillow behavior: stackers (23%), plumpers (20%), rollers or folders (16%), cuddlers (16%), and smashers, who pound their pillows into a more comfy shape (10%). Women were more likely to plump, whereas men were more likely to fold. The prevalence of stackers led the company to sell more pillows packaged as pairs, as well as to market different levels of softness or firmness.[3]

Marketers also have extensive information about how consumption patterns vary across countries. On a per capita basis within Western Europe, for example, the Swiss consume the most chocolate, the Greeks eat the most cheese, the Irish drink the most tea, and the Austrians smoke the most cigarettes.

Nevertheless, many business firms are not sophisticated about gathering information. Many do not have a marketing research department. Others have a department that limits its work to routine forecasting, sales analysis, and occasional surveys. Many managers complain about not knowing where critical information is located in the company; getting too much information that they cannot use and too little that they really need; getting important information too late; and doubting the information's accuracy. Companies with superior information enjoy a competitive advantage. The company can choose its markets better, develop better offerings, and execute better marketing planning.

TABLE 3.1

Information Needs Probes

1. What decisions do you regularly make?
2. What information do you need to make these decisions?
3. What information do you regularly get?
4. What special studies do you periodically request?
5. What information would you want that you are not getting now?
6. What information would you want daily? Weekly? Monthly? Yearly?
7. What magazines and trade reports would you like to see on a regular basis?
8. What topics would you like to be kept informed of?
9. What data analysis programs would you want?
10. What are the four most helpful improvements that could be made in the present marketing information system?

Every firm must organize and distribute a continuous flow of information to its marketing managers. Companies study their managers' information needs and design marketing information systems (MIS) to meet these needs. A **marketing information system (MIS)** consists of people, equipment, and procedures to gather, sort, analyze, evaluate, and distribute needed, timely, and accurate information to marketing decision makers. A marketing information system is developed from internal company records, marketing intelligence activities, and marketing research. The first two topics are discussed here; the latter topic is reviewed in the next chapter.

The company's marketing information system should be a cross between what managers think they need, what managers really need, and what is economically feasible. An internal MIS committee can interview a cross section of marketing managers to discover their information needs. Table 3.1 displays some useful questions.

::: Internal Records and Marketing Intelligence

Marketing managers rely on internal reports on orders, sales, prices, costs, inventory levels, receivables, payables, and so on. By analyzing this information, they can spot important opportunities and problems.

The Order-to-Payment Cycle

The heart of the internal records system is the order-to-payment cycle. Sales representatives, dealers, and customers send orders to the firm. The sales department prepares invoices and transmits copies to various departments. Out-of-stock items are back ordered. Shipped items are accompanied by shipping and billing documents that are sent to various departments.

Today's companies need to perform these steps quickly and accurately. Customers favor firms that can promise timely delivery. Customers and sales representatives fax or e-mail their orders. Computerized warehouses quickly fill these orders. The billing department sends out invoices as quickly as possible. An increasing number of companies are using the Internet and extranets to improve the speed, accuracy, and efficiency of the order-to-payment cycle.

Sales Information Systems

Marketing managers need timely and accurate reports on current sales. Wal-Mart, for example, knows the sales of each product by store and total each evening. This enables it to transmit nightly orders to suppliers for new shipments of replacement stock. Wal-Mart shares its sales data with its larger suppliers such as P&G and expects P&G to re-supply Wal-Mart stores in a timely manner. Wal-Mart has entrusted P&G with the management of its inventory.[4]

Companies must carefully interpret the sales data so as not to get the wrong signals. Michael Dell gave this illustration: "If you have three yellow Mustangs sitting on a dealer's lot and a customer wants a red one, the salesman may be really good at figuring out how to sell the yellow Mustang. So the yellow Mustang gets sold, and a signal gets sent back to the factory that, hey, people want yellow Mustangs."

Technological gadgets are revolutionizing sales information systems and allowing representatives to have up-to-the-second information. In visiting one of the 10,000 golf shops around the country, sales reps for TaylorMade used to spend up to two hours counting golf clubs in stock before filling new orders by hand. Since the company gave its reps handheld devices with bar-code readers and Internet connections, the reps now simply point their handhelds at the bar codes and automatically tally inventory. By using the two hours they save to focus on boosting sales to retail customers, sales reps improved productivity by 20 percent.[5]

Databases, Data Warehousing, and Data Mining

Today companies organize their information in databases—customer databases, product databases, salesperson databases—and then combine data from the different databases. For example, the customer database will contain every customer's name, address, past transactions, and even demographics and psychographics (activities, interests, and opinions) in some instances. Instead of a company sending a mass "carpet bombing" mailing of a new offer to every customer in its database, it will score the different customers according to purchase recency, frequency, and monetary value. It will send the offer only to the highest scoring customers. Besides saving on mailing expenses, this will often achieve a double-digit response rate.

PIZZA HUT

Pizza Hut claims to have the largest fast-food customer data warehouse in the world, with 40 million U.S. households—or between 40 and 50 percent of the U.S. market. The millions of customer records are gleaned from point-of-sale transactions at its restaurants. Pizza Hut can slice and dice data by favorite toppings, date of last order, or by whether you order a salad with your pepperoni pizza. Using its Teradata Warehouse Miner, Pizza Hut has not only been able to purge expensive duplicates from its direct-mail campaigns, but can also target its marketing to find the best coupon offers for each household and predict the success of campaigns.[6]

Companies warehouse these data and make them easily accessible to decision makers. Furthermore, by hiring analysts skilled in sophisticated statistical methods, they can "mine" the data and garner fresh insights into neglected customer segments, recent customer trends, and other useful information. The customer information can be cross-tabbed with product and salesperson information to yield still deeper insights. To manage all the different databases efficiently and effectively, more firms are using business integration software (see "Marketing Insight: Putting Data to Work with Business Integration Software").

Using its own in-house technology, for example, Wells Fargo has developed the ability to track and analyze every bank transaction made by its 10 million retail customers—whether at ATMs, bank branches, or online. When transaction data are combined with personal information provided by customers, Wells Fargo can come up with targeted offerings to coincide with a customer's life-changing event. As a result, compared with the industry average of 2.2 products per customer, Wells Fargo sells 4.[7]

The Marketing Intelligence System

The internal records system supplies *results* data, but the marketing intelligence system supplies *happenings* data. A **marketing intelligence system** is a set of procedures and sources managers use to obtain everyday information about developments in the marketing environment. Marketing managers collect marketing intelligence by reading books, newspapers, and trade publications; talking to customers, suppliers, and distributors; and meeting with other company managers.

A company can take several steps to improve the quality of its marketing intelligence.

- ***A company can train and motivate the sales force to spot and report new developments.*** Sales representatives are positioned to pick up information missed by other means, yet they often fail to pass on that information. The company must "sell" its sales force on their impor-

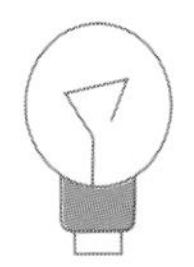

MARKETING INSIGHT | PUTTING DATA TO WORK WITH BUSINESS INTEGRATION SOFTWARE

In the 1990s, companies spent billions installing giant databases and data warehouses and then enormous sums on consultants trying to make sense of it all. A typical large retailer now has 80 terabytes worth of stored information—equivalent to 16 million digital photos or 320 miles of bookshelves. Wal-Mart has a staggering 285 terabytes in its data warehouse.

But data have value only if they can be used. As one analyst put it, "It's like having a bank account with millions of dollars in it but no ATM card. If you can't get it out and can't make it work for you, then it is not really useful." Business integration (BI) software is designed to analyze and interpret massive quantities of data. Typical BI applications cull information out of giant databases and put them into "data marts"—smaller clusters of similar information. Breaking data down in this way helps to more easily and thoroughly diffuse information through the organization.

Consider how business integration software allows Ben & Jerry's to monitor a pint of ice cream from inception to consumption. At Ben & Jerry's headquarters in Burlington, Vermont, each pint of ice cream is stamped after manufacture and its tracking number put in an Oracle database. Using Business Objects software, the sales team can then see which flavors are generating the most sales (Cherry Garcia is a perennial favorite). The marketing department can check to see whether orders online require additional philanthropic donations. The finance people are able to record sales and close their books more quickly. Consumer affairs can match up the pints with the roughly 225 calls and e-mails the company receives each week to make sure there are not systematic problems with any particular ingredients.

BI software is seen as relatively inexpensive and convenient to install, and the results can show up quickly. The Sesame Workshop installed the software for the 2003 holiday season to track its Elmo dolls and was able to cut its back orders by a third. Red Robin Gourmet Burgers, a 196-location chain, used BI software to fine-tune its marketing and operations. It found it was wasting thousands on unused sauces. Staples long devoted space to high-margin furniture. With BI, it found that small items were more profitable. Successes like these are why the market for business integration software is expected to reach $7.5 billion in 2006.

Source: Adapted from Julie Schlosser, "Looking for Intelligence in Ice Cream," *Fortune,* March 17, 2003, pp. 114–120.

tance as intelligence gatherers. Sales reps should know which types of information to send to which managers. Grace Performance Chemicals, a division of W. R. Grace, supplies materials and chemicals to the construction and packaging industries. Grace sales reps were instructed to observe the innovative ways customers used its products to suggest possible new products. For example, some customers were using Grace waterproofing materials to soundproof their cars and patch boots and tents. Seven new-product ideas emerged in total, worth millions in sales to the company.[8]

- ***A company can motivate distributors, retailers, and other intermediaries to pass along important intelligence.*** Many companies hire specialists to gather marketing intelligence. Service providers often send mystery shoppers to their stores to assess how employees treat customers. Mystery shoppers for McDonald's discovered that only 46 percent of its restaurants nationwide met internal speed-of-service standards, forcing the company to rethink processes and training.[9] Retailers also use mystery shoppers. Neiman Marcus employs a professional shopper agency to shop at its stores nationwide. It finds stores that consistently score high on the service have the best sales. Typical questions their mystery shoppers report on are: How long before a sales associate greeted you? Did the sales associate act as if he or she wanted your business? Was the sales associate knowledgeable about products in stock?[10]

- ***A company can network externally.*** It can purchase competitors' products; attend open houses and trade shows; read competitors' published reports; attend stockholders' meetings; talk to employees, dealers, distributors, suppliers, and freight agents; collect competitors' ads; and look up news stories about competitors. Software developer Cognos created an internal Web site called Street Fighter where any of the firm's 3,000 workers can submit scoops about competitors and win prizes.[11] Competitive intelligence must be done legally and ethically, though. Procter & Gamble reportedly paid a multimillion-dollar settlement to Unilever when some external operatives hired as part of a P&G corporate intelligence program to learn about Unilever's hair care products were found to have engaged in such unethical behavior as "dumpster diving."[12]

- ***A company can set up a customer advisory panel.*** Members might include representative customers or the company's largest customers or its most outspoken or sophisticated customers. Many business schools have advisory panels made up of alumni and recruiters who provide valuable feedback on the curriculum.

TABLE 3.2

Secondary Commercial Data Sources

- Nielsen Company: Data on products and brands sold through retail outlets (Retail Index Services), supermarket scanner data (Scantrack), data on television audiences (Media Research Services), magazine circulation data (Neodata Services, Inc.), and others.
- MRCA Information Services: Data on weekly family purchases of consumer products (National Consumer Panel) and data on home food consumption (National Menu Census).
- Information Resources, Inc.: Supermarket scanner data (InfoScan) and data on the impact of supermarket promotions (PromotioScan).
- SAMI/Burke: Reports on warehouse withdrawals to food stores in selected market areas (SAMI reports) and supermarket scanner data (Samscam).
- Simmons Market Research Bureau (MRB Group): Annual reports covering television markets, sporting goods, and proprietary drugs, with demographic data by sex, income, age, and brand preferences (selective markets and media reaching them).
- Other commercial research houses selling data to subscribers include the Audit Bureau of Circulation: Arbitron, Audits and Surveys; Dun & Bradstreet's; National Family Opinion; Standard Rate & Data Service; and Starch.

- ***A company can take advantage of government data resources.*** The 2000 U.S. census provides an in-depth look at the population swings, demographic groups, regional migrations, and changing family structure of 281,421,906 people. Census marketer Claritas cross-references census figures with consumer surveys and its own grassroots research for clients such as Procter & Gamble, Dow Jones, and Ford Motor. Partnering with "list houses" that provide customer phone and address information, Claritas can help firms select and purchase mailing lists with specific clusters.[13]
- ***A company can purchase information from outside suppliers.*** Well-known data suppliers include the A.C. Nielsen Company and Information Resources, Inc. (see Table 3.2). These research firms gather consumer-panel data at a much lower cost than the company could manage on its own. Biz360 has specialized databases to provide reports from 7,000 sources on the extent and nature of media coverage a company is receiving.[14]
- ***A company can use online customer feedback systems to collect competitive intelligence.*** Online customer feedback facilitates collection and dissemination of information on a global scale, usually at low cost. Through online customer review boards or forums, one customer's evaluation of a product or a supplier can be distributed to a large number of other potential buyers and, of course, to marketers seeking information on the competition. Currently existing channels for feedback include message boards, threaded discussion forums that allow users to post new and follow up existing posts; discussion forums, which are more like bulletin boards; opinion forums, which feature more in-depth, lengthy reviews; and chat rooms. While chat rooms have the advantage of allowing users to share experiences and impressions, their unstructured nature makes it difficult for marketers to find relevant messages. To address this issue, various companies have adopted structured systems, such as customer discussion boards or customer reviews. See "Marketing Memo: Clicking on the Competition" for a summary of the major categories of structured online feedback systems.[15]

Some companies circulate marketing intelligence. The staff scans the Internet and major publications, abstracts relevant news, and disseminates a news bulletin to marketing managers. It collects and files relevant information and assists managers in evaluating new information.

::: Analyzing the Macroenvironment

Successful companies recognize and respond profitably to unmet needs and trends. Companies could make a fortune if they could solve any of these problems: a cure for cancer; chemical cures for mental diseases; desalinization of seawater; nonfattening, tasty nutritious food; practical electric cars; and affordable housing.

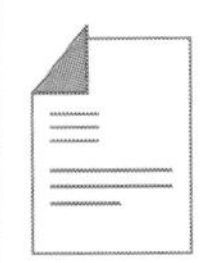

MARKETING **MEMO** | **CLICKING ON THE COMPETITION**

There are four main ways marketers can find relevant online information on competitors' product strengths and weaknesses, and summary comments and overall performance rating of a product, service, or supplier.

- ***Independent customer goods and service review forums.*** These forums include well-known Web sites such as Epinions.com, Rateital.com, Consumerreview.com, and Bizrate.com. Bizrate.com combines consumer feedback from two sources: its 1.2 million members who have volunteered to provide ratings and feedback to assist other shoppers, and survey results on service quality collected from customers of stores listed in Bizrate. These sites have the advantage of being independent from the goods and service providers, which may reduce bias.
- ***Distributor or sales agent feedback sites.*** These sites offer both positive and negative product or service reviews, but the stores or distributors have built the sites themselves. Amazon.com, for instance, offers an interactive feedback opportunity through which buyers, readers, editors, and others may review all products listed in the site, especially books. Elance.com is an online professional services provider that allows contractors to describe their level of satisfaction with subcontractors and provide details of their experiences.
- ***Combo-sites offering customer reviews and expert opinions.*** This type of site is concentrated in financial services and high-tech products that require professional knowledge. Zdnet.com, an online advisor on technology products, offers customer comments and evaluations based on ease of use, features, and stability, along with expert reviews. Zdnet summarizes the number of positive and negative evaluations and total download numbers within a certain period (commonly a week or a month) for each software program. The advantage of this type of review site lies in the fact that a product supplier can compare opinions from the experts with those from consumers.
- ***Customer complaint sites.*** These forums are designed mainly for dissatisfied customers. Reviewers at most opinion sites tend to offer positive comments due to financial incentives and potential lawsuits for slanderous or libelous negative comments. In contrast, some Web sites offer a complaining forum with a moderator. For instance, Planetfeedback.com allows customers to voice unfavorable experiences with specific companies. Another site, Complaints.com, is devoted to customers who want to vent their frustrations with particular firms or their offerings.

Source: Adapted from Robin T. Peterson and Zhilin Yang, "Web Product Reviews Help Strategy," *Marketing News*, April 7, 2004, p. 18.

Needs and Trends

Enterprising individuals and companies manage to create new solutions to unmet needs. FedEx was created to meet the need for next-day mail delivery. Dockers was created to meet the needs of baby boomers who could no longer really wear—or fit into!—their jeans and wanted a physically and psychologically comfortable pair of pants. Amazon was created to offer more choice and information for books and other products.

We can draw distinctions among fads, trends, and megatrends. A **fad** is "unpredictable, short-lived, and without social, economic, and political significance." A company can cash in on a fad such as Beanie Babies, Furbies, and Tickle Me Elmo dolls, but this is more a matter of luck and good timing than anything else.[16]

A **trend** is a direction or sequence of events that has some momentum and durability. Trends are more predictable and durable than fads. A trend reveals the shape of the future and provides many opportunities. For example, the percentage of people who value physical fitness and well-being has risen steadily over the years, especially in the under-30 group, the young women and upscale group, and people living in the West. Marketers of health foods and exercise equipment cater to this trend with appropriate products and communications.

Megatrends have been described as "large social, economic, political and technological changes [that] are slow to form, and once in place, they influence us for some time—between seven and ten years, or longer."[17] See "Marketing Insight: Ten Megatrends Shaping the Consumer Landscape" for a look into the forces in play during the next decade or so.

Trends and megatrends merit close attention. A new product or marketing program is likely to be more successful if it is in line with strong trends rather than opposed to them, but detecting a new market opportunity does not guarantee success, even if it is technically feasible. For example, today some companies sell portable "electronic books"; but there may not be a sufficient number of people interested in reading a book on a computer screen or willing to pay the required price. This is why market research is necessary to determine an opportunity's profit potential.

To help marketers spot cultural shifts that might bring new opportunities or threats, several firms offer social-cultural forecasts. The Yankelovich Monitor interviews 2,500 people nationally

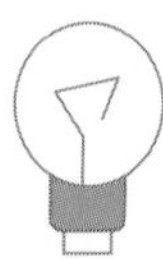

MARKETING INSIGHT | TEN MEGATRENDS SHAPING THE CONSUMER LANDSCAPE

- ***Aging Boomers.*** As baby boomers grow older, their impact on consumer spending can hardly be overstated. That's because unlike previous generations, boomers are deciding to delay the aging process and will continue to earn and spend as they age.
- ***Delayed Retirement.*** Baby boomers have delayed every life stage transition, such as getting married and having children. So it's highly likely that they will also delay their retirement. Between 2000 and 2010, the Bureau of Labor Statistics forecasts a 33 percent increase in the number of people ages 65 to 74 in the workforce.
- ***The Changing Nature of Work.*** More than half of all U.S. workers are employed in management, in professional or related occupations, or in a sales or other office-based position.
- ***Greater Educational Attainment—Especially Among Women.*** With so many jobs requiring intellectual skills, the number of high school graduates attending college is rising. While men and women are equally likely to graduate from high school, women are more likely to attend college. The long-term implications of this trend are that people with a college education will have higher lifetime incomes, and there should be an increase in women's earning power.
- ***Labor Shortages.*** Although more service workers are needed in suburban areas, fewer people can afford to live there. Suburban locales will turn to service automation or a greater reliance on immigrant labor.
- ***Increased Immigration.*** Based on Census 2000, the Census Bureau estimated that 40 percent of the nation's population growth was due to immigration. As our citizens age, the population growth for newborns will be outpaced by the growth due to immigration.
- ***Rising Hispanic Influence.*** Already the largest minority group in the United States, with 35 million people, the Hispanic population is projected by the Census Bureau to increase 35 percent in this decade. Though Hispanic households represented only 9 percent of U.S. households in 2000, they accounted for 20 percent of the 4 million children born in this country that year.
- ***Shifting Birth Trends.*** These are represented by three minitrends: (1) the increasing incidence of births by older women—35 and older—who have higher spending power, (2) the declining number of births by teenagers, and (3) the rising diversity among young children. About two-thirds of women of childbearing age are non-Hispanic whites, but they accounted for less than half (43.5%) of births in 2000.
- ***Widening Geographic Differences.*** This trend has two elements. There is an increasing demographic difference between cities, suburbs, and rural areas, along with a rise in distinctive regional consumer markets. For example, the very low population growth in New England has led to a median age of 37.1 in that region compared to a median age of 32.3 in Texas or 33.3 in California. Non-Hispanic whites make up 84 percent of total population in New England but only 53 percent of population in the West.
- ***Changing Age Structure.*** In the future the differences in size between one age cohort and the next will be much smaller. Over the next decade there is likely to be only a slight change, 1 percent or less annually, in the number of consumers in each age cohort younger than 35.

Source: Adapted from Peter Francese, "Top Trends for 2003," *American Demographics* (December 2002/January 2003): 48–51.

each year and has tracked 35 social trends since 1971, such as "anti-bigness," "mysticism," "living for today," "away from possessions," and "sensuousness." It describes the percentage of the population who share the attitude as well as the percentage who do not.

Identifying the Major Forces

Companies and their suppliers, marketing intermediaries, customers, competitors, and publics all operate in a macroenvironment of forces and trends that shape opportunities and pose threats. These forces represent "noncontrollables," which the company must monitor and to which it must respond. In the economic arena, companies and consumers are increasingly affected by global forces (see Table 3.3).

The beginning of the new century brought a series of new challenges: the steep decline of the stock market, which affected savings, investment, and retirement funds; increasing unemployment; corporate scandals; and of course, the rise of terrorism. These dramatic events were accompanied by the continuation of other, already-existing longer-term trends that have profoundly influenced the global landscape.

Within the rapidly changing global picture, the firm must monitor six major forces: demographic, economic, social-cultural, natural, technological, and political-legal. Although these forces will be described separately, marketers must pay attention to their interactions, because these will lead to new opportunities and threats. For example, explosive population growth (demographic) leads to more resource depletion and pollution (natural), which leads consumers to call for more laws (political-legal), which stimulate new technological solutions and products (technological), which, if they are affordable (economic), may actually change attitudes and behavior (social-cultural).

TABLE 3.3

Global Forces Affecting Marketing

1. The substantial speedup of international transportation, communication, and financial transactions, leading to the rapid growth of world trade and investment, especially tripolar trade (North America, Western Europe, Far East).
2. The movement of manufacturing capacity and skills to lower-cost countries.
3. The rise of trade blocs such as the European Union and the NAFTA signatories.
4. The severe debt problems of a number of countries, along with the increasing fragility of the international financial system.
5. The increasing use of barter and countertrade to support international transactions.
6. The move toward market economies in formerly socialist countries along with rapid privatization of publicly owned companies.
7. The rapid dissemination of global lifestyles.
8. The development of emerging markets, namely, China, India, Eastern Europe, the Arab countries, and Latin America.
9. The increasing tendency of multinationals to transcend locational and national characteristics and become transnational firms.
10. The increasing number of cross-border corporate strategic alliances—for example, airlines.
11. The increasing ethnic and religious conflicts in certain countries and regions.
12. The growth of global brands across a wide variety of industries such as autos, food, clothing, and electronics.

::: The Demographic Environment

Demographic trends are highly reliable for the short and intermediate run. There is little excuse for a company's being suddenly surprised by demographic developments. The Singer Company should have known for years that its sewing machine business would be hurt by smaller families and more working wives, yet it was slow in responding.

The main demographic force that marketers monitor is *population,* because people make up markets. Marketers are keenly interested in the size and growth rate of population in cities, regions, and nations; age distribution and ethnic mix; educational levels; household patterns; and regional characteristics and movements.

Worldwide Population Growth

The world population is showing explosive growth: It totaled 6.1 billion in 2000 and will exceed 7.9 billion by the year 2025.[18] Here is an interesting picture:

> If the world were a village of 1,000 people, it would consist of 520 women and 480 men, 330 children, and 60 people over age 65, 10 college graduates and 335 illiterate adults. The village would contain 52 North Americans, 55 Russians, 84 Latin Americans, 95 East and West Europeans, 124 Africans, and 584 Asians. Communication would be difficult because 165 people would speak Mandarin, 86 English, 83 Hindi/Urdu, 64 Spanish, 58 Russian, and 37 Arabic, and the rest would speak one of over 200 other languages. There would be 329 Christians, 178 Moslems, 132 Hindus, 62 Buddhists, 3 Jews, 167 nonreligious, 45 atheists, and 86 others.[19]

The population explosion has been a source of major concern. Unchecked population growth and consumption could eventually result in insufficient food supply, depletion of key minerals, overcrowding, pollution, and an overall deterioration in the quality of life. Moreover, population growth is highest in countries and communities that can least afford it. The less developed regions of the world currently account for 76 percent of the world population and are growing at 2 percent per year, whereas the population in the more developed countries is growing at only 0.6 percent per year. In developing countries, the death rate has been falling as a result of modern medicine, but the birthrate has remained fairly stable. Feeding, clothing, and educating children, while also providing a rising standard of living, is nearly impossible in these countries.

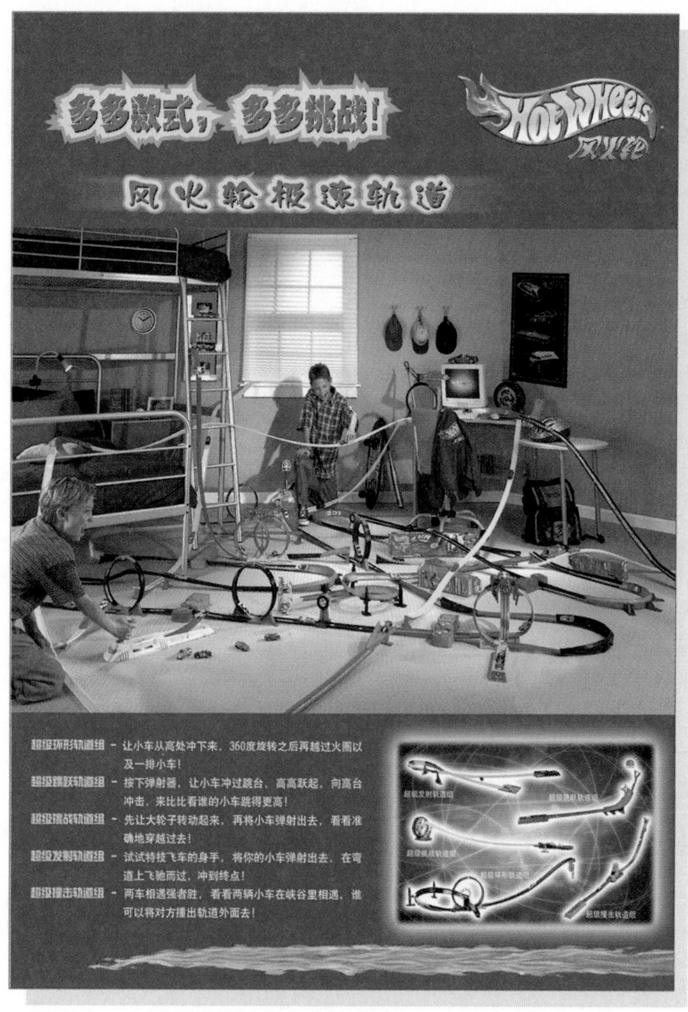

A Mattel ad in Chinese for its Hot Wheels toy. The headline reads: "Hot Wheels Performance Tracks—Great Varieties, Great Challenges!"

Explosive population growth has major implications for business. A growing population does not mean growing markets unless these markets have sufficient purchasing power. Nonetheless, companies that carefully analyze their markets can find major opportunities. For example, to curb its skyrocketing population, the Chinese government has passed regulations limiting families to one child. One consequence of these regulations: These children are spoiled and fussed over as never before. Known in China as "little emperors," Chinese children are being showered with everything from candy to computers as a result of the "six pocket syndrome." As many as six adults—parents, grandparents, great-grandparents, and aunts and uncles—may be indulging the whims of each child. This trend has encouraged toy companies, such as Japan's Bandai Company, Denmark's Lego Group, and the U.S.'s Hasbro and Mattel to aggressively enter the Chinese market.[20]

Population Age Mix

National populations vary in their age mix. At one extreme is Mexico, a country with a very young population and rapid population growth. At the other extreme is Japan, a country with one of the world's oldest populations. Milk, diapers, school supplies, and toys would be important products in Mexico. Japan's population would consume many more adult products.

However, there is a global trend toward an aging population. According to a survey in *The Economist,* more people will grow old in this century than ever before. In 2004 or 2005, the population of people aged 60 or over will surpass the proportion of under fives, and there are unlikely to ever again be more toddlers than seniors. It is the start of what the Japanese are calling The Silver Century. The graying of the population is affected by another trend, the widespread fall in fertility rates. In most countries, women are not having enough babies to replace the people who die. The result will be fewer working people to replace those who retire. In a decade's time, many countries—Japan, the United States, and the European countries, for instance—will face the huge problem of having to support a vastly larger population of elderly people.[21]

A population can be subdivided into six age groups: preschool, school-age children, teens, young adults age 25 to 40, middle-aged adults age 40 to 65, and older adults age 65 and up. For marketers, the most populous age groups shape the marketing environment. In the United States, the "baby boomers," the 78 million people born between 1946 and 1964, are one of the most powerful forces shaping the marketplace. Baby boomers are fixated on their youth, not their age.

With many baby boomers well into their fifties and even the last wave turning 40, demand for products to turn back the hands of time has exploded. According to one survey, half of all boomers were depressed that they were no longer young and nearly one in five were actively resisting the aging process. The 40-plus age group will be 60 percent bigger than the 18 to 39 group by 2010, and it now controls three-quarters of the country's wealth. As they search for the fountain of youth, sales of hair replacement and coloring aids, health club memberships, home gym equipment, skin-tightening creams, nutritional supplements, and organic foods have all soared.[22]

Boomers grew up with TV advertising, so they are an easier market to reach than the 45 million born between 1965 and 1976, dubbed Generation X (and also the shadow generation, twenty-somethings, and baby busters).[23] Generation-Xers are typically cynical about hard-sell marketing pitches that promise more than they can deliver, but some marketers have been able to break through.

VW

Volkswagen sales in the United States rose from under 50,000 cars in 1993 to over 300,000 a decade later partly as a result of a "Drivers Wanted" ad campaign that targeted fun-loving or youthful drivers. Rather than appealing to the mass market, VW went after a younger demographic willing to spend a little extra on a Volkswagen because of the car's German engineering, sportier image, and versatility. The voiceover on the introductory TV spot identifies the target audience by saying, "On the road of life, there are passengers and there are drivers."[24]

Both baby boomers and Generation-Xers will be passing the torch to the latest demographic group, Generation Y or the echo boomers, born between 1977 and 1994. Now numbering 72 million, this group is almost equal in size to baby boomers. One distinguishing characteristic of this age group is their utter fluency and comfort with computer and Internet technology. Don Tapscott has christened them "Net-Gens" for this reason. He says: "To them, digital technology is no more intimidating than a VCR or a toaster."[25]

Ethnic and Other Markets

Countries also vary in ethnic and racial makeup. At one extreme is Japan, where almost everyone is Japanese; at the other is the United States, where people come from virtually all nations. The United States was originally called a "melting pot," but there are increasing signs that the melting didn't occur. Now people call the United States a "salad bowl" society, with ethnic groups maintaining their ethnic differences, neighborhoods, and cultures.

According to the 2000 census, the U.S. population of 276.2 million was 72 percent white. African Americans constituted 13 percent, and Latinos 11 percent. The Latino population had been growing fast, with the largest subgroups of Mexican (5.4 percent), Puerto Rican (1.1 percent), and Cuban (0.4 percent) descent. Asian Americans constituted 3.8 percent of the U.S. population, with the Chinese as the largest group, followed by the Filipinos, Japanese, Asian Indians, and Koreans, in that order. Latino and Asian American consumers are concentrated in the far western and southern parts of the country, although some dispersal is taking place. Moreover, there were nearly 25 million people living in the United States—more than 9 percent of the population—who were born in another country.

A frequently noted megatrend, the increase in the percentage of Hispanics in the total population, represents a major shift in the nation's center of gravity. Hispanics made up half of all new workers in the past decade and will bump up to 25 percent of workers in two generations. Despite their lagging family incomes, Hispanic buying power is soaring. Disposable income has jumped 29 percent since 2001, to $652 billion in 2003—double the pace of the rest of the population. From the food Americans eat, to the clothing they wear, the music they listen to, and the cars they buy, Hispanics are having a huge impact. Companies are scrambling to refine their products and their marketing to reach this fastest-growing and most influential consumer group:[26]

- ***Procter & Gamble.*** In 2000 the company set up a 65-person bilingual team to better target Latino consumers. Now the company tailors its products to appeal to Latino tastes. For example, it added a third scent to its Gain detergent called "White Water Fresh" after finding that 57 percent of Latinos like to smell their purchases.
- ***Kroger.*** The nation's number-one grocery chain spent $1.8 million to convert its 59,000 square-foot Houston store into a *Supermercado* with Spanish-language signage and products such as plantain leaves and Mexican cocoa. The company has also expanded its private-label Buena Comida line to 105 different items.
- ***PacifiCare Health Systems.*** When this Cypress, California–based insurance company found that 20 percent of its 3 million policyholders are Hispanic, it set up a new unit, Latino Health Solutions. The unit markets PacifiCare health insurance products in Spanish, directs Hispanics to Spanish-speaking doctors, and translates documents into Spanish for Hispanic workers.

Ethnic groups have certain specific wants and buying habits. Several food, clothing, and furniture companies have directed their products and promotions to one or more of these groups.[27] Charles Schwab is one of the leading financial services firms serving Asian Americans with a carefully targeted marketing program.[28]

CHARLES SCHWAB

San Francisco–based Charles Schwab recognized the growing power of the Asian consumer after the 1990 census. It now employs over 200 people who speak Chinese, Korean, and Vietnamese at call centers dedicated to Asian American customers who either want to communicate in their own languages or to whom cultural affinity is important. There is a Chinese-language Web site for trading, research, and online news service. Fourteen Schwab branches are found in predominantly Asian neighborhoods across the country. The company also advertises on Asian TV channels, in newspapers, on radio, and at online community Web sites.

Yet marketers must be careful not to overgeneralize about ethnic groups. Within each ethnic group are consumers who are quite different from each other. "There is really no such thing as an Asian market," says Greg Macabenta, whose ethnic advertising agency specializes in the Filipino market. Macabenta emphasizes that the five major Asian American groups have their own very specific market characteristics, speak different languages, consume different cuisines, practice different religions, and represent very distinct national cultures.[29]

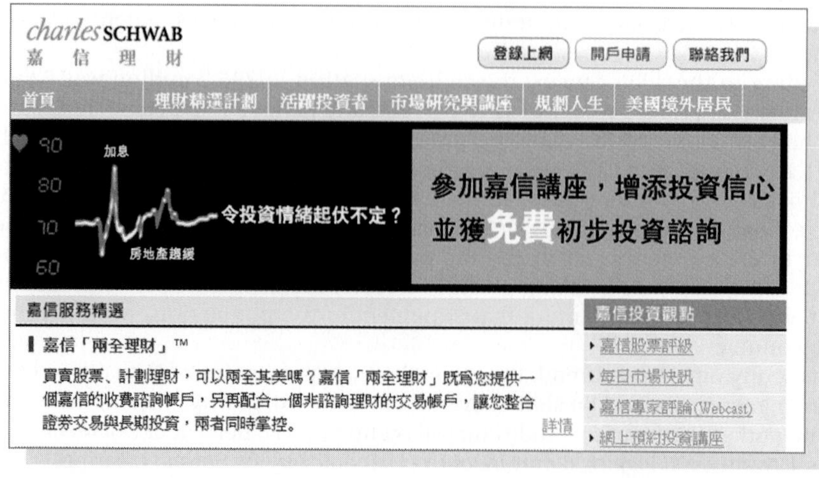

The home page of Schwab's Chinese-language Web site. Customers who prefer to use Chinese can trade, do research, and get the latest news.

Diversity goes beyond ethnic and racial markets. More than 50 million Americans have disabilities, and they constitute a market for home delivery companies such as Peapod, and for various medical services.

Educational Groups

The population in any society falls into five educational groups: illiterates, high school dropouts, high school diplomas, college degrees, and professional degrees. In Japan, 99 percent of the population is literate, whereas in the United States 10 to 15 percent of the population may be functionally illiterate. However, the United States has one of the world's highest percentages of college-educated citizens, around 36 percent. The high number of educated people in the United States spells a high demand for quality books, magazines, and travel, and a high supply of skills.

BRAND NAME UNIVERSITIES

The higher levels of educational attainment in the United States have led to both an increased emphasis on marketing to college students and the increased marketing of colleges and universities as definable "brands." Heightened competition for the top students and concerns about institutions' reputations and rankings are prompting these institutions to create a brand image. No one disputes the strength of the "Harvard" name as a symbol of educational excellence and preeminence. Bottom-line pressures due to tuition discounting and comparative shopping by prospective students and their parents are encouraging lesser-known colleges to take a market-oriented approach. Georgia Tech defines itself as the "twenty-first-century technology university" by focusing on its quality programs, cutting-edge research, and aggressive technology transfer. Clark University in Worcester, Massachusetts, emphasizes its size (Clark is among the smallest of the major research universities), its history as an innovator, and a student body comprised of individuals who are obsessed with their own areas of interest.[30]

Household Patterns

The "traditional household" consists of a husband, wife, and children (and sometimes grandparents). Yet, in the United States today, one out of eight households is "diverse" or "nontraditional," and includes single live-alones, adult live-togethers of one or both sexes, single-parent families, childless married couples, and empty-nesters. More people are divorcing or separating, choosing not to marry, marrying later, or marrying without the intention to have children. Each group has a distinctive set of needs and buying habits. For example, people in the SSWD group (single, separated, widowed, divorced) need smaller apartments; inexpensive and smaller appliances, furniture, and furnishings; and smaller-size food packages. Marketers must increasingly consider the special needs of nontraditional households, because they are now growing more rapidly than traditional households.

Married couple households—the dominant cohort since the formation of the United States—have slipped from nearly 80 percent in the 1950s to around 50 percent today. Americans are delaying marriage longer than ever, cohabiting in greater numbers, forming more same-sex partnerships, living far longer, and remarrying less after splitting up. By 2010, nearly 30 percent of homes will be inhabited by someone who lives alone. A record number of children—33 percent—are now born to single parents, many of them underemployed mothers. But singles can also have much buying power and spend more on themselves than those who live in larger households. Products such as the George Foreman grill that target people who live alone and value convenience can be successful.[31]

A study by Cava Research Group at the University of Leeds in the United Kingdom emphasizes that single doesn't necessarily mean "alone." Researchers interviewed hundreds of people between the ages of 25 and 60 and concluded that "friends are the new family." They observed a growing trend for "neo-tribes" of 20-somethings to live communally. At the other end of the spectrum, older divorced people were seen centering their lives on their children and friends and keeping their romantic lives separate. This emphasis on friendship can influence marketers in everything from whom they target to how they craft their marketing messages. Travel with friends or with a group, for instance, now appeals to a wider swath of singles than college students on spring break or seniors going off to an elderhostel.[32] Online services are recognizing this trend.

FRIENDSTER.COM

Founded in Sunnyvale, California, in 2003, Friendster connects people for dating, making friends, business propositions, and plain old online voyeurism. The founder of Friendster created it after trying an online dating service and finding that he was not "keen on messaging random weirdoes." The premise of Friendster is that it's better to connect to new people through people you already know. It's the old friend of a friend of a friend strategy for meeting and dating. Users can browse through the profiles of their friends, friends' friends, and so on in their network. With just 20 friends, a user can be linked to 50,000 or more people. The profiles include photos, favorite books, and other interests, along with pictures of their friends on the network. When users find someone interesting, they can see how they are connected and write a note. It's like being the star of your own game of "Six Degrees of Separation"—the notion that anyone can be linked to anyone else in the world via six connections. The site, which is free to members, has about 7 million users and has spawned a number of knock-off social networking sites such as Tribe, Rise, and Google's Orkut.[33]

The gay market is a particularly lucrative segment. Academics and marketing experts estimate that the gay and lesbian population ranges between 4 and 8 percent of the total U.S. population, with an even higher percentage in urban areas.[34] Compared to the average American, respondents who classify themselves as gay are over 10 times more likely to be in professional jobs, almost twice as likely to own a vacation home, eight times more likely to own a computer notebook, and twice as likely to own individual stocks.[35] Companies such as Absolut, American Express, IKEA, Procter & Gamble, and Subaru have recognized the potential of this market and the nontraditional household market as a whole.

GAY.COM

Gays and lesbians are also the perfect online consumer group since they spend up to 10 times longer online than the average Internet user, according to a recent Forrester Research study. It shouldn't be surprising, then, that the number-one American Web site to reach single men with household incomes over $75,000 is *not* CNN sports, but Gay.com. The site pulls in big-name mainstream advertisers such as American Airlines, Viacom, Procter & Gamble, General Motors, and IBM. These smart marketers know that gays and lesbians are among the most brand-loyal of consumers, with 87 percent more likely to give their business to companies that target them specifically. That's why Gay.com's parent company, PlanetOutPartners, has taken an aggressive approach toward advertisers with this pitch: "The average middle-class family spends over $1 million to raise a child through age 22. Some gay people have kids. Most don't. Where are they spending their money? On your products."[36]

Geographical Shifts in Population

This is a period of great migratory movements between and within countries. Forward-looking companies and entrepreneurs are taking advantage of the growth in immigrant populations and marketing their wares specifically to these new members of the population.

Within countries, population movement also occurs as people migrate from rural to urban areas, and then to suburban areas. Although the United States experienced a rural rebound in the 1990s as nonmetropolitan counties attracted large numbers of urban refugees, the twenty-first century saw urban markets grow more rapidly again due to a higher birth rate, a lower death rate, and rapid growth from foreign immigration.[37]

Location makes a difference in goods and service preferences. The movement to the Sunbelt states has lessened the demand for warm clothing and home heating equipment and increased the demand for air conditioning. Those who live in large cities such as New York, Chicago, and San Francisco account for most of the sales of expensive furs, perfumes, luggage, and works of art. These cities also support the opera, ballet, and other forms of culture. Americans living in the suburbs lead more casual lives, do more outdoor living, and have greater neighbor interaction, higher incomes, and younger families. Suburbanites buy vans, home workshop equipment, outdoor furniture, lawn and gardening tools, and outdoor cooking equipment. There are also regional differences: People in Seattle buy more toothbrushes per capita than people in any other U.S. city; people in Salt Lake City eat more candy bars; people from New Orleans use more ketchup; and people in Miami drink more prune juice.

Suburban growth and a disdain for commuting has helped those businesses that cater to the growing SOHO (small office—home office) segment. Nearly 40 million Americans are working out of their homes with the help of electronic conveniences like computers, cell phones, fax machines, and personal organizers. Makers of RTA (ready to assemble) furniture might find a strong consumer base among all the cashed-out former city residents setting up offices in small towns or telecommuting from there to larger companies. One company that is shifting gears to appeal to the SOHO segment is Kinko's Copy Centers.

KINKO'S COPY CENTERS

Founded in the 1970s as a campus photocopying business, Kinko's is now reinventing itself as the well-appointed office outside the home. Where once there were copy machines, the 1,200 Kinko's stores in this country and abroad now feature a mix of fax machines, ultra-fast color printers, and networks of computers equipped with popular software programs and high-speed Internet connections. Kinko's is now a $2 billion company that offers an unprecedented array of office services. People can come to a Kinko's store to do all their office jobs: copy, send and receive faxes, use various programs on the computer, go on the Internet, order stationery and other printed supplies, and even teleconference. And as more people work at home, Kinko's offers an escape from the isolation of the home office. Kinko's acquisition by FedEx in early 2004 resulted in further integration with the overnight delivery pioneer.[38]

Marketers also look at where consumers are gathering. Almost one in two people over the age of five (120 million) moved at least one time between 1995 and 2000, according to a Census 2000 brief. The brief's state-by-state analysis clearly shows that the shift has been toward the Sunbelt states, away from the Midwest and Northeast.[39] From Virginia on down to Florida, and western Sunbelt states such as Texas, Nevada, or Arizona, these "hot" states are luring more roamers. An interesting facet of this trend is that these Sunbelt states are no longer seen solely as retiree meccas, but are luring young people to settle there, too. Naples, Florida, is a case in point.

NAPLES, FLORIDA

The most recent U.S. census found that Naples, Florida, a city of 21,000, and surrounding Collier County have been acquiring young, single, college-educated residents at a faster clip than any other part of the United States. Once young people might have just visited their retired parents in Naples or helped them move there. Now, they may move in. Aside from being drawn by the balmy weather—Naples has 333 days of sunshine a year and an average temperature of 75 degrees—they are tempted by employment. There are jobs in companies catering to the needs of well-to-do seasonal residents and retirees as well as new technology ventures based in and around Naples that have won national, even international, clients and reputations. Entrepreneurs, many relatively young themselves, have been moving to Naples and its environs to launch companies in telecommunications, computer software, marketing, and other fields. Young people are asking themselves "why wait to retire here. I want this quality of life now."[40]

::: Other Major Macroenvironments

Other macroenvironment forces profoundly affect the fortunes of marketers. Here we review developments in the economic, social-cultural, natural, technological, and political-legal environments.

Economic Environment

Markets require purchasing power as well as people. The available purchasing power in an economy depends on current income, prices, savings, debt, and credit availability. Marketers must pay careful attention to trends affecting purchasing power because they can have a strong impact on business, especially for companies whose products are geared to high-income and price-sensitive consumers.

INCOME DISTRIBUTION Nations vary greatly in level and distribution of income and industrial structure. There are four types of industrial structures: *subsistence economies* (few opportunities for marketers); *raw-material-exporting economies* like Zaire (copper) and Saudi Arabia (oil), with good markets for equipment, tools, supplies, and luxury goods for the rich; *industrializing economies,* like India, Egypt, and the Philippines, where a new rich class and a growing middle class demand new types of goods; and *industrial economies,* which are rich markets for all sorts of goods.

In a global economy, marketers need to pay attention to the shifting income distribution in countries around the world, particularly countries where affluence levels are rising.

INDIA

With its surfeit of low-cost, high-IQ, English-speaking employees, India is snapping up programming and call-center jobs once held by Americans in a wave of outsourcing that shows no signs of stopping. By 2008, IT services and back-office work in India will swell fivefold, to a $57 billion annual export industry employing 4 million people and accounting for 7 percent of India's gross domestic product. While India's ascendance inevitably means lost jobs and anguish for American white-collar workers, it also means a larger market for American and Western goods—and anguish for traditional Indian families. Along with training in American accents and geography, India's legions of call-center employees are absorbing new ideas about family, material possessions, and romance. "I call these kids 'liberalization children,' " says Rama Bijapurkar, a Bombay-based marketing consultant. "This generation has a hunger in the belly for achievement." Liberalization children are questioning conservative traditions such as arranged marriages and no public kissing. They want to watch Hollywood movies, listen to Western music, chat on cell phones, buy on credit—rather than saving—and eat out in restaurants or cafés. And they are being targeted relentlessly by companies that have waited to see India develop a Western-style consumer class.[41]

Marketers often distinguish countries with five different income-distribution patterns: (1) very low incomes; (2) mostly low incomes; (3) very low, very high incomes; (4) low, medium, high incomes; and (5) mostly medium incomes. Consider the market for Lamborghinis, an automobile costing more than $150,000. The market would be very small in countries with type (1) or (2) income patterns. One of the largest single markets for Lamborghinis turns out to be Portugal [income pattern (3)]—one of the poorer countries in Western Europe, but one with enough wealthy families to afford expensive cars.

Over the past three decades in the United States, the rich have grown richer, the middle class has shrunk, and the poor have remained poor. From 1973 to 1999, earnings for U.S. households in the top 5 percent of the income distribution grew 65 percent, compared with growth of 11 percent for the middle fifth households during the same period. This is leading to a two-tier U.S. market, with affluent people able to buy expensive goods and working-class people having to spend more carefully, shopping at discount stores and factory outlet malls, and selecting less expensive store brands. Conventional retailers who offer medium-priced goods are the most vulnerable to these changes. Companies that respond to the trend by tailoring their products and pitches to these two very different Americas stand to gain.[42]

GAP

GAP pursues a segmented market strategy with three tiers of retail clothing stores: the upscale Banana Republic, the mid-market GAP, and the budget-priced Old Navy. Jeans sell for $70 at Banana Republic stores and for as much as $50 at GAP stores. Old Navy jeans sell for under $25. Each store has its own look, its own clothing lines, and its own in-house advertising. This segmented strategy helped GAP grow from a $7 billion to a $14 billion business between 1996 and 2003.[43]

SAVINGS, DEBT, AND CREDIT AVAILABILITY Consumer expenditures are affected by savings, debt, and credit availability. U.S. consumers have a high debt-to-income ratio, which slows down further expenditures on housing and large-ticket items. Credit is very available in the United States but at fairly high interest rates, especially to lower-income borrowers. Here the Internet can offer a helping hand: Consumers seeking a mortgage can go to lendingtree.com, fill out a single loan application, and receive several loan package proposals from competing banks within 48 hours.

OUTSOURCING AND FREE TRADE An economic issue of increasing importance is the migration of manufacturers and service jobs off shore. Outsourcing is seen as a competitive necessity by many firms, but as a cause of unemployment by many domestic workers. For example, in December 2003, IBM decided to move the jobs of nearly 5,000 programmers to India and China. GE has moved much of its research and development overseas. Microsoft, Dell, American Express, and virtually every major multinational from Accenture to Yahoo! have already offshored work or are considering doing so.

The savings are dramatic, with companies cutting 20 to 70 percent of their labor costs, assuming the work is of comparable quality. However, beyond the short-term gain for employers and pain for displaced domestic white-collar employees is the scarier long-term prospect. The exodus of programming work, in particular, throws the future of America's tech dominance into doubt. Many wonder whether the United States can continue to lead the industry as software programming spreads around the globe from India to Bulgaria. In Bombay, for example, there is high-speed Internet access, a world-class university, and a venture capital industry—all the ingredients you need to spawn the next earthshaking technology innovation.[44]

Outside the labor market, advocates for and against free trade debate the merits of protective tariffs.

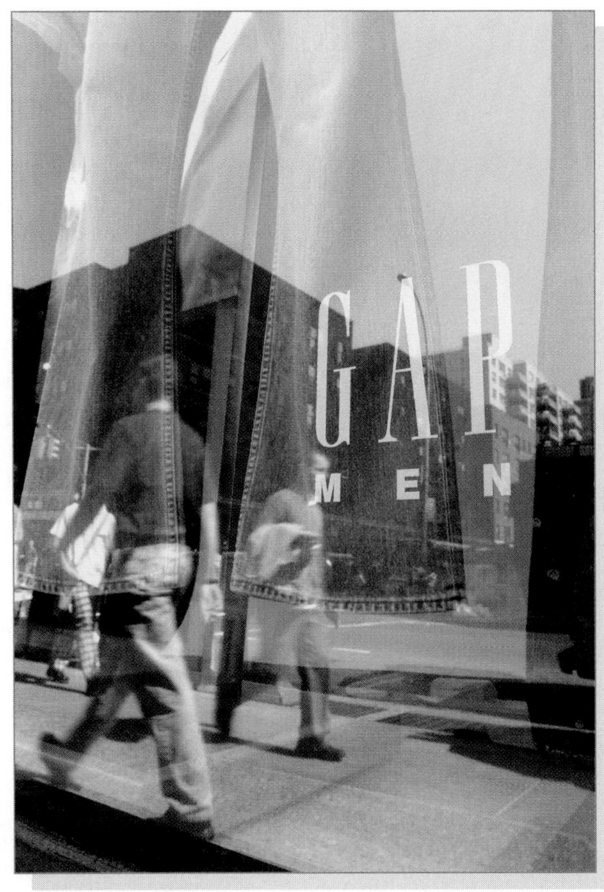

A GAP storefront displays the familiar, recognizable GAP "look."

FAIR TRADE COFFEE

Activist group Global Exchange, a human rights organization dedicated to promoting environmental, political, and social justice around the world, has pressured the coffee industry to support Fair Trade Certified coffee. More than 500,000 farmers around the world produce and sell more than 170 million pounds of coffee each year through the Fair Trade network. Over 100 Fair Trade coffee brands are sold worldwide in approximately 35,000 retail outlets (7,000 in the United States). To become Fair Trade certified, an importer must meet stringent international criteria, such as paying a minimum price per pound of $1.26. Global Exchange chose to target Starbucks to participate in the network, given its high profile. A grassroots campaign led to the introduction of whole bean Fair Trade Certified coffee at over 2,300 Starbucks stores as part of a broader corporate social responsibility initiative on the part of the company.[45]

Social-Cultural Environment

Purchasing power is directed toward certain goods and services and away from others according to people's tastes and preferences. Society shapes the beliefs, values, and norms that largely define these tastes and preferences. People absorb, almost unconsciously, a worldview that defines their relationships to themselves, to others, to organizations, to society, to nature, and to the universe.

- ***Views of themselves.*** People vary in the relative emphasis they place on self-gratification. In the United States during the 1960s and 1970s, "pleasure seekers" sought fun, change, and escape. Others sought "self-realization." People bought dream cars and dream vacations and spent more time in health activities (jogging, tennis), in introspection, and in arts and crafts (see Table 3.4 for a current profile). Today, some people are adopting more conservative behaviors and ambitions. Marketers must recognize that there are many different groups with different views of themselves.

- ***Views of others.*** People are concerned about the homeless, crime and victims, and other social problems. They would like to live in a more humane society. At the same time, people are seeking out their "own kind" and avoiding strangers. They hunger for serious and long-lasting relationships with a few others. These trends portend a growing market for social-support products and services that promote direct relations between human beings, such as health clubs, cruises, and religious activity. They also suggest a growing market for "social surrogates," things that allow people who are alone to feel that they are not, such as television, home video games, and chat rooms on the Internet.

- ***Views of organizations.*** People vary in their attitudes toward corporations, government agencies, trade unions, and other organizations. Most people are willing to work for these organizations, but there has been an overall decline in organizational loyalty. The massive wave of company downsizings and corporate accounting scandals such as those at Enron, WorldCom, and Tyco has bred cynicism and distrust.[46] Many people today see work not as a source of satisfaction, but as a required chore to earn money to enjoy their nonwork hours. This outlook has several marketing implications. Companies need to find new ways to win back consumer and employee confidence. They need to make sure that they are good corporate citizens and that their consumer messages are honest.

- ***Views of society.*** People vary in their attitudes toward their society. Some defend it (preservers), some run it (makers), some take what they can from it (takers), some want to change it (changers), some are looking for something deeper (seekers), and some want to leave it (escapers).[47] Consumption patterns often reflect social attitude. Makers tend to be high achievers who eat, dress, and live well. Changers usually live more frugally, drive smaller cars, and wear simpler clothes. Escapers and seekers are a major market for movies, music, surfing, and camping.

- ***Views of nature.*** People vary in their attitudes toward nature. Some feel subjugated by it, others feel in harmony with it, and still others seek mastery over it. A long-term trend has been humankind's growing mastery of nature through technology. More recently, however, people have awakened to nature's fragility and finite resources. They recognize that nature can be destroyed by human activities. Business has responded to increased interest in camping, hiking, boating, and fishing with hiking boots, tenting equipment, and other gear. Tour operators are packaging tours to wilderness areas and to places like Antarctica.

- ***Views of the universe.*** People vary in their beliefs about the origin of the universe and their place in it. Most Americans are monotheistic, although religious conviction and practice have been waning through the years. Certain evangelical movements are reaching out to bring people back into organized religion. Some of the religious impulse has been redirected into an interest in Eastern religions, mysticism, the occult, and the human potential movement.

As people lose their religious orientation, they seek self-fulfillment and immediate gratification. At the same time, every trend seems to breed a countertrend, as indicated by a worldwide rise in religious fundamentalism. Here are some other cultural characteristics of interest to marketers: the persistence of core cultural values, the existence of subcultures, and shifts of values through time.

HIGH PERSISTENCE OF CORE CULTURAL VALUES The people living in a particular society hold many *core beliefs* and values that tend to persist. Most Americans still believe in work, in getting married, in giving to charity, and in being honest. Core beliefs and values are passed on from parents to children and are reinforced by major social institutions—schools, churches, businesses, and governments. *Secondary beliefs* and values are more open to change. Believing in the institution of marriage is a core belief; believing that people ought to get married early is a secondary belief. Thus family-planning marketers could make some

TABLE 3.4

Most Popular American Leisure Activities (percent of adults who participate)

Walking for exercise	59%
Gardening	45%
Swimming	35%
Photography	26%
Bicycling	25%
Fishing	23%
Bowling	21%
Camping	21%
Jogging or running	18%
Free weights or circuit training	17%
Golf	16%
Adult continuing education	16%
Hiking/backpacking	14%
Power boating	9%

Source: Scarborough Research, 2001, as summarized in "Where Does the Time Go?" *American Demographics* (April 2002) 56.

headway arguing that people should get married later, rather than that they should not get married at all.

Marketers have some chance of changing secondary values but little chance of changing core values. For instance, the nonprofit organization Mothers Against Drunk Drivers (MADD) does not try to stop the sale of alcohol, but it does promote the idea of appointing a designated driver who will not drink that evening. The group also lobbies to raise the legal drinking age.

EXISTENCE OF SUBCULTURES Each society contains **subcultures**, groups with shared values emerging from their special life experiences or circumstances. Members of subcultures share common beliefs, preferences, and behaviors. To the extent that subcultural groups exhibit different wants and consumption behavior, marketers can choose particular subcultures as target markets.

Marketers sometimes reap unexpected rewards in targeting subcultures. Marketers have always loved teenagers because they are society's trendsetters in fashion, music, entertainment, ideas, and attitudes. Marketers also know that if they attract someone as a teen, there is a good chance they will keep the person as a customer later in life. Frito-Lay, which draws 15 percent of its sales from teens, said it saw a rise in chip-snacking by grown-ups. "We think it's because we brought them in as teenagers," said Frito-Lay's marketing director.[48]

SHIFTS OF SECONDARY CULTURAL VALUES THROUGH TIME Although core values are fairly persistent, cultural swings do take place. In the 1960s, hippies, the Beatles, Elvis Presley, and other cultural phenomena had a major impact on young people's hairstyles, clothing, sexual norms, and life goals. Today's young people are influenced by new heroes and new activities: U2's Bono, the NBA's LeBron James, golf's Tiger Woods, and skateboarder Tony Hawk.

Natural Environment

The deterioration of the natural environment is a major global concern. In many world cities, air and water pollution have reached dangerous levels. There is great concern about "greenhouse gases" in the atmosphere due to the burning of fossil fuels; about the depletion of the ozone layer due to certain chemicals; and about growing shortages of water. In Western Europe, "green" parties have vigorously pressed for public action to reduce industrial pollution. In the United States, experts have documented ecological deterioration, and watchdog groups such as the Sierra Club and Friends of the Earth carry these concerns into political and social action.

New regulations hit certain industries very hard. Steel companies and public utilities have had to invest billions of dollars in pollution-control equipment and more environmentally friendly fuels. The auto industry has had to introduce expensive emission controls in cars. The soap industry has had to increase its products' biodegradability. The major hope is that companies will adopt practices that will protect the natural environment. Great opportunities await companies and marketers who can create new solutions that promise to reconcile prosperity with environmental protection.

Consumers often appear conflicted about the natural environment. One research study showed that although 80 percent of U.S. consumers stated that whether or not a product is safe for the environment influenced their decision to buy that product, only a little over half asserted that they bought recycled or environmentally safe products.[49] Young people especially were more likely to feel that nothing that they did personally made a difference. Increasing the number of green products that are bought requires breaking consumers' loyalty habits, overcoming consumer skepticism about the motives behind the introduction of green products and their quality level, and changing consumer attitudes about the role they play in environmental protection. (See "Marketing Insight: Green Marketing".)

Marketers need to be aware of the threats and opportunities associated with four trends in the natural environment: the shortage of raw materials, especially water; the increased cost of energy; increased pollution levels; and the changing role of governments.

SHORTAGE OF RAW MATERIALS The earth's raw materials consist of the infinite, the finite renewable, and the finite nonrenewable. *Infinite resources,* such as air and water, are becoming a problem. Water shortages are already a political issue, and the danger is no longer long term. *Finite renewable resources,* such as forests and food, must be used wisely. Forestry companies are required to reforest timberlands in order to protect the soil and to ensure sufficient wood to meet future demand. Because the amount of arable land is fixed and urban areas are constantly encroaching on farmland, food supply can also be a major problem. *Finite nonrenewable resources*—oil, coal, platinum, zinc, silver—will pose a serious problem as the point of depletion approaches. Firms making products that require these increasingly scarce minerals face substantial cost increases. Firms engaged in research and development have an excellent opportunity to develop substitute materials.

INCREASED ENERGY COSTS One finite nonrenewable resource, oil, has created serious problems for the world economy. In October 2004, oil prices shot up to over $55 a barrel, reinforcing the need for alternative energy forms. Companies are searching for practical means to harness solar, nuclear, wind, and other forms of energy. In the solar energy field alone, hundreds of firms introduced first-generation products to harness solar energy for heating homes and other uses. Other firms are engaged in building practical electric automobiles, with a potential prize of billions for the winner. Practical combination vehicles, like the Toyota Prius, *Motor Trend* magazine's 2004 Car of the Year, are already available.

ANTI-POLLUTION PRESSURES Some industrial activity will inevitably damage the natural environment. Consider the dangerous mercury levels in the ocean, the quantity of DDT and other chemical pollutants in the soil and food supply, and the littering of the environment with bottles, plastics, and other packaging materials. A large market has been created for pollution-control solutions, such as scrubbers, recycling centers, and landfill systems. Its existence leads to a search for alternative ways to produce and package goods. 3M runs a Pollution Prevention Pays program that has led to a substantial reduction in pollution and costs. Dow Chemical built a new ethylene plant in Alberta that uses 40 percent less energy and releases 97 percent less wastewater. AT&T uses a special

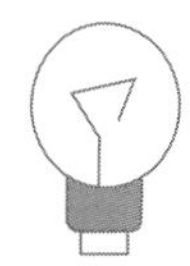

MARKETING INSIGHT | GREEN MARKETING

Although environmental issues have long affected marketing practices, especially in Europe, their relevance has increased in the last decade or so. With the well-publicized Earth Day activities in the United States in April 1990, the "green marketing" movement was born. An explosion of "environmentally friendly" products and marketing programs appeared as firm after firm tried to capitalize on consumers' perceived increased sensitivity to environmental issues.

From a branding perspective, however, "green marketing" programs have not been entirely successful. For example, in 1994, Philips Electronics NV branded its eco-friendly, energy-saving fluorescent bulbs as "Earthlight." Due to a lack of sales success, the product was repackaged in 2000 as convenient, seven-year life "Marathon" bulbs, and sales grew steadily at 7 percent annually. Faced with slumping sales, Ben & Jerry's dropped its "Rainforest Crunch" flavor of ice cream, introduced on Earth Day in 1990 to tout conservation and nuts from rainforest trees. Despite a concerted marketing effort, Green Mountain Energy has found it difficult to sell electricity from eco-friendly power plants.

Many other marketers tried and failed with green sales pitches over the last decade. What obstacles did this movement encounter?

- ***Overexposure and lack of credibility.*** So many companies made environmental claims that the public became skeptical of their validity. Government investigations into some "green" claims (e.g., the degradability of trash bags) and media reports of the spotty environmental track records behind others only increased consumers' doubts. This backlash resulted in many consumers thinking environmental claims were just marketing gimmicks.
- ***Consumer behavior.*** Research studies have shown that consumers as a whole may not be willing to pay a premium for environmental benefits, although certain market segments will be. Most consumers appear unwilling to give up the benefits of other alternatives to choose green products. For example, some consumers dislike the performance, appearance, or texture of recycled paper and household products. And some consumers are unwilling to give up the convenience of disposable products such as diapers.
- ***Poor implementation.*** In jumping on the green marketing bandwagon, many firms did a poor job implementing their marketing program. Products were poorly designed in terms of environmental worthiness, overpriced, and inappropriately promoted. Some ads failed to make the connection between what the company was doing for the environment and how it affected individual consumers.

To get around these obstacles and make sure environmental initiatives are implemented, some companies recommend relying on the efforts of a "Green Champion"—an environmentalist who works internally to make companies greener. Jean Palmateer, an environmental engineer, is a "green champion" for DePuy Orthopaedics, a division of Johnson & Johnson. She recommends getting broad goals accomplished by personalizing the issue. For instance, when Palmeteer wanted to keep the medical device makers' wastewater tanks clean, she told workers that better maintained tanks would not just help the earth, but save them from 3:00 A.M. phone calls when the tanks failed to discharge. Now the tanks are cleaner and workers are sleeping better at night.

There have been some notable green marketing successes through the years. Chevron' s highly visible "People Do" ad campaign attempted to transform consumers' negative perceptions of oil companies and their effect on the environment by describing specific Chevron programs designed to save wildlife, preserve seashores, and so on.

McDonald's has introduced a number of well-publicized environmental initiatives through the years, such as unbleached paper carry-out bags and replacing polystyrene foam sandwich clamshells with paper wraps and lightweight recycled boxes. McDonald's received the EPA WasteWise Partner of the Year award for waste reduction efforts that: (1) conserved 3,200 tons of paper and cardboard by replacing sandwich containers with single-layer flexible sandwich wraps; (2) eliminated 1,100 tons of cardboard materials that would have been used for shipping by switching to light drink cups; and (3) resulted in spending $355 million on recycled content products.

Sources: Jacquelyn Ottman, *Green Marketing: Opportunity for Innovation,* 2nd ed. (Chicago: NTC/Contemporary Publishing Company, 1998); Geoffrey Fowler, "'Green' Sales Pitch Isn't Moving Many Products," *Wall Street Journal,* March 6, 2002, p. B4; Lynn J. Cook, "Our Electrons Are Greener," *Forbes,* June 23, 2003, p. 101; Kevin Lane Keller, *Strategic Brand Management,* 2nd ed. (Upper Saddle River, NJ: Prentice Hall, 2003); Maggie Jackson, "Earth-Friendly Company Changes Come from One 'Green Champion' at a Time," *Boston Globe,* May 9, 2004, p. G1.

software package to choose the least harmful materials, cut hazardous waste, reduce energy use, and improve product recycling in its operations.[50]

CHANGING ROLE OF GOVERNMENTS Governments vary in their concern and efforts to promote a clean environment. For example, the German government is vigorous in its pursuit of environmental quality, partly because of the strong green movement in Germany and partly because of the ecological devastation in the former East Germany. Many poor nations are doing little about pollution, largely because they lack the funds or the political will. It is in the richer nations' interest to help the poorer nations control their pollution, but even the richer nations today lack the necessary funds.

Technological Environment

One of the most dramatic forces shaping people's lives is technology. Technology has released such wonders as penicillin, open-heart surgery, and the birth control pill. It has released such horrors as the hydrogen bomb, nerve gas, and the submachine gun. It has also released such mixed blessings as the automobile and video games.

Every new technology is a force for "creative destruction." Transistors hurt the vacuum-tube industry, xerography hurt the carbon paper business, autos hurt the railroads, and television hurt the newspapers. Instead of moving into the new technologies, many old industries fought or ignored them, and their businesses declined. Yet it is the essence of market capitalism to be dynamic and tolerate the creative destructiveness of technology as the price of progress.

Look out Dell, HP, Apple, and Microsoft: According to some seers, "smart" mobile phones will eventually eclipse the PC.

SMART PHONES

"One day, 2 or 3 billion people will have cell phones, and they are all not going to have PCs," says Jeff Hawkins, inventor of the Palm Pilot and chief technology officer for PalmOne. "The mobile phone will become their digital life," Hawkins predicts. After a slow start, mobile phones have become more ubiquitous—there are 1.5 billion in the world today—and smarter. Today's most sophisticated phones already have the processing power of a mid-1990s PC while consuming 100 times less electricity. The phones are used to send e-mail, browse the Web, take pictures, and play video games. Hawkins predicts that within the next few decades all phones will be mobile phones, capable of receiving voice and Internet signals at broadband speeds, and that mobile-phone bills will shrink to a few dollars a month as phone companies pay off their investment in new networks. New smart phones in the works include Palm's pocket-size Treo600, with a tiny keyboard, a built-in digital camera, and slots for added memory; and Motorola's MPx, which features a "dual-hinge" design. The handset opens in one direction and appears to be a regular phone, but it also flips open on another axis to look like an e-mail device, with the expanded phone keypad serving as a small, conventional qwerty keypad.[51]

The economy's growth rate is affected by how many major new technologies are discovered. Unfortunately, technological discoveries do not arise evenly through time—the railroad industry created a lot of investment, and then investment petered out until the auto industry emerged. Later, radio created a lot of investment, which then petered out until television appeared. In the time between major innovations, an economy can stagnate. In the meantime, minor innovations fill the gap: freeze-dried coffee, combination shampoo and conditioner, antiperspirants and deodorants, and the like. They involve less risk, but they also divert research effort away from major breakthroughs.

New technology also creates major long-run consequences that are not always foreseeable. The contraceptive pill, for example, led to smaller families, more working wives, and larger discretionary incomes—resulting in higher expenditures on vacation travel, durable goods, and luxury items.

The marketer should monitor the following trends in technology: the pace of change, the opportunities for innovation, varying R&D budgets, and increased regulation.

ACCELERATING PACE OF CHANGE Many of today's common products were not available 40 years ago. John F. Kennedy did not know personal computers, digital wristwatches, video recorders, fax machines, personal digital assistants, or the Internet; nor has the pace of technological change slowed down. The Human Genome project promises to usher in the Biological Century as biotech workers create new medical cures, new foods, and new materials. Electronic researchers are building smarter chips to make our cars, homes, and offices more responsive to changing conditions. The blending of personal computers, scanners, fax and copy machines, wireless phones, the Internet, and e-mail has made it possible for people to *telecommute*—that is, work at home or on the road instead of traveling to an office. This trend may reduce auto pollution, bring the family closer together, and create more home-centered shopping and entertainment.

An increasing number of ideas are being worked on, and the time between the appearance of new ideas and their successful implementation is all but disappearing. So is the time between introduction and peak production. Ninety percent of all the scientists who ever lived are alive today, and technology feeds upon itself.

UNLIMITED OPPORTUNITIES FOR INNOVATION Scientists today are working on a startling range of new technologies that will revolutionize products and production processes. Some of the most exciting work is being done in biotechnology, computers, microelectronics, telecommunications, robotics, and designer materials. Researchers are working on AIDS cures, happiness pills, painkillers, totally safe contraceptives, and nonfattening foods. They are designing robots for firefighting, underwater exploration, and home nursing. In addition, scientists also work on fantasy products, such as small flying cars, three-dimensional television, and space colonies. The challenge in each case is to develop affordable versions of these products.

SAMSUNG

In an ambitious endeavor, Samsung has launched a digital home business. In Korea, Samsung has 6,000 networked homes that are outfitted with Internet-enabled ovens, refrigerators, security cameras, and wall-mounted flat-panel displays. Samsung is looking to take the idea abroad. Wiring homes in the United States will cost from $2,000 to $10,000, making adoption relatively affordable. Besides overcoming a few technical challenges, however, Samsung must also contend with consumers who worry about the complexity or even need for such products. But experts look to the further penetration of broadband access to propel the adoption of the digital home as consumers learn to access digital media and commerce from more devices.[52]

Companies are already harnessing the power of *virtual reality (VR),* the combination of technologies that allows users to experience three-dimensional, computer-generated environments through sound, sight, and touch. Virtual reality has already been applied to gathering consumer reactions to new automobile designs, kitchen layouts, exterior home designs, and other potential offerings.

VARYING R&D BUDGETS Although the United States leads the world in annual R&D expenditures, a growing portion of U.S. R&D expenditures is going into the development side of R&D, raising concerns about whether the United States can maintain its lead in basic science. Many companies are content to put their money into copying competitors' products and making minor feature and style improvements. Even basic research companies such as DuPont, Bell Laboratories, and Pfizer are proceeding cautiously, and more research directed toward major breakthroughs is being conducted by consortiums of companies rather than by single companies.

INCREASED REGULATION OF TECHNOLOGICAL CHANGE As products become more complex, the public needs to be assured of its safety. Consequently, government agencies' powers to investigate and ban potentially unsafe products have been expanded. In the United States, the Federal Food and Drug Administration must approve all drugs before they can be sold. Safety and health regulations have also increased in the areas of food, automobiles, clothing, electrical appliances, and construction. Marketers must be aware of these regulations when proposing, developing, and launching new products.

Political-Legal Environment

Marketing decisions are strongly affected by developments in the political and legal environment. This environment is composed of laws, government agencies, and pressure groups that influence and limit various organizations and individuals. Sometimes these laws also create new opportunities for business. For example, mandatory recycling laws have given the recycling industry a major boost and spurred the creation of dozens of new companies making new products from recycled materials. Two major trends deal with the increase in business legislation and the growth of special interest groups.

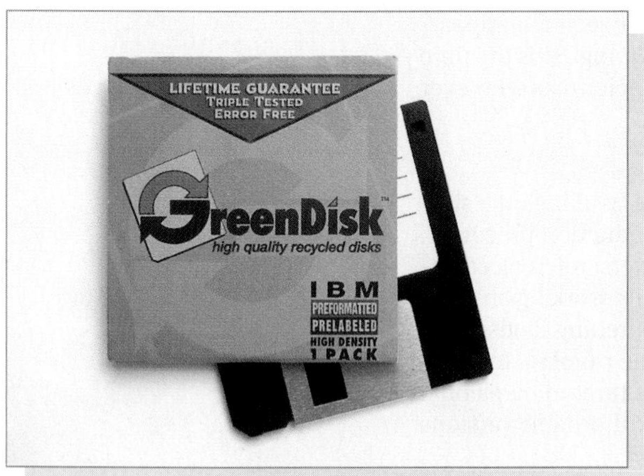

GreenDisk, a company that produces high-quality recycled disks.

INCREASE IN BUSINESS LEGISLATION Business legislation has three main purposes: to protect companies from unfair competition, to protect consumers from unfair business practices, and to protect the interests of society from unbridled business behavior. A major purpose of business legislation and enforcement is to charge businesses with the social costs created by their products or production processes. A central concern is this: At what point do the costs of regulation exceed the benefits? The laws are not always administered fairly; regulators and enforcers may be lax or overzealous. Although each new law may have a legitimate rationale, it may have the unintended effect of sapping initiative and retarding economic growth.

Legislation affecting business has increased steadily over the years. The European Commission has been active in establishing a new framework of laws covering competitive behavior, product standards, product liability, and commercial transactions for the 25 member nations of the European Union. The United States has many laws on its books covering such issues as competition, product safety and liability, fair trade and credit practices, and packaging and labeling.[53]

Several countries have gone further than the United States in passing strong consumer protection legislation. Norway bans several forms of sales promotion—trading stamps, contests, premiums—as inappropriate or "unfair" instruments for promoting products. Thailand requires food processors selling national brands to market low-price brands also, so that low-income consumers can find economy brands. In India, food companies need

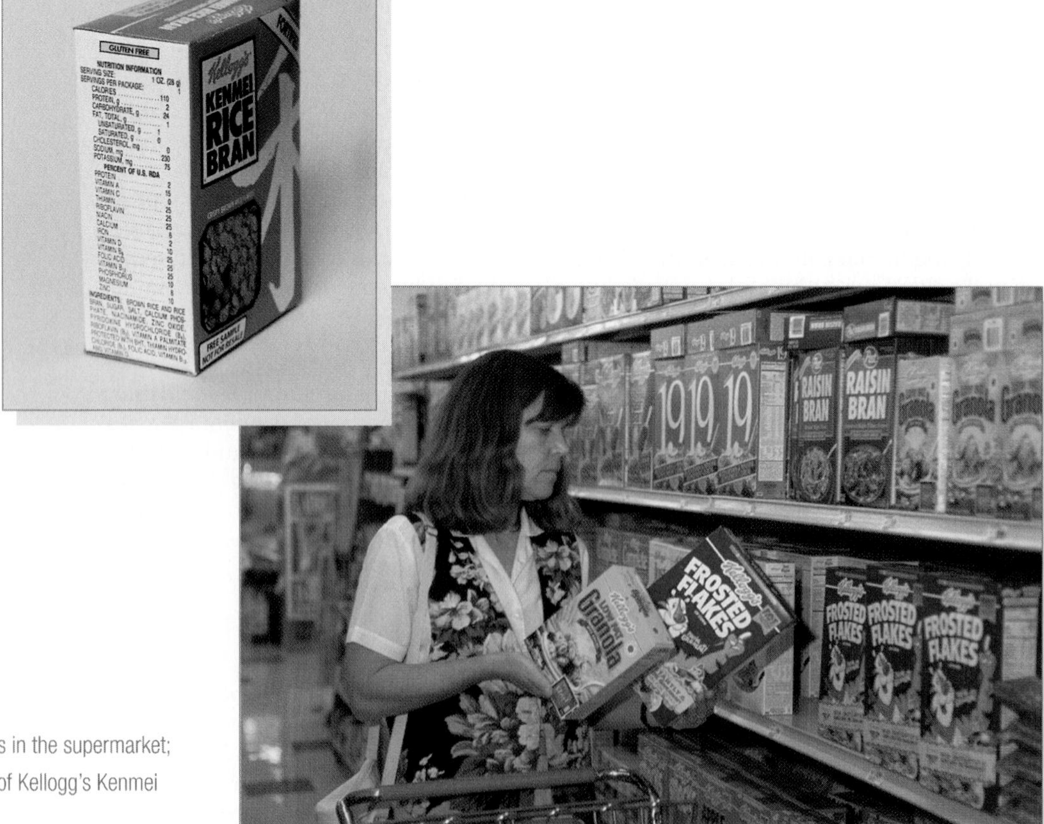

Checking the nutrition labels in the supermarket; the nutrition label on a box of Kellogg's Kenmei Rice Bran.

special approval to launch brands that duplicate what already exists on the market, such as another cola drink or brand of rice.

Marketers must have a good working knowledge of the major laws protecting competition, consumers, and society. Companies generally establish legal review procedures and promulgate ethical standards to guide their marketing managers, and as more business takes place in cyberspace, marketers must establish new parameters for doing electronic business ethically.

Unit pricing labels for cereals on a supermarket shelf.

GROWTH OF SPECIAL-INTEREST GROUPS

The number and power of special-interest groups have increased over the past three decades. Political action committees (PACs) lobby government officials and pressure business executives to pay more attention to consumers' rights, women's rights, senior citizens' rights, minority rights, and gay rights.

Many companies have established public affairs departments to deal with these groups and issues. An important force affecting business is the **consumerist movement**—an organized movement of citizens and government to strengthen the rights and powers of buyers in relation to sellers. Consumerists have advocated and won the right to know the true interest cost of a loan, the true cost per standard unit of competing brands (unit pricing), the basic ingredients in a product, the nutritional quality of food, the freshness of products, and the true benefits of a product.

With consumers increasingly willing to swap personal information for customized products from firms—as long as they can be trusted—privacy issues will continue to be a public policy hot button.[54] Consumer concerns are that they will be robbed or cheated; that private information will be used against them; that someone will steal their identity; that they will be bombarded with solicitations; and that children will be targeted.[55] Several companies have established consumer affairs departments to help formulate policies and respond to consumer complaints. Companies are careful to answer their e-mail and to resolve and learn from any customer complaints.

Clearly, new laws and growing numbers of pressure groups have put more restraints on marketers. Marketers have to clear their plans with the company's legal, public relations, public affairs, and consumer affairs departments. Insurance companies directly or indirectly affect the design of smoke detectors; scientific groups affect the design of spray products by condemning aerosols. In essence, many private marketing transactions have moved into the public domain.

SUMMARY :::

1. To carry out their analysis, planning, implementation, and control responsibilities, marketing managers need a marketing information system (MIS). The role of the MIS is to assess the managers' information needs, develop the needed information, and distribute that information in a timely manner.
2. An MIS has three components: (a) an internal records system, which includes information on the order-to-payment cycle and sales reporting systems; (b) a marketing intelligence system, a set of procedures and sources used by managers to obtain everyday information about pertinent developments in the marketing

environment; and (c) a marketing research system that allows for the systematic design, collection, analysis, and reporting of data and findings relevant to a specific marketing situation.

3. Many opportunities are found by identifying trends (directions or sequences of events that have some momentum and durability) and megatrends (major social, economic, political, and technological changes that have long-lasting influence).
4. Within the rapidly changing global picture, marketers must monitor six major environmental forces: demographic, economic, social-cultural, natural, technological, and political-legal.
5. In the demographic environment, marketers must be aware of worldwide population growth; changing mixes of age, ethnic composition, and educational levels; the rise of nontraditional families; large geographic shifts in population; and the move to micromarketing and away from mass marketing.
6. In the economic arena, marketers need to focus on income distribution and levels of savings, debt, and credit availability.
7. In the social-cultural arena, marketers must understand people's views of themselves, others, organizations, society, nature, and the universe. They must market products that correspond to society's core and secondary values, and address the needs of different subcultures within a society.
8. In the natural environment, marketers need to be aware of raw materials shortages, increased energy costs and pollution levels, and the changing role of governments in environmental protection.
9. In the technological arena, marketers should take account of the accelerating pace of technological change, opportunities for innovation, varying R&D budgets, and the increased governmental regulation brought about by technological change.
10. In the political-legal environment, marketers must work within the many laws regulating business practices and with various special-interest groups.

APPLICATIONS :::

Marketing Debate Is Consumer Behavior More a Function of a Person's Age or Generation?

One of the widely debated issues in developing marketing programs that target certain age groups is how much consumers change over time. Some marketers maintain that age differences are critical and that the needs and wants of a 25-year-old in 2002 are not that different from those of a 25-year-old in 1972. Others dispute that contention and argue that cohort and generation effects are critical and that marketing programs must therefore suit the times.

Take a position: Age differences are fundamentally more important than cohort effects versus Cohort effects can dominate age differences.

Marketing Discussion

What brands and products do you feel successfully "speak to you" and effectively target your age group? Why? Which ones do not? What could they do better?

IN THIS CHAPTER, WE WILL ADDRESS THE FOLLOWING QUESTIONS:

1. What constitutes good marketing research?
2. What are good metrics for measuring marketing productivity?
3. How can marketers assess their return on investment of marketing expenditures?
4. How can companies more accurately measure and forecast demand?

CHAPTER 4 :::

CONDUCTING MARKETING RESEARCH AND FORECASTING DEMAND

four

In addition to monitoring a changing marketing environment, marketers also need to develop specific knowledge about their particular markets. Good marketers want information to help them interpret past performance as well as plan future activities. Marketers need timely, accurate, and actionable information on consumers, competition, and their brands. They need to make the best possible tactical decisions in the short run and strategic decisions in the long run. Discovering a consumer insight and understanding its marketing implications can often lead to a successful product launch or spur the growth of a brand.

St. Louis-based Build-A-Bear Workshop has cleverly capitalized on the "kiddie-craft" trend in children's toys as well as the trend for interactive entertainment retailing. Instead of making pottery or play jewelry, the chain, with more than 160 stores in the United States, Canada, the United Kingdom, Japan, Denmark, and Korea, allows kids (and adults too) to design their own teddy bears and other stuffed animals, complete with clothing, shoes, and accessories. The chain boasts an average of over $500 per square foot in annual revenue, double the U.S. mall average. Ten percent of sales in 2003 came from hosting nearly 100,000 parties at a cost to customers of approximately $250 for two hours, which includes a stuffed animal for each child. Build-A-Bear has created a database on 9 million kids and their households by inviting customers to register their bears: >>>

A Build-A-Bear Workshop customer leaving the store.

By including a barcode inside the bear, the company can reunite the owner with the bear if it gets lost. The database allows Build-A-Bear to contact customers by surface and e-mail with gift certificates, promotions, and party reminders.[1]

In this chapter, we review the steps involved in the marketing research process. We also consider how marketers can develop effective metrics for measuring marketing productivity. Finally, we outline how marketers can develop good sales forecasts.

::: The Marketing Research System

Marketing managers often commission formal marketing studies of specific problems and opportunities. They may request a market survey, a product-preference test, a sales forecast by region, or an advertising evaluation. It is the job of the marketing researcher to produce insight into the customer's attitudes and buying behavior. We define **marketing research** as the systematic design, collection, analysis, and reporting of data and findings relevant to a specific marketing situation facing the company. Marketing research is now about a $16.5 billion industry globally, according to ESOMAR, the World Association of Opinion and Market Research Professionals.

A company can obtain marketing research in a number of ways. Most large companies have their own marketing research departments, which often play crucial roles within the organization.[2]

PROCTER & GAMBLE

P&G's large market research function is called Consumer & Market Knowledge (CMK). Its goal is to bring consumer insight to decision making at all levels. Dedicated CMK groups work for P&G businesses around the world, including Global Business Units (GBUs), which focus on long-term brand equity and initiative development, and Market Development Organizations (MDOs), which focus on local market expertise and retail partnerships. There is also a relatively smaller, centralized corporate CMK group which, in partnership with the line businesses, focuses on three kinds of work: (1) proprietary research methods development, (2) expert application of, and cross-business learning from, core research competencies, and (3) shared services and infrastructure. CMK leverages traditional research basics such as brand tracking. CMK also finds, invents, or co-develops leading-edge research approaches such as experiential consumer contacts, proprietary modeling methods, and scenario-planning or knowledge synthesis events. CMK professionals connect market insights from all these sources to shape company strategies and decisions. They influence day-to-day operational choices, such as which product formulations are launched, as well as long-term plans, such as which corporate acquisitions best round out the product portfolio.

Yet, marketing research is not limited to large companies with big budgets and marketing research departments. At much smaller companies, marketing research is often carried out by everyone in the company—and by customers, too.

KARMALOOP.COM

Karmaloop bills itself as an online urban boutique, and it has built its reputation as a top shop for Fashionistas because of its relentless tracking of trendsetters. The five-year-old Boston company has made streetwear fashion a science by keeping tabs on young tastemakers' buying habits. In addition to its crew of 15 moonlighting artists, DJs, and designers, Karmaloop recruits street team members to ferret out new trends and to spread the word about Karmaloop brands. The street teams, which now boast 3,000 reps, pass out fliers and stickers at nightclubs, concerts, and on the street, but also report on what they see at events, in the way of trends.[3]

Companies normally budget marketing research at 1 to 2 percent of company sales. A large percentage of that is spent on the services of outside firms. Marketing research firms fall into three categories:

1. ***Syndicated-service research firms*** – These firms gather consumer and trade information, which they sell for a fee. Examples: Nielsen Media Research, SAMI/Burke.
2. ***Custom marketing research firms*** – These firms are hired to carry out specific projects. They design the study and report the findings.
3. ***Specialty-line marketing research firms*** – These firms provide specialized research services. The best example is the field-service firm, which sells field interviewing services to other firms.

Small companies can hire the services of a marketing research firm or conduct research in creative and affordable ways, such as:

1. ***Engaging students or professors to design and carry out projects*** – One Boston University MBA project helped American Express develop a successful advertising campaign geared toward young professionals. The cost: $15,000.
2. ***Using the Internet*** – A company can collect considerable information at very little cost by examining competitors' Web sites, monitoring chat rooms, and accessing published data.
3. ***Checking out rivals*** – Many small companies routinely visit their competitors. Tom Coohill, a chef who owns two Atlanta restaurants, gives managers a food allowance to dine out and bring back ideas. Atlanta jeweler Frank Maier Jr., who often visits out-of-town rivals, spotted and copied a dramatic way of lighting displays.[4]

Most companies, such as Fuji Photo Film, use a combination of marketing research resources to study their industries, competitors, audiences, and channel strategies:

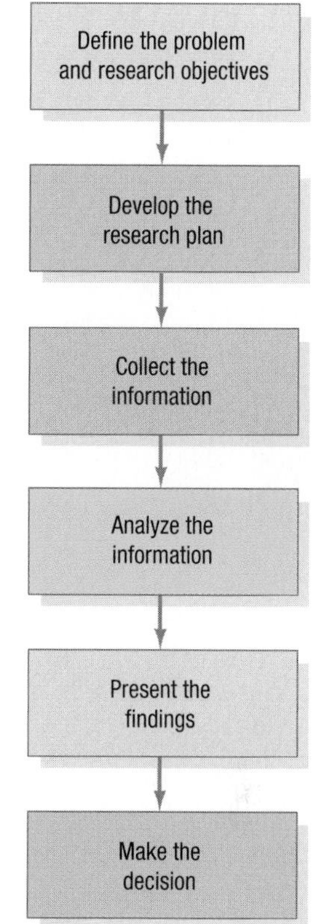

FIG. 4.1

The Marketing Research Process

FUJI PHOTO FILM

At the highest level, Fuji relies on data from market research syndicate NDP Group to study the market for products ranging from digital cameras to ink jet photo paper. Fuji also does custom research with a variety of research partners, and it conducts internal research for projects requiring quick information, such as changes to package design. Regardless of how the marketing research data are collected, it is a top priority for Fuji, which has had to adapt its film and digital imaging products to a rapidly changing marketplace. "If you don't have market research to help you figure out what is changing and what the future will be, you will be left behind," says Fuji's director of category management and trade marketing.[5]

::: The Marketing Research Process

Effective marketing research involves the six steps shown in Figure 4.1. We will illustrate these steps with the following situation:

> American Airlines (AA) is constantly looking for new ways to serve its passengers; it was one of the first companies to install phone handsets. Now it is reviewing many new ideas, especially to cater to its first-class passengers on very long flights, many of whom are businesspeople whose high-priced tickets pay most of the freight. Among these ideas are: (1) to supply an Internet connection with limited access to Web pages and e-mail messaging; (2) to offer 24 channels of satellite cable TV; and (3) to offer a 50-CD audio system that lets each passenger create a customized play list of music and movies to enjoy during the flight. The marketing research manager was assigned to investigate how first-class passengers would rate these services and how much extra they would be willing to pay if a charge was made. He was asked to focus specifically on the Internet connection. One estimate says that airlines might realize revenues of $70 billion over the next decade from in-flight Internet access, if enough first-class passengers would be willing to pay $25 for it. AA could thus recover its costs in a reasonable time. Making the connection available would cost the airline $90,000 per plane.[6]

Step 1: Define the Problem, the Decision Alternatives, and the Research Objectives

Marketing management must be careful not to define the problem too broadly or too narrowly for the marketing researcher. A marketing manager who instructs the marketing researcher to "Find out everything you can about first-class air travelers' needs," will collect a lot of unnecessary information. One who says, "Find out if enough passengers aboard a B747 flying direct between Chicago and Tokyo would be willing to pay $25 for an Internet connection so that American Airlines would break even in one year on the cost of offering this service," is taking too narrow a view of the problem. The marketing researcher might even raise this question: "Why does the Internet connection have to be priced at $25 as opposed to $10, $50, or some other price? Why does American have to break even on the cost of the service, especially if it attracts new users to AA?"

In discussing the problem, American's managers discover another issue. If the new service were successful, how fast could other airlines copy it? Airline marketing research is replete with examples of new services that have been so quickly copied by competitors that no airline has gained a sustainable competitive advantage. How important is it to be first, and how long could the lead be sustained?

The marketing manager and marketing researcher agreed to define the problem as follows: "Will offering an in-flight Internet service create enough incremental preference and profit for American Airlines to justify its cost against other possible investments American might make?" To help in designing the research, management should first spell out the decisions it might face and then work backward. Suppose management spells out these decisions: (1) Should American offer an Internet connection? (2) If so, should the service be offered to first-class only, or include business class, and possibly economy class? (3) What price(s) should be charged? (4) On what types of planes and lengths of trips should it be offered?

Now management and marketing researchers are ready to set specific research objectives: (1) What types of first-class passengers would respond most to using an in-flight Internet service? (2) How many first-class passengers are likely to use the Internet service at different price levels? (3) How many extra first-class passengers might choose American because of this new service? (4) How much long-term goodwill will this service add to American Airlines' image? (5) How important is Internet service to first-class passengers relative to providing other services such as a power plug, or enhanced entertainment?

Not all research projects can be this specific. Some research is exploratory—its goal is to shed light on the real nature of the problem and to suggest possible solutions or new ideas. Some research is descriptive—it seeks to ascertain certain magnitudes, such as how many first-class passengers would purchase in-flight Internet service at $25. Some research is causal—its purpose is to test a cause-and-effect relationship.

Step 2: Develop the Research Plan

The second stage of marketing research calls for developing the most efficient plan for gathering the needed information. The marketing manager needs to know the cost of the research plan before approving it. Suppose the company made a prior estimate that launching the in-flight Internet service would yield a long-term profit of $50,000. The manager believes that doing the research would lead to an improved pricing and promotional plan and a long-term profit of $90,000. In this case, the manager should be willing to spend up to $40,000 on this research. If the research would cost more than $40,000, it is not worth doing.[7] Designing a research plan calls for decisions on the data sources, research approaches, research instruments, sampling plan, and contact methods.

DATA SOURCES The researcher can gather secondary data, primary data, or both. *Secondary data* are data that were collected for another purpose and already exist somewhere. *Primary data* are data freshly gathered for a specific purpose or for a specific research project.

Researchers usually start their investigation by examining some of the rich variety of secondary data to see whether the problem can be partly or wholly solved without collecting costly primary data. Secondary data provide a starting point and offer the advantages of low cost and ready availability. When the needed data do not exist or are dated, inaccurate, incomplete, or unreliable, the researcher will have to collect primary data. Most marketing research projects involve some primary-data collection. The normal procedure is to interview some people individually or in groups, to get a sense of how people feel about the topic in question, and then develop a formal research instrument, debug it, and carry it into the field.

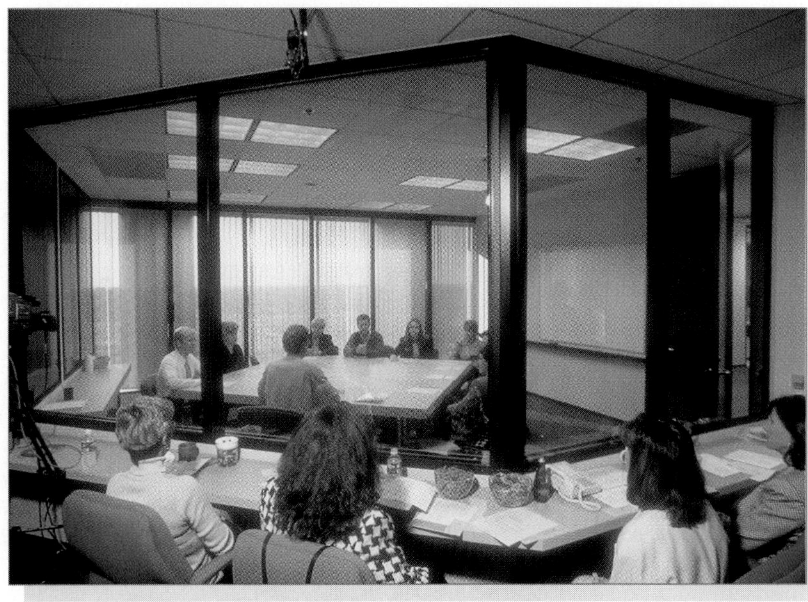
A focus group in session, with marketing people observing through a two-way mirror.

RESEARCH APPROACHES Primary data can be collected in five main ways: through observation, focus groups, surveys, behavioral data, and experiments.

Observational Research Fresh data can be gathered by observing the relevant actors and settings.[8] Consumers can be unobtrusively observed as they shop or as they consume products. Ogilvy & Mather's Discovery Group creates documentary-style videos by sending researchers into consumers' homes with handheld video cameras. Hours of footage are edited to a 30-minute "highlight reel" which the group uses to analyze consumer behavior. Other researchers equip consumers with pagers and instruct them to write down what they are doing whenever prompted, or hold more informal interview sessions at a café or bar. The American Airlines researchers might meander around first-class lounges to hear how travelers talk about the different carriers and their features. They can fly on competitors' planes to observe in-flight service.

Focus Group Research A **focus group** is a gathering of six to ten people who are carefully selected based on certain demographic, psychographic, or other considerations and brought together to discuss at length various topics of interest. Participants are normally paid a small sum for attending. A professional research moderator provides questions and probes based on a discussion guide or agenda prepared by the responsible marketing managers to ensure that the right material gets covered.

Moderators attempt to track down potentially useful insights as they try to discern the real motivations of consumers and why they are saying and doing certain things. The sessions are typically recorded in some fashion, and marketing managers often remain behind two-way mirrors in the next room. In the American Airlines research, the moderator might start with a broad question, such as, "How do you feel about first-class air travel?" Questions then move to how people view the different airlines, different existing services, different proposed services, and specifically, Internet service. Although focus-group research has been shown to be a useful exploratory step, researchers must avoid generalizing the reported feelings of the focus-group participants to the whole market, because the sample size is too small and the sample is not drawn randomly. "Marketing Insight: Conducting Informative Focus Groups" has some practical tips to improve the quality of focus groups.

Survey Research Companies undertake surveys to learn about people's knowledge, beliefs, preferences, and satisfaction, and to measure these magnitudes in the general population. A company such as American Airlines might prepare its own survey instrument to gather the information it needs, or it might add questions to an omnibus survey that carries the questions of several companies, at a much lower cost. It can also put the questions to an ongoing consumer panel run by itself or another company. It may do a mall intercept study by having researchers approach people in a shopping mall and ask them questions.

Behavioral Data Customers leave traces of their purchasing behavior in store scanning data, catalog purchases, and customer databases. Much can be learned by analyzing these data. Customers' actual purchases reflect preferences and often are more reliable than statements they offer to market researchers. People may report preferences for popular brands, and yet the data show them actually buying other brands. For example, grocery

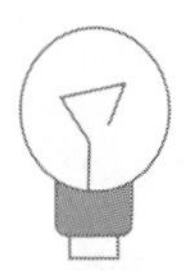

MARKETING INSIGHT | CONDUCTING INFORMATIVE FOCUS GROUPS

Focus groups allow marketers to observe how and why consumers accept or reject concepts, ideas, or any specific notion. The key to using focus groups successfully is to *listen*. It is critical to eliminate biases as much as possible. Although many useful insights can emerge from thoughtfully run focus groups, there can be questions as to their validity, especially in today's marketing environment.

Some researchers believe that consumers have been so bombarded with ads, they unconsciously (or perhaps cynically) parrot back what they have already heard as compared to what they think. There is also always a concern that participants are just trying to maintain their self-image and public persona or have a need to identify with the other members of the group. Participants may not be willing to admit in public—or may not even recognize—their behavior patterns and motivations. There is also always the "loudmouth" problem—when one highly opinionated person drowns out the rest of the group. It may be expensive to recruit qualified subjects ($3,000 to $5,000 per group), but getting the right participants is crucial.

Even when multiple groups are involved, it may be difficult to generalize the results to a broader population. For example, within the United States, focus-group findings often vary from region to region. One firm specializing in focus-group research claimed that the best city to conduct focus groups was Minneapolis because it could get a fairly well-educated sample of people who were honest and forthcoming about their opinions. Many marketers interpret focus groups carefully in New York and other northeastern cities because the people in these areas tend to be highly critical and generally do not report that they like much. Too often, managers become comfortable with a particular focus-group format and apply it generally and automatically to every circumstance. Europeans typically need more time than American marketers are usually willing to give—a focus group there rarely takes less than two hours and often more than four.

Participants must feel as relaxed as possible and feel a strong obligation to "speak the truth." Physical surroundings can be crucial. Researchers at one agency knew they had a problem when a fight broke out between participants at one of their sessions. As one executive noted, "we wondered why people always seemed grumpy and negative—people were resistant to any idea we showed them." The problem was the room itself: cramped, stifling, forbidding: "It was a cross between a hospital room and a police interrogation room." To fix the problem, the agency gave the room a makeover. Other firms are adapting the look of the room to fit the theme of the topic—like designing the room to look like a playroom when speaking to children.

Although many firms are substituting observational research for focus groups, ethnographic research can be expensive and tricky: Researchers have to be highly skilled, participants have to be on the level, and mounds of data have to be analyzed. The beauty of focus groups, as one marketing executive noted, is that "it's still the most cost-effective, quickest, dirtiest way to get information in rapid time on an idea." In analyzing the pros and cons, Wharton's Americus Reed might have said it best: "A focus group is like a chain saw. If you know what you're doing, it's very useful and effective. If you don't, you could lose a limb."

Sources: Sarah Stiansen, "How Focus Groups Can Go Astray," *Adweek,* December 5, 1988, pp. FK 4–6; Jeffrey Kasner, "Fistfights and Feng Shui," *Boston Globe,* July 21, 2001, pp. C1–C2; Leslie Kaufman, "Enough Talk," *Newsweek,* August 18, 1997, pp. 48–49; Linda Tischler, "Every Move You Make," *Fast Company,* April 2004, pp. 73–75; Alison Stein Wellner, "The New Science of Focus Groups," *American Demographics* (March 2003): 29–33; Dennis Rook, "Out-of-Focus Groups," *Marketing Research* 15; no. 2 (Summer 2003): 11; Dennis W. Rook, "Loss of Vision; Focus Groups Fail to Connect Theory, Current Practice," *Marketing News,* September 15, 2003, p. 40.

shopping data show that high-income people do not necessarily buy the more expensive brands, contrary to what they might state in interviews; and many low-income people buy some expensive brands. Clearly, American Airlines can learn many useful things about its passengers by analyzing ticket purchase records.

Experimental Research The most scientifically valid research is experimental research. The purpose of experimental research is to capture cause-and-effect relationships by eliminating competing explanations of the observed findings. To the extent that the design and execution of the experiment eliminate alternative hypotheses that might explain the results, research and marketing managers can have confidence in the conclusions.

Experiments call for selecting matched groups of subjects, subjecting them to different treatments, controlling extraneous variables, and checking whether observed response differences are statistically significant. To the extent that extraneous factors are eliminated or controlled, the observed effects can be related to the variations in the treatments. American Airlines might introduce in-flight Internet service on one of its regular flights from Chicago to Tokyo. It might charge $25 one week and charge only $15 the next week. If the plane carried approximately the same number of first-class passengers each week and the particular weeks made no difference, any significant difference in the number of calls made could be related to the different prices charged. The experimental design could be elaborated by trying other prices and including other air routes.

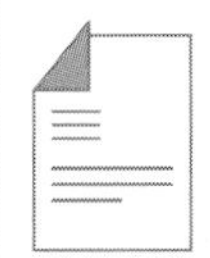

MARKETING MEMO | QUESTIONNAIRE DOS AND DON'TS

1. ***Ensure that questions are without bias.*** Do not lead the respondent into an answer.
2. ***Make the questions as simple as possible.*** Questions that include multiple ideas or two questions in one will confuse respondents.
3. ***Make the questions specific.*** Sometimes it is advisable to add memory cues. For example, it is good practice to be specific with time periods.
4. ***Avoid jargon or shorthand.*** Avoid trade jargon, acronyms, and initials not in everyday use.
5. ***Steer clear of sophisticated or uncommon words.*** Only use words in common speech.
6. ***Avoid ambiguous words.*** Words such as "usually" or "frequently" have no specific meaning.
7. ***Avoid questions with a negative in them.*** It is better to say "Do you ever . . . ?" than "Do you never . . . ?"
8. ***Avoid hypothetical questions.*** It is difficult to answer questions about imaginary situations. Answers cannot necessarily be trusted.
9. ***Do not use words that could be misheard.*** This is especially important when the interview is administered over the telephone. "What is your opinion of sects?" could yield interesting but not necessarily relevant answers.
10. ***Desensitize questions by using response bands.*** For questions that ask people their age or companies their employee turnover, it is best to offer a range of response bands.
11. ***Ensure that fixed responses do not overlap.*** Categories used in fixed response questions should be sequential and not overlap.
12. ***Allow for "other" in fixed response questions.*** Precoded answers should always allow for a response other than those listed.

Source: Adapted from Paul Hague and Peter Jackson, *Market Research: A Guide to Planning, Methodology, and Evaluation* (London: Kogan Page, 1999). See also, Hans Baumgartner and Jan-Benedict E. M. Steenkamp, "Response Styles in Marketing Research: A Cross-National Investigation," *Journal of Marketing Research* (May 2001): 143–156.

RESEARCH INSTRUMENTS Marketing researchers have a choice of three main research instruments in collecting primary data: questionnaires, qualitative measures, and mechanical devices.

Questionnaires A questionnaire consists of a set of questions presented to respondents. Because of its flexibility, the questionnaire is by far the most common instrument used to collect primary data. Questionnaires need to be carefully developed, tested, and debugged before they are administered on a large scale. In preparing a questionnaire, the researcher carefully chooses the questions and their form, wording, and sequence. The form of the question can influence the response. Marketing researchers distinguish between closed-end and open-end questions. Closed-end questions specify all the possible answers and provide answers that are easier to interpret and tabulate. Open-end questions allow respondents to answer in their own words and often reveal more about how people think. They are especially useful in exploratory research, where the researcher is looking for insight into how people think rather than measuring how many people think a certain way. Table 4.1 provides examples of both types of questions; and see "Marketing Memo: Questionnaire Dos and Don'ts."

Qualitative Measures Some marketers prefer more qualitative methods for gauging consumer opinion because consumer actions do not always match their answers to survey questions. *Qualitative research techniques* are relatively unstructured measurement approaches that permit a range of possible responses, and they are a creative means of ascertaining consumer perceptions that may otherwise be difficult to uncover. The range of possible qualitative research techniques is limited only by the creativity of the marketing researcher. Here are seven techniques employed by design firm IDEO for understanding the customer experience:[9]

- ***Shadowing***—observing people using products, shopping, going to hospitals, taking the train, using their cell phones.
- ***Behavior mapping***—photographing people within a space, such as a hospital waiting room, over two or three days.
- ***Consumer journey***—keeping track of all the interactions a consumer has with a product, service, or space.

TABLE 4.1 Types of Questions

Name	Description	Example
A. Closed-end Questions		
Dichotomous	A question with two possible answers.	In arranging this trip, did you personally phone American? Yes No
Multiple choice	A question with three or more answers.	With whom are you traveling on this flight? ☐ No one ☐ Children only ☐ Spouse ☐ Business associates/friends/relatives ☐ Spouse and children ☐ An organized tour group
Likert scale	A statement with which the respondent shows the amount of agreement/disagreement.	Small airlines generally give better service than large ones. Strongly disagree 1___ Disagree 2___ Neither agree nor disagree 3___ Agree 4___ Strongly agree 5___
Semantic differential	A scale connecting two bipolar words. The respondent selects the point that represents his or her opinion.	American Airlines Large -------------------------Small Experienced -------------------------Inexperienced Modern -------------------------Old-fashioned
Importance scale	A scale that rates the importance of some attribute.	Airline food service to me is Extremely important 1___ Very important 2___ Somewhat important 3___ Not very important 4___ Not at all important 5___
Rating scale	A scale that rates some attribute from "poor" to "excellent."	American food service is Excellent 1___ Very Good 2___ Good 3___ Fair 4___ Poor 5___
Intention-to-buy scale	A scale that describes the respondent's intention to buy.	If an in-flight telephone were available on a long flight, I would Definitely buy 1___ Probably buy 2___ Not sure 3___ Probably not buy 4___ Definitely not buy 5___
B. Open-end Questions		
Completely unstructured	A question that respondents can answer in an almost unlimited number of ways.	What is your opinion of American Airlines?
Word association	Words are presented, one at a time, and respondents mention the first word that comes to mind.	What is the first word that comes to your mind when you hear the following? Airline ______________ American ______________ Travel ______________
Sentence completion	An incomplete sentence is presented and respondents complete the sentence.	When I choose an airline, the most important consideration in my decision is ______________.
Story completion	An incomplete story is presented, and respondents are asked to complete it.	"I flew American a few days ago. I noticed that the exterior and interior of the plane had very bright colors. This aroused in me the following thoughts and feelings. . . . " Now complete the story.
Picture	A picture of two characters is presented, with one making a statement. Respondents are asked to identify with the other and fill in the empty balloon.	
Thematic Apperception Test (TAT)	A picture is presented and respondents are asked to make up a story about what they think is happening or may happen in the picture.	

- ***Camera journals***—asking consumers to keep visual diaries of their activities and impressions relating to a product.
- ***Extreme user interviews***—talking to people who really know—or know nothing—about a product or service and evaluating their experience using it.
- ***Storytelling***—prompting people to tell personal stories about their consumer experiences.
- ***Unfocus groups***—interviewing a diverse group of people: To explore ideas about sandals, IDEO gathered an artist, a bodybuilder, a podiatrist, and a shoe fetishist.

Because of the freedom afforded both researchers in their probes and consumers in their responses, qualitative research can often be a useful first step in exploring consumers' brand and product perceptions. There are also drawbacks to qualitative research. The in-depth insights that emerge have to be tempered by the fact that the samples involved are often very small and may not necessarily generalize to broader populations. Moreover, given the qualitative nature of the data, there may also be questions of interpretation. Different researchers examining the same results from a qualitative research study may draw very different conclusions. "Marketing Insight: Getting into Consumers' Heads with Qualitative Research" describes some popular approaches.

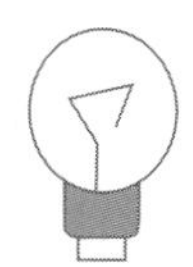

MARKETING **INSIGHT** | GETTING INTO CONSUMERS' HEADS WITH QUALITATIVE RESEARCH

Here are some commonly used qualitative research approaches to getting inside consumers' minds and finding out what they are thinking or feeling about brands and products:

1. ***Word associations.*** People can be asked what words come to mind when they hear the brand's name. "What does the Timex name mean to you? Tell me what comes to mind when you think of Timex watches." The primary purpose of free association tasks is to identify the range of possible brand associations in consumers' minds. But they may also provide some rough indication of the relative strength, favorability, and uniqueness of brand associations too.
2. ***Projective techniques.*** People are presented an incomplete stimulus and asked to complete it or given an ambiguous stimulus that may not make sense in and of itself and are asked to make sense of it. The argument is that people will reveal their true beliefs and feelings. One such approach is "bubble exercises" based on cartoons or photos. Different people are depicted buying or using certain products or services. Empty bubbles, like those found in cartoons, are placed in the scenes to represent the thoughts, words, or actions of one or more of the participants. People are then asked to "fill in the bubble" by indicating what they believed was happening or being said. Another technique is comparison tasks. People are asked to convey their impressions by comparing brands to people, countries, animals, activities, fabrics, occupations, cars, magazines, vegetables, nationalities, or even other brands.
3. ***Visualization.*** People can be asked to create a collage from magazine photos or drawings to depict their perceptions. ZMET is a research technique that starts with a group of participants, who are asked in advance to select a minimum of 12 images from their own sources (e.g., magazines, catalogs, and family photo albums) that represent their thoughts and feelings about the research topic. The participants bring these images to a personal one-on-one interview with a study administrator, who uses advanced interview techniques to explore the images with the participant and reveal hidden meanings. Finally, the participants use a computer program to create a collage with these images that communicates their subconscious thoughts and feelings about the topic. One ZMET study probed what women thought of panty hose. Twenty hose-wearing women were asked to collect pictures that captured their feelings about wearing panty hose. Some of the pictures showed fence posts encased in plastic wrap or steel bands strangling trees, suggesting that panty hose are tight and inconvenient. Another picture showed tall flowers in a vase, suggesting that the product made a woman feel thin, tall, and sexy.
4. ***Brand personification.*** People can be asked to describe what kind of person they think of when the brand is mentioned: "If the brand were to come alive as a person, what would it be like, what would it do, where would it live, what would it wear, who would it talk to if it went to a party (and what would it talk about)?" For example, they may say that the John Deere brand makes them think of a rugged Midwestern male who is hardworking and trustworthy. The brand personality delivers a picture of the more human qualities of the brand.
5. ***Laddering.*** A series of increasingly more specific "why" questions can be used to gain insight into consumer motivation and consumers' deeper, more abstract goals. Ask why someone wants to buy a Nokia cellular phone. "They look well built" (attribute). "Why is it important that the phone be well built?" "It suggests that the Nokia is reliable" (a functional benefit). "Why is reliability important?" "Because my colleagues or family can be sure to reach me" (an emotional benefit). "Why must you be available to them at all times?" "I can help them if they are in trouble" (brand essence). The brand makes this person feel like a Good Samaritan, ready to help others.

Sources: Allen Adamson, "Why Traditional Brand Positioning Can't Last," *Brandweek,* November 17, 2003, pp. 38–40; Todd Wasserman, "Sharpening the Focus," *Brandweek,* November 3, 2003, pp. 28–32; Linda Tischler, "Every Move You Make," *Fast Company,* April 2004, pp. 73–75; Gerald Zaltman, *How Customers Think: Essential Insights into the Mind of the Market* (Boston: Harvard Business School Press, 2003).

Mechanical Devices Mechanical devices are occasionally used in marketing research. For example, galvanometers can measure the interest or emotions aroused by exposure to a specific ad or picture. The tachistoscope flashes an ad to a subject with an exposure interval that may range from less than one hundredth of a second to several seconds. After each exposure, the respondent describes everything he or she recalls. Eye cameras study respondents' eye movements to see where their eyes land first, how long they linger on a given item, and so on. As one would expect, in recent years technology has advanced to such a degree that now devices like skin sensors, brain wave scanners, and full body scanners are being used to get consumer responses.[10]

Technology has replaced the diaries that participants in media surveys used to have to keep. Audiometers can be attached to television sets in participating homes to record when the set is on and to which channel it is tuned. Electronic devices can record the number of radio programs a person is exposed to during the day or, using Global Positioning System (GPS) technology, how many billboards a person may walk by or drive by during a day.

SAMPLING PLAN After deciding on the research approach and instruments, the marketing researcher must design a sampling plan. This calls for three decisions:

1. ***Sampling unit: Who is to be surveyed?*** The marketing researcher must define the target population that will be sampled. In the American Airlines survey, should the sampling unit be only first-class business travelers, first-class vacation travelers, or both? Should travelers under age 18 be interviewed? Should both husbands and wives be interviewed? Once the sampling unit is determined, a sampling frame must be developed so that everyone in the target population has an equal or known chance of being sampled.
2. ***Sample size: How many people should be surveyed?*** Large samples give more reliable results than small samples. However, it is not necessary to sample the entire target population or even a substantial portion to achieve reliable results. Samples of less than 1 percent of a population can often provide good reliability, with a credible sampling procedure.
3. ***Sampling procedure: How should the respondents be chosen?*** To obtain a representative sample, a probability sample of the population should be drawn. Probability sampling allows the calculation of confidence limits for sampling error. Thus, one could conclude after the sample is taken that "the interval 5 to 7 trips per year has 95 chances in 100 of containing the true number of trips taken annually by first-class passengers flying between Chicago and Tokyo." Three types of probability sampling are described in Table 4.2 part A. When the cost or time involved in probability sampling is too high, marketing researchers will take nonprobability samples. Table 4.2 part B describes three types. Some marketing researchers feel that nonprobability

TABLE 4.2

Probability and Nonprobability Samples

A. Probability Sample	
Simple random sample	Every member of the population has an equal chance of selection.
Stratified random sample	The population is divided into mutually exclusive groups (such as age groups), and random samples are drawn from each group.
Cluster (area) sample	The population is divided into mutually exclusive groups (such as city blocks), and the researcher draws a sample of the groups to interview.
B. Nonprobability Sample	
Convenience sample	The researcher selects the most accessible population members.
Judgment sample	The researcher selects population members who are good prospects for accurate information.
Quota sample	The researcher finds and interviews a prescribed number of people in each of several categories.

samples are very useful in many circumstances, even though they do not allow sampling error to be measured.

CONTACT METHODS Once the sampling plan has been determined, the marketing researcher must decide how the subject should be contacted: mail, telephone, personal, or online interview.

Mail Questionnaire The *mail questionnaire* is the best way to reach people who would not give personal interviews or whose responses might be biased or distorted by the interviewers. Mail questionnaires require simple and clearly worded questions. Unfortunately, the response rate is usually low or slow.

Telephone Interview *Telephone interviewing* is the best method for gathering information quickly; the interviewer is also able to clarify questions if respondents do not understand them. The response rate is typically higher than in the case of mailed questionnaires. The main drawback is that the interviews have to be short and not too personal. Telephone interviewing is getting more difficult because of consumers' growing antipathy toward telemarketers calling them in their homes and interrupting their lives. In late 2003, Congress passed legislation allowing the Federal Trade Commission to restrict telemarketing calls to consumers through its "Do Not Call" registry. Even though marketing research firms are exempt, many think that the legislation spells the beginning of the end of telephone surveys as a marketing research method.

Personal Interview *Personal interviewing* is the most versatile method. The interviewer can ask more questions and record additional observations about the respondent, such as dress and body language. At the same time, personal interviewing is the most expensive method and requires more administrative planning and supervision than the other three. It is also subject to interviewer bias or distortion. Personal interviewing takes two forms. In *arranged interviews*, respondents are contacted for an appointment, and often a small payment or incentive is offered. *Intercept interviews* involve stopping people at a shopping mall or busy street corner and requesting an interview. Intercept interviews can have the drawback of being nonprobability samples, and the interviews must not require too much time.

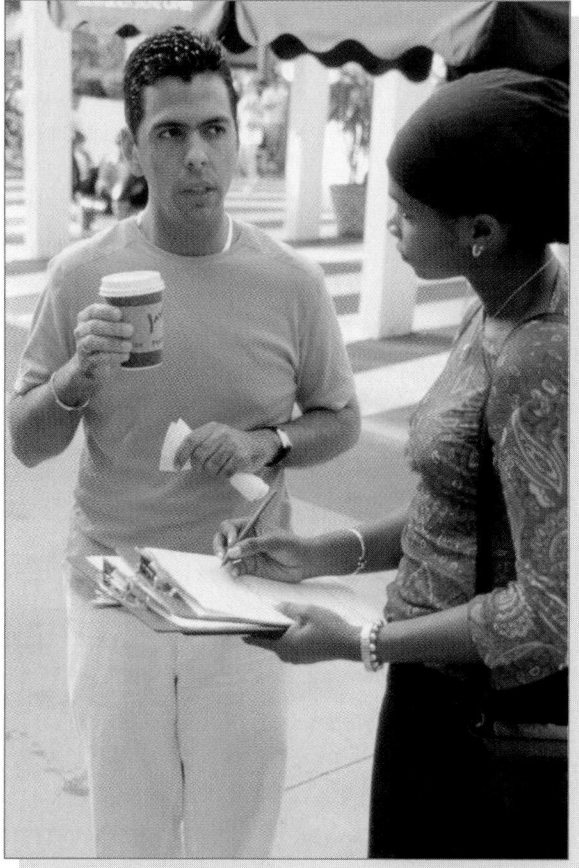

An intercept interview at a mall.

Online Interview There is increased use of online methods. Online research was up 20 to 30 percent in 2003 and was expected to continue along the same growth trajectory in 2004. Furthermore, online research is estimated to make up 25 percent of all survey-based research in 2004.[11]

There are so many ways to use the Net to do research. A company can include a questionnaire on its Web site and offer an incentive to answer the questionnaire; or it can place a banner on some frequently visited site such as Yahoo!, inviting people to answer some questions and possibly win a prize. The company can sponsor a chat room or bulletin board and introduce questions from time to time, or host a real-time panel or virtual focus group. A company can learn about individuals who visit its site by following how they *clickstream* through the Web site and move to other sites. A company can post different prices, use different headlines, offer different product features on different Web sites or at different times to learn the relative effectiveness of its offerings.

Online product testing, in which companies float trial balloons for new products, is also growing and providing information much faster than traditional marketing research techniques used to develop new products. For instance, marketers for Mattel's Hot Wheels toys rely heavily on the Web to interact with collectors to help develop new products, promotions, and licensed goods.

Following one fan survey, marketing executives learned that they could expand licensed offerings to boys ages 11 to 16 to keep them in the brand franchise, resulting in extended partnerships with Bell Motorcycles and BMX bikes.[12]

HERSHEY'S FOOD CORP.

Candymaker Hershey was an early innovator in the area of online product testing. In 1999 through 2000, the company moved its new product testing online along with its entire historical product testing. It combined more than 1,200 historical concept tests with about 300 to 400 online test results to create an online "turnkey" system that works both as a reporting tool and as an archival system. The move to online product testing has cut Hershey's new product development process by two-thirds—a strategic advantage in a mature market—and keeps a wealth of institutional data on hand even as research personnel change over the years.[13]

While marketers are right to be infatuated with the possibilities of online research, it's important to remember that the field is still in its infancy and is constantly evolving to meet the needs of companies, advertising agencies, and consumers. "Marketing Memo: Pros and Cons of Online Research" outlines some of the advantages and disadvantages of online research thus far.

Step 3: Collect the Information

The data collection phase of marketing research is generally the most expensive and the most prone to error. In the case of surveys, four major problems arise. Some respondents will not be at home and must be contacted again or replaced. Other respondents will refuse to cooperate. Still others will give biased or dishonest answers. Finally, some interviewers will be biased or dishonest. Getting the right respondents is critical.

MEDIAMARK RESEARCH

Mediamark Research interviews 26,000 Americans in their homes on the kinds of media they use, the brands and products they use, and their attitudes toward topics such as sports and politics. Up until 2002, however, the company had tended to exclude non-English-speaking Hispanics from the research. As the Hispanic population increased in numbers and buying power, the company recognized that it could no longer afford this limiting and potentially biased approach. Mediamark recruited a bilingual traveling task force so that when interviewers come to a Hispanic household, respondents can answer the survey in English or Spanish. They also are creating a more seamless interviewing database by asking the same questions to all people no matter what language they speak and what level of acculturation they have.[14]

Data collection methods are rapidly improving thanks to computers and telecommunications. Some research firms interview from a centralized location. Professional interviewers sit in booths and draw telephone numbers at random. When the phone is answered, the interviewer reads a set of questions from a monitor and types the respondents' answers into a computer. This procedure eliminates editing and coding, reduces errors, saves time, and produces all the required statistics. Other research firms have set up interactive terminals in shopping centers. Persons willing to be interviewed sit at a terminal, read the questions from the monitor, and type in their answers.

One savvy marketer gets primary data via online surveys from a highly coveted demographic as they play games.

NEOPETS.COM

With more than 22 million members and 27,000 new ones joining every day, Neopets is one of the most popular children's Web sites. The Web site is free, and it allows users to create, nurture, and care for cyberpets as they earn "neopoints." They raise their neopet in a virtual neighborhood that includes eating at

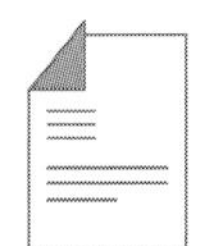

MARKETING MEMO | PROS AND CONS OF ONLINE RESEARCH

Advantages

- ***Online research is inexpensive.*** The cost of gathering survey information electronically is much less expensive than by traditional means. A typical e-mail survey costs about half what a conventional survey costs, and return rates can be as high as 50 percent. For instance, Virgin.net used online research to launch its broadband service in the United Kingdom in 2002. Now the company does all its research online. The brand has seen an increase in response rates from 17 percent with paper-based research to almost 72 percent and costs have dropped 90 percent.
- ***Online research is faster.*** Online surveys are faster to complete since the survey can automatically direct respondents to applicable questions and be sent electronically to the research supplier once finished. One estimate is that 75 to 80 percent of a survey's targeted response can be generated in 48 hours using online methods, as compared to a telephone survey that can take 70 days to obtain 150 interviews.
- ***People tend to be more honest online than they are in personal or telephone interviews.*** Britain's online polling company YouGov.com took 500 people and surveyed half via intercom in a booth and the other half online, asking them politically correct questions such as "Should there be more aid to Africa?" Online answers were deemed much more honest. People may be more open about their opinions when they can respond to a survey privately and not to another person whom they feel might be judging them, especially on sensitive topics.
- ***Online research is more versatile.*** The multimedia applications of online research are especially advantageous. For instance, virtual reality software lets visitors inspect 3-D models of products such as cameras, cars, and medical equipment, and product characteristics can be easily manipulated online. Even at the most basic level, online surveys make answering a questionnaire easier and more fun than paper-and-pencil versions.

Disadvantages

- ***Samples can be small and skewed.*** Perhaps the largest criticism leveled against online research is that not everyone is online. Research subjects who respond to online surveys are more likely to be tech-savvy middle-class males. Some 40 percent of households are without Internet access in the United States—and there is an even higher percentage without access when you reach out to international markets. These people are likely to differ in socioeconomic and education levels from those online. While marketers can be certain that more and more people will go online, it is important for online market researchers to find creative ways to reach certain population segments that are less likely to be online, such as older Americans or Hispanics. One option is to combine offline sources with online findings. Providing temporary Internet access at locations such as malls and recreation centers is another strategy. Some research firms use statistical models to fill in the gaps in market research left by offline consumer segments.
- ***Online market research is prone to technological problems and inconsistencies.*** Because online research is a relatively new method, many market researchers have not gotten survey designs right. A common error occurs in transferring a written survey to the screen. Others overuse technology, concentrating on the bells and whistles and graphics, while ignoring basic survey design guidelines. Problems also arise because browser software varies. The Web designer's final product may be seen very differently depending upon the research subject's screen and operating system.

Sources: Catherine Arnold, "Not Done Net; New Opportunities Still Exist in Online Research," *Marketing News,* April 1, 2004, p. 17; Nima M. Ray and Sharon W. Tabor, "Contributing Factors; Several Issues Affect e-Research Validity," *Marketing News,* September 15, 2003, p. 50; Louella Miles, "Online, On Tap," *Marketing,* June 16, 2004, pp. 39–40; Joe Dysart, "Cutting Market Research Costs with On-Site Surveys," *The Secured Lender* (March/April 2004): 64–67; Suzy Bashford, "The Opinion Formers," *Revolution,* May 2004, pp. 42–46; Bob Lamons, "Eureka! Future of B-to-B Research is Online," *Marketing News,* September 24, 2001, pp. 9–10.

McDonald's, watching Disney movie clips, feeding pets General Mills cereal, or playing Reese's Puffs Mini Golf with them. In this unique form of interactive product placement, advertisers pay to become part of the branded Neopet environment. In return, they get increased exposure to their products or services and data on their target market's consumer behavior. "We live and breathe market research," says Rik Kinney, executive vice president of the Glendale, California, company. The primary research mechanism at Neopets is a link to an online survey, prominently displayed on the homepage. Members are rewarded with Neopoints for answering questions about their shopping habits, and users complete 6,000 to 8,000 surveys a day. Interestingly, despite building a profitable business around selling information on its loyal users, Neopets has won kudos from privacy advocates because the company only releases data about its user base as a whole or about certain segments, but does not reveal any facts on individual users.[15]

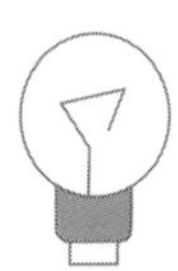

MARKETING INSIGHT | GLOBAL ONLINE MARKET RESEARCH CHALLENGES

When chipmaker Intel Research wanted to know how people in countries around the world use technology, it sent an anthropologist to find out. Dr. Genevieve Bell visited 100 households in 19 cities in 7 countries in Asia and the Pacific. She came back to Intel with 20 gigabytes of digital photos, 19 field notebooks, and insights about technology, culture, and design that would challenge company assumptions about digital technology.

It stands to reason that Intel—a global tech powerhouse—would want to know how technology is used in its international markets. Yet all companies have a stake in knowing how the rest of the world sees and uses what most Westerners take for granted: Internet technology. With online research becoming the fastest-growing market research tool, marketers with global ambitions need to know which countries are online and why, or why not.

Internet penetration is low in most parts of Asia, Latin America, and Central and Eastern Europe. In Brazil, for example, only 7 percent of the population is online. While most people assume that the low penetration is due to economies that don't support an expensive technological infrastructure, there are other factors involved. There's climate, for one. In Malaysia, power surges caused by monsoons can fry computer motherboards. Government is also a powerful spur or barrier to Internet penetration. While the Chinese economy is zooming ahead, it's unlikely the authoritarian Chinese government will feel comfortable with market researchers gathering information from its citizens via the Internet. Contrast this with South Korea, where the government has made widespread broadband Internet access a priority, and has provided incentives to PC makers to bring cheaper models to market.

Other significant factors that can keep computers and Wi-Fi and data ports from crossing the threshold are religion and culture. Dr. Bell found that values of humility and simplicity are deemed incompatible with Internet technology and make it less welcome in some Hindu homes in India or Muslim homes in Malaysia and Indonesia. She also noted that while Americans have private space in the home for leisure activities, Japan's tighter quarters afford little privacy. This may explain the huge popularity of text messaging on mobile phones among Japan's young people.

Dr. Bell's findings on global responses to technology point up one of the biggest obstacles to conducting international research, whether online or not: a lack of consistency. Nan Martin, global accounts director for Synovate Inc., a market research firm with offices in 46 countries, says: "In global research, we have to adapt culturally to how, where and with whom we are doing the research . . . A simple research study conducted globally becomes much more complicated as a result of the cultural nuances, and it's necessary for us to be sensitive to those nuances in data collection and interpretation." For instance, suppose Internet penetration is equal. In Latin America, where consumers are uncomfortable with the impersonal nature of the Internet, researchers might need to incorporate interactive elements into a survey so participants feel they are talking to a real person. In Asia, focus groups are challenging because of the cultural tendency to conform. Online surveys may bring more honest responses and keep respondents from "losing face."

And what if a researcher collects data face-to-face in Mexico, but by Internet in the United States? Nan Martin says that, "not only are the subjects answering the question differently because of cultural difference, but the data are being collected by a different method. That can shake the underpinnings of how research scientists feel about collecting data: that every time you change a variable, you're making interpretation of the results more challenging. It is so challenging, in fact, that some say this is an area where global marketers are best served by hiring an expert—an outside research firm with an expertise in acquiring and analyzing international data."

Sources: Arundhati Parmar, "Stumbling Blocks; Net Research Is Not Quite Global," *Marketing News,* March 3, 2003, p. 51; Catherine Arnold, "Global Perspective; Synovate Exec Discusses Future of International Research," *Marketing News,* May 15, 2004, p. 43; Michael Erard, "For Technology, No Small World After All," *New York Times,* May 6, 2004, p. G5; Deborah L. Vence, "Global Consistency: Leave It to the Experts," *Marketing News,* April 28, 2003, p. 37.

It is important to recognize that not everyone in the sample population will be online. (See "Marketing Insight: Global Online Market Research Challenges.")

Step 4: Analyze the Information

The next-to-last step in the process is to extract findings from the collected data. The researcher tabulates the data and develops frequency distributions. Averages and measures of dispersion are computed for the major variables. The researcher will also apply some advanced statistical techniques and decision models in the hope of discovering additional findings.

Step 5: Present the Findings

As the last step, the researcher presents the findings. The researcher should present findings that are relevant to the major marketing decisions facing management. The main survey findings for the American Airlines case show that:

1. The chief reasons for using in-flight Internet service are to pass the time surfing, and to send and receive messages from colleagues and family. The charge would be put on passengers' charge accounts and paid by their companies.

2. About 5 first-class passengers out of every 10 would use the Internet service during a flight at $25; about 6 would use it at $15. Thus, a charge of $15 would produce less revenue ($90 = 6 × $15) than $25 ($125 = 5 × $25). By charging $25, AA would collect $125 per flight. Assuming that the same flight takes place 365 days a year, AA would annually collect $45,625 (= $125 × 365). Since the investment is $90,000, it will take approximately two years before American Airlines breaks even.
3. Offering in-flight service would strengthen the public's image of American Airlines as an innovative and progressive airline. American would gain some new passengers and customer goodwill.

Step 6: Make the Decision

The managers who commissioned the research need to weigh the evidence. If their confidence in the findings is low, they may decide against introducing the in-flight Internet service. If they are predisposed to launching the service, the findings support their inclination. They may even decide to study the issues further and do more research. The decision is theirs, but hopefully the research provided them with insight into the problem. (See Table 4.3.)[16]

A growing number of organizations are using a marketing decision support system to help their marketing managers make better decisions. MIT's John Little defines a **marketing decision support system (MDSS)** as a coordinated collection of data, systems, tools, and techniques with supporting software and hardware by which an organization gathers and interprets relevant information from business and environment and turns it into a basis for marketing action.[17]

A classic MDSS example is the CALLPLAN model which helps salespeople determine the number of calls to make per period to each prospect and current client. The model takes into account travel time as well as selling time. When launched, the model was tested at United Airlines with an experimental group that managed to increase its sales over a matched control group by 8 percentage points.[18] Once a year, *Marketing News* lists hundreds of current marketing and sales software programs that assist in designing marketing research studies, segmenting markets, setting prices and advertising budgets, analyzing media, and planning sales force activity.

TABLE 4.3

The Seven Characteristics of Good Marketing Research

1. Scientific method.	Effective marketing research uses the principles of the scientific method: careful observation, formulation of hypotheses, prediction, and testing.
2. Research creativity.	At its best, marketing research develops innovative ways to solve a problem: a clothing company catering to teenagers gave several young men video cameras, then used the videos for focus groups held in restaurants and other places teens frequent.
3. Multiple methods.	Marketing researchers shy away from overreliance on any one method. They also recognize the value of using two or three methods to increase confidence in the results.
4. Interdependence of models and data.	Marketing researchers recognize that data are interpreted from underlying models that guide the type of information sought.
5. Value and cost of information.	Marketing researchers show concern for estimating the value of information against its cost. Costs are typically easy to determine, but the value of research is harder to quantify. It depends on the reliability and validity of the findings and management's willingness to accept and act on those findings.
6. Healthy skepticism.	Marketing researchers show a healthy skepticism toward glib assumptions made by managers about how a market works. They are alert to the problems caused by "marketing myths."
7. Ethical marketing.	Marketing research benefits both the sponsoring company and its customers. The misuse of marketing research can harm or annoy consumers, increasing resentment at what consumers regard as an invasion of their privacy or a disguised sales pitch.

Overcoming Barriers to the Use of Marketing Research

In spite of the rapid growth of marketing research, many companies still fail to use it sufficiently or correctly, for several reasons:[19]

- ***A narrow conception of the research.*** Many managers see marketing research as a fact-finding operation. They expect the researcher to design a questionnaire, choose a sample, conduct interviews, and report results, often without a careful definition of the problem or of the decisions facing management. When fact-finding fails to be useful, management's idea of the limited usefulness of marketing research is reinforced.
- ***Uneven caliber of researchers.*** Some managers view marketing research as little more than a clerical activity and treat it as such. Less competent marketing researchers are hired, and their weak training and deficient creativity lead to unimpressive results. The disappointing results reinforce management's prejudice against marketing research. Management continues to pay low salaries to its market researchers, thus perpetuating the basic problem.
- ***Poor framing of the problem.*** In the famous case where Coca-Cola introduced the New Coke after much research, the failure of the New Coke was largely due to not setting up the research problem correctly, from a marketing perspective. The issue was how consumers felt about Coca-Cola as a brand and not necessarily the taste in isolation.
- ***Late and occasionally erroneous findings.*** Managers want results that are accurate and conclusive. They may want the results tomorrow. Yet good marketing research takes time and money. Managers are disappointed when marketing research costs too much or takes too much time.
- ***Personality and presentational differences.*** Differences between the styles of line managers and marketing researchers often get in the way of productive relationships. To a manager who wants concreteness, simplicity, and certainty, a marketing researcher's report may seem abstract, complicated, and tentative. Yet in the more progressive companies, marketing researchers are being included as members of the product management team, and their influence on marketing strategy is growing.

Failure to use marketing research properly has led to numerous gaffes, including this historic one:

STAR WARS

In the 1970s, a successful research executive left General Foods for a daring gambit: Bring market research to Hollywood to give film studios access to the same research that had spurred General Foods' success. A major studio handed him a science fiction film proposal and asked him to research and predict its success or failure: His views would inform their decision about whether or not to back the film. He concluded the film would fail. For one, he argued, Watergate had made America less trusting of its institutions and, as a result, Americans in the 1970s prized realism and authenticity over science fiction. This particular film also had the word "war" in its title; he reasoned that America, suffering from its post-Vietnam hangover, would stay away in droves. The film was *Star Wars*. What this researcher delivered was information, not insight. He failed to study the script itself, to see that it was a fundamentally human story—of love, conflict, loss, and redemption—that merely played out against the backdrop of space.[20]

::: Measuring Marketing Productivity

An important task of marketing research is to assess the efficiency and effectiveness of marketing activities. Marketers increasingly are being held accountable for their investments and must be able to justify marketing expenditures to senior management.[21] In a recent Accenture survey, 70 percent of marketing executives stated that they did not have a handle on the return on their marketing investments.[22] Another study revealed that 63 percent of senior management said they were dissatisfied with their marketing performance measurement system and wanted marketing to supply prior and posterior estimates of the impact of marketing programs.[23] With marketing costs already high and continuing to rise, senior executives are tired of seeing what they consider to be wasteful marketing—failed new products and lavish ad campaigns, extensive sales calls, and expensive promotions that are unable to move the sales needle.

Marketing research can help address this increased need for accountability. Two complementary approaches to measure marketing productivity are: (1) marketing metrics to assess marketing effects and (2) marketing-mix modeling to estimate causal relationships and how marketing activity affects outcomes. Some developments in the financial tools that can be used to measure key marketing assets are described in "Marketing Insight: Seeing the Big Picture and Getting to the Bottom Line in Marketing."

Marketing Metrics

Marketers employ a wide variety of measures to assess marketing effects. **Marketing metrics** is the set of measures that helps firms to quantify, compare, and interpret their marketing performance. Marketing metrics can be used by brand managers to design marketing programs and by senior management to decide on financial allocations. When marketers can estimate the dollar contribution of marketing activities, they are better able to justify the value of marketing investments to senior management.[24]

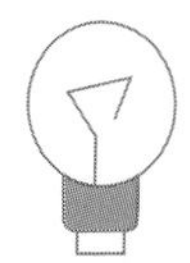

MARKETING INSIGHT | SEEING THE BIG PICTURE AND GETTING TO THE BOTTOM LINE IN MARKETING

To provide a financial overview of marketing activity, several authors have developed new approaches to thinking about marketing. Here are three notable ones.

Peter Doyle maintains that:

> value-based marketing is not primarily about numbers. . . . [Rather,] it consists of three main elements. First is a set of beliefs about the objectives of marketing. The . . . primary task is to develop strategies that will maximize shareholder return. . . . Second is a set of principles for choosing marketing strategies and making marketing decisions that are consistent with these beliefs. These principles are based on estimating the future cash flow associated with a strategy to calculate the shareholder value added. Finally, it is a set of processes that ensure that marketing develops, selects, and implements a strategy that is consistent with these beliefs and principles. These processes concern management of the financial, marketing and organizational value drivers of the business. The financial value drivers are those key ratios that have the most significant impact on shareholder value. The marketing drivers are the customer-oriented plans necessary to drive improvement in the financial ratios. The organizational value drivers are the core capabilities, systems and leadership styles needed to create and implement the shareholder value orientation in the business.

According to Doyle, financial value drivers relate to sales growth, operating margin, and investment; marketing value drivers relate to strong brands, customer loyalty, strategic relationships, market selection, and differential advantage.

Roger Best maintains that:

> Market-based management is at the base of a business with a strong market orientation. A strong market orientation translates into a strong customer focus, competitor orientation, and a team approach that cuts across organizational functions. The result is a market-based business that is in a strong position to develop and deliver market-based strategies designed to attract, satisfy, and retain customers. Implemented successfully across a wide range of market situations, a market-based approach . . . will deliver higher levels of profitability, cash flow, and shareholder value than will a cost-based approach.

Best maintains that the only source of positive cash flow is the customer and therefore the customer must be the focus of market-based management.

Tim Ambler suggests that if firms think they are already measuring marketing performance adequately, they should ask themselves five questions:

1. Do you routinely research consumer behavior (retention, acquisition, usage, etc.) and why consumers behave that way (awareness, satisfaction, perceived quality, etc.)?
2. Are the results of this research routinely reported to the board in a format integrated with financial marketing metrics?
3. In those reports, are the results compared with the levels previously forecasted in the business plans?
4. Are they also compared with the levels achieved by your key competitor using the same indicators?
5. Is short-term performance adjusted according to the change in your marketing-based asset(s)?

Ambler believes firms must give priority to measuring and reporting marketing performance through marketing metrics. He believes evaluation can be split into two parts: (1) short-term results and (2) changes in brand equity. Short-term results often reflect profit-and-loss concerns as shown by sales turnover, shareholder value, or some combination of the two. Brand-equity measures include awareness, market share, relative price, number of complaints, distribution and availability, total number of customers, perceived quality, and loyalty/retention. Ambler also recommends developing employee measures and metrics, arguing that "End users are the ultimate customers, but your own staff are your first; you need to measure the health of the internal market."

Sources: Peter Doyle, *Value-Based Marketing: Marketing Strategies for Corporate Growth and Shareholder Value* (Chichester, England: John Wiley & Sons, 2000); Roger J. Best, *Market-Based Management: Strategies for Growing Customer Value and Profitability*, 2nd ed. (Upper Saddle River, NJ: Prentice Hall, 2000); Tim Ambler, *Marketing and the Bottom Line: The New Methods of Corporate Wealth* (London: Financial Times/Prentice Hall, 2000).

TABLE 4.4

Sample Marketing Metrics

I. External	II. Internal
Awareness	Awareness of goals
Market share (volume or value)	Commitment to goals
Relative price (market share value/volume)	Active innovation support
Number of complaints (level of dissatisfaction)	Resource adequacy
Consumer satisfaction	Staffing/skill levels
Distribution/availability	Desire to learn
Total number of customers	Willingness to change
Perceived quality/esteem	Freedom to fail
Loyalty/retention	Autonomy
Relative perceived quality	Relative employee satisfaction

Source: Tim Ambler, "What Does Marketing Success Look Like?" *Marketing Management* (Spring 2001): 13–18.

Many marketing metrics relate to customer-level concerns such as their attitudes and behavior; others relate to brand-level concerns such as market share, relative price premium, or profitability.[25] Companies can also monitor an extensive set of metrics internal to the company. One important set of measures relates to a firm's innovativeness. For example, 3M tracks the proportion of sales resulting from its recent innovations. Another key set relates to employees. Table 4.4 summarizes a list of popular internal and external marketing metrics from a survey in the United Kingdom.[26]

Amazon.com is a firm renowned for constantly monitoring its marketing activities. CEO Jeff Bezos wants to know average customer contacts per order, average time per contact, the breakdown of e-mail versus telephone contacts, and the total cost to the company of each. The man in charge of Amazon's customer service and its warehouse and distribution operations looks at about 300 charts a week for his division.[27]

Firms are also employing organizational processes and systems to make sure that the value of all of these different metrics is maximized by the firm. A summary set of relevant internal and external measures can be assembled in a *marketing dashboard* for synthesis and interpretation. Some companies are also appointing marketing controllers to review budget items and expenses. Increasingly, these controllers are using business intelligence software to create digital versions of marketing dashboards that aggregate data from disparate internal and external sources.

MILWAUKEE ELECTRIC TOOL CORP.

Milwaukee Electric Tool is a manufacturer of items ranging from screwdrivers to gaskets and drill bits to heavy industrial machinery. For years, the company had deployed a data platform that let it gather information on its distribution, financials, manufacturing, sales, marketing, payables, receivables, and manufacturing operation. The company needed a way to bring all the data together and match trends. After the company changed to a new software package, Essbase XTD Analytic Server and Customer Focus Suite, its marketing manager could understand the mix of products a specific customer group was ordering and develop programs to promote more sales.[28]

As input to the marketing dashboard, companies can prepare two market-based scorecards that reflect performance and provide possible early warning signals. A **customer-performance scorecard** records how well the company is doing year after year on such customer-based measures as shown in Table 4.5. Norms should be set for each measure, and management should take action when results get out of bounds.

The second measure is called a **stakeholder-performance scorecard**. Companies need to track the satisfaction of various constituencies who have a critical interest in and impact on the company's performance: employees, suppliers, banks, distributors, retailers, stockholders. Again, norms should be set for each group and management should take action when one or more groups register increased levels of dissatisfaction.[29] Consider Hewlett-Packard's program.

TABLE 4.5

Sample Customer-Performance Scorecard Measures

- Percentage of new customers to average number of customers.
- Percentage of lost customers to average number of customers.
- Percentage of win-back customers to average number of customers.
- Percentage of customers falling into very dissatisfied, dissatisfied, neutral, satisfied, and very satisfied categories.
- Percentage of customers who say they would repurchase the product.
- Percentage of customers who say they would recommend the product to others.
- Percentage of target market customers who have brand awareness or recall.
- Percentage of customers who say that the company's product is the most preferred in its category.
- Percentage of customers who correctly identify the brand's intended positioning and differentiation.
- Average perception of company's product quality relative to chief competitor.
- Average perception of company's service quality relative to chief competitor.

HEWLETT-PACKARD

Each division of Hewlett-Packard evaluates its performance on a customer-based scorecard that monitors 18 to 20 "business fundamentals." Some, such as customer satisfaction and on-time delivery, are rated for all divisions; other indicators are tracked according to the nature of the division's business. The company is thus able to gauge the effects of its marketing strategies on sales and profits and to identify areas where improvements in performance can lead to improved quantitative results.[30]

Measuring Marketing Plan Performance

Marketers today have better marketing metrics for measuring the performance of marketing plans.[31] They can use four tools to check on plan performance: sales analysis, market share analysis, marketing expense-to-sales analysis, and financial analysis.

SALES ANALYSIS **Sales analysis** consists of measuring and evaluating actual sales in relation to goals. Two specific tools are used in sales analysis.

Sales-variance analysis measures the relative contribution of different factors to a gap in sales performance. Suppose the annual plan called for selling $4,000 widgets in the first quarter at $1 per widget, for total revenue of $4,000. At quarter's end, only 3,000 widgets were sold at $.80 per widget, for total revenue of $2,400. How much of the sales performance is due to the price decline and how much to the volume decline? The following calculation answers this question:

Variance due to price decline =	(\$1.00−\$.80) (3,000) =	\$ 600	37.5%
Variance due to volume decline =	(\$1.00) (4,000−3,000) =	\$1,000	62.5%
		\$1,600	100.0%

Almost two-thirds of the variance is due to failure to achieve the volume target. The company should look closely at why it failed to achieve expected sales volume.

Microsales analysis looks at specific products, territories, and so forth that failed to produce expected sales. Suppose the company sells in three territories and expected sales were 1,500 units, 500 units, and 2,000 units, respectively. The actual sales volume was 1,400 units, 525 units, and 1,075 units, respectively. Thus territory 1 showed a 7 percent shortfall in terms of expected sales; territory 2, a 5 percent improvement over expectations; and territory 3, a 46 percent shortfall! Territory 3 is causing most of the trouble. The sales vice president needs to check into territory 3: Maybe territory 3's sales rep is underperforming; a major competitor has entered this territory; or business is in a recession in this territory.

MARKET SHARE ANALYSIS Company sales do not reveal how well the company is performing relative to competitors. For this purpose, management needs to track its market share.

Market share can be measured in three ways: **Overall market share** is the company's sales expressed as a percentage of total market sales. **Served market share** is its sales expressed as a percentage of the total sales to its served market. Its **served market** is all the buyers who are able and willing to buy its product. Served market share is always larger than overall market share. A company could capture 100 percent of its served market and yet have a relatively small share of the total market. **Relative market share** can be expressed as market share in relation to its largest competitor. A relative market share over 100 percent indicates a market leader. A relative market share of exactly 100 percent means that the company is tied for the lead. A rise in relative market share means a company is gaining on its leading competitor.

Conclusions from market share analysis, however, are subject to certain qualifications:

- ***The assumption that outside forces affect all companies in the same way is often not true.*** The U.S. Surgeon General's Report on the harmful consequences of cigarette smoking caused total cigarette sales to falter, but not equally for all companies.
- ***The assumption that a company's performance should be judged against the average performance of all companies is not always valid.*** A company's performance should be judged against the performance of its closest competitors.
- ***If a new firm enters the industry, then every existing firm's market share might fall.*** A decline in market share might not mean that the company is performing any worse than other companies. Share loss depends on the degree to which the new firm hits the company's specific markets.
- ***Sometimes a market share decline is deliberately engineered to improve profits.*** For example, management might drop unprofitable customers or products.
- ***Market share can fluctuate for many minor reasons.*** For example, it can be affected by whether a large sale occurs on the last day of the month or at the beginning of the next month. Not all shifts in market share have marketing significance.[32]

A useful way to analyze market share movements is in terms of four components:

Overall market share = *Customer penetration* × *Customer loyalty* × *Customer selectivity* × *Price selectivity*

where:

Customer penetration: percentage of all customers who buy from the company.

Customer loyalty: purchases from the company by its customers expressed as a percentage of their total purchases from all suppliers of the same products.

Customer selectivity: size of the average customer purchase from the company expressed as a percentage of the size of the average customer purchase from an average company.

Price selectivity: average price charged by the company expressed as a percentage of the average price charged by all companies.

Now suppose the company's dollar market share falls during the period. The overall market share equation provides four possible explanations: The company lost some of its customers (lower customer penetration); existing customers are buying less from the company (lower customer loyalty); the company's remaining customers are smaller in size (lower customer selectivity); or the company's price has slipped relative to competition (lower price selectivity).

MARKETING EXPENSE-TO-SALES ANALYSIS Annual-plan control requires making sure that the company is not overspending to achieve sales goals. The key ratio to watch is *marketing expense-to-sales.* In one company, this ratio was 30 percent and consisted of five component expense-to-sales ratios: sales force-to-sales (15 percent); advertising-to-sales (5 percent); sales promotion-to-sales (6 percent); marketing research-to-sales (1 percent); and sales administration-to-sales (3 percent).

Management needs to monitor these ratios. Fluctuations outside the normal range are cause for concern. The period-to-period fluctuations in each ratio can be tracked on a *control chart* (see Figure 4.2). This chart shows that the advertising expense-to-sales ratio normally fluctuates between 8 and 12 percent, say 99 out of 100 times. In the fifteenth period, however, the ratio exceeded the upper control limit. One of two hypotheses can

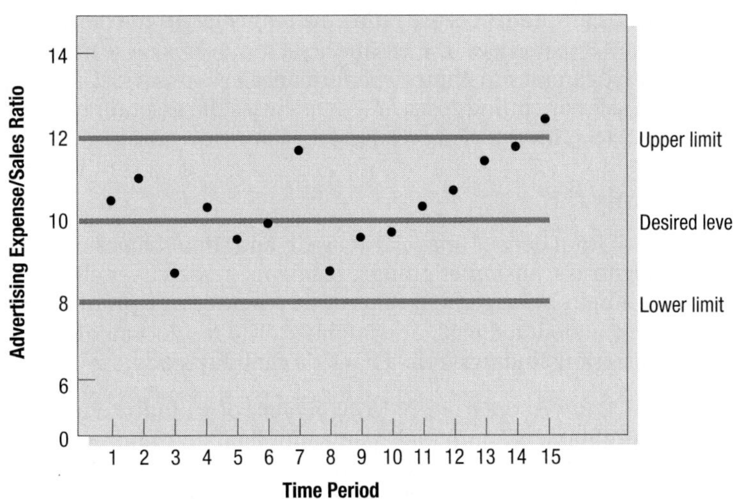

FIG. 4.2

The Control-Chart Model

explain this occurrence: (1) The company still has good expense control, and this situation represents a rare chance event. (2) The company has lost control over this expense and should find the cause. If no investigation is made, the risk is that some real change might have occurred, and the company will fall behind. If the environment is investigated, the risk is that the investigation will uncover nothing and be a waste of time and effort.

The behavior of successive observations even within the upper and lower control limits should be watched. Note in Figure 4.2 that the level of the expense-to-sales ratio rose steadily from the ninth period onward. The probability of encountering six successive increases in what should be independent events is only 1 in 64.[33] This unusual pattern should have led to an investigation sometime before the fifteenth observation.

FINANCIAL ANALYSIS The expense-to-sales ratios should be analyzed in an overall financial framework to determine how and where the company is making its money. Marketers are increasingly using financial analysis to find profitable strategies beyond sales building.

Management uses financial analysis to identify the factors that affect the company's *rate of return on net worth.*[34] The main factors are shown in Figure 4.3, along with illustrative numbers for a large chain-store retailer. The retailer is earning a 12.5 percent return on net worth. The return on net worth is the product of two ratios, the company's *return on assets* and its *financial leverage.* To improve its return on net worth, the company must increase its ratio of net profits to its assets or increase the ratio of its assets to its net worth. The company should analyze the composition of its assets (i.e., cash, accounts receivable, inventory, and plant and equipment) and see if it can improve its asset management.

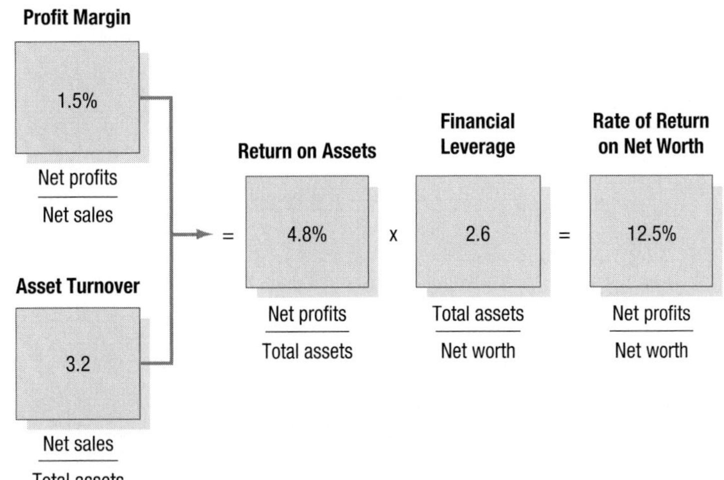

FIG. 4.3

Financial Model of Return on Net Worth

The return on assets is the product of two ratios, the *profit margin* and the *asset turnover*. The profit margin in Figure 4.3 seems low, whereas the asset turnover is more normal for retailing. The marketing executive can seek to improve performance in two ways: (1) Increase the profit margin by increasing sales or cutting costs; and (2) increase the asset turnover by increasing sales or reducing assets (e.g., inventory, receivables) that are held against a given level of sales.[35]

Profitability Analysis

Companies can benefit from deeper financial analysis, and should measure the profitability of their products, territories, customer groups, segments, trade channels, and order sizes. This information can help management determine whether any products or marketing activities should be expanded, reduced, or eliminated. The results can often be surprising. Here are some disconcerting findings from a bank profitability study:

> We have found that anywhere from 20 to 40 percent of an individual institution's products are unprofitable, and up to 60 percent of their accounts generate losses. Our research has shown that, in most firms, more than half of all customer relationships are not profitable, and 30 to 40 percent are only marginally so. It is frequently a mere 10 to 15 percent of a firm's relationships that generate the bulk of its profits. Our profitability research into the branch system of a regional bank produced some surprising results . . . 30 percent of the bank's branches were unprofitable.[36]

MARKETING-PROFITABILITY ANALYSIS We will illustrate the steps in marketing-profitability analysis with the following example:

The marketing vice president of a lawnmower company wants to determine the profitability of selling its lawnmower through three types of retail channels: hardware stores, garden supply shops, and department stores. The company's profit-and-loss statement is shown in Table 4.6.

Step 1: Identifying Functional Expenses Assume that the expenses listed in Table 4.6 are incurred to sell the product, advertise it, pack and deliver it, and bill and collect for it. The first task is to measure how much of each expense was incurred in each activity.

Suppose that most of the salary expense went to sales representatives and the rest went to an advertising manager, packing and delivery help, and an office accountant. Let the breakdown of the $9,300 be $5,100, $1,200, $1,400, and $1,600, respectively. Table 4.7 shows the allocation of the salary expense to these four activities.

Table 4.7 also shows the rent account of $3,000 allocated to the four activities. Because the sales reps work away from the office, none of the building's rent expense is assigned to selling. Most of the expenses for floor space and rented equipment are for packing and delivery. The supplies account covers promotional materials, packing materials, fuel purchases for delivery, and home office stationery. The $3,500 in this account is reassigned to the functional uses made of the supplies.

TABLE 4.6

A Simplified Profit-and-Loss Statement

Sales		$60,000
Cost of goods sold		39,000
Gross margin		$21,000
Expenses		
Salaries	$9,300	
Rent	3,000	
Supplies	3,500	
		15,800
Net profit		$5,200

Natural Accounts	Total	Selling	Advertising	Packing and Delivery	Billing and Collecting
Salaries	$9,300	$5,100	$1,200	$1,400	$1,600
Rent	3,000	—	400	2,000	600
Supplies	3,500	400	1,500	1,400	200
	$15,800	$5,500	$3,100	$4,800	$2,400

TABLE 4.7

Mapping Natural Expenses into Functional Expenses

Step 2: Assigning Functional Expenses to Marketing Entities The next task is to measure how much functional expense was associated with selling through each type of channel. Consider the selling effort. The selling effort is indicated by the number of sales made in each channel. This number is found in the selling column of Table 4.8. Altogether, 275 sales calls were made during the period. Because the total selling expense amounted to $5,500 (see Table 4.8), the selling expense averaged $20 per call.

Advertising expense can be allocated according to the number of ads addressed to different channels. Because there were 100 ads altogether, the average ad cost $31.

The packing and delivery expense is allocated according to the number of orders placed by each type of channel. This same basis was used for allocating billing and collection expense.

Step 3: Preparing a Profit-and-Loss Statement for Each Marketing Entity A profit-and-loss statement can now be prepared for each type of channel (see Table 4.9). Because hardware stores accounted for half of total sales ($30,000 out of $60,000), this channel is charged with half the cost of goods sold ($19,500 out of $39,000). This leaves a gross margin from hardware stores of $10,500. From

Channel Type	Selling	Advertising	Packing and Delivery	Billing and Collecting
Hardware	200	50	50	50
Garden supply	65	20	21	21
Department stores	10	30	9	9
	275	**100**	**80**	**80**
Functional expense	$5,500	$3,100	$4,800	$2,400
÷ No. of Units	275	100	80	80
Equals	**$ 20**	**$ 31**	**$ 60**	**$ 30**

TABLE 4.8

Bases for Allocating Functional Expenses to Channels

	Hardware	Garden Supply	Dept. Stores	Whole Company
Sales	$30,000	$10,000	$20,000	$60,000
Cost of goods sold	19,500	6,500	13,000	39,000
Gross margin	$10,500	$ 3,500	$ 7,000	$21,000
Expenses				
Selling ($20 per call)	$ 4,000	$ 1,300	$ 200	$ 5,500
Advertising ($31 per advertisement)	1,550	620	930	3,100
Packing and delivery ($60 per order)	3,000	1,260	540	4,800
Billing ($30 per order)	1,500	630	270	2,400
Total Expenses	$10,050	$ 3,810	$ 1,940	$ 15,800
Net profit or loss	$ 450	$ (310)	$ 5,060	$ 5,200

TABLE 4.9

Profit-and-Loss Statements for Channels

this must be deducted the proportions of the functional expenses hardware stores consumed. According to Table 4.8, hardware stores received 200 out of 275 total sales calls. At an imputed value of $20 a call, hardware stores have to be charged with a $4,000 selling expense. Table 4.8 also shows that hardware stores were the target of 50 ads. At $31 an ad, the hardware stores are charged with $1,550 of advertising. The same reasoning applies in computing the share of the other functional expenses to charge to hardware stores. The result is that hardware stores gave rise to $10,050 of the total expenses. Subtracting this from the gross margin, the profit of selling through hardware stores is only $450.

This analysis is repeated for the other channels. The company is losing money in selling through garden supply shops and makes virtually all of its profits through department stores. Notice that gross sales is not a reliable indicator of the net profits for each channel.

DETERMINING CORRECTIVE ACTION It would be naive to conclude that the company should drop garden supply shops and possibly hardware stores so that it can concentrate on department stores. The following questions need to be answered first:

- To what extent do buyers buy on the basis of type of retail outlet versus brand?
- What are the trends with respect to the importance of these three channels?
- How good are the company marketing strategies directed at the three channels?

On the basis of the answers, marketing management can evaluate five alternatives:

1. Establish a special charge for handling smaller orders.
2. Give more promotional aid to garden supply shops and hardware stores.
3. Reduce the number of sales calls and the amount of advertising going to garden supply shops and hardware stores.
4. Do not abandon any channel entirely, but only the weakest retail units in each channel.
5. Do nothing.

In general, marketing-profitability analysis indicates the relative profitability of different channels, products, territories, or other marketing entities. It does not prove that the best course of action is to drop the unprofitable marketing entities, nor does it capture the likely profit improvement if these marginal marketing entities are dropped.

DIRECT VERSUS FULL COSTING Like all information tools, marketing-profitability analysis can lead or mislead marketing executives, depending on how well they understand its methods and limitations. The lawnmower company showed some arbitrariness in its choice of bases for allocating the functional expenses to its marketing entities. "Number of sales calls" was used to allocate selling expenses, when in principle "number of sales working hours" is a more accurate indicator of cost. The former base was used because it involves less record keeping and computation.

Far more serious is another judgmental element affecting profitability analysis. The issue is whether to allocate full costs or only direct and traceable costs in evaluating a marketing entity's performance. The lawnmower company sidestepped this problem by assuming only simple costs that fit in with marketing activities, but the question cannot be avoided in real-world analyses of profitability. Three types of costs have to be distinguished:

1. ***Direct costs*** – These are costs that can be assigned directly to the proper marketing entities. Sales commissions are a direct cost in a profitability analysis of sales territories, sales representatives, or customers. Advertising expenditures are a direct cost in a profitability analysis of products to the extent that each advertisement promotes only one product. Other direct costs for specific purposes are sales force salaries and traveling expenses.
2. ***Traceable common costs*** – These are costs that can be assigned only indirectly, but on a plausible basis, to the marketing entities. In the example, rent was analyzed this way.
3. ***Nontraceable common costs*** – These are common costs whose allocation to the marketing entities is highly arbitrary. To allocate "corporate image" expenditures equally to all products would be arbitrary, because all products do not benefit equally. To allocate them proportionately to the sales of the various products would be arbitrary because relative product sales reflect many factors besides corporate image making. Other examples are top management salaries, taxes, interest, and other overhead.

No one disputes the inclusion of direct costs in marketing cost analysis. There is a small amount of controversy about including traceable common costs, which lump together costs that would change with the scale of marketing activity and costs that would not change. If the lawnmower company drops garden supply shops, it would probably continue to pay the same rent. In this event, its profits would not rise immediately by the amount of the present loss in selling to garden supply shops ($310).

The major controversy concerns whether the nontraceable common costs should be allocated to the marketing entities. Such allocation is called the *full-cost approach*, and its advocates argue that all costs must ultimately be imputed in order to determine true profitability. However, this argument confuses the use of accounting for financial reporting with its use for managerial decision making. Full costing has three major weaknesses:

1. The relative profitability of different marketing entities can shift radically when one arbitrary way to allocate nontraceable common costs is replaced by another.
2. The arbitrariness demoralizes managers, who feel that their performance is judged adversely.
3. The inclusion of nontraceable common costs could weaken efforts at real cost control.

Operating management is most effective in controlling direct costs and traceable common costs. Arbitrary assignments of nontraceable common costs can lead managers to spend their time fighting arbitrary cost allocations instead of managing controllable costs well.

Companies are showing a growing interest in using marketing-profitability analysis or its broader version, activity-based cost accounting (ABC), to quantify the true profitability of different activities.[37] To improve profitability, managers can then examine ways to reduce the resources required to perform various activities, or make the resources more productive or acquire them at lower cost. Alternatively, management may raise prices on products that consume heavy amounts of support resources. The contribution of ABC is to refocus management's attention away from using only labor or material standard costs to allocate full cost, and toward capturing the actual costs of supporting individual products, customers, and other entities.

Marketing-Mix Modeling

Marketing accountability also means that marketers can more precisely estimate the effects of different marketing investments. *Marketing-mix models* analyze data from a variety of sources, such as retailer scanner data, company shipment data, pricing, media, and promotion spending data, to understand more precisely the effects of specific marketing activities. To deepen understanding, multivariate analyses are conducted to sort through how each marketing element influences marketing outcomes of interest such as brand sales or market share.[38]

Especially popular with packaged-goods marketers such as Procter & Gamble, Clorox, and Colgate, the findings from marketing-mix modeling are used to allocate or reallocate expenditures. Analyses explore which part of ad budgets are wasted, what optimal spending levels are, and what minimum investment levels should be.[39] Although marketing-mix modeling helps to isolate effects, it is less effective at assessing how different marketing elements work in combination.

::: Forecasting and Demand Measurement

One major reason for undertaking marketing research is to identify market opportunities. Once the research is complete, the company must measure and forecast the size, growth, and profit potential of each market opportunity. Sales forecasts are used by finance to raise the needed cash for investment and operations; by the manufacturing department to establish capacity and output levels; by purchasing to acquire the right amount of supplies; and by human resources to hire the needed number of workers. Marketing is responsible for preparing the sales forecasts. If its forecast is far off the mark, the company will be saddled with excess inventory or have inadequate inventory. Sales forecasts are based on estimates of demand. Managers need to define what they mean by market demand. Here is a good example of the importance of defining the market correctly:

COCA-COLA

When Roberto Goizueta became CEO of Coca-Cola, many people thought that Coke's sales were maxed out. Goizueta, however, reframed the view of Coke's market share. He said Coca-Cola accounted for less than 2 ounces of the 64 ounces of fluid that each of the world's 4.4 billion people drank on average every day. "The enemy is coffee, milk, tea, water," he told his people at Coke, and he ushered in a huge period of growth.

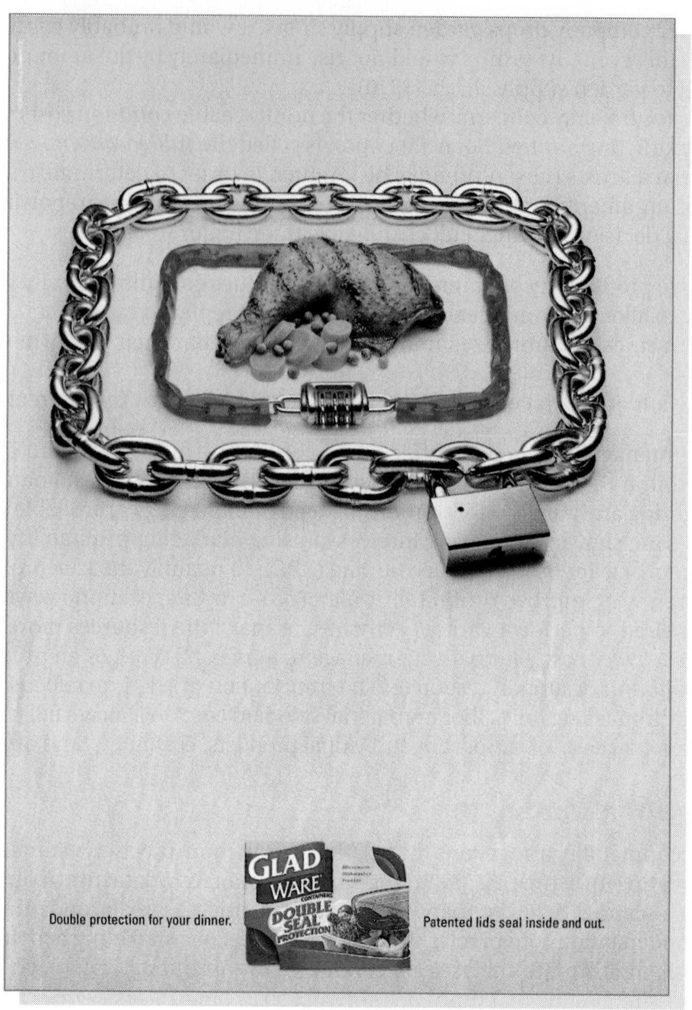

An ad for a Clorox product, Gladware. Clorox is one of the companies that uses marketing-mix modeling to test the effectiveness of its advertising.

The Measures of Market Demand

Companies can prepare as many as 90 different types of demand estimates (see Figure 4.4). Demand can be measured for six different product levels, five different space levels, and three different time levels.

Each demand measure serves a specific purpose. A company might forecast short-run demand for a particular product for the purpose of ordering raw materials, planning production, and borrowing cash. It might forecast regional demand for its major product line to decide whether to set up regional distribution.

Forecasts also depend on which type of market is being considered. The size of a market hinges on the number of buyers who might exist for a particular market offer. But there are many productive ways to break down the market:

- The **potential market** is the set of consumers who profess a sufficient level of interest in a market offer. However, consumer interest is not enough to define a market. Potential consumers must have enough income and must have access to the product offer.
- The **available market** is the set of consumers who have interest, income, and access to a particular offer. For some market offers, the company or government may restrict sales to certain groups. For example, a particular state might ban motorcycle sales to anyone under 21 years of age. The eligible adults constitute the *qualified available market*—the set of consumers who have interest, income, access, and qualifications for the particular market offer.
- The **target market** is the part of the qualified available market the company decides to pursue. The company might decide to concentrate its marketing and distribution effort on the East Coast. The company will end up selling to a certain number of buyers in its target market.
- The **penetrated market** is the set of consumers who are buying the company's product.

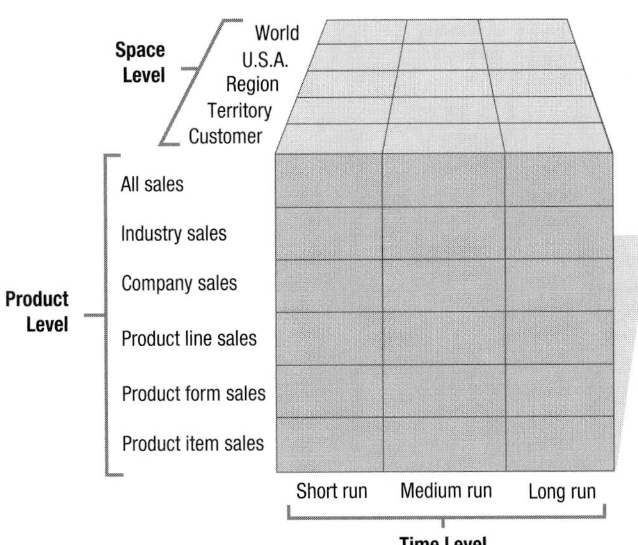

FIG. 4.4

Ninety Types of Demand Measurement (6 × 5 × 3)

These definitions are a useful tool for market planning. If the company is not satisfied with its current sales, it can take a number of actions. It can try to attract a larger percentage of buyers from its target market. It can lower the qualifications for potential buyers. It can expand its available market by opening distribution elsewhere or lowering its price; or it can reposition itself in the minds of its customers. Consider the case of Target Stores.

TARGET

Facing stiff competition from top retailers Wal-Mart and Kmart, Target Stores decided to reach more affluent shoppers and woo them away from department stores. The Midwestern discount retailer ran an unusual advertising campaign in some unusual spots: the Sunday magazines of the *New York Times*, the *Los Angeles Times*, and the *San Francisco Examiner*. One ad showed a woman riding a vacuum cleaner through the night sky. The ad simply said "Fashion and Housewares," with the Target logo in the lower right-hand corner. These hip spots gained Target Stores a reputation as the "upstairs" mass retailer, or "Kmart for Yuppies," as one shopper put it. In 2001, Target brought "fashion to food" by adding grocery sections to its retail concept and creating 175,000-square-foot SuperTargets. By 2004, there were 1,249 Target stores in 47 states (with 119 SuperTarget stores).[40]

A Vocabulary for Demand Measurement

The major concepts in demand measurement are market demand and company demand. Within each, we distinguish among a demand function, a sales forecast, and a potential.

MARKET DEMAND As we have seen, the marketer's first step in evaluating marketing opportunities is to estimate total market demand. **Market demand** for a product is the total volume that would be bought by a defined customer group in a defined geographical area in a defined time period in a defined marketing environment under a defined marketing program.

Market demand is not a fixed number, but rather a function of the stated conditions. For this reason, it can be called the *market demand function*. The dependence of total market demand on underlying conditions is illustrated in Figure 4.5(a). The horizontal axis shows different possible levels of industry marketing expenditure in a given time period. The vertical axis shows the resulting demand level. The curve represents the estimated market demand associated with varying levels of industry marketing expenditure.

Some base sales (called the *market minimum*, labeled *Q1* in the figure) would take place without any demand-stimulating expenditures. Higher levels of industry marketing expenditures would yield higher levels of demand, first at an increasing rate, then at a decreasing rate. Marketing expenditures beyond a certain level would not stimulate much further demand, thus suggesting an upper limit to market demand called the *market potential* (labeled *Q2* in the figure).

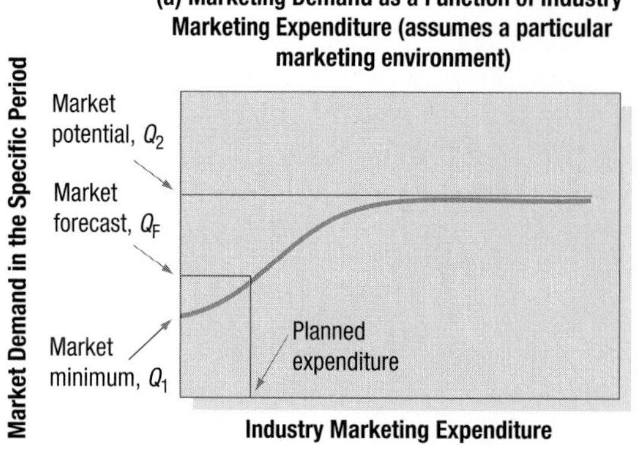

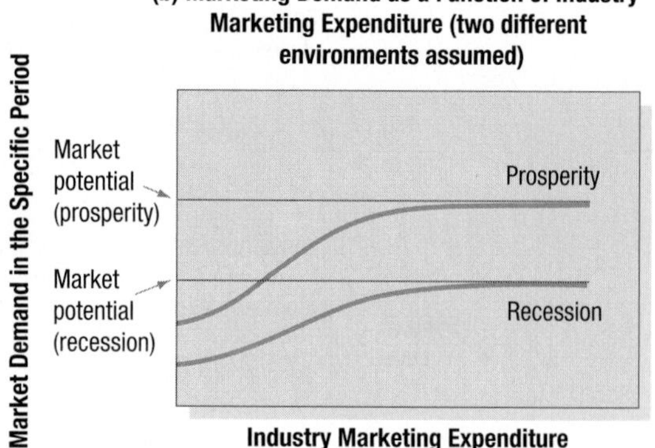

FIG. **4.5** Market Demand Functions

The distance between the market minimum and the market potential shows the overall *marketing sensitivity of demand.* We can think of two extreme types of markets, the expansible and the nonexpansible. An *expansible market,* such as the market for racquetball playing, is very much affected in its total size by the level of industry marketing expenditures. In terms of Figure 4.5(a), the distance between *Q*1 and *Q*2 is relatively large. A *nonexpansible market*—for example, the market for opera—is not much affected by the level of marketing expenditures; the distance between *Q*1 and *Q*2 is relatively small. Organizations selling in a nonexpansible market must accept the market's size (the level of *primary demand* for the product class) and direct their efforts to winning a larger **market share** for their product (the level of selective demand for the company's product).

It pays to compare the current level of market demand to the potential demand level. The result is called the **market penetration index**. A low market penetration index indicates substantial growth potential for all the firms. A high market penetration index suggests that there will be increased costs in attracting the few remaining prospects. Generally, price competition increases and margins fall when the market penetration index is already high.

A company should also compare its current market share to its potential market share. The result is called the company's **share penetration index**. A low share penetration index indicates that the company can greatly expand its share. The underlying factors holding it back could be many: low brand awareness, low brand availability, benefit deficiencies, too high a price. A firm should calculate the share penetration increases that would occur with investments to remove each deficiency, to see which investments would produce the greatest improvement in share penetration.[41]

It is important to remember that the market demand function is not a picture of market demand over time. Rather, the curve shows alternative current forecasts of market demand associated with alternative possible levels of industry marketing effort in the current period.

MARKET FORECAST Only one level of industry marketing expenditure will actually occur. The market demand corresponding to this level is called the **market forecast**.

MARKET POTENTIAL The market forecast shows expected market demand, not maximum market demand. For the latter, we have to visualize the level of market demand resulting from a "very high" level of industry marketing expenditure, where further increases in marketing effort would have little effect in stimulating further demand. **Market potential** is the limit approached by market demand as industry marketing expenditures approach infinity for a given marketing environment.

The phrase "for a given market environment" is crucial. Consider the market potential for automobiles in a period of recession versus a period of prosperity. The market potential is higher during prosperity. The dependence of market potential on the environment is illustrated in Figure 4.5(b). Market analysts distinguish between the position of the market demand function and movement along it. Companies cannot do anything about the posi-

One of the highest percentages of ownership/use of a product in the U.S. is that for television: 98% of Americans own a TV, and most families own more than one. (a) The big TV in the family/living room; (b) doing homework with the bedroom TV; (c) following a cooking show in the kitchen.

tion of the market demand function, which is determined by the marketing environment. However, companies influence their particular location on the function when they decide how much to spend on marketing.

Companies interested in market potential have a special interest in the **product penetration percentage**, which is the percentage of ownership or use of a product or service in a population. Here are some U.S. percentages: television (98%), health insurance (84%), car (81%), home ownership (67%), PC (54%), stock ownership (48%), gun ownership (41%), and fax (12%).[42] Companies assume that the lower the product penetration percentage, the higher the market potential, although this assumes that everyone will eventually be in the market for every product.

COMPANY DEMAND We are now ready to define company demand: **Company demand** is the company's estimated share of market demand at alternative levels of company marketing effort in a given time period. The company's share of market demand depends on how its products, services, prices, communications, and so on are perceived relative to the competitors'. If other things are equal, the company's market share would depend on the size and effectiveness of its market expenditures relative to competitors. Marketing model builders have developed sales response functions to measure how a company's sales are affected by its marketing expenditure level, marketing mix, and marketing effectiveness.[43]

COMPANY SALES FORECAST Once marketers have estimated company demand, their next task is to choose a level of marketing effort. The chosen level will produce an expected level of sales. The **company sales forecast** is the expected level of company sales based on a chosen marketing plan and an assumed marketing environment.

The company sales forecast is represented graphically with company sales on the vertical axis and company marketing effort on the horizontal axis, as in Figure 4.5. Too often the sequential relationship between the company forecast and the company marketing plan is confused. One frequently hears that the company should develop its marketing plan on the basis of its sales forecast. This forecast-to-plan sequence is valid if "forecast" means an estimate of national economic activity or if company demand is nonexpansible. The sequence is not valid, however, where market demand is expansible or where "forecast" means an estimate of company sales. The company sales forecast does not establish a basis for deciding what to spend on marketing. On the contrary, the sales forecast is the result of an assumed marketing expenditure plan.

Two other concepts are worth mentioning in relation to the company sales forecast. A **sales quota** is the sales goal set for a product line, company division, or sales representative. It is primarily a managerial device for defining and stimulating sales effort. Management sets sales quotas on the basis of the company sales forecast and the psychology of stimulating its achievement. Generally, sales quotas are set slightly higher than estimated sales to stretch the sales force's effort.

A **sales budget** is a conservative estimate of the expected volume of sales and is used primarily for making current purchasing, production, and cash flow decisions. The sales budget is based on the sales forecast and the need to avoid excessive risk. Sales budgets are generally set slightly lower than the sales forecast.

COMPANY SALES POTENTIAL Company sales potential is the sales limit approached by company demand as company marketing effort increases relative to that of competitors. The absolute limit of company demand is, of course, the market potential. The two would be equal if the company got 100 percent of the market. In most cases, company sales potential is less than the market potential, even when company marketing expenditures increase considerably, relative to competitors. The reason is that each competitor has a hard core of loyal buyers who are not very responsive to other companies' efforts to woo them.

Estimating Current Demand

We are now ready to examine practical methods for estimating current market demand. Marketing executives want to estimate total market potential, area market potential, and total industry sales and market shares.

TOTAL MARKET POTENTIAL Total market potential is the maximum amount of sales that might be available to all the firms in an industry during a given period, under a given level of industry marketing effort and environmental conditions. A common way to estimate total market potential is as follows: Estimate the potential number of buyers times the average quantity purchased by a buyer times the price.

If 100 million people buy books each year, and the average book buyer buys three books a year, and the average price of a book is $20, then the total market potential for books is $6 billion (100 million × 3 × $20). The most difficult component to estimate is the number of buyers for the specific product or market. One can always start with the total population in the nation, say, 261 million people. The next step is to eliminate groups that obviously would not buy the product. Let us assume that illiterate people and children under 12 do not buy books, and they constitute 20 percent of the population.

This means that only 80 percent of the population, or approximately 209 million people, would be in the suspect pool. We might do further research and find that people of low income and low education do not read books, and they constitute over 30 percent of the suspect pool. Eliminating them, we arrive at a prospect pool of approximately 146.3 million book buyers. We would use this number of potential buyers to calculate total market potential.

A variation on this method is the *chain-ratio method.* It involves multiplying a base number by several adjusting percentages. Suppose a brewery is interested in estimating the market potential for a new light beer. An estimate can be made by the following calculation:

> Demand for the new light beer = Population × personal discretionary income per capita average percentage of discretionary income spent on food × average percentage of amount spent on food that is spent on beverages × average percentage of amount spent on beverages that is spent on alcoholic beverages × average percentage of amount spent on alcoholic beverages that is spent on beer × expected percentage of amount spent on beer that will be spent on light beer.

AREA MARKET POTENTIAL Companies face the problem of selecting the best territories and allocating their marketing budget optimally among these territories. Therefore, they need to estimate the market potential of different cities, states, and nations. Two major methods of assessing area market potential are available: the market-buildup method, which is used primarily by business marketers, and the multiple-factor index method, which is used primarily by consumer marketers.

Market-Buildup Method The **market-buildup method** calls for identifying all the potential buyers in each market and estimating their potential purchases. This method produces accurate results if we have a list of all potential buyers and a good estimate of what each will buy. Unfortunately, this information is not always easy to gather.

Consider a machine-tool company that wants to estimate the area market potential for its wood lathe in the Boston area. Its first step is to identify all potential buyers of wood lathes in the area. The buyers consist primarily of manufacturing establishments that have to shape or ream wood as part of their operation, so the company could compile a list from a directory of all manufacturing establishments in the Boston area. Then it could estimate the number of lathes each industry might purchase based on the number of lathes per thousand employees or per $1 million of sales in that industry.

An efficient method of estimating area market potentials makes use of the *North American Industry Classification System (NAICS)*, developed by the U.S. Bureau of the Census in conjunction with the Canadian and Mexican governments.[44] The NAICS classifies all manufacturing into 20 major industry sectors. Each sector is further broken into a six-digit, hierarchical structure as follows (illustrated with paging).

51	Industry Sector (Information)
513	Industry Subsector (Broadcasting and telecommunications)
5133	Industry Group (Telecommunications)
51332	Industry (Wireless telecommunications carriers, except satellite)
513321	National Industry (U.S. Paging)

For each six-digit NAICS number, a company can purchase CD-ROMs of business directories that provide complete company profiles of millions of establishments, subclassified by location, number of employees, annual sales, and net worth.

To use the NAICS, the lathe manufacturer must first determine the six-digit NAICS codes that represent products whose manufacturers are likely to require lathe machines. To get a full picture of all six-digit NAICS industries that might use lathes, the company can (1) determine past customers' NAICS codes; (2) go through the NAICS manual and check off all the six-digit industries that might have an interest in lathes; (3) mail questionnaires to a wide range of companies inquiring about their interest in wood lathes.

The company's next task is to determine an appropriate base for estimating the number of lathes that will be used in each industry. Suppose customer industry sales are the most appropriate base. Once the company estimates the rate of lathe ownership relative to the customer industry's sales, it can compute the market potential.

Multiple-Factor Index Method Like business marketers, consumer companies also have to estimate area market potentials, but the customers of consumer companies are too numerous to be listed. The method most commonly used in consumer markets is a straightforward index method. A drug manufacturer, for example, might assume that the market potential for drugs is directly related to population size. If the state of Virginia has 2.28 percent of the U.S. population, the company might assume that Virginia will be a market for 2.28 percent of total drugs sold.

A single factor, however, is rarely a complete indicator of sales opportunity. Regional drug sales are also influenced by per capita income and the number of physicians per 10,000 people. Thus it makes sense to develop a multiple-factor index, with each factor assigned a specific weight. The numbers are the weights attached to each variable. For example, suppose Virginia has 2.00 percent of the U.S. disposable personal income, 1.96 percent of U.S. retail sales, and 2.28 percent of U.S. population, and the respective weights are 0.5, 0.3, and 0.2. The buying-power index for Virginia would be 2.04 [0.5(2.00) + 0.3(1.96) + 0.2(2.28)]. Thus 2.04 percent of the nation's drug sales might be expected to take place in Virginia.

The weights used in the buying-power index are somewhat arbitrary. Other weights can be assigned if appropriate. Furthermore, a manufacturer would want to adjust the market potential for additional factors, such as competitors' presence in that market, local promotional costs, seasonal factors, and local market idiosyncrasies.

Many companies compute other area indexes as a guide to allocating marketing resources. Suppose the drug company is reviewing the six cities listed in Table 4.10. The first two columns show its percentage of U.S. brand and category sales in these six cities. Column 3 shows the **brand development index (BDI)**, which is the index of brand sales to category sales. Seattle, for example, has a BDI of 114 because the brand is relatively more developed than the category in Seattle. Portland has a BDI of 65, which means that the brand in Portland is relatively underdeveloped. Normally, the lower the BDI, the higher the market opportunity, in that there is room to grow the brand. However, other marketers would argue the opposite, that marketing funds should go into the brand's strongest markets—where it might be important to reinforce loyalty or more easily capture additional brand share.[45]

TABLE 4.10

Calculating the Brand Development Index (BDI)

Territory	(a) Percent of U.S. Brand Sales	(b) Percent of U.S. Category Sales	BDI (a ÷ b) × 100
Seattle	3.09	2.71	114
Portland	6.74	10.41	65
Boston	3.49	3.85	91
Toledo	.97	.81	120
Chicago	1.13	.81	140
Baltimore	3.12	3.00	104

After the company decides on the city-by-city allocation of its budget, it can refine each city allocation down to census tracts or zip+4 code centers. *Census tracts* are small, locally defined statistical areas in metropolitan areas and some other counties. They generally have stable boundaries and a population of about 4,000. Zip+4 code centers (which were designed by the U.S. Post Office) are a little larger than neighborhoods. Data on population size, median family income, and other characteristics are available for these geographical units. Marketers have found these data extremely useful for identifying high-potential retail areas within large cities or for buying mailing lists to use in direct-mail campaigns (see Chapter 8).

INDUSTRY SALES AND MARKET SHARES Besides estimating total potential and area potential, a company needs to know the actual industry sales taking place in its market. This means identifying competitors and estimating their sales.

The industry trade association will often collect and publish total industry sales, although it usually does not list individual company sales separately. With this information, each company can evaluate its performance against the whole industry. Suppose a company's sales are increasing by 5 percent a year, and industry sales are increasing by 10 percent. This company is actually losing its relative standing in the industry.

Another way to estimate sales is to buy reports from a marketing research firm that audits total sales and brand sales. Nielsen Media Research audits retail sales in various product categories in supermarkets and drugstores and sells this information to interested companies. These audits can give a company valuable information about its total product-category sales as well as brand sales. It can compare its performance to the total industry or any particular competitor to see whether it is gaining or losing share.

Business-goods marketers typically have a harder time estimating industry sales and market shares. Business marketers have no Nielsens to rely on. Distributors typically will not supply information about how much of competitors' products they are selling. Business-goods marketers therefore operate with less knowledge of their market share results.

Estimating Future Demand

Very few products or services lend themselves to easy forecasting; those that do generally involve a product whose absolute level or trend is fairly constant and where competition is nonexistent (public utilities) or stable (pure oligopolies). In most markets, total demand and company demand are not stable. Good forecasting becomes a key factor in company success. The more unstable the demand, the more critical is forecast accuracy, and the more elaborate is forecasting procedure.

Companies commonly use a three-stage procedure to prepare a sales forecast. They prepare a macroeconomic forecast first, followed by an industry forecast, followed by a company sales forecast. The macroeconomic forecast calls for projecting inflation, unemployment, interest rates, consumer spending, business investment, government expenditures, net exports, and other variables. The end result is a forecast of gross national product, which is then used, along with other environmental indicators, to forecast industry sales. The company derives its sales forecast by assuming that it will win a certain market share.

How do firms develop their forecasts? Firms may do it internally or buy forecasts from outside sources such as marketing research firms, which develop a forecast by interviewing customers, distributors, and other knowledgeable parties. Specialized forecasting firms produce long-range forecasts of particular macroenvironmental components, such as population, natural resources, and technology. Some examples are Global Insight (a merger of Data Resources and Wharton Econometric Forecasting Associates), Forrester Research, and the Gartner Group. Futurist research firms produce speculative scenarios; three examples are the Institute for the Future, Hudson Institute, and the Futures Group.

All forecasts are built on one of three information bases: what people say, what people do, or what people have done. The first basis—what people say—involves surveying the opinions of buyers or those close to them, such as salespeople or outside experts. It includes three methods: surveys of buyer's intentions, composites of sales force opinions, and expert opinion. Building a forecast on what people do involves another method—putting the product into a test market to measure buyer response. The final basis—what people have done—involves analyzing records of past buying behavior or using time-series analysis or statistical demand analysis.

SURVEY OF BUYERS' INTENTIONS **Forecasting** is the art of anticipating what buyers are likely to do under a given set of conditions. Because buyer behavior is so important, buyers should be surveyed. For major consumer durables (for example, major appliances), several research organizations conduct periodic surveys of consumer buying intentions. These organizations ask questions like the following:

Do you intend to buy an automobile within the next six months?

0.00	0.20	0.40	0.60	0.80	1.00
No chance	Slight possibility	Fair possibility	Good possibility	High possibility	Certain

This is called a **purchase probability scale**. The various surveys also inquire into consumers' present and future personal finances and their expectations about the economy. The various bits of information are then combined into a consumer confidence (Conference Board) or consumer sentiment measure (Survey Research Center of the University of Michigan). Consumer durable-goods producers subscribe to these indexes in the hope of anticipating major shifts in buying intentions so they can adjust production and marketing plans accordingly.

For business buying, research firms can carry out buyer-intention surveys regarding plant, equipment, and materials. Their estimates tend to fall within a 10 percent error band of the actual outcomes. Buyer-intention surveys are particularly useful in estimating demand for industrial products, consumer durables, product purchases where advanced planning is required, and new products. The value of a buyer-intention survey increases to the extent that the cost of reaching buyers is small, the buyers are few, they have clear intentions, they implement their intentions, and they willingly disclose their intentions.

COMPOSITE OF SALES FORCE OPINIONS When buyer interviewing is impractical, the company may ask its sales representatives to estimate their future sales. Each sales representative estimates how much each current and prospective customer will buy of each of the company's products.

Few companies use sales force estimates without making some adjustments. Sales representatives might be pessimistic or optimistic, or they might go from one extreme to another because of a recent setback or success. Furthermore, they are often unaware of larger economic developments and do not know how their company's marketing plans will influence future sales in their territory. They might deliberately underestimate demand so that the company will set a low sales quota, or they might lack the time to prepare careful estimates or might not consider the effort worthwhile. To encourage better estimating, the company could offer certain aids or incentives. For example, sales reps might receive a record of their past forecasts compared with actual sales and also a description of company assumptions on the business outlook, competitor behavior, and marketing plans.

Involving the sales force in forecasting brings a number of benefits. Sales reps might have better insight into developing trends than any other single group. After participating in the forecasting process, reps might have greater confidence in their sales quotas and more incentive to achieve them. Also, a "grassroots" forecasting procedure provides detailed estimates broken down by product, territory, customer, and sales rep.

EXPERT OPINION Companies can also obtain forecasts from experts, including dealers, distributors, suppliers, marketing consultants, and trade associations. Large appliance companies periodically survey dealers for their forecasts of short-term demand, as do car companies. Dealer estimates are subject to the same strengths and weaknesses as sales force estimates. Many companies buy economic and industry forecasts from well-known economic-forecasting firms. These specialists are able to prepare better economic forecasts than the company because they have more data available and more forecasting expertise.

Occasionally, companies will invite a group of experts to prepare a forecast. The experts exchange views and produce a group estimate (*group-discussion method*); or the experts supply their estimates individually, and an analyst combines them into a single estimate (*pooling of individual estimates*). Alternatively, the experts supply individual estimates and assumptions that are reviewed by the company, then revised. Further rounds of estimating and refining follow (this is the Delphi method).[46]

PAST-SALES ANALYSIS Sales forecasts can be developed on the basis of past sales. *Time-series analysis* consists of breaking down past time series into four components (trend, cycle, seasonal, and erratic) and projecting these components into the future. *Exponential smoothing* consists of projecting the next period's sales by combining an average of past sales and the most recent sales, giving more weight to the latter. *Statistical demand analysis* consists of measuring the impact level of each of a set of causal factors (e.g., income, marketing expenditures, price) on the sales level. Finally, *econometric analysis* consists of building sets of equations that describe a system, and proceeding to fit the parameters statistically.

MARKET-TEST METHOD When buyers do not plan their purchases carefully or experts are not available or reliable, a direct-market test is desirable. A direct-market test is especially desirable in forecasting new-product sales or established product sales in a new distribution channel or territory. (We discuss market testing in detail in Chapter 20.)

SUMMARY :::

1. Companies can conduct their own marketing research or hire other companies to do it for them. Good marketing research is characterized by the scientific method, creativity, multiple research methods, accurate model building, cost-benefit analysis, healthy skepticism, and an ethical focus.
2. The marketing research process consists of defining the problem and research objective, developing the research plan, collecting the information, analyzing the information, presenting the findings to management, and making the decision.
3. In conducting research, firms must decide whether to collect their own data or use data that already exist. They must also decide which research approach (observational, focus-group, survey, behavioral data, or experimental) and which research instruments (questionnaire or mechanical instruments) to use. In addition, they must decide on a sampling plan and contact methods.
4. Analysis should ensure that the company achieves the sales, profits, and other goals established in its annual plan. The main tools are sales analysis, market share analysis, marketing expense-to-sales analysis, and financial analysis of the marketing plan.
5. Profitability analysis seeks to measure and control the profitability of various products, territories, customer groups, trade channels, and order sizes. An important part of controlling for profitability is assigning costs and generating profit-and-loss statements.
6. There are two types of demand: market demand and company demand. To estimate current demand, companies attempt to determine total market potential, area market potential, industry sales, and market share. To estimate future demand, companies survey buyers' intentions, solicit their sales force's input, gather expert opinions, or engage in market testing. Mathematical models, advanced statistical techniques, and computerized data collection procedures are essential to all types of demand and sales forecasting.

APPLICATIONS :::

Marketing Debate What is the Best Type of Marketing Research?

Many market researchers have their favorite research approaches or techniques, although different researchers often have different preferences. Some researchers maintain that the only way to really learn about consumers or brands is through in-depth, qualitative research. Others contend that the only legitimate and defensible form of marketing research involves quantitative measures.

Take a position: Marketing research should be quantitative versus Marketing research should be qualitative.

Marketing Discussion

When was the last time you participated in a survey? How helpful do you think was the information you provided? How could the research have been done differently to make it more effective?

PART

3

CONNECTING WITH CUSTOMERS

IN THIS CHAPTER, WE WILL ADDRESS THE FOLLOWING QUESTIONS:

1. What are customer value, satisfaction, and loyalty, and how can companies deliver them?
2. What is the lifetime value of customers?
3. How can companies both attract and retain customers?
4. How can companies cultivate strong customer relationships?
5. How can companies deliver total quality?
6. What is database marketing?

CHAPTER 5 ::: CREATING CUSTOMER VALUE, SATISFACTION, AND LOYALTY

five

Today, companies face their toughest competition ever. Moving from a product and sales philosophy to a marketing philosophy, however, gives a company a better chance of outperforming competition. And the cornerstone of a well-conceived marketing orientation is strong customer relationships. Marketers must connect with customers—informing, engaging, and maybe even energizing them in the process. John Chambers, CEO of Cisco Systems, put it well: "Make your customer the center of your culture." Customer-centered companies are adept at building customer relationships, not just products; they are skilled in market engineering, not just product engineering.

Walk into most banks, and you'll notice that human contact is kept to a minimum. The scenario at a branch of Washington Mutual, known affectionately as "WaMu" (Wa-moo) by its employees and loyal customers, is a sharp contrast. There are no teller windows. No ropes. If you need to open a checking account (with free checking), you step right up to the concierge station and a friendly person directs you to the right "nook." WaMu gets cozier with customers by training its sales associates to be approachable and to find out about customers' needs. If a customer's child just got into college, they can walk him or her over to a loan officer or they can steer a prospective homeowner to the mortgage desk. If your children are with you and get restless, you can send them to the WaMu Kids® corner >>>

Employee welcomes customers to a Las Vegas WaMu bank: Washington Mutual prides itself on being customer-friendly.

to play. The bank's format, known as its Occasio™ style, which is Latin for "favorable opportunity," is carefully designed to facilitate cross-selling of products. This is important, because when customers buy multiple products, they are more likely to remain a customer of the bank and are far more profitable. After four years, the average customer who opens a free checking account and then purchases additional products has an exponentially more profitable relationship with the bank, and this is reflected in higher than average deposit, investment, consumer-loan, and mortgage-loan bank balances. This kind of growth has propelled the formerly unknown Seattle thrift bank into a $268 billion major player in under a decade. "WaMu" is now the nation's largest thrift bank and the sixth-largest bank overall.[1]

As Washington Mutual's experience shows, successful marketers are the ones that fully satisfy their customers. In this chapter, we spell out in detail the ways companies can go about winning customers and beating competitors. The answer lies largely in doing a better job of meeting or exceeding customer expectations.

::: Building Customer Value, Satisfaction, and Loyalty

Managers who believe the customer is the company's only true "profit center" consider the traditional organization chart in Figure 5.1a—a pyramid with the president at the top, management in the middle, and front-line people and customers at the bottom—obsolete. Successful marketing companies invert the chart (Figure 5.1b). At the top are customers; next in importance are front-line people who meet, serve, and satisfy customers; under them are the middle managers, whose job is to support the front-line people so they can serve customers well; and at the base is top management, whose job is to hire and support

| FIG. 5.1 |

Traditional Organization Versus Modern Customer-Oriented Company Organization

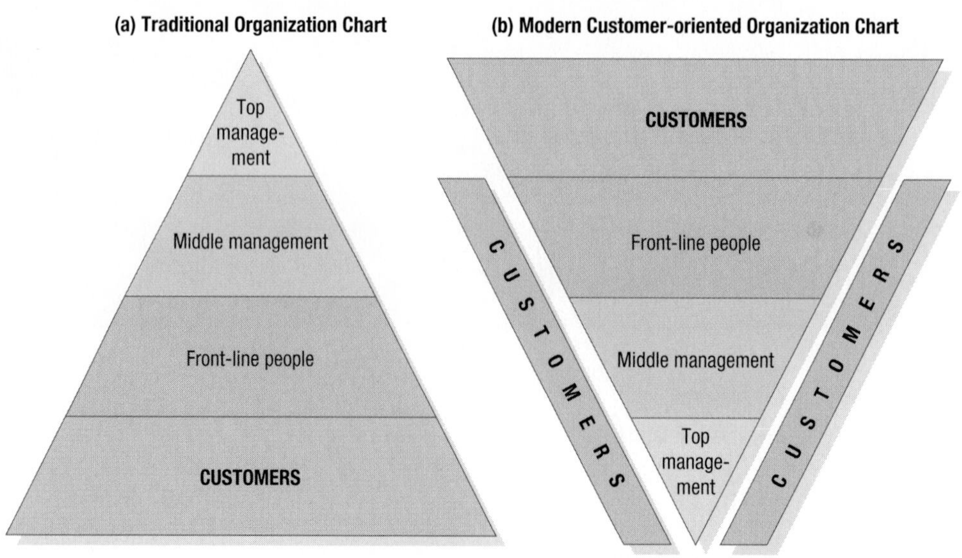

good middle managers. We have added customers along the sides of Figure 5.1(b) to indicate that managers at every level must be personally involved in knowing, meeting, and serving customers.

Some companies have been founded with the customer-on-top business model and customer advocacy has been their strategy—and competitive advantage—all along. Online auction giant eBay Inc., epitomizes this New World Order:

EBAY

eBay helped facilitate the exchange of $20 billion of goods in 2003. Consumer trust is the key element of that success, which enabled the company to grow and support commerce between millions of anonymous buyers and sellers. To establish trust, eBay tracks and publishes the reputations of both buyers and sellers on the basis of feedback from each transaction, and eBay's millions of passionate users have come to demand a voice in all major decisions the company makes. eBay sees listening, adapting, and enabling as its main roles. This is clear in one of the company's most cherished institutions: the Voice of the Customer program. Every few months, eBay brings in as many as a dozen sellers and buyers and asks them questions about how they work and what else eBay needs to do. At least twice a week the company holds hour-long teleconferences to poll users on almost every new feature or policy. The result is that users (eBay's customers) feel like owners, and they have taken the initiative to expand the company into ever-new territory.[2]

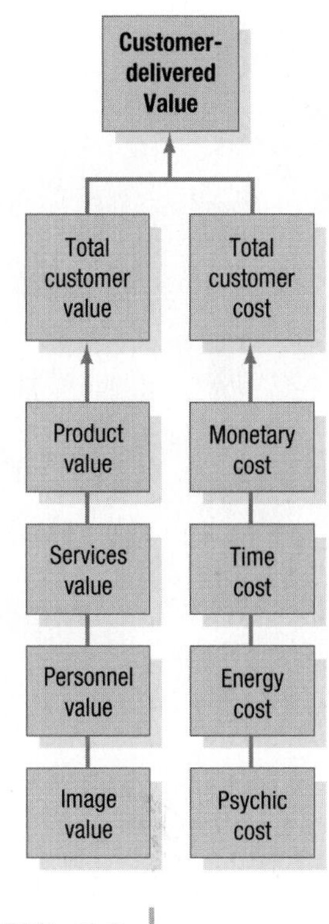

FIG. 5.2

Determinants of Customer-Delivered Value

With the rise of digital technologies like the Internet, today's increasingly informed consumers expect companies to do more than connect with them, more than satisfy them, and even more than delight them. For instance, customers now have a quick and easy means of doing comparison shopping through sites like Biz.rate, Shopping.com, and Pricegrabber.com. The Internet also facilitates communication between customers. Web sites like Epinions.com and Amazon.com enable customers to share information about their experiences in using various products and services.

Customer Perceived Value

Consumers are more educated and informed than ever, and they have the tools to verify companies' claims and seek out superior alternatives.[3] How then do they ultimately make choices? Customers tend to be value-maximizers, within the bounds of search costs and limited knowledge, mobility, and income. Customers estimate which offer will deliver the most perceived value and act on it (Figure 5.2). Whether or not the offer lives up to expectation affects customer satisfaction and the probability that he or she will purchase the product again.

Customer perceived value (CPV) is the difference between the prospective customer's evaluation of all the benefits and all the costs of an offering and the perceived alternatives. **Total customer value** is the perceived monetary value of the bundle of economic, functional, and psychological benefits customers expect from a given market offering. **Total customer cost** is the bundle of costs customers expect to incur in evaluating, obtaining, using, and disposing of the given market offering, including monetary, time, energy, and psychic costs.

Customer perceived value is thus based on the difference between what the customer gets and what he or she gives for different possible choices. The customer gets benefits and assumes costs. The marketer can increase the value of the customer offering by some combination of raising functional or emotional benefits and/or reducing one or more of the various types of costs. The customer who is choosing between two value offerings, V1 and V2, will examine the ratio V1:V2 and favor V1 if the ratio is larger than one, favor V2 if the ratio is smaller than one, and will be indifferent if the ratio equals one.

APPLYING VALUE CONCEPTS An example will help here. Suppose the buyer for a large construction company wants to buy a tractor from Caterpillar or Komatsu. The competing salespeople carefully describe their respective offers. The buyer wants to use the tractor in residential construction work. He would like the tractor to deliver certain levels of reliability, durability, performance, and resale value. He evaluates the tractors and decides that Caterpillar has a higher product value based on perceptions of those attributes. He also perceives differences in the accompanying services—delivery, training, and maintenance—and decides that Caterpillar provides better service and more knowledgeable and responsive personnel. Finally, he places higher value on Caterpillar's corporate image. He adds up all

Caterpillar sells tractors like this one not just on the product's attributes, but also on the value of the services, personnel, and image the company offers.

the values from these four sources—product, services, personnel, and image—and perceives Caterpillar as delivering greater customer value.

Does he buy the Caterpillar tractor? Not necessarily. He also examines his total cost of transacting with Caterpillar versus Komatsu, which consists of more than the money. As Adam Smith observed over two centuries ago, "The real price of anything is the toil and trouble of acquiring it." Total customer cost includes the buyer's time, energy, and psychic costs. The buyer evaluates these elements together with the monetary cost to form a total customer cost. Then the buyer considers whether Caterpillar's total customer cost is too high in relation to the total customer value Caterpillar delivers. If it is, the buyer might choose the Komatsu tractor. The buyer will choose whichever source he thinks delivers the highest customer perceived value.

Now let us use this decision-making theory to help Caterpillar succeed in selling to this buyer. Caterpillar can improve its offer in three ways. First, it can increase total customer value by improving product, services, personnel, and/or image benefits. Second, it can reduce the buyer's nonmonetary costs by reducing the time, energy, and psychic costs. Third, it can reduce its product's monetary cost to the buyer.

Suppose Caterpillar concludes that the buyer sees its offer as worth $20,000. Further, suppose Caterpillar's cost of producing the tractor is $14,000. This means that Caterpillar's offer potentially generates $6,000 over the company's cost, so Caterpillar needs to charge a price between $14,000 and $20,000. If it charges less than $14,000, it won't cover its costs; if it charges more than $20,000, it will price itself out of the market.

The price Caterpillar charges will determine how much value will be delivered to the buyer and how much will flow to Caterpillar. For example, if Caterpillar charges $19,000, it is creating $1,000 of customer perceived value and keeping $5,000 for itself. The lower Caterpillar sets its price, the higher the customer perceived value and, therefore, the higher the customer's incentive to purchase. To win the sale, Caterpillar must offer more customer perceived value than Komatsu does.[4]

CHOICES AND IMPLICATIONS Some marketers might argue that the process we have described is too rational. Suppose the customer chooses the Komatsu tractor. How can we explain this choice? Here are three possibilities.

1. ***The buyer might be under orders to buy at the lowest price.*** The Caterpillar salesperson's task is to convince the buyer's manager that buying on price alone will result in lower long-term profits.
2. ***The buyer will retire before the company realizes that the Komatsu tractor is more expensive to operate.*** The buyer will look good in the short run; he or she is maximizing personal benefit. The Caterpillar salesperson's task is to convince other people in the customer company that Caterpillar delivers greater customer value.
3. ***The buyer enjoys a long-term friendship with the Komatsu salesperson.*** In this case, Caterpillar's salesperson needs to show the buyer that the Komatsu tractor will draw complaints from the tractor operators when they discover its high fuel cost and need for frequent repairs.

The point of these examples is clear: Buyers operate under various constraints and occasionally make choices that give more weight to their personal benefit than to the company's benefit.

Customer perceived value is a useful framework that applies to many situations and yields rich insights. Here are its implications: First, the seller must assess the total customer value and total customer cost associated with each competitor's offer in order to know how his or her offer rates in the buyer's mind. Second, the seller who is at a customer perceived value disadvantage has two alternatives: to increase total customer value or to decrease total customer cost. The former calls for strengthening or augmenting the offer's product, services, personnel, and image benefits. The latter calls for reducing the buyer's costs by reducing the price, simplifying the ordering and delivery process, or absorbing some buyer risk by offering a warranty.[5]

DELIVERING HIGH CUSTOMER VALUE Consumers have varying degrees of loyalty to specific brands, stores, and companies. Oliver defines **loyalty** as "A deeply held commitment to re-buy or re-patronize a preferred product or service in the future despite situational influences and marketing efforts having the potential to cause switching behavior."[6] A 2002 survey of American consumers revealed that some of the brands that have great consumer loyalty include Avis rental cars, Sprint long-distance service, Nokia mobile phones, Ritz-Carlton hotels, and Miller Genuine Draft beer.[7]

The key to generating high customer loyalty is to deliver high customer value. Michael Lanning, in his *Delivering Profitable Value,* says that a company must design a competitively superior value proposition aimed at a specific market segment, backed by a superior value-delivery system.[8]

The **value proposition** consists of the whole cluster of benefits the company promises to deliver; it is more than the core positioning of the offering. For example, Volvo's core positioning has been "safety," but the buyer is promised more than just a safe car; other benefits include a long-lasting car, good service, and a long warranty period. Basically, the value proposition is a statement about the resulting experience customers will gain from the company's market offering and from their relationship with the supplier. The brand must represent a promise about the total experience customers can expect. Whether the promise is kept depends on the company's ability to manage its value-delivery system. The **value-delivery system** includes all the experiences the customer will have on the way to obtaining and using the offering.

BRITISH AIRWAYS

British Airways and American Airlines may use the same kind of aircraft to fly executives first class between New York and London, but British Airways (BA) beats American Airlines by meeting customers' needs for convenience and rest at every step of the journey. BA's value-delivery system includes a separate first-class express check-in and security clearance, plus a pre-flight express meal service in the first-class lounge so that time-pressed executives can maximize sleep time on the plane without the distraction of in-flight meals. BA was the first to put seats that recline into perfectly flat beds in its first-class section, and in the United Kingdom a fast-track customs area speeds busy executives on their way.[9]

A similar theme is emphasized by Simon Knox and Stan Maklan in their *Competing on Value.*[10] Too many companies create a value gap by failing to align brand value with customer value. Brand marketers try to distinguish their brand from others by a slogan ("washes whiter") or a unique selling proposition ("A Mars a day helps you work, rest, and play"), or by augmenting the basic offering with added services ("Our hotel will provide a computer upon request"). Yet, they are less successful in delivering distinctive customer value, primarily because their marketing people focus on the brand image and not enough on actual product or service performance. Whether customers will actually receive the promised value proposition will depend on the marketer's ability to influence various core business processes. Knox and Maklan want company marketers to spend as much time influencing the company's core processes as they do designing the brand profile. Here is an example of a company that is a master at delivering customer value.

SUPERQUINN

Superquinn is Ireland's largest supermarket chain and its founder, Feargal Quinn, is Ireland's master marketer. A greeter is posted at the store entrance to welcome and help customers and even offer coffee, and to provide umbrellas in case of rain and carryout service to customers' cars. Department managers post themselves in the aisles to interact with customers and answer questions. There is a high-quality salad bar, fresh bread baked every four hours, and indications of when produce arrived, including the farmers' pictures. Superquinn also operates a child-care center. It offers a loyalty program that gives points for the amount purchased and for discovering anything wrong with the store, such as dented cans or bad tomatoes. The loyalty card is recognized by a dozen other firms (a bank, gas station, etc.) who give points for purchasing at their establishments. Because everything is done to exceed normal customer expectations, Superquinn stores enjoy an almost-cult following.[11]

Total Customer Satisfaction

Whether the buyer is satisfied after purchase depends on the offer's performance in relation to the buyer's expectations. In general, **satisfaction** is a person's feelings of pleasure or disappointment resulting from comparing a product's perceived performance (or outcome) in relation to his or her expectations. If the performance falls short of expectations, the customer is dissatisfied. If the performance matches the expectations, the customer is satisfied. If the performance exceeds expectations, the customer is highly satisfied or delighted.[12]

Although the customer-centered firm seeks to create high customer satisfaction, that is not its ultimate goal. If the company increases customer satisfaction by lowering its price or increasing its services, the result may be lower profits. The company might be able to increase its profitability by means other than increased satisfaction (for example, by improving manufacturing processes or investing more in R&D). Also, the company has many stakeholders, including employees, dealers, suppliers, and stockholders. Spending more to increase customer satisfaction might divert funds from increasing the satisfaction of other "partners." Ultimately, the company must operate on the philosophy that it is trying to deliver a high level of customer satisfaction subject to delivering acceptable levels of satisfaction to the other stakeholders, given its total resources.

CUSTOMER EXPECTATIONS How do buyers form their expectations? From past buying experience, friends' and associates' advice, and marketers' and competitors' information and promises. If marketers raise expectations too high, the buyer is likely to be disappointed. However, if the company sets expectations too low, it won't attract enough buyers (although it will satisfy those who do buy).[13] Some of today's most successful companies are raising expectations and delivering performances to match. When General Motors launched the Saturn car division, it changed the whole buyer–seller relationship with a New Deal for car buyers: There would be a fixed price (none of the traditional haggling); a 30-day guarantee or money back; and salespeople on salary, not on commission (none of the traditional hard sell).[14] Look at what high satisfaction can do.

JETBLUE

JetBlue Airways, founded in New York in 1999, significantly raised customer expectations of low-fare carriers. With its brand new Airbus jets, comfy leather seats, live satellite TV, free wireless Internet access, and a consumer-friendly policy of never bumping a passenger, it has inspired lots of low-fare/high-service copycats. Like pioneer Southwest, where JetBlue's CEO David Neeleman tried out his wings, JetBlue finds employees who know how to keep customers coming back. He asks each person he hires to follow a few corporate commandments known as the Values, including safety, caring, integrity, fun, and passion. Even CEO Neeleman and the pilots get on their hands and knees to pick trash out from between seats and scrub the restrooms to prep planes for the next trip. The pitch-in prepping keeps turnaround time down, another reason more and more customers come to JetBlue. The proof is in the numbers: While almost every other airline is drowning in red ink, JetBlue is in the black. In 2003 the airline pulled in a $104 million profit on revenues of $998 million. It now carries more people from New York to Fort Lauderdale than any other airline.[15]

A customer's decision to be loyal or to defect is the sum of many small encounters with the company. Consulting firm Forum Corporation says that in order for all these small encounters to add up to customer loyalty, companies need to create a "branded customer experience." Here is how San Francisco's Joie de Vivre chain does this.

The Perpetually Late Girl
The 205-horsepower Saturn ION Red Line
When you put people first, you try to get them there first, too.
With its supercharged 205-hp engine, sport-tuned suspension and 17" forged alloy wheels,
the ION™ Red Line quad coupe might even make you perpetually early.
See more at Saturn.com
People first.

This Saturn Ion ad looks like a lot of other car ads. But buying a Saturn has unique advantages: no haggling over price, a 30-day money-back guarantee, and salespeople on salary, not commission.

JOIE DE VIVRE

Joie de Vivre Hospitality Inc., operates a chain of boutique hotels, restaurants, and resorts in the San Francisco area. Each property's unique décor, quirky amenities, and thematic style are often loosely based on popular magazines. For example, the Hotel del Sol—a converted motel bearing a yellow exterior and surrounded by palm trees wrapped with festive lights—is described as "kind of *Martha Stewart Living* meets *Islands* magazine."[16] Two Silicon Valley hotels offer guests high-speed Internet connections in their rooms and by the pool.[17] The boutique concept enables the hotels to offer personal touches such as vitamins in place of chocolates on pillows. Joie de Vivre now owns the largest number of independent hotel properties in the Bay Area.

Measuring Satisfaction

Many companies are systematically measuring customer satisfaction and the factors shaping it. For example, IBM tracks how satisfied customers are with each IBM salesperson they encounter, and makes this a factor in each salesperson's compensation.

A company would be wise to measure customer satisfaction regularly because one key to customer retention is customer satisfaction. A highly satisfied customer generally stays loyal longer, buys more as the company introduces new products and upgrades existing products, talks favorably about the company and its products, pays less attention to competing brands and is less sensitive to price, offers product or service ideas to the company, and costs less to serve than new customers because transactions are routine.

The link between customer satisfaction and customer loyalty, however, is not proportional. Suppose customer satisfaction is rated on a scale from one to five. At a very low level of customer satisfaction (level one), customers are likely to abandon the company and even bad-mouth it. At levels two to four, customers are fairly satisfied but still find it easy to switch when a better offer comes along. At level five, the customer is very likely to repurchase and even spread good word of mouth about the company. High satisfaction or delight creates an emotional bond with the brand or company, not just a rational preference. Xerox's senior management found out that its "completely satisfied" customers were six times more likely to repurchase Xerox products over the following 18 months than its "very satisfied" customers.[18]

When customers rate their satisfaction with an element of the company's performance—say, delivery—the company needs to recognize that customers vary in how they define good delivery. It could mean early delivery, on-time delivery, order completeness, and so on. The company must also realize that two customers can report being "highly satisfied" for different reasons. One may be easily satisfied most of the time and the other might be hard to please but was pleased on this occasion.[19]

A number of methods exist to measure customer satisfaction. *Periodic surveys* can track customer satisfaction directly. Respondents can also be asked additional questions to measure repurchase intention and the likelihood or willingness to recommend the company and brand to others. Paramount attributes the success of its five theme parks to the thousands of Web-based guest surveys it sends to customers who have agreed to be contacted. During the past year, the company conducted more than 55 Web-based surveys and netted 100,000 individual responses that described guest satisfaction on topics including rides, dining, shopping, games, and shows.[20]

Companies can monitor the *customer loss rate* and contact customers who have stopped buying or who have switched to another supplier to learn why this happened. Finally, companies can hire *mystery shoppers* to pose as potential buyers and report on strong and weak points experienced in buying the company's and competitors' products. Managers themselves can enter company and competitor sales situations where they are unknown and experience firsthand the treatment they receive, or phone their own company with questions and complaints to see how the calls are handled.

For customer satisfaction surveys, it's important that companies ask the right questions. Frederick Reichheld suggests that perhaps only one question really matters: "Would you recommend this product or service to a friend?" He maintains that marketing departments typically focus surveys on the areas they can control, such as brand image, pricing, and product features. According to Reichheld, a customer's willingness to recommend to a friend results from how well the customer is treated by front-line employees, which in turn is determined by all the functional areas that contribute to a customer's experience.[21]

In addition to tracking customer value expectations and satisfaction, companies need to monitor their competitors' performance in these areas. One company was pleased to find that 80 percent of its customers said they were satisfied. Then the CEO found out that its leading competitor had a 90 percent customer satisfaction score. He was further dismayed when he learned that this competitor was aiming for a 95 percent satisfaction score.

For customer-centered companies, customer satisfaction is both a goal and a marketing tool. Companies need to be especially concerned today with their customer satisfaction level because the Internet provides a tool for consumers to spread bad word of mouth—as well as good word of mouth—to the rest of the world. On Web sites like troublebenz.com and lemonmb.com, angry Mercedes-Benz owners have been airing their complaints on everything from faulty key fobs and leaky sunroofs to balky electronics that leave drivers and their passengers stranded.[22]

Companies that do achieve high customer satisfaction ratings make sure their target market knows it. When J. D. Power began to rate national home mortgage leaders, Countrywide was quick to advertise its number-one ranking in customer satisfaction. Dell Computer's meteoric growth in the computer systems industry can be partly attributed to achieving and advertising its number-one rank in customer satisfaction.

The University of Michigan's Claes Fornell has developed the American Customer Satisfaction Index (ACSI) to measure the perceived satisfaction consumers feel with different firms, industries, economic sectors, and national economies.[23] Examples of firms that led their respective industries with high ACSI scores in 2003 are Dell (78), Cadillac (87), FedEx (82), Google (82), Heinz (88), Kenmore (84), Southwest Airlines (75), and Yahoo! (78).

Product and Service Quality

Satisfaction will also depend on product and service quality. What exactly is quality? Various experts have defined it as "fitness for use," "conformance to requirements," "freedom from variation," and so on.[24] We will use the American Society for Quality Control's definition: **Quality** is the totality of features and characteristics of a product or service that bear on its ability to satisfy stated or implied needs.[25] This is clearly a customer-centered definition. We

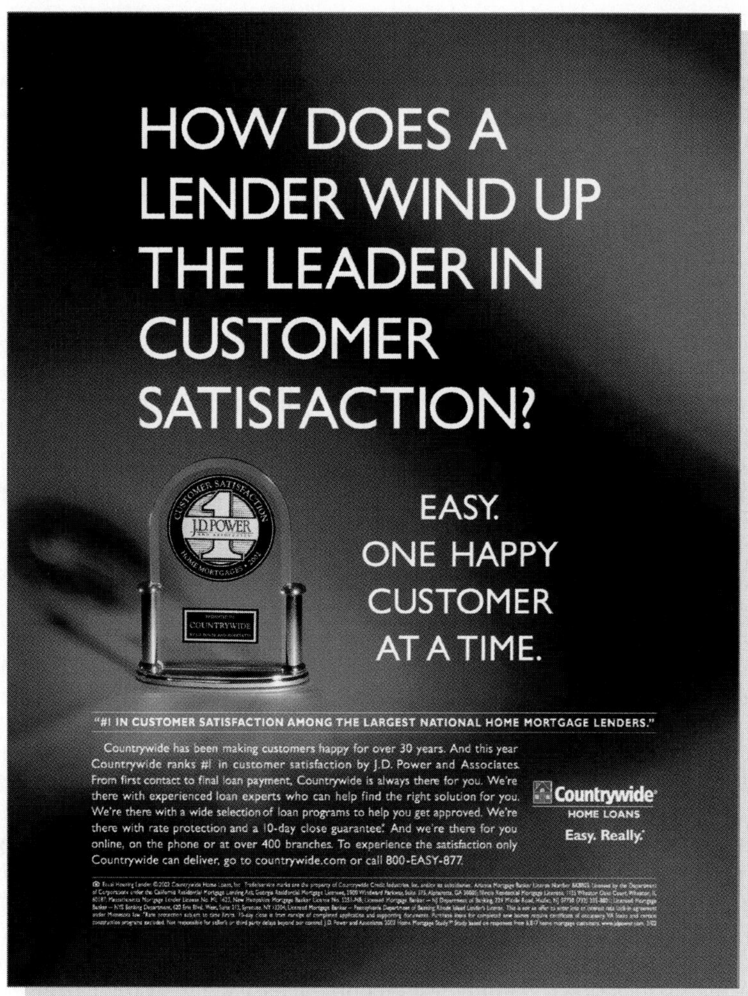

A Countrywide ad touts its #1 Customer Satisfaction rating from J. D. Power and Associates. Ratings like these are important to a customer-centered company, because word of mouth, good and bad, spreads so quickly on the Internet.

can say that the seller has delivered quality whenever the seller's product or service meets or exceeds the customers' expectations. A company that satisfies most of its customers' needs most of the time is called a quality company, but it is important to distinguish between *conformance* quality and *performance* quality (or grade). A Lexus provides higher performance quality than a Hyundai: The Lexus rides smoother, goes faster, and lasts longer. Yet both a Lexus and a Hyundai can be said to deliver the same conformance quality if all the units deliver their respective promised quality.

Total quality is the key to value creation and customer satisfaction. Total quality is everyone's job, just as marketing is everyone's job. This idea was expressed well by Daniel Beckham:

> Marketers who don't learn the language of quality improvement, manufacturing, and operations will become as obsolete as buggy whips. The days of functional marketing are gone. We can no longer afford to think of ourselves as market researchers, advertising people, direct marketers, strategists—we have to think of ourselves as customer satisfiers—customer advocates focused on whole processes.[26]

Marketing managers have two responsibilities in a quality-centered company. First, they must participate in formulating strategies and policies to help the company win through total quality excellence. Second, they must deliver marketing quality alongside production quality. Each marketing activity—marketing research, sales training, advertising, customer service, and so on—must be performed to high standards.

Total Quality Management

The quest to maximize customer satisfaction led some firms to adopt total quality management principles. **Total quality management (TQM)** is an organization-wide approach to continuously improving the quality of all the organization's processes, products, and services.

According to GE's former chairman, John F. Welch Jr., "Quality is our best assurance of customer allegiance, our strongest defense against foreign competition, and the only path to sustained growth and earnings."[27] The drive to produce goods that are superior in world markets has led some countries—and groups of countries—to recognize or award prizes to companies that exemplify the best quality practices (e.g., the Deming Prize in Japan, the Malcolm Baldridge National Quality Award in the United States, and the European Quality Award).

Product and service quality, customer satisfaction, and company profitability are intimately connected. Higher levels of quality result in higher levels of customer satisfaction, which support higher prices and (often) lower costs. Studies have shown a high correlation between relative product quality and company profitability.[28]

In practicing TQM, however, some firms ran into implementation problems as they became overly focused—perhaps even obsessed—with processes and *how* they were doing business. They lost sight of the needs and wants of customers and *why* they were doing business. In some cases, companies were able to achieve benchmarks against top quality standards, but only by incurring prohibitive increases in costs. For example, scientific equipment maker Varian embraced TQM principles but found itself rushing to meet production schedules and deadlines that managers now feel may not have been that important to their customers to begin with.

In a reaction to this somewhat myopic behavior, some companies now concentrate their efforts on "return on quality" or ROQ. ROQ adherents advocate improving quality only on those dimensions that produce tangible customer benefits, lower costs, or increased sales. This bottom-line orientation forces companies to make sure that the quality of the product offerings is in fact the quality consumers actually want.[29]

Rust, Moorman, and Dickson studied managers seeking to increase their financial returns from quality improvements.[30] They found that firms that adopted primarily a revenue expansion emphasis (externally focusing on growing demand through catering to and increasing consumers' preferences for quality) performed better as compared to firms that adopted primarily a cost-reduction emphasis (internally focusing on improving the efficiency of internal processes) or firms that attempted to adopt both emphases simultaneously.

Marketers play several roles in helping their companies define and deliver high-quality goods and services to target customers. First, they bear the major responsibility for correctly identifying the customers' needs and requirements. Second, they must communicate customer expectations properly to product designers. Third, they must make sure that customers' orders are filled correctly and on time. Fourth, they must check that customers have received proper instructions, training, and technical assistance in the use of the product. Fifth, they must stay in touch with customers after the sale to ensure that they are satisfied and remain satisfied. Sixth, they must gather customer ideas for product and service improvements and convey them to the appropriate departments. When marketers do all this, they are making substantial contributions to total quality management and customer satisfaction, as well as to customer and company profitability.

::: Maximizing Customer Lifetime Value

Ultimately, marketing is the art of attracting and keeping profitable customers. According to James V. Putten of American Express, the best customers outspend others by ratios of 16 to 1 in retailing, 13 to 1 in the restaurant business, 12 to 1 in the airline business, and 5 to 1 in the hotel and motel industry.[31] Yet every company loses money on some of its customers. The well-known 20–80 rule says that the top 20 percent of the customers may generate as much as 80 percent of the company's profits. Sherden suggested amending the rule to read 20–80–30, to reflect the idea that the top 20 percent of customers generate 80 percent of the company's profits, half of which are lost serving the bottom 30 percent of unprofitable customers.[32] The implication is that a company could improve its profits by "firing" its worst customers.

Furthermore, it is not necessarily the company's largest customers who yield the most profit. The largest customers demand considerable service and receive the deepest discounts. The smallest customers pay full price and receive minimal service, but the costs of transacting with small customers reduce their profitability. The midsize customers receive good service and pay nearly full price and are often the most profitable. This fact helps explain why many large firms are now invading the middle market. Major air express carriers, for instance, are finding that it does not pay to ignore small and midsize international shippers. Programs geared toward smaller customers provide a network of drop boxes, which allow for substantial discounts over letters and packages picked up at the shipper's place of business. United Parcel Service (UPS) conducts seminars to instruct exporters in the finer points of shipping overseas.[33]

Customer Profitability

What makes a customer profitable? A **profitable customer** is a person, household, or company that over time yields a revenue stream that exceeds by an acceptable amount the company's cost stream of attracting, selling, and servicing that customer. Note that the emphasis is on the lifetime stream of revenue and cost, not on the profit from a particular transaction.[34] Customer profitability can be assessed individually, by market segment, or by channel.

Although many companies measure customer satisfaction, most companies fail to measure individual customer profitability. Banks claim that this is a difficult task because a customer uses different banking services and the transactions are logged in different departments. However, banks that have succeeded in linking customer transactions have been appalled by the number of unprofitable customers in their customer base. Some banks report losing money on over 45 percent of their retail customers. There are only two solutions to handling unprofitable customers: Raise fees or reduce service support.[35]

CUSTOMER PROFITABILITY ANALYSIS A useful type of profitability analysis is shown in Figure 5.3.[36] Customers are arrayed along the columns and products along the rows. Each cell contains a symbol for the profitability of selling that product to that customer. Customer 1 is very profitable; he buys three profit-making products (P1, P2, and P4). Customer 2 yields a picture of mixed profitability; he buys one profitable product and one unprofitable product. Customer 3 is a losing customer because he buys one profitable product and two unprofitable products.

What can the company do about customers 2 and 3? (1) It can raise the price of its less profitable products or eliminate them, or (2) it can try to sell them its profit-making products. Unprofitable customers who defect should not concern the company. In fact, the company should encourage these customers to switch to competitors.

Customer profitability analysis (CPA) is best conducted with the tools of an accounting technique called Activity-Based Costing (ABC). The company estimates all revenue coming from the customer, less all costs. The costs should include not only the cost of making and distributing the products and services, but also such costs as taking phone calls from the customer, traveling to visit the customer, entertainment and gifts—all the company's resources that went into serving that customer. When this is done for each customer, it is possible to classify customers into different profit tiers: platinum customers (most profitable), gold customers (profitable), iron customers (low profitability but desirable), and lead customers (unprofitable and undesirable).

The company's job is to move iron customers into the gold tier and gold customers into the platinum tier, while dropping the lead customers or making them profitable by raising their prices or lowering the cost of serving them. More generally, marketers must segment customers into those worth pursuing versus those potentially less lucrative customers that should receive less attention, if any at all.

Dhar and Glazer make an interesting analogy between the individuals that make up the firm's customer portfolio for a firm and the stocks that make up an investment portfolio.[37] Just as with the latter, it is important to calculate the beta, or risk-reward value, for each customer and diversify the customer portfolio accordingly. From their perspective, firms

Products	Customers C_1	C_2	C_3	
P_1	+	+	+	Highly profitable product
P_2	+			Profitable product
P_3		–	–	Losing product
P_4	+		–	Mixed-bag product
	High-profit customer	Mixed-bag customer	Losing customer	

FIG. 5.3

Customer–Product Profitability Analysis

should assemble portfolios of negatively correlated individuals so that the financial contributions of one offset the deficits of another to maximize the portfolio's risk-adjusted lifetime value.

COMPETITIVE ADVANTAGE Companies must not only be able to create high absolute value, but also high value relative to competitors at a sufficiently low cost. **Competitive advantage** is a company's ability to perform in one or more ways that competitors cannot or will not match. Michael Porter urged companies to build a sustainable competitive advantage.[38] But few competitive advantages are sustainable. At best, they may be leverageable. A *leverageable advantage* is one that a company can use as a springboard to new advantages, much as Microsoft has leveraged its operating system to Microsoft Office and then to networking applications. In general, a company that hopes to endure must be in the business of continuously inventing new advantages.

Any competitive advantage must be seen by customers as a *customer advantage.* For example, if a company delivers faster than its competitors, this will not be a customer advantage if customers do not value speed. Companies must focus on building customer advantages. Then they will deliver high customer value and satisfaction, which leads to high repeat purchases and ultimately to high company profitability.

Measuring Customer Lifetime Value

The case for maximizing long-term customer profitability is captured in the concept of customer lifetime value. **Customer lifetime value (CLV)** describes the net present value of the stream of future profits expected over the customer's lifetime purchases. The company must subtract from the expected revenues the expected costs of attracting, selling, and servicing that customer, applying the appropriate discount rate (e.g., 10%–20%, depending on cost of capital and risk attitudes). Various CLV estimates have been made for different products and services.

- Carl Sewell, in *Customers for Life* (with Paul Brown), estimated that a customer entering his car dealership for the first time represents a potential lifetime value of over $300,000.[39] If the satisfied customer brings in other customers, the figure would be higher. Similarly, General Motors estimates its lifetime customers to be worth $276,000 on average. These six-figure values are a graphic illustration of the importance of keeping the customer satisfied for the life of the automobile to better the chances of a repeat purchase.[40]
- Even though tacos may cost less than a dollar each, executives at Taco Bell have determined that a repeat customer is worth as much as $11,000. By sharing such estimates of customer lifetime value with its employees, Taco Bell's managers help employees understand the value of keeping customers satisfied.[41]
- Mark Grainer, former chairman of the Technical Assistance Research Programs Institute (TARP), estimated that a loyal supermarket customer is worth $3,800 annually.[42]

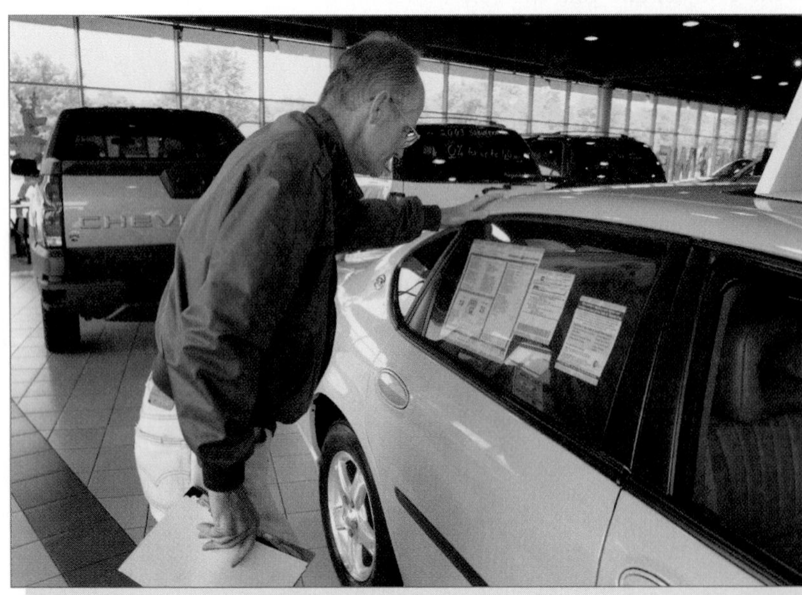
A GM customer shops the showroom at Hoskins Chevrolet in Elk Grove Village, Illinois. What GM wants is to satisfy him so he comes back to Hoskins and GM each time he needs a car.

We can work out an example of estimating CLV. Suppose a company analyzes its new-customer acquisition cost:

- Cost of average sales call (including salary, commission, benefits, and expenses): $300
- Average number of sales calls to convert an average prospect into a customer: 4
- Cost of attracting a new customer: $1,200

This is an underestimate because we are omitting the cost of advertising and promotion, plus the fact that only a fraction of all pursued prospects end up being converted into customers.

Now suppose the company estimates average customer lifetime value as follows:

- Annual customer revenue: $500
- Average number of loyal years: 20
- Company profit margin: .10
- Customer lifetime value: $1,000

This company is spending more to attract new customers than they are worth. Unless the company can sign up customers with fewer sales calls, spend less per sales call, stimulate higher new-customer annual spending, retain customers longer, or sell them higher-profit products, it is headed for bankruptcy. Of course, in addition to an average customer estimate, a company needs a way of estimating CLV for each individual customer to decide how much to invest in each customer.

CLV calculations provide a formal quantitative framework for planning customer investment and help marketers to adopt a long-term perspective. One challenge in applying CLV concepts, however, is to arrive at reliable cost and revenue estimates. Marketers who use CLV concepts must also be careful to not forget the importance of short-term, brand-building marketing activities that will help to increase customer loyalty.

Customer Equity

The aim of customer relationship management (CRM) is to produce high customer equity. **Customer equity** is the total of the discounted lifetime values of all of the firm's customers.[43] Clearly, the more loyal the customers, the higher the customer equity. Rust, Zeithaml, and Lemon distinguish three drivers of customer equity: value equity, brand equity, and relationship equity.[44]

- ***Value equity*** is the customer's objective assessment of the utility of an offering based on perceptions of its benefits relative to its costs. The sub-drivers of value equity are quality, price, and convenience. Each industry has to define the specific factors underlying each sub-driver in order to find programs to improve value equity. An airline passenger might define quality as seat width; a hotel guest might define quality as room size. Value equity makes the biggest contribution to customer equity when products are differentiated and when they are more complex and need to be evaluated. Value equity especially drives customer equity in business markets.
- ***Brand equity*** is the customer's subjective and intangible assessment of the brand, above and beyond its objectively perceived value. The sub-drivers of brand equity are customer brand awareness, customer attitude toward the brand, and customer perception of brand ethics. Companies use advertising, public relations, and other communication tools to affect these sub-drivers. Brand equity is more important than the other drivers of customer equity where products are less differentiated and have more emotional impact. We consider brand equity in detail in Chapter 9.
- ***Relationship equity*** is the customer's tendency to stick with the brand, above and beyond objective and subjective assessments of its worth. Sub-drivers of relationship equity include loyalty programs, special recognition and treatment programs, community-building programs, and knowledge-building programs. Relationship equity is especially important where personal relationships count for a lot and where customers tend to continue with suppliers out of habit or inertia.

This formulation integrates *value management, brand management,* and *relationship management* within a customer-centered focus. Companies can decide which driver(s) to strengthen for the best payoff. The researchers believe they can measure and compare the financial return of alternative investments to help choose strategies and actions based on which would provide the best return on marketing investments.

An alternative formulation to customer equity is provided by Blattberg, Getz, and Thomas. They view customer equity as driven by three components: acquisition, retention, and add-on selling.[45] Acquisition is affected by the number of prospects, the acquisition probability of a prospect, and acquisition spending per prospect. Retention is influenced by the retention rate and retention spending level. Add-on spending is a function of the efficiency of add-on selling, the number of add-on selling offers given to existing customers, and the response rate to new offers. Marketing activities can then be judged by how they affect these three components.

Customer equity represents a promising approach to marketing management. "Marketing Insight: Progress and Priorities in Customer Equity Management" highlights some recent academic thinking on the subject. Note too that customer equity notions can be extended. Mohan Sawhney defines the **relational equity** of the firm as the cumulative value of the firm's network of relationships with its customers, partners, suppliers, employees, and investors.[46] Relational equity depends on the company's ability to attract and retain talent, customers, investors, and partners.

::: Cultivating Customer Relationships

Maximizing customer value means cultivating long-term customer relationships. In the past, producers customized their offerings to each customer: The tailor fitted a suit and a cobbler made shoes for each individual. The Industrial Revolution ushered in an era of mass production. To maximize economies of scale, companies made standard goods in advance of orders and left it to individuals to fit into whatever was available. Producers moved from *built-to-order* marketing to *built-to-stock* marketing.

Companies are now moving away from wasteful mass marketing to more precision marketing designed to build strong customer relationships.[47] Today's economy is supported by information businesses. Information has the advantages of being easy to differentiate, customize, personalize, and dispatch over networks at incredible speed.

As companies have grown proficient at gathering information about individual customers and business partners (suppliers, distributors, retailers), and as their factories are designed more flexibly, they have increased their ability to individualize market offerings, messages, and media. **Mass customization** is the ability of a company to meet each customer's requirements—to prepare on a mass basis individually designed products, services, programs, and communications.[48] While Levi's and Lands' End were among the first clothing manufacturers to introduce custom jeans, now there are many players in the mass-customization market:

- Nike lets consumers customize athletic shoes for $10 more. A shopper with two different size feet can even get a nonmatching pair.
- At Reflect.com, the Web site for Procter & Gamble spin-off Reflect True Custom Beauty, consumers answer a set of questions and then get custom-blended foundation, moisturizer, shampoo, or other cosmetics and skin-care products.
- Interactive Custom Clothes, which began making made-to-order jeans and pants in 1996, has grown so fast that it had to stop taking orders in 2003. The company is now trying to find an apparel manufacturer or retailer partner to help ease the load.

Customer Relationship Management (CRM)

In addition to working with partners—called **partner relationship management (PRM)**—many companies are intent on developing stronger bonds with their customers—called **customer relationship management (CRM)**. This is the process of managing detailed information about individual customers and carefully managing all customer "touch points" to maximize customer loyalty. A *customer touch point* is any occasion on which a customer encounters the brand and product—from actual experience to personal or mass communications to casual observation. For a hotel, the touch points include reservations, check-in and check-out, frequent-stay programs, room service, business services, exercise facilities, laundry service, restaurants, and bars. For instance, the Four Seasons relies on personal touches, such as a staff that always addresses guests by name, high-powered employees who understand the needs of sophisticated business travelers, and at least one best-in-region facility, such as a premier restaurant or spa.[49]

Customer relationship management enables companies to provide excellent real-time customer service through the effective use of individual account information. Based on

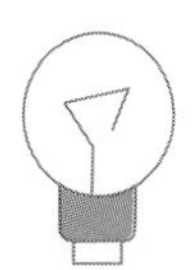

MARKETING INSIGHT | PROGRESS AND PRIORITIES IN CUSTOMER EQUITY MANAGEMENT

Customer equity has roots in many different marketing concepts—direct marketing and database marketing, service quality, relationship marketing, brand equity. Its unique focus, however, is on understanding the value of the customer to the firm and how to manage the customer as a strategic asset to increase overall firm value for shareholders.

Customer equity can be seen as the expected lifetime value of a firm's existing customer base plus the expected future lifetime value of newly acquired customers. This basic CLV model can be modified to incorporate several other dimensions, such as individual customer risk, the social effects of the word of mouth, and competitive and environmental effects that can dampen customer retention rates.

A special issue of the *Journal of Service Research* devoted to articles on the topic of customer equity included contributions by top academics working on that topic. The papers covered a wide range of issues, among them how to implement customer equity management:

1. ***Assemble individual-level, industry-wide consumer data.*** Pooled customer information by all industry competitors can provide insight into crucial considerations such as an individual's share of requirements. The benefits of broad industry cooperation can offset the costs from the loss of company-specific knowledge.
2. ***Track marketing's effect on the balance sheet, not just the income statement.*** Accounting principles that recognize the customer asset are needed. The challenge is that CLV calculations depend on assumptions about a host of factors, such as the future income stream from a customer, appropriate cost allocations to a customer, discount factors, and the expected economic life of a customer.
3. ***Model future revenues appropriately.*** Decisions about the timing and probability of revenue flows have important implications.
4. ***Maximize (don't just measure) CLV.*** Marketers must implement marketing initiatives to maximize the value of the customer franchise (e.g., loyalty programs, customer reactivations, and cross-selling).
5. ***Align the organization with customer management activities.*** For example, some catalog retailers or credit card companies commonly separate the prospect acquisition team from a customer conversion team from those responsible for ongoing customer retention and servicing. Another team may even be assigned to work on reactivation of dormant accounts.
6. ***Respect the sensitivity of customer information.*** Consider decentralizing customer information storage and having data reside with the consumer, on personal computers or smart cards. Also, allow consumers the right to audit and contest the accuracy of their profiles.
7. ***Develop CRM from an efficiency tool into a service improvement tool.*** The most successful CRM implementations reevaluate and refine all customer-facing business processes; develop and motivate all service and support personnel; and select and tailor appropriate technologies.

Source: Special Issue on Customer Equity Management, *Journal of Services Research* 5, no.1 (August 2002).

what they know about each valued customer, companies can customize market offerings, services, programs, messages, and media. CRM is important because a major driver of company profitability is the aggregate value of the company's customer base.[50] A pioneer in the application of CRM techniques is Harrah's Entertainment.

HARRAH'S

In 1997, Harrah's Entertainment Inc., in Las Vegas, launched a pioneering loyalty program that pulled all customer data into a centralized warehouse and provided sophisticated analysis to better understand the value of the investments the casino makes in its customers. Harrah's now has fine-tuned its Total Rewards system to achieve near-real-time analysis: As customers interact with slot machines, check into casinos or buy meals, they receive reward offers based on the predictive analyses. The company has now identified hundreds of customer segments among its more than 25 million slot players. By targeting offers to highly specific customer segments, Harrah's boosted its market share by six percentage points and increased net income by 12.4 percent, even during the difficult post-9/11 market in 2002.[51]

Some of the groundwork for customer relationship management was laid by Don Peppers and Martha Rogers in a series of books.[52] Peppers and Rogers outline a four-step framework for one-to-one marketing that can be adapted to CRM marketing as follows:

- ***Identify your prospects and customers.*** Do not go after everyone. Build, maintain, and mine a rich customer database with information derived from all the channels and customer touch points.

Playing the slots at Harrah's Cherokee Casino in North Carolina These customers are probably part of a sophisticated segmenting system that lets Harrah's target offers to hundreds of customer segments among its 25 million slot players.

- ***Differentiate customers in terms of (1) their needs and (2) their value to your company.*** Spend proportionately more effort on the most valuable customers (MVCs). Apply Activity Based Costing and calculate customer lifetime value. Estimate net present value of all future profits coming from purchases, margin levels, and referrals, less customer-specific servicing costs.
- ***Interact with individual customers to improve your knowledge about their individual needs and to build stronger relationships.*** Formulate customized offerings that are communicated in a personalized way.
- ***Customize products, services, and messages to each customer.*** Facilitate customer/company interaction through the company contact center and Web site.

Table 5.1 lists the main differences between mass marketing and one-to-one marketing.

A key driver of shareholder value is the aggregate value of the customer base. Winning companies improve the value of their customer base by excelling at strategies such as the following:

- ***Reducing the rate of customer defection.*** Whole Foods, the world's largest retailer of natural and organic foods, woos customers with a commitment to marketing the best foods and a team concept for employees. Selecting and training employees to be knowledgeable and friendly increases the likelihood that the inevitable shopping questions from customers will be answered satisfactorily.
- ***Increasing the longevity of the customer relationship.*** The more involved a customer is with the company, the more likely he or she is to stick around. Some companies treat their customers as partners—especially in business-to-business markets—soliciting their help in the design of new products or improving their customer service. Instant Web Companies (IWCO), a Chanhassen, Minnesota, direct-mail printer, launched a monthly Customer Spotlight program where guest companies provide an overview of their business and direct-mail programs and comment on IWCO practices, products, and services. IWCO's staff not only gains exposure to customers, but also develops a broader perspective on customers' business and marketing objectives and how to add value and identify options that help meet their customers' goals.[53]
- ***Enhancing the growth potential of each customer through "share-of-wallet," cross-selling, and up-selling.***[54] Harley-Davidson sells more than motorcycles and riding supplements (such as gloves, leather jackets, helmets, and sunglasses). Harley dealerships sell more than 3,000 items of clothing—some even have their own fitting rooms. Licensed goods sold by others range from the predictable (shot glasses, cue balls, and Zippo cigarette lighters) to the more surprising items (cologne, dolls, and cell phones). Harley-branded merchandise amounted to more than $211 million in company sales in 2003.
- ***Making low-profit customers more profitable or terminating them.*** To avoid the direct need for termination, unprofitable customers can be made to buy more or in larger quantities, forgo certain features or services, or pay higher amounts or fees. Banks, phone companies, and travel agencies are all now charging for once-free services to ensure minimum customer revenue levels.
- ***Focusing disproportionate effort on high-value customers.*** The most valuable customers can be treated in a special way. Thoughtful gestures such as birthday greetings, small gifts, or invitations to special sports or arts events can send a strong signal to the customer.

Attracting, Retaining, and Growing Customers

Customers are becoming harder to please. They are smarter, more price conscious, more demanding, less forgiving, and they are approached by many more competitors with equal or better offers. The challenge, according to Jeffrey Gitomer, is not necessarily to produce

TABLE 5.1

Mass Marketing Versus One-to-One Marketing

Mass Marketing	One-to-One Marketing
Average customer	Individual customer
Customer anonymity	Customer profile
Standard product	Customized market offering
Mass production	Customized production
Mass distribution	Individualized distribution
Mass advertising	Individualized message
Mass promotion	Individualized incentives
One-way message	Two-way messages
Economies of scale	Economies of scope
Share of market	Share of customer
All customers	Profitable customers
Customer attraction	Customer retention

Source: Adapted from Don Peppers and Martha Rogers, *The One-to-One Future* (New York: Doubleday/Currency, 1993). See their Web site www.1to1.com.

satisfied customers; several competitors can do this. The challenge is to produce delighted and loyal customers.[55]

Companies seeking to expand their profits and sales have to spend considerable time and resources searching for new customers. To generate leads, the company develops ads and places them in media that will reach new prospects; it sends direct mail and makes phone calls to possible new prospects; its salespeople participate in trade shows where they might find new leads; it purchases names from list brokers; and so on. All this activity produces a list of suspects. *Suspects* are people or organizations who might conceivably have an interest in buying the company's product or service, but may not have the means or real intention to buy. The next task is to identify which suspects are really good *prospects*—customers with the motivation, ability, and opportunity to make a purchase—by interviewing them, checking on their financial standing, and so on. Then it is time to send out the salespeople.

It is not enough, however, to attract new customers; the company must keep them and increase their business. Too many companies suffer from high **customer churn**—high customer defection. It is like adding water to a leaking bucket. Cellular carriers, for example, are plagued with "spinners," customers who switch carriers at least three times a year looking for the best deal. Many lose 25 percent of their subscribers each year at an estimated cost of $2 billion to $4 billion. Unfortunately, much marketing theory and practice centers on the art of attracting new customers, rather than on retaining and cultivating existing ones. The emphasis traditionally has been on making sales rather than building relationships; on preselling and selling rather than caring for the customer afterward.

There are two main ways to strengthen customer retention. One is to erect high switching barriers. Customers are less inclined to switch to another supplier when this would involve high capital costs, high search costs, or the loss of loyal-customer discounts. The better approach is to deliver high customer satisfaction. This makes it harder for competitors to offer lower prices or inducements to switch.

Some companies think they are getting a sense of customer satisfaction by tallying complaints, but 96 percent of dissatisfied customers don't complain; they just stop buying.[56] The best thing a company can do is to make it easy for the customer to complain. Suggestion forms, toll-free numbers, Web sites, and e-mail addresses allow for quick, two-way communication. The 3M Company claims that over two-thirds of its product improvement ideas come from listening to customer complaints.

Listening is not enough, however; the company must respond quickly and constructively to any complaint (see "Marketing Memo: How to Handle Customer Complaints"):

> Of the customers who register a complaint, between 54 and 70% will do business again with the organization if their complaint is resolved. The figure goes up to a staggering

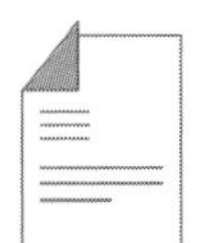

MARKETING MEMO | HOW TO HANDLE CUSTOMER COMPLAINTS

No matter how perfectly designed and implemented a marketing program is, mistakes will happen. Given the potential downside of having an unhappy customer, it is critical that the negative experience be dealt with properly. As with any marketing crisis large or small, swiftness and sincerity are the key watchwords. Customers must feel an immediate sense that the company truly cares. Beyond that, the following procedures can help to recover customer goodwill:

1. Set up a 7-day, 24-hour toll-free "hotline" (by phone, fax, or e-mail) to receive and act on customer complaints.
2. Contact the complaining customer as quickly as possible. The slower the company is to respond, the more dissatisfaction may grow and lead to negative word of mouth.
3. Accept responsibility for the customer's disappointment; don't blame the customer.
4. Use customer service people who are empathic.
5. Resolve the complaint swiftly and to the customer's satisfaction. Some complaining customers are not looking for compensation so much as a sign that the company cares.

Source: Philip Kotler, *Kotler on Marketing* (New York: The Free Press, 1999), pp. 21–22.

95% if the customer feels that the complaint was resolved quickly. Customers who have complained to an organization and had their complaints satisfactorily resolved tell an average of five people about the good treatment they received.[57]

Dell Computer Corp. quickly yanked its corporate PC tech support out of India and placed it in a domestic call center when its U.S-based customers complained about the quality of help they received: rigid, "by-the-book" technicians who wasted their time wading through fixes they had already tried, problems with poor phone connections, and strongly accented English that was hard to understand.[58]

More companies now recognize the importance of satisfying and retaining customers. Satisfied customers constitute the company's *customer relationship capital.* If the company were to be sold, the acquiring company would have to pay not only for the plant and equipment and the brand name, but also for the delivered *customer base,* the number and value of the customers who would do business with the new firm. Here are some interesting facts that bear on customer retention:[59]

1. Acquiring new customers can cost five times more than the costs involved in satisfying and retaining current customers. It requires a great deal of effort to induce satisfied customers to switch away from their current suppliers.
2. The average company loses 10 percent of its customers each year.
3. A 5 percent reduction in the customer defection rate can increase profits by 25 percent to 85 percent, depending on the industry.
4. The customer profit rate tends to increase over the life of the retained customer.

Figure 5.4 shows the main steps in the process of attracting and keeping customers. The starting point is everyone who might conceivably buy the product or service (*suspects*). From these the company determines the most likely *prospects,* which it hopes to convert into *first-time customers,* and then into *repeat customers,* and then into *clients*—people to whom the company gives very special and knowledgeable treatment. The next challenge is to turn clients into *members* by starting a membership program that offers benefits to customers who join, and then into *advocates,* customers who enthusiastically recommend the company and its products and services to others. The ultimate challenge is to turn advocates into *partners.*

Markets can be characterized by their long-term buying dynamics and how easily and often customers can enter and leave.[60]

1. ***Permanent capture markets.*** Once a customer, always a customer (e.g., nursing homes, trust funds, and medical care).
2. ***Simple retention markets.*** Customers can permanently be lost after each period (e.g., telecom, cable, financial services, other services, subscriptions).
3. ***Customer migration markets.*** Customers can leave and come back (e.g., catalogs, consumer products, retail, and airlines).

Some customers inevitably become inactive or drop out. The challenge is to reactivate dissatisfied customers through win-back strategies. It is often easier to re-attract ex-customers (because the company knows their names and histories) than to find new ones. The key is to analyze the causes of customer defection through exit interviews and lost-customer surveys. The aim is to win back only those customers who have strong profit potential.

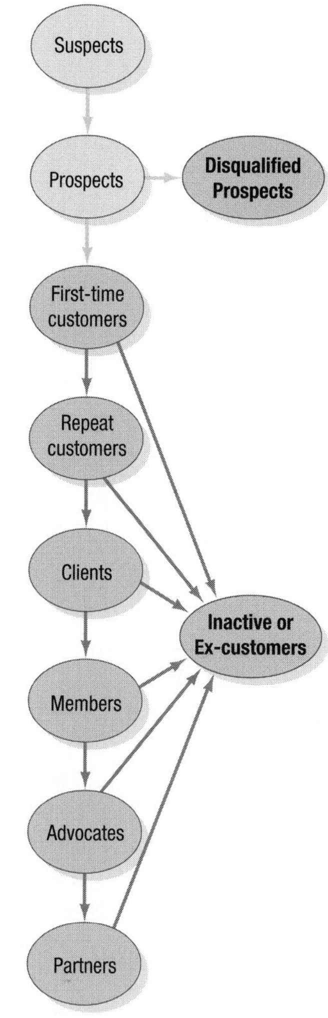

FIG. 5.4

The Customer-Development Process

Source: See Jill Griffin, *Customer Loyalty: How to Earn It, How to Keep It* (New York: Lexington Books, 1995). p. 36. Also see Murray Raphel and Neil Raphel, *Up the Loyalty Ladder Turning Sometime Customers into Full-Time Advocates of Your Business* (New York: HarperBusiness, 1995).

Building Loyalty

How much should a company invest in building loyalty so that the costs do not exceed the gains? We need to distinguish five different levels of investment in customer relationship building:

1. ***Basic marketing.*** The salesperson simply sells the product.
2. ***Reactive marketing.*** The salesperson sells the product and encourages the customer to call if he or she has questions, comments, or complaints.
3. ***Accountable marketing.*** The salesperson phones the customer to check whether the product is meeting expectations. The salesperson also asks the customer for any product or service improvement suggestions and any specific disappointments.
4. ***Proactive marketing.*** The salesperson contacts the customer from time to time with suggestions about improved product uses or new products.
5. ***Partnership marketing.*** The company works continuously with its large customers to help improve their performance. (General Electric, for example, has stationed engineers at large utilities to help them produce more power.)

Most companies practice only basic marketing when their markets contain many customers and their unit profit margins are small. Whirlpool is not going to phone each washing machine buyer to express appreciation. It may set up a customer hot line. In markets with few customers and high profit margins, most sellers will move toward partnership marketing. Boeing, for example, works closely with American Airlines to design airplanes that fully satisfy American's requirements. As Figure 5.5 shows, the likely level of relationship marketing depends on the number of customers and the profit margin level.

An increasingly essential ingredient for the best relationship marketing today is the right technology. Table 5.2 highlights five imperatives of CRM and where technology fits in. GE Plastics could not target its e-mail effectively to different customers if it were not for advances in database software. Dell Computer could not customize computer ordering for its global corporate customers without advances in Web technology. Companies are using e-mail, Web sites, call centers, databases, and database software to foster continuous contact between company and customer. Here is how one company used technology to build customer value:

AMERITRADE

The discount brokerage service Ameritrade provides detailed information to its customers, which helps to create strong bonds. It provides customized alerts to the device of the customer's choice, detailing stock movements and analysts' recommendations. The company's Web site permits online trading and provides access to a variety of research tools. Ameritrade developed an investing tutorial called Darwin, which it offered free on CD-ROM to its customers. Customers responded to this new focus on their needs: Ameritrade grew from fewer than 100,000 accounts in 1997 to 2.9 million in 2003.[61]

	High Margin	Medium Margin	Low Margin
Many customers/ distributors	Accountable	Reactive	Basic or reactive
Medium number of customers/ distributors	Proactive	Accountable	Reactive
Few customers/ distributors	Partnership	Proactive	Accountable

FIG. 5.5

Levels of Relationship Marketing

TABLE 5.2 Breaking Down Customer Relationship Management: What Customer Relationship Management Really Comprises

CRM Imperative				
Acquiring the right customer	Crafting the right value proposition	Instituting the best processes	Motivating employees	Learning to retain customers
You Get It When . . .				
■ You've identified your most valuable customers. ■ You've calculated your share of their wallet for your goods and services.	■ You've studied what products or services your customers need today and will need tomorrow. ■ You've surveyed what products or services your competitors offer today and will offer tomorrow. ■ You've spotted what products or services you should be offering.	■ You've researched the best way to deliver your products or services to customers, including the alliances you need to strike, the technologies you need to invest in, and the service capabilities you need to develop or acquire.	■ You know what tools your employees need to foster customer relationships. ■ You've identified the HR systems you need to institute in order to boost employee loyalty.	■ You've learned why customers defect and how to win them back. ■ You've analyzed what your competitors are doing to win your high-value customers. ■ Your senior management monitors customer defection metrics.
CRM Technology Can Help . . .				
■ Analyze customer revenue and cost data to identify current and future high-value customers. ■ Target your direct-marketing efforts better.	■ Capture relevant product and service behavior data. ■ Create new distribution channels. ■ Develop new pricing models. ■ Build communities.	■ Process transactions faster. ■ Provide better information to the front line. ■ Manage logistics and the supply chain more efficiently. ■ Catalyze collaborative commerce.	■ Align incentives and metrics. ■ Deploy knowledge management systems.	■ Track customer defection and retention levels. ■ Track customer service satisfaction levels.

Source: Darrel K. Rigby, Frederick F. Reichheld, and Phil Schefter, "Avoid the Four Perils of CRM," *Harvard Business Review* (February 2002): 106.

At the same time, online companies need to make sure their attempts to create relationships with customers don't backfire, as when customers are bombarded by computer-generated recommendations that consistently miss the mark. Buy a lot of baby gifts on Amazon, and your personalized recommendations suddenly don't look so personal. E-tailers need to recognize the limitations of online personalization at the same time that they try harder to find technology and processes that really work.[62]

Companies are also recognizing the importance of the personal component to CRM and what happens once customers make actual contact. As Stanford's business guru Jeffrey Pfeffer puts it, "the best companies build cultures in which front-line people are empowered to do what's needed to take care of the customer." He cites examples of firms like SAS, the Scandinavian airline, which engineered a turnaround in part based on the insight that a customer's impressions of a company are formed through a myriad of small interactions—checking in, boarding the plane, eating a meal, and so on.[63]

Reducing Customer Defection

There are five main steps a company can take to reduce the defection rate.

First, the company must define and measure its retention rate. For a magazine, the renewal rate is a good measure of retention. For a college, it could be the first- to second-year retention rate, or the class graduation rate.

Second, the company must distinguish the causes of customer attrition and identify those that can be managed better. (See "Marketing Memo: Asking Questions When Customers Leave.") The Forum Corporation analyzed the customers lost by 14 major companies for reasons other than leaving the region or going out of business: 15 percent switched because they found a better product; another 15 percent found a cheaper product; and 70 percent left because of poor or little attention from the supplier. Not much can be done about customers who leave the region or go out of business, but much can be done about those who leave because of poor service, shoddy products, or high prices.[64]

Third, the company needs to estimate how much profit it loses when it loses customers. In the case of an individual customer, the lost profit is equal to the customer's lifetime value—that is, the present value of the profit stream that the company would have realized if the customer had not defected prematurely—through some of the calculations outlined above.

Fourth, the company needs to figure out how much it would cost to reduce the defection rate. As long as the cost is less than the lost profit, the company should spend the money.

And finally, nothing beats listening to customers. Some companies have created an ongoing mechanism that keeps senior managers permanently plugged in to front-line customer feedback. MBNA, the credit card giant, asks every executive to listen in on telephone conversations in the customer service area or customer recovery units. Deere & Company, which makes John Deere tractors and has a superb record of customer loyalty—nearly 98 percent annual retention in some product areas—uses retired employees to interview defectors and customers.[65]

Forming Strong Customer Bonds

"Marketing Memo: Forming Strong Customer Bonds" offers some tips on connecting with customers. Berry and Parasuraman have identified three retention-building approaches:[66] adding financial benefits, adding social benefits, and adding structural ties.

ADDING FINANCIAL BENEFITS Two financial benefits that companies can offer are frequency programs and club marketing programs. **Frequency programs (FPs)** are designed to provide rewards to customers who buy frequently and in substantial amounts.[67] Frequency marketing is an acknowledgment of the fact that 20 percent of a company's customers might account for 80 percent of its business. Frequency programs are seen as a way to build long-term loyalty with these customers, potentially creating cross-selling opportunities in the process.

American Airlines was one of the first companies to pioneer a frequency program in the early 1980s, when it decided to offer free mileage credit to its customers. Hotels next adopted FPs, with Marriott taking the lead with its Honored Guest Program, followed by car rental firms. Then credit card companies began to offer points based on card usage level. Sears offers rebates to its Discover cardholders; and today most supermarket chains offer price club cards, which provide member customers with discounts on particular items.[68]

Typically, the first company to introduce an FP gains the most benefit, especially if competitors are slow to respond. After competitors respond, FPs can become a financial burden to all the offering companies, but some companies are more efficient and creative in

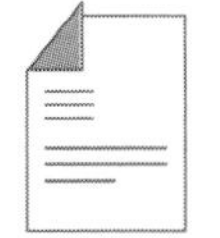

MARKETING MEMO | ASKING QUESTIONS WHEN CUSTOMERS LEAVE

To create effective retention programs, marketing managers need to identify customer defection patterns. This analysis should start with internal records, such as sales logs, pricing records, and customer survey results. The next step is to extend defection research to outside sources, such as benchmarking studies and statistics from trade associations. Some key questions to ask:

1. Do customers defect at different rates during the year?
2. Does retention vary by office, region, sales representative, or distributor?
3. What is the relationship between retention rates and changes in prices?
4. What happens to lost customers, and where do they usually go?
5. What are the retention norms for your industry?
6. Which company in your industry retains customers the longest?

Source: Reprinted from William A. Sherden, "When Customers Leave," *Small Business Reports* (November 1994): 45.

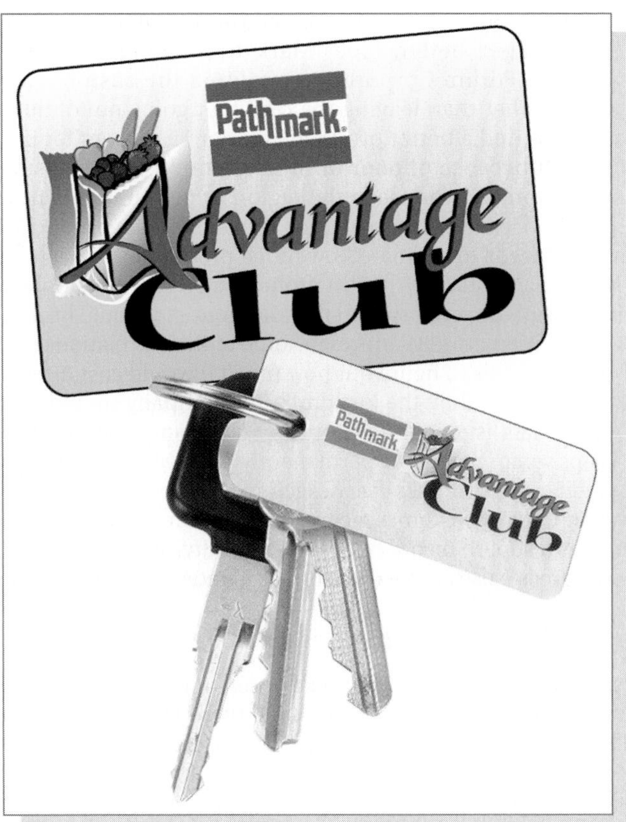

Pathmark Advantage Club cards: one for the wallet, one for the keyring.

managing FPs. For example, airlines run tiered loyalty programs in which they offer different levels of rewards to different travelers. They may offer one frequent-flier mile for every mile flown to occasional travelers and two frequent-flier miles for every mile flown to top customers.

Many companies have created club membership programs. Club membership can be open to everyone who purchases a product or service, or it can be limited to an affinity group or to those willing to pay a small fee. Although open clubs are good for building a database or snagging customers from competitors, limited membership clubs are more powerful long-term loyalty builders. Fees and membership conditions prevent those with only a fleeting interest in a company's products from joining. These clubs attract and keep

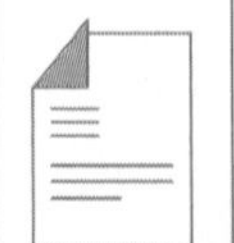

MARKETING MEMO — FORMING STRONG CUSTOMER BONDS

Companies that want to form strong customer bonds need to attend to the following basics:

- Get cross-departmental participation in planning and managing the customer satisfaction and retention process.
- Integrate the "Voice of the Customer" to capture their stated and unstated needs or requirements in all business decisions.
- Create superior products, services, and experiences for the target market.
- Organize and make accessible a database of information on individual customer needs, preferences, contacts, purchase frequency, and satisfaction.
- Make it easy for customers to reach appropriate company personnel and express their needs, perceptions, and complaints.
- Run award programs recognizing outstanding employees.

those customers who are responsible for the largest portion of business. Some highly successful clubs include the following:

APPLE

Apple encourages owners of its computers to form local Apple-user groups. By 2001, there were over 600 groups ranging in size from fewer than 25 members to over 1,000 members. The user groups provide Apple owners with opportunities to learn more about their computers, share ideas, and get product discounts. They sponsor special activities and events and perform community service. A visit to Apple's Web site will help a customer find a nearby user group.[69]

HARLEY-DAVIDSON

The world-famous motorcycle company sponsors the Harley Owners Group (H.O.G.), which now numbers 650,000 members in over 1,200 chapters. The first-time buyer of a Harley-Davidson motorcycle gets a free one-year membership. H.O.G. benefits include a magazine called *Hog Tales,* a touring handbook, emergency road service, a specially designed insurance program, theft reward service, discount hotel rates, and a Fly & Ride program enabling members to rent Harleys while on vacation. The company also maintains an extensive Web site devoted to H.O.G., which includes information on club chapters, events, and a special members-only section.[70]

ADDING SOCIAL BENEFITS Company personnel work on cementing social bonds with customers by individualizing and personalizing customer relationships. In essence, thoughtful companies turn their customers into clients. Donnelly, Berry, and Thompson draw this distinction:

> Customers may be nameless to the institution; clients cannot be nameless. Customers are served as part of the mass or as part of larger segments; clients are served on an individual basis. Customers are served by anyone who happens to be available; clients are served by the professional assigned to them.[71]

E-commerce companies looking to attract and retain customers are discovering that personalization goes beyond creating customized information.[72] For example, the Lands' End Live Web site offers visitors the opportunity to talk with a customer service representative. Nordstrom takes a similar approach with its Web site to ensure that online buyers are as satisfied with the company's customer service as the in-store visitors; and, with the click of a button, Eddie Bauer's e-commerce site connects shoppers to customer service representatives (CSRs) with a text-based chat feature.

A 2001 survey of 3,500 Web shoppers found that 77 percent of online shoppers have at least once selected an item for purchase but failed to complete the transaction.[73] Jupiter Media Metrix has reported that two-thirds of Web shoppers abandon shopping carts.[74] Worse, only 1.8 percent of visits to online retailers lead to sales, compared with 5 percent of visits to department stores. Analysts attribute this behavior partly to a general absence of interactive customer service in e-commerce. Customers looking for help are often sent to a text help file rather than a live sales representative. This can be frustrating and may prompt a customer to exit the site without buying. Another benefit of providing

Member of the Westsachsen, Germany, chapter of an H.O.G. club at a gathering in Hamburg to celebrate Harley-Davidson's 100th anniversary. Harley-Davidson uses its Web site to run one of the most successful club membership programs.

live sales assistance is the ability to sell additional items. When a representative is involved in the sale, the average amount per order is typically higher.

THE CONTAINER STORE

Dallas-based specialty chain The Container Store reaps the benefit of using live customer service personnel to augment its online orders. A Container Store representative speaks on the phone with each customer who submits an online request for custom closet planning. More importantly, phone calls don't end at the order initiation stage. An individual carefully reviews every Internet order before it is fulfilled. If it seems that certain parts of an order don't fit together, the customer representative calls to make sure that what is ordered is what the customer wants. In this way, The Container Store catches many mistakes that customers have made unknowingly long before orders are shipped. This both saves on returns and gives customers a more positive overall experience.[75]

Not all customer service features involve live personnel. Both Macys.com and gap.com offer prerecorded customer service information. Gap's Web site includes a "zoom" feature, which shoppers can use to get a close look at every detail of a garment, from elastic waistbands to fabric prints. Lands' End Live allows customers to "try on" clothes online using virtual models based on measurements supplied by customers.

ADDING STRUCTURAL TIES The company may supply customers with special equipment or computer links that help customers manage orders, payroll, and inventory. A good example is McKesson Corporation, a leading pharmaceutical wholesaler, which invested millions of dollars in EDI capabilities to help independent pharmacies manage inventory, order-entry processes, and shelf space. Another example is Milliken & Company, which provides proprietary software programs, marketing research, sales training, and sales leads to loyal customers.

Lester Wunderman, an astute observer of contemporary marketing, thinks talk about "loyalizing" customers misses the point.[76] People can be loyal to country, family, and beliefs, but less so to their toothpaste, soap, or even beer. The marketer's aim should be to increase the consumer's *proclivity to repurchase* the company's brand.

Here are his suggestions for creating structural ties with the customer:

1. ***Create long-term contracts.*** A newspaper subscription replaces the need to buy a newspaper each day. A 20-year mortgage replaces the need to re-borrow the money each year. A home heating oil agreement assures continuous delivery without renewing the order.
2. ***Charge a lower price to consumers who buy larger supplies.*** Offer lower prices to people who agree to be supplied regularly with a certain brand of toothpaste, detergent, or beer.
3. ***Turn the product into a long-term service.*** DaimlerChrysler could sell "miles of reliable transportation" instead of cars, with the consumer able to lease different cars at different times or for different occasions such as a station wagon for shopping and a convertible for the weekend. Gaines, the dog food company, could offer a Pet Care service that includes kennels, insurance, and veterinary care along with food.

::: Customer Databases and Database Marketing

Marketers must know their customers. And in order to know the customer, the company must collect information and store it in a database and do database marketing: A **customer database** is an organized collection of comprehensive information about individual customers or prospects that is current, accessible, and actionable for such marketing purposes as lead generation, lead qualification, sale of a product or service, or maintenance of customer relationships. **Database marketing** is the process of building, maintaining, and using customer databases and other databases (products, suppliers, resellers) for the purpose of contacting, transacting, and building customer relationships.

Customer Databases

As the former chief marketing officer of Amazon liked to point out, when you walk through the door at Macy's, the retailer has no idea who you are. When you log on to Amazon, however, you are greeted by name, presented a customized set of product purchase suggestions based on your past purchase choices, and offered an accompanying series of frank customer reviews. As you log off the site, you are also asked permission to be e-mailed special offers.[77]

Many companies confuse a customer mailing list with a customer database. A **customer mailing list** is simply a set of names, addresses, and telephone numbers. A customer database contains much more information, accumulated through customer transactions, registration information, telephone queries, cookies, and every customer contact.

Ideally, a customer database contains the consumer's past purchases, demographics (age, income, family members, birthdays), psychographics (activities, interests, and opinions), mediagraphics (preferred media), and other useful information. The catalog company Fingerhut possesses some 1,400 pieces of information about each of the 30 million households in its massive customer database.

Ideally, a **business database** would contain business customers' past purchases; past volumes, prices, and profits; buyer team member names (and ages, birthdays, hobbies, and favorite foods); status of current contracts; an estimate of the supplier's share of the customer's business; competitive suppliers; assessment of competitive strengths and weaknesses in selling and servicing the account; and relevant buying practices, patterns, and policies. For example, a Latin American unit of the Swiss pharmaceutical firm Novartis keeps data on 100,000 of Argentina's farmers, knows their crop protection chemical purchases, groups them by value, and treats each group differently.

Figure 5.6 displays a method for selectively gaining greater share of a customer's business, based on the presumption that the firm has gained a deep understanding of the customer.

Data Warehouses and Datamining

Savvy companies are capturing information every time a customer comes into contact with any of its departments. Touch points include a customer purchase, a customer-requested service call, an online query, or a mail-in rebate card. Banks and credit card companies, telephone companies, catalog marketers, and many other companies have a great deal of information about their customers, including not only addresses and phone numbers, but also their transactions and enhanced data on age, family size, income, and other demographic information.

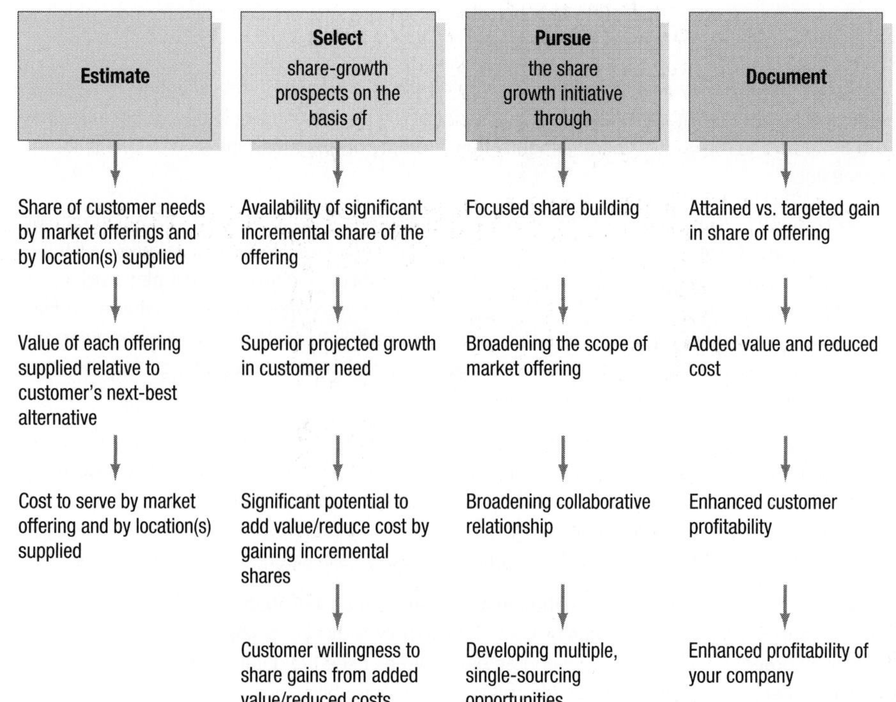

FIG. 5.6

Increasing Customer Share of Requirements

Source: James C. Anderson and James A. Narus, *MIT Sloan Management Review* (Spring 2003): 45.

These data are collected by the company's contact center and organized into a **data warehouse**. Company personnel can capture, query, and analyze the data. Inferences can be drawn about an individual customer's needs and responses. Telemarketers can respond to customer inquiries based on a total picture of the customer relationship.

Through **datamining**,[78] marketing statisticians can extract useful information about individuals, trends, and segments from the mass of data. Datamining involves the use of sophisticated statistical and mathematical techniques such as cluster analysis, automatic interaction detection, predictive modeling, and neural networking.[79]

Some observers believe that a proprietary database can provide a company with a significant competitive advantage. MCI Communications Corporation, the long-distance carrier, sifts through 1 trillion bytes of customer phoning data to craft new discount calling plans for different types of customers. Lands' End can tell which of its 2 million customers should receive special mailings of specific clothing items that would fit their wardrobe needs. (See Figure 5.7 for additional examples.)

USING THE DATABASE In general, companies can use their databases in five ways:

1. ***To identify prospects.*** Many companies generate sales leads by advertising their product or service. The ads generally contain a response feature, such as a business reply card or toll-free phone number. The database is built from these responses. The company sorts through the database to identify the best prospects, then contacts them by mail, phone, or personal call in an attempt to convert them into customers.
2. ***To decide which customers should receive a particular offer.*** Companies are interested in selling, up-selling, and cross-selling their products and services. Companies set up criteria describing the ideal target customer for a particular offer. Then they search their customer databases for those who most closely resemble the ideal type. By noting

| FIG. 5.7 |

Examples of Database Marketing

Qwest Twice a year Qwest sifts through its customer list looking for customers that have the potential to be more profitable. The company's database contains as many as 200 observations about each customer's calling patterns. By looking at demographic profiles, plus the mix of local versus long-distance calls or whether a consumer has voice mail, Qwest can estimate potential spending. Next, the company determines how much of the customer's likely telecom budget is already coming its way. Armed with that knowledge, Qwest sets a cutoff point for how much to spend on marketing to this customer.

Royal Caribbean Royal Caribbean uses its database to offer spur-of-the-moment cruise packages to fill all the berths on its ships. It focuses on retired people and single people because they are more able to make quick commitments. Fewer empty berths mean maximized profits for the cruise line.

Fingerhut The skillful use of database marketing and relationship building has made catalog house Fingerhut one of the nation's largest direct-mail marketers. Not only is its database full of demographic details such as age, marital status, and number of children, but it also tracks customers' hobbies, interests, and birthdays. Fingerhut tailors mail offers based on what each customer is likely to buy. Fingerhut stays in continuous touch with customers through regular and special promotions, such as annual sweepstakes, free gifts, and deferred billing. Now the company has applied its database marketing to its Web sites.

Mars Mars is a market leader not only in candy, but also in pet food. In Germany, Mars has compiled the names of virtually every cat-owning family by contacting veterinarians and by advertising a free booklet titled "How to Take Care of Your Cat." Those who request the booklet fill out a questionnaire, so Mars knows the cat's name, age, and birthday. Mars now sends a birthday card to each cat each year, along with a new-cat-food sample or money-saving coupons for Mars brands.

American Express It is no wonder that, at its secret location in Phoenix, security guards watch over American Express's 500 billion bytes of data on how its customers have used the company's 35 million green, gold, and platinum charge cards. Amex uses the database to include precisely targeted offers in its monthly mailing of millions of customer bills.

response rates, a company can improve its targeting precision over time. Following a sale, it can set up an automatic sequence of activities: One week later, send a thank-you note; five weeks later, send a new offer; ten weeks later (if customer has not responded), phone the customer and offer a special discount.

3. ***To deepen customer loyalty.*** Companies can build interest and enthusiasm by remembering customer preferences; by sending appropriate gifts, discount coupons, and interesting reading material.
4. ***To reactivate customer purchases.*** Companies can install automatic mailing programs (automatic marketing) that send out birthday or anniversary cards, Christmas shopping reminders, or off-season promotions. The database can help the company make attractive or timely offers.
5. ***To avoid serious customer mistakes.*** A major bank confessed to a number of mistakes that it had made by not using its customer database well. In one case, the bank charged a customer a penalty for late payment on his mortgage, failing to note that he headed a company that was a major depositor in this bank. He quit the bank. In a second case, two different staff members of the bank phoned the same mortgage customer offering a home equity loan at different prices. Neither knew that the other had made the call. In a third case, a bank gave a premium customer only standard service in another country.

The Downside of Database Marketing and CRM

Having covered the good news about database marketing, we also have to cover the bad news. Four problems can deter a firm from effectively using CRM. The first is that building and maintaining a customer database requires a large investment in computer hardware, database software, analytical programs, communication links, and skilled personnel. It is difficult to collect the right data, especially to capture all the occasions of company interaction with individual customers. Building a customer database would not be worthwhile in the following cases: (1) where the product is a once-in-a-lifetime purchase (e.g., a grand piano); (2) where customers show little loyalty to a brand (i.e., there is lots of customer churn); (3) where the unit sale is very small (e.g., a candy bar); and (4) where the cost of gathering information is too high.

The second problem is the difficulty of getting everyone in the company to be customer-oriented and to use the available information. Employees find it far easier to carry on traditional transaction marketing than to practice customer relationship marketing. Effective database marketing requires managing and training employees as well as dealers and suppliers.

The third problem is that not all customers want a relationship with the company, and they may resent knowing that the company has collected that much personal information about them. Marketers must be concerned about customer attitudes toward privacy and security. American Express, long regarded as a leader on privacy issues, does not sell information on specific customer transactions. However, American Express found itself the target of consumer outrage when it announced a partnership with KnowledgeBase Marketing, Inc., that would have made data on 175 million Americans available to any merchant who accepts American Express cards. American Express killed the partnership. AOL, also targeted by privacy advocates, junked a plan to sell subscribers' telephone numbers. Online companies would be smart to explain their privacy policies, and give consumers the right not to have their information stored in a database. European countries do not look favorably upon database marketing. The European Union passed a law handicapping the growth of database marketing in its 15 member countries. Europeans are more protective of their private information than are U.S. citizens.

A fourth problem is that the assumptions behind CRM may not always hold true.[80] For example, it may not be the case that it costs less to serve more loyal customers. High-volume customers often know their value to a company and can leverage it to extract premium service and/or price discounts. Loyal customers may expect and demand more from the firm and resent any attempt by the firm to receive full or higher prices. They may also be jealous of attention lavished on other customers. When eBay began to chase big corporate customers such as IBM, Disney, and Sears, some small mom-and-pop businesses who helped to build the brand felt abandoned.[81] Loyal customers may not necessarily be the best ambassadors for the brand. One study found that customers who scored high on behavioral loyalty and bought a lot of a company' products were less active word-of-mouth

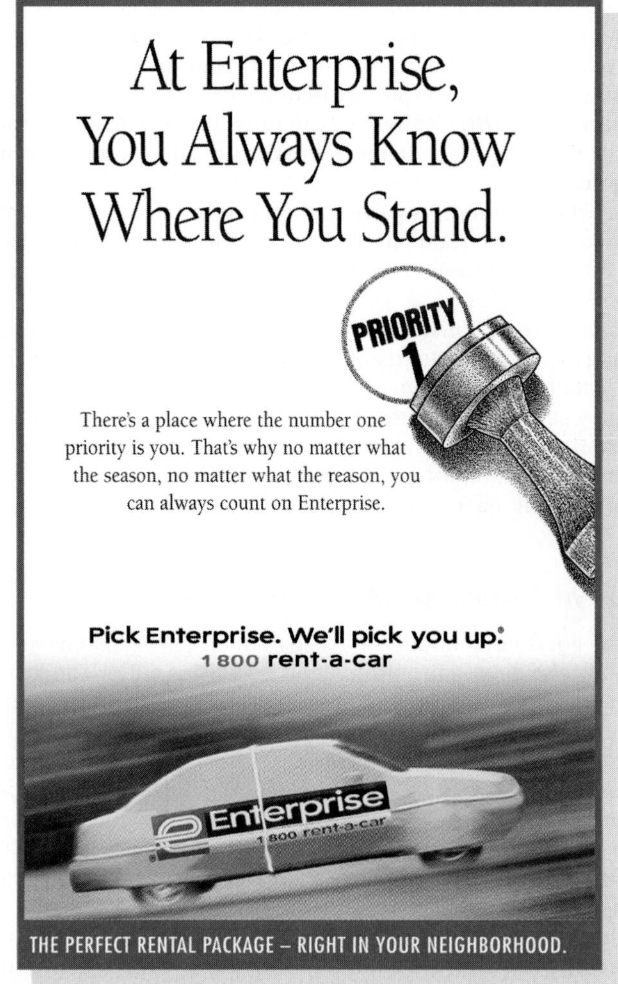

This Enterprise Rent-A-Car ad focuses on CRM: "There's a place where the number one priority is you."

marketers to others than customers who scored high on attitudinal loyalty and expressed greater commitment to the firm.

Thus, the benefits of database marketing do not come without heavy costs, not only in collecting the original customer data, but also in maintaining them and mining them. Yet, when it works, a data warehouse yields more than it costs. A 1996 study by DWI estimated that the average return on investment for a data warehouse over the course of three years is more than 400 percent, but the data have to be in good condition, and the discovered relationships must be valid. Consider the following cases were database marketing went awry:

CNA INSURANCE

At CNA Insurance, five programmers worked for nine months loading five years of claims data into a computer, only to discover that the data had been miscoded. Even if coded correctly, the data must be updated continuously because people move, drop out, or change their interests.

BRITISH COLUMBIA TELECOM

This company decided to invite 100 of its best customers to a Vancouver Grizzlies basketball game and selected customers who were heavy 900-number users. The invitations were already at the printer when the marketing staff discovered that heavy 900-number users included sex-line enthusiasts. They quickly added other criteria to search for a revised list of guests.

Database marketing is most frequently used by business marketers and service providers (hotels, banks, airlines; and insurance, credit card, and telephone companies) that normally and easily collect a lot of customer data. Other types of companies that are in the best position to invest in CRM are companies that do a lot of cross-selling and up-selling (e.g., GE and Amazon) or companies whose customers have highly differentiated needs and are of highly differentiated value to the company. It is used less often by packaged-goods retailers and consumer packaged-goods companies, though some companies (Kraft, Quaker Oats, Ralston Purina, and Nabisco) have built databases for certain brands. Businesses where the CLV is low, those who have high churn, and where there is no direct contact between the seller and ultimate buyer may not benefit as much from CRM. Some businesses cited as CRM successes include Enterprise Rent-A-Car, Pioneer Hi-bred Seeds, Fidelity Investments, Lexus, Intuit, and Capital One.[82]

Deloitte Consulting reported in 1999 that 70 percent of firms found little or no improvement through CRM implementation. The reasons are many: The system was poorly designed, it became too expensive, users didn't make much use of it or report much benefit, and collaborators ignored the system. One set of business commentators suggested the following as the four main perils of CRM:[83]

1. Implementing CRM before creating a customer strategy.
2. Rolling out CRM before changing organization to match.
3. Assuming more CRM technology is better.
4. Stalking, not wooing customers.

All this points to the need for each company to determine how much to invest in building and using database marketing to conduct its customer relationships. "Marketing Insight: Succeeding at CRM" provides some best-practice guidelines.

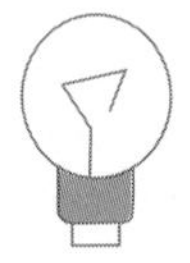

MARKETING **INSIGHT** | SUCCEEDING AT CRM

Based on a comprehensive survey of leading companies, Wharton's George Day concludes that superior CRM performance comes from integrating three components of the customer-relating capability: an organizational orientation that makes customer retention a priority and gives employees wide latitude to satisfy customers; information about relationships, including the quality of relevant customer data and the systems for sharing this information across the firm; and configuration, the alignment of the organization toward building customer relationships, achieved through incentives, metrics, organization structure, and accountabilities.

Configuration was the factor that most separated good firms from bad firms. Day observed that relatively few businesses in the survey emphasized customer satisfaction and retention in their incentives. An exception was Siebel Systems which tied 50 percent of management's incentive compensation and 25 percent of salespeople's compensation to measures of customer satisfaction. The real payoff, he notes, is when all the elements of a configuration—metrics, incentives, and structures—are properly aligned, citing General Electric Aircraft Engine Business Group's attempts to improve service for its jet engine customers. A study of customer needs led GE to assign a corporate vice president to each of the top 50 customers, putting leaders of its quality program on-site with customers, using the Internet to personalize delivery of parts, and incorporating customer service metrics into employee evaluation criteria.

Day also found that information was less important than orientation and configuration in distinguishing leaders from followers. He concluded that big investments in CRM technology were yielding negligible competitive advantages. He also concluded that one of the reasons many CRM failures occur is because companies concentrate on customer contact processes without making corresponding changes in internal structures and systems. His recommendation? Change the configuration before installing CRM: "Our survey results confirm that a superior customer relating capability has everything to do with how a business builds and manages its organization and not much to do with the CRM tools and technologies it employs."

Sources: George S. Day, "Creating a Superior Customer-Relating Capability," *Sloan Management Review* 44, no. 3 (2003): 77–82; George S. Day, "Creating a Superior Customer-Relating Capability," *MSI Report No. 03–101,* Marketing Science Institute, Cambridge, MA; "Why Some Companies Succeed at CRM (and Many Fail)," *Knowledge at Wharton,* http://knowledge.wharton.upenn.edu, January 15, 2003.

SUMMARY :::

1. Customers are value-maximizers. They form an expectation of value and act on it. Buyers will buy from the firm that they perceive to offer the highest customer-delivered value, defined as the difference between total customer value and total customer cost.

2. A buyer's satisfaction is a function of the product's perceived performance and the buyer's expectations. Recognizing that high satisfaction leads to high customer loyalty, many companies today are aiming for TCS—total customer satisfaction. For such companies,

customer satisfaction is both a goal and a marketing tool.

3. Losing profitable customers can dramatically affect a firm's profits. The cost of attracting a new customer is estimated to be five times the cost of keeping a current customer happy. The key to retaining customers is relationship marketing.
4. Quality is the totality of features and characteristics of a product or service that bear on its ability to satisfy stated or implied needs. Today's companies have no choice but to implement total quality management programs if they are to remain solvent and profitable.
5. Marketing managers have two responsibilities in a quality-centered company. First, they must participate in formulating strategies and policies designed to help the company win through total quality excellence. Second, they must deliver marketing quality alongside production quality.
6. Companies are also becoming skilled in Customer Relationship Management (CRM), which focuses on meeting the individual needs of valued customers. The skill requires building a customer database and doing datamining to detect trends, segments, and individual needs.

APPLICATIONS :::

Marketing Debate Online Versus Offline Privacy?

As more and more firms practice relationship marketing and develop customer databases, privacy issues are emerging as an important topic. Consumers and public interest groups are scrutinizing—and sometimes criticizing—the privacy policies of firms. Concerns are also being raised about potential theft of online credit card information or other potentially sensitive or confidential financial information. Others maintain that the online privacy fears are unfounded and that security issues are every bit as much a concern in the offline world. They argue that the opportunity to steal information exists virtually everywhere and that it is up to the consumer to protect his or her interests.

Take a position: (1) Privacy is a bigger issue in the online world than the offline world versus Privacy is no different online than offline. (2) Consumers on the whole receive more benefit than risk from marketers knowing their personal information.

Marketing Discussion

Consider the lifetime value of customers (CLV). Choose a business and show how you would go about developing a quantitative formulation that captures the concept. How would organizations change if they totally embraced the customer equity concept and maximized CLV?

IN THIS CHAPTER, WE WILL ADDRESS THE FOLLOWING QUESTIONS:

1. How do consumer characteristics influence buying behavior?
2. What major psychological processes influence consumer responses to the marketing program?
3. How do consumers make purchasing decisions?
4. How do marketers analyze consumer decision making?

CHAPTER 6 ::: ANALYZING CONSUMER MARKETS

six

The aim of marketing is to meet and satisfy target customers' needs and wants better than competitors. **Consumer behavior** is the study of how individuals, groups, and organizations select, buy, use, and dispose of goods, services, ideas, or experiences to satisfy their needs and wants. Studying consumers provides clues for improving or introducing products or services, setting prices, devising channels, crafting messages, and developing other marketing activities. Marketers are always looking for emerging trends that suggest new marketing opportunities. The metrosexual is one:

In the summer of 2003, some marketing pundits proclaimed the existence of a new male market—the "metrosexual"—which was defined as straight urban men who enjoy such things as shopping and using grooming products and services. English soccer star David Beckham, with his carefully crafted fashion look, has been touted as the quintessential metrosexual icon. He's not afraid to wear either nail polish or sarongs (off the field, that is). One researcher estimated that 30 to 35 percent of young American men exhibited metrosexual tendencies, as evidenced in part by their purchase of products such as skin care cream and fragrances. Another study found "an emerging wave of men who chafe against the restrictions of traditional male roles and do what they want, buy what they want, enjoy what they want—regardless of whether some people might consider them unmanly." The emergence of this market has been a boon for >>>

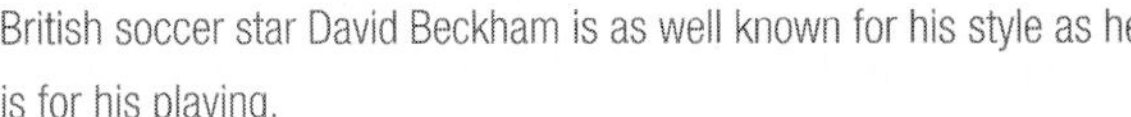
British soccer star David Beckham is as well known for his style as he is for his playing.

men's grooming products, fueling the success of brands such as Unilever's Axe, a fragrant all-over body spray, The Body Shop's "For Men" line, and U.K. drugstore chain Boots' newly opened Men's Zones.[1]

Successful marketing requires that companies fully connect with their customers. Adopting a holistic marketing orientation means understanding consumers—gaining a 360-degree view of both their daily lives and the changes that occur during their lifetimes. Gaining a thorough, in-depth consumer understanding helps to ensure that the right products are marketed to the right consumers in the right way. This chapter explores individual consumer buying dynamics; the next chapter explores the buying dynamics of business buyers.

::: What Influences Consumer Behavior?

Marketers must fully understand both the theory and reality of consumer behavior. Table 6.1 includes some interesting facts about the American consumer in 2001, and "Marketing Insight: Consumer Trends for the Future" gives an idea of what marketers can expect to encounter in the year 2025.

A consumer's buying behavior is influenced by cultural, social, and personal factors. Cultural factors exert the broadest and deepest influence.

Cultural Factors

Culture, subculture, and social class are particularly important influences on consumer buying behavior. **Culture** is the fundamental determinant of a person's wants and behavior. The growing child acquires a set of values, perceptions, preferences, and behaviors through his or her family and other key institutions. A child growing up in the United States is exposed to the following values: achievement and success, activity, efficiency and practicality, progress, material comfort, individualism, freedom, external comfort, humanitarianism, and youthfulness.[2]

Each culture consists of smaller **subcultures** that provide more specific identification and socialization for their members. Subcultures include nationalities, religions, racial groups, and geographic regions. When subcultures grow large and affluent enough, companies often design specialized marketing programs to serve them. *Multicultural marketing* grew out of careful marketing research, which revealed that different ethnic and demographic niches did not always respond favorably to mass-market advertising.

Companies have capitalized on well-thought-out multicultural marketing strategies in recent years (see "Marketing Insight: Marketing to Cultural Market Segments"). For instance, many banks and life insurance companies are focusing on Hispanic Americans because although their income level is rising, the 40 million Hispanic Americans living in the United States have not yet become big consumers of financial services:

GE FINANCIAL

GE Financial has taken slow and careful steps to woo the Hispanic market. It spent more than two years researching and planning its Hispanic initiative, working closely with key people in the Hispanic community. It set up a Spanish-language call center, launched a Web site and tapped bilingual agents in key cities to sell GE products. It drafted financial commentator Julie Stav, a Latino personal finance guru, to make a series of information spots that run in English on GE's NBC station in Miami and in Spanish on Telemundo.[3]

TABLE 6.1

American Consumer Almanac

Personal Care

Amount spent per consumer unit on personal care products and services in 1999: **$408**

Food

Average annual expenditure on all food per household in 1999: **$5,031**

Number of eggs consumed per capita in 2000: **258**

Pounds of coffee (bean equivalent) consumed per capital 1999: **10**

Eating Out

Percentage of adults who eat out on a typical day: **44%**

Most popular month and day of the week to eat out: **August; Saturday**

Gum, Chocolate, and Candy

The average American chews **300** sticks of gum a year.

Wine (gallons per capita wine consumption)

France: **16.1** United States: **2.1**

Cars and Light Trucks

Median age of vehicles in operation in the U.S. in 2000: **Cars 8.3 years; Trucks 6.9 years**

Estimated percentage of U.S. households with three or more vehicles in 2000: **21%**

With 2 vehicles: **42%** With 1 vehicle: **31%** With no vehicles: **6%**

Travel and Lodging

Average annual number of trips per person of more than 100 miles: **3.9**

The number of nights the average traveler spends in a hotel, motel, or bed and breakfast annually: **3.3**

Leisure Time

Average number of times a U.S. adult goes out to a movie annually: **9**

Average number of times a U.S. adult attends a sporting event annually: **7**

Percentage of U.S. adults who visit an art museum, historical park, or monument or arts/crafts fair annually: **66%**

Consumer Electronics (percentage of household penetration)

VCR: **93%** Personal computer: **61%**

Wireless Phones

Percentage of U.S. drivers who usually have some type of wireless phone in their vehicle: **54%**

Percentage of U.S. households with cellular phones: **59%**

Of *those*, the percentage who report using their wireless phone while driving: **73%**

Virtually all human societies exhibit *social stratification.* Stratification sometimes takes the form of a caste system where the members of different castes are reared for certain roles and cannot change their caste membership. More frequently, it takes the form of **social classes**, relatively homogeneous and enduring divisions in a society, which are hierarchically ordered and whose members share similar values, interests, and behavior. One classic depiction of social classes in the United States defined seven ascending levels, as follows: (1) lower lowers, (2) upper lowers, (3) working class, (4) middle class, (5) upper middles, (6) lower uppers, and (7) upper uppers.[4]

Social classes have several characteristics. First, those within each class tend to behave more alike than persons from two different social classes. Social classes differ in dress, speech patterns, recreational preferences, and many other characteristics. Second, persons are perceived as occupying inferior or superior positions according to social class. Third,

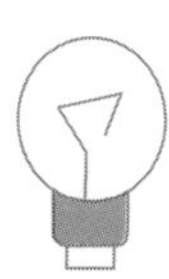

MARKETING INSIGHT | CONSUMER TRENDS FOR THE FUTURE

What fundamental demographic trends will shape the consumer market over the next 25 years? To help answer that question, *American Demographics* teamed up with MapInfo, a Troy, New York–based market research firm, to create population projections to 2025. They found that the trends most likely to influence the business agendas of tomorrow are already gaining momentum today, and the smartest marketers have started developing strategies for the three largest and most likely demographic trends that will shape the marketplace of tomorrow:

America the Crowded

- More opportunity, more niche markets
- Environmental concerns moving front and center

By the year 2025, the U.S. population is expected to exceed 350 million people—an increase of about 70 million and a boost of 25 percent. Expect record-shattering growth to continue, as Americans live longer, birth rates hold steady, and immigration continues apace. However, this massive market does not herald a return to the mass market. As the population increases, niche markets may become unwieldy for businesses to target with a single marketing strategy. As a result, the niche market of today, such as Hispanic Americans, will become a mass market in its own right, segmented not only by nationality (i.e., Mexican, Guatemalan), but also by spending behavior and other psychographic characteristics. Of course, population growth will present some challenges. Natural resources will be stretched, so we can expect to see escalating conflicts at the local level over the use of land, water, and power. Products and services will be scrutinized more closely for their environmental impact.

The Mighty Mature Market

- The senior market gaining new allure
- Creating ageless, multigenerational brands

By 2025, as baby boomers age and life expectancy continues to increase, the number of seniors will double to more than 70 million people. The graying of America means that companies will have to do more than pay lip service to the idea of marketing to older people. Yet, businesses are not going to suddenly lose all interest in the 18 to 34 demographic. Instead, companies will have to learn to establish brands that attract older consumers without alienating younger ones. One example: A recent Pepsi commercial features a teenage boy in the middle of a mosh pit at a rock concert. He turns around to discover his father rocking out nearby. People at 50 aren't considered over the hill anymore. Smart marketers will capitalize on this knowledge and create the image of an ageless society where people define themselves more by the activities they're involved in than by their age. For instance, college students can be 20, 30, or 60 years old.

The Consumer Kaleidoscope

- Devising campaigns that appeal to many demographic segments
- Figuring out how to address the shrinking white majority

By 2025, the term "minority," as it's currently used, will be virtually obsolete. As the share of non-Hispanic whites falls to 60 percent from 70 percent today, the Hispanic population will almost double and the number of Asians in the United States will also double. As one executive at a trends consulting firm said, companies that have not yet developed a multicultural marketing strategy have to "wake up and smell the Thai tacos." Yet it's hard to know whether tomorrow's multicultural marketing strategies will continue to be segmented by race or whether an increasingly multicultural population prefers inclusive "fusion" strategies that attempt to encompass many different nationalities or racial identities in one campaign. Think Benetton and GAP for this latter strategy. To figure this out, companies will have to rely more heavily on ethnographic research. And yet, they can't ignore the dwindling white majority. If the current gap in wealth and income between white and nonwhite consumers holds for the next 25 years, businesses will have ample reason to target the nation's 210 million non-Hispanic white consumers.

Source: Adapted from Alison Stein Wellner, "The Next 25 Years," *American Demographics* (April 2003): 24–27.

social class is indicated by a cluster of variables—for example, occupation, income, wealth, education, and value orientation—rather than by any single variable. Fourth, individuals can move up or down the social-class ladder during their lifetimes. The extent of this mobility varies according to how rigid the social stratification is in a given society.

Social classes show distinct product and brand preferences in many areas, including clothing, home furnishings, leisure activities, and automobiles. Social classes differ in media preferences, with upper-class consumers often preferring magazines and books and lower-class consumers often preferring television. Even within a media category such as TV, upper-class consumers tend to prefer news and drama, and lower-class consumers tend to prefer soap operas and sports programs. There are also language differences among the social classes. Advertising copy and dialogue must ring true to the targeted social class.

Social Factors

In addition to cultural factors, a consumer's behavior is influenced by such social factors as reference groups, family, and social roles and statuses.

REFERENCE GROUPS A person's **reference groups** consist of all the groups that have a direct (face-to-face) or indirect influence on his/her attitudes or behavior. Groups having a direct influence on a person are called **membership groups**. Some membership groups are **primary groups**, such as family, friends, neighbors, and co-workers, those with whom the person interacts fairly continuously and informally. People also belong to **secondary groups**, such as religious, professional, and trade-union groups, which tend to be more formal and require less continuous interaction.

People are significantly influenced by their reference groups in at least three ways. Reference groups expose an individual to new behaviors and lifestyles, and influence attitudes and self-concept; they create pressures for conformity that may affect actual product and brand choices. People are also influenced by groups to which they do not belong. **Aspirational groups** are those a person hopes to join; **dissociative groups** are those whose values or behavior an individual rejects.

Manufacturers of products and brands where group influence is strong must determine how to reach and influence opinion leaders in these reference groups. An **opinion leader** is the person in informal, product-related communications who offers advice or information about a specific product or product category, such as which of several brands is best or how a particular product may be used.[5] Marketers try to reach opinion leaders by identifying demographic and psychographic characteristics associated with opinion leadership, identifying the media read by opinion leaders, and directing messages at opinion leaders.

NESTLÉ

Prior to the launch of its KitKat Kubes, a variant of the popular KitKat brand, Nestlé hired an agency to create a buzz among opinion leaders in the age 16 to 25 market. A database of about 20,000 was sent text messages and then this database was whittled down to 100 opinion leaders by a phone questionnaire. The opinion leaders were then sent a large box of KitKat Kubes. As one project manager at Nestlé Rowntree said: "It only takes 50 people to make a craze." But of course, it has to be the right fifty people.[6]

In Japan, high school girls have often been credited with creating the buzz that makes products such as Shiseido's Neuve nail polish a big hit.[7] In the United States, the hottest trends in teenage music, language, and fashion often start in the inner cities. Clothing companies like Hot Topic, which hope to appeal to the fickle and fashion-conscious youth market, have made a concerted effort to monitor urban opinion leaders' style and behavior.

HOT TOPIC

With 494 stores in malls in 49 states and Puerto Rico, Hot Topic has been hugely successful at using anti-establishment style in its fashions. Hot Topic's tagline, "everything about the music," reflects its operating premise: Music is the primary influence on teen fashion. Whether a teen is into rock, pop-punk, emo, acid rap, rave, or rockabilly—or even more obscure musical tastes—Hot Topic has the T-shirt for him or her. T-shirts featuring bands are the company's bread and butter. In order to keep up with music trends, all Hot Topic staffers, from the CEO to the lowliest store employee, regularly attend concerts by up-and-coming and established bands to scout who's wearing what. It's a perk for store clerks because they get reimbursed for concert tickets if they turn in a fashion write-up later. Hot Topic uses customer input too. Store managers keep comment cards near the till for shoppers to fill out. Hot Topic's Web site solicits e-mailed suggestions, and the CEO reads more than 1,000 customer comment cards and e-mails a month.[8]

FAMILY The family is the most important consumer buying organization in society, and family members constitute the most influential primary reference group.[9] We can distinguish between two families in the buyer's life. The **family of orientation** consists of parents and siblings. From parents a person acquires an orientation toward religion, politics, and economics, and a sense of personal ambition, self-worth, and love.[10] Even if the buyer no longer interacts very much with his or her parents, their influence on behavior can be significant. In countries where parents live with grown children, their influence can be substantial. A more direct influence on everyday buying behavior is the **family of procreation**—namely, one's spouse and children.

The makeup of the American family, however, has changed dramatically.[11] The U.S. Census Bureau's newest numbers show that married-couple households—the dominant

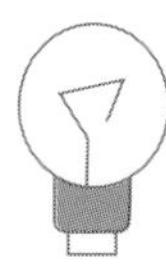

MARKETING INSIGHT | MARKETING TO CULTURAL MARKET SEGMENTS

Hispanic Americans

Expected to account for a quarter of the U.S. population by 2050, Hispanic Americans are the fastest-growing minority, and soon will be the largest minority in the country. Already with a population the same size as Canada, annual Hispanic American purchasing power in 2002 was $646 billion (total consumer spending by white Americans was $6.3 trillion). The Hispanic American segment can be difficult for marketers. Roughly two dozen nationalities can be classified as "Hispanic American," including Cuban, Mexican, Puerto Rican, Dominican, and other Central and South American groups. The Hispanic American group contains a mix of cultures, physical types, racial backgrounds, and aspirations.

Nickelodeon has been hugely successful in creating a "Pan-Latina" character, Dora the Explorer, that appeals to the increasing Hispanic preschool population in all these groups. The character is bilingual and the show displays aspects of many different Hispanic cultures. Dora's creators enlisted the help of a team of consultants with Latin American backgrounds. As a result, kids might see Dora up in the Andes or with a cocky, a frog that's an important part of Puerto Rican folklore. The research has paid off; the show is the most watched preschool show on commercial television, not only by Hispanic Americans but also by all preschoolers.

Yet despite their differences, Hispanic Americans often share strong family values, a need for respect, brand loyalty, and a strong interest in product quality. Marketers are reaching out to Hispanic Americans with targeted promotions, ads, or Web sites, but need to be careful to capture the nuances of cultural and market trends. For example, recognizing the fact that Hispanic consumers make twice as many trips to the grocery store per week and are less likely to eat out, Goya Foods has captured whole sections of large supermarkets, offering all the different goods Hispanic consumers might want. Other food companies have also introduced products targeting Hispanics, such as Frito-Lay with a lineup of spicy snacks sold in a rack emblazoned with the slogan "A Todo Sabor" (roughly, In Full Flavor).

African Americans

The purchasing power of the country's 34 million African Americans exploded during the prosperous 1990s. Based on survey findings, African Americans are the most fashion-conscious of all racial and ethnic groups. They also tend to be strongly motivated by quality and selection, and shop more at neighborhood stores. A telling testament to the growing power of African American consumers is their influence on white consumers, particularly those ages 12 to 34. Often fashion, dining, entertainment, sports, and music tastes emerge first from African American communities and make their way to the mainstream suburban mall. Think of rap- and hip-hop–inspired clothing, for instance.

Many companies have been successful at tailoring products to meet the needs of African Americans. In 1987, Hallmark Cards, Inc., launched its Afrocentric brand, Mahogany, with only 16 cards; it offers 800 cards today. Other companies offer more inclusive product lines within the same brand. Sara Lee Corporation's L'eggs discontinued its separate line of pantyhose for black women and now offers shades and styles popular among black women as half of the company's general-focus sub-brands. Finally, America's biggest packaged goods marketer, the Procter & Gamble Company, is teaming up its ad agencies specializing in campaigns aimed at African Americans with their general-market counterparts. By taking what used to be separate efforts through ethnic agencies and making them part of the company's core marketing effort, Procter & Gamble is moving the African American market from being largely an afterthought to being the name of the game.

Asian Americans

According to the U.S. Census Bureau, "Asian" refers to people having origins in any of the original peoples of the Far East, Southeast Asia, or the Indian subcontinent. Six countries represent 79 percent of the Asian U.S. population: China (21%), the Philippines (18%), India (11%), Vietnam (10%), Korea (10%), and Japan (9%).

Asian Americans tend to be more brand conscious than other minority groups, but yet are the least loyal to particular brands. Compared to other minority groups, they also tend to care more about what others think (e.g., whether their neighbors will approve). Asian Americans are the most wired and computer literate group too, and are more likely to use the Internet on a daily basis. Asian Americans often live with a larger extended family and may resonate to those types of depictions in advertising. Bank of America prospered by targeting Asians in San Francisco with separate TV campaigns aimed at Chinese, Korean, and Vietnamese consumers.

Sources: Rebecca Gardyn and John Fetto "The Way We Shop," *American Demographics* (February 2003): 33–34; Leon E. Wynter, "Business & Race: Hispanic Buying Habits Become More Diverse," *Wall Street Journal,* January 8, 1997, p. B1; Lisa A. Yorgey, "Hispanic Americans," *Target Marketing* (February 1998): 67; Carole Radice, "Hispanic Consumers: Understanding a Changing Market," *Progressive Grocer* (February 1997): 109–114; Alejandro Bianchi and Gabriel Sama, "Goya Foods Leads an Ethnic Sales Trend," *Wall Street Journal,* July 9, 2002, p. B2; Eduardo Porter and Betsy Mckay, "Frito-Lay Adds Spanish Accent to Snacks," *Wall Street Journal,* May 22, 2002, p. B3; Valerie Lynn Gray, "Going After Our Dollars," *Black Enterprise* (July 1997): 68–78; David Kiley, "Black Surfing," *Brandweek,* November 17, 1997, p. 36; Dana Canedy, "The Courtship of Black Consumers," *New York Times,* August 11, 1998, p. D1; Paula Lyon Andrus, "Mass Appeal: 'Dora' Translates Well," *Marketing News,* October 13, 2003, p. 8. Mindy Charski, "Old Navy to Tailor Message to Hispanics," *Adweek,* August 4, 2003, p. 9.

cohort since the country's founding—have slipped from nearly 80 percent in the 1950s to roughly 50 percent today. That means that the United States' 86 million single adults could soon define the new majority. Already, unmarrieds make up 42 percent of the workforce, 40 percent of homebuyers, 35 percent of voters, and one of the most powerful consumer groups on record. Marketers will have to pay attention not only to the buying habits of "singletons" who have delayed marriage, but also to families once considered on the fringe: cohabiting partners, divorced parents who share custody, single parents by choice, and same-sex couples who may or may not have children.

Marketers are interested in the roles and relative influence of family members in the purchase of a large variety of products and services. In the United States, husband–wife involvement has traditionally varied widely by product category. The wife has usually acted as the family's main purchasing agent, especially for food, sundries, and staple-clothing items. Now traditional purchasing roles are changing, and marketers would be wise to see both men and women as possible targets.

With expensive products and services like cars, vacations, or housing, the vast majority of husbands and wives engage in more joint decision making.[12] Given women's increasing wealth and income-generating ability, financial service firms such as Citigroup, Charles Schwab, and Merrill Lynch have expanded their efforts to attract women investors and business owners.[13] And marketers are realizing that men aren't the main buyers of high-tech gizmos and gadgets these days. Women actually buy more technology than men do, but consumer electronics stores have been slow to catch on to this fact. Some savvy electronics stores are starting to heed women's complaints of being ignored, patronized, or offended by salespeople. RadioShack Corp., a 7,000-store chain, began actively recruiting female store managers so that now a woman manages about one out of every seven stores.[14]

Nevertheless, men and women may respond differently to marketing messages.[15] One study showed that women valued connections and relationships with family and friends and placed a high priority on people. Men, on the other hand, related more to competition and placed a high priority on action. Marketers are taking more direct aim at women with new products such as Quaker's Nutrition for Women cereals and Crest Rejuvenating Effects toothpaste. Gillette Co. researched psychological issues specific to women and came out with an ergonomically designed razor, Venus, that fit more easily in a woman's hand. Sherwin-Williams recently designed a Dutch Boy easy-to-use "Twist and Pour" paint can targeted specifically at women.

Another shift in buying patterns is an increase in the amount of dollars spent and the direct and indirect influence wielded by children and teens.[16] Direct influence describes children's hints, requests, and demands—"I want to go to McDonald's." Direct influence of kids between the ages of 4 and 12 totaled around $275 billion in 1999. Their indirect influence on parental spending accounted for another $312 billion of household purchases.[17] Indirect influence means that parents know the brands, product choices, and preferences of their children without hints or outright requests. One research study showed that teenagers were playing a more active role than before in helping parents choose a car, audio/video equipment, or a vacation spot.[18]

Marketers use every possible channel of communication to reach kids, especially such popular media as Nickelodeon, Cartoon Network, or the Disney Channel on TV and magazines such as *Nickelodeon, Sports Illustrated for Kids,* and *Disney Adventures.*

DISNEY CHANNEL

After being considered an unprofitable stepchild of the Disney empire, the Disney Channel has become the company's cash cow solely from its ability to reach the underserved "tween market"—the 29 million 8 to 14-year-olds—and leverage its success through Disney's other divisions. In 2000, on the lookout for hip programming that would appeal to both tweens and their parents, the Disney Channel cast a then-obscure 12-year-old in the title role of a new weekly series, Lizzie McGuire. This sitcom about an everyday middle-schooler became a huge hit, and a year later Disney began running it on Saturday mornings on ABC, another Disney property. Then, in 2002, Disney unleashed a continuous stream of Lizzie spinoffs: Disney Press began publishing Lizzie books; its Buena Vista Music Group released the soundtrack for the series, which went platinum the following July; and Lizzie began airing every single day on the Disney Channel. That same year Disney's consumer products division began marketing everything from Lizzie dolls and sleeping bags to Lizzie pencils and notebooks. The Lizzie franchise has probably earned Disney about $100 million.[19]

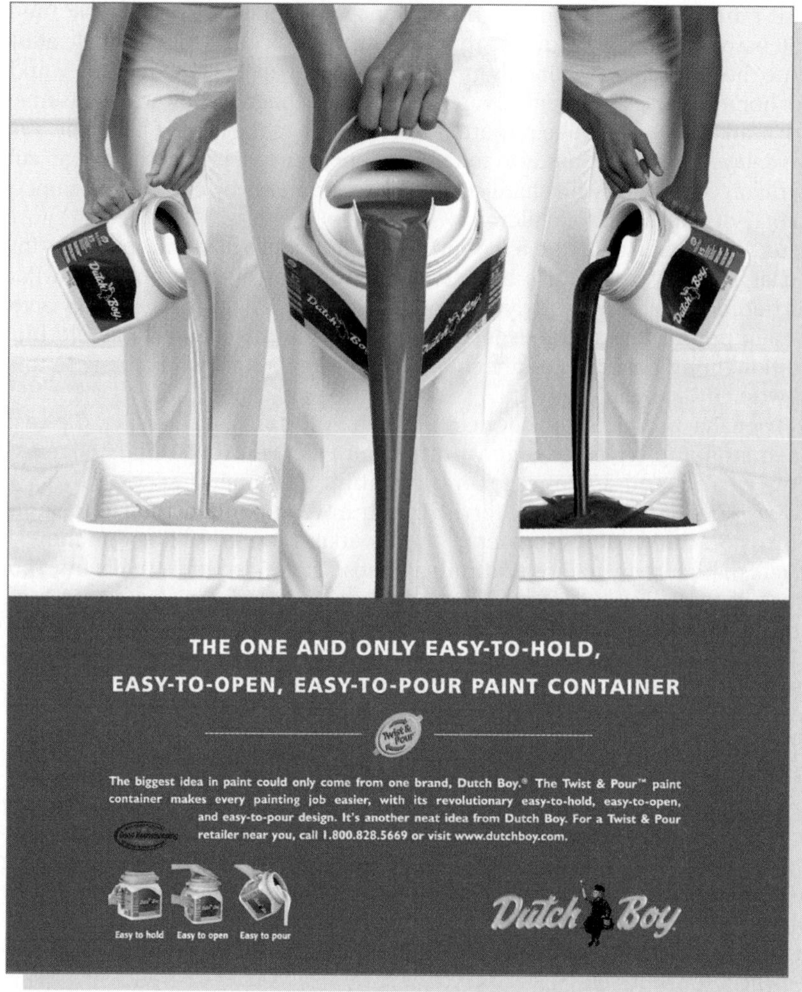

Marketers are focusing more closely on women and their needs: This Dutch Boy "Twist and Pour" ad, which features a new, easy to use paint container, is targeted specifically at women.

The Lizzie McGuire juggernaut demonstrates how powerful television can be in reaching children, and marketers are using television to target children at younger ages than ever before. By the time children are around 2 years old, they can often recognize characters, logos, and specific brands. Marketers are tapping into that audience with product tie-ins, placed at a child's eye level, on just about everything—from Scooby Doo vitamins to Elmo juice and cookies.[20]

Today companies are also likely to use the Internet to show products to children and solicit marketing information from them. Millions of kids under the age of 17 are online. Marketers have jumped online with them, offering freebies in exchange for personal information. Many have come under fire for this practice and for not clearly differentiating ads from games or entertainment.

ROLES AND STATUSES A person participates in many groups—family, clubs, organizations. The person's position in each group can be defined in terms of role and status. A **role** consists of the activities a person is expected to perform. Each role carries a **status**. A senior vice president of marketing has more status than a sales manager, and a sales manager has more status than an office clerk. People choose products that reflect and communicate their role and actual or desired status in society. Company presidents often drive Mercedes, wear expensive suits, and drink expensive wines. Marketers must be aware of the status symbol potential of products and brands.

Personal Factors

A buyer's decisions are also influenced by personal characteristics. These include the buyer's age and stage in the life cycle; occupation and economic circumstances; personality and self-concept; and lifestyle and values. Because many of these characteristics have a very

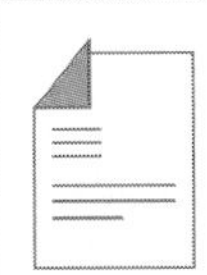

MARKETING MEMO | THE AVERAGE AMERICAN CONSUMER QUIZ

Statements	Percent of consumers agreeing % Men	Percent of consumers agreeing % Women
1. A store's brand is usually a better buy than a nationally advertised brand.	______	______
2. I went fishing at least once in the past 12 months.	______	______
3. I am a homebody.	______	______
4. Information from advertising helps me make better buying decisions.	______	______
5. I like to pay cash for everything I buy.	______	______
6. A woman's place is in the home.	______	______
7. I am interested in spices and seasonings.	______	______
8. The father should be the boss in the house.	______	______
9. You have to use disinfectants to get things really clean.	______	______
10. I believe beings from other planets have visited Earth.	______	______

Note: Listed above are a series of statements that have been used in attitude surveys of American consumers. Only *married* U.S. men and women participated in these surveys. The people were selected because they were representative of a broad cross section of American consumers. The survey respondents were selected through a quota sample, balanced on age, income, geographical area, and population density. Consumers were asked whether they agreed or disagreed with each statement. For each statement, please estimate what percent of *married* American men and women agreed with each statement in 2004. Write a number between 0% and 100% in the columns to the right to indicate the percentage agreement. The correct answers can be found in the following footnote.*

* 1. M=57%, W=57%; 2. M=34%, W=24%; 3. M=64%, W=66%; 4. M=57%, W=61%; 5. M=60%, W=58%; 6. M=25%, W=23%; 7. M=70%, W=77%; 8. M=47%, W=29%; 9. M=58%, W=62%; 10. M=40%, W=35%. These numbers are based on DDB Life Style Study™. For an interesting application and analysis of the quiz, see Stephen J. Hoch, "Who Do We Know: Predicting the Interests and Opinions of the American Consumer," *Journal of Consumer Research*, 15 (December, 1998): 315–324.

direct impact on consumer behavior, it is important for marketers to follow them closely. See how well you do with "Marketing Memo: The Average American Consumer Quiz."

AGE AND STAGE IN THE LIFE CYCLE People buy different goods and services over a lifetime. Taste in food, clothes, furniture, and recreation is often age related. Consumption is also shaped by the *family life cycle* and the number, age, and gender of people in the household at any point in time. American households are increasingly fragmented—the traditional family of four with a husband, wife, and two kids makes up a much smaller percentage of total households than it once did. In addition, *psychological* life-cycle stages may matter. Adults experience certain "passages" or "transformations" as they go through life.[21]

Marketers should also consider *critical life events or transitions*—marriage, childbirth, illness, relocation, divorce, career change, widowhood—as giving rise to new needs. These should alert service providers—banks, lawyers, and marriage, employment, and bereavement counselors—to ways they can help.[22]

BANK OF AMERICA (BOA)

BOA is using "event-based triggers" to help its premier customers. BOA, using NCR's "Relationship Optimizer" solution, monitors large deposits, withdrawals, insufficient funds, and other events that deviate from a customer's normal behavior. Client managers are alerted to these events and phone the client to see if they can be of any assistance. For example, if a client has withdrawn a large sum of money to buy a home, the client manager offers to help the client find the best mortgage.

OCCUPATION AND ECONOMIC CIRCUMSTANCES Occupation also influences consumption patterns. A blue-collar worker will buy work clothes, work shoes, and lunchboxes. A company president will buy dress suits, air travel, and country club memberships. Marketers try to identify the occupational groups that have above-average interest in their products and services. A company can even tailor its products for certain occupational groups: Computer software companies, for example, design different products for brand managers, engineers, lawyers, and physicians.

Product choice is greatly affected by economic circumstances: spendable income (level, stability, and time pattern), savings and assets (including the percentage that is liquid), debts, borrowing power, and attitudes toward spending and saving. Luxury-goods makers such as Gucci, Prada, and Burberry can be vulnerable to an economic downturn. If economic indicators point to a recession, marketers can take steps to redesign, reposition, and reprice their products or introduce or increase the emphasis on discount brands so that they can continue to offer value to target customers.

PERSONALITY AND SELF-CONCEPT Each person has personality characteristics that influence his or her buying behavior. By **personality**, we mean a set of distinguishing human psychological traits that lead to relatively consistent and enduring responses to environmental stimuli. Personality is often described in terms of such traits as self-confidence, dominance, autonomy, deference, sociability, defensiveness, and adaptability.[23] Personality can be a useful variable in analyzing consumer brand choices. The idea is that brands also have personalities, and consumers are likely to choose brands whose personalities match their own. We define **brand personality** as the specific mix of human traits that may be attributed to a particular brand.

Stanford's Jennifer Aaker conducted research into brand personalities and identified the following five traits:[24]

1. Sincerity (down-to-earth, honest, wholesome, and cheerful)
2. Excitement (daring, spirited, imaginative, and up-to-date)
3. Competence (reliable, intelligent, and successful)
4. Sophistication (upper-class and charming)
5. Ruggedness (outdoorsy and tough)

She proceeded to analyze some well-known brands and found that a number of them tended to be strong on one particular trait: Levi's with "ruggedness"; MTV with "excitement"; CNN with "competence"; and Campbell's with "sincerity." The implication is that these brands will attract persons who are high on the same personality traits. A brand personality may have several attributes: Levi's suggests a personality that is also youthful, rebellious, authentic, and American. The company utilizes product features, services, and image making to transmit the product's personality.

A Levi's ad expresses the brand personality: youthful, rebellious, authentic, American.

Consumers often choose and use brands that have a brand personality consistent with their own *actual self-concept* (how one views oneself), although in some cases the match may be based on the consumer's *ideal self-concept* (how one would like to view oneself) or even *others' self-concept* (how one thinks others see one) rather than actual self-image.[25] These effects may also be more pronounced for publicly consumed products as compared to privately consumed goods.[26] On the other hand, consumers who are high "self-monitors"—that is, sensitive to how others see them—are more likely to choose brands whose personalities fit the consumption situation.[27]

LIFESTYLE AND VALUES People from the same subculture, social class, and occupation may lead quite different lifestyles. A **lifestyle** is a person's pattern of living in the world as expressed in activities, interests, and opinions. Lifestyle portrays the "whole person" interacting with his or her environment. Marketers search for relationships between their products and lifestyle groups. For example, a computer manufacturer might find that most computer buyers are achievement-oriented. The marketer may then aim the brand more clearly at the achiever lifestyle. Marketers are always uncovering new trends in consumer lifestyles. Here's an example of one of the latest lifestyle trends businesses are currently targeting:

LOHAS

Consumers who worry about the environment, want products to be produced in a sustainable way, and spend money to advance their personal development and potential have been named "LOHAS." The name is an acronym standing for *lifestyles of health and sustainability.* The market for LOHAS products encompasses things like organic foods, energy-efficient appliances and sonar panels, as well as alternative medicine, yoga tapes, and ecotourism. Taken together, they accounted for a $230 billion market in 2000. Rather than looking at discrete product categories like cars or organic foods, it is more important to look at the common factors linking these product groups—for example, at cars, or energy and household products that are perceived as better for the environment and society.[28]

Lifestyles are shaped partly by whether consumers are *money-constrained* or *time-constrained.* Companies aiming to serve money-constrained consumers will create lower-cost products and services. By appealing to the money-constrained, Wal-Mart has become the largest company in the world. Its "everyday low prices" have wrung tens of billions of dollars out of the retail supply chain, passing the larger part of savings along to shoppers with rock-bottom bargain prices.[29]

Consumers who experience time famine are prone to **multitasking**, that is, doing two or more things at the same time. They will phone or eat while driving, or bicycle to work to get exercise. They will also pay others to perform tasks because time is more important than money. They may prefer bagels to breakfast cereals because they are quicker. Companies aiming to serve them will create convenient products and services for this group. Much of the wireless revolution is fueled by the multitasking trend. Texas Instruments recently unveiled a product design called WANDA, short for Wireless Any Network Digital Assistant, that allows users to talk on a cell phone while Web browsing over Wi-fi while conducting business via Bluetooth.

In some categories, notably food processing, companies targeting time-constrained consumers need to be aware that these very same consumers seek the illusion that they are not operating within time constraints. The food processing industry has a name for those who seek both convenience and some involvement in the cooking process: the "convenience involvement segment."[30]

HAMBURGER HELPER

Launched in 1971 in response to tough economic times, the inexpensive pasta-and-powdered mix Hamburger Helper was designed to quickly and inexpensively stretch a pound of meat into a family meal. With an estimated 44 percent of evening meals prepared in under 30 minutes and strong competition from fast-food drive-through windows, restaurant deliveries, and precooked grocery store dishes, Hamburger Helper's days of prosperity might seem numbered. Market researchers found, however, that some consumers do not necessarily want the fastest microwaveable meal solution possible—they also want to feel good about how they prepare a meal. In fact, on average, they would prefer to use at least one pot or pan and 15 minutes of time. To remain attractive to the segment who want to spend less time in the kitchen without totally abandoning their traditional roles as family mealmakers, marketers of Hamburger Helper are always introducing new flavors to tap into the latest consumer taste trends.[31]

Consumer decisions are also influenced by **core values**, the belief systems that underlie consumer attitudes and behaviors. Core values go much deeper than behavior or attitude, and determine, at a basic level, people's choices and desires over the long term. Marketers who target consumers on the basis of their values believe that by appealing to people's inner selves, it is possible to influence their outer selves—their purchase behavior.

::: Key Psychological Processes

The starting point for understanding consumer behavior is the stimulus-response model shown in Figure 6.1. Marketing and environmental stimuli enter the consumer's consciousness. A set of psychological processes combine with certain consumer characteristics to result in decision processes and purchase decisions. The marketer's task is to understand what happens in the consumer's consciousness between the arrival of the outside marketing stimuli and the ultimate purchase decisions. Four key psychological processes—motivation, perception, learning, and memory—fundamentally influence consumer responses to the various marketing stimuli.

Motivation: Freud, Maslow, Herzberg

A person has many needs at any given time. Some needs are *biogenic;* they arise from physiological states of tension such as hunger, thirst, or discomfort. Other needs are *psychogenic;* they arise from psychological states of tension such as the need for recognition, esteem, or belonging. A need becomes a motive when it is aroused to a sufficient level of intensity. A **motive** is a need that is sufficiently pressing to drive the person to act.

Three of the best-known theories of human motivation—those of Sigmund Freud, Abraham Maslow, and Frederick Herzberg—carry quite different implications for consumer analysis and marketing strategy.

FREUD'S THEORY Sigmund Freud assumed that the psychological forces shaping people's behavior are largely unconscious, and that a person cannot fully understand his or her own motivations. When a person examines specific brands, he or she will react not only to their stated capabilities, but also to other, less conscious cues. Shape, size, weight, material, color, and brand name can all trigger certain associations and emotions. A technique called *laddering* can be used to trace a person's motivations from the stated instrumental ones to the more terminal ones. Then the marketer can decide at what level to develop the message and appeal.[32]

Motivation researchers often collect "in-depth interviews" with a few dozen consumers to uncover deeper motives triggered by a product. They use various *projective techniques* such as word association, sentence completion, picture interpretation, and role playing. Many of these techniques were pioneered by Ernest Dichter, a Viennese psychologist who settled in America.[33]

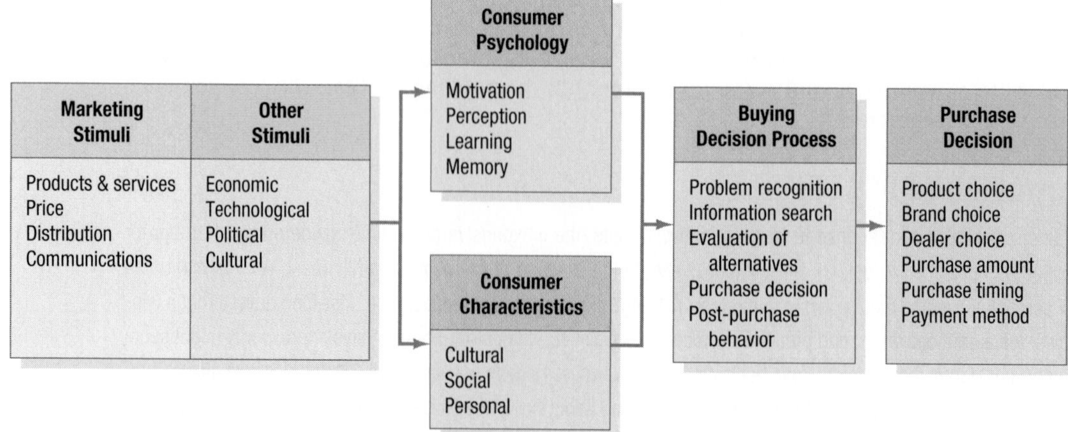

FIG. 6.1 Model of Consumer Behavior

Today motivational researchers continue the tradition of Freudian interpretation. Jan Callebaut identifies different motives a product can satisfy. For example, whisky can meet the need for social relaxation, status, or fun. Different whisky brands need to be motivationally positioned in one of these three appeals.[34] Another motivation researcher, Clotaire Rapaille, works on breaking the "code" behind a lot of product behavior. Research analyzing paper towels, according to Rapaille, revealed that its appeal to mothers is in how cleanliness plays into their instinctive desire to have their genes survive. "You are not just cleaning the table. You are saving the whole family," asserts the researcher.[35]

MASLOW'S THEORY Abraham Maslow sought to explain why people are driven by particular needs at particular times.[36] Why does one person spend considerable time and energy on personal safety and another on pursuing the high opinion of others? Maslow's answer is that human needs are arranged in a hierarchy, from the most pressing to the least pressing. In order of importance, they are physiological needs, safety needs, social needs, esteem needs, and self-actualization needs (see Figure 6.2). People will try to satisfy their most important needs first. When a person succeeds in satisfying an important need, he or she will then try to satisfy the next-most-important need. For example, a starving man (need 1) will not take an interest in the latest happenings in the art world (need 5), nor in how he is viewed by others (need 3 or 4), nor even in whether he is breathing clean air (need 2); but when he has enough food and water, the next-most-important need will become salient.

Maslow's theory helps marketers understand how various products fit into the plans, goals, and lives of consumers.

HERZBERG'S THEORY Frederick Herzberg developed a two-factor theory that distinguishes *dissatisfiers* (factors that cause dissatisfaction) and *satisfiers* (factors that cause satisfaction).[37] The absence of dissatisfiers is not enough; satisfiers must be present to motivate a purchase. For example, a computer that does not come with a warranty would be a dissatisfier. Yet the presence of a product warranty would not act as a satisfier or motivator of a purchase, because it is not a source of intrinsic satisfaction. Ease of use would be a satisfier.

Herzberg's theory has two implications. First, sellers should do their best to avoid dissatisfiers (for example, a poor training manual or a poor service policy). Although these things will not sell a product, they might easily unsell it. Second, the seller should identify the major satisfiers or motivators of purchase in the market and then supply them. These satisfiers will make the major difference as to which brand the customer buys.

Perception

A motivated person is ready to act. How the motivated person actually acts is influenced by his or her view or perception of the situation. **Perception** is the process by which an individual selects, organizes, and interprets information inputs to create a meaningful picture of

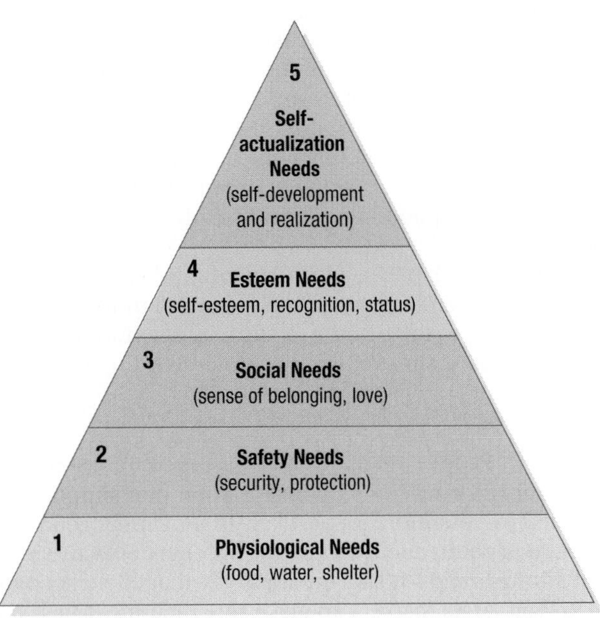

FIG. 6.2

Maslow's Hierarchy of Needs

Source: Motivation and Personality, 2nd ed., by A. H. Maslow, 1970. Reprinted by permission of Prentice Hall, Inc., Upper Saddle River, New Jersey.

the world.[38] Perception depends not only on the physical stimuli, but also on the stimuli's relation to the surrounding field and on conditions within the individual. The key point is that perceptions can vary widely among individuals exposed to the same reality. One person might perceive a fast-talking salesperson as aggressive and insincere; another, as intelligent and helpful. Each will respond differently to the salesperson.

In marketing, perceptions are more important than the reality, as it is perceptions that will affect consumers' actual behavior. People can emerge with different perceptions of the same object because of three perceptual processes: selective attention, selective distortion, and selective retention.

SELECTIVE ATTENTION It has been estimated that the average person may be exposed to over 1,500 ads or brand communications a day. Because a person cannot possibly attend to all of these, most stimuli will be screened out—a process called **selective attention**. Selective attention means that marketers have to work hard to attract consumers' notice. The real challenge is to explain which stimuli people will notice. Here are some findings:

1. ***People are more likely to notice stimuli that relate to a current need.*** A person who is motivated to buy a computer will notice computer ads; he or she will be less likely to notice DVD ads.
2. ***People are more likely to notice stimuli that they anticipate.*** You are more likely to notice computers than radios in a computer store because you do not expect the store to carry radios.
3. ***People are more likely to notice stimuli whose deviations are large in relation to the normal size of the stimuli.*** You are more likely to notice an ad offering $100 off the list price of a computer than one offering $5 off.

Although people screen out much of the surrounding stimuli, they are influenced by unexpected stimuli, such as sudden offers in the mail, over the phone, or from a salesperson. Marketers may attempt to promote their offers intrusively to bypass selective attention filters.

SELECTIVE DISTORTION Even noticed stimuli do not always come across in the way the senders intended. **Selective distortion** is the tendency to interpret information in a way that will fit our preconceptions. Consumers will often distort information to be consistent with prior brand and product beliefs.[39]

A stark demonstration of the power of consumer brand beliefs is the typical result of product sampling tests. In "blind" taste tests, one group of consumers samples a product without knowing which brand it is, whereas another group of consumers samples the product knowing which brand it is. Invariably, differences arise in the opinions of the two groups despite the fact that the two groups are *literally consuming exactly the same product*!

When consumers report different opinions between branded and unbranded versions of identical products, it must be the case that the brand and product beliefs, created by whatever means (e.g., past experiences, marketing activity for the brand, etc.), have somehow changed their product perceptions. Examples of branded differences can be found with virtually every type of product. For example, one study found that consumers were equally split in their preference for Diet Coke versus Diet Pepsi when tasting both on a blind basis.[40] When tasting the branded versions, however, consumers preferred Diet Coke by 65 percent and Diet Pepsi by only 23 percent (with the remainder seeing no difference).

Selective distortion can work to the advantage of marketers with strong brands when consumers distort neutral or ambiguous brand information to make it more positive. In other words, beer may seem to taste better, a car may seem to drive more smoothly, the wait in a bank line may seem shorter, and so on, depending on the particular brands involved.

SELECTIVE RETENTION People will fail to register much information to which they are exposed in memory, but will tend to retain information that supports their attitudes and beliefs. Because of **selective retention**, we are likely to remember good points about a product we like and forget good points about competing products. Selective retention again works to the advantage of strong brands. It also explains why marketers need to use repetition in sending messages to their target market—to make sure their message is not overlooked.

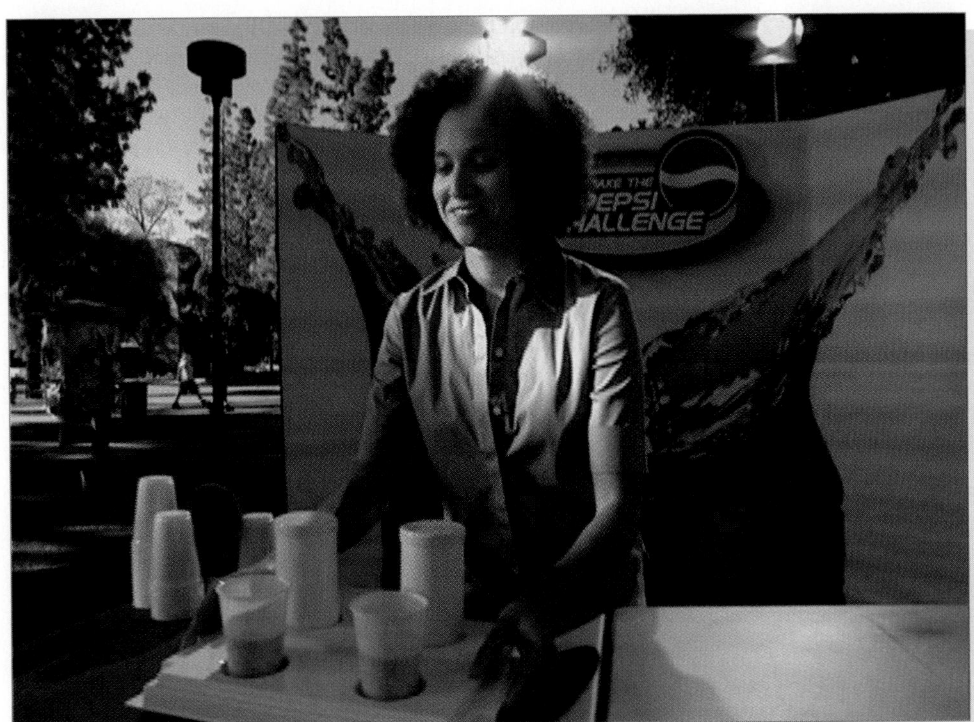

A Pepsi Challenge taste test in New York's Central Park. Companies like Pepsi often do taste tests of their products against other branded products to see if brand really makes a difference in customer preferences.

SUBLIMINAL PERCEPTION The selective perception mechanisms require active engagement and thought by consumers. A topic that has fascinated armchair marketers for ages is **subliminal perception**. The argument is that marketers embed covert, subliminal messages in ads or packages. Consumers are not consciously aware of these messages, but yet they affect their behavior. Although it is clear many subtle subconscious effects can exist with consumer processing,[41] no evidence supports the notion that marketers can systematically control consumers at that level.[42]

Learning

When people act, they learn. **Learning** involves changes in an individual's behavior arising from experience. Most human behavior is learned. Learning theorists believe that learning is produced through the interplay of drives, stimuli, cues, responses, and reinforcement.

A **drive** is a strong internal stimulus impelling action. **Cues** are minor stimuli that determine when, where, and how a person responds. Suppose you buy a Dell computer. If your experience is rewarding, your response to computers and Dell will be positively reinforced. Later on, when you want to buy a printer, you may assume that because Dell makes good computers, Dell also makes good printers. In other words, you *generalize* your response to similar stimuli. A countertendency to generalization is discrimination. **Discrimination** means that the person has learned to recognize differences in sets of similar stimuli and can adjust responses accordingly.

Learning theory teaches marketers that they can build demand for a product by associating it with strong drives, using motivating cues, and providing positive reinforcement. A new company can enter the market by appealing to the same drives that competitors use and by providing similar cue configurations, because buyers are more likely to transfer loyalty to similar brands (generalization); or the company might design its brand to appeal to a different set of drives and offer strong cue inducements to switch (discrimination).

Memory

All the information and experiences individuals encounter as they go through life can end up in their long-term memory. Cognitive psychologists distinguish between **short-term memory (STM)**—a temporary repository of information—and **long-term memory (LTM)**—a more permanent repository.

Most widely accepted views of long-term memory structure involve some kind of associative model formulation.[43] For example, the **associative network memory model** views LTM as consisting of a set of nodes and links. *Nodes* are stored information connected by *links* that vary in strength. Any type of information can be stored in the memory network, including information that is verbal, visual, abstract, or contextual. A spreading activation process from node to node determines the extent of retrieval and what information can actually be recalled in any given situation. When a node becomes activated because external information is being encoded (e.g., when a person reads or hears a word or phrase) or internal information is retrieved from LTM (e.g., when a person thinks about some concept), other nodes are also activated if they are sufficiently strongly associated with that node.

Consistent with the associative network memory model, consumer brand knowledge in memory can be conceptualized as consisting of a brand node in memory with a variety of linked associations. The strength and organization of these associations will be important determinants of the information that can be recalled about the brand. **Brand associations** consist of all brand-related thoughts, feelings, perceptions, images, experiences, beliefs, attitudes, and so on that become linked to the brand node.

Marketing can be seen as making sure that consumers have the right types of product and service experiences such that the right brand knowledge structures are created and maintained in memory.

GODIVA CHOCOLATIER

Godiva Chocolatier's success is based on the appeal of emotional brand associations. In 1994, when the recession slowed sales of super premium goods, such as chocolates that sold for as much as $45 a pound, Godiva underwent a marketing makeover in its retail stores. The idea was to define, through store design, what the experience of eating chocolate felt like—sensual, indulgent, even sinful. In its multimillion-dollar redesign Godiva created elegant Art Noveau–style stores with bleached wood floors and wood and glass display cases. Customers were able to sample chocolates and find price lists instead of having to ask the salesperson the prices (which they might have found embarrassing). As redesigned "test" stores began to post significantly higher sales, Godiva rolled out the whole redesign and now the brand's associations of luxurious indulgence and sensuality have become ingrained in consumers' minds.[44]

Companies such as Procter & Gamble like to create mental maps of consumers that depict their knowledge of a particular brand in terms of the key associations that are likely to

FIG. 6.3

Hypothetical Dole Mental Map

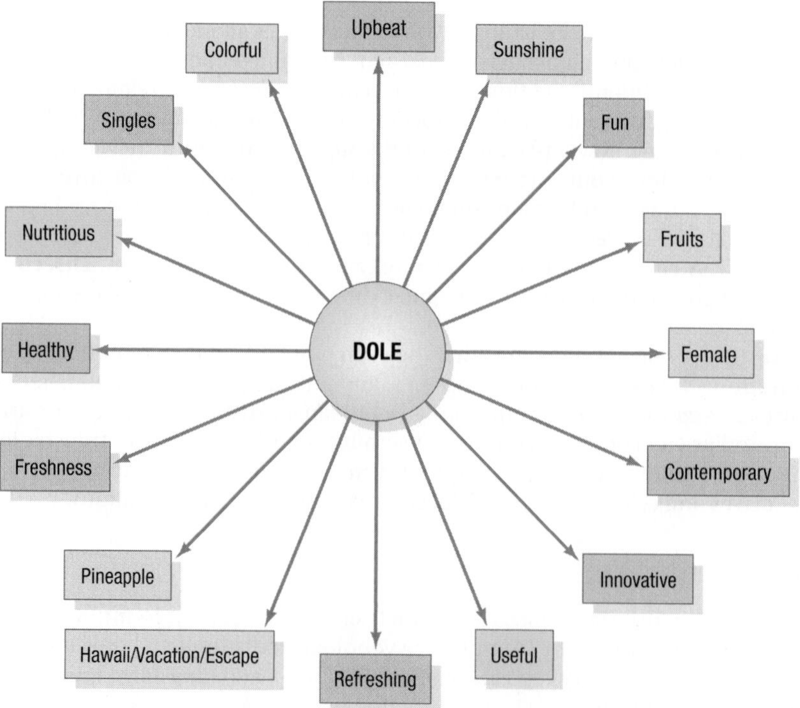

be triggered in a marketing setting and their relative strength, favorability, and uniqueness to consumers. Figure 6.3 displays a very simple mental map highlighting brand beliefs for a hypothetical consumer for the Dole brand.

MEMORY PROCESSES: ENCODING **Memory encoding** refers to how and where information gets into memory. Memory encoding can be characterized according to the amount or quantity of processing that information receives at encoding (i.e., how much a person thinks about the information) and the nature or quality of processing that information receives at encoding (i.e., the manner in which a person thinks about the information). The quantity and quality of processing will be an important determinant of the strength of an association.[45]

In general, the more attention placed on the meaning of information during encoding, the stronger the resulting associations in memory will be.[46] When a consumer actively thinks about and "elaborates" on the significance of product or service information, stronger associations are created in memory. Another key determinant of the strength of a newly formed association will be the content, organization, and strength of existing brand associations in memory. It will be easier for consumers to create an association to new information when extensive, relevant knowledge structures already exist in memory. One reason why personal experiences create such strong brand associations is that information about the product is likely to be related to existing knowledge.

Consider the brand associations that might be created by a new TV ad campaign, employing a popular celebrity endorser, designed to create a new benefit association for a well-known brand. For example, assume Bruce Springsteen and his classic songs "Born in the USA" and "Born to Run" were jointly used to promote the "American heritage" and "Patriotic appeal" of New Balance athletic shoes, a Massachusetts-based company that

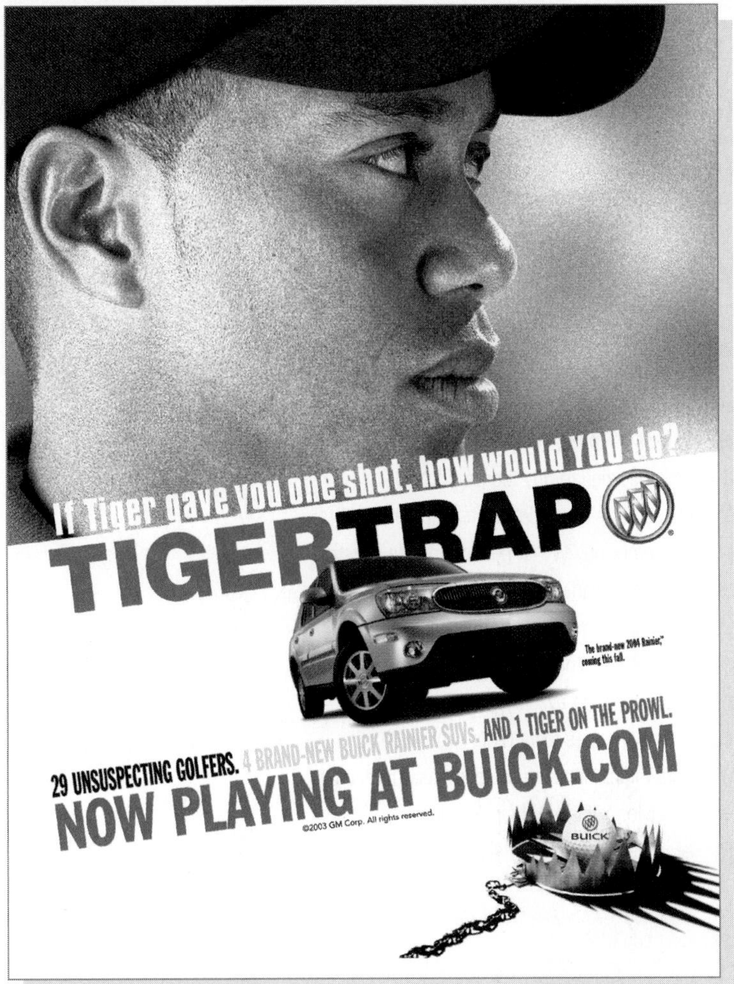

A Buick ad campaign features a popular celebrity endorser, the golfer Tiger Woods. Buick wants to appeal to younger drivers with a campaign designed to create a new benefit association for this well-known brand.

still manufactures in its local area. A number of different scenarios characterize how consumers might process such an ad:

1. Some consumers may barely notice the ads so that the amount of processing devoted to the ads is extremely low, resulting in weak to nonexistent brand associations.
2. The ads may catch the attention of other consumers, resulting in sufficient processing, but these consumers may devote most of the time during the ads thinking about the song and wondering why Springsteen decided to endorse New Balance (and whether he actually wore them), resulting in strong associations to Springsteen, but not to New Balance.
3. Another group of consumers may not only notice the ads but may think of how they had a wrong impression of New Balance and that it is "different" from the way they thought and that they would feel good about wearing the shoe. The endorsement by Springsteen in this case helped to transfer and create positive associations.

In addition to congruency or consistency with existing knowledge, the ease with which new information can be integrated into established knowledge structures clearly depends on the nature of that information, in terms of characteristics such as simplicity, vividness, and concreteness.

Repeated exposures to information provide greater opportunity for processing and thus the potential for stronger associations. Recent advertising research in a field setting, however, suggests that qualitative considerations and the manner or style of consumer processing engendered by an ad are generally more important than the cumulative total of ad exposures.[47] In other words, high levels of repetition for an uninvolving, unpersuasive ad is unlikely to have as much sales impact as lower levels of repetition for an involving, persuasive ad.

MEMORY PROCESSES: RETRIEVAL **Memory retrieval** refers to how information gets out of memory. According to the associative network memory model, the strength of a brand association increases both the likelihood that that information will be accessible and the ease with which it can be recalled by "spreading activation." Successful recall of brand information by consumers does not depend only on the initial strength of that information in memory. Three factors are particularly important.

First, the presence of *other* product information in memory can produce interference effects. It may cause the information to be either overlooked or confused. One challenge in a category crowded with many competitors—for example, airlines, financial services, and insurance companies—is that consumers may mix up brands.

TABLE 6.2

Understanding Consumer Behavior

Who buys our product or service?
Who makes the decision to buy the product?
Who influences the decision to buy the product?
How is the purchase decision made? Who assumes what role?
What does the customer buy? What needs must be satisfied?
Why do customers buy a particular brand?
Where do they go or look to buy the product or service?
When do they buy? Any seasonality factors?
How is our product perceived by customers?
What are customers' attitudes toward our product?
What social factors might influence the purchase decision?
Do customers' lifestyles influence their decisions?
How do personal or demographic factors influence the purchase decision?

Source: Based on list from George Belch and Michael Belch, *Advertising and Communication Management,* 6th ed. (Homewood, IL: Irwin, 2003).

Second, the time since exposure to information at encoding affects the strength of a new association—the longer the time delay, the weaker the association. The time elapsed since the last exposure opportunity, however, has been shown generally to produce only gradual decay. Cognitive psychologists believe that memory is extremely durable, so that once information becomes stored in memory, its strength of association decays very slowly.[48]

Third, information may be "available" in memory (i.e., potentially recallable) but may not be "accessible" (i.e., unable to be recalled) without the proper retrieval cues or reminders. The particular associations for a brand that "come to mind" depend on the context in which the brand is considered. The more cues linked to a piece of information, however, the greater the likelihood that the information can be recalled. The effectiveness of retrieval cues is one reason why marketing *inside* a supermarket or any retail store is so critical—in terms of the actual product packaging, the use of in-store mini-billboard displays, and so on. The information they contain and the reminders they provide of advertising or other information already conveyed outside the store will be prime determinants of consumer decision making.

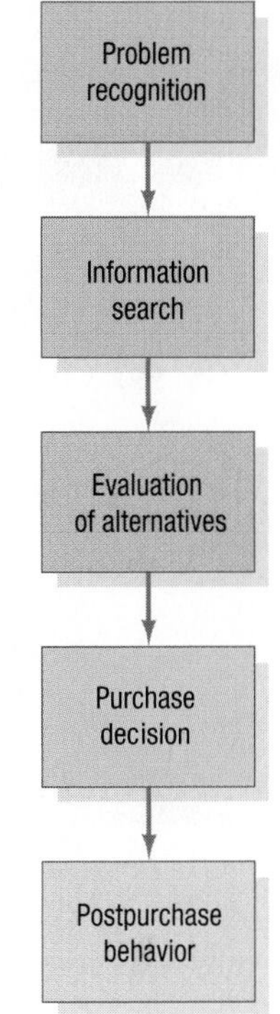

FIG. 6.4

Five-Stage Model of the Consumer Buying Process

::: The Buying Decision Process: The Five-Stage Model

These basic psychological processes play an important role in understanding how consumers actually make their buying decisions. Marketers must understand every facet of consumer behavior. Table 6.2 provides a list of some key consumer behavior questions in terms of "who, what, when, where, how, and why." Smart companies try to fully understand the customers' buying decision process—all their experiences in learning, choosing, using, and even disposing of a product.[49]

Honda engineers took videos of shoppers loading groceries into car trunks to observe their frustrations and generate possible design solutions. Intuit, the maker of Quicken financial software, watched first-time buyers try to learn Quicken to sense their problems in learning how to use the product. Bissel developed its Steam n' Clean vacuum cleaner based on the product trial experiences of a local PTA group near corporate headquarters in Grand Rapids, Michigan. The result was a name change, color-coded attachments, and an infomercial highlighting its special features.[50]

Marketing scholars have developed a "stage model" of the buying decision process (see Figure 6.4). The consumer passes through five stages: problem recognition, information search, evaluation of alternatives, purchase decision, and postpurchase behavior. Clearly, the buying process starts long before the actual purchase and has consequences long afterward.[51]

But consumers do not always pass through all five stages in buying a product. They may skip or reverse some stages. A woman buying her regular brand of toothpaste goes directly from the need for toothpaste to the purchase decision, skipping information search and evaluation. The model in Figure 6.4 provides a good frame of reference, however, because it captures the full range of considerations that arise when a consumer faces a highly involving new purchase.[52]

Problem Recognition

The buying process starts when the buyer recognizes a problem or need. The need can be triggered by internal or external stimuli. With an internal stimulus, one of the person's normal needs—hunger, thirst, sex—rises to a threshold level and becomes a drive; or a need can be aroused by an external stimulus. A person may admire a neighbor's new car or see a television ad for a Hawaiian vacation, which triggers thoughts about the possibility of making a purchase. A believer in "retail theater," Krispy Kreme lights a neon "HOT NOW" sign to get attention—and purchase interest—each time a new batch of doughnuts is baked.

Marketers need to identify the circumstances that trigger a particular need by gathering information from a number of consumers. They can then develop marketing strategies that trigger consumer interest. This is particularly important with discretionary purchases such as luxury goods, vacation packages, and entertainment options. Consumer motivation may need to be increased so that a potential purchase is even given serious consideration.

Information Search

An aroused consumer will be inclined to search for more information. We can distinguish between two levels of arousal. The milder search state is called *heightened attention.* At this level a person simply becomes more receptive to information about a product. At the next

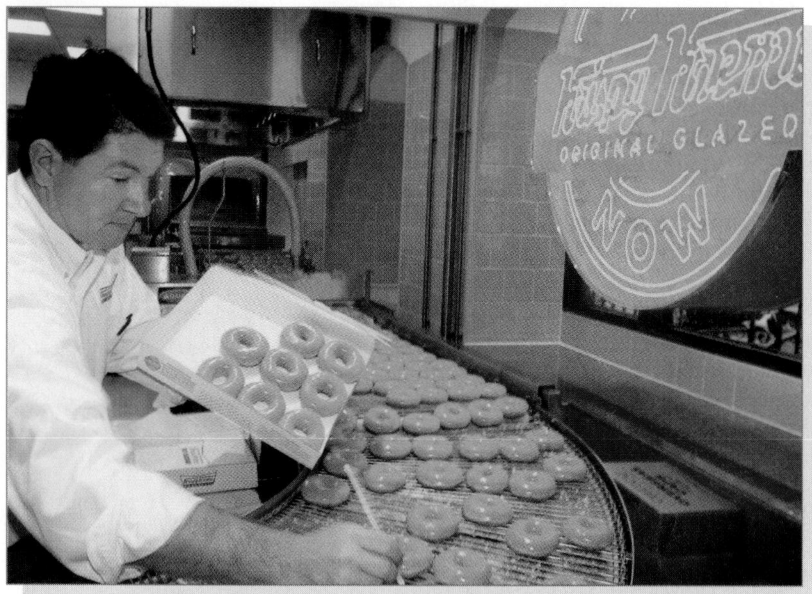

Triggering need: The "HOT NOW" sign is lit at this new Krispy Kreme store at Harrod's in London to signal the arrival of a batch of freshly baked doughnuts.

level, the person may enter an *active information search:* looking for reading material, phoning friends, going online, and visiting stores to learn about the product.

Of key interest to the marketer are the major information sources to which the consumer will turn and the relative influence each will have on the subsequent purchase decision. These information sources fall into four groups:

- ***Personal.*** Family, friends, neighbors, acquaintances
- ***Commercial.*** Advertising, Web sites, salespersons, dealers, packaging, displays
- ***Public.*** Mass media, consumer-rating organizations
- ***Experiential.*** Handling, examining, using the product

The relative amount and influence of these sources vary with the product category and the buyer's characteristics. Generally speaking, the consumer receives the most information about a product from commercial sources—that is, marketer-dominated sources. However, the most effective information often comes from personal sources or public sources that are independent authorities. More than 40 percent of all car shoppers consult *Consumer Reports,* making it the biggest single source of information.[53] Each information source performs a different function in influencing the buying decision. Commercial sources normally perform an information function, whereas personal sources perform a legitimizing or evaluation function. For example, physicians often learn of new drugs from commercial sources but turn to other doctors for evaluations.

The Internet has changed the process of information search. Today's marketplace is made up of traditional consumers (who do not shop online), cyber-consumers (who mostly shop online), and hybrid consumers (who do both).[54] Most consumers are hybrid: They shop in grocery stores but occasionally order from Peapod; they shop for books in Barnes & Noble bookstores but also sometimes order books from bn.com. People still like to squeeze the tomatoes, touch the fabric, smell the perfume, and interact with salespeople. They are motivated by more than shopping efficiency. Most companies will need a presence both offline and online to cater to these hybrid consumers.

ZAGAT

Based on the principle of organized word of mouth, husband and wife team Tim and Nina Zagat have recruited thousands of reviewers to rate restaurants in the world's top cities. These surveys were compiled into guidebooks that have sold millions. Now they have expanded their scope to include hotels, resorts, spas, and other services. Zagat's Web site has created an online community of reviewers, who are motivated in part by award prizes for the wittiest comments. Providing content online has actually helped sales of guidebooks offline. The New York guide has remained the number-one book sold in the city (with sales surpassing the Bible).[55]

Through gathering information, the consumer learns about competing brands and their features. The first box in Figure 6.5 shows the *total set* of brands available to the consumer. The individual consumer will come to know only a subset of these brands (*awareness set*). Some brands will meet initial buying criteria (*consideration set*). As the consumer gathers more information, only a few will remain as strong contenders (*choice set*). The consumer makes a final choice from this set.[56]

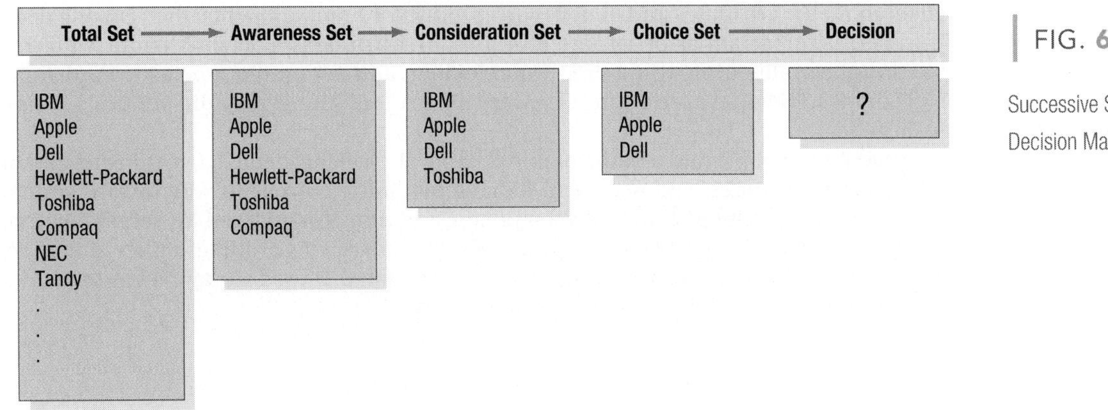

FIG. 6.5

Successive Sets Involved in Consumer Decision Making

Figure 6.5 makes it clear that a company must strategize to get its brand into the prospect's awareness set, consideration set, and choice set. Food companies might work with supermarkets, for instance, in changing the way they display products. If a storeowner arranges yogurt first by brand (like Dannon and Yoplait) and then by flavor within each brand, consumers will tend to select their flavors from the same brand. However, if the products had been displayed with all the strawberry yogurts together, then all the vanilla yogurts and so forth, consumers would probably choose which flavors they wanted first, and then choose which brand name they would most like for that particular flavor. Australian supermarkets arrange meats by the way they might be cooked, and stores use more descriptive labels, like "a 10-minute herbed beef roast." The result is that Australians buy a greater variety of meats than Americans, who choose from meats laid out by animal type—beef, chicken, pork, and so on.[57]

The company must also identify the other brands in the consumer's choice set so that it can plan the appropriate competitive appeals. In addition, the company should identify the consumer's information sources and evaluate their relative importance. Consumers should be asked how they first heard about the brand, what information came later, and the relative importance of the different sources. The answers will help the company prepare effective communications for the target market.

Evaluation of Alternatives

How does the consumer process competitive brand information and make a final value judgment? No single process is used by all consumers or by one consumer in all buying situations. There are several processes, the most current models of which see the process as cognitively oriented. That is, they see the consumer as forming judgments largely on a conscious and rational basis.

Some basic concepts will help us understand consumer evaluation processes: First, the consumer is trying to satisfy a need. Second, the consumer is looking for certain benefits from the product solution. Third, the consumer sees each product as a bundle of attributes with varying abilities for delivering the benefits sought to satisfy this need. The attributes of interest to buyers vary by product—for example:

1. ***Cameras.*** Picture sharpness, camera speeds, camera size, price
2. ***Hotels.*** Location, cleanliness, atmosphere, price
3. ***Mouthwash.*** Color, effectiveness, germ-killing capacity, price, taste/flavor
4. ***Tires.*** Safety, tread life, ride quality, price

Consumers will pay the most attention to attributes that deliver the sought-after benefits. The market for a product can often be segmented according to attributes that are important to different consumer groups.

BELIEFS AND ATTITUDES Evaluations often reflect beliefs and attitudes. Through experience and learning, people acquire beliefs and attitudes. These in turn influence buying behavior. A **belief** is a descriptive thought that a person holds about something. People's beliefs about the attributes and benefits of a product or brand influence their buying decisions. Just as important as beliefs are attitudes. An **attitude** is a person's enduring favorable or unfavorable evaluation, emotional feeling, and action tendencies toward some object or idea.[58] People have attitudes toward almost everything: religion, politics, clothes, music, food.

Attitudes put people into a frame of mind: liking or disliking an object, moving toward or away from it. Attitudes lead people to behave in a fairly consistent way toward similar objects. Because attitudes economize on energy and thought, they can be very difficult to change. A company is well-advised to fit its product into existing attitudes rather than to try to change attitudes. Here is an example of an organization that used ad campaigns to remind consumers of their attitudes, with handsome results:

CALIFORNIA MILK PROCESSOR BOARD

After a 20-year decline in milk consumption among Californians, in 1993 milk processors from across the state formed the California Milk Processor Board (CMPB) with one goal in mind: to get people to drink more milk. The ad agency commissioned by the CMPB developed a novel approach to pitching milk's benefits. Research had shown that most consumers already believed milk was good for them. So the campaign would remind consumers of the inconvenience and annoyance of running out of milk, which became known as "milk deprivation." The "Got Milk?" tagline served to remind consumers to make sure they had milk in their refrigerators. In the year prior to the campaign's launch, California milk processors experienced a decline in sales volume of 1.67 percent. A year after the launch, sales volume increased 1.07 percent. In 1995, the "Got Milk?" campaign was licensed to the National Dairy Board. In 1998, the National Fluid Milk Processor Education Program, which had been using the "milk mustache" campaign since 1994 to boost sales, bought the rights to the "Got Milk?" tagline. The "Got Milk?" campaign continues to pay strong dividends. For 2002 and the first half of 2003, milk sales in California, where the ad campaign is centered, increased roughly 1.5 percent, whereas sales in the rest of the country remained flat.[59]

EXPECTANCY-VALUE MODEL The consumer arrives at attitudes (judgments, preferences) toward various brands through an attribute evaluation procedure.[60] He or she develops a set of beliefs about where each brand stands on each attribute. The **expectancy-value model** of attitude formation posits that consumers evaluate products and services by combining their brand beliefs—the positives and negatives—according to importance.

Suppose Linda Brown has narrowed her choice set to four laptop computers (A, B, C, D). Assume that she is interested in four attributes: memory capacity, graphics capability, size and weight, and price. Table 6.3 shows her beliefs about how each brand rates on the four attributes. If one computer dominated the others on all the criteria, we could predict that Linda would choose it. But, as is often the case, her choice set consists of brands that vary in their appeal. If Linda wants the best memory capacity, she should buy A; if she wants the best graphics capability, she should buy C; and so on.

TABLE 6.3

A Consumer's Brand Beliefs about Computers

Computer	Attribute			
	Memory Capacity	Graphics Capability	Size and Weight	Price
A	10	8	6	4
B	8	9	8	3
C	6	8	10	5
D	4	3	7	8

Note: Each attribute is rated from 0 to 10, where 10 represents the highest level on that attribute. Price, however, is indexed in a reverse manner, with a 10 representing the lowest price, because a consumer prefers a low price to a high price.

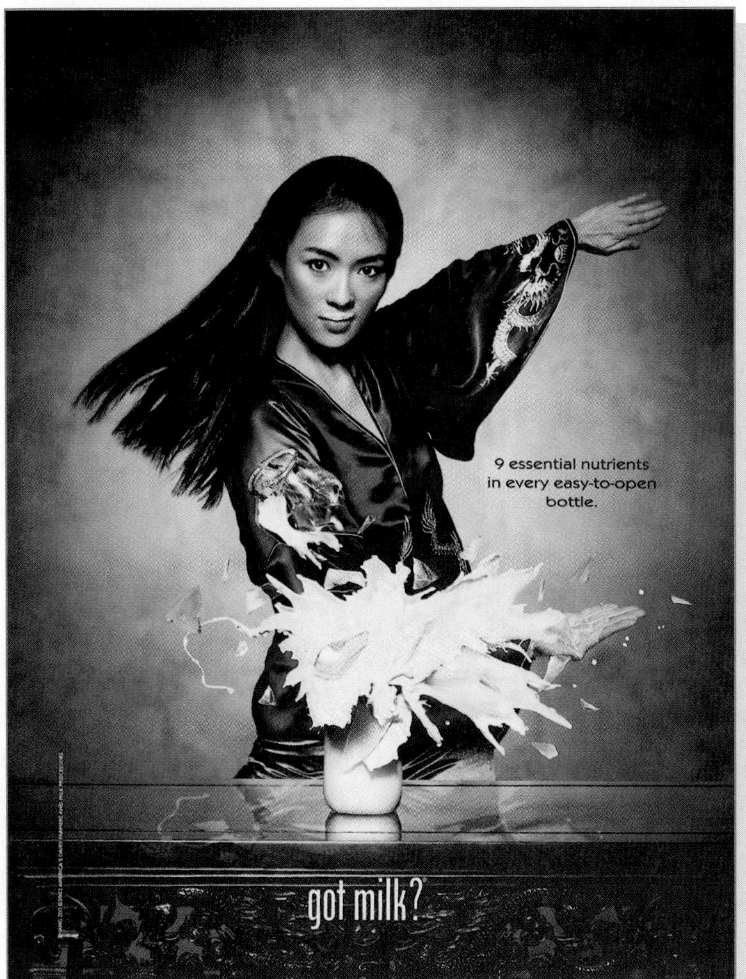

A "Got Milk" ad from the very successful campaign features Hong Kong star Zhang Ziyi from the film "Crouching Tiger, Hidden Dragon."

Most buyers consider several attributes in their purchase decision. If we knew the weights that Linda Brown attaches to the four attributes, we could more reliably predict her computer choice. Suppose Linda assigned 40 percent of the importance to the computer's memory capacity, 30 percent to graphics capability, 20 percent to size and weight, and 10 percent to price. To find Linda's perceived value for each computer, according to the expectancy-value model, we multiply her weights by her beliefs about each computer's attributes. This computation leads to the following perceived values:

$$\text{Computer A} = 0.4(8) + 0.3(9) + 0.2(6) + 0.1(9) = 8.0$$

$$\text{Computer B} = 0.4(7) + 0.3(7) + 0.2(7) + 0.1(7) = 7.0$$

$$\text{Computer C} = 0.4(10) + 0.3(4) + 0.2(3) + 0.1(2) = 6.0$$

$$\text{Computer D} = 0.4(5) + 0.3(3) + 0.2(8) + 0.1(5) = 5.0$$

An expectancy-model formulation would predict that Linda will favor computer A, which (at 8.0) has the highest perceived value.[61]

Suppose most computer buyers form their preferences the same way. Knowing this, a computer manufacturer can do a number of things to influence buyer decisions. The marketer of computer B, for example, could apply the following strategies to stimulate greater interest in brand B:

- ***Redesign the computer.*** This technique is called real repositioning.
- ***Alter beliefs about the brand.*** Attempting to alter beliefs about the brand is called psychological repositioning.
- ***Alter beliefs about competitors' brands.*** This strategy, called competitive depositioning, makes sense when buyers mistakenly believe a competitor's brand has more quality than it actually has.

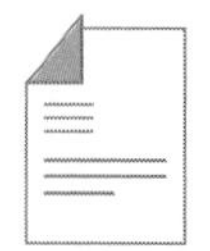

MARKETING MEMO | APPLYING CUSTOMER VALUE ANALYSIS

A useful technique to gain consumer insight is customer value analysis. *Customer value analysis* assumes that customers choose between competitive brand offerings on the basis of which delivers the most customer value. Customer value is given by:

Customer Value = Customer Benefits − Customer Costs

Customer benefits include *product benefits*, *service benefits*, *personnel benefits*, and *image benefits*. Assume customers can judge the relative benefit level or worth of different brands. Suppose a customer is considering three brands, A, B, and C, and judges the customer benefits to be worth $150, $140, and $135, respectively. If the customer costs are the same, the customer would clearly choose brand A.

However, the costs are rarely the same. In addition to *purchase price*, costs include *acquisition costs*, *usage costs*, *maintenance costs*, *ownership costs*, and *disposal costs*. Often a customer will buy a more expensive brand because that particular brand will impose lower costs of other kinds. Consider Table 6.4. A, the highest-priced brand, also involves a lower total cost than lower-priced brands B and C. Clearly, supplier A has done a good job of reducing customers' other costs. Now we can compare the customer value of the three brands:

Customer value of A = $150 − $130 = $20

Customer value of B = $140 − $135 = $5

Customer value of C = $135 − $140 = −$5

The customer will prefer brand A both because the benefit level is higher and because the customer costs are lower, but this does not have to be the case. Suppose A decided to charge $120 instead of $100 to take advantage of its higher perceived benefit level. Then A's customer cost would have been $150 instead of $130 and just offset its higher perceived benefit. Brand A, because of its greed, would lose the sale to brand B.

Very often, managers conduct a **customer value analysis** to reveal the company's strengths and weaknesses relative to various competitors. The major steps in such an analysis are:

TABLE 6.4 | Customer Costs of Three Brands

	A	B	C
Price	$100	$ 90	$ 80
Acquisition costs	15	25	30
Usage costs	4	7	10
Maintenance costs	2	3	7
Ownership costs	3	3	5
Disposal costs	6	5	8
Total Cost	$130	$135	$140

1. ***Identify the major attributes customers value.*** Customers are asked what attributes and performance levels they look for in choosing a product and vendors.
2. ***Assess the quantitative importance of the different attributes.*** Customers are asked to rate the importance of the different attributes. If the customers diverge too much in their ratings, they should be clustered into different segments.
3. ***Assess the company's and competitors' performances on the different customer values against their rated importance.*** Customers describe where they see the company's and competitors' performances on each attribute.
4. ***Examine how customers in a specific segment rate the company's performance against a specific major competitor on an attribute-by-attribute basis.*** If the company's offer exceeds the competitor's offer on all important attributes, the company can charge a higher price (thereby earning higher profits), or it can charge the same price and gain more market share.
5. ***Monitor customer values over time.*** The company must periodically redo its studies of customer values and competitors' standings as the economy, technology, and features change.

- ***Alter the importance weights.*** The marketer could try to persuade buyers to attach more importance to the attributes in which the brand excels.
- ***Call attention to neglected attributes.*** The marketer could draw buyers' attention to neglected attributes, such as styling or processing speed.
- ***Shift the buyer's ideals.*** The marketer could try to persuade buyers to change their ideal levels for one or more attributes.[62]

"Marketing Memo: Applying Customer Value Analysis" describes a cost–benefit technique that provides additional insight into consumer decision making in a competitive setting.

Purchase Decisions

In the evaluation stage, the consumer forms preferences among the brands in the choice set. The consumer may also form an intention to buy the most preferred brand. In executing a purchase intention, the consumer may make up to five sub-decisions: *brand* (brand

A), *dealer* (dealer 2), *quantity* (one computer), *timing* (weekend), and *payment method* (credit card). Purchases of everyday products involve fewer decisions and less deliberation. For example, in buying sugar, a consumer gives little thought to vendor or payment method.

In some cases, consumers may decide not to formally evaluate each and every brand; in other cases, intervening factors may affect the final decision.

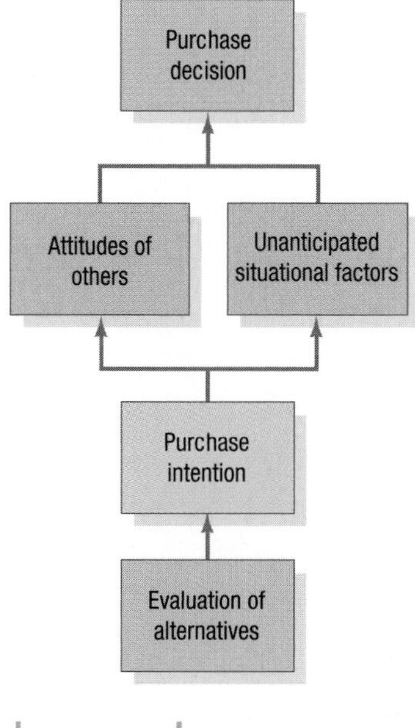

FIG. 6.6

Steps Between Evaluation of Alternatives and a Purchase Decision

NONCOMPENSATORY MODELS OF CONSUMER CHOICE The expectancy-value model is a compensatory model in that perceived good things for a product can help to overcome perceived bad things. But consumers may not want to invest so much time and energy to evaluate brands. They often take "mental shortcuts" that involve various simplifying *choice heuristics.*

With **noncompensatory models** of consumer choice, positive and negative attribute considerations do not necessarily net out. Evaluating attributes more in isolation makes decision making easier for a consumer, but also increases the likelihood that the person would have made a different choice if he or she had deliberated in greater detail. We highlight three such choice heuristics here.

1. With the **conjunctive heuristic**, the consumer sets a minimum acceptable cutoff level for each attribute and chooses the first alternative that meets the minimum standard for all attributes. For example, if Linda Brown decided that all attributes had to be rated at least a 7, she would choose computer B.
2. With the **lexicographic heuristic**, the consumer chooses the best brand on the basis of its perceived most important attribute. With this decision rule, Linda Brown would choose computer C.
3. With the **elimination-by-aspects heuristic**, the consumer compares brands on an attribute selected probabilistically—where the probability of choosing an attribute is positively related to its importance—and brands are eliminated if they do not meet minimum acceptable cutoff levels.

Characteristics of the person (e.g., brand or product knowledge), the purchase decision task and setting (e.g., number and similarity of brand choices and time pressure involved), and social context (e.g., need for justification to a peer or boss) all may affect if and how choice heuristics are used.[63]

Consumers do not necessarily adopt only one type of choice rule in making purchase decisions. In some cases, they adopt a phased decision strategy that combines two or more decision rules. For example, they might use a noncompensatory decision rule such as the conjunctive heuristic to reduce the number of brand choices to a more manageable number and then evaluate the remaining brands. Understanding if and how consumers screen brands can be critical. One reason for the runaway success of the Intel Inside campaign in the 1990s was that it made the brand the first cutoff for many consumers—they would only buy a PC which had an Intel microprocessor. PC makers such as IBM, Dell, and Gateway had no choice but to support Intel's marketing efforts.

INTERVENING FACTORS Even if consumers form brand evaluations, two general factors can intervene between the purchase intention and the purchase decision (Figure 6.6).[64] The first factor is the *attitudes of others.* The extent to which another person's attitude reduces the preference for an alternative depends on two things: (1) the intensity of the other person's negative attitude toward the consumer's preferred alternative and (2) the consumer's motivation to comply with the other person's wishes.[65] The more intense the other person's negativism and the closer the other person is to the consumer, the more the consumer will adjust his or her purchase intention. The converse is also true: A buyer's preference for a brand will increase if someone he or she respects favors the same brand strongly.

Related to the attitudes of others is the role played by infomediaries who publish their evaluations. Examples include *Consumer Reports,* which provides unbiased expert reviews of all types of products and services; J.D. Powers, which provides consumer-based ratings of cars, financial services, and travel products and services; professional movie, book, and music reviewers; customer reviews of books and music on Amazon.com; and the increasing number of chat rooms where people discuss products, services, and companies. Consumers are undoubtedly influenced by these evaluations, as evidenced by the success of a small-budget movie like *My Big Fat Greek Wedding,* which received a slew of favorable reviews by moviegoers on many Web sites.

The second factor is *unanticipated situational factors* that may erupt to change the purchase intention. Linda Brown might lose her job, some other purchase might become more urgent, or a store salesperson may turn her off. Preferences and even purchase intentions are not completely reliable predictors of purchase behavior.

A consumer's decision to modify, postpone, or avoid a purchase decision is heavily influenced by *perceived risk*.[66] There are many different types of risks that consumers may perceive in buying and consuming a product:

1. ***Functional risk*** – the product does not perform up to expectations.
2. ***Physical risk*** – the product poses a threat to the physical well-being or health of the user or others.
3. ***Financial risk*** – the product is not worth the price paid.
4. ***Social risk*** – the product results in embarrassment from others.
5. ***Psychological risk*** – the product affects the mental well-being of the user.
6. ***Time risk*** – the failure of the product results in an opportunity cost of finding another satisfactory product.

The amount of perceived risk varies with the amount of money at stake, the amount of attribute uncertainty, and the amount of consumer self-confidence. Consumers develop routines for reducing risk, such as decision avoidance, information gathering from friends, and preference for national brand names and warranties. Marketers must understand the factors that provoke a feeling of risk in consumers and provide information and support to reduce perceived risk.

Postpurchase Behavior

After the purchase, the consumer might experience dissonance that stems from noticing certain disquieting features or hearing favorable things about other brands, and will be alert to information that supports his or her decision. Marketing communications should supply beliefs and evaluations that reinforce the consumer's choice and help him or her feel good about the brand.

The marketer's job therefore does not end with the purchase. Marketers must monitor postpurchase satisfaction, postpurchase actions, and postpurchase product uses.

POSTPURCHASE SATISFACTION What determines customer satisfaction with a purchase? Satisfaction is a function of the closeness between expectations and the product's perceived performance.[67] If performance falls short of expectations, the consumer is *disappointed;* if it meets expectations, the consumer is *satisfied;* if it exceeds expectations, the consumer is *delighted.* These feelings make a difference in whether the customer buys the product again and talks favorably or unfavorably about it to others.

Consumers form their expectations on the basis of messages received from sellers, friends, and other information sources. The larger the gap between expectations and performance, the greater the dissatisfaction. Here the consumer's coping style comes into play. Some consumers magnify the gap when the product is not perfect, and they are highly dissatisfied; others minimize the gap and are less dissatisfied.[68]

The importance of postpurchase satisfaction suggests that product claims must truthfully represent the product's likely performance. Some sellers might even understate performance levels so that consumers experience higher-than-expected satisfaction with the product.

POSTPURCHASE ACTIONS Satisfaction or dissatisfaction with the product will influence subsequent behavior. If the consumer is satisfied, he or she will exhibit a higher probability of purchasing the product again. For example, data on automobile brand choice show a high correlation between being highly satisfied with the last brand bought and intention to buy the brand again. One survey showed that 75 percent of Toyota buyers were highly satisfied and about 75 percent intended to buy a Toyota again; 35 percent of Chevrolet buyers were highly satisfied and about 35 percent intended to buy a Chevrolet again. The satisfied customer will also tend to say good things about the brand to others. Marketers say: "Our best advertisement is a satisfied customer."[69]

Dissatisfied consumers may abandon or return the product. They may seek information that confirms its high value. They may take public action by complaining to the company, going to a lawyer, or complaining to other groups (such as business, private, or government

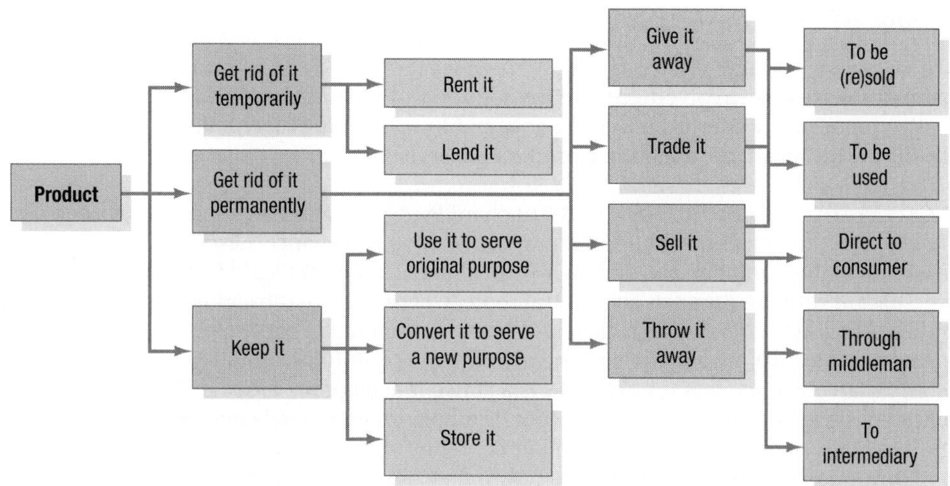

FIG. 6.7

How Customers Use or Dispose of Products

Source: From Jacob Jacoby, Carol K. Berning, and Thomas F. Dietvorst, "What about Disposition?" *Journal of Marketing* (July 1977): 23. Reprinted with permission of the American Marketing Association.

agencies). Private actions include making a decision to stop buying the product (*exit option*) or warning friends (*voice option*).[70] In all these cases, the seller has done a poor job of satisfying the customer.[71]

Chapter 5 described CRM programs designed to build long-term brand loyalty. Postpurchase communications to buyers have been shown to result in fewer product returns and order cancellations.[72] Computer companies, for example, can send a letter to new owners congratulating them on having selected a fine computer. They can place ads showing satisfied brand owners. They can solicit customer suggestions for improvements and list the location of available services. They can write intelligible instruction booklets. They can send owners a magazine containing articles describing new computer applications. In addition, they can provide good channels for speedy redress of customer grievances.

POSTPURCHASE USE AND DISPOSAL Marketers should also monitor how buyers use and dispose of the product (Figure 6.7). A key driver of sales frequency is product consumption rate—the more quickly buyers consume a product, the sooner they may be back in the market to repurchase it.

One potential opportunity to increase frequency of product use is when consumers' perceptions of their usage differ from the reality. Consumers may fail to replace products with relatively short life spans in a timely manner because of a tendency to underestimate product life.[73] One strategy to speed up replacement is to tie the act of replacing the product to a certain holiday, event, or time of year.

For example, several brands have run promotions tied in with the springtime switch to daylight savings time (e.g., Oral-B toothbrushes). Another strategy might be to provide consumers with better information as to either: (1) when the product was first used or would need to be replaced or (2) the current level of performance. For example, batteries offer built-in gauges that show how much power they have left; toothbrushes have color indicators on their bristles to indicate when they are too worn; and so on. Perhaps the simplest way to increase usage is when actual usage of a product is less than optimal or recommended. In this case, consumers must be persuaded of the merits of more regular usage, and potential hurdles to increased usage must be overcome.

If consumers throw the product away, the marketer needs to know how they dispose of it, especially if it can damage the environment (as in the case with batteries, beverage containers, and disposable diapers). Increased public awareness of recycling and ecological concerns as well as consumer complaints about having to throw away beautiful bottles led French perfume maker Rochas to think about introducing a refillable fragrance line.

::: Other Theories of Consumer Decision Making

The consumer decision process may not always develop in a carefully planned fashion. It is important to understand other theories and approaches to how consumers make decisions and when they might apply.

Level of Consumer Involvement

The expectancy-value model assumes a high level of involvement on the part of the consumer. **Consumer involvement** can be defined in terms of the level of engagement and active processing undertaken by the consumer in responding to a marketing stimulus (e.g., from viewing an ad or evaluating a product or service).

ELABORATION LIKELIHOOD MODEL Richard Petty and John Cacioppo's *elaboration likelihood model,* an influential model of attitude formation and change, describes how consumers make evaluations in both low- and high-involvement circumstances.[74] There are two means of persuasion with their model: The central route, where attitude formation or change involves much thought and is based on a diligent, rational consideration of the most important product or service information; and the peripheral route, where attitude formation or change involves comparatively much less thought and is a consequence of the association of a brand with either positive or negative peripheral cues. Examples of peripheral cues for consumers might be a celebrity endorsement, a credible source, or any object that engendered positive feelings.

Consumers follow the central route only if they possess sufficient *motivation, ability,* and *opportunity.* In other words, consumers must want to evaluate a brand in detail, must have the necessary brand and product or service knowledge in memory, and must be given sufficient time and the proper setting to actually do so. If any one of those three factors is lacking, consumers will tend to follow the peripheral route and consider less central, more extrinsic factors in their decisions.

LOW-INVOLVEMENT MARKETING STRATEGIES Many products are bought under conditions of low involvement and the absence of significant brand differences. Consider salt. Consumers have little involvement in this product category. They go to the store and reach for the brand. If they keep reaching for the same brand, it is out of habit, not strong brand loyalty. There is good evidence that consumers have low involvement with most low-cost, frequently purchased products.

Marketers use four techniques to try to convert a low-involvement product into one of higher involvement. First, they can link the product to some involving issue, as when Crest toothpaste is linked to avoiding cavities. Second, they can link the product to some involving personal situation—for example, fruit juice makers began to include vitamins such as calcium to fortify their drinks. Third, they might design advertising to trigger strong emotions related to personal values or ego defense, as when cereal makers began to advertise the heart-healthy nature of cereals to adults and the importance of living a long time to enjoy family life. Fourth, they might add an important feature—for example, when GE light bulbs introduced "Soft White" versions. These strategies at best raise consumer involvement from a low to a moderate level; they do not necessarily propel the consumer into highly involved buying behavior.

If, regardless of what the marketer can do, consumers will have low involvement with a purchase decision, they are likely to follow the peripheral route. Marketers must pay special attention to giving consumers one or more positive cues that they can use to justify their brand choice. Brand familiarity can be important if consumers decide to just buy the brand about which they have heard or seen the most. Frequent ad repetition, visible sponsorships, and vigorous PR are all ways to enhance brand familiarity. Other peripheral cues can also be used. A beloved celebrity endorser, attractive packaging, or an appealing promotion all might tip the balance in favor of the brand.[75]

VARIETY-SEEKING BUYING BEHAVIOR Some buying situations are characterized by low involvement but significant brand differences. Here consumers often do a lot of brand switching. Think about cookies. The consumer has some beliefs about cookies, chooses a brand of cookies without much evaluation, and evaluates the product during consumption. Next time, the consumer may reach for another brand out of a wish for a different taste. Brand switching occurs for the sake of variety rather than dissatisfaction.

The market leader and the minor brands in this product category have different marketing strategies. The market leader will try to encourage habitual buying behavior by dominating the shelf space with a variety of related but different product versions, avoiding out-of-stock conditions, and sponsoring frequent reminder advertising. Challenger firms will encourage variety seeking by offering lower prices, deals, coupons, free samples, and advertising that tries to break the consumer's purchase and consumption cycle and presents reasons for trying something new.

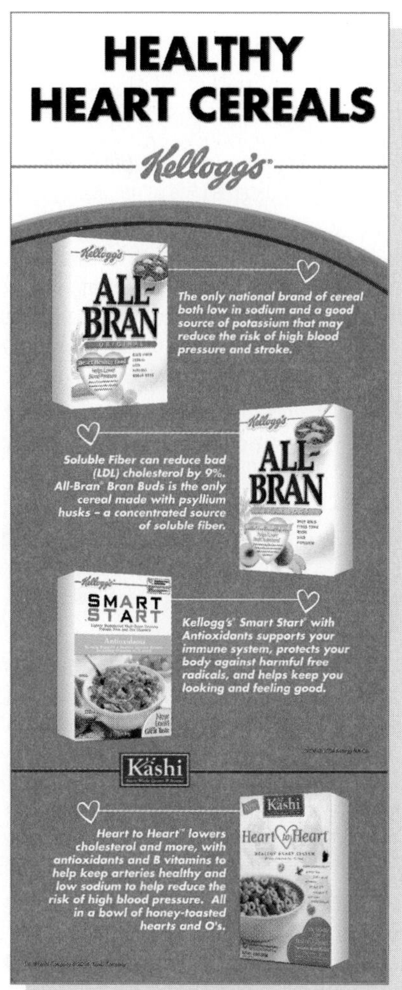

Converting a low-involvement product to a higher-involvement product: Kellogg's now advertises its products as "healthy heart cereals" to make consumers aware that which cereal you eat matters.

Decision Heuristics and Biases

As the low-involvement and noncompensatory model discussions suggest, consumers do not always process information or make decisions in a deliberate, rational manner. Behavioral decision theory is a thriving area in consumer research. Behavioral decision theorists have identified many different heuristics and biases in everyday consumer decision making. **Heuristics** are rules of thumb or mental shortcuts in the decision process.

Heuristics can come into play when consumers forecast the likelihood of future outcomes or events.[76]

1. The **availability heuristic**: Consumers base their predictions on the quickness and ease with which a particular example of an outcome comes to mind. If an example comes to mind too easily, consumers might overestimate the likelihood of the outcome or event happening. For example, a recent product failure may lead a consumer to inflate the likelihood of a future product failure and make him or her more inclined to purchase a product warranty.
2. The **representativeness heuristic**: Consumers base their predictions on how representative or similar the outcome is to other examples. One reason that package appearances may be so similar for different brands in the same product category is that they want to be seen as representative of the category as a whole.
3. The **anchoring and adjustment heuristic**: Consumers arrive at an initial judgment and then make adjustments of that first impression based on additional information. For services marketers, it is critical to make a strong first impression to establish a favorable anchor so that subsequent experiences are interpreted in a more favorable light.

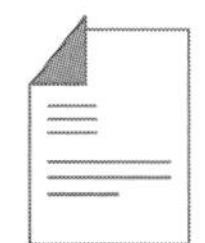

MARKETING MEMO | DECISION TRAPS

In *Decision Traps,* Jay Russo and Paul Schoemaker reveal the 10 most common mistakes managers make in their decisions.

1. ***Plunging In***—Beginning to gather information and reach conclusions without taking a few minutes to think about the crux of the issue you're facing or to think through how you believe decisions like this one should be made.
2. ***Frame Blindness***—Setting out to solve the wrong problem because you've created a mental framework for your decision, with little thought, that causes you to overlook the best options or lose sight of important objectives.
3. ***Lack of Frame Control***—Failing to consciously define the problem in more ways than one or being unduly influenced by the frames of others.
4. ***Overconfidence in Your Judgment***—Failing to collect key factual information because you are too sure of your assumptions and opinions.
5. ***Shortsighted Shortcuts***—Relying inappropriately on "rules of thumb" such as implicitly trusting the most readily available information or anchoring too much on convenient facts.
6. ***Shooting from the Hip***—Believing you can keep straight in your head all the information you've discovered, and therefore "winging it" rather than following a systematic procedure when making the final choice.
7. ***Group Failure***—Assuming that with many smart people involved, good choices will follow automatically, and therefore failing to manage the group decision-making process.
8. ***Fooling Yourself About Feedback***—Failing to interpret the evidence from past outcomes for what it really says, either because you are protecting your ego or because you are tricked by hindsight effects.
9. ***Not Keeping Track***—Assuming that experience will make its lessons available automatically, and therefore failing to keep systematic records to track the results of your decisions and failing to analyze these results in ways that reveal their key lessons.
10. ***Failure to Audit Your Decision Process***—Failing to create an organized approach to understanding your own decision making, so you remain constantly exposed to all the other nine decision traps.

Sources: J. Edward Russo and Paul J. H. Schoemaker, *Decision Traps: Ten Barriers to Brilliant Decision-Making and How to Overcome Them* (New York: Doubleday, 1990); see also, J. Edward Russo and Paul J. H. Schoemaker, *Winning Decisions: Getting It Right the First Time* (New York: Doubleday, 2001).

Note that marketing managers also may use heuristics and be subject to biases in their decision making. "Marketing Memo: Decision Traps" reveals 10 common mistakes managers make in their decisions.

Mental Accounting

Researchers have found that consumers use mental accounting when they handle their money.[77] **Mental accounting** refers to the manner by which consumers code, categorize, and evaluate financial outcomes of choices. Formally, it has been defined in terms of, "The tendency to categorize *funds* or items of value even though there is no logical *basis* for the categorization, e.g., individuals often segregate their savings into separate accounts to meet different goals even though funds from any of the accounts can be applied to any of the goals."[78]

For example, assume you spend $50 to buy a ticket to see a concert.[79] As you arrive at the show, you realize you've lost your ticket. You may be unsure about purchasing another ticket for $50. Assume, on the other hand, that you realized you had lost $50 on the way to buy the ticket. You might be much more likely to go ahead and buy the ticket anyway. Although the amount lost in each case was the same—$50—the reactions were very different. In the first case, you may have mentally allocated $50 for going to a concert. Buying another ticket would therefore exceed your mental concert budget. In the second case, the money that was lost did not belong to any account, so the mental concert budget had not yet been exceeded.

According to Chicago's Richard Thaler, mental accounting is based on a set of key core principles:

1. Consumers tend to *segregate gains.* When a seller has a product with more than one positive dimension, it is desirable to have each dimension evaluated separately. Listing multiple benefits of a large industrial product, for example, can make the sum of the parts seem greater than the whole.
2. Consumers tend to *integrate losses.* Marketers have a distinct advantage in selling something if its cost can be added to another large purchase. House buyers are more inclined to view additional expenditures favorably given the high price of buying a house.
3. Consumers tend to *integrate smaller losses with larger gains.* The "cancellation" principle might explain why withholding taxes taken from monthly paychecks are less aversive

than large, lump-sum tax payments—they are more likely to be absorbed by the larger pay amount.

4. Consumers tend to *segregate small gains from large losses.* The "silver lining" principle might explain the popularity of rebates on big-ticket purchases such as cars.

The principles of mental accounting are derived in part from prospect theory. **Prospect theory** maintains that consumers frame decision alternatives in terms of gains and losses according to a value function. Consumers are generally loss averse. They tend to overweight very low probabilities and underweight very high probabilities.

Profiling the Customer Buying Decision Process

How can marketers learn about the stages in the buying process for their product? They can think about how they themselves would act (*introspective method*). They can interview a small number of recent purchasers, asking them to recall the events leading to their purchase (*retrospective method*). They can locate consumers who plan to buy the product and ask them to think out loud about going through the buying process (*prospective method*); or they can ask consumers to describe the ideal way to buy the product (*prescriptive method*). Each method yields a picture of the steps in the process.

Trying to understand the customer's behavior in connection with a product has been called mapping the customer's *consumption system,*[80] *customer activity cycle,*[81] or *customer scenario.*[82] This can be done for such activity clusters as doing laundry, preparing for a wedding, or buying a car. Buying a car, for example, involves a whole cluster of activities, including choosing the car, financing the purchase, buying insurance, buying accessories, and so on.

SUMMARY :::

1. Consumer behavior is influenced by three factors: cultural (culture, subculture, and social class); social (reference groups, family, and social roles and statuses); and personal (age, stage in the life cycle, occupation, economic circumstances, lifestyle, personality, and self-concept). Research into all these factors can provide marketers with clues to reach and serve consumers more effectively.
2. Four main psychological processes affect consumer behavior: motivation, perception, learning, and memory.
3. To understand how consumers actually make buying decisions, marketers must identify who makes and has input into the buying decision; people can be initiators, influencers, deciders, buyers, or users. Different marketing campaigns might be targeted to each type of person.
4. The typical buying process consists of the following sequence of events: problem recognition, information search, evaluation of alternatives, purchase decision, and postpurchase behavior. The marketers' job is to understand the behavior at each stage. The attitudes of others, unanticipated situational factors, and perceived risk may all affect the decision to buy, as will consumers' levels of postpurchase satisfaction and postpurchase actions on the part of the company.

APPLICATIONS :::

Marketing Debate Is Target Marketing Ever Bad?

As marketers increasingly develop marketing programs tailored to certain target market segments, some critics have denounced these efforts as exploitative. For example, the preponderance of billboards advertising cigarettes, alcohol, and other vices in low-income urban areas is seen as taking advantage of a vulnerable market segment. Critics can be especially harsh in evaluating marketing programs that target African Americans and other minority groups, claiming that they often employ clichéd stereotypes and inappropriate depictions. Others counter with the point of view that targeting and positioning is critical to marketing and that these marketing programs are an attempt to be relevant to a certain consumer group.

Take a position: Targeting minorities is exploitative versus Targeting minorities is a sound business practice.

Marketing Discussion What Are Your Mental Accounts?

What mental accounts do you have in your mind about purchasing products or services? Do you have any rules you employ in spending money? Are they different from what other people do? Do you follow Thaler's four principles in reacting to gains and losses?

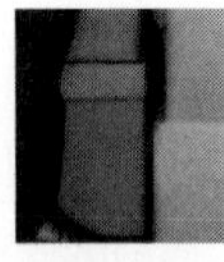

IN THIS CHAPTER, WE WILL ADDRESS THE FOLLOWING QUESTIONS:

1. What is the business market, and how does it differ from the consumer market?
2. What buying situations do organizational buyers face?
3. Who participates in the business-to-business buying process?
4. How do business buyers make their decisions?
5. How can companies build strong relationships with business customers?
6. How do institutional buyers and government agencies do their buying?

What if you're onto something big, but aren't big yet? Start with SAP® solutions for small and midsize companie Solutions designed to fit any size business – and any size budget. And because they're built with expansion in mind, they won't just help you grow, they will grow with you. Visit sap.com/ideas or call 800 880 1727, because we have a few big ideas of our own.

CHAPTER 7 ::: ANALYZING BUSINESS MARKETS

seven

Business organizations do not only sell; they also buy vast quantities of raw materials, manufactured components, plant and equipment, supplies, and business services. There are over 13 million buying organizations in the United States alone. To create and capture value, sellers need to understand these organizations' needs, resources, policies, and buying procedures.

German software company SAP has become a leading seller to the business market by specializing in software to automate business functions, such as finance and factory management. It owns over half the market. SAP's leadership strategy is to focus carefully on what customers want, and show them how SAP's software applications can improve profits, raise revenue, or reduce costs. Partly through acquisitions, SAP offers IT customers one-stop shopping to standardize business processes.[1]

Some of the world's most valuable brands belong to business marketers: ABB, Caterpillar, DuPont, FedEx, GE, Hewlett-Packard, IBM, Intel, and Siemens. Much of basic marketing also applies to business marketers. They need to embrace holistic marketing principles, such as building strong relationships with their customers, just like any marketer. But there are some unique considerations in selling to other businesses.[2] In this chapter, we will highlight some of the crucial differences for marketing in business markets.

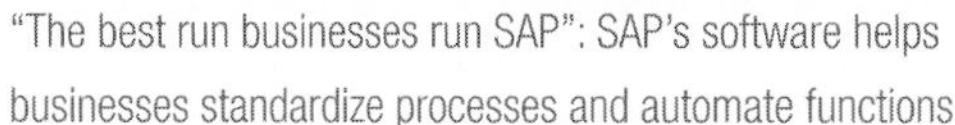
"The best run businesses run SAP": SAP's software helps businesses standardize processes and automate functions.

::: What Is Organizational Buying?

Webster and Wind define **organizational buying** as the decision-making process by which formal organizations establish the need for purchased products and services and identify, evaluate, and choose among alternative brands and suppliers.[3]

The Business Market Versus the Consumer Market

The **business market** consists of all the organizations that acquire goods and services used in the production of other products or services that are sold, rented, or supplied to others. The major industries making up the business market are agriculture, forestry, and fisheries; mining; manufacturing; construction; transportation; communication; public utilities; banking, finance, and insurance; distribution; and services.

More dollars and items are involved in sales to business buyers than to consumers. Consider the process of producing and selling a simple pair of shoes. Hide dealers must sell hides to tanners, who sell leather to shoe manufacturers, who sell shoes to wholesalers, who sell shoes to retailers, who finally sell them to consumers. Each party in the supply chain also has to buy many other goods and services.

Business markets have several characteristics that contrast sharply with those of consumer markets:

- ***Fewer, larger buyers.*** The business marketer normally deals with far fewer, much larger buyers than the consumer marketer does. The fate of Goodyear Tire Company and other

MARKETING INSIGHT | BIG SALES TO SMALL BUSINESS

Like millions of Americans, Ken Kantor likes to shop on eBay. However, he isn't looking for collectible Barbies, Batman cards, or gently used roller blades. Co-owner of a small audio design company, Intelligent Audio Systems, Kantor bids on business equipment, and he was pleased as punch to purchase some nearly new testing meters for $100 each, which would have easily gone for $4,700 retail.

Business owners like Kantor represent not only a sweet spot for eBay but also for behemoths such as IBM, American Express, and Microsoft. According to the Small Business Administration's Office of Advocacy, 550,000 small businesses opened in the United States in 2002. Those new ventures need capital equipment, technology, supplies, and services. Look beyond the United States to new ventures around the world and you have a huge new B2B growth market. Here's how some companies are reaching it:

- With its new suite of run-your-business software, **Microsoft** is counting on sales to 45 million small to midsize businesses worldwide to add $10 billion to annual revenue by 2010. Yet even with all its cash, Microsoft can't afford to send reps to all of them. Instead, Microsoft is unleashing an army of independent computer consulting companies—24,000 in all—known as value-added resellers. It has also added 300 sales managers to help educate and support both resellers and customers.
- **IBM** counts small to midsize businesses as 20 percent of its business and has launched Express, a line of hardware, software services, and financing, for this market. IBM sells through regional reps as well as independent software vendors and resellers, and it supports its small-midsize push with millions of dollars in advertising annually. Ads include TV spots and print ads in publications such as *American Banker* and *Inc.* The company also directly targets gay business owners with ads in *The Advocate* and *Out.* To reach other minority segments, such as African Americans and Hispanics, IBM partners with nonprofits.
- **American Express** has been steadily adding new features to its credit card for small business, which some small companies use to cover hundreds of thousands of dollars a month in cash needs. In addition to its credit card, American Express has been expanding its leading operations for small business. It has created a small business network called OPEN (www.openamericanexpress.com) to bring together various services, Web tools, and discount programs with other giants like ExxonMobil, Dell, FedEx, and Staples. With OPEN, American Express not only allows customers to save money on common expenses; it also encourages them to do much of their recordkeeping on its Web site.

Yet while small to midsize businesses present a huge opportunity, they also present huge challenges. The market is large and fragmented by industry, size, and number of years in operation. And once you reach them, it's hard to persuade them to buy. Small business owners are notably averse to long-range planning and have an "I'll buy it when I need it" decision-making style. Fortunately, however, those new to this market can tap into the growing body of experience from the likes of IBM, Microsoft, Hewlett-Packard, American Express, and others who have honed their small business marketing strategies.

Sources: Based on Barnaby J. Feder, "When Goliath Comes Knocking on David's Door," *New York Times,* May 6, 2003, p. G13; Jay Greene, "Small Biz: Microsoft's Next Big Thing?" *BusinessWeek,* April 21, 2003, pp. 72–73; Jennifer Gilbert, "Small but Mighty," *Sales& Marketing Management* (January 2004): 30–35; Verne Kopytoff, "Businesses Click on eBay," *San Francisco Chronicle,* July 28, 2003, p. E1; Matt Krantz, "Firms Jump on the eBay Wagon," *USA Today,* May 3, 2004, pp. 1B, 2B.

automotive part suppliers depends on getting contracts from a few major automakers. A few large buyers do most of the purchasing in such industries as aircraft engines and defense weapons. Although it should be noted that as a slowing economy has put a stranglehold on large corporations' purchasing departments, the small and midsize business market is offering new opportunities for suppliers.[4] See "Marketing Insight: Big Sales to Small Business," for more on this promising new B2B market, and see "Marketing Memo: Guidelines for Selling to Small Business" for some "do's and don'ts."

- ***Close supplier–customer relationship.*** Because of the smaller customer base and the importance and power of the larger customers, suppliers are frequently expected to customize their offerings to individual business customer needs. Business buyers often select suppliers who also buy from them. An example would be a paper manufacturer that buys chemicals from a chemical company that buys a considerable amount of its paper.

- ***Professional purchasing.*** Business goods are often purchased by trained purchasing agents, who must follow their organizations' purchasing policies, constraints, and requirements. Many of the buying instruments—for example, requests for quotations, proposals, and purchase contracts—are not typically found in consumer buying. Professional buyers spend their careers learning how to buy better. Many belong to the National Association of Purchasing Managers (NAPM), which seeks to improve professional buyers' effectiveness and status. This means that business marketers have to provide greater technical data about their product and its advantages over competitors' products.

- ***Several buying influences.*** More people typically influence business buying decisions. Buying committees consisting of technical experts and even senior management are common in the purchase of major goods. Business marketers have to send well-trained sales representatives and sales teams to deal with the well-trained buyers.

- ***Multiple sales calls.*** Because more people are involved in the selling process, it takes multiple sales calls to win most business orders, and some sales cycles can take years. A study by McGraw-Hill found that it takes four to four and a half calls to close an average industrial sale. In the case of capital equipment sales for large projects, it may take multiple attempts to fund a project, and the sales cycle—between quoting a job and delivering the product—is often measured in years.[5]

- ***Derived demand.*** The demand for business goods is ultimately derived from the demand for consumer goods. For this reason, the business marketer must closely monitor the buying patterns of ultimate consumers. For instance, the Big Three automakers in Detroit have been driving the boom in demand for steel-bar products. Much of that demand is derived from consumers' continued love affair with minivans and other light trucks, which consume far more steel than cars. Business buyers must also pay close attention to current and expected economic factors, such as the level of production, investment, consumer spending, and the interest rate. In a recession, business buyers reduce their investment in plant, equipment, and inventories. Business marketers can do little to stimulate total demand in this environment. They can only fight harder to increase or maintain their share of demand.

- ***Inelastic demand.*** The total demand for many business goods and services is inelastic—that is, not much affected by price changes. Shoe manufacturers are not going to buy much more leather if the price of leather falls, nor will they buy much less leather if the price rises, unless they can find satisfactory substitutes. Demand is especially inelastic in the short run because producers cannot make quick changes in production methods. Demand is also inelastic for business goods that represent a small percentage of the item's total cost, such as shoelaces.

- ***Fluctuating demand.*** The demand for business goods and services tends to be more volatile than the demand for consumer goods and services. A given percentage increase in consumer demand can lead to a much larger percentage increase in the demand for plant and equipment necessary to produce the additional output. Economists refer to this as the *acceleration effect.* Sometimes a rise of only 10 percent in consumer demand can cause as much as a 200 percent rise in business demand for products in the next period; a 10 percent fall in consumer demand may cause a complete collapse in business demand.

- ***Geographically concentrated buyers.*** More than half of U.S. business buyers are concentrated in seven states: New York, California, Pennsylvania, Illinois, Ohio, New Jersey, and Michigan. The geographical concentration of producers helps to reduce selling costs. At the same time, business marketers need to monitor regional shifts of certain industries.

- ***Direct purchasing.*** Business buyers often buy directly from manufacturers rather than through intermediaries, especially items that are technically complex or expensive (such as mainframes or aircraft).

Buying Situations

The business buyer faces many decisions in making a purchase. The number of decisions depends on the buying situation: complexity of the problem being solved, newness of the buying requirement, number of people involved, and time required. Patrick Robinson and others distinguish three types of buying situations: the straight rebuy, modified rebuy, and new task.[6]

STRAIGHT REBUY The purchasing department reorders on a routine basis (e.g., office supplies, bulk chemicals) and chooses from suppliers on an "approved list." The suppliers make an effort to maintain product and service quality and often propose automatic reordering systems to save time. "Out-suppliers" attempt to offer something new or to exploit dissatisfaction with a current supplier. Out-suppliers try to get a small order and then enlarge their purchase share over time.

MODIFIED REBUY The buyer wants to modify product specifications, prices, delivery requirements, or other terms. The modified rebuy usually involves additional participants on both sides. The in-suppliers become nervous and have to protect the account. The out-suppliers see an opportunity to propose a better offer to gain some business.

NEW TASK A purchaser buys a product or service for the first time (e.g., office building, new security system). The greater the cost or risk, the larger the number of participants and the greater their information gathering—and therefore the longer the time to a decision.[7]

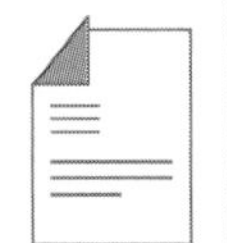

MARKETING MEMO | GUIDELINES FOR SELLING TO SMALL BUSINESS

- ***Don't lump small and midsize businesses together.*** There's a big gap between $1 million in revenue and $50 million or between a start-up with 10 employees and a more mature business with 100. IBM customizes its small and midsize business portal (www-ibm.com/businesscenter/us) with call-me or text-chat buttons that are connected to products for different market segments.
- ***Don't waste their time.*** That means no cold calls, entertaining sales shows, or sales pitches over long, boozy lunches.
- ***Do keep it simple.*** This could be a corollary to "don't waste their time." Simplicity means one point of contact with a supplier for all service problems or one single bill for all services and products. AT&T corporation, which serves 3.9 million businesses with fewer than 100 employees, bundles data management, networking, and other abilities into convenient single packages for this market.
- ***Do use the Internet.*** In its research on buying patterns of small business owners, Hewlett-Packard found that these time-strapped decision makers prefer to buy, or at least research, products and services online. To that end, HP has designed a site targeted to small and midsize businesses and pulls business owners to the site through extensive advertising, direct mail, e-mail campaigns, catalogs, and events. IBM prospects via eBay by selling refurbished or phased-out equipment on its new B2B site. About 80 percent of IBM's equipment is sold to small businesses that are new to IBM—half of which have agreed to receive calls with other offers.
- ***Don't forget about direct contact.*** Even if a small business owner's first point of contact is via the Internet, you still need to offer phone or face time. Sprint connects with small businesses through its Sprint Experience Centers. Located in major metropolitan areas, these centers bring Sprint's products to life and serve as a place where Sprint reps or dealer reps can invite prospects and let them interact with the technologies.
- ***Do provide support after the sale.*** Small businesses want partners, not pitchmen. When The DeWitt Company, a 100-employee landscaping products business, purchased a large piece of machinery from Moeller, a German company, the company's president paid DeWitt's CEO a personal visit and stayed until the machine was up and running properly.
- ***Do your homework.*** The realities of small or midsize business management are different from those of a large corporation. Microsoft created a small, fictional executive research firm, Southridge, and baseball-style trading cards of its key decision makers in order to help Microsoft employees tie sales strategies to small business realities.

Sources: Based on Barnaby J. Feder, "When Goliath Comes Knocking on David's Door," *New York Times,* May 6, 2003, p. G13; Jay Greene, "Small Biz: Microsoft's Next Big Thing?" *BusinessWeek,* April 21, 2003, pp. 72–73; Jennifer Gilbert, "Small but Mighty," *Sales& Marketing Management* (January 2004): 30–35; Verne Kopytoff, "Businesses Click on eBay," *San Francisco Chronicle,* July 28, 2003, p. E1.

The business buyer makes the fewest decisions in the straight rebuy situation and the most in the new-task situation. Over time, new-buy situations become straight rebuys and routine purchase behavior. New-task buying passes through several stages: awareness, interest, evaluation, trial, and adoption.[8] The effectiveness of communication tools varies at each stage. Mass media are most important during the initial awareness stage; salespeople have their greatest impact at the interest stage; and technical sources are the most important during the evaluation stage.

In the new-task situation, the buyer has to determine product specifications, price limits, delivery terms and times, service terms, payment terms, order quantities, acceptable suppliers, and the selected supplier. Different participants influence each decision, and the order in which these decisions are made varies. This situation is the marketer's greatest opportunity and challenge. Because of the complicated selling involved, many companies use a *missionary sales force* consisting of their most effective salespeople. The brand promise and the manufacturer's brand name recognition will be important in establishing trust and the customer's willingness to consider change. The marketer also tries to reach as many key participants as possible and provide helpful information and assistance.

Once a customer is acquired, in-suppliers are continually seeking ways to add value to their market offer to facilitate rebuys. Often they do this by giving customers customized information:

ORICA LTD.

Orica Ltd., formerly ICI Australia, competes in the cutthroat commercial explosives business. Its customers are quarries that use explosives to blast solid rock face into aggregate of a specified size. Orica is constantly trying to minimize the cost of explosives. As a supplier, Orica realized it could create significant value by improving the efficiency of the blast. To do this, it established over 20 parameters that influenced the success of the blast and began collecting data from customers on the input parameters as well as the outcomes of individual blasts. By collating the data, Orica engineers came to understand the conditions that produced different outcomes. It then could offer customers a contract for "broken rock" that would almost guarantee the desired outcome. The success of Orica's approach—of managing the entire blast for the quarry rather than simply selling explosives—entrenched the company as the world's leading supplier of commercial explosives.[9]

Customers considering dropping six or seven figures on one transaction for big-ticket goods and services want all the information they can get. One way to entice new buyers is to create a customer reference program in which satisfied existing customers act in concert with the company's sales and marketing department by agreeing to serve as references. Companies that have such programs are Siebel Systems, J.D. Edwards, and Sun Microsystems:

J.D. EDWARDS

Denver-based software developer J.D. Edwards invites customers with a story that's "relevant to new customers" to join its reference program and specify the level at which they would like to participate. Customers might agree to take phone calls from potential customers, host a site visit, or simply lend their names or blurbs to press releases and other copy. J.D. Edwards' corporate communications director says that hearing other customers' stories is crucial for prospective buyers. The company evaluates the benefit of those customer references by tracking sales generated in the earlier stages of the prospect's contact with the program. For a seven-month period in 2002–2003, the reference program helped generate more than $35 million in software licensing fees.

Systems Buying and Selling

Many business buyers prefer to buy a total solution to a problem from one seller. Called *systems buying,* this practice originated with government purchases of major weapons and communications systems. The government would solicit bids from *prime contractors,* who assembled the package or system. The contractor who was awarded the contract would be responsible for bidding out and assembling the system's subcomponents from *second-tier contractors.* The prime contractor would thus provide a turnkey solution, so-called because the buyer simply had to turn one key to get the job done.

FORD

Ford has transformed itself from being mainly a car manufacturer to being mainly a car assembler. Ford relies primarily on a few major systems suppliers to provide seating systems, braking systems, door systems, and other major assemblies. In designing a new automobile, Ford works closely with (say) its seat manufacturer and creates a *black box specification* of the basic seat dimensions and performance that it needs, and then waits for the seat supplier to propose the most cost-effective design. When they agree, the seat supplier subcontracts with parts suppliers to produce and deliver the needed components.

Sellers have increasingly recognized that buyers like to purchase in this way, and many have adopted systems selling as a marketing tool. One variant of systems selling is *systems contracting,* where a single supplier provides the buyer with his or her entire requirement of MRO (maintenance, repair, operating) supplies. During the contract period, the supplier manages the customer's inventory. For example, Shell Oil manages the oil inventory of many of its business customers and knows when it requires replenishment. The customer benefits from reduced procurement and management costs and from price protection over the term of the contract. The seller benefits from lower operating costs because of a steady demand and reduced paperwork.

Systems selling is a key industrial marketing strategy in bidding to build large-scale industrial projects, such as dams, steel factories, irrigation systems, sanitation systems, pipelines, utilities, and even new towns. Project engineering firms must compete on price, quality, reliability, and other attributes to win contracts. Consider the following example.

JAPAN AND INDONESIA

The Indonesian government requested bids to build a cement factory near Jakarta. A U.S. firm made a proposal that included choosing the site, designing the cement factory, hiring the construction crews, assembling the materials and equipment, and turning over the finished factory to the Indonesian government. A Japanese firm, in outlining its proposal, included all of these services, plus hiring and training the workers to run the factory, exporting the cement through its trading companies, and using the cement to build roads and new office buildings in Jakarta. Although the Japanese proposal involved more money, it won the contract. Clearly, the Japanese viewed the problem not just as one of building a cement factory (the narrow view of systems selling) but as one of contributing to Indonesia's economic development. They took the broadest view of the customer's needs. This is true systems selling.

::: Participants in the Business Buying Process

Who buys the trillions of dollars' worth of goods and services needed by business organizations? Purchasing agents are influential in straight-rebuy and modified-rebuy situations, whereas other department personnel are more influential in new-buy situations. Engineering personnel usually have a major influence in selecting product components, and purchasing agents dominate in selecting suppliers.[10]

The Buying Center

Webster and Wind call the decision-making unit of a buying organization *the buying center.* It is composed of "all those individuals and groups who participate in the purchasing decision-making process, who share some common goals and the risks arising from the decisions."[11] The buying center includes all members of the organization who play any of seven roles in the purchase decision process.[12]

1. ***Initiators.*** Those who request that something be purchased. They may be users or others in the organization.
2. ***Users.*** Those who will use the product or service. In many cases, the users initiate the buying proposal and help define the product requirements.
3. ***Influencers.*** People who influence the buying decision. They often help define specifications and also provide information for evaluating alternatives. Technical personnel are particularly important influencers.
4. ***Deciders.*** People who decide on product requirements or on suppliers.
5. ***Approvers.*** People who authorize the proposed actions of deciders or buyers.

6. ***Buyers.*** People who have formal authority to select the supplier and arrange the purchase terms. Buyers may help shape product specifications, but they play their major role in selecting vendors and negotiating. In more complex purchases, the buyers might include high-level managers.
7. ***Gatekeepers.*** People who have the power to prevent sellers or information from reaching members of the buying center. For example, purchasing agents, receptionists, and telephone operators may prevent salespersons from contacting users or deciders.

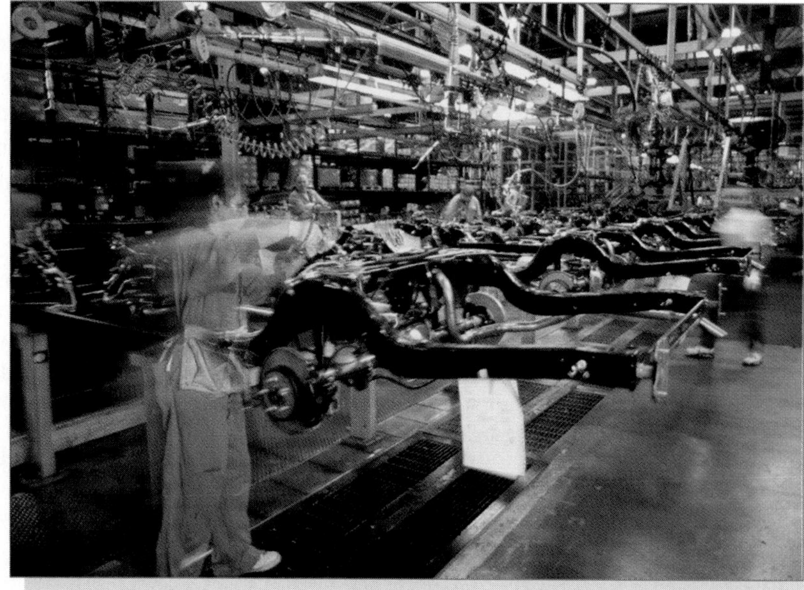

Ford assembly line in action: Worker assembling autos at Ford Motor Company's St. Thomas Auto Plant in Ontario, Canada.

Several individuals can occupy a given role (e.g., there may be many users or influencers), and the individual may occupy multiple roles.[13] A purchasing manager, for example, often occupies the roles of buyer, influencer, and gatekeeper simultaneously: he or she can determine which sales reps can call on other people in the organization; what budget and other constraints to place on the purchase; and which firm will actually get the business, even though others (deciders) might select two or more potential vendors who can meet the company's requirements.

The typical buying center has a minimum of five or six members and often has dozens. The buying center may include people outside the target customer organization, such as government officials, consultants, technical advisors, and other members of the marketing channel.

Buying Center Influences

Buying centers usually include several participants with differing interests, authority, status, and persuasiveness. Each member of the buying center is likely to give priority to very different decision criteria. For example, engineering personnel may be concerned primarily with maximizing the actual performance of the product; production personnel may be concerned mainly with ease of use and reliability of supply; financial personnel may focus on the economics of the purchase; purchasing may be concerned with operating and replacement costs; union officials may emphasize safety issues, and so on.

Business buyers also respond to many influences when they make their decisions. Each buyer has personal motivations, perceptions, and preferences, which are influenced by the buyer's age, income, education, job position, personality, attitudes toward risk, and culture. Buyers definitely exhibit different buying styles. There are "keep-it-simple" buyers, "own-expert" buyers, "want-the-best" buyers, and "want-everything-done" buyers. Some younger, highly educated buyers are computer experts who conduct rigorous analyses of competitive proposals before choosing a supplier. Other buyers are "toughies" from the old school and pit the competing sellers against one another.

Webster cautions that ultimately, individuals, not organizations, make purchasing decisions.[14] Individuals are motivated by their own needs and perceptions in attempting to maximize the rewards (pay, advancement, recognition, and feelings of achievement) offered by the organization. Personal needs "motivate" the behavior of individuals but organizational needs "legitimate" the buying decision process and its outcomes. People are not buying "products." They are buying solutions to two problems: the organization's economic and strategic problem and their own personal "problem" of obtaining individual achievement and reward. In this sense, industrial buying decisions are both "rational" and "emotional," as they serve both the organization's and the individual's needs.[15]

Buying Center Targeting

To target their efforts properly, business marketers have to figure out: Who are the major decision participants? What decisions do they influence? What is their level of influence? What evaluation criteria do they use? Consider the following example:

A company sells nonwoven disposable surgical gowns to hospitals. The hospital personnel who participate in this buying decision include the vice president of purchasing, the operating-room administrator, and the surgeons. The vice president of purchasing analyzes whether the hospital should buy disposable gowns or reusable gowns. If the findings favor disposable gowns, then the operating-room administrator compares various competitors' products and prices and makes a choice. This administrator considers absorbency, antiseptic quality, design, and cost, and normally buys the brand that meets the functional requirements at the lowest cost. Surgeons influence the decision retroactively by reporting their satisfaction with the particular brand.

The business marketer is not likely to know exactly what kind of group dynamics take place during the decision process, although whatever information he or she can obtain about personalities and interpersonal factors is useful.

Small sellers concentrate on reaching the *key buying influencers*. Larger sellers go for *multilevel in-depth selling* to reach as many participants as possible. Their salespeople virtually "live" with high-volume customers. Companies will have to rely more heavily on their communications programs to reach hidden buying influences and keep current customers informed.[16]

SYMANTEC CORPORATION

Internet security provider Symantec Corporation has moved from being primarily a provider of consumer software (under the Norton name) to a provider of enterprise security solutions for financial services, health care, and utilities industries, as well as key accounts for the U.S. Department of Defense. To reach these new markets, Symantec had to restructure its sales force to develop high-level relationships. So Symantec launched the Executive Sponsorship Program in 2003. The 13 Symantec executives enrolled in the program are paired with vice presidents or C-level executives within 19 key customer organizations in industries ranging from banking to telecommunications and manufacturing. The goal of the program is to foster better understanding of Symantec's customers and their business concerns. So far the program has enabled Symantec to be seen as a valued partner and enabled the Symantec executives to gain insights into how they can develop products that fit customers' needs.[17]

Business marketers must periodically review their assumptions about buying center participants. For years, Kodak sold X-ray film to hospital lab technicians. Kodak research indicated that professional administrators were increasingly making purchasing decisions. As a result, Kodak revised its marketing strategy and developed new advertising to reach out to these decision makers.

In defining target segments, four types of business customers can often be identified, with corresponding marketing implications.

1. ***Price-oriented customers*** (transactional selling). Price is everything.
2. ***Solution-oriented customers*** (consultative selling). They want low prices but will respond to arguments about lower total cost or more dependable supply or service.
3. ***Gold-standard customers*** (quality selling). They want the best performance in terms of product quality, assistance, reliable delivery, and so on.
4. ***Strategic-value customers*** (enterprise selling). They want a fairly permanent sole-supplier relationship with your company.

Some companies are willing to handle price-oriented buyers by setting a lower price, but establishing restrictive conditions: (1) limiting the quantity that can be purchased; (2) no refunds; (3) no adjustments; and (4) no services.[18]

- ***Cardinal Health*** set up a bonus dollars scheme at one time and gave points according to how much the business customer purchased. The points could be turned in for extra goods or free consulting.
- ***GE*** is installing diagnostic sensors in its airline engines and railroad engines. It is now compensated for hours of flight or railroad travel.
- ***IBM*** is now more of a service company aided by products than a product company aided by services. It may offer to sell computer power on demand (like video on demand) as an alternative to selling computers.

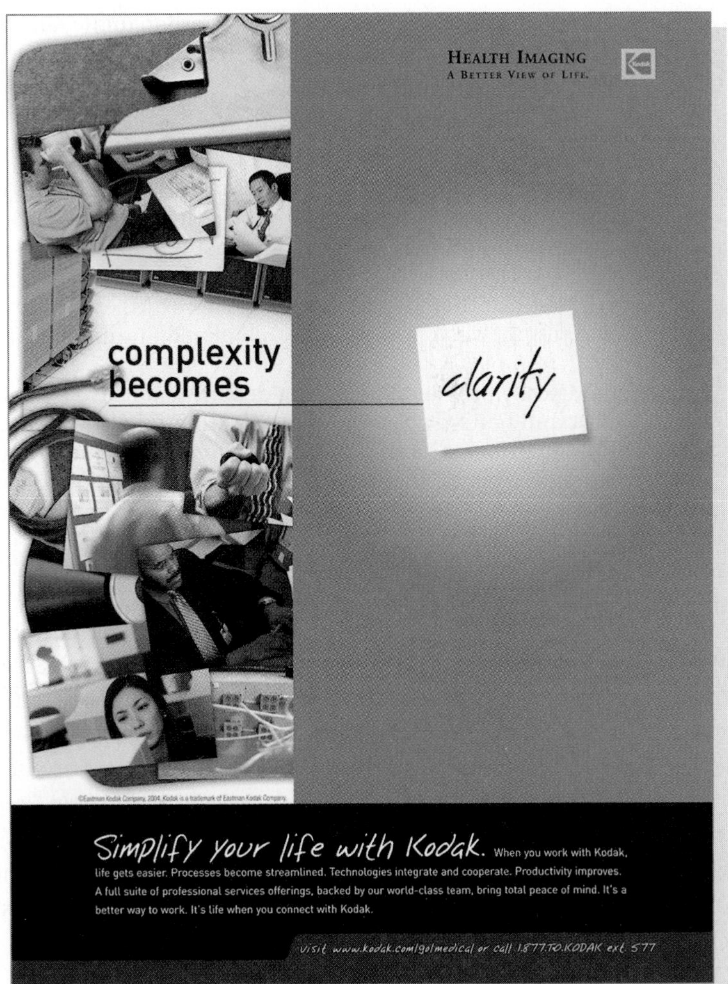

Kodak ad that targets hospital administrators by offering services that streamline processes, integrate technologies, and improve productivity.

Risk and gain sharing can be used to offset requested price reductions from customers. For example, say Medline, a hospital supplier, signs an agreement with Highland Park Hospital promising $350,000 in savings over the first 18 months in exchange for a tenfold increase in the hospitals' share of supplies. If Medline achieves less than this promised savings, it will make up the difference. If Medline achieves substantially more than this promise, it participates in the extra savings. To make such arrangements work, the supplier must be willing to help the customer to build a historical database, reach an agreement for measuring benefits and costs, and devise a dispute resolution mechanism.

Solution selling can also alleviate price pressure and comes in different forms. Here are three examples.[19]

- ***Solutions to Enhance Customer Revenues.*** Hendrix Voeders used its sales consultants to help farmers deliver an incremental animal weight gain of 5 to 10 percent over competitors.
- ***Solutions to Decrease Customer Risks.*** ICI Explosives formulated a safer way to ship explosives for quarries.
- ***Solutions to Reduce Customer Costs.*** W.W. Grainger employees work at large customer facilities to reduce materials-management costs.

::: The Purchasing/Procurement Process

Every organization has specific purchasing objectives, policies, procedures, organizational structures, and systems. In principle, business buyers seek to obtain the highest benefit package (economic, technical, service, and social) in relation to a market offering's costs. A business buyer's incentive to purchase will be greater in proportion to the ratio of perceived benefits to costs. The marketer's task is to construct a profitable offering that delivers superior customer value to the target buyers.

Purchasing Orientations

In the past, purchasing departments occupied a low position in the management hierarchy, in spite of often managing more than half the company's costs. Recent competitive pressures have led many companies to upgrade their purchasing departments and elevate administrators to vice presidential rank. Today's purchasing departments are staffed with MBAs who aspire to be CEOs—like Thomas Stallkamp, Chrysler's former executive vice president of procurement and supply, who cut costs and streamlined the automaker's manufacturing processes.[20]

These new, more strategically oriented purchasing departments have a mission to seek the best value from fewer and better suppliers. Some multinationals have even elevated them to "strategic supply departments" with responsibility for global sourcing and partnering. At Caterpillar, for example, purchasing, inventory control, production scheduling, and traffic have been combined into one department. Lockheed Martin is another firm that has improved its business buying practices.

LOCKHEED MARTIN

Defense contractor Lockheed Martin, which spends $13.2 billion annually, created a Strategic Sourcing Solutions Group to centralize the company's purchasing functions across divisions and consolidate redundancies. The group is comprised of 52 employees with cross-functional experience, and their mission is "to be an integrated, leading edge team that provides industry-recognized supply chain intelligence and innovative sourcing strategies, while fully optimizing customer value." As an example of the group's strategic focus, Lockheed Martin found it was spending roughly 25 to 40 percent more than it should on machining. A machining council was assigned to look into driving down the number of suppliers and consolidating among the preferred ones. The supply base was reduced by a combination of driving more business to preferred suppliers, increasing the frequency of negotiating, and introducing reverse auctions where appropriate.[21]

The upgrading of purchasing means that business marketers must upgrade their sales personnel to match the higher caliber of the business buyers. Formally, we can distinguish three company purchasing orientations:[22]

- ***Buying Orientation.*** The purchaser's focus is short term and tactical. Buyers are rewarded on their ability to obtain the lowest price from suppliers for the given level of quality and availability. Buyers use two tactics: *commoditization,* where they imply that the product is a commodity and care only about price; and *multisourcing,* where they use several sources and make them compete for shares of the company's purchases.
- ***Procurement Orientation.*** Here buyers simultaneously seek quality improvements and cost reductions. Buyers develop collaborative relationships with major suppliers and seek savings through better management of acquisition, conversion, and disposal costs. They encourage early supplier involvement in materials handling, inventory levels, just-in-time management, and even product design. They negotiate long-term contracts with major suppliers to ensure the timely flow of materials. They work closely with their manufacturing group on materials requirement planning (MRP) to make sure supplies arrive on time.
- ***Supply Chain Management Orientation.*** Here purchasing's role is further broadened to become a more strategic, value-adding operation. Purchasing executives at the firm work with marketing and other company executives to build a seamless supply chain management system from the purchase of raw materials to the on-time arrival of finished goods to the end users.

Types of Purchasing Processes

Marketers need to understand how business purchasing departments work. These departments purchase many types of products, and the purchasing process will vary depending on the types of products involved. Peter Kraljic distinguished four product-related purchasing processes:[23]

1. ***Routine products.*** These products have low value and cost to the customer and involve little risk (e.g., office supplies). Customers will seek the lowest price and emphasize routine ordering. Suppliers will offer to standardize and consolidate orders.
2. ***Leverage products.*** These products have high value and cost to the customer but involve little risk of supply (e.g., engine pistons) because many companies make them. The supplier knows that the customer will compare market offerings and costs, and it needs to show that its offering minimizes the customer's total cost.
3. ***Strategic products.*** These products have high value and cost to the customer and also involve high risk (e.g., mainframe computers). The customer will want a well-known and trusted supplier and be willing to pay more than the average price. The supplier should seek strategic alliances that take the form of early supplier involvement, co-development programs, and co-investment.
4. ***Bottleneck products.*** These products have low value and cost to the customer but they involve some risk (e.g., spare parts). The customer will want a supplier who can guarantee a steady supply of reliable products. The supplier should propose standard parts and offer a tracking system, delivery on demand, and a help desk.

Purchasing Organization and Administration

Most purchasing professionals describe their jobs as more strategic, technical, team-oriented, and involving more responsibility than ever before. "Purchasing is doing more cross-functional work than it did in the past," says David Duprey, a buyer for Anaren Microwave, Inc. Sixty-one percent of buyers surveyed said the buying group was more involved in new-product design and development than it was five years ago; and more than half of the buyers participate in cross-functional teams, with suppliers well represented.[24]

In multidivisional companies, most purchasing is carried out by separate divisions. Some companies, however, have started to centralize purchasing. Headquarters identifies materials purchased by several divisions and buys them centrally, thereby gaining more purchasing clout. The individual divisions can buy from another source if they can get a better deal, but in general, centralized purchasing produces substantial savings. For the business marketer, this development means dealing with fewer and higher-level buyers and using a national account sales group to deal with large corporate buyers.

At the same time, companies are decentralizing some purchasing operations by empowering employees to purchase small-ticket items such as special binders, coffeemakers, or Christmas trees. This has come about through the availability of corporate purchasing cards issued by credit card organizations. Companies distribute the cards to foremen, clerks, and secretaries; the cards incorporate codes that set credit limits and restrict where they can be used. National Semiconductor's purchasing chief has noted that the cards have cut processing costs from $30 an order to a few cents. The additional benefit is that buyers and suppliers now spend less time on paperwork.

::: Stages in the Buying Process

At this point we are ready to describe the general stages in the business buying decision process. Robinson and Associates have identified eight stages and called them *buyphases*.[25] The stages are shown in Table 7.1. This model is called the *buygrid* framework.

Table 7.1 describes the buying stages involved in a new-task buying situation. In modified-rebuy or straight-rebuy situations, some stages are compressed or bypassed. For example, in a straight-rebuy situation, the buyer normally has a favorite supplier or a ranked list of suppliers. Thus the supplier search and proposal solicitation stages would be skipped.

The eight-stage buyphase model describes the major steps in the business buying process. Tracing out a buyflow map can provide many clues to the business marketer. A buyflow map for the purchase of a packaging machine in Japan is shown in Figure 7.1. The numbers within the icons are defined at the right. The italicized numbers between icons show the flow of events. Over 20 people in the purchasing company were involved, including the production

TABLE 7.1

Buygrid Framework: Major Stages (Buyphases) of the Industrial Buying Process in Relation to Major Buying Situations (Buyclasses)

		Buyclasses		
		New Task	**Modified Rebuy**	**Straight Rebuy**
	1. Problem recognition	Yes	Maybe	No
	2. General need description	Yes	Maybe	No
	3. Product specification	Yes	Yes	Yes
BUYPHASES	4. Supplier search	Yes	Maybe	No
	5. Proposal solicitation	Yes	Maybe	No
	6. Supplier selection	Yes	Maybe	No
	7. Order-routine specification	Yes	Maybe	No
	8. Performance review	Yes	Yes	Yes

manager and staff, new-product committee, company laboratory, marketing department, and the department for market development. The entire decision-making process took 121 days. There are important considerations in each of the eight stages.

Problem Recognition

The buying process begins when someone in the company recognizes a problem or need that can be met by acquiring a good or service. The recognition can be triggered by internal or external stimuli. Internally, some common events lead to problem recognition. The company decides to develop a new product and needs new equipment and materials. A machine breaks down and requires new parts. Purchased material turns out to be unsatisfactory, and

FIG. 7.1

Organizational Buying Behavior in Japan: Packaging-Machine Purchase Process

Source: "Japanese Firms Use Unique Buying Behavior." *The Japan Economic Journal*, December 23, 1980, p. 29. Reprinted by permission.

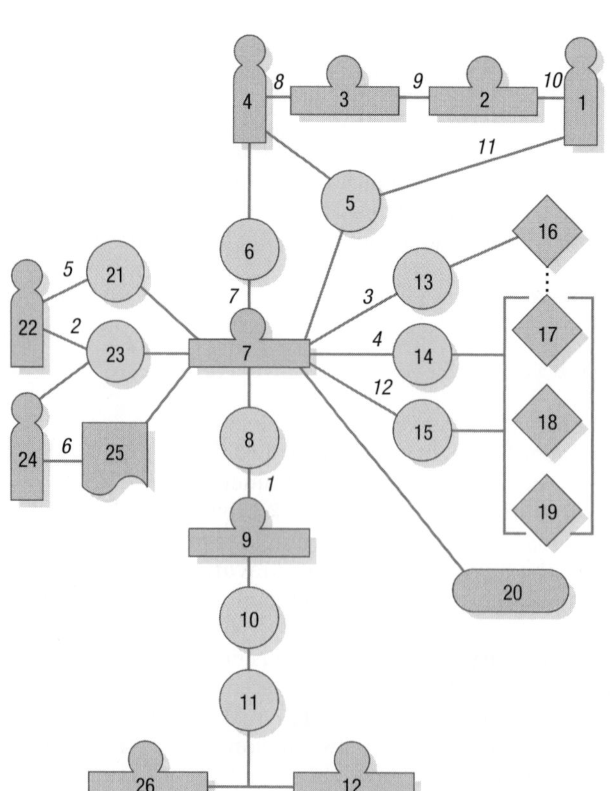

the company searches for another supplier. A purchasing manager senses an opportunity to obtain lower prices or better quality. Externally, the buyer may get new ideas at a trade show, see an ad, or receive a call from a sales representative who offers a better product or a lower price. Business marketers can stimulate problem recognition by direct mail, telemarketing, and calling on prospects.

General Need Description and Product Specification

Next, the buyer determines the needed item's general characteristics and required quantity. For standard items, this is simple. For complex items, the buyer will work with others—engineers, users—to define characteristics like reliability, durability, or price. Business marketers can help by describing how their products meet or even exceed the buyer's needs. Here is an example of how a supplier is using value-added services to gain a competitive edge.

HEWLETT-PACKARD

Hewlett-Packard's marketing division has developed a concept called "trusted advisor." The marketers felt HP needed to move beyond selling systems to selling itself as an advisor and offering specific solutions to unique problems. What HP discovered is that some companies want a partner and others simply want a product that works. HP assumes an advisory role when it sells complex products like a network computer system. HP estimates that the new way of selling has contributed to a 60 percent growth of the high-end computer business. The company has increased its consulting business and is working on enterprise-wide projects through a series of partnerships with systems integrators and software companies.[26]

One of a series of Hewlett Packard ads with the theme "+ hp = everything is possible" that focus on its consulting and advisory capabilities. Through a joint venture with the Hong Kong Special Administrative Region government, hp created a Web portal that gives Hong Kong's citizens 24-hour access to government services.

The buying organization now develops the item's technical specifications. Often, the company will assign a product-value-analysis engineering team to the project. *Product value analysis (PVA)* is an approach to cost reduction in which components are studied to determine if they can be redesigned or standardized or made by cheaper methods of production. The PVA team will examine the high-cost components in a given product. The team will also identify overdesigned components that last longer than the product itself. Tightly written specifications will allow the buyer to refuse components that are too expensive or that fail to meet specified standards. Suppliers can use product value analysis as a tool for positioning themselves to win an account.

Supplier Search

The buyer next tries to identify the most appropriate suppliers through trade directories, contacts with other companies, trade advertisements, and trade shows. Business marketers also put products, prices, and other information on the Internet.[27] While B2B electronic commerce has not delivered on its early promise, it still far outstrips B2C commerce. According to market research firm eMarketer, U.S. businesses spent about $482 billion on online transactions with other businesses in 2002—up 242 percent from $141 billion spent two years earlier. By comparison, consumers spent only $71 billion on goods and services online in 2002.[28] The move to Internet purchasing has far-reaching implications for suppliers and will change the shape of purchasing for years to come. (See "Marketing Insight: The Business-to-Business Cyberbuying Bazaar.")

E-Procurement

Web sites are organized around two types of e-hubs: *vertical hubs* centered on industries (plastics, steel, chemicals, paper) and *functional hubs* (logistics, media buying, advertising, energy management). In addition to using these Web sites, companies can do e-procurement in other ways:

- ***Direct extranet links to major suppliers.*** A company can set up extranet links to its major suppliers. For example, it can set up a direct e-procurement account at Dell or Office Depot, and its employees can make their purchases this way.
- ***Buying alliances.*** Coca-Cola, Sara Lee, Kraft, PepsiCo, Gillette, P&G, and several other companies joined forces to form a buying alliance called Transora to use their combined leverage to obtain lower prices for raw materials. Transora members also share data on less expensive ways to ship products and track inventory. Several auto companies (GM, Ford, DaimlerChrysler) formed Covisint for the same reason. They believe they can save as much as $1,200 per car.

Covisint's home page: "Solutions and services to . . . Connect. Communicate. Collaborate."

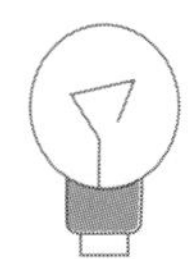

MARKETING INSIGHT | THE BUSINESS-TO-BUSINESS (B2B) CYBERBUYING BAZAAR

With the growth of consumer online shopping, it is easy to lose sight of one of the most significant trends in e-commerce: the growth of business-to-business e-procurement. In addition to posting their own Web pages on the Internet, companies have established intranets for employees to communicate with one another, and extranets to link a company's communications and data with regular suppliers and distributors.

So far, most of the products that businesses are buying electronically are MRO materials (maintenance, repair, and operations) and travel and entertainment services. MRO materials make up 30 percent of business purchases, and the transaction costs for order processing are high, which means there is a huge incentive to streamline the process. Here are some examples: Los Angeles County purchases everything from chickens to condoms over the Internet. National Semiconductor has automated almost all of the company's 3,500 monthly requisitions to buy materials ranging from the sterile booties worn in its fabrication plants to state-of-the-art software. GE buys not only general operating supplies, but also industrial supplies online. Now that GE Information Services (GEIS) has opened its buying site to other companies, the company is well on its way to creating a vast electronic clearinghouse. Hundreds of thousands of firms will exchange trillions of dollars of industrial inputs—with GEIS running the show.

Many brick-and-mortar companies have expanded their online presence by building their business-to-business operations and targeting small businesses, which account for 98 percent of all U.S. employers. The 54 percent of companies that now purchase over the Internet are utilizing electronic marketplaces that are popping up in several forms:

- ***Catalog sites.*** Companies can order thousands of items through electronic catalogs distributed by e-procurement software, such as Grainger's.
- ***Vertical markets.*** Companies buying industrial products such as plastics, steel, or chemicals, or services such as logistics or media can go to specialized Web sites (called e-hubs). For example, Plastics.com allows plastics buyers to search for the best prices from the thousands of plastics sellers.
- ***"Pure Play" auction sites.*** These are online marketplaces such as eBay and Freemarkets.com that could not have been realized without the Internet and for which no business model existed before their formation. Freemarkets.com provides online auctions for buyers and sellers of industrial parts, raw materials, commodities, and services in over 50 product categories, and has facilitated over $40 billion worth of commerce since 1995.
- ***Spot (or exchange) markets.*** On spot electronic markets, prices change by the minute. ChemConnect.com is an exchange for buyers and sellers of bulk chemicals such as benzine and is a B2B success in an arena littered with failed online exchanges. First to market, it is now the biggest online exchange for chemical trading, with volume of $8.8 billion in 2002. Customers like Vanguard Petroleum Corp. in Houston conduct about 15 percent of their spot purchases and sales of natural gas liquids on ChemConnect's commodities trading site.
- ***Private exchanges.*** Hewlett-Packard, IBM, and Wal-Mart operate private exchanges to link with specially invited groups of suppliers and partners over the Web.
- ***Barter markets.*** In these markets, participants offer to trade goods or services.
- ***Buying alliances.*** Several companies buying the same goods join together to form purchasing consortia and gain deeper discounts on volume purchases (Transora, Covisint).

Online business buying offers several advantages: It shaves transaction costs for both buyers and suppliers, reduces time between order and delivery, consolidates purchasing systems, and forges more intimate relationships between partners and buyers. On the downside, it may help to erode supplier–buyer loyalty and create potential security problems. Businesses also face a technological dilemma because no single system yet dominates.

Sources: Robert Yoegel, "The Evolution of B-to-B Selling on the 'Net,"' *Target Marketing* (August 1998): 34; Andy Reinhardt, "Extranets: Log On, Link Up, Save Big," *BusinessWeek,* June 22, 1998, p. 134; "To Byte the Hand that Feeds," *The Economist,* June 17, 1998, pp. 61–62; John Evan Frook, "Buying Behemoth—By Shifting $5B in Spending to Extranets, GE Could Ignite a Development Frenzy," *Internetweek,* August 17, 1998, p. 1; Nicole Harris, "'Private Exchanges' May Allow B-to-B Commerce to Thrive After All," *Wall Street Journal,* March 16, 2001, pp. B1, B4; Olga Kharif, "B2B, Take 2," *BusinessWeek,* November 25, 2003; George S. Day, Adam J. Fein, and Gregg Ruppersberger, "Shakeouts in Digital Markets: Lessons from B2B Exchanges," *California Management Review* 45, no. 2 (Winter 2003): 131–151; Julia Angwin, "Top Online Chemical Exchange Is Unlikely Success Story," *Wall Street Journal,* January 8, 2004, p. A15.

- ***Company buying sites.*** General Electric formed the Trading Process Network (TPN) where it posts *requests for proposals (RFPs),* negotiates terms, and places orders.

Moving into e-procurement involves more than acquiring software; it requires changing purchasing strategy and structure. However, the benefits are many: Aggregating purchasing across multiple departments gains larger, centrally negotiated volume discounts. There is less buying of substandard goods from outside the approved list of suppliers, and a smaller purchasing staff is required.

OWENS-CORNING

In 2001, the Owens-Corning purchasing organization set a goal of wiping out 80 percent of its paper invoices by the end of 2004. The strategic objectives underlying this goal were cost reduction, supply chain visibility, business process integration, and a common standardized process for all suppliers. To accomplish these objectives, Owens-Corning signed on with Advanced Data Exchange (ADX), an outsourced provider of EDI and XML, which takes whatever suppliers have to work with and effectively translates it into a usable electronic format for Owens-Corning. The electronic invoicing initiative worked with the company's use of e-auctions. Starting in 2004, all suppliers participating in e-auctions were told that as part of online auction bids they must agree to exchange invoices and purchase orders electronically if they are awarded the contract. With a $3 billion annual spending budget, Owens-Corning has the kind of clout to ensure suppliers get online.[29]

The supplier's task is to get listed in major online catalogs or services, develop a strong advertising and promotion program, and build a good reputation in the marketplace. This often means creating a well-designed and easy-to-use Web site.

HEWLETT-PACKARD

In 2003, Hewlett-Packard Co. was named number one in *BtoB* magazine's annual ranking of the top B-to-B Web sites. The site (www.hp.com) was launched after HP's merger with Compaq Computer and has 2.5 million pages and roughly 1,900 site areas. The challenge for HP was to integrate this enormous amount of information and present it coherently. Upon entering the site, users can click directly into their customer segment and search for information by product or by solution or click into a product category. The site allows companies to create customized catalogs for frequently purchased products, set up automatic approval routing for orders, and conduct end-to-end transaction processing. To further build relationships with customers, HP.com features Flash demos that show how to use the site, e-newsletters, live chats with sales reps, online classes, and real-time customer support. HP's Web efforts are paying off big: roughly 55 percent of the company's total sales come from the Web site.[30]

Suppliers who lack the required production capacity or suffer from a poor reputation will be rejected. Those who qualify may be visited by the buyer's agents, who will examine the suppliers' manufacturing facilities and meet their personnel. After evaluating each company, the buyer will end up with a short list of qualified suppliers. Many professional buyers have forced suppliers to change their marketing to increase their likelihood of making the cut.

CUTLER-HAMMER

Pittsburgh-based Cutler-Hammer supplies circuit breakers, motor starters, and other electrical equipment to industrial manufacturers such as Ford Motor Company. In response to the growing complexity and proliferation of its products, C-H developed "pods" of salespeople focused on a particular geographic region, industry, or market concentration. Each person brings a degree of expertise about a product or service. Now the salespeople can leverage the knowledge of co-workers to sell to increasingly sophisticated buying teams instead of working in isolation.[31]

Proposal Solicitation

The buyer invites qualified suppliers to submit proposals. If the item is complex or expensive, the buyer will require a detailed written proposal from each qualified supplier. After evaluating the proposals, the buyer will invite a few suppliers to make formal presentations.

Business marketers must be skilled in researching, writing, and presenting proposals. Written proposals should be marketing documents that describe value and benefits in customer terms. Oral presentations should inspire confidence, and position the company's capabilities and resources so that they stand out from the competition.

Consider the hurdles that Xerox has set up in qualifying suppliers.

XEROX

Xerox qualifies only suppliers who meet the ISO 9000 quality standards, but to win the company's top award—certification status—a supplier must first complete the Xerox Multinational Supplier Quality Survey. The survey requires the supplier to issue a quality assurance manual, to adhere to continuous improvement principles, and to demonstrate effective systems implementation. Once qualified, a supplier must participate in Xerox's Continuous Supplier Involvement process: The two companies work together to create specifications for quality, cost, delivery times, and process capability. The final step toward certification requires a supplier to undergo additional, rigorous quality training and an evaluation based on the same criteria as the Malcolm Baldridge National Quality Award. Not surprisingly, only 176 suppliers worldwide have achieved the 95 percent rating required for certification as a Xerox supplier.[32]

Supplier Selection

Before selecting a supplier, the buying center will specify desired supplier attributes and indicate their relative importance. To rate and identify the most attractive suppliers, buying centers often use a supplier-evaluation model such as the one shown in Table 7.2.

Business marketers need to do a better job of understanding how business buyers arrive at their valuations.[33] Anderson, Jain, and Chintagunta conducted a study of the main methods business marketers use to assess customer value and found eight different *customer value assessment (CVA)* methods. Companies tended to use the simpler methods, although the more sophisticated ones promise to produce a more accurate picture of customer perceived value. (See "Marketing Memo: Methods of Assessing Customer Value.")

The choice and importance of different attributes varies with the type of buying situation.[34] Delivery reliability, price, and supplier reputation are important for routine-order products. For procedural-problem products, such as a copying machine, the three most important attributes are technical service, supplier flexibility, and product reliability. For political-problem products that stir rivalries in the organization (such as the choice of a computer system), the most important attributes are price, supplier reputation, product reliability, service reliability, and supplier flexibility.

TABLE 7.2

An Example of Vendor Analysis

Attributes	Rating Scale				
	Importance Weights	Poor (1)	Fair (2)	Good (3)	Excellent (4)
Price	.30				X
Supplier reputation	.20			X	
Product reliability	.30				X
Service reliability	.10		X		
Supplier flexibility	.10			X	
Total score: .30(4) + .20(3) + .30(4) + .10(2) + .10(3) = 3.5					

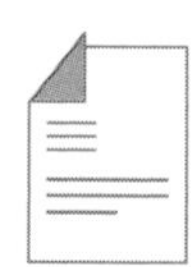

MARKETING MEMO | METHODS OF ASSESSING CUSTOMER VALUE

1. ***Internal engineering assessment.*** Company engineers use laboratory tests to estimate the product's performance characteristics. Weakness: Ignores the fact that in different applications, the product will have different economic value.
2. ***Field value-in-use assessment.*** Customers are interviewed about cost elements associated with using the new-product offering compared to an incumbent product. The task is to assess how much each element is worth to the buyer.
3. ***Focus-group value assessment.*** Customers in a focus group are asked what value they would put on potential market offerings.
4. ***Direct survey questions.*** Customers are asked to place a direct dollar value on one or more changes in the market offering.
5. ***Conjoint analysis.*** Customers are asked to rank their preference for alternative market offerings or concepts. Statistical analysis is used to estimate the implicit value placed on each attribute.
6. ***Benchmarks.*** Customers are shown a "benchmark" offering and then a new-market offering. They are asked how much more they would pay for the new offering or how much less they would pay if certain features were removed from the benchmark offering.
7. ***Compositional approach.*** Customers are asked to attach a monetary value to each of three alternative levels of a given attribute. This is repeated for other attributes. The values are then added together for any offer configuration.
8. ***Importance ratings.*** Customers are asked to rate the importance of different attributes and the supplier firms' performance on these attributes.

Source: James C. Anderson, Dipak C. Jain, and Pradeep K. Chintagunta, "A Customer Value Assessment in Business Markets: A State-of-Practice Study," *Journal of Business-to-Business Marketing* 1, no. 1 (1993): 3–29.

The buying center may attempt to negotiate with preferred suppliers for better prices and terms before making the final selection. Despite moves toward strategic sourcing, partnering, and participation in cross-functional teams, buyers still spend a large chunk of their time haggling with suppliers on price. In 1998, 92 percent of buyers responding to a *Purchasing* magazine survey cited negotiating price as one of their top responsibilities. Nearly as many respondents said price remains a key criterion they use to select suppliers.[35]

Marketers can counter the request for a lower price in a number of ways. They may be able to show evidence that the "total cost of ownership," that is, the "life-cycle cost" of using their product is lower than that of competitors' products. They can also cite the value of the services the buyer now receives, especially if those services are superior to those offered by competitors.

Other approaches may also be used to counter intense price pressure. Consider the following example.

LINCOLN ELECTRIC

Lincoln Electric has a decades-long tradition of working with its customers to reduce costs through its Guaranteed Cost Reduction Program. When a customer insists that a Lincoln distributor lower prices to match Lincoln's competitors, the company and the particular distributor may guarantee that, during the coming year, they will find cost reductions in the customer's plant that meet or exceed the price difference between Lincoln's products and the competition's. If an independent audit at the end of the year does not reveal the promised cost savings, Lincoln Electric and the distributor compensate the customer for the difference. In all the years the program has been in existence, Lincoln has only had to write a check once or twice.[36]

As part of the buyer selection process, buying centers must decide how many suppliers to use. Companies are increasingly reducing the number of suppliers. Ford, Motorola, and Honeywell have cut the number of suppliers by anywhere from 20 to 80 percent. These companies want their chosen suppliers to be responsible for a larger component system; they want them to achieve continuous quality and performance improvement and at the same time lower the supply price each year by a given percentage. These companies expect their suppliers to work closely with them during product development, and they value their suggestions. There is even a trend toward single sourcing.

Companies that use multiple sources often cite the threat of a labor strike as the biggest deterrent to single sourcing. Another reason companies may be reluctant to use a single source is that they fear they will become too comfortable in the relationship and lose their competitive edge.

Order-Routine Specification

After selecting suppliers, the buyer negotiates the final order, listing the technical specifications, the quantity needed, the expected time of delivery, return policies, warranties, and so on. Many industrial buyers lease heavy equipment like machinery and trucks. The lessee gains a number of advantages: conserving capital, getting the latest products, receiving better service, and some tax advantages. The lessor often ends up with a larger net income and the chance to sell to customers who could not afford outright purchase.

In the case of maintenance, repair, and operating items, buyers are moving toward blanket contracts rather than periodic purchase orders. A blanket contract establishes a long-term relationship in which the supplier promises to resupply the buyer as needed, at agreed-upon prices, over a specified period of time. Because the stock is held by the seller, blanket contracts are sometimes called *stockless purchase plans.* The buyer's computer automatically sends an order to the seller when stock is needed. This system locks suppliers in tighter with the buyer and makes it difficult for out-suppliers to break in unless the buyer becomes dissatisfied with the in-supplier's prices, quality, or service.

Companies that fear a shortage of key materials are willing to buy and hold large inventories. They will sign long-term contracts with suppliers to ensure a steady flow of materials. DuPont, Ford, and several other major companies regard long-term supply planning as a major responsibility of their purchasing managers. For example, General Motors wants to buy from fewer suppliers who are willing to locate close to its plants and produce high-quality components. In addition, business marketers are using the Internet to set up extranets with important customers to facilitate and lower the cost of transactions. The customers enter orders directly on the computer, and these orders are automatically transmitted to the supplier. Some companies go further and shift the ordering responsibility to their suppliers in systems called *vendor-managed inventory.* These suppliers are privy to the customer's inventory levels and take responsibility to replenish it automatically through *continuous replenishment programs.*

"OTIFNE" is a term that summarizes three desirable outcomes of a B-to-B transaction:

- OT—deliver on time
- IF—in full
- NE—no error

All three matter. If a supplier achieves on-time compliance of only 80 percent, in-full compliance of 90 percent, and no error compliance of 70 percent, overall performance computes at 80% × 90% × 70%—only 50%!

Performance Review

The buyer periodically reviews the performance of the chosen supplier(s). Three methods are commonly used. The buyer may contact the end users and ask for their evaluations; the buyer may rate the supplier on several criteria using a weighted score method; or the buyer might aggregate the cost of poor performance to come up with adjusted costs of purchase, including price. The performance review may lead the buyer to continue, modify, or end a supplier relationship.

Many companies have set up incentive systems to reward purchasing managers for good buying performance, in much the same way that sales personnel receive bonuses for good selling performance. These systems are leading purchasing managers to increase pressure on sellers for the best terms.

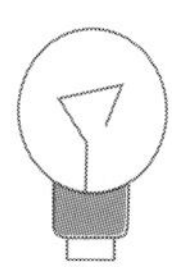

MARKETING INSIGHT | ESTABLISHING CORPORATE TRUST AND CREDIBILITY

Strong bonds and relationships between firms depend on their perceived credibility. *Corporate credibility* refers to the extent to which customers believe that a firm can design and deliver products and services that satisfy their needs and wants. Corporate credibility relates to the reputation that a firm has achieved in the marketplace and is the foundation for a strong relationship. It is difficult for a firm to develop strong ties with another firm unless it is seen as highly credible.

Corporate credibility, in turn, depends on three factors:

- ***Corporate expertise***—the extent to which a company is seen as able to make and sell products or conduct services.
- ***Corporate trustworthiness***—the extent to which a company is seen as motivated to be honest, dependable, and sensitive to customer needs.
- ***Corporate likability***—the extent to which a company is seen as likable, attractive, prestigious, dynamic, and so on.

In other words, a credible firm is seen as being good at what it does; it keeps its customers' best interests in mind and is enjoyable to work with.

Trust is a particularly important determinant of credibility and a firm's relationships with other firms. Trust is reflected in the willingness and confidence of a firm to rely on a business partner. A number of interpersonal and interorganizational factors affect trust in a business-to-business relationship, such as the perceived competence, integrity, honesty, and benevolence of the firm. Trust will be affected by personal interactions between employees of a firm as well as opinions about the company as a whole, and perceptions of trust will evolve with more experience with a company.

Trust can be especially tricky in online settings, and firms often impose more stringent requirements on their online business partners. Business buyers worry that they won't get products of the right quality delivered to the right place at the right time. Sellers worry about getting paid on time—or at all—and how much credit they should extend. Some firms, such as transportation and supply chain management company Ryder System, are using tools such as automated credit-checking applications and online trust services to help determine the credibility of trading partners.

Sources: Robert M. Morgan and Shelby D. Hunt, "The Commitment–Trust Theory of Relationship Marketing," *Journal of Marketing* 58, no. 3 (1994): 20–38; Christine Moorman, Rohit Deshpande, and Gerald Zaltman, "Factors Affecting Trust in Market Research Relationships," *Journal of Marketing* 57 (January 1993): 81–101; Kevin Lane Keller and David A. Aaker, "Corporate-Level Marketing: The Impact of Credibility on a Company's Brand Extensions," *Corporate Reputation Review* 1 (August 1998): 356–378; Bob Violino, "Building B2B Trust," *Computerworld,* June 17, 2002, p. 32; Richard E. Plank, David A. Reid, and Ellen Bolman Pullins, "Perceived Trust in Business-to-Business Sales: A New Measure," *Journal of Personal Selling and Sales Management* 19, no. 3 (Summer 1999): 61–72.

::: Managing Business-to-Business Customer Relationships

To improve effectiveness and efficiency, business suppliers and customers are exploring different ways to manage their relationships. Closer relationships are driven in part by trends related to supply chain management, early supplier involvement, purchasing alliances, and so on.[37] Cultivating the right relationships with business is paramount with any holistic marketing program.

The Benefits of Vertical Coordination

Much research has advocated greater vertical coordination between buying partners and sellers so that they transcend mere transactions to engage in activities that create more value for both parties. Building trust between parties is often seen as one prerequisite to healthy long-term relationships.[38] "Marketing Insight: Establishing Corporate Trust and Credibility" identifies some key dimensions of those concepts. Consider the mutual benefits from the following arrangement.

MOTOMAN INC. AND STILLWATER TECHNOLOGIES

Motoman Inc., a leading supplier of industry robotic systems, and Stillwater Technologies, a contract tooling and machinery company and a key supplier to Motoman, are tightly integrated. Not only do they occupy office and manufacturing space in the same facility, but their telephone and computer systems are linked, and they share a common lobby, conference room, and employee cafeteria. Philip V. Morrison, chairman and

CEO of Motoman, says it is like "a joint venture without the paperwork." Short delivery distances are just one benefit of the unusual partnership. Also key is the fact that employees of both companies have ready access to one another and can share ideas on improving quality and reducing costs. This close relationship has opened the door to new opportunities. Both companies had been doing work for Honda Motor Company, and Honda suggested that they work together on systems projects. The integration makes the two bigger than they are individually.[39]

One historical study of four very different business-to-business relationships found that several factors, by affecting partner interdependence and/or environmental uncertainty, influenced the development of a relationship between business partners.[40] The relationship between advertising agencies and clients illustrates these findings:

1. ***In the relationship formation stage, one partner experienced substantial market growth.*** Manufacturers capitalizing on mass-production techniques developed national brands, which increased the importance and amount of mass-media advertising.
2. ***Information asymmetry between partners was such that a partnership would generate more profits than if the partner attempted to invade the other firm's area.*** Advertising agencies had specialized knowledge that their clients would have had difficulty obtaining.
3. ***At least one partner had high barriers to entry that would prevent the other partner from entering the business.*** Advertising agencies could not easily become national manufacturers, and for years, manufacturers were not eligible to receive media commissions.
4. ***Dependence asymmetry existed such that one partner was more able to control or influence the other's conduct.*** Advertising agencies had control over media access.
5. ***One partner benefited from economies of scale related to the relationship.*** Ad agencies gained by providing the same market information to multiple clients.

Cannon and Perreault found that buyer–supplier relationships differed according to four factors: availability of alternatives; importance of supply; complexity of supply; and supply market dynamism. Based on these four factors, they classified buyer–supplier relationships into eight different categories:[41]

1. ***Basic buying and selling*** – relatively simple, routine exchanges with moderately high levels of cooperation and information exchange.
2. ***Bare bones*** – similar to basic buying and selling but more adaptation by the seller and less cooperation and information exchange.
3. ***Contractual transaction*** – generally low levels of trust, cooperation, and interaction; exchange is defined by formal contract.
4. ***Customer supply*** – traditional custom supply situation where competition rather than cooperation is the dominant form of governance.
5. ***Cooperative systems*** – although coupled closely in operational ways, neither party demonstrates structural commitment through legal means or adaptation approaches.
6. ***Collaborative*** – much trust and commitment leading to true partnership.
7. ***Mutually adaptive*** – much relationship-specific adaptation for buyer and seller, but without necessarily strong trust or cooperation.
8. ***Customer is king*** – although bonded by a close, cooperative relationship, the seller adapts to meet the customer's needs without expecting much adaptation or change on the part of the customer in exchange.

Some firms find that their needs can be satisfied with fairly basic supplier performance. They do not want or require a close relationship with a supplier. Alternatively, some suppliers may not find it worth their while to invest in customers with limited growth potential. One study found that the closest relationships between customers and suppliers arose when the supply was important to the customer and when there were procurement obstacles such as complex purchase requirements and few alternative suppliers.[42] Another study suggested that greater vertical coordination between buyer and seller through information exchange and planning is usually necessary only when high environmental uncertainty exists and specific investments are modest.[43]

Business Relationships: Risks and Opportunism

Buvik and John note that in establishing a customer–supplier relationship, there is tension between safeguarding and adaptation. Vertical coordination can facilitate stronger customer–seller ties but at the same time may increase the risk to the customer's and supplier's specific investments. *Specific investments* are those expenditures tailored to a particular company and value chain partner (e.g., investments in company-specific training, equipment, and operating procedures or systems).[44] Specific investments help firms grow profits and achieve their positioning.[45] For example, Xerox has worked closely with its suppliers to develop customized processes and components that reduced its copier-manufacturing costs by 30 to 40 percent. In return, suppliers received sales and volume guarantees, an enhanced understanding of their customer needs, and a strong position with Xerox for future sales.[46]

Specific investments, however, also entail considerable risk to both customer and supplier. Transaction theory from economics maintains that because these investments are partially sunk, they lock in the firms that make the investments to a particular relationship. Sensitive cost and process information may need to be exchanged. A buyer may be vulnerable to holdup because of switching costs; a supplier may be more vulnerable to holdup in future contracts because of dedicated assets and/or expropriation of technology/knowledge. In terms of the latter risk, consider the following example.[47]

An automobile component manufacturer wins a contract to supply an under-hood component to an original equipment manufacturer (OEM). A one-year, sole-source contract safeguards the supplier's OEM-specific investments in a dedicated production line. However, the supplier may also be obliged to work (noncontractually) as a partner with the OEM's internal engineering staff (using linked computing facilities) to exchange detailed engineering information and coordinate frequent design and manufacturing changes over the term of the contract. These interactions could reduce costs and/or increase quality by improving the firm's responsiveness to marketplace changes. Such interactions could also potentially magnify the threat to the supplier's intellectual property.

When buyers cannot easily monitor supplier performance, the supplier might shirk or cheat and not deliver the expected value. *Opportunism* can be thought of as "some form of cheating or undersupply relative to an implicit or explicit contract."[48] It may involve blatant self-interest and deliberate misrepresentation that violates contractual agreements. In creating the 1996 version of the Ford Taurus, Ford Corporation chose to outsource the whole process to one supplier, Lear Corporation. Lear committed to a contract that, for various reasons, it knew it was unable to fulfill. According to Ford, Lear missed deadlines, failed to meet weight and price objectives, and furnished parts that did not work.[49] A more passive form of opportunism might involve a refusal or unwillingness to adapt to changing circumstances.

Opportunism is a concern because firms must devote resources to control and monitoring that otherwise could be allocated to more productive purposes. Contracts may become inadequate to govern supplier transactions when supplier opportunism becomes difficult to detect; as firms make specific investments in assets that cannot be used elsewhere; and as contingencies are harder to anticipate. Customers and suppliers are more likely to form a joint venture (versus a simple contract) when the supplier's degree of asset specificity is high, monitoring the supplier's behavior is difficult, and the supplier has a poor reputation.[50] When a supplier has a good reputation, for example, it is more likely to avoid opportunism to protect this valuable intangible asset.

The presence of a significant future time horizon and/or strong solidarity norms so that customers and suppliers are willing to strive for joint benefits can cause a shift in the effect of specific investments, from expropriation (increased opportunism on the receiver's part) to bonding (reduced opportunism).[51]

::: Institutional and Government Markets

Our discussion has concentrated largely on the buying behavior of profit-seeking companies. Much of what we have said also applies to the buying practices of institutional and government organizations. However, we want to highlight certain special features of these markets.

The **institutional market** consists of schools, hospitals, nursing homes, prisons, and other institutions that must provide goods and services to people in their care. Many of these organizations are characterized by low budgets and captive clienteles. For example, hospitals have to decide what quality of food to buy for patients. The buying objective here is not profit, because the food is provided as part of the total service package; nor is cost minimization the sole objective, because poor food will cause patients to complain and hurt the hospital's reputation. The hospital purchasing agent has to search for institutional-food vendors whose quality meets or exceeds a certain minimum standard and whose prices are low. In fact, many food vendors set up a separate division to sell to institutional buyers because of these buyers' special needs and characteristics. Heinz produces, packages, and prices its ketchup differently to meet the requirements of hospitals, colleges, and prisons. Aramark Corp., has a competitive advantage when it comes to providing food for the nation's prisons, a direct result of refining its purchasing practices and its supply chain management:

ARAMARK CORP.

Where Aramark once merely selected products from lists provided by potential suppliers, it now collaborates with suppliers to develop products that Aramark customizes to meet the needs of individual segments. In the corrections segment, quality has historically been sacrificed to meet food costs operators outside that market would find impossible to work with. "When you go after business in the corrections field, you are making bids that are measured in hundredths of a cent," says John Zillmer, president of Aramark's Food & Support Services, "So any edge we can gain on the purchasing side is extremely valuable." Aramark took a series of protein products and sourced them with unique partners at price points it never could have imagined before. It was able to drive costs down by working with partners who understood the chemistry of proteins and knew how to do things to lower the price but which could still create a product very acceptable to Aramark's customers. Then Aramark replicated this process with 163 different items formulated exclusively for corrections. Rather than reduce food costs by increments of a penny or so a meal, which was the previous norm for this market, Aramark succeeded in taking 5 to 9 cents off a meal—while maintaining or even improving quality.[52]

Being a supplier of choice for the nation's schools or hospitals means big business:

CARDINAL HEALTH

A spinoff of Baxter Healthcare Corporation, Cardinal Health has become the largest supplier of medical, surgical, and laboratory products in the United States. The company's stockless inventory program, known as ValueLink, was cited as a "best practice" by Arthur Andersen's business consulting practice. Currently in service at over 150 acute-care hospitals in the United States, this program supplies hospital personnel with the products they need when and where they need them. An integrated system meets the needs of customers who deal with life-and-death situations every minute. In the old system, an 18-wheeler simply dropped off a week's or a month's worth of supplies at the back door of a hospital. It inevitably turned out that the items most in demand were the ones in short supply, whereas the ones the hospital never used were available in great number. Cardinal Health estimates that its ValueLink system saves customers an average of $500,000 or more each year.[53]

In most countries, government organizations are a major buyer of goods and services. Government organizations typically require suppliers to submit bids, and normally they award the contract to the lowest bidder. In some cases, the government unit will make allowance for the supplier's superior quality or reputation for completing contracts on time. Governments will also buy on a negotiated contract basis, primarily in the case of complex projects involving major R&D costs and risks and in cases where there is little competition. Government organizations tend to favor domestic suppliers. A major complaint of multinationals operating in Europe was that each country showed favoritism toward its nationals in spite of superior offers available from foreign firms. The European Union is removing this bias.

Because their spending decisions are subject to public review, government organizations require considerable paperwork from suppliers, who often complain about excessive paperwork, bureaucracy, regulations, decision-making delays, and frequent shifts in procurement personnel. Given all the red tape, why would any firm want to do business

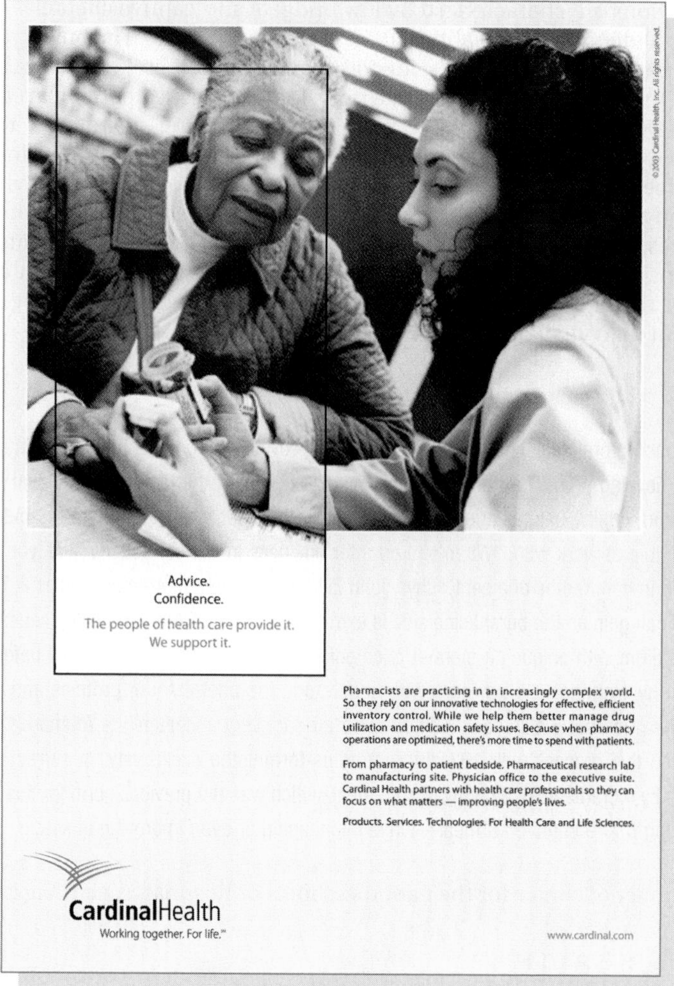

Advice.
Confidence.
The people of health care provide it.
We support it.
Pharmacists are practicing in an increasingly complex world. So they rely on our innovative technologies for effective, efficient inventory control. While we help them better manage drug utilization and medication safety issues. Because when pharmacy operations are optimized, there's more time to spend with patients.
From pharmacy to patient bedside. Pharmaceutical research lab to manufacturing site. Physician office to the executive suite. Cardinal Health partners with health care professionals so they can focus on what matters — improving people's lives.
Products. Services. Technologies. For Health Care and Life Sciences.
CardinalHealth
Working together. For life.℠
www.cardinal.com

Cardinal Health ad directed to pharmacists that focuses on its ability to partner with customers to help them manage inventory, drug utilization, and medication safety issues.

with the U.S. government? Here is how Paul E. Goulding, a Washington, DC–based consultant who has helped clients obtain more than $30 billion in government contracts, answers that question:[54]

> When I hear that question, I tell the story of the businessman who buys a hardware store after moving to a small town. He asks his new employees who the biggest hardware customer in town is. He is surprised to learn that the customer isn't doing business with his store. When the owner asks why not, his employees say the customer is difficult to do business with and requires that a lot of forms be filled out. I point out that the same customer is probably very wealthy, doesn't bounce his checks, and usually does repeat business when satisfied. That's the type of customer the federal government can be.

The U.S. government buys goods and services valued at $200 billion. That makes Uncle Sam the largest customer in the world. It is not just the dollar figure that is large, but the number of individual acquisitions. According to the General Sources Administration Procurement Data Center, over 20 million individual contract actions are processed every year. Although most items purchased are between $2,500 and $25,000, the government also makes purchases in the billions, many of them in technology. But government decision makers often think that technology vendors have not done their homework. In addition, vendors do not pay enough attention to cost justification, which is a major activity for government procurement professionals. Companies hoping to be government contractors need to help government agencies see the bottom-line impact of products.

Just as companies provide government agencies with guidelines on how best to purchase and use their products, governments provide would-be suppliers with detailed guidelines describing how to sell to the government. Not following the guidelines properly and filling out forms and contracts incorrectly can create a legal nightmare.[55] Suppliers have to master the system and try to find ways to cut through the red tape. Goulding says that it requires an investment of time, money, and resources not unlike what is required for entering a new market overseas.

ADI TECHNOLOGY

The federal government has always been ADI Technology Corporation's most important client: Federal contracts account for about 90 percent of its nearly $6 million in annual revenues. Yet managers at this professional services company often shake their heads at all the work that goes into winning the coveted government contracts. A comprehensive bid proposal will run from 500 to 700 pages because of federal paperwork requirements. The company's president estimates that the firm has spent as much as $20,000, mostly in worker hours, to prepare a single bid proposal.

Fortunately for businesses of all sizes, the federal government has been trying to simplify the contracting procedure and make bidding more attractive. Some reforms place more emphasis on buying commercial off-the-shelf items instead of items built to the government's specs; online communication with vendors to eliminate the massive paperwork; and a "debriefing" from the appropriate government agency for vendors who lose a bid, enabling them to increase their chances of winning the next time around.[56] The government's goal is to get all purchases online. To do this, the government is likely to bet on Web-based forms, digital signatures, and electronic procurement cards (P-cards).[57]

Several federal agencies that act as purchasing agents for the rest of the government have launched Web-based catalogs that allow authorized defense and civilian agencies to buy everything from medical and office supplies to clothing online. "Marketing Memo: Selling Tech to the Government" provides some tips for attacking that multibillion-dollar market. The General Services Administration, for example, not only sells stocked merchandise through its Web site, but also creates direct links between buyers and contract suppliers.

In spite of these reforms, for a number of reasons many companies that sell to the government have not used a marketing orientation. The government's procurement policies have traditionally emphasized price, leading suppliers to invest considerable effort in bringing costs down. Where product characteristics are carefully specified, product differentia-

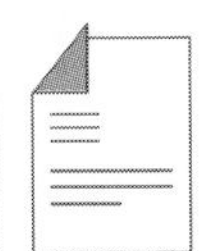

MARKETING MEMO | SELLING TECH TO THE GOVERNMENT

The U.S. government is projected to spend $65.9 billion on IT in fiscal year 2006. A large chunk of this U.S. government business, however, isn't contracted out at all. Through the General Services Administration (GSA) and other government organizations, companies can sell directly to agencies without having to go to formal bidding. Here are three tips for how to tap into that market.

1. ***Get in the Government IT Catalog.*** The GSA runs an online catalog of goods and services for government agencies. About 28 percent of federal spending flows through the catalog's Schedule 70, which includes more than 2000 tech vendors. Getting a business listed can be important. Applications can be done electronically. Remember to spell out pricing structure carefully.
2. ***Work Your Way In.*** Small businesses—especially those owned by women and minorities—are often needed by large businesses to satisfy small business set-asides. To maximize that probability:
   - ***Make sure contractors can find you.*** Get listed on the Small Business Administration's Subcontracting Network (wed.sba.gov/subnet) or use the U.S. Chamber of Commerce Web site.
   - ***Stay on top of key contracts.*** Several Web sites provide updates for the latest deals that might provide opportunities (www.fedbizopps.gov; www.dodbusopps.com; prod.nais.nasa.gov/pub/fedproc/home.hml).
   - ***Work the angles.*** Meet with prospective bidders and explain your qualifications.
3. ***Network Actively.*** Attend one of the large trade shows, such as FOSE, GSA Expo, or E-Gov.

Source: Owen Thomas, "How to Sell Tech to the Feds," *Business 2.0,* March 2003, pp. 111–112.

tion is not a marketing factor; nor are advertising and personal selling of much consequence in winning bids. Some companies have pursued government business by establishing separate government marketing departments.

Companies such as Gateway, Rockwell, Kodak, and Goodyear anticipate government needs and projects, participate in the product specification phase, gather competitive intelligence, prepare bids carefully, and produce strong communications to describe and enhance their companies' reputations.

SUMMARY :::

1. Organizational buying is the decision-making process by which formal organizations establish the need for purchased products and services, then identify, evaluate, and choose among alternative brands and suppliers. The business market consists of all the organizations that acquire goods and services used in the production of other products or services that are sold, rented, or supplied to others.
2. Compared to consumer markets, business markets generally have fewer and larger buyers, a closer customer–supplier relationship, and more geographically concentrated buyers. Demand in the business market is derived from demand in the consumer market and fluctuates with the business cycle. Nonetheless, the total demand for many business goods and services is quite price-inelastic. Business marketers need to be aware of the role of professional purchasers and their influencers, the need for multiple sales calls, and the importance of direct purchasing, reciprocity, and leasing.
3. The buying center is the decision-making unit of a buying organization. It consists of initiators, users, influencers, deciders, approvers, buyers, and gatekeepers. To influence these parties, marketers must be aware of environmental, organizational, interpersonal, and individual factors.
4. The buying process consists of eight stages called buyphases: (1) problem recognition, (2) general need description, (3) product specification, (4) supplier search, (5) proposal solicitation, (6) supplier selection, (7) order-routine specification, and (8) performance review.
5. Business marketers must form strong bonds and relationships with their customers and provide them added value. Some customers, however, may prefer more of a transactional relationship.
6. The institutional market consists of schools, hospitals, nursing homes, prisons, and other institutions that provide goods and services to people in their care. Buyers for government organizations tend to require a great deal of paperwork from their vendors and to favor open bidding and domestic companies. Suppliers must be prepared to adapt their offers to the special needs and procedures found in institutional and government markets.

APPLICATIONS :::

Marketing Debate How Different is Business-to-Business Marketing?

Many business-to-business marketing executives lament the challenges of business-to-business marketing, maintaining that many traditional marketing concepts and principles do not apply. For a number of reasons, they assert that selling products and services to a company is fundamentally different from selling to individuals. Others disagree, claiming that marketing theory is still valid and only involves some adaptation in the marketing tactics.

Take a position: Business-to-business marketing requires a special, unique set of marketing concepts and principles versus Business-to-business marketing is really not that different and the basic marketing concepts and principles apply.

Marketing Discussion

Consider some of the consumer behavior topics from Chapter 6. How might you apply them to business-to-business settings? For example, how might noncompensatory models of choice work?

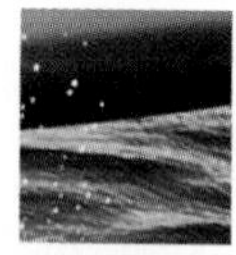

IN THIS CHAPTER, WE WILL ADDRESS THE FOLLOWING QUESTIONS:

1. What are the different levels of market segmentation?
2. How can a company divide a market into segments?
3. How should a company choose the most attractive target markets?
4. What are the requirements for effective segmentation?

CHAPTER 8 ::: IDENTIFYING MARKET SEGMENTS AND TARGETS

eight

Markets are not homogeneous. A company cannot connect with all customers in large, broad, or diverse markets. Consumers vary on many dimensions and often can be grouped according to one or more characteristics. A company needs to identify which market segments it can serve effectively. Such decisions require a keen understanding of consumer behavior and careful strategic thinking. Marketers sometimes mistakenly pursue the same market segment as many other firms and overlook some potentially more lucrative segments.

The magnitude and wealth of older consumers, for example, should be important to many different marketers.[1] The population of mature consumers, those 50 and older, will swell to 115 million in the next 25 years. Yet, not only have youth-obsessed marketers traditionally neglected this huge market, they have also turned them off with stereotypes of grandmas and grandpas living on fixed incomes.[2] "To young product managers, everyone over 45 is lumped into a category called old," says Lori Bitter, partner at J. Walter Thompson's Mature Marketing Group. "They want to put swing music in the background of an ad targeted at 50-year-olds. We have to say, 'No, let's try Sting'." Seniors, particularly boomers-turned-seniors, often make buying decisions based on lifestyle, not age. But don't expect them to remain loyal once they've made a decision. Although highly brand-conscious and brand-aware, baby boomers are not necessarily as brand loyal as traditionally was the case >>>

A rapidly growing target market: Mature consumers who live active lives and who make buying decisions based not on age, but on lifestyle.

with older consumers.[3] With their allegiances potentially up for grabs, astute markets would be wise to keep their eyes on them.[4]

To compete more effectively, many companies are now embracing target marketing. Instead of scattering their marketing effort (a "shotgun" approach), they focus on those consumers they have the greatest chance of satisfying (a "rifle" approach).

Effective target marketing requires that marketers:

1. Identify and profile distinct groups of buyers who differ in their needs and preferences (market segmentation).
2. Select one or more market segments to enter (market targeting).
3. For each target segment, establish and communicate the distinctive benefit(s) of the company's market offering (market positioning).

This chapter will focus on the first two steps. Chapter 10 discusses brand and market positioning.

::: Levels of Market Segmentation

The starting point for discussing segmentation is **mass marketing**. In mass marketing, the seller engages in the mass production, mass distribution, and mass promotion of one product for all buyers. Henry Ford epitomized this strategy when he offered the Model-T Ford in one color, black. Coca-Cola also practiced mass marketing when it sold only one kind of Coke in a 6.5-ounce bottle.

The argument for mass marketing is that it creates the largest potential market, which leads to the lowest costs, which in turn can lead to lower prices or higher margins. However, many critics point to the increasing splintering of the market, which makes mass marketing more difficult. The proliferation of advertising media and distribution channels is making it difficult and increasingly expensive to reach a mass audience. Some claim that mass marketing is dying. Most companies are turning to *micromarketing* at one of four levels: segments, niches, local areas, and individuals.

Segment Marketing

A market segment consists of a group of customers who share a similar set of needs and wants. Thus we distinguish between car buyers who are primarily seeking low-cost basic transportation, those seeking a luxurious driving experience, and those seeking driving thrills and performance. We must be careful not to confuse a *segment* and a *sector.* A car company might say that it will target young, middle-income car buyers. The problem is that young, middle-income car buyers will differ about what they want in a car. Some will want a low-cost car and others will want an expensive car. Young, middle-income car buyers are a sector, not a segment.

The marketer does not create the segments; the marketer's task is to identify the segments and decide which one(s) to target. Segment marketing offers key benefits over mass marketing. The company can presumably better design, price, disclose and deliver the product or service to satisfy the target market. The company also can fine-tune the marketing program and activities to better reflect competitors' marketing.

The Model T: Henry Ford was the first to mass-market automobiles. Ford mass-produced by assembly line, mass-distributed through dealers, and mass-promoted one product for all buyers in ads like these.

However, even a segment is partly a fiction, in that not everyone wants exactly the same thing. Anderson and Narus have urged marketers to present flexible market offerings to all members of a segment.[5]

A **flexible market offering** consists of two parts: a *naked solution* containing the product and service elements that all segment members value, and *discretionary options* that some segment members value. Each option might carry an additional charge. For example, Delta Airlines offers all economy passengers a seat and soft drinks. It charges economy passengers extra for alcoholic beverages. Siemens Electrical Apparatus Division sells metal-clad boxes to small manufacturers whose price includes free delivery and a warranty, but also offers installation, tests, and communication peripherals as extra-cost options.

Market segments can be defined in many different ways. One way to carve up a market is to identify *preference segments.* Suppose ice cream buyers are asked how much they value sweetness and creaminess as two product attributes. Three different patterns can emerge.

1. ***Homogeneous preferences*** – Figure 8.1(a) shows a market where all the consumers have roughly the same preferences. The market shows no natural segments. We would predict that existing brands would be similar and cluster around the middle of the scale in both sweetness and creaminess.
2. ***Diffused preferences*** – At the other extreme, consumer preferences may be scattered throughout the space (Figure 8.1[b]), indicating that consumers vary greatly in their preferences. The first brand to enter the market is likely to position itself to appeal to the most people. A second competitor could locate next to the first brand and fight for market share, or it could locate in a corner to attract a customer group that was not satisfied with the center brand. If several brands are in the market, they are likely to position themselves throughout the space and show real differences to match differences in consumer preference.

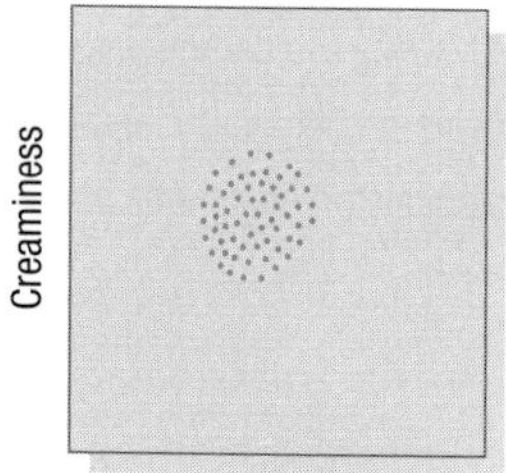

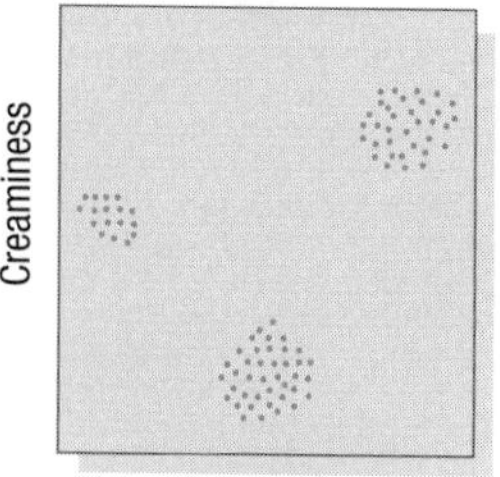

FIG. 8.1

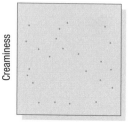

Basic Market-Preference Patterns

3. ***Clustered preferences*** – The market might reveal distinct preference clusters, called *natural market segments* (Figure 8.1[c]). The first firm in this market has three options. It might position in the center, hoping to appeal to all groups. It might position in the largest market segment (*concentrated marketing*). It might develop several brands, each positioned in a different segment. If the first firm developed only one brand, competitors would enter and introduce brands in the other segments.

Later in this chapter, we will consider various ways to segment and compete in a market.

Niche Marketing

A niche is a more narrowly defined customer group seeking a distinctive mix of benefits. Marketers usually identify niches by dividing a segment into subsegments. For example, Progressive, a Cleveland auto insurer, sells "nonstandard" auto insurance to risky drivers with a record of auto accidents, charges a high price for coverage and makes a lot of money in the process.

An attractive niche is characterized as follows: The customers in the niche have a distinct set of needs; they will pay a premium to the firm that best satisfies their needs; the niche is not likely to attract other competitors; the nicher gains certain economies through specialization; and the niche has size, profit, and growth potential. Whereas segments are fairly large and normally attract several competitors, niches are fairly small and normally attract only one or two.

ENTERPRISE

Enterprise Rent-A-Car has challenged Hertz's supremacy in the rental car market by tailoring its marketing program to a relatively neglected target market.[6] While Hertz, Avis, Alamo, and others specialize in airport rental cars for business and leisure travelers, Enterprise has attacked the low-budget, insurance-replacement market by primarily renting to customers whose cars have been wrecked or stolen. Enterprise charges low rental rates by avoiding expensive airport and downtown locations, by only opening for daylight hours, and by holding on to its fleet of cars for a longer period of time before replacing them. Enterprise also distinguishes itself, in part, by offering to pick up customers. Enterprise has a limited advertising budget, relying more on a grassroots marketing push based on referrals from insurance agents and adjusters, car dealers, body shops, and garages. By creating unique associations to low cost and convenience in an overlooked niche market, Enterprise has been highly profitable.

Larger companies, such as IBM, have lost pieces of their market to nichers: This confrontation has been labeled "guerrillas against gorillas."[7] Some large companies have even turned to niche marketing. Hallmark commands a 55 percent share of the $7.8 billion global greeting card market by rigorously segmenting its greeting card business. In addition to popular sub-branded card lines like the humorous Shoebox Greetings, Hallmark has introduced lines targeting specific market segments. Fresh Ink targets 18- to 39-year-old women, Hallmark En Espanol targets Hispanic card givers, and Out of the Blue targets those who want inexpensive cards that can be sent for no reason.[8]

Niche marketers presumably understand their customers' needs so well that the customers willingly pay a premium. Tom's of Maine all-natural personal care products sometimes commands a 30 percent premium on its toothpaste because its unique, environmentally friendly products and charitable donation programs appeal to consumers who have been turned off by big businesses.[9] As marketing efficiency increases, niches that were seemingly too small may become more profitable.[10]

In the world of pharmaceuticals, biotech company Genentech stands out for developing drugs that target tiny niche markets instead of going after blockbusters like Pfizer's Lipitor or Merck's Zocor, cholesterol medications that rack up billions of dollars in sales:

GENENTECH

San Francisco–based Genentech pursues "targeted therapies," drugs aimed at relatively small subsets of patients. The drugs produce the same kind of dramatic benefit doctors get when they identify the specific type of bacteria causing an infection and slam it with the right antibiotic. A few years ago, the company launched the first highly targeted therapy—Herceptin, a breast-cancer drug that is prescribed only to the

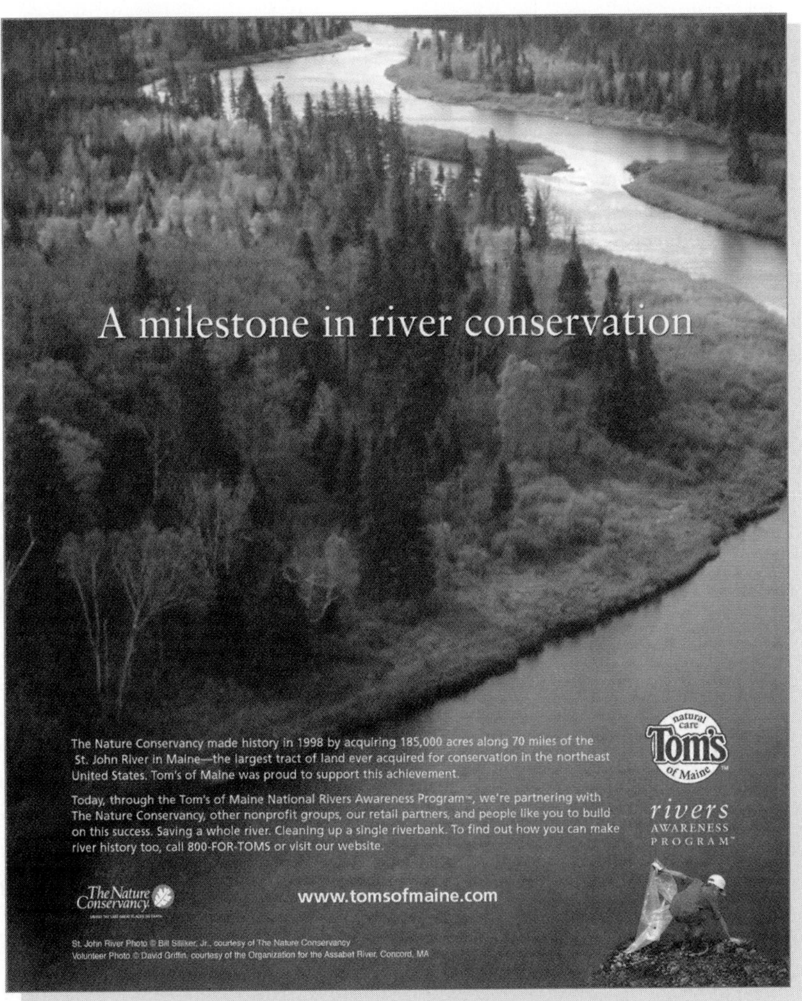

A milestone in river conservation
The Nature Conservancy made history in 1998 by acquiring 185,000 acres along 70 miles of the St. John River in Maine—the largest tract of land ever acquired for conservation in the northeast United States. Tom's of Maine was proud to support this achievement.
Today, through the Tom's of Maine National Rivers Awareness Program™, we're partnering with The Nature Conservancy, other nonprofit groups, our retail partners, and people like you to build on this success. Saving a whole river. Cleaning up a single riverbank. To find out how you can make river history too, call 800-FOR-TOMS or visit our website.
natural care
Tom's
of Maine
rivers
AWARENESS
PROGRAM™
The Nature Conservancy
www.tomsofmaine.com
St. John River Photo © Bill Silliker, Jr., courtesy of The Nature Conservancy
Volunteer Photo © David Griffin, courtesy of the Organization for the Assabet River, Concord, MA

Niche marketer Tom's of Maine makes environmentally friendly products and participates in a number of environmental action programs, like the Tom's of Maine National Rivers Awareness Program™

25 percent or so of patients whose tumors harbor a particular genetic quirk—and it hasn't looked back. Genentech's targeted therapies make economic sense because the company is small, doesn't need to sell billions of dollars of drugs each year to support an army of sales reps or marketing executives, and can charge premium prices because its anti-cancer drugs really work. Genentech's revenues were $3.3 billion in 2003, up 24 percent from 2001.[11]

Globalization has facilitated niche marketing. For example, the German economy has more than 300,000 small and midsize companies (known as *the Mittelstand*). Many enjoy over 50 percent market share in well-defined global niches. Hermann Simon dubbed these global niche leaders "hidden champions."[12] Here are some examples:

- Tetra Food supplies 80 percent of the food for feeding pet tropical fish.
- Hohner has 85 percent of the world harmonica market.
- Becher has 50 percent of the world's oversized umbrella market.
- Steiner Optical has 80 percent of the world's military field glasses market.

These hidden champions tend to be found in stable markets, are typically family owned or closely held, and are long lived. They are dedicated to their customers and offer superior performance, responsive service, and punctual delivery (rather than low price) as well as customer intimacy. Senior management emphasizes continuous innovation and stays in direct and regular contact with top customers.

The low cost of setting up shop on the Internet has also led to many small business start-ups aimed at niches. The recipe for Internet niching success: Choose a hard-to-find product that customers do not need to see and touch. This "Webpreneur" followed the recipe with astonishing results:[13]

OSTRICHESONLINE.COM

Whereas Internet giants like Amazon.com struggled to realize a profit, Steve Warrington is earning a six-figure income selling ostriches—and every product derived from them—online (www.ostrichesonline.com). Since the site was launched for next to nothing in 1996, Warrington's business has sold to over 20,000 clients in over 125 countries from a catalog of more than 17,500 ostrich-related products. Visitors to the site can buy ostrich meat, feathers, leather jackets, videos, eggshells, and subscribe to a newsletter devoted to ostriches.[14]

Local Marketing

Target marketing is leading to marketing programs tailored to the needs and wants of local customer groups (trading areas, neighborhoods, even individual stores). Citibank provides different mixes of banking services in its branches, depending on neighborhood demographics. Kraft helps supermarket chains identify the cheese assortment and shelf positioning that will optimize cheese sales in low-, middle-, and high-income stores, and in different ethnic neighborhoods.

AMERICAN DRUG

American Drug, one of the largest U.S. drugstore retailers, had its marketing team assess shopping patterns at hundreds of its Osco and Sav-on Drug Stores on a market-by-market basis. Using scanned data, the company fine-tuned the stores' product mix, revamped store layout, and refocused marketing efforts to more closely align with local consumer demand. Depending on the local demographics, each store unit varies the amount and type of merchandise in such categories as hardware, electrical supplies, automotive supplies, cookware, over-the-counter drugs, and convenience goods.[15]

Local marketing reflects a growing trend called grassroots marketing. Marketing activities concentrate on getting as close and personally relevant to individual customers as possible. Much of Nike's initial success has been attributed to the ability to engage target consumers through grassroots marketing such as sponsorship of local school teams, expert-conducted clinics, and provision of shoes, clothing, and equipment.

A large part of local, grassroots marketing is experiential marketing, which promotes a product or service not just by communicating its features and benefits, but by also connecting it with unique and interesting experiences. One marketing commentator describes experiential marketing this way: "The idea is not to sell something, but to demonstrate how a brand can enrich a customer's life."[16] "Marketing Insight: Experiential Marketing" describes the concept of Customer Experience Management.

Holiday Inn Hotels and Resorts is trying to recharge its faded brand image through experiential marketing aimed not only at creating new customer experiences, but also at getting customers to kindle nostalgia for their own childhood experiences with the brand:

HOLIDAY INN HOTELS AND RESORTS

The chain that grew up with the Interstate System and defined the overnight roadside experience is trying to push itself back into Americans' consciousness. The marketing push is geared at evoking the good old days when its popularity was reflected in stolen towels—the chain claims it still loses 560,000 towels annually. So in 2003, Holiday Inn designated August 28 as "National Towel Amnesty Day." Extending through Labor Day weekend, each Holiday Inn distributed 50 limited edition towels that read, "100 percent cotton, 100 percent guilt-free, 100 percent yours." In addition, the chain created an Internet site at www.holiday-inn.com/towels where visitors could share towel stories. For each story collected, $1 was donated to a charity benefiting children with life-threatening diseases who wish to visit central Florida attractions. By getting customers involved in swapping stories, the hotel chain hopes to play up the emotional connection many Americans still have with its simple, dependable, white-bread image.[17]

Pine and Gilmore, who are pioneers on the topic, have argued that we are on the threshold of the "Experience Economy," a new economic era in which all businesses must orchestrate memorable events for their customers.[18] They assert:

- If you charge for stuff, then you are in the *commodity business.*
- If you charge for tangible things, then you are in the *goods business.*
- If you charge for the activities you perform, then you are in the *service business.*
- If you charge for the time customers spend with you, then and only then are you in the *experience* business.

Citing examples of a range of companies from Disney to AOL, they maintain that salable experiences come in four varieties: entertainment, education, esthetic, and escapist. VANS, which pioneered slip-on sneakers for skateboarding, has succeeded in that market with an offbeat marketing mix of events, sponsorships, and even a documentary film, all celebrating the skateboard culture.[19] VANS' CEO Gary Schoenfeld proclaims, "Our vision is not to hit our

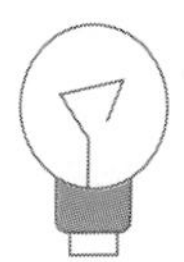

MARKETING **INSIGHT** | EXPERIENTIAL MARKETING

Through several books and papers, Columbia University's Bernd Schmitt has developed the concept of *Customer Experience Management (CEM)*—the process of strategically managing a customer's entire experience with a product or company. According to Schmitt, brands can help to create five different types of experiences: (1) Sense, (2) Feel, (3) Think, (4) Act, (5) Relate. In each case, Schmitt distinguishes between hard-wired and acquired experiential response levels. He maintains that marketers can provide experiences for customers through a set of experience providers.

1. ***Communications:*** advertising, public relations, annual reports, brochures, newsletters, and magalogs.
2. ***Visual/verbal identity:*** names, logos, signage, and transportation vehicles.
3. ***Product presence:*** product design, packaging, and point-of-sale displays.
4. ***Co-branding:*** event marketing and sponsorships, alliances and partnerships, licensing, and product placement in movies or TV.
5. ***Environments:*** retail and public spaces, trade booths, corporate buildings, office interiors, and factories.
6. ***Web sites and electronic media:*** corporate sites, product or service sites, CD-ROMs, automated e-mails, online advertising, and intranets.
7. ***People:*** salespeople, customer service representatives, technical support or repair providers, company spokepersons, and CEOs and other executives.

The CEM framework is made up of five basic steps:

1. ***Analyzing the experiential world of the customer:*** gaining insights into the sociocultural context of consumers or the business context of business customers.
2. ***Building the experiential platform:*** developing a strategy that includes the positioning for the kind of experience the brand stands for ("what"), the value proposition of what relevant experience to deliver ("why"), and the overall implementation theme that will be communicated ("how").
3. ***Designing the brand experience:*** implementing their experiential platform in the look and feel of logos and signage, packaging, and retail spaces, in advertising, collaterals, and online.
4. ***Structuring the customer interface:*** implementing the experiential platform in the dynamic and interactive interfaces including face-to-face, in stores, during sales visits, at the check-in desk of a hotel, or the e-commerce engine of a Web site.
5. ***Engaging in continuous innovation:*** implementing the experiential platform in new-product development, creative marketing events for customers, and fine-tuning the experience at every point of contact.

Schmitt cites Pret A Manger, the U.K.-based sandwich company, as an example of a company that provides an attractive brand experience, customer interface, and ongoing innovation: "The Pret A Manger brand is about great tasting, handmade, natural products served by amazing people who are passionate about their work. The sandwiches and stores look appealing and attractive. The company hires only 5% of those who apply and only after they have worked for a day in the shop. This process ensures good fit and good teamwork." He also offers Singapore Airlines, Starbucks, and Amazon.com as outstanding providers of customer experiences.

Sources: www.exgroup.com; Bernd Schmitt, *Customer Experience Management: A Revolutionary Approach to Connecting with Your Customers* (New York: John Wiley and Sons, 2003); Bernd Schmitt, David L. Rogers, and Karen Vrotsos, *There's No Business That's Not Show Business: Marketing in an Experience Culture* (Upper Saddle River, NJ: Prentice Hall, 2003); Bernd Schmitt, *Experiential Marketing: How to Get Companies to Sense, Feel, Think, Act, and Relate to Your Company and Brands* (New York: Free Press, 1999); Bernd Schmitt and Alex Simonson, *Marketing Aesthetics: The Strategic Management of Brands, Identity and Image* (New York: Free Press, 1997).

Pro skateboarders Darrell Stanton and Scott Kane in a VANS ad. Both Stanton and Kane are part of a VANS-sponsored team.

target audience over the head with our ads, but to integrate ourselves into the places they are most likely to be."

Those who favor localized marketing see national advertising as wasteful because it is too "arm's length" and fails to address local needs. Those against local marketing argue that it drives up manufacturing and marketing costs by reducing economies of scale. Logistical problems are magnified. A brand's overall image might be diluted if the product and message are different in different localities.

Customerization

The ultimate level of segmentation leads to "segments of one," "customized marketing," or "one-to-one marketing."[20]

Today customers are taking more individual initiative in determining what and how to buy. They log onto the Internet; look up information and evaluations of product or service offers; dialogue with suppliers, users, and product critics; and in many cases, design the product they want. More online companies today are offering customers a Choiceboard, an interactive online system that allows individual customers to design their own products and services by choosing from a menu of attributes, components, prices, and delivery options. The customer's selections send signals to the supplier's manufacturing system that set in motion the wheels of procurement, assembly, and delivery.[21]

Wind and Rangaswamy see the Choiceboard as a movement toward "customerizing" the firm.[22] **Customerization** combines operationally driven mass customization with customized marketing in a way that empowers consumers to design the product and service offering of their choice. The firm no longer requires prior information about the customer, nor does the firm need to own manufacturing. The firm provides a platform and tools and "rents" out to customers the means to design their own products. A company is customerized when it is able to respond to individual customers by customizing its products, services, and messages on a one-to-one basis.[23]

Each business unit will have to decide whether it would gain more by designing its business system to create offerings for *segments* or for *individuals*. Companies that favor segmentation see it as more efficient, as requiring less customer information, and as permitting more standardization of market offerings. Those who favor individual marketing claim that segments are a fiction, that individuals within so-called segments differ greatly, and that marketers can achieve much more precision and effectiveness by addressing individual needs.

Customization is certainly not for every company: It may be very difficult to implement for complex products such as automobiles. Customization can raise the cost of goods by

Acumins Internet-based vitamin company Acumins blends vitamins, herbs, and minerals according to a customer's instructions, compressing up to 95 ingredients into three to five "personalized pills." The Acumins premise is simple and attractive: Why swallow dozens of pills when you can take three pills with dozens of ingredients of your choosing?

Paris Miki The Japanese company Paris Miki, one of the largest eyeglass retailers in the world, uses a design tool that takes a digital picture of the customer's face. The customer describes the style he or she wants—sports, elegant, traditional—and the system displays alternatives on the computerized photograph. After selecting the frame, the customer also chooses nosepieces, hinges, and arms. The glasses are ready within an hour.

DeBeers With DeBeers' Design Your Own Ring program, customers can design their own diamond rings by choosing from any of 189 unique combinations of center stone and side stone shapes and weights and band metal, as well as connect with a local jeweler who can help them buy it.

Andersen Windows Andersen Windows of Bayport, Minnesota, the home-building industry's leading window and patio door manufacturer, has developed an interactive computer version of its catalogs for distributors and retailers that is linked directly to the factory. With this system, now in 650 showrooms, salespeople can help customers customize each window, check the design for structural soundness, and generate a price quote. From there Andersen went on to develop a "batch of one" manufacturing process in which every window and door part is made to order, thus reducing its finished parts inventory (a major cost to the company).

ChemStation Based in Dayton, Ohio, ChemStation offers customized soap formulas to its industrial customers, who range from car washes to the U.S. Air Force. What cleans a car will not clean an airplane or equipment in a mine shaft. Salespeople visit customer sites to gather information. All the data from the company's chemical lab and its field studies are kept in a central database called Tank Management System (TMS). TMS is linked directly to both the lab and the company's 40 plants across the country, where computer-operated machines mix each customer's special formula.

FIG. 8.2

Examples of Marketing Customization

Sources: "Creating Greater Customer Value May Require a Lot of Changes," *Organizational Dynamics* (Summer 1998): 26; Erick Schonfeld, "The Customized, Digitized, Have-It-Your-Way Economy," *Fortune,* September 28, 1998, pp. 115–124; Jim Barlow, "Individualizing Mass Production," *Houston Chronicle,* April 13, 1997, p. E1; Sarah Schafer, "Have It Your Way," *Inc.,* November 18, 1997, pp. 56–64; Jim Christie, "Mass Customization: The New Assembly Line?" *Investor's Daily,* February 25, 2000.

more than the customer is willing to pay. Some customers do not know what they want until they see actual products. Customers cannot cancel the order after the company has started to work on the product. The product may be hard to repair and have little sales value. In spite of this, customization has worked well for some products. Figure 8.2 shows examples of companies that employ customization.

::: Segmenting Consumer Markets

Two broad groups of variables are used to segment consumer markets. Some researchers try to form segments by looking at descriptive characteristics: geographic, demographic, and psychographic. Then they examine whether these customer segments exhibit different needs or product responses. For example, they might examine the differing attitudes of "professionals," "blue collars," and other groups toward, say, "safety" as a car benefit.

Other researchers try to form segments by looking at "behavioral" considerations, such as consumer responses to benefits, use occasions, or brands. Once the segments are formed, the researcher sees whether different characteristics are associated with each consumer-response segment. For example, the researcher might examine whether people who want "quality" rather than "low price" in buying an automobile differ in their geographic, demographic, and psychographic makeup.

Regardless of which type of segmentation scheme is employed, the key is that the marketing program can be profitably adjusted to recognize customer differences. The major segmentation variables—geographic, demographic, psychographic, and behavioral segmentation—are summarized in Table 8.1.

Geographic Segmentation

Geographic segmentation calls for dividing the market into different geographical units such as nations, states, regions, counties, cities, or neighborhoods. The company can operate in one or a few areas, or operate in all but pay attention to local variations. For example, Hilton Hotels customizes rooms and lobbies according to location. Northeastern hotels are sleeker and more cosmopolitan. Southwestern hotels are more rustic. Major retailers such as Wal-Mart, Sears, Roebuck & Co., and Kmart all allow local managers to stock products that suit the local community.[24]

TABLE 8.1

Major Segmentation Variables for Consumer Markets

Geographic region	Pacific, Mountain, West North Central, West South Central, East North Central, East South Central, South Atlantic, Middle Atlantic, New England
City or metro size	Under 5,000; 5,000–20,000; 20,000–50,000; 50,000–100,000; 100,000–250,000; 250,000–500,000; 500,000–1,000,000; 1,000,000–4,000,000; 4,000,000 or over
Density	Urban, suburban, rural
Climate	Northern, southern
Demographic age	Under 6, 6–11, 12–19, 20–34, 35–49, 50–64, 65+
Family size	1-2, 3-4, 5+
Family life cycle	Young, single; young, married, no children; young, married, youngest child under 6; young, married, youngest child 6 or over; older, married, with children; older, married, no children under 18; older, single; other
Gender	Male, female
Income	Under $10,000; $10,000–$15,000; $15,000–$20,000; $20,000–$30,000; $30,000–$50,000; $50,000–$100,000; $100,000 and over
Occupation	Professional and technical; managers, officials, and proprietors; clerical sales; craftspeople; forepersons; operatives; farmers; retired; students; homemakers; unemployed
Education	Grade school or less; some high school; high school graduate; some college; college graduate
Religion	Catholic, Protestant, Jewish, Muslim, Hindu, other
Race	White, Black, Asian, Hispanic
Generation	Baby boomers, Generation Xers
Nationality	North American, South American, British, French, German, Italian, Japanese
Social class	Lower lowers, upper lowers, working class, middle class, upper middles, lower uppers, upper uppers
Psychographic lifestyle	Culture-oriented, sports-oriented, outdoor-oriented
Personality	Compulsive, gregarious, authoritarian, ambitious
Behavioral occasions	Regular occasion, special occasion
Benefits	Quality, service, economy, speed
User status	Nonuser, ex-user, potential user, first-time user, regular user
Usage rate	Light user, medium user, heavy user
Loyalty status	None, medium, strong, absolute
Readiness stage	Unaware, aware, informed, interested, desirous, intending to buy
Attitude toward product	Enthusiastic, positive, indifferent, negative, hostile

BED BATH & BEYOND

Home furnishing retailer Bed Bath & Beyond's ability to cater to local tastes has fueled its phenomenal growth. Bed Bath & Beyond's managers pick 70 percent of their own merchandise, and this fierce local focus has helped the chain evolve from one that began selling little more than bed linens to the "beyond" part—products ranging from picture frames and pot holders to imported olive oil and designer door mats. In Manhattan stores, for instance, managers are beginning to stock wall paint. You won't find paint in suburban stores where customers can go to Home Depot or Lowe's. One Bed Bath manager says that several customers have been surprised when they found out that the store is part of a national chain and not a mom-and-pop operation. That's the ultimate compliment.[25]

More and more, regional marketing means marketing right down to a specific zip code.[26] Many companies use mapping software to show the geographic locations of their customers. The software may show a retailer that most of his customers are within only a 10-mile radius of his store, and further concentrated with certain zip+4 areas. By mapping the densest areas, the retailer can resort to *customer cloning*, assuming that the best prospects live where most of his customers come from.

Some approaches combine geographic data with demographic data to yield even richer descriptions of consumers and neighborhoods. Claritas, Inc., has developed a geoclustering approach called PRIZM (Potential Rating Index by Zip Markets) that classifies over half a million U.S. residential neighborhoods into 15 distinct groups and 66 distinct lifestyle segments called PRIZM Clusters.[27] The groupings take into consideration 39 factors in 5 broad categories: (1) education and affluence, (2) family life cycle, (3) urbanization, (4) race and ethnicity, and (5) mobility. The neighborhoods are broken down by zip code, zip+4, or census tract and block group. The clusters have descriptive titles such as *Blue Blood Estates, Winner's Circle, Hometown Retired, Latino America, Shotguns and Pickups,* and *Back Country Folks.* The inhabitants in a cluster tend to lead similar lives, drive similar cars, have similar jobs, and read similar magazines. Here are four new PRIZM clusters:[28]

- ***Young Digerati.*** Couples or single-headed households, most of them with kids, who have decided to stay in urban centers rather than flee to the suburbs. This sector includes a high proportion of affluent, tech-savvy, 20-somethings, who tend to hold master's degrees and live in fashionable neighborhoods on the urban fringe. They are staking out territory in once-forgotten neighborhoods in cities such as New York, Chicago, and Atlanta.
- ***Beltway Boomers.*** Now in their forties and fifties, these college-educated, upper-middle-class homeowners married late and are still raising children. They live in comfortable suburban subdivisions and are still pursuing kid-centered lifestyles.
- ***The Cosmopolitans.*** Continued gentrification of the nation's cities has resulted in the emergence of this segment, concentrated in America's fast-growing metro areas such as Las Vegas, Miami, and Albuquerque. These households feature older homeowners, empty nesters, and college graduates who enjoy leisure-intensive lifestyles.
- ***Old Milltowns.*** Just as America's once thriving factory towns have aged, so have their residents. Old Milltowns reflects the decline of these small, once-industrial communities, now filled with retired singles and couples living quietly on fixed incomes. These home-centered residents make up one of the top segments for daytime television.

Marketers can use PRIZM to answer such questions as these: Which geographic areas (neighborhoods or zip codes) contain our most valuable customers? How deeply have we already penetrated these segments? Which distribution channels and promotional media work best in reaching our target clusters in each area? Geoclustering captures the increasing diversity of the American population. Upscale sportswear retailer Eddie Bauer has used geoclustering information to better locate stores and serve customers. Based on a successful pilot with *Veggie Tales* concerts, Clear Channel Communications is using geoclustering information to send targeted e-mails to prospects for national tours in all entertainment venues.[29] Marketing to microsegments has become accessible even to small organizations as database costs decline, PCs proliferate, software becomes easier to use, data integration increases, and the Internet grows.[30]

Demographic Segmentation

In demographic segmentation, the market is divided into groups on the basis of variables such as age, family size, family life cycle, gender, income, occupation, education, religion, race, generation, nationality, and social class. There are several reasons for the popularity of demographic variables to distinguish customer groups. One reason is that consumer needs, wants, and usage rates and product and brand preferences are often associated with demographic variables. Another is that demographic variables are easier to measure. Even when the target market is described in nondemographic terms (say, a personality type), the link back to demographic characteristics may be needed in order to estimate the size of the market and the media that should be used to reach it efficiently.

Here is how certain demographic variables have been used to segment markets.

AGE AND LIFE-CYCLE STAGE Consumer wants and abilities change with age. Toothpaste brands such as Crest and Colgate offer three main lines of products to target kids, adults, and older consumers. Age segmentation can be even more refined. Pampers divides its market into prenatal, newborn (0–1 month), infant (2–5 months), cruiser (6–12 months), toddler (13–18 months), explorer (19–23 months), and preschooler (24 months+).

Nevertheless, age and life cycle can be tricky variables.[31] In some cases, the target market for products may be the psychologically young. For example, Honda tried to target 21-year-olds with its boxy Element, which company officials described as a "dorm room on wheels." So many baby boomers were attracted to the car's ads depicting sexy college kids partying near the car at a beach, however, that the average age of buyers turned out to be 42! Nostalgia can also play a role. Chrysler had a young target market in mind for the PT Cruiser, but found that lots of older consumers were reminded of hot rods from their youth. Toyota has been more successful with its younger pitch for Scion.[32]

SCION

Named for wealthy offspring, Scion is an attempt by Toyota to attract the Gen Y audience, which might see Toyota as their parents' brand. The Scion has a hip look and feel—and an industrial strength stereo—and is sold in chrome and black showrooms tucked inside Toyota dealerships. Priced at under $15,000 and sold on a fixed price basis (no haggling), the marketing strategy is to go underground and link the brand to up-and-coming entertainment and events, allowing the youthful target to "discover" the brand.

LIFE STAGE Persons in the same part of the life cycle may differ in their life stage. **Life stage** defines a person's major concern, such as going through a divorce, going into a second marriage, taking care of an older parent, deciding to cohabit with another person, deciding to buy a new home, and so on. These life stages present opportunities for marketers who can help people cope with their major concerns.

NEWLYWEDS

It has been estimated that newlyweds in the United States spend a total of $70 billion on their households in the first year after marriage—and they buy more in the first six months of marriage than an established household does in five years! Marketers know that marriage often means that two sets of shopping habits and brand preferences have to be blended into one. Companies such as Procter & Gamble, Clorox, and Colgate-Palmolive include their products in "Newlywed Kits" that are distributed when couples apply for their marriage license. JC Penney has identified "Starting Outs" as one of its two major customer groups. Marketers pay companies a premium for name lists to assist their direct marketing because, as one marketer noted, newlywed names "are like gold."[33]

GENDER Men and women tend to have different attitudinal and behavioral orientations, based partly on genetic makeup and partly on socialization. For example, women tend to be more communal-minded and men tend to be more self-expressive and goal-directed; women tend to take in more of the data in their immediate environment; men tend to focus on the part of the environment that helps them achieve a goal. A research study examining how men and women shop found that men often need to be invited to touch a product, while women are likely to pick it up without prompting. Men often like to read product information; women may relate to a product on a more personal level.[34]

Gender differentiation has long been applied in clothing, hairstyling, cosmetics, and magazines. Avon has built a $6 billion-plus business selling beauty products to women. Some products have been positioned as more masculine or feminine. Gillette's Venus is the most successful female shaving line ever, with over 70 percent of the market, and has appropriate product design, packaging, and advertising cues to reinforce a female image; Camel Cigarettes emphasizes men and surrounds the brand with more masculine, rugged cues.

Media have emerged to facilitate gender targeting. Women can be more easily reached on Lifetime, Oxygen, and WE television networks and through scores of women's magazines; men are more likely to be found at ESPN, Comedy Central, Fuel, and Spike TV channels, and reading magazines such as *Maxim* and *Men's Health*.[35]

Some traditionally more male-oriented markets, such as the automobile industry, are beginning to recognize gender segmentation, and are changing how they design and sell cars. For example, armed with research suggesting that 80 percent of home improvement projects are now initiated by women, Lowe's designed its stores with wider aisles—to make it easier for shopping carts to get around—and to include more big-ticket appliances and high-margin home furnishings. Half of its clientele is now female, forcing its more traditional competitor, Home Depot, to introduce "Ladies Night at the Depot" to appeal to women.[36] Many others are recognizing the opportunities to target women.

An ad for financial services firm Paine Webber features a picture of two women: one clearly the mother, the other her 20-something-year-old daughter. The copy reads, "You're psyched about the future. You're full of new ideas. You're looking to start a business. You're the one on the right." The one on the right is the older woman. Paine Webber is one of a handful of companies—including Chico's, the hugely successful women's clothing chain, and New Balance sneakers—that are targeting one of the biggest, richest, most lucrative and most ignored markets: boomer women. Women control or influence 80 percent of both consumer and business goods and services. They have sole or joint ownership of 87 percent of homes and account for over 60 percent of all home improvement, home computer, and health care services purchases. And they start 70 percent of all new businesses. In short, women are spending the money and boomer women have more of it to spend.

INCOME Income segmentation is a long-standing practice in such product and service categories as automobiles, clothing, cosmetics, financial services, and travel.

WACHOVIA CORP.

Like many banks, Wachovia is trying to determine who its "sweet spot" clients are and deliver specialized services for those individuals. Wachovia's wealth management unit has determined that executives and professionals with between $2.5 million and $15 million of assets are the bank's most attractive customers. These customers are not the affluent or "ultra-wealthy" and, by and large, did not inherit their wealth. The bank plans to become extremely focused on this segment, with the idea of helping them move from creating wealth to leveraging that wealth and then, finally, to preserving it.[37]

However, income does not always predict the best customers for a given product. Blue-collar workers were among the first purchasers of color television sets; it was cheaper for them to buy these sets than to go to movies and restaurants.

Increasingly, companies are finding that their markets are "hourglass-shaped" as middle-market Americans migrate toward more premium products.[38] When Whirlpool launched a pricey Duet washer line, sales doubled forecasts in a weak economy, due primarily to middle-class shoppers who traded up. Michael Silverstein, a senior vice president and director for the Boston Consulting Group, and former BCG partner Neil Fiske have been studying this phenomenon, which they call "trading up." Their new book, *Trading Up: The New American Luxury,* documents their investigation into the forces driving the trend and points out companies that have cracked the code for success in this market:[39]

PANERA BREAD

While lunch at Panera's bakery cafés costs twice as much as at Burger King, customers don't mind paying because the cafés deliver all three benefits that Silverstein and Fiske say are common to successful new-luxury goods: *technical benefits* (how a product is engineered), *functional benefits* (the experience it provides the customer), and *emotional benefits* (how it makes the customer feel). Getting a smoked turkey breast with chipotle mayonnaise on Asiago cheese focaccia and a chai latte in a pleasing café atmosphere is the kind of satisfying experience "trading-up" customers crave. And being able to deliver that experience quickly and relatively inexpensively has spurred the growth of Panera and others in the so-called "fast casual" dining segment.

According to Silverstein and Fiske, companies that make a concerted effort to reinvent their products and come up with something genuinely better will find a huge potential market. The trading-up universe generally begins with households earning at least $50,000. In the United States, more than 47 million households have that kind of spending power. Of course, if companies miss out on this new market, they risk being "trapped in the middle" and seeing their market share steadily decline. General Motors was caught in the middle, between highly engineered German imports in the luxury market and high-value Japanese and Korean models in the economy class.[40]

GENERATION Each generation is profoundly influenced by the times in which it grows up—the music, movies, politics, and defining events of that period. Demographers call these groups *cohorts.* Members of a cohort share the same major cultural, political, and economic

FIG. 8.3

Profiling American Generations

Source: Bonnie Tsui, "Generation Next," *Advertising Age,* January 15, 2001, pp. 14–16.

GI generation (16 million people)
Born 1901–1924
Shaped by hard times and the Great Depression, financial security is one of their core values. Conservative spenders and civic-minded, they are team-oriented and patriotic.
Silent Generation (35 million people)
Born 1925–1945
Trusting conformists who value stability, they are now involved in civic life and extended families.
Baby Boomers (78 million people)
Born 1946–1964
Great acquisitors, they are value- and cause-driven despite indulgences and hedonism.
Generation X (57 million people)
Born 1965–1977
Cynical and media-savvy, they are more alienated and individualistic.
Generation Y (60 million)
Born 1978–1994
Edgy, focused on urban style, they are more idealistic than Generation X.
Millennials (42 million people)
Born 1995–2002
Multicultural, they will be tech-savvy, educated, grow up in affluent society, and have big spending power.

experiences. They have similar outlooks and values. Marketers often advertise to a cohort group by using the icons and images prominent in their experiences. Figure 8.3 depicts six well-established cohort groups. "Marketing Insight: Marketing to Generation Y" provides insight into that key age cohort. "Marketing Memo: Cheat Sheet for 21-Year-Olds" provides insights into a key part of Gen Y.

Yet, while distinctions can be made between different cohorts, generational cohorts also influence each other. For instance, because so many members of Generation Y—"Echo Boomers"—are living with their boomer parents, the parents are being influenced and exhibiting what demographers are calling a "boom-boom effect." The same products that appeal to 21-year-olds are appealing to youth-obsessed baby boomers. Boomer parents are watching MTV's *The Osbournes,* the reality show based on heavy-metal rocker Ozzy Osbourne and his family, right alongside their children.

Meredith, Schewe, and Karlovich developed a framework called The Lifestage Analytic Matrix, which combines information on cohorts, life stages, physiographics, emotional effects, and socioeconomics in analyzing a segment or individual.[41] For example, two individuals from the same cohort may differ in their *life stages* (having a divorce, getting remarried), *physiographics* (coping with hair loss, menopause, arthritis, or osteoporosis), *emotional effects* (nostalgia for the past, wanting experiences instead of things), or *socioeconomics* (losing a job, receiving an inheritance). The authors believe this analysis will lead to more efficient targeting and messages.

SOCIAL CLASS Social class has a strong influence on preference in cars, clothing, home furnishings, leisure activities, reading habits, and retailers. Many companies design products and services for specific social classes. The tastes of social classes change with the years. The 1990s were about greed and ostentation for the upper classes. Affluent tastes now run more conservatively, although luxury goods makers such as Coach, Tiffany, Burberry, TAG Heuer, and Louis Vuitton still successfully sell to those seeking the good life.[42]

Psychographic Segmentation

Psychographics is the science of using psychology and demographics to better understand consumers. In *psychographic segmentation,* buyers are divided into different groups on the basis of psychological/personality traits, lifestyle, or values. People within the same demographic group can exhibit very different psychographic profiles.

One of the most popular commercially available classification systems based on psychographic measurements is SRI Consulting Business Intelligence's (SRIC-BI) VALS™ framework. VALS classifies U.S. adults into eight primary groups based on personality traits and key demographics. The segmentation system is based on responses to a questionnaire featuring 4 demographic and 35 attitudinal questions. The VALS system is continually updated with new data from more than 80,000 surveys per year (see Figure 8.4).[43]

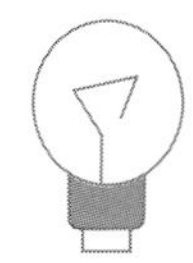

MARKETING INSIGHT | MARKETING TO GENERATION Y

They're dubbed "Echo Boomers" or "Generation Y." They grew up during times of economic abundance followed by years of economic recession. Their world was defined by long years of national calm and peace disrupted by events like Columbine and 9/11. They have been "wired" almost from birth—playing computer games, navigating the World Wide Web, downloading music, connecting with friends via instant messaging and mobile phones. They have a sense of entitlement and abundance from having grown up during the economic boom and being pampered by their boomer parents. They are selective, confident, and also impatient. They "want what they want when they want it"—and they often get it by using plastic. The average 21-year-old is carrying almost $3,000 in credit card debt (see "Marketing Memo: A Cheat Sheet for 21-Year-Olds" for more fast facts about 21-year-olds within the Gen Y cohort).

The influences that have shaped the Gen Y cohort are incredibly important to marketers because Generation Y is the force that will shape consumer and business markets for years to come. Born between 1977 and 1994, Generation Y is three times the size of Generation X. Roughly 78 million Americans belong to this group, the largest generational cohort in American history. Their spending power is estimated at $187 billion annually. If you take that $187 billion, factor in career growth, household and family formation, and multiply by another 53 years of life expectancy, you're in the $10 trillion range in consumer spending over the life span of today's 21-year-olds.

It's not surprising, then, that market researchers and advertisers are racing to get a bead on Gen Y's buying behavior. Because they are often turned off by overt branding practices and a "hard sell," marketers have tried many different approaches to reach and persuade Generation Y.[70]

1. ***Online buzz***—Rock band Foo Fighters created a digital street team that sends targeted e-mail blasts to members who "get the latest news, exclusive audio/video sneak previews, tons of chances to win great Foo Fighters prizes, and become part of the Foo Fighters Family."
2. ***Student ambassadors***—Red Bull enlists college students as Red Bull Student Brand Managers to distribute samples, research drinking trends, design on-campus marketing initiatives, and write stories for student newspapers.
3. ***Unconventional sports***—Dodge automobiles sponsors the World Dodgeball Association, which is taking the sport "to a new level by emphasizing teamwork, strategy, and skill."
4. ***Cool events***—The U.S. Open of Surfing attracted sponsors such as Honda, Philips Electronics and, of course, O'Neill Clothing, originators of the first wet suit. Spring break in Florida has been the place for the launch of such products as Old Spice Cool Contact Refreshment Towels and Calvin Klein's CK swimwear line.
5. ***Computer games***—Product placement is not restricted to movies or TV: Mountain Dew, Oakley, and Harley-Davidson all made deals to put logos on Tony Hawk's Pro Skater 3 from Activision.
6. ***Videos***—Burton snowboards ensures that its boards and riders are clearly visible in any videos that are shot.
7. ***Street teams***—As part of an anti-smoking crusade, The American Legacy hires teens as the "Truth Squad" to hand out T-shirts, bandanas, and dog tags at teen-targeted events

Sources: J. M. Lawrence, "Trends: X-ed Out: Gen Y Takes Over," *Boston Herald,* February 2, 1999, p. 243; Martha Irvine, "Labels Don't Fit Us, Gen Y Insists," *Denver Post,* April 19, 2001, p. A9; Anonymous, "Gen Y and the Future of Mall Retailing," *American Demographics* (December 2002/January 2003): J1–J4; Michael J. Weiss, "To Be about to Be," *American Demographics* (September 2003): 28–36; John Leo, "The Good-News Generation," *U.S. News & World Report,* November 3, 2003, p. 60; Kelly Pate, "Not 'X,' but 'Y' Marks the Spot: Young Generation a Marketing Target," *Denver Post,* August 17, 2003, p. K1; Bruce Horovitz, "Gen Y: A Tough Crowd to Sell," *USA Today,* April 22, 2002, pp. 1B–2B; Bruce Horovitz, "Marketers Revel with Spring Breakers," *USA Today,* March 12, 2002, p. 3B.

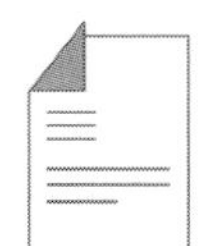

MARKETING MEMO | CHEAT SHEET FOR 21-YEAR-OLDS

In 2003, 4.1 million Americans turned 21. Here are some facts you need to know about them.

41%—Share of 21-year-olds who currently live with mom and/or dad.

60%—Share of college students who plan to move back home after graduation.

1-in-4—Odds that a 21-year-old was raised by a single parent.

70%—Share of 21-year-olds who have a full- or part-time job.

47%—Share of 21-year-olds who own a mobile phone.

23 million—Number of ad impressions received thus far by the average 21-year-old.

$2,241,141—Amount the average 21-year-old will spend between now and the end of his or her life.

$3,000—Credit card debt of the average 21-year-old.

5.8—Years until the average 21-year-old man marries for the first time.

4.1—Years until the average 21-year-old woman marries for the first time.

10—Years until the average 21-year-old buys his or her first vacation home.

43%—Share of 21-year-olds who have a tattoo or a body piercing.

62%—Share of 21-year-olds who are non-Hispanic whites.

Source: John Fetto, "Twenty-One, and Counting . . . ," *American Demographics* (September 2003): 48.

FIG. 8.4

The VALS Segmentation System: An 8-Part Typology

Source: © 2004 by SRI Consulting Business Intelligence. All rights reserved. Printed by permission.

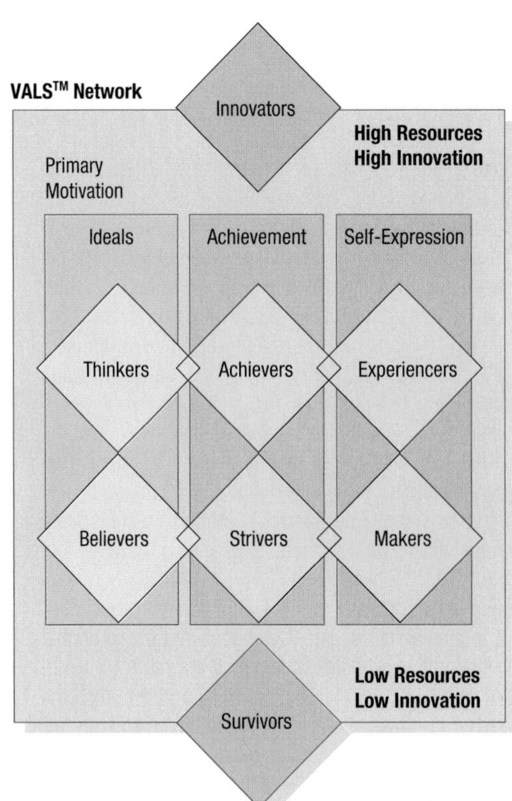

The major tendencies of the four groups with higher resources are:

1. ***Innovators*** – Successful, sophisticated, active, "take-charge" people with high self-esteem. Purchases often reflect cultivated tastes for relatively upscale, niche-oriented products and services.
2. ***Thinkers*** – Mature, satisfied, and reflective people who are motivated by ideals and value order, knowledge, and responsibility. Favor durability, functionality, and value in products.
3. ***Achievers*** – Successful goal-oriented people who focus on career and family. Favor premium products that demonstrate success to their peers.
4. ***Experiencers*** – Young, enthusiastic, impulsive people who seek variety and excitement. Spend a comparatively high proportion of income on fashion, entertainment, and socializing.

The major tendencies of the four groups with lower resources are:

1. ***Believers*** – Conservative, conventional, and traditional people with concrete beliefs. Favor familiar, American products and are loyal to established brands.
2. ***Strivers*** – Trendy and fun-loving people who are resource-constrained. Favor stylish products that emulate the purchases of those with greater material wealth.
3. ***Makers*** – Practical, down-to-earth, self-sufficient people who like to work with their hands. Favor American-made products with a practical or functional purpose.
4. ***Survivors*** – Elderly, passive people who are concerned about change. Loyal to their favorite brands.

You can find out which VALS type you are by going to SRIC-BI's Web site (www.sric-bi.com).

Psychographic segmentation schemes are often customized by culture. The Japanese version of VALS, Japan VALS™, divides society into 10 consumer segments on the basis of two key consumer concepts: life orientation (traditional ways, occupations, innovation, and self-expression) and attitudes to social change (sustaining, pragmatic, adapting, and innovating).

Behavioral Segmentation

In behavioral segmentation, buyers are divided into groups on the basis of their knowledge of, attitude toward, use of, or response to a product.

Once cranberries were used only for holiday dinner at Thanksgiving and Christmas. Ocean Spray cranberry-based juice drinks have given the company a year-round market for its product.

DECISION ROLES It is easy to identify the buyer for many products. In the United States, men normally choose their shaving equipment, and women choose their pantyhose; but even here marketers must be careful in making their targeting decisions, because buying roles change. When ICI, the giant British chemical company, discovered that women made 60 percent of the decisions on the brand of household paint, it decided to advertise its DuLux brand to women.

People play five roles in a buying decision: *Initiator, Influencer, Decider, Buyer, User.* For example, assume a wife initiates a purchase by requesting a new treadmill for her birthday. The husband may then seek information from many sources, including his best friend who has a treadmill and is a key influencer in what models to consider. After presenting the alternative choices to his wife, he then purchases her preferred model which, as it turns out, ends up being used by the entire family. Different people are playing different roles, but all are crucial in the decision process and ultimate consumer satisfaction.

BEHAVIORAL VARIABLES Many marketers believe that behavioral variables—occasions, benefits, user status, usage rate, loyalty status, buyer-readiness stage, and attitude—are the best starting points for constructing market segments.

Occasions Occasions can be defined in terms of the time of day, week, month, year, or in terms of other well-defined temporal aspects of a consumer's life. Buyers can be distinguished according to the occasions when they develop a need, purchase a product, or use a product. For example, air travel is triggered by occasions related to business, vacation, or family. Occasion segmentation can help firms expand product usage. For example, the Florida Citrus Growers ran an ad campaign—"Orange Juice. It's Not Just For Breakfast Anymore"— to expand its usage to other day parts. During the 1960s and 1970s, Ocean Spray Cranberries, Inc., was essentially a single-purpose, single-usage product: Consumption of cranberries was almost entirely confined to the serving of cranberry sauce as a side dish with Thanksgiving and Christmas holiday dinners. After a pesticide scare one Thanksgiving drastically cut sales and almost put growers out of business, the cooperative embarked on a program to diversify and create a year-round market by producing cranberry-based juice drinks and other products.[44]

Marketers also can try to extend activities associated with certain holidays to other times of the year. For instance, while Christmas, Mother's Day, and Valentine's Day are the three major gift-giving holidays, these and other holidays account for just over half of the gifters' budgets. That leaves the rest available throughout the year for occasion-driven gift-giving: birthdays, weddings, anniversaries, housewarming, and new babies.[45]

Benefits Buyers can be classified according to the benefits they seek. Even car drivers who want to stop for gas may seek different benefits. Through its research, Mobil identified five different benefit segments and their sizes:

1. ***Road Warriors*** – premium products and quality service. (16%)
2. ***Generation F*** – fast fuel, fast service, and fast food. (27%)
3. ***True Blues*** – branded products and reliable service. (16%)
4. ***Home Bodies*** – convenience. (21%)
5. ***Price Shoppers*** – low price. (20%)

Surprisingly, although gasoline is largely a commodity, price shoppers constituted only 20 percent of the buyers. Mobil decided to focus on the less price-sensitive segments, and rolled out *Friendly Serve:* cleaner property, bathrooms, better lighting, well-stocked stores, and friendlier personnel. Although Mobil charged 2 cents per gallon more than its competitors, sales increased by 20 to 25 percent.[46]

User Status Markets can be segmented into nonusers, ex-users, potential users, first-time users, and regular users of a product. Blood banks cannot rely only on regular donors to supply blood; they must also recruit new first-time donors and contact ex-donors. Each will require a different marketing strategy. Included in the potential user group are consumers who will become users in connection with some life stage or life event. Mothers-to-be are potential users who will turn into heavy users. Producers of infant products and services learn their names and shower them with products and ads to capture a share of their future purchases. Market-share leaders tend to focus on attracting potential users because they have the most to gain. Smaller firms focus on trying to attract current users away from the market leader.

Usage Rate Markets can be segmented into light, medium, and heavy product users. Heavy users are often a small percentage of the market but account for a high percentage of total consumption. For example, heavy beer drinkers account for 87 percent of the beer consumed—almost seven times as much as the light beer drinkers. Marketers would rather attract one heavy user than several light users. A potential problem, however, is that heavy users often either are extremely loyal to one brand, or never stay loyal to a brand and are always looking for the lowest price.

Buyer-Readiness Stage A market consists of people in different stages of readiness to buy a product. Some are unaware of the product, some are aware, some are informed, some are interested, some desire the product, and some intend to buy. The relative numbers make a big difference in designing the marketing program. Suppose a health agency wants to encourage women to have an annual Pap test to detect possible cervical cancer. At the beginning, most women may be unaware of the Pap test. The marketing effort should go into awareness-building advertising using a simple message. Later, the advertising should dramatize the benefits of the Pap test and the risks of not taking it. A special offer of a free health examination might motivate women to actually sign up for the test.

Loyalty Status Buyers can be divided into four groups according to brand loyalty status:

1. ***Hard-core loyals*** – Consumers who buy only one brand all the time.
2. ***Split loyals*** – Consumers who are loyal to two or three brands.

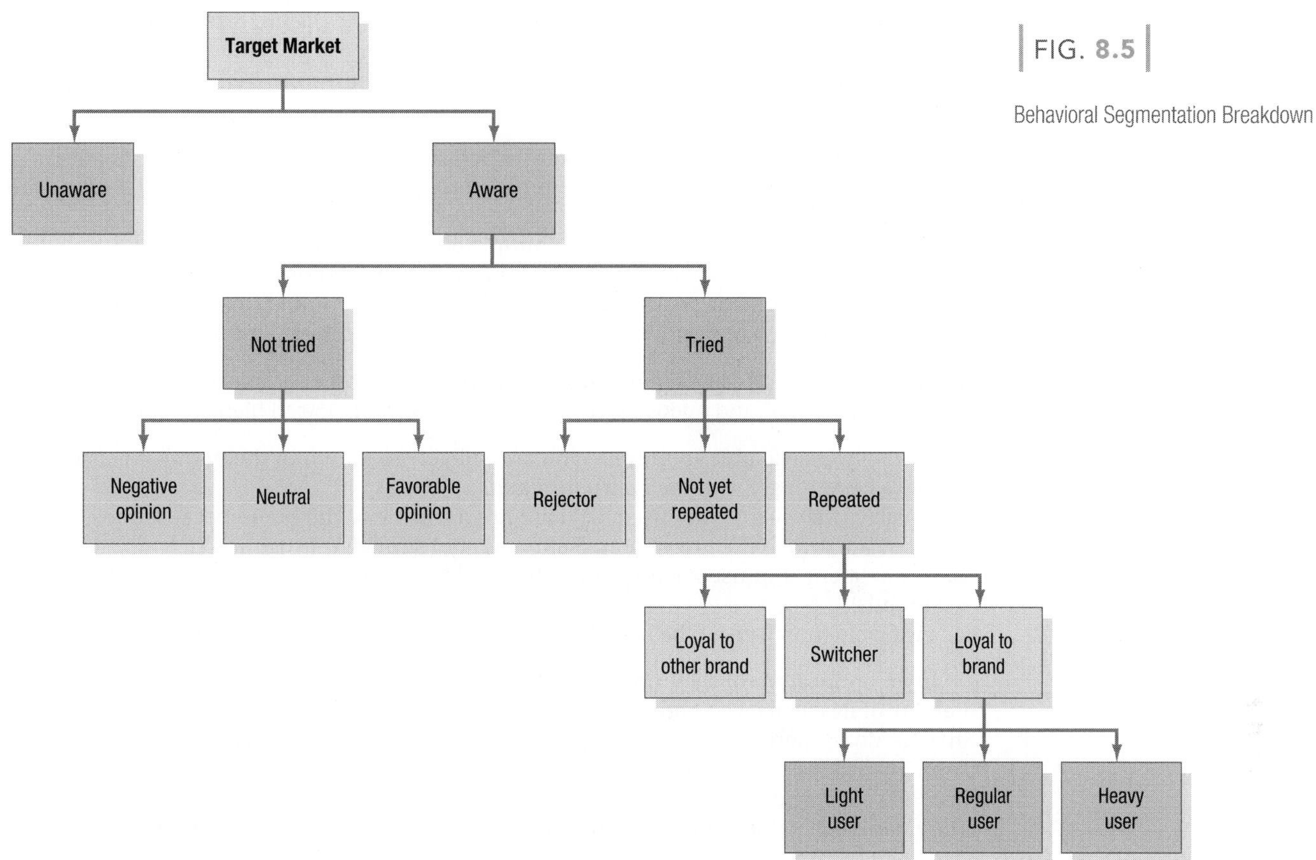

FIG. 8.5

Behavioral Segmentation Breakdown

3. ***Shifting loyals*** – Consumers who shift loyalty from one brand to another.
4. ***Switchers*** – Consumers who show no loyalty to any brand.[47]

A company can learn a great deal by analyzing the degrees of brand loyalty: (1) By studying its hard-core loyals, the company can identify its products' strengths. (2) By studying its split loyals, the company can pinpoint which brands are most competitive with its own. (3) By looking at customers who are shifting away from its brand, the company can learn about its marketing weaknesses and attempt to correct them.

Companies selling in a market dominated by switchers may have to rely more on price-cutting. If mistreated, they can also turn on the company. One caution: What appear to be brand-loyal purchase patterns may reflect habit, indifference, a low price, a high switching cost, or the nonavailability of other brands.

Attitude Five attitude groups can be found in a market: enthusiastic, positive, indifferent, negative, and hostile. Door-to-door workers in a political campaign use voter attitude to determine how much time to spend with that voter. They thank enthusiastic voters and remind them to vote; they reinforce those who are positively disposed; they try to win the votes of indifferent voters; they spend no time trying to change the attitudes of negative and hostile voters.

Combining different behavioral bases can help to provide a more comprehensive and cohesive view of a market and its segments. Figure 8.5 depicts one possible way to break down a target market by various behavioral segmentation bases.

THE CONVERSION MODEL The Conversion Model has been developed to measure the strength of the psychological commitment between brands and consumers and their openness to change.[48] To determine the ease with which a consumer can be converted to another choice, the model assesses commitment based on factors such as consumer attitudes toward and satisfaction with current brand choices in a category and the importance of the decision to select a brand in the category.[49]

The model segments *users* of a brand into four groups based on strength of commitment, from low to high, as follows:

1. Convertible (users who are most likely to defect).
2. Shallow (consumers who are uncommitted to the brand and could switch—some are actively considering alternatives).
3. Average (consumers who are also committed to the brand they are using, but not as strongly—they are unlikely to switch brands in the short term).
4. Entrenched (consumers who are strongly committed to the brand they are currently using—they are highly unlikely to switch brands in the foreseeable future).

The model also classifies *nonusers* of a brand into four other groups based on their "balance of disposition" and openness to trying the brand, from low to high, as follows:

1. Strongly Unavailable (nonusers who are unlikely to switch to the brand—their preference lies strongly with their current brands).
2. Weakly Unavailable (nonusers who are not available to the brand because their preference lies with their current brand, although not strongly).
3. Ambivalent (nonusers who are as attracted to the brand as they are to their current brands).
4. Available (nonusers of the brand who are most likely to be acquired in the short run).

In an application of the Conversion Model, Lloyds TSB bank discovered that the profitability of its clients who had been identified as "least committed" had fallen by 14 percent in a 12-month period, whereas those that were "most committed" had increased by 9 percent. Those who were "committed" were 20 percent more likely to increase the number of products they held during the 12-month period. As a result, the bank took action to attract and retain high-value committed customers, which resulted in increased profitability.

::: Bases for Segmenting Business Markets

Business markets can be segmented with some of the same variables used in consumer market segmentation, such as geography, benefits sought, and usage rate, but business marketers also use other variables. Bonoma and Shapiro proposed segmenting the business market with the variables shown in Table 8.2. The demographic variables are the most important, followed by the operating variables—down to the personal characteristics of the buyer.

The table lists major questions that business marketers should ask in determining which segments and customers to serve. A rubber-tire company should first decide which industries it wants to serve. It can sell tires to manufacturers of automobiles, trucks, farm tractors, forklift trucks, or aircraft. Within a chosen target industry, a company can further segment by company size. The company might set up separate operations for selling to large and small customers. Consider how Dell is organized.

DELL

Dell is divided into two direct sales divisions: One sells to consumers and small businesses; another manages the company's corporate accounts. Three key segments are included under the corporate accounts umbrella: the enterprise group (*Fortune* 500 companies), large corporate accounts (multinational companies in what would be the *Fortune* 501 to 2000 range), and preferred accounts (medium businesses with 200 to 2,000 employees).

Marketing to Small Businesses

Small businesses, in particular, have become a Holy Grail for business marketers.[50] In the United States, small businesses are now responsible for 50 percent of the gross national product, according to the U.S. Small Business Administration, and this segment is growing at 11 percent annually, three percentage points higher than the growth of large companies. Here are two examples of companies focusing on small businesses.

TABLE 8.2

Major Segmentation Variables for Business Markets

Demographic

1. *Industry:* Which industries should we serve?
2. *Company size:* What size companies should we serve?
3. *Location:* What geographical areas should we serve?

Operating Variables

4. *Technology:* What customer technologies should we focus on?
5. *User or nonuser status:* Should we serve heavy users, medium users, light users, or nonusers?
6. *Customer capabilities:* Should we serve customers needing many or few services?

Purchasing Approaches

7. *Purchasing-function organization:* Should we serve companies with highly centralized or decentralized purchasing organizations?
8. *Power structure:* Should we serve companies that are engineering dominated, financially dominated, and so on?
9. *Nature of existing relationships:* Should we serve companies with which we have strong relationships or simply go after the most desirable companies?
10. *General purchase policies:* Should we serve companies that prefer leasing? Service contracts? Systems purchases? Sealed bidding?
11. *Purchasing criteria:* Should we serve companies that are seeking quality? Service? Price?

Situational Factors

12. *Urgency:* Should we serve companies that need quick and sudden delivery or service?
13. *Specific application:* Should we focus on certain applications of our product rather than all applications?
14. *Size of order:* Should we focus on large or small orders?

Personal Characteristics

15. *Buyer-seller similarity:* Should we serve companies whose people and values are similar to ours?
16. *Attitudes toward risk:* Should we serve risk-taking or risk-avoiding customers?
17. *Loyalty:* Should we serve companies that show high loyalty to their suppliers?

Source: Adapted from Thomas V. Bonoma and Benson P. Shapiro, *Segmenting the Industrial Market* (Lexington, MA: Lexington Books, 1983).

BB&T

BB&T Corporation, headquartered in Winston-Salem, North Carolina, is positioning itself as a powerful local bank with a down-home approach. It launched a business-to-business (B2B) advertising campaign depicting various Carolina businesses and their owners. Each entrepreneur is a BB&T small business customer, and the ads reinforce the bank's commitment to small business.[51]

PENN NATIONAL INSURANCE

With 82 percent of its commercial business coming from small businesses, Penn National Insurance decided it needed to identify the different classes of business that offer the greatest opportunity for profit. Working with a commercial insurance database, the company was able to categorize such key information as exposure data, growth, and employment information by business classification, size, and location. Beyond making it easier for agents to pinpoint prospects, the segmentation scheme also helped Penn National diversify beyond its concentration in the construction business. Overall, some 244 small business segments (based on SIC codes) were identified.[52]

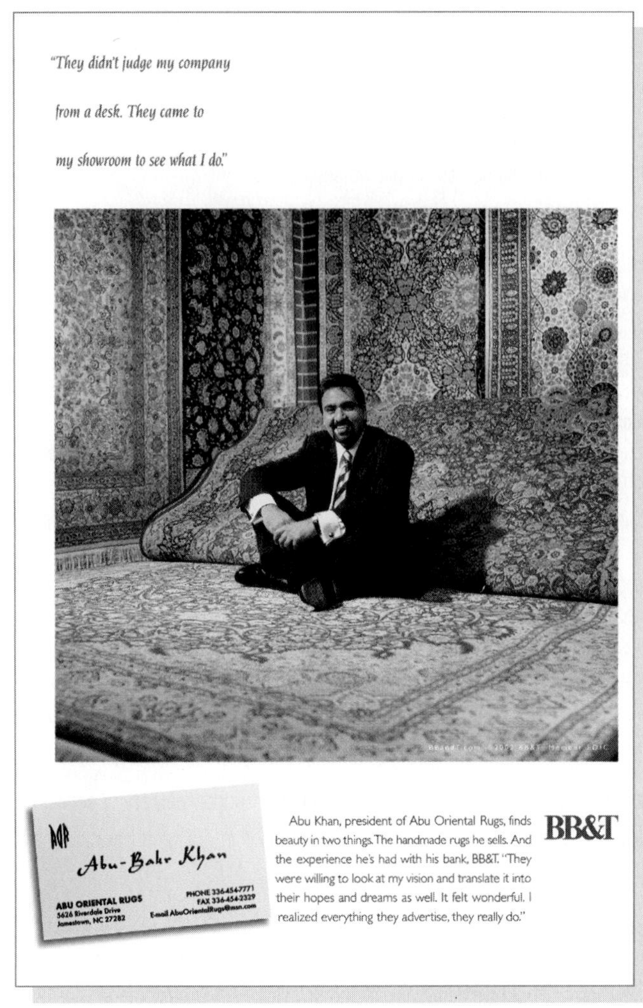

One of North Carolina BB&T bank's B to B ads featuring local businesses and their owners: "They didn't judge my company from a desk. They came to my showroom to see what I do."

Within a given target industry and customer size, a company can segment by purchase criteria. For example, government laboratories need low prices and service contracts for scientific equipment; university laboratories need equipment that requires little service; and industrial laboratories need equipment that is highly reliable and accurate.

Sequential Segmentation

Business marketers generally identify segments through a sequential process. Consider an aluminum company: The company first undertook macrosegmentation. It looked at which end-use market to serve: automobile, residential, or beverage containers. It chose the residential market, and needed to determine the most attractive product application: semifinished material, building components, or aluminum mobile homes. Deciding to focus on building components, it considered the best customer size and chose large customers. The second stage consisted of microsegmentation. The company distinguished among customers buying on price, service, or quality. Because the aluminum company had a high-service profile, it decided to concentrate on the service-motivated segment of the market.

Business buyers seek different benefit bundles based on their stage in the purchase decision process:[53]

1. ***First-time prospects*** – Customers who have not yet purchased but want to buy from a vendor who understands their business, who explains things well, and whom they can trust.
2. ***Novices*** – Customers who are starting their purchasing relationship want easy-to-read manuals, hot lines, a high level of training, and knowledgeable sales reps.
3. ***Sophisticates*** – Established customers want speed in maintenance and repair, product customization, and high technical support.

These segments may also have different channel preferences. First-time prospects would prefer to deal with a company salesperson instead of a catalog or direct-mail channel, because the latter provides too little information. Sophisticates, on the other hand, may want to conduct more of their buying over electronic channels.

One proposed segmentation scheme classifies business buyers into three groups, each warranting a different type of selling:[54]

- ***Price-oriented customers (transactional selling).*** They want value through lowest price.
- ***Solution-oriented customers (consultative selling).*** They want value through more benefits and advice.
- ***Strategic-value customers (enterprise selling).*** They want value through the supplier co-investing and participating in the customer's business.

The authors cite several cases of mismanagement by companies that did not understand the business buyer:

- A packaging manufacturer decided to upgrade and rename sales reps as packaging consultants at a cost of $10 million, but 90 percent of its customers bought transactionally. The company failed and was acquired by a major competitor who reintroduced a transactional selling effort.
- A consulting firm replaced its long-term consultants with salespeople to sell quick consulting projects. They acquired many new clients but lost most of their old clients, who wanted consultative selling.
- A container manufacturer selling consultatively to a major food company was asked to join in some risk and gain sharing involving co-development of radically new packaging approaches. It refused and lost the account.

::: Market Targeting

Once the firm has identified its market-segment opportunities, it has to decide how many and which ones to target. Marketers are increasingly combining several variables in an effort to identify smaller, better-defined target groups. Thus, a bank may not only identify a group of wealthy retired adults, but within that group distinguish several segments depending on current income, assets, savings, and risk preferences. This has led some market researchers to advocate a *needs-based market segmentation approach.* Roger Best proposed the seven-step approach shown in Table 8.3.

TABLE 8.3

Steps in the Segmentation Process

	Description
1. Needs-Based Segmentation	Group customers into segments based on similar needs and benefits sought by customer in solving a particular consumption problem.
2. Segment Identification	For each needs-based segment, determine which demographics, lifestyles, and usage behaviors make the segment distinct and identifiable (actionable).
3. Segment Attractiveness	Using predetermined segment attractiveness criteria (such as market growth, competitive intensity, and market access), determine the overall attractiveness of each segment.
4. Segment Profitability	Determine segment profitability.
5. Segment Positioning	For each segment, create a "value proposition" and product-price positioning strategy based on that segment's unique customer needs and characteristics.
6. Segment "Acid Test"	Create "segment storyboards" to test the attractiveness of each segment's positioning strategy.
7. Marketing-Mix Strategy	Expand segment positioning strategy to include all aspects of the marketing mix: product, price, promotion, and place.

Source: Adapted from Robert J. Best, *Market-Based Management* (Upper Saddle River, NJ: Prentice Hall, 2000).

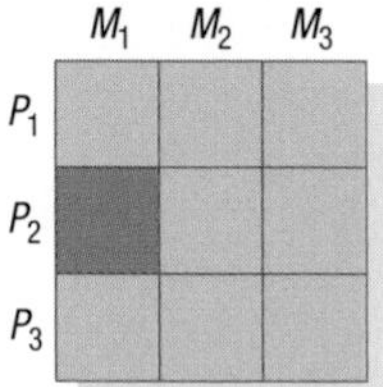

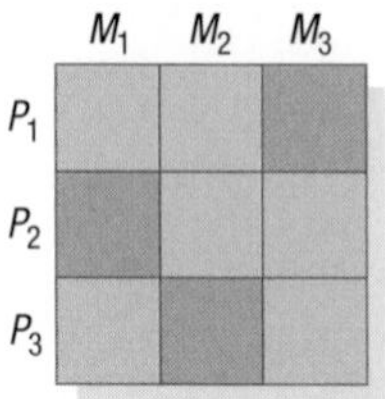

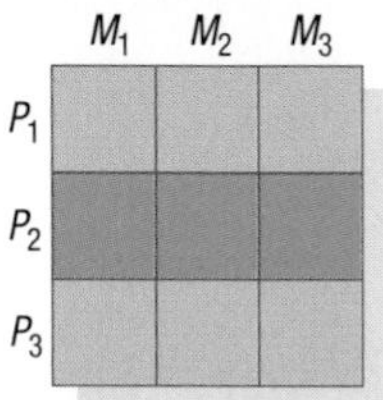

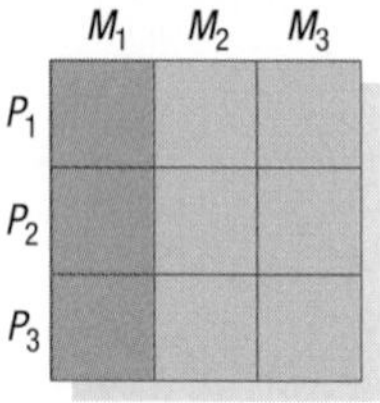

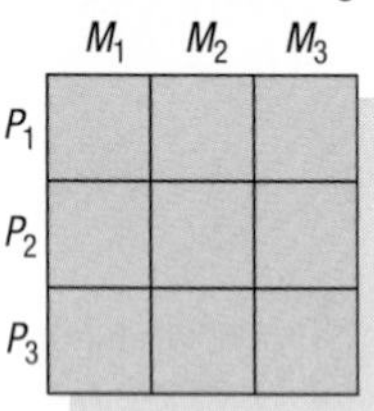

P = Product M = Market

FIG. 8.6

Five Patterns of Target Market Selection

Source: Adapted from Derek F. Abell, *Defining the Business: The Starting Point of Strategic Planning* (Upper Saddle River, NJ: Prentice Hall, 1980), ch. 8, pp. 192–196.

Effective Segmentation Criteria

Not all segmentation schemes are useful. For example, table salt buyers could be divided into blond and brunette customers, but hair color is undoubtedly irrelevant to the purchase of salt. Furthermore, if all salt buyers buy the same amount of salt each month, believe all salt is the same, and would pay only one price for salt, this market would be minimally segmentable from a marketing point of view.

To be useful, market segments must rate favorably on five key criteria:

- ***Measurable.*** The size, purchasing power, and characteristics of the segments can be measured.
- ***Substantial.*** The segments are large and profitable enough to serve. A segment should be the largest possible homogeneous group worth going after with a tailored marketing program. It would not pay, for example, for an automobile manufacturer to develop cars for people who are under four feet tall.
- ***Accessible.*** The segments can be effectively reached and served.
- ***Differentiable.*** The segments are conceptually distinguishable and respond differently to different marketing-mix elements and programs. If married and unmarried women respond similarly to a sale on perfume, they do not constitute separate segments.
- ***Actionable.*** Effective programs can be formulated for attracting and serving the segments.

Evaluating and Selecting the Market Segments

In evaluating different market segments, the firm must look at two factors: the segment's overall attractiveness and the company's objectives and resources. How well does a potential segment score on the five criteria? Does a potential segment have characteristics that make it generally attractive, such as size, growth, profitability, scale economies, and low risk? Does investing in the segment make sense given the firm's objectives, competencies, and resources? Some attractive segments may not mesh with the company's long-run objectives, or the company may lack one or more necessary competencies to offer superior value.

After evaluating different segments, the company can consider five patterns of target market selection, shown in Figure 8.6.

SINGLE-SEGMENT CONCENTRATION Volkswagen concentrates on the small-car market and Porsche on the sports car market. Through concentrated marketing, the firm gains a strong knowledge of the segment's needs and achieves a strong market presence. Furthermore, the firm enjoys operating economies through specializing its production, distribution, and promotion. If it captures segment leadership, the firm can earn a high return on its investment.

However, there are risks. A particular market segment can turn sour or a competitor may invade the segment: When digital camera technology took off, Polaroid's earnings fell sharply. For these reasons, many companies prefer to operate in more than one segment. If selecting more than one segment to serve, a company should pay close attention to segment interrelationships on the cost, performance, and technology side. A company carrying fixed costs (sales force, store outlets) can add products to absorb and share some costs. The sales force will sell additional products, and a fast-food outlet will offer additional menu items. Economies of scope can be just as important as economies of scale.

Companies can try to operate in supersegments rather than in isolated segments. A **supersegment** is a set of segments sharing some exploitable similarity. For example, many symphony orchestras target people who have broad cultural interests, rather than only those who regularly attend concerts.

SELECTIVE SPECIALIZATION A firm selects a number of segments, each objectively attractive and appropriate. There may be little or no synergy among the segments, but each promises to be a moneymaker. This multisegment strategy has the advantage of diversifying the firm's risk. When Procter & Gamble launched Crest Whitestrips, initial target segments included newly engaged women and brides-to-be as well as gay males.

PRODUCT SPECIALIZATION The firm makes a certain product that it sells to several different market segments. An example would be a microscope manufacturer who sells to university, government, and commercial laboratories. The firm makes different microscopes for the different customer groups and builds a strong reputation in the specific product area. The downside risk is that the product may be supplanted by an entirely new technology.

MARKET SPECIALIZATION The firm concentrates on serving many needs of a particular customer group. An example would be a firm that sells an assortment of products only to university laboratories. The firm gains a strong reputation in serving this customer group and becomes a channel for additional products the customer group can use. The downside risk is that the customer group may suffer budget cuts or shrink in size.

FULL MARKET COVERAGE The firm attempts to serve all customer groups with all the products they might need. Only very large firms such as IBM (computer market), General Motors (vehicle market), and Coca-Cola (nonalcoholic beverage market) can undertake a full market coverage strategy. Large firms can cover a whole market in two broad ways: through undifferentiated marketing or differentiated marketing.

In *undifferentiated marketing,* the firm ignores segment differences and goes after the whole market with one offer. It designs a product and a marketing program that will appeal to the broadest number of buyers. It relies on mass distribution and advertising. It aims to endow the product with a superior image. Undifferentiated marketing is "the marketing counterpart to standardization and mass production in manufacturing."[55] The narrow product line keeps down costs of research and development, production, inventory, transportation, marketing research, advertising, and product management. The undifferentiated advertising program keeps down advertising costs. Presumably, the company can turn its lower costs into lower prices to win the price-sensitive segment of the market.

In *differentiated marketing,* the firm operates in several market segments and designs different products for each segment. Cosmetics firm Estée Lauder markets brands that appeal to women (and men) of different tastes: The flagship brand, the original Estée Lauder, appeals to older consumers; Clinique caters to middle-aged women; M.A.C. to youthful hipsters; Aveda to aromatherapy enthusiasts; and Origins to ecoconscious consumers who want cosmetics made from natural ingredients.[56]

EMMIS BROADCASTING

Emmis Communications owns three different radio stations in New York with three different distinct targets and positions: WQHT-FM ("Hot 97") proclaims that it plays "blazin' hip-hop (urban street music) and R&B," and is popular with listeners in the under-25 crowd. WRKS-FM (98.7 KISS-FM) describes itself as "offering the best variety of old school and today's R&B [rhythm and blues]," and appeals to older listeners. WQCD-FM (CD 101.9) is the country's largest smooth jazz radio station and targets adults age 25 to 54, who want a radio station to relax to and to listen to at work.[57] If one of the formats falls out of fashion, the fact that the other stations tap into different market segments provides a potential buffer to ratings and sales.

MANAGING MULTIPLE SEGMENTS The best way to manage multiple segments is to appoint segment managers with sufficient authority and responsibility for building the segment's business. At the same time, segment managers should not be so focused as to resist cooperating with other groups in the company. Consider the following situation.

BAXTER

Baxter operates several divisions selling different products and services to hospitals. Each division sends out its own invoices. Some hospitals complain about receiving as many as seven different Baxter invoices each month. Baxter's marketers finally convinced the separate divisions to send the invoices to headquarters so that Baxter could send one invoice a month to its customers.

Differentiated marketing: Emmis Broadcasting's WRKS (98.7 KISS-FM) appeals to older listeners with old school and today's R&B; its other stations in the New York market target under-25s with hip-hop (WQHT-FM) and adults 25-54 with smooth jazz (CD 101.9).

DIFFERENTIATED MARKETING COSTS Differentiated marketing typically creates more total sales than undifferentiated marketing. However, it also increases the costs of doing business. The following costs are likely to be higher:

- ***Product modification costs.*** Modifying a product to meet different market-segment requirements usually involves R&D, engineering, and special tooling costs.
- ***Manufacturing costs.*** It is usually more expensive to produce 10 units of 10 different products than 100 units of one product. The longer the production setup time and the smaller the sales volume of each product, the more expensive the product becomes. However, if each model is sold in sufficiently large volume, the higher setup costs may be quite small per unit.
- ***Administrative costs.*** The company has to develop separate marketing plans for each market segment. This requires extra marketing research, forecasting, sales analysis, promotion, planning, and channel management.
- ***Inventory costs.*** It is more costly to manage inventories containing many products.
- ***Promotion costs.*** The company has to reach different market segments with different promotion programs. The result is increased promotion-planning costs and media costs.

Because differentiated marketing leads to both higher sales and higher costs, nothing general can be said regarding the profitability of this strategy. Companies should be cautious about oversegmenting their markets. If this happens, they may want to turn to *countersegmentation* to broaden the customer base. For example, Johnson & Johnson broadened its target market for its baby shampoo to include adults. Smith Kline Beecham launched its Aquafresh toothpaste to attract three benefit segments simultaneously: those seeking fresh breath, whiter teeth, and cavity protection.

Additional Considerations

Three other considerations must be taken into account in evaluating and selecting segments: segment-by-segment invasion plans, updating segmentation schemes, and ethical choice of market targets.

SEGMENT-BY-SEGMENT INVASION PLANS A company would be wise to enter one segment at a time. Competitors must not know to what segment(s) the firm will move next.

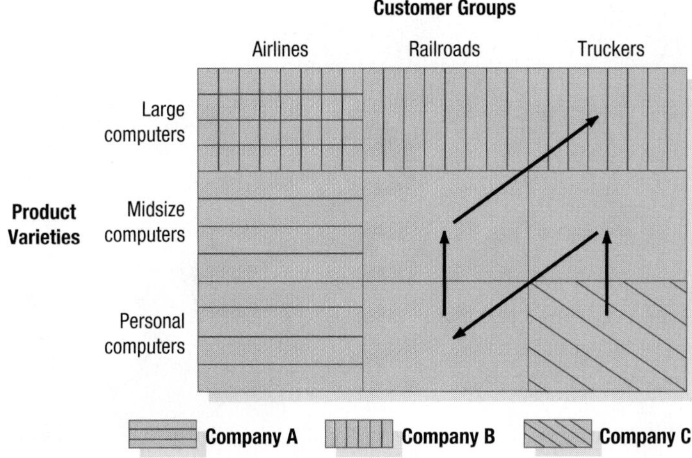

FIG. 8.7

Segment-by-Segment Invasion Plan

Segment-by-segment invasion plans are illustrated in Figure 8.7. Three firms, A, B, and C, have specialized in adapting computer systems to the needs of airlines, railroads, and trucking companies. Company A meets all the computer needs of airlines. Company B sells large computer systems to all three transportation sectors. Company C sells personal computers to trucking companies.

Where should company C move next? Arrows have been added to the chart to show the planned sequence of segment invasions. Company C will next offer midsize computers to trucking companies. Then, to allay company B's concern about losing some large computer business with trucking companies, C's next move will be to sell personal computers to railroads. Later, C will offer midsize computers to railroads. Finally, it may launch a full-scale attack on company B's large computer position in trucking companies. Of course, C's hidden planned moves are provisional in that much depends on competitors' segment moves and responses.

Unfortunately, too many companies fail to develop a long-term invasion plan. PepsiCo is an exception. It first attacked Coca-Cola in the grocery market, then in the vending-machine market, then in the fast-food market, and so on. Japanese firms also plot their invasion sequence. They first gain a foothold in a market, then enter new segments with products. Toyota began by introducing small cars (Tercel, Corolla), then expanded into midsize cars (Camry, Avalon), and finally into luxury cars (Lexus).

A company's invasion plans can be thwarted when it confronts blocked markets. The invader must then figure out a way to break in. The problem of entering blocked markets calls for a megamarketing approach. **Megamarketing** is the strategic coordination of economic, psychological, political, and public relations skills, to gain the cooperation of a number of parties in order to enter or operate in a given market. Pepsi used megamarketing to enter the Indian market.

PEPSICO

After Coca-Cola left India, Pepsi worked with an Indian business group to gain government approval for its entry, over the objections of domestic soft drink companies and anti-multinational legislators. Pepsi offered to help India export some agricultural products in a volume that would more than cover the cost of importing soft-drink concentrate. Pepsi also promised to help rural areas in their economic development. It further offered to transfer food-processing, packaging, and water-treatment technology to India. Pepsi's bundle of benefits won the support of various Indian interest groups.

Once in, a multinational must be on its best behavior. This calls for well-thought-out *civic positioning.*

A Pepsi ad from India. To enter the Indian market, Pepsi used megamarketing: With the aid of an Indian business group, it offered a package of benefits that gained it acceptance.

HEWLETT-PACKARD

Hewlett-Packard positions itself as a company implementing "e-inclusion,"— the attempt to help bring the benefits of technology to the poor. Toward that end, HP has begun a three-year project designed to create jobs, improve education, and provide better access to government services in the Indian state of Kuppam. Working with the local government, as well as a branch of HP Labs based in India, the company is helping to provide the rural poor with access to government records, schools, health information, crop prices, and so forth. Its hope is to stimulate small, tech-based businesses. Not only does this build goodwill and the HP brand in India, but it will also help the company discover new, profitable lines of business.[58]

UPDATING SEGMENTATION SCHEMES Market segmentation analysis must be done periodically because segments change. At one time the personal computer industry segmented its products purely on speed and power. Later, PC marketers recognized an emerging "Soho" market, named for "small office and home office." Mail-order companies such as Dell and Gateway appealed to this market's requirement for high performance coupled with low price and user-friendliness. Shortly thereafter, PC makers began to see Soho as comprised of smaller segments. "Small-office needs might be very different from home-office needs," says one Dell executive.[59]

One way to discover new segments is to investigate the hierarchy of attributes consumers examine in choosing a brand if they use phased decision strategies. This process is called **market partitioning**. Years ago, most car buyers first decided on the manufacturer and then on one of its car divisions (*brand-dominant hierarchy*). A buyer might favor General Motors cars and, within this set, Pontiac. Today, many buyers decide first on the nation from which they want to buy a car (*nation-dominant hierarchy*). Buyers may first decide they want to buy a Japanese car, then Toyota, and then the Corolla model of Toyota. Companies must monitor potential shifts in consumers' hierarchy of attributes and adjust to changing priorities.

The hierarchy of attributes can reveal customer segments. Buyers who first decide on price are price dominant; those who first decide on the type of car (e.g., sports, passenger, station wagon) are type dominant; those who first decide on the car brand are brand dominant. Those who are type/price/brand dominant make up a segment; those who are quality/service/type dominant make up another segment. Each segment may have distinct demographics, psychographics, and mediagraphics.[60]

ETHICAL CHOICE OF MARKET TARGETS Market targeting sometimes generates public controversy.[61] The public is concerned when marketers take unfair advantage of vulnerable groups (such as children) or disadvantaged groups (such as inner-city poor people), or promote potentially harmful products. The cereal industry has been heavily criticized for marketing efforts directed toward children. Critics worry that high-powered appeals presented through the mouths of lovable animated characters will overwhelm children's defenses and lead them to want sugared cereals or poorly balanced breakfasts. Toy marketers have been similarly criticized. McDonald's and other chains have drawn criticism for pitching their high-fat, salt-laden fare to low-income, inner-city residents.

Internal documents from R. J. Reynolds and Brown & Williamson Tobacco Corporation (marketer of the Kool brand) have revealed the extent to which these companies targeted black youths age 16 to 25, particularly with their menthol brands.[62] G. Heileman Brewing drew fire when it extended its Colt 45 malt liquor line with Powermaster, a new high-test malt (5.9 alcohol). Malt liquor is consumed primarily by blacks, and by targeting blacks extensively Heileman was itself targeted by federal officials, industry leaders, black activists, and the media.[63]

Not all attempts to target children, minorities, or other special segments draw criticism. Colgate-Palmolive's Colgate Junior toothpaste has special features designed to get children to brush longer and more often. Other companies are responding to the special needs of minority segments. Black-owned ICE theaters noticed that although moviegoing by blacks has surged, there were few inner-city theaters. Starting in Chicago, ICE partnered with the black communities in which it operates theaters, using local radio stations to promote films and featuring favorite food items at concession stands.[64] Thus the issue is not who is targeted, but rather, how and for what. Socially responsible marketing calls for targeting that serves not only the company's interests, but also the interests of those targeted.

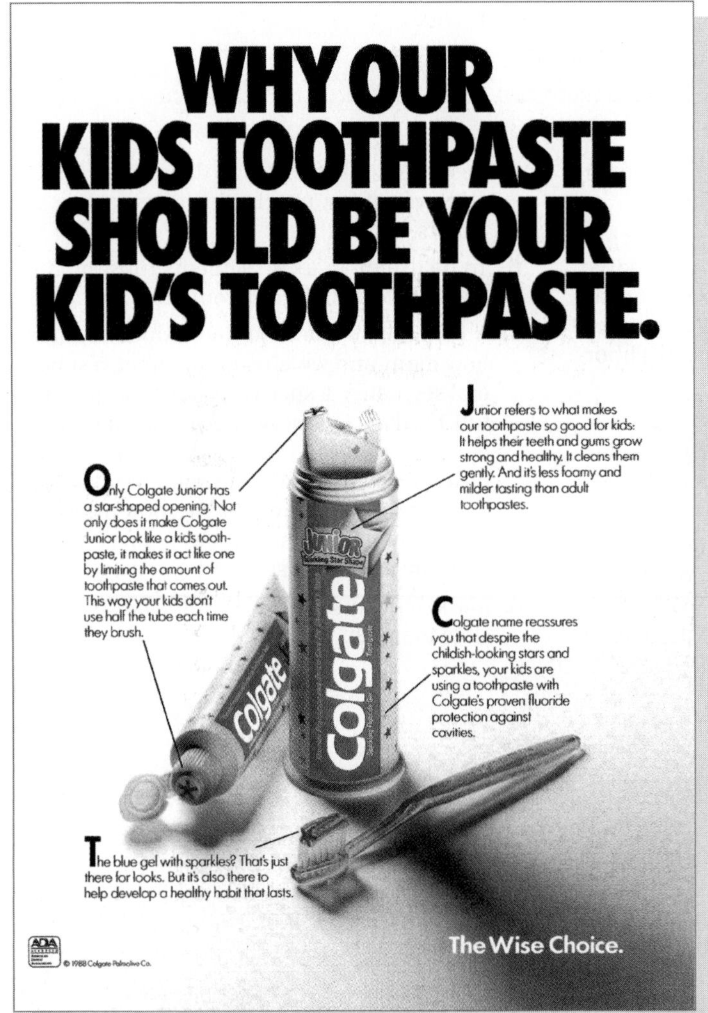

Socially responsible marketing: Colgate Junior Toothpaste ads promote special features designed to get children to brush more often.

This is the case being made by many companies marketing to the nation's preschoolers. With nearly 4 million youngsters attending some kind of organized child care, the potential market—including both kids and parents—is too great to pass up. So in addition to stocking the usual standards like art easels, gerbil cages, and blocks, the nation's preschools are likely to have Care Bear worksheets, Pizza Hut reading programs, and Nickelodeon magazines.

NICKELODEON, PIZZA HUT, FORD MOTOR CORP.

Cable TV station Nickelodeon was one of the first companies to capitalize on the preschool market when it launched *Nick Jr.* family magazine in 1999. It distributes half of the magazine's 1 million copies to preschools free and makes no bones about the fact that it is trying to sell parents on Nickelodeon shows and licensed products. In contrast, other corporations insist that their preschool products are designed purely to meet a social need. Pizza Hut is one. Its preschool program offers each student a certificate for a personal pizza if his or her teacher spends at least 60 minutes a week reading to the class for four consecutive weeks. In 2002, 1.6 million preschoolers in 33,800 child-care facilities participated. Likewise, automaker Ford says it sends posters to 100,000 preschools, child-care centers, and kindergarten classes to encourage children ages 2 to 5 to think about safety. The poster is an alphabet of safety tips with, not surprisingly, A for automobile (but no F for Ford).

Teachers and parents are divided in their feelings about the ethics of this increasing preschool marketing push. Some side with groups like Stop Commercial Exploitation of Children who feel that preschoolers are incredibly susceptible to advertising and that schools' endorsements of products make children believe the product is good for them—no matter what it is. Yet, many preschools and day care centers operating on tight budgets welcome the free resources.[65]

SUMMARY :::

1. Target marketing involves three activities: market segmentation, market targeting, and market positioning.
2. Markets can be targeted at four levels: segments, niches, local areas, and individuals. Market segments are large, identifiable groups within a market. A niche is a more narrowly defined group. Marketers appeal to local markets through grassroots marketing for trading areas, neighborhoods, and even individual stores.
3. More companies now practice individual and mass customization. The future is likely to see more self-marketing, a form of marketing in which individual consumers take the initiative in designing products and brands.
4. There are two bases for segmenting consumer markets: consumer characteristics and consumer responses. The major segmentation variables for consumer markets are geographic, demographic, psychographic, and behavioral. These variables can be used singly or in combination.
5. Business marketers use all these variables along with operating variables, purchasing approaches, and situational factors.
6. To be useful, market segments must be measurable, substantial, accessible, differentiable, and actionable.
7. A firm has to evaluate the various segments and decide how many and which ones to target: a single segment, several segments, a specific product, a specific market, or the full market. If it serves the full market, it must choose between differentiated and undifferentiated marketing. Firms must also monitor segment relationships, and seek economies of scope and the potential for marketing to supersegments. They should develop segment-by-segment invasion plans.
8. Marketers must choose target markets in a socially responsible manner.

APPLICATIONS :::

Marketing Debate Is Mass Marketing Dead?

With marketers increasingly adopting more and more refined market segmentation schemes—fueled by the Internet and other customization efforts—some critics claim that mass marketing is dead. Others counter that there will always be room for large brands that employ marketing programs targeting the mass market.

Take a position: Mass marketing is dead versus Mass marketing is still a viable way to build a profitable brand.

Marketing Discussion

Descriptive versus Behavioral Market Segmentation Schemes Think of various product categories. How would you classify yourself in terms of the various segmentation schemes? How would marketing be more or less effective for you depending on the segment involved? How would you contrast demographic versus behavioral segment schemes? Which ones do you think would be most effective for marketers trying to sell to you?

PART 4

BUILDING STRONG BRANDS

IN THIS CHAPTER, WE WILL ADDRESS THE FOLLOWING QUESTIONS:

1. What is a brand and how does branding work?
2. What is brand equity?
3. How is brand equity built, measured, and managed?
4. What are the important decisions in developing a branding strategy?

nine

Building a strong brand requires careful planning and a great deal of long-term investment. At the heart of a successful brand is a great product or service, backed by creatively designed and executed marketing. One of the hottest brands around is Google:

Founded in 1998 by two Stanford University Ph.D. students, search engine Google's name is a play on the word googol—the number represented by a 1 followed by 100 zeroes—a reference to the huge amount of data online. With 200 million search requests daily, the company has turned a profit by focusing on searches alone and not adding other services, as was the case with many other portals. By focusing on plain text, avoiding ads, and using sophisticated search algorithms, Google provides fast and reliable service. Google makes money from paid listings relevant to a searcher's query, and by licensing its technology to firms such as AOL and the Washington Post. In perhaps the ultimate sign of success, the brand is now often used as a verb—"to google" is to search online. Based on a public poll of the brand that had made the most impact in their lives, Google was named "Brand of the Year" in 2002 by Interbrand branding consultants. This success has not gone unnoticed, however, and has led to strong competitive responses from industry giants Yahoo! and Microsoft.[1]

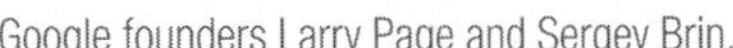
Google founders Larry Page and Sergey Brin.

Perhaps the most distinctive skill of professional marketers is their ability to create, maintain, enhance, and protect brands. Branding has become a marketing priority. Successful brands such as Starbucks, Sony, and Nike command a price premium and elicit much loyalty. New brands such as Krispy Kreme, Red Bull, and JetBlue capture the imagination of consumers and the financial community alike. Marketers of successful twenty-first-century brands must excel at the strategic brand management process. *Strategic brand management* involves the design and implementation of marketing activities and programs to build, measure, and manage brands to maximize their value. The strategic brand management process involves four main steps:

- Identifying and establishing brand positioning.
- Planning and implementing brand marketing.
- Measuring and interpreting brand performance.
- Growing and sustaining brand value.

Chapter 10 deals with brand positioning. The remaining topics are discussed in this chapter. Chapter 11 reviews important concepts dealing with competition.

::: What Is Brand Equity?

The American Marketing Association defines a **brand** as "a name, term, sign, symbol, or design, or a combination of them, intended to identify the goods or services of one seller or group of sellers and to differentiate them from those of competitors." A brand is thus a product or service that adds dimensions that differentiate it in some way from other products or services designed to satisfy the same need. These differences may be functional, rational, or tangible—related to product performance of the brand. They may also be more symbolic, emotional or intangible—related to what the brand represents.

Branding has been around for centuries as a means to distinguish the goods of one producer from those of another.[2] The earliest signs of branding in Europe were the medieval guilds' requirement that craftspeople put trademarks on their products to protect themselves and consumers against inferior quality. In the fine arts, branding began with artists signing their works. Brands today play a number of important roles that improve consumers' lives and enhance the financial value of firms.

The Role of Brands

Brands identify the source or maker of a product and allow consumers—either individuals or organizations—to assign responsibility to a particular manufacturer or distributor. Consumers may evaluate the identical product differently depending on how it is branded. Consumers learn about brands through past experiences with the product and its marketing program. They find out which brands satisfy their needs and which ones do not. As consumers' lives become more complicated, rushed, and time-starved, the ability of a brand to simplify decision making and reduce risk is invaluable.[3]

Brands also perform valuable functions for firms.[4] First, they simplify product handling or tracing. Brands help to organize inventory and accounting records. A brand also offers the firm legal protection for unique features or aspects of the product.[5] The brand name can be protected through registered trademarks; manufacturing processes can be protected through patents; and packaging can be protected through copyrights and designs. These intellectual property rights ensure that the firm can safely invest in the brand and reap the benefits of a valuable asset.

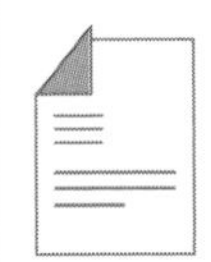

MARKETING MEMO | THE BRAND REPORT CARD

The world's strongest brands share 10 attributes:

1. ***The brand excels at delivering the benefits consumers truly desire.*** Do you focus relentlessly on maximizing customers' product and service experiences?
2. ***The brand stays relevant.*** Are you in touch with your customers' tastes, current market conditions, and trends?
3. ***The pricing strategy is based on consumer perceptions of value.*** Have you optimized price, cost, and quality to meet or exceed customer expectations?
4. ***The brand is properly positioned.*** Have you established necessary and competitive points of parity with competitors? Have you established desirable and deliverable points of difference?
5. ***The brand is consistent.*** Are you sure that your marketing programs are not sending conflicting messages?
6. ***The brand portfolio and hierarchy makes sense.*** Can the corporate brand create a seamless umbrella for all the brands in the portfolio? Do you have a brand hierarchy that is well thought out and well understood?
7. ***The brand makes use of and coordinates a full repertoire of marketing activities to build equity.*** Have you capitalized on the unique capabilities of each communication option while ensuring that the meaning of the brand is consistently represented?
8. ***The brand's managers understand what the brand means to consumers.*** Do you know what customers like and do not like about your brand? Have you created detailed, research-driven portraits of your target customers?
9. ***The brand is given proper, sustained support.*** Are the successes or failures of marketing programs fully understood before they are changed? Is the brand given sufficient R&D support?
10. ***The company monitors sources of brand equity.*** Have you created a brand charter that defines the meaning and equity of the brand and how it should be treated? Have you assigned explicit responsibility for monitoring and preserving brand equity?

Source: Adapted from Kevin Lane Keller, "The Brand Report Card," *Harvard Business Review* (January 1, 2000): 147–157

Brands can signal a certain level of quality so that satisfied buyers can easily choose the product again.[6] Brand loyalty provides predictability and security of demand for the firm and creates barriers to entry that make it difficult for other firms to enter the market. Loyalty also can translate into a willingness to pay a higher price—often 20 to 25 percent more.[7] Although competitors may easily duplicate manufacturing processes and product designs, they cannot easily match lasting impressions in the minds of individuals and organizations from years of marketing activity and product experience. In this sense, branding can be seen as a powerful means to secure a competitive advantage.[8]

To firms, brands thus represent enormously valuable pieces of legal property that can influence consumer behavior, be bought and sold, and provide the security of sustained future revenues to their owner.[9] Large earning multiples have been paid for brands in mergers or acquisitions, starting with the boom years of the mid-1980s. The price premium is often justified on the basis of assumptions of the extra profits that could be extracted and sustained from the brands, as well as the tremendous difficulty and expense of creating similar brands from scratch. Wall Street believes that strong brands result in better earnings and profit performance for firms, which, in turn, creates greater value for shareholders. Much of the recent interest in brands by senior management has been a result of these bottom-line financial considerations. "Marketing Memo: The Brand Report Card" lists 10 key characteristics based on a review of the world's strongest brands.[10]

The Scope of Branding

How then do you "brand" a product? Although firms provide the impetus to brand creation through marketing programs and other activities, ultimately a brand is something that resides in the minds of consumers. A brand is a perceptual entity that is rooted in reality but reflects the perceptions and perhaps even the idiosyncrasies of consumers.

Branding is endowing products and services with the power of a brand. Branding is all about creating differences. To brand a product, it is necessary to teach consumers "who" the product is—by giving it a name and using other brand elements to help identify it—as well as "what" the product does and "why" consumers should care. Branding involves creating mental structures and helping consumers organize their knowledge about products and services in a way that clarifies their decision making and, in the process, provides value to the firm.

For branding strategies to be successful and brand value to be created, consumers must be convinced that there are meaningful differences among brands in the product or service category. The key to branding is that consumers must not think that all brands in the category are the same.

Brand differences often are related to attributes or benefits of the product itself. Gillette, Merck, Sony, 3M, and others have been leaders in their product categories for decades due, in part, to continual innovation. Other brands create competitive advantages through non-product-related means. Coca-Cola, Calvin Klein, Gucci, Tommy Hilfiger, Marlboro, and others have become leaders in their product categories by understanding consumer motivations and desires and creating relevant and appealing images around their products.

Branding can be applied virtually anywhere a consumer has a choice. It is possible to brand a physical good (Campbell's soup, Pantene shampoo, or Ford Mustang automobiles), a service (Singapore Airlines, Bank of America, or BlueCross/BlueShield medical insurance), a store (Nordstrom department store, Foot Locker specialty store, or Safeway supermarket), a person (Tom Clancy, Britney Spears, or Andre Agassi), a place (the city of Sydney, state of Texas, or country of Spain), an organization (UNICEF, American Automobile Association, or The Rolling Stones), or an idea (abortion rights, free trade, or freedom of speech).

Defining Brand Equity

Brand equity is the added value endowed to products and services. This value may be reflected in how consumers think, feel, and act with respect to the brand, as well as the prices, market share, and profitability that the brand commands for the firm. Brand equity is an important intangible asset that has psychological and financial value to the firm.

Marketers and researchers use various perspectives to study brand equity.[11] Customer-based approaches view brand equity from the perspective of the consumer—either an individual or an organization.[12] The premise of customer-based brand equity models is that the power of a brand lies in what customers have seen, read, heard, learned, thought, and felt about the brand over time. In other words, the power of a brand lies in the minds of existing or potential customers and what they have experienced directly and indirectly about the brand.[13]

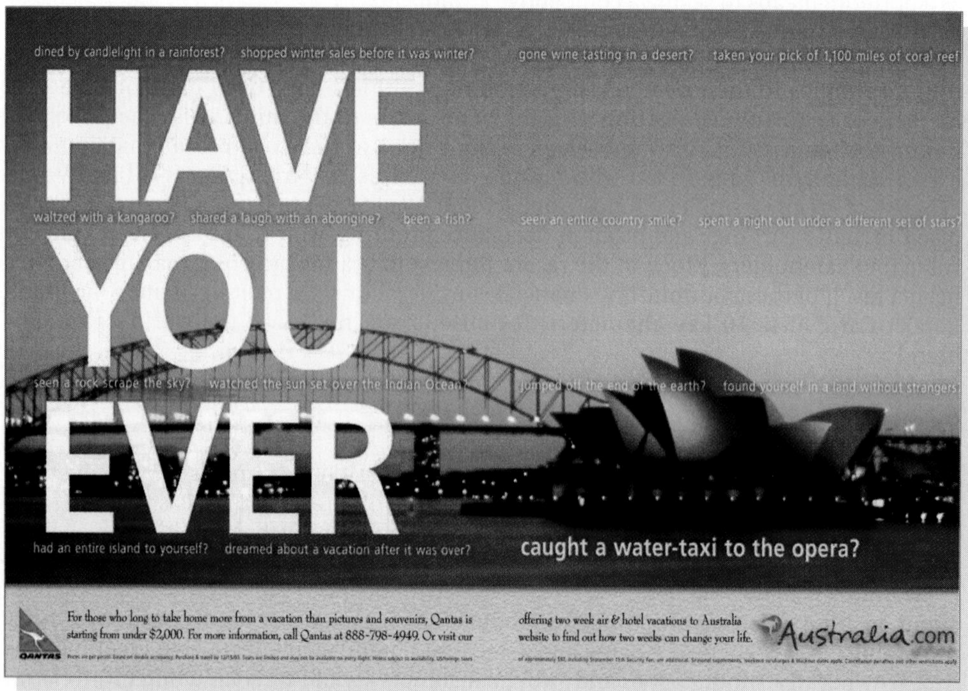

Branding a place: ad for Australia tourism focusing on the city of Sydney with its signature opera house.

Customer-based brand equity can be defined as the differential effect that brand knowledge has on consumer response to the marketing of that brand.[14] A brand is said to have positive customer-based brand equity when consumers react more favorably to a product and the way it is marketed when the brand is identified as compared to when it is not. A brand is said to have negative customer-based brand equity if consumers react less favorably to marketing activity for the brand under the same circumstances.

There are three key ingredients to this definition. First, brand equity arises from differences in consumer response. If no differences occur, then the brand name product can essentially be classified as a commodity or generic version of the product. Competition would then probably be based on price.

Second, these differences in response are a result of consumer's knowledge about the brand. **Brand knowledge** consists of all the thoughts, feelings, images, experiences, beliefs, and so on that become associated with the brand. In particular, brands must create strong, favorable, and unique brand associations with customers, as has been the case with Volvo (*safety*), Hallmark (*caring*), and Harley-Davidson (*adventure*). Third, the differential response by consumers that makes up the brand equity is reflected in perceptions, preferences, and behavior related to all aspects of the marketing of a brand. Table 9.1 summarizes some of these key benefits of brand equity.

The challenge for marketers in building a strong brand is therefore ensuring that customers have the right type of experiences with products and services and their marketing programs to create the desired brand knowledge structures for the brand.

APPLE COMPUTER

Apple Computer is recognized as a master at building a strong brand that resonates with customers across generations and national boundaries. Named "2003 Marketer of the Year" by *Advertising Age* magazine, Apple achieves incredible brand loyalty largely by delivering on its mission as defined by CEO Steven Jobs: "To create great things that change people's lives." It has created an army of Apple evangelists not just because of its great advertising but also because it focuses on the consumer in everything it does. Some of its biggest buzz campaigns don't even originate with the company: In a trendy club in Manhattan's meatpacking district, two DJs host Tuesday night "Open iPod DJ Parties." Yet, the company doesn't rely on customers to do its marketing. Apple spent $293 million to create 73 retail stores to fuel excitement for the brand, including a store in New York's SoHo that drew over 14 million visitors in 2003. The rationale behind the move to retail is that the more people can see and touch Apple products—and see what Apple can do for them—the more likely Apple is to increase its market share, which is still a tiny slice of the PC market.[15]

Consumer knowledge is what drives the differences that manifest themselves in brand equity. In an abstract sense, brand equity can be seen as providing marketers with a vital strategic "bridge" from their past to their future.

TABLE 9.1

Marketing Advantages of Strong Brands

Marketing Advantages of Strong Brands
Improved Perceptions of Product Performance
Greater Loyalty
Less Vulnerability to Competitive Marketing Actions
Less Vulnerability to Marketing Crises
Larger Margins
More Inelastic Consumer Response to Price Increases
More Elastic Consumer Response to Price Decreases
Greater Trade Cooperation and Support
Increased Marketing Communications Effectiveness
Possible Licensing Opportunities
Additional Brand Extension Opportunities

Brand Equity as a Bridge

From the perspective of brand equity, all the marketing dollars spent each year on products and services should be thought of as investments in consumer brand knowledge. The *quality* of the investment in brand building is the critical factor, not necessarily the *quantity*, beyond some minimal threshold amount.

It is actually possible to "overspend" on brand building if money is not spent wisely. In the beverage category, brands such as Michelob, Miller Lite, and 7Up saw sales decline in the 1990s despite sizable marketing support, arguably because of poorly targeted and delivered marketing campaigns. And there are numerous examples of brands that amass a great deal of brand equity by spending on marketing activities that create valuable, enduring memory traces in the consumers' minds. Despite being outspent by such beverage brand giants as Coca-Cola, Pepsi, and Budweiser, the California Milk Processor Board was able to reverse a decades-long decline in consumption of milk in California partly through its well-designed and executed "Got Milk?" campaign.

At the same time, the brand knowledge created by these marketing investments dictates appropriate future directions for the brand. Consumers will decide, based on what they think and feel about the brand, where (and how) they believe the brand should go and grant permission (or not) to any marketing action or program. New products such as Crystal Pepsi, Levi's Tailored Classic suits, Fruit of the Loom laundry detergent, and Cracker Jack cereal failed because consumers found them inappropriate.

A brand is essentially a marketer's promise to deliver predictable product or service performance. A **brand promise** is the marketer's vision of what the brand must be and do for consumers. At the end of the day, the true value and future prospects of a brand rest with consumers, their knowledge about the brand, and their likely response to marketing activity as a result of this knowledge. Understanding consumer brand knowledge—all the different things that become linked to the brand in the minds of consumers—is thus of paramount importance because it is the foundation of brand equity.

Virgin, the brainchild of England's flamboyant Richard Branson, vividly illustrates the power enjoyed and responsibility assumed by a strong brand.[16]

VIRGIN

Starting with Virgin Music, Branson's Virgin Group Ltd., now spans three continents and 200 businesses, including Virgin Atlantic Airways, Virgin Mobile (cell phones), Virgin Energy, Virgin Rail, Virgin Direct (insurance, mortgages, and investment funds), and Virgin Hotels. Clearly, Branson can create interest in almost any business he wants by simply attaching the name "Virgin" to it. Virgin Mobile exemplifies this strategy. Branson supplies the brand, a small initial investment, and takes a majority control while big-name partners come up with the cash. Some marketing and financial critics point out that he is diluting the brand, that it covers too many businesses. Branson has had some fumbles: Virgin Cola, Virgin Cosmetics, and Virgin Vodka have all but disappeared. But Branson replies: "We have a strategy of using the credibility of our brand to challenge the dominant players in a range of industries where we believe the consumer is not getting value for money. . . . If the consumer benefits, I see no reason why we should be frightened about launching new products." One of Branson's newest ventures: He's jumping into the fiercely competitive discount airline business in the United States with Virgin USA in 2005.

Brand Equity Models

Although there is agreement about basic principles, a number of models of brand equity offer some different perspectives. Here we briefly highlight four of the more established ones.

BRAND ASSET VALUATOR Advertising agency Young and Rubicam (Y&R) developed a model of brand equity called Brand Asset Valuator (BAV). Based on research with almost 200,000 consumers in 40 countries, BAV provides comparative measures of the brand equity of thousands of brands across hundreds of different categories. There are four key components—or pillars—of brand equity, according to BAV:

- ***Differentiation*** measures the degree to which a brand is seen as different from others.
- ***Relevance*** measures the breadth of a brand's appeal.

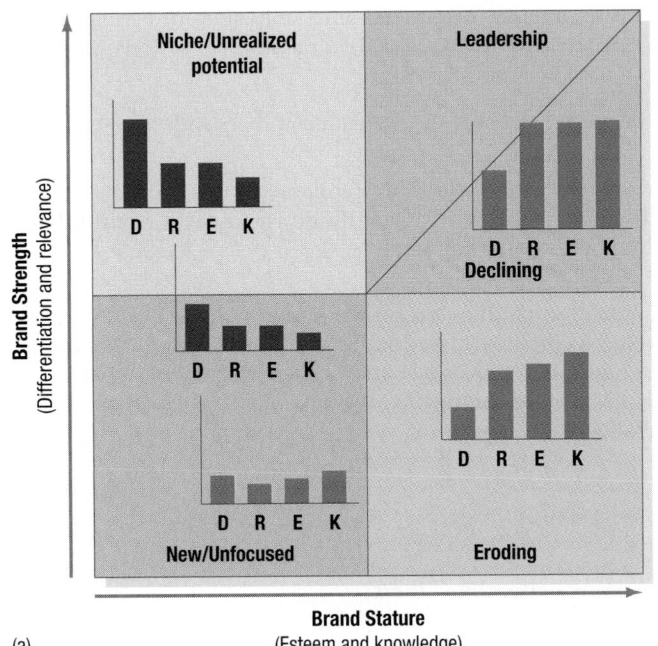

(a)

Niche/Unrealized potential
Tamiflu
Dolce & Gabbana
IKEA
Gevalia
PayPal.com
FX

Leadership
Disney
Hallmark
7Up
Subway
Nike
Lego

Declining
Kmart
Xerox
Pillsbury
Burger King
Gillette

New/Unfocused
Benson & Hedges
Air France
Optimum Online
National Car Rental
Golf Digest
HSBC

Eroding
U-Haul
Friskies
Northwest Airlines
Prudential Insurance

Brand Strength
(Differentiation and relevance)

Brand Stature
(Esteem and knowledge)

(b)

FIG. 9.1

BAV Power Grid

- ***Esteem*** measures how well the brand is regarded and respected.
- ***Knowledge*** measures how familiar and intimate consumers are with the brand.

Differentiation and Relevance combine to determine *Brand Strength.* These two pillars point to the brand's future value, rather than just reflecting its past. Esteem and Knowledge together create *Brand Stature,* which is more of a "report card" on past performance.

Examining the relationships among these four dimensions—a brand's "pillar pattern"—reveals much about its current and future status. Brand Strength and Brand Stature can be combined to form a Power Grid that depicts the stages in the cycle of brand development—each with its characteristic pillar patterns—in successive quadrants (see Figure 9.1). New brands, just after they are launched, show low levels on all four pillars. Strong new brands tend to show higher levels of Differentiation than Relevance, while both Esteem and Knowledge are lower still. Leadership brands show high levels on all four pillars. Finally, declining brands show high Knowledge—evidence of past performance—relative to a lower level of Esteem, and even lower Relevance and Differentiation.

AAKER MODEL Former UC-Berkeley marketing professor David Aaker views brand equity as a set of five categories of brand assets and liabilities linked to a brand that add to or subtract from the value provided by a product or service to a firm and/or to that firm's customers. These categories of brand assets are: (1) brand loyalty, (2) brand awareness, (3) perceived quality, (4) brand associations, and (5) other proprietary assets such as patents, trademarks, and channel relationships.

According to Aaker, a particularly important concept for building brand equity is *brand identity*—the unique set of brand associations that represent what the brand stands for and promises to customers.[17] Aaker sees brand identity as consisting of 12 dimensions organized around 4 perspectives: *brand-as-product* (product scope, product attributes, quality/value, uses, users, country of origin); *brand-as-organization* (organizational attributes, local versus global); *brand-as-person* (brand personality, brand–customer relationships); and *brand-as-symbol* (visual imagery/metaphors and brand heritage).

Aaker also conceptualizes brand identity as including a core and an extended identity. The core identity—the central, timeless essence of the brand—is most likely to remain constant as the brand travels to new markets and products. The extended identity includes various brand identity elements, organized into cohesive and meaningful groups. If we apply this approach to Saturn, the newest General Motors car division might yield the following:[18]

- ***Core Identity.*** A world-class car with employees who treat customers with respect and as friends.
- ***Extended Identity.*** U.S. subcompact with Spring Hill, Tennessee, plant; no pressure, no haggling, informative retail experience; thoughtful, friendly, down-to-earth, youthful and lively personality; committed employees and loyal users.

BRANDZ Marketing research consultants Millward Brown and WPP have developed the BRANDZ model of brand strength, at the heart of which is the BrandDynamics pyramid. According to this model, brand building involves a sequential series of steps, where each step is contingent upon successfully accomplishing the previous step. The objectives at each step, in ascending order, are as follows:

- ***Presence.*** Do I know about it?
- ***Relevance.*** Does it offer me something?
- ***Performance.*** Can it deliver?
- ***Advantage.*** Does it offer something better than others?
- ***Bonding.*** Nothing else beats it.

Research has shown that bonded consumers, those at the top level of the pyramid, build stronger relationships with the brand and spend more of their category expenditures on the brand than those at lower levels of the pyramid. More consumers, however, will be found at the lower levels. The challenge for marketers is to develop activities and programs that help consumers move up the pyramid.

BRAND RESONANCE The brand resonance model also views brand building as an ascending, sequential series of steps, from bottom to top: (1) ensuring identification of the brand with customers and an association of the brand in customers' minds with a specific product class or customer need; (2) firmly establishing the totality of brand meaning in the minds of customers by strategically linking a host of tangible and intangible brand associations; (3) eliciting the proper customer responses in terms of brand-related judgment and feelings; and (4) converting brand response to create an intense, active loyalty relationship between customers and the brand. According to this model, enacting the four steps involves establishing six "brand building blocks" with customers. These brand building blocks can be assembled in terms of a brand pyramid, as illustrated in Figure 9.2. The model emphasizes the duality of brands—the rational route to brand building is the left-hand side of the pyramid, whereas the emotional route is the right-hand side.[19]

MasterCard is an example of a brand with duality, as it emphasizes both the rational advantage to the credit card, through its acceptance at establishments worldwide, and the emotional advantage through its award-winning "priceless" advertising campaign, which shows people buying items to reach a certain goal. The goal itself—a feeling, an accomplishment, or other intangible—is "priceless" ("There are some things money can't buy, for everything else, there's MasterCard.").

The creation of significant brand equity involves reaching the top or pinnacle of the brand pyramid, and will occur only if the right building blocks are put into place.

- ***Brand salience*** relates to how often and easily the brand is evoked under various purchase or consumption situations.
- ***Brand performance*** relates to how the product or service meets customers' functional needs.
- ***Brand imagery*** deals with the extrinsic properties of the product or service, including the ways in which the brand attempts to meet customers' psychological or social needs.
- ***Brand judgments*** focus on customers' own personal opinions and evaluations.
- ***Brand feelings*** are customers' emotional responses and reactions with respect to the brand.
- ***Brand resonance*** refers to the nature of the relationship that customers have with the brand and the extent to which customers feel that they are "in sync" with the brand.

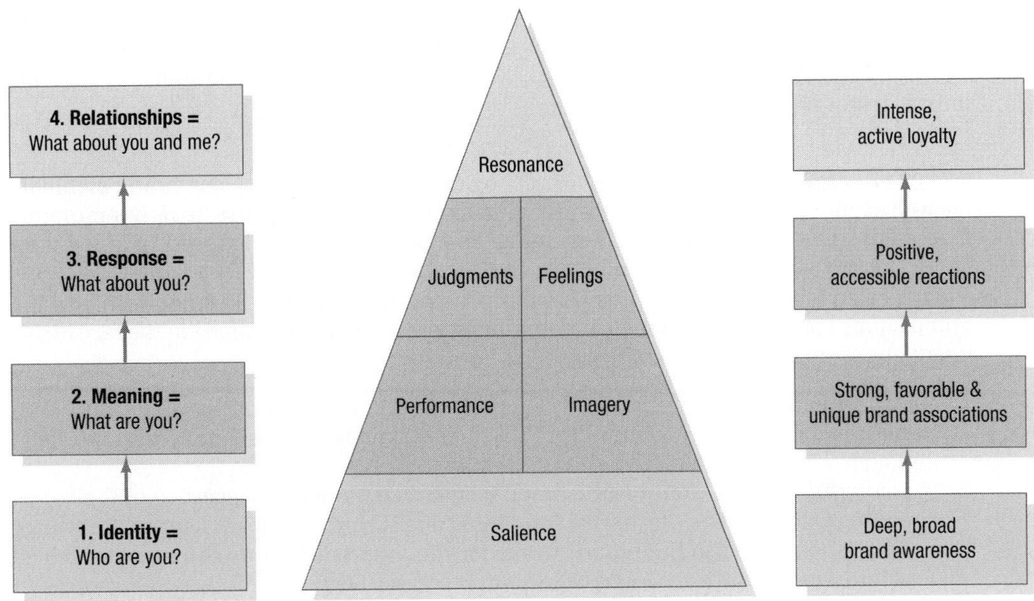

FIG. 9.2 | Brand Resonance Pyramid

Resonance is characterized in terms of the intensity or depth of the psychological bond customers have with the brand, as well as the level of activity engendered by this loyalty. Examples of brands with high resonance include Harley-Davidson, Apple, and eBay.

::: Building Brand Equity

Marketers build brand equity by creating the right brand knowledge structures with the right consumers. This process depends on *all* brand-related contacts—whether marketer-initiated or not. From a marketing management perspective, however, there are three main sets of *brand equity drivers:*

1. ***The initial choices for the brand elements or identities making up the brand (e.g., brand names, URLs, logos, symbols, characters, spokespeople, slogans, jingles, packages, and signage).*** Old Spice uses bright-red packaging and its familiar ocean schooner to reinforce its nautical theme while also launching deodorant and antiperspirant extensions adding the High Endurance and Red Zone brand names.[20]
2. ***The product and service and all accompanying marketing activities and supporting marketing programs.*** Joe Boxer made its name selling colorful underwear with its signature yellow smiley face, Mr. Licky, in a hip, fun way. The company spent almost zero on advertising; clever stunts and events garnered publicity and word of mouth. An exclusive deal with Kmart has generated strong retail support.[21]
3. ***Other associations indirectly transferred to the brand by linking it to some other entity (e.g., a person, place, or thing).*** Subaru used the rugged Australian Outback and actor Paul Hogan of *Crocodile Dundee* movie fame in ads to help craft the brand image of the Subaru Outback line of sports utility wagons.

Choosing Brand Elements

Brand elements are those trademarkable devices that serve to identify and differentiate the brand. Most strong brands employ multiple brand elements. Nike has the distinctive "swoosh" logo, the empowering "Just Do It" slogan, and the mythological "Nike" name based on the winged goddess of victory.

Brand elements can be chosen to build as much brand equity as possible. The test of the brand-building ability of these elements is what consumers would think or feel about the product *if* they only knew about the brand element. A brand element that provides a positive contribution to brand equity, for example, would be one where consumers assumed or inferred certain valued associations or responses. Based on its name alone, a consumer might expect ColorStay lipsticks to be long-lasting and SnackWell to be healthful snack foods.

BRAND ELEMENT CHOICE CRITERIA There are six criteria in choosing brand elements (as well as more specific choice considerations in each case). The first three (memorable, meaningful, and likable) can be characterized as "brand building" in terms of how brand equity can be built through the judicious choice of a brand element. The latter three (protectable, adaptable, and transferable) are more "defensive" and are concerned with how the brand equity contained in a brand element can be leveraged and preserved in the face of different opportunities and constraints.

1. ***Memorable.*** How easily is the brand element recalled? How easily recognized? Is this true at both purchase and consumption? Short brand names such as Tide, Crest, and Puffs can help.
2. ***Meaningful.*** To what extent is the brand element credible and suggestive of the corresponding category? Does it suggest something about a product ingredient or the type of person who might use the brand? Consider the inherent meaning in names such as DieHard auto batteries, Mop & Glo floor wax, and Lean Cuisine low-calorie frozen entrees.
3. ***Likeability.*** How aesthetically appealing do consumers find the brand element? Is it inherently likable visually, verbally, and in other ways? Concrete brand names such as Sunkist, Spic and Span, and Firebird evoke much imagery.
4. ***Transferable.*** Can the brand element be used to introduce new products in the same or different categories? To what extent does the brand element add to brand equity across geographic boundaries and market segments? Volkswagen chose to name its new SUV, Touareg, after a tribe of colorful Saharan nomads. Unfortunately, historically they were also notorious slave owners, which created a negative press backlash in the United States.[22]
5. ***Adaptable.*** How adaptable and updatable is the brand element? Betty Crocker has received over eight makeovers through the years—although she is over 75 years old, she doesn't look a day over 35!
6. ***Protectible.*** How legally protectible is the brand element? How competitively protectible? Can it be easily copied? It is important that names that become synonymous with product categories—such as Kleenex, Kitty Litter, Jell-O, Scotch Tape, Xerox, and Fiberglass—retain their trademark rights and not become generic.

DEVELOPING BRAND ELEMENTS In creating a brand, marketers have many choices of brand elements to identify their products. Before, companies chose brand names by generating a list of possible names, debating their merits, eliminating all but a few, testing them with target consumers, and making a final choice.[23] Today, many companies hire a marketing research firm to develop and test names. These companies use human brainstorming sessions and vast computer databases, cataloged by association, sounds, and other qualities. Name-research procedures include *association tests* (What images come to mind?), *learning tests* (How easily is the name pronounced?), *memory tests* (How well is the name remembered?), and *preference tests* (Which names are preferred?). Of course, the firm must also conduct searches to make sure the chosen name has not already been registered.

Brand elements can play a number of brand-building roles. If consumers do not examine much information in making their product decisions, brand elements should be easily recognized and recalled and inherently descriptive and persuasive. Memorable or meaningful brand elements can reduce the burden on marketing communications to build awareness and link brand associations. The different associations that arise from the likeability and appeal of brand elements may also play a critical role in the equity of a brand. The Keebler elves reinforce home-style baking quality and a sense of magic and fun for their line of cookies. Ads featuring the Buddy Lee doll character for Lee's Jeans helped to make the brand popular with a younger audience that had not yet connected to the brand.

Brand names are not the only important brand element. Often, the less concrete brand benefits are, the more important it is that brand elements capture the brand's intangible

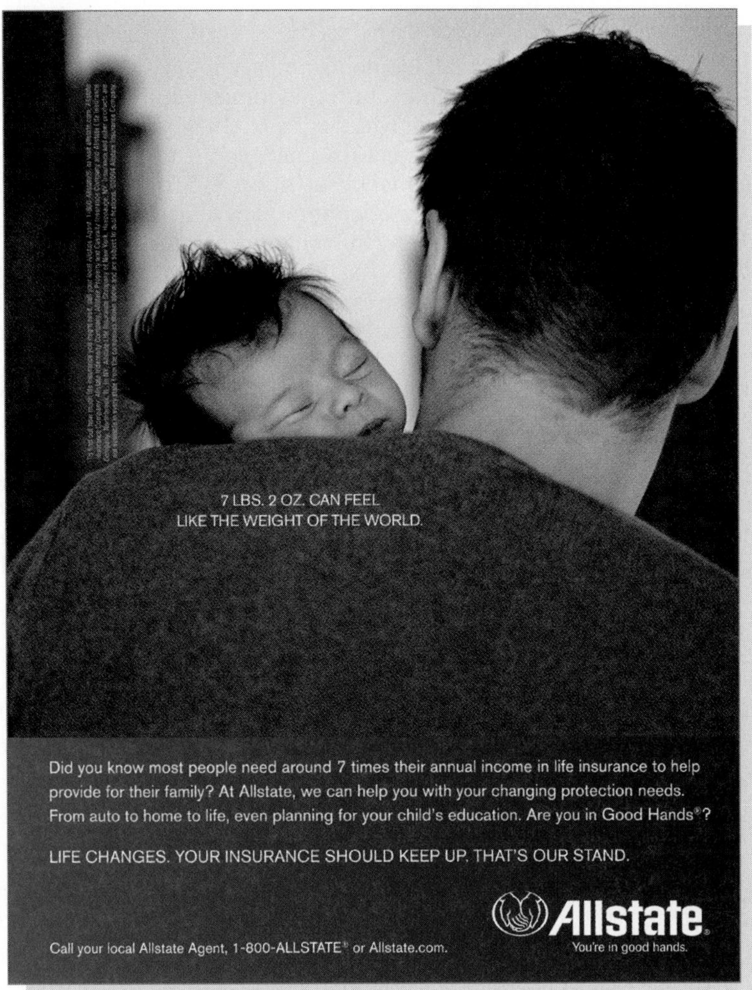

7 LBS. 2 OZ. CAN FEEL
LIKE THE WEIGHT OF THE WORLD.
Did you know most people need around 7 times their annual income in life insurance to help provide for their family? At Allstate, we can help you with your changing protection needs. From auto to home to life, even planning for your child's education. Are you in Good Hands®?
LIFE CHANGES. YOUR INSURANCE SHOULD KEEP UP. THAT'S OUR STAND.
Allstate.
You're in good hands.
Call your local Allstate Agent, 1-800-ALLSTATE® or Allstate.com.

Building a brand with elements that capture the brand's intangible characteristics: An Allstate ad, with the graphic symbol of cupped hands and the tagline, "You're in good hands."

characteristics. Many insurance firms use symbols of strength (the Rock of Gibraltar for Prudential and the stag for Hartford), security (the "good hands" of Allstate, Traveller's umbrella, and the hard hat of Fireman's Fund), or some combination of the two (the castle for Fortis).

A powerful—but sometimes overlooked—brand element is slogans. Like brand names, slogans are an extremely efficient means to build brand equity. Slogans can function as useful "hooks" or "handles" to help consumers grasp what the brand is and what makes it special. They are an indispensable means of summarizing and translating the intent of a marketing program. Think of the inherent brand meaning in slogans such as, "Like a Good Neighbor, State Farm is There," "Nothing Runs Like a Deere," and "Help is Just Around the Corner. Tru Value Hardware."

AVIS GROUP HOLDINGS INC.

A classic case of a company using a slogan to build brand equity is that of Avis's 41-year-old "We Try Harder" ad campaign. In 1963, when the campaign was developed, Avis was losing money and widely considered the number-two car rental company next to market leader Hertz. When account executives from DDB ad agency met with Avis managers, they asked: "What can you do that we can say you do better than your competitors?" An Avis manager replied, "We try harder because we have to." Someone at DDB wrote this down and it became the heart of the campaign. Avis was hesitant to air the campaign because of its blunt, break-the-rules honesty, but also because the company had to deliver on that promise. Yet, by creating buy-in on "We Try Harder" from all Avis employees, especially its front-line employees at the rental desks, the company was able to create a company culture and brand image from an advertising slogan.[24]

Designing Holistic Marketing Activities

Although the judicious choice of brand elements and secondary associations can make important contributions to building brand equity, the primary input comes from the product or service and supporting marketing activities.

Brands are not built by advertising alone. Customers come to know a brand through a range of contacts and touch points: personal observation and use, word of mouth, interactions with company personnel, online or telephone experiences, and payment transactions. A **brand contact** can be defined as any information-bearing experience a customer or prospect has with the brand, the product category, or the market that relates to the marketer's product or service.[25] Any of these experiences can be positive or negative. The company must put as much effort into managing these experiences as it does in producing its ads.[26]

The strategy and tactics behind marketing programs have changed dramatically in recent years.[27] Marketers are creating brand contacts and building brand equity through many avenues, such as clubs and consumer communities, trade shows, event marketing, sponsorship, factory visits, public relations and press releases, and social cause marketing. To market its cereals, General Mills supplemented traditional advertising and promotion with, among other things, a family-themed, entertainment-based retail destination, Cereal Adventure, inside Minneapolis's Mall of America, the world's largest shopping mall.[28] Chupa Chups has developed an extensive marketing program.

CHUPA CHUPS

Who says lollipops are just for kids? Not Spanish Chupa Chups, the world's largest maker of lollipops. In order to extend the Chupa Chups brand beyond children, Chupa Chups is taking a truly holistic approach, which includes savvy—and totally free—product placement, fresh marketing ideas, and even its own line of retail boutiques. An internal task force, dubbed 4C for Chupa Chups Corporate Communications, is charged with raising brand awareness among fashion-conscious and media-saturated teens and youth. One example: When he learned that the coach of Barcelona's soccer team was struggling to quit smoking, a 4C sports fan sent him a complimentary box of Chupa Chups. For the rest of the season, the coach was rarely seen on the sidelines without a lollipop in his mouth. Chupa Chups sales in soccer-crazed Catalonia doubled that year. The company also gains visibility at high-profile awards ceremonies. When A-list stars come out at such events as the Venice Film Festival or the Grammys, a scantily clad "Chupa Chick" in a lollipop-studded bra top is there to greet them. So far Chupa's "celebrity suckers"—those caught on camera sucking a Chupa Chups—include Jerry Seinfeld, Elton John, Georgio Armani, Sheryl Crow, and Magic Johnson. Once Chupa Chups has caught teens' attention via these "nonendorser endorsers," they can point them to Chupa Chups packed in makeup kits or to clothing, eyewear, motorcycle helmets, and other items bearing the brand name.[29]

Regardless of the particular tools or approaches they choose, holistic marketers emphasize three important new themes in designing brand-building marketing programs: personalization, integration, and internalization.

PERSONALIZATION The rapid expansion of the Internet has created opportunities to personalize marketing.[30] Marketers are increasingly abandoning the mass-market practices that built brand powerhouses in the 1950s, 1960s, and 1970s for new approaches that are in fact a throwback to marketing practices from a century ago, when merchants literally knew their customers by name. To adapt to the increased consumer desire for personalization, marketers have embraced concepts such as experiential marketing, one-to-one marketing, and permission marketing. Chapter 5 summarized some of these concepts; "Marketing Insight: Applying Permission Marketing" highlights key principles with that particular approach.

From a branding point of view, these concepts are about getting consumers more actively involved with a brand by creating an intense, active relationship. *Personalizing marketing* is about making sure that the brand and its marketing are as relevant as possible to as many customers as possible—a challenge, given that no two customers are identical.

JONES SODA

Peter van Stolk founded Jones Soda on the premise that Gen Y consumers would be more accepting of a new soft-drink brand if they felt they discovered it themselves. Jones Soda initially was sold only in shops that sell surfboards, snowboards, and skateboards. The Jones Soda Web site encourages fans to send in personal photos for possible use on Jones Soda labels. Although only maybe 40 or so are picked annually from the tens of thousands of entries, the approach helps to create relevance and an emotional connection.[31]

INTEGRATION One implication of these new marketing approaches is that the traditional "marketing-mix" concept and the notion of the "4 Ps" may not adequately describe modern marketing programs. **Integrating marketing** is about mixing and matching marketing activities to maximize their individual and collective effects.[32] As part of integrated marketing, marketers need a variety of different marketing activities that reinforce the brand promise. The Olive Garden has become the second-largest casual dining restaurant chain in the United States, with $2 billion in sales and over 500 restaurants, in part through a fully integrated marketing program.

THE OLIVE GARDEN

The Olive Garden brand promise is "the idealized Italian family meal" characterized by "fresh, simple delicious Italian food," "complimented by a great glass of wine," "welcomed by people who treat you like family," "in a comfortable home-like setting." To live up to that brand promise, The Olive Garden sends select managers and servers on cultural immersion trips to Italy; launched the Culinary Institute of Tuscany in Italy to inspire new dishes; conducts wine training workshops for employees and in-restaurant wine sampling for customers; and remodeled restaurants to give them a Tuscan farmhouse look. Communications include in-store, employee, and mass-media messages that all reinforce the brand promise and ad slogan, "When You're Here, You're Family."[33]

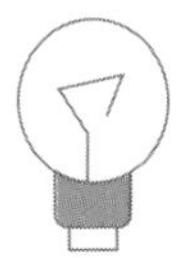

MARKETING INSIGHT | APPLYING PERMISSION MARKETING

Permission marketing, the practice of marketing to consumers only after gaining their express permission, is a tool companies can use to break through clutter and build customer loyalty. With the help of large databases and advanced software, companies can store gigabytes of customer data and send targeted, personalized marketing messages to customers.

Seth Godin, a pioneer in the technique, estimates that each American receives about 3,000 marketing messages daily. He maintains that marketers can no longer use "interruption marketing" via mass-media campaigns. Marketers can develop stronger consumer relationships by respecting consumers' wishes and sending messages only when they express a willingness to become more involved with the brand. According to Godin, effective permission marketing works because it is "anticipated, personal, and relevant."

Godin identifies five steps to effective permission marketing:

1. Offer the prospect an incentive to volunteer (e.g., free sample, sales promotion, or contest).
2. Offer the interested prospect a curriculum over time that teaches the consumer about the product or service.
3. Reinforce the incentive to guarantee that the prospect maintains the permission.
4. Offer additional incentives to get more permission from the consumer.
5. Over time, leverage the permission to change consumer behavior toward profits.

Permission marketing does have drawbacks. One is that it presumes consumers to some extent "know what they want." But in many cases, consumers have undefined, ambiguous, or conflicting preferences. In applying permission marketing, consumers may need to be given assistance in forming and conveying their preferences. "Participatory marketing" may be a more appropriate concept because marketers and consumers need to work together to find out how the firm can best satisfy consumers.

Sources: Seth Godin, *Permission Marketing: Turning Strangers into Friends, and Friends into Customers* (New York: Simon & Schuster, 1999); Susan Fournier, Susan Dobscha, and David Mick, "Preventing the Premature Death of Relationship Marketing," *Harvard Business Review* (January–February, 1998): 42–51.

The Olive Garden's integrated marketing program includes sending managers and servers to Italy on cultural immersion trips. Part of the trip is training classes at the Olive Garden's Culinary Institute of Tuscany. In this photo, they are learning about pasta.

Integration is especially critical with marketing communications. From the perspective of brand building, all communication options should be evaluated in terms of ability to affect brand equity. Each communication option can be judged in terms of the effectiveness and efficiency with which it affects brand awareness and with which it creates, maintains, or strengthens brand image. **Brand awareness** is consumers' ability to identify the brand under different conditions, as reflected by their brand recognition or recall performance. **Brand image** is the perceptions and beliefs held by consumers, as reflected in the associations held in consumer memory.

As we discuss in Chapter 17, different communication options have different strengths and can accomplish different objectives. It is important to employ a mix of different communication options, each of which plays a specific role in building or maintaining brand equity. Although Michelin may invest in R&D and engage in advertising, promotions, and other communications to reinforce the tires' "safety" association, it may also choose to sponsor events to make sure Michelin is seen as contemporary and up-to-date. The marketing communication program should be put together so that the whole is greater than the sum of the parts. In other words, as much as possible, there should be a match among certain communication options so that the effects of any one option are enhanced by the presence of another.

INTERNALIZATION Marketers must now "walk the walk" to deliver the brand promise. They must adopt an *internal* perspective to consider what steps to take to be sure employees and marketing partners appreciate and understand basic branding notions, and how they can help—or hurt—brand equity.[34] **Internal branding** is activities and processes that help to inform and inspire employees.[35] It is critical for service companies and retailers that all employees have an up-to-date, deep understanding of the brand and its promise.

Brand bonding occurs when customers experience the company as delivering on its brand promise. All of the customers' contacts with company employees and company communications must be positive. *The brand promise will not be delivered unless everyone in the company lives the brand.* One of the most potent influences on brand perception is the experience customers have with company personnel.

ELI LILLY

In 2000, Eli Lilly launched a new brand-building initiative with the slogan, "Answers that Matter." The aim was to establish Eli Lilly as a pharmaceutical firm that could give doctors, patients, hospitals, HMOs, and government trustworthy answers to questions of concern to them. To make sure that everyone at Eli Lilly had the knowledge to be able to deliver the right answers, Lilly developed a comprehensive Brand-to-Action training program.[36]

Companies need to engage in continual open dialogue with employees. Some firms have pushed "B2E" (business-to-employee) programs through corporate intranets and other means. Disney is so successful at internal branding and having employees support its brand that it even holds seminars at the Disney Institute on the "Disney Style" for employees from other companies.

Holistic marketers must go even further and train and encourage distributors and dealers to serve their customers well. Poorly trained dealers can ruin the best efforts to build a strong brand image.

Leveraging Secondary Associations

The third and final way to build brand equity is, in effect, to "borrow" it. That is, brand associations may themselves be linked to other entities that have their own associations, creating "secondary" brand associations. In other words, brand equity may be created by linking the brand to other information in memory that conveys meaning to consumers (see Figure 9.3).

The brand may be linked to certain source factors, such as the company (through branding strategies), countries or other geographical regions (through identification of product origin), and channels of distribution (through channel strategy); as well as to other brands (through ingredient or co-branding), characters (through licensing), spokespeople (through endorsements), sporting or cultural events (through sponsorship), or some other third-party sources (through awards or reviews).

For example, assume Burton—makers of snowboards as well as ski boots, bindings, clothing, and outerwear—decided to introduce a new surfboard called "The Dominator." Burton has gained over a third of the snowboard market by closely aligning itself with top professional riders and creating a strong amateur snowboarder community around the country. In creating the marketing program to support the new Dominator surfboard, Burton could attempt to leverage secondary brand knowledge in a number of different ways:

- Burton could leverage associations to the corporate brand by "sub-branding" the product, calling it "Dominator by Burton." Consumers' evaluations of the new product would be influenced by how they felt about Burton and how they felt that such knowledge predicted the quality of a Burton surfboard.
- Burton could try to rely on its rural New England origins, but such a geographical location would seem to have little relevance to surfing.

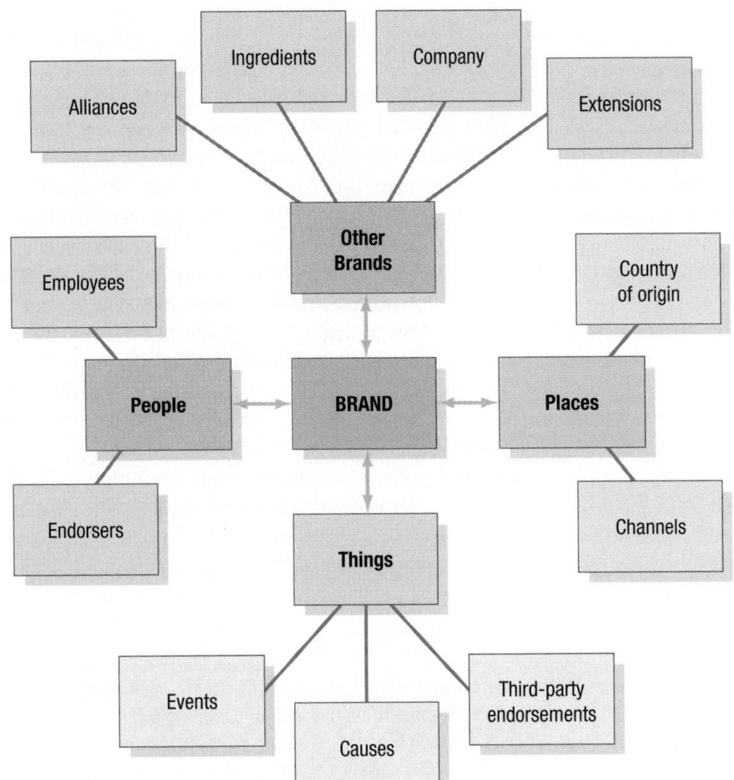

FIG. 9.3

Secondary Sources of Brand Knowledge

- Burton could also try to sell through popular surf shops in a hope that its credibility would "rub off" on the Dominator brand.
- Burton could attempt to co-brand by identifying a strong ingredient brand for its foam or fiberglass materials (as Wilson did by incorporating Goodyear tire rubber on the soles of its ProStaff Classic tennis shoes).
- Burton could attempt to find one or more top professional surfers to endorse the surfboard or choose to become a sponsor of a surfing competition or even the entire Association of Surfing Professionals (ASP) World Tour.
- Burton could attempt to secure and publicize favorable ratings from third-party sources like *Surfer* or *Surfing* magazine.

Thus, independent of the associations created by the surfboard itself, its brand name, or any other aspects of the marketing program, Burton may be able to build equity by linking the brand to these other entities.

::: Measuring Brand Equity

Given that the power of a brand resides in the minds of consumers and how it changes their response to marketing, there are two basic approaches to measuring brand equity. An *indirect* approach assesses potential sources of brand equity by identifying and tracking consumer brand knowledge structures. A *direct* approach assesses the actual impact of brand knowledge on consumer response to different aspects of the marketing. "Marketing Insight: The Brand Value Chain" shows how the two measurement approaches can be linked.

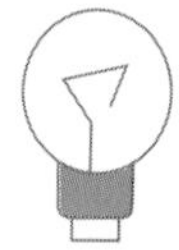

MARKETING INSIGHT | THE BRAND VALUE CHAIN

The **brand value chain** is a structured approach to assessing the sources and outcomes of brand equity and the manner in which marketing activities create brand value. The brand value chain is based on several basic premises.

The brand value creation process begins when the firm invests in a marketing program targeting actual or potential customers. Any marketing program investment that can be attributed to brand value development, either intentional or not, falls into this category—product research, development, and design; trade or intermediary support; and marketing communications.

The marketing activity associated with the program affects the customer "mind-set" with respect to the brand. The issue is, in what ways have customers been changed as a result of the marketing program? This mind-set, across a broad group of customers, then results in certain outcomes for the brand in terms of how it performs in the marketplace. This is the collective impact of individual customer actions regarding how much and when they purchase, the price that they pay, and so on. Finally, the investment community considers market performance and other factors such as replacement cost and purchase price in acquisitions to arrive at an assessment of shareholder value in general and the value of a brand in particular.

The model also assumes that a number of linking factors intervene between these stages and determine the extent to which value created at one stage transfers to the next stage. Three sets of multipliers moderate the transfer between the marketing program and the subsequent three value stages—the program multiplier, the customer multiplier, and the market multiplier. The *program multiplier* determines the ability of the marketing program to affect the customer mind-set and is a function of the quality of the program investment. The *customer multiplier* determines the extent to which value created in the minds of customers affects market performance. This result depends on contextual factors external to the customer. Three such factors are competitive superiority (how effective is the quantity and quality of the marketing investment of other competing brands), channel and other intermediary support (how much brand reinforcement and selling effort is being put forth by various marketing partners), and customer size and profile (how many and what types of customers, profitable or not, are attracted to the brand). The *market multiplier* determines the extent to which the value shown by the market performance of a brand is manifested in shareholder value. It depends, in part, on the actions of financial analysts and investors.

Sources: Kevin Lane Keller and Don Lehmann, "How Do Brands Create Value," *Marketing Management* (May/June 2003): 27–31. See also, Rajendra K. Srivastava, Tasadduq A. Shervani, and Liam Fahey, "Market-Based Assets and Shareholder Value." *Journal of Marketing* 62, no. 1 (1998): 2–18, and M. J. Epstein and R. A. Westbrook, "Linking Actions to Profits in Strategic Decision Making," *MIT Sloan Management Review* (Spring 2001): 39–49. In terms of related empirical insights, see Manoj K. Agrawal and Vithala Rao "An Empirical Comparison of Consumer-Based Measures of Brand Equity," *Marketing Letters* 7, no. 3 (1996): 237–247, and Walfried Lassar, Banwari Mittal, and Arun Sharma, "Measuring Customer-Based Brand Equity," *Journal of Consumer Marketing* 12, no. 4 (1995): 11–19.

The two general approaches are complementary, and marketers can employ both. In other words, for brand equity to perform a useful strategic function and guide marketing decisions, it is important for marketers to (1) fully understand the sources of brand equity and how they affect outcomes of interest, as well as (2) how these sources and outcomes change, if at all, over time. Brand audits are important for the former; brand tracking is important for the latter.

Brand Audits

To better understand their brands, marketers often need to conduct brand audits. A **brand audit** is a consumer-focused exercise that involves a series of procedures to assess the health of the brand, uncover its sources of brand equity, and suggest ways to improve and leverage its equity.

The brand audit can be used to set strategic direction for the brand. Are the current sources of brand equity satisfactory? Do certain brand associations need to be strengthened? Does the brand lack uniqueness? What brand opportunities exist and what potential challenges exist for brand equity? As a result of this strategic analysis, the marketer can develop a marketing program to maximize long-term brand equity.

Marketers should conduct a brand audit whenever they consider important shifts in strategic direction. With newspapers experiencing declining circulation as more people rely on radio, TV, and the Internet for their news, some publishers are now commissioning brand audits and attempting to redesign newspapers to be contemporary, relevant, and interesting to readers. Conducting brand audits on a regular basis (e.g., annually) allows marketers to keep their fingers on the pulse of their brands so that they can manage them more proactively and responsively. Audits are particularly useful background for managers as they set up their marketing plans.

Brand audits can have profound implications for strategic direction and brands' resulting performance.[37]

POLAROID

The results of a brand audit in Western Europe led Polaroid to decide to try to change its conventional photography image there to emphasize the "fun side" of its cameras. Polaroid gave one group of consumers 35 mm cameras and another group Polaroid cameras. Both groups went to a wedding and were told to shoot a roll of film. The 35 mm photos were typical wedding fare—posed and proper. The Polaroid photos were completely different—spontaneous and spirited. Those consumers with the Polaroids began to tell stories of the amusing antics that happened when the camera appeared. Polaroid learned from this research that its cameras could be a social stimulant and catalyst, bringing fun into people's lives, a theme that was picked up in advertising and that suggested new distribution strategies.

A brand audit requires the understanding of sources of brand equity from the perspective of both the firm and the consumer.[38] From the perspective of the firm, it is necessary to understand exactly what products and services are currently being offered to consumers and how they are being marketed and branded. From the perspective of the consumer, it is necessary to uncover the true meaning of brands and products to the consumer. Brand audits consist of two steps: the brand inventory and the brand exploratory.

BRAND INVENTORY The purpose of the *brand inventory* is to provide a current, comprehensive profile of how all the products and services sold by a company are marketed and branded. Profiling each product or service requires identifying all associated brand elements as well as the supporting marketing program. This information should be accurate, comprehensive, and timely, and summarized in both visual and verbal form. As part of the brand inventory, it is also advisable to profile competitive brands, in as much detail as possible, in terms of their branding and marketing efforts.

The brand inventory helps to suggest what consumers' current perceptions *may* be based on. Although the brand inventory is primarily a descriptive exercise, some useful analysis can be conducted too. For example, marketers can assess the consistency of all the different products or services sharing a brand name. Are the different brand elements used in a consistent way or are there many different variations and versions—perhaps for no obvious reason—depending on geographical market, market segment, and so on? Similarly, are the supporting marketing programs logical and consistent across related brands?

BRAND EXPLORATORY The *brand exploratory* is research activity conducted to understand what consumers think and feel about the brand and its corresponding product category to identify sources of brand equity.

Several preliminary activities are useful for the brand exploratory. A number of prior research studies may be relevant. It is also useful to interview company personnel to gain an understanding of their beliefs about consumer perceptions. The diversity of opinion that typically emerges from these internal interviews serves several functions: It increases the likelihood that useful insights or ideas will be generated; it also points out any internal inconsistencies or misconceptions

Although these preliminary activities may yield useful findings and suggest certain hypotheses, they are often incomplete. Additional research may be required to better understand how customers shop for and use products and services and what they think of various brands. To allow a broad range of issues to be covered and to permit certain issues to be pursued in greater depth, the brand exploratory often employs qualitative research techniques, such as word associations, projective techniques, visualization, brand personification, and laddering (see Chapter 4).

Many firms are now using ethnography to supplement traditional focus groups. They study consumers in their everyday habitats at home, at work, at play, or shopping. Based on ethnographic research, Duracell, for example, learned that people had trouble removing a tab from its hearing aid batteries. The result was the introduction of a new product, Easy Tab. Whirlpool learned that people didn't want to wait for their dishwashers to fill up before running the machine, so its Kitchen Aid unit introduced a smaller version called Briva.

E! NETWORK

E! Network's sister station, The Style Network, has recently undergone a metamorphosis as a result of a brand audit. The Style Network was once known for its emphasis on haute couture, but a brand audit revealed that Style viewers wanted to watch shows that were more applicable to their lives. In response, Style phased in makeover shows with new twists. For instance, in "Guess Who's Coming to Decorate?" the contestant chooses between, say, his mother, a friend, or a designer for an interior overhaul. To tout Style's own "makeover," there's a $10 million ad campaign with the tagline "Where life gets a new look."[39]

Brand Tracking

Tracking studies collect information from consumers on a routine basis over time. Tracking studies typically employ quantitative measures to provide marketers with current information as to how their brands and marketing programs are performing on the basis of a number of key dimensions. Tracking studies are a means of understanding where, how much, and in what ways brand value is being created.

These studies perform an important function for managers by providing consistent baseline information to facilitate day-to-day decision making. As more varied marketing activity surrounds the brand, it becomes difficult and expensive to research each individual marketing action. Tracking studies provide valuable diagnostic insights into the collective effects of a host of marketing activities. Regardless of how few or many changes are made in the marketing program over time, it is important to monitor the health of the brand and its equity so that proper adjustments can be made.

Brand Valuation

Brand equity needs to be distinguished from **brand valuation**, which is the job of estimating the total financial value of the brand. Certain companies base their growth on acquiring and building rich brand portfolios. Nestlé has acquired Rowntree (U.K.), Carnation (U.S.), Stouffer (U.S.), Buitoni-Perugina (Italy), and Perrier (France), making it the world's largest food company.

Table 9.2 displays the world's most valuable brands in 2004 according to one ranking.[40] With these well-known companies, brand value is typically over one-half of the total company market capitalization. John Stuart, co-founder of Quaker Oats, said: "If this business were split up, I would give you the land and bricks and mortar, and I would take the brands

TABLE 9.2

The World's 10 Most Valuable Brands

Rank	Brand	2004 Brand Value (Billions)
1	Coca-Cola	$67.39
2	Microsoft	$61.37
3	IBM	$53.79
4	GE	$44.11
5	Intel	$33.50
6	Disney	$27.11
7	McDonald's	$25.00
8	Nokia	$24.04
9	Toyota	$22.67
10	Marlboro	$22.13

and trade marks, and I would fare better than you." U.S. companies do not list brand equity on their balance sheets because of the arbitrariness of the estimate. However, brand equity is given a value by some companies in the United Kingdom, Hong Kong, and Australia. "Marketing Insight: What Is a Brand Worth?" reviews one popular valuation approach, based in part on the price premium the brand commands times the extra volume it moves over an average brand.[41]

::: Managing Brand Equity

Effective brand management requires a long-term view of marketing decisions. Because consumer responses to marketing activity depend on what they know and remember about a brand, short-term marketing actions, by changing brand knowledge, necessarily increase or decrease the success of future marketing actions. Additionally, a long-term view results in proactive strategies designed to maintain and enhance customer-based brand equity over time in the face of external changes in the marketing environment and internal changes in a firm's marketing goals and programs.

Brand Reinforcement

As a company's major enduring asset, a brand needs to be carefully managed so that its value does not depreciate. Many brand leaders of 70 years ago are still today's brand leaders: Kodak, Wrigley's, Coca-Cola, Heinz, and Campbell Soup, but only by constantly striving to improve their products, services, and marketing. "Marketing Memo: Twenty-First-Century Branding" offers some contemporary perspectives on enduring brand leadership.

Brand equity is reinforced by marketing actions that consistently convey the meaning of the brand to consumers in terms of: (1) What products the brand represents; what core benefits it supplies; and what needs it satisfies; as well as (2) how the brand makes those products superior and which strong, favorable, and unique brand associations should exist in the minds of consumers. Nivea, one of Europe's strongest brands, has expanded its scope from a skin-cream brand to a skin-care and personal-care brand through carefully designed and implemented brand extensions reinforcing the Nivea brand promise of "mild," "gentle," and "caring" in a broader arena.

Reinforcing brand equity requires innovation and relevance throughout the marketing program. Marketers must introduce new products and conduct new marketing activities that truly satisfy their target markets. The brand must always be moving forward—but moving forward in the right direction. Marketing must always find new and compelling offerings and ways to market them. Brands that fail to do so—such as Kmart, Levi Strauss, Montgomery Ward, Oldsmobile, and Polaroid—find that their market leadership dwindles or even disappears.

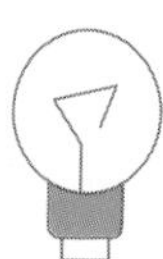

MARKETING INSIGHT | WHAT IS A BRAND WORTH?

According to top brand valuation firm Interbrand, brand valuation is based on an assessment of what the value is today of the earnings or cash flow the brand can be expected to generate in the future. To estimate brand value, it is necessary to: (1) identify the true earnings that can be attributed strictly to the brand and (2) capitalize the earnings by applying a multiple to historic earnings as a discount rate to future cash flow.

Brand earnings. Interbrand maintains that not all of a brand's profitability can necessarily be applied to the valuation of that brand. A brand may essentially be a commodity or derive much of its profitability from non-brand-related considerations (like its distribution system). Elements of profitability that do not result from the brand's identity must therefore be excluded. Because the valuation may be adversely affected by using a single year's profit, Interbrand uses a three-year weighted average of historical profit.

Brand earnings are calculated by subtracting a number of items from brand sales: (1) costs of brand sales, (2) marketing costs, (3) variable and fixed overheads including depreciation and central overhead allocation, (4) remuneration of capital charge (a 5%–10% rental charge on the replacement value of the capital employed in the line of production), and (5) taxation.

Brand strength. To adjust these earnings, Interbrand conducts an in-depth assessment of brand strength. The assessment involves a detailed review of the brand, its positioning, the market in which it operates, competition, past performance, future plans, and risks to the brand. Interbrand administers a detailed questionnaire to collect the information from managers and customers. It also examines annual reports and other printed materials, and even conducts inspection visits to distributors and retail outlets.

Brand strength is a composite of seven weighted factors, each of which is scored according to established guidelines (see below). The resulting total, known as the *brand strength score,* is expressed as a percentage. This score is converted to an earnings multiple to be used against the brand-related profits. Certain adjustments are made to create a weighted average of post-tax brand profitability against which the brand multiplier is applied. Interbrand makes the comparison between the reciprocal of these multipliers and typical discount rates (or interest rates): A so-called perfect brand with a brand strength score of 100 would have a discount rate of 5 percent (1 over 20), which would be the typical return on a fairly low risk investment; a weaker brand with a lower multiplier would have a higher discount rate to reflect the greater risk.

Interbrand Brand Strength Formula (Weights in Parentheses)

1. ***Leadership*** (25%)—The brand's ability to influence its market and be a dominant force with a strong market share such that it can set price points, command distribution, and resist competitive invasions. A brand that leads its market or market sector is a more stable and valuable property than a brand lower down the order.
2. ***Stability*** (15%)—The ability of the brand to survive over a long period of time based on consumer loyalty and past history. Long-established brands that have become part of the "fabric" of their markets are particularly valuable.
3. ***Market*** (10%)—The brand's trading environment in terms of growth prospects, volatility, and barriers to entry. Brands in markets such as foods, drinks, and publishing are intrinsically more valuable than brands in, for example, high-tech or clothing areas, as the latter markets are more vulnerable to technological or fashion changes.
4. ***Geographic Spread*** (25%)—The ability of the brand to cross geographic and cultural borders. Brands that are international are inherently more valuable than national or regional brands, due in part to their economies of scale.
5. ***Trend*** (10%)—The ongoing direction and ability of the brand to remain contemporary and relevant to consumers.
6. ***Support*** (10%)—The amount and consistency of marketing and communication activity. Those brand names that have received consistent investment and focused support must be regarded as more valuable than those that have not. While the amount spent in supporting a brand is important, the quality of this support is equally significant.
7. ***Protection*** (5%)—The brand owner's legal titles. A registered trademark is a statutory monopoly in a name, device, or in a combination of these two. Other protection may exist in common law, at least in certain countries. The strength and breadth of the brand's protection is critical in assessing its worth.

Sources: Michael Birkin, "Assessing Brand Value," in *Brand Power,* edited by Paul Sobart (New York: Macmillan); Simon Mottram, "The Power of the Brand," ARF Brand Equity Conference, February 15–16, 1994; John Murphy, *Brand Valuation* (London: Hutchinson Business Books, 1989); Jean-Noel Kapferer, *Strategic Brand Management* (London: Kogan Page Limited, 1992); Noel Penrose and Martin Moorhouse, "The Valuation of Brands," *Trademark World,* no. 17 (February 1989); Tom Blackett, "The Role of Brand Valuation in Marketing Strategy," *Marketing Research Today* 17, no. 4 (November 1989): 245–248.

KELLOGG

After experiencing falling market share and profits through the 1990s, Kellogg was able to reestablish market leadership in the cereal business by getting consumers to pay more for their high-profit brands. The secret? Adding new features to old favorites such as Special K Red Berries cereal with freeze-dried berries, priced at nearly double the price of Raisin Bran cereal, or putting toys and computer CDs inside boxes of kids' cereals.[42]

An important consideration in reinforcing brands is the consistency of the marketing support the brand receives, in terms of both amount and kind. Consistency does not mean uniformity and no changes: Many tactical changes may be necessary to maintain the strate-

Campbell's Soup continually updates its marketing and its ads: This ad for its new "Soup at Hand" product features Bucky Lasek, a top pro skateboarder.

gic thrust and direction of the brand. Unless there is some change in the marketing environment, however, there is little need to deviate from a successful positioning. In such cases, sources of brand equity should be vigorously preserved and defended.

VOLVO

In an attempt to woo a different audience, Volvo drifted away from its heritage of safety in the late 1990s to push driving fun, speed, and performance. Purchased by Ford in 1999, the company dropped its ReVOLVOlution-themed ad campaign for the brand and went back to its roots in an attempt to revive sagging sales. Volvo's positioning was updated, however, to convey "active safety" to transcend the brand's boxy, sturdy "passive safety" image. With product introductions that maximized safety but that still encompassed style, performance, and luxury, Volvo's sales set records in 2003.[43]

In managing brand equity, it is important to recognize the trade-offs between those marketing activities that fortify the brand and reinforce its meaning and those that attempt to leverage or borrow from existing brand equity to reap some financial benefit.[44] At some point, failure to reinforce the brand will diminish brand awareness and weaken brand image.

THE HOME DEPOT

Since The Home Depot opened its first store in 1978 in Atlanta, the company has emphasized exemplary customer service. Its sales staff is trained to offer on-the-spot lessons in laying tile, electrical installations, and other

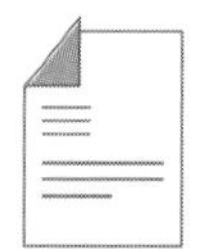

MARKETING MEMO | TWENTY-FIRST-CENTURY BRANDING

One of the most successful marketers of the last fifteen years, Scott Bedbury played a key role in the rise of both Nike and Starbucks. In his insightful book, *A New Brand World,* he offers the following branding principles:

1. ***Relying on brand awareness has become marketing fool's gold***—Smart brands are more concerned with brand relevance and brand resonance.
2. ***You have to know it before you can grow it***—Most brands don't know who they are, where they've been, and where they're going.
3. ***Always remember the Spandex rule of brand expansion***—Just because you can doesn't mean you should.
4. ***Great brands establish enduring customer relationships***—They have more to do with emotions and trust than with footwear cushioning or the way a coffee bean is roasted.
5. ***Everything matters***—Even your restroom.
6. ***All brands need good parents***—Unfortunately, most brands come from troubled homes.
7. ***Big is no excuse for being bad***—Truly great brands use their superhuman powers for good and place people and principles before profits.
8. ***Relevance, simplicity, and humanity***—Rather than technology—will distinguish brands in the future.

Source: Scott Bedbury, *A New Brand World* (New York: Viking Press, 2002).

projects; they are experienced tradespersons—plumbers, electricians, and carpenters. In recent years, however, there were customer complaints about clutter in the aisles and salespeople stocking items instead of providing service. Starting in 2001, The Home Depot gave its stores a makeover called Service Performance Improvement (SPI). SPI limits restocking to off-peak hours and prohibits forklifts in store aisles during the day. The program resulted in up to a 70 percent increase in employee interactions with customers. Before SPI was introduced, employees spent as little as 40 percent of their time with customers. ■

Brand Revitalization

Changes in consumer tastes and preferences, the emergence of new competitors or new technology, or any new development in the marketing environment could potentially affect the fortunes of a brand. In virtually every product category, there are examples of once prominent and admired brands—such as Smith Corona, Zenith, and TWA—that have fallen on hard times or, in some cases, disappeared.[45] Nevertheless, a number of these brands have managed to make impressive comebacks in recent years, as marketers have breathed new life into their customer franchises. Brands such as Breck, Dr. Scholl's and Fanta have all seen their brand fortunes successfully turned around to varying degrees.

Reversing a fading brand's fortunes requires either that it "returns to its roots" and lost sources of brand equity are restored, or that new sources of brand equity are established. Regardless of which approach is taken, brands on the comeback trail have to make more "revolutionary" changes than the "evolutionary" changes.

Often, the first thing to do in turning around the fortunes of a brand is to understand what the sources of brand equity were to begin with. Are positive associations losing their strength or uniqueness? Have negative associations become linked to the brand? Decisions must then be made as to whether to retain the same positioning or create a new positioning, and, if so, which positioning to adopt. Sometimes the positioning is still appropriate; it's the actual marketing program that is the source of the problem because it is failing to deliver on the brand promise. In those instances, a "back to basics" strategy may make sense, as was the case with Harley-Davidson.

HARLEY-DAVIDSON

Founded in 1903 in Milwaukee, WI, Harley-Davidson has twice narrowly escaped bankruptcy but is today one of the most-recognized motor vehicle brands in the world. In dire financial straits in the 1980s, it desperately licensed its name for such ill-advised ventures as Harley-Davidson cigarettes and wine coolers.

Although consumers loved the brand, sales were depressed by product quality problems. Harley's return to greatness was begun by improving manufacturing processes. Harley also developed a strong brand community in the form of an owners' club, called the Harley Owners Group (HOG), which sponsors bike rallies, charity rides, and other motorcycle events. Harley-Davidson has continued to promote its brand with grassroots marketing efforts and finds itself in the enviable position of having consumer demand exceed what it can supply.

In other cases, however, the old positioning is just no longer viable and a "reinvention" strategy is necessary. Mountain Dew completely overhauled its brand image to become a soft-drink powerhouse. As its history reveals, it is often easiest to revive a brand that is around, but has just more or less been forgotten.

MOUNTAIN DEW

Pepsi initially introduced Mountain Dew in 1969 and marketed it with the countrified tagline "Yahoo Mountain Dew! It'll Tickle Your Innards." By the 1990s, the brand was languishing on store shelves despite an attempt to evolve the image with outdoor action scenes. To turn the brand around, Mountain Dew updated the packaging and launched ads featuring a group of anonymous young males—the "Dew Dudes"—participating in extreme sports such as bungee jumping, skydiving, and snowboarding while consuming Mountain Dew. The brand slogan became "Do the Dew." The brand's successful pursuit of young soda drinkers led to Mountain Dew challenging Diet Coke to become the number-three selling soft drink in terms of market share by 2000.

There is obviously a continuum involved with revitalization strategies, with pure "back to basics" at one end and pure "reinvention" at the other end. Many revitalizations combine elements of both strategies. To refresh old sources of brand equity or create new sources, two main approaches are possible:

1. Expand the depth and/or breadth of brand awareness by improving consumer recall and recognition of the brand during purchase or consumption settings.
2. Improve the strength, favorability, and uniqueness of brand associations making up the brand image. This approach may involve programs directed at existing or new brand associations.

Brand revitalizations of almost any kind start with the product. General Motors' turnaround with its fading Cadillac brand was fueled by new model designs that redefined the Cadillac look and styling, such as with the CTS sedan, XLR roadster, and ESV sport utility vehicle.[46]

Brand Crisis

Marketing managers must assume that at some point in time, some kind of brand crisis will arise. Diverse brands such as Jack in the Box restaurants, Firestone tires, Exxon oil, Suzuki Samurai sport utility vehicles, and Martha Stewart have all experienced a serious, potentially crippling brand crisis. In general, the more that brand equity and a strong corporate image has been established—especially with respect to corporate credibility and trustworthiness—the more likely it is that the firm can weather the storm. Careful preparation and a well-managed crisis management program, however, are also critical. As Johnson & Johnson's nearly flawless handling of the Tylenol product-tampering incident suggests, the key to managing a crisis is that consumers see the response by the firm as both *swift* and *sincere.*

In terms of swiftness, the longer it takes a firm to respond to a marketing crisis, the more likely it is that consumers can form negative impressions as a result of unfavorable media coverage or word of mouth. Perhaps even worse, consumers may find out that they do not really like the brand that much after all and permanently switch to alternative brands or products.

PERRIER

Perrier was forced to halt production worldwide and recall all of its existing bottles in February 1994, when traces of benzene, a known carcinogen, were found in excessive quantities in the bottled water. Over the course of the next few weeks, several explanations were offered as to how the contamination occurred, creating confusion and skepticism. Perhaps even more damaging, the product itself was off the shelves until May 1994.

Despite an expensive relaunch featuring ads and promotions, the brand struggled to regain lost market share, and a full year later found sales less than half of what they once had been. Part of the problem was that during the time the product was unavailable, consumers and retailers found satisfactory substitutes. With its key "purity" association tarnished—the brand had been advertised as the "Earth's First Soft Drink" and "It's Perfect. It's Perrier."—the brand had no other compelling points-of-difference over these competitors.[47] Eventually, the company was taken over by Nestlé SA.

Second, swift actions must also come across as sincere. The more sincere the response by the firm—in terms of public acknowledgment of the severity of the impact on consumers and a willingness of the firm to take whatever steps are necessary and feasible to solve the crisis—the less likely it is that consumers will form negative attributions.

GERBER

Although Gerber had established a strong image of trust with consumers, baby food is a product category characterized by an extremely high level of involvement and need for reassurance. When consumers reported finding shards of glass in some jars of its baby food, Gerber tried to reassure the public that there were no problems in its manufacturing plants. But the company adamantly refused to have its baby food withdrawn from food stores. Some consumers clearly found Gerber's response unsatisfactory: Its market share slumped from 66 percent to 52 percent within a couple of months. As one company official admits, "Not pulling our baby food off the shelf gave the appearance that we aren't a caring company."[48]

::: Devising a Branding Strategy

The **branding strategy** for a firm reflects the number and nature of common and distinctive brand elements applied to the different products sold by the firm. In other words, devising a branding strategy involves deciding the nature of new and existing brand elements to be applied to new and existing products.

The decision as to how to brand new products is especially critical. When a firm introduces a new product, it has three main choices:

1. It can develop new brand elements for the new product.
2. It can apply some of its existing brand elements.
3. It can use a combination of new and existing brand elements.

When a firm uses an established brand to introduce a new product, it is called a **brand extension**. When a new brand is combined with an existing brand, the brand extension can also be called a **sub-brand**, as with Hershey Kisses candy, Adobe Acrobat software, Toyota Camry automobiles, and American Express Blue cards. An existing brand that gives birth to a brand extension is referred to as the **parent brand**. If the parent brand is already associated with multiple products through brand extensions, then it may also be called a **family brand**.

Brand extensions can be broadly classified into two general categories:[49] In a **line extension**, the parent brand is used to brand a new product that targets a new market segment within a product category currently served by the parent brand, such as through new flavors, forms, colors, added ingredients, and package sizes. Dannon has introduced several types of Dannon yogurt line extensions through the years—Fruit on the Bottom, Natural Flavors, Fruit Blends, and Whipped. In a **category extension**, the parent brand is used to enter a different product category from that currently served by the parent brand, such as Swiss Army watches. Honda has used its company name to cover such different products as automobiles, motorcycles, snowblowers, lawnmowers, marine engines, and snowmobiles. This allows Honda to advertise that it can fit "six Hondas in a two-car garage."

A **brand line** consists of all products—original as well as line and category extensions—sold under a particular brand. A **brand mix** (or brand assortment) is the set of all brand lines that a particular seller makes available to buyers. Many companies are now introducing **branded variants**, which are specific brand lines supplied to specific retailers or distribution channels. They result from the pressure retailers put on manufacturers to provide distinctive offerings. A camera company may supply its low-end cameras to mass merchandisers while limiting its higher-priced items to specialty camera shops. Valentino may design and supply different lines of suits and jackets to different department stores.[50]

A **licensed product** is one whose brand name has been licensed to other manufacturers who actually make the product. Corporations have seized on licensing to push the company name and image across a wide range of products—from bedding to shoes—making it a $35 billion business.[51] Jeep's licensing program added up to $400 million in global sales in 2002 and included everything from strollers (built for a father's longer arms) to apparel (with teflon in the denim)—as long they fit the brand's positioning of "Life Without Limits."[52]

Branding Decision: To Brand or Not to Brand?

The first branding strategy decision is whether to develop a brand name for a product. Today, branding is such a strong force that hardly anything goes unbranded. So-called commodities do not have to remain commodities. A *commodity* is a product presumably so basic that it cannot be physically differentiated in the minds of consumers. Over the years, a number of products that at one time were seen as essentially commodities have become highly differentiated as strong brands have emerged in the category.[53] Some notable examples (with brand pioneers in parentheses) are: coffee (Maxwell House), bath soap (Ivory), flour (Gold Medal), beer (Budweiser), oatmeal (Quaker), pickles (Vlasic), bananas (Chiquita), pineapples (Dole), and even salt (Morton).

Assuming a firm decides to brand its products or services, it must then choose which brand names to use. Four general strategies are often used:

- ***Individual names.*** This policy is followed by General Mills (Bisquick, Gold Medal flour, Nature Valley granola bars, Old El Paso Mexican foods, Pop Secret popcorn, Wheaties cereal, and Yoplait yogurt). A major advantage of an individual-names strategy is that the company does not tie its reputation to the product's. If the product fails or appears to have low quality, the company's name or image is not hurt. Companies often use different brand names for different quality lines within the same product class. Delta branded its low-fare air carrier Song in part to protect the equity of its Delta Airlines brand.[54]
- ***Blanket family names.*** This policy is followed by Heinz and General Electric. A blanket family name also has advantages. Development cost is less because there is no need for "name" research or heavy advertising expenditures to create brand-name recognition. Furthermore, sales of the new product are likely to be strong if the manufacturer's name is good. Campbell's introduces new soups under its brand name with extreme simplicity and achieves instant recognition.
- ***Separate family names for all products.*** This policy is followed by Sears (Kenmore for appliances, Craftsman for tools, and Homart for major home installations). If a company produces quite different products, it is not desirable to use one blanket family name. Swift and Company developed separate family names for its hams (Premium) and fertilizers (Vigoro).
- ***Corporate name combined with individual product names.*** This sub-branding policy is followed by Kellogg (Kellogg's Rice Krispies, Kellogg's Raisin Bran, and Kellogg's Corn Flakes), as well as Honda, Sony, and Hewlett-Packard. The company name legitimizes, and the individual name individualizes, the new product.

The first two strategies are sometimes referred to as a "house of brands" and a "branded house," respectively, and can be seen as representing two ends of a brand relationship continuum, with the latter two strategies as being in between and combinations of the two. Although firms rarely adopt a pure example of any of the four strategies, deciding which general strategy to emphasize depends on several factors, as evidenced by Table 9.3.

Two key components of virtually any branding strategy are brand extensions and brand portfolios.

Brand Extensions

Recognizing that one of their most valuable assets is their brands, many firms have decided to leverage that asset by introducing a host of new products under some of their strongest brand names. Most new products are in fact line extensions—typically 80 to 90% in any one year. Moreover, many of the most successful new products, as rated by various sources, are extensions (e.g., Microsoft Xbox video game system, Apple iPod digital music player, and Nokia 6800 cell phone). Nevertheless, many new products are introduced each year as new brands (e.g., Zyprexa mood stabilizer drug, TiVo digital video recorders, and Mini automobile).

TABLE 9.3

Selecting a Brand Relationship Spectrum Position

Toward a Branded House	Toward a House of Brands
Does the parent brand contribute to the offering by adding:	**Is there a compelling need for a separate brand because it will:**
—Associations enhancing the value proposition?	—Create and own an association?
—Credibility through organizational associations?	—Represent a new, different offering?
—Visibility?	—Retain/capture customer/brand bond?
—Communication efficiencies?	—Deal with channel conflict?
Will the master brand be strengthened by associating with the new offering?	**Will the business support a new brand name?**

Source: Adapted from David A. Aaker and Erich Joachimsthaler, *Brand Leadership* (New York: Free Press, 2000), Figure 4-6, p. 120.

ADVANTAGES OF BRAND EXTENSIONS Two main advantages of brand extensions are that they can facilitate new-product acceptance, as well as provide positive feedback to the parent brand and company.

New-Product Success Brand extensions improve the odds of new-product success in a number of ways. With a brand extension, consumers can make inferences and form expectations as to the likely composition and performance of a new product based on what they already know about the parent brand itself and the extent to which they feel this information is relevant to the new product.[55] For example, when Sony introduced a new personal computer tailored for multimedia applications, Vaio, consumers may have been more likely to feel comfortable with its anticipated performance because of their experience with and knowledge of other Sony products.

By setting up positive expectations, extensions reduce risk.[56] Because of the potentially increased consumer demand resulting from introducing a new product as an extension, it also may be easier to convince retailers to stock and promote a brand extension. From a marketing communications perspective, an introductory campaign for an extension does not have to create awareness of both the brand and the new product but instead can concentrate on the new product itself.[57]

Extensions can thus result in reduced costs of the introductory launch campaign, important given that establishing a new brand name in the U.S. marketplace for a mass-consumer-packaged good can cost $100 million! They also can avoid the difficulty—and expense—of coming up with a new name. Extensions allow for packaging and labeling efficiencies. Similar or virtually identical packages and labels for extensions can result in lower production costs and, if coordinated properly, more prominence in the retail store by creating a "billboard" effect. For example, Stouffers offers a variety of frozen entrees with identical orange packaging that increases their visibility when they are stocked together in the freezer. By offering consumers a portfolio of brand variants within a product category, consumers who need a change—because of boredom, satiation, or whatever—can switch to a different product type without having to leave the brand family.

SUAVE

The low-priced family brand, Suave, sold by Helene-Curtis, includes a variety of personal-care products such as shampoo and conditioners, baby products, skin lotions, antiperspirants and deodorants, and so on. Given the amount of brand switching and the large number of personal care product brands kept by consumers in general—and of shampoos in particular—the ability of Suave to offer a full product line is a competitive advantage. By continually line extending, Suave keeps up with any new market trend or shift in consumer demand.[58]

Positive Feedback Effects Besides facilitating acceptance of new products, brand extensions can also provide feedback benefits.[59] They can help to clarify the meaning of a brand and its core brand values or improve consumer perceptions of the credibility of the company behind the extension. Thus, through brand extensions, Crayola means

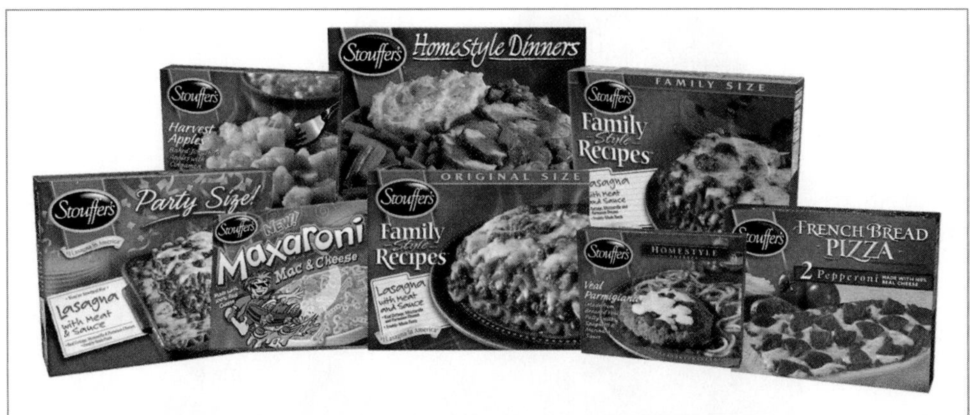

Brand extensions allow for packaging and labeling efficiency: Stouffer's distinctive orange packaging lets consumers switch to a different product without leaving the brand.

"colorful crafts for kids," Aunt Jemima means "breakfast foods," and Weight Watchers means "weight loss and maintenance."

Line extensions can renew interest and liking for the brand and benefit the parent brand by expanding market coverage. Kimberly-Clark's Kleenex unit has a goal of having facial tissue in every room of the home. This philosophy has led to a wide variety of Kleenex facial tissues and packaging, including scented, ultra-soft and lotion-impregnated tissues; boxes with drawings of dinosaurs and dogs for children's rooms, or colorful, stylish designs to match room décor; and a "man-sized" box with tissues 50 percent larger than regular Kleenex. One benefit of a successful extension is that it may also serve as the basis for subsequent extensions. During the 1970s and 1980s, Billabong established its brand credibility with the young surfing community as a designer and producer of quality surf apparel. This success permitted it to extend into other youth-oriented areas, such as snowboarding and skateboarding.

DISADVANTAGES OF BRAND EXTENSIONS On the downside, line extensions may cause the brand name to not be as strongly identified with any one product.[60] Ries and Trout call this the "line-extension trap."[61] By linking its brand to mainstream food products such as mashed potatoes, powdered milk, soups, and beverages, Cadbury ran the risk of losing its more specific meaning as a chocolates and candy brand.[62] **Brand dilution** occurs when consumers no longer associate a brand with a specific product or highly similar products and start thinking less of the brand.

If a firm launches extensions consumers deem inappropriate, they may question the integrity and competence of the brand. Different varieties of line extensions may confuse and perhaps even frustrate consumers: Which version of the product is the "right one" for them? As a result, they may reject new extensions for "tried-and-true" favorites or all-purpose versions. Retailers have to reject many new products and brands because they do not have the shelf or display space for them.

The worst possible scenario with an extension is that not only does it fail, but it harms the parent brand image in the process. Fortunately, such events are rare. "Marketing failures," where insufficient consumers were attracted to a brand, are typically much less damaging than "product failures," where the brand fundamentally fails to live up to its promise. Even then, product failures dilute brand equity only when the extension is seen as very similar to the parent brand. The Audi 5000 car suffered from a tidal wave of negative publicity and word of mouth in the mid-1980s when it was alleged to have a "sudden acceleration" problem. The adverse publicity also spilled over to the 4000 model. But the Quattro was relatively more insulated from negative repercussions, because it was distanced from the 5000 by its more distinct branding and advertising strategy.[63]

Even if sales of a brand extension are high and meet targets, it is possible that this revenue may have resulted from consumers switching to the extension from existing product offerings of the parent brand—in effect *cannibalizing* the parent brand. Intrabrand shifts in sales may not necessarily be so undesirable, as they can be thought of as a form of *preemptive cannibalization.* In other words, consumers might have switched to a competing brand instead of the line extension if it had not been introduced into the category. Tide laundry detergent maintains the same market share now compared as it did 50 years ago because of the sales contributions of the various line extensions (scented and unscented powder, tablet, liquid, and other forms).

Crest White Strips leverages the strong reputation of Crest in dental care.

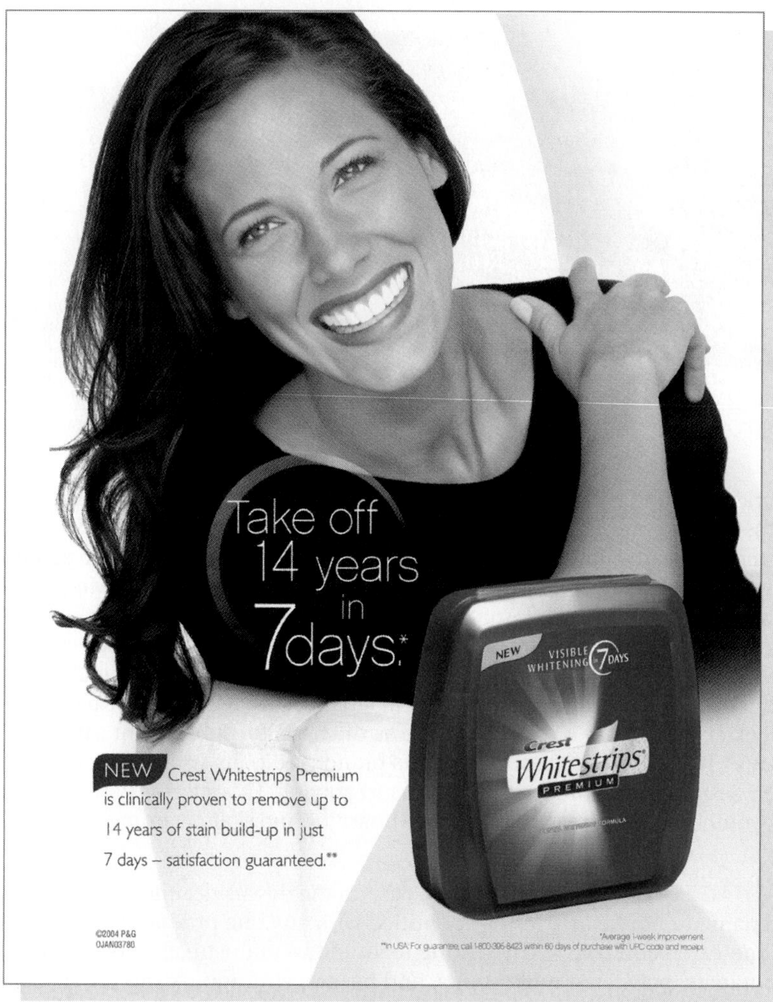

One easily overlooked disadvantage to brand extensions is that by introducing a new product as a brand extension, the firm forgoes the chance to create a new brand with its own unique image and equity. Consider the advantages to Disney of having introduced more adult-oriented Touchstone films; to Levi's of having introduced casual Dockers pants; and to Black and Decker of having introduced high-end Dewalt power tools.

SUCCESS CHARACTERISTICS A potential new-product extension for a brand must be judged by how effectively it leverages existing brand equity from the parent brand to the new product, as well as how effectively the extension, in turn, contributes to the equity of the parent brand.[64] Crest White Strips leveraged the strong reputation of Crest and dental care to provide reassurance in the teeth-whitening arena, while also reinforcing its dental authority image. The most important consideration with extensions is that there is "fit" in the mind of the consumer. Consumers may see a basis of fit for an extension in many ways—common physical attributes, usage situations, or user types.

One major mistake in evaluating extension opportunities is failing to take *all* of consumers' brand knowledge structures into account. Often marketers mistakenly focus on one or perhaps a few brand associations as a potential basis of fit and ignore other, possibly more important, associations in the process.

BIC

The French company Societe Bic, by emphasizing inexpensive, disposable products, was able to create markets for nonrefillable ball-point pens in the late 1950s; disposable cigarette lighters in the early 1970s; and disposable razors in the early 1980s. It unsuccessfully tried the same strategy in marketing Bic perfumes in the

United States and Europe in 1989. The perfumes—two for women ("Nuit" and "Jour") and two for men ("Bic for Men" and "Bic Sport for Men")—were packaged in quarter-ounce glass spray bottles that looked like fat cigarette lighters and sold for $5 each. The products were displayed on racks at checkout counters throughout Bic's extensive distribution channels. At the time, a Bic spokeswoman described the new products as extensions of the Bic heritage—"high quality at affordable prices, convenient to purchase, and convenient to use." The brand extension was launched with a $20 million advertising and promotion campaign containing images of stylish people enjoying themselves with the perfume and using the tagline "Paris In Your Pocket." Nevertheless, Bic was unable to overcome its lack of cachet and negative image associations, and the extension was a failure.[65]

"Marketing Memo: Research Insights on Brand Extensions" outlines a number of academic research findings on brand extensions.

Brand Portfolios

All brands have boundaries—a brand can only be stretched so far. Multiple brands are often necessary to pursue multiple market segments. Any one brand is not viewed equally favorably by all the different market segments that the firm would like to target. Some other reasons for introducing multiple brands in a category include:[66]

1. To increase shelf presence and retailer dependence in the store;
2. To attract consumers seeking variety who may otherwise have switched to another brand;
3. To increase internal competition within the firm; and
4. To yield economies of scale in advertising, sales, merchandising, and physical distribution.

The **brand portfolio** is the set of all brands and brand lines a particular firm offers for sale to buyers in a particular category. Different brands may be designed and marketed to appeal to different market segments.

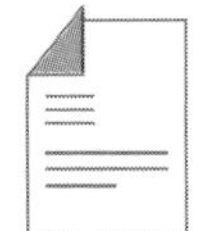

MARKETING MEMO | RESEARCH INSIGHTS ON BRAND EXTENSIONS

Academics have studied brand extensions closely. Here is a summary of some of their key research findings.

- Successful brand extensions occur when the parent brand is seen as having favorable associations and there is a perception of fit between the parent brand and the extension product.
- There are many bases of fit: product-related attributes and benefits, as well as non-product-related attributes and benefits related to common usage situations or user types.
- Depending on consumer knowledge of the categories, perceptions of fit may be based on technical or manufacturing commonalties or more surface considerations such as necessary or situational complementarity.
- High-quality brands stretch farther than average-quality brands, although both types of brands have boundaries.
- A brand that is seen as prototypical of a product category can be difficult to extend outside the category.
- Concrete attribute associations tend to be more difficult to extend than abstract benefit associations.
- Consumers may transfer associations that are positive in the original product class but become negative in the extension context.
- Consumers may infer negative associations about an extension, perhaps even based on other inferred positive associations.
- It can be difficult to extend into a product class that is seen as easy to make.
- A successful extension can not only contribute to the parent brand image but also enable a brand to be extended even farther.
- An unsuccessful extension hurts the parent brand only when there is a strong basis of fit between the two.
- An unsuccessful extension does not prevent a firm from "backtracking" and introducing a more similar extension.
- Vertical extensions can be difficult and often require sub-branding strategies.
- The most effective advertising strategy for an extension emphasizes information about the extension (rather than reminders about the parent brand).

Source: Kevin Lane Keller, *Strategic Brand Management,* 2nd ed. (Upper Saddle River, NJ: Prentice Hall, 2003).

GAP

Founded in 1969 and named after the "generation gap," retail clothing manufacturer GAP grew by selling colorful GAP-branded clothing positioned as casual, functional, and "basic with attitude." GAP expanded beyond its flagship stores though acquisitions and extensions. GAPKids is a highly successful extension that was introduced in 1986. GAP bought Banana Republic and its unique travel and safari-themed stores and catalogs in 1983, and reformulated the clothing to reflect more urban tastes. In March 1994, GAP introduced Old Navy clothing stores to sell GAP-like men's, women's, and children's apparel at lower prices in large, warehouse-style outlets.

A brand portfolio must be judged by its ability to maximize brand equity. The optimal brand portfolio is one where each brand maximizes equity in combination with all other brands in the portfolio. In designing the optimal brand portfolio, marketers generally need to trade off market coverage and these other considerations with costs and profitability. If profits can be increased by dropping brands a portfolio is too big; if profits can be increased by adding brands, a portfolio is not big enough. In general, the basic principle in designing a brand portfolio is to *maximize market coverage,* so that no potential customers are being ignored, but to *minimize brand overlap,* so brands are not competing to gain customer approval. Each brand should be clearly differentiated and appealing to a sizable enough marketing segment to justify its marketing and production costs.[67]

Brand portfolios need to be carefully monitored over time to identify weak brands and kill unprofitable ones.[68]

ELECTROLUX

In the late 1990s, consumer durables manufacturer Electrolux offered a range of professional food service equipment in Western Europe. By 1996, the company had 15 brands in the professional food service equipment market, but only one, Zanussi, was sold in more than one country in Europe. By moving from a segmentation scheme based on price—low, medium, and high—to one based on consumer needs—from basic solutions to prestige gourmet—Electrolux was able to go from 15 local brands to having four pan-European brands. The resulting economies of scale and scope helped turn Electrolux's fortunes around, so even though it deleted many brands, its professional kitchenware division's sales never dwindled and it was finally able to turn a profit in 2001.

Brand lines with poorly differentiated brands are likely to be characterized by much cannibalization and require pruning.[69] Kellogg's Eggo waffles come in 16 flavors. Investors can choose among 8,000 mutual funds. Students can choose among hundreds of business schools. For the seller, this may spell hypercompetition. For the buyer, this may spell too much choice.

Besides these considerations, there are a number of specific roles brands can play as part of a brand portfolio.

FLANKERS Flanker or "fighter" brands are positioned with respect to competitors' brands so that more important (and more profitable) *flagship brands* can retain their desired positioning. Procter & Gamble markets Luvs diapers in a way that flanks the more premium positioned Pampers. In designing these fighter brands, marketers must walk a fine line. Fighter brands must not be so attractive that they take sales away from their higher-priced comparison brands or referents. At the same time, if fighter brands are seen as connected to other brands in the portfolio in any way (e.g., by virtue of a common branding strategy), then fighter brands must not be designed so cheaply that they reflect poorly on these other brands.

CASH COWS Some brands may be kept around despite dwindling sales because they still manage to hold on to a sufficient number of customers and maintain their profitability with virtually no marketing support. These "cash cow" brands can be effectively "milked" by capitalizing on their reservoir of existing brand equity. For example, despite the fact that technological advances have moved much of its market to the newer Mach III brand of razors, Gillette still sells the older Trac II, Atra, and Sensor brands. Because withdrawing these brands may not necessarily result in customers switching to another Gillette brand, it may be more profitable for Gillette to keep them in its brand portfolio for razor blades.

LOW-END ENTRY-LEVEL The role of a relatively low-priced brand in the brand portfolio often may be to attract customers to the brand franchise. Retailers like to feature these "traffic builders" because they are able to "trade up" customers to a higher-priced brand. For example, BMW introduced certain models into its 3-series automobiles in part as a means of bringing new customers into the brand franchise with the hope of later "moving them up" to higher-priced models when they later decided to trade in their cars.

HIGH-END PRESTIGE The role of a relatively high-priced brand in the brand family often is to add prestige and credibility to the entire portfolio. For example, one analyst argued that the real value of its Corvette high performance sports car to Chevrolet was in "its ability to lure curious customers into showrooms and at the same time help improve the image of other Chevrolet cars. It does not mean a hell of a lot for GM profitability, but there is no question that it is a traffic builder."[70] Corvette's technological image and prestige were meant to cast a halo over the entire Chevrolet line.

SUMMARY :::

1. A brand is a name, term, sign, symbol, or design, or some combination of these elements, intended to identify the goods and services of one seller or group of sellers and to differentiate them from those of competitors. The different components of a brand—brand names, logos, symbols, package designs, and so on—are brand elements.
2. Brands offer a number of benefits to customers and firms. Brands are valuable intangible assets that need to be managed carefully. The key to branding is that consumers perceive differences among brands in a product category.
3. Brand equity should be defined in terms of marketing effects uniquely attributable to a brand. That is, brand equity relates to the fact that different outcomes result in the marketing of a product or service because of its brand, as compared to the results if that same product or service was not identified by that brand.
4. Building brand equity depends on three main factors: (1) The initial choices for the brand elements or identities making up the brand; (2) the way the brand is integrated into the supporting marketing program; and (3) the associations indirectly transferred to the brand by linking the brand to some other entity (e.g., the company, country of origin, channel of distribution, or another brand).
5. Brand equity needs to be measured in order to be managed well. Brand audits are in-depth examinations of the health of a brand and can be used to set strategic direction for the brand. Tracking studies involve information collected from consumers on a routine basis over time and provide valuable tactical insights into the short-term effectiveness of marketing programs and activities. Brand audits measure "where the brand has been," and tracking studies measure "where the brand is now" and whether marketing programs are having the intended effects.
6. A branding strategy for a firm identifies which brand elements a firm chooses to apply across the various products it sells. In a brand extension, a firm uses an established brand name to introduce a new product. Potential extensions must be judged by how effectively they leverage existing brand equity to a new product, as well as how effectively the extension, in turn, contributes to the equity of the existing parent brand.
7. Brands can play a number of different roles within the brand portfolio. Brands may expand coverage, provide protection, extend an image, or fulfill a variety of other roles for the firm. Each brand name product must have a well-defined positioning. In that way, brands can maximize coverage and minimize overlap and thus optimize the portfolio.

APPLICATIONS :::

Marketing Debate Are Brand Extensions Good or Bad?

Some critics vigorously denounce the practice of brand extensions, as they feel that too often companies lose focus and consumers become confused. Other experts maintain that brand extensions are a critical growth strategy and source of revenue for the firm.

Take a position: Brand extensions can endanger brands versus brand extensions are an important brand-growth strategy.

Marketing Discussion

How can you relate the different models of brand equity presented in this chapter? How are they similar? How are they different? Can you construct a brand equity model that incorporates the best aspects of each model?

IN THIS CHAPTER, WE WILL ADDRESS THE FOLLOWING QUESTIONS:

1. How can a firm choose and communicate an effective positioning in the market?
2. How are brands differentiated?
3. What marketing strategies are appropriate at each stage of the product life cycle?
4. What are the implications of market evolution for marketing strategies?

CHAPTER 10 ::: CRAFTING THE BRAND POSITIONING

ten

No company can win if its products and offerings resemble every other product and offering. Companies must pursue relevant positioning and differentiation. As part of the strategic brand management process, each company and offering must represent a distinctive big idea in the mind of the target market.

The Public Broadcasting Service finds its brand in a difficult position. The average nightly prime-time ratings for public television's 349 stations declined 23 percent from 1993 to 2002. During that same period, cable networks such as Discovery Channel, History Channel, A&E, and Fox News siphoned off PBS viewers and experienced a 122 percent growth. PBS's loyal audience is aging—the average age of a prime-time PBS viewer is the mid-fifties. The challenge is to attract new, younger viewers while still maintaining the quality programming that is its mission. PBS's identity crisis caused CEO Pat Mitchell to proclaim in 2002: "For public broadcasting to be vital and viable, we are going to have to embrace some changes."[1]

>>>

A recent PBS fund drive on New York's Channel Thirteen. Channel Thirteen is adjusting its programming to attract a more diverse audience.

As the plight of PBS demonstrates, even when a company succeeds in distinguishing itself, differences can be short-lived. Companies normally reformulate their marketing strategies and offerings several times. Economic conditions change, competitors launch new assaults, and products pass through new stages of buyer interest and requirements. Marketers must develop strategies for each stage in the product's life cycle. The goal is to extend the product's life and profitability, keeping in mind that products do not last forever. This chapter explores specific ways a company can effectively position and differentiate its offerings to achieve a competitive advantage throughout the life cycle of a product or an offering.

::: Developing and Communicating a Positioning Strategy

All marketing strategy is built on STP—Segmentation, Targeting, and Positioning. A company discovers different needs and groups in the marketplace, targets those needs and groups that it can satisfy in a superior way, and then positions its offering so that the target market recognizes the company's distinctive offering and image. If a company does a poor job of positioning, the market will be confused. This happened when National Car Company and Alamo Rent-a-Car were combined by their former parent, ANC Rental Corp., following its Chapter 11 bankruptcy court filing in 2001.

NATIONAL CAR RENTAL AND ALAMO RENT-A-CAR

Premium brand National traditionally catered to business travelers, whereas Alamo Rent-a-Car has been getting 90 percent of its business from leisure travelers. After the two merged, the dual Alamo/National logos were plastered on everything from airport shuttle buses to workers' polo shirts. Customers of both Alamo and National had problems distinguishing between the brands, even though National's cars typically rent for 10 to 20 percent more than Alamo's. After all, the customers had to stand in the same line behind the same airport counter, receive service from the same rental agents, ride the same shuttle buses, and drive cars from the same fleet. National was most hurt by the lack of differentiation at these key touchpoints, and its market share fell 5 to 10 percent. Interestingly, after consolidation of the brands, shuttle bus frequency improved 38 percent and business travelers were given even more options to bypass the rental counter entirely. Still, in surveys, National renters *perceived* the buses to be slower, the lines longer, and customer service poorer. The clear implication was that in order for the two brands to maintain their integrity and their positioning with their respective market segments, they had to be separated.[2] ■

If a company does an excellent job of positioning, then it can work out the rest of its marketing planning and differentiation from its positioning strategy. We define positioning as follows: **Positioning** is the act of designing the company's offering and image to occupy a distinctive place in the mind of the target market. The goal is to locate the brand in the minds of consumers to maximize the potential benefit to the firm. A good brand positioning helps guide marketing strategy by clarifying the brand's essence, what goals it helps the consumer achieve, and how it does so in a unique way. The result of positioning is the successful creation of a *customer-focused value proposition,* a cogent reason why the target market should buy the product. Table 10.1 shows how three companies—Perdue, Volvo, and Domino's—defined their value proposition given their target customers, benefits, and prices.

The word "positioning" was popularized by two advertising executives, Al Ries and Jack Trout. They see positioning as a creative exercise done with an existing product:

TABLE 10.1 Examples of Value Propositions Demand States and Marketing Tasks

Company and Product	Target Customers	Benefits	Price	Value Proposition
Perdue (chicken)	Quality-conscious consumers of chicken	Tenderness	10% premium	More tender golden chicken at a moderate premium price
Volvo (station wagon)	Safety-conscious "upscale" families	Durability and safety	20% premium	The safest, most durable wagon in which your family can ride
Domino's (pizza)	Convenience-minded pizza lovers	Delivery speed and good quality	15% premium	A good hot pizza, delivered to your door within 30 minutes of ordering, at a moderate price

> Positioning starts with a product. A piece of merchandise, a service, a company, an institution, or even a person. . . . But positioning is not what you do to a product. Positioning is what you do to the mind of the prospect. That is, you position the product in the mind of the prospect.[3]

"Marketing Insight: Value Disciplines Positioning" offers another point of view about positioning. According to virtually all approaches, positioning requires that similarities and differences between brands be defined and communicated. Specifically, deciding on a positioning requires determining a frame of reference by identifying the target market and the competition, and identifying the ideal points-of-parity and points-of-difference brand associations.

Competitive Frame of Reference

A starting point in defining a competitive frame of reference for a brand positioning is to determine **category membership**—the products or sets of products with which a brand competes and which function as close substitutes. As we discuss in Chapter 11, competitive analysis will consider a whole host of factors—including the resources, capabilities, and likely intentions of various other firms—in choosing those markets where consumers can be profitably serviced.

Target market decisions are often a key determinant of the competitive frame of reference. Deciding to target a certain type of consumer can define the nature of competition because certain firms have decided to target that segment in the past (or plan to do so in the

MARKETING INSIGHT | VALUE DISCIPLINES POSITIONING

Two consultants, Michael Treacy and Fred Wiersema, proposed a positioning framework called *value disciplines.* Within its industry, a firm could aspire to be the *product leader*, the *operationally excellent firm*, or the *customer-intimate firm.* This framework is based on the notion that in every market there is a mix of three types of customers. Some customers favor the firm that is on the technological frontier (product leadership); other customers want highly reliable performance (operational excellence); and still others want high responsiveness in meeting their individual needs (customer intimacy).

A firm cannot normally be best in all three ways, or even in two ways. Each value discipline requires different managerial mind-sets and investments that often conflict. Thus McDonald's excels at operational excellence, but could not afford to slow down its service to prepare hamburgers differently for each customer. Nor could McDonald's lead in new products because each addition would disrupt the smooth functioning of normal operations. Even within a large company, such as GE, each division might follow a different value discipline: GE's major appliance division pursues operational excellence, its engineered plastics division pursues customer intimacy, and its jet engine division pursues product leadership.

Treacy and Wiersema propose that a business should follow four rules for success:

1. Become best at one of the three value disciplines.
2. Achieve an adequate performance level in the other two disciplines.
3. Keep improving one's superior position in the chosen discipline so as not to lose out to a competitor.
4. Keep becoming more adequate in the other two disciplines, because competitors keep raising customers' expectations.

Source: Michael Treacy and Fred Wiersema, *The Disciplines of Market Leaders* (Reading, MA: Addison-Wesley, 1994).

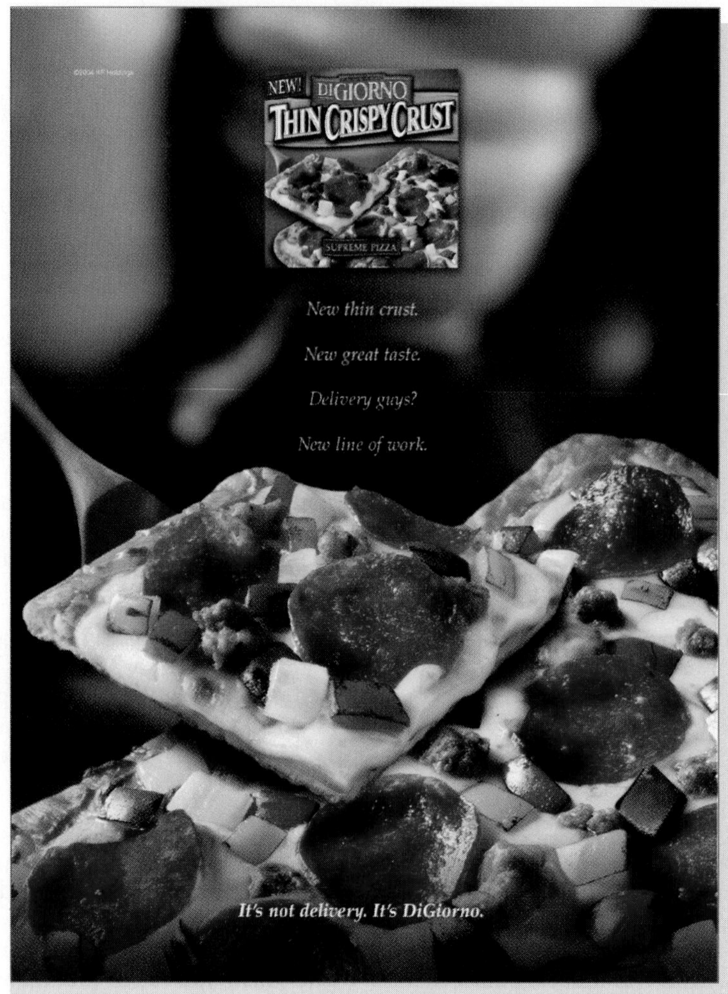

"It's not delivery, it's DiGiorno." DiGiorno print ad that carries through on the delivered pizza positioning, which helped make it the frozen pizza leader.

future), or consumers in that segment already may look to certain brands in their purchase decisions. Determining the proper competitive frame of reference requires understanding consumer behavior and the consideration sets consumers use in making brand choices. In the United Kingdom, for example, the Automobile Association has positioned itself as the fourth "emergency service"—along with police, fire, and ambulance—to convey greater credibility and urgency. And look at how DiGiorno's positioned itself:

DIGIORNO'S PIZZA

DiGiorno's is a frozen pizza whose crust rises when the pizza is heated. Instead of putting it in the frozen pizza category, the marketers positioned it in the delivered pizza category. One of their ads shows party guests asking which pizza delivery service the host used. Then he says: "It's not delivery, its DiGiorno!" This helped highlight DiGiorno's fresh quality and superior taste. Through this clever positioning, DiGiorno's sales went from essentially nothing in 1995 to $382 million in 2002, making it the frozen pizza leader.[4]

Points-of-Parity and Points-of-Difference

Once the competitive frame of reference for positioning has been fixed by defining the customer target market and nature of competition, marketers can define the appropriate points-of-difference and points-of-parity associations.[5]

POINTS-OF-DIFFERENCE Points-of-difference (PODs) are attributes or benefits consumers strongly associate with a brand, positively evaluate, and believe that they could not find to the same extent with a competitive brand. Strong, favorable, and unique brand associations that make up points-of-difference may be based on virtually any type of attribute or benefit. Examples are FedEx (*guaranteed overnight delivery*), Nike (*performance*), and Lexus (*quality*).

Creating strong, favorable, and unique associations as points-of-difference is a real challenge, but essential in terms of competitive brand positioning. Consider the success of IKEA.

IKEA

Swedish retailer IKEA took a luxury product—home furnishings and furniture—and made it a reasonably priced alternative for the mass market. IKEA supports its low prices by having customers self-serve, deliver, and assemble the products themselves. IKEA also gains a point-of-difference through its product offerings. As one commentator noted, "IKEA built its reputation on the notion that Sweden produces good, safe, well-built things for the masses. It has some of the most innovative designs at the lowest cost out there." It also operates an excellent restaurant in each store (rare among furniture stores); offers child-care services while the parents shop; offers a membership program entitling members to special discounts on their purchases beyond the normal low price; and mails out millions of catalogs featuring the latest furniture.[6]

POINTS-OF-PARITY Points-of-parity (POPs), on the other hand, are associations that are not necessarily unique to the brand but may in fact be shared with other brands. These types of associations come in two basic forms: category and competitive.

Category points-of-parity are associations consumers view as essential to be a legitimate and credible offering within a certain product or service category. In other words, they represent necessary—but not necessarily sufficient—conditions for brand choice. Consumers might not consider a travel agency truly a travel agency unless it is able to make air and hotel reservations, provide advice about leisure packages, and offer various ticket payment and delivery options. Category points-of-parity may change over time due to technological advances, legal developments, or consumer trends, but they are the "greens fees" to play the marketing game.

Competitive points-of-parity are associations designed to negate competitors' points-of-difference. If, in the eyes of consumers, the brand association designed to be the competitor's point-of-difference is as strong for a brand as for competitors *and* the brand is able to establish another association as strong, favorable, and unique as part of its point-of-difference, then the brand should be in a superior competitive position. In other words, if a brand can "break even" in those areas where the competitors are trying to find an advantage *and* can achieve advantages in other areas, the brand should be in a strong—and perhaps unbeatable—competitive position. While other luxury-goods makers slumped in 2000, Coach saw its sales zoom ahead by adding style and fashion to its legendary rugged bags and briefcases.[7] As another example, consider the introduction of Miller Lite beer.[8]

MILLER LITE

The initial advertising strategy for Miller Lite beer had two goals—assuring parity with key competitors in the category by stating that it "tastes great," while at the same time creating a point-of-difference: It contained one-third less calories and was thus "less filling" than regular, full-strength beers. As is often the case, the point-of-parity and point-of-difference were somewhat conflicting, as consumers tend to equate taste with calories. To overcome potential resistance, Miller employed credible spokespeople, primarily popular former professional athletes, who would presumably not drink a beer unless it tasted good. These ex-jocks humorously debated which of the two product benefits—"tastes great" or "less filling"—was more descriptive of the beer. The ads ended with the clever tagline "Everything You've Always Wanted In a Beer . . . And Less."

POINTS-OF-PARITY VERSUS POINTS-OF-DIFFERENCE To achieve a point-of-parity (POP) on a particular attribute or benefit, a sufficient number of consumers must believe that the brand is "good enough" on that dimension. There is a "zone" or "range of tolerance or acceptance" with points-of-parity. The brand does not literally have to be seen as equal to competitors, but consumers must feel that the brand does well enough on that particular attribute or benefit. If consumers feel that way, they may be willing to base their evaluations and decisions on other factors potentially more favorable to the brand. A light beer presumably would never taste as good as a full-strength beer, but it would have to taste close enough to be able to effectively compete. With points-of-difference, however, the brand must demonstrate clear superiority. Consumers must be convinced that Louis Vuitton has the most stylish handbags, Energizer is the longest-lasting battery, and Merrill Lynch offers the best financial advice and planning.

Often, the key to positioning is not so much in achieving a point-of-difference (POD) as in achieving points-of-parity!

VISA VERSUS AMERICAN EXPRESS

Visa's POD in the credit card category is that it is the most widely available card, which underscores the category's main benefit of convenience. American Express, on the other hand, has built the equity of its brand by highlighting the prestige associated with the use of its card. Having established their PODs, Visa and American Express now compete by attempting to blunt each others' advantage to create POPs. Visa offers gold and platinum cards to enhance the prestige of its brand and advertises, "It's Everywhere You Want to Be" in settings that reinforce exclusivity and acceptability. American Express has substantially increased the number of vendors that accept its cards and created other value enhancements through its "Make Life Rewarding" program.

Establishing Category Membership

Target customers are aware that Maybelline is a leading brand of cosmetics, Cheerios is a leading brand of cereal, Accenture is a leading consulting firm, and so on. Often, however, marketers must inform consumers of a brand's category membership. Perhaps the most obvious situation is the introduction of new products, especially when the category membership is not apparent. This uncertainty can be a special problem for high-tech products. There are also situations where consumers know a brand's category membership, but may not be convinced that the brand is a valid member of the category. For example, consumers may be aware that Hewlett-Packard produces digital cameras, but they may not be certain whether Hewlett-Packard cameras are in the same class as Sony, Olympus, Kodak, and Nikon. In this instance, HP might find it useful to reinforce category membership.

Brands are sometimes affiliated with categories in which they do not hold membership. This approach is one way to highlight a brand's point-of-difference, providing that consumers know the brand's actual membership. With this approach, however, it is important that consumers understand what the brand stands for, and not just what it is *not.* It is important to not be trapped between categories. The Konica e-mini M digital camera and MP3 player was marketed as the "four-in-one entertainment solution," but suffered from functional deficiencies in each of its product applications and languished in the marketplace.[9]

The preferred approach to positioning is to inform consumers of a brand's membership before stating its point-of-difference. Presumably, consumers need to know what a product is and what function it serves before deciding whether it dominates the brands against which it competes. For new products, initial advertising often concentrates on creating brand awareness and subsequent advertising attempts to craft the brand image.

Occasionally, a company will try to straddle two frames of reference:

BMW

When BMW first made a strong competitive push into the U.S. market in the early 1980s, it positioned the brand as being the only automobile that offered both luxury *and* performance. At that time, American luxury cars were seen by many as lacking performance, and American performance cars were seen as lacking luxury. By relying on the design of its cars, its German heritage, and other aspects of a well-conceived marketing program, BMW was able to simultaneously achieve: (1) a point-of-difference on luxury and a point-of-parity on performance with respect to performance cars and (2) a point-of-difference on performance and a point-of-parity on luxury with respect to luxury cars. The clever slogan "The Ultimate Driving Machine" effectively captured the newly created umbrella category—luxury performance cars.

While a straddle positioning often is attractive as a means of reconciling potentially conflicting consumer goals, it also carries an extra burden. If the points-of-parity and points-of-difference with respect to both categories are not credible, the brand may not be viewed as a legitimate player in either category. Many early PDAs that unsuccessfully tried to straddle categories ranging from pagers to laptop computers provide a vivid illustration of this risk.

There are three main ways to convey a brand's category membership:

1. ***Announcing category benefits.*** To reassure consumers that a brand will deliver on the fundamental reason for using a category, benefits are frequently used to announce category membership. Thus, industrial tools might claim to have durability and antacids might announce their efficacy. A brownie mix might attain membership in the baked desserts category by claiming the benefit of great taste and support this benefit claim by possessing high-quality ingredients (performance) or by showing users delighting in its consumption (imagery).
2. ***Comparing to exemplars.*** Well-known, noteworthy brands in a category can also be used to specify category membership. When Tommy Hilfiger was an unknown, advertising announced his membership as a great American designer by associating him with Geoffrey Beene, Stanley Blacker, Calvin Klein, and Perry Ellis, who were recognized members of that category.
3. ***Relying on the product descriptor.*** The product descriptor that follows the brand name is often a concise means of conveying category origin. Ford Motor Co., invested more than $1 billion on a radical new 2004 model called the X-Trainer, which combines the attributes of an SUV, a minivan, and a station wagon. To communicate its unique position—and to avoid association with its Explorer and Country Squire models—the vehicle is designated a "sports wagon."[10]

Choosing POPs and PODs

Points-of-parity are driven by the needs of category membership (to create category POPs) and the necessity of negating competitors' PODs (to create competitive POPs). In choosing points-of-difference, two important considerations are that consumers find the POD desirable and that the firm has the capabilities to deliver on the POD.

There are three key consumer desirability criteria for PODs.

1. ***Relevance.*** Target consumers must find the POD personally relevant and important. The Westin Stamford hotel in Singapore advertised that it was the world's tallest hotel, but a hotel's height is not important to many tourists.
2. ***Distinctiveness.*** Target consumers must find the POD distinctive and superior. When entering a category where there are established brands, the challenge is to find a viable basis for differentiation. Splenda sugar substitute overtook Equal and Sweet 'n Low to become the leader in its category in 2003 by differentiating itself on its authenticity as a product derived from sugar, without any of the associated drawbacks.[11]
3. ***Believability.*** Target consumers must find the POD believable and credible. A brand must offer a compelling reason for choosing it over the other options. Mountain Dew may argue that it is more energizing than other soft drinks and support this claim by noting that it has a higher level of caffeine. Chanel No. 5 perfume may claim to be the quintessential elegant French perfume and support this claim by noting the long association between Chanel and haute couture.

There are three key deliverability criteria.

1. ***Feasibility.*** The firm must be able to actually create the POD. The product design and marketing offering must support the desired association. Does communicating the desired association involve real changes to the product itself, or just perceptual ones as to how the consumer thinks of the product or brand? It is obviously easier to convince consumers of some fact about the brand that they were unaware of and may have overlooked than to make changes in the product *and* convince consumers of these changes. General Motors has had to work to overcome public perceptions that Cadillac is not a youthful, contemporary brand.
2. ***Communicability.*** It is very difficult to create an association that is not consistent with existing consumer knowledge or that consumers, for whatever reason, have trouble believing. Consumers must be given a compelling reason and understandable rationale as to why the brand can deliver the desired benefit. What factual, verifiable evidence or "proof points" can be given as support so that consumers will actually believe in the brand and its desired associations? Substantiators often come in the form of patented, branded ingredients, such as Nivea Wrinkle Control Crème with Q10 co-enzyme or Herbal Essences hair conditioner with Hawafena.

3. ***Sustainability.*** Is the positioning preemptive, defensible, and difficult to attack? Can the favorability of a brand association be reinforced and strengthened over time? If yes, the positioning is likely to be enduring. Sustainability will depend on internal commitment and use of resources as well as external market forces. It is generally easier for market leaders such as Gillette, Intel, and Microsoft, whose positioning is based in part on demonstrable product performance, to sustain their positioning than for market leaders such as Gucci, Prada, and Hermes, whose positioning is based on fashion and is thus subject to the whims of a more fickle market.

Marketers must decide at which level(s) to anchor the brand's points-of-differences. At the lowest level are the *brand attributes,* at the next level are the *brand's benefits,* and at the top are the *brand's values.* Thus marketers of Dove soap can talk about its attribute of one-quarter cleansing cream; or its benefit of softer skin; or its value, being more attractive. Attributes are typically the least desirable level to position. First, the buyer is more interested in benefits. Second, competitors can easily copy attributes. Third, the current attributes may become less desirable.

Research has shown, however, that brands can sometimes be successfully differentiated on seemingly irrelevant attributes *if* consumers infer the proper benefit.[12] Procter & Gamble differentiates its Folger's instant coffee by its "flaked coffee crystals," created through a "unique patented process." In reality, the shape of the coffee particles is irrelevant because the crystals immediately dissolve in the hot water. Saying that a brand of coffee is "mountain grown" is irrelevant because most coffee is mountain grown. "Marketing Memo: Writing a Positioning Statement" outlines how positioning can be expressed formally.

Creating POPs and PODs

One common difficulty in creating a strong, competitive brand positioning is that many of the attributes or benefits that make up the points-of-parity and points-of-difference are negatively correlated. If consumers rate the brand highly on one particular attribute or benefit, they also rate it poorly on another important attribute. For example, it might be difficult to position a brand as "inexpensive" and at the same time assert that it is "of the highest quality." Table 10.2 displays some other examples of negatively correlated attributes and benefits. Moreover, individual attributes and benefits often have positive *and* negative aspects. For example, consider a long-lived brand that is seen as having a great deal of heritage. Heritage could suggest experience, wisdom, and expertise. On the other hand, it could also easily be seen as a negative: It might imply being old-fashioned and not up-to-date.

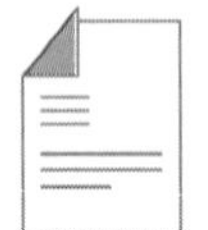

MARKETING **MEMO** | WRITING A POSITIONING STATEMENT

To communicate a company or brand positioning, marketing plans often include a *positioning statement.* The statement should follow the form: To *(target group and need)* our *(Brand)* is *(concept)* that *(point-of-difference).* For example: "To *busy professionals who need to stay organized, Palm Pilot* is *an electronic organizer* that *allows you to back up files on your PC more easily and reliably than competitive products.*" Sometimes the positioning statement is more detailed:

> *Mountain Dew:* To young, active soft-drink consumers who have little time for sleep, Mountain Dew is the soft drink that gives you more energy than any other brand because it has the highest level of caffeine. With Mountain Dew, you can stay alert and keep going even when you haven't been able to get a good night's sleep.

Note that the positioning first states the product's membership in a category (e.g., Mountain Dew is a soft drink) and then shows its point-of-difference from other members of the group (e.g., has more caffeine). The product's membership in the category suggests the points-of-parity that it might have with other products in the category, but the case for the product rests on its points-of-difference. Sometimes the marketer will put the product in a surprisingly different category before indicating the points of difference.

Sources: Bobby J. Calder and Steven J. Reagan, "Brand Design," in *Kellogg on Marketing,* edited by Dawn Iacobucci (New York: John Wiley & Sons, 2001), p. 61; Alice M. Tybout and Brian Sternthal, "Brand Positioning," in *Kellogg on Marketing,* edited by Dawn Iacobucci (New York: John Wiley & Sons, 2001), p. 54.

TABLE 10.2

Examples of Negatively Correlated Attributes and Benefits

Low Price vs. High Quality	Powerful vs. Safe
Taste vs. Low Calories	Strong vs. Refined
Nutritious vs. Good Tasting	Ubiquitous vs. Exclusive
Efficacious vs. Mild	Varied vs. Simple

BROOKS BROTHERS

In the late 1990s, Brooks Brothers found its heritage to be a deficit rather than a plus. The American retailer's starched shirts and pinstriped suits seemed an anachronism in a world of jeans, khakis, polo tops, and casual Fridays. The company tried to downplay its heritage by stocking trendier sweaters and slacks. The move both alienated loyal customers and failed to attract new ones, and the company lost share. In 2001, Italian-born Claudio Del Vecchio bought the company for $225 million, and began using the Brooks Brothers heritage as a positive point-of-difference. The look is more sophisticated, quality is back, and prices are higher. For now, Brooks Brothers is focused on wooing its traditional customers. The store has published a book chronicling its history. It is inviting select customers to a series of 185th anniversary events and reintroducing pieces from its past, including the Shetland sweater introduced in 1904 and the sack suit JFK loved. As a sign that the beleaguered company must be doing something right, other stores are copying it by mining their own heritage: Coach is bringing back its bucket-shaped "feed bag" purse, Eddie Bauer is reintroducing the 1936 quilted Skyliner jacket, and J. Crew is making its classic tweed jacket and roll-neck sweater again.[13]

Unfortunately, consumers typically want to maximize *both* attributes and benefits. Much of the art and science of marketing is dealing with trade-offs, and positioning is no different. The best approach clearly is to develop a product or service that performs well on both dimensions. BMW was able to establish its "luxury and performance" straddle positioning due in large part to product design and the fact that the car was seen as both luxurious and high performance. Gore-Tex was able to overcome the seemingly conflicting product image of "breathable" and "waterproof" through technological advances. There are additional ways to address the problem of negatively correlated POPs and PODs.

PRESENT SEPARATELY An expensive but sometimes effective approach to addressing negatively correlated attributes and benefits is to launch two different marketing campaigns, each one devoted to a different brand attribute or benefit. These campaigns may run together at one point in time or sequentially over time. Head & Shoulders shampoo met success in Europe with a dual campaign where one campaign emphasized its dandruff removal efficacy while another emphasized the appearance and beauty of hair after its use. The hope is that consumers will be less critical when judging the POP and POD benefits in isolation. The downside with such an approach is that you need two strong campaigns. Moreover, if marketers do not address the negative correlation head-on, consumers may not develop the desired positive associations.

LEVERAGE EQUITY OF ANOTHER ENTITY In the Miller Lite example above, the brand "borrowed" or leveraged the equity of well-known and well-liked celebrities to lend credibility to a negatively correlated benefit. Brands can potentially link themselves to any kind of entity that possesses the right kind of equity as a means to establish an attribute or benefit as a POP or POD. Branded ingredients may also lend some credibility to a questionable attribute in consumers' minds. Borrowing equity, however, is not riskless. Personal computer manufacturers such as IBM and Compaq found that the Intel Inside co-op advertising program, which gave Intel exposure in the PC makers' ad, resulted in consumers seeking Intel-based computers.

REDEFINE THE RELATIONSHIP Another potentially powerful but often difficult way to address the negative relationship between attributes and benefits is to convince consumers that in fact the relationship is positive. This redefinition can be accomplished by providing consumers with a different perspective and suggesting that they may be overlooking or ignoring certain considerations.

APPLE COMPUTERS

When Apple Computers launched MacIntosh, its key point-of-difference was "user friendly." Many consumers valued ease of use, especially those who bought personal computers for the home. One drawback with a "user-friendly" association was that customers who bought personal computers for business applications thought that if a personal computer was easy to use, then it must not be very powerful. Recognizing this potential problem, Apple ran a clever ad campaign with the tag line "The Power to Be Your Best." The strategy behind the ads was that because Apple was easy to use, people in fact did just that—they used it!—a simple but important indication of "power." In other words, the most powerful computers were ones people actually used.

::: Differentiation Strategies

To avoid the commodity trap, marketers must start with the belief that you can differentiate anything. (See "Marketing Memo: How to Derive Fresh Consumer Insights to Differentiate Products and Services.") Brands can be differentiated on the basis of many variables. Southwest Airlines has differentiated itself in several different ways.

SOUTHWEST AIRLINES

The Dallas-based airline carved its niche in short-haul flights with low prices, reliable service, and a healthy sense of humor. Southwest keeps costs low by offering only basic in-flight service (no meals, no movies) and rapid turnaround at the gates to keep the planes in the air. Southwest knew that it could not differentiate on price alone because competitors could try to muscle into the market with their own cheaper versions. The airline has also distinguished itself as a "fun" airline, noted for humorous in-flight commentary from pilots and cabin crew members. Another popular feature of Southwest flights is the first-come, first-served open seating: Passengers are given numbered cards based on when they arrive at the gate. Southwest is now the nation's sixth-largest airline in revenue, and holds the distinction of being the only low-fare airline to achieve long-term success.[14]

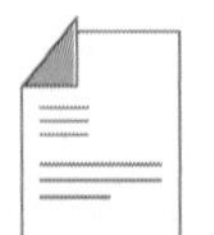

MARKETING MEMO | HOW TO DERIVE FRESH CONSUMER INSIGHTS TO DIFFERENTIATE PRODUCTS AND SERVICES

In "Discovering New Points of Differentiation," Ian C. MacMillan and Rita Gunther McGrath argue that if companies examine customers' entire experience with a product or service—the consumption chain—they can uncover opportunities to position their offerings in ways that neither they nor their competitors thought possible. MacMillan and McGrath list a set of questions marketers can use to help them identify new, consumer-based points of differentiation.

- How do people become aware of their need for your product and service?
- How do consumers find your offering?
- How do consumers make their final selection?
- How do consumers order and purchase your product or service?
- What happens when your product or service is delivered?
- How is your product installed?
- How is your product or service paid for?
- How is your product stored?
- How is your product moved around?
- What is the consumer really using your product for?
- What do consumers need help with when they use your product?
- What about returns or exchanges?
- How is your product repaired or serviced?
- What happens when your product is disposed of or no longer used?

Source: Ian C. MacMillan and Rita Gunther McGrath, "Discovering New Points of Differentiation," *Harvard Business Review* (July–August 1997): 133–145.

The obvious means of differentiation, and often most compelling ones to consumers, relate to aspects of the product and service. Swatch offers colorful, fashionable watches. Subway differentiates itself in terms of healthy sandwiches as an alternative to fast food. Method built a $10 million business in a year by creating a line of nontoxic household cleaning products with bright colors and sleek designs totally unique to the category.[15] In competitive markets, however, firms may need to go beyond these. Among the other dimensions a company can use to differentiate its market offering are personnel, channel, and image. This section highlights these four different differentiation strategies.

Product Differentiation

As Chapter 12 describes, brands can be differentiated on the basis of a number of different product or service dimensions: product form, features, performance, conformance, durability, reliability, repairability, style, and design, as well as such service dimensions as ordering ease, delivery, installation, customer training, customer consulting, and maintenance and repair.

Besides these specific concerns, one more general positioning for brands is as "best quality." How important is a high-quality product positioning? The Strategic Planning Institute studied the impact of higher relative product quality and found a significantly positive correlation between relative product quality and return on investment (ROI).[16] High-quality business units earned more because premium quality allowed them to charge a premium price; they benefited from more repeat purchase, consumer loyalty, and positive word of mouth; and the costs of delivering more quality were not much higher than for business units producing low quality.

Quality will depend on actual product performance, but it is also communicated by choosing physical signs and cues. Here are some examples:

- A lawnmower manufacturer that claims its lawnmower is "powerful" has given it a noisy motor because buyers think noisy lawnmowers are more powerful.
- A truck manufacturer undercoats the chassis not because it needs undercoating but because undercoating suggests concern for quality.
- A car manufacturer makes sure its car doors make a solid sound when they slam shut because many buyers slam the doors in the showroom to test how well the car is built.
- Ritz Carlton hotels signal high quality by training employees to answer calls within three rings, to answer with a genuine "smile" in their voices, and to be extremely knowledgeable about all hotel services.

Quality is also communicated through other marketing elements. A high price usually signals premium quality. Quality image is also affected by packaging, distribution, advertising, and promotion. Here are some cases where a brand's quality image was hurt:

- A well-known frozen-food brand lost its prestige image by being on sale too often.
- A premium beer's image was hurt when it switched from bottles to cans.
- A highly regarded television receiver lost its quality image when mass-merchandise outlets began to carry it.

A manufacturer's reputation also contributes to the perception of quality. Certain companies are sticklers for quality; consumers expect Nestlé and IBM products to be well made. Smart companies communicate quality to buyers and guarantee "customer satisfaction or your money back."

Becoming a Singapore Airlines flight attendant is not easy: company requirements are strict. But Singapore Airlines has a worldwide reputation for excellent service, built largely on the customer relations skills of its flight attendants.

Personnel Differentiation

Companies can gain a strong competitive advantage through having better-trained people. Singapore Airlines enjoys an excellent reputation in large part because of its flight attendants.

McDonald's people are courteous, IBM people are professional, and Disney people are upbeat. The sales forces of such companies as General Electric, Cisco, Frito-Lay, Northwestern Mutual Life, and Pfizer enjoy an excellent reputation.[17] Better-trained personnel exhibit six characteristics: *Competence*: They possess the required skill and knowledge; *courtesy*: They are friendly, respectful, and considerate; *credibility*: They are trustworthy; *reliability*: They perform the service consistently and accurately; *responsiveness*: They respond quickly to customers' requests and problems; and *communication*: They make an effort to understand the customer and communicate clearly.[18] Retailers, in particular, are likely to use their front-line employees as a means of differentiating and positioning their brand. This is certainly true of large chain bookstores like Barnes & Noble and Borders:[19]

BARNES & NOBLE AND BORDERS

Barnes & Noble and Borders superstores certainly look eerily similar: large comfy chairs, mahogany bookshelves, tasteful décor, and the scent of fresh-brewed coffee. However, the stores have very different business philosophies and both use their employees as "missionaries" for widely different inventory and business models. Borders, which has 32,000 employees and 445 U.S. superstores, focuses on offering the widest assortment of titles and tailoring its inventory to each store's location. Barnes & Noble, which has 40,000 employees in 800 U.S. stores, attracts customers with low prices and the most popular books. While both companies say that "passion" is the most important quality in their booksellers, that passion is expressed in different ways. Barnes & Noble hires people with a passion for customer service and a general love of books. They are clean cut and wear collared shirts. Putting the book in the customer's hand and fast cashiering are their mandates. Borders employees are likely to be tattooed or have multiple body piercings. The company prides itself on the diversity of its employees and hires people who radiate excitement about particular books and music, relying on them to suggest topics and titles rather than simply find a book for a customer.

Channel Differentiation

Companies can achieve competitive advantage through the way they design their distribution channels' *coverage, expertise,* and *performance.* Caterpillar's success in the construction-equipment industry is based partly on superior channel development. Its dealers are found in more locations than competitors' dealers, and they are typically better trained and perform more reliably. Dell in computers and Avon in cosmetics distinguish themselves by developing and managing high-quality direct-marketing channels. Back in 1946, pet food was cheap, not too nutritious, and sold exclusively in supermarkets and the occasional feed store: Dayton, Ohio–based Iams found success selling premium pet food through regional veterinarians, breeders, and pet stores.

APOLLO GROUP INC.

Apollo Group Inc., has turned conventional higher education on its head by launching an online university geared toward the neglected market of working adults. University of Phoenix Online is one of Apollo's most successful ventures, with 50,000 students, and in the past year UOP's enrollment surged by 70 percent. In addition to differentiating based on delivering education through a different channel—online classes—Apollo charges only $10,000 for yearly tuition, 55 percent of what a typical private college charges.[20]

Image Differentiation

Buyers respond differently to company and brand images. The primary way to account for Marlboro's extraordinary worldwide market share (around 30 percent) is that Marlboro's "macho cowboy" image has struck a responsive chord with much of the cigarette-smoking public. Wine and liquor companies also work hard to develop distinctive images for their brands.

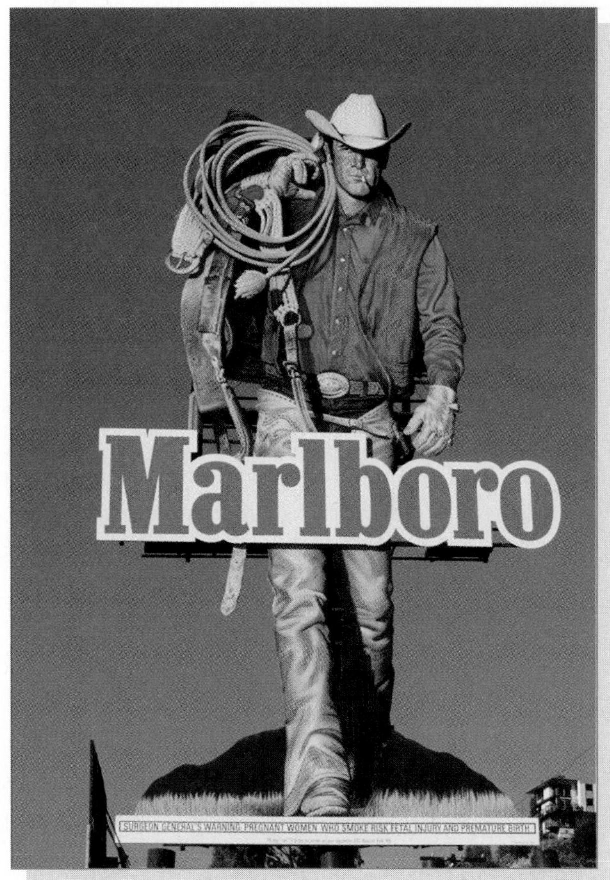

Image differentiation: The world-famous "Marlboro Man" image is instantly recognizable on billboards and in print ads.

Identity and image need to be distinguished. *Identity* is the way a company aims to identify or position itself or its product. *Image* is the way the public perceives the company or its products. An effective identity does three things: It establishes the product's character and value proposition. It conveys this character in a distinctive way. It delivers emotional power beyond a mental image. For the identity to work, it must be conveyed through every available communication vehicle and brand contact. It should be diffused in ads, annual reports, brochures, catalogs, packaging, company stationery, and business cards. If "IBM means service," this message must be expressed in symbols, colors and slogans, atmosphere, events, and employee behavior.

Even a seller's physical space can be a powerful image generator. Hyatt Regency hotels developed a distinctive image through its atrium lobbies. Companies can create a strong image by inviting prospects and customers to visit their headquarters and factories. Boeing, Ben & Jerry's, Hershey's, Saturn, and Crayola all sponsor excellent company tours that draw millions of visitors a year.[21] Companies such as Hallmark and Kohler have built corporate museums at their headquarters that display their history and the drama of producing and marketing their products.

"Marketing Memo: Exceeding Customer Expectations" describes one systematic approach to developing a differentiated, customer-oriented offering.

::: Product Life-Cycle Marketing Strategies

A company's positioning and differentiation strategy must change as the product, market, and competitors change over the *product life cycle* (PLC). To say that a product has a life cycle is to assert four things:

1. Products have a limited life.
2. Product sales pass through distinct stages, each posing different challenges, opportunities, and problems to the seller.

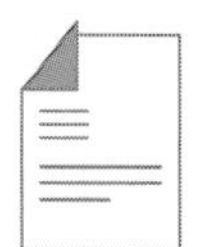

MARKETING MEMO | EXCEEDING CUSTOMER EXPECTATIONS

Crego and Schiffrin have proposed that customer-centered organizations should study what customers value and then prepare an offering that exceeds their expectations. They see this as a three-step process:

1. ***Defining the customer value model:*** The company first lists all the product and service factors that might influence the target customers' perception of value.
2. ***Building the customer value hierarchy:*** The company now assigns each factor to one of four groups: basic, expected, desired, and unanticipated. Consider the set of factors at a fine restaurant:
   - ***Basic:*** The food is edible and delivered in a timely fashion. (If this is all the restaurant does right, the customer would normally not be satisfied.)
   - ***Expected:*** There is good china and tableware, a linen tablecloth and napkin, flowers, discreet service, and well-prepared food. (These factors make the offering acceptable, but not exceptional.)
   - ***Desired:*** The restaurant is pleasant and quiet, and the food is especially good and interesting.
   - ***Unanticipated:*** The restaurant serves a complimentary sorbet between the courses and places candy on the table after the last course is served.
3. ***Deciding on the customer value package:*** Now the company chooses that combination of tangible and intangible items, experiences, and outcomes designed to outperform competitors and win the customers' delight and loyalty.

Sources: Edwin T. Crego Jr. and Peter D. Schiffrin, *Customer Centered Reengineering* (Homewood, IL: Irwin, 1995).

3. Profits rise and fall at different stages of the product life cycle.
4. Products require different marketing, financial, manufacturing, purchasing, and human resource strategies in each life-cycle stage.

Product Life Cycles

Most product life-cycle curves are portrayed as bell-shaped (see Figure 10.1). This curve is typically divided into four stages: introduction, growth, maturity, and decline.[22]

1. ***Introduction*** – A period of slow sales growth as the product is introduced in the market. Profits are nonexistent because of the heavy expenses of product introduction.
2. ***Growth*** – A period of rapid market acceptance and substantial profit improvement.
3. ***Maturity*** – A slowdown in sales growth because the product has achieved acceptance by most potential buyers. Profits stabilize or decline because of increased competition.
4. ***Decline*** – Sales show a downward drift and profits erode.

The PLC concept can be used to analyze a product category (liquor), a product form (white liquor), a product (vodka), or a brand (Smirnoff). Not all products exhibit a bell-shaped PLC.[23] Three common alternate patterns are shown in Figure 10.2.

FIG. 10.1

Sales and Profit Life Cycles

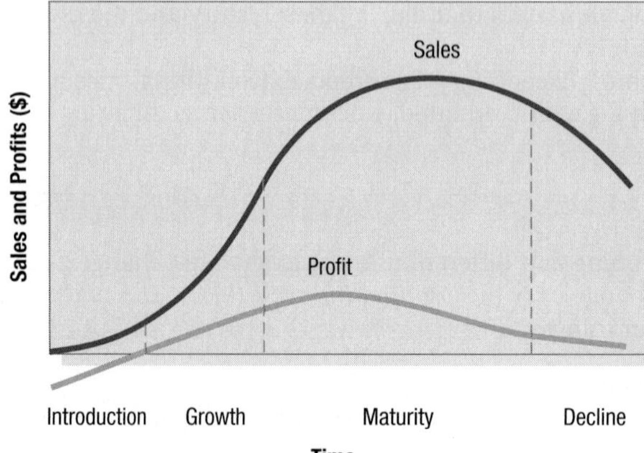

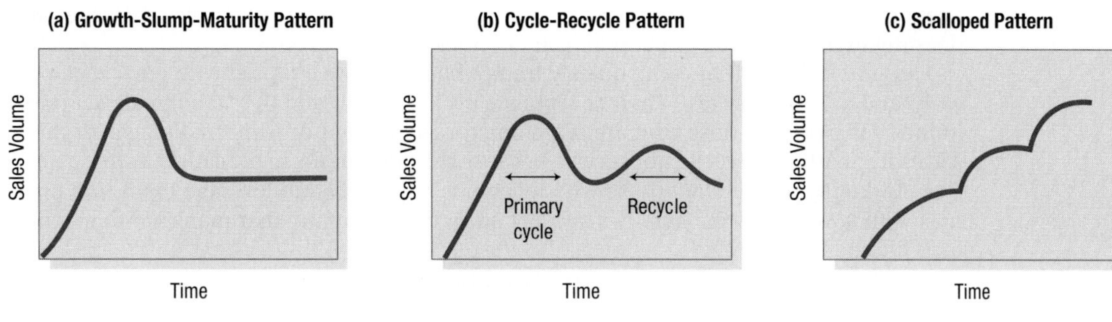

FIG. 10.2 Common Product Life-Cycle Patterns

Figure 10.2(a) shows a *growth-slump-maturity pattern*, often characteristic of small kitchen appliances such as handheld mixers and bread makers. Sales grow rapidly when the product is first introduced and then fall to a "petrified" level that is sustained by late adopters buying the product for the first time and early adopters replacing the product.

The *cycle-recycle pattern* in Figure 10.2(b) often describes the sales of new drugs. The pharmaceutical company aggressively promotes its new drug, and this produces the first cycle. Later, sales start declining and the company gives the drug another promotion push, which produces a second cycle (usually of smaller magnitude and duration).[24]

Another common pattern is the *scalloped PLC* in Figure 10.2(c). Here sales pass through a succession of life cycles based on the discovery of new-product characteristics, uses, or users. The sales of nylon, for example, show a scalloped pattern because of the many new uses—parachutes, hosiery, shirts, carpeting, boat sails, automobile tires—that continue to be discovered over time.[25]

Style, Fashion, and Fad Life Cycles

We need to distinguish three special categories of product life cycles—styles, fashions, and fads (Figure 10.3). A style is a basic and distinctive mode of expression appearing in a field of human endeavor. Styles appear in homes (colonial, ranch, Cape Cod); clothing (formal, casual, funky); and art (realistic, surrealistic, abstract). A style can last for generations, and go in and out of vogue. A fashion is a currently accepted or popular style in a given field. Fashions pass through four stages: distinctiveness, emulation, mass fashion, and decline.[26]

The length of a fashion cycle is hard to predict. One point of view is that fashions end because they represent a purchase compromise, and consumers start looking for missing attributes.[27] For example, as automobiles become smaller, they become less comfortable, and then a growing number of buyers start wanting larger cars. Furthermore, too many consumers adopt the fashion, thus turning others away. Another observation is that the length of a particular fashion cycle depends on the extent to which the fashion meets a genuine

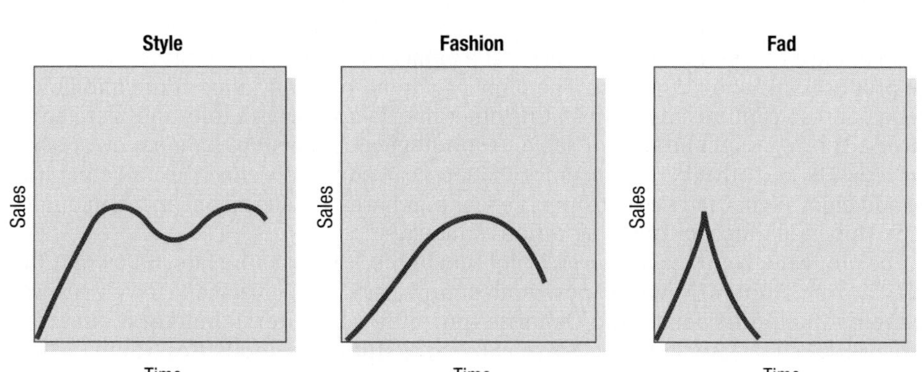

FIG. 10.3 Style, Fashion, and Fad Life Cycles

need, is consistent with other trends in the society, satisfies societal norms and values, and does not exceed technological limits as it develops.[28]

Fads are fashions that come quickly into public view, are adopted with great zeal, peak early, and decline very fast. Their acceptance cycle is short, and they tend to attract only a limited following of those who are searching for excitement or want to distinguish themselves from others. Fads do not survive because they do not normally satisfy a strong need. The marketing winners are those who recognize fads early and leverage them into products with staying power. Here is a success story of a company that managed to extend a fad's life span:

TRIVIAL PURSUIT

Since its debut at the International Toy Fair in 1982, Trivial Pursuit has sold 65 million copies in 18 languages in 32 countries, and it remains one of the best-selling adult games. Parker Brothers has kept the product's popularity going by making a new game with updated questions every year. It also keeps creating offshoots—travel packs, a children's version, Trivial Pursuit Genus IV, and an interactive CD-ROM from Virgin Entertainment Interactive. The game has its own Web site (www.trivialpursuit.com), which received 100,000 visitors in its initial two-month test period. If you are having trouble making dinner conversation on a date—no problem: NTN Entertainment Network has put Trivial Pursuit in about 3,000 restaurants.[29]

Marketing Strategies: Introduction Stage and the Pioneer Advantage

Because it takes time to roll out a new product, work out the technical problems, fill dealer pipelines, and gain consumer acceptance, sales growth tends to be slow at this stage.[30] Sales of expensive new products such as high-definition TV are slowed by additional factors such as product complexity and fewer potential buyers.

Profits are negative or low in the introduction stage. Promotional expenditures are at their highest ratio to sales because of the need to (1) inform potential consumers, (2) induce product trial, and (3) secure distribution in retail outlets.[31] Firms focus on those buyers who are the most ready to buy, usually higher-income groups. Prices tend to be high because costs are high.

Companies that plan to introduce a new product must decide when to enter the market. To be first can be rewarding, but risky and expensive. To come in later makes sense if the firm can bring superior technology, quality, or brand strength.

Speeding up innovation time is essential in an age of shortening product life cycles. Being early can pay off. One study found that products that came out six months late—but on budget—earned an average of 33 percent less profit in their first five years; products that came out on time but 50 percent over budget cut their profits by only 4 percent.

Most studies indicate that the market pioneer gains the most advantage. Companies like Campbell, Coca-Cola, Hallmark, and Amazon.com developed sustained market dominance.[32] Carpenter and Nakamoto found that 19 out of 25 companies who were market leaders in 1923 were still the market leaders in 1983, 60 years later.[33] Robinson and Min found that in a sample of industrial-goods businesses, 66 percent of pioneers survived at least 10 years, versus 48 percent of the early followers.[34]

What are the sources of the pioneer's advantage?[35] Early users will recall the pioneer's brand name if the product satisfies them. The pioneer's brand also establishes the attributes the product class should possess. The pioneer's brand normally aims at the middle of the market and so captures more users. Customer inertia also plays a role; and there are producer advantages: economies of scale, technological leadership, patents, ownership of scarce assets, and other barriers to entry. Pioneers can have more effective marketing spending and enjoy higher rates of consumer repeat purchases. An alert pioneer can maintain its leadership indefinitely by pursuing various strategies.[36]

The pioneer advantage, however, is not inevitable.[37] Look at the fate of Bowmar (hand calculators), Apple's Newton (personal digital assistant), Netscape (Web browser), Reynolds (ballpoint pens), and Osborne (portable computers), market pioneers who were overtaken by later entrants. Steven Schnaars studied 28 industries where the imitators surpassed the innovators.[38] He found several weaknesses among the failing pioneers, including new products that were too crude, were improperly positioned, or appeared before there was strong demand; product-development costs that exhausted the innovator's resources; a lack of resources to compete against entering larger firms; and managerial incompetence or unhealthy complacency. Successful imitators thrived by offering lower prices, improving the product more continuously, or using brute market power to overtake the pioneer. None of the companies that now dominate in the manufacture of personal computers—including Dell, Gateway, and Compaq—were first movers.[39]

Golder and Tellis raise further doubts about the pioneer advantage.[40] They distinguish between an *inventor* (first to develop patents in a new-product category), a *product pioneer* (first to develop a working model), and a *market pioneer* (first to sell in the new-product category). They also include nonsurviving pioneers in their sample. They conclude that although pioneers may still have an advantage, a larger number of market pioneers fail than has been reported and a larger number of early market leaders (though not pioneers) succeed. Examples of later entrants overtaking market pioneers are IBM over Sperry in mainframe computers, Matsushita over Sony in VCRs, and GE over EMI in CAT scan equipment. In a more recent study, Tellis and Golder identify the following five factors as underpinning long-term market leadership: vision of a mass market, persistence, relentless innovation, financial commitment, and asset leverage.[41]

The pioneer should visualize the various product markets it could initially enter, knowing that it cannot enter all of them at once. Suppose market-segmentation analysis reveals the product market segments shown in Figure 10.4. The pioneer should analyze the profit potential of each product market singly and in combination and decide on a market expansion path. Thus the pioneer in Figure 10.4 plans first to enter product market P_1M_1, then move the product into a second market (P_1M_2), then surprise the competition by developing a second product for the second market (P_2M_2), then take the second product back into the first market (P_2M_1), and then launch a third product for the first market (P_3M_1). If this game plan works, the pioneer firm will own a good part of the first two segments and serve them with two or three products.

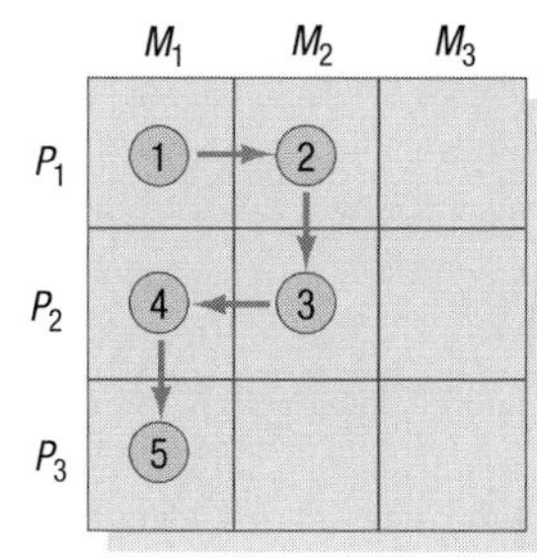

FIG. 10.4

Long-Range Product Market Expansion Strategy (P_i = product i; M_j = Market j)

Marketing Strategies: Growth Stage

The growth stage is marked by a rapid climb in sales. Early adopters like the product, and additional consumers start buying it. New competitors enter, attracted by the opportunities. They introduce new product features and expand distribution.

Prices remain where they are or fall slightly, depending on how fast demand increases. Companies maintain their promotional expenditures at the same or at a slightly increased level to meet competition and to continue to educate the market. Sales rise much faster than promotional expenditures, causing a welcome decline in the promotion–sales ratio. Profits increase during this stage as promotion costs are spread over a larger volume and unit manufacturing costs fall faster than price declines owing to the producer learning effect. Firms have to watch for a change from an accelerating to a decelerating rate of growth in order to prepare new strategies.

During this stage, the firm uses several strategies to sustain rapid market growth:

- It improves product quality and adds new product features and improved styling.
- It adds new models and flanker products (i.e., products of different sizes, flavors, and so forth that protect the main product).
- It enters new market segments.
- It increases its distribution coverage and enters new distribution channels.
- It shifts from product-awareness advertising to product-preference advertising.
- It lowers prices to attract the next layer of price-sensitive buyers.

These market expansion strategies strengthen the firm's competitive position. Consider how Yahoo! has fueled growth.

YAHOO!

Founded in 1994 by Web-surfing Stanford University grad students, Yahoo! has become the number-one place to be on the Web, averaging 120 million visitors in a month. The company grew into more than just a search engine; it became a portal, offering a full-blown package of information and services, from e-mail to online shopping malls. Yahoo!'s revenues, which exceeded $1.3 billion in 2003, come from a number of sources—banner ads, paid search, subscriptions for services such as personals, and a broadband partnership with SBC Communications. Yahoo!'s $1.6 billion acquisition of Overture Services, a key paid search competitor of Google, helped strengthen its claim as a one-stop shop for advertisers. Yahoo! also continued to grow globally with strong emphasis on Europe and Asia.[42]

A firm in the growth stage faces a trade-off between high market share and high current profit. By spending money on product improvement, promotion, and distribution, it can capture a dominant position. It forgoes maximum current profit in the hope of making even greater profits in the next stage.

Marketing Strategies: Maturity Stage

At some point, the rate of sales growth will slow, and the product will enter a stage of relative maturity. This stage normally lasts longer than the previous stages and poses big challenges to marketing management. *Most products are in the maturity stage of the life cycle, and most marketing managers cope with the problem of marketing the mature product.*

The maturity stage divides into three phases: growth, stable, and decaying maturity. In the first phase, the sales growth rate starts to decline. There are no new distribution channels to fill. In the second phase, sales flatten on a per capita basis because of market saturation. Most potential consumers have tried the product, and future sales are governed by population growth and replacement demand. In the third phase, decaying maturity, the absolute level of sales starts to decline, and customers begin switching to other products.

The sales slowdown creates overcapacity in the industry, which leads to intensified competition. Competitors scramble to find niches. They engage in frequent markdowns. They increase advertising and trade and consumer promotion. They increase R&D budgets to develop product improvements and line extensions. They make deals to supply private brands. A shakeout begins, and weaker competitors withdraw. The industry eventually consists of well-entrenched competitors whose basic drive is to gain or maintain market share.

Sustaining rapid market growth by adding new models and flanker products: the Snapple product line.

Dominating the industry are a few giant firms—perhaps a quality leader, a service leader, and a cost leader—that serve the whole market and make their profits mainly through high volume and lower costs. Surrounding these dominant firms is a multitude of market nichers, including market specialists, product specialists, and customizing firms. The issue facing a firm in a mature market is whether to struggle to become one of the "big three" and achieve profits through high volume and low cost or to pursue a niching strategy and achieve profits through low volume and a high margin.

Some companies abandon weaker products and concentrate on more profitable products and on new products. Yet they may be ignoring the high potential many mature markets and old products still have. Industries widely thought to be mature—autos, motorcycles, television, watches, cameras—were proved otherwise by the Japanese, who found ways to offer new value to customers. Seemingly moribund brands like

RCA, Jell-O, and Ovaltine have achieved sales revivals through the exercise of marketing imagination.[43] The resurgence in Hush Puppies' popularity in the footwear category is a case study in reviving an old, nearly forgotten brand.

HUSH PUPPIES

Hush Puppies' suede shoes, symbolized by the cuddly, rumpled, droopy-eyed dog, were a kid's favorite in the 1950s and 1960s. Changes in fashion trends and a series of marketing mishaps eventually resulted in an out-of-date image and diminished sales. Wolverine World Wide, makers of Hush Puppies, made a number of marketing changes in the early 1990s to reverse the sales slide. New product designs and numerous offbeat color combinations, such as powder blue, lime green, and electric orange, enhanced the brand's fashion appeal. Popular designers began to use the shoes in their fashion shows. Wolverine also jacked the price up from $40 to $70, and showered free shoes on Hollywood celebrities. Once the shoes had garnered enough buzz, the company made them more widely available by distributing them to better department stores. Hush Puppies sales rose from 30,000 pairs in 1994 to more than 1.7 million pairs in 1996. When fashions shifted a few years later, Hush Puppies expanded into sandals and walking shoes, and new international markets, and experienced an all-time sales high in 2002.[44]

MARKET MODIFICATION A company might try to expand the market for its mature brand by working with the two factors that make up sales volume:

Volume = number of brand users × usage rate per user

It can try to expand the number of brand users by *converting nonusers.* The key to the growth of air freight service is the constant search for new users to whom air carriers can demonstrate the benefits of using air freight rather than ground transportation.

DENTAL FLOSS

Despite the fact that the Academy of General Dentistry touts brushing and flossing as the best methods for fighting tooth decay, only 24 percent of households use floss. Several oral care marketers see this as a golden opportunity to convert the floss-averse. Aquafresh, owned by GlaxoSmithKline, has created Aquafresh Floss 'N' Cap which combines toothpaste and floss with a cap that doubles as a built-in floss dispenser. Johnson & Johnson, the market leader in this category, has developed a special handheld flosser called the Reach Access Daily Flosser. Glide, newly acquired by Procter & Gamble and the most recommended brand by dentists, perhaps has the easiest job convincing people to floss; the company got a boost when hygiene-obsessed Jerry Seinfeld used Glide on his hugely popular TV show.[45]

It can also try to expand the number of brand users by *entering new market segments.* When Goodyear decided to sell its tires via Wal-Mart, Sears, and Discount Tire, it boosted market share from 14 to 16 percent in the first year.[46] In recent years AARP has tried the tack of reaching out to new market segments:[47]

AARP

AARP, the American Association for Retired Persons, is a mature brand in more ways than one. The $625 million, 35-million-member organization serves people age 50 and over by offering advocacy efforts, products, services, and benefits. Yet, the organization has been dogged by the perception that it is only for elderly people living in retirement communities. With the boomer population expected to double in the next 30 years, AARP is repositioning itself to appeal to people in their late fifties who still have an active lifestyle. AARP's goal is to recruit 50 percent of people age 50 and over by 2003 and to that end it is hosting a number of activities. These include triathlons in several cities to promote fitness, a touring exhibit of Grandma Moses' art to inspire creativity, and an education campaign to prevent predatory mortgage lending and home improvement fraud. The challenge for AARP, however, is creating a single brand that not only attracts new members but also continues to appeal to those in the age 65 and over segment. As part of that effort, AARP is publishing several editions of its newly titled *AARP: The Magazine* (formerly called *Modern Maturity*): one for 50 to 59-year-old boomers, an edition for 60 to 69-year-olds, and one for those 70 and older.

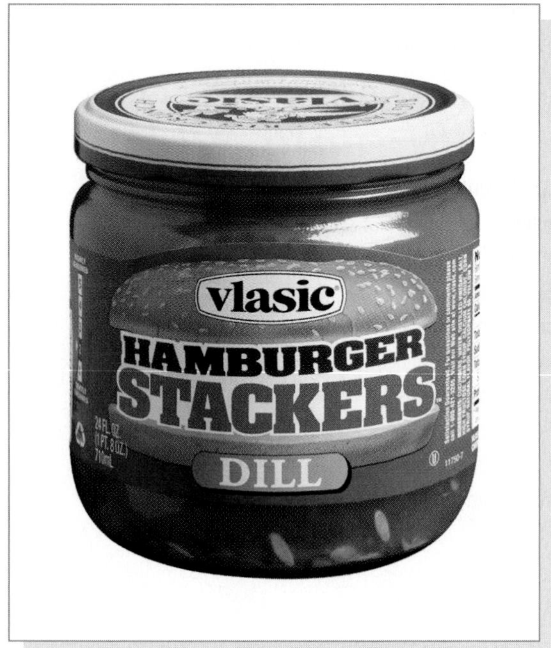

Feature improvement: Vlasic Hamburger Stackers.

A third way to expand the number of brand users is *winning competitors' customers*. Examples of this approach abound. Marketers of Puffs facial tissues are always wooing Kleenex customers. Volume can also be increased by convincing current users to increase their brand usage: (1) *Use the product on more occasions.* Serve Campbell's soup for a snack. Use Heinz vinegar to clean windows. Take Kodak pictures of your pets. (2) *Use more of the product on each occasion.* Drink a larger glass of orange juice. (3) *Use the product in new ways.* Use Tums antacid as a calcium supplement.[48]

PRODUCT MODIFICATION Managers also try to stimulate sales by modifying the product's characteristics through quality improvement, feature improvement, or style improvement.

Quality improvement aims at increasing the product's functional performance. A manufacturer can often overtake its competition by launching a "new and improved" product. Grocery manufacturers call this a "plus launch" and promote a new additive or advertise something as "stronger," "bigger," or "better." This strategy is effective to the extent that the quality is improved, buyers accept the claim of improved quality, and a sufficient number of buyers will pay for higher quality. In the case of the canned coffee industry, manufacturers are using "freshness" to better position their brands in the face of fierce competition from premium rivals, such as store brands where customers grind their own beans in the store. Kraft's Maxwell House will tout coffee sold in its new Fresh Seal packaging and P&G's Folger's ads will show how its AromaSeal canisters—plastic, peel-top, resealable and easy-grip packages—will make its ground beans fresher.[49]

However, customers are not always willing to accept an "improved" product, as the classic tale of New Coke illustrates.

COCA-COLA

Battered by competition from the sweeter Pepsi-Cola, Coca-Cola decided in 1985 to replace its old formula with a sweeter variation, dubbed the New Coke. Coca-Cola spent $4 million on market research. Blind taste tests showed that Coke drinkers preferred the new, sweeter formula, but the launch of New Coke provoked a national uproar. Market researchers had measured the taste but had failed to measure the emotional attachment consumers had to Coca-Cola. There were angry letters, formal protests, and even lawsuit threats, to force the retention of "The Real Thing." Ten weeks later, the company withdrew New Coke and reintroduced its century-old formula as "Classic Coke," giving the old formula even stronger status in the marketplace.

Feature improvement aims at adding new features (for example, size, weight, materials, additives, accessories) that expand the product's performance, versatility, safety, or convenience. In 1998, after years of research and development, Vlasic created a cucumber 10 times larger than the traditional pickle cucumber. The chips, sold as "Hamburger Stackers," are large enough to cover the entire surface of a hamburger and are stacked a dozen high in jars.[50]

Pfizer also embarked on feature improvement for its Listerine brand.

PFIZER INC.

"Obviously it's very difficult for people to walk down the street with a bottle of Listerine, take a swig and spit it out," says Dermot Boden, vice president for global oral care at Pfizer Inc., which owns the Listerine brand. This is the rationale behind Cool Mint Listerine's PocketPak, oral care strips which dissolve instantly in the mouth, allowing for oral care on the go. Six years in the making, this new, convenient form of Listerine not only enabled the brand to reach younger consumers, but it also generated a hefty $120 million in less than a year after its release.[51]

This strategy has several advantages. New features build the company's image as an innovator and win the loyalty of market segments that value these features. They provide an opportunity for free publicity and they generate sales force and distributor enthusiasm. The chief disadvantage is that feature improvements are easily imitated; unless there is a permanent gain from being first, the feature improvement might not pay off in the long run.[52]

Style improvement aims at increasing the product's esthetic appeal. The periodic introduction of new car models is largely about style competition, as is the introduction of new packaging for consumer products. A style strategy might give the product a unique market identity. Yet style competition has problems. First, it is difficult to predict whether people—and which people—will like a new style. Second, a style change usually requires discontinuing the old style, and the company risks losing customers.

MARKETING PROGRAM MODIFICATION Product managers might also try to stimulate sales by modifying other marketing program elements. They should ask the following questions:

- ***Prices.*** Would a price cut attract new buyers? If so, should the list price be lowered, or should prices be lowered through price specials, volume or early purchase discounts, freight cost absorption, or easier credit terms? Or would it be better to raise the price to signal higher quality?
- ***Distribution.*** Can the company obtain more product support and display in existing outlets? Can more outlets be penetrated? Can the company introduce the product into new distribution channels?
- ***Advertising.*** Should advertising expenditures be increased? Should the message or copy be changed? Should the media mix be changed? Should the timing, frequency, or size of ads be changed?
- ***Sales promotion.*** Should the company step up sales promotion—trade deals, cents-off coupons, rebates, warranties, gifts, and contests?
- ***Personal selling.*** Should the number or quality of salespeople be increased? Should the basis for sales force specialization be changed? Should sales territories be revised? Should sales force incentives be revised? Can sales-call planning be improved?
- ***Services.*** Can the company speed up delivery? Can it extend more technical assistance to customers? Can it extend more credit?

Marketers often debate which tools are most effective in the mature stage. For example, would the company gain more by increasing its advertising or its sales promotion budget? Sales promotion has more impact at this stage because consumers have reached an equilibrium in their buying habits and preferences, and psychological persuasion (advertising) is not as effective as financial persuasion (sales promotion deals). Many consumer-packaged-goods companies now spend over 60 percent of their total promotion budget on sales promotion to support mature products. Other marketers argue that brands should be managed as capital assets and supported by advertising. Advertising expenditures should be treated as a capital investment. Brand managers use sales promotion because its effects are quicker and more visible to their superiors; but excessive sales promotion activity can hurt the brand's image and long-run profit performance.

Marketing Strategies: Decline Stage

Sales decline for a number of reasons, including technological advances, shifts in consumer tastes, and increased domestic and foreign competition. All lead to overcapacity, increased price-cutting, and profit erosion. The decline might be slow, as in the case of sewing machines; or rapid, as in the case of the 5.25 floppy disks. Sales may plunge to zero, or they may petrify at a low level.

As sales and profits decline, some firms withdraw from the market. Those remaining may reduce the number of products they offer. They may withdraw from smaller market segments and weaker trade channels, and they may cut their promotion budgets and reduce prices further. Unfortunately, most companies have not developed a policy for handling aging products.

Unless strong reasons for retention exist, carrying a weak product is very costly to the firm—and not just by the amount of uncovered overhead and profit: There are many hidden costs. Weak products often consume a disproportionate amount of management's time; require frequent price and inventory adjustments; generally involve short production runs in spite of expensive setup times; require both advertising and sales force attention that might be better used to make the healthy products more profitable; and can cast a shadow on the company's image. The biggest cost might well lie in the future. Failing to eliminate weak products delays the aggressive search for replacement products. The weak products create a lopsided product mix, long on yesterday's breadwinners and short on tomorrow's.

In handling aging products, a company faces a number of tasks and decisions. The first task is to establish a system for identifying weak products. Many companies appoint a product-review committee with representatives from marketing, R&D, manufacturing, and finance. The controller's office supplies data for each product showing trends in market size, market share, prices, costs, and profits. A computer program then analyzes this information. The managers responsible for dubious products fill out rating forms showing where they think sales and profits will go, with and without any changes in marketing strategy. The product-review committee makes a recommendation for each product—leave it alone, modify its marketing strategy, or drop it.[53]

Some firms abandon declining markets earlier than others. Much depends on the presence and height of exit barriers in the industry.[54] The lower the exit barriers, the easier it is for firms to leave the industry, and the more tempting it is for the remaining firms to stay and attract the withdrawing firms' customers. For example, Procter & Gamble stayed in the declining liquid-soap business and improved its profits as others withdrew.

According to one study of company strategies in declining industries, five strategies are available to the firm:

1. Increasing the firm's investment (to dominate the market or strengthen its competitive position).
2. Maintaining the firm's investment level until the uncertainties about the industry are resolved.
3. Decreasing the firm's investment level selectively, by dropping unprofitable customer groups, while simultaneously strengthening the firm's investment in lucrative niches.
4. Harvesting ("milking") the firm's investment to recover cash quickly.
5. Divesting the business quickly by disposing of its assets as advantageously as possible.[55]

The appropriate strategy depends on the industry's relative attractiveness and the company's competitive strength in that industry. A company that is in an unattractive industry but possesses competitive strength should consider shrinking selectively. A company that is in an attractive industry and has competitive strength should consider strengthening its investment. Look what Quaker Oats has done with oatmeal.

QUAKER OATS

After being banished to the cupboard for years, instant oatmeal has staged a comeback with campaigns emphasizing health (for all) and fun (for kids) as oatmeal sales shot up in the late 1990s. The category turnaround began in January 1997 when the FDA permitted manufacturers to state that "diets low in saturated fat and cholesterol that include soluble fiber from oatmeal may reduce the risk of heart disease." Quaker Oats, which owns almost two-thirds of the category, capitalized on the opportunity to target kids by infusing fun with nutrition through new oatmeal products such as Sea Adventures and Dinosaur Eggs.[56]

If the company were choosing between harvesting and divesting, its strategies would be quite different. *Harvesting* calls for gradually reducing a product or business's costs while trying to maintain sales. The first step is to cut R&D costs and plant and equipment investment. The company might also reduce product quality, sales force size, marginal services, and advertising expenditures. It would try to cut these costs without letting customers, competitors, and employees know what is happening. Harvesting is difficult to execute. Yet many mature products warrant this strategy. Harvesting can substantially increase the company's current cash flow.[57]

Companies that successfully restage or rejuvenate a mature product often do so by adding value to the original product. Consider the experience of Pitney Bowes, the dominant producer of postage meters.

PITNEY BOWES

In 1996, critics, and even Pitney Bowes insiders, predicted that faxes would kill regular mail, on which Pitney's business relies. Then they predicted that e-mail would kill faxes and that all these technological advances combined would kill Pitney's profits. As it happens, the surge in direct mail and Internet-related bills has generated more mail, not less, but the Internet also enabled new companies such as e-Stamps and stamps.com to enter Pitney's territory by offering a way to download stamps over the Internet. Pitney recast itself as a messaging company—its slogan became "Engineering the Flow of Communication." It developed software products that let customers track incoming materials and outgoing products, convert bills and print files to fax or e-mail, and track when a document has been acted upon. Pitney also provides electronic billing services for e-commerce companies and even added an electronic-stamp business to compete with the stamp start-ups. Pitney's view: The Internet is not the enemy; rather, it is a vehicle for becoming a broad-based messaging company.[58]

When a company decides to drop a product, it faces further decisions. If the product has strong distribution and residual goodwill, the company can probably sell it to another firm. If the company can't find any buyers, it must decide whether to liquidate the brand quickly or slowly. It must also decide on how much inventory and service to maintain for past customers.

The Product Life-Cycle Concept: Critique

The PLC concept helps marketers interpret product and market dynamics. It can be used for planning and control, although it is useful as a forecasting tool. PLC theory has its share of critics. They claim that life-cycle patterns are too variable in shape and duration. Critics charge that marketers can seldom tell what stage the product is in. A product may appear to be mature when actually it has reached a plateau prior to another upsurge. They charge that the PLC pattern is the result of marketing strategies rather than an inevitable course that sales must follow:

> Suppose a brand is acceptable to consumers but has a few bad years because of other factors—for instance, poor advertising, delisting by a major chain, or entry of a "me-too" competitive product backed by massive sampling. Instead of thinking in terms of corrective measures, management begins to feel that its brand has entered a declining stage. It therefore withdraws funds from the promotion budget to finance R&D on new items. The next year the brand does even worse, panic increases. . . . Clearly, the PLC is a dependent variable which is determined by marketing actions; it is not an independent variable to which companies should adapt their marketing programs.[59]

Table 10.3 summarizes the characteristics, marketing objectives, and marketing strategies of the four stages of the PLC.

::: Market Evolution

Because the PLC focuses on what is happening to a particular product or brand rather than on what is happening to the overall market, it yields a product-oriented picture rather than a market-oriented picture. Firms need to visualize a *market's* evolutionary path as it is affected by new needs, competitors, technology, channels, and other developments.[60]

In the course of a product's or brand's existence, its positioning must change to keep pace with market developments. Consider the case of Lego.

TABLE 10.3 | Summary of Product Life-Cycle Characteristics, Objectives, and Strategies

	Introduction	**Growth**	**Maturity**	**Decline**
Characteristics				
Sales	Low sales	Rapidly rising sales	Peak sales	Declining sales
Costs	High cost per customer	Average cost per customer	Low cost per customer	Low cost per customer
Profits	Negative	Rising profits	High profits	Declining profits
Customers	Innovators	Early adopters	Middle majority	Laggards
Competitors	Few	Growing number	Stable number beginning to decline	Declining number
Marketing Objectives				
	Create product awareness and trial	Maximize market share	Maximize profit while defending market share	Reduce expenditure and milk the brand
Strategies				
Product	Offer a basic product	Offer product extensions, service, warranty	Diversify brands and items models	Phase out weak
Price	Charge cost-plus	Price to penetrate market	Price to match or best competitors'	Cut price
Distribution	Build selective distribution	Build intensive distribution	Build more intensive distribution	Go selective: phase out unprofitable outlets
Advertising	Build product awareness among early adopters and dealers	Build awareness and interest in the mass market	Stress brand differences and benefits	Reduce to level needed to retain hard-core loyals
Sales Promotion	Use heavy sales promotion to entice trial	Reduce to take advantage of heavy consumer demand	Increase to encourage brand switching	Reduce to minimal level

Sources: Chester R. Wasson, *Dynamic Competitive Strategy and Product Life Cycles* (Austin, TX: Austin Press, 1978); John A. Weber, "Planning Corporate Growth with Inverted Product Life Cycles," *Long Range Planning* (October 1976): 12–29; Peter Doyle, "The Realities of the Product Life Cycle," *Quarterly Review of Marketing* (Summer 1976).

LEGO GROUP

LEGO Group, the Danish toy company, enjoyed a 72 percent global market share of the construction-toy market; but children were spending more of their spare time with video games, computers, and television and less time with traditional toys. Lego recognized the need to change or expand its market space. It redefined its market space as "family edutainment," which included toys, education, interactive technology, software, computers, and consumer electronics. All involved exercising the mind and having fun. Part of LEGO Group's plan is to capture an increasing share of customer spending as children become young adults and then parents.

Like products, markets evolve through four stages: emergence, growth, maturity, and decline.

EMERGENCE Before a market materializes, it exists as a latent market. For example, for centuries people have wanted faster means of calculation. The market satisfied this need with abacuses, slide rules, and large adding machines. Suppose an entrepreneur recognizes

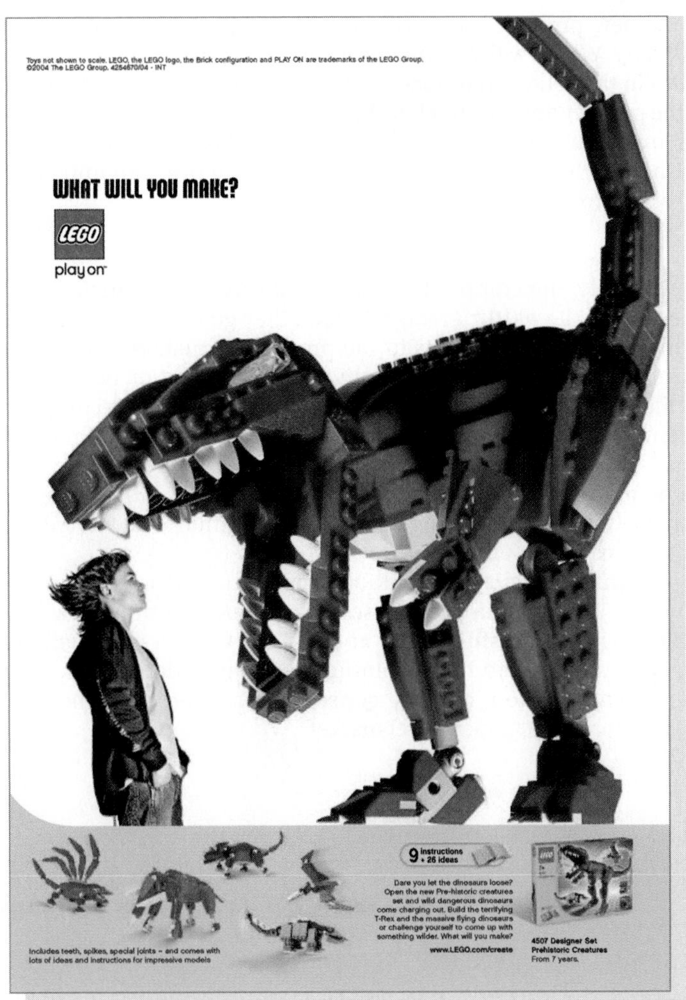

An ad to the trade for the LEGO 2004 product line. LEGO is redefining its market space as "family edutainment," not just children's construction toys.

this need and imagines a technological solution in the form of a small, handheld electronic calculator. He now has to determine the product attributes, including physical size and number of mathematical functions. Because he is market-oriented, he interviews potential buyers and finds that target customers vary greatly in their preferences. Some want a four-function calculator (adding, subtracting, multiplying, and dividing) and others want more functions (calculating percentages, square roots, and logs). Some want a small hand calculator and others want a large one. This type of market, in which buyer preferences scatter evenly, is called a *diffused-preference market.*

The entrepreneur's problem is to design an optimal product for this market. He or she has three options:

1. The new product can be designed to meet the preferences of one of the corners of the market (*a single-niche strategy*).
2. Two or more products can be simultaneously launched to capture two or more parts of the market (*a multiple-niche strategy*).
3. The new product can be designed for the middle of the market (*a mass-market strategy*).

For small firms, a single-niche market strategy makes the most sense. A small firm does not have the resources for capturing and holding the mass market. A large firm might go after the mass market by designing a product that is medium in size and number of functions. Assume that the pioneer firm is large and designs its product for the mass market. On launching the product, the *emergence* stage begins.[61]

(a) Market-fragmentation Stage

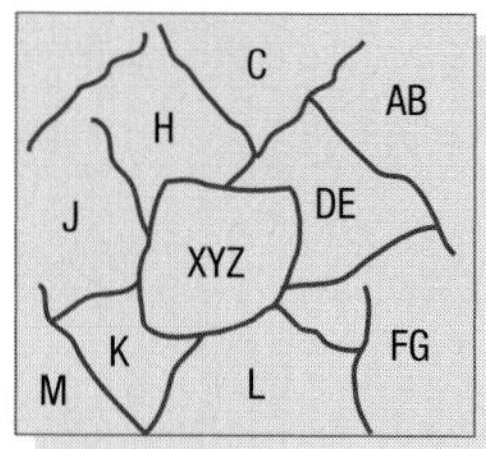

(b) Market-consolidation Stage

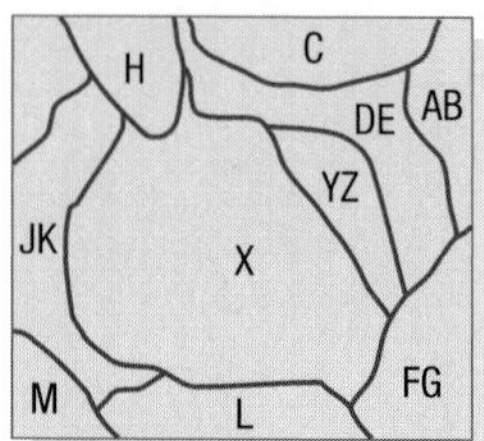

FIG. 10.5

Market-Fragmentation and Market-Consolidation Strategies

GROWTH If the new product sells well, new firms will enter the market, ushering in a *market-growth stage.* Where will a second firm enter the market, assuming that the first firm established itself in the center? If the second firm is small, it is likely to avoid head-on competition with the pioneer and to launch its brand in one of the market corners. If the second firm is large, it might launch its brand in the center against the pioneer. The two firms can easily end up sharing the mass market. Or a large second firm can implement a multiple-niche strategy and surround and box in the pioneer.

MATURITY Eventually, the competitors cover and serve all the major market segments and the market enters the *maturity stage.* In fact, they go further and invade each others' segments, reducing everyone's profits in the process. As market growth slows down, the market splits into finer segments and high *market fragmentation* occurs. This situation is illustrated in Figure 10.5(a) where the letters represent different companies supplying various segments. Note that two segments are unserved because they are too small to yield a profit.

Market fragmentation is often followed by a *market consolidation* caused by the emergence of a new attribute that has strong appeal. This situation is illustrated in Figure 10.5(b) and the expansive size of the X territory.

"Marketing Insight: Dynamics of Attribute Competition" discusses how new attributes emerge in a market. However, even a consolidated market condition will not last. Other companies will copy a successful brand, and the market will eventually splinter again. Mature markets swing between fragmentation and consolidation. The fragmentation is brought about by competition, and the consolidation is brought about by innovation. Consider the evolution of the paper towel market.

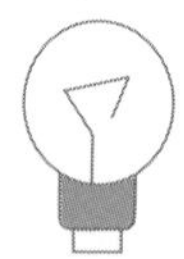

MARKETING INSIGHT | DYNAMICS OF ATTRIBUTE COMPETITION

Competition produces a continuous round of new product attributes. If a new attribute succeeds, several competitors soon offer it. To the extent that oil companies all offer credit card payment at gas station pumps, payment methods are no longer a basis for choosing a gas station. *Customer expectations are progressive.* This fact underlines the strategic importance of maintaining the lead in introducing new attributes. Each new attribute, if successful, creates a competitive advantage for the firm, leading to temporarily higher-than-average market share and profits. The market leader must learn to routinize the innovation process.

Can a firm look ahead and anticipate the succession of attributes that are likely to win favor and be technologically feasible? How can the firm discover new attributes? There are four approaches.

1. ***A customer-survey process:*** The company asks consumers what benefits they would like added to the product and their desire level for each. The firm also examines the cost of developing each new attribute and likely competitive responses.
2. ***An intuitive process:*** Entrepreneurs get hunches and undertake product development without much marketing research. Natural selection determines winners and losers. If a manufacturer has intuited an attribute that the market wants, that manufacturer is considered smart or lucky.
3. ***A dialectical process:*** Innovators should not march with the crowd. Thus blue jeans, which began as an inexpensive article of clothing, over time became fashionable and more expensive. This unidirectional movement, however, contains the seeds of its own destruction. Eventually, the price falls again or some manufacturer introduces another cheap material for pants.
4. ***A needs-hierarchy process:*** (See Maslow's theory in Chapter 6.) We would predict that the first automobiles would provide basic transportation and be designed for safety. Later, automobiles would start appealing to social acceptance and status needs. Still later, automobiles would be designed to help people "fulfill" themselves. The innovator's task is to assess when the market is ready to satisfy a higher-order need.

The actual unfolding of new attributes in a market is more complex than simple theories suggest. We should not underestimate the role of technology and societal processes. For example, the strong consumer wish for portable computers remained unmet until miniaturization technology was sufficiently developed. Developments such as inflation, shortages, environmentalism, consumerism, and new lifestyles lead consumers to reevaluate product attributes. Inflation increases the desire for a smaller car, and a desire for car safety increases the desire for a heavier car. The innovator must use marketing research to gauge the strength of different attributes to determine the company's best move.

Source: Marnik G. Dekimpe and Dominique M. Hanssens, "Empirical Generalizations about Market Evolution and Stationarity," *Marketing Science* 14, no. 3, pt. 1 (1995): G109–121.

PAPER TOWELS

Originally, homemakers used cotton and linen dishcloths and towels in their kitchens. A paper company, looking for new markets, developed paper towels. This development crystallized a latent market. Other manufacturers entered the market. The number of brands grew and created market fragmentation. Industry overcapacity led manufacturers to search for new features. One manufacturer, hearing consumers complain that paper towels were not absorbent, introduced "absorbent" towels and increased its market share. This market consolidation did not last long because competitors came out with their own versions of absorbent paper towels. The market fragmented again. Then another manufacturer introduced a "superstrength" towel. It was soon copied. Another manufacturer introduced a "lint-free" paper towel, which was subsequently copied. Thus paper towels evolved from a single product to one with various absorbencies, strengths, and applications. Market evolution was driven by the forces of innovation and competition.

DECLINE Eventually, demand for the present products will begin to decrease, and the market will enter the *decline stage.* Either society's total need level declines or a new technology replaces the old. For example, shifts in tradition and a trend toward cremation have caused casket makers and funeral homes to reconsider how to conduct their business.[62]

SUMMARY :::

1. Deciding on positioning requires the determination of a frame of reference—by identifying the target market and the nature of the competition—and the ideal points-of-parity and points-of-difference brand associations. To determine the proper competitive frame of reference, one must understand consumer behavior and the considerations consumers use in making brand choices.
2. Points-of-difference are those associations unique to the brand that are also strongly held and favorably evaluated by consumers. Points-of-parity are those associations not necessarily unique to the brand but perhaps shared with other brands. Category point-of-parity associations are associations consumers view as being necessary to a legitimate and credible product offering within a certain category. Competitive point-of-parity associations are those associations designed to negate competitors' points-of-difference.
3. The key to competitive advantage is product differentiation. A market offering can be differentiated along five dimensions: product (form, features, performance quality, conformance quality, durability, reliability, repairability, style, design); services (order ease, delivery, installation, customer training, customer consulting, maintenance and repair, miscellaneous services); personnel, channel, or image (symbols, media, atmosphere, and events).
4. Because economic conditions change and competitive activity varies, companies normally find it necessary to reformulate their marketing strategy several times during a product's life cycle. Technologies, product forms, and brands also exhibit life cycles with distinct stages. The general sequence of stages in any life cycle is introduction, growth, maturity, and decline. The majority of products today are in the maturity stage.
5. Each stage of the product life cycle calls for different marketing strategies. The introduction stage is marked by slow growth and minimal profits. If successful, the product enters a growth stage marked by rapid sales growth and increasing profits. There follows a maturity stage in which sales growth slows and profits stabilize. Finally, the product enters a decline stage. The company's task is to identify the truly weak products; develop a strategy for each one; and phase out weak products in a way that minimizes the hardship to company profits, employees, and customers.
6. Like products, markets evolve through four stages: emergence, growth, maturity, and decline.

APPLICATIONS :::

Marketing Debate Do Brands Have Finite Lives?

Often, after a brand begins to slip in the marketplace or disappears altogether, commentators observe, "all brands have their day." Their rationale is that all brands, in some sense, have a finite life and cannot be expected to be leaders forever. Other experts contend, however, that brands can live forever, and their long-term success depends on the skill and insight of the marketers involved.

Take a position: Brands cannot be expected to last forever versus There is no reason for a brand to ever become obsolete.

Marketing Discussion

Identify other negatively correlated attributes and benefits not included in Table 10.2. What strategies do firms use to try to position themselves on the basis of pairs of attributes and benefits?

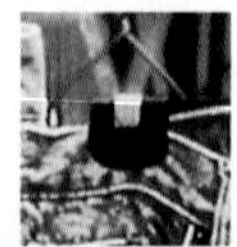

IN THIS CHAPTER, WE WILL ADDRESS THE FOLLOWING QUESTIONS:

1. How do marketers identify primary competitors?
2. How should we analyze competitors' strategies, objectives, strengths, and weaknesses?
3. How can market leaders expand the total market and defend market share?
4. How should market challengers attack market leaders?
5. How can market followers or nichers compete effectively?

CHAPTER 11 ::: DEALING WITH COMPETITION

eleven

Building strong brands requires a keen understanding of competition, and competition grows more intense every year. New competition is coming from all directions—from global competitors eager to grow sales in new markets; from online competitors seeking cost-efficient ways to expand distribution; from private label and store brands designed to provide low-price alternatives; and from brand extensions from strong megabrands leveraging their strengths to move into new categories. Consider how competition has intensified in the jeans market.

Levi Strauss has seen its sales plummet from a peak of $7.1 billion in 1996 to about $4 billion in 2003 in part because of fierce competition. Its jeans brands, exemplified by the classic 501, are being hit from all sides: above, from trendy, high-end designer lines such as Calvin Klein, Tommy Hilfiger, and GAP; below, from popular, lower-priced private labels such as JC Penney's Arizona and Sears' Canyon River Blues; from one side by traditional, entrenched brands such as the western Wranglers and urban Lee's; and from another other side by hip, youthful lines such as American Eagle, Bugle Boy, JNCO, Lucky, and Diesel. Levi's is being hit from so many directions, it is hard for the company to know in which direction to turn! To better compete, it recently introduced the Signature line to be sold at discount stores such as Wal-Mart and the more expensive Premium Red >>>

Levi's competition: Some of the many brands and styles of jeans.

Tab line to be sold at upscale department stores such as Nordstrom and Neiman Marcus. Many marketing pundits wondered, however, whether it was too little too late, and if the brand could ever reclaim its lofty position.[1]

To effectively devise and implement the best possible brand positioning strategies, companies must pay keen attention to their competitors.[2] Markets have become too competitive to just focus on the consumer alone. This chapter examines the role competition plays and how marketers can best manage their brands, depending on their market position.

::: Competitive Forces

Michael Porter has identified five forces that determine the intrinsic long-run attractiveness of a market or market segment: industry competitors, potential entrants, substitutes, buyers, and suppliers. His model is shown in Figure 11.1. The threats these forces pose are as follows:

1. ***Threat of intense segment rivalry*** – A segment is unattractive if it already contains numerous, strong, or aggressive competitors. It is even more unattractive if it is stable or declining, if plant capacity additions are done in large increments, if fixed costs are high, if exit barriers are high, or if competitors have high stakes in staying in the segment. These conditions will lead to frequent price wars, advertising battles, and new-product introductions, and will make it expensive to compete. The cellular phone market has seen fierce competition due to segment rivalry.
2. ***Threat of new entrants*** – A segment's attractiveness varies with the height of its entry and exit barriers.[3] The most attractive segment is one in which entry barriers are high and exit barriers are low. Few new firms can enter the industry, and poor-performing firms can easily exit. When both entry and exit barriers are high, profit potential is high, but firms face more risk because poorer-performing firms stay in and fight it out. When both entry and exit barriers are low, firms easily enter and leave the industry, and the returns are stable and low. The worst case is when entry barriers are low and exit barriers are high: Here firms enter during good times but find it hard to leave during bad times.

FIG. 11.1

Five Forces Determining Segment Structural Attractiveness

Source: Reprinted with the permission of the Free Press, an imprint of Simon & Schuster, from Michael E. Porter, *Competitive Advantage: Creating and Sustaining Superior Performance*. Copyright 1985 by Michael E. Porter.

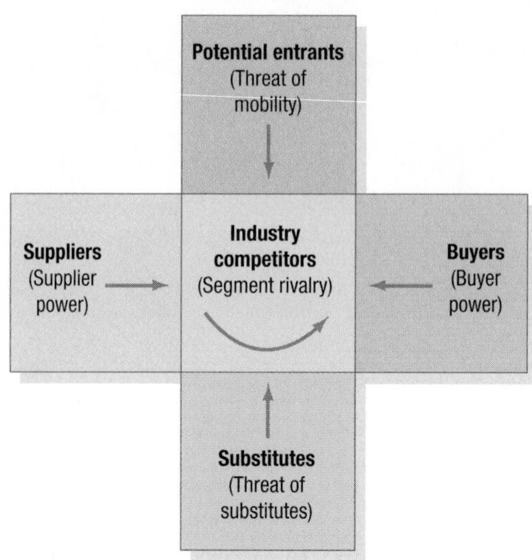

The result is chronic overcapacity and depressed earnings for all. The airline industry has low entry barriers but high exit barriers, leaving all the companies struggling during economic downturns.

3. ***Threat of substitute products*** – A segment is unattractive when there are actual or potential substitutes for the product. Substitutes place a limit on prices and on profits. The company has to monitor price trends closely. If technology advances or competition increases in these substitute industries, prices and profits in the segment are likely to fall. Greyhound buses and Amtrak trains have seen profitability threatened by the rise of air travel.
4. ***Threat of buyers' growing bargaining power*** – A segment is unattractive if buyers possess strong or growing bargaining power. The rise of retail giants such as Wal-Mart has led some analysts to conclude that the potential profitability of packaged-goods companies will become curtailed. Buyers' bargaining power grows when they become more concentrated or organized, when the product represents a significant fraction of the buyers' costs, when the product is undifferentiated, when the buyers' switching costs are low, when buyers are price sensitive because of low profits, or when buyers can integrate upstream. To protect themselves, sellers might select buyers who have the least power to negotiate or switch suppliers. A better defense consists of developing superior offers that strong buyers cannot refuse.
5. ***Threat of suppliers' growing bargaining power*** – A segment is unattractive if the company's suppliers are able to raise prices or reduce quantity supplied. Oil companies such as ExxonMobil, Shell, BP, and Chevron-Texaco are at the mercy of the amount of oil reserves and the actions of oil supplying cartels like OPEC. Suppliers tend to be powerful when they are concentrated or organized, when there are few substitutes, when the supplied product is an important input, when the costs of switching suppliers are high, and when the suppliers can integrate downstream. The best defenses are to build win–win relations with suppliers or use multiple supply sources.

::: Identifying Competitors

It would seem a simple task for a company to identify its competitors. PepsiCo knows that Coca-Cola's Dasani is the major bottled water competitor for its Aquafina brand; Citigroup knows that Bank of America is a major banking competitor; and PetSmart.com knows that its major online competitor for pet food and supplies is Petco.com. However, the range of a company's actual and potential competitors can be much broader. And a company is more likely to be hurt by emerging competitors or new technologies than by current competitors. This certainly has been true for Toys "R" Us and other major toy retailers:

TOYS "R" US AND KB TOYS

Pricing pressure from discounters Wal-Mart, Target, and even electronics vendors such as Best Buy and Circuit City has pummeled the toy chains and sent some of them into bankruptcy. During the 2004 holiday season, Wal-Mart made its most aggressive move yet into the toy business, drastically reducing prices and undercutting Toys "R" Us and KB Toys by 20 percent. At Wal-Mart, one of the season's hottest toys, Hokey-Pokey Elmo, sold for $19.46, whereas at KB Toys it cost $24.99. With their bare bones prices, the discounters have higher sales, more locations, and the flexibility, if necessary, to break even or even lose money in areas such as toys while falling back on other product revenue. In response, some chains, such as venerable FAO Schwartz, have filed for bankruptcy, while others, such as Toys "R" Us, are contracting. The company closed 182 freestanding Kids "R" Us stores as well as its Imaginarium chain. KB Toys may try specializing in order to survive and become a niche provider.[4]

Many businesses failed to look to the Internet for their most formidable competitors. Web sites that offer jobs, real estate listings, and automobiles online threaten newspapers, which derive a huge portion of their revenue from classified ads. The businesses with the most to fear from Internet technology are the world's middlemen. A few years back, Barnes & Noble and Borders bookstore chains were competing to see who could build the most megastores, where book browsers could sink into comfortable couches and sip cappuccino. While they were deciding which products to stock, Jeffrey Bezos was building an online empire called Amazon.com. Bezos's cyber-bookstore had the advantage of offering an almost unlimited selection of books without the expense of stocking inventory. Now both Barnes & Noble and Borders are playing catch-up in building their own online stores. "Competitor myopia"—a focus on current competitors rather than latent ones—has rendered some businesses extinct:[5]

ENCYCLOPAEDIA BRITANNICA

In 1996, 230-year-old Encyclopaedia Britannica dismissed its entire home sales force after the arrival of its $5-per-month subscription Internet site made the idea of owning a 32-volume set of books for $1,250 less appealing to parents. Britannica decided to create an online site after realizing that computer-savvy kids most often sought information online or on CD-ROMs such as Microsoft's Encarta, which sold for $50. What really smarts is that Britannica had the opportunity to partner with Microsoft in providing content for Encarta but refused. Britannica now sells print sets and offers online access to premium subscribers on its Web site.[6]

We can examine competition from both an industry and a marketing point of view.[7]

Industry Concept of Competition

What exactly is an industry? An **industry** is a group of firms that offer a product or class of products that are close substitutes for one another. Industries are classified according to number of sellers; degree of product differentiation; presence or absence of entry, mobility, and exit barriers; cost structure; degree of vertical integration; and degree of globalization.

NUMBER OF SELLERS AND DEGREE OF DIFFERENTIATION The starting point for describing an industry is to specify the number of sellers and whether the product is homogeneous or highly differentiated. These characteristics give rise to four industry structure types:

1. ***Pure monopoly*** – Only one firm provides a certain product or service in a certain country or area (a local water or cable company). An unregulated monopolist might charge a high price, do little or no advertising, and offer minimal service. If partial substitutes are available and there is some danger of competition, the monopolist might invest in more service and technology. A regulated monopolist is required to charge a lower price and provide more service as a matter of public interest.
2. ***Oligopoly*** – A small number of (usually) large firms produce products that range from highly differentiated to standardized. *Pure oligopoly* consists of a few companies producing essentially the same commodity (oil, steel). Such companies would find it hard to charge anything more than the going price. If competitors match on price and services, the only way to gain a competitive advantage is through lower costs. *Differentiated oligopoly* consists of a few companies producing products (autos, cameras) partially differentiated along lines of quality, features, styling, or services. Each competitor may seek leadership in one of these major attributes, attract the customers favoring that attribute, and charge a price premium for that attribute.
3. ***Monopolistic competition*** – Many competitors are able to differentiate their offers in whole or in part (restaurants, beauty shops). Competitors focus on market segments where they can meet customer needs in a superior way and command a price premium.
4. ***Pure competition*** – Many competitors offer the same product and service (stock market, commodity market). Because there is no basis for differentiation, competitors' prices will be the same. No competitor will advertise unless advertising can create psychological differentiation (cigarettes, beer), in which case it would be more proper to describe the industry as monopolistically competitive.

An industry's competitive structure can change over time. For instance, the media industry has continued to consolidate, turning from monopolistic into a differentiated oligopoly:

MEDIA INDUSTRY

For more than a decade, the media business has been steadily consolidating to the point that four media empires can now vertically integrate content with distribution: Rupert Murdoch's $30 billion News Corp., Time Warner at $39.9 billion, $26.6 billion Viacom and, the smallest, $6.9 billion NBC. Combining the studios that produce pro-

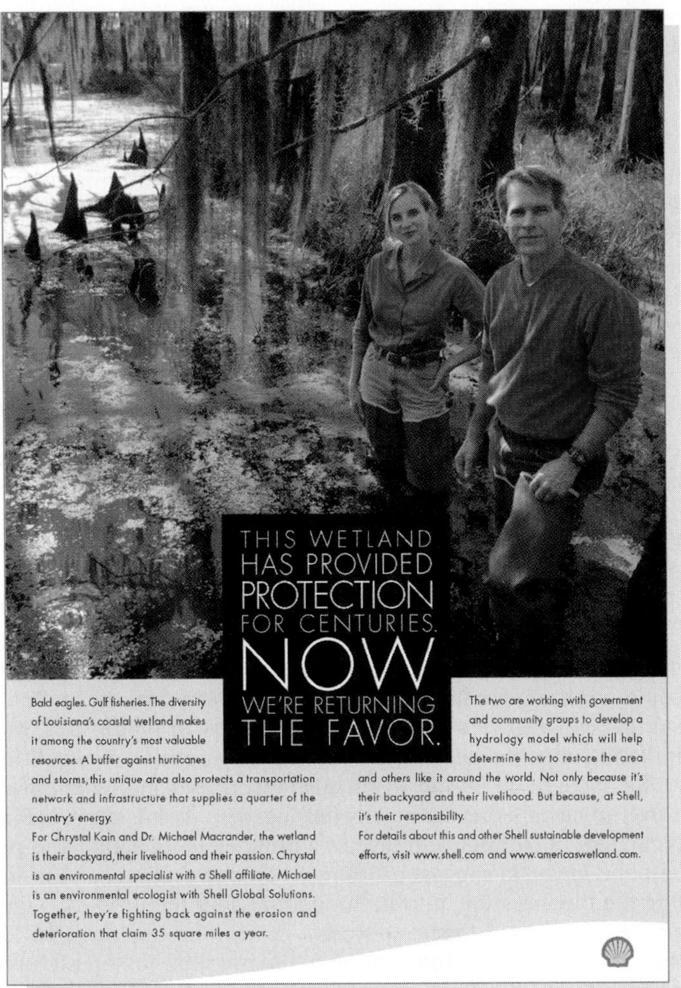

THIS WETLAND
HAS PROVIDED
PROTECTION
FOR CENTURIES.
NOW
WE'RE RETURNING
THE FAVOR.
Bald eagles. Gulf fisheries. The diversity of Louisiana's coastal wetland makes it among the country's most valuable resources. A buffer against hurricanes and storms, this unique area also protects a transportation network and infrastructure that supplies a quarter of the country's energy.
For Chrystal Kain and Dr. Michael Macrander, the wetland is their backyard, their livelihood and their passion. Chrystal is an environmental specialist with a Shell affiliate. Michael is an environmental ecologist with Shell Global Solutions. Together, they're fighting back against the erosion and deterioration that claim 35 square miles a year.
The two are working with government and community groups to develop a hydrology model which will help determine how to restore the area and others like it around the world. Not only because it's their backyard and their livelihood. But because, at Shell, it's their responsibility.
For details about this and other Shell sustainable development efforts, visit www.shell.com and www.americaswetland.com.

Shell Oil is a vertically integrated firm that is also today becoming an environmentally friendly firm. This ad is one of a series in a campaign to spotlight Shell's sustainable development program.

gramming with cable and broadcasting units that distribute content saves money and benefits shareholders. However, consumers are concerned by the effects of dwindling competition. With fewer people deciding on programming, quality and variety could suffer, and less competition may mean higher prices for cable and satellite subscribers. Also, most important, if a few media giants control content and distribution, smaller, more innovative programs could be squeezed out.[8]

ENTRY, MOBILITY, AND EXIT BARRIERS Industries differ greatly in ease of entry. It is easy to open a new restaurant but difficult to enter the aircraft industry. Major *entry barriers* include high capital requirements; economies of scale; patents and licensing requirements; scarce locations, raw materials, or distributors; and reputation requirements. Even after a firm enters an industry, it might face *mobility barriers* when it tries to enter more attractive market segments.

Firms often face *exit barriers,* such as legal or moral obligations to customers, creditors, and employees; government restrictions; low asset-salvage value due to overspecialization or obsolescence; lack of alternative opportunities; high vertical integration; and emotional barriers.[9] Many firms stay in an industry as long as they cover their variable costs and some or all of their fixed costs. Their continued presence, however, dampens profits for everyone. Even if some firms do not want to exit the industry, they might decrease their size. Companies can try to reduce shrinkage barriers to help ailing competitors get smaller gracefully.[10]

COST STRUCTURE Each industry has a certain cost burden that shapes much of its strategic conduct. For example, steelmaking involves heavy manufacturing and raw material costs; toy manufacturing involves heavy distribution and marketing costs. Firms strive to reduce their largest costs. The integrated steel company with the most cost-efficient plant will have a great advantage over other integrated steel companies; but even it has higher costs than the new steel mini-mills.

DEGREE OF VERTICAL INTEGRATION Companies find it advantageous to integrate backward or forward (**vertical integration**). Major oil producers carry on oil exploration, oil drilling, oil refining, chemical manufacture, and service-station operation. Vertical integration often lowers costs, and the company gains a larger share of the value-added stream. In addition, vertically integrated firms can manipulate prices and costs in different parts of the value chain to earn profits where taxes are lowest. There can be disadvantages, such as high costs in certain parts of the value chain and a lack of flexibility. Companies are increasingly questioning how vertical they should be. Many are outsourcing more activities, especially those that can be done better and more cheaply by specialist firms.

DEGREE OF GLOBALIZATION Some industries are highly local (such as lawn care); others are global (such as oil, aircraft engines, cameras). Companies in global industries need to compete on a global basis if they are to achieve economies of scale and keep up with the latest advances in technology.[11]

Market Concept of Competition

Using the market approach, competitors are companies that satisfy the same customer need. For example, a customer who buys a word-processing package really wants "writing ability"—a need that can also be satisfied by pencils, pens, or typewriters. Marketers must overcome "marketing myopia" and stop defining competition in traditional category terms.[12] Coca-Cola, focused on its soft-drink business, missed seeing the market for coffee bars and fresh-fruit-juice bars that eventually impinged on its soft-drink business.

The market concept of competition reveals a broader set of actual and potential competitors. Rayport and Jaworski suggest profiling a company's direct and indirect competitors by mapping the buyer's steps in obtaining and using the product. Figure 11.2 illustrates their *competitor map* of Eastman Kodak in the film business. In the center is a listing of consumer activities: buying a camera, buying film, taking pictures, and so on. The first outer ring lists Kodak's main competitors with respect to each consumer activity:

FIG. 11.2

Competitor Map—Eastman Kodak

Source: Jeffrey F. Rayport and Bernard J. Jaworski, *e-Commerce* (New York: McGraw-Hill, 2001), p. 53.

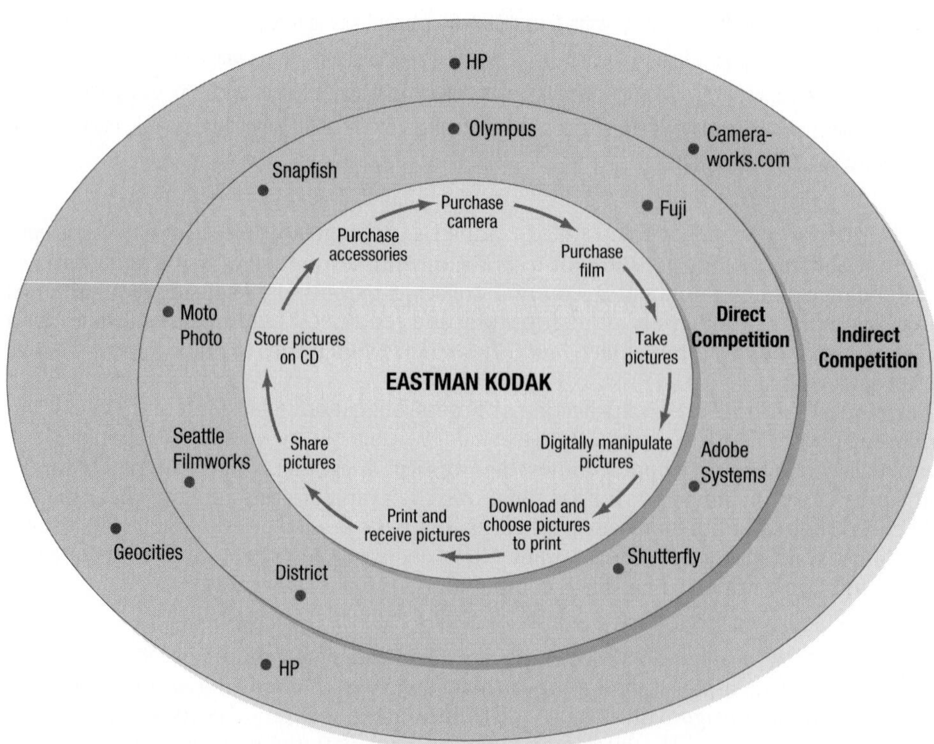

Olympus for buying a camera, Fuji for purchasing film, and so on. The second outer ring lists indirect competitors—HP, Intel, cameraworks.com—who in Kodak's case are increasingly becoming direct competitors. This type of analysis highlights both the opportunities and the challenges a company faces.[13]

::: Analyzing Competitors

Once a company identifies its primary competitors, it must ascertain their strategies, objectives, strengths, and weaknesses.

Strategies

A group of firms following the same strategy in a given target market is called a **strategic group**.[14] Suppose a company wants to enter the major appliance industry. What is its strategic group? It develops the chart shown in Figure 11.3 and discovers four strategic groups based on product quality and level of vertical integration. Group A has one competitor (Maytag); group B has three (General Electric, Whirlpool, and Sears); group C has four; and group D has two. Important insights emerge from this exercise. First, the height of the entry barriers differs for each group. Second, if the company successfully enters a group, the members of that group become its key competitors.

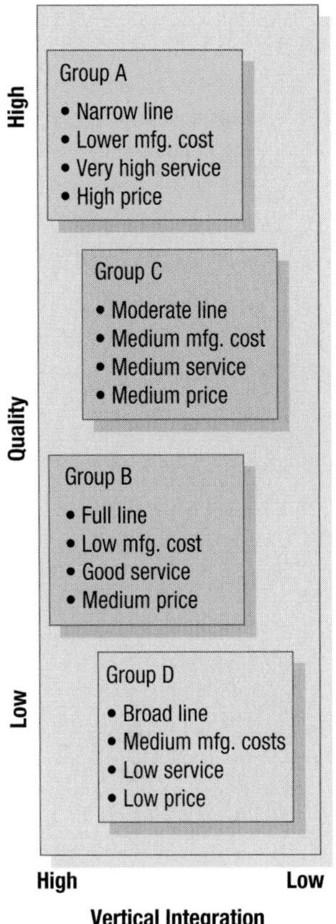

FIG. 11.3

Strategic Groups in the Major Appliance Industry

Objectives

Once a company has identified its main competitors and their strategies, it must ask: What is each competitor seeking in the marketplace? What drives each competitor's behavior? Many factors shape a competitor's objectives, including size, history, current management, and financial situation. If the competitor is a division of a larger company, it is important to know whether the parent company is running it for growth, profits, or milking it.[15]

One useful initial assumption is that competitors strive to maximize profits. However, companies differ in the emphasis they put on short-term versus long-term profits. Many U.S. firms have been criticized for operating on a short-run model, largely because current performance is judged by stockholders who might lose confidence, sell their stock, and cause the company's cost of capital to rise. Japanese firms operate largely on a market-share-maximization model. They receive much of their funds from banks at a lower interest rate and in the past have readily accepted lower profits. An alternative assumption is that each competitor pursues some mix of objectives: current profitability, market share growth, cash flow, technological leadership, or service leadership.

Finally, a company must monitor competitors' expansion plans. Figure 11.4 shows a product-market battlefield map for the personal computer industry. Dell, which started out as a strong force in selling personal computers to individual users, is now a major force in the commercial and industrial market. Other incumbents may try to set up mobility barriers to Dell's further expansion.

Strengths and Weaknesses

A company needs to gather information on each competitor's strengths and weaknesses. Table 11.1 shows the results of a company survey that asked customers to rate its three competitors, A, B, and C, on five attributes. Competitor A turns out to be well known and

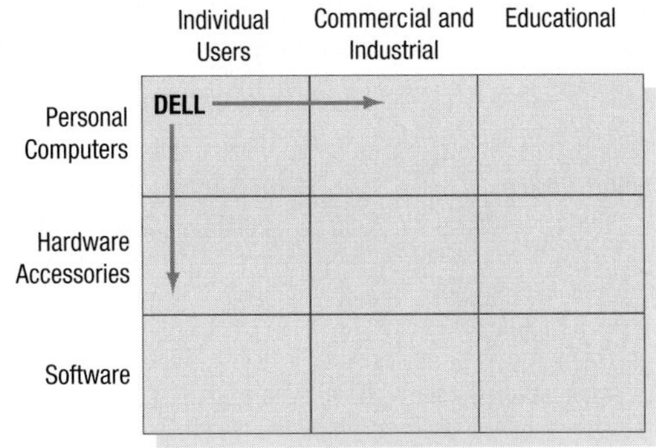

FIG. 11.4

A Competitor's Expansion Plans

TABLE 11.1

Customers' Ratings of Competitors on Key Success Factors

	Customer Awareness	Product Quality	Product Availability	Technical Assistance	Selling Staff
Competitor A	E	E	P	P	G
Competitor B	G	G	E	G	E
Competitor C	F	P	G	F	F

Note: E = excellent, G = good, F = fair, P = poor.

respected for producing high-quality products sold by a good sales force. Competitor A is poor at providing product availability and technical assistance. Competitor B is good across the board and excellent in product availability and sales force. Competitor C rates poor to fair on most attributes. This suggests that the company could attack Competitor A on product availability and technical assistance and Competitor C on almost anything, but should not attack B, which has no glaring weaknesses.

In general, a company should monitor three variables when analyzing competitors:

1. ***Share of market*** – The competitor's share of the target market.
2. ***Share of mind*** – The percentage of customers who named the competitor in responding to the statement, "Name the first company that comes to mind in this industry."
3. ***Share of heart*** – The percentage of customers who named the competitor in responding to the statement, "Name the company from which you would prefer to buy the product."

There is an interesting relationship among these three measures. Table 11.2 shows the numbers for these three measures for the three competitors listed in Table 11.1. Competitor A enjoys the highest market share but is slipping. Its mind share and heart share are also slipping, probably because it is not providing good product availability and technical assistance. Competitor B is steadily gaining market share, probably due to strategies that are increasing its mind share and heart share. Competitor C seems to be stuck at a low level of market share, mind share, and heart share, probably because of its poor product and marketing attributes. We could generalize as follows: *Companies that make steady gains in mind share and heart share will inevitably make gains in market share and profitability.*

To improve market share, many companies benchmark their most successful competitors, as well as world-class performers. The technique and its benefits are described in "Marketing Memo: Benchmarking To Improve Competitive Performance."

Selecting Competitors

After the company has conducted customer value analysis and examined competitors carefully, it can focus its attack on one of the following classes of competitors: strong versus weak, close versus distant, and "good" versus "bad."

- ***Strong versus Weak.*** Most companies aim their shots at weak competitors, because this requires fewer resources per share point gained. Yet, the firm should also compete with strong competitors to keep up with the best. Even strong competitors have some weaknesses.
- ***Close versus Distant.*** Most companies compete with competitors who resemble them the most. Chevrolet competes with Ford, not with Ferrari. Yet companies should also recognize distant competitors. Coca-Cola states that its number-one competitor is tap water, not

TABLE 11.2

Market Share, Mind Share, and Heart Share

	Market Share			Mind Share			Heart Share		
	2000	2001	2002	2000	2001	2002	2000	2001	2002
Competitor A	50%	47%	44%	60%	58%	54%	45%	42%	39%
Competitor B	30	34	37	30	31	35	44	47	53
Competitor C	20	19	19	10	11	11	11	11	8

Pepsi. U.S. Steel worries more about plastic and aluminum than about Bethlehem Steel; museums now worry about theme parks and malls.

- ***"Good" versus "Bad".*** Every industry contains "good" and "bad" competitors.[16] A company should support its good competitors and attack its bad competitors. Good competitors play by the industry's rules; they make realistic assumptions about the industry's growth potential; they set prices in reasonable relation to costs; they favor a healthy industry; they limit themselves to a portion or segment of the industry; they motivate others to lower costs or improve differentiation; and they accept the general level of their share and profits. Bad competitors try to buy share rather than earn it; they take large risks; they invest in overcapacity; and they upset industrial equilibrium.

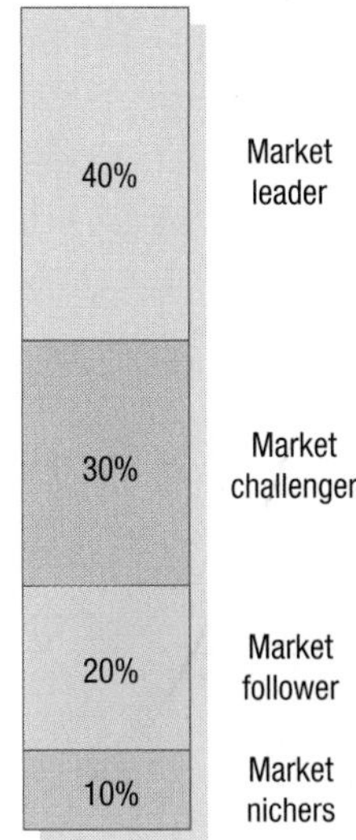

FIG. 11.5

Hypothetical Market Structure

::: Competitive Strategies for Market Leaders

We can gain further insight by classifying firms by the roles they play in the target market: leader, challenger, follower, or nicher. Suppose a market is occupied by the firms shown in Figure 11.5. Forty percent of the market is in the hands of a *market leader;* another 30 percent is in the hands of a *market challenger;* another 20 percent is in the hands of a *market follower,* a firm that is willing to maintain its market share and not rock the boat. The remaining 10 percent is in the hands of *market nichers,* firms that serve small market segments not being served by larger firms.

Many industries contain one firm that is the acknowledged market leader. This firm has the largest market share in the relevant product market, and usually leads the other firms in price changes, new-product introductions, distribution coverage, and promotional intensity. Some well-known market leaders are Microsoft (computer software), Intel (microprocessors), Gatorade (sports drinks), Best Buy (retail electronics), McDonald's (fast food), Gillette (razor blades), UnitedHealth (health insurance), and Visa (credit cards).

Ries and Trout argue that well-known products generally hold a distinctive position in consumers' minds. Nevertheless, unless a dominant firm enjoys a legal monopoly, its life is not altogether easy. It must maintain constant vigilance. A product innovation may come along and hurt the leader (Nokia's and Ericsson's digital cell phones took over from Motorola's analog models). The leader might spend conservatively whereas a challenger spends liberally (Montgomery Ward's lost its retail dominance to Sears after World War II). The leader might misjudge its competition and find itself left behind (as Sears did when it underestimated Kmart and later Wal-Mart). The dominant firm might look old-fashioned against new and peppier rivals (Pepsi has attempted to take share from Coke by portraying itself as the more youthful brand). The dominant firm's costs might rise excessively and

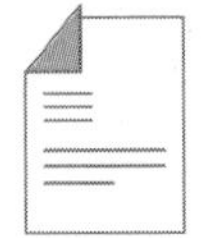

MARKETING MEMO | BENCHMARKING TO IMPROVE COMPETITIVE PERFORMANCE

Benchmarking is the art of learning from companies that perform certain tasks better than other companies. There can be as much as a tenfold difference between the quality, speed, and cost performance of a world-class company and an average company. The aim of benchmarking is to copy or improve on "best practices," either within an industry or across industries. Benchmarking involves seven steps:

1. Determine which functions to benchmark;
2. Identify the key performance variables to measure;
3. Identify the best-in-class companies;
4. Measure performance of best-in-class companies;
5. Measure the company's performance;
6. Specify programs and actions to close the gap; and
7. Implement and monitor results.

How can companies identify best-practice companies? A good starting point is asking customers, suppliers, and distributors whom they rate as doing the best job.

Sources: Robert C. Camp, *Benchmarking: The Search for Industry-Best Practices that Lead to Superior Performance* (White Plains, NY: Quality Resources, 1989); Michael J. Spendolini, *The Benchmarking Book* (New York: Amacom, 1992); Stanley Brown, "Don't Innovate—Imitate!" *Sales & Marketing Management* (January 1995): 24–25; Tom Stemerg, "Spies Like Us," *Inc.* (August 1998): 45–49. See also, <www.benchmarking.org>; Michael Hope, "Contrast and Compare," *Marketing,* August 28, 1997, pp. 11–13; Robert Hiebeler, Thomas B. Kelly, and Charles Ketteman, *Best Practices: Building Your Business with Customer-Focused Solutions* (New York: Arthur Andersen/Simon & Schuster, 1998).

hurt its profits, or a discount competitor can undercut prices. "Marketing Insight: When Your Competitor Delivers More for Less" describes how leaders can respond to an aggressive competitive price discounter.

Consider how hard Hershey is working to maintain its leadership position in the U.S. chocolate candy market.[17]

HERSHEY

Under constant pressure from fast-growing snack makers of all kinds, Hershey Foods Corp., has found that domination of the U.S. chocolate candy business is not enough. Increasingly, consumers are passing up Hershey's candies for chips, sports bars, cereal bars, or granola bars. To maintain profit targets, Hershey has cut costs, dropped weak product lines such as Luden's throat lozenges, cut hundreds of slow-selling package sizes, improved distribution by increasing high-margin convenience store presence, and introduced extensions of its strongest brands such as Reese's Inside Out Cups. To more broadly compete and sustain growth, however, Hershey's is even considering other new snack products. ■

Remaining number one calls for action on three fronts. First, the firm must find ways to expand total market demand. Second, the firm must protect its current market share through good defensive and offensive actions. Third, the firm can try to increase its market share, even if market size remains constant.

Expanding the Total Market

The dominant firm normally gains the most when the total market expands. If Americans increase their consumption of ketchup, Heinz stands to gain the most because it sells almost two-thirds of the country's ketchup. If Heinz can convince more Americans to use ketchup, or to use ketchup with more meals, or to use more ketchup on each occasion, Heinz will benefit considerably. In general, the market leader should look for new customers or more usage from existing customers.

NEW CUSTOMERS Every product class has the potential of attracting buyers who are unaware of the product or who are resisting it because of price or lack of certain features. A company can search for new users among three groups: those who might use it but do not *(market-penetration strategy),* those who have never used it *(new-market segment strategy),* or those who live elsewhere *(geographical-expansion strategy).*

Starbucks Coffee is one of the best-known brands in the world. Starbucks is able to sell a cup of coffee for $3 while the store next door can only get $1. And if you want the popular café latte, it's $4. Starbucks has more than 7,200 locations throughout North America, the Pacific Rim, Europe, and the Middle East, and its annual revenue for 2002 topped $3.3 billion. Its corporate Web site gives a peek into its multipronged approach to growth.[18]

> Starbucks purchases and roasts high-quality whole bean coffees and sells them along with fresh, rich-brewed, Italian style espresso beverages, a variety of pastries and confections, and coffee-related accessories and equipment—primarily through its company-operated retail stores. In addition, Starbucks sells whole bean coffees through a specialty sales group and supermarkets. Additionally, Starbucks produces and sells bottled Frappuccino® coffee drinks and a line of premium ice creams through its joint venture partnerships and offers a line of innovative premium teas produced by its wholly owned subsidiary, Tazo Tea Company. The company's objective is to establish Starbucks as the most recognized and respected brand in the world. To achieve this goal, the company plans to continue to rapidly expand its retail operations, grow its specialty sales and other operations, and selectively pursue opportunities to leverage the Starbucks brand through the introduction of new products and the development of new distribution channels.

MORE USAGE Usage can be increased by increasing the *level* or *quantity* of consumption or increasing the *frequency* of consumption.

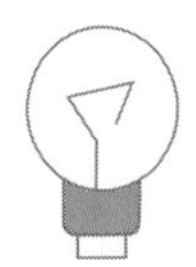

MARKETING INSIGHT | WHEN YOUR COMPETITOR DELIVERS MORE FOR LESS

Companies offering the powerful combination of low prices and high quality are capturing the hearts and wallets of consumers in Europe and the United States, where more than half of the population now shops weekly at mass merchants like Wal-Mart and Target, up from 25 percent in 1996. These and similar value players, such as Aldi, ASDA, Dell, E*TRADE Financial, JetBlue Airways, Ryanair, and Southwest Airlines, are transforming the way consumers of nearly every age and income purchase groceries, apparel, airline tickets, financial services, and computers.

The market share gains of value-based players give their higher-priced rivals definite cause for alarm. After years of near-exclusive sway over all but the most discount-minded consumers, many mainstream companies now face steep cost disadvantages and lack the product and service superiority that once set them apart from low-priced competitors. Today, as value-driven companies in a growing number of industries move from competing solely on price to catching up on attributes such as quality, service, and convenience, traditional players are right to feel threatened.

To compete with value-based rivals, mainstream companies must reconsider the perennial routes to business success: keeping costs in line, finding sources of differentiation, and managing prices effectively. To succeed in value-based markets, companies are required to infuse these timeless strategies with greater intensity and focus and then execute them flawlessly. Differentiation, for example, becomes less about the abstract goal of rising above competitive clutter and more about identifying opportunities left open by the value players' business models. Effective pricing means waging a transaction-by-transaction perception battle to win over those consumers who are predisposed to believe that value-oriented competitors are always cheaper.

Competitive outcomes will be determined, as always, on the ground—in product aisles, merchandising displays, process rethinks, and pricing stickers. When it comes to value-based competition, traditional players can't afford to drop a stitch. Value-driven competitors have changed the expectations of consumers about the trade-off between quality and price. This shift is gathering momentum, placing a new premium on—and adding new twists to—the old imperatives of differentiation and execution.

Differentiation

To counter value-based players, it will be necessary to focus on areas where their business models give other companies room to maneuver. Instead of trying to compete with Wal-Mart and other value retailers on price, for example, Walgreens emphasizes convenience across all elements of its business. It has expanded rapidly to make its stores ubiquitous, meanwhile ensuring that most of them are on corner locations with easy parking. In addition, Walgreens has overhauled its in-store layouts to speed consumers in and out, placing key categories such as convenience foods and one-hour photo services near the front. To protect pharmacy sales, the company has implemented a simple telephone and online preordering system, made it easy to transfer prescriptions between locations around the country, and installed drive-through windows at most freestanding stores. These steps helped Walgreens double its revenue from 1998 to 2002—to over $32 billion, from $15 billion.

Execution

Value-based markets also place a premium on execution, particularly in prices and costs. Kmart's disastrous experience in trying to compete head-on with Wal-Mart highlights the difficulty of challenging value leaders on their own terms. Matching or even beating a value player's prices—as Kmart briefly did—won't necessarily win the battle of consumer perceptions against companies with reputations for the lowest prices. Value players tend to price frequently purchased, easy-to-compare products and services aggressively and to make up for lost margins by charging more for higher-end offerings. Focused advertising to showcase "special buys" and the use of simple, prominent signage enable retailers to get credit for the value they offer and will probably become an ever-more-visible feature of the competitive landscape.

Ultimately, of course, the ability to offer even selectively competitive prices depends on keeping costs in line. Continual improvement is necessary, suggesting an increasing role, in a variety of industries, for Toyota's lean-manufacturing methods, which aim to reduce costs and improve quality constantly and simultaneously. In financial services, for example, banks have used lean techniques to speed check processing and mortgage approvals and to improve call-center performance. Lean operations will probably emerge in more industries. Companies have no choice—those that fail to constantly take out costs may perish.

Source: Adapted from Robert J. Frank, Jeffrey P. George, and Laxman Narasimhan, "When Your Competitor Delivers More for Less," *McKinsey Quarterly* (Winter 2004): 48–59.

The amount of consumption can sometimes be increased through packaging or product design. Larger package sizes have been shown to increase the amount of product that consumers use at one time.[19] The usage of "impulse" consumption products such as soft drinks and snacks increases when the product is made more available.

Increasing frequency of use, on the other hand, involves identifying additional opportunities to use the brand in the same basic way or identifying completely new and different ways to use the brand. In some cases, the product may be seen as useful only in certain places and at certain times, especially if it has strong brand associations to particular usage situations or user types.

To generate additional usage opportunities, a marketing program can communicate the appropriateness and advantages of using the brand more frequently in new or existing situations and/or remind consumers to actually use the brand as close as possible to those situations. The wine industry launched a number of initiatives in the late 1990s to attract Gen-Xers and convince them wine was a "casual, every day libation to be drunk like bottled water, beer or soda."[20]

Another potential opportunity to increase frequency of use is when consumers' perceptions of their usage differs from the reality of their usage. For many products with relatively short life spans, consumers may fail to replace the product when they should because of a tendency to overestimate the length of productive usage.[21] One strategy to speed up product replacement is to tie the act of replacing the product to a certain holiday, event, or time of year. Another strategy might be to provide consumers with better information as to either: (1) when the product was first used or would need to be replaced or (2) the current level of product performance. Each Gillette Mach3 cartridge features a blue stripe that slowly fades with repeated use. After about a dozen shaves, it fades away, signaling the user to move on to the next cartridge.

The second approach is to identify completely new and different applications. For example, food product companies have long advertised new recipes that use their branded products in entirely different ways. Given that the average American eats dry breakfast cereal three mornings a week, cereal manufacturers would gain if they could promote cereal eating on other occasions—perhaps as a snack.

ARM & HAMMER

After discovering that consumers used Arm & Hammer baking soda brand as a refrigerator deodorant, a heavy promotion campaign was launched focusing on this single use. After succeeding in getting half of the homes in America to place an open box of baking soda in the refrigerator, the brand was then extended into a variety of new product categories, such as toothpaste, antiperspirant, and laundry detergent.

Product development can spur new uses. Chewing gum manufacturers are exploring ways to make "nutracuetical" products as a cheap, effective delivery mechanism for medicine. The majority of Adam's chewing gums (number two in the world) claim health benefits. Aquafresh and Arm & Hammer are two dental gums that both achieved some success.[22]

Defending Market Share

While trying to expand total market size, the dominant firm must continuously defend its current business. The leader is like a large elephant being attacked by a swarm of bees. Tropicana must constantly guard against Minute Maid orange juice; Duracell against Energizer batteries; Hertz against Avis rental cars; Kodak against Fuji film.[23] Sometimes the competitor is domestic; sometimes it is foreign.

What can the market leader do to defend its terrain? The most constructive response is *continuous innovation.* The leader leads the industry in developing new product and customer services, distribution effectiveness, and cost cutting. It keeps increasing its competitive strength and value to customers.

Consider how Caterpillar has become dominant in the construction-equipment industry despite charging a premium price and being challenged by a number of able competitors, including John Deere, J. I. Case, Komatsu, and Hitachi. Several policies combine to explain Caterpillar's success:[24]

- ***Premium performance.*** Caterpillar produces high-quality equipment known for its reliability and durability—key buyer considerations in the choice of heavy industrial equipment.
- ***Extensive and efficient dealership system.*** Caterpillar maintains the largest number of independent construction-equipment dealers in the industry, all of whom carry a complete line of Caterpillar equipment.
- ***Superior service.*** Caterpillar has built a worldwide parts and service system second to none in the industry.

- ***Full-line strategy.*** Caterpillar produces a full line of construction equipment to enable customers to do one-stop buying.
- ***Good financing.*** Caterpillar provides a wide range of financial terms for customers who buy its equipment.

Akio Morita and an early Walkman. Morita refused to abandon his idea for a portable cassette player, saying Sony doesn't serve markets, Sony creates markets. And he was certainly right: by the twentieth anniversary of the Walkman, Sony had sold over 250 million units.

In satisfying customer needs, a distinction can be drawn between responsive marketing, anticipative marketing, and creative marketing. A *responsive* marketer finds a stated need and fills it. An *anticipative* marketer looks ahead into what needs customers may have in the near future. A *creative* marketer discovers and produces solutions customers did not ask for but to which they enthusiastically respond.

Sony exemplifies creative marketing. It has introduced many successful new products that customers never asked for or even thought were possible: Walkmans, VCRs, videocameras, CDs. Sony is a *market-driving firm,* not just a market-driven firm. Akio Morita, its founder, once proclaimed that Sony doesn't serve markets; Sony creates markets.[25] The Walkman is a classic example: In the late 1970s, Akio Morita was working on a pet project that would revolutionize the way people listened to music: a portable cassette player he called the Walkman. Engineers at the company insisted there was little demand for such a product, but Morita refused to part with his vision. By the twentieth anniversary of the Walkman, Sony had sold over 250 million in nearly 100 different models.[26]

Even when it does not launch offensives, the market leader must not leave any major flanks exposed. It must consider carefully which terrains are important to defend, even at a loss, and which can be surrendered.[27] The aim of defensive strategy is to reduce the probability of attack, divert attacks to less threatening areas, and lessen their intensity. The defender's speed of response can make an important difference in the profit consequences. A dominant firm can use the six defense strategies summarized in Figure 11.6.[28]

POSITION DEFENSE Position defense involves occupying the most desirable market space in the minds of the consumers, making the brand almost impregnable, like Tide laundry detergent with cleaning; Crest toothpaste with cavity prevention; and Pampers diapers with dryness.

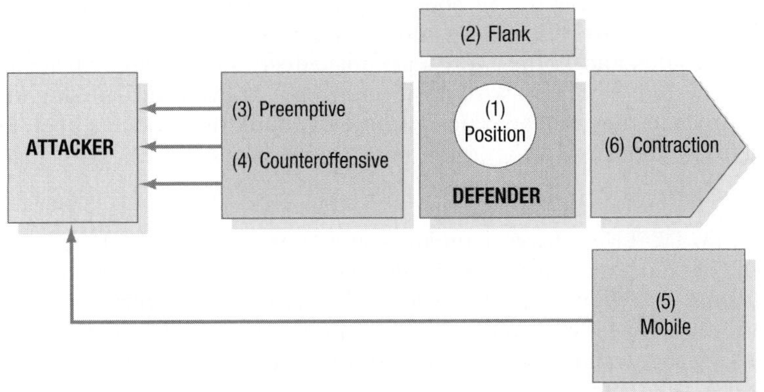

FIG. 11.6

Six Types of Defense Strategies

FLANK DEFENSE Although position defense is important, the market leader should also erect outposts to protect a weak front or possibly serve as an invasion base for counterattack. When Heublein's brand Smirnoff, which had 23 percent of the U.S. vodka market, was attacked by low-priced competitor Wolfschmidt, Heublein actually *raised* the price and put the increased revenue into advertising. At the same time, Heublein introduced another brand, Relska, to compete with Wolfschmidt and still another, Popov, to sell for less than Wolfschmidt. This strategy effectively bracketed Wolfschmidt and protected Smirnoff's flanks.

PREEMPTIVE DEFENSE A more aggressive maneuver is to attack *before* the enemy starts its offense. A company can launch a preemptive defense in several ways. It can wage guerrilla action across the market—hitting one competitor here, another there—and keep everyone off balance; or it can try to achieve a grand market envelopment. Bank of America's 13,000 ATMs and 4,500 branches nationwide now provide steep competition to local and regional banks. It can send out market signals to dissuade competitors from attacking.[29] It can introduce a stream of new products, making sure to precede them with *preannouncements*—deliberate communications regarding future actions.[30] Preannouncements can signal to competitors that they will have to fight to gain market share.[31] If Microsoft announces plans for a new-product development, smaller firms may choose to concentrate their development efforts in other directions to avoid head-to-head competition. Some high-tech firms have even been accused of engaging in "vaporware"—preannouncing products that miss delivery dates or are not even ever introduced.[32]

COUNTEROFFENSIVE DEFENSE When attacked, most market leaders will respond with a counterattack. Counterattacks can take many forms. In a *counteroffensive,* the leader can meet the attacker frontally or hit its flank or launch a pincer movement. An effective counterattack is to invade the attacker's main territory so that it will have to pull back to defend the territory. After FedEx watched UPS successfully invade its airborne delivery system, FedEx invested heavily in ground delivery service through a series of acquisitions to challenge UPS on its home turf.[33] Another common form of counteroffensive is the exercise of economic or political clout. The leader may try to crush a competitor by subsidizing lower prices for the vulnerable product with revenue from its more profitable products; or the leader may prematurely announce that a product upgrade will be available, to prevent customers from buying the competitor's product; or the leader may lobby legislators to take political action to inhibit the competition.

MOBILE DEFENSE In mobile defense, the leader stretches its domain over new territories that can serve as future centers for defense and offense through market broadening and market diversification. *Market broadening* involves shifting focus from the current product to the underlying generic need. The company gets involved in R&D across the whole range of technology associated with that need. Thus "petroleum" companies sought to recast themselves into "energy" companies. Implicitly, this change demanded that they dip their research fingers into the oil, coal, nuclear, hydroelectric, and chemical industries. *Market diversification* involves shifting into unrelated industries. When U.S. tobacco companies like Reynolds and Philip Morris acknowledged the growing curbs on cigarette smoking, they were not content with position defense or even with looking for cigarette substitutes. Instead they moved quickly into new industries, such as beer, liquor, soft drinks, and frozen foods.

CONTRACTION DEFENSE Large companies sometimes recognize that they can no longer defend all of their territory. The best course of action then appears to be *planned contraction* (also called *strategic withdrawal*): giving up weaker territories and reassigning resources to stronger territories. Diageo acquired most of Seagram's brands in 2001 and spun off Pillsbury and Burger King so it could concentrate on powerhouse alcoholic beverage brands such as Smirnoff vodka, J&B scotch, and Tanqueray gin.[34]

Expanding Market Share

Market leaders can improve their profitability by increasing their market share. In many markets, one share point is worth tens of millions of dollars. A one-share-point gain in coffee is worth $48 million; and in soft drinks, $120 million! No wonder normal competition has turned into marketing warfare.

Gaining increased share in the served market, however, does not automatically produce higher profits—especially for labor-intensive service companies that may not experience many economies of scale. Much depends on the company's strategy.

Because the cost of buying higher market share may far exceed its revenue value, a company should consider four factors before pursuing increased market share:

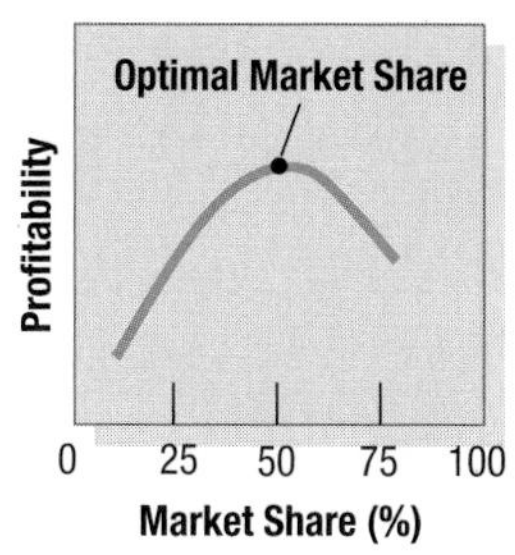

FIG. 11.7

The Concept of Optimal Market Share

- The possibility of provoking antitrust action, such as recently occurred with investigations of Microsoft and Intel. Jealous competitors are likely to cry "monopoly" if a dominant firm makes further inroads. This rise in risk would diminish the attractiveness of pushing market share gains too far.
- Economic cost. Figure 11.7 shows that profitability might fall with further market share gains after some level. In the illustration, the firm's *optimal market share* is 50 percent. The cost of gaining further market share might exceed the value. The "holdout" customers may dislike the company, be loyal to competitive suppliers, have unique needs, or prefer dealing with smaller suppliers. The cost of legal work, public relations, and lobbying rises with market share. Pushing for higher market share is less justified when there are few scale or experience economies, unattractive market segments exist, buyers want multiple sources of supply, and exit barriers are high. Some market leaders have even increased profitability by selectively decreasing market share in weaker areas.[35]
- Pursuing the wrong marketing-mix strategy. Miller Brewing spent *$1.5 billion* on measured advertising during the 1990s but still managed to lose market share. Its ad campaigns were highly distinctive but, unfortunately, also largely irrelevant to its targeted customer base.[36] When it was acquired by SAB in 2002, new management overhauled marketing operations.[37] Companies successfully gaining share typically outperform competitors in three areas: new-product activity, relative product quality, and marketing expenditures.[38] Companies that cut prices more deeply than competitors typically do not achieve significant gains, as enough rivals meet the price cuts and others offer other values so that buyers do not switch. Competitive rivalry and price cutting have been shown to be most intense in industries with high fixed costs, high inventory costs, and stagnant primary demand, such as steel, auto, paper, and chemicals.[39]
- The effect of increased market share on actual and perceived quality.[40] Too many customers can put a strain on the firm's resources, hurting product value and service delivery. America Online experienced growing pains when its customer base expanded, resulting in system outages and access problems. Consumers may also infer that "bigger is not better" and assume that growth will lead to a deterioration of quality. If "exclusivity" is a key brand benefit, existing customers may resent additional new customers.

::: Other Competitive Strategies

Firms that occupy second, third, and lower ranks in an industry are often called runner-up, or trailing firms. Some, such as Colgate, Ford, Avis, and PepsiCo, are quite large in their own right. These firms can adopt one of two postures. They can attack the leader and other competitors in an aggressive bid for further market share (market challengers), or they can play ball and not "rock the boat" (market followers).

Market-Challenger Strategies

Many market challengers have gained ground or even overtaken the leader. Toyota today produces more cars than General Motors and British Airways flies more international passengers than the former leader, Pan Am, did in its heyday. Airbus delivers more aircraft than Boeing.

BOEING AND AIRBUS

When it closed the books on December 31, 2003, Airbus, the company that began in 1970 as an unwieldy confederation of European aerospace firms, had replaced 89-year-old Boeing as the world's largest manufacturer of commercial aircraft. Airbus was on course to deliver 300 new airplanes in 2003 versus 280 from Boeing—just five years earlier in 1998 Boeing delivered twice as many as Airbus. What happened? Challenger Airbus began with a clean slate. It created an innovative new product line equipped with modern features—the massive A380 designed to carry 555 passengers at only 2.5 cents per seat mile. In contrast, Boeing had an arcane production system developed in World War II, and it couldn't match Airbus's advances without redesigning aircraft at prohibitive costs. Once the manufacturing marvel of the world, Boeing fell behind in both technology and manufacturing efficiency during the 1990s. "A new player that's aggressive and focused will almost always gain ground on an established player," says Dean Headley, co-author of a national airline quality report. And in the aircraft business, when it can take nearly a decade to go from design to launch, lost ground can be incredibly difficult to regain.[41]

Challengers like Airbus set high aspirations, leveraging their resources while the market leader often runs the business as usual. That's why the CEO of Airbus, Noel Foregard, vows to keep what he calls the "mentality of a challenger." Now let's examine the competitive attack strategies available to market challengers.

DEFINING THE STRATEGIC OBJECTIVE AND OPPONENT(S) A market challenger must first define its strategic objective. Most aim to increase market share. The challenger must decide whom to attack:

- ***It can attack the market leader.*** This is a high-risk but potentially high-payoff strategy and makes good sense if the leader is not serving the market well. The alternative strategy is to out-innovate the leader across the whole segment. Xerox wrested the copy market from 3M by developing a better copying process. Later, Canon grabbed a large chunk of Xerox's market by introducing desk copiers.
- ***It can attack firms of its own size that are not doing the job and are underfinanced.*** These firms have aging products, are charging excessive prices, or are not satisfying customers in other ways.
- ***It can attack small local and regional firms.*** Several major banks grew to their present size by gobbling up smaller regional banks, or "guppies."

If the attacking company goes after the market leader, its objective might be to gain a certain share. Miller Brewing is under no illusion that it can topple Anheuser-Busch's Budweiser in the domestic premium beer market—it is simply seeking a larger share. If the attacking company goes after a small local company, its objective might be to drive that company out of existence.

CHOOSING A GENERAL ATTACK STRATEGY Given clear opponents and objectives, what attack options are available? We can distinguish among five attack strategies: frontal, flank, encirclement, bypass, and guerilla attacks.

Frontal Attack In a pure *frontal attack,* the attacker matches its opponent's product, advertising, price, and distribution. The principle of force says that the side with the greater manpower (resources) will win. A modified frontal attack, such as cutting price vis-à-vis the opponent's, can work if the market leader does not retaliate and if the competitor convinces the market that its product is equal to the leader's. Helene Curtis is a master at convincing the market that its brands—such as Suave and Finesse—are equal in quality but a better value than higher-priced brands.

Flank Attack An enemy's weak spots are natural targets. A *flank attack* can be directed along two strategic dimensions—geographic and segmental. In a geographic attack, the challenger spots areas where the opponent is underperforming. For example, some of IBM's former mainframe rivals, such as Honeywell, chose to set up strong sales branches in medium- and smaller-sized cities that were relatively neglected by IBM. The other flanking strategy is to serve uncovered market needs, as Japanese automakers did when they developed more fuel-efficient cars.

A flanking strategy is another name for identifying shifts in market segments that are causing gaps to develop, then rushing in to fill the gaps and develop them into strong segments.

LEAPFROG ENTERPRISES INC.

Based in Emeryille, California, this small "David" of a toy company succeeded in using a flank attack against "Goliath" Mattel. In 1999, when the educational toy category couldn't have been drearier, LeapFrog unleashed a product it touted as "a toy in its shape, but an educational product in its soul." LeapFrog's toy, the LeapPad, is a laptop-like device that teaches children age 4 to 8 reading, math, spelling, and geography in a fun way. Parents happily paid $50 for the LeapPad consoles and $15 for content cartridges. In December 2000, the product raced past Razor scooter to become the top-selling toy—the first time in at least 15 years that an educational toy was number one. In 2001, LeapPad was the number-one selling toy in the nation, and so far the company has sold more than 8.6 million systems. Of course, its success has spurred Mattel to compete head-on by launching its own version of LeapPad, an easy-to-use Power Touch Learning System.[42]

Flanking is in the best tradition of modern marketing, which holds that the purpose of marketing is to discover needs and satisfy them. Flank attacks are particularly attractive to a challenger with fewer resources than its opponent and are much more likely to be successful than frontal attacks.

Encirclement Attack The encirclement maneuver is an attempt to capture a wide slice of the enemy's territory through a "blitz." It involves launching a grand offensive on several fronts. Encirclement makes sense when the challenger commands superior resources and believes a swift encirclement will break the opponent's will. In making a stand against arch rival Microsoft, Sun Microsystems licensed its Java software to hundreds of companies and millions of software developers for all sorts of consumer devices. As consumer electronics products began to go digital, Java started appearing in a wide range of gadgets.

Bypass Attack The most indirect assault strategy is the *bypass.* It means bypassing the enemy and attacking easier markets to broaden one's resource base. This strategy offers three lines of approach: diversifying into unrelated products, diversifying into new geographical markets, and leapfrogging into new technologies to supplant existing products. Pepsi used a bypass strategy against Coke by purchasing: (1) orange juice giant Tropicana for $3.3 billion in 1998, which owned almost twice the market share of Coca-Cola's Minute Maid, and (2) The Quaker Oats Company for $14 billion in 2000. (The Quaker Oats Company owns Gatorade Thirst Quenchers, which boasts a huge market share lead over the Coca-Cola Company's Powerade.)[43]

Technological leapfrogging is a bypass strategy practiced in high-tech industries. The challenger patiently researches and develops the next technology and launches an attack, shifting the battleground to its territory, where it has an advantage. Nintendo's successful attack in the video-game market was precisely about wresting market share by introducing a superior technology and redefining the "competitive space." Then Sega/Genesis did the same with more advanced technology, and now Sony's PlayStation has grabbed the technological lead to gain almost 60 percent of the video-game market.[44] Challenger Google used technological leapfrogging to overtake Yahoo! and become the market leader in search. Now another company is using the same tactic to try to become the "Google" of e-mail:

STATA LABS

If Raymie Stata, co-founder of San Mateo–based Stata Labs, has his way you will "bloomba" your e-mail in the same way that you "google" a company name or product on the Internet. He created his Bloomba e-mail management system in response to flaws in Microsoft's Outlook, which is used by 50 percent of office workers. Stata feels that people waste precious time adapting to what he sees as a counterintuitive e-mail management system. Rather than using folders or other complicated filing systems, Bloomba features a powerful search function that indexes all of your messages—even attachments—and lets you search for them in seconds. While it has yet to overtake Microsoft's Outlook, business journalists are hailing Bloomba's technology as the wave of the future for serious e-mail communicators.[45]

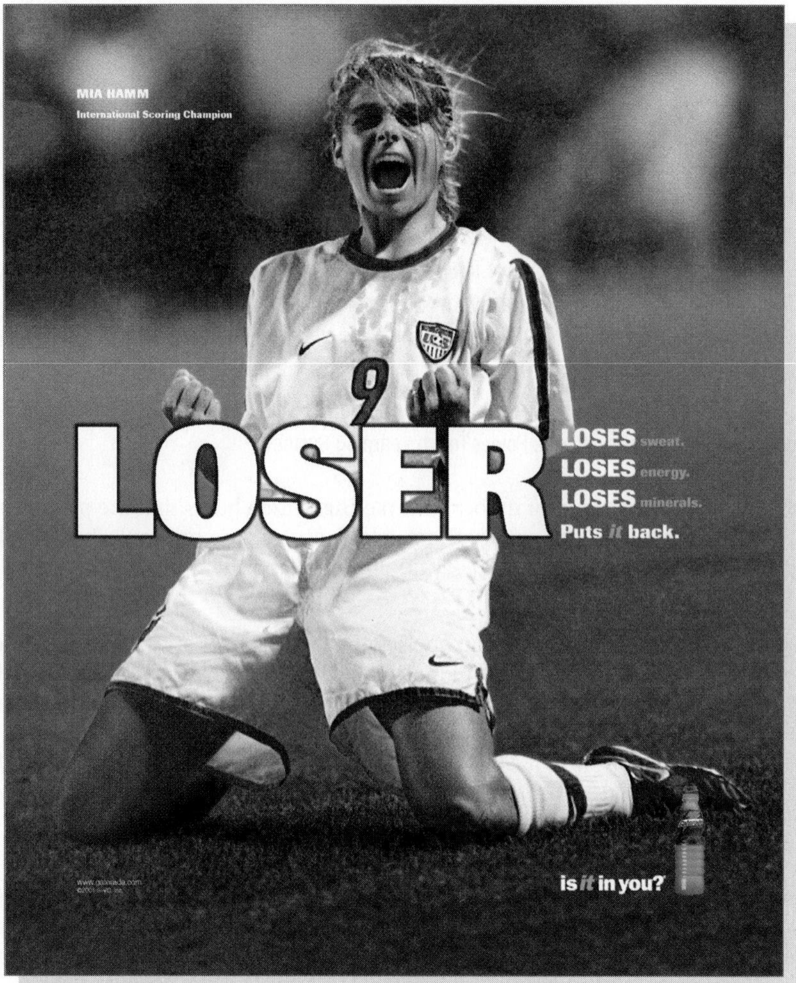

A Gatorade ad with the soccer star Mia Hamm. In a bypass strategy against Coca-Cola, Pepsi bought The Quaker Oats Company, owner of Gatorade Thirst Quenchers, which has a much larger share of the sports drink market than Coca-Cola's Powerade.

Guerrilla Warfare Guerrilla warfare consists of waging small, intermittent attacks to harass and demoralize the opponent and eventually secure permanent footholds. The guerrilla challenger uses both conventional and unconventional means of attack. These include selective price cuts, intense promotional blitzes, and occasional legal action. Princeton Review successfully challenged Kaplan Educational Centers, the largest test-preparation business in the United States, through e-mail horror stories about Kaplan and brash ads—"Stanley's a wimp," or "Friends don't let friends take Kaplan"—while always touting the Princeton Review's smaller, livelier classes.

Normally, guerrilla warfare is practiced by a smaller firm against a larger one. The smaller firm launches a barrage of attacks in random corners of the larger opponent's market in a manner calculated to weaken the opponent's market power. Military dogma holds that a continual stream of minor attacks usually creates more cumulative impact, disorganization, and confusion in the enemy than a few major attacks. A guerrilla campaign can be expensive, although admittedly less expensive than a frontal, encirclement, or flank attack. Guerrilla warfare is more a preparation for war than a war itself. Ultimately, it must be backed by a stronger attack if the challenger hopes to beat the opponent.

CHOOSING A SPECIFIC ATTACK STRATEGY The challenger must go beyond the five broad strategies and develop more specific strategies:

- ***Price discount.*** The challenger can offer a comparable product at a lower price. This is the strategy of discount retailers. Three conditions must be fulfilled. First, the challenger must convince buyers that its product and service are comparable to the leader's. Second, buyers must be price sensitive. Third, the market leader must refuse to cut its price in spite of the competitor's attack.

- ***Lower price goods.*** The challenger can offer an average- or lower-quality product at a much lower price. Little Debbie Snack Cakes were priced lower than Drake's and outsold Drake's by 20 to 1. Firms that establish themselves through a lower-price strategy, however, can be attacked by firms whose prices are even lower.
- ***Value-priced goods and services.*** In recent years companies ranging from retailers such as Target and airlines such as Southwest are combining low prices and high quality to snag market share from market leaders. In the United Kingdom, premium retailers like Boots and Sainsbury are now scrambling to meet intensifying price—and quality—competition from ASDA and Tesco.[46]
- ***Prestige goods.*** A market challenger can launch a higher-quality product and charge a higher price than the leader. Mercedes gained on Cadillac in the U.S. market by offering a car of higher quality at a higher price.
- ***Product proliferation.*** The challenger can attack the leader by launching a larger product variety, thus giving buyers more choice. Baskin-Robbins achieved its growth in the ice cream business by promoting more flavors—31—than its larger competitors.
- ***Product innovation.*** The challenger can pursue product innovation. 3M typically enters new markets by introducing a product improvement or breakthrough.
- ***Improved services.*** The challenger can offer new or better services to customers. Avis's famous attack on Hertz, "We're only second. We try harder," was based on promising and delivering cleaner cars and faster service than Hertz.
- ***Distribution innovation.*** A challenger might develop a new channel of distribution. Avon became a major cosmetics company by perfecting door-to-door selling instead of battling other cosmetic firms in conventional stores.
- ***Manufacturing-cost reduction.*** The challenger might achieve lower manufacturing costs than its competitors through more efficient purchasing, lower labor costs, and more modern production equipment.
- ***Intensive advertising promotion.*** Some challengers attack the leader by increasing expenditures on advertising and promotion. Substantial promotional spending, however, is usually not a sensible strategy unless the challenger's product or advertising message is superior.

A challenger's success depends on combining several strategies to improve its position over time.

SAMSUNG

Korean consumer electronics giant Samsung has used many of the challenger strategies to take on Japanese manufacturers and begin outselling them across a wide range of products. Like many other Asian companies, Samsung used to stress volume and market domination rather than profitability. Yet during the Asian financial crisis of the late 1990s, when other Korean *chaobols* collapsed beneath a mountain of debt, Samsung took a different tack. It cut costs and placed new emphasis on manufacturing flexibility, which allows its consumer electronics goods to go from project phase to store shelves within six months. It also began a serious focus on innovation, using technological leapfrogging to produce state-of-the-art mobile telephone handsets that are big sellers not only across Asia but also in Europe and the United States.[47]

"Marketing Memo: Making Smaller Better" provides some additional tips for challenger brands.

Market-Follower Strategies

Some years ago, Theodore Levitt wrote an article entitled "Innovative Imitation," in which he argued that a strategy of *product imitation* might be as profitable as a strategy of *product innovation*.[48] The innovator bears the expense of developing the new product, getting it into distribution, and informing and educating the market. The reward for all this work and risk is normally market leadership. However, another firm can come along and copy or improve on the new product. Although it probably will not overtake the leader, the follower can achieve high profits because it did not bear any of the innovation expense.

S&S CYCLE

S&S Cycle is the biggest supplier of complete engines and major motor parts to more than 15 companies that build several thousand Harley-like cruiser bikes each year. These cloners charge as much as $30,000 for their customized creations. S&S has built its name by improving on Harley-Davidson's handiwork. Its customers are often would-be Harley buyers frustrated by long waiting lines at the dealers. Other customers simply want the incredibly powerful S&S engines. S&S stays abreast of its evolving market by ordering a new Harley bike every year and taking apart the engine to see what it can improve upon.[49]

Many companies prefer to follow rather than challenge the market leader. Patterns of "conscious parallelism" are common in capital-intensive, homogeneous-product industries, such as steel, fertilizers, and chemicals. The opportunities for product differentiation and image differentiation are low; service quality is often comparable; and price sensitivity runs high. The mood in these industries is against short-run grabs for market share because that strategy only provokes retaliation. Most firms decide against stealing one anothers' customers. Instead, they present similar offers to buyers, usually by copying the leader. Market shares show high stability.

This is not to say that market followers lack strategies. A market follower must know how to hold current customers and win a fair share of new customers. Each follower tries to bring distinctive advantages to its target market—location, services, financing. Because the follower is often a major target of attack by challengers, it must keep its manufacturing costs low and its product quality and services high. It must also enter new markets as they open up. The follower has to define a growth path, but one that does not invite competitive retaliation. Four broad strategies can be distinguished:

1. ***Counterfeiter*** – The counterfeiter duplicates the leader's product and package and sells it on the black market or through disreputable dealers. Music record firms, Apple Computer, and Rolex have been plagued with the counterfeiter problem, especially in Asia.

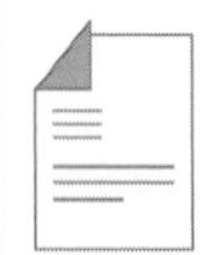

MARKETING MEMO — MAKING SMALLER BETTER

Adam Morgan offers eight suggestions on how small brands can better compete:

1. ***Break with your immediate past***—Don't be afraid to ask "dumb" questions to challenge convention and view your brand differently.
2. ***Build a "lighthouse identity"***—Establish values and communicate who and why you are (e.g., Apple).
3. ***Assume thought leadership of the category***—Break convention in terms of representation (what you say about yourself), where you say it (medium), and experience (what you do beyond talk).
4. ***Create symbols of reevaluation***—A rocket uses half of its fuel in the first mile to break loose from the gravitational pull—you may need to polarize people.
5. ***Sacrifice***—Focus your target, message, reach and frequency, distribution, and line extensions and recognize that less can be more.
6. ***Overcommit***—Although you may do fewer things, do "big" things when you do them.
7. ***Use publicity and advertising to enter popular culture***—Unconventional communications can get people talking.
8. ***Be idea-centered, not consumer-centered***—Sustain challenger momentum by not losing sight of what the brand is about and can be, and redefine marketing support and the center of the company to reflect this vision.

Source: Adam Morgan, *Eating the Big Fish: How Challenger Brands Can Compete Against Brand Leaders* (New York: John Wiley & Sons, 1999).

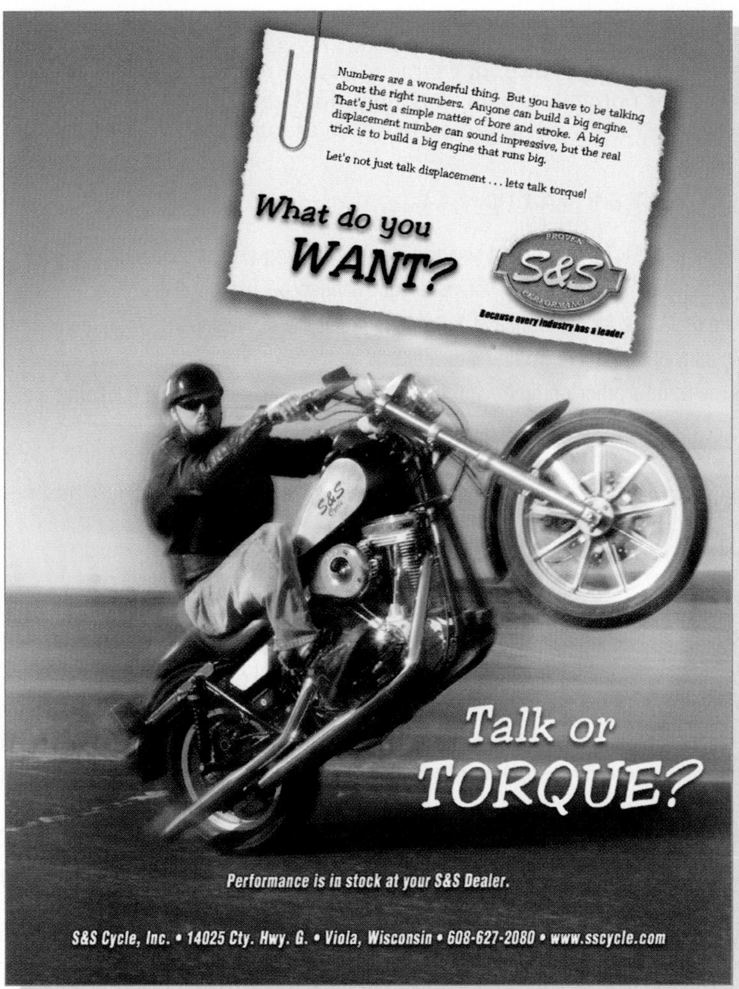

Market follower strategies: S&S Cycle supplies engines and parts to companies that build Harley-Davidson clones. S&S has a reputation for building powerful engines that improve on the Harley product.

2. ***Cloner*** – The cloner emulates the leader's products, name, and packaging, with slight variations. For example, Ralcorp Holding Inc., sells imitations of name-brand cereals in lookalike boxes. Its Tasteeos, Fruit Rings, and Corn Flakes sell for nearly $1 a box less than the leading name brands.
3. ***Imitator*** – The imitator copies some things from the leader but maintains differentiation in terms of packaging, advertising, pricing, or location. The leader does not mind the imitator as long as the imitator does not attack the leader aggressively. Fernandez Pujals grew up in Fort Lauderdale, Florida, and took Domino's home delivery idea to Spain, where he borrowed $80,000 to open his first store in Madrid. His TelePizza chain now operates almost 1,000 stores in Europe and Latin America.
4. ***Adapter*** – The adapter takes the leader's products and adapts or improves them. The adapter may choose to sell to different markets, but often the adapter grows into the future challenger, as many Japanese firms have done after adapting and improving products developed elsewhere.

What does a follower earn? Normally, less than the leader. For example, a study of food-processing companies showed the largest firm averaging a 16 percent return on investment; the number-two firm, 6 percent; the number-three firm, −1 percent, and the number-four firm, −6 percent. In this case, only the top two firms have profits. No wonder Jack Welch, former CEO of GE, told his business units that each must reach the number-one or -two position in its market or else! Followership is often not a rewarding path.

Market-Nicher Strategies

An alternative to being a follower in a large market is to be a leader in a small market, or niche. Smaller firms normally avoid competing with larger firms by targeting small markets of little or no interest to the larger firms. Here is an example.

LOGITECH INTERNATIONAL

Logitech has become a $1.3 billion global success story by making every variation of computer mouse imaginable. The company turns out mice for left- and right-handed people, cordless mice that use radio waves, mice shaped like real mice for children, and 3-D mice that let the user appear to move behind screen objects. It sells to OEMs as well as via its own brand at retail. Its global dominance in the mouse category enabled the company to expand into other computer peripherals, such as PC headsets, PC gaming peripherals, and Webcams.[50]

Even large, profitable firms use niching strategies for some of their business units or companies.

ITW

Illinois Tool Works (ITW) manufactures thousands of products, including nails, screws, plastic six-pack holders for soda cans, bicycle helmets, backpacks, plastic buckles for pet collars, resealable food packages, and more. Since the late 1980s, the company has made between 30 and 40 acquisitions each year, which added new products to the product line. ITW has more than 500 highly autonomous and decentralized business units. When one division commercializes a new product, the product and personnel are spun off into a new entity.[51]

Firms with low shares of the total market can be highly profitable through smart niching. A. T. Cross niched itself in the high-price writing instruments market with its famous gold and silver items. Family-run Tire Rack sells 2 million specialty tires a year through the Internet, telephone, and mail, from its South Bend, Indiana, location.[52] Such companies tend to offer high value, charge a premium price, achieve lower manufacturing costs, and shape a strong corporate culture and vision. New Balance is a classic example of a small company that has successfully used market-nicher strategies to establish a strong market position.

NEW BALANCE

Despite the fact that it has no celebrity endorsers and does comparatively little advertising, New Balance has achieved more customer loyalty than any other athletic shoe brand. Its secret? A truly distinctive product. New Balance offers customers athletic shoes of varying widths. It targets the relatively neglected older market segment of fairly serious athletes age 25 to 45. Its low-key advertising appears in niche magazines like *Outside*, *New England Runner*, and *Prevention*, and on cable TV channels such as CNN, Golf Channel, and A&E. Consistency and focus have paid dividends. With only 3.7 percent of the market in 1999, sales grew to almost a billion dollars by 2002, making the brand the number-three player in the category.[53]

In a study of hundreds of business units, the Strategic Planning Institute found that the return on investment averaged 27 percent in smaller markets, but only 11 percent in larger markets.[54] Why is niching so profitable? The main reason is that the market nicher ends up knowing the target customers so well that it meets their needs better than other firms selling to this niche casually. As a result, the nicher can charge a substantial price over costs. The nicher achieves *high margin,* whereas the mass marketer achieves *high volume.*

Nichers have three tasks: creating niches, expanding niches, and protecting niches. Niching carries a major risk in that the market niche might dry up or be attacked. The company is then stuck with highly specialized resources that may not have high-value alternative uses.

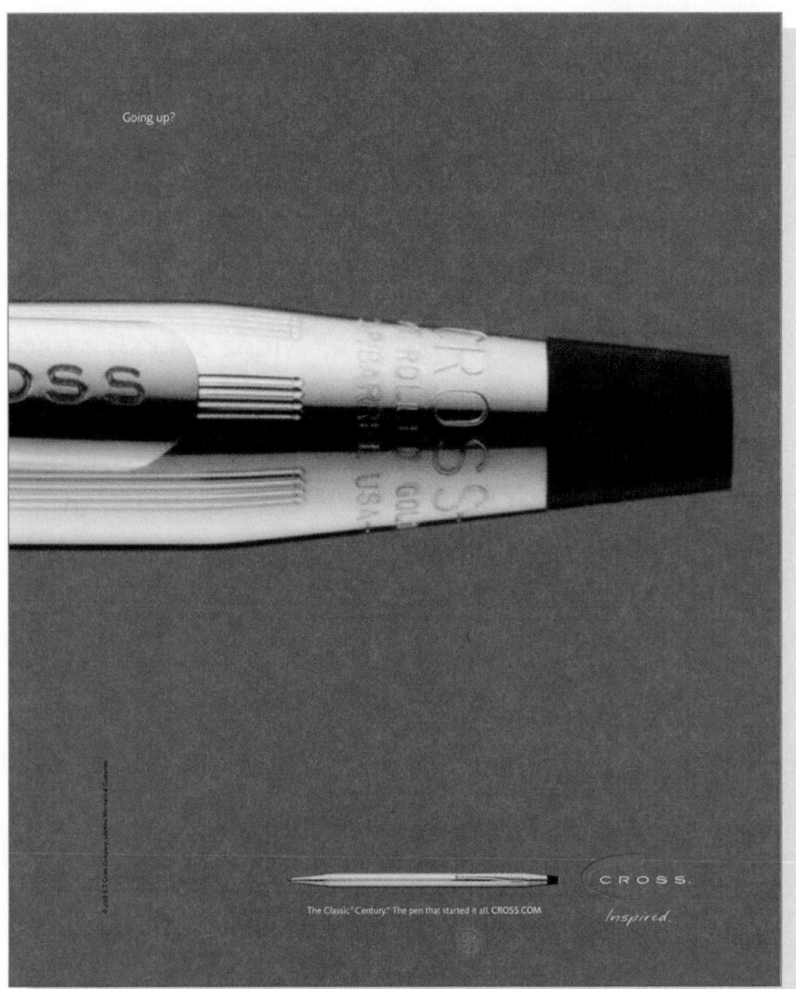

Going up?
CROSS
The Classic® Century.® The pen that started it all. CROSS.COM
CROSS.
Inspired.

Market nicher strategies: A.T. Cross's famous gold and silver pens are in the high-priced writing instruments niche.

ZIPPO

With smoking on a steady decline, Bradford, Pennsylvania–based Zippo Manufacturing is finding the market for its iconic metal cigarette lighter drying up. Zippo marketers now find themselves needing to diversify and to broaden their focus to "selling flame." With a goal of reducing reliance on tobacco-related products to 50 percent of revenue by 2010, the company introduced a long, slender multipurpose lighter for candles, grills, and fireplaces in 2001; has explored licensing arrangements with suppliers of flame-related outdoor products; and has acquired Case Cutlery, a knifemaker.[55]

Because niches can weaken, the firm must continually create new ones. "Marketing Memo: Niche Specialist Roles" outlines some options. The firm should "stick to its niching" but not necessarily to its niche. That is why *multiple niching* is preferable to *single niching*. By developing strength in two or more niches, the company increases its chances for survival.

Firms entering a market should aim at a niche initially rather than the whole market. (See "Marketing Memo: Strategies for Entering Markets Held by Incumbent Firms.") The cell phone industry has experienced phenomenal growth but is now facing fierce competition as the number of new potential users dwindles. Through innovative marketing, Boost Mobile and Virgin have successfully tapped into one of the few remaining high-growth segments: Generation Y customers entering the market.[56]

VIRGIN GROUP LTD.

While Virgin is a big player in music, air travel, and other industries, it is the new kid on the block in the wireless business. Yet, rather than launch a frontal attack on AT&T Wireless, Cingular, or Verizon, Virgin Mobile is targeting young phone users and was the first wireless company to expressly target this group. Virgin Mobile offers one of the simplest prepaid plans around with no contracts and no hidden fees. The company touts cool features such as a "rescue ring" to escape a boring date or the voice of Isaac Hayes or Grandpa Munster for the greet-

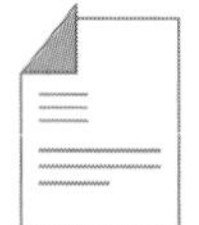

MARKETING MEMO — NICHE SPECIALIST ROLES

The key idea in successful nichemanship is specialization. Here are some possible niche roles:

- ***End-user specialist:*** The firm specializes in serving one type of end-use customer. For example, a *value-added reseller (VAR)* customizes the computer hardware and software for specific customer segments and earns a price premium in the process.
- ***Vertical-level specialist:*** The firm specializes at some vertical level of the production-distribution value chain. A copper firm may concentrate on producing raw copper, copper components, or finished copper products.
- ***Customer-size specialist:*** The firm concentrates on selling to either small, medium-sized, or large customers. Many nichers specialize in serving small customers who are neglected by the majors.
- ***Specific-customer specialist:*** The firm limits its selling to one or a few customers. Many firms sell their entire output to a single company, such as Sears or General Motors.
- ***Geographic specialist:*** The firm sells only in a certain locality, region, or area of the world.
- ***Product or product-line specialist:*** The firm carries or produces only one product line or product. A firm may produce only lenses for microscopes. A retailer may carry only ties.
- ***Product-feature specialist:*** The firm specializes in producing a certain type of product or product feature. Rent-a-Wreck, for example, is a California car-rental agency that rents only "beat-up" cars.
- ***Job-shop specialist:*** The firm customizes its products for individual customers.
- ***Quality-price specialist:*** The firm operates at the low- or high-quality ends of the market. Hewlett-Packard specializes in the high-quality, high-price end of the hand-calculator market.
- ***Service specialist:*** The firm offers one or more services not available from other firms. An example would be a bank that takes loan requests over the phone and hand-delivers the money to the customer.
- ***Channel specialist:*** The firm specializes in serving only one channel of distribution. For example, a soft-drink company decides to make a very large-sized soft drink available only at gas stations.

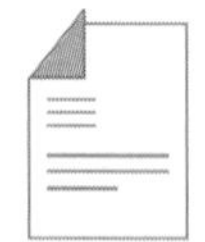

MARKETING MEMO — STRATEGIES FOR ENTERING MARKETS HELD BY INCUMBENT FIRMS

Carpenter and Nakamoto examined strategies for launching a new product into a market dominated by one brand, such as Jell-O or FedEx. (These brands, which include many market pioneers, are particularly difficult to attack because many are the standard against which others are judged.) They identified four strategies that have good profit potential in this situation:

1. ***Differentiation:*** Positioning away from the dominant brand with a comparable or premium price and heavy advertising spending to establish the new brand as a credible alternative. Example: Honda's motorcycle challenges Harley-Davidson.
2. ***Challenger:*** Positioning close to the dominant brand with heavy advertising spending and comparable or premium price to challenge the dominant brand as the category standard. Example: Pepsi competing against Coke.
3. ***Niche:*** Positioning away from the dominant brand with a high price and a low advertising budget to exploit a profitable niche. Example: Tom's of Maine all-natural toothpaste competing against Crest.
4. ***Premium:*** Positioning near the dominant brand with little advertising spending but a premium price to move "up market" relative to the dominant brand. Examples: Godiva chocolate and Häagen-Dazs ice cream competing against standard brands.

Sources: Gregory S. Carpenter and Kent Nakamoto, "Competitive Strategies for Late Entry into a Market with a Dominant Brand," *Management Science* (October 1990): 1268–1278; Gregory S. Carpenter and Kent Nakamoto, "The Impact of Consumer Preference Formation on Marketing Objectives and Competitive Second Mover Strategies," *Journal of Consumer Psychology* 5, no. 4 (1996): 325–358; Venkatesh Shankar, Gregory Carpenter, and Lakshman Krishnamurthi, "Late Mover Advantage: How Innovative Late Entrants Outsell Pioneers," *Journal of Marketing Research* 35 (February 1998): 54–70.

ing. And, to emphasize that the phone plan has "nothing to hide," Virgin runs provocative ads featuring nude actors. Branson himself even showed up half-naked in New York's Times Square to kick off the company's 50–50 joint venture with Sprint PCS Group. The niching strategy seems to be working; in a very short period of time, Virgin Mobile gained more than 1 million users.[57]

::: Balancing Customer and Competitor Orientations

We have stressed the importance of a company's positioning itself competitively as a market leader, challenger, follower, or nicher. Yet a company must not spend all its time focusing on competitors.

Competitor-Centered Companies

A *competitor-centered company* sets its course as follows:

Situation

- Competitor W is going all out to crush us in Miami.
- Competitor X is improving its distribution coverage in Houston and hurting our sales.
- Competitor Y has cut its price in Denver, and we lost three share points.
- Competitor Z has introduced a new service feature in New Orleans, and we are losing sales.

Reactions

- We will withdraw from the Miami market because we cannot afford to fight this battle.
- We will increase our advertising expenditure in Houston.
- We will meet competitor Y's price cut in Denver.
- We will increase our sales promotion budget in New Orleans.

This kind of planning has some pluses and minuses. On the positive side, the company develops a fighter orientation. It trains its marketers to be on constant alert, to watch for weaknesses in its competitors' and its own position. On the negative side, the company is too reactive. Rather than formulating and executing a consistent, customer-oriented strategy, it determines its moves based on its competitors' moves. It does not move toward its own goals. It does not know where it will end up, because so much depends on what its competitors do.

Customer-Centered Companies

A *customer-centered company* focuses more on customer developments in formulating its strategies.

Situation

- The total market is growing at 4 percent annually.
- The quality-sensitive segment is growing at 8 percent annually.
- The deal-prone customer segment is also growing fast, but these customers do not stay with any supplier very long.
- A growing number of customers have expressed an interest in a 24-hour hot line, which no one in the industry offers.

Reactions

- We will focus more effort on reaching and satisfying the quality segment of the market. We will buy better components, improve quality control, and shift our advertising theme to quality.
- We will avoid cutting prices and making deals because we do not want the kind of customer that buys this way.
- We will install a 24-hour hot line if it looks promising.

Clearly, the customer-centered company is in a better position to identify new opportunities and set a course that promises to deliver long-run profits. By monitoring customer needs, it can decide which customer groups and emerging needs are the most important to serve, given its resources and objectives. Jeff Bezos, founder of Amazon.com, strongly favors a customer-centered orientation: "Amazon.com's mantra has been that we were going to obsess over our customers and not our competitors. We watch our competitors, learn from them, see the things that they [were doing for customers] and copy those things as much as we can. But we were never going to obsess over them."[58]

SUMMARY :::

1. To prepare an effective marketing strategy, a company must study competitors as well as actual and potential customers. Companies need to identify competitors' strategies, objectives, strengths, and weaknesses.
2. A company's closest competitors are those seeking to satisfy the same customers and needs and making similar offers. A company should also pay attention to latent competitors, who may offer new or other ways to satisfy the same needs. A company should identify competitors by using both industry and market-based analyses.
3. A market leader has the largest market share in the relevant product market. To remain dominant, the leader looks for ways to expand total market demand, attempts to protect its current market share, and perhaps tries to increase its market share.
4. A market challenger attacks the market leader and other competitors in an aggressive bid for more market share. Challengers can choose from five types of general attack; challengers must also choose specific attack strategies.
5. A market follower is a runner-up firm that is willing to maintain its market share and not rock the boat. A follower can play the role of counterfeiter, cloner, imitator, or adapter.
6. A market nicher serves small market segments not being served by larger firms. The key to nichemanship is specialization. Nichers develop offerings to fully meet a certain group of customers' needs, commanding a premium price in the process.
7. As important as a competitive orientation is in today's global markets, companies should not overdo the emphasis on competitors. They should maintain a good balance of consumer and competitor monitoring.

APPLICATIONS :::

Marketing Debate How Do You Attack a Category Leader?

Attacking a leader is always difficult. Some strategists recommend attacking a leader "head-on" by targeting its strengths. Other strategists disagree and recommend flanking and attempting to avoid the leader's strengths.

Take a position: The best way to challenge a leader is to attack its strengths versus The best way to attack a leader is to avoid a head-on assault and to adopt a flanking strategy.

Marketing Discussion

Pick an industry. Classify firms according to the four different roles they might play: leader, challenger, follower, and nicher. How would you characterize the nature of competition? Do the firms follow the principles described in this chapter?

PART

5

SHAPING THE MARKET OFFERINGS

IN THIS CHAPTER, WE WILL ADDRESS THE FOLLOWING QUESTIONS:

1. What are the characteristics of products and how can they be classified?
2. How can companies differentiate products?
3. How can a company build and manage its product mix and product lines?
4. How can companies combine products to create strong co-brands or ingredient brands?
5. How can companies use packaging, labeling, warranties, and guarantees as marketing tools?

CHAPTER 12 ::: SETTING PRODUCT STRATEGY

twelve

At the heart of a great brand is a great product. Product is a key element in the market offering. Market leaders generally offer products and services of superior quality.

Perhaps no other high-end product combines the skilled craftsmanship, market dominance, and longevity of Steinway pianos. One-hundred-fifty years old, the family-run company retains many of the same manufacturing processes from its humble origins in New York City. Although mass-produced pianos take roughly 20 days to build, building a Steinway takes nine months to a year. A Steinway piano requires 12,000 parts, most of them handcrafted, and relies on 120 technical patents and innovations. Despite the fact that it can produce only a few thousand pianos a year and has only 2 percent of all keyboard unit sales in the United States, Steinway commands 25 percent of the sales dollars and 35 percent of the profits. Not surprisingly, Steinway owns the market in concert halls (where it has a market share over 95 percent) and with composers and musicians.[1]

A Steinway concert grand: the great product at the heart of a great brand.

Marketing planning begins with formulating an offering to meet target customers' needs or wants. The customer will judge the offering by three basic elements: product features and quality, services mix and quality, and price (see Figure 12.1). In this chapter, we examine product; in Chapter 13, services; and in Chapter 14, prices. All three elements must be meshed into a competitively attractive offering.

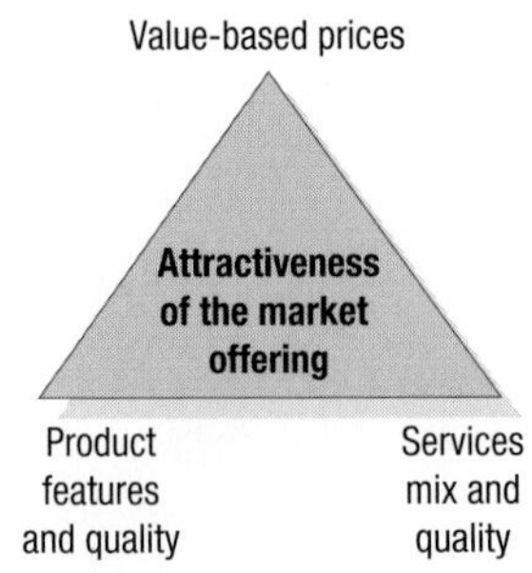

FIG. 12.1

Components of the Market Offering

::: Product Characteristics and Classifications

Many people think that a product is a tangible offering, but a product can be more than that. A **product** is anything that can be offered to a market to satisfy a want or need. Products that are marketed include physical goods, services, experiences, events, persons, places, properties, organizations, information, and ideas.

Product Levels: The Customer Value Hierarchy

In planning its market offering, the marketer needs to address five product levels (see Figure 12.2).[2] Each level adds more customer value, and the five constitute a **customer value hierarchy**. The fundamental level is the **core benefit**: the service or benefit the customer is really buying. A hotel guest is buying "rest and sleep." The purchaser of a drill is buying "holes." Marketers must see themselves as benefit providers.

At the second level, the marketer has to turn the core benefit into a **basic product**. Thus a hotel room includes a bed, bathroom, towels, desk, dresser, and closet.

At the third level, the marketer prepares an **expected product**, a set of attributes and conditions buyers normally expect when they purchase this product. Hotel guests expect a clean bed, fresh towels, working lamps, and a relative degree of quiet. Because most hotels can meet this minimum expectation, the traveler normally will settle for whichever hotel is most convenient or least expensive.

At the fourth level, the marketer prepares an **augmented product** that exceeds customer expectations. In developed countries, brand positioning and competition take place at this level. In developing countries and emerging markets such as China and India, however, competition takes place mostly at the expected product level.

Differentiation arises on the basis of product augmentation. Product augmentation also leads the marketer to look at the user's total **consumption system**: the way the user performs the tasks of getting and using products and related services.[3] As Levitt observed long ago:

FIG. 12.2

Five Product Levels

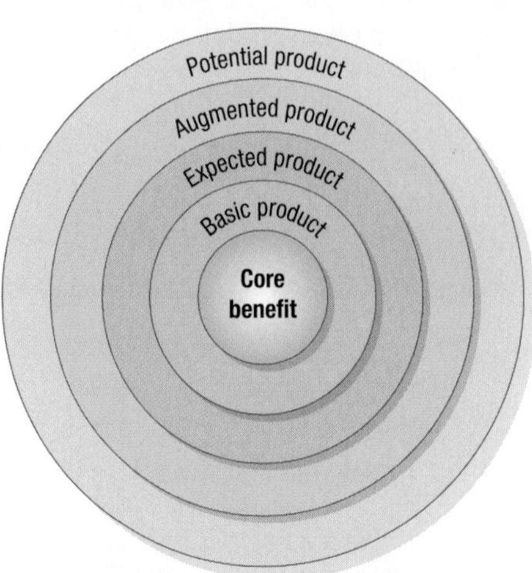

> The new competition is not between what companies produce in their factories, but between what they add to their factory output in the form of packaging, services, advertising, customer advice, financing, delivery arrangements, warehousing, and other things that people value.[4]

Some things should be noted about product-augmentation strategy. First, each augmentation adds cost. Second, augmented benefits soon become expected benefits and necessary points-of-parity. Today's hotel guests expect cable or satellite television with a remote control and high-speed Internet access or two phone lines. This means competitors will have to search for still other features and benefits. Third, as companies raise the price of their augmented product, some competitors offer a "stripped-down" version at a much lower price. Thus, alongside the growth of fine hotels like Four Seasons and Ritz Carlton, we see the emergence of lower-cost hotels and motels like Motel 6 and Comfort Inn, which cater to clients who simply want the basic product.

JAMESTOWN CONTAINER CO.

What could be harder to differentiate than corrugated cardboard? Yet, Jamestown Container Company, the lead supplier of corrugated products for companies such as 3M, has formed strategic partnerships with area manufacturers to provide every part of the shipping system. It not only provides boxes, but also offers tape, shrinkwrap, and everything else needed either to display or to ship a customer's final product. "It's a combination for survival," says the company's Chief Operating Officer. "More customers want to call one place for everything. We have to keep reinventing ourselves and form these kinds of relationships to remain competitive."[5]

At the fifth level stands the **potential product**, which encompasses all the possible augmentations and transformations the product or offering might undergo in the future. Here is where companies search for new ways to satisfy customers and distinguish their offer. For instance, in an era when customers are demanding ever-faster Internet and wireless connections, Verizon is investing its capital in creating a raft of potential products:

VERIZON

Rather than be seen as a follower in the highly competitive telecom industry, Verizon is pushing fast into totally new territory. For one thing, Verizon is rolling out fiber-optic connections to every home and business in its 29-state territory over the next 10 to 15 years. This will allow the lightning-fast transmission of everything from traditional phone service to HDTV. The company is no less aggressive when it comes to wireless technology. Verizon has covered Manhattan with more than 1,000 Wi-Fi hot spots that lets any Verizon broadband subscriber use a laptop to tap into the Net wirelessly when near a Verizon pay phone. The company is also deploying 3G, a third-generation wireless service that lets customers make super-speedy Net connections from their mobile phones. In short, the company is investing billions in services customers don't even know they want yet, but which—Verizon is betting—will set the standard for the entire industry.[6]

Also consider the customization platforms new e-commerce sites are offering, from which companies can learn by seeing what different customers prefer. Proctor & Gamble, for example, has developed Reflect.com, which offers customized beauty products created interactively on the Web site.

Product Classifications

Marketers have traditionally classified products on the basis of characteristics: durability, tangibility, and use (consumer or industrial). Each product type has an appropriate marketing-mix strategy.[7]

DURABILITY AND TANGIBILITY Products can be classified into three groups, according to durability and tangibility:

1. ***Nondurable goods*** are tangible goods normally consumed in one or a few uses, like beer and soap. Because these goods are consumed quickly and purchased frequently, the appropriate strategy is to make them available in many locations, charge only a small markup, and advertise heavily to induce trial and build preference.

2. ***Durable goods*** are tangible goods that normally survive many uses: refrigerators, machine tools, and clothing. Durable products normally require more personal selling and service, command a higher margin, and require more seller guarantees.
3. ***Services*** are intangible, inseparable, variable, and perishable products. As a result, they normally require more quality control, supplier credibility, and adaptability. Examples include haircuts, legal advice, and appliance repairs.

CONSUMER-GOODS CLASSIFICATION The vast array of goods consumers buy can be classified on the basis of shopping habits. We can distinguish among convenience, shopping, specialty, and unsought goods.

The consumer usually purchases **convenience goods** frequently, immediately, and with a minimum of effort. Examples include tobacco products, soaps, and newspapers. Convenience goods can be further divided. *Staples* are goods consumers purchase on a regular basis. A buyer might routinely purchase Heinz ketchup, Crest toothpaste, and Ritz crackers. *Impulse goods* are purchased without any planning or search effort. Candy bars and magazines are impulse goods. *Emergency goods* are purchased when a need is urgent—umbrellas during a rainstorm, boots and shovels during the first winter snowstorm. Manufacturers of impluse and emergency goods will place them in those outlets where consumers are likely to experience an urge or compelling need to make a purchase.

Shopping goods are goods that the consumer, in the process of selection and purchase, characteristically compares on such bases as suitability, quality, price, and style. Examples include furniture, clothing, used cars, and major appliances. Shopping goods can be further divided. *Homogeneous shopping goods* are similar in quality but different enough in price to justify shopping comparisons. *Heterogeneous shopping goods* differ in product features and services that may be more important than price. The seller of heterogeneous shopping goods carries a wide assortment to satisfy individual tastes and must have well-trained salespeople to inform and advise customers.

Specialty goods have unique characteristics or brand identification for which a sufficient number of buyers are willing to make a special purchasing effort. Examples include cars, stereo components, photographic equipment, and men's suits. A Mercedes is a specialty good because interested buyers will travel far to buy one. Specialty goods do not involve making comparisons; buyers invest time only to reach dealers carrying the wanted products. Dealers do not need convenient locations, although they must let prospective buyers know their locations.

Unsought goods are those the consumer does not know about or does not normally think of buying, like smoke detectors. The classic examples of known but unsought goods are life insurance, cemetery plots, gravestones, and encyclopedias. Unsought goods require advertising and personal-selling support.

INDUSTRIAL-GOODS CLASSIFICATION Industrial goods can be classified in terms of how they enter the production process and their relative costliness. We can distinguish three groups of industrial goods: materials and parts, capital items, and supplies and business services. **Materials and parts** are goods that enter the manufacturer's product completely. They fall into two classes: raw materials and manufactured materials and parts. *Raw materials* fall into two major groups: *farm products* (e.g., wheat, cotton, livestock, fruits, and vegetables) and *natural products* (e.g., fish, lumber, crude petroleum, iron ore). Farm products are supplied by many producers, who turn them over to marketing intermediaries, who provide assembly, grading, storage, transportation, and selling services. Their perishable and seasonal nature gives rise to special marketing practices. Their commodity character results in relatively little advertising and promotional activity, with some exceptions. At times, commodity groups will launch campaigns to promote their product—potatoes, cheese, and beef. Some producers brand their products—Dole salads, Mott's apples, and Chiquita bananas.

Natural products are limited in supply. They usually have great bulk and low unit value and must be moved from producer to user. Fewer and larger producers often market them directly to industrial users. Because the users depend on these materials, long-term supply contracts are common. The homogeneity of natural materials limits the amount of demand-creation activity. Price and delivery reliability are the major factors influencing the selection of suppliers.

Manufactured materials and parts fall into two categories: component materials (iron, yarn, cement, wires) and component parts (small motors, tires, castings). *Component materials* are usually fabricated further—pig iron is made into steel, and yarn is woven into cloth.

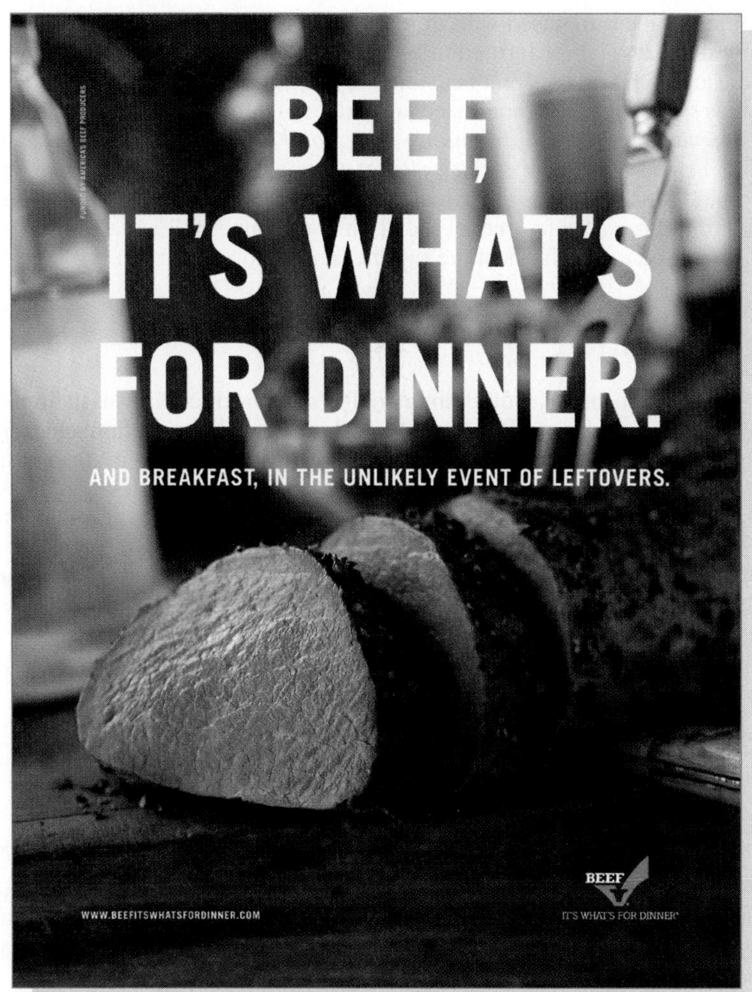

A Beef Council ad, part of the "Beef, It's What's for Dinner" campaign of TV and print ads designed to promote beef as a good food.

The standardized nature of component materials usually means that price and supplier reliability are key purchase factors. *Component parts* enter the finished product with no further change in form, as when small motors are put into vacuum cleaners, and tires are put on automobiles. Most manufactured materials and parts are sold directly to industrial users. Price and service are major marketing considerations, and branding and advertising tend to be less important.

Capital items are long-lasting goods that facilitate developing or managing the finished product. They include two groups: installations and equipment. *Installations* consist of buildings (factories, offices) and heavy equipment (generators, drill presses, mainframe computers, elevators). Installations are major purchases. They are usually bought directly from the producer, with the typical sale preceded by a long negotiation period. The producer's sales force includes technical personnel. Producers have to be willing to design to specification and to supply postsale services. Advertising is much less important than personal selling.

Equipment comprises portable factory equipment and tools (hand tools, lift trucks) and office equipment (personal computers, desks). These types of equipment do not become part of a finished product. They have a shorter life than installations but a longer life than operating supplies. Although some equipment manufacturers sell direct, more often they use intermediaries, because the market is geographically dispersed, the buyers are numerous, and the orders are small. Quality, features, price, and service are major considerations. The sales force tends to be more important than advertising, although the latter can be used effectively.

Supplies and business services are short-term goods and services that facilitate developing or managing the finished product. Supplies are of two kinds: *maintenance and repair items* (paint, nails, brooms), and *operating supplies* (lubricants, coal, writing paper, pencils). Together, they go under the name of MRO goods. Supplies are the equivalent of convenience goods; they are usually purchased with minimum effort on a straight rebuy basis. They are normally marketed through intermediaries because of their low unit value and the great number and geographic dispersion of customers. Price and service are important considerations, because suppliers are standardized and brand preference is not high.

Business services include *maintenance and repair services* (window cleaning, copier repair) and *business advisory services* (legal, management consulting, advertising). Maintenance and repair services are usually supplied under contract by small producers or are available from the manufacturers of the original equipment. Business advisory services are usually purchased on the basis of the supplier's reputation and staff.

::: Differentiation

To be branded, products must be differentiated. Physical products vary in their potential for differentiation. At one extreme, we find products that allow little variation: chicken, aspirin, and steel. Yet even here, some differentiation is possible: Perdue chickens, Bayer aspirin, and India's Tata Steel have carved out distinct identities in their categories. Procter & Gamble makes Tide, Cheer, and Gain laundry detergents, each with a separate brand identity. At the other extreme are products capable of high differentiation, such as automobiles, commercial buildings, and furniture. Here the seller faces an abundance of design parameters, including form, features, performance quality, conformance quality, durability, reliability, repairability, and style.[8]

Marketers are always looking for new dimensions of differentiation. Otis Elevator Company has upped the ante in its category by making its elevators smarter:

OTIS ELEVATOR COMPANY

At a typical bank of elevators in an office building lobby, you press the "up" button and take the first elevator that comes, with no idea how many stops there will be until you get to your floor. Now Otis has developed a "smart" elevator. You key in your floor on a centralized panel. The panel tells you which elevator is going to take you to your floor. Your elevator takes you right to your floor and races back to the lobby. With this simple change, Otis has managed to turn every elevator into an express. This remarkable differentiator means a speedier ride and less groaning and sighing by riders, but it also has big benefits for builders. Buildings need fewer elevators for a given density of people, so builders can use the extra space for people rather than people conveyers.[9]

Product Differentiation

FORM Many products can be differentiated in **form**—the size, shape, or physical structure of a product. Consider the many possible forms taken by products such as aspirin. Although aspirin is essentially a commodity, it can be differentiated by dosage size, shape, color, coating, or action time.

FEATURES Most products can be offered with varying **features** that supplement its basic function. A company can identify and select appropriate new features by surveying recent buyers and then calculating *customer value* versus *company cost* for each potential feature. The company should also consider how many people want each feature, how long it would take to introduce each feature, and whether competitors could easily copy the feature. Companies must also think in terms of feature bundles or packages. Auto companies often manufacture cars at several "trim levels." This lowers manufacturing and inventory costs. Each company must decide whether to offer feature customization at a higher cost or a few standard packages at a lower cost.

PERFORMANCE QUALITY Most products are established at one of four performance levels: low, average, high, or superior. **Performance quality** is the level at which the product's primary characteristics operate. Firms should not necessarily design the highest performance level possible. The manufacturer must design a performance level appropriate to the target market and competitors' performance levels. A company must also manage performance quality through time. Continuously improving the product can produce the high returns and market share. Lowering quality in an attempt to cut costs often has dire consequences. Schlitz, the number-two beer brand in the United States in the 1960s and 1970s, was driven into the dust because management adopted a financially motivated strategy to increase its short-term profits and curry favor with shareholders. In fact, quality is becoming an increasingly important parameter for differentiation as companies adopt a value model and provide higher quality for less money. Cataloger J. Crew is raising the prices of its merchandise as it raises the quality bar higher:

J. CREW

J. Crew is returning to a tradition of preppy quality goods. It is adding pleats to the backs of its shirts and having them made in Italy instead of China. Its shoes are also being made in Italy, and the company is tailoring trousers to fit better. The cover of the Fall 2003 catalog reflected the company's emphasis on quality by crisply portraying each color-dyed stitch, the weave of the wool, and each tiny pearl collar button.[10]

CONFORMANCE QUALITY Buyers expect products to have a high **conformance quality**, which is the degree to which all the produced units are identical and meet the promised specifications. Suppose a Porsche 944 is designed to accelerate to 60 miles per hour within 10 seconds. If every Porsche 944 coming off the assembly line does this, the model is said to have high conformance quality. The problem with low conformance quality is that the product will disappoint some buyers.

DURABILITY **Durability**, a measure of the product's expected operating life under natural or stressful conditions, is a valued attribute for certain products. Buyers will generally pay more for vehicles and kitchen appliances that have a reputation for being long lasting. However, this rule is subject to some qualifications. The extra price must not be excessive. Furthermore, the product must not be subject to rapid technological obsolescence, as is the case with personal computers and video cameras.

RELIABILITY Buyers normally will pay a premium for more reliable products. **Reliability** is a measure of the probability that a product will not malfunction or fail within a specified time period. Maytag, which manufactures major home appliances, has an outstanding reputation for creating reliable appliances.

REPAIRABILITY **Repairability** is a measure of the ease of fixing a product when it malfunctions or fails. Ideal repairability would exist if users could fix the product themselves with little cost in money or time. Some products include a diagnostic feature that allows service people to correct a problem over the telephone or advise the user how to correct it. Many computer hardware and software companies offer technical support over the phone, or by fax or e-mail. Cisco put together a Knowledge Base of Frequently Asked Questions (FAQs) on its Web site which it estimates handles about 80 percent of the roughly 4 million monthly requests for information, and saves the company $250 million annually. Each new call and solution goes to a tech writer who adds the solution to the FAQs, thus reducing the number of future phone calls.[11]

STYLE **Style** describes the product's look and feel to the buyer. Car buyers pay a premium for Jaguars because of their extraordinary look. Aesthetics play a key role in such brands as Absolut vodka, Apple computers, Montblanc pens, Godiva chocolate, and Harley-Davidson motorcycles.[12] Style has the advantage of creating distinctiveness that is difficult to copy. On the negative side, strong style does not always mean high performance. A car may look sensational but spend a lot of time in the repair shop.

Design: The Integrative Force

As competition intensifies, design offers a potent way to differentiate and position a company's products and services.[13] In increasingly fast-paced markets, price, and technology are not enough. Design is the factor that will often give a company its competitive edge. **Design** is the totality of features that affect how a product looks and functions in terms of customer requirements.

Design is particularly important in making and marketing retail services, apparel, packaged goods, and durable equipment. All the qualities we have discussed are design parameters. The designer has to figure out how much to invest in form, feature development, performance, conformance, durability, reliability, repairability, and style. To the company, a well-designed product is one that is easy to manufacture and distribute. To the customer, a well-designed product is one that is pleasant to look at and easy to open, install, use, repair, and dispose of. The designer has to take all these factors into account.

The arguments for good design are particularly compelling for smaller consumer-products companies and start-ups that don't have big advertising dollars. That's how one small brewery got noticed.

FLYING FISH BREWING CO.

Before he started his company, founder Gene Muller sent Pentagram Design Company a case of beer bottles with blank labels and a note that said, "This space available for good design." He told Pentagram partner Michael Beirut that he wanted something a breed apart from the usual mountain-range motif themes that everyone else seemed to be doing. The Pentagram design Muller liked most and picked for his start-up was a fish-bone propeller plane. Flying Fish Brewing Company was born. Not only has the eye-catching image helped sell the beer, but the company's merchandise sales (T-shirts, hats, and pint glasses) have been surprisingly strong, especially at music festivals.[14]

Certain countries are winning on design: Italian design in apparel and furniture; Scandinavian design for functionality, aesthetics, and environmental consciousness. Braun, a German division of Gillette, has elevated design to a high art in its electric shavers, coffeemakers, hair dryers, and food processors. The company's design department enjoys equal status with engineering and manufacturing. The Danish firm Bang & Olufsen has received many kudos for the design of its stereos, TV equipment, and telephones. "Marketing Insight: Design as a Powerful Marketing Tool" describes some successes and failures in design.

Services Differentiation

When the physical product cannot easily be differentiated, the key to competitive success may lie in adding valued services and improving their quality. The main service differentiators are: ordering ease, delivery, installation, customer training, customer consulting, and maintenance and repair.

ORDERING EASE **Ordering ease** refers to how easy it is for the customer to place an order with the company. Baxter Healthcare has eased the ordering process by supplying hospitals with computer terminals through which they send orders directly to Baxter. Many banks now provide home banking software to help customers get information and do transactions more efficiently. Consumers are now able to order and receive groceries without going to the supermarket.

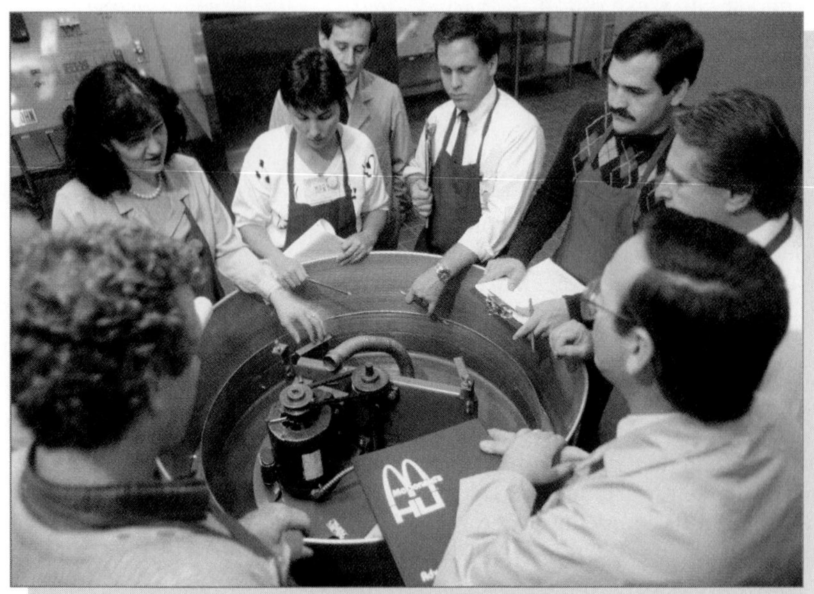

A group of franchisees learning the business at McDonald's Hamburger U. in Oak Brook, Illinois.

DELIVERY **Delivery** refers to how well the product or service is delivered to the customer. It includes speed, accuracy, and care attending the delivery process. Today's customers have grown to expect delivery speed: pizza delivered in one-half hour, film developed in one hour, eyeglasses made in one hour, cars lubricated in 15 minutes. Levi Strauss, Benetton, and The Limited have adopted computerized *quick response systems* (QRS) that link the information systems of their suppliers, manufacturing plants, distribution centers, and retailing outlets. Cemex, a giant cement company based in Mexico, has transformed the cement busi-

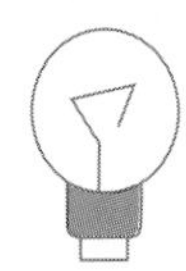

MARKETING INSIGHT | DESIGN AS A POWERFUL MARKETING TOOL

Manufacturers, service providers, and retailers seek new designs to create differentiation and establish a more complete connection with consumers. Holistic marketers recognize the emotional power of design and the importance to consumers of how things look and feel. Design is now more fully integrated into the marketing management process. For example:

- After seeing some of their brands lose share to competitors with stronger designs and aesthetics, Procter & Gamble appointed a Chief Design Officer in 2001 and now hands out an A. G. Lafley Design award each Fall. Lafley, P&G's CEO, is credited with pushing for more products to involve design at the front end—not as an afterthought. These products, such as Crest Whitestrips, Olay Daily Facials, and the whole line of Swiffer Quick Clean products, have generated more trials, more repurchases, and more sales.
- Sweden's IKEA has become one of the top furniture retailers in the world in part through its ability to design and manufacture inexpensive furniture that doesn't seem cheap. Another Scandinavian company, Finland's Nokia, is credited with taking a little black blob with tiny buttons and turning it into an object of desire. Nokia was the first to introduce user-changeable covers for cellphones, the first to have elliptical-shaped, soft, and friendly forms, and the first with big screens. In the early 1990s, Nokia controlled only 12 percent of the global market for cell phones. Today, it is the world leader in handsets, with 38 percent of the market.

With an increasingly visually oriented culture, translating brand meaning and positioning through design is critical. "In a crowded marketplace," writes Virginia Postrel in *The Substance of Style,* "aesthetics is often the only way to make a product stand out." Design can shift consumer perceptions to make brand experiences more rewarding. Consider the lengths Boeing went to to make its 777 airplane seem roomier and more comfortable. Raised center bins, side luggage bins, divider panels, gently arched ceilings, and raised seats make the aircraft interior seem bigger. As one design engineer noted, "If we do our jobs, people don't realize what we have done. They just say they feel more comfortable."

Designers sometimes put a human face—literally—on their products. The Porsche Boxster's bulges and curves can be seen as suggestive of muscle; the Apple iMac was thought by one designer to be "a head stuck to a body via a long skinny arm"; and Microsoft's optical mouse can be seen as an outstretched hand. When Frog Design set out to make a Disney cordless phone for kids, it wanted the design to live up to the famed Disney imagery. After exhaustive study, Frog defined the composite elements of a Disney character and applied it to the phone. The eyes were interpreted in terms of the LCD screen and were made as big as possible; the torso was interpreted in terms of the housing of the phone and was S-shaped, with a roundness in the top front and bottom back; and the feet were interpreted in terms of the base and charger stand, which used built-up plastic to emulate a sock pushed up around an ankle.

A bad design can also ruin a product's prospects. Sony's e-Villa Internet appliance was intended to allow consumers to have Internet access from their kitchens. But at nearly 32 pounds and 16 inches, the mammoth product was so awkward and heavy that the owner's manual recommended customers bend their legs, not their back, to pick it up. The product was eventually withdrawn after three months.

Sources: A. G. Lafley, "Delivering Delight," *Fast Company,* June 2004, p. 51; Frank Nuovo, "A Call for Fashion," *Fast Company,* June 2004, p. 52; Bobbie Gossage, "Strategies: Designing Success," *Inc. Magazine,* May 2004, pp. 27–29; Jim Hopkins, "When the Devil Is in the Design," *USA Today,* December 31, 2001, p. 3B; J. Lynn Lunsford and Daniel Michaels, "Masters of Illusion," *Wall Street Journal,* November 25, 2002, pp. B1, B5; Jerome Kathman, "Building Leadership Brands by Design," *Brandweek,* December 1, 2003, p. 20; Bob Parks, "Deconstructing Cute," *Business 2.0,* December 2002/January 2003, pp. 47–50; Lisa Margonelli, "How Ikea Designs Its Sexy Price Tags," *Business 2.0,* October 2002, pp. 106–112.

ness by promising to deliver concrete faster than pizza. Cemex equips every truck with a *global positioning system* (GPS) so that its real-time location is known and full information is available to drivers and dispatchers. Cemex is able to promise that if your load is more than 10 minutes late, you get a 20 percent discount.[15]

INSTALLATION **Installation** refers to the work done to make a product operational in its planned location. Buyers of heavy equipment expect good installation service. Differentiating at this point in the consumption chain is particularly important for companies with complex products. Ease of installation becomes a true selling point, especially when the target market is technology novices. For customers wishing to connect to the Internet using a high-speed digital subscriber line (DSL), Pacific Bell developed installation kits that included an interactive software setup program so customers could complete their DSL setup in less than an hour.[16]

CUSTOMER TRAINING **Customer training** refers to training the customer's employees to use the vendor's equipment properly and efficiently. General Electric not only sells and installs expensive X-ray equipment in hospitals; it also gives extensive training to users of this equipment. McDonald's requires its new franchisees to attend Hamburger University in Oak Brook, Illinois, for two weeks, to learn how to manage the franchise properly.

CUSTOMER CONSULTING **Customer consulting** refers to data, information systems, and advice services that the seller offers to buyers.

HERMAN MILLER INC.

Herman Miller, a large office furniture company, has partnered with a California firm to show corporate clients how to get the full benefits out of its furnishings. The firm, Future Industrial Technologies, specializes in workplace ergonomics training. Working through Herman Miller's dealership network, customers can arrange two-hour training sessions for small groups of employees. The sessions are run by some of the 1,200 physical therapists, occupational therapists, registered nurses, and chiropractors who work under contract to Future Industrial Technologies. While customer ergonomics training results in only modest revenue gains for Herman Miller, the company feels that teaching healthy work habits creates higher levels of satisfaction for customers and sets Herman Miller products apart.[17]

MAINTENANCE AND REPAIR **Maintenance and repair** describes the service program for helping customers keep purchased products in good working order. Hewlett-Packard offers online technical support, or "e-support," for its customers. In the event of a service problem, customers can use various online tools to find a solution. Those aware of the specific problem can search an online database for fixes; those unaware can use diagnostic software that finds the problem and searches the online database for an automatic fix. Customers can also seek online help from a technician.[18]

BEST BUY

As consolidation and competitive pricing among electronics retailers continues, companies are increasingly looking for new ways to stand out in the crowd. That's why Best Buy contracted with the Geek Squad, a small residential computer services company in its home market of Minnesota's twin cities, to revamp the chain's in-store computer repair services. Previously, PCs were sent to regional repair facilities, a process that was time-consuming and ultimately contributed to a high degree of consumer dissatisfaction. Now about half of all repairs are made in Best Buy stores. But the real differentiator is the Geek Squad's ability to make house calls (at a higher fee). Geek Squad house calls are called a "Beetle Roll" because of the squad's signature fleet of hip VW Beetles. Geek Squad employees even dress differently for house calls—they wear a distinctive "geek" look as opposed to the traditional Best Buy blue they wear at the in-store service centers.[19]

::: Product and Brand Relationships

Each product can be related to other products.

The Product Hierarchy

The product hierarchy stretches from basic needs to particular items that satisfy those needs. We can identify six levels of the product hierarchy (using life insurance as an example):

1. ***Need family*** – The core need that underlies the existence of a product family. Example: security.
2. ***Product family*** – All the product classes that can satisfy a core need with reasonable effectiveness. Example: savings and income.
3. ***Product class*** – A group of products within the product family recognized as having a certain functional coherence. Also known as product category. Example: financial instruments.

4. ***Product line*** – A group of products within a product class that are closely related because they perform a similar function, are sold to the same customer groups, are marketed through the same outlets or channels, or fall within given price ranges. A product line may be composed of different brands or a single family brand or individual brand that has been line extended. Example: life insurance.
5. ***Product type*** – A group of items within a product line that share one of several possible forms of the product. Example: term life insurance.
6. ***Item (also called stockkeeping unit or product variant)*** – A distinct unit within a brand or product line distinguishable by size, price, appearance, or some other attribute. Example: Prudential renewable term life insurance.

Product Systems and Mixes

A **product system** is a group of diverse but related items that function in a compatible manner. For example, PalmOne handheld and smartphone product lines come with attachable products including headsets, cameras, keyboards, presentation projectors, e-books, MP3 players, and voice recorders. A **product mix** (also called a **product assortment**) is the set of all products and items a particular seller offers for sale. A product mix consists of various product lines. In General Electric's Consumer Appliance Division, there are product-line managers for refrigerators, stoves, and washing machines. NEC's (Japan) product mix consists of communication products and computer products. Michelin has three product lines: tires, maps, and restaurant-rating services. At Northwestern University, there are separate academic deans for the medical school, law school, business school, engineering school, music school, speech school, journalism school, and liberal arts school.

A company's product mix has a certain width, length, depth, and consistency. These concepts are illustrated in Table 12.1 for selected Procter & Gamble consumer products.

- The *width* of a product mix refers to how many different product lines the company carries. Table 12.1 shows a product-mix width of five lines. (In fact, P&G produces many additional lines.)
- The *depth* of a product mix refers to the total number of items in the mix. In Table 12.1, it is 20. We can also talk about the average length of a line. This is obtained by dividing the total length (here 20) by the number of lines (here 5), or an average product length of 4.
- The *width* of a product mix refers to how many variants are offered of each product in the line. If Tide comes in two scents (Mountain Spring and Regular), two formulations (liquid and powder), and two additives (with or without bleach), Tide has a depth of eight as there are eight distinct variants. The average depth of P&G's product mix can be calculated by averaging the number of variants within the brand groups.
- The *consistency* of the product mix refers to how closely related the various product lines are in end use, production requirements, distribution channels, or some other way. P&G's product lines are consistent insofar as they are consumer goods that go through the same distribution channels. The lines are less consistent insofar as they perform different functions for the buyers.

These four product-mix dimensions permit the company to expand its business in four ways. It can add new product lines, thus widening its product mix. It can lengthen each product line. It can add more product variants to each product and deepen its product mix. Finally, a company can pursue more product-line consistency. To make these product and brand decisions, it is useful to conduct product-line analysis.

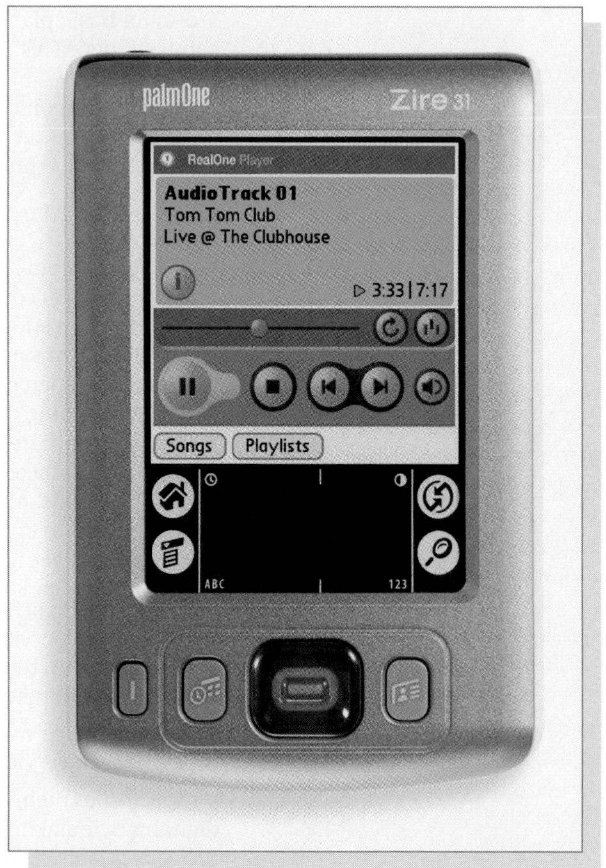

The PalmOne Zire 31 handheld. Owners can select from more than 20,000 available applications and use the expansion slot to add more memory, applications, or MP3 tunes.

TABLE 12.1 Product-Mix Width and Product-Line Length for Procter & Gamble Products (including Dates of Introduction)

	Product-Mix Width				
	Detergents	Toothpaste	Bar Soap	Disposable Diapers	Paper Products
PRODUCT LINE LENGTH	Ivory Snow (1930)	Gleem (1952)	Ivory (1879)	Pampers (1961)	Charmin (1928)
	Dreft (1933)	Crest (1955)	Camay (1926)	Luvs (1976)	Puffs (1960)
	Tide (1946)		Zest (1952)		Bounty (1965)
	Cheer (1950)		Safeguard (1963)		
	Dash (1954)		Oil of Olay (1993)		
	Bold (1965)				
	Gain (1966)				
	Era (1972)				

Product-Line Analysis

In offering a product line, companies normally develop a basic platform and modules that can be added to meet different customer requirements. Car manufacturers build their cars around a basic platform. Homebuilders show a model home to which additional features can be added. This modular approach enables the company to offer variety while lowering production costs.

Product-line managers need to know the sales and profits of each item in their line in order to determine which items to build, maintain, harvest, or divest.[20] They also need to understand each product line's market profile.

SALES AND PROFITS Figure 12.3 shows a sales and profit report for a five-item product line. The first item accounts for 50 percent of total sales and 30 percent of total profits. The first two items account for 80 percent of total sales and 60 percent of total profits. If these two items were suddenly hurt by a competitor, the line's sales and profitability could collapse. These items must be carefully monitored and protected. At the other end, the last item delivers only 5 percent of the product line's sales and profits. The product-line manager may consider dropping this item unless it has strong growth potential.

Every company's product portfolio contains products with different margins. Supermarkets make almost no margin on bread and milk; reasonable margins on canned and frozen foods; and even better margins on flowers, ethnic food lines, and freshly baked goods. A local telephone company makes different margins on its core telephone service, call waiting, caller ID, and voice mail.

A company can classify its products into four types that yield different gross margins, depending on sales volume and promotion. To illustrate with personal computers:

- ***Core product.*** Basic computers that produce high sales volume and are heavily promoted but with low margins because they are viewed as undifferentiated commodities.
- ***Staples.*** Items with lower sales volume and no promotion, such as faster CPUs or bigger memories. These yield a somewhat higher margin.
- ***Specialties.*** Items with lower sales volume but which might be highly promoted, such as digital moviemaking equipment; or might generate income for services, such as personal delivery, installation, or on-site training.
- ***Convenience items.*** Peripheral items that sell in high volume but receive less promotion, such as computer monitors, printers, upscale video or sound cards, and software. Consumers tend to buy them where they buy the original equipment because it is more convenient than making further shopping trips. These items can carry higher margins.

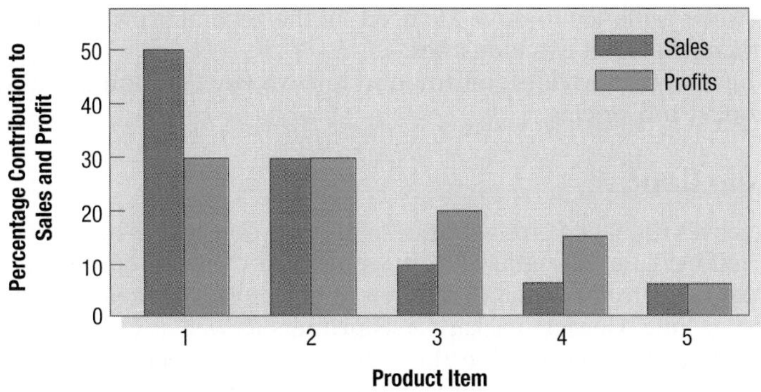

FIG. 12.3

Product-Item Contributions to a Product Line's Total Sales and Profits

The main point is that companies should recognize that these items differ in their potential for being priced higher or advertised more as ways to increase their sales, margins, or both.[21]

MARKET PROFILE The product-line manager must review how the line is positioned against competitors' lines. Consider paper company X with a paperboard product line.[22] Two paperboard attributes are weight and finish quality. Paper weight is usually offered at standard levels of 90, 120, 150, and 180 weight. Finish quality is offered at low, medium, and high levels. Figure 12.4 shows the location of the various product-line items of company X and four competitors, A, B, C, and D. Competitor A sells two product items in the extra-high weight class ranging from medium to low finish quality. Competitor B sells four items that vary in weight and finish quality. Competitor C sells three items in which the greater the weight, the greater the finish quality. Competitor D sells three items, all lightweight but varying in finish quality. Company X offers three items that vary in weight and finish quality.

The product map shows which competitors' items are competing against company X's items. For example, company X's low-weight, medium-quality paper competes against competitor D's and B's papers, but its high-weight, medium-quality paper has no direct competitor. The map also reveals possible locations for new items. No manufacturer offers a high-weight, low-quality paper. If company X estimates a strong unmet demand and can produce and price this paper at low cost, it could consider adding this item to its line.

Another benefit of product mapping is that it identifies market segments. Figure 12.4 shows the types of paper, by weight and quality, preferred by the general printing industry, the point-of-purchase display industry, and the office supply industry. The map shows that

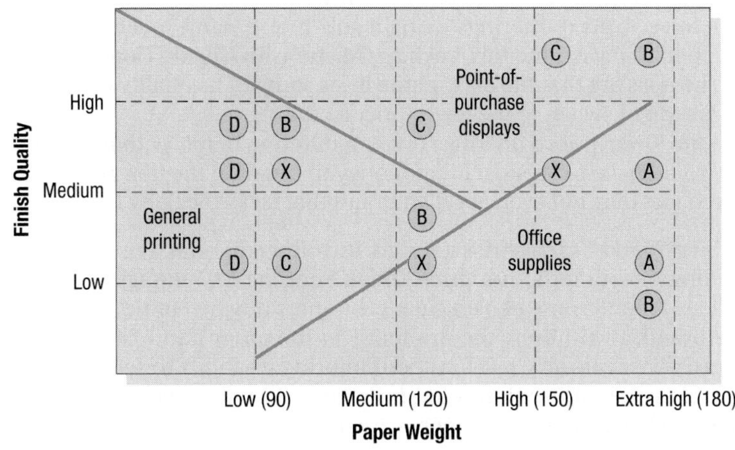

FIG. 12.4

Product Map for a Paper-Product Line

Source: Benson P. Shapiro, *Industrial Product Policy: Managing the Existing Product Line.* (Cambridge, MA: Marketing Science Institute Report No. 77-110).

company X is well positioned to serve the needs of the general printing industry but is less effective in serving the other two industries.

Product-line analysis provides information for two key decision areas—product-line length and product-mix pricing.

Product-Line Length

Company objectives influence product-line length. One objective is to create a product line to induce upselling: Thus General Motors would like to move customers up from the Chevrolet to the Buick to the Cadillac. A different objective is to create a product line that facilitates cross-selling: Hewlett-Packard sells printers as well as computers. Still another objective is to create a product line that protects against economic ups and downs; Electrolux offers white goods such as refrigerators, dishwashers, and vacuum cleaners under different brand names in the discount, middle-market, and premium segments, in part in case the economy moves up or down.[23] Companies seeking high market share and market growth will generally carry longer product lines. Companies that emphasize high profitability will carry shorter lines consisting of carefully chosen items.

Product lines tend to lengthen over time. Excess manufacturing capacity puts pressure on the product-line manager to develop new items. The sales force and distributors also pressure the company for a more complete product line to satisfy customers. But as items are added, costs rise: design and engineering costs, inventory-carrying costs, manufacturing-changeover costs, order-processing costs, transportation costs, and new-item promotional costs. Eventually, someone calls a halt: Top management may stop development because of insufficient funds or manufacturing capacity. The controller may call for a study of money-losing items. A pattern of product-line growth followed by massive pruning may repeat itself many times.

A company lengthens its product line in two ways: by line stretching and line filling.

LINE STRETCHING Every company's product line covers a certain part of the total possible range. For example, BMW automobiles are located in the upper price range of the automobile market. **Line stretching** occurs when a company lengthens its product line beyond its current range. The company can stretch its line down-market, up-market, or both ways.

Down-Market Stretch A company positioned in the middle market may want to introduce a lower-priced line for any of three reasons:

1. The company may notice strong growth opportunities as mass retailers such as Wal-Mart, Best Buy, and others attract a growing number of shoppers who want value-priced goods.
2. The company may wish to tie up lower-end competitors who might otherwise try to move up-market. If the company has been attacked by a low-end competitor, it often decides to counterattack by entering the low end of the market.
3. The company may find that the middle market is stagnating or declining.

A company faces a number of naming choices in deciding to move down-market. Sony, for example, faced three choices:

1. Use the name Sony on all of its offerings. (Sony did this.)
2. Introduce lower-priced offerings using a sub-brand name, such as Sony Value Line. Other companies have done this, such as Gillette with Gillette Good News and Ramada Limited. The risks are that the Sony name loses some of its quality image and that some Sony buyers might switch to the lower-priced offerings.
3. Introduce the lower-priced offerings under a different name, without mentioning Sony; but Sony would have to spend a lot of money to build up the new brand name, and the mass merchants may not even accept a brand that lacks the Sony name.

Moving down-market carries risks. Kodak introduced Kodak Funtime film to counter lower-priced brands, but it did not price Kodak Funtime low enough to match the lower-priced film. It also found some of its regular customers buying Funtime, so it was cannibalizing its core brand. It withdrew the product. On the other hand, Mercedes successfully introduced its C-Class cars at $30,000 without injuring its ability to sell other Mercedes cars for $100,000 and up. John Deere introduced a lower-priced line of lawn tractors called Sabre from John Deere while still selling its more expensive tractors under the John Deere name.

A print ad for Gallo of Sonoma showing members of the younger generation of the Gallo family, with the tagline: "New Generation. World Class."

Up-Market Stretch Companies may wish to enter the high end of the market for more growth, higher margins, or simply to position themselves as full-line manufacturers. Many markets have spawned surprising upscale segments: Starbucks in coffee, Häagen-Dazs in ice cream, and Evian in bottled water. The leading Japanese auto companies have each introduced an upscale automobile: Toyota's Lexus; Nissan's Infiniti; and Honda's Acura. Note that they invented entirely new names rather than using or including their own names.

Other companies have included their own name in moving up-market. Gallo introduced Gallo of Sonoma (priced at $10 to $30 a bottle) to compete in the premium wine segment, using the founder's grandchildren as spokespeople in an intensive push-and-pull campaign. With a hip, young, and fun image, case sales volume tripled to 680,000 in 1999. General Electric introduced the GE Profile brand for its large appliance offerings in the upscale market.[24] Some brands have used modifiers to signal a noticeable, although presumably not dramatic, quality improvement, such as Ultra Dry Pampers, Extra Strength Tylenol, or PowerPro Dustbuster Plus.

Two-Way Stretch Companies serving the middle market might decide to stretch their line in both directions. Texas Instruments (TI) introduced its first calculators in the medium-price-medium-quality end of the market. Gradually, it added calculators at the lower end, taking market share away from Bowmar, and at the higher end to compete with Hewlett-Packard. This two-way stretch won TI early market leadership in the hand-calculator market.

Holiday Inn Worldwide also has performed a two-way stretch of its hotel product line. The hotel chain broke its domestic hotels into five separate chains to tap into five different benefit segments—the upscale Crowne Plaza, the traditional Holiday Inn, the budget Holiday Inn Express, and the business-oriented Holiday Inn Select and Holiday Inn Suites & Rooms. Different branded chains received different marketing programs and emphasis. Holiday Inn Express has been advertised with the humorous "Stay Smart" advertising campaign showing the brilliant feats that ordinary people could attempt after staying at the chain. By basing the development of these brands on distinct consumer targets with unique needs, Holiday Inn is able to ensure against overlap between brands.

LINE FILLING A product line can also be lengthened by adding more items within the present range. There are several motives for *line filling:* reaching for incremental profits, trying to satisfy dealers who complain about lost sales because of missing items in the line, trying to utilize excess capacity, trying to be the leading full-line company, and trying to plug holes to keep out competitors.

BMW AG

In four years BMW has morphed from a one-brand, five-model carmaker into a three-brand, 10-model powerhouse. Not only has the carmaker expanded BMW's product range downward with Mini Coopers and its compact 1-series models, but it has also built it upward with Rolls-Royce, while filling the gaps in between with its X3 Sports Activity Vehicle, and a 6-series coupe. The company has used line filling successfully to boost its appeal to the wannabe-rich, the rich, and the super-rich, all without departing from its pure premium positioning.[25]

Line filling is overdone if it results in self-cannibalization and customer confusion. The company needs to differentiate each item in the consumer's mind. Each item should possess a *just-noticeable difference.* According to Weber's law, customers are more attuned to relative than to absolute difference.[26] They will perceive the difference between boards 2 and 3 feet long and boards 20 and 30 feet long but not between boards 29 and 30 feet long. The company should also check that the proposed item meets a market need and is not being added simply to satisfy an internal need. The infamous Edsel automobile, on which Ford lost $350 million in the late 1950s, met Ford's internal positioning needs for a car between its Ford and Lincoln lines but not the market's needs.

LINE MODERNIZATION, FEATURING, AND PRUNING Product lines need to be modernized. A company's machine tools might have a 1970s look and lose out to newer-styled competitors' lines. The issue is whether to overhaul the line piecemeal or all at once. A piecemeal approach allows the company to see how customers and dealers take to the new style. It is also less draining on the company's cash flow, but it allows competitors to see changes and to start redesigning their own lines.

In rapidly changing product markets, modernization is continuous. Companies plan improvements to encourage customer migration to higher-valued, higher-priced items. Microprocessor companies such as Intel and AMD, and software companies such as Microsoft and Oracle, continually introduce more advanced versions of their products. A major issue is timing improvements so they do not appear too early (damaging sales of the current line) or too late (after the competition has established a strong reputation for more advanced equipment).

The product-line manager typically selects one or a few items in the line to feature. Sears will announce a special low-priced washing machine to attract customers. At other times, managers will feature a high-end item to lend prestige to the product line. Sometimes a company finds one end of its line selling well and the other end selling poorly. The company may try to boost demand for the slower sellers, especially if they are produced in a factory that is idled by lack of demand; but it could be counterargued that the company should promote items that sell well rather than try to prop up weak items.

Product-line managers must periodically review the line for deadwood that is depressing profits. "Marketing Insight: Rationalizing Brand Portfolios for Growth" describes some

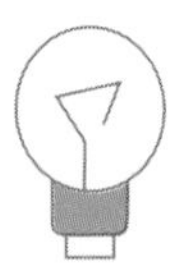

MARKETING INSIGHT | RATIONALIZING BRAND PORTFOLIOS FOR GROWTH

In 1999, Unilever owned more than 1,600 distinct brands. Some of Unilever's famed brands include Lipton tea, Snuggle fabric softener, Ragu pasta sauces, Bird's-Eye frozen foods, Close-Up toothpaste, Calvin Klein fragrances, and Dove personal-care products. But more than 90 percent of its profits came from just 400 brands. That year, the company announced its "Path to Growth" program designed to get the most value from its brand portfolio by eliminating three-quarters of its brands by 2003. The company intended to retain global brands such as Lipton, as well as regional brands and "local jewels" such as Persil, the leading detergent in the United Kingdom. Unilever co-chairman Niall FitzGerald likened the brand reduction to weeding a garden so "the light and air get in to the blooms which are likely to grow the best."

Unilever is not alone. Multibrand companies all over the world are attempting to optimize their brand portfolios. In many cases, this has led to a greater focus on core brand growth and to concentrating energy and resources on the biggest and most established brands. Hasbro has designated a set of core toy brands, including GI Joe, Transformers, and My Little Pony, to emphasize in its marketing. Procter & Gamble's "back to basics strategy" concentrates on its thirteen $1 billion-plus brands, such as Tide, Crest, Pampers, and Pringles.

At the same time, firms have to be careful to avoid overreliance on existing brands at the expense of any new brands. Kraft spent the early part of the 2000s introducing one line extension after another of its established brands, such as Oreo cookies, Chips Ahoy, and Jell-O. Some extensions failed. A Chips Ahoy extension, Gooey Warm n' Chewy, turned out to be tricky to eat and too pricey. Extension proliferation meant that the company missed out on important health and nutrition trends in the marketplace. Stagnant sales led to the ouster of co-CEO Betsy Holden in December 2003.

Sources: John Willman, "Leaner, Cleaner, and Healthier Is the Stated Aim," *Financial Times,* February 23, 2000; John Thornhill, "A Bad Time to Be in Consumer Goods," *Financial Times,* September 28, 2000; "Unilever's Goal: 'Power Brands'," *Advertising Age,* January 3, 2000; "Unilever Axes 25,000 Jobs," *CNNfn,* February 22, 2000; Harriet Marsh, "Unilever a Year Down the 'Path'," *Marketing,* February 22, 2001, p. 30. Patricia O'Connell, "A Chat with Unilever's Niall Fitzgerald," *BusinessWeek Online,* August 2, 2001; Nirmalya Kumar, "Kill a Brand, Keep a Customer," *Harvard Business Review* (December 2003): 86–95; Sarah Ellison, "Kraft's Stale Strategy," *Wall Street Journal,* December 18, 2003, pp. B1, B6; Brad Stone, "Back to Basics," *Newsweek,* August 4, 2003, pp. 42–44.

developments with that strategy. The weak items can be identified through sales and cost analysis. A chemical company cut down its line from 217 to the 93 products with the largest volume, the largest contribution to profits, and the greatest long-term potential. Pruning is also done when the company is short of production capacity. Companies typically shorten their product lines in periods of tight demand and lengthen their lines in periods of slow demand.

Product-Mix Pricing

Chapter 14 describes pricing concepts, strategies, and tactics in detail, but it is useful to consider some basic product-mix pricing issues here. Price-setting logic must be modified when the product is part of a product mix. In this case, the firm searches for a set of prices that maximizes profits on the total mix. Pricing is difficult because the various products have demand and cost interrelationships and are subject to different degrees of competition. We can distinguish six situations involving product-mix pricing: product-line pricing, optional-feature pricing, captive-product pricing, two-part pricing, by-product pricing, and product-bundling pricing.

PRODUCT-LINE PRICING Companies normally develop product lines rather than single products and introduce price steps.

INTEL

Intel has segmented its product line into microprocessors aimed at specific markets, such as cheap PCs, mid-tier "performance" PCs, and powerful servers. This strategy let Intel balance thin profits from chips like the Celeron—new models of which sell for as little as $150 and go into low-priced PCs—with cash cows like the Itanium workstation and server chips, which cost up to $4,200 each. The company's most profitable chips are the Pentium 4 chips, priced between $300 and $600, depending on processor speed.[27]

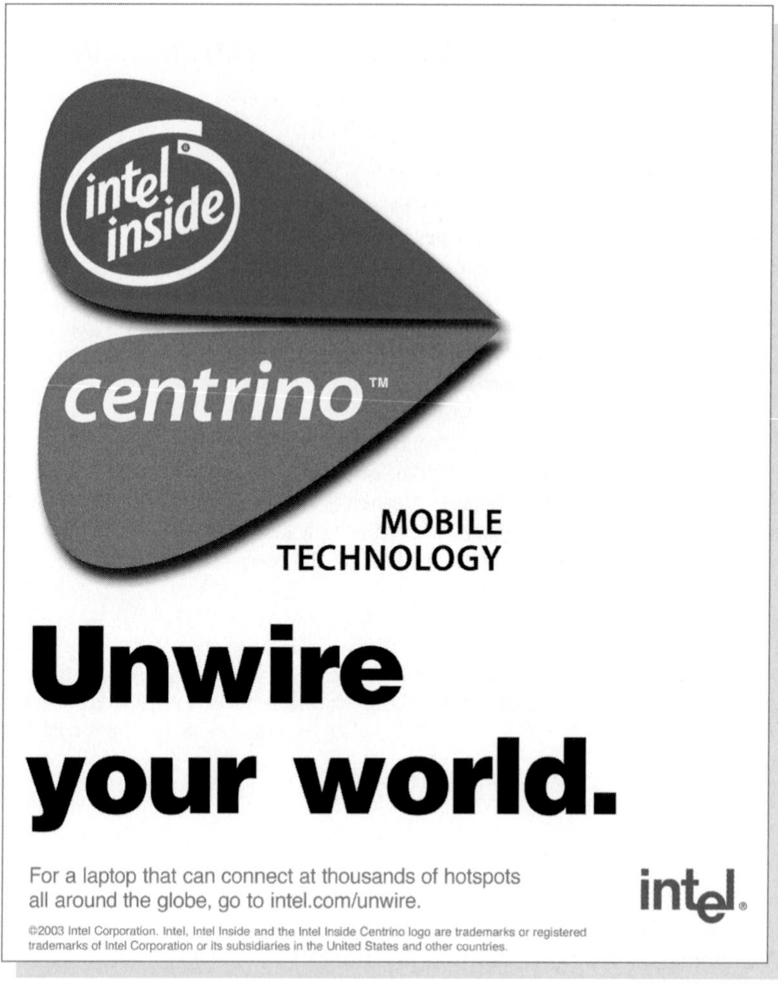

Print ad for Intel® Centrino™, part of Intel's product line of microprocessors segmented by market. Centrino mobile technology is a set of notebook technologies designed specifically for wireless notebook PCs, and for the top of the market.

In many lines of trade, sellers use well-established price points for the products in their line. A men's clothing store might carry men's suits at three price levels: $200, $400, and $600. Customers will associate low-, average-, and high-quality suits with the three price points. The seller's task is to establish perceived quality differences that justify the price differences.

OPTIONAL-FEATURE PRICING Many companies offer optional products, features, and services along with their main product. The automobile buyer can order electric window controls, defoggers, light dimmers, and an extended warranty. Pricing is a sticky problem, because companies must decide which items to include in the standard price and which to offer as options. For many years, U.S. auto companies advertised a stripped-down model for $10,000 to pull people into showrooms. The economy model was stripped of so many features that most buyers left the showroom spending $13,000.

Restaurants face a similar pricing problem. Customers can often order liquor in addition to the meal. Many restaurants price their liquor high and their food low. The food revenue covers costs, and the liquor produces the profit. This explains why servers often press hard to get customers to order drinks. Other restaurants price their liquor low and food high to draw in a drinking crowd.

CAPTIVE-PRODUCT PRICING Some products require the use of ancillary, or **captive, products**. Manufacturers of razors, digital phones, and cameras often price them low and set high markups on razor blades and film, respectively. AT&T may give a cellular phone free if the person commits to buying two years of phone service.

HEWLETT-PACKARD

In 1996, Hewlett-Packard (HP) began drastically cutting prices on its printers, by as much as 60 percent in some cases. HP could afford to make such dramatic cuts because customers typically spend twice as much on replacement ink cartridges, toner, and specialty paper as on the actual printer over the life of the product. As the price of printers dropped, printer sales rose, as did the number of aftermarket sales. HP now owns about 40 percent of the worldwide printer business. Its inkjet supplies carry 35 percent profit margins and generated \$2.2 billion in operating profits in 2002—over 70 percent of the company's total.[28]

There is a danger in pricing the captive product too high in the aftermarket. Caterpillar, for example, makes high profits in the aftermarket by pricing its parts and service high. This practice has given rise to "pirates," who counterfeit the parts and sell them to "shady tree" mechanics who install them, sometimes without passing on the cost savings to customers. Meanwhile, Caterpillar loses sales.[29]

TWO-PART PRICING Service firms often engage in **two-part pricing**, consisting of a fixed fee plus a variable usage fee. Telephone users pay a minimum monthly fee plus charges for calls beyond a certain area. Amusement parks charge an admission fee plus fees for rides over a certain minimum. The service firm faces a problem similar to captive-product pricing—namely, how much to charge for the basic service and how much for the variable usage. The fixed fee should be low enough to induce purchase of the service; the profit can then be made on the usage fees.

BY-PRODUCT PRICING The production of certain goods—meats, petroleum products, and other chemicals—often results in by-products. If the by-products have value to a customer group, they should be priced on their value. Any income earned on the by-products will make it easier for the company to charge a lower price on its main product if competition forces it to do so. Australia's CSR was originally named Colonial Sugar Refinery and its early reputation was formed as a sugar company. The company began to sell by-products of its sugar cane: waste sugar cane fiber was used to manufacture wallboard. By the mid 1990s, through product development and acquisition, CSR had become one of the top 10 companies in Australia selling building and construction materials.

PRODUCT-BUNDLING PRICING Sellers often bundle products and features. **Pure bundling** occurs when a firm only offers its products as a bundle. Michael Ovitz's former company, Artists Management Group, would sign up a "hot" actor if the film company would also accept other talents that Ovitz represented (directors, writers, scripts). This is a form of *tied-in sales*. In **mixed bundling**, the seller offers goods both individually and in bundles. When offering a mixed bundle, the seller normally charges less for the bundle than if the items were purchased separately. An auto manufacturer might offer an option package at less than the cost of buying all the options separately. A theater company will price a season subscription at less than the cost of buying all the performances separately. Because customers may not have planned to buy all the components, the savings on the price bundle must be substantial enough to induce them to buy the bundle.[30]

Some customers will want less than the whole bundle. Suppose a medical-equipment supplier's offer includes free delivery and training. A particular customer might ask to forgo the free delivery and training in exchange for a lower price. The customer is asking the seller to "unbundle" or "rebundle" its offer. If a supplier saves \$100 by not supplying delivery and reduces the customer's price by \$80, the supplier has kept the customer happy while increasing its profit by \$20.

Studies have shown that as promotional activity increases on individual items in the bundle, buyers perceive less saving on the bundle and are less apt to pay for the bundle. This research has offered the following three suggested guidelines for correctly implementing a bundling strategy:[31]

- Don't promote individual products in a package as frequently and cheaply as the bundle. The bundle price should be much lower than the sum of individual products or the consumer will not perceive its attractiveness.

Co-branding: Part of a video ad directed at children for two General Mills products, Trix cereal and Yoplait yogurt.

■ Limit promotions to a single item in the mix if you still want to promote individual products. Another option: alternate promotions, one after another, in order to avoid conflicting promotions.

■ If you decide to offer large rebates on individual products, it must be the absolute exception and done with discretion. Otherwise, the consumer uses the price of individual products as an external reference for the bundle, which then loses value.

Co-Branding and Ingredient Branding

CO-BRANDING Products are often combined with products from other companies in various ways. A rising phenomenon is the emergence of **co-branding**—also called dual branding or brand bundling—in which two or more well-known existing brands are combined into a joint product and/or marketed together in some fashion.[32] One form of co-branding is *same-company co-branding*, as when General Mills advertises Trix and Yoplait yogurt. Still another form is *joint-venture co-branding*, as in the case of General Electric and Hitachi lightbulbs in Japan and the Citibank AAdvantage credit card. There is *multiple-sponsor co-branding*, as in the case of Taligent, a technological alliance of Apple, IBM, and Motorola.[33] Finally, there is *retail co-branding* where two retail establishments, such as fast-food restaurants, use the same location as a way to optimize both space and profits:

CINNABON

When you think of Cinnabon, you think of—or catch a whiff of—only one thing: cinnamon rolls. However, this 18-year-old chain needed to add a new dimension in order to spark sales at its franchises, all tucked into shopping malls. To do that Cinnabon is now co-branding with Freshen, a seller of smoothie drinks. The two concepts work well because people get thirsty while eating a cinnamon roll and Freshen offers a healthy alternative to soda. The match has already "freshened" Cinnabon's sales, which have spiked 3 to 4 percent at the co-branded locations.[34]

The main advantage to co-branding is that a product may be convincingly positioned by virtue of the multiple brands involved. Co-branding can generate greater sales from the existing target market as well as open additional opportunities with new consumers and channels. Co-branding also can reduce the cost of product introduction because two well-known images are combined, accelerating potential adoption. And co-branding may be a valuable means to learn about consumers and how other companies approach them. Companies within the automotive industry have reaped all of these benefits of co-branding.

The potential disadvantages of co-branding are the risks and lack of control from becoming aligned with another brand in the minds of consumers. Consumer expectations about the level of involvement and commitment with co-brands are likely to be high, so unsatisfactory performance could have negative repercussions for the brands involved. If the other brand has entered into a number of co-branding arrangements, there may be a risk that overexposure will dilute the transfer of any association. It may also result in a lack of focus on existing brands.

A necessary condition for co-branding success is that the two brands separately have brand equity—adequate brand awareness and a sufficiently positive brand image. The most important requirement is that there is a logical fit between the two brands such that the combined brand or marketing activity maximizes the advantages of the individual brands while minimizing the disadvantages. Research studies show that consumers are more apt to perceive co-brands favorably if the two brands are complementary rather than similar:[35]

GODIVA AND SLIM-FAST

Godiva (fine chocolate) rates high on taste and richness, whereas Slim-Fast (weight-loss products) rates favorably on calorie content and value. In an academic research study, a hypothetical cake-mix extension of either brand alone was judged by sample consumers to be similar to the parent brand. For instance, Godiva cake mix was judged to be good tasting but high on calories, whereas Slim-Fast cake mix was perceived to be low on both calories and taste. In contrast, co-brands such as Slim-Fast cake mix by Godiva or Godiva cake mix by Slim-Fast were judged to possess the desirable attributes of *both* brands.

Besides these strategic considerations, co-branding ventures must be entered into and executed carefully. There must be the right kind of fit in values, capabilities, and goals, in addition to an appropriate balance of brand equity. There must be detailed plans to legalize contracts, make financial arrangements, and coordinate marketing programs. As one executive at Nabisco put it, "Giving away your brand is a lot like giving away your child—you want to make sure everything is perfect." The financial arrangement between brands may vary, although one common approach involves a licensing fee and royalty from the brand more involved in the production process.

Brand alliances involve a number of decisions.[36] What capabilities do you not have? What resource constraints are you faced with (people, time, money, etc.)? What growth goals or revenue needs do you have? In assessing a joint branding opportunity, a number of questions need to be asked. Is it a profitable business venture? How does it help to maintain or strengthen brand equity? Is there any possible risk of dilution of brand equity? Does it offer any extrinsic advantages (e.g., learning opportunities)?

INGREDIENT BRANDING **Ingredient branding** is a special case of co-branding. It involves creating brand equity for materials, components, or parts that are necessarily contained within other branded products. Some successful ingredient brands include Dolby noise reduction, Gore-Tex water-resistant fibers, and Scotchgard fabrics. Some popular ingredient-branded products are Betty Crocker baking mixes with Hershey's chocolate syrup, Lunchables lunch combinations with Taco Bell tacos, and Lay's potato chips made with KC Masterpiece barbecue sauce.

An interesting take on ingredient branding is "self-branding" in which companies advertise and even trademark their own branded ingredients. For instance, Westin Hotels advertises its "Heavenly Bed" and "Heavenly Shower." The Heavenly Bed has been so successful that Westin now sells the bed, pillows, sheets, and blankets via an online catalog, along with other "Heavenly" gifts and bath items. If you can do it well, it makes much more sense to self-brand ingredients because you have more control and can develop the ingredient to suit your purposes.[37]

Ingredient brands attempt to create sufficient awareness and preference for their product such that consumers will not buy a "host" product that does not contain the ingredient. DuPont has achieved success in marketing its products as ingredient brands.

DUPONT

Over the years, DuPont has introduced a number of innovative products, such as Corian® solid-surface material, for use in markets ranging from apparel to aerospace. Many of these products, such as Lycra® and Stainmaster® fabrics, Teflon® coating, and Kevlar® fiber, became household names as ingredient brands in consumer products manufactured by other companies. Several recent ingredient brands include Supro® isolated soy proteins used in food products and RiboPrinter® genetic fingerprinting technology.[38]

Many manufacturers make components or materials that enter into final branded products, but whose individual identity normally gets lost. One of the few component branders who have succeeded in building a separate identity is Intel. Intel's consumer-directed brand campaign convinced many personal computer buyers to buy only computer brands with "Intel Inside." As a result, major PC manufacturers—IBM, Dell, Compaq—purchase their chips from Intel at a premium price rather than buy equivalent chips from an unknown supplier. Most component manufacturers, however, would find it difficult to create a successful ingredient brand. "Marketing Memo: Making Ingredient Branding Work" outlines the characteristics of successful ingredient branding.

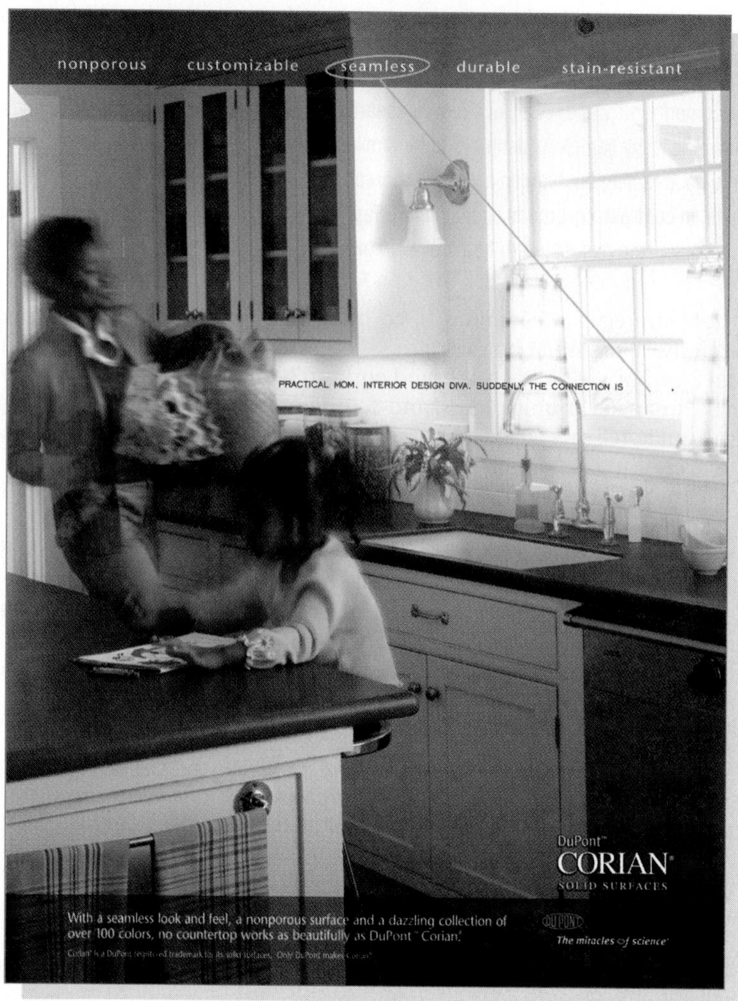

A DuPont ad for its Corian® solid-surface material, used here in a familiar household application as a kitchen countertop.

::: Packaging, Labeling, Warranties, and Guarantees

Most physical products have to be packaged and labeled. Some packages—such as the Coke bottle and the L'eggs container—are world famous. Many marketers have called packaging a fifth P, along with price, product, place, and promotion. Most marketers,

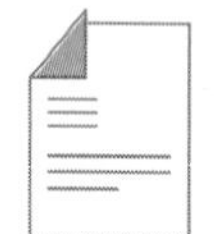

MARKETING MEMO | MAKING INGREDIENT BRANDING WORK

What are the requirements for success in ingredient branding?

1. Consumers must perceive that the ingredient matters to the performance and success of the end product. Ideally, this intrinsic value is easily visible or experienced.
2. Consumers must be convinced that not all ingredient brands are the same and that the ingredient is superior.
3. A distinctive symbol or logo must clearly signal to consumers that the host product contains the ingredient. Ideally, the symbol or logo would function like a "seal" and would be simple and versatile and credibly communicate quality and confidence.
4. A coordinated "pull" and "push" program must help consumers understand the importance and advantages of the branded ingredient. Channel members must offer full support. Often this will involve consumer advertising and promotions and—sometimes in collaboration with manufacturers—retail merchandising and promotion programs.

Sources: Kevin Lane Keller, *Strategic Brand Management,* 2nd ed. (Upper Saddle River, NJ: Prentice Hall, 2003); Paul F. Nunes, Stephen F. Dull, and Patrick D. Lynch, "When Two Brands Are Better Than One," *Outlook,* No. 1 (2003): 14–23.

however, treat packaging and labeling as an element of product strategy. Warranties and guarantees can also be an important part of the product strategy, which often appear on the package.

Packaging

We define **packaging** as all the activities of designing and producing the container for a product. Packages might include up to three levels of material. Paco Rabanne cologne comes in a bottle (*primary package*) that is in a cardboard box (*secondary package*) that is in a corrugated box (*shipping package*) containing six dozen boxes of Paco Rabanne.

Well-designed packages can create convenience and promotional value. We must include packaging as a styling weapon, especially in food products, cosmetics, toiletries, and small consumer appliances. The package is the buyer's first encounter with the product and is capable of turning the buyer on or off. For Arizona Iced Tea, packaging is definitely a turn-on.[39]

ARIZONA ICED TEA

Arizona Iced Tea marketer Ferolito, Vultaggio, & Sons has gained success by taking a rather straightforward drink—tea—and putting it into unusual bottles with elaborate designs. The wide-mouthed, long-necked bottles have been trendsetters in the New Age beverage category, and customers often buy the tea just for the bottle. Because consumers are known to hang on to their empties or convert them into lamps and other household objects, the company uses unique bottle shapes for its line extensions. It uses a ridged grip design on Arizona Rx Elixirs, miniature jugs for Arizona Iced Coffees, and a pint-sized, deep-blue urn for Blue Luna Café Latte.[40]

Various factors have contributed to the growing use of packaging as a marketing tool:

- ***Self-service.*** An increasing number of products are sold on a self-service basis. In an average supermarket, which stocks 15,000 items, the typical shopper passes by some 300 items per minute. Given that 53 percent of all purchases are made on impulse, the effective package must perform many of the sales tasks: attract attention, describe the product's features, create consumer confidence, and make a favorable overall impression. A good example is the book publishing industry, where customers often quite literally choose a book by its cover: The number-one classics publisher, Penguin Books Ltd., is repackaging most of its titles and spending $500,000 to promote them under the banner, "Classic Books, Fresh Looks." Sales have increased 400 percent for Dorothy Parker's *Complete Stories,* 50 percent for a new translation of *Don Quixote,* 43 percent for *Pride and Prejudice.*[41]
- ***Consumer affluence.*** Rising consumer affluence means consumers are willing to pay a little more for the convenience, appearance, dependability, and prestige of better packages.
- ***Company and brand image.*** Packages contribute to instant recognition of the company or brand.
- ***Innovation opportunity.*** Innovative packaging can bring large benefits to consumers and profits to producers. Companies are incorporating unique materials and features such as resealable spouts and openings. Heinz's unique, colorful EZ Squirt ketchup revitalized that brand's sales. Dutch Boy developed the award-winning Twist & Pour paint container, an easy-to-carry, easy-to-open, easy-to-pour-and-close paint jug. Not only did the new packaging increase sales, but it also gave Dutch Boy more distribution at higher retail prices.[42]

Developing an effective package requires a number of decisions. From the perspective of both the firm and consumers, packaging must achieve a number of objectives:[43]

1. Identify the brand,
2. Convey descriptive and persuasive information,
3. Facilitate product transportation and protection,
4. Assist at-home storage, and
5. Aid product consumption.

To achieve the marketing objectives for the brand and satisfy the desires of consumers, the aesthetic and functional components of packaging must be chosen correctly. Aesthetic considerations relate to a package's size and shape, material, color, text and graphics. Color must be carefully chosen: Blue is cool and serene, red is active and lively, yellow is medicinal and weak, pastel colors are feminine and dark colors are masculine. Functionally, structural design is crucial. For example, packaging innovations with food products over the years have resulted in packages becoming resealable, tamper-proof, and more convenient to use (easy-to-hold, easy-to-open, or squeezable). Changes in canning have made vegetables crunchier, and special wraps have extended the life of refrigerated food.[44]

The various packaging elements must be harmonized. The packaging elements must also be harmonized with decisions on pricing, advertising, and other parts of the marketing program. Packaging changes can have immediate impact on sales. For example, sales of the Heath candy bar increased 25 percent after its wrapper was redone.

After packaging is designed, it must be tested. *Engineering tests* are conducted to ensure that the package stands up under normal conditions; *visual tests,* to ensure that the script is legible and the colors harmonious; *dealer tests,* to ensure that dealers find the packages attractive and easy to handle; and *consumer tests,* to ensure favorable consumer response.

Developing effective packaging may cost several hundred thousand dollars and take several months to complete. Companies must pay attention to growing environmental and safety concerns about packaging. Shortages of paper, aluminum, and other materials suggest that marketers should try to reduce packaging. Many packages end up as broken bottles and crumpled cans littering the streets and countryside. Packaging creates a major problem for solid waste disposal, requiring huge amounts of labor and energy. Fortunately, many companies have gone "green."

TETRA PAK

Tetra Pak, a major Swedish multinational, provides an example of the power of innovative packaging and customer thinking. Tetra Pak invented an "aseptic" package that enables milk, fruit juice, and other perishable liquid foods to be distributed without refrigeration, so dairies can distribute milk over a wider area without investing in refrigerated trucks and facilities. Supermarkets can carry Tetra Pak packaged products on ordinary shelves, allowing them to save expensive refrigerator space. Tetra's motto is "the package should save more than it costs." Tetra Pak advertises the benefits of its packaging to consumers directly and even initiates recycling programs to save the environment. Its new American headquarters in Vernon Hills, Illinois, was built using recycled materials and other environmentally sensitive building products and techniques.[45]

Labeling

Sellers must label products. The label may be a simple tag attached to the product or an elaborately designed graphic that is part of the package. The label might carry only the brand name or a great deal of information. Even if the seller prefers a simple label, the law may require additional information.

Labels perform several functions. First, the label *identifies* the product or brand—for instance, the name Sunkist stamped on oranges. The label might also *grade* the product; canned peaches are grade labeled A, B, and C. The label might *describe* the product: who made it, where it was made, when it was made, what it contains, how it is to be used, and how to use it safely. Finally, the label might *promote* the product through attractive graphics. New technology allows for 360-degree shrink-wrapped labels to surround containers with bright graphics and accommodate more on-pack product information, replacing paper labels glued on to cans and bottles.[46]

Labels eventually become outmoded and need freshening up. The label on Ivory soap has been redone at least 18 times since the 1890s, with gradual changes in the size and design of the letters. The label for Milk Bone dog biscuits was redesigned to emphasize the key visual elements that emerged from consumer research—the dog, the biscuit, and the bone shape—and helped to stem a sales slide for the brand.[47] Companies with labels that have become icons need to tread very carefully when initiating a redesign:

Ivory soap labels through the years: the label in 1882, and the three-bar package label in 2003.

CAMPBELL SOUP COMPANY

The Campbell Soup Company has estimated that the average shopper sees its familiar red-and-white can 76 times a year, creating the equivalent of millions of dollars worth of advertising. Its label is such an icon that pop artist Andy Warhol immortalized it in one of his silk screens in the 1960s. The original Campbell's Soup label—with its scripted name and signature red-and-white—was designed in 1898, and the company did not redesign it until more than a century later, in 1999. With the goal of making the label more contemporary and making it easier for customers to find individual soups, Campbell made the famous script logo smaller and featured a photo of a steaming bowl of the soup flavor inside. In addition to the new graphic, the company put nutritional information on the packaging, serving suggestions, quick dinner ideas, and colored bands that identify the six subgroups of condensed soup, that is, creams, broths, and so on.[48]

There is a long history of legal concerns surrounding labels, as well as packaging. In 1914, the Federal Trade Commission Act held that false, misleading, or deceptive labels or packages constitute unfair competition. The Fair Packaging and Labeling Act, passed by Congress in 1967, set mandatory labeling requirements, encouraged voluntary industry packaging standards, and allowed federal agencies to set packaging regulations in specific industries.

The Food and Drug Administration (FDA) has required processed-food producers to include nutritional labeling that clearly states the amounts of protein, fat, carbohydrates, and calories contained in products, as well as their vitamin and mineral content as a percentage of the recommended daily allowance.[49] The FDA recently launched a drive to control health claims in food labeling by taking action against the potentially misleading use of such descriptions as "light," "high fiber," and "low fat." Consumerists have lobbied for additional labeling laws to require *open dating* (to describe product freshness), *unit pricing* (to state the product cost in standard measurement units), *grade labeling* (to rate the quality level), and *percentage labeling* (to show the percentage of each important ingredient).

Warranties and Guarantees

All sellers are legally responsible for fulfilling a buyer's normal or reasonable expectations. Warranties are formal statements of expected product performance by the manufacturer. Products under warranty can be returned to the manufacturer or designated repair center for repair, replacement, or refund. Warranties, whether expressed or implied, are legally enforceable.

MITSUBISHI MOTORS NORTH AMERICA

To counter consumer perceptions that Mitsubishi lags behind competitors when it comes to quality, the company has begun offering a new 10-year, 100,000-mile Powertrain warranty. This warranty, which is retroactive on all 2004 vehicles, replaces its 7-year, 60,000-mile warranty. Mitsubishi hopes that the new, longer-term warranty will signal to consumers that the company has confidence in the quality and reliability of its vehicles.[50]

Many sellers offer either general guarantees or specific guarantees.[51] A company such as Procter & Gamble promises general or complete satisfaction without being more specific—"If you are not satisfied for any reason, return for replacement, exchange, or refund." Other companies offer specific guarantees and in some cases, extraordinary guarantees:

- General Motors' Saturn car division will accept the return of a new car within 30 days if the buyer is not satisfied.
- Hampton Inn motels guarantees a restful night or the customer does not have to pay.
- A. T. Cross guarantees its Cross pens and pencils for life. The customer mails the pen to A. T. Cross (mailing envelopes are provided at stores selling Cross writing instruments), and the pen is repaired or replaced at no charge.
- FedEx won its place in the minds and hearts of mailers by promising next-day delivery "absolutely, positively by 10:30 A.M."
- Oakley Millwork, a Chicago supplier of construction-industry products, has a "no back-order guarantee" that promises that if any item in its catalog was unavailable for immediate delivery, the customer would get the item free.
- BBBK, a pest extermination company, offers the following guarantee: (1) no payment until all pests are eradicated; (2) if the effort fails, the customer receives a full refund to pay the next exterminator; (3) if guests on the client's premises spot a pest, BBBK will pay for the guest's room and send an apology letter; and (4) if the client's facility is closed down, BBBK will pay all fines, lost profits, and $5,000.

Guarantees reduce the buyer's perceived risk. They suggest that the product is of high quality and that the company and its service performance are dependable. All this enables the company to charge a higher price than a competitor who is not offering an equivalent guarantee.

Guarantees are most effective in two situations. The first is where the company or the product is not well known. For example, a company might sell a liquid claiming to remove the toughest spots. A "money-back guarantee if not satisfied" would provide buyers with some confidence in purchasing the product. The second situation is where the product's quality is superior to the competition. The company can gain by guaranteeing superior performance, knowing that competitors cannot match its guarantee.

SUMMARY :::

1. Product is the first and most important element of the marketing mix. Product strategy calls for making coordinated decisions on product mixes, product lines, brands, and packaging and labeling.
2. In planning its market offering, the marketer needs to think through the five levels of the product: the core benefit, the basic product, the expected product, the augmented product, and the potential product, which encompasses all the augmentations and transformations the product might ultimately undergo.
3. Products can be classified in several ways. In terms of durability and reliability, products can be nondurable goods, durable goods, or services. In the consumer-goods category, products are convenience goods (staples, impulse goods, emergency goods), shopping goods (homogeneous and heterogeneous), specialty goods, or unsought goods. In the industrial-goods category, products fall into one of three categories: materials and parts (raw materials and manufactured materials and parts), capital items (installations and equipment), or supplies and business services (operating supplies, maintenance and repair items, maintenance and repair services, and business advisory services).
4. Brands can be differentiated on the basis of a number of different product or service dimensions: product form, features, performance, conformance, durability, reliability, repairability, style, and design, as well as such service dimensions as ordering ease, delivery, installation, customer training, customer consulting, and maintenance and repair.
5. Most companies sell more than one product. A product mix can be classified according to width, length, depth, and consistency. These four dimensions are the tools for developing the company's marketing strategy and deciding which product lines to grow, maintain, harvest, and divest. To analyze a product line and decide how many resources should be invested in that line, product-line managers need to look at sales and profits and market profile.
6. A company can change the product component of its marketing mix by lengthening its product via line stretching (down-market, up-market, or both) or line filling, by modernizing its products, by featuring certain products, and by pruning its products to eliminate the least profitable.
7. Brands are often sold or marketed jointly with other brands. Ingredient brands and co-brands can add value

assuming they have equity and are perceived as fitting appropriately.

8. Physical products have to be packaged and labeled. Well-designed packages can create convenience value for customers and promotional value for producers. In effect, they can act as "five-second commercials" for the product. Warranties and guarantees can offer further assurance to consumers.

APPLICATIONS :::

Marketing Debate With Products, Is It Form or Function?

The "form versus function" debate applies in many arenas, including marketing. Some marketers believe that product performance is the end all and be all. Other marketers maintain that the looks, feel, and other design elements of products are what really make the difference.

Take a position: Product functionality is the key to brand success versus Product design is the key to brand success.

Marketing Discussion

Consider the different means of differentiating products and services. Which ones have the most impact on your choices? Why? Can you think of certain brands that excel on a number of these different means of differentiation?

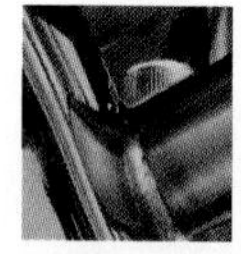

IN THIS CHAPTER, WE WILL ADDRESS THE FOLLOWING QUESTIONS:

1. How are services defined and classified, and how do they differ from goods?
2. How are services marketed?
3. How can service quality be improved?
4. How do services marketers create strong brands?
5. How can goods-producing companies improve customer support services?

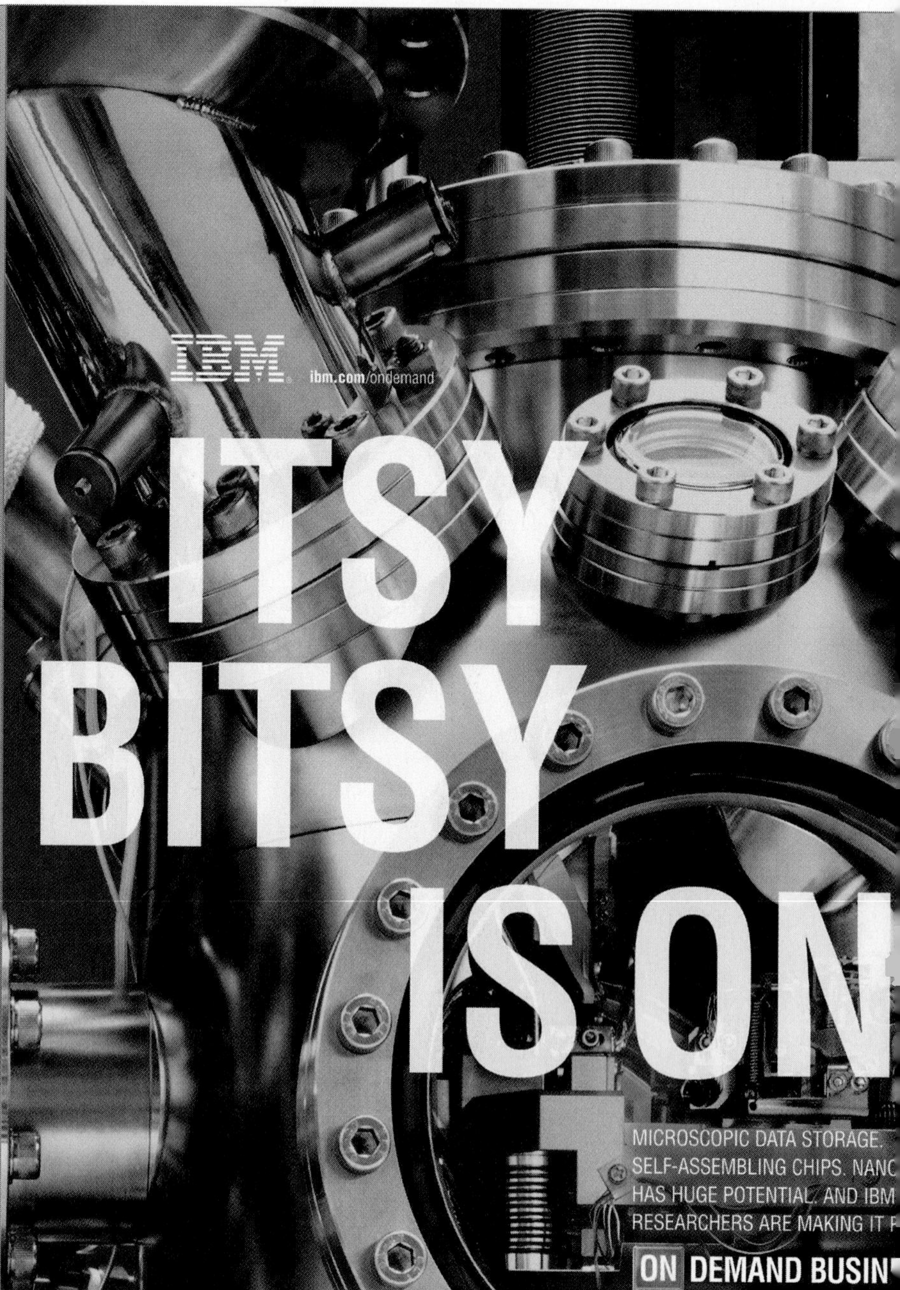

CHAPTER 13 ::: DESIGNING AND MANAGING SERVICES

thirteen

As companies find it harder and harder to differentiate their physical products, they turn to service differentiation. Many books point out the significant profitability of companies that manage to deliver superior service.[1] Companies seek to develop a reputation for superior performance in on-time delivery, better and faster answering of inquiries, and quicker resolution of complaints. Service becomes the mantra. Perhaps the most dramatic example of how the growth of services has changed the face of business is what has happened to one of the world's most successful companies, IBM.

Famous for its accomplishments in computer hardware and software, IBM has undergone a massive transformation. Currently, almost half of its $81 billion in annual revenues comes from global services. Companies such as American Express are signing up for consulting engagements that involve customized software, hardware, and systems solutions worth literally billions of dollars to IBM. IBM's "e-business on demand" initiative is a company-wide effort to help other companies harness the power of technology through IBM products and services. To fulfill its service promises, IBM has had to develop new skills and become more customer focused. The $3.5 billion acquisition of PriceWaterhouseCoopers Consulting in October 2002 has provided valuable strategic expertise. To help improve R&D designs and service implementation, Big Blue is now sending hundreds >>>

A print ad from IBM's "On Demand" campaign, which focuses on customizing hardware, software, and systems to help other companies harness the power of technology with IBM products and services.

of its brightest researchers to visit customers to better understand how they actually use information technology. "The aim is to create a very deep connection between IBM and its customers. . . ," said David B. Yoffie, a Harvard Business School Professor, "But it's making IBM more like a service business with technology thrown in than a technology business."[2]

Service businesses increasingly fuel the world economy. Because it is critical to understand the special nature of services and what that means to marketers, in this chapter we systematically analyze services and how to market them most effectively.

::: The Nature of Services

The Bureau of Labor Statistics reports that the service-producing sector will continue to be the dominant employment generator in the economy, adding 20.5 million jobs by 2010. Employment in the service-producing sector is expected to increase by 19 percent over the 2000–2010 period, whereas manufacturing employment is expected to increase by only 3 percent. In fact, manufacturing's share of total jobs is expected to decline from 13 percent in 2000 to 11 percent in 2010.[3] These numbers and others have led to a growing interest in the special problems of marketing services.[4]

Service Industries Are Everywhere

The *government sector,* with its courts, employment services, hospitals, loan agencies, military services, police and fire departments, postal service, regulatory agencies, and schools, is in the service business. The *private nonprofit sector,* with its museums, charities, churches, colleges, foundations, and hospitals, is in the service business. A good part of the *business sector,* with its airlines, banks, hotels, insurance companies, law firms, management consulting firms, medical practices, motion picture companies, plumbing repair companies, and real estate firms, is in the service business. Many workers in the *manufacturing sector,* such as computer operators, accountants, and legal staff, are really service providers. In fact, they make up a "service factory" providing services to the "goods factory." And those in the *retail sector,* such as cashiers, clerks, salespeople, and customer service representatives, are also providing a service.

We define a service as follows: A **service** is any act or performance that one party can offer to another that is essentially intangible and does not result in the ownership of anything. Its production may or may not be tied to a physical product.

Manufacturers, distributors, and retailers can provide value-added services or simply excellent customer service to differentiate themselves.

ONSTAR

General Motors has gone a step further with its OnStar service, which helps customers with related tasks including emergency services dispatch, stolen vehicle location, roadside assistance, remote diagnostics, and route support. Every month OnStar unlocks about 28,000 car doors, dispatches 13,000 roadside assistance vehicles, and locates 700 lost vehicles. While the first year of OnStar is free to GM car owners, it now claims renewal rates as high as 80% at annual subscription fees ranging from $200 to more than $800. By 2005, OnStar is projected to bring in more than $2 billion for GM.[5]

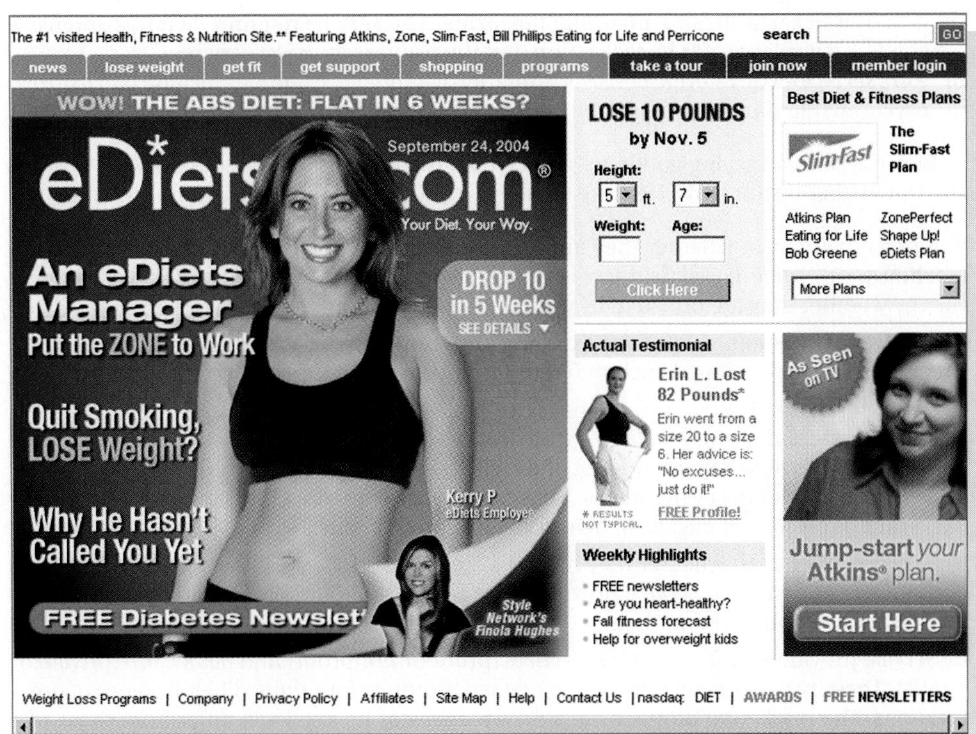

The home page from eDiets.com's award-winning site is easy to look at and easy to customize, making it one of the most popular diet sites on the Web.

Many pure service firms are now using the Internet to reach customers. A little surfing on the Web will turn up a large number of virtual service providers. Here's what the judges of the 2003 Webby Business awards said about one of their winners:

eDIETS.COM

A Google search under "diet" generates a staggering 8,530,000 responses, suggesting that America's fixation on its collective girth has become decidedly more high-tech. Of the many diet sites, eDiets has done the best job of compiling information and cementing partnerships (with weight-loss specialists like Atkins and healthy-eating magazines like Cooking Light) most desired by dieters. Add in exercise guides as well as sections that account for a host of medical conditions (diabetes, high cholesterol, lactose intolerance), and eDiets is by far the most customizable—and cleanly designed—dieting resource on the web.[6]

Categories of Service Mix

A company's offerings often include some services. The service component can be a minor or a major part of the total offering. Five categories of offerings can be distinguished:

1. ***Pure tangible good*** – The offering consists primarily of a tangible good such as soap, toothpaste, or salt. No services accompany the product.
2. ***Tangible good with accompanying services*** – The offering consists of a tangible good accompanied by one or more services. Levitt observes that "the more technologically sophisticated the generic product (e.g., cars and computers), the more dependent are its sales on the quality and availability of its accompanying customer services (e.g., display rooms, delivery, repairs and maintenance, application aids, operator training, installation advice, warranty fulfillment). In this sense, General Motors is probably more service intensive than manufacturing intensive. Without its services, its sales would shrivel."[7]
3. ***Hybrid*** – The offering consists of equal parts of goods and services. For example, people patronize restaurants for both food and service.
4. ***Major service with accompanying minor goods and services*** – The offering consists of a major service along with additional services or supporting goods. For example, airline passengers buy transportation. The trip includes some tangibles, such as food and

drinks, a ticket stub, and an airline magazine. The service requires a capital-intensive good—an airplane—for its realization, but the primary item is a service.

5. ***Pure service*** – The offering consists primarily of a service. Examples include baby-sitting, psychotherapy, and massage.

Because of this varying goods-to-service mix, it is difficult to generalize about services without further distinctions. Here are some additional distinctions that can be helpful:

- Services vary as to whether they are *equipment-based* (automated car washes, vending machines) or *people-based* (window washing, accounting services). People-based services vary by whether they are provided by unskilled, skilled, or professional workers.
- Service companies can choose among different *processes* to deliver their service. Restaurants have developed such different formats as cafeteria-style, fast-food, buffet, and candlelight service.
- Some services require the *client's presence* and some do not. Brain surgery involves the client's presence, a car repair does not. If the client must be present, the service provider has to be considerate of his or her needs. Thus beauty salon operators will invest in décor, play background music, and engage in light conversation with the client.
- Services differ as to whether they meet a *personal need* (personal services) or a *business need* (business services). Service providers typically develop different marketing programs for personal and business markets.
- Service providers differ in their *objectives* (profit or nonprofit) and *ownership* (private or public). These two characteristics, when crossed, produce four quite different types of organizations. The marketing programs of a private investor hospital will differ from those of a private charity hospital or a Veterans' Administration hospital.[8]

The nature of the service mix also has implications for how consumers evaluate quality. For some services, customers cannot judge the technical quality even after they have received the service. Figure 13.1 shows various products and services according to difficulty of evaluation.[9] At the left are goods high in *search qualities*—that is, characteristics the buyer can evaluate before purchase. In the middle are goods and services high in *experience qualities*—characteristics the buyer can evaluate after purchase. At the right are goods and services high in *credence qualities*—characteristics the buyer normally finds hard to evaluate even after consumption.[10]

Because services are generally high in experience and credence qualities, there is more risk in purchase. This has several consequences. First, service consumers generally rely on word of mouth rather than advertising. Second, they rely heavily on price, personnel, and physical cues to judge quality. Third, they are highly loyal to service providers who satisfy

FIG. 13.1

Continuum of Evaluation for Different Types of Products

Source: Valarie A. Zeithaml, "How Consumer Evaluation Processes Differ between Goods and Services," in *Marketing of Services,* edited by James H. Donnelly and William R. George. Reprinted with permission of the American Marketing Association (Chicago: American Marketing Association, 1981).

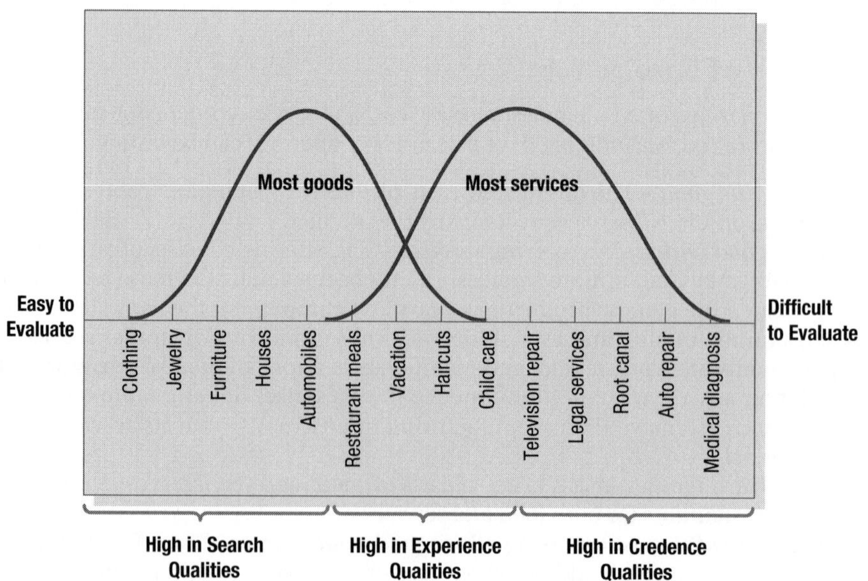

them. Fourth, because of the switching costs involved, much consumer inertia can exist. It can be challenging to entice a customer away from a competitor. Wachovia Bank's slogan, "Let's Get Started," was a call to action to new and existing customers alike.

Distinctive Characteristics of Services

Services have four distinctive characteristics that greatly affect the design of marketing programs: *intangibility, inseparability, variability,* and *perishability.*

INTANGIBILITY Unlike physical products, services cannot be seen, tasted, felt, heard, or smelled before they are bought. The person getting a face-lift cannot see the results before the purchase, and the patient in the psychiatrist's office cannot know the exact outcome.

To reduce uncertainty, buyers will look for evidence of quality. They will draw inferences about quality from the place, people, equipment, communication material, symbols, and price that they see. Therefore, the service provider's task is to "manage the evidence," to "tangibilize the intangible."[11] Whereas product marketers are challenged to add abstract ideas, service marketers are challenged to add physical evidence and imagery to abstract offers.

Service companies can try to demonstrate their service quality through *physical evidence* and *presentation.*[12] A hotel will develop a look and a style of dealing with customers that realizes its intended customer value proposition, whether it is cleanliness, speed, or some other benefit. Suppose a bank wants to position itself as the "fast" bank. It could make this positioning strategy tangible through a number of marketing tools:

1. ***Place*** – The exterior and interior should have clean lines. The layout of the desks and the traffic flow should be planned carefully. Waiting lines should not get overly long.
2. ***People*** – Personnel should be busy. There should be a sufficient number of employees to manage the workload.
3. ***Equipment*** – Computers, copying machines, desks should be and look "state of the art."
4. ***Communication material*** – Printed materials—text and photos—should suggest efficiency and speed.
5. ***Symbols*** – The name and symbol should suggest fast service.
6. ***Price*** – The bank could advertise that it will deposit $5 in the account of any customer who waits in line for more than five minutes.

Service marketers must be able to transform intangible services into concrete benefits. To aid in "tangibilizing the intangible," Carbone and Haeckel propose a set of concepts called *customer experience engineering.*[13] Companies must first develop a clear picture of what they want the customer's perception of an experience to be and then design a consistent set of *performance and context clues* to support that experience. In the case of a bank, whether the teller dispensed the right amount of cash is a performance clue; a context clue is whether the teller was properly dressed. The context clues in a bank are delivered by people (*humanics*) and things (*mechanics*). The company assembles the clues in an *experience blueprint,* a pictorial representation of the various clues. To the extent possible, the clues should address all five senses. The Disney Company is a master at developing *experience blueprints* in its theme parks; so are companies such as Jamba Juice and Barnes & Noble in their respective retail stores.[14] The Mayo Clinic has set new standards in the health care industry.

THE MAYO CLINIC

The Mayo Clinic carefully manages a set of visual and experiential clues to tell a consistent and compelling story about its service. Mayo's credo is "the patient comes first." From public exam rooms to laboratories, Mayo facilities have been designed so that, in the words of the architect who designed one of the buildings, "patients feel a little better before they see their doctors." The 20-story Gonda Building in Rochester, Minnesota, has spectacular wide-open spaces, and the lobby of the Mayo Clinic hospital in Scottsdale, Arizona, has an indoor waterfall and a wall of windows overlooking mountains. Hospital rooms feature microwave ovens and chairs that really do convert to beds because, as one staff member explained, "People don't come to the hospital alone." In pediatric exam rooms, resuscitation equipment is hidden behind a large cheery picture.[15]

INSEPARABILITY Services are typically produced and consumed simultaneously. This is not true of physical goods, which are manufactured, put into inventory, distributed through multiple resellers, and consumed later. If a person renders the service, then the provider is part of the service. Because the client is also present as the service is produced, provider–client interaction is a special feature of services marketing.

In the case of entertainment and professional services, buyers are very interested in the specific provider. It is not the same concert if Madonna is indisposed and replaced by Shania Twain, or if a legal defense will be supplied by John Nobody because antitrust expert David Boies is unavailable. When clients have strong provider preferences, price is raised to ration the preferred provider's limited time.

Several strategies exist for getting around this limitation. The service provider can learn to work with larger groups. Psychotherapists have moved from one-on-one therapy to small-group therapy to groups of over 300 people in a large hotel ballroom. The service provider can learn to work faster—the psychotherapist can spend 30 more-efficient minutes with each patient instead of 50 less-structured minutes and can see more patients. The service organization can train more service providers and build up client confidence, as H&R Block has done with its national network of trained tax consultants. Creative artists have also developed techniques to overcome the limits of inseparability.

BLUE MAN GROUP

The Blue Man Group got its start in 1988 when the three original members—Matt Goldman, Phil Stanton, and Chris Wink—began performing on the streets of New York City. The company eventually moved into a theater, and the three performed every show for three straight years without the help of understudies. When the group opened a second show in Boston, the founders decided to add more Blue Men to help carry the weight. Today 33 different performers, including one woman, enable the Blue Man Group to take on various projects, such as performing in Las Vegas, recording a Grammy-nominated album, and starring in a series of commercials for Intel's Pentium processors.[16]

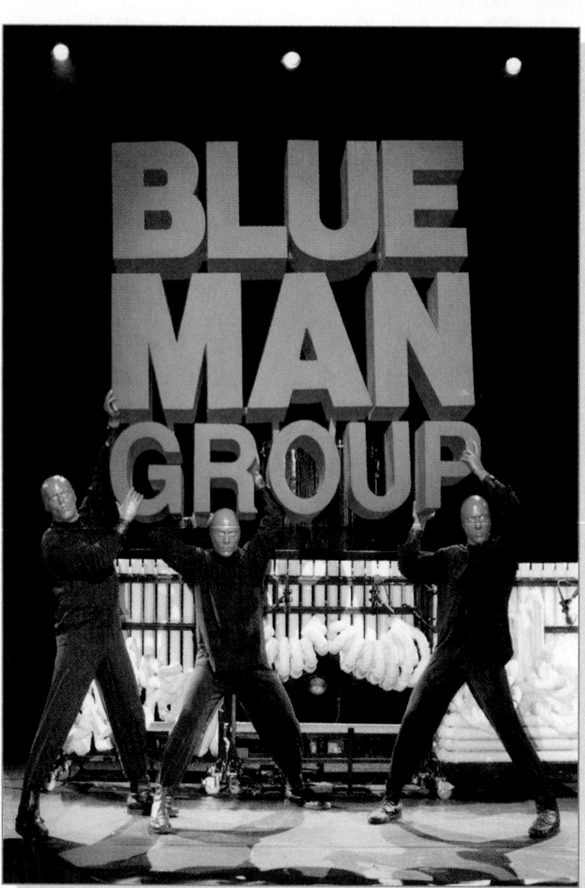

The Blue Man Group, with three of its thirty-three performers.

VARIABILITY Because services depend on who provides them and when and where they are provided, they are highly variable. Some doctors have an excellent bedside manner; others are less patient with their patients. Some surgeons are very successful in performing a certain operation; others are not. Service buyers are aware of this variability and often talk to others before selecting a service provider. Here are three steps service firms can take to increase quality control.

1. ***Invest in good hiring and training procedures.*** Recruiting the right employees and providing them with excellent training is crucial, regardless of whether employees are highly skilled professionals or low-skilled workers. Ideally, employees should exhibit competence, a caring attitude, responsiveness, initiative, problem-solving ability, and goodwill. Service companies such as FedEx and Marriott empower their front-line personnel to spend up to $100 to resolve a customer problem.
2. ***Standardize the service-performance process throughout the organization.*** This is done by preparing a *service blueprint* that depicts events and processes in a flowchart, with the objective of recognizing potential fail points. Figure 13.2 shows a service blueprint for a nationwide floral-delivery organization.[17] The customer's experience is limited to dialing the phone, making choices, and placing an order. Behind the scenes, the floral organization gathers the flowers, places them in a vase, delivers them, and collects payment. Any one of these activities can be done well or poorly.
3. ***Monitor customer satisfaction.*** Employ suggestion and complaint systems, customer surveys, and comparison shopping. General Electric sends out 700,000 response cards a year asking households to rate its service people's performance. Citibank

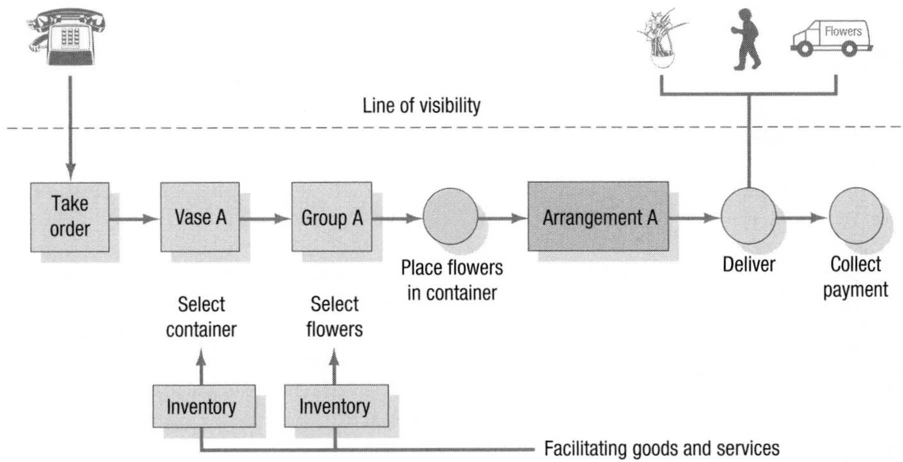

FIG. 13.2

A Service-Performance-Process Map: Nationwide Floral Delivery

Source: Adapted from G. Lynn Shostack, "Service Positioning Through Structural Change," *Journal of Marketing* (January 1987): 39. Reprinted with permission of the American Marketing Association.

checks continuously on measures of ART (accuracy, responsiveness, and timeliness). Firms can also develop customer information databases and systems to permit more personalized, customized service.[18]

PERISHABILITY Services cannot be stored. Perishability is not a problem when demand is steady. When demand fluctuates, service firms have problems. For example, public transportation companies have to own much more equipment because of rush-hour demand than if demand were even throughout the day. Some doctors charge patients for missed appointments because the service value exists only at that point.

Several strategies can produce a better match between demand and supply in a service business.[19] On the demand side:

- ***Differential pricing*** will shift some demand from peak to off-peak periods. Examples include low early evening movie prices and weekend discount prices for car rentals.
- ***Nonpeak demand*** can be cultivated. McDonald's pushes breakfast service, and hotels promote mini-vacation weekends.
- ***Complementary*** services can be developed to provide alternatives to waiting customers, such as cocktail lounges in restaurants and automatic teller machines in banks.
- ***Reservation systems*** are a way to manage the demand level. Airlines, hotels, and physicians employ them extensively.

On the supply side:

- ***Part-time employees*** can be hired to serve peak demand. Colleges add part-time teachers when enrollment goes up, and restaurants call in part-time servers when needed.
- ***Peak-time efficiency*** routines can be introduced. Employees perform only essential tasks during peak periods. Paramedics assist physicians during busy periods.
- ***Increased consumer participation*** can be encouraged. Consumers fill out their own medical records or bag their own groceries.
- ***Shared*** services can be developed. Several hospitals can share medical-equipment purchases.
- ***Facilities for future expansion*** can be developed. An amusement park buys surrounding land for later development.

Many airlines, hotels, and resorts have e-mail alerts to self-selected segments of their customer base that offer special short-term discounts and promotions. Club Med uses early to midweek e-mails to people in its database to pitch unsold weekend packages, typically 30 to 40 percent off the standard package price.[20] After 40 years of making people stand in line at its theme parks, Disney instituted Fastpass, which allows visitors to reserve a spot in line and eliminate the wait. When polled, it turns out that 95 percent of visitors like the change. Disney's vice president, Dale Stafford, told a reporter, "We have

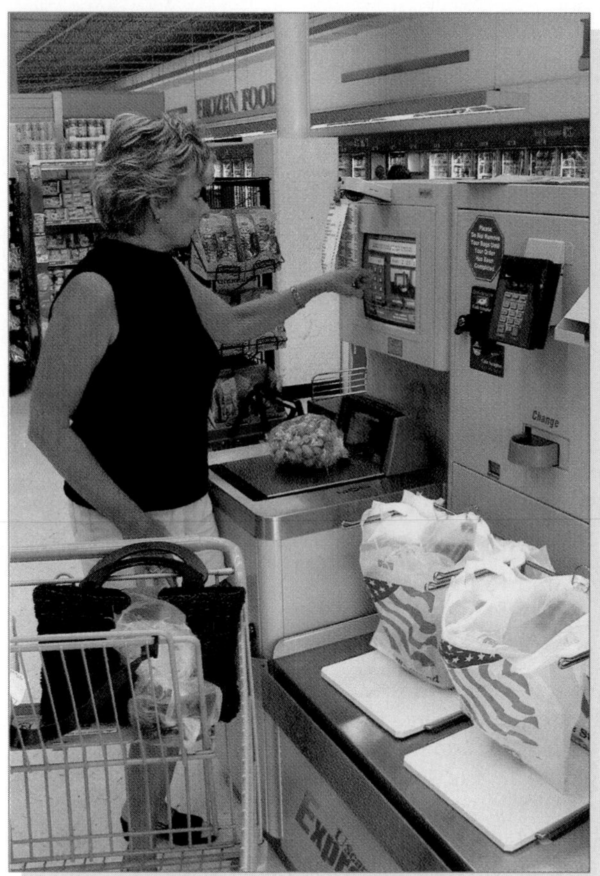

A shopper uses the automatic express checkout to pay for and bag purchases herself. These computerized checkout systems allow the shopper to pay with a credit card, a debit card, or cash.

been teaching people how to stand in line since 1955, and now we are telling them they don't have to. Of all the things we can do and all the marvels we can create with the attractions, this is something that will have a profound effect on the entire industry."[21]

::: Marketing Strategies for Service Firms

At one time, service firms lagged behind manufacturing firms in their use of marketing because they were small, or they were professional businesses that did not use marketing, or they faced large demand or little competition. This has certainly changed. "Marketing Memo: A Service Marketing Checklist" outlines the questions top service marketing organizations should be asking.

A Shifting Customer Relationship

Not all companies, however, have invested in providing superior service, at least not to all customers. *BusinessWeek,* in its October 23, 2000, issue, carried a cover story called "Why Service Stinks," based in part on the fact that from 1994 to 2000, customer satisfaction in the United States dropped 12.5 percent for airlines, 8.1 percent for banks, 6.5 percent for stores, and 4 percent for hotels.[22] Customers complained about inaccurate information; unresponsive, rude, or poorly trained personnel; and long wait times. And the picture doesn't look any rosier now. Customer service complaints are on the rise, even though many complaints never actually reach a live human being. Here are some statistics that should give service companies and customer service departments pause:[23]

- ***On the phone.*** Some 80 percent of the nation's companies haven't figured out how to get customers the assistance they need.
- ***Online.*** Forrester Research estimates that 35 percent of all e-mail inquiries to companies don't get a response within 7 days and about 25 percent don't get a response at all.
- ***Interactive Voice Response.*** While many of America's largest companies have installed call routing software called Interactive Voice Response Systems, more than 90 percent of financial services consumers say they don't like them.

In former times, service companies held out a welcoming hand to all customers, but these companies now have so much data on individuals that they are able to classify their customers into profit tiers. So service is not uniformly bad for all customers. Airlines, hotels, and banks all pamper good customers. Big spenders get special discounts, promotional offers, and lots of special service. The rest of their customers get higher fees, stripped-down service, and at best a voice message to answer inquiries.

Financial services giants have installed special software that tells them—in an instant—when a lucrative customer is on the phone. Such systems immediately send the call ahead of dozens—even hundreds—of other callers who must wait while the big spender gets special attention.[24] Charles Schwab's best customers get their calls answered in 15 seconds; other customers can wait 10 minutes or more. Sears sends a repairperson to its best customers within two hours; other customers wait four hours.

This shift from a customer service democracy to a meritocracy is also a response to lower profit margins resulting from customers becoming more price-driven and less loyal. Companies are now driven to seek ways to squeeze more profit out of the different customer tiers. Firms have decided to raise fees and lower service to customers who barely pay their way, and to coddle big spenders to retain their patronage as long as possible.

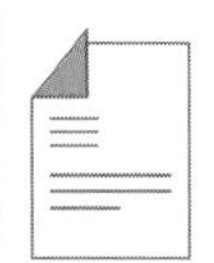

MARKETING MEMO | A SERVICE MARKETING CHECKLIST

Customers' expectations are the true standards for judging service quality. Berry and Parasuraman propose that marketing managers ask the following questions as they seek to manage and exceed expectations:

1. ***Do we strive to present a realistic picture of our service to customers?*** Do we always check the accuracy of our promotional messages? Is there regular communication between employees who serve customers and those who make promises to customers? Do we assess the impact of cues such as price on customer expectations?
2. ***Is performing the service right the first time a top priority?*** Are our employees trained and rewarded for delivering error-free service? Do we regularly evaluate our service designs to identify and correct potential flaws?
3. ***Do we communicate effectively with customers?*** Do we periodically contact customers to ascertain their needs and let them know we appreciate their business? Do we train and require employees to demonstrate to customers that we care about and value them?
4. ***Do we surprise customers during the service process?*** Are our employees aware that the service delivery process is our prime opportunity to exceed customers' expectations? Do we take specific steps to encourage excellence?
5. ***Do our employees regard service problems as opportunities to impress customers?*** Do we prepare and encourage employees to excel in the service recovery process? Do we reward them for providing exceptional recovery service?
6. ***Do we continuously evaluate and improve our performance against customers' expectations?*** Do we perform consistently above the adequate service level? Do we capitalize on opportunities to exceed the desired service level?

Sources: Excerpted from Leonard L. Berry and A. Parasuraman, *Marketing Services: Competing Through Quality* (New York: The Free Press, 1991), pp. 72–73. Also see Leonard L. Berry, *On Great Service: A Framework for Action* (New York: The Free Press, 1995); and his *Discovering the Soul of Service* (New York: The Free Press, 1999).

Companies that provide differentiated levels of service, however, must be careful about claiming superior service—the customers who receive poor treatment will bad-mouth the company and injure its reputation. Delivering services that maximize both customer satisfaction and company profitability can be challenging. Upstart airline JetBlue is a recent success story.

JETBLUE

While other airlines have lost millions of dollars and even declared bankruptcy, JetBlue has managed to head in a different direction. It has attempted to create a more contemporary alternative to Southwest Airlines. Like Southwest, it uses a single type of airplane, avoids "hub" cities to fly "point-to-point," and keeps turnaround time to a bare minimum. Unlike Southwest, however, JetBlue uses larger Airbus A320 planes, which permit longer-haul flights; adorns planes with cushy leather seats and seat-back TVs; and permits seat reservations. Slick advertising, nattily attired flight attendants, and a state-of-art Web site help to produce a very consumer-friendly, up-market image. JetBlue did share one other thing with Southwest Airlines—they were the only airlines to turn a profit in 2002.[25] JetBlue also recorded a profit in 2003 before encountering some financial turbulence in 2004.

There are also shifts that favor the customer in the client relationship. Customers are becoming more sophisticated about buying product support services and are pressing for "services unbundling." They want separate prices for each service element and the right to select the elements they want. Customers also increasingly dislike having to deal with a multitude of service providers handling different types of equipment. Some third-party service organizations now service a greater range of equipment.[26]

Most important, the Internet has empowered customers by letting them vent their rage about bad service—or reward good service—and have their comments beamed around the world with a mouse click. See "Marketing Insight: Voice Mail Hell" for a look at some ways in which the scales are tipping in the customer's favor and why service industries should take heed.

Holistic Marketing for Services

Because service encounters are complex interactions affected by multiple elements, adopting a holistic marketing perspective is especially important. The service outcome, and whether or not people will remain loyal to a service provider, is influenced by a host of variables. Keaveney identified more than 800 critical behaviors that cause customers to switch services.[27] These behaviors can be placed into one of eight categories (see Table 13.1).

Holistic marketing for services requires external, internal, and interactive marketing (see Figure 13.3).[28] *External marketing* describes the normal work of preparing, pricing, distributing, and promoting the service to customers. *Internal marketing* describes training and motivating employees to serve customers well. Berry has argued that the most important contribution the marketing department can make is to be "exceptionally clever in getting everyone else in the organization to practice marketing."[29]

SINGAPORE AIRLINES (SIA)

Singapore Airlines is consistently recognized as the world's "best" airline in large part due to its stellar efforts at internal marketing. SIA strives to create a "wow effect" and regularly surprise its customers. It does this by listening intensely and constantly identifying opportunities generated by customer feedback.

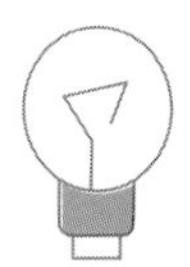

MARKETING INSIGHT | VOICE MAIL HELL

As anyone who has ever spent 15 minutes in Interactive Voice Mail "hell" knows, customer rage is a fact of twenty-first-century life. While we have ever more products that are supposed to make our lives more convenient, there are ever more companies we need to deal with to install and set up those products or fix a problem when they fail. In the past, we used to interact with a human being; now we are more likely to interact with a prerecorded voice message or a remote "online technical help" center. The result: more customer rage than ever. In fact, Virginia-based Customer Care Alliance, in a survey of 1,094 households, has concluded that U.S. companies are driving their customers crazy.

Of the 45 percent of households that reported at least one "serious problem" with a product or service in the past year, more than two-thirds of those customers experienced "rage" over the way the incident was handled. Sixteen percent of respondents said they wanted "revenge" on the company, and 3 percent took legal action.

Rising frustration levels come at a price for companies. Angry customers can damage a brand or company with bad word of mouth. Ninety percent of angry customers reported that they shared their story with a friend. Now, they can share their stories with strangers via the Internet. "The Internet is word of mouth on steroids," Pete Blackshaw likes to say, and he should know. Blackshaw is chief marketing and customer satisfaction officer for Intelliseek, a company that has made a profit by allowing consumers to rant—or rave—on its Planetfeedback.com site. With a few clicks on the Planetfeedback site, shoppers can send an e-mail, complaint, compliment, suggestion, or question directly to a company with the option to post comments publicly at the site as well.

That's what Beth Heckel, a Colorado preschool aide did, after she received a series of threatening letters from CD club, Columbia House, a full six years after her daughter's membership expired. Heckel couldn't get a response from the company by phone or mail and was on the verge of sending in the disputed $40 just to salvage her credit rating. When Heckel sent her complaint to Columbia House via Planetfeedback.com, she got an e-mail conceding the company's error and the letters stopped. The likelihood of finally getting some action—or just the satisfaction of venting publicly—is why consumers sent 67,000 e-mails to 15,000 companies via Planetfeedback last year alone. Sue MacDonald, an Intelliseek spokesperson, said: "About 80 percent of the companies respond to the complaints, some within an hour."

More important than simply responding to a disgruntled customer, however, is preventing dissatisfaction from occurring in the future. Ironically, Blackshaw says, "a company will spend hundreds of dollars per customer to attract people to its business, but far less to keep that customer once he or she has been acquired." That may mean simply taking the time to nurture customer relationships and give customers attention from an actual living, breathing human being. Columbia Records claims it is now spending $10 million to improve its call center and customers who phone the company can now "opt out" to reach an operator at any point in their calls.

Sources: Jane Spencer, "Cases of Customer Rage Mount as Bad Service Prompts Venting," *Wall Street Journal,* September 17, 2003, p. D4; Judi Ketteler, "Grumbling Groundswell," *Cincinnati Business Courier,* September 8, 2003; Richard Halicks, "You Can Count on Customer Disservice," *Atlanta Journal Constitution,* June 29, 2003, p. D4; Michelle Slatella, "Toll-Free Apology Soothes Savage Beast," *New York Times,* February 12, 2004, p. G4; Bruce Horovitz, "Whatever Happened to Customer Service?" *USA Today,* September 26, 2003, p. A1.

TABLE 13.1

Factors Leading to Customer Switching Behavior

Pricing
- High Price
- Price Increases
- Unfair Pricing
- Deceptive Pricing

Inconvenience
- Location/Hours
- Wait for Appointment
- Wait for Service

Core Service Failure
- Service Mistakes
- Billing Errors
- Service Catastrophe

Service Encounter Failures
- Uncaring
- Impolite
- Unresponsive
- Unknowledgeable

Response to Service Failure
- Negative Response
- No Response
- Reluctant Response

Competition
- Found Better Service

Ethical Problems
- Cheat
- Hard Sell
- Unsafe
- Conflict of Interest

Involuntary Switching
- Customer Moved
- Provider Closed

Source: Susan M. Keaveney, "Customer Switching Behavior in Service Industries: An Exploratory Study," *Journal of Marketing* (April 1995): 71–82.

Some examples of this are SIA's new lighter, more nutritious fare and its in-flight e-mail service. SIA places a high emphasis on training. Its latest initiative, called "Transforming Customer Service (TCS)," involves staff in five key operational areas: cabin crew, engineering, ground services, flight operations, and sales support. The TCS culture is embedded in all management training, company-wide. TCS also uses a 40-30-30 rule in its holistic approach to people, processes and products: 40 percent of resources go to training and invigorating staff, 30 percent is spent on reviewing process and procedures, and the last 30 percent on creating new product and service ideas.[30]

Interactive marketing describes the employees' skill in serving the client. Clients judge service not only by its *technical quality* (e.g., Was the surgery successful?), but also by its *functional quality* (e.g., Did the surgeon show concern and inspire confidence?).[31] Technology has great power to make service workers more productive.[32] Respiratory therapists at the University of California at San Diego Medical Center now carry miniature computers in their coat pockets so that they can call up patient records on handheld computers and therefore spend more time working directly with patients.

Companies must avoid pushing productivity so hard, however, that they reduce perceived quality. Some methods lead to too much standardization. Service providers must deliver "high-touch" as well as "high-tech."[33] Consider Schwab.

SCHWAB.COM

Charles Schwab, the nation's largest discount brokerage house, uses the Web to create an innovative combination of high-tech and high-touch services. One of the first major brokerage houses to provide online trading, Schwab today services 8 million accounts. It has avoided competing on price with low-priced competitors (e.g., Ameritrade.com) and instead has assembled the most comprehensive financial and company information

FIG. 13.3

Three Types of Marketing in Service Industries

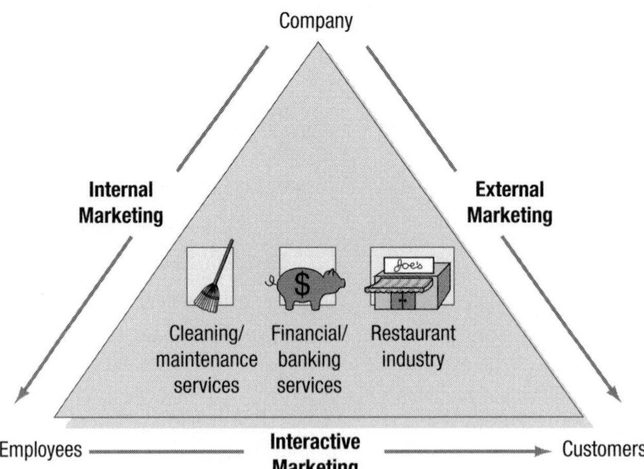

resources to be found online. It offers account information and proprietary research from retail brokers; real-time quotes; an after-hours trading program; the Schwab learning center; live events; online chats with customer service representatives; a global investing service; and market updates delivered by e-mail. Schwab continues to lead its competitors by applying the three principles of superior service (online, via phone, and in local branch offices), innovative products, and discount prices.[34]

::: Managing Service Quality

The service quality of a firm is tested at each service encounter. If retail clerks are bored, cannot answer simple questions, or are visiting with each other while customers are waiting, customers will think twice about doing business again with that seller.

Customer Expectations

Customers form service expectations from many sources, such as past experiences, word of mouth, and advertising. In general, customers compare the *perceived service* with the *expected service*.[35] If the perceived service falls below the expected service, customers are disappointed. If the perceived service meets or exceeds their expectations, they are apt to use the provider again. Successful companies add benefits to their offering that not only *satisfy* customers but surprise and *delight* them. Delighting customers is a matter of exceeding expectations.

RITZ-CARLTON HOTELS

Ritz-Carlton Hotels legendary service starts with 100 hours of training annually for every employee. The company empowers employees to make decisions and spend money to solve customer service issues. Guestrooms are exhaustively reviewed every 90 days and guaranteed to be defect free, check-in time has been cut in half, and special programs created for family travelers and weddings. It's perhaps no surprise that Ritz-Carlton was the first two-time winner of the Malcolm Baldridge National Quality Award.[36]

Parasuraman, Zeithaml, and Berry formulated a service-quality model that highlights the main requirements for delivering high service quality.[37] The model, shown in Figure 13.4, identifies five gaps that cause unsuccessful delivery:

1. ***Gap between consumer expectation and management perception*** – Management does not always correctly perceive what customers want. Hospital administrators may think that patients want better food, but patients may be more concerned with nurse responsiveness.

2. ***Gap between management perception and service-quality specification*** – Management might correctly perceive customers' wants but not set a performance standard. Hospital administrators may tell the nurses to give "fast" service without specifying it in minutes.
3. ***Gap between service-quality specifications and service delivery*** – Personnel might be poorly trained, or incapable of or unwilling to meet the standard; or they may be held to conflicting standards, such as taking time to listen to customers and serving them fast.
4. ***Gap between service delivery and external communications*** – Consumer expectations are affected by statements made by company representatives and ads. If a hospital brochure shows a beautiful room, but the patient arrives and finds the room to be cheap and tacky looking, external communications have distorted the customer's expectations.
5. ***Gap between perceived service and expected service*** – This gap occurs when the consumer misperceives the service quality. The physician may keep visiting the patient to show care, but the patient may interpret this as an indication that something really is wrong.

Based on this service-quality model, these researchers identified the following five determinants of service quality, in order of importance.[38]

1. ***Reliability*** – The ability to perform the promised service dependably and accurately.
2. ***Responsiveness*** – The willingness to help customers and to provide prompt service.
3. ***Assurance*** – The knowledge and courtesy of employees and their ability to convey trust and confidence.
4. ***Empathy*** – The provision of caring, individualized attention to customers.

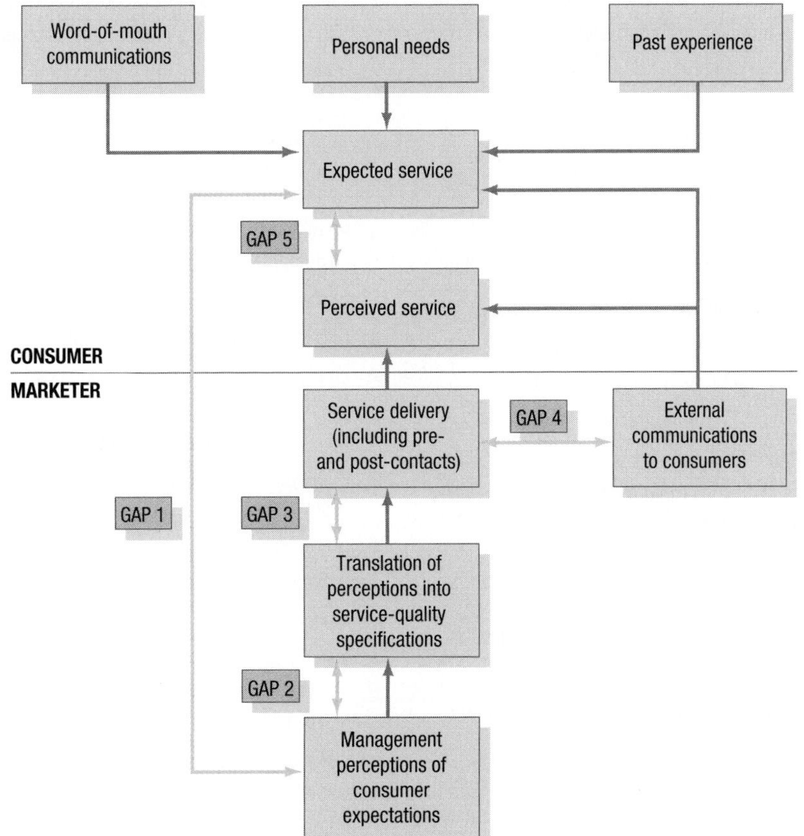

FIG. 13.4

Service-Quality Model

Sources: A. Parasuraman, Valarie A. Zeithaml, and Leonard L. Berry, "A Conceptual Model of Service Quality and its implications for Future Research," *Journal of Marketing* (Fall 1985): 44. Reprinted with permission of the American Marketing Association. The model is more fully discussed or elaborated in Valarie A. Zeithaml and Mary Jo Bitner, *Services Marketing* (New York: McGraw-Hill, 1996), ch. 2.

5. ***Tangibles*** – The appearance of physical facilities, equipment, personnel, and communication materials.

Based on these five factors, the researchers developed the 21-item SERVQUAL scale (see Table 13.2).[39] They also note that there is a *zone of tolerance* or range where consumer perceptions on a service dimension would be deemed satisfactory, anchored by the minimum level consumers would be willing to accept and the level that customers believe can and should be delivered. "Marketing Insight: The Role of Expectations in Service-Quality Perceptions" describes important recent research on services marketing. "Marketing Memo: Assessing E-Service Quality" reviews models of online service quality.

Best Practices of Service-Quality Management

Various studies have shown that well-managed service companies share the following common practices: a strategic concept, a history of top-management commitment to quality, high standards, self-service technologies, systems for monitoring service performance and customer complaints, and an emphasis on employee satisfaction. "Marketing Memo: Recommendations for Improving Service Quality" also offers a comprehensive set of guidelines for service marketers. Rackspace, a San Antonio–based Web-hosting company, embodies many of these practices.

RACKSPACE

In 1999, the Rackspace tech support team was lax about delivering great service and, indeed, was often hostile to customers. Its turnaround began with a new company mantra—to provide *fanatical* support. This concept was backed by a few simple rules: Criticizing a customer is a firing offense. Be reliable. No news is not good news. In other words, you must communicate frequently with customers. Remove all obstacles that make it hard for customers to do business with you. Rackspace also broke down departmental silos and created eight "pods." These clusters include a team leader, two or three account managers, billing personnel, and several tech-support specialists. Each pod serves a group of customers sorted by size and complexity. With this setup, every Rackspace customer calls the

TABLE 13.2

SERVQUAL Attributes

Reliability

- Providing service as promised
- Dependability in handling customers' service problems
- Performing services right the first time
- Providing services at the promised time
- Maintaining error-free records

Responsiveness

- Keeping customer informed as to when services will be performed
- Prompt service to customers
- Willingness to help customers
- Readiness to respond to customers' requests

Assurance

- Employees who instill confidence in customers
- Making customers feel safe in their transactions
- Employees who are consistently courteous
- Employees who have the knowledge to answer customer questions

Empathy

- Giving customers individual attention
- Employees who deal with customers in a caring fashion
- Having the customer's best interests at heart
- Employees who understand the needs of their customers
- Convenient business hours

Tangibles

- Modern equipment
- Visually appealing facilities
- Employees who have a neat, professional appearance
- Visually appealing materials associated with the service

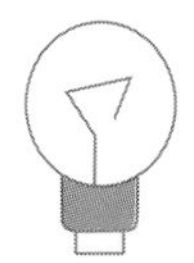

MARKETING INSIGHT | THE ROLE OF EXPECTATIONS IN SERVICE-QUALITY PERCEPTIONS

The Parasuraman, Ziethaml, and Berry service-quality model highlights some of the gaps that cause unsuccessful service delivery. Subsequent research has extended the model to incorporate additional considerations. Boulding, Kalra, Staelin, and Zeithaml have developed a dynamic process model of service quality. The model is based on the premise that customer perceptions and expectations of service quality change over time, but at any one point in time are a function of prior expectations of what *will* and what *should* happen during the service encounter, as well as the *actual* service delivered during the last contact. The researchers' empirically tested model contends that the two different types of expectations have opposing effects on perceptions of service quality.

1. *Increasing* customer expectations of what the firm *will* deliver can lead to improved perceptions of overall service quality.
2. *Decreasing* customer expectations of what the firm *should* deliver can lead to improved perceptions of overall service quality.

Much work has validated the role of expectations in consumers' interpretations and evaluations of the service encounter and the relationship they adopt with a firm over time. Consumers are often forward-looking with respect to their decision to keep or switch from a service relationship. Any marketing activity that affects current or expected future usage can help to solidify a service relationship.

With continuously provided services, such as public utilities, health care, financial services, computing services, insurance, and other professional, membership, or subscription services, customers have been observed to mentally calculate their *payment equity*—the perceived fairness of the level of economic benefits derived from service usage in relation to the level of economic costs. Payment costs typically consist of some combination of an initial payment such as a membership fee or retainer; a fixed, periodic fee such as a monthly service charge; and a variable fee such as usage-based charges. Payment benefits depend on current payment and usage levels. The perceived fairness of the exchange determines service satisfaction and future usage. In other words, it is as if customers ask themselves, "Am I using this service enough, given what I pay for it?" Customers may be satisfied even with low usage *if* that is their expectation.

There can be a dark side to long-term service relationships. For example, with an ad agency, the client may feel that over time, the agency loses objectivity and becomes stale in its thinking or begins to take advantage of the relationship.

Sources: William Boulding, Ajay Kalra, Richard Staelin, and Valarie A. Zeithaml, "A Dynamic Model of Service Quality: From Expectations to Behavioral Intentions," *Journal of Marketing Research* 30 (February 1993): 7–27; Katherine N. Lemon, Tiffany Barnett White, and Russell S. Winer, "Dynamic Customer Relationship Management: Incorporating Future Considerations into the Service Retention Decision," *Journal of Marketing* 6 (January 2002): 1–14; Ruth N. Bolton and Katherine N. Lemon, "A Dynamic Model of Customers' Usage of Services: Usage as an Antecedent and Consequence of Satisfaction," *Journal of Marketing* 36 (May 1999): 171–186; Kent Grayson and Tim Ambler, "The Dark Side of Long-Term Relationships in Marketing Services," *Journal of Marketing Research* 36 (February 1999): 132–141.

same person every time and gets a problem solved quickly. Every month Rackspace gives the "straightjacket award" to the employee who best lives up to the company's "fanatical customer support" motto. Public recognition of employee achievement includes customer compliments posted on the walls and a "FANATIC" sign hanging prominently above the desk of straightjacket award winners. When the company received its first gift from a customer a few months after these rules and procedures were set in stone, it knew it was on the right track.[40] ■

STRATEGIC CONCEPT Top service companies are "customer obsessed." They have a clear sense of their target customers and their needs. They have developed a distinctive strategy for satisfying these needs. While most brokerage firms chase after an older, wealthier customer base, online brokers E*TRADE targets 24- to 37-year-old Gen Xers who are technologically savvy and self-sufficient but largely ignored by other firms. As CEO Christos Cotsakos observes, "There's this whole generation that's very computer literate, that's building wealth and looking for solutions that aren't like their grandfathers'. If we can identify with this new class of individuals and provide them with the best value, we think we can own that space."[41]

TOP-MANAGEMENT COMMITMENT Companies such as Marriott, Disney, and USAA have a thorough commitment to service quality. Their managements look not only at financial performance on a monthly basis, but also at service performance. Ray Kroc of McDonald's insisted on continually measuring each McDonald's outlet on its conformance to QSCV: quality, service, cleanliness, and value. Some companies insert a reminder along with employees' paychecks: BROUGHT TO YOU BY THE CUSTOMER. Sam Walton of Wal-Mart required the following employee pledge: "I solemnly swear and declare that every customer that comes within 10 feet of me, I will smile, look them in the eye, and greet them, so help me Sam."

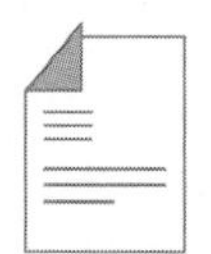

MARKETING MEMO | ASSESSING E-SERVICE QUALITY

Zeithaml, Parasuraman, and Malhotra define online service quality as the extent to which a Web site facilitates efficient and effective shopping, purchasing, and delivery. They identified 11 dimensions of perceived e-service quality: access, ease of navigation, efficiency, flexibility, reliability, personalization, security/privacy, responsiveness, assurance/trust, site aesthetics, and price knowledge. Some of these service-quality dimensions were the same online as offline, but some specific underlying attributes were different. Different dimensions emerged with e-service quality too. They also found that empathy didn't seem to be as important online, unless there were service problems. Core dimensions of regular service quality were efficiency, fulfillment, reliability, and privacy; core dimensions of service recovery were responsiveness, compensation, and real-time access to help.

Wolfinbarger and Gilly developed a reduced scale of online service quality with four key dimensions: reliability/fulfillment, Web site design, security/privacy, and customer service. The researchers interpret their study findings to suggest that the most basic building blocks of a "compelling online experience" are reliability and outstanding Web site functionality in terms of time savings, easy transactions, good selection, in-depth information, and the "right level" of personalization. Their 14-item scale is displayed here:

Reliability/Fulfillment

The product that came was represented accurately by the Web site.
You get what you ordered from this Web site.
The product is delivered by the time promised by the company.

Web Site Design

This Web site provides in-depth information.
The site doesn't waste my time.
It is quick and easy to complete a transaction at this Web site.
The level of personalization at this site is about right, not too much or too little.
This Web site has good selection.

Security/Privacy

I feel that my privacy is protected at this site.
I feel safe in my transactions with this Web site.
This Web site has adequate security transactions.

Customer Service

The company is willing and ready to respond to customer needs.
When you have a problem, the Web site shows a sincere interest in solving it.
Inquiries are answered promptly.

Sources: Valarie A. Zeithaml, A. Parsu Parasuraman, and Arvind Malhotra, "A Conceptual Framework for Understanding e-Service Quality: Implications for Future Research and Managerial Practice," *Marketing Science Institute Working Paper,* Report No. 00-115, 2000; Mary Wolfinbarger and Mary C. Gilly, ".comQ: Dimensionalizing, Measuring, and Predicting Quality of the E-tail Experience," *Marketing Science Institute Working Paper,* Report No. 02-100, 2002.

HIGH STANDARDS The best service providers set high service-quality standards. Citibank aims to answer phone calls within 10 seconds and customer letters within 2 days. The standards must be set *appropriately* high. A 98 percent accuracy standard may sound good, but it would result in FedEx losing 64,000 packages a day; 6 misspelled words on each page of a book; 400,000 mis-filled prescriptions daily; and unsafe drinking water 8 days a year. One can distinguish between companies offering "merely good" service and those offering "breakthrough" service, aimed at being 100 percent defect-free.[42]

A service company can differentiate itself by designing a better and faster delivery system. There are three levels of differentiation.[43] The first is *reliability:* Some suppliers are more reliable in their on-time delivery, order completeness, and order-cycle time. The second is *resilience:* Some suppliers are better at handling emergencies, product recalls, and answering inquiries. The third is *innovativeness:* Some suppliers create better information systems, introduce bar coding and mixed pallets, and in other ways help the customer.

Many distribution experts say that a company's money would be better spent on improving delivery performance than on advertising. They say that superior service performance is a more effective differentiator than image expenditures. Furthermore, it is harder for a competitor to duplicate a superior distribution system than to copy an advertising campaign.

DIAL-A-MATTRESS

Napoleon Barragan started Dial-A-Mattress in 1976; by 1999, it had generated $80 million in annual sales. Customers can call a toll-free number (1-800-Mattres) 24 hours a day, seven days a week, talk to a bedding consultant, have the right mattress delivered the same day, and receive a 30-day customer satisfaction guarantee trial period. The company also sells mattresses via a successful Web site, mattress.com, as well as in its own showrooms around the country.

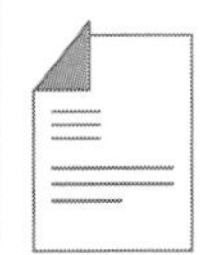

MARKETING MEMO | RECOMMENDATIONS FOR IMPROVING SERVICE QUALITY

Parasuraman, Berry, and Zeithaml, who are academic research pioneers on services, offer 10 lessons that they maintain are essential for improving service quality across service industries.

1. ***Listening***—Understand what customers really want through continuous learning about the expectations and perceptions of customers and noncustomers (e.g., by means of a service-quality information system).
2. ***Reliability***—Reliability is the single most important dimension of service quality and must be a service priority.
3. ***Basic service***—Service companies must deliver the basics and do what they are supposed to do—keep promises, use common sense, listen to customers, keep customers informed, and be determined to deliver value to customers.
4. ***Service design***—Develop a holistic view of the service while managing its many details.
5. ***Recovery***—To satisfy customers who encounter a service problem, service companies should encourage customers to complain (and make it easy for them to do so), respond quickly and personally, and develop a problem resolution system.
6. ***Surprising customers***—Although reliability is the most important dimension in *meeting* customers' service expectations, process dimensions (e.g., assurance, responsiveness, and empathy) are most important in *exceeding* customer expectations, for example, by surprising them with uncommon swiftness, grace, courtesy, competence, commitment, and understanding.
7. ***Fair play***—Service companies must make special efforts to be fair and to demonstrate fairness to customers and employees.
8. ***Teamwork***—Teamwork is what enables large organizations to deliver service with care and attentiveness by improving employee motivation and capabilities.
9. ***Employee researc***—Conduct research with employees to reveal why service problems occur and what companies must do to solve problems.
10. ***Servant leadership***—Quality service comes from inspired leadership throughout the organization; from excellent service-system design; from the effective use of information and technology; and from a slow-to-change, invisible, all-powerful, internal force called corporate culture.

Source: Leonard L. Berry, A. Parasuraman, and Valarie A. Zeithaml, "Ten Lessons for Improving Service Quality," *MSI Reports Working Paper Series, No. 03-001,* 2003 (Cambridge, MA: Marketing Science Institute), pp. 61–82.

SELF-SERVICE TECHNOLOGIES (SSTS) As is the case with products, consumers value convenience in services.[44] Many person-to-person service interactions are being replaced by self-service technologies.[45] To the traditional vending machines we can add Automated Teller Machines (ATMs), self-pumping at gas stations, self-checkout at hotels, self-ticket purchasing on the Internet, and self-customization of products on the Internet.

Not all SSTs improve service quality, but they have the potential of making service transactions more accurate, convenient, and faster. Every company needs to think about improving its service using SSTs. Companies would be smart to enable customers to call the company when they need more information than the SST provides. Online hotel reservation Web sites often include a "Call Me" button. If the customer clicks on it, a service rep will immediately phone the person to answer a question. Even banks miss an opportunity to use their ATMs. A customer might draw money from the ATM and see the message: "Call 1-800-123-4567 to earn more interest"; but the customer goes home and forgets to call. The ATM's message could have been: "You have $6,000 over the required balance."

Imagine an auto insurance company wanting to improve its claim service and assistance. Normally, a driver involved in an accident has to wait for a claims adjuster to show up, assess the damage, and offer a settlement. The insurance company's Web site could include step-by-step guidelines telling the insured person what to do. It would list the kinds of documents needed by the police, and by the hospital; suggest the names of reliable medical and legal professionals; and list reputable car-rental firms and repair shops in the customer's area. Claim forms would be filled out on the Web site. The claims adjuster, when he or she visits the driver, can use a handheld mobile computing device and digital camera to photograph the damage, send a streaming video back to headquarters, get approval, and print out a check for car repair on the spot.

When initiating self-service technologies, some companies have found that the biggest obstacle is not the technology itself, but convincing customers to use it. "Marketing Memo: Getting Self-Service Kiosks off the Ground" offers some tips.

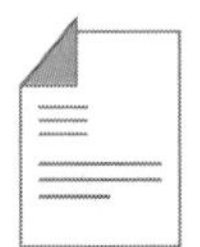

MARKETING MEMO | GETTING SELF-SERVICE KIOSKS OFF THE GROUND

With air travelers already skittish about security-imposed delays, the idea that a self-service kiosk will malfunction with no one around to help can make them avoid self-service altogether, even if they have to wait longer. Delta has been successful in getting customers to use its self-service kiosks by employing a number of tactics.

1. ***Advertise the advantages.*** Delta initiated a major ad campaign to make customers aware of the advantages of self-service. Ads saying "Experience Waitlessness" and "Delta Air Lines" with "Lines" crossed out appeared all over New York City. Once at the airport, customers in check-in lines are approached by customer reps who direct them to the kiosks.
2. ***Be there to help.*** First-time users, in particular, need handholding, so an employee should be available to show them the ropes and to help if a machine malfunctions. If people have a good experience the first time, they will become kiosk converts.
3. ***Maintain the machines.*** Machines break down, particularly in a rugged, heavy-use environment like an airport. Delta tries to prevent self-service kiosk breakdowns instead of having to put up an "out of order" sign.

Source: John McCormick, "Roadblock: The Customer; Airlines, Railroads, Grocery Stores and Hotels Racing to Deploy Self-Service Check-In Devices Have Discovered Two Things," *Baseline,* April 1, 2003.

MONITORING SYSTEMS Top firms audit service performance, both their own and competitors', on a regular basis. They collect *voice of the customer (VOC) measurements* to probe customer satisfiers and dissatisfiers. They use comparison shopping, ghost shopping, customer surveys, suggestion and complaint forms, service-audit teams, and letters to the president. The First Chicago Bank employs a weekly Performance Measurement Program charting its performance on a large number of customer-sensitive issues. Figure 13.5 shows a typical chart that tracks speed in answering customer service phone inquiries. The bank will take action whenever performance falls below the minimum acceptable level. It also raises its performance goal over time.

Mystery shopping—the use of undercover shoppers who are paid to report back to the company—is now big business: $300 million in the United States and $500 million worldwide. Fast-food chains, big-box stores, gas stations, and even large government agencies are using mystery shoppers to pinpoint and fix customer service problems.

Services can be judged on *customer importance* and *company performance. Importance-performance analysis* is used to rate the various elements of the service bundle and identify what actions are required. Table 13.3 shows how customers rated 14 service elements (attributes) of an automobile dealer's service department on importance and performance. For example, "Job done right the first time" (attribute 1) received a mean importance rating of 3.83 and a mean performance rating of 2.63, indicating that customers felt it was highly important but not performed well.

The ratings of the 14 elements are displayed in Figure 13.6 and divided into four sections. Quadrant A shows important service elements that are not being performed at the desired levels; they include elements 1, 2, and 9. The dealer should concentrate on improving the service department's performance on these elements. Quadrant B shows important service elements that are being performed well; the company needs to maintain the high performance. Quadrant C shows minor service elements that are being delivered in a mediocre

FIG. 13.5

Tracking Customer Service Performance

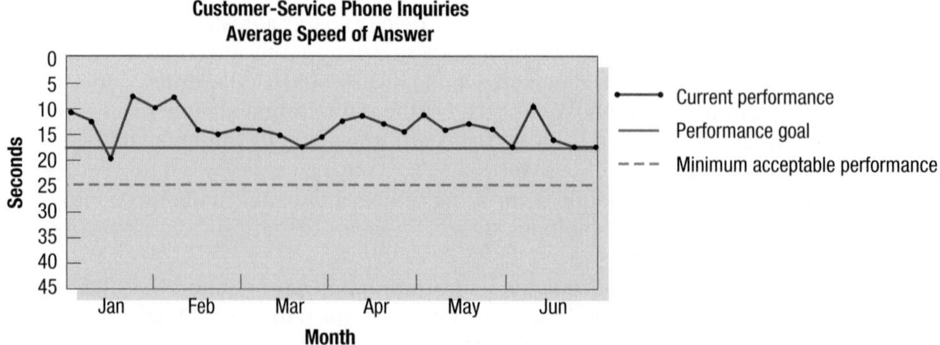

TABLE 13.3

Customer Importance and Performance Ratings for an Auto Dealership

Attribute Number	Attribute Description	Mean Importance Rating[a]	Mean Performance Rating[b]
1	Job done right the first time	3.83	2.63
2	Fast action on complaints	3.63	2.73
3	Prompt warranty work	3.60	3.15
4	Able to do any job needed	3.56	3.00
5	Service available when needed	3.41	3.05
6	Courteous and friendly service	3.41	3.29
7	Car ready when promised	3.38	3.03
8	Perform only necessary work	3.37	3.11
9	Low prices on service	3.29	2.00
10	Clean up after service work	3.27	3.02
11	Convenient to home	2.52	2.25
12	Convenient to work	2.43	2.49
13	Courtesy buses and cars	2.37	2.35
14	Send out maintenance notices	2.05	3.33

[a]Ratings obtained from a four-point scale of "extremely important" (4), "important" (3), "slightly important" (2), and "not important" (1).

[b]Ratings obtained from a four-point scale of "excellent" (4), "good" (3), "fair" (2), and "poor" (1). A "no basis for judgment" category was also provided.

way but do not need any attention. Quadrant D shows that a minor service element, "Send out maintenance notices," is being performed in an excellent manner. Perhaps the company should spend less on sending out maintenance notices and use the savings to improve performance on important elements. The analysis can be enhanced by checking on the competitors' performance levels on each element.[46]

SATISFYING CUSTOMER COMPLAINTS Studies of customer dissatisfaction show that customers are dissatisfied with their purchases about 25 percent of the time but that only about 5 percent complain. The other 95 percent either feel complaining is not worth the effort, or they do not know how or to whom to complain.

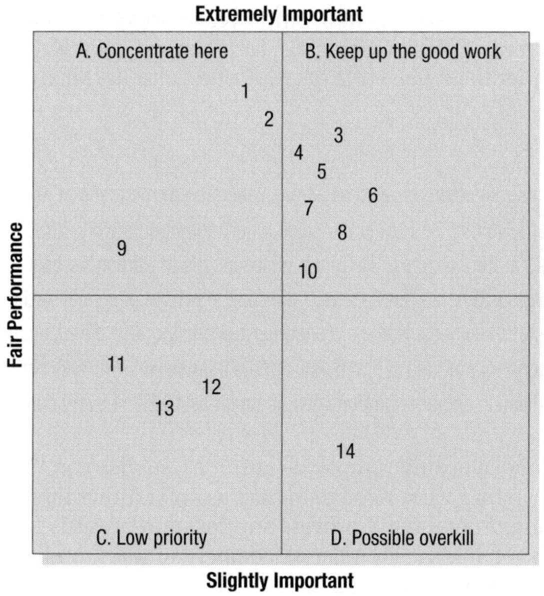

FIG. 13.6

Importance-Performance Analysis

Of the 5 percent who complain, only about 50 percent report a satisfactory problem resolution. Yet the need to resolve a customer problem in a satisfactory manner is critical. On average, a satisfied customer tells three people about a good product experience. The average dissatisfied customer gripes to 11 people. If each of them tells still other people, the number of people exposed to bad word of mouth may grow exponentially.

Customers whose complaints are satisfactorily resolved often become more company-loyal than customers who were never dissatisfied.[47] About 34 percent of customers who register major complaints will buy again from the company if their complaint is resolved, and this number rises to 52 percent for minor complaints. If the complaint is resolved quickly, between 52 percent (major complaints) and 95 percent (minor complaints) will buy again from the company.[48]

Every complaint is a gift if handled well. Companies that encourage disappointed customers to complain—and also empower employees to remedy the situation on the spot—have been shown to achieve higher revenues and greater profits than companies that do not have a systematic approach for addressing service failures.[49] Pizza Hut prints its toll-free number on all pizza boxes. When a customer complains, Pizza Hut sends voice mail to the store manager, who must call the customer within 48 hours and resolve the complaint. Hyatt Hotels gets high marks on many of these criteria.

HYATT HOTELS

Hyatt Hotels excels at answering complaints in an extraordinarily short time. One business customer, for example, checked into the Denver Hyatt but did not like his room. He turned on the television and was greeted by a screen with the Hyatt customer survey. Using the TV remote, he punched in his evaluations. To his surprise and delight, within five minutes of receiving the electronic communication, the hotel manager called him to say that because the hotel was entirely booked and the room could not be changed, the guest could expect a hospitality gift for his inconvenience.[50]

Research has shown that customers evaluate complaint incidents in terms of the outcomes they receive, the procedures used to arrive at those outcomes, and the nature of the interpersonal treatment during the process.[51]

Getting front-line employees to adopt *extra-role behaviors* and to advocate the interests and image of the firm to consumers as well as take initiative and engage in conscientious behavior in dealing with customers can be a critical asset in handling complaints.[52] Companies also are increasing the quality of their *call centers* and their *customer service representatives* (CSRs). Handling phone calls more efficiently can improve service, reduce complaints, and extend customer longevity.

SATISFYING EMPLOYEES AS WELL AS CUSTOMERS Excellent service companies know that positive employee attitudes will promote stronger customer loyalty. Sears found a high correlation between customer satisfaction, employee satisfaction, and store profitability. In companies such as Hallmark, John Deere, and Four Seasons Hotels, employees exhibit real company pride. Consider the crucial role of employees with Re/Max:[53]

RE/MAX

Re/Max has actually made its real estate brokers and franchisees the prime focus of its marketing. As one industry observer noted, "Agents perceive that Re/Max is the place where top agents work. That message is very clear and it's a powerful one to people in the business." Re/Max's philosophy is to attract the best agents who in turn attract the best and most profitable customers—an approach that has led Re/Max agents to the highest average annual commissions in the real estate business. National consumer advertising and the distinctive Re/Max logo—a red, white, and blue hot air balloon—are funded in part by the agents themselves, who also benefit from the fact that they pay a flat fee for Re/Max affiliation and are compensated as much as 100% of every commission.

Given the importance of positive employee attitudes, service companies must attract the best employees they can find. They need to market a career rather than just a job. They must design a sound training program and provide support and rewards for good performance. They can use the intranet, internal newsletters, daily reminders, and employee roundtables to reinforce customer-centered attitudes.

Outstanding Agents.
Outstanding Results.
RE/MAX agents average more experience and more sales than other real estate agents.
That's good news for you and your family – whether you're hoping to buy or looking to sell.
RE/MAX
www.remax.com
RE/MAX Community
555-1212
Each RE/MAX® real estate office is independently owned and operated.

Agents are the focus of RE/MAX marketing, as this print ad shows. Advertising like this is paid for in part by the agents themselves.

It is important to audit employee job satisfaction regularly. Karl Albrecht observed that unhappy employees can be "terrorists." Rosenbluth and Peters went so far as to say that the company's employees, not the company's customers, have to be made number one if the company hopes to truly satisfy its customers.[54] A company must be careful in training its employees to be friendly:

SAFEWAY STORES

In the 1990s, supermarket chain Safeway instituted "Superior Service," an unusually aggressive program to build employee friendliness toward customers. Among the rules: Make eye contact with all customers, smile, greet each one, offer samples of products, make suggestions about other possible items to purchase. To ensure compliance, "mystery shoppers" secretly graded workers. Those who received poor grades were sent to a training program. Although surveys showed that customers were pleased with the program, many employees admitted to being stressed out and several quit in protest over the plan. "It's so artificial, it's unreal," said one second-generation Safeway employee who quit her job as cashier after 20 years with the chain, partly out of frustration with the Superior Service program. Several female employees even filed sexual harassment suits against Safeway, charging that the forced smiles were misinterpreted and led to unwelcome advances from male customers.[55]

::: Managing Service Brands

Some of the world's strongest brands are services—consider financial service leaders such as Citibank, American Express, JP Morgan, HSBC, and Goldman Sachs. Several hospitals have attained "megabrand" reputations for being the best in their field, such as the Mayo Clinic,

Massachusetts General, and Sloan-Kettering. These hospitals could open clinics in other cities and attract patients on the strength of their brand reputation. As with any brand, service brands must be skillful at differentiating themselves and developing appropriate brand strategies.

Differentiating Services

Service marketers frequently complain about the difficulty of differentiating their services. The deregulation of several major service industries—communications, transportation, energy, banking—has resulted in intense price competition. To the extent that customers view a service as fairly homogeneous, they care less about the provider than the price.

PROGRESSIVE CORP.

Ranked number one in *BusinessWeek*'s Top 50 Performers for 2004, Progressive shows how a service company can stand out from the pack by constantly asking—and answering—the question, "Is there an even better way?" Auto insurers have never been known as a customer-friendly bunch, but Progressive used this dismal history to its advantage. From its start in the 1990s, the company gained notice for offering prospective customers price quotes from up to three rival insurers, as well as its own. This move gained it thousands of new accounts. Then, once Progressive won new customers' business, it mobilized an army of 12,000 claims adjusters who speed right to an accident scene—and often cut a check right on the spot. Its latest new service is one that lets drivers involved in a small accident drop off their banged-up car, pick up a rental—and then come back to a fully repaired car a couple of days later. All of these nontraditional moves have paid off big time: While others in the industry are just coming out of a slump, Progressive's profits have soared an average annual 183 percent over the past three years to $1.3 billion in 2003.[56]

Service offerings, however, can be differentiated in many ways. The offering can include innovative features. What the customer expects is called the *primary service package*. Vanguard, the second-largest no-load mutual fund company, has a unique client ownership structure that lowers costs and permits better fund returns. Strongly differentiated from many competitors, the brand grew through word of mouth, PR, and viral marketing.[57]

The provider can add *secondary service features* to the package. In the airline industry, various carriers have introduced such secondary service features as movies, merchandise for sale, air-to-ground telephone service, and frequent-flier award programs. Marriott is setting up hotel rooms for high-tech travelers who need accommodations that will support computers, fax machines, and e-mail. Many companies are using the Web to offer secondary service features that were never possible before:

KAISER PERMANENTE

Like many health maintenance organizations (HMOs), Kaiser Permanente is seeking value-added services that will not break the bank. The largest nonprofit health plan in the United States, with 8 million members in 11 states, the Kaiser Permanente award-winning Web site lets members register for office visits, e-mail questions to nurses and pharmacists (and get responses within 24 hours), participate in discussions monitored by health care professionals, and search for information in drug and health encyclopedias. Soon members will be able to directly access their own medical records.[58]

Conversely, other service providers are adding a human element to combat competition from online businesses. This is happening in many large drugstores. As in-store pharmacies see competition from low-cost online mail-order drugstores, they are playing up the presence of on-site health care professionals. For instance, Brooks Pharmacy is establishing "RX Care Centers" in many of its remodeled stores. There are private consulting rooms where pharmacists can speak at length with patients about complicated prescription benefit plans, potentially dangerous drug interactions, and embarrassing subjects like urinary incontinence. CVS is giving its pharmacists more time to speak to customers by investing in machines that count pills and fill pill bottles, a time-consuming and tedious task for most pharmacists.[59]

Sometimes the company achieves differentiation through the sheer range of its service offerings and the success of its cross-selling efforts. The major challenge is that most service offerings and innovations are easily copied. Still, the company that regularly introduces innovations will gain a succession of temporary advantages over competitors.

SCHNEIDER NATIONAL

Schneider National is the world's largest long-haul truckload freight carrier, with more than 40,000 bright orange trailers on the roads. Although the core benefit is to move freight from one location to another, Don Schneider is in the *customer solutions* business. His company is expert at providing a cost-minimizing trailer for each load. He offers service guarantees backed by monetary incentives for meeting tight schedules. He runs driver-training programs to improve driver performance. Dispatchers are assigned to large customers. Schneider was the first to introduce a computerized tracking system in each truck. Even painting the trucks orange was part of the branding strategy. If further innovations come into this industry, they will probably come from Schneider.

Developing Brand Strategies for Services

Developing brand strategies for a service brand requires special attention to choosing brand elements, establishing image dimensions, and devising the branding strategy.

CHOOSING BRAND ELEMENTS The intangibility of services has implications for the choice of brand elements. Because service decisions and arrangements are often made away from the actual service location itself (e.g., at home or at work), brand recall becomes critically important. In such cases, an easy-to-remember brand name is critical.

Other brand elements—logos, symbols, characters, and slogans—can also "pick up the slack" and complement the brand name to build brand awareness and brand image. These other brand elements often attempt to make the service and some of its key benefits more tangible, concrete, and real—for example, the "friendly skies" of United, the "good hands" of Allstate, and the "bullish" nature of Merrill Lynch.

Because a physical product does not exist, the physical facilities of the service provider—its primary and secondary signage, environmental design and reception area, apparel, collateral material, and so on—are especially important. All aspects of the service delivery process can be branded, which is why Allied Van Lines is concerned about the appearance of its drivers and laborers; why UPS has developed such strong equity with its brown trucks, and why DoubleTree hotels offers warm, fresh-baked cookies as a means of symbolizing care and friendliness.

ESTABLISHING IMAGE DIMENSIONS Organizational associations—such as perceptions about the people who make up the organization and who provide the service—are likely to be particularly important brand associations that may affect evaluations of service quality directly or indirectly. One particularly important association is company credibility and perceived expertise, trustworthiness, and likability.

Service firms must therefore design marketing communication and information programs so that consumers learn more about the brand than the information they get from service encounters alone. These programs may involve marketing communications which may be particularly effective at helping the firm to develop the proper brand personality. In 2003, State Farm launched a major new image-building marketing campaign.

STATE FARM

State Farm, ranked number 25 on the *Fortune* 500 list of largest companies, has a network of nearly 17,000 agents serving an estimated 28 million households in the United States and Canada. In 2003, a multimedia, multifaceted campaign was introduced with the theme, "We Live Where You Live." Backed by an integrated marketing campaign featuring print, TV, radio, direct mail, agent sales materials, point-of-sale pieces, a redesigned Web site, Internet banner ads, and billboards, the campaign was intended to reinforce its "good neighbor" image while also conveying that State Farm had expanded beyond its traditional lines of business of automotive, home, and life insurance into fields like health insurance, mutual funds, and even banking. The campaign was designed to show that State Farm financial services could offer support through life's transitions and that its agents are the source of these services. "With all that has happened in the markets in recent years, consumers today demand integrity, stability and a personal relationship from those who seek to help them with their financial needs," said Jack Weekes, vice president of marketing at State Farm.[60]

DEVISING BRANDING STRATEGY Finally, services also must consider developing a brand hierarchy and brand portfolio that permits positioning and targeting of different market segments. Classes of service can be branded vertically on the basis of price and quality. Vertical extensions often require sub-branding strategies where the corporate name is combined with

A print ad that is part of State Farm's "We Live Where You Live" multimedia image-building campaign. The ad also contains the familiar tagline, "LIKE A GOOD NEIGHBOR STATE FARM IS THERE.™"

an individual brand name or modifier. In the hotel and airlines industries, brand lines and portfolios have been created by brand extension and introductions. For example, Delta Airlines brands its business-class service as BusinessElite, its frequent-flier program as Sky Miles, its in-flight magazine as *Sky* magazine, its airport lounges as Crown Room Clubs, and its short-haul airlines as Song. Hilton Hotels has a portfolio of brands that includes Hilton Garden Inns to target budget-conscious business travelers and compete with the popular Courtyard by Marriott chain, as well as DoubleTree, Embassy Suites, Homewood Suites, and Hampton Inn. The circus Cirque du Soleil has adopted a very strict branding strategy.[61]

CIRQUE DU SOLEIL

Cirque du Soleil (French for "circus of the sun") has broken loose from circus convention. It takes traditional ingredients like trapeze artists, clowns, muscle men, and contortionists but places them in a nontraditional setting with lavish costumes, New Age music, and spectacular stage designs. Each production is loosely tied together with a theme such as "a tribute to the nomadic soul" (*Varekai*) or "a phantasmagoria of urban life" (*Saltimbanco*). Given that most theatrical productions fail, the fact that all 15 of Cirque du Soleil's productions have succeeded and that the firm nets $100 million a year is impressive. Part of the success is a company culture that encourages creativity and innovation and carefully safeguards the brand. Each production is created in-house—roughly one a year—and is unique: There are no duplicate touring companies.

::: Managing Product Support Services

Thus far we have focused on service industries. No less important are product-based industries that must provide a service bundle. Manufacturers of equipment—small appliances, office machines, tractors, mainframes, airplanes—all have to provide *product support services.*

Product support service is becoming a major battleground for competitive advantage. Chapter 12 described how products could be augmented with key service differentiators—ordering ease, delivery, installation, customer training, customer consulting, and maintenance and repair. Some equipment companies, such as Caterpillar Tractor and John Deere, make over 50 percent of their profits from these services. In the global marketplace, companies that make a good product but provide poor local service support are seriously disadvantaged. Firms that provide high-quality service outperform their less-service-oriented competitors.

Identifying and Satisfying Customer Needs

The company must define customer needs carefully in designing a service support program. Customers have three specific worries:[62]

- They worry about reliability and *failure frequency.* A farmer may tolerate a combine that will break down once a year, but not two or three times a year.
- They worry about *downtime.* The longer the downtime, the higher the cost. The customer counts on the seller's *service dependability*—the seller's ability to fix the machine quickly, or at least provide a loaner.[63]
- They worry about *out-of-pocket costs.* How much does the customer have to spend on regular maintenance and repair costs?

A buyer takes all these factors into consideration in choosing a vendor. The buyer tries to estimate the **life-cycle cost**, which is the product's purchase cost plus the discounted cost of maintenance and repair less the discounted salvage value. Buyers ask for hard data in choosing among vendors.

The importance of reliability, service dependability, and maintenance vary. A one-computer office will need higher product reliability and faster repair service than an office where other computers are available if one breaks down. An airline needs 100 percent reliability in the air. Where reliability is important, manufacturers or service providers can offer guarantees to promote sales.

To provide the best support, a manufacturer must identify the services customers value most and their relative importance. In the case of expensive equipment, manufacturers offer *facilitating services* such as installation, staff training, maintenance and repair services, and financing. They may also add *value-augmenting services.* Herman Miller, a major office furniture company, offers the Herman Miller promise to buyers: (1) five-year product warranties; (2) quality audits after project installation; (3) guaranteed move-in dates; (4) trade-in allowances on systems products.

A manufacturer can offer and charge for product support services in different ways. One specialty organic-chemical company provides a standard offering plus a basic level of services. If the customer wants additional services, it can pay extra or increase its annual purchases to a higher level, in which case additional services would be included. As another alternative, many companies offer *service contracts* (also called *extended warranties*), in which sellers agree to provide free maintenance and repair services for a specified period of time at a specified contract price. Service contracts often have variable lengths and different deductibles so that customers can choose the service level they want beyond the basic service package.

Companies need to plan product design and service-mix decisions in tandem. Design and quality-assurance managers should be part of the new-product development team. Good product design will reduce the amount of subsequent servicing. The Canon home copier uses a disposable toner cartridge that greatly reduces the need for service calls. Kodak and 3M designed equipment allowing the user to "plug in" to a central diagnostic facility that performs tests, locates the trouble, and fixes the equipment over the telephone lines. Companies are adding modularity and disposability to facilitate self-servicing.

Postsale Service Strategy

The quality of customer service departments varies greatly. At one extreme are departments that simply transfer customer calls to the appropriate person or department for action, with little follow-up. At the other extreme are departments eager to receive customer requests, suggestions, and even complaints and handle them expeditiously.

In providing service, most companies progress through a series of stages. Manufacturers usually start out by running their own parts-and-service departments. They want to stay close to the equipment and know its problems. They also find it expensive and time-consuming to train others, and discover that they can make good money running the parts-and-service business. As long as they are the only supplier of the needed parts, they can charge a premium price. In fact, many equipment manufacturers price their equipment low and compensate by charging high prices for parts and service. (This explains why competitors manufacture the same or similar parts and sell them to customers or intermediaries for less.)

Over time, manufacturers switch more maintenance and repair service to authorized distributors and dealers. These intermediaries are closer to customers, operate in more locations, and can offer quicker service. Manufacturers still make a profit on the parts but leave the servicing profit to intermediaries. Still later, independent service firms emerge. Over 40 percent of auto-service work is now done outside franchised automobile dealerships by independent garages and chains such as Midas Muffler, Sears, and JCPenney. Independent service organizations handle mainframes, telecommunications equipment, and a variety of other equipment lines. They typically offer a lower price or faster service than the manufacturer or authorized intermediaries.

Customer service choices are increasing rapidly, however, and this is holding down prices and profits on service. Equipment manufacturers increasingly have to figure out how to make money on their equipment, independent of service contracts. Some new car warranties now cover 100,000 miles before servicing. The increase in disposable or never-fail equipment makes customers less inclined to pay from 2 percent to 10 percent of the purchase price every year for a service. Some large customers handle their own maintenance and repair. A company with several hundred personal computers, printers, and related equipment might find it cheaper to have its own service personnel on-site. These companies typically press the manufacturer for a lower price, because they are providing their own services.

SUMMARY :::

1. A service is any act or performance that one party can offer to another that is essentially intangible and does not result in the ownership of anything. It may or may not be tied to a physical product.
2. Services are intangible, inseparable, variable, and perishable. Each characteristic poses challenges and requires certain strategies. Marketers must find ways to give tangibility to intangibles; to increase the productivity of service providers; to increase and standardize the quality of the service provided; and to match the supply of services with market demand.
3. In the past service industries lagged behind manufacturing firms in adopting and using marketing concepts and tools, but this situation has now changed. Service marketing must be done holistically: It calls not only for external marketing but also for internal marketing to motivate employees, and interactive marketing to emphasize the importance of both "high-tech" and "high-touch."
4. Customers' expectations play a critical role in their service experiences and evaluations. Companies must manage service quality by understanding the effects of each service encounter.
5. Top service companies excel at the following practices: a strategic concept, a history of top-management commitment to quality, high standards, self-service technologies, systems for monitoring service performance and customer complaints, and an emphasis on employee satisfaction.
6. To brand a service organization effectively, the company must differentiate its brand through primary and secondary service features and develop appropriate brand strategies. Effective branding programs for services often employ multiple brand elements. They also develop brand hierarchies and portfolios and establish image dimensions to reinforce or complement service offerings.
7. Even product-based companies must provide postpurchase service. To provide the best support, a manufacturer must identify the services customers value most and their relative importance. The service mix includes both presale services (facilitating and value-augmenting services) and postsale services (customer service departments, repair and maintenance services).

APPLICATIONS :::

Marketing Debate Is Service Marketing Different from Product Marketing?

Some service marketers vehemently maintain that service marketing is fundamentally different from product marketing and that different skills are involved. Some traditional product marketers disagree, saying "good marketing is good marketing."

Take a position: Product and service marketing are fundamentally different versus Product and service marketing are highly related.

Marketing Discussion

Colleges, universities, and other educational institutions can be classified as service organizations. How can you apply the marketing principles developed in this chapter to your school? Do you have any advice as to how it could become a better service marketer?

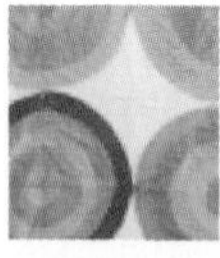

IN THIS CHAPTER, WE WILL ADDRESS THE FOLLOWING QUESTIONS:

1. How do consumers process and evaluate prices?
2. How should a company set prices initially for products or services?
3. How should a company adapt prices to meet varying circumstances and opportunities?
4. When should a company initiate a price change?
5. How should a company respond to a competitor's price change?

LARGER LOADS
MEAN
FEWER LOADS.

THE DUET® WASHER AND DRYER

Imagine a washer that can handle up to 16 pairs of jeans at once.* And a dryer that can dry clothes faster than you ever thought possible. Do more in the same space. Get more done in the same time. The Duet washer and dryer from Whirlpool. Giving you the power to get more done. JUST IMAGINE®

www.whirlpool.com *Various sizes. ®Registered trademark/™ Trademark of Whirlpool, U.S.A. ©2004 Whirlpool Corporation.

CHAPTER 14 ::: DEVELOPING PRICING STRATEGIES AND PROGRAMS

fourteen

Price is the one element of the marketing mix that produces revenue; the other elements produce costs. Prices are perhaps the easiest element of the marketing program to adjust; product features, channels, and even promotion take more time. Price also communicates to the market the company's intended value positioning of its product or brand. A well-designed and marketed product can command a price premium and reap big profits. Consider Whirlpool.

Washers and dryers traditionally were seen as utilitarian products that could never justify a high price. In 2001, Whirlpool introduced the Duet, a front-loading washer-dryer combo that retailed at $2,300—nearly four times the price of comparative models. How did Whirlpool do it? The Duet was a truly unique offering that promised "performance and efficiency without compromise." Its huge capacities could wash and dry big loads, yet it used much less water and electricity than competitors. It also washed all types of clothing—from silks and lace to sleeping bags and comforters. Duet also could claim an emotional benefit for users—bigger loads meant fewer loads and therefore more time and freedom to do other things.[1]

>>>

A print ad for the Whirlpool Duet, a premium-priced washer-dryer combo that retails for nearly four times the price of comparative models.

The Duet pricing plan was the result of a broader shift in Whirlpool's pricing strategy to reduce the frequency of costly and potentially confusing discounts. It wanted to find the optimal prices for its products. Many marketers, however, neglect their pricing strategies—one survey found that managers spent less than 10 percent of their time on pricing.[2]

Pricing decisions are clearly complex and difficult. Holistic marketers must take into account many factors in making pricing decisions—the company, the customers, the competition, and the marketing environment. Pricing decisions must be consistent with the firm's marketing strategy and its target markets and brand positionings.

In this chapter, we provide concepts and tools to facilitate the setting of initial prices and adjusting prices over time and markets.

::: Understanding Pricing

Price is not just a number on a tag or an item:

> Price is all around us. You pay rent for your apartment, tuition for your education, and a fee to your physician or dentist. The airline, railway, taxi, and bus companies charge you a fare; the local utilities call their price a rate; and the local bank charges you interest for the money you borrow. The price for driving your car on Florida's Sunshine Parkway is a toll, and the company that insures your car charges you a premium. The guest lecturer charges an honorarium to tell you about a government official who took a bribe to help a shady character steal dues collected by a trade association. Clubs or societies to which you belong may make a special assessment to pay unusual expenses. Your regular lawyer may ask for a retainer to cover her services. The "price" of an executive is a salary, the price of a salesperson may be a commission, and the price of a worker is a wage. Finally, although economists would disagree, many of us feel that income taxes are the price we pay for the privilege of making money.[3]

Throughout most of history, prices were set by negotiation between buyers and sellers. "Bargaining" is still a sport in some areas. Setting one price for all buyers is a relatively modern idea that arose with the development of large-scale retailing at the end of the nineteenth century. F. W. Woolworth, Tiffany and Co., John Wanamaker, and others advertised a "strictly one-price policy," because they carried so many items and supervised so many employees.

Today the Internet is partially reversing the fixed pricing trend. Computer technology is making it easier for sellers to use software that monitors customers' movements over the Web and allows them to customize offers and prices. New software applications are also allowing buyers to compare prices instantaneously through online robotic shoppers or "shopbots." As one industry observer noted, "We are moving toward a very sophisticated economy. It's kind of an arms race between merchant technology and consumer technology."[4] (See "Marketing Insight: The Internet and Pricing Effects on Sellers and Buyers.")

Traditionally, price has operated as the major determinant of buyer choice. This is still the case in poorer nations, among poorer groups, and with commodity-type products. Although nonprice factors have become more important in recent decades, price still remains one of the most important elements determining market share and profitability. Consumers and purchasing agents have more access to price information and price discounters. Consumers put pressure on retailers to lower their prices. Retailers put pressure on manufacturers to lower their prices. The result is a marketplace characterized by heavy discounting and sales promotion.

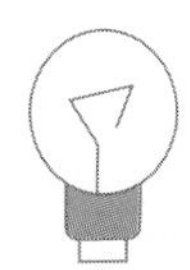

MARKETING **INSIGHT**

THE INTERNET AND PRICING EFFECTS ON SELLERS AND BUYERS

E-commerce has been arguably the Web's hottest application. Yet the Internet is more than simply a new "marketspace." Internet-based technologies are actually changing the rules of the market. Here is a short list of how the Internet allows sellers to discriminate between buyers and buyers to discriminate between sellers.

Buyers can:

- ***Get instant price comparisons from thousands of vendors.*** One site, PriceScan.com, lures thousands of visitors a day, most of them corporate buyers. Intelligent shopping agents ("bots") take price comparison a step further and seek out products, prices, and reviews from as many as 2,000 merchants. Whether they use "bots" or not, consumers now regularly check online prices, compare them with those in their local stores and may well take a peek at what customers in other countries are paying and order from overseas. Consumers also may unbundle product information from the transaction themselves. For instance, someone might use the Internet to research digital cameras, but visit an electronics store for a hands-on demonstration, then walk out of the store without buying, go home to use a search engine to find the lowest price, and buy a camera online.
- ***Name their price and have it met.*** On Priceline.com, the customer states the price he wants to pay for an airline ticket, hotel, or rental car and Priceline checks whether any seller is willing to meet that price. Consumers can fix their own prices, and sellers can use it too: Airlines can fill in demand for empty seats, and hotels welcome the chance to sell vacant rooms. Volume-aggregating sites combine the orders of many customers and press the supplier for a deeper discount.
- ***Get products free.*** Open Source, the free software movement that started with Linux, will erode margins for just about any company doing software. Open-source software is popping up everywhere. It's in PCs and cell phones and set-top boxes. It's in servers that power the world's Web sites, such as Google and Amazon, and in giant corporate and government systems. The biggest challenge confronting Microsoft, Oracle, IBM, and virtually every other major software producer is now: How do you compete with programs that can be had free?

Sellers can:

- ***Monitor customer behavior and tailor offers to individuals.*** Although shopping agent software and price comparison Web sites provide published prices, consumers may be missing out on the special deals they can get with the help of new technologies. GE Lighting, which gets 55,000 pricing requests a year, has Web programs that evaluate 300 factors that go into a pricing quote, such as past sales data and discounts, so that it can reduce processing time from up to 30 days to 6 hours.
- ***Give certain customers access to special prices.*** CDNOW, an online vendor of music albums, e-mails certain buyers a special Web site address with lower prices. Unless you know the secret address, you pay full price. Business marketers are already using extranets to get a precise handle on inventory, costs, and demand at any given moment in order to adjust prices instantly.

Both buyers and sellers can:

- ***Negotiate prices in online auctions and exchanges.*** Want to sell hundreds of excess and slightly worn widgets? Post a sale on eBay. Want to purchase vintage baseball cards at a bargain price? Go to www.baseballplanet.com.

Sources: Amy E. Cortese, "Good-Bye to Fixed Pricing?" *BusinessWeek,* May 4, 1998, pp. 71–84; Michael Menduno, "Priced to Perfection," *Business 2.0,* March 6, 2001, pp. 40–42; Faith Keenan, "The Price Is Really Right," *BusinessWeek,* March 31, 2003, pp. 61–67; Paul Markillie, "A Perfect Market: A Survey of E-Commerce," *The Economist,* May 15, 2004, pp. 3–20; David Kirpatrick, "How the Open-Source World Plans to Smack Down Microsoft, and Oracle, and . . .", *Fortune,* February 23, 2004, pp. 92–100. For a discussion of some of the academic issues involved, see Florian Zettelmeyer, "Expanding to the Internet: Pricing and Communication Strategies when Firms Compete on Multiple Channels," *Journal of Marketing Research* 37 (August 2000): 292–308; John G. Lynch Jr. and Dan Ariely, "Wine Online: Search Costs Affect Competition on Price, Quality, and Distribution," *Marketing Science* (Winter 2000): 83–103; Rajiv Lal and Miklos Sarvary, "When and How Is the Internet Likely to Decrease Price Competition?" *Marketing Science* 18, no.4 (1999): 485–503.

How Companies Price

Companies do their pricing in a variety of ways. In small companies, prices are often set by the boss. In large companies, pricing is handled by division and product-line managers. Even here, top management sets general pricing objectives and policies and often approves the prices proposed by lower levels of management. In industries where pricing is a key factor (aerospace, railroads, oil companies), companies will often establish a pricing department to set or assist others in determining appropriate prices. This department reports to the marketing department, finance department, or top management. Others who exert an influence on pricing include sales managers, production managers, finance managers, and accountants.

Executives complain that pricing is a big headache—and one that is getting worse by the day. Many companies do not handle pricing well, and throw up their hands at "strategies" like this: "We determine our costs and take our industry's traditional margins." Other common mistakes are: Price is not revised often enough to capitalize on market changes; price is set independently of the rest of the marketing mix rather than as an intrinsic element of market-positioning strategy; and price is not varied enough for different product items, market segments, distribution channels, and purchase occasions.

Others have a different attitude: They use price as a key strategic tool. These "power pricers" have discovered the highly leveraged effect of price on the bottom line.[5] They customize prices and offerings based on segment value and costs.

PROGRESSIVE INSURANCE

Progressive Insurance collects and analyzes loss data in automobile insurance better than anyone else. Its understanding of what it costs to service various types of customers enables it to serve the lucrative high-risk customer no one else wants to insure. Free of competition and armed with a solid understanding of costs, Progressive makes good profits serving this customer base.[6]

The importance of pricing for profitability was demonstrated in a 1992 study by McKinsey & Company. Examining 2,400 companies, McKinsey concluded that a 1 percent improvement in price created an improvement in operating profit of 11.1 percent. By contrast, 1 percent improvements in variable cost, volume, and fixed cost produced profit improvements, respectively, of only 7.8 percent, 3.3 percent, and 2.3 percent.

Effectively designing and implementing pricing strategies requires a thorough understanding of consumer pricing psychology and a systematic approach to setting, adapting, and changing prices.

Consumer Psychology and Pricing

Many economists assume that consumers are "price takers" and accept prices at "face value" or as given. Marketers recognize that consumers often actively process price information, interpreting prices in terms of their knowledge from prior purchasing experience, formal communications (advertising, sales calls, and brochures), informal communications (friends, colleagues, or family members), and point-of-purchase or online resources.[7] Purchase decisions are based on how consumers perceive prices and what they consider to be the current actual price—*not* the marketer's stated price. They may have a lower price threshold below which prices may signal inferior or unacceptable quality, as well as an upper price threshold above which prices are prohibitive and seen as not worth the money.

Understanding how consumers arrive at their perceptions of prices is an important marketing priority. Here we consider three key topics—reference prices, price–quality inferences, and price endings.

REFERENCE PRICES Prior research has shown that although consumers may have fairly good knowledge of the range of prices involved, surprisingly few can recall specific prices of products accurately.[8] When examining products, however, consumers often employ **reference prices**. In considering an observed price, consumers often compare it to an internal reference price (pricing information from memory) or an external frame of reference (such as a posted "regular retail price").[9]

All types of reference prices are possible (see Table 14.1). Sellers often attempt to manipulate reference prices. For example, a seller can situate its product among expensive products to imply that it belongs in the same class. Department stores will display women's apparel in separate departments differentiated by price; dresses found in the more expensive department are assumed to be of better quality.

Reference-price thinking is also encouraged by stating a high manufacturer's suggested price, or by indicating that the product was priced much higher originally, or by pointing to a competitor's high price.[10]

CONSUMER ELECTRONICS

On JVC's Web site, the manufacturer's suggested retail price often bears no relationship to what you would be charged by a retailer for the same item. For instance, for a model of mini-digital video camcorder that doubles as a digital still camera, JVC suggests a retail price of $1,099.95, but Circuit City was selling it for $799.99 and Amazon.com for $699.99. Compared with other consumer items, from clothing to cars to furniture to toothbrushes, the gap between the prices routinely quoted by manufacturer and retailer in consumer electronics is

TABLE 14.1

Possible Consumer Reference Prices

- "Fair Price" (what the product should cost)
- Typical Price
- Last Price Paid
- Upper-Bound Price (reservation price or what most consumers would pay)
- Lower-Bound Price (lower threshold price or the least consumers would pay)
- Competitor Prices
- Expected Future Price
- Usual Discounted Price

Source: Adapted from Russell S. Winer, "Behavioral Perspectives on Pricing: Buyers' Subjective Perceptions of Price Revisited," in *Issues in Pricing: Theory and Research*, edited by Timothy Devinney (Lexington, MA: Lexington Books, 1988), pp. 35–57.

large. "The simplest thing to say is that we have trained the consumer electronics buyer to think he is getting 20 or 30 or 40 percent off," said Robert Atkins, a vice president at Mercer Management Consulting. A product manager for Olympus America, primarily known for its cameras, defends the practice by saying that the high manufacturer's suggested retail price is a psychological tool, a reference price that makes people see they are getting something of value for less than top price.[11]

Clever marketers try to frame the price to signal the best value possible. For example, a relatively more expensive item can be seen as less expensive by breaking the price down into smaller units. A $500 annual membership may be seen as more expensive than "under $50 a month" even if the totals are the same.[12]

When consumers evoke one or more of these frames of reference, their perceived price can vary from the stated price.[13] Research on reference prices has found that "unpleasant surprises"—when perceived price is lower than the stated price—can have a greater impact on purchase likelihood than pleasant surprises.[14]

PRICE–QUALITY INFERENCES Many consumers use price as an indicator of quality. Image pricing is especially effective with ego-sensitive products such as perfumes and expensive cars. A $100 bottle of perfume might contain $10 worth of scent, but gift givers pay $100 to communicate their high regard for the receiver.

Price and quality perceptions of cars interact.[15] Higher-priced cars are perceived to possess high quality. Higher-quality cars are likewise perceived to be higher priced than they actually are. Table 14.2 shows how consumer perceptions about cars can differ from reality. When alternative information about true quality is available, price becomes a less significant indicator of quality. When this information is not available, price acts as a signal of quality.

CKE RESTAURANTS

In the fast-food business, rampant price wars are seen by some as a symptom of erosion in quality. That's why CKE Restaurants, parent company of Carl Jr.'s and Hardee's, is bucking the "dollar menu" trend and upping the price of its burgers. Its president and CEO Andrew F. Puzder says: "The problem is if you start selling something for 99 cents, then people assume its worth 99 cents. And those are the least profitable customers." When Puzder bought the troubled Hardee's chain, part of his overhaul was to focus on quality and standout menus for both chains. He created a $3.95 hamburger that is advertised as the "Six Dollar Burger" to connote both quality and value.[16]

Some brands adopt scarcity as a means to signify quality and justify premium pricing. Some automakers have bucked the massive discounting craze that shook the industry and are producing smaller batches of new models, creating a buzz around them, and using the demand to raise the sticker price.[17] Waiting lists, once reserved for limited-edition cars like Ferraris, are becoming more common for mass-market models, including Volkswagen and Acura SUVs and Toyota and Honda minivans.

TABLE 14.2

Consumer Perceptions Versus Reality for Cars

Wall Street firm Morgan Stanley used J.D. Power and Associates' 2003 Vehicle Dependability Study, which tracks reliability over three years, and CNW Market Research's Perceived Quality Survey to find out which car brands were potentially over- and undervalued.

Overvalued: Brands whose perceived quality exceeds actual quality by percentage	
Land Rover	75.3%
Kia	66.6%
Volkswagen	58.3%
Volvo	36.0%
Mercedes	34.2%
Undervalued: Brands whose actual quality exceeds perceived quality by percentage	
Mercury	42.3%
Infiniti	34.1%
Buick	29.7%
Lincoln	25.3%
Chrysler	20.8%

Source: David Kiley, "U.S. Automakers Get a Bum Rap," *USA Today*, January 15, 2004, p. B5.

As the Beanie Baby craze demonstrated, scarcity combined with strong demand can lead to high market prices. Here is another example:

DREW ESTATES

Produced in Nicaragua, flavored with wine, oil, and herbs, and packed in boxes with graffiti-like labels, Drew Estates' cigars are sold in only 500 U.S. stores. Atypical blends, colorful off-beat marketing, and limited production of the three main lines of cigars—Acid, Natural, and Ambrosia—have contributed to premium prices of approximately $10 per cigar. Drew Estates is happy to keep customers guessing about the brand. As co-founder, Jonathan Drew says, "The day I go mass market, I'm out of business. When people are in a store, they'll buy a $150 box because they don't know if they will see one again for another three months."[18]

PRICE CUES Consumer perceptions of prices are also affected by alternative pricing strategies. Many sellers believe that prices should end in an odd number. Many customers see a stereo amplifier priced at $299 instead of $300 as a price in the $200 range rather than $300 range. Research has shown that consumers tend to process prices in a "left-to-right" manner rather than by rounding.[19] Price encoding in this fashion is important if there is a mental price break at the higher, rounded price. Another explanation for "9" endings is that they convey the notion of a discount or bargain, suggesting that if a company wants a high-price image, it should avoid the odd-ending tactic.[20] One study even showed that demand was actually increased one-third by *raising* the price of a dress from $34 to $39, but demand was unchanged when the price was increased from $34 to $44.[21]

Prices that end with "0" and "5" are also common in the marketplace as they are thought to be easier for consumers to process and retrieve from memory.[22] "Sale" signs next to prices have been shown to spur demand, but only if not overused: Total category sales are highest when some, but not all, items in a category have sale signs; past a certain point, use of additional sale signs will cause total category sales to fall.[23] "Marketing Memo: When to Use Price Cues" provides some guidelines.

::: Setting the Price

A firm must set a price for the first time when it develops a new product, when it introduces its regular product into a new distribution channel or geographical area, and when it enters bids on new contract work. The firm must decide where to position its product on quality and price. In some markets, like the auto market, as many as eight *price points* or price tiers and levels can be found:

Segment	Example
Ultimate	Rolls-Royce
Gold Standard	Mercedes-Benz
Luxury	Audi
Special Needs	Volvo
Middle	Buick
Ease/Convenience	Ford Escort
Me Too, but Cheaper	Hyundai
Price Alone	Kia

Most markets have three to five price points or tiers. Marriott Hotels is good at developing different brands for different price points: Marriott Vacation Club—Vacation Villas (highest price), Marriott Marquis (high price), Marriott (high-medium price), Renaissance (medium-high price), Courtyard (medium price), Towne Place Suites (medium-low price), and Fairfield Inn (low price).

Consumers often rank brands according to price tiers in a category.[24] For example, Figure 14.1 shows the three price tiers that resulted from a study of the ice cream market.[25] In that market, as the figure shows, there is also a relationship between price and quality. Within any tier, as the figure shows, there is a range of acceptable prices, called *price bands*. The price bands provide managers with some indication of the flexibility and breadth they can adopt in pricing their brands within a particular price tier.

The firm has to consider many factors in setting its pricing policy.[26] We will describe a six-step procedure: (1) selecting the pricing objective; (2) determining demand; (3) estimating costs; (4) analyzing competitors' costs, prices, and offers; (5) selecting a pricing method; and (6) selecting the final price.

Step 1: Selecting the Pricing Objective

The company first decides where it wants to position its market offering. The clearer a firm's objectives, the easier it is to set price. A company can pursue any of five major objectives through pricing: survival, maximum current profit, maximum market share, maximum market skimming, or product-quality leadership.

SURVIVAL Companies pursue *survival* as their major objective if they are plagued with overcapacity, intense competition, or changing consumer wants. As long as prices cover variable costs and some fixed costs, the company stays in business. Survival is a short-run objective; in the long run, the firm must learn how to add value or face extinction.

MAXIMUM CURRENT PROFIT Many companies try to set a price that will *maximize current profits*. They estimate the demand and costs associated with alternative prices and choose the price that produces maximum current profit, cash flow, or rate of return on investment. This strategy assumes that the firm has knowledge of its demand and cost functions; in reality,

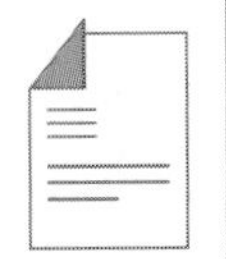

MARKETING MEMO | WHEN TO USE PRICE CUES

Pricing cues, such as sale signs and prices that end in 9, become less effective the more they are employed. Anderson and Simester maintain that they must be used judiciously on those items where consumers' price knowledge may be poor. They cite the following examples:

1. Customers purchase the item infrequently.
2. Customers are new.
3. Product designs vary over time.
4. Prices vary seasonally.
5. Quality or sizes vary across stores.

Source: Adapted from Eric Anderson and Duncan Simester, "Mind Your Pricing Cues," *Harvard Business Review* (September 2003): 96–103.

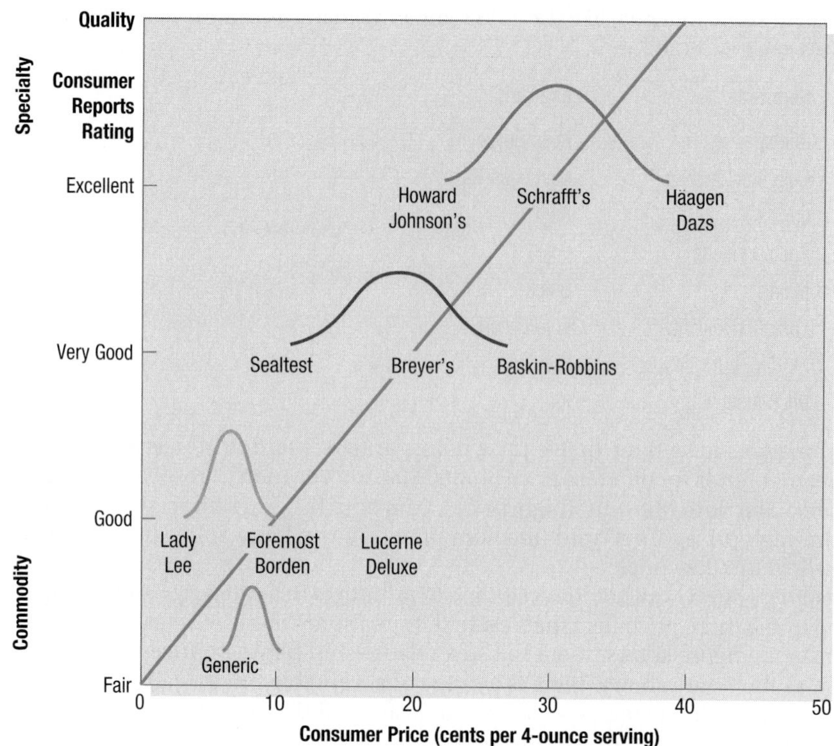

FIG. 14.1

Price Tiers in the Ice Cream Market

these are difficult to estimate. In emphasizing current performance, the company may sacrifice long-run performance by ignoring the effects of other marketing-mix variables, competitors' reactions, and legal restraints on price.

MAXIMUM MARKET SHARE Some companies want to *maximize their market share.* They believe that a higher sales volume will lead to lower unit costs and higher long-run profit. They set the lowest price, assuming the market is price sensitive. Texas Instruments (TI) has practiced this **market-penetration pricing**. TI would build a large plant, set its price as low as possible, win a large market share, experience falling costs, and cut its price further as costs fall.

The following conditions favor setting a low price: (1) The market is highly price sensitive, and a low price stimulates market growth; (2) production and distribution costs fall with accumulated production experience; and (3) a low price discourages actual and potential competition.

MAXIMUM MARKET SKIMMING Companies unveiling a new technology favor setting high prices to *maximize market skimming.* Sony is a frequent practitioner of **market-skimming pricing**, where prices start high and are slowly lowered over time. When Sony introduced the world's first high-definition television (HDTV) to the Japanese market in 1990, it was priced at $43,000. So that Sony could "skim" the maximum amount of revenue from the various segments of the market, the price dropped steadily through the years—a 28-inch HDTV cost just over $6,000 in 1993 and a 42-inch HDTV cost about $1,200 in 2004.[27]

Market skimming makes sense under the following conditions: (1) A sufficient number of buyers have a high current demand; (2) the unit costs of producing a small volume are not so high that they cancel the advantage of charging what the traffic will bear; (3) the high initial price does not attract more competitors to the market; (4) the high price communicates the image of a superior product.

PRODUCT-QUALITY LEADERSHIP A company might aim to be the *product-quality leader* in the market. Many brands strive to be "affordable luxuries"—products or services characterized by high levels of perceived quality, taste, and status with a price just high enough not to be out of consumers' reach. Brands such as Starbucks coffee, Aveda shampoo, Victoria's Secret lingerie, BMW cars, and Viking ranges have been able to position themselves as quality leaders in their categories, combining quality, luxury, and premium prices with an intensely loyal customer base.[28] Grey Goose and Absolut carved out a superpremium niche in the essentially odorless, colorless, and tasteless vodka category through clever on-premise and off-premise marketing that made the brands seem hip and exclusive.[29]

OTHER OBJECTIVES Nonprofit and public organizations may have other pricing objectives. A university aims for *partial cost recovery,* knowing that it must rely on private gifts and public grants to cover the remaining costs. A nonprofit hospital may aim for full cost recovery in its pricing. A nonprofit theater company may price its productions to fill the maximum number of theater seats. A social service agency may set a service price geared to client income.

Whatever the specific objective, businesses that use price as a strategic tool will profit more than those who simply let costs or the market determine their pricing.

Step 2: Determining Demand

Each price will lead to a different level of demand and therefore have a different impact on a company's marketing objectives. The relation between alternative prices and the resulting current demand is captured in a demand curve (see Figure 14.2). In the normal case, demand and price are inversely related: The higher the price, the lower the demand. In the case of prestige goods, the demand curve sometimes slopes upward. A perfume company raised its price and sold more perfume rather than less! Some consumers take the higher price to signify a better product. However, if the price is too high, the level of demand may fall.

PRICE SENSITIVITY The demand curve shows the market's probable purchase quantity at alternative prices. It sums the reactions of many individuals who have different price sensitivities. The first step in estimating demand is to understand what affects price sensitivity. Generally speaking, customers are most price sensitive to products that cost a lot or are bought frequently. They are less price sensitive to low-cost items or items they buy infrequently. They are also less price sensitive when price is only a small part of the total cost of obtaining, operating, and servicing the product over its lifetime. A seller can charge a higher price than competitors and still get the business if the company can convince the customer that it offers the lowest *total cost of ownership* (TCO).

Companies, of course, prefer customers who are less price sensitive. Table 14.3 lists some characteristics that are associated with decreased price sensitivity. On the other hand, the Internet has the potential to increase customers' price sensitivity. In buying a specific book online, for example, a customer can compare the prices offered by over two dozen online bookstores by just clicking mySimon.com. These prices can differ by as much as 20 percent.

Although the Internet increases the opportunity for price-sensitive buyers to find and favor lower-price sites, many buyers may not be that price sensitive. McKinsey conducted a study and found that 89 percent of a sample of Internet customers visited only one book site, 84 percent visited only one toy site, and 81 percent visited only one music site, which indicates that there is less price-comparison shopping taking place on the Internet than is possible.

Companies need to understand the price sensitivity of their customers and prospects and the trade-offs people are willing to make between price and product characteristics. Targeting only price-sensitive consumers may in fact be "leaving money on the table."

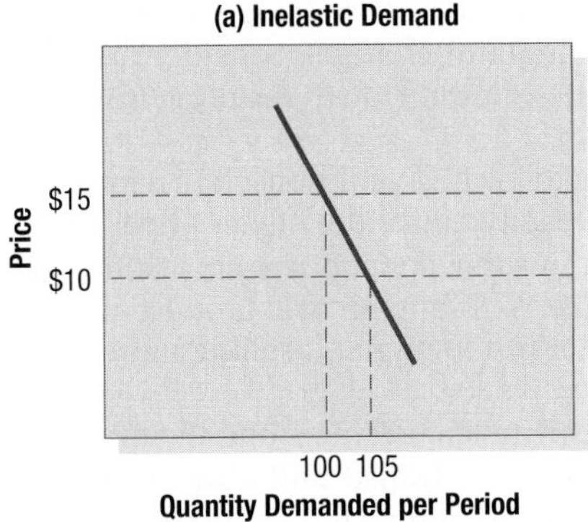

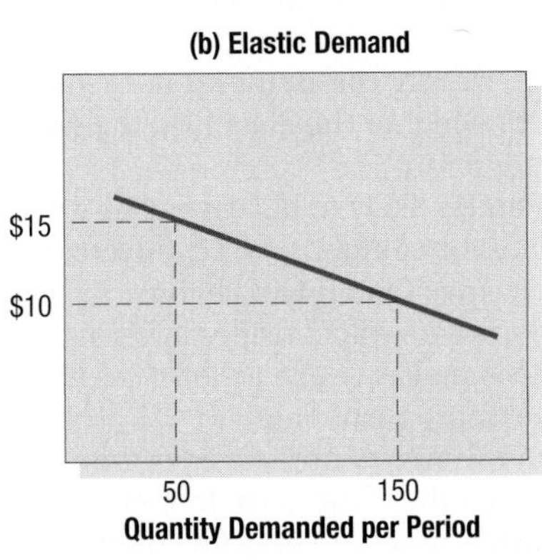

FIG. 14.2

Inelastic and Elastic Demand

TABLE 14.3

Factors Leading to Less Price Sensitivity

- The product is more distinctive.
- Buyers are less aware of substitutes.
- Buyers cannot easily compare the quality of substitutes.
- The expenditure is a smaller part of the buyer's total income.
- The expenditure is small compared to the total cost of the end product.
- Part of the cost is borne by another party.
- The product is used in conjunction with assets previously bought.
- The product is assumed to have more quality, prestige, or exclusiveness.
- Buyers cannot store the product.

Source: Adapted from Thomas T. Nagle and Reed K. Holden, *The Strategy and Tactics of Pricing*, 3rd ed. (Upper Saddle River, NJ: Prentice Hall, 2001), ch. 4.

ESTIMATING DEMAND CURVES Most companies make some attempt to measure their demand curves using several different methods.

- ***Statistical analysis*** of past prices, quantities sold, and other factors can reveal their relationships. The data can be longitudinal (over time) or cross-sectional (different locations at the same time). Building the appropriate model and fitting the data with the proper statistical techniques calls for considerable skill.
- ***Price experiments*** can be conducted. Bennett and Wilkinson systematically varied the prices of several products sold in a discount store and observed the results.[30] An alternative approach is to charge different prices in similar territories to see how sales are affected. Still another approach is to use the Internet. An e-business could test the impact of a 5 percent price increase by quoting a higher price to every fortieth visitor to compare the purchase response. However, it must do this carefully and not alienate customers, as happened when Amazon price-tested discounts of 30 percent, 35 percent, and 40 percent for DVD buyers, only to find that those receiving the 30 percent discount were upset.[31]
- ***Surveys*** can explore how many units consumers would buy at different proposed prices, although there is always the chance that they might understate their purchase intentions at higher prices to discourage the company from setting higher prices.[32]

In measuring the price–demand relationship, the market researcher must control for various factors that will influence demand. The competitor's response will make a difference. Also, if the company changes other marketing-mix factors besides price, the effect of the price change itself will be hard to isolate. Nagle presents an excellent summary of the various methods for estimating price sensitivity and demand.[33]

PRICE ELASTICITY OF DEMAND Marketers need to know how responsive, or elastic, demand would be to a change in price. Consider the two demand curves in Figure 14.2. With demand curve (a), a price increase from $10 to $15 leads to a relatively small decline in demand from 105 to 100. With demand curve (b), the same price increase leads to a substantial drop in demand from 150 to 50. If demand hardly changes with a small change in price, we say the demand is *inelastic*. If demand changes considerably, demand is *elastic*. The higher the elasticity, the greater the volume growth resulting from a 1 percent price reduction.

Demand is likely to be less elastic under the following conditions: (1) There are few or no substitutes or competitors; (2) buyers do not readily notice the higher price; (3) buyers are slow to change their buying habits; (4) buyers think the higher prices are justified. If demand is elastic, sellers will consider lowering the price. A lower price will produce more total revenue. This makes sense as long as the costs of producing and selling more units do not increase disproportionately.[34]

It is a mistake to not consider the price elasticity of customers and their needs in developing marketing programs. In 1997, the Metropolitan Transit Authority in New York introduced a new purchase plan for subway riders that discounted fares after passes were used 47 times in a month. Critics pointed out that the special fare did not benefit those customers whose demand was most elastic, suburban off-peak riders who used the subway the least. Commuters' demand curve is perfectly inelastic; no matter what happens to the fare, these people must get to work and get back home.[35]

Price elasticity depends on the magnitude and direction of the contemplated price change. It may be negligible with a small price change and substantial with a large price change. It may differ for a price cut versus a price increase, and there may be a *price indifference band* within which price changes have little or no effect. A McKinsey pricing study estimated that the price indifference band can range as large as 17 percent for mouthwash, 13 percent for batteries, 9 percent for small appliances, and 2 percent for certificates of deposit.

Finally, long-run price elasticity may differ from short-run elasticity. Buyers may continue to buy from a current supplier after a price increase, but they may eventually switch suppliers. Here demand is more elastic in the long run than in the short run, or the reverse may happen: Buyers may drop a supplier after being notified of a price increase but return later. The distinction between short-run and long-run elasticity means that sellers will not know the total effect of a price change until time passes.

Step 3: Estimating Costs

Demand sets a ceiling on the price the company can charge for its product. Costs set the floor. The company wants to charge a price that covers its cost of producing, distributing, and selling the product, including a fair return for its effort and risk. Yet, when companies price products to cover full costs, the net result is not always profitability. See "Marketing Memo: Three Myths About Pricing Strategy," for more on common pricing strategy errors.

TYPES OF COSTS AND LEVELS OF PRODUCTION A company's costs take two forms, fixed and variable. **Fixed costs** (also known as **overhead**) are costs that do not vary with production or sales revenue. A company must pay bills each month for rent, heat, interest, salaries, and so on, regardless of output.

Variable costs vary directly with the level of production. For example, each hand calculator produced by Texas Instruments involves the cost of plastic, microprocessor chips, packaging, and the like. These costs tend to be constant per unit produced. They are called variable because their total varies with the number of units produced.

MARKETING MEMO | THREE MYTHS ABOUT PRICING STRATEGY

According to George E. Cressman Jr., senior pricer at Strategic Pricing Group, marketers nurture three major myths about pricing strategy:

- ***Pricing our products to cover full costs will make us profitable.*** Marketers often do not realize the value they actually do provide but think in terms of product features. They frequently treat the service elements in a product offering as sales incentives rather than value-enhancing augmentations for which they can charge. Says Cressman, "When we price to cover costs, there is an underlying assumption that customers value us for our costs. Then the logical conclusions would be that we should increase costs so we can increase price, and customers will love us even more!" Marketers should instead determine how many customers will ascribe how much value to their offerings, then ask, "Given our cost structure, what volume changes are necessary to make price changes profitable?"
- ***Pricing our products to grow market share will make us profitable.*** Cressman reminds marketers that share is determined by value delivery at competitive advantage, not just price cuts. Therefore, "The correct question is not: 'What level of price will enable us to achieve our sales and market share objectives?' but 'What shares of the market can we most profitably serve?' "
- ***Pricing our products to meet customer demands will make us profitable.*** Cutting prices to keep customers or beat competitive offers encourages customers to demand price concessions and trains salespeople to offer them. "When you're tempted to ask what customers will pay," says Cressman, "don't ask them. You know you won't like the answer. Instead, marketers should ask, "What prices can we convince customers are supported by the value of our products and services?" and "How can we better segment the market to reflect differences in value delivered to different types of customers?" Create different levels of value and price options for different market segments and their respective value needs. And to finesse a price cut, provide a reduced-priced option. "That makes the demand for a price concession the customer's problem, for it must then choose which benefits to forgo."

Source: Adapted from Bob Donath, "Dispel Major Myths About Pricing," *Marketing News,* February 3, 2003, p. 10.

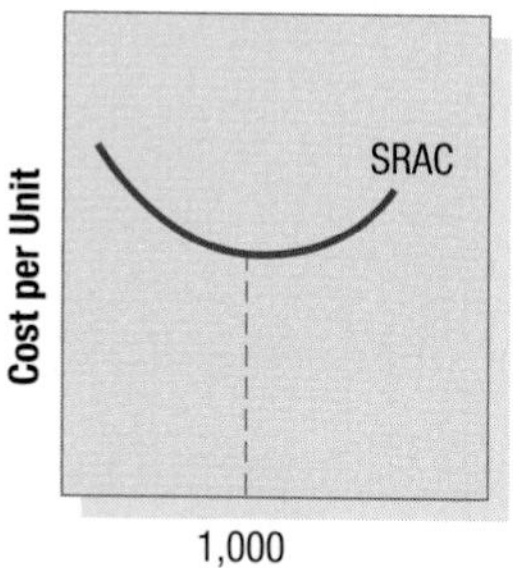

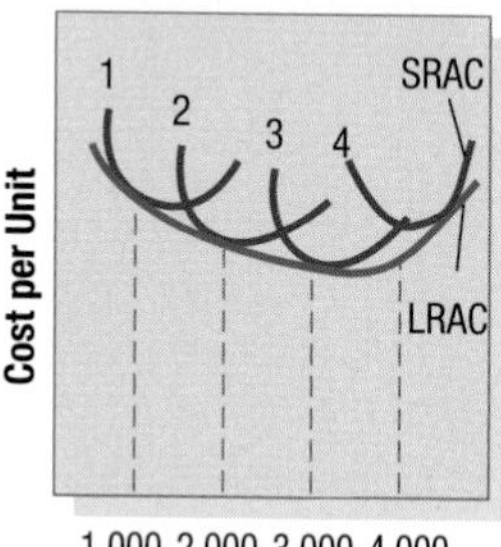

FIG. 14.3

Cost per Unit at Different Levels of Production per Period

Total costs consist of the sum of the fixed and variable costs for any given level of production. **Average cost** is the cost per unit at that level of production; it is equal to total costs divided by production. Management wants to charge a price that will at least cover the total production costs at a given level of production.

To price intelligently, management needs to know how its costs vary with different levels of production. Take the case in which a company such as TI has built a fixed-size plant to produce 1,000 hand calculators a day. The cost per unit is high if few units are produced per day. As production approaches 1,000 units per day, the average cost falls because the fixed costs are spread over more units. Short-run average cost increases after 1,000 units, because the plant becomes inefficient: Workers have to line up for machines, machines break down more often, and workers get in each others' way (see Figure 14.3 [a]).

If TI believes it can sell 2,000 units per day, it should consider building a larger plant. The plant will use more efficient machinery and work arrangements, and the unit cost of producing 2,000 units per day will be less than the unit cost of producing 1,000 units per day. This is shown in the long-run average cost curve (LRAC) in Figure 14.3 [b]. In fact, a 3,000-capacity plant would be even more efficient according to Figure 14.3 [b], but a 4,000-daily production plant would be less efficient because of increasing diseconomies of scale: There are too many workers to manage, and paperwork slows things down. Figure 14.3 [b] indicates that a 3,000-daily production plant is the optimal size if demand is strong enough to support this level of production.

ACCUMULATED PRODUCTION Suppose TI runs a plant that produces 3,000 hand calculators per day. As TI gains experience producing hand calculators, its methods improve. Workers learn shortcuts, materials flow more smoothly, and procurement costs fall. The result, as Figure 14.4 shows, is that average cost falls with accumulated production experience. Thus the average cost of producing the first 100,000 hand calculators is $10 per calculator. When the company has produced the first 200,000 calculators, the average cost has fallen to $9. After its accumulated production experience doubles again to 400,000, the average cost is $8. This decline in the average cost with accumulated production experience is called the **experience curve** or **learning curve**.

Now suppose three firms compete in this industry, TI, A, and B. TI is the lowest-cost producer at $8, having produced 400,000 units in the past. If all three firms sell the calculator for $10, TI makes $2 profit per unit, A makes $1 per unit, and B breaks even. The smart move for TI would be to lower its price to $9. This will drive B out of the market, and even A may consider leaving. TI will pick up the business that would have gone to B (and possibly A). Furthermore, price-sensitive customers will enter the market at the lower price. As production increases beyond 400,000 units, TI's costs will drop still further and faster and more than restore its profits, even at a price of $9. TI has used this aggressive pricing strategy repeatedly to gain market share and drive others out of the industry.

Experience-curve pricing, nevertheless, carries major risks. Aggressive pricing might give the product a cheap image. The strategy also assumes that competitors are weak followers. It leads the company into building more plants to meet demand, while a competitor innovates a lower-cost technology. The market leader is now stuck with the old technology.

Most experience-curve pricing has focused on manufacturing costs, but all costs can be improved on, including marketing costs. If three firms are each investing a large sum of money in telemarketing, the firm that has used it the longest might achieve the lowest costs. This firm can charge a little less for its product and still earn the same return, all other costs being equal.[36]

FIG. 14.4

Cost per Unit as a Function of Accumulated Production: The Experience Curve

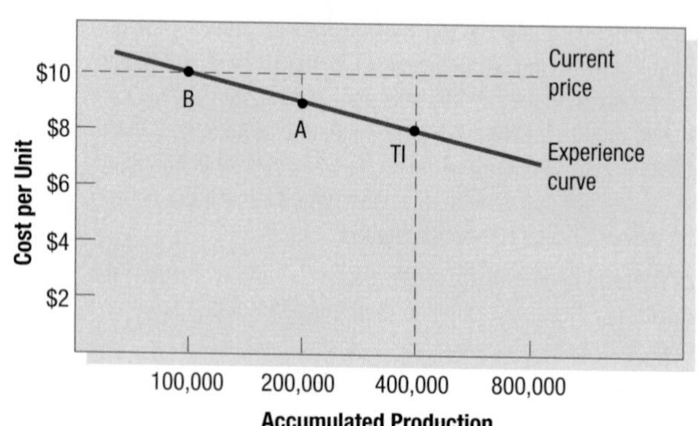

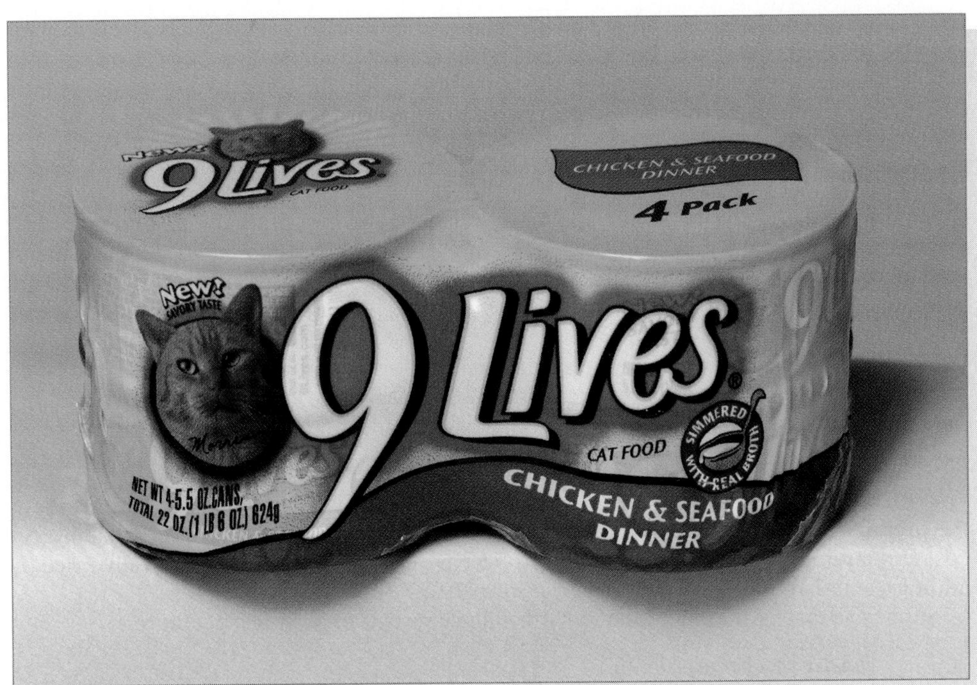

The redesigned 9Lives® four-pack package.

ACTIVITY-BASED COST ACCOUNTING Today's companies try to adapt their offers and terms to different buyers. A manufacturer, for example, will negotiate different terms with different retail chains. One retailer may want daily delivery (to keep inventory lower) while another may accept twice-a-week delivery in order to get a lower price. The manufacturer's costs will differ with each chain, and so will its profits. To estimate the real profitability of dealing with different retailers, the manufacturer needs to use **activity-based cost (ABC) accounting** instead of standard cost accounting.[37]

ABC accounting tries to identify the real costs associated with serving each customer. It allocates indirect costs like clerical costs, office expenses, supplies, and so on, to the activities that use them, rather than in some proportion to direct costs. Both variable and overhead costs are tagged back to each customer. Companies that fail to measure their costs correctly are not measuring their profit correctly and are likely to misallocate their marketing effort. The key to effectively employing ABC is to define and judge "activities" properly. One proposed time-based solution calculates the cost of one minute of overhead and then decides how much of this cost each activity uses.[38]

TARGET COSTING Costs change with production scale and experience. They can also change as a result of a concentrated effort by designers, engineers, and purchasing agents to reduce them through **target costing**.[39] Market research is used to establish a new product's desired functions and the price at which the product will sell, given its appeal and competitors' prices. Deducting the desired profit margin from this price leaves the target cost that must be achieved. Each cost element—design, engineering, manufacturing, sales—must be examined, and different ways to bring down costs must be considered. The objective is to bring the final cost projections into the target cost range. If this is not possible, it may be necessary to stop developing the product because it could not sell for the target price and make the target profit.

To hit price and margin targets, marketers of 9Lives® brand of cat food employed target costing to bring their price down to "four cans for a dollar" via a reshaped package and redesigned manufacturing processes. Even with lower prices, profits for the brand doubled.

Step 4: Analyzing Competitors' Costs, Prices, and Offers

Within the range of possible prices determined by market demand and company costs, the firm must take competitors' costs, prices, and possible price reactions into account. The firm should first consider the nearest competitor's price. If the firm's offer contains features not offered by the nearest competitor, their worth to the customer should be evaluated and added to the

FIG. 14.5

The Three Cs Model for Price Setting

competitor's price. If the competitor's offer contains some features not offered by the firm, their worth to the customer should be evaluated and subtracted from the firm's price. Now the firm can decide whether it can charge more, the same, or less than the competitor. But competitors can change their prices in reaction to the price set by the firm, as we'll see later in this chapter.

Step 5: Selecting a Pricing Method

Given the three Cs—the customers' demand schedule, the cost function, and competitors' prices—the company is now ready to select a price. Figure 14.5 summarizes the three major considerations in price setting. Costs set a floor to the price. Competitors' prices and the price of substitutes provide an orienting point. Customers' assessment of unique features establishes the price ceiling.

Companies select a pricing method that includes one or more of these three considerations. We will examine six price-setting methods: markup pricing, target-return pricing, perceived-value pricing, value pricing, going-rate pricing, and auction-type pricing.

MARKUP PRICING The most elementary pricing method is to add a standard **markup** to the product's cost. Construction companies submit job bids by estimating the total project cost and adding a standard markup for profit. Lawyers and accountants typically price by adding a standard markup on their time and costs.

Suppose a toaster manufacturer has the following costs and sales expectations:

Variable cost per unit	$10
Fixed cost	$300,000
Expected unit sales	50,000

The manufacturer's unit cost is given by:

$$\text{Unit cost} = \text{variable cost} + \frac{\text{fixed cost}}{\text{unit sales}} = \$10 + \frac{\$300{,}000}{50{,}000} = \$16$$

Now assume the manufacturer wants to earn a 20 percent markup on sales. The manufacturer's markup price is given by:

$$\text{Markup price} = \frac{\text{unit cost}}{(1 - \text{desired return on sales})} = \frac{\$16}{1 - 0.2} = \$20$$

The manufacturer would charge dealers $20 per toaster and make a profit of $4 per unit. The dealers in turn will mark up the toaster. If dealers want to earn 50 percent on their selling price, they will mark up the toaster to $40. This is equivalent to a cost markup of 100 percent. Markups are generally higher on seasonal items (to cover the risk of not selling), specialty items, slower-moving items, items with high storage and handling costs, and demand-inelastic items, such as prescription drugs.

Does the use of standard markups make logical sense? Generally, no. Any pricing method that ignores current demand, perceived value, and competition is not likely to lead to the optimal price. Markup pricing works only if the marked-up price actually brings in the expected level of sales.

Companies introducing a new product often price it high, hoping to recover their costs as rapidly as possible. But this strategy could be fatal if a competitor is pricing low. This happened to Philips, the Dutch electronics manufacturer, in pricing its videodisc players. Philips wanted to make a profit on each player. Japanese competitors priced low and succeeded in building their market share rapidly, which in turn pushed down their costs substantially.

Still, markup pricing remains popular. First, sellers can determine costs much more easily than they can estimate demand. By tying the price to cost, sellers simplify the pricing task. Second, where all firms in the industry use this pricing method, prices tend to be similar. Price competition is therefore minimized. Third, many people feel that cost-plus pricing is fairer to both buyers and sellers. Sellers do not take advantage of buyers when the latter's demand becomes acute, and sellers earn a fair return on investment.

TARGET-RETURN PRICING In **target-return pricing**, the firm determines the price that would yield its target rate of return on investment (ROI). Target pricing is used by General

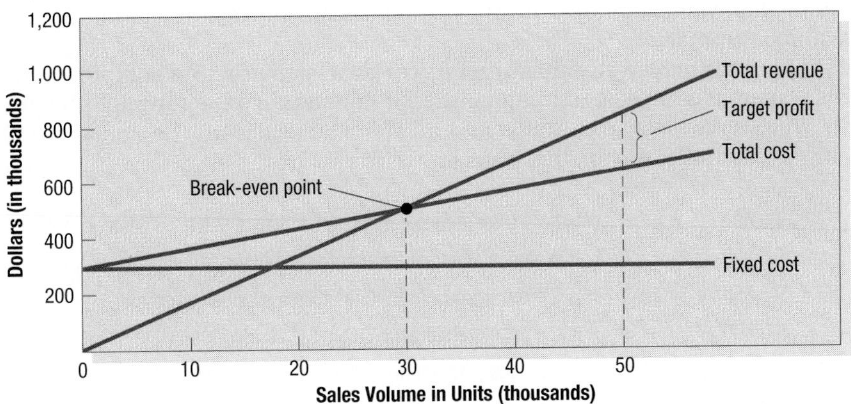

FIG. 14.6

Break-Even Chart for Determining Target-Return Price and Break-Even Volume

Motors, which prices its automobiles to achieve a 15 to 20 percent ROI. This method is also used by public utilities, which need to make a fair return on investment.

Suppose the toaster manufacturer has invested $1 million in the business and wants to set a price to earn a 20 percent ROI, specifically $200,000. The target-return price is given by the following formula:

$$\text{Target-return price} = \text{unit cost} + \frac{\text{desired return} \times \text{invested capital}}{\text{unit sales}}$$

$$= \$16 + \frac{.20 \times \$1{,}000{,}000}{50{,}000} = \$20$$

The manufacturer will realize this 20 percent ROI provided its costs and estimated sales turn out to be accurate. But what if sales do not reach 50,000 units? The manufacturer can prepare a break-even chart to learn what would happen at other sales levels (see Figure 14.6). Fixed costs are $300,000 regardless of sales volume. Variable costs, not shown in the figure, rise with volume. Total costs equal the sum of fixed costs and variable costs. The total revenue curve starts at zero and rises with each unit sold.

The total revenue and total cost curves cross at 30,000 units. This is the break-even volume. It can be verified by the following formula:

$$\text{Break-even volume} = \frac{\text{fixed cost}}{(\text{price} - \text{variable cost})} = \frac{\$300{,}000}{\$20 - \$10} = 30{,}000$$

The manufacturer, of course, is hoping that the market will buy 50,000 units at $20, in which case it earns $200,000 on its $1 million investment, but much depends on price elasticity and competitors' prices. Unfortunately, target-return pricing tends to ignore these considerations. The manufacturer needs to consider different prices and estimate their probable impacts on sales volume and profits. The manufacturer should also search for ways to lower its fixed or variable costs, because lower costs will decrease its required break-even volume.

PERCEIVED-VALUE PRICING An increasing number of companies now base their price on the customer's **perceived value**. They must deliver the value promised by their value proposition, and the customer must perceive this value. They use the other marketing-mix elements, such as advertising and sales force, to communicate and enhance perceived value in buyers' minds.[40]

Perceived value is made up of several elements, such as the buyer's image of the product performance, the channel deliverables, the warranty quality, customer support, and softer attributes such as the supplier's reputation, trustworthiness, and esteem. Furthermore, each potential customer places different weights on these different elements, with the result that some will be *price buyers*, others will be *value buyers*, and still others will be *loyal buyers*. Companies need different strategies for these three groups. For price buyers, companies need to offer stripped-down products and reduced services. For value buyers, companies must keep innovating new value and aggressively reaffirming their value. For loyal buyers, companies must invest in relationship building and customer intimacy.

Caterpillar uses perceived value to set prices on its construction equipment. It might price its tractor at $100,000, although a similar competitor's tractor might be priced at $90,000. When a prospective customer asks a Caterpillar dealer why he should pay $10,000 more for the Caterpillar tractor, the dealer answers:

$ 90,000	is the tractor's price if it is only equivalent to the competitor's tractor
$ 7,000	is the price premium for Caterpillar's superior durability
$ 6,000	is the price premium for Caterpillar's superior reliability
$ 5,000	is the price premium for Caterpillar's superior service
$ 2,000	is the price premium for Caterpillar's longer warranty on parts
$110,000	is the normal price to cover Caterpillar's superior value
−$10,000	discount
$100,000	final price

The Caterpillar dealer is able to indicate why Caterpillar's tractor delivers more value than the competitor's. Although the customer is asked to pay a $10,000 premium, he is actually getting $20,000 extra value! He chooses the Caterpillar tractor because he is convinced that its lifetime operating costs will be lower.

Yet even when a company claims that its offering delivers more total value, not all customers will respond positively. There is always a segment of buyers who care only about the price. There are other buyers who suspect that the company is exaggerating its product quality and services. One company installed its software system in one or two plants operated by a company. The substantial and well-documented cost savings convinced the customer to buy the software for its other plants.

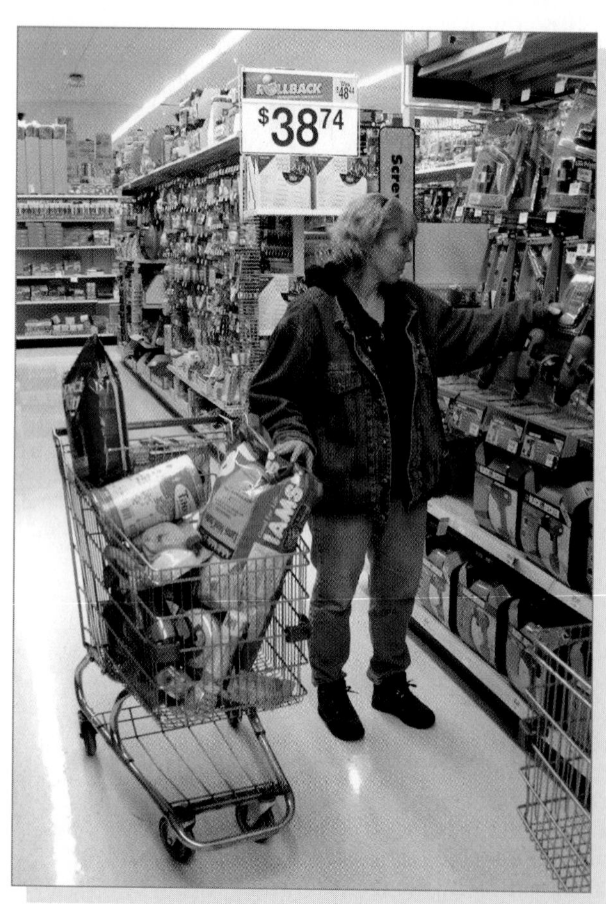

Shoppers at Wal-Mart get EDLP—everyday low pricing—on major brands.

The key to perceived-value pricing is to deliver more value than the competitor and to demonstrate this to prospective buyers. Basically, a company needs to understand the customer's decision-making process. The company can try to determine the value of its offering in several ways: managerial judgments within the company, value of similar products, focus groups, surveys, experimentation, analysis of historical data, and conjoint analysis.[41]

For example, DuPont educated its customers about the true value of its higher-grade polyethylene resin called Alathon. Instead of claiming only that pipes made from it were 5 percent more durable, DuPont produced a detailed analysis of the comparative costs of installing and maintaining in-ground irrigation pipe. The real savings came from the diminished need to pay the labor and crop-damage costs associated with digging up and replacing the underground pipe. DuPont was able to charge 7 percent more and still see its sales double the following year.

VALUE PRICING In recent years, several companies have adopted **value pricing**: They win loyal customers by charging a fairly low price for a high-quality offering. Among the best practitioners of value pricing are IKEA and Southwest Airlines.

In the early 1990s, Procter & Gamble created quite a stir when it reduced prices on supermarket staples such as Pampers and Luvs diapers, liquid Tide detergent, and Folger's coffee to value price them. In the past, a brand-loyal family had to pay what amounted to a $725 premium for a year's worth of P&G products versus private-label or low-priced brands. To offer value prices, P&G underwent a major overhaul. It redesigned the way it developed, manufactured, distributed, priced, marketed, and sold products to deliver better value at every point in the supply chain.[42]

Value pricing is not a matter of simply setting lower prices; it is a matter of reengineering the company's operations to become a low-cost producer without sacrificing quality, and lowering prices significantly to attract a large number of value-conscious customers.

An important type of value pricing is **everyday low pricing (EDLP)**, which takes place at the retail level. A retailer who holds to an EDLP pricing policy charges a constant low price with little or no price promotions and special sales. These constant prices eliminate week-to-week price uncertainty and can be contrasted to the "high-low" pricing of promotion-oriented competitors. In **high-low pricing**, the retailer charges higher prices on an everyday basis but then runs frequent promotions in which prices are temporarily lowered below the EDLP level.[43] The two different pricing strategies have been shown to affect consumer price judgments—deep discounts (EDLP) can lead to lower perceived prices by consumers over time than frequent, shallow discounts (high-low), even if the actual averages are the same.[44]

In recent years, high-low pricing has given way to EDLP at such widely different venues as General Motors' Saturn car dealerships and upscale department stores such as Nordstrom; but the king of EDLP is surely Wal-Mart, which practically defined the term. Except for a few sale items every month, Wal-Mart promises everyday low prices on major brands. "It's not a short-term strategy," says one Wal-Mart executive. "You have to be willing to make a commitment to it, and you have to be able to operate with lower ratios of expense than everybody else."

Some retailers have even based their entire marketing strategy around what could be called *extreme* everyday low pricing. Partly fueled by an economic downturn, once unfashionable "dollar stores" are gaining in popularity:

DOLLAR GENERAL CORP. FAMILY DOLLAR

Dollar stores are shedding their stigma, stocking name brands, and attracting younger and more affluent shoppers. These ultra-discounters have developed a successful formula for drawing shoppers from Target and even Wal-Mart: Build small, easy-to-navigate stores with parking handy; keep overhead low by limiting inventory; and spend sparingly on store décor and get free word-of-mouth publicity. I.J. Rosenberg attracted more than 3,000 customers to the grand opening of his second Little Bucks store in suburban Atlanta by handing out fliers promising to sell nine televisions, nine Game-boys, and nine Razor scooters each for 99 cents. While most extreme-value stores are still regional, chains like Little Bucks, Dollar Tree, Family Dollar, and Big Lots now operate in at least 40 states. The two biggest chains, Dollar General and Family Dollar, are breaking ground on new stores at a pace of more than one each day. These two companies operate more than 10,000 stores nationwide, nearly twice as many as six years ago.[45]

The most important reason retailers adopt EDLP is that constant sales and promotions are costly and have eroded consumer confidence in the credibility of everyday shelf prices. Consumers also have less time and patience for such time-honored traditions as watching for supermarket specials and clipping coupons. Yet, there is no denying that promotions create excitement and draw shoppers. For this reason, EDLP is not a guarantee of success. As supermarkets face heightened competition from their counterparts and from alternative channels, many find that the key to drawing shoppers is using a combination of high-low and everyday low pricing strategies, with increased advertising and promotions.[46]

GOING-RATE PRICING In **going-rate pricing**, the firm bases its price largely on competitors' prices. The firm might charge the same, more, or less than major competitor(s). In oligopolistic industries that sell a commodity such as steel, paper, or fertilizer, firms normally charge the same price. The smaller firms "follow the leader," changing their prices when the market leader's prices change rather than when their own demand or costs change. Some firms may charge a slight premium or slight discount, but they preserve the amount of difference. Thus minor gasoline retailers usually charge a few cents less per gallon than the major oil companies, without letting the difference increase or decrease.

Going-rate pricing is quite popular. Where costs are difficult to measure or competitive response is uncertain, firms feel that the going price is a good solution because it is thought to reflect the industry's collective wisdom.

AUCTION-TYPE PRICING Auction-type pricing is growing more popular, especially with the growth of the Internet. There are over 2,000 electronic marketplaces selling everything from pigs to used vehicles to cargo to chemicals. One major purpose of auctions is to dispose of excess inventories or used goods. Companies need to be aware of the three major types of auctions and their separate pricing procedures.

- ***English auctions (ascending bids).*** One seller and many buyers. On sites such as Yahoo! and eBay, the seller puts up an item and bidders raise the offer price until the top price is reached. English auctions are being used today for selling antiques, cattle, real estate, and used equipment and vehicles. After seeing ticket brokers and scalpers reap millions by charging what the market would bear, Ticketmaster Corp. began auctioning the best seats to concerts in late 2003 through its Web site, ticketmaster.com.[47]
- ***Dutch auctions (descending bids).*** One seller and many buyers, or one buyer and many sellers. In the first kind, an auctioneer announces a high price for a product and then slowly decreases the price until a bidder accepts the price. In the other, the buyer announces something that he wants to buy and then potential sellers compete to get the sale by offering the lowest price. Each seller sees what the last bid is and decides whether to go lower. FreeMarkets.com helped Royal Mail Group plc, the United Kingdom's public mail service company, save approximately 2.5 million pounds in part via an auction where 25 airlines bid for its international freight business.[48]
- ***Sealed-bid auctions.*** Would-be suppliers can submit only one bid and cannot know the other bids. The U.S. government often uses this method to procure supplies. A supplier will not bid below its cost but cannot bid too high for fear of losing the job. The net effect of these two pulls can be described in terms of the bid's *expected profit.* Using expected profit for setting price makes sense for the seller that makes many bids. The seller who bids only occasionally or who needs a particular contract badly will not find it advantageous to use expected profit. This criterion does not distinguish between a $1,000 profit with a 0.10 probability and a $125 profit with a 0.80 probability. Yet the firm that wants to keep production going would prefer the second contract to the first.

Step 6: Selecting the Final Price

Pricing methods narrow the range from which the company must select its final price. In selecting that price, the company must consider additional factors, including the impact of other marketing activities, company pricing policies, gain-and-risk-sharing pricing, and the impact of price on other parties.

IMPACT OF OTHER MARKETING ACTIVITIES The final price must take into account the brand's quality and advertising relative to the competition. In a classic study, Farris and Reibstein examined the relationships among relative price, relative quality, and relative advertising for 227 consumer businesses, and found the following:

- Brands with average relative quality but high relative advertising budgets were able to charge premium prices. Consumers apparently were willing to pay higher prices for known products than for unknown products.
- Brands with high relative quality and high relative advertising obtained the highest prices. Conversely, brands with low quality and low advertising charged the lowest prices.
- The positive relationship between high prices and high advertising held most strongly in the later stages of the product life cycle for market leaders.[49]

These findings suggest that price is not as important as quality and other benefits in the market offering. One study asked consumers to rate the importance of price and other attributes in using online retailing. Only 19 percent cared about price; far more cared about customer support (65 percent), on-time delivery (58 percent), and product shipping and handling (49 percent).[50]

COMPANY PRICING POLICIES The price must be consistent with company pricing policies. At the same time, companies are not averse to establishing pricing penalties under certain circumstances.[51]

Airlines charge $150 to those who change their reservations on discount tickets. Banks charge fees for too many withdrawals in a month or for early withdrawal of a certificate of deposit. Car rental companies charge $50 to $100 penalties for no-shows for specialty vehicles. Although these policies are often justifiable, they must be used judiciously so as not to unnecessarily alienate customers. (See "Marketing Insight: Stealth Price Increases.")

Many companies set up a pricing department to develop policies and establish or approve decisions. The aim is to ensure that salespeople quote prices that are reasonable to customers and profitable to the company. Dell Computer has developed innovative pricing techniques.

DELL

Dell uses a high-tech "cost-forecasting" system that enables it to scale its selling prices[52] based on consumer demand and the company's own costs. The company instituted this flexible pricing model in 2001 to maximize its margins during the economic slowdown. Dell managers get cost information from suppliers, which they then combine with knowledge about profit targets, delivery dates, and competition to set prices for business segments. On any given day, the same computer might sell at different prices depending on whether the purchaser is a government, small business, or home PC buyer. The cost-forecasting system may help to explain why Dell was the only U.S. PC maker among the top six to report a profit for the first quarter of 2001.[53]

GAIN-AND-RISK-SHARING PRICING Buyers may resist accepting a seller's proposal because of a high perceived level of risk. The seller has the option of offering to absorb part or all of the risk if it does not deliver the full promised value. Consider the following.

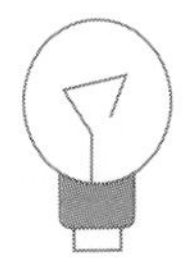

MARKETING INSIGHT | STEALTH PRICE INCREASES

With consumers stubbornly resisting higher prices, companies are trying to figure out how to increase revenue without really raising prices. Increasingly, the solution has been through the addition of fees for what had once been free features. Although some consumers abhor "nickel-and-dime" pricing strategies, small additional charges can add up to a substantial source of revenue.

The numbers can be staggering. Fees for consumers who pay bills online, bounce checks, or use automated teller machines bring banks an estimated $30 billion annually. Retailers Target and Best Buy charge a 15 percent "restocking fee" for returning electronic products. Credit card late payments—up by 11 percent in 2003—exceed $10 billion in total. The telecommunications industry in general has been aggressive at adding fees for setup, change-of-service, service termination, directory assistance, regulatory assessment, number portability, and cable hookup and equipment, costing consumers billions of dollars. By charging its long-distance customers a new 99-cent monthly "regulatory assessment fee," AT&T could bring in as much as $475 million.

This explosion of fees has a number of implications. Given that list prices stay fixed, they may result in inflation being understated. They also make it harder for consumers to compare competitive offerings. Although various citizen groups have been formed to pressure companies to roll back some of these fees, they don't always get a sympathetic ear from state and local governments who have been guilty of their own array of fees, fines, and penalties to raise necessary revenue.

Companies justify the extra fees as the only fair and viable way to cover expenses without losing customers. Many argue that it makes sense to charge a premium for added services that cost more to provide, rather than charge all customers the same amount regardless of whether or not they use the extra service. Breaking out charges and fees according to the services involved is seen as a way to keep the basic costs low. Companies also use fees as a means to weed out unprofitable customers or change their behavior. Some airlines now charge passengers $50 for paper tickets and $25 for every bag over 50 pounds.

Ultimately, the viability of extra fees will be decided in the marketplace and by the willingness of consumers to vote with their wallets and pay the fees or vote with their feet and move on.

Source: Adapted from Michael Arndt, "Fees! Fees! Fees!" *BusinessWeek,* September 29, 2003, pp. 99–104; "The Price Is Wrong," *The Economist,* May 25, 2002, pp. 59–60.

BAXTER HEALTHCARE

Baxter, a leading medical products firm, approached Columbia/HCA, a leading health care provider, with an offer to develop an information management system that would save Columbia several million dollars over an eight-year period. When Columbia balked, Baxter offered to guarantee the savings; if they were not realized, Baxter would write a check for the difference. Baxter got the order!

Baxter could have gone further and proposed that if Baxter's information system saved Columbia more than the targeted amount, Baxter's share of the additional savings would be 30 percent. An increasing number of companies, especially business marketers who promise great savings with their equipment, may have to stand ready to guarantee the promised savings, and possibly participate if the gains are much greater than expected.

IMPACT OF PRICE ON OTHER PARTIES Management must also consider the reactions of other parties to the contemplated price.[54] How will distributors and dealers feel about it? If they do not make enough profit, they may not choose to bring the product to market. Will the sales force be willing to sell at that price? How will competitors react? Will suppliers raise their prices when they see the company's price? Will the government intervene and prevent this price from being charged?

While Wal-Mart's relentless drive to squeeze out costs and lower prices has benefited consumers, the downward price pressure is taking a big toll on suppliers such as Vlasic.[55]

VLASIC

In the late 1990s, when Wal-Mart offered gallon-sized jars of Vlasic pickles for only $2.97, customers were overjoyed—even though they couldn't possibly eat them fast enough. Yet, what was lauded as a "statement item" for Wal-Mart—the kind of item that trumpets the company's commitment to low prices—reshaped every aspect of Vlasic's pickle business, and with devastating results. Here's the math: Vlasic's gallon jar of pickles went into every one of Wal-Mart's 3,000 stores for $2.97. At that price, Vlasic and Wal-Mart were making only a penny or two a jar. Yet, by selling 80 jars a week in every store, you're talking 240,000 gallons of pickles every week. Quickly, the gallon jar started cannibalizing Vlasic's non-Wal-Mart business, since the company had to struggle to get enough pickles to fill the jars. The gallon jar chewed up the profit margins of its Wal-Mart account, which grew to 30 percent of Vlasic's business. While the sheer volume of pickles going out of Vlasic's plants gave Vlasic strong sales numbers, strong growth numbers, and a vaunted place in the world of pickles at Wal-Mart, the company's profits shriveled to 25 percent or more. Eventually, Vlasic was able to get the jar size to just over one-half gallon for $2.97.

Marketers need to know the laws regulating pricing. U.S. legislation states that sellers must set prices without talking to competitors: Price-fixing is illegal. Many federal and state statutes protect consumers against deceptive pricing practices. For example, it is illegal for a company to set artificially high "regular" prices, then announce a "sale" at prices close to previous everyday prices.

::: Adapting the Price

Companies usually do not set a single price, but rather a pricing structure that reflects variations in geographical demand and costs, market-segment requirements, purchase timing, order levels, delivery frequency, guarantees, service contracts, and other factors. As a result of discounts, allowances, and promotional support, a company rarely realizes the same profit from each unit of a product that it sells. Here we will examine several price-adaptation strategies: geographical pricing, price discounts and allowances, promotional pricing, and differentiated pricing.

Geographical Pricing (Cash, Countertrade, Barter)

In geographical pricing the company decides how to price its products to different customers in different locations and countries.

PROCTER & GAMBLE

China is P&G's sixth-largest market, yet two-thirds of China's population earns less than $25 per month. So in 2003, P&G developed a tiered pricing initiative to help compete against cheaper local brands while still protecting the value of its global brands. P&G introduced a 320-gram bag of Tide Clean White for 23 cents, compared with 33 cents for 350 grams of Tide Triple Action. The Clean White version doesn't offer such benefits as stain removal and fragrance, but it costs less to make and, according to P&G, outperforms every other brand at that price level.[56]

Should the company charge higher prices to distant customers to cover the higher shipping costs or a lower price to win additional business? How should exchange rates and the strength of different currencies be accounted for? A weak dollar in the summer of 2003 allowed some U.S. companies to mark up prices and still match more expensive imports. During this time, Dow Chemical was able to achieve price increases of almost 15 percent for 2003.[57]

Another issue is how to get paid. This issue is critical when buyers lack sufficient hard currency to pay for their purchases. Many buyers want to offer other items in payment, a practice known as **countertrade**. American companies are often forced to engage in countertrade if they want the business. Countertrade may account for 15 to 25 percent of world trade and takes several forms:[58] barter, compensation deals, buyback agreements, and offset.

- ***Barter.*** The direct exchange of goods, with no money and no third party involved. In 1993, Eminence S.A., one of France's major clothing makers, launched a five-year deal to barter $25 million worth of U.S.–produced underwear and sportswear to customers in eastern Europe, in exchange for a variety of goods and services, including global transportation and advertising space in eastern European magazines.
- ***Compensation deal.*** The seller receives some percentage of the payment in cash and the rest in products. A British aircraft manufacturer sold planes to Brazil for 70 percent cash and the rest in coffee.
- ***Buyback arrangement.*** The seller sells a plant, equipment, or technology to another country and agrees to accept as partial payment products manufactured with the supplied equipment. A U.S. chemical company built a plant for an Indian company and accepted partial payment in cash and the remainder in chemicals manufactured at the plant.
- ***Offset.*** The seller receives full payment in cash but agrees to spend a substantial amount of the money in that country within a stated time period. For example, PepsiCo sells its cola syrup to Russia for rubles and agrees to buy Russian vodka at a certain rate for sale in the United States.

Price Discounts and Allowances

Most companies will adjust their list price and give discounts and allowances for early payment, volume purchases, and off-season buying (see Table 14.4).[59] Companies must do this carefully or find that their profits are much less than planned.[60]

Discount pricing has become the modus operandi of a surprising number of companies offering both products and services. Some product categories tend to self-destruct by always being on sale. Salespeople, in particular, are quick to give discounts in order to close a sale. But word can get around fast that the company's list price is "soft," and discounting becomes the norm. The discounts undermine the value perceptions of the offerings.

Some companies in an overcapacity situation are tempted to give discounts or even begin to supply a retailer with a store brand version of their product at a deep discount. Because the store brand is priced lower, however, it may start making inroads on the manufacturer's brand. Manufacturers should stop to consider the implications of supplying products at a discount to retailers because they may end up losing long-run profits in an effort to meet short-run volume goals.

When automakers get rebate-happy, the market just sits back and waits for a deal. When Ford was able to buck that trend, it achieved positive results.

TABLE 14.4

Price Discounts and Allowances

Cash Discount:	A price reduction to buyers who pay bills promptly. A typical example is "2/10, net 30," which means that payment is due within 30 days and that the buyer can deduct 2 percent by paying the bill within 10 days.
Quantity Discount:	A price reduction to those who buy large volumes. A typical example is "$10 per unit for less than 100 units; $9 per unit for 100 or more units." Quantity discounts must be offered equally to all customers and must not exceed the cost savings to the seller. They can be offered on each order placed or on the number of units ordered over a given period.
Functional Discount:	Discount (also called *trade discount*) offered by a manufacturer to trade-channel members if they will perform certain functions, such as selling, storing, and recordkeeping. Manufacturers must offer the same functional discounts within each channel.
Seasonal Discount:	A price reduction to those who buy merchandise or services out of season. Hotels, motels, and airlines offer seasonal discounts in slow selling periods.
Allowance:	An extra payment designed to gain reseller participation in special programs. *Trade-in allowances* are granted for turning in an old item when buying a new one. *Promotional allowances* reward dealers for participating in advertising and sales support programs.

FORD

In 2003, at a time when other American auto companies were emphasizing rebates and 0 percent loans, Ford Motor Company actually raised average prices through "smart pricing." The company analyzed sales data from dealerships to predict which prices and incentives would be the most effective for different models in different markets. More marketing funds were allocated to high-margin but slow-selling models, such as the F-150 truck, as well as to push lucrative options and extras. Ford offered only a $1,000 rebate on the Escape, a small sport utility vehicle, but $3,000 on the slower-selling Explorer model.[61] Ford actually increased market share during this time and estimated that smart pricing contributed one-third of its profit.

Kevin Clancy, chairman of Copernicus, a major marketing research and consulting firm, found that only between 15 and 35 percent of buyers in most categories are price sensitive. People with higher incomes and higher product involvement willingly pay more for features, customer service, quality, added convenience, and the brand name. So it can be a mistake for a strong, distinctive brand to plunge into price discounting to respond to low-price attacks.[62] At the same time, discounting can be a useful tool if the company can gain concessions in return, such as when the customer agrees to sign a three-year contract, is willing to order electronically, thus saving the company money, or agrees to buy in truckload quantities.

Sales management needs to monitor the proportion of customers who are receiving discounts, the average discount, and the particular salespeople who are overrelying on discounting. Higher levels of management should conduct a **net price analysis** to arrive at the "real price" of their offering. The real price is affected not only by discounts, but by many other expenses (see promotional pricing below) that reduce the realized price: Suppose the company's list price is $3,000. The average discount is $300. The company's promotional spending averages $450 (15% of the list price). Co-op advertising money of $150 is given to retailers to back the product. The company's net price is $2,100, not $3,000.

Promotional Pricing

Companies can use several pricing techniques to stimulate early purchase:

- ***Loss-leader pricing.*** Supermarkets and department stores often drop the price on well-known brands to stimulate additional store traffic. This pays if the revenue on the additional sales compensates for the lower margins on the loss-leader items. Manufacturers of loss-leader brands typically object because this practice can dilute the brand image and bring complaints from retailers who charge the list price. Manufacturers have tried to restrain intermediaries from loss-leader pricing through lobbying for retail-price-maintenance laws, but these laws have been revoked.

- ***Special-event pricing.*** Sellers will establish special prices in certain seasons to draw in more customers. Every August, there are back-to-school sales.
- ***Cash rebates.*** Auto companies and other consumer-goods companies offer cash rebates to encourage purchase of the manufacturers' products within a specified time period. Rebates can help clear inventories without cutting the stated list price.
- ***Low-interest financing.*** Instead of cutting its price, the company can offer customers low-interest financing. Automakers have even announced no-interest financing to attract customers.
- ***Longer payment terms.*** Sellers, especially mortgage banks and auto companies, stretch loans over longer periods and thus lower the monthly payments. Consumers often worry less about the cost (i.e., the interest rate) of a loan and more about whether they can afford the monthly payment.
- ***Warranties and service contracts.*** Companies can promote sales by adding a free or low-cost warranty or service contract.
- ***Psychological discounting.*** This strategy involves setting an artificially high price and then offering the product at substantial savings; for example, "Was $359, now $299." Illegitimate discount tactics are fought by the Federal Trade Commission and Better Business Bureaus. Discounts from normal prices are a legitimate form of promotional pricing.

Promotional-pricing strategies are often a zero-sum game. If they work, competitors copy them and they lose their effectiveness. If they do not work, they waste money that could have been put into other marketing tools, such as building up product quality and service or strengthening product image through advertising.

Differentiated Pricing

Companies often adjust their basic price to accommodate differences in customers, products, locations, and so on. Lands' End creates men's shirts in many different styles, weights, and levels of quality. A men's white button-down shirt may cost as little as $18.50 or as much as $48.00.[63]

GATEWAY COUNTRY

In its more than 200 Country Stores, Gateway has initiated a new four-tiered pricing strategy: market pricing, which will place products within 5 percent of the going rate, competitive pricing, very competitive, and finally disruptive pricing. Disruptive pricing will position the price of a device as much as 50 percent below the market. The point of disruptive pricing is to gain market share in high-growth categories. Gateway has already tested the disruptive-pricing waters by introducing a 42-inch plasma TV at $2,999. The company claims that despite the low price, there was still a healthy margin.[64]

Price discrimination occurs when a company sells a product or service at two or more prices that do not reflect a proportional difference in costs. In first-degree price discrimination, the seller charges a separate price to each customer depending on the intensity of his or her demand. In second-degree price discrimination, the seller charges less to buyers who buy a larger volume. In third-degree price discrimination, the seller charges different amounts to different classes of buyers, as in the following cases:

- ***Customer-segment pricing.*** Different customer groups are charged different prices for the same product or service. For example, museums often charge a lower admission fee to students and senior citizens.
- ***Product-form pricing.*** Different versions of the product are priced differently but not proportionately to their respective costs. Evian prices a 48-ounce bottle of its mineral water at $2.00. It takes the same water and packages 1.7 ounces in a moisturizer spray for $6.00. Through product-form pricing, Evian manages to charge $3.00 an ounce in one form and about $.04 an ounce in another.

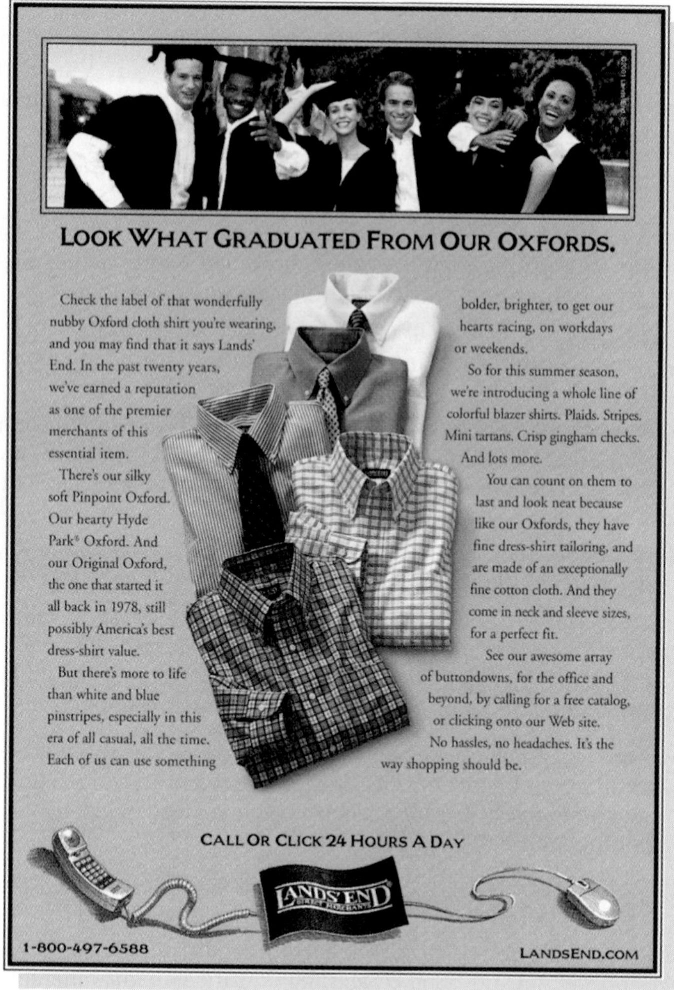

Lands' End print ad for its Oxford shirts spells out the array of styles, colors, weights, and quality levels it makes to meet the needs of many different customers.

- ***Image pricing.*** Some companies price the same product at two different levels based on image differences. A perfume manufacturer can put the perfume in one bottle, give it a name and image, and price it at $10 an ounce. It can put the same perfume in another bottle with a different name and image and price it at $30 an ounce.
- ***Channel pricing.*** Coca-Cola carries a different price depending on whether it is purchased in a fine restaurant, a fast-food restaurant, or a vending machine.
- ***Location pricing.*** The same product is priced differently at different locations even though the cost of offering at each location is the same. A theater varies its seat prices according to audience preferences for different locations.
- ***Time pricing.*** Prices are varied by season, day, or hour. Public utilities vary energy rates to commercial users by time of day and weekend versus weekday. Restaurants charge less to "early bird" customers. Hotels charge less on weekends.

The airline and hospitality industries use yield management systems and **yield pricing**, by which they offer discounted but limited early purchases, higher-priced late purchases, and the lowest rates on unsold inventory just before it expires.[65] Airlines charge different fares to passengers on the same flight, depending on the seating class; the time of day (morning or night coach); the day of the week (workday or weekend); the season; the person's company, past business, or status (youth, military, senior citizen); and so on.

That's why on a flight from New York City to Miami you might have paid $200 and be sitting across from someone who has paid $1,290. Take Continental Airlines: It launches 2,000 flights a day and each flight has between 10 and 20 prices. Continental starts booking flights 330 days in advance, and every flying day is different from every other flying day. At any given moment the market has more than 7 million prices. And in a system that tracks the difference in prices and the price of competitors' offerings, airlines collectively change

75,000 prices a day! It's a system designed to punish procrastinators by charging them the highest possible prices.

The phenomenon of offering different pricing schedules to different consumers and dynamically adjusting prices is exploding.[66] See "Marketing Insight: Smart Pricing Takes Off," for more on how companies are using software packages that provide real-time controlled tests of actual consumer response to different pricing schedules.

Most consumers are probably not even aware of the degree to which they are the targets of discriminatory pricing. For instance, catalog retailers like Victoria's Secret routinely send out catalogs that sell identical goods except at different prices. Consumers who live in a more free-spending zip code may see only the higher prices. Office product superstore Staples also sends out office supply catalogs with different prices.

Some forms of price discrimination (in which sellers offer different price terms to different people within the same trade group) are illegal. However, price discrimination is legal if the seller can prove that its costs are different when selling different volumes or different qualities of the same product to different retailers. Predatory pricing—selling below cost with the intention of destroying competition—is unlawful.[67] Even if legal, some differentiated pricing may meet with a hostile reaction. Coca-Cola considered raising its vending machine soda prices on hot days using wireless technology, and lowering the price on cold days. Customers so disliked the idea that Coke abandoned it.

For price discrimination to work, certain conditions must exist. First, the market must be segmentable and the segments must show different intensities of demand. Second, members in the lower-price segment must not be able to resell the product to the higher-price segment. Third, competitors must not be able to undersell the firm in the higher-price segment. Fourth, the cost of segmenting and policing the market must not exceed the extra revenue derived from price discrimination. Fifth, the practice must not breed customer resentment and ill will. Sixth, the particular form of price discrimination must not be illegal.[68]

::: Initiating and Responding to Price Changes

Companies often face situations where they may need to cut or raise prices.

Initiating Price Cuts

Several circumstances might lead a firm to cut prices. One is excess plant capacity: The firm needs additional business and cannot generate it through increased sales effort, product improvement, or other measures. It may resort to aggressive pricing, but in initiating a price cut, the company may trigger a price war.

Companies sometimes initiate price cuts in a *drive to dominate the market through lower costs.* Either the company starts with lower costs than its competitors or it initiates price cuts in the hope of gaining market share and lower costs. A price-cutting strategy involves possible traps:

- ***Low-quality trap.*** Consumers will assume that the quality is low.
- ***Fragile-market-share trap.*** A low price buys market share but not market loyalty. The same customers will shift to any lower-priced firm that comes along.
- ***Shallow-pockets trap.*** The higher-priced competitors may cut their prices and may have longer staying power because of deeper cash reserves.

Initiating Price Increases

A successful price increase can raise profits considerably. For example, if the company's profit margin is 3 percent of sales, a 1 percent price increase will increase profits by 33 percent if sales volume is unaffected. This situation is illustrated in Table 14.5. The assumption is that a company charged $10 and sold 100 units and had costs of $970, leaving a profit of $30, or 3 percent on sales. By raising its price by 10 cents (1 percent price increase), it boosted its profits by 33 percent, assuming the same sales volume.

A major circumstance provoking price increases is *cost inflation.* Rising costs unmatched by productivity gains squeeze profit margins and lead companies to regular rounds of price increases. Companies often raise their prices by more than the cost

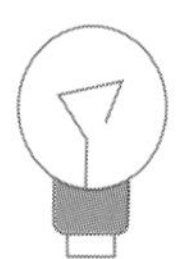

MARKETING INSIGHT | SMART PRICING TAKES OFF

Stelios Haji-Ioannou has made a fortune with easyJet, the eight-year-old airline that offers dynamically priced discount fares. In a nutshell, passengers pay less for a seat the earlier they buy. Stelios, as he's universally known, has applied the same yield management formula with varying degrees of success to car rentals, credit cards, and even Internet cafés. Now he's taking the concept to the movies. In 2003 he launched easyCinema, a 2,000-seat, 10-screen complex outside London. It is founded on the premise that 80 percent of cinema seats never see a bottom. At easyCinema tickets start at about 30 cents and rise with demand, rewarding patrons who book in advance or enjoy off-peak screenings. But the same system that netted a fortune for easyJet is facing hurdles: Britain's big movie distributors don't like getting a lump sum from Stelios rather than creaming off a high percentage of box office revenue in the first weeks of a film's run (the least revenue-producing for Stelios). Still, Stelios isn't giving up, and under the umbrella of easyGroup, the entrepreneur also plans to launch a cruise ship (easyCruise), a hotel chain (easyDorm), and even fast food (easyPizza)!

Stelios's easyGroup leads the field in what has been alternately called revenue management or yield management—pricing a perishable resource in accordance with demand from multiple customer segments to maximize revenue or profit. Prices are adjusted dynamically as a function of inventory level and time left in the selling season. Yet, "dynamic pricing" (or "smart pricing" or "scientific pricing") is not only the province of those with perishable inventory, such as the airline and hospitality industries. With the advent of Internet technology, there has been an explosion of information about customers and their preferences. Combine this capacity with businesses' pressing needs and you can see why we are entering a new era of pricing. In a sluggish economy, companies haven't been able to raise prices for years. Like easyGroup, they are taking a page from the airlines, which have been using revenue management techniques for 25 years.

The new dynamic pricing systems, produced by SAP and start-ups like DemandTec and ProfitLogic Inc., sift through massive databases available on a corporate intranet. These databases include up-to-date information about orders, promotions, product revenue, and stock levels in warehouses. Early adopters using Web-based pricing tools include Saks, Best Buy, Ford Motor Co., The Home Depot, JC Penney, Safeway, and General Electric. Here are two success stories:

CASUAL MALE

A retail chain offering clothing to big and tall men, Casual Male analyzed sales data to determine exactly how to "slice and dice" markets to offer the right prices at the right time. Using two years' worth of sales data on 40,000 items, from ties to sweaters, in 410 stores, the company is able to estimate when and how much to cut prices. Pricing could reflect the fact that people in the Northeast stopped buying bathing suits in July, while demand stayed strong in some Midwestern markets through August, and never really stopped in the Sunbelt. As a result of more flexible and responsive pricing, gross margins rose 25 percent in 2002.

DHL WORLDWIDE EXPRESS INC.

DHL used to have one-price-fits-all list prices for shipping packages in the United States and around the world, and when potential customers called for rates DHL scared them off by asking for more than FedEx or UPS. With Web pricing tools, DHL tested the market by offering cold callers different prices to see how low prices could go and still make a profit. In the end, DHL wound up changing hundreds of prices. There were plenty of surprises. Most prices did go down, but the company didn't have to match the competition. In fact, by lowering prices a bit, DHL's "ad hoc" business not only stabilized but it also grew. For instance, of people who called to get a quote, 17 percent actually shipped prior to the pricing overhaul. The new prices have increased the ratio to nearly 25 percent.

Constant price variation, however, can be tricky where consumer relationships are concerned. Research shows it tends to work best in situations where there's no bond between the buyer and the seller. One way to make it work is to offer customers a unique bundle of products and services to meet their needs precisely, making it harder for them to make price comparisons. This tactic is being used to sell software, which is vulnerable to price wars because the cost of producing more copies is near zero. Application service providers are "renting" their software and support by the month instead of selling an unlimited-use license.

The tactic most companies favor, however, is to market perfect pricing as a reward for good behavior rather than as a penalty. For instance, shipping company APL, Inc., rewards customers who can better predict how much cargo space they'll need with cheaper rates for booking early. Customers are getting savvier about how to avoid buyer's remorse. They are changing their buying behavior to accommodate the new realities of dynamic pricing—where prices vary frequently by channels, products, customers, and time.

Sources: Ajit Kambil, "Are You Leaving Money on the Table?" *Journal of Business Strategy* (January/February 2002): 40–43; Peter Coy, "The Power of Smart Pricing," *BusinessWeek,* April 10, 2000, pp. 160–164; Charles Fishman, "Which Price Is Right?" *Fast Company,* March 2003, pp. 92–102; Mark Ritson, "Stelios Shows There's an 'Easy' Way to a Smart Pricing Strategy," *Marketing,* April 10, 2003, p. 16; Ian Wylie, "In Movieland, Not So Easy," *Fast Company,* October 2003, p. 35; Bob Tedeschi, "E-Commerce Report," *New York Times,* September 2, 2002, p. C5; Faith Keenan, "The Price Is Really Right," *BusinessWeek,* March 31, 2003, pp. 62–67. For a review of recent and seminal work linking pricing decisions with operational insights, see: Moritz Fleischmann, Joseph M. Hall, and David F. Pyke, "Research Brief: Smart Pricing," *MIT Sloan Management Review* (Winter 2004): 9–13.

TABLE 14.5

Profits Before and After a Price Increase

	Before	After	
Price	$ 10	$10.10	(a 1 percent price increase)
Units sold	100	100	
Revenue	$1000	$1010	
Costs	–970	–970	
Profit	$ 30	$ 40	(a 33⅓ percent profit increase)

increase, in anticipation of further inflation or government price controls, in a practice called *anticipatory pricing.*

Another factor leading to price increases is *overdemand.* When a company cannot supply all of its customers, it can raise its prices, ration supplies to customers, or both. The price can be increased in the following ways. Each has a different impact on buyers.

- ***Delayed quotation pricing.*** The company does not set a final price until the product is finished or delivered. This pricing is prevalent in industries with long production lead times, such as industrial construction and heavy equipment.
- ***Escalator clauses.*** The company requires the customer to pay today's price and all or part of any inflation increase that takes place before delivery. An escalator clause bases price increases on some specified price index. Escalator clauses are found in contracts for major industrial projects, like aircraft construction and bridge building.
- ***Unbundling.*** The company maintains its price but removes or prices separately one or more elements that were part of the former offer, such as free delivery or installation. Car companies sometimes add antilock brakes and passenger-side airbags as supplementary extras to their vehicles.
- ***Reduction of discounts.*** The company instructs its sales force not to offer its normal cash and quantity discounts.

A company needs to decide whether to raise its price sharply on a one-time basis or to raise it by small amounts several times. Generally, consumers prefer small price increases on a regular basis to sudden, sharp increases.

In passing price increases on to customers, the company must avoid looking like a price gouger.[69] Companies also need to think of who will bear the brunt of increased prices. Customer memories are long, and they can turn against companies they perceive as price gougers. A vivid illustration of such reactions was the experience of Marlboro, Philip Morris's leading cigarette brand.[70]

MARLBORO

On April 2, 1993, or "Marlboro Friday," Philip Morris announced plans to "increase market share and grow long-term profitability in a highly price sensitive market environment." A price cut of 40 cents in Marlboro cigarettes was to be initiated, matched by increased expenditures in retail promotions and consumer continuity programs. A prime impetus for these dramatic price cuts was Philip Morris's hefty price increases, which had often occurred two to three times a year and had been above the rate of inflation (as much as 10% in a year). The price gap between Marlboro and discount brands rose to as much as $1 and resulted in steady sales increases for discount brands at the expense of Marlboro market share. By day's end on Friday, Philip Morris stock price declined 23 percent, representing a one-day loss of $13 billion in shareholder equity. By significantly cutting the difference between Marlboro and discount cigarettes, however, Philip Morris was able to woo back many customers. Within nine months after the price drop, Marlboro's market share increased to almost 27 percent, eventually rising to almost 30 percent.[71]

The Marlboro episode reinforces the fact that although strong brands can command price premiums, the premiums cannot be excessive. Price hikes without corresponding investments in the value of the brand increases vulnerability to lower-priced competition. Consumers may be willing to "trade down" because they no longer can justify to themselves that the higher-priced brand is worth it. This also happened to Kraft.

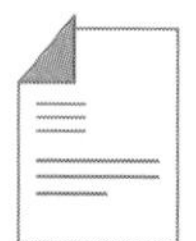

MARKETING MEMO | MARKETING STRATEGIES TO AVOID RAISING PRICES

Given strong consumer resistance to price hikes, marketers go to great lengths to find alternative approaches that will allow them to avoid increasing prices when they otherwise would have done so. Here are a few popular ones.

- Shrinking the amount of product instead of raising the price. (Hershey Foods maintained its candy bar price but trimmed its size. Nestlé maintained its size but raised the price.)
- Substituting less expensive materials or ingredients. (Many candy bar companies substituted synthetic chocolate for real chocolate to fight price increases in cocoa.)
- Reducing or removing product features. (Sears engineered down a number of its appliances so they could be priced competitively with those sold in discount stores.)
- Removing or reducing product services, such as installation or free delivery.
- Using less expensive packaging material or larger package sizes.
- Reducing the number of sizes and models offered.
- Creating new economy brands. (Jewel food stores introduced 170 generic items selling at 10 percent to 30 percent less than national brands.)

KRAFT FOODS INC.

Early in 2003, Kraft responded to increasing commodity costs for coffee and cheese by raising its own prices. The move widened the gap between Kraft's brand-name items and its generic competitors, many of which held the line on price increases. Recession-weary consumers flocked to the cheaper choices. As sales fell, Kraft backpedaled, rolling back many prices and flooding the market with new coupons and promotions. It was a costly misstep. Kraft, which typically spends about $900 million a year on marketing, spent an extra $200 million to lure back lost customers. Analysts and other observers questioned whether the company would have been better off boosting margins through additional cost-cutting, including reduced ad spending.[72]

Several techniques help consumers avoid sticker shock and a hostile reaction when prices rise: One is that a sense of fairness must surround any price increase, and customers must be given advance notice so they can do forward buying or shop around. Sharp price increases need to be explained in understandable terms. Making low-visibility price moves first is also a good technique: Eliminating discounts, increasing minimum order sizes, and curtailing production of low-margin products are some examples; and contracts or bids for long-term projects should contain escalator clauses based on such factors as increases in recognized national price indexes.[73] "Marketing Memo: Marketing Strategies to Avoid Raising Prices" describes other means by which companies can respond to higher costs or overdemand without raising prices.

Reactions to Price Changes

Any price change can provoke a response from customers, competitors, distributors, suppliers, and even government.

CUSTOMER REACTIONS Customers often question the motivation behind price changes.[74] A price cut can be interpreted in different ways: The item is about to be replaced by a new model; the item is faulty and is not selling well; the firm is in financial trouble; the price will come down even further; the quality has been reduced. A price increase, which would normally deter sales, may carry some positive meanings to customers: The item is "hot" and represents an unusually good value.

COMPETITOR REACTIONS Competitors are most likely to react when the number of firms are few, the product is homogeneous, and buyers are highly informed. Competitor reactions can be a special problem when they have a strong value proposition.

Print ad for Zantac, which took market leadership from competitor Tagamet despite being introduced at a price premium.

ZANTAC VERSUS TAGAMET

Pharmaceutical company Glaxo introduced its ulcer medication Zantac to attack market incumbent Tagamet. The conventional wisdom was that, as the "second one in," Glaxo should price Zantac 10 percent below Tagamet. CEO Paul Girolam knew that Zantac was superior to Tagamet in terms of fewer drug interactions and side effects and more convenient dosing. Glaxo introduced Zantac at a significant price premium over Tagamet and still gained the market-leader position.[75]

How can a firm anticipate a competitor's reactions? One way is to assume that the competitor reacts in a set way to price changes. The other is to assume that the competitor treats each price change as a fresh challenge and reacts according to self-interest at the time. Now the company will need to research the competitor's current financial situation, recent sales, customer loyalty, and corporate objectives. If the competitor has a market share objective, it is likely to match the price change.[76] If it has a profit-maximization objective, it may react by increasing the advertising budget or improving product quality.

The problem is complicated because the competitor can put different interpretations on a price cut: that the company is trying to steal the market, that the company is doing poorly and trying to boost its sales, or that the company wants the whole industry to reduce prices to stimulate total demand.

Responding to Competitors' Price Changes

How should a firm respond to a price cut initiated by a competitor? In markets characterized by high product homogeneity, the firm should search for ways to enhance its augmented product. If it cannot find any, it will have to meet the price reduction. If the competitor raises its price in a homogeneous product market, other firms might not match it unless the increase will benefit the industry as a whole. Then the leader will have to roll back the increase.

In nonhomogeneous product markets, a firm has more latitude. It needs to consider the following issues: (1) Why did the competitor change the price? To steal the market, to utilize excess capacity, to meet changing cost conditions, or to lead an industry-wide price change? (2) Does the competitor plan to make the price change temporary or permanent? (3) What will happen to the company's market share and profits if it does not respond? Are other companies going to respond? (4) What are the competitors' and other firms' responses likely to be to each possible reaction?

Market leaders frequently face aggressive price-cutting by smaller firms trying to build market share. Using price, Fuji attacks Kodak, Schick attacks Gillette, and AMD attacks Intel. Brand leaders also face lower-priced private-store brands. The brand leader can respond in several ways:

- ***Maintain price.*** The leader might maintain its price and profit margin, believing that (1) it would lose too much profit if it reduced its price, (2) it would not lose much market share, and (3) it could regain market share when necessary. However, the argument against price maintenance is that the attacker gets more confident, the leader's sales force gets demoralized, and the leader loses more share than expected. The leader panics, lowers price to regain share, and finds that regaining its market position is more difficult than expected.
- ***Maintain price and add value.*** The leader could improve its product, services, and communications. The firm may find it cheaper to maintain price and spend money to improve perceived quality than to cut price and operate at a lower margin.
- ***Reduce price.*** The leader might drop its price to match the competitor's price. It might do so because (1) its costs fall with volume, (2) it would lose market share because the market is price sensitive, and (3) it would be hard to rebuild market share once it is lost. This action will cut profits in the short run.
- ***Increase price and improve quality.*** The leader might raise its price and introduce new brands to bracket the attacking brand.
- ***Launch a low-price fighter line.*** It might add lower-priced items to the line or create a separate, lower-priced brand.

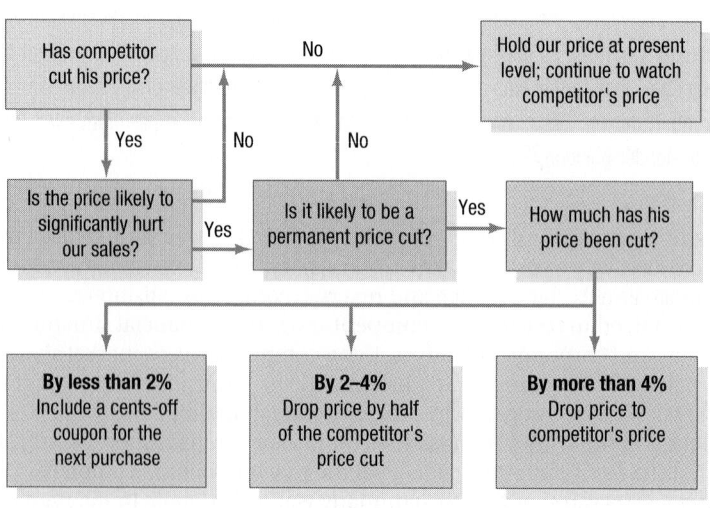

FIG. 14.7

Price-Reaction Program for Meeting a Competitor's Price Cut

The best response varies with the situation. The company has to consider the product's stage in the life cycle, its importance in the company's portfolio, the competitor's intentions and resources, the market's price and quality sensitivity, the behavior of costs with volume, and the company's alternative opportunities.

An extended analysis of alternatives may not be feasible when the attack occurs. The company may have to react decisively within hours or days. It would make better sense to anticipate possible competitors' price changes and to prepare contingent responses. Figure 14.7 shows a *price-reaction program* to be used if a competitor cuts prices. Reaction programs for meeting price changes find their greatest application in industries where price changes occur with some frequency and where it is important to react quickly—for example, in the meatpacking, lumber, and oil industries.

SUMMARY :::

1. Despite the increased role of nonprice factors in modern marketing, price remains a critical element of the marketing mix. Price is the only element that produces revenue; the others produce costs.
2. In setting pricing policy, a company follows a six-step procedure. It selects its pricing objective. It estimates the demand curve, the probable quantities it will sell at each possible price. It estimates how its costs vary at different levels of output, at different levels of accumulated production experience, and for differentiated marketing offers. It examines competitors' costs, prices, and offers. It selects a pricing method. It selects the final price.
3. Companies do not usually set a single price, but rather a pricing structure that reflects variations in geographical demand and costs, market-segment requirements, purchase timing, order levels, and other factors. Several price-adaptation strategies are available: (1) geographical pricing; (2) price discounts and allowances; (3) promotional pricing; and (4) discriminatory pricing.
4. After developing pricing strategies, firms often face situations in which they need to change prices. A price decrease might be brought about by excess plant capacity, declining market share, a desire to dominate the market through lower costs, or economic recession. A price increase might be brought about by cost inflation or overdemand. Companies must carefully manage customer perceptions in raising prices.
5. Companies must anticipate competitor price changes and prepare contingent response. A number of responses are possible in terms of maintaining or changing price or quality.
6. The firm facing a competitor's price change must try to understand the competitor's intent and the likely duration of the change. Strategy often depends on whether a firm is producing homogeneous or nonhomogeneous products. Market leaders attacked by lower-priced competitors can choose to maintain price, raise the perceived quality of their product, reduce price, increase price and improve quality, or launch a low-priced fighter line.

APPLICATIONS :::

Marketing Debate Is the Right Price a Fair Price?

Prices are often set to satisfy demand or to reflect the premium that consumers are willing to pay for a product or service. Some critics shudder, however, at the thought of $2 bottles of water, $150 running shoes, and $500 concert tickets.

Take a position: Prices should reflect the value that consumers are willing to pay versus Prices should primarily just reflect the cost involved in making a product or service.

Marketing Discussion

Think of the various pricing methods described above—markup pricing, target-return pricing, perceived-value pricing, value pricing, going-rate pricing, and auction-type pricing. As a consumer, which method do you personally prefer to deal with? Why? If the average price were to stay the same, which would you prefer: (1) for firms to set one price and not deviate or (2) to employ slightly higher prices most of the year, but slightly lower discounted prices or specials for certain occasions?

PART

DELIVERING VALUE

IN THIS CHAPTER, WE WILL ADDRESS THE FOLLOWING QUESTIONS:

1. What is a marketing channel system and value network?
2. What work do marketing channels perform?
3. How should channels be designed?
4. What decisions do companies face in managing their channels?
5. How should companies integrate channels and manage channel conflict?
6. What is the future for e-commerce?

CHAPTER 15 ::: DESIGNING AND MANAGING VALUE NETWORKS AND CHANNELS

fifteen

Successful value creation needs successful value delivery. Holistic marketers are increasingly taking a value network view of their businesses. Instead of limiting their focus to their immediate suppliers, distributors, and customers, they are examining the whole supply chain that links raw materials, components, and manufactured goods and shows how they move toward the final consumers. Companies are looking at their suppliers' suppliers upstream and at their distributors' customers downstream. They are looking at customer segments and how company resources can best be organized to meet needs. Failure to coordinate the value network properly can have dire consequences.

Discount chain Kmart's rise in the 1970s was characterized by its blue light specials and famous (or infamous) in-store announcement, "Attention Kmart Shoppers!" But suffering from poor locations, an unfavorable image, and deteriorating sales, Kmart decided to try to match Wal-Mart's everyday low prices. This move, however, forced the company to drop the widely distributed Sunday newspaper circulars that promoted sales and drove store traffic. Even worse, a terrible replenishment system also resulted in numerous hot sellers being out of stock. Kmart filed for Chapter 11 bankruptcy on January 22, 2002, the biggest retailer to have done so up to that time.[1]

>>>

A Blue Light Shop Online kiosk at Kmart.

Companies today must build and manage a continuously evolving value network. In this chapter, we consider strategic and tactical issues with marketing channels and value networks. We will examine marketing channel issues from the perspective of retailers, wholesalers, and physical-distribution agencies in Chapter 16.

::: Marketing Channels and Value Networks

Most producers do not sell their goods directly to the final users; between them stands a set of intermediaries performing a variety of functions. These intermediaries constitute a marketing channel (also called a trade channel or distribution channel). Formally, **marketing channels** are sets of interdependent organizations involved in the process of making a product or service available for use or consumption. They are the set of pathways a product or service follows after production, culminating in purchase and use by the final end user.[2]

Some intermediaries—such as wholesalers and retailers—buy, take title to, and resell the merchandise; they are called *merchants.* Others—brokers, manufacturers' representatives, sales agents—search for customers and may negotiate on the producer's behalf but do not take title to the goods; they are called *agents.* Still others—transportation companies, independent warehouses, banks, advertising agencies—assist in the distribution process but neither take title to goods nor negotiate purchases or sales; they are called *facilitators.*

The Importance of Channels

A **marketing channel system** is the particular set of marketing channels employed by a firm. Decisions about the marketing channel system are among the most critical facing management. In the United States, channel members collectively earn margins that account for 30 to 50 percent of the ultimate selling price. In contrast, advertising typically accounts for less than 5 to 7 percent of the final price.[3] Marketing channels also represent a substantial opportunity cost. One of the chief roles of marketing channels is to convert potential buyers into profitable orders. Marketing channels must not just *serve* markets, they must also *make* markets.[4]

The channels chosen affect all other marketing decisions. The company's pricing depends on whether it uses mass merchandisers or high-quality boutiques. The firm's sales force and advertising decisions depend on how much training and motivation dealers need. In addition, channel decisions involve relatively long-term commitments to other firms as well as a set of policies and procedures. When an automaker signs up independent dealers to sell its automobiles, the automaker cannot buy them out the next day and replace them with company-owned outlets.[5]

In managing its intermediaries, the firm must decide how much effort to devote to push versus pull marketing. A **push strategy** involves the manufacturer using its sales force and trade promotion money to induce intermediaries to carry, promote, and sell the product to end users. Push strategy is appropriate where there is low brand loyalty in a category, brand choice is made in the store, the product is an impulse item, and product benefits are well understood. A **pull strategy** involves the manufacturer using advertising and promotion to persuade consumers to ask intermediaries for the product, thus inducing the intermediaries to order it. Pull strategy is appropriate when there is high brand loyalty and high involvement in the category, when people perceive differences between brands, and when people choose the brand before they go to the store. Top marketing companies such as Nike, Intel, and Coca-Cola skillfully employ both push and pull strategies.

Channel Development

A new firm typically starts as a local operation selling in a limited market, using existing intermediaries. The number of such intermediaries is apt to be limited: a few manufacturers' sales agents, a few wholesalers, several established retailers, a few trucking companies, and a few warehouses. Deciding on the best channels might not be a problem; the problem might be to convince the available intermediaries to handle the firm's line.

If the firm is successful, it might branch into new markets and use different channels in different markets. In smaller markets, the firm might sell directly to retailers; in larger markets, it might sell through distributors. In rural areas, it might work with general-goods merchants; in urban areas, with limited-line merchants. In one part of the country, it might grant exclusive franchises; in another, it might sell through all outlets willing to handle the merchandise. In one country it might use international sales agents; in another, it might partner with a local firm.[6] In short, the channel system evolves in response to local opportunities and conditions.

This entrepreneur started by developing channels in a small niche and then expanding slowly into new channels.

SEAYU ENTERPRISES INC.

SeaYu is taking a slow and steady approach to channel development for its pioneering product "Petrotech Odor Eliminator." Designed to eliminate the odors that pets generate—from wet doggy smell to kitty litter box aroma—Petrotech Odor Eliminator was first sold across the country at small pet specialty retailers and kennels, through breeders, and animal rescue centers. Once it established a reputation in these specialized channels and gained some publicity, SeaYu signed a contract with the huge PetSmart chain. SeaYu's product will first begin selling only in PetSmart's mail-order catalog and then will be rolled out to its retail locations. In the meantime, customers have given SeaYu feedback that the product not only eliminates pet odors, but is also useful for clearing the air of other annoying smells such as bacon cooking or cigarette smoke. SeaYu plans to eventually broaden distribution into other markets like housewares and the automotive aftermarket. This, in turn, could lead to deals with larger discount chains such as Wal-Mart or Target.[7]

Today's successful companies are also multiplying the number of "go-to-market" or **hybrid channels** in any one market area:

- IBM uses its sales force to sell to large accounts, outbound telemarketing to sell to medium-sized accounts, direct mail with an inbound number for small accounts, retailers to sell to still smaller accounts, and the Internet to sell specialty items.
- Charles Schwab enables its customers to do transactions in its branches, over the phone, or on the Internet.
- Staples markets through its traditional retail channel, a direct-response Internet site, virtual malls, and thousands of links on affiliated sites.

Companies that manage hybrid channels must make sure these channels work well together and match each target customer's preferred ways of doing business. Customers expect *channel integration*, characterized by the following features:

- The ability to order a product online and pick it up at a convenient retail location.
- The ability to return an online-ordered product to a nearby store of the retailer.
- The right to receive discounts based on total online and offline purchases.

"Marketing Memo: Multichannel Shopping Checklist" offers some concrete advice on channel integration. Here's a specific example of a company that has carefully managed its multiple channels.

REI

What's more frustrating: Buying hiking boots that cripple your feet or trying on the perfect hiking boots only to find that the store is out of stock in the size or style you want? At Recreational Equipment Inc. (REI), outdoor enthusiasts can easily avoid both frustrations. In 59 REI stores across the country, customers are lighting up gas stoves, pitching tents, and snuggling deep into sleeping bags. If an item is out of stock, all customers need do is tap into the store's Internet kiosk to order it from REI's Web site. Less Internet savvy

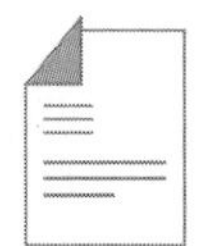

MARKETING MEMO | MULTICHANNEL SHOPPING CHECKLIST

During the 2003 "back-to-school" season, the e-tailing group, an e-commerce consulting firm in Chicago, sent mystery shoppers to visit retail locations of 16 e-tailers to test their claims of an integrated shopping experience in the online/retail returns process. Overall, the study found that 44 percent of in-store returns of merchandise purchased online required a store manager to override the retail system in order to accept the return. In response to this and several other inadequacies revealed by the study, the e-tailing group created a "Best of Breed Multi-channel Shopping Checklist" to help marketers better integrate online and offline channels:

- Train all store associates on processes for online merchandise returns.
- List your company's 800 number on the Web homepage, and be sure your customer service hours of operation are easily accessible.
- Provide an information center that is easy to navigate and includes contact information, FAQs, guarantees, return policies, and tips for first-time customers.
- Implement a store locator feature that includes store locations, hours, and events.
- Make store pickup for purchases an option and include real-time inventory levels, where applicable.
- Post the store's weekly circular online for a more complete multichannel experience.
- Offer gift certificates that can be redeemed online and offline.
- Send e-mail notifications of the order, shipping, and return credit; include a reminder of the returns process in notifications as well as a link to your store locator.
- Suppy all pertinent/compatible information for store return of merchandise on the packing slip or invoice.

Source: Excerpted from Hallie Mummert, "Multi-Channel Marketers Earn a 'C+' on Returns," *Target Marketing* (October 2003): 158.

customers can even get clerks to place the order for them from the checkout counters. For its seamless integration of retail store, Web site, Internet kiosks, mail-order catalogs, value-priced outlets, and toll-free order number, REI has been named today's top multichannel marketer by Forrester Research. And REI not only generates store-to-Internet traffic, it also sends Internet shoppers into its stores. If a customer browses REI's site and stops to read an REI "Learn and Share" article on backpacking, the site might highlight an in-store promo on hiking boots. Linking all its channels has produced outstanding results: In a 24-month period, REI found that dual-channel shoppers spent 114 percent more than single-channel ones and that tri-channel shoppers spent 48 percent more than dual-channel shoppers.[8] ■

Different consumers, however, have different needs during the purchase process. Nunes and Cespedes argue that in many markets, buyers fall into one of four categories.[9]

1. ***Habitual shoppers*** – Purchase from the same places in the same manner over time.
2. ***High value deal seekers*** – Know their needs and "channel surf" a great deal before buying at the lowest possible price.
3. ***Variety-loving shoppers*** – Gather information in many channels, take advantage of high-touch services, and then buy in their favorite channel, regardless of price.
4. ***High-involvement shoppers*** – Gather information in all channels, make their purchase in a low-cost channel, but take advantage of customer support from a high-touch channel.

The same consumer may choose to use different channels for different functions in making a purchase. A consumer may choose to browse through a catalog before visiting a store or take a test drive at a dealer before ordering a car online.

Consumers may seek different types of channels depending on the particular types of goods involved. Some consumers are willing to "trade up" to retailers offering higher-end goods such as TAG Heuer watches or Callaway golf clubs; these same consumers are also willing to "trade down" to discount retailers to buy private-label paper towels, detergent, or vitamins.[10]

Value Networks

A supply chain view of a firm sees markets as destination points and amounts to a linear view of the flow. The company should first think of the target market, however, and then design the supply chain backward from that point. This view has been called **demand chain planning**. Northwestern's Don Schultz says: "A demand chain management approach doesn't just push things through the system. It emphasizes what solutions consumers are looking for, not what

Sales channel for Bowflex fitness equipment: a print ad with a coupon and an 800 number for phone calls.

products we are trying to sell them." Schultz has suggested that the traditional marketing "four P's" be replaced by a new acronym, SIVA, which stands for solutions, information, value, and access.[11]

An even broader view sees a company at the center of a **value network**—a system of partnerships and alliances that a firm creates to source, augment, and deliver its offerings. A value network includes a firm's suppliers and its suppliers' suppliers, and its immediate customers and their end customers. The value network includes valued relations with others such as university researchers and government approval agencies.

A company needs to orchestrate these parties to enable it to deliver superior value to the target market. Palm, the leading manufacturer of handheld devices, consists of a whole community of suppliers and assemblers of semiconductor components, plastic cases, LCD displays, and accessories; of offline and online resellers; and of 275,000 developers who have created over 21,000 software programs and 100 hardware add-ons for the Palm operating systems for hand-held computers and smartphones.

Demand chain planning yields several insights. First, the company can estimate whether more money is made upstream or downstream, in case it might want to integrate backward or forward. Second, the company is more aware of disturbances anywhere in the supply chain that might cause costs, prices, or supplies to change suddenly. Third, companies can go online with their business partners to carry on faster and more accurate communications, transactions, and payments to reduce costs, speed up information, and increase accuracy. With the advent of the Internet, companies are forming more numerous and complex relationships with other firms. For example, Ford not only manages numerous supply chains, but also sponsors or transacts on many B2B Web sites and exchanges as needs arise.

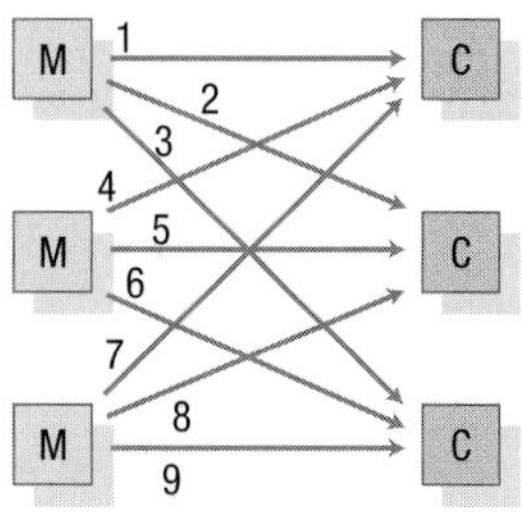

(a) Number of Contacts
M x C = 3 x 3 = 9

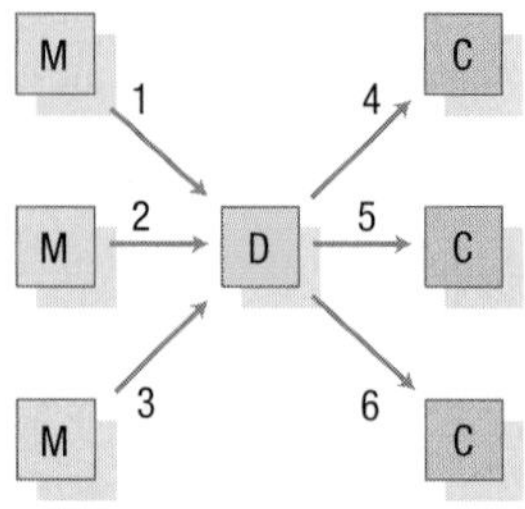

(b) Number of Contacts
M + C = 3 + 3 = 6

M = Manufacturer
C = Customer
D = Distributor

FIG. 15.1

How a Distributor Increases Efficiency

Managing this value network has required companies to make increasing investments in information technology (IT) and software. They have invited such software firms as SAP and Oracle to design comprehensive *enterprise resource planning* (ERP) systems to manage cash flow, manufacturing, human resources, purchasing, and other major functions within a unified framework. They hope to break up department silos and carry out core business processes more seamlessly. In most cases, however, companies are still a long way from truly comprehensive ERP systems.

Marketers, for their part, have traditionally focused on the side of the value network that looks toward the customer. In the future, they will increasingly participate in and influence their companies' upstream activities and become network managers, not only product and customer managers.

::: The Role of Marketing Channels

Why would a producer delegate some of the selling job to intermediaries? Delegation means relinquishing some control over how and to whom the products are sold. Producers do gain several advantages by using intermediaries:

- ***Many producers lack the financial resources to carry out direct marketing.*** For example, General Motors sells its cars through more than 8,000 dealer outlets in North America alone. Even General Motors would be hard-pressed to raise the cash to buy out its dealers.
- ***Producers who do establish their own channels can often earn a greater return by increasing investment in their main business.*** If a company earns a 20 percent rate of return on manufacturing and a 10 percent return on retailing, it does not make sense to do its own retailing.
- ***In some cases direct marketing simply is not feasible.*** The William Wrigley Jr. Company would not find it practical to establish small retail gum shops throughout the world or to sell gum by mail order. It would have to sell gum along with many other small products and would end up in the drugstore and grocery store business. Wrigley finds it easier to work through the extensive network of privately owned distribution organizations.

Intermediaries normally achieve superior efficiency in making goods widely available and accessible to target markets. Through their contacts, experience, specialization, and scale of operation, intermediaries usually offer the firm more than it can achieve on its own. According to Stern and his colleagues:

> Intermediaries smooth the flow of goods and services. . . . This procedure is necessary in order to bridge the discrepancy between the assortment of goods and services generated by the producer and the assortment demanded by the consumer. The discrepancy results from the fact that manufacturers typically produce a large quantity of a limited variety of goods, whereas consumers usually desire only a limited quantity of a wide variety of goods.[12]

Figure 15.1 shows one major source of cost savings using intermediaries. Part (a) shows three producers, each using direct marketing to reach three customers. This system requires nine different contacts. Part (b) shows the three producers working through one distributor, who contacts the three customers. This system requires only six contacts. In this way, intermediaries reduce the number of contacts and the work.

Channel Functions and Flows

A marketing channel performs the work of moving goods from producers to consumers. It overcomes the time, place, and possession gaps that separate goods and services from those who need or want them. Members of the marketing channel perform a number of key functions (see Table 15.1).

Some functions (physical, title, promotion) constitute a *forward flow* of activity from the company to the customer; other functions (ordering and payment) constitute a *backward flow* from customers to the company. Still others (information, negotiation, finance, and risk taking) occur in both directions. Five flows are illustrated in Figure 15.2 for the marketing of forklift trucks. If these flows were superimposed in one diagram, the tremendous complexity of even simple marketing channels would be apparent. A manufacturer selling a physical product and services might require three channels: a *sales*

TABLE 15.1

Channel Member Functions

- Gather information about potential and current customers, competitors, and other actors and forces in the marketing environment.
- Develop and disseminate persuasive communications to stimulate purchasing.
- Reach agreements on price and other terms so that transfer of ownership or possession can be effected.
- Place orders with manufacturers.
- Acquire the funds to finance inventories at different levels in the marketing channel.
- Assume risks connected with carrying out channel work.
- Provide for the successive storage and movement of physical products.
- Provide for buyers' payment of their bills through banks and other financial institutions.
- Oversee actual transfer of ownership from one organization or person to another.

channel, a *delivery channel,* and a *service channel.* To sell its Bowflex fitness equipment, the Nautilus Group has used television infomercials, the telephone, and the Internet as sales channels; UPS ground service as the delivery channel; and local repair people as the service channel. When sales failed to meet goals, Nautilus added retail stores to its sales channels in 2003. When a competitor infringed on the Bowflex patent by placing an imitation product into retail stores, Nautilus began selling Bowflex home gyms through the retail channel.

The question is not *whether* various channel functions need to be performed—they must be—but rather, *who* is to perform them. All channel functions have three things in common: They use up scarce resources; they can often be performed better through specialization; and they can be shifted among channel members. When the manufacturer shifts some functions to intermediaries, the producer's costs and prices are lower, but the intermediary must add a charge to cover its work. If the intermediaries are more efficient than the manufacturer, prices to consumers should be lower. If consumers perform some functions themselves, they should enjoy even lower prices.

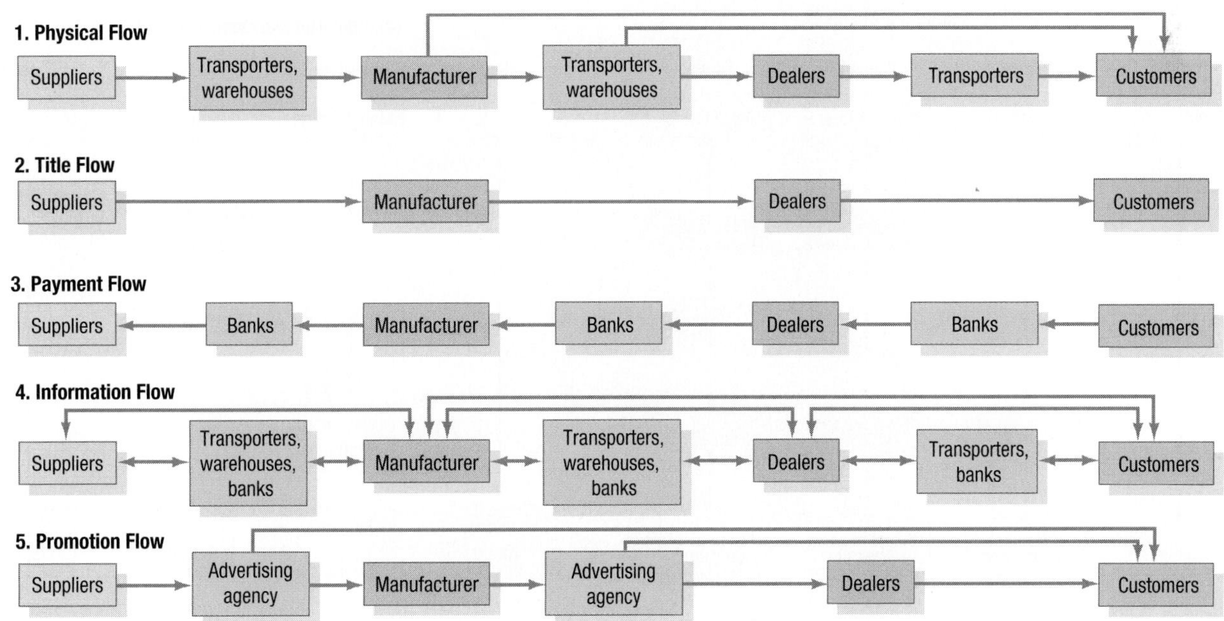

FIG. 15.2 Five Marketing Flows in the Marketing Channel for Forklift Trucks

Marketing functions, then, are more basic than the institutions that perform them at any given time. Changes in channel institutions largely reflect the discovery of more efficient ways to combine or separate the economic functions that provide assortments of goods to target customers.

Channel Levels

The producer and the final customer are part of every channel. We will use the number of intermediary levels to designate the length of a channel. Figure 15.3(a) illustrates several consumer-goods marketing channels of different lengths.

A **zero-level channel** (also called a **direct-marketing channel**) consists of a manufacturer selling directly to the final customer. The major examples are door-to-door sales, home parties, mail order, telemarketing, TV selling, Internet selling, and manufacturer-owned stores. Avon sales representatives sell cosmetics door-to-door; Tupperware representatives sell kitchen goods through home parties; Franklin Mint sells collectibles through mail order; AT&T uses the telephone to prospect for new customers or to sell enhanced services to existing customers; Time-Life sells music and video collections through TV commercials or longer "infomercials"; Red Envelope sells gifts online; and Gateway sells computers and other consumer electronics through its own stores. "Marketing Insight: M-Commerce Opens Up New Opportunities for Marketers" describes new developments in that area.

A *one-level channel* contains one selling intermediary, such as a retailer. A *two-level channel* contains two intermediaries. In consumer markets, these are typically a wholesaler and a retailer. A *three-level channel* contains three intermediaries. In the meatpacking industry, wholesalers sell to jobbers, who sell to small retailers. In Japan, food distribution may involve as many as six levels. From the producer's point of view, obtaining information about end users and exercising control becomes more difficult as the number of channel levels increases.

Figure 15.3(b) shows channels commonly used in industrial marketing. An industrial-goods manufacturer can use its sales force to sell directly to industrial customers; or it can sell to industrial distributors, who sell to the industrial customers; or it can sell through manufacturer's representatives or its own sales branches directly to industrial customers, or indirectly to industrial customers through industrial distributors. Zero-, one-, and two-level marketing channels are quite common.

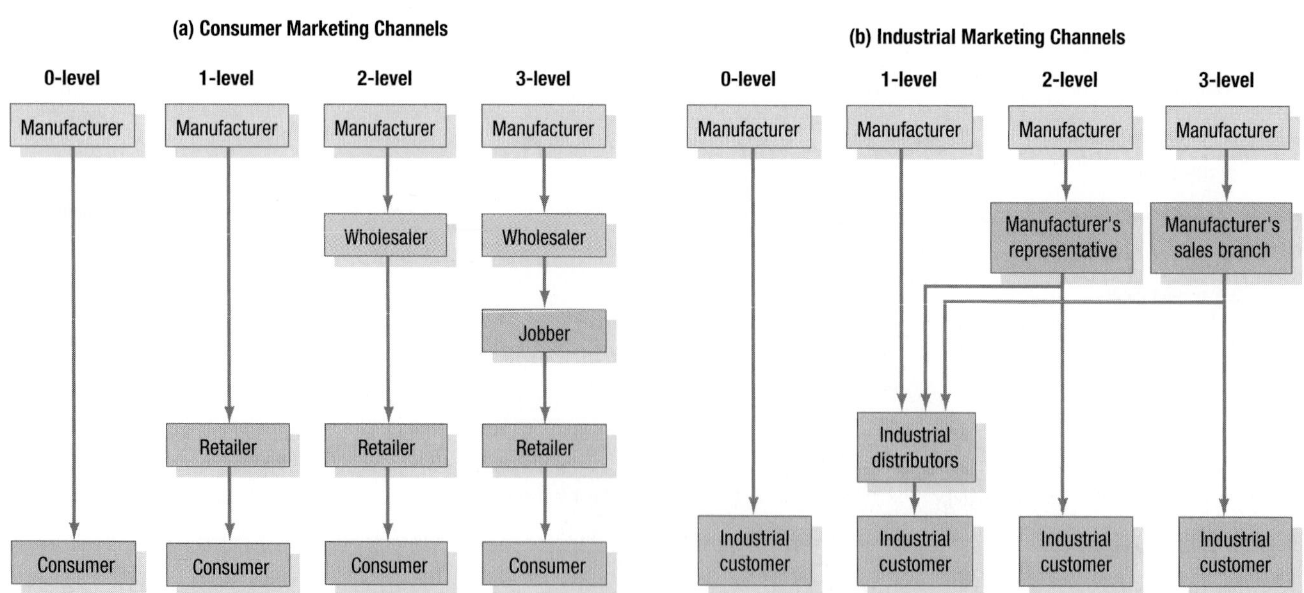

FIG. 15.3 | Consumer and Industrial Marketing Channels

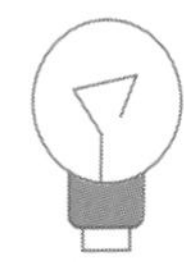

MARKETING INSIGHT | M-COMMERCE OPENS UP NEW OPPORTUNITIES FOR MARKETERS

Consumers and businesspeople no longer need to be near a computer to send and receive information. All they need is a cellular phone or personal digital assistant (PDA). While they are on the move, they can connect with the Internet to check stock prices, the weather, sports scores; send and receive e-mail messages; and place online orders. A whole field called *telematics* involves placing wireless Internet-connected computers in the dashboards of cars and trucks, and making more home appliances (such as computers) wireless so that they can be used anywhere in or near the home. Many see a big future in what is now called *m-commerce* (m for mobile). Consider the fast growth of Internet-connected phones.

In Japan, millions of teenagers carry DoCoMo phones available from NTT (Nippon Telephone and Telegraph). They can also use their phone to order goods. Each month, the subscriber receives a bill from NTT listing the monthly subscriber fee, the usage fee, and the cost of all the transactions. The person can then pay the bill at the nearest 7-11 store. In the United States, Conversagent (formerly ActiveBuddy) creates software applications that connect Instant Messaging users to marketer-created data using conversational language.

The potential market opportunities for location-based services are enormous. Consider some possibilities:

- Getting a Coke by pointing and clicking the phone at a vending machine. The bottle drops down and an appropriate amount is deducted from the owner's bank account.
- Using the phone to search for a nearby restaurant that meets the customer's entered criteria.
- Watching stock prices while sitting in the restaurant and deciding to place a purchase order.
- Clicking the phone to pay the bill for the meal; the cellular phone replaces the credit card.
- Coming home and clicking a combination of keys on the phone to open the door.

Some see positive benefits, such as locating people making emergency 911 calls or checking on the whereabouts of one's children late at night. Others worry about privacy issues. What if an employer learns that an employee is being treated for AIDS at a local clinic, or a wife finds out her husband is out clubbing? Like so many new technologies, location-based services have potential for good or harm, and ultimately will warrant public scrutiny and regulation.

Sources: Douglas Lamont, *Conquering the Wireless World: The Age of M-Commerce* (New York: Wiley, 2001); Marc Weingarten, "The Medium Is the Instant Message," *Business 2.0,* February 2002, pp. 98–99.

Channels normally describe a forward movement of products from source to user. One can also talk about *reverse-flow channels.* They are important in the following cases: (1) to reuse products or containers (such as refillable chemical-carrying drums); (2) to refurbish products (such as circuit boards or computers) for resale; (3) to recycle products (such as paper); and (4) to dispose of products and packaging (waste products). Several intermediaries play a role in reverse-flow channels, including manufacturers' redemption centers, community groups, traditional intermediaries such as soft-drink intermediaries, trash-collection specialists, recycling centers, trash-recycling brokers, and central-processing warehousing.[13]

HEWLETT-PACKARD

Each month Hewlett-Packard, the world's second-largest computer maker, sends 1.7 million tons of broken-down and unwanted electronics to meet their end—or their new beginning—at its Roseville, California, recycling center. Yet the company, in conjunction with recycling partner Noranda Inc., still only recycles less than 1 percent of the hardware it makes. Pressured by complaints about how they dispose of products—including shipping old machines to be broken down in Asian countries with less strict environmental laws—computer makers have joined with the EPA, environmental groups, and a nonprofit group called Product Stewardship Institute. These groups created the National Electronics Product Stewardship Initiative, but the process of creating a nationwide recycling standard is incredibly slow. Without a system in place, electronics makers like HP and Dell have launched inventive PR campaigns to spur the public to recycle. On Earth Day 2003, at a Starbucks support center in Seattle and the following day in New York's Grand Central Terminal, HP accepted computer hardware made by any manufacturer and recycled it at no charge. HP also boosted the incentive for consumers and small businesses to hire HP to recycle old PCs and monitors through its recycle-by-mail program, which costs $15 to $46 depending on the size of the equipment.[14]

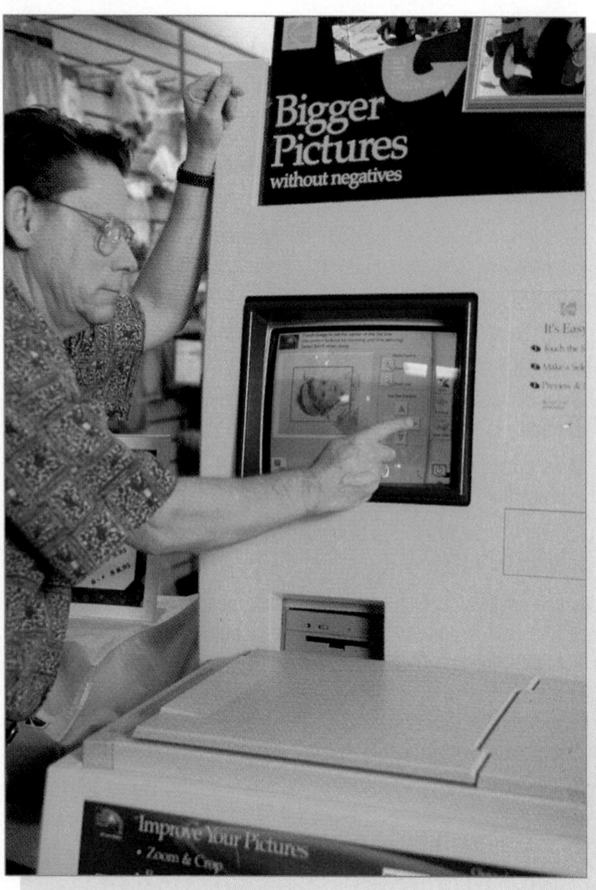

A customer operates a Kodak minilab in a retail outlet. Minilabs often appear in retail stores that also have photo processing departments, like Walgreens and CVS stores.

Service Sector Channels

Marketing channels are not limited to the distribution of physical goods. Producers of services and ideas also face the problem of making their output available and accessible to target populations. Schools develop "educational-dissemination systems" and hospitals develop "health-delivery systems." These institutions must figure out agencies and locations for reaching a population spread out over an area.

Marketing channels also keep changing in "person" marketing. Before 1940, professional comedians could reach audiences through vaudeville houses, special events, nightclubs, radio, movies, carnivals, and theaters. Vaudeville houses have vanished and been replaced by comedy clubs and cable television stations. Politicians also must choose a mix of channels—mass media, rallies, coffee hours, spot TV ads, direct mail, billboards, faxes, e-mail, Web sites—for delivering their messages to voters.[15]

As Internet and other technology advance, service industries such as banking, insurance, travel, and stock buying and selling are operating through new channels. Kodak offers its customers four different ways to print their digital photos—minilabs in retail outlets, home printers, online services with the Ofoto Web site, and self-service kiosks.[16]

Reaching the right customers was a key factor in one of the biggest financial services merger ever.

CITICORP

Distribution strategy and the blend of different customer segment targets was a stated objective of the $70 billion merger between Citicorp and Travelers Group. Citicorp was one of the world's largest banks, while Travelers focused on insurance, mutual funds, and investment banking businesses. One of the major stated goals of the merger was the ability of each organization to cross-sell the other's products to its customers and to exploit the two organizations' distribution channels to maximize the penetration of the merged companies' products throughout the world.[17]

::: Channel-Design Decisions

Designing a marketing channel system involves analyzing customer needs, establishing channel objectives, identifying major channel alternatives, and evaluating major channel alternatives.

Analyzing Customers' Desired Service Output Levels

In designing the marketing channel, the marketer must understand the service output levels desired by target customers. Channels produce five service outputs:

1. ***Lot size*** – The number of units the channel permits a typical customer to purchase on one occasion. In buying cars for its fleet, Hertz prefers a channel from which it can buy a large lot size; a household wants a channel that permits buying a lot size of one.
2. ***Waiting and delivery time*** – The average time customers of that channel wait for receipt of the goods. Customers increasingly prefer faster and faster delivery channels.
3. ***Spatial convenience*** – The degree to which the marketing channel makes it easy for customers to purchase the product. Chevrolet, for example, offers greater spatial conve-

nience than Cadillac, because there are more Chevrolet dealers. Chevrolet's greater market decentralization helps customers save on transportation and search costs in buying and repairing an automobile.

4. ***Product variety*** – The assortment breadth provided by the marketing channel. Normally, customers prefer a greater assortment because more choices increase the chance of finding what they need.
5. ***Service backup*** – The add-on services (credit, delivery, installation, repairs) provided by the channel. The greater the service backup, the greater the work provided by the channel.[18]

The marketing-channel designer knows that providing greater service outputs means increased channel costs and higher prices for customers. Different customers have different service needs. The success of discount stores indicates that many consumers are willing to accept smaller service outputs if they can save money.

Establishing Objectives and Constraints

Channel objectives should be stated in terms of targeted service output levels. Under competitive conditions, channel institutions should arrange their functional tasks to minimize total channel costs and still provide desired levels of service outputs.[19] Usually, planners can identify several market segments that want different service levels. Effective planning requires determining which market segments to serve and the best channels for each.

Channel objectives vary with product characteristics. Perishable products require more direct marketing. Bulky products, such as building materials, require channels that minimize the shipping distance and the amount of handling. Nonstandard products, such as custom-built machinery and specialized business forms, are sold directly by company sales representatives. Products requiring installation or maintenance services, such as heating and cooling systems, are usually sold and maintained by the company or by franchised dealers. High-unit-value products such as generators and turbines are often sold through a company sales force rather than intermediaries.

Channel design must take into account the strengths and weaknesses of different types of intermediaries. For example, manufacturers' reps are able to contact customers at a low cost per customer because the total cost is shared by several clients, but the selling effort per customer is less intense than if company sales reps did the selling. Channel design is also influenced by competitors' channels.

Channel design must adapt to the larger environment. When economic conditions are depressed, producers want to move their goods to market using shorter channels and without services that add to the final price of the goods. Legal regulations and restrictions also affect channel design. U.S. law looks unfavorably on channel arrangements that may tend to substantially lessen competition or create a monopoly.

Identifying Major Channel Alternatives

Companies can choose from a wide variety of channels for reaching customers—from sales forces to agents, distributors, dealers, direct mail, telemarketing, and the Internet. Each channel has unique strengths as well as weaknesses. Sales forces can handle complex products and transactions, but they are expensive. The Internet is much less expensive, but it cannot handle complex products. Distributors can create sales, but the company loses direct contact with customers.

The problem is further complicated by the fact that most companies now use a mix of channels. Each channel hopefully reaches a different segment of buyers and delivers the right products to each at the least cost. When this does not happen, there is usually channel conflict and excessive cost.

A channel alternative is described by three elements: the types of available business intermediaries, the number of intermediaries needed, and the terms and responsibilities of each channel member.

TYPES OF INTERMEDIARIES A firm needs to identify the types of intermediaries available to carry on its channel work.

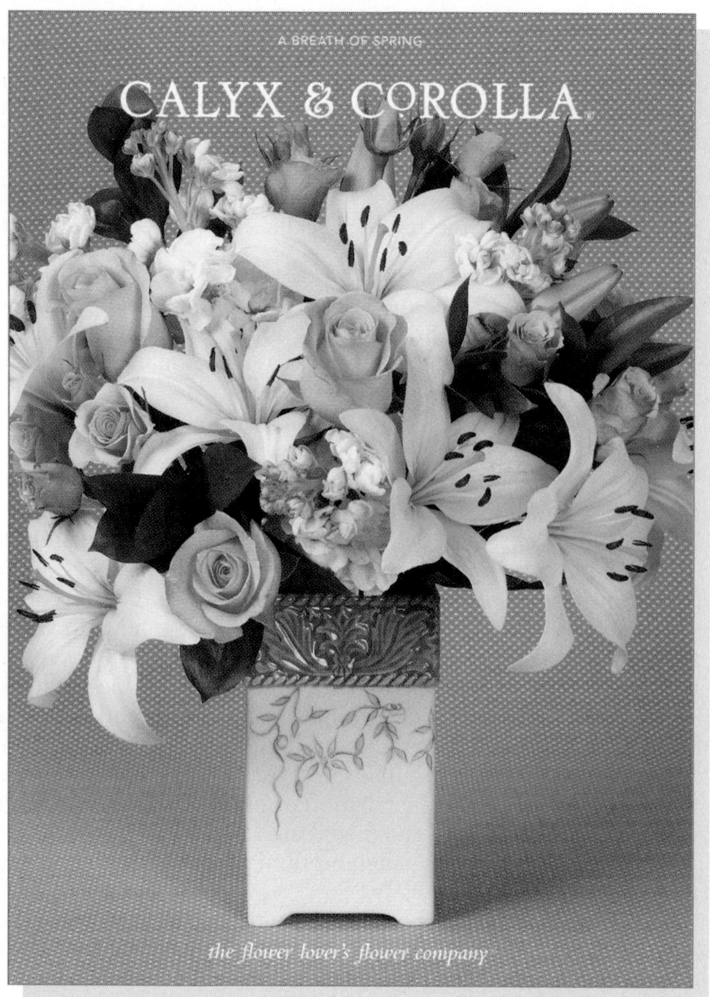

Innovative marketing channels: Calyx and Corolla sells flowers through direct delivery with a print catalog and an online store.

For example, a test-equipment manufacturer developed an audio device for detecting poor mechanical connections in machines with moving parts. Company executives felt this product would sell in all industries where electric, combustion, or steam engines were used, such as aviation, automobiles, railroads, food canning, construction, and oil. The sales force was small. The problem was how to reach these diverse industries effectively. The following alternatives were identified:

- Expand the company's direct sales force. Assign sales representatives to contact all prospects in an area, or develop separate sales forces for the different industries.
- Hire manufacturers' agents in different regions or end-use industries to sell the new equipment.
- Find distributors in the different regions or end-use industries that will buy and carry the device. Give them exclusive distribution, adequate margins, product training, and promotional support.

Table 15.2 lists channel alternatives identified by a consumer electronics company that produces cellular car phones.

Companies should search for innovative marketing channels. Medion sold 600,000 PCs in Europe, mostly via major one- or two-week "burst promotions" at Aldi's supermarkets.[20] Columbia House has successfully merchandised music albums through the mail. Other sellers such as Harry and David and Calyx & Corolla have creatively sold fruit and flowers, respectively, through direct delivery. (See "Marketing Insight: How CarMax Is Transforming the Auto Business.")

TABLE **15.2**

Channel Alternatives for a Cellular Car Phone Maker

- The company could sell its car phones to automobile manufacturers to be installed as original equipment.
- The company could sell its car phones to auto dealers.
- The company could sell its car phones to retail automotive-equipment dealers through a direct sales force or through distributors.
- The company could sell its car phones to car phone specialist dealers through a direct sales force or dealers.
- The company could sell its car phones through mail-order catalogs.
- The company could sell its car phones through mass merchandisers such as Best Buy or Circuit City.

Bank One is letting Avon literally open doors for wider distribution of its credit cards:

BANK ONE CORP, AVON PRODUCTS INC.

A new partnership between Bank One and Avon marks the first time a card issuer has employed another company's distribution network—Avon representatives—as part of an affinity program to put plastic in more purses and wallets. Several factors are in the partnership's favor. First, the Avon reps alone make up a lucrative target market. Avon reps get the same rewards as consumers when using the Platinum Visa and they also reap a $25 credit toward their Avon business account once each approved customer they sign up makes a purchase. If each rep gets just one account holder signed up, that's 600,000 cards right there. Avon representatives and customers are largely women, and Avon says that women control 81 percent of family purchasing decisions and 85 percent of them manage the household checkbook. By partnering with Avon, Bank

MARKETING **INSIGHT** | HOW CARMAX IS TRANSFORMING THE AUTO BUSINESS

For years, buying a used car was considered a dangerous and risky business; used-car salesmen were stock figures in comedy routines. Then CarMax emerged to change the face of the industry and its standards. Circuit City, a major retailer of electronic products, started CarMax, the Auto Superstore, in 1993. The first superstore opened in Richmond, Virginia, where its headquarters are located, and CarMax is now the nation's leading specialty retailer of used cars; it operates 50 used-car superstores in 24 markets. CarMax also operates 12 new-car franchises, which are integrated or co-located with its used-car superstores.

What is so special about CarMax? The company locates its used-car superstores, each carrying around 500 cars, on large lots on the outskirts of a city near a major highway. Customers enter an attractive display room, where a sales associate finds out what kind of car they want and then escorts them to a computer kiosk. Using a touch screen, the associate retrieves a full listing of the cars in stock that meet the customer's criteria. A color display of each car can be shown along with the vehicle's features and its fixed selling price. The company has over 15,000 cars in all, nearly every make and model.

There is no price negotiation. The salesperson, paid a commission on the number of cars sold rather than their value, has no incentive to push higher-priced cars. The customer is informed that CarMax mechanics have carried out a 110-point inspection and made any necessary repairs beforehand. Furthermore, a car buyer receives a 5-day money-back guarantee and a 30-day comprehensive warranty. If the buyer wants financing, the CarMax associate can arrange it in 20 minutes. The entire process typically takes less than one hour.

The company's niche has to been to focus on the used-car market. Given that today's cars are better and have longer life expectancies, many buyers now prefer to save money by buying a used car, and the substantial growth of car leasing has greatly inflated the supply of used cars. Banks are more willing to offer low-cost financing for used cars, especially when research revealed that default rates were lower for used-car buyers. Finally, dealers have reported earning a higher profit on used cars, up to $100 more than for a new car.

CarMax has been very successful in achieving even greater margins: The company's average selling price for a used vehicle is $15,000 and its average profit margin is 13 percent, compared with industry averages of $13,650 and 11 percent, respectively. Although the major auto makes experienced a decline in sales and profitability in 2003 with new cars, CarMax experienced sales and revenue growth.

Sources: Gregory J. Gilligan, "Circuit City's CarMax Superstores Pass $300 Million in Yearly Sales," *Knight-Ridder/Tribune Business News,* April 5, 1997, p. 19; Arlena Sawyers, "CarMax Is Out of the Red, in the Pink," *Automotive News,* April 16, 2001, p. 28; Laura Heller, "Circuit City Restructures, Spins Off CarMax Unit," *DSN Retailing Today,* March 11, 2002, pp. 3–4.

One goes directly to the person who holds the purse strings. The benefits go two ways, however, since the partnership will spur brand awareness for Avon. "Every time someone takes the Avon card out of the wallet, it will remind them that we are around," says Avon's senior manager of credit card operations.[21]

Sometimes a company chooses an unconventional channel because of the difficulty or cost of working with the dominant channel. The advantage is that the company will encounter less competition during the initial move into this channel. After trying to sell its inexpensive Timex watches through regular jewelry stores, the U.S. Time Company placed its watches in fast-growing mass-merchandise outlets. Avon chose door-to-door selling because it was not able to break into regular department stores. The company made more money than most firms selling through department stores.

NUMBER OF INTERMEDIARIES Companies have to decide on the number of intermediaries to use at each channel level. Three strategies are available: exclusive distribution, selective distribution, and intensive distribution.

Exclusive distribution means severely limiting the number of intermediaries. It is used when the producer wants to maintain control over the service level and outputs offered by the resellers. Often it involves *exclusive dealing* arrangements. By granting exclusive distribution, the producer hopes to obtain more dedicated and knowledgeable selling. It requires greater partnership between seller and reseller and is used in the distribution of new automobiles, some major appliances, and some women's apparel brands. When the legendary Italian designer label Gucci found its image severely tarnished by overexposure from licensing and discount stores, Gucci decided to end contracts with third-party suppliers, control its distribution, and open its own stores to bring back some of the luster.[22] Exclusive deals between suppliers and retailers are becoming a mainstay for specialists looking for an edge in a business world that is increasingly driven by price.[23]

- Disney Consumer Products and Wal-Mart signed a landmark pact in 2003 giving Wal-Mart a six-month exclusive on sales of toys and merchandise from Disney's new Kim Possible franchise.
- When Scholastic Entertainment relaunched its Clifford the Big Red Dog kids' franchise after leaving it neglected for years, the company used exclusive deals with Target and JC Penney to enjoy a comfort zone it wouldn't have had if the product had been launched across several channels.

Selective distribution involves the use of more than a few but less than all of the intermediaries who are willing to carry a particular product. It is used by established companies and by new companies seeking distributors. The company does not have to worry about too many outlets; it can gain adequate market coverage with more control and less cost than intensive distribution. Disney is a good example of selective distribution.

DISNEY

Disney sells its videos through five main channels: Movie rental stores like Blockbuster; the company's proprietary retail stores, called Disney Stores; retail stores like Best Buy; online retailers like Amazon.com and Disney's own online Disney Stores; the Disney catalog and other catalog sellers. These varied channels afford Disney maximum market coverage, and enable the company to offer its videos at a number of price points.[24]

Intensive distribution consists of the manufacturer placing the goods or services in as many outlets as possible. This strategy is generally used for items such as tobacco products, soap, snack foods, and gum, products for which the consumer requires a great deal of location convenience.

Manufacturers are constantly tempted to move from exclusive or selective distribution to more intensive distribution to increase coverage and sales. This strategy may help in the short term, but often hurts long-term performance. Intensive distribution increases product and service availability but may also result in retailers competing aggressively. If price wars ensue, retailer profitability may also decline, potentially dampening retailer interest in supporting the product. It may also harm brand equity, as the Calvin Klein experience illustrates.

CALVIN KLEIN

In May 2000, designer Calvin Klein sued Linda Wachner, CEO of Warnaco Group Inc., for selling his jeans to cut-rate, mass-market outlets without his permission. Warnaco, which has the license to make and distribute the jeans, was accused by Calvin Klein of making lower-quality jeans for these outlets, and therefore hurting his image. The suit was settled out of court in January 2001, and both sides said they "look forward to expanding jeans wear sales consistent with the image and prestige of Calvin Klein products." Warnaco would limit distributing jeans wear products to department and specialty stores.

TERMS AND RESPONSIBILITIES OF CHANNEL MEMBERS The producer must determine the rights and responsibilities of participating channel members. Each channel member must be treated respectfully and given the opportunity to be profitable.[25] The main elements in the "trade-relations mix" are price policies, conditions of sale, territorial rights, and specific services to be performed by each party.

Price policy calls for the producer to establish a price list and schedule of discounts and allowances that intermediaries see as equitable and sufficient.

Conditions of sale refers to payment terms and producer guarantees. Most producers grant cash discounts to distributors for early payment. Producers might also provide distributors a guarantee against defective merchandise or price declines. A guarantee against price declines gives distributors an incentive to buy larger quantities.

Distributors' territorial rights define the distributors' territories and the terms under which the producer will enfranchise other distributors. Distributors normally expect to receive full credit for all sales in their territory, whether or not they did the selling.

Mutual services and responsibilities must be carefully spelled out, especially in franchised and exclusive-agency channels. McDonald's provides franchisees with a building, promotional support, a recordkeeping system, training, and general administrative and technical assistance. In turn, franchisees are expected to satisfy company standards regarding physical facilities, cooperate with new promotional programs, furnish requested information, and buy supplies from specified vendors.

Evaluating the Major Alternatives

Each channel alternative needs to be evaluated against economic, control, and adaptive criteria.

ECONOMIC CRITERIA Each channel alternative will produce a different level of sales and costs. Figure 15.4 shows how six different sales channels stack up in terms of the value added per sale and the cost per transaction. For example, in selling industrial products costing between $2,000 and $5,000, the cost per transaction has been estimated as $500 (field sales),

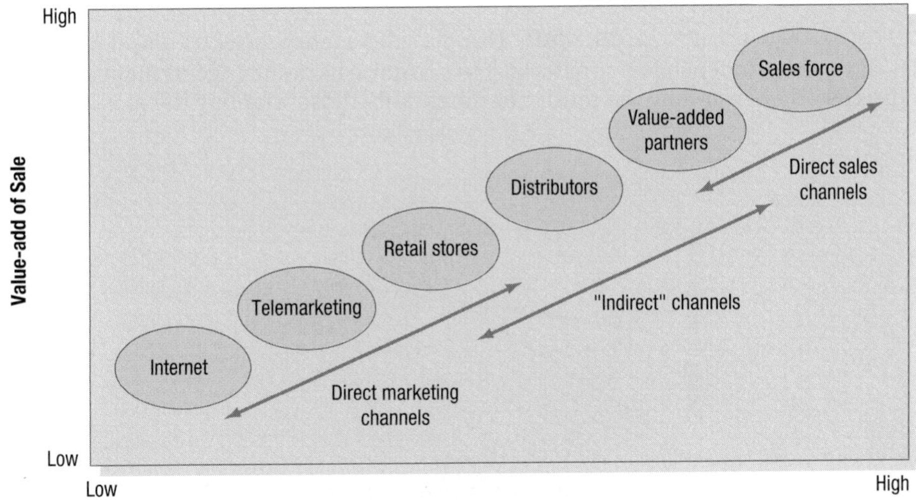

FIG. 15.4

The Value-Adds Versus Costs of Different Channels

Source: Oxford Associates, adapted from Dr. Rowland T. Moriarty, Cubex Corp.

$200 (distributors), $50 (telesales), and $10 (Internet). Banks claim that in selling retail banking services, the cost per transaction is $2 (teller), $.50 (ATM), and $.10 (Internet). Clearly, sellers would try to replace high-cost channels with low-cost channels when the value added per sale was sufficient. The lower-cost channels tend to be low-touch channels. This is not important in ordering commodity items, but buyers who are shopping for more complex products may prefer high-touch channels such as salespeople.

When sellers discover a convenient lower-cost channel, they try to get their customers to use it. The company may reward customers for switching. Many airlines initially gave bonus frequent flier mileage awards when customers booked reservations on line. Other companies may raise the fees on customers using their higher-cost channels to get them to switch. Companies that are successful in switching their customers to lower-cost channels, assuming no loss of sales or deterioration in service quality, will gain a **channel advantage**.[26]

As an example of an economic analysis of channel choices, consider the following situation:

> A North Carolina furniture manufacturer wants to sell its line to retailers on the West Coast. The manufacturer is trying to decide between two alternatives: One calls for hiring 10 new sales representatives who would operate out of a sales office in San Francisco. They would receive a base salary plus commissions. The other alternative would be to use a San Francisco manufacturers' sales agency that has extensive contacts with retailers. The agency has 30 sales representatives, who would receive a commission based on their sales.

The first step is to determine whether a company sales force or a sales agency will produce more sales. Most marketing managers believe that a company sales force will sell more. They concentrate on the company's products; they are better trained to sell those products; they are more aggressive because their future depends on the company's success; and they are more successful because many customers prefer to deal directly with the company. However, the sales agency could conceivably sell more. First, the agency has 30 representatives, not just 10. This sales force might be just as aggressive as a direct sales force, depending on the commission level. Some customers prefer dealing with agents who represent several manufacturers rather than with salespersons from one company; and the agency has extensive contacts and marketplace knowledge, whereas a company sales force would need to build these from scratch.

The next step is to estimate the costs of selling different volumes through each channel. The cost schedules are shown in Figure 15.5. The fixed costs of engaging a sales agency are lower than those of establishing a company sales office, but costs rise faster through an agency because sales agents get a larger commission than company salespeople. The final step is comparing sales and costs. As Figure 15.5 shows, there is one sales level (S_B) at which selling costs are the same for the two channels. The sales agency is thus the better channel for any sales volume below S_B, and the company sales branch is better at any volume above S_B. Given this information, it is not surprising that sales agents tend to be used by smaller firms, or by large firms in smaller territories where the volume is low.

CONTROL AND ADAPTIVE CRITERIA Using a sales agency poses a control problem. A sales agency is an independent firm seeking to maximize its profits. Agents may concentrate on the customers who buy the most, not necessarily those who buy the manufacturer's

FIG. 15.5

Break-even Cost Chart for the Choice Between a Company Sales Force and a Manufacturer's Sales Agency

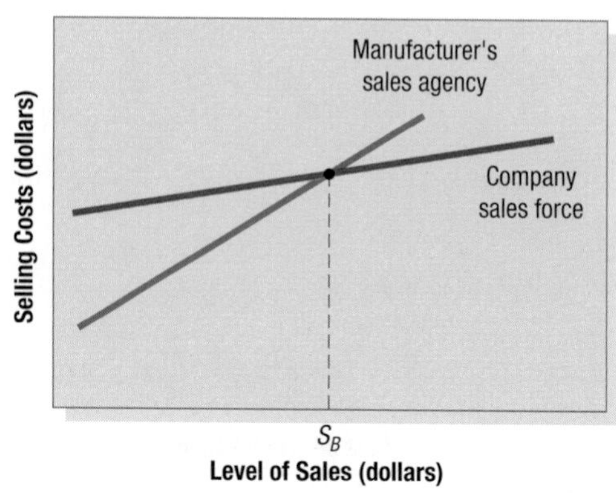

goods. Furthermore, agents might not master the technical details of the company's product or handle its promotion materials effectively.

To develop a channel, members must make some degree of commitment to each other for a specified period of time. Yet these commitments invariably lead to a decrease in the producer's ability to respond to a changing marketplace. In rapidly changing, volatile, or uncertain product markets, the producer needs channel structures and policies that provide high adaptability.

::: Channel-Management Decisions

After a company has chosen a channel alternative, individual intermediaries must be selected, trained, motivated, and evaluated. Channel arrangements must be modified over time.

Selecting Channel Members

Companies need to select their channel members carefully. To customers, the channels are the company. Consider the negative impression customers would get of McDonald's, Shell Oil, or Mercedes-Benz if one or more of their outlets or dealers consistently appeared dirty, inefficient, or unpleasant.

To facilitate channel member selection, producers should determine what characteristics distinguish the better intermediaries. They should evaluate the number of years in business, other lines carried, growth and profit record, financial strength, cooperativeness, and service reputation. If the intermediaries are sales agents, producers should evaluate the number and character of other lines carried and the size and quality of the sales force. If the intermediaries are department stores that want exclusive distribution, the producer should evaluate locations, future growth potential, and type of clientele.

Training Channel Members

Companies need to plan and implement careful training programs for their intermediaries. Fast-growing Culver's restaurants requires its Midwestern franchisees to work 60 hours in one of the 5 restaurants Culver owns and then work 12-hour days, 6 days a week for 4 months at headquarters, learning every facet of how Culver operates logistically and financially.[27]

Microsoft requires third-party service engineers to complete a set of courses and take certification exams. Those who pass are formally recognized as Microsoft Certified Professionals, and they can use this designation to promote business. Others use customer surveys rather than exams.

KYOCERA MITA CORPORATION

In 2003, Kyocera Mita America commissioned J.D. Power and Associates to develop a program to survey Kyocera Mita dealers' customers and certify those dealers that met or exceeded national benchmarks for sales and service customer satisfaction. Certification is based on customer satisfaction with an office equipment dealer's product knowledge, expertise in machine operation, ability to advise customers about their specific needs, and timely delivery of the equipment. Additional areas covered by the program are ability to schedule service appointments in a timely manner, concern for customer needs, and clear explanations of services performed. "The J.D. Power and Associates certification recognizes Kyocera Mita Total Solution Provider dealers for outstanding customer experience, and allows them to differentiate within the dealer marketplace, helping to contribute to increased customer traffic and higher sales," said Michael Pietrunti, vice president of marketing at Kyocera Mita America. "This certification positions dealers as industry-wide leaders in customer satisfaction."[28]

Motivating Channel Members

A company needs to view its intermediaries in the same way it views its end users. It needs to determine intermediaries' needs and construct a channel positioning such that its channel offering is tailored to provide superior value to these intermediaries.

Being able to stimulate channel members to top performance starts with understanding their needs and wants. The company should provide training programs, market research programs, and other capability-building programs to improve intermediaries' performance.

The company must constantly communicate its view that the intermediaries are partners in a joint effort to satisfy end users of the product.

Producers vary greatly in skill in managing distributors. **Channel power** can be defined as the ability to alter channel members' behavior so that they take actions they would not have taken otherwise.[29] Manufacturers can draw on the following types of power to elicit cooperation:

- ***Coercive power.*** A manufacturer threatens to withdraw a resource or terminate a relationship if intermediaries fail to cooperate. This power can be effective, but its exercise produces resentment and can generate conflict and lead the intermediaries to organize countervailing power.
- ***Reward power.*** The manufacturer offers intermediaries an extra benefit for performing specific acts or functions. Reward power typically produces better results than coercive power, but can be overrated. The intermediaries may come to expect a reward every time the manufacturer wants a certain behavior to occur.
- ***Legitimate power.*** The manufacturer requests a behavior that is warranted under the contract. As long as the intermediaries view the manufacturer as a legitimate leader, legitimate power works.
- ***Expert power.*** The manufacturer has special knowledge that the intermediaries value. Once the expertise is passed on to the intermediaries, however, this power weakens. The manufacturer must continue to develop new expertise so that the intermediaries will want to continue cooperating.
- ***Referent power.*** The manufacturer is so highly respected that intermediaries are proud to be associated with it. Companies such as IBM, Caterpillar, and Hewlett-Packard have high referent power.[30]

Coercive and reward power are objectively observable; legitimate, expert, and referent power are more subjective and dependent on the ability and willingness of parties to recognize them.

Most producers see gaining intermediaries' cooperation as a huge challenge.[31] They often use positive motivators, such as higher margins, special deals, premiums, cooperative advertising allowances, display allowances, and sales contests. At times they will apply negative sanctions, such as threatening to reduce margins, slow down delivery, or terminate the relationship. The weakness of this approach is that the producer is using crude, stimulus-response thinking.

The children's corner in an Apple retail store. Apple stores are designed to be a complete technology experience for the customer, who has access to every Apple product, to in-store presentations and workshops, and to expert advice.

More sophisticated companies try to forge a long-term partnership with distributors. The manufacturer clearly communicates what it wants from its distributors in the way of market coverage, inventory levels, marketing development, account solicitation, technical advice and services, and marketing information. The manufacturer seeks distributor agreement with these policies and may introduce a compensation plan for adhering to the policies. Here are three examples of successful partner-building practices:

- Timken Corporation (roller bearings) has its sales reps make multilevel calls on its distributors.
- DuPont has a distributor marketing steering committee that meets regularly.
- Rust-Oleum introduces a menu of marketing programs each quarter; distributors choose the programs that fit their needs.

Evaluating Channel Members

Producers must periodically evaluate intermediaries' performance against such standards as sales-quota attainment, average inventory levels, customer delivery time, treatment of damaged and lost goods, and cooperation in promotional and training programs. A producer will occasionally discover that it is paying too much to particular intermediaries for what they are actually doing. One manufacturer that was compensating a distributor for holding inventories found that the inventories were actually held in a public warehouse at its expense. Producers should set up functional discounts in which they pay specified amounts for the trade channel's performance of each agreed-upon service. Underperformers need to be counseled, retrained, motivated, or terminated.

Modifying Channel Arrangements

A producer must periodically review and modify its channel arrangements. Modification becomes necessary when the distribution channel is not working as planned, consumer buying patterns change, the market expands, new competition arises, innovative distribution channels emerge, and the product moves into later stages in the product life cycle. Consider Apple.

APPLE

To combat its lowly 3.4 percent share of the U.S. personal computer market, Apple has opened more than 75 retail locations since 2001. The stores sell Apple products exclusively and target tech-savvy customers with in-store product presentations and workshops; a full line of Apple products, software, and accessories; and a "Genius Bar" staffed by an Apple specialist. Although the move upset existing retailers, Apple explained that since www.apple.com generated roughly 25 percent of sales, its own retail chain was a natural extension.[32]

No marketing channel will remain effective over the whole product life cycle. Early buyers might be willing to pay for high value-added channels, but later buyers will switch to lower-cost channels. Small office copiers were first sold by manufacturers' direct sales forces, later through office equipment dealers, still later through mass merchandisers, and now by mail-order firms and Internet marketers.

In competitive markets with low entry barriers, the optimal channel structure will inevitably change over time. The change could involve adding or dropping individual channel members, adding or dropping particular market channels, or developing a totally new way to sell goods.

Adding or dropping individual channel members requires an incremental analysis. What would the firm's profits look like with and without this intermediary? An automobile manufacturer's decision to drop a dealer requires subtracting the dealer's sales and estimating the possible sales loss or gain to the manufacturer's other dealers.

Sometimes a producer considers dropping all intermediaries whose sales are below a certain amount. Look at Navistar:

A Navistar truck, one of the many models the company produces and sells through a network of dealerships that have the technical expertise and local contacts to keep Navistar in markets both large and small.

NAVISTAR

Navistar's operating company, International Truck and Engine Corporation, noted at one time that 5 percent of its dealers were selling fewer than three or four trucks a year. It cost the company more to service these dealers than their sales were worth, but dropping these dealers could have repercussions on the system as a whole. The unit costs of producing trucks would be higher, because the overhead would be spread over fewer trucks; some employees and equipment would be idled; some business in these markets would go to competitors; and other dealers might become insecure. Other factors include nonrepresentation in smaller markets, longtime loyal customers not being serviced appropriately, and overall fewer dealers with technical knowledge to serve the current customer base. All these factors must be taken into account.

The most difficult decision involves revising the overall channel strategy.[33] Distribution channels clearly become outmoded, and a gap arises between the existing distribution system and the ideal system that would satisfy target customers' needs and desires (see "Marketing Memo: Designing a Customer-Driven Distribution System"). Examples abound: Avon's door-to-door system for selling cosmetics had to be modified as more women entered the workforce; IBM's exclusive reliance on a field sales force had to be modified with the introduction of low-priced personal computers; and in retail banking the trend toward opening branches has now come full circle within just a decade:

BRANCH BANKING

Just ten years ago bank branches seemed to be a dying breed, a casualty of banking industry consolidation and the belief that automated teller machines, online banking, and telephone call centers would reduce customers' reliance on their neighborhood branches. In Manhattan alone, the number of branches and bank offices dropped from 607 to 459 between June 1994 and June 2001. Yet now bankers say that the industry overestimated the attraction of electronic banking and the profitability of retail banking. Many people want "high-touch" over "high-tech," or at least the choice, and banks are responding by opening branches at a breakneck clip. Bank of America, for instance, plans to open 550 branches over the next three years. Bank One Corp., which lopped off 80 of its branches between 2000 and 2002, is expanding again. Banking analysts caution, however, that the expansion of the branch distribution channel, if not well thought out, could dilute banks' earnings. The banks that will succeed, they say, are those that are fully committed to the retail strategy, such as Seattle-based Washington Mutual, and Cherry Hill, New Jersey's, Commerce Bancorp Inc. According to Commerce's CEO, simply building a branch system is not enough. Banks need a proven, "value-added" business model to entice customers and cross- and up-sell their products.[34]

::: Channel Integration and Systems

Distribution channels do not stand still. New wholesaling and retailing institutions emerge, and new channel systems evolve. We will look at the recent growth of vertical, horizontal, and multichannel marketing systems; the next section examines how these systems cooperate, conflict, and compete.

Vertical Marketing Systems

One of the most significant recent channel developments is the rise of vertical marketing systems. A **conventional marketing channel** comprises an independent producer, wholesaler(s), and retailer(s). Each is a separate business seeking to maximize its own profits,

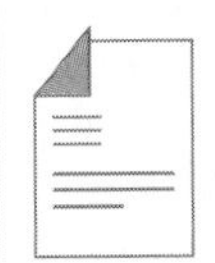

MARKETING MEMO | DESIGNING A CUSTOMER-DRIVEN DISTRIBUTION SYSTEM

Stern and Sturdivant have outlined an excellent framework, called Customer-Driven Distribution System Design, for moving a poorly functioning distribution system closer to a customer's ideal system. Companies have to reduce the gaps between the service outputs that target customers' desires, those the existing channel system delivers, and those management thinks are feasible within the existing constraints. Six steps are involved:

1. Research target customers' value perceptions, needs, and desires regarding channel service outputs.
2. Examine the performance of the company's and competitors' existing distribution systems in relation to customer desires.
3. Find service output gaps that need corrective action.
4. Identify major constraints that will limit possible corrective actions.
5. Design a "management-bounded" channel solution.
6. Implement the reconfigured distribution system.

Source: Anne T. Coughlan, Erin Anderson, Louis W. Stern, and Adel I. El-Ansary, *Marketing Channels*, 6th ed. (Upper Saddle River, NJ: Prentice Hall, 2001).

even if this goal reduces profit for the system as a whole. No channel member has complete or substantial control over other members.

A **vertical marketing system (VMS)**, by contrast, comprises the producer, wholesaler(s), and retailer(s) acting as a unified system. One channel member, the *channel captain*, owns the others or franchises them or has so much power that they all cooperate. The channel captain can be the producer, the wholesaler, or the retailer. Notable producer channel captains are Coca-Cola with soft drinks, Gillette with shaving products, and Procter & Gamble with detergents.

VMSs arose as a result of strong channel members' attempts to control channel behavior and eliminate the conflict that results when independent members pursue their own objectives. VMSs achieve economies through size, bargaining power, and elimination of duplicated services. They have become the dominant mode of distribution in the U.S. consumer marketplace, serving between 70 and 80 percent of the total market. There are three types of VMS: corporate, administered, and contractual.

CORPORATE VMS A *corporate VMS* combines successive stages of production and distribution under single ownership. For example, Sears obtains over 50 percent of the goods it sells from companies that it partly or wholly owns. Sherwin-Williams makes paint but also owns and operates 2,000 retail outlets. Giant Food Stores operates an ice-making facility, a soft-drink bottling operation, an ice cream plant, and a bakery that supplies Giant stores with everything from bagels to birthday cakes.

ADMINISTERED VMS An *administered VMS* coordinates successive stages of production and distribution through the size and power of one of the members. Manufacturers of a dominant brand are able to secure strong trade cooperation and support from resellers. Thus Kodak, Gillette, and Campbell Soup are able to command high levels of cooperation from their resellers in connection with displays, shelf space, promotions, and price policies.

The most advanced supply-distributor arrangement for administered VMSs involve **distribution programming**, which can be defined as building a planned, professionally managed, vertical marketing system that meets the needs of both manufacturer and distributors. The manufacturer establishes a department within the company called *distributor-relations planning*. Its job is to identify distributor needs and build up merchandising programs to help each distributor operate as efficiently as possible. This department and the distributors jointly plan merchandising goals, inventory levels, space and visual merchandising plans, sales-training requirements, and advertising and promotion plans. The aim is to convert the distributors from thinking that they make their money primarily on the buying side (through tough negotiation with the manufacturer) to seeing that they make their money on the selling side (by being part of a sophisticated, vertical marketing system). Kraft and Procter & Gamble are two companies with excellent distributor-relations planning.

CONTRACTUAL VMS A *contractual VMS* consists of independent firms at different levels of production and distribution integrating their programs on a contractual basis to obtain more economies or sales impact than they could achieve alone. Johnston and Lawrence call them "value-adding partnerships" (VAPs).[35] Contractual VMSs now constitute one of the most significant developments in the economy. They are of three types:

1. ***Wholesaler-sponsored voluntary chains*** – Wholesalers organize voluntary chains of independent retailers to help them compete with large chain organizations. The wholesaler develops a program in which independent retailers standardize their selling practices and achieve buying economies that enable the group to compete effectively with chain organizations.
2. ***Retailer cooperatives*** – Retailers take the initiative and organize a new business entity to carry on wholesaling and possibly some production. Members concentrate their purchases through the retailer co-op and plan their advertising jointly. Profits are passed back to members in proportion to their purchases. Nonmember retailers can also buy through the co-op but do not share in the profits.
3. ***Franchise organizations*** – A channel member called a *franchisor* might link several successive stages in the production-distribution process. Franchising has been the fastest-growing retailing development in recent years. Although the basic idea is an old one, some forms of franchising are quite new.

The traditional system is the *manufacturer-sponsored retailer franchise*. Ford, for example, licenses dealers to sell its cars. The dealers are independent businesspeople who agree to meet specified conditions of sales and services. Another is the *manufacturer-sponsored wholesaler franchise*. Coca-Cola, for example, licenses bottlers (wholesalers) in various markets who buy its syrup concentrate and then carbonate, bottle, and sell it to retailers in local markets. A newer system is the *service-firm-sponsored retailer franchise*. A service firm organizes a whole system for bringing its service efficiently to consumers. Examples are found in the auto-rental business (Hertz, Avis), fast-food-service business (McDonald's, Burger King), and motel business (Howard Johnson, Ramada Inn).

THE NEW COMPETITION IN RETAILING Many independent retailers that have not joined VMSs have developed specialty stores that serve special market segments. The result is a polarization in retailing between large vertical marketing organizations and independent specialty stores, which creates a problem for manufacturers. They are strongly tied to independent intermediaries, but must eventually realign themselves with the high-growth vertical marketing systems on less attractive terms. Furthermore, vertical marketing systems constantly threaten to bypass large manufacturers and set up their own manufacturing. *The new competition in retailing is no longer between independent business units but between whole systems of centrally programmed networks (corporate, administered, and contractual) competing against one another to achieve the best cost economies and customer response.*

Horizontal Marketing Systems

Another channel development is the **horizontal marketing system**, in which two or more unrelated companies put together resources or programs to exploit an emerging marketing opportunity. Many supermarket chains have arrangements with local banks to offer in-store banking. Citizen Bank has 256 in-store branches in supermarkets in New England. Each company lacks the capital, know-how, production, or marketing resources to venture alone, or it is afraid of the risk. The companies might work with each other on a temporary or permanent

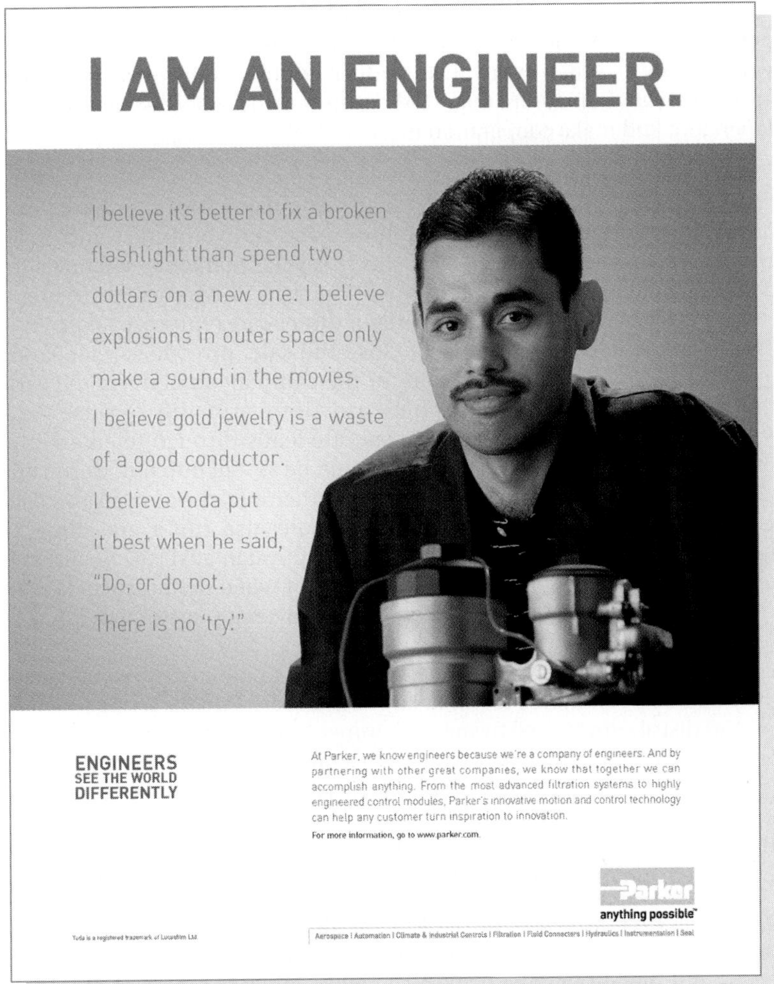

A Parker-Hannifin ad that stresses its engineering expertise in many applications.

basis or create a joint venture company. H&R Block, Inc., for example, entered into an agreement with GEICO insurance to provide car insurance information to Block customers. Customers now can contact GEICO through a special toll-free number.

Multichannel Marketing Systems

Once, many companies sold to a single market through a single channel. Today, with the proliferation of customer segments and channel possibilities, more companies have adopted multichannel marketing. **Multichannel marketing** occurs when a single firm uses two or more marketing channels to reach one or more customer segments.

PARKER-HANNIFIN

The Parker-Hannifin Corporation (PHC) sells fluid power and electromechanical motion and control systems to a variety of mobile and stationary equipment markets through distributors and direct OEM sales. There appears to be little conflict between channels selling to separate target market segments such as forestry, marine, industrial, agricultural, mining, and many others.

By adding more channels, companies can gain three important benefits. The first is increased market coverage. The second is lower channel cost—selling by phone rather than personal visits to small customers. The third is more customized selling—adding a technical sales force to sell more complex equipment. The gains from adding new channels come at a price, however. New channels typically introduce conflict and control problems. Two or more channels may end up competing for the same customers. The new channels may be more independent and make cooperation more difficult.

PLANNING CHANNEL ARCHITECTURE Clearly, companies need to think through their channel architecture. Moriarty and Moran propose using the hybrid grid shown in Figure 15.6 to plan the channel architecture.[36] The grid shows several marketing channels (rows) and several demand-generation tasks (columns). The grid illustrates why using only one channel is not efficient. Consider using only a direct sales force. A salesperson would have to find leads, qualify them, presell, close the sale, provide service, and manage account growth. It would be more efficient for the company to perform the earlier tasks, leaving the salesperson to invest his or her costly time primarily to close the sale. The company's marketing department would generate leads through telemarketing, direct mail, advertising, and trade shows. The leads would be sorted into hot, warm, and cool by using qualifying techniques such as checking whether a lead wants a sales call and has adequate purchasing power. The department would also run a preselling campaign informing prospects about the company's products through advertising, direct mail, and telemarketing. The salesperson comes to the prospect when the prospect is ready to talk business. This multichannel architecture optimizes coverage, customization, and control while minimizing cost and conflict.

Companies should use different channels for selling to different size customers. A company can use its direct sales force to sell to large customers, telemarketing to sell to midsize customers, and distributors to sell to small customers; but these gains can be compromised by an increased level of conflict over who has account ownership. For example, territory-based sales representatives may want credit for all sales in their territories, regardless of the marketing channel used.

Multichannel marketers also need to decide how much of their product to offer in each of the channels. There are many different approaches to take—consider the following two:[37]

- ***J&R Music and Computer World,*** the $292 million marketer of consumer electronics, offers its entire product line in its catalog, on its Web site, and in its store to give customers the same view of its goods regardless of which channel they choose to shop. J&R sees offer-

FIG. 15.6

The Hybrid Grid

Source: Rowland T. Moriarty and Ursula Moran, "Marketing Hybrid Marketing Systems," *Harvard Business Review* (November–December 1990): 150.

Demand-generation Tasks

Marketing Channels and Methods (VENDOR)	Lead generation	Qualifying sales	Presales	Close of sale	Postsales service	Account management	CUSTOMER
Internet							
National account management							
Direct sales							
Telemarketing							
Direct mail							
Retail stores							
Distributors							
Dealers and value-added resellers							
Advertising							

ing everything in all three channels as a competitive advantage and feels that making sure customers are treated equally well is what makes the store unique. Yet not every retailer has the luxury of huge stand-alone stores such as J&R's 300,000-square-foot Manhattan emporium. In addition, bulky catalogs cost more to print and mail.

- ***Patagonia Inc.,*** views the Web as the ideal channel for showing off its entire line of goods and is limited by space in its 14 stores (and 5 outlet stores) to offering a selection of its entire outdoorwear line. Similarly, Patagonia offers less than 70 percent of merchandise in its print catalogs. Other marketers prefer to limit their online offerings on the theory that customers look to Web sites and catalogs for a "best of" array of merchandise and don't want to have to click through dozens of pages.

::: Conflict, Cooperation, and Competition

No matter how well channels are designed and managed, there will be some conflict, if for no other reason than that the interests of independent business entities do not always coincide. **Channel conflict** is generated when one channel member's actions prevent the channel from achieving its goal. **Channel coordination** occurs when channel members are brought together to advance the goals of the channel, as opposed to their own potentially incompatible goals.[38] Here we examine three questions: What types of conflict arise in channels? What causes channel conflict? What can be done to resolve conflict situations?

Types of Conflict and Competition

Suppose a manufacturer sets up a vertical channel consisting of wholesalers and retailers. The manufacturer hopes for channel cooperation that will produce greater profits for each channel member. Yet vertical, horizontal, and multichannel conflict can occur.

Vertical channel conflict means conflict between different levels within the same channel. General Motors came into conflict with its dealers in trying to enforce policies on service, pricing, and advertising. Coca-Cola came into conflict with bottlers who also agreed to bottle Dr. Pepper.

Horizontal channel conflict involves conflict between members at the same level within the channel. Some Ford car dealers in Chicago complained about other Chicago Ford dealers advertising and pricing too aggressively. Some Pizza Inn franchisees complained about other Pizza Inn franchisees cheating on ingredients, providing poor service, and hurting the overall Pizza Inn image.

Multichannel conflict exists when the manufacturer has established two or more channels that sell to the same market. Multichannel conflict is likely to be especially intense when the members of one channel get a lower price (based on larger volume purchases) or work with a lower margin. When Goodyear began selling its popular tire brands through Sears, Wal-Mart, and Discount Tire, it angered its independent dealers. It eventually placated them by offering exclusive tire models that would not be sold in other retail outlets. Such a strategy does not always work. When Pacific Cycles purchased Schwinn, it decided to supplement the brand's higher-end 2,700-dealer network with some of its own channels where it sold its own mid-tier bikes through large retail chains such as Toys "R" Us, Target, and Wal-Mart. Even though Pacific Cycles offered exclusive models to the existing Schwinn network, over 1,700 dealers pedaled away. A key question was whether the sales gains from the big retail chains would offset the loss from the dealer defections.[39]

Causes of Channel Conflict

It is important to identify the causes of channel conflict. Some are easy to resolve, others are not.

One major cause is *goal incompatibility.* For example, the manufacturer may want to achieve rapid market penetration through a low-price policy. Dealers, in contrast, may prefer to work with high margins and pursue short-run profitability. Sometimes conflict arises from *unclear roles and rights.* HP may sell personal computers to large accounts through its own sales force, but its licensed dealers may also be trying to sell to large accounts. Territory boundaries and credit for sales often produce conflict.

Conflict can also stem from *differences in perception*. The manufacturer may be optimistic about the short-term economic outlook and want dealers to carry higher inventory. Dealers may be pessimistic. In the beverage category, it is not uncommon for disputes to arise between manufacturers and their distributors about the optimal advertising strategy. Conflict might also arise because of the intermediaries' *dependence* on the manufacturer. The fortunes of exclusive dealers, such as auto dealers, are profoundly affected by the manufacturer's product and pricing decisions. This situation creates a high potential for conflict.

Managing Channel Conflict

As companies add channels to grow sales, they run the risk of creating channel conflict. Some channel conflict can be constructive and lead to better adaptation to a changing environment, but too much is dysfunctional. The challenge is not to eliminate conflict but to manage it better. Here's an example of how one B2B company added a potentially conflicting e-commerce channel and still managed to build trust—not stir up conflict—with its distributors:[40]

AB DICK

Printing equipment manufacturer AB Dick was on the verge of bypassing an important distributor channel for a direct e-commerce channel. Instead, the company developed a tiered dealer model and formed strategic supply chain partnerships with influential distributors. AB Dick would deal directly via the Web with all customers in a respective dealer's territory for sales of supplies. The dealer would act as the distribution point, bill and collect from the customer, maintain the relationship in terms of high-end equipment sales, earn incremental margins from the online sales of supplies (even though the transaction would be direct from AB Dick to the end user), and remain the local contact for equipment sales. According to AB Dick's Vice President of Technology, the dealers were happy because they picked up margin on business they never had, but they also picked up collections, freight, transportation, and labor. AB Dick benefited from reduced costs per online transaction and incremental sales. It had to balance the efficiencies and convenience of direct online ordering for its end users with the need to maintain its dealers as local points-of-distribution and customer contact.

There are several mechanisms for effective conflict management.[41] One is the adoption of superordinate goals. Channel members come to an agreement on the fundamental goal they are jointly seeking, whether it is survival, market share, high quality, or customer satisfaction. They usually do this when the channel faces an outside threat, such as a more efficient competing channel, an adverse piece of legislation, or a shift in consumer desires.

A useful step is to exchange persons between two or more channel levels. General Motors executives might agree to work for a short time in some dealerships, and some dealership owners might work in GM's dealer policy department. Hopefully, the participants will grow to appreciate the other's point of view.

Co-optation is an effort by one organization to win the support of the leaders of another organization by including them in advisory councils, boards of directors, and the like. As long as the initiating organization treats the leaders seriously and listens to their opinions, co-optation can reduce conflict, but the initiating organization may have to compromise its policies and plans to win their support.

Much can be accomplished by encouraging joint membership in and between trade associations. For example, there is good cooperation between the Grocery Manufacturers of America and the Food Marketing Institute, which represents most of the food chains; this cooperation led to the development of the universal product code (UPC). Presumably, the associations can consider issues between food manufacturers and retailers and resolve them in an orderly way.

When conflict is chronic or acute, the parties may have to resort to diplomacy, mediation, or arbitration. *Diplomacy* takes place when each side sends a person or group to meet with its counterpart to resolve the conflict. *Mediation* means resorting to a neutral third party who is skilled in conciliating the two parties' interests. *Arbitration* occurs when the two parties agree to present their arguments to one or more arbitrators and accept the arbitration decision. Sometimes, when none of these methods proves effective, a company or a channel partner may choose to file a lawsuit. Levi Strauss and U.K. retailer Tesco became locked in a legal battle beginning in 1999.

LEVI'S

Levi-Strauss filed a suit with the European Court of Justice against Tesco claiming the retailer's selling of low-priced Levi's jeans imported from outside Britain "undermines the product experience." Tesco had offered genuine Levis at roughly half the price of other U.K. retailers. Levi-Strauss also objected to the fact that its jeans appear in the same stores that sell produce and other food items. After much legal wrangling, the courts decided in favor of Levi-Strauss in November 2001. Levi-Strauss subsequently decided to introduce a much less expensive value line of Signature jeans that could be sold in Asda supermarkets in the United Kingdom, as well as in Wal-Mart in the United States.[42]

Legal and Ethical Issues in Channel Relations

For the most part, companies are legally free to develop whatever channel arrangements suit them. In fact, the law seeks to prevent companies from using exclusionary tactics that might keep competitors from using a channel. Here we briefly consider the legality of certain practices, including exclusive dealing, exclusive territories, tying agreements, and dealers' rights.

Many producers like to develop exclusive channels for their products. A strategy in which the seller allows only certain outlets to carry its products is called exclusive distribution. When the seller requires that these dealers not handle competitors' products, this is called exclusive dealing. Both parties benefit from exclusive arrangements: The seller obtains more loyal and dependable outlets, and the dealers obtain a steady source of supply of special products and stronger seller support. Exclusive arrangements are legal as long as they do not substantially lessen competition or tend to create a monopoly, and as long as both parties enter into the agreement voluntarily.

Exclusive dealing often includes exclusive territorial agreements. The producer may agree not to sell to other dealers in a given area, or the buyer may agree to sell only in its own territory. The first practice increases dealer enthusiasm and commitment. It is also perfectly legal—a seller has no legal obligation to sell through more outlets than it wishes. The second practice, whereby the producer tries to keep a dealer from selling outside its territory, has become a major legal issue. An example of bitter lawsuits is one brought by GT Bicycles of Santa Ana, California, against the giant Price-Costco chain, which sold 2,600 of its high-priced mountain bikes at a huge discount, thus upsetting GTs other U.S. dealers. GT alleges that it first sold the bikes to a dealer in Russia and that they were meant for sale only in Russia. GT maintains that it constitutes fraud when discounters work with middlemen to get exclusive goods.[43]

Producers of a strong brand sometimes sell it to dealers only if they will take some or all of the rest of the line. This practice is called full-line forcing. Such **tying agreements** are not necessarily illegal, but they do violate U.S. law if they tend to lessen competition substantially.

Producers are free to select their dealers, but their right to terminate dealers is somewhat restricted. In general, sellers can drop dealers "for cause," but they cannot drop dealers if, for example, the dealers refuse to cooperate in a doubtful legal arrangement, such as exclusive dealing or tying agreements.

::: E-Commerce Marketing Practices

E-business describes the use of electronic means and platforms to conduct a company's business.[44] **E-commerce** means that the company or site offers to transact or facilitate the selling of products and services online. E-commerce has given rise in turn to e-purchasing and e-marketing. **E-purchasing** means companies decide to purchase goods, services, and information from various online suppliers. Smart e-purchasing has already saved companies millions of dollars. **E-marketing** describes company efforts to inform buyers, communicate, promote, and sell its products and services over the Internet. The *e* term is also used in terms such as e-finance, e-learning, and e-service. But as someone observed, the *e* will eventually be dropped when most business practice is online.

We can distinguish between **pure-click** companies, those that have launched a Web site without any previous existence as a firm, and **brick-and-click** companies, existing companies that have added an online site for information and/or e-commerce.

Pure-Click Companies

There are several kinds of pure-click companies: Search engines, Internet Service Providers (ISPs), commerce sites, transaction sites, content sites, and enabler sites. Commerce sites sell all types of products and services, notably books, music, toys, insurance, stocks, clothes, financial services, and so on. Among the most prominent commerce sites are Amazon, eBay, and Expedia. Commerce sites use various strategies to compete: AutoNation, a leading metamediary of car buying and related services; Hotels, the information leader in hotel reservations; Buy.com, the low-price leader; Winespectator, the single category specialist; and Reflect.com, the most personalized site for skin and hair care.

The Internet is most useful for products and services when the shopper seeks greater ordering convenience (e.g., books and music) or lower cost (e.g., stock trading or news reading). It is also useful when buyers need information about product features and prices (e.g., automobiles or computers). The Internet is less useful for products that must be touched or examined in advance. But even this has exceptions. People can order furniture from EthanAllen.com, major appliances from Sears.com, and expensive computers from Dell or Gateway without trying them in advance.

THE DOT-COM BUBBLE Pure-click Web businesses reached astronomical capitalization levels in the late 1990s, in some cases far exceeding the capitalization of major companies such as United Airlines or PepsiCo. They were considered a major threat to traditional businesses until the investing frenzy collapsed in 2000. "Marketing Insight: Burst of the Dot-Com Bubble" describes the decline in dot-com fortunes. As much as the Internet boom was overhyped, its demise may have also been greatly exaggerated. Table 15.3 displays some common misperceptions as to the current state of e-business and e-commerce.

Companies must set up and operate their e-commerce Web sites carefully. Customer service is critical. Firms such as Ritz Camera use live online chat to give potential customers immediate advice about products for sale on their Web sites.[45] Asset manager Vanguard's service representatives train customers to use its Web sites over the telephone. As a result, Vanguard was able to cut staff in half, an important accomplishment given that a phone call to a rep cost the company $9 versus pennies for a Web login.[46]

BUSINESS-TO-BUSINESS E-COMMERCE Although the popular press has given the most attention to business-to-consumer (B2C) Web sites, even more activity is being conducted on business-to-business (B2B) sites. The B2B sites are changing the supplier–customer rela-

TABLE 15.3 | E-Business Perception versus Reality

Perception	Reality
Profitable Internet companies are rare.	About 40% of 200-plus public Net companies made a fourth-quarter profit in 2003.
Companies ditched Web efforts amid the tech recession.	Spending on e-business projects has risen every year since the bust, now comprising 27% of all tech spending.
Broadband has not gained traction.	U.S. subscriptions have doubled since 2001 and are growing at 56%.
The productivity gain from e-business turned out to be modest.	Productivity growth doubled as the Net proliferated, but most of the acceleration was in industries that use tech a lot, such as autos.
Online advertising died.	The popularity of banner ads gave way to ads tied to search results, boosting online advertising to $6.6 billion this year.
IPO investors in e-tailors lost lots of money.	An investment of $1,000 in every e-tail IPO, good or bad, would have increased about 35%.
B2B e-commerce never really happened.	Although hundreds of B2B exchanges failed, $3.9 trillion worth of e-commerce was conducted in 2003.
Web-era productivity gains are confined to tech companies.	More than 80% of post-1995 acceleration is in nontech industries.

Source: Adapted from Timothy J. Mullaney, "The E-Biz Surprise," *BusinessWeek,* May 12, 2003, pp. 60–68.

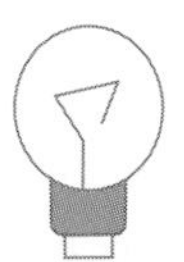

MARKETING **INSIGHT** | **BURST OF THE DOT-COM BUBBLE**

Although the Internet ushered in a new era, many businesses did not capitalize on the initial opportunities and made a host of errors. Dot-coms failed for a variety of reasons: Many rushed into the market without proper research or planning. They had poorly designed Web sites with problems of complexity, poor navigation, and downtime. They lacked adequate infrastructures for shipping on time and for answering customer inquiries. They believed that the first company entering a category would win category leadership. These companies wanted to exploit network economies, namely, the fact that the value of a network to each of its members is proportional to the number of other users (Metcalfe's Law). Some just rushed into the market in the hope of launching an initial public offering (IPO) while the market was hot.

Many dot-coms did not build a sound business model that would deliver eventual profits. The ease of entry of competitors and the ease of customers switching Web sites in search of better prices forced them to accept margin-killing low prices. To acquire customers, dot-coms spent large amounts on mass marketing and offline advertising. They relied on spin and buzz instead of target marketing and word-of-mouth marketing, and they devoted too much effort to acquiring customers instead of building loyal and more frequent users among current customers. They did not understand customer behavior when it came to online surfing and purchasing.

Bottom line: Building an effective online business requires much of the same hard work, careful planning and patience as a traditional business.

Source: Adapted from Timothy J. Mullaney, "The E-Biz Surprise," *BusinessWeek,* May 12, 2003, pp. 60–68.

tionship in profound ways. Firms are using B2B auction sites, spot exchanges, online product catalogs, barter sites, and other online resources to obtain better prices. In 2002, LendingTree brokered 1.5 million loans on behalf of 170 lenders. Retail loans are an ideal commodity to trade online: Loans are highly standardized, the lending industry is fragmented, and large volumes of transactions allow small profit margins to add up.[47]

The purpose of B2B sites is to make markets more efficient. In the past, buyers had to exert a lot of effort to gather information on worldwide suppliers. With the Internet, buyers have easy access to a great deal of information. They can get information from: (1) supplier Web sites; (2) *infomediaries,* third parties that add value by aggregating information about alternatives; (3) *market makers,* third parties that create markets linking buyers and sellers; and (4) *customer communities* which are Web sites where buyers can swap stories about suppliers' products and services.[48]

The net impact of these mechanisms is to make prices more transparent. In the case of undifferentiated products, price pressure will increase. In the case of highly differentiated products, buyers will gain a better picture of their true value. Suppliers of superior products will be able to offset price transparency with value transparency; suppliers of undifferentiated products will have to drive down their costs in order to compete.

Brick-and-Click Companies

Many brick-and-mortar companies have agonized over whether to add an online e-commerce channel. Many companies moved quickly to open Web sites describing their businesses but resisted adding e-commerce to their sites. They felt that selling their products or services online would produce channel conflict—they would be competing with their offline retailers, agents, or their own stores.[49] Compaq feared, for example, that its retailers would drop its line of computers if Compaq offered to sell the same computers directly online. Merrill Lynch hesitated to introduce online stock trading to compete with E*TRADE, Schwab, and other online brokerages, fearing that its own brokers would rebel. Even the store-based bookseller Barnes & Noble delayed opening an online site to challenge Amazon. All eventually succumbed after seeing how much business was rushing to its online competitors.

Yet adding an e-commerce channel creates the threat of a backlash from retailers, brokers, agents, and other intermediaries. The question is how to sell both through intermediaries and online. There are at least three strategies for trying to gain acceptance from intermediaries. One, offer different brands or products on the Internet. Two, offer the offline partners higher commissions to cushion the negative impact on sales. Three, take orders on the Web site but have retailers deliver and collect payment. Harley-Davidson treaded carefully before going online.

HARLEY-DAVIDSON

Given that Harley sells more than $500 million worth of parts and accessories to its loyal followers, an online venture was an obvious next step to generate even more revenue. Harley needed to be careful, however, to avoid the wrath of 650 dealers who benefited from the high margins on those sales. Harley's solution was to send customers seeking to buy accessories online to the company's Web site. Before they can buy anything, they are prompted to select a participating Harley-Davidson dealer. When the customer places the order, it is transmitted to the selected dealer for fulfillment, ensuring that the dealer still remains the focal point of the customer experience. Dealers, in turn, had to agree to a number of standards, such as checking for orders twice a day and shipping orders promptly. The Web site now gets more than 1 million visitors a month.[50]

Some pure or predominantly online companies have invested in brick-and-mortar sites. Dell introduced kiosks into big-name chains such as Sears to better target consumers and allow product trial. Dell was rebuffed by some retailers, such as Best Buy and CompUSA, who viewed the company as a competitor.[51]

Most companies brand their online ventures under their existing brand names. It is difficult to launch a new brand successfully, as Bank One discovered.

WINGSPANBANK.COM

In June 1999, Bank One launched a spin-off venture called WingspanBank to get into the online banking business, but it developed WingspanBank as a separate entity. WingspanBank customers could not use Bank One branches to do their banking in person. No wonder it garnered only 144,000 accounts and had to be closed down as a separate venture.

Ultimately, companies may need to decide whether to drop some or all of their retailers and go direct. Banks, however, have found that despite the convenience of online services, some customers still prefer to conduct certain transactions at the bank itself—80 percent of new checking and savings accounts are still opened in physical bank branches.[52]

ONLINE GROCERS

Despite the demise of online grocer Webvan—after burning through $1 billion—some traditional brick-and-mortar supermarket chains such as Publix, Safeway, and Albertson's are finding success with their online ventures. Royal Ahold bought a controlling interest in one-time online star Peapod as a service complement for its Giant and Stop & Shop chains. These chains find online sales a good way to satisfy their more affluent customers and compete with discounters such as Wal-Mart. Although the chains incur delivery costs, marketing expenses are minimal. Because of its convenience to customers, the average online order at Safeway is $120, twice that of the average in-store ticket. Annual online grocery sales for Britain's biggest grocery chain, Tesco, stood at over 500 million pounds ($947.1 million), making it the world's largest online grocer. Tesco covers 96 percent of the United Kingdom and delivers over 110,000 orders per week.[53]

Not everyone, however, has embraced the Internet as a channel. Consider Stihl.

STIHL

Stihl manufactures handheld outdoor power equipment. All Stihl products are branded under one name and Stihl does not do private labels for other companies. Stihl is best known for chain saws, but has expanded into string trimmers, blowers, hedge trimmers, and cut-off machines. It sells exclusively to seven independent U.S. distributors and five Stihl-owned marketing and distribution centers, who sell Stihl products to a nationwide network of more than 8,000 servicing retail dealers. It also is a worldwide exporter of U.S.–manufactured Stihl products to 130 countries. Stihl is one of the few outdoor-power-equipment companies that does not sell its products through mass merchants, catalogs, or the Internet.[54]

Stihl print ad focuses on the value of its nationwide network of retail dealers, who sell and service its products exclusively. If you want a Stihl product, you have to go to a Stihl dealer.

SUMMARY :::

1. Most producers do not sell their goods directly to final users. Between producers and final users stands one or more marketing channels, a host of marketing intermediaries performing a variety of functions.
2. Marketing-channel decisions are among the most critical decisions facing management. The company's chosen channel(s) profoundly affect all other marketing decisions.
3. Companies use intermediaries when they lack the financial resources to carry out direct marketing, when direct marketing is not feasible, and when they can earn more by doing so. The most important functions performed by intermediaries are information, promotion, negotiation, ordering, financing, risk taking, physical possession, payment, and title.
4. Manufacturers have many alternatives for reaching a market. They can sell direct or use one-, two-, or three-level channels. Deciding which type(s) of channel to use calls for analyzing customer needs, establishing channel objectives, and identifying and evaluating the major alternatives, including the types and numbers of intermediaries involved in the channel.
5. Effective channel management calls for selecting intermediaries and training and motivating them. The goal is to build a long-term partnership that will be profitable for all channel members.
6. Marketing channels are characterized by continuous and sometimes dramatic change. Three of the most important trends are the growth of vertical marketing systems, horizontal marketing systems, and multichannel marketing systems.
7. All marketing channels have the potential for conflict and competition resulting from such sources as goal incompatibility, poorly defined roles and rights, perceptual differences, and interdependent relationships. Companies can manage conflict by striving for superordinate goals, exchanging people among two or more channel levels, coopting the support of leaders in different parts of the channel, and encouraging joint membership in and between trade associations.

8. Channel arrangements are up to the company, but there are certain legal and ethical issues to be considered with regard to practices such as exclusive dealing or territories, tying agreements, and dealers' rights.

9. E-commerce has grown in importance as companies have adopted "brick-and-click" channel systems. Channel integration must recognize the distinctive strengths of online and offline selling and maximize their joint contributions.

APPLICATIONS :::

Marketing Debate Does It Matter Where You Are Sold?

Some marketers feel that the image of the particular channel in which they sell their products does not matter—all that matters is that the right customers shop there and the product is displayed in the right way. Others maintain that channel images—such as a retail store—can be critical and must be consistent with the image of the product.

Take a position: Channel images do not really affect the brand images of the products they sell that much versus Channel images must be consistent with the brand image.

Marketing Discussion

Think of your favorite retailers. How have they integrated their channel system? How would you like their channels to be integrated? Do you use multiple channels from them? Why?

IN THIS CHAPTER, WE WILL ADDRESS THE FOLLOWING QUESTIONS:

1. What major types of marketing intermediaries occupy this sector?
2. What marketing decisions do these marketing intermediaries make?
3. What are the major trends with marketing intermediaries?

CHAPTER 16 ::: MANAGING RETAILING, WHOLESALING, AND LOGISTICS

sixteen

In the previous chapter, we examined marketing intermediaries from the viewpoint of manufacturers who wanted to build and manage marketing channels. In this chapter, we view these intermediaries—retailers, wholesalers, and logistical organizations—as requiring and forging their own marketing strategies. Intermediaries must strive for marketing excellence like any company, or suffer the consequences.

In late December 2003, Manifest Discs and Tapes, a music lover's mecca in two North and South Carolina towns, shocked loyal customers by announcing it would close all its locations and lay off all 100 of its employees. Even though there were still plenty of consumers eager to browse Manifest's stock of 85,000 albums, the popular chain was bowing to powerful forces hitting music retailers across the country. Tower Records, Musicland, and Wherehouse were all either filing for bankruptcy or up for sale at bargain prices. Shifts in consumer tastes, rampant ripping and burning of CDs, and an explosion of online downloads, fueled by Apple's popular iTunes site, led to declining CD sales. Competition from discounters, which treated CDs as loss leaders to generate store traffic, and online giant Amazon left traditional music retailers frequently overpriced. Struggling to create a shopping experience that would justify consumers' time and money, some retailers have experimented with in-store technology such as Internet-connect kiosks and >>>

Opening day at new Starbucks Hear Music Coffeehouse, March 2004, Santa Monica, California, a joint venture with Hewlett Packard and its wholly owned subsidiary Hear Music.

portable Wi-Fi devices that allowed music sampling while roaming the store. In conjunction with its wholly owned subsidiary, retailer Hear Music, Starbucks is opening Hear Music Coffeehouses, fully integrated café-music stores that offer 3,000 square feet of warmly lit space where you can buy regular old CDs or linger with a latte while you listen to music and sift through thousands of songs stored in a computer database to create your own personalized masterpiece. In about five minutes a freshly burned CD, complete with your chosen title and funky artwork on the disc and the jacket (plus liner notes), is ready to take home.[1]

During this same time, department stores also found themselves contending with a dwindling customer base. But not all retailers have found themselves falling behind. Some intermediaries dominate the manufacturers who deal with them. Many use strategic planning, advanced information systems, and sophisticated marketing tools. They measure performance more on a return-on-investment basis than on a profit-margin basis. They segment their markets, improve their market targeting and positioning, and aggressively pursue market expansion and diversification strategies. In this chapter, we consider marketing excellence in retailing, wholesaling, and logistics.

::: Retailing

Retailing includes all the activities involved in selling goods or services directly to final consumers for personal, nonbusiness use. A **retailer** or **retail store** is any business enterprise whose sales volume comes primarily from retailing.

Any organization selling to final consumers—whether it is a manufacturer, wholesaler, or retailer—is doing retailing. It does not matter *how* the goods or services are sold (by person, mail, telephone, vending machine, or Internet) or *where* they are sold (in a store, on the street, or in the consumer's home).

Types of Retailers

Consumers today can shop for goods and services in a wide variety of retail organizations. There are store retailers, nonstore retailers, and retail organizations. Perhaps the best-known type of retailer is the department store. Japanese department stores such as Takashimaya and Mitsukoshi attract millions of shoppers each year. These stores feature art galleries, restaurants, cooking classes, and children's playgrounds.

Retail-store types pass through stages of growth and decline that can be described as the *retail life cycle*.[2] A type emerges, enjoys a period of accelerated growth, reaches maturity, and then declines. Department stores took 80 years to reach maturity, whereas warehouse retail outlets reached maturity in 10 years. The most important retail-store types are described in Table 16.1.

LEVELS OF SERVICE The *wheel-of-retailing* hypothesis explains one reason that new store types emerge.[3] Conventional retail stores typically increase their services and raise their prices to cover the costs. These higher costs provide an opportunity for new store forms to offer lower prices and less service. New store types meet widely different consumer preferences for service levels and specific services.

TABLE 16.1

Major Retailer Types

Specialty store: Narrow product line. Athlete's Foot, Tall Men, The Limited, The Body Shop.

Department store: Several product lines. Sears, JCPenney, Nordstrom, Bloomingdale's.

Supermarket: Large, low-cost, low-margin, high-volume, self-service store designed to meet total needs for food and household products. Kroger, Jewel, Food Emporium.

Convenience store: Small store in residential area, often open 24/7, limited line of high-turnover convenience products plus takeout. 7-Eleven, Circle K.

Discount store: Standard or specialty merchandise; low-price, low-margin, high-volume stores. Wal-Mart, Kmart, Circuit City, Crown Bookstores.

Off-price retailer: Leftover goods, overruns, irregular merchandise sold at less than retail. Factory outlets, independent off-price retailers. Filene's Basement, T.J. Maxx, warehouse clubs Sam's Clubs, Price-Costco, BJ's Wholesale.

Superstore: Huge selling space, routinely purchased food and household items, plus services (laundry, shoe repair, dry cleaning, check cashing). Category killer (deep assortment in one category) such as Petsmart, Staples, Home Depot; combination store such as Jewel, Osco; hypermarket (huge stores that combine supermarket, discount, and warehouse retailing), such as Carrefour in France, Pyrca in Spain, and Meijer's in the Netherlands.

Catalog showroom: Broad selection of high-markup, fast-moving, brand-name goods sold by catalog at discount. Customers pick up merchandise at the store. Inside Edge Ski and Bike.

Retailers can position themselves as offering one of four levels of service:

1. ***Self-service*** – Self-service is the cornerstone of all discount operations. Many customers are willing to carry out their own locate-compare-select process to save money.
2. ***Self-selection*** – Customers find their own goods, although they can ask for assistance.
3. ***Limited service*** – These retailers carry more shopping goods, and customers need more information and assistance. The stores also offer services (such as credit and merchandise-return privileges).
4. ***Full service*** – Salespeople are ready to assist in every phase of the locate-compare-select process. Customers who like to be waited on prefer this type of store. The high staffing cost, along with the higher proportion of specialty goods and slower-moving items and the many services, results in high-cost retailing.

By combining these different service levels with different assortment breadths, we can distinguish the four broad positioning strategies available to retailers, as shown in Figure 16.1:

1. ***Bloomingdale's*** – Stores that feature a broad product assortment and high value added. Stores in this quadrant pay close attention to store design, product quality, service, and

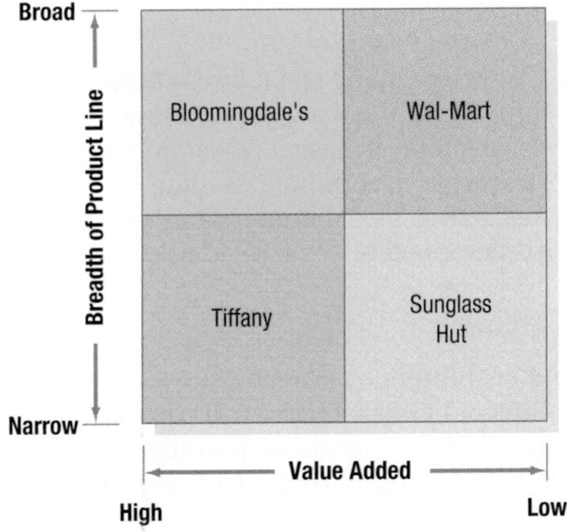

FIG. 16.1

Retail Positioning Map

Source: William T. Gregor and Eileen M. Friars, *Money Merchandising: Retail Revolution in Consumer Financial Service* (Cambridge, MA: The MAC Group, 1982).

image. Their profit margin is high, and if they are fortunate enough to have high volume, they will be very profitable.
2. ***Tiffany*** – Stores that feature a narrow product assortment and high value added. Such stores cultivate an exclusive image and tend to operate on a high margin and low volume.
3. ***Sunglass Hut*** – Stores that feature a narrow line and low value added. Such stores keep their costs and prices low by centralizing buying, merchandising, advertising, and distribution.
4. ***Wal-Mart*** – Stores that feature a broad line and low value added. They focus on keeping prices low so that they have an image of being a place for good buys. They make up for low margin by high volume.

Although the overwhelming bulk (97 percent) of goods and services is sold through stores, *nonstore retailing* has been growing much faster than store retailing. Nonstore retailing falls into four major categories: direct selling, direct marketing (which includes telemarketing and Internet selling), automatic vending, and buying services:

1. ***Direct selling*** (also called *multilevel selling, network marketing*) is a $9 billion industry, with over 600 companies selling door-to-door or at home sales parties. Well-known in one-to-one selling are Avon, Electrolux, and Southwestern Company of Nashville (Bibles). Tupperware and Mary Kay Cosmetics are sold one-to-many: A salesperson goes to the home of a host who has invited friends; the salesperson demonstrates the products and takes orders. Pioneered by Amway, the multilevel (network) marketing sales system consists of recruiting independent businesspeople who act as distributors. The distributor's compensation includes a percentage of sales of those the distributor recruits as well as earnings on direct sales to customers. These direct-selling firms, now finding fewer consumers at home, are developing multidistribution strategies.
2. ***Direct marketing*** has roots in direct-mail and catalog marketing (Lands' End, L.L. Bean); it includes *telemarketing* (1-800-FLOWERS), *television direct-response marketing* (Home Shopping Network, QVC), and *electronic shopping* (Amazon.com, Autobytel.com). Of these, electronic shopping experienced a major take-off in the late 1990s as consumers flocked to dot-com sites to buy books, music, toys, electronics, and other products.
3. ***Automatic vending*** is used for a variety of merchandise, including impulse goods like cigarettes, soft drinks, coffee, candy, newspapers, magazines, and other products like hosiery, cosmetics, hot food, condoms, and paperbacks. Vending machines are found in factories, offices, large retail stores, gasoline stations, hotels, restaurants, and many other places. They offer 24-hour selling, self-service, and merchandise that is always fresh. Japan has the most vending machines per person—Coca-Cola has over 1 million there, and annual vending sales of $50 billion—twice that of the United States. These reliable, high-tech machines allow consumers to buy products ranging from blue jeans to expensive lunches. Some U.S. retailers are now trying to emulate Japan's success with a new generation of vending machines in high-traffic areas. All over South Florida, machines are popping up that dispense Banana Boat sunscreen to travelers and outdoor enthusiasts where they need it most.[4]
4. ***Buying service*** is a storeless retailer serving a specific clientele—usually employees of large organizations—who are entitled to buy from a list of retailers that have agreed to give discounts in return for membership.

CORPORATE RETAILING Although many retail stores are independently owned, an increasing number are part of some form of **corporate retailing**. Corporate retail organizations achieve economies of scale, greater purchasing power, wider brand recognition, and better-trained employees. The major types of corporate retailing—corporate chain stores, voluntary chains, retailer cooperatives, franchises, and merchandising conglomerates—are described in Table 16.2. Franchising is described in detail in "Marketing Insight: Franchise Fever."

New Models for Success

In the past, retailers held customers by offering convenient location, special or unique assortments of goods, greater or better services than competitors, and store credit cards. All of this has changed. Today, national brands such as Ralph Lauren Polo, Calvin Klein, and Levi's are found in department stores, in their own shops, in merchandise outlets, and in

TABLE 16.2

Major Types of Corporate Retail Organizations

Corporate chain store: Two or more outlets owned and controlled, employing central buying and merchandising, and selling similar lines of merchandise. GAP, Pottery Barn, Hold Everything.

Voluntary chain: A wholesaler-sponsored group of independent retailers engaged in bulk buying and common merchandising. Independent Grocers Alliance (IGA).

Retailer cooperative: Independent retailers using a central buying organization and joint promotion efforts. Associated Grocers, ACE Hardware.

Consumer cooperative: A retail firm owned by its customers. Members contribute money to open their own store, vote on its policies, elect a group to manage it, and receive dividends.

Franchise organization: Contractual association between a franchiser and franchisees, popular in a number of product and service areas. McDonald's, Subway, Pizza Hut, Jiffy Lube, 7-Eleven.

Merchandising conglomerate: A corporation that combines several diversified retailing lines and forms under central ownership, with some integration of distribution and management. Allied Domeq PLC with Dunkin' Donuts and Baskin-Robbins, plus a number of British retailers and a wine and spirits group.

off-price discount stores. In their drive for volume, national-brand manufacturers have placed their branded goods everywhere. The result is that retail-store assortments have grown more alike.

Service differentiation also has eroded. Many department stores have trimmed services, and many discounters have increased services. Customers have become smarter shoppers. They do not want to pay more for identical brands, especially when service differences have diminished; nor do they need credit from a particular store, because bank credit cards are almost universally accepted.

In the face of increased competition from discount houses and specialty stores, department stores are waging a comeback war. In addition to locations in the centers of cities, many have branches in suburban shopping centers, where parking is plentiful and family incomes are higher. Bloomingdale's opened a store in downtown SoHo to attract young, well-heeled New Yorkers who would rarely venture up to their flagship midtown store.[5] To better compete, other department stores update merchandise more frequently, remodel their stores, introduce their own brands, and experiment with mail-order and online marketing, and telemarketing.[6]

Two models for department store success seem to be emerging:[7]

- ***Strong retail brand approach.*** In this type of department store, typified by Marks and Spencer in the United Kingdom and Kohl's in the United States, in-house brands feature strongly and managers take an active roll in choosing inventory. Kohl's and Marks and Spencer are more interested in promoting themselves as brands than promoting any particular brand within them. While these stores tend to have high operating costs, they usually command high margins if their in-house brands are both fashionable and popular.
- ***The showcase store.*** Typified by Galeries Lafayette in Paris and Selfridges in London, this type of store not only sells other people's brands but often gets the vendors of those brands to take responsibility for stock, staff, and even the selling space. The vendors then hand over a percentage of the sales to the store's owner. This translates into lower gross

Wall poster ads for Bloomingdale's new SoHo store in New York.

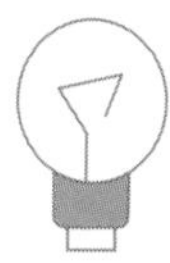

MARKETING INSIGHT | FRANCHISE FEVER

Franchising accounts for more than $1 trillion of annual U.S. sales and nearly one-third of all retail transactions. More than 320,000 small businesses are franchises, employing one in every 16 workers in the country. This figure should not come as a surprise in a society where it is nearly impossible to stroll down a city block or drive on a suburban thoroughfare without seeing a McDonald's, a Jiffy-Lube, a Supercuts, or a 7-Eleven.

In a franchising system, individual *franchisees* are a tightly knit group of enterprises whose systematic operations are planned, directed, and controlled by the operation's innovator, called a *franchiser.* Franchises are distinguished by three characteristics:

1. The franchiser owns a trade or service mark and licenses it to franchisees in return for royalty payments.
2. The franchisee pays for the right to be part of the system. Start-up costs include rental and lease equipment and fixtures, and usually a regular license fee. McDonald's franchisees may invest as much as $1.6 million in total start-up costs and fees. The franchisee then pays McDonald's a certain percentage of sales plus a monthly rent.
3. The franchiser provides its franchisees with a system for doing business. McDonald's requires franchisees to attend "Hamburger University" in Oak Brook, Illinois, for three weeks to learn how to manage the business. Franchisees must follow certain procedures in buying materials.

Franchising is mutually beneficial to both franchiser and franchisee. Among the benefits reaped by franchisers are the motivation and hard work of employees who are entrepreneurs rather than "hired hands," the franchisees' familiarity with local communities and conditions, and the enormous purchasing power of the franchiser. Franchisees benefit from buying into a business with a well-known and accepted brand name. They find it easier to borrow money from financial institutions, and they receive support in areas ranging from marketing and advertising to site selection and staffing.

Franchisees do walk a line between being independent and loyal to the franchiser. Their independence can allow them more flexibility. When Mike Roper opened his first Quiznos Sub franchise south of Chicago in the fall of 2000, the restaurant industry was about to collapse into its longest slump in nearly 30 years. Yet, his sales leapt 40 percent in his store's second year, far exceeding his projection of only 4 percent growth. Whenever business slows, he pretends it is "grand-opening day" again, with coupons and cookie giveaways to draw more traffic. "When you have your own money on the line, you act a little differently," he says. "You tend to be a little more aggressive on the day to day."

The franchise explosion in recent years, however, has increasingly saturated the domestic market. To sustain growth, firms are looking overseas (McDonald's has over 30,000 restaurants in 119 countries outside the United States) or in nontraditional site locations in the United States. Franchises are opening in airports, sports stadiums, college campuses, hospitals, gambling casinos, theme parks, convention halls, and even riverboats.

Sources: Norman D. Axelrad and Robert E. Weigand, "Franchising—A Marriage of System Members," in *Marketing Managers Handbook,* 3rd ed., edited by Sidney Levy, George Frerichs, and Howard Gordon (Chicago: Dartnell, 1994), pp. 919–934; Meg Whittemore, "New Directions in Franchising," *Nation's Business* (January 1995): 45–52; "Trouble in Franchise Nation," *Fortune,* March 6, 1995, pp. 115–129; Carol Steinberg, "Millionaire Franchisees," *Success* (March 1995): 65–69; Richard Gibson, "Even 'Copycat' Businesses Require Creativity and Flexibility," *Wall Street Journal Online,* March 2004; <http://www.entrepreneur.com>.

margins for the department store but also lower operating costs. The showcase store needs to keep droves of customers coming in, and that means it needs to be an entertainment destination in its own right. Galeries Lafayette's flagship Paris store recently offered free lessons from professional striptease artists to promote the opening of its huge new lingerie department.

Supermarkets have opened larger stores, carry a larger number and variety of items, and upgrade facilities. Supermarkets have also increased their promotional budgets and moved heavily into private brands. Others have sought to create stronger differentiation.

WHOLE FOODS MARKET

In 157 stores in 28 states, the District of Columbia, Canada, and Great Britain, Whole Foods creates celebrations of food. The markets are bright and well staffed, and food displays are bountiful and seductive. Whole Foods is the largest organic and natural foods grocer in the country and offers lots of information about its food. If you want to know, for instance, whether the chicken in the display case lived a happy, free-roaming life, you get a 16-page booklet and an invitation to visit the farm in Pennsylvania where it was raised. If you can't find the information you need, you have only to ask a well-trained and knowledgeable employee. Whole Foods' approach is working, especially for consumers who view organic and artisanal food as an affordable luxury. In each of the last four years, Whole Foods beat Wal-Mart in both overall and comparable-store, year-to-year sales growth.[8]

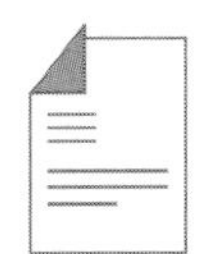

MARKETING **MEMO** | **HELPING STORES TO SELL**

In the pursuit of higher sales volume, retailers are studying their store environments for ways to improve the shopper experience. Paco Underhill, managing director of the retail consultant Envirosell Inc., offers the following advice for fine-tuning retail space in order to keep shoppers spending:

- ***Attract shoppers and keep them in the store:*** The amount of time shoppers spend in a store is perhaps the single most important factor in determining how much they will buy.
- ***Honor the "transition zone":*** On entering a store, people need to slow down and sort out the stimuli, which means that shoppers will likely be moving too fast to respond positively to signs, merchandise, or sales clerks in the zone they cross before making that transition. Make sure there are clear sight lines.
- ***Don't make them hunt:*** Put the most popular products up front to reward busy shoppers and encourage leisurely shoppers to look more. At Staples, ink cartridges are one of the first products shoppers encounter after entering.
- ***Make merchandise available to the reach and touch:*** It is hard to overemphasize the importance of customers' hands. A store can offer the finest, cheapest, sexiest goods, but if the shopper cannot reach or pick them up, much of their appeal can be lost.
- ***Men do not ask questions:*** Men always move faster than women do through a store's aisles. In many settings, it is hard to get them to look at anything they had not intended to buy. Men also do not like asking where things are. If a man cannot find the section he is looking for, he will wheel about once or twice, then leave the store without ever asking for help.
- ***Women need space:*** A shopper, especially a woman, is far less likely to buy an item if her derriere is brushed, even lightly, by another customer when she is looking at a display. Keeping aisles wide and clear is crucial.
- ***Make checkout easy:*** Be sure to have the right high-margin goods near cash registers to satisfy impulse shoppers. And people love to buy candy when they check out—so satisfy their sweet tooth.

Source: Paco Underhill, *Why We Buy: The Science of Shopping* (New York: Simon & Schuster, 1999); Keith Hammonds, "How We Sell," *Fast Company,* November 1999, p. 294; Paul Keegan, "The Architect of Happy Customers," *Business 2.0,* August 2002, pp. 85–87; Bob Parks, "5 Rules of Great Design," *Business 2.0,* March 2003, pp. 47–49.

Marketing Decisions

We will examine retailers' marketing decisions in the areas of target market, product assortment and procurement, services and store atmosphere, price, communication, and location. (See also "Marketing Memo: Helping Stores to Sell.")

TARGET MARKET A retailer's most important decision concerns the target market. Until the target market is defined and profiled, the retailer cannot make consistent decisions on product assortment, store decor, advertising messages and media, price, and service levels. Some retailers have defined their target markets quite well:

CHRISTOPHER & BOND

Apparel retailer Christopher & Bond bucked a downward retail sales trend to generate increased sales in 2002–2003 by shunning trendy fashions to target a more mature consumer less concerned about the latest and greatest. Christopher & Bond decided to appeal to 40-something moms—a traditionally overlooked market segment—who preferred classic looks in their clothing. They even created a prototype to help focus their efforts: "Mary" is a 48-year-old suburban mother of two who works as a teacher, nurse, or bank teller. By compiling a rich profile of the target—right down to her physical measurements—they could then go about designing and making clothes to fill her closet, something few other retailers were bothering to do.[9]

Retailers are slicing the market into finer and finer segments and introducing new lines of stores to provide a more relevant set of offerings to exploit niche markets. Gymboree launched Janie and Jack, selling apparel and gifts for babies and toddlers; Hot Topic introduced Torrid, selling fashions for plus-sized teen girls; and Chico's added Pazo, selling casual apparel for working women in their thirty's.[10]

PRODUCT ASSORTMENT The retailer's product assortment must match the target market's shopping expectations. The retailer has to decide on product-assortment *breadth* and *depth.* A restaurant can offer a narrow and shallow assortment (small lunch counters), a

TABLE 16.3 Retail Category Management

Step	What It Means	How Borders Applied It
1. Define the category.	Decide where you draw the line between product categories. For example, do your customers view alcohol and soft drinks as one beverage category, or should you manage them separately?	Named the cookbook section Food and Cooking because consumers expected to see books on nutrition there as well.
2. Figure out its role.	Determine how the category fits into the whole store. For example, "destination" categories lure folks in, so they get maximum marketing push, while "fill-ins" carry a minimal assortment.	Decided to make Food and Cooking a destination category.
3. Assess performance.	Analyze sales data from ACNielsen, Information Resources Inc., and others. Identify opportunities.	Learned that cookbooks sell faster than expected during holidays. Responded by creating gift promotions.
4. Set goals.	Agree on the category's objectives, including sales, profit, and average-transaction targets, as well as customer satisfaction levels.	Aimed to grow cookbook sales faster than the store average and to grab market share from competition.
5. Choose the audience.	Sharpen your focus within the category for maximum effect.	Decided to go after repeat buyers. "Since 30% of shoppers buy 70% of the cookbooks sold, we are aiming at the enthusiast," says Borders' Chief Marketing Officer Mike Spinozzi.
6. Figure out tactics.	Decide the best product selection, promotion merchandising, and pricing to achieve the category's goals.	Gave more prominent display to books by celebrity chefs like Mario Batali. Created a more approachable product selection by reducing the number of titles on certain subjects.
7. Implement the plan.	Set the timetable and execute the tactics.	Introduced changes to its cooking sections as of November 2002.

Source: Andrew Raskin, "Who's Minding the Store," *Business 2.0,* February 2003, p. 73.

narrow and deep assortment (delicatessen), a broad and shallow assortment (cafeteria), or a broad and deep assortment (large restaurant). Table 16.3 provides an illustration of how Borders developed category assortment within a section of its stores. New York–based retailer Aeropostale was named the top retailer in *Business-Week*'s 2004 "Hot Growth" list mainly by carefully matching its product assortment to young teen target market needs.

AEROPOSTALE INC.

Rather than compete head-on with trend-setting Abercrombie and Fitch or American Eagle Outfitters Inc., Aeropostale has chosen to embrace a key reality of its target market: teens, and especially those on the young end, often want to look like other teens. So while Abercrombie and American Eagle reduced the number of cargo pants on the sales floor in the fall of 2003, Aeropostale kept the cargos coming and at a price that wouldn't bust teens' wallets. Piggybacking on the right trends doesn't come cheaply. Aeropostale is among the most diligent of teen retailers when it comes to consumer research. In addition to high school focus groups and in-store product tests, Aeropostale launched an Internet-based program that seeks online shoppers' input in creating new styles. The company targets 10,000 of its best customers for each of these tests and averages 3,500 participants in each of 20 tests a year. Aeropostale has gone from being a lackluster performer with only 100 stores to a powerhouse with 494 mall stores and earnings that have jumped an average of 88 percent over the past three years.[11]

The real challenge begins after defining the store's product assortment, and that is to develop a product-differentiation strategy. Here are some possibilities:

- ***Feature exclusive national brands that are not available at competing retailers.*** Saks might get exclusive rights to carry the dresses of a well-known international designer.

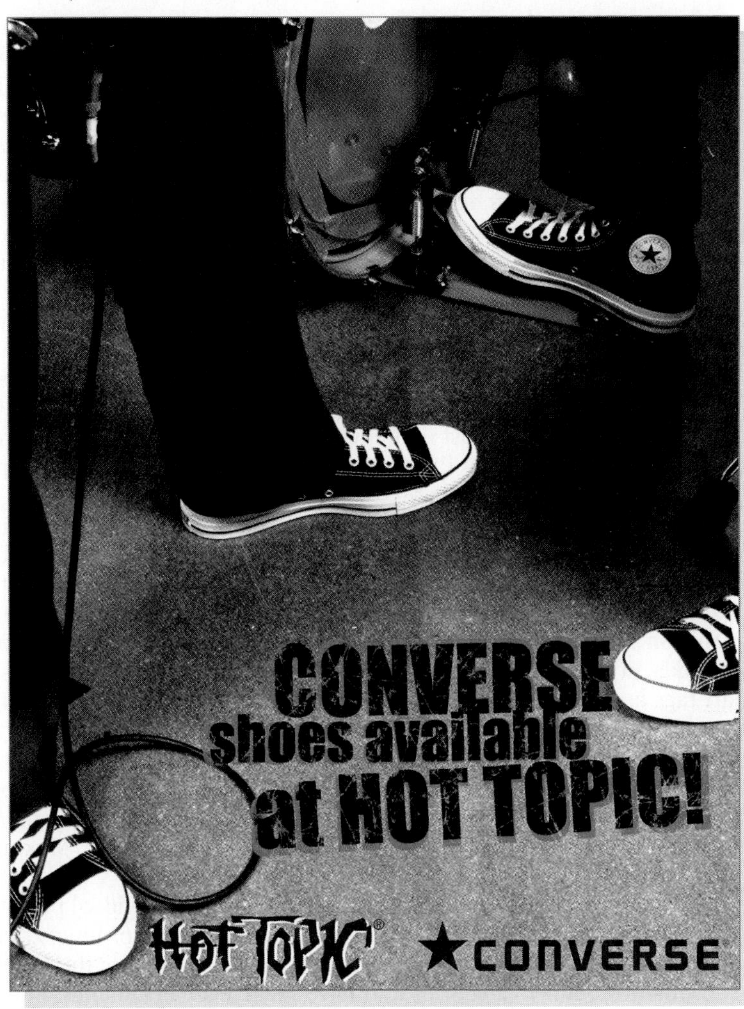

Print ad for Hot Topic and Converse shoes: Hot Topic features the merchandise teens want, usually before the competition does.

- ***Feature mostly private branded merchandise.*** Benetton and GAP design most of the clothes carried in their stores. Many supermarket and drug chains carry private branded merchandise.
- ***Feature blockbuster distinctive merchandise events.*** Bloomingdale's will run month-long shows featuring the goods of another country, such as India or China, throughout the store.
- ***Feature surprise or ever-changing merchandise.*** Off-price apparel retailer T.J. Maxx offers surprise assortments of distress merchandise (goods the owner must sell immediately because it needs cash), overstocks, and closeouts, totaling 10,000 new items each week.
- ***Feature the latest or newest merchandise first.*** Hot Topic sells hip clothing and hard-to-find pop culture merchandise to teens, catching trends to launch new products in six to eight weeks, literally months before traditional competitors using off-shore suppliers.[12]
- ***Offer merchandise customizing services.*** Harrod's of London will make custom-tailored suits, shirts, and ties for customers, in addition to ready-made menswear.
- ***Offer a highly targeted assortment.*** Lane Bryant carries goods for the larger woman. Brookstone offers unusual tools and gadgets for the person who wants to shop in an "adult toy store."[13]

Merchandise may vary by geographical market. In 2003, electronics superstore Best Buy reviewed each of its 25,000 SKUs to adjust its merchandise according to income level and buying habits of shoppers.[14] Bed Bath & Beyond allows store managers to pick 70 percent of their own merchandise to make stores cater to local interests.[15]

PROCUREMENT After deciding on the product-assortment strategy, the retailer must establish merchandise sources, policies, and practices. In the corporate headquarters of a supermarket chain, specialist buyers (sometimes called *merchandise managers*) are responsible for developing brand assortments and listening to salespersons' presentations. In some chains, buyers have the authority to accept or reject new items. In other chains, they are limited to screening "obvious rejects" and "obvious accepts"; they bring other items to the buying committee for approval. Even when an item is accepted by a chain-store buying committee, individual stores in the chain may not carry it. About one-third of the items must be stocked and about two-thirds are stocked at the discretion of each store manager.

Manufacturers face a major challenge trying to get new items onto store shelves. They offer the nation's supermarkets between 150 and 250 new items each week, of which store buyers reject over 70 percent. Manufacturers need to know the acceptance criteria used by buyers, buying committees, and store managers. A. C. Nielsen Company interviewed store managers and found that they are most influenced (in order of importance) by strong evidence of consumer acceptance, a well-designed advertising and sales promotion plan, and generous financial incentives to the trade.

Retailers are rapidly improving their skills in demand forecasting, merchandise selection, stock control, space allocation, and display. They are using computers to track inventory, compute economic order quantities, order goods, and analyze dollars spent on vendors and products. Supermarket chains are using scanner data to manage their merchandise mix on a store-by-store basis and soon all stores will probably be using "smart tags" to track goods, in real time, as they move from factories to supermarkets to shopping baskets. Smart tags are based on inexpensive versions of Radio Frequency Identification (RFID) tracking technology. RFID systems are made up of readers and "smart tags"—microchips attached to antennas. When a tag nears a reader, it broadcasts the information in the chip. Smart tags contain unique numbers to identify products and to provide a means to look up detailed additional information stored in the computer. For more on the possible uses—and abuses—of this technology, see "Marketing Insight: Making Labels Smarter."

When retailers do study the economics of buying and selling individual products, they typically find that a third of their square footage is being tied up by products that do not make an economic profit (above the cost of capital) for the store. Another third of the space is typically allocated to product categories that have break-even economics. And the final third of the space actually creates more than 100 percent of the economic profit. Yet, most retailers are unaware of which third of their products is generating the profit.[16]

Stores are using **direct product profitability (DPP)** to measure a product's handling costs (receiving, moving to storage, paperwork, selecting, checking, loading, and space cost) from the time it reaches the warehouse until a customer buys it in the retail store. Resellers who have adopted DPP learn to their surprise that the gross margin on a product often bears little relation to the direct product profit. Some high-volume products may have such high handling costs that they are less profitable and deserve less shelf space than low-volume products. Clearly, vendors are facing increasingly sophisticated retailers.

To better differentiate themselves and generate consumer interest, some luxury retailers are attempting to make their stores and merchandise more varied. Burberry's sells antique cufflinks and made-to-measure Scottish kilts only in London and customized trench coats only in New York.[17]

Trader Joe's is one store that has differentiated itself largely via its innovative procurement strategy.

TRADER JOE'S INC.

Los Angeles–based Trader Joe's began 45 years ago as a convenience store and has carved out a special niche. It has been dubbed a "gourmet food outlet discount warehouse hybrid," for selling a constantly rotating assortment of upscale specialty food and wine at lower-than-average prices. Trader Joe's also sells roughly 80 percent of what it stocks under private labels (compared to only 16 percent at most supermarkets). When it comes to procurement, Trader Joe's has adopted a "less is more" philosophy. Every store carries about 2,500 products, compared to 25,000 at a conventional supermarket, and it carries only those products it can buy and sell at a good price, even if it means changing stock weekly. Each of its 18 expert buyers go directly to hundreds of sup-

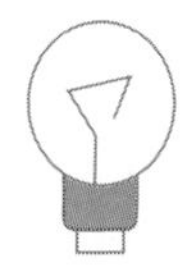

MARKETING INSIGHT | MAKING LABELS SMARTER

In April 2004, several pallets of toilet paper arrived at Wal-Mart's Sanger, Texas, distribution center. This seemingly mundane event actually heralded a revolution in retailing technology. With a small electronic tag affixed to each crate of Kimberly-Clark goods, the toilet tissue announced its own arrival to the distribution center at the same time that a computer checked that the crates were the exact same ones that rumbled out of Kimberly-Clark's plant. If any crates were missing, the computer would issue an alert.

Radio Frequency Identification (RFID) or "smart" tags have been around for decades. Wal-Mart's widespread adoption of them, however, could make them as common as bar codes. For just as the pallets of tissue paper, shampoo, and other goods were announcing their own arrival in Wal-Mart's distribution center, Wal-Mart stunned the retailing world by announcing that it expects—no, demands—its top 100 suppliers implement RFID technology by January 2005. And what Wal-Mart demands, suppliers *do.* If Wal-Mart's suppliers meet the deadline, the megaretailer stands to save as much as $8 billion a year. Here's just a snapshot of how RFID will change the business landscape

A key rationale for RFID tags is that retailers can alert manufacturers before shelves go bare, and consumer-goods manufacturers can further perfect their supply chain so that they don't produce or distribute too few or too many goods. Gillette maintains that retailers and consumer-goods firms lose around $30 billion a year from being out-of-stock on crucial items. Gillette is using smart tags to let store owners know that they need to reorder more stock, as well as to provide alerts if a large decrease on a shelf may be the result of shoplifting. Gillette also is using smart tags to improve logistics and shipping from factories versus traditional bar code scanning. IBM consultants assert that smart tags can shrink inventories by 5 to 25 percent.

RFID technology has the potential to transform our relationship to the objects around us and the relationship of objects to each other. For instance, your clothes might soon be able to tell your washing machine what settings to use. Frozen dinners may be able to tell the microwave what setting to use. "RFID could help give inanimate objects the power to sense, reason, communicate and even act," says Glover Ferguson, chief scientist for consulting firm Accenture.

The ability to link product IDs with databases containing the life histories and whereabouts of products makes RFID useful for preventing counterfeiting and even ensuring food and drug safety. A food company could program a system to alert plant managers when cases of meat sit too long unrefrigerated. The FDA is already pushing for the widespread tagging of medicines to keep counterfeit pharmaceuticals from entering the market. Some retailers are using RFID to prevent shoplifting.

Although a potential boon to marketers, smart tags raise issues of consumer privacy. Take the example of tagged medications. Electronic readers in office buildings might detect the type of medication carried by employees—an invasion of privacy. Or what about RFID-enabled customer loyalty cards that encode all sorts of personal and financial data? Already a group of more than 40 public-interest groups has called for strict public-notification rules, the right to demand deactivation of the tag when people leave stores, and overall limits on the technology's use until privacy concerns have been better addressed. Privacy advocates have ample time to organize. So far the price of RFID technology is too prohibitive to tag individual items. At a price of between 25 and 50 cents per tag, it is not yet worth it to put them on every can of soda or tube of toothpaste.

Sources: Christine Y. Chen, "Wal-Mart Drives a New Tech Boom," *Fortune,* June 28, 2004, p. 202; Rana Foroohar, "The Future of Shopping," *Newsweek,* June 7, 2004, p. 74; Jonathan Krim, "Embedding Their Hopes in RFID. Tagging Technology Promises Efficiency but Raises Privacy Issue," *Washington Post,* June 23, 2004, p. E01; Barbara Rose, "Smart-Tag Wave About to Wash over Retailing," *Chicago Tribune,* April 18, 2004, p. 5; "The Best Thing Since Bar Code," *The Economist,* February 8, 2003, pp. 57–58.

pliers, not to intermediaries, and 20 to 25 percent of its suppliers are overseas. With thousands of vendor relationships all around the world, Trader Joe's success formula is a difficult one to copy. In addition, a product finds a space on the shelf only if it's approved by a tasting panel, and there is a tasting panel on each coast to address regional tastes. Even if a product makes it onto the shelf, there is no guarantee it will be popular. The company introduces as many as 20 products a week to replace unpopular items.[18]

SERVICES AND STORE ATMOSPHERE The services mix is a key tool for differentiating one store from another. Retailers must decide on the *services mix* to offer customers:

- Prepurchase services include accepting telephone and mail orders, advertising, window and interior display, fitting rooms, shopping hours, fashion shows, trade-ins.
- Postpurchase services include shipping and delivery, gift wrapping, adjustments and returns, alterations and tailoring, installations, engraving.
- Ancillary services include general information, check cashing, parking, restaurants, repairs, interior decorating, credit, rest rooms, baby-attendant service.

Retailers also need to consider differentiating based on unerringly reliable customer service. Pressed by discounters and by shoppers who are increasingly blasé about brands, retailers are rediscovering the usefulness of customer service as a point of differentiation, whether it is face-to-face, across phone lines, or even via a technological innovation:

- GAP clerks are getting twice as much training as in the past and are encouraged to help customers plan outfits that could mean more items rung up at the register.
- Wal-Mart has installed self-checkout lanes in some stores to speed harried customers through the final stage of shopping.
- Grocery stores have started zeroing in on customers and asking what they want to see in the store. New England–based chain Hannaford Brothers has done just that and has expanded its organic and natural food selection as a result.

Whatever retailers do to enhance customer service, they will have to keep women in mind. Approximately 85 percent of everything sold in this country is bought or influenced by a woman, and women are fed up with the decline in customer service. They are finding every possible way to get around the system, from ordering online, to resisting fake sales or just doing without.[19] See "Marketing Memo: What Women Want from Customer Service," for guidelines on making the shopping experience more rewarding for women—and for your bottom line.

Atmosphere is another element in the store arsenal. Every store has a physical layout that makes it hard or easy to move around. Every store has a "look." The store must embody a planned atmosphere that suits the target market and draws consumers toward purchase. Consider Kohl's floor plan.

KOHL'S

Retail giant Kohl's employs a floor plan modeled after a racetrack. Designed to convey customers smoothly past all the merchandise in the store, an eight-foot-wide main aisle moves them in a circle around the store. The design also includes a middle aisle that hurried shoppers can use as a shortcut. The racetrack loop yields higher spending levels than many competitors: Kohl's stores take in an average $279 per square foot, compared with $220 a square foot for Target and $147 for Dillard's.[20]

Supermarkets have found that varying the tempo of music affects the average time spent in the store and the average expenditures. Retailers are now adding fragrances to stimulate certain moods in shoppers. London's Heathrow Airport sprays the scent of pine needles because it stimulates the sense of holidays and weekend walks. Automobile dealers will spray a "leather" scent in second-hand cars to make them smell "new."[21]

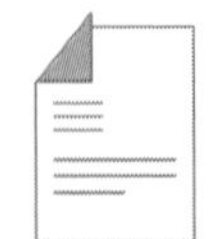

MARKETING MEMO | WHAT WOMEN WANT FROM CUSTOMER SERVICE

1. ***Start at the end: speed up the checkout.*** Don't tempt a woman to walk out by wasting her time. Whole Foods guarantees a maximum four-minute wait at its supermarkets. National Car Rental has eliminated waiting in line by allowing customers to reserve their vehicles online. So think a minute: What are you doing for your "big order" customers while the "10 item" dabblers whisk right through the turnstile?
2. ***Make the experience worth having.*** Figure out a way to teach anyone who's stationed near a store entrance the basic skills of saying "hello" and knowing the store layout. Wal-Mart and Old Navy have permanent greeters. If you can't afford extra people, ensure that the nicer staff work near the front door.
3. ***Assign patrolling customer-care watchdogs on the sales floor.*** Many women answer, "May I help you?" with "Just looking." She probably is. But watch when her head jerks up suddenly and her eyes scan the horizon looking for assistance. She is ready for help and she wants it NOW. It's the moment of truth, and if you miss it, you lose.
4. ***Know who you are.*** There's a reason that retailers like Chico's, The Limited, and Kohl's have been able to consistently turn in good numbers. Not only are their brands integrated (merchandise, environment, service, and pricing), but they also cater to the expectations of the customers who want them. Too many retailers covet "new" customers (read younger, thinner, hipper, richer), and ignore their core shoppers. Be proud of who you are—and love the one you're with.

Source: Adapted from Mary Lou Quinlan, "Women Aren't Buying It," *Brandweek,* June 2, 2003, pp. 20–22.

STORE ACTIVITIES AND EXPERIENCES The growth of e-commerce has forced traditional brick-and-mortar retailers to respond. In addition to their natural advantages, such as products that shoppers can actually see, touch, and test, real-life customer service, and no delivery lag time for small or medium-sized purchases, they also provide a shopping experience as a strong differentiator.[22]

To entice Internet-savvy consumers to visit their stores, real-life retailers are developing new services and promotions. The change in strategy can be noticed in practices as simple as calling each shopper a "guest" (as many stores are beginning to do) or as grandiose as building an indoor amusement park.

For example, REI applies the principle of "experiential retailing" in selling outdoor gear and clothing products: Consumers are able to test climbing equipment on 25-foot or even 65-foot walls in the store and can test Gore-Tex raincoats by going under a simulated rain shower.[23] Victoria's Secret stores work on the concept of "retail theater": Customers feel they are in a romance novel, with lush music and faint floral scents in the background.

There has been a marked rise in establishments that provide a place for people to congregate, such as cafés, juice bars, bookshops, and brew pubs. Bass Pro Shops, a retailer of outdoor sports equipment, features giant aquariums, waterfalls, trout ponds, archery and rifle ranges, putting greens, and classes in everything from ice fishing to conservation—all free. The Discovery Zone, a chain of children's play spaces, offers indoor spaces where kids can go wild without breaking anything and stressed-out parents can exchange stories.

Retailers are also creating in-store entertainment in the hope of attracting customers who want fun and excitement. In the United Kingdom, Selfridges is the champion of the showcase business model and the retail theme park. Selfridges also carves out areas within stores for outside manufacturers to control and display their brands as they see fit. Selfridges encourages these vendors to create vibrant, exciting areas that not only look very different, but do different things. As the retailer strives to get "a younger center of gravity," Selfridges' sales have increased 10.6 percent from 2002 to 2003.

Even manufacturers such as Maytag are realizing the power of adding retail theater to their brand and have created showcase stores. At the grand opening of Maytag's Costa Mesa, California, store, customers were invited to "Bake cookies, clean your dishes. Take our washer for a spin. . . . Stop in and test-drive your new appliance today." Test-driving appliances is not just an opening day gig for Maytag, but an everyday occurrence. Customers sit and eat pastries in Maytag's well-appointed kitchens and then see how clean the dishwasher can get their plates. They bring in their dirty laundry to try out a Maytag stackable washer/dryer while their children watch cartoons on TV.[24]

Super-regional malls are anchoring themselves with unique and interesting shops, rather than the brand-name department stores and national retailers that fill most traditional malls. Says Laurence C. Siegel, chairman and CEO at Mills Corp., "There are no Macy's at our centers. We want to create destination retail." The Sony Style store, where Sony entertainment and electronics products are displayed in environments that encourage customers to test them, is an example of a megamall store.

PRICE DECISION Prices are a key positioning factor and must be decided in relation to the target market, the product-and-service assortment mix, and the competition. All retailers would like to achieve high volumes and high gross margins. They would like high *Turns x Earns,* but the two usually do not go together. Most retailers fall into the *high-markup, lower-volume* group (fine specialty stores) or the *low-markup, higher-volume* group (mass merchandisers and discount stores). Within each of these groups are further gradations. Bijan's on Rodeo Drive in Beverly Hills prices suits starting at $1,000 and shoes at $400. At the other end, Target has skillfully combined a hip image with discount prices to offer customers a strong value proposition.

Retailers must also pay attention to pricing tactics. Most retailers will put low prices on some items to serve as traffic builders or loss leaders. They will run storewide sales. They will plan markdowns on slower-moving merchandise. Shoe retailers, for example, expect to sell 50 percent of their shoes at the normal markup, 25 percent at a 40 percent markup, and the remaining 25 percent at cost.

As Chapter 14 notes, some retailers such as Wal-Mart have abandoned "sales pricing" in favor of everyday low pricing (EDLP). EDLP could lead to lower advertising costs, greater pricing stability, a stronger image of fairness and reliability, and higher retail profits.

Research has shown that supermarket chains practicing everyday low pricing can be more profitable than those practicing Hi-Lo sales pricing, but only in certain circumstances.[25]

COMMUNICATION DECISION Retailers use a wide range of communication tools to generate traffic and purchases. They place ads, run special sales, issue money-saving coupons, and run frequent shopper-reward programs, in-store food sampling, and coupons on shelves or at checkout points. Each retailer must use communications that support and reinforce its image positioning. Fine stores will place tasteful, full-page ads in magazines such as *Vogue, Vanity Fair,* or *Esquire*. They will carefully train salespeople to greet customers, interpret their needs, and handle complaints. Off-price retailers will arrange their merchandise to promote the idea of bargains and large savings, while conserving on service and sales assistance.

BLOOMINGDALE'S AND LIMITED TOO

In order to avoid skyrocketing advertising costs and to subtly highlight certain brands, retailers are publishing glossy magazines—dubbed "magalogs"—or even books, and sometimes charging the customer for them. Upscale New York retailer Bloomingdale's rolled out *B* in 2003, a 130-page glossy magazine with about 80 percent editorial content highlighting fashion, travel destinations, entertaining, and celebrity profiles. About 270,000 customers in Bloomingdale's loyalty program get *B* by mail quarterly at no charge, but the magalog is available for sale for $3.95 at Bloomingdale's or by subscription. Limited Too is taking an even subtler approach. The retailer for clothing and accessories for girls 8 to 14 recently started selling "Tuned In," a series of fiction books by Julia De Villers. The books are sold for $5.50 only at the retailer. While the series is not intended as an ad for Limited's products, the first book, *Fast Friends,* mentioned fashion throughout and included a back-to-school shopping list for the central character. These and other retailer publications don't have 800-numbers in them or store Web site URLs, but are geared more toward getting the reader to absorb the lifestyle that the store's brands or the store itself portrays.[26]

LOCATION DECISION Retailers are accustomed to saying that the three keys to success are "location, location, and location." Department store chains, oil companies, and fast-food franchisers exercise great care in selecting locations. The problem breaks down into selecting regions of the country in which to open outlets, then particular cities, and then particular sites. A supermarket chain might decide to operate in the Midwest; in the cities of Chicago, Milwaukee, and Indianapolis; and in 14 locations, mostly suburban, within the Chicago area.

Retailers can locate their stores in the central business district, a regional shopping center, a community shopping center, a shopping strip, or within a larger store:

- ***General business districts.*** This is the oldest and most heavily trafficked city area, often known as "downtown." Store and office rents are normally high. Most downtown areas were hit by a flight to the suburbs in the 1960s, resulting in deteriorated retailing facilities; but in the 1990s, a minor renaissance of interest in downtown apartments, stores, and restaurants began in many cities.
- ***Regional shopping centers.*** These are large suburban malls containing 40 to 200 stores. They usually draw customers from a 5- to 20-mile radius. Typically, malls featured one or two nationally known anchor stores, such as JCPenney or Lord & Taylor, and a great number of smaller stores, many under franchise operation. The department store's role, however, is increasingly taken over by a combination of big box stores such as Petco, Circuit City, Bed Bath & Beyond.[27] Malls are attractive because of generous parking, one-stop shopping, restaurants, and recreational facilities. Successful malls charge high rents and may get a share of stores' sales.
- ***Community shopping centers.*** These are smaller malls with one anchor store and between 20 and 40 smaller stores.
- ***Strip malls (also called shopping strips).*** These contain a cluster of stores, usually housed in one long building, serving a neighborhood's needs for groceries, hardware, laundry, shoe repair, and dry cleaning. They usually serve people within a 5- to 10-minute driving range.
- ***A location within a larger store.*** Certain well-known retailers—McDonald's, Starbucks, Nathan's, Dunkin' Donuts—locate new, smaller units as concession space within larger stores or operations, such as airports, schools, or department stores.

In view of the relationship between high traffic and high rents, retailers must decide on the most advantageous locations for their outlets. They can use a variety of methods to assess locations, including traffic counts, surveys of consumer shopping habits, and analysis of competitive locations.[28] Several models for site location have also been formulated.[29]

Retailers can assess a particular store's sales effectiveness by looking at four indicators: (1) number of people passing by on an average day; (2) percentage who enter the store; (3) percentage of those entering who buy; and (4) average amount spent per sale.

Trends in Retailing

At this point, we can summarize the main developments retailers and manufacturers need to take into account in planning competitive strategies.

- ***New Retail Forms and Combinations.*** Some supermarkets include bank branches. Bookstores feature coffee shops. Gas stations include food stores. Loblaw's Supermarkets have added fitness clubs to their stores. Shopping malls and bus and train stations have peddlers' carts in their aisles. Retailers are also experimenting with limited-time-only stores called "pop-ups" that let retailers promote brands, reach seasonal shoppers for a few weeks in busy areas, and create buzz. When Target launched its line of clothes designed by Isaac Mizrahi, it set up a temporary Target store at Rockefeller Center in New York City, which sold only the Mizrahi line. The publicity convinced shoppers to make the trek to the Target store in Queens, an outer borough of New York City. JCPenney has taken a page from Target's book and unveiled designer Chris Madden's home, bath, and kitchen line in a 2,500-square-foot Rockefeller Center space for one month only. The pop-up offered four PCs for Web buying, so that customers were exposed to a wider selection of JCPenney merchandise.[30]
- ***Growth of Intertype Competition.*** Different types of stores—discount stores, catalog showrooms, department stores—all compete for the same consumers by carrying the same type of merchandise. Retailers that have helped shoppers to be economically cautious, to simplify their increasingly busy and complicated lives and provide an emotional connection, are the winners in the new retailing landscape of the twenty-first century. The biggest winners: supercenters, dollar stores, warehouse clubs, and the Internet.[31]
- ***Competition Between Store-based and Non-store-based Retailing.*** Consumers now receive sales offers through direct-mail letters and catalogs, and over television, computers, and telephones. These non-store-based retailers are taking business away from store-based retailers. Some store-based retailers initially saw online retailing as a definite threat. Home Depot shocked its top vendors (Black & Decker, Stanley Tools, etc.) by issuing a memo implying that if they started to sell online, Home Depot might drop them as suppliers. Now Home Depot is finding it advantageous to work with online retailers. Wal-Mart recently joined with America Online (AOL) so that AOL will provide a low-cost Internet access service that carries the Wal-Mart brand, and Wal-Mart will promote the service and AOL in its stores and through TV advertising. Stores such as Wal-Mart and Kmart have developed their own Web sites, and some online retailers are finding it advantageous to own or manage physical outlets, either retail stores or warehouses.
- ***Growth of Giant Retailers.*** Through their superior information systems, logistical systems, and buying power, giant retailers are able to deliver good service and immense volumes of product at appealing prices to masses of consumers. They are crowding out smaller manufacturers who cannot deliver enough quantity and often dictating to the most powerful manufacturers what to make, how to price and promote, when and how to ship, and even how to improve production and management. Manufacturers need these accounts; otherwise they would lose 10 to 30 percent of the market. Some giant retailers are *category killers* that concentrate on one product category, such as toys (Toys "R" Us), home improvement (Home Depot), or office supplies (Staples). Others are *supercenters* that combine grocery items with a huge selection of nonfood merchandise (Wal-Mart). The supercenter is becoming the premier retail format in the United States: 63 percent of American women shopped at supercenters in the last 90 days of 2003 compared to only 32 percent in 2000.[32]
- ***Decline of Middle Market Retailers.*** Increasingly, the retail market can be characterized as being hourglass or dog-bone shaped: Growth seems to be centered at the top (with luxury offerings) or at the bottom (with discount pricing). Opportunities are scarcer in the middle where retailers such as Sears and JCPenney have struggled. Montgomery Ward actually went

out of business. Supermarkets, department stores, and drugstores are most at risk or on the brink—since 2000, fewer consumers have shopped these channels weekly, as newer, more relevant places have come to serve their needs.[33] As discount retailers improve their quality and image, consumers have been willing to trade down. Target offers Todd Oldham designs and Kmart sells an extensive line of Joe Boxer underwear and sleepwear.[34] To better compete, Sears adjusted its merchandise, service, and prices in an attempt to provide a more compelling alternative to discounters and department stores.[35]

- ***Growing Investment in Technology.*** Retailers are using computers to produce better forecasts, control inventory costs, order electronically from suppliers, send e-mail between stores, and even sell to customers within stores. They are adopting checkout scanning systems,[36] electronic funds transfer, electronic data interchange,[37] in-store television, store traffic radar systems,[38] and improved merchandise-handling systems.
- ***Global Presence of Major Retailers.*** Retailers with unique formats and strong brand positioning are increasingly appearing in other countries.[39] U.S. retailers such as McDonald's, The Limited, GAP, and Toys "R" Us have become globally prominent. Wal-Mart operates over 700 stores abroad. Among foreign-based global retailers in the United States are Britain's Marks and Spencer, Italy's Benetton, France's Carrefour hypermarkets, Sweden's IKEA home furnishings stores, and Japan's Yaohan supermarkets.[40]

::: Private Labels

A growing trend and major marketing decision for retailers concerns private labels. A **private label brand** (also called reseller, store, house, or distributor brand) is one retailers and wholesalers develop. Retailers such as Benetton, The Body Shop, and Marks and Spencer carry mostly own-brand merchandise. In Britain, the largest food chains, Sainsbury and Tesco, sell 50 and 45 percent store-label goods, respectively. In the United States, store brands now account for one of every five items sold, a $51.6 billion business last year, according to the Private Label Manufacturers' Association.

Some experts believe that 50 percent is the natural limit for carrying private brands because (1) consumers prefer certain national brands, and (2) many product categories are not feasible or attractive on a private-brand basis. If that's the case, then Target has reached the "limit." An estimated 50 percent of Target's products are private brands, including the hugely popular housewares designed by Michael Graves and Todd Oldham.

Indeed, private brands are rapidly gaining ascendance in a way that has manufacturers of name brands running scared. Consider the following:[41]

- Wal-Mart's Ol'Roy dog food has surpassed Nestlé's venerable Purina brand as the top-selling dog chow.
- One in every two ceiling fans sold in the United States is from Home Depot and most of those are its own Hampton Bay brand.
- *Consumer Reports* rated Winn-Dixie supermarket's chocolate ice cream ahead of brand name Breyer's.
- Grocery giant Kroger cranks out 4,300 of its own label food and drink items from the 41 factories it owns and operates.

Private labels can be found in many categories. When they found the computer selections on their shelves shrinking, big electronics retailers such as Best Buy and Radio Shack launched their own house brand PCs.[42]

House Brands

Why do intermediaries bother to sponsor their own brands? First, they are more profitable. Intermediaries search for manufacturers with excess capacity who will produce the private label at a low cost. Other costs, such as research and development, advertising, sales promotion, and physical distribution are also much lower. This means that the private brander can charge a lower price and yet make a higher profit margin. Second, retailers develop exclusive store brands to differentiate themselves from competitors. Many consumers develop a preference for store brands in certain categories.

LOBLAW

Since 1984, when its President's Choice line of foods made its debut, it has been difficult to say "private label" without Loblaw and President's Choice coming instantly to mind. Toronto-based Loblaw's Decadent Chocolate Chip Cookie quickly became a Canadian leader and showed how innovative store brands could compete effectively with national brands by matching or even exceeding their quality. A finely tuned brand strategy involving its premium President's Choice line and no-frills, yellow-labeled No Name line has helped differentiate its stores and build Loblaw into a powerhouse in Canada and the United States. The President's Choice line of products has become so successful that Loblaw is licensing it to noncompetitive retailers in other countries, thus turning a local store brand into—believe it or not—a global brand. Today, private label sales make up 30 percent of Loblaw's total sales, compared with a Canadian average of 20 percent.[43]

That's how store brands were "born." More and more chains are looking to distinguish themselves in a crowded retail field with a brand that is available nowhere else:

RH MACY & CO.

Thanks to a creative private brand strategy conceived by Macy's parent company, Federated Department Stores, teens are forgoing the hip, vintage-apparel shops of New York's lower east side for Macy's American Rag clothing. Federated created the vintage-inspired apparel in an atmosphere intentionally designed to reflect a flea market or second-hand store. Before American Rag's launch, Federated carefully sowed the seeds of authenticity by sponsoring a Lollapalooza music tour and using a design and brand specialist.[44]

In some cases, there has even been a return to "no branding" of certain staple consumer goods and pharmaceuticals. Carrefours, the originator of the French hypermarket, introduced a line of "no brands" or generics in its stores in the early 1970s. **Generics** are unbranded, plainly packaged, less expensive versions of common products such as spaghetti, paper towels, and canned peaches. They offer standard or lower quality at a price that may be as much as 20 percent to 40 percent lower than nationally advertised brands and 10 percent to 20 percent lower than retailer private label brands. The lower price of generics is made possible by lower-quality ingredients, lower-cost labeling and packaging, and minimal advertising.

The Private Label Threat

In the confrontation between manufacturers' and private brands, retailers have many advantages and increasing market power. Because shelf space is scarce, many supermarkets now charge a *slotting fee* for accepting a new brand, to cover the cost of listing and stocking it. Retailers also charge for special display space and in-store advertising space. They typically give more prominent display to their own brands and make sure they are well stocked. Retailers are now building better quality into their store brands.

The growing power of store brands is not the only factor weakening national brands. Consumers are more price sensitive. They are noting better quality as competing manufacturers and national retailers copy and duplicate the qualities of the best brands. The continuous barrage of coupons and price specials has trained a generation of shoppers to buy on price. The fact that companies have reduced advertising to 30 percent of their

Company-supplied photo for the introduction of three new colors of Heinz EZ Squirt: children and parents don't have a clue to what's inside until they squirt it or draw with it on their favorite foods. The colors: Passion Pink, Awesome Orange, and Totally Teal.

total promotion budget has weakened their brand equity. The endless stream of brand extensions and line extensions has blurred brand identity and led to a confusing amount of product proliferation.

Manufacturers have reacted to the private label threat, in part, by spending substantial amounts of money on consumer-directed advertising and promotion to maintain strong brand preference. The prices have to be somewhat higher to cover the higher promotion cost. At the same time, mass distributors pressure manufacturers to put more promotional money into trade allowances and deals if they want adequate shelf space. Once manufacturers start giving in, they have less to spend on advertising and consumer promotion, and their brand leadership spirals down. This is the national-brand manufacturers' dilemma.

To maintain their power, leading brand marketers should invest in heavy and continuous R&D to bring out new brands, line extensions, features, and quality improvements. They must sustain a strong "pull" advertising program to maintain high consumer brand recognition and preference. They must find ways to partner with major mass distributors in a joint search for logistical economies and competitive strategies that produce savings. It is imperative to cut all unnecessary costs to have more competitive prices. National brands may command a price premium, but not one that exceeds the value perceptions of consumers.[45] Here is an example of what leading brand marketers must do:

HEINZ

H.J. Heinz has retained market leadership in the ketchup category by combining a distinctive, slightly sweet-tasting product; a carefully monitored price gap with competitors; and aggressive packaging, product development, and promotional efforts (e.g., squeezable, "no drips" bottles, flavored and colored (Blastin' Green) ketchup, and "hipper" advertising).

::: Wholesaling

Wholesaling includes all the activities involved in selling goods or services to those who buy for resale or business use. Wholesaling excludes manufacturers and farmers because they are engaged primarily in production, and it excludes retailers. Wholesalers (also called *distributors*) differ from retailers in a number of ways. First, wholesalers pay less attention to promotion, atmosphere, and location because they are dealing with business customers rather than final consumers. Second, wholesale transactions are usually larger than retail transactions, and wholesalers usually cover a larger trade area than retailers. Third, the government deals with wholesalers and retailers differently in terms of legal regulations and taxes.

Why are wholesalers used at all? Why do manufacturers not sell directly to retailers or final consumers? In general, wholesalers are used when they are more efficient in performing one or more of the following functions:

- ***Selling and promoting.*** Wholesalers' sales forces help manufacturers reach many small business customers at a relatively low cost. Wholesalers have more contacts, and often buyers trust wholesalers more than they trust a distant manufacturer.
- ***Buying and assortment building.*** Wholesalers are able to select items and build the assortments their customers need, saving the customers considerable work.
- ***Bulk breaking.*** Wholesalers achieve savings for their customers through buying in large carload lots and breaking the bulk into smaller units.
- ***Warehousing.*** Wholesalers hold inventories, thereby reducing inventory costs and risks to suppliers and customers.
- ***Transportation.*** Wholesalers can often provide quicker delivery to buyers because they are closer to the buyers.
- ***Financing.*** Wholesalers finance customers by granting credit, and finance suppliers by ordering early and paying bills on time.
- ***Risk bearing.*** Wholesalers absorb some risk by taking title and bearing the cost of theft, damage, spoilage, and obsolescence.

- ***Market information.*** Wholesalers supply information to suppliers and customers regarding competitors' activities, new products, price developments, and so on.
- ***Management services and counseling.*** Wholesalers often help retailers improve their operations by training sales clerks, helping with store layouts and displays, and setting up accounting and inventory-control systems. They may help industrial customers by offering training and technical services.

The Growth and Types of Wholesaling

Wholesaling has grown in the United States in recent years.[46] A number of factors explain this: the growth of larger factories located some distance from the principal buyers; production in advance of orders rather than in response to specific orders; an increase in the number of levels of intermediate producers and users; and the increasing need for adapting products to the needs of intermediate and final users in terms of quantities, packages, and forms. The major types of wholesalers are described in Table 16.4.

Wholesaler Marketing Decisions

Wholesaler-distributors have faced mounting pressures in recent years from new sources of competition, demanding customers, new technologies, and more direct-buying programs by large industrial, institutional, and retail buyers. They have had to develop appropriate strategic responses. One major drive has been to increase asset productivity by managing their inventories and receivables better. They also have had to improve their strategic decisions on target markets, product assortment and services, price, promotion, and place.

TABLE 16.4

Major Wholesaler Types

Merchant wholesalers: Independently owned businesses that take title to the merchandise they handle. They are full-service and limited-service jobbers, distributors, mill supply houses.

Full-service wholesalers: Carry stock, maintain a sales force, offer credit, make deliveries, provide management assistance. Wholesale merchants sell primarily to retailers: Some carry several merchandise lines, some carry one or two lines, others carry only part of a line. Industrial distributors sell to manufacturers and also provide services like credit and delivery.

Limited-service wholesalers: *Cash and carry wholesalers* sell a limited line of fast-moving goods to small retailers for cash. *Truck wholesalers* sell and deliver a limited line of semiperishable goods to supermarkets, grocery stores, hospitals, restaurants, hotels. *Drop shippers* serve bulk industries such as coal, lumber, heavy equipment. They assume title and risk from the time an order is accepted to its delivery. *Rack jobbers* serve grocery retailers in nonfood items. Delivery people set up displays, price goods, keep inventory records; they retain title to goods and bill retailers only for goods sold to end of year. *Producers' cooperatives* assemble farm produce to sell in local markets. *Mail-order wholesalers* send catalogs to retail, industrial, and institutional customers; orders are filled and sent by mail, rail, plane, or truck.

Brokers and agents: Facilitate buying and selling, on commission of 2 to 6 percent of the selling price; limited functions; generally specialize by product line or customer type. *Brokers* bring buyers and sellers together and assist in negotiation; paid by the party hiring them. Food brokers, real estate brokers, insurance brokers. *Agents* represent buyers or sellers on a more permanent basis. Most manufacturers' agents are small businesses, with a few skilled salespeople: Selling agents have contractual authority to sell a manufacturer's entire output; purchasing agents make purchases for buyers and often receive, inspect, warehouse, and ship merchandise; commission merchants take physical possession of products and negotiate sales.

Manufacturers' and retailers' branches and offices: Wholesaling operations conducted by sellers or buyers themselves rather than through independent wholesalers. Separate branches and offices are dedicated to sales or purchasing. Many retailers set up purchasing offices in major market centers.

Specialized wholesalers: Agricultural assemblers (buy the agricultural output of many farms), petroleum bulk plants and terminals (consolidate the output of many wells), and auction companies (auction cars, equipment, etc., to dealers and other businesses).

TARGET MARKET Wholesalers need to define their target markets. They can choose a target group of customers by size (only large retailers), type of customer (convenience food stores only), need for service (customers who need credit), or other criteria. Within the target group, they can identify the most profitable customers and design stronger offers to build better relationships with them. They can propose automatic reordering systems, set up management-training and advisory systems, and even sponsor a voluntary chain. They can discourage less profitable customers by requiring larger orders or adding surcharges to smaller ones.

PRODUCT ASSORTMENT AND SERVICES The wholesalers' "product" is their assortment. Wholesalers are under great pressure to carry a full line and maintain sufficient stock for immediate delivery, but the costs of carrying huge inventories can kill profits. Wholesalers today are reexamining how many lines to carry and are choosing to carry only the more profitable ones. They are also examining which services count most in building strong customer relationships and which ones should be dropped or charged for. The key is to find a distinct mix of services valued by their customers.

PRICE DECISION Wholesalers usually mark up the cost of goods by a conventional percentage, say 20 percent, to cover their expenses. Expenses may run 17 percent of the gross margin, leaving a profit margin of approximately 3 percent. In grocery wholesaling, the average profit margin is often less than 2 percent. Wholesalers are beginning to experiment with new approaches to pricing. They might cut their margin on some lines in order to win important new customers. They will ask suppliers for a special price break when they can turn it into an opportunity to increase the supplier's sales.

PROMOTION DECISION Wholesalers rely primarily on their sales force to achieve promotional objectives. Even here, most wholesalers see selling as a single salesperson talking to a single customer, instead of a team effort to sell, build, and service major accounts. Wholesalers would benefit from adopting some of the image-making techniques used by retailers. They need to develop an overall promotion strategy involving trade advertising, sales promotion, and publicity. They also need to make greater use of supplier promotion materials and programs.

PLACE DECISION In the past, wholesalers were typically located in low-rent, low-tax areas and put little money into their physical setting and offices. Often the materials-handling systems and order-processing systems lagged behind the available technologies. Today, progressive wholesalers have been improving materials-handling procedures and costs by developing *automated warehouses* and improving their supply capabilities through advanced information systems. Here is an example.[47]

MCKESSON

McKesson Corporation is a leading health care services company providing pharmaceutical and medical-surgical supply management, information solutions, pharmacy automation, and sales and marketing services to the health care industry. The company has unmatched depth, breadth, and reach delivering unique cost-saving and quality improvement solutions to pharmacies, hospitals, physicians, extended care sites, payor sites, and pharmaceutical and medical-surgical manufacturers. McKesson maintains a strong presence on the Internet through its Web site www.mckesson.com. The site offers access to information about the company, its people, products, and services. McKesson customers can use the Web site to access the company's health care software applications as well as order and track pharmaceutical and medical-surgical products.[48]

Trends in Wholesaling

Manufacturers always have the option of bypassing wholesalers or replacing inefficient wholesalers with better ones. Manufacturers' major complaints against wholesalers are as follows: They do not aggressively promote the manufacturer's product line, and act more like order takers; they do not carry enough inventory and therefore fail to fill customers' orders fast enough; they do not supply the manufacturer with up-to-date market, customer, and competitive information; they do not attract high-caliber managers and bring down their own costs; and they charge too much for their services.

It even appeared that wholesalers were headed for a significant decline as large manufacturers and retailers moved aggressively into direct-buying programs. Savvy wholesalers rallied to the challenge and began to reengineer their businesses. The most successful wholesaler-distributors adapted their services to meet their suppliers' and target customers' changing needs. They recognized that they had to add value to the channel. They also had to reduce their operating costs by investing in more advanced materials-handling technology, information systems, and the Internet.

GRAINGER

W. W. Grainger, Inc., is the leading broad line supplier of facilities maintenance products in North America. Sales for 2002 were $4.6 billion. Grainger serves customers through a network of nearly 600 branches, 17 distribution centers, and four Web sites to guarantee product availability and quick service. The distribution centers are linked by satellite network, which has reduced customer-response time and boosted sales. It offers over 500,000 supplies and 2.5 million repair parts to clients.[49]

Narus and Anderson interviewed leading industrial distributors and identified four ways they strengthened their relationships with manufacturers:

1. They sought a clear agreement with their manufacturers about their expected functions in the marketing channel.
2. They gained insight into the manufacturers' requirements by visiting their plants and attending manufacturer association conventions and trade shows.
3. They fulfilled their commitments to the manufacturer by meeting the volume targets, paying bills promptly, and feeding back customer information to their manufacturers.
4. They identified and offered value-added services to help their suppliers.[50]

The wholesaling industry remains vulnerable to one of the most enduring trends—fierce resistance to price increases and the winnowing out of suppliers based on cost and quality. The trend toward vertical integration, in which manufacturers try to control or own their intermediaries, is still strong. "Marketing Memo: Strategies of High-Performance Wholesaler-Distributors" outlines some of the strategies used by successful wholesale organizations.

::: Market Logistics

Physical distribution starts at the factory. Managers choose a set of warehouses (stocking points) and transportation carriers that will deliver the goods to final destinations in the desired time or at the lowest total cost. Physical distribution has now been expanded into the broader concept of **supply chain management (SCM)**. Supply chain management starts before physical distribution: It involves procuring the right inputs (raw materials, components, and capital equipment); converting them efficiently into finished products; and dispatching them to the final destinations. An even broader perspective calls for studying how the company's suppliers themselves obtain their inputs. The supply chain perspective can help a company identify superior suppliers and distributors and help them improve productivity, which ultimately brings down the company's costs.

Market logistics involves planning the infrastructure to meet demand, then implementing and controlling the physical flows of materials and final goods from points of origin to points of use, to meet customer requirements at a profit.

Market logistics planning has four steps:[51]

1. Deciding on the company's value proposition to its customers. (What on-time delivery standard should be offered? What levels should be attained in ordering and billing accuracy?)
2. Deciding on the best channel design and network strategy for reaching the customers. (Should the company serve customers directly or through intermediaries? What products should it source from which manufacturing facilities? How many warehouses should it maintain and where should they be located?)

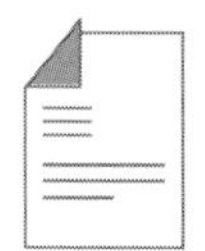

MARKETING MEMO | STRATEGIES FOR HIGH-PERFORMANCE WHOLESALER-DISTRIBUTORS

Lusch, Zizzo, and Kenderine studied 136 wholesalers in North America and concluded that the progressive ones are renewing themselves in five ways:

1. ***Strengthening core operations:*** Wholesalers develop such expertise in distributing their particular product line that manufacturers and retailers cannot duplicate the efficiency.
2. ***Expanding into global markets:*** Wholesalers, especially in the chemical, electronics, and computer fields, have been expanding not only to Canada and Mexico, but also in Europe and Asia.
3. ***Doing more with less:*** Wholesalers have been investing heavily in technology, including bar coding and scanning, fully automated warehouses, electronic data interchange (EDI), and advanced information technology.
4. ***Committing to TQM:*** Progressive wholesalers are moving toward managing processes to improve outcomes as perceived by customers, including performing quality assessment of suppliers' products and thereby adding value. As wholesalers move toward zero-defect customer service, manufacturers and retailers see this trend as contributing to their own capacity to satisfy customers.
5. ***Marketing support philosophy:*** Wholesalers recognize that their role is not simply to represent the suppliers' interests, or their customers' interests, but to support both, by acting as a valued member of the marketing value chain.

Sources: Robert F. Lusch, Deborah Zizzo, and James M. Kenderdine, "Strategic Renewal in Distribution," *Marketing Management*, no. 2 (1993): 20–29. Also see their *Foundations of Wholesaling—A Strategic and Financial Chart Book, Distribution Research Program* (Norman: College of Business Administration, University of Oklahoma, 1996).

3. Developing operational excellence in sales forecasting, warehouse management, transportation management, and materials management.
4. Implementing the solution with the best information systems, equipment, policies, and procedures.

Market logistics leads to an examination of the most efficient way to deliver value:

- A software company normally sees its challenge as producing and packaging software disks and manuals, then shipping them to wholesalers—who ship them to retailers, who sell them to customers. Customers bring the software package to home or office and download the software onto a hard drive. Market logistics would look at two superior delivery systems. The first involves ordering the software to be downloaded onto the customer's hard drive. The second system allows software to be loaded onto a computer by the computer manufacturer. Both solutions eliminate the need for printing, packaging, shipping, and stocking millions of disks and manuals. The same solutions are available for distributing music, newspapers, video games, films, and other products that deliver voice, text, data, or images.
- The IKEA Retailers, franchisees of the world-famous IKEA concept for retail sale of furniture and home furnishings, are able to sell good-quality furniture and home furnishings at 20 percent less than competitors. The cost savings stem from several sources: (1) The IKEA Retailers buy in such large volume that they get lower prices; (2) the furniture and home furnishings are designed in "knock-down" form and shipped flat at a much lower transportation cost; (3) the customer drives the furniture home, which saves delivery cost; (4) the customer assembles the furniture. The IKEA concept works on a low markup and high volume.

Integrated Logistics Systems

The market logistics task calls for **integrated logistics systems (ILS)**, involving materials management, material flow systems, and physical distribution, abetted by information technology (IT). Third-party suppliers, such as FedEx Logistics Services or Ryder Integrated Logistics, often participate in designing or managing these systems. Volvo, working with FedEx, set up a warehouse in Memphis with a complete stock of truck parts. A dealer, needing a part in an emergency, phones a toll-free number, and the part is flown out the same day and delivered that night either at the airport or at the dealer's office or even at the roadside repair site.

Information systems play a critical role in managing market logistics, especially computers, point-of-sale terminals, uniform product bar codes, satellite tracking, electronic data interchange (EDI), and electronic funds transfer (EFT). These developments have shortened the order-cycle time, reduced clerical labor, reduced the error rate in documents, and provided improved control of operations. They have enabled companies to make promises such as "the product will be at dock 25 at 10:00 A.M. tomorrow," and control this promise through information.

Market logistics involves several activities. The first is sales forecasting, on the basis of which the company schedules distribution, production, and inventory levels. Production plans indicate the materials the purchasing department must order. These materials arrive through inbound transportation, enter the receiving area, and are stored in raw-material inventory. Raw materials are converted into finished goods. Finished-goods inventory is the link between customer orders and manufacturing activity. Customers' orders draw down the finished-goods inventory level, and manufacturing activity builds it up. Finished goods flow off the assembly line and pass through packaging, in-plant warehousing, shipping-room processing, outbound transportation, field warehousing, and customer delivery and servicing.

Management has become concerned about the total cost of market logistics, which can amount to 30 to 40 percent of the product's cost. The grocery industry alone thinks it can decrease its annual operating costs by 10 percent, or $30 billion, by revamping its market logistics. A typical box of breakfast cereal takes 104 days to get from factory to supermarket, chugging through a labyrinth of wholesalers, distributors, brokers, and consolidators.[52] With inefficiencies like these, it is no wonder that experts call market logistics "the last frontier for cost economies." Lower market-logistics costs will permit lower prices, yield higher profit margins, or both. Even though the cost of market logistics can be high, a well-planned program can be a potent tool in competitive marketing. Companies can attract additional customers by offering better service, faster cycle time, or lower prices through market-logistics improvements.

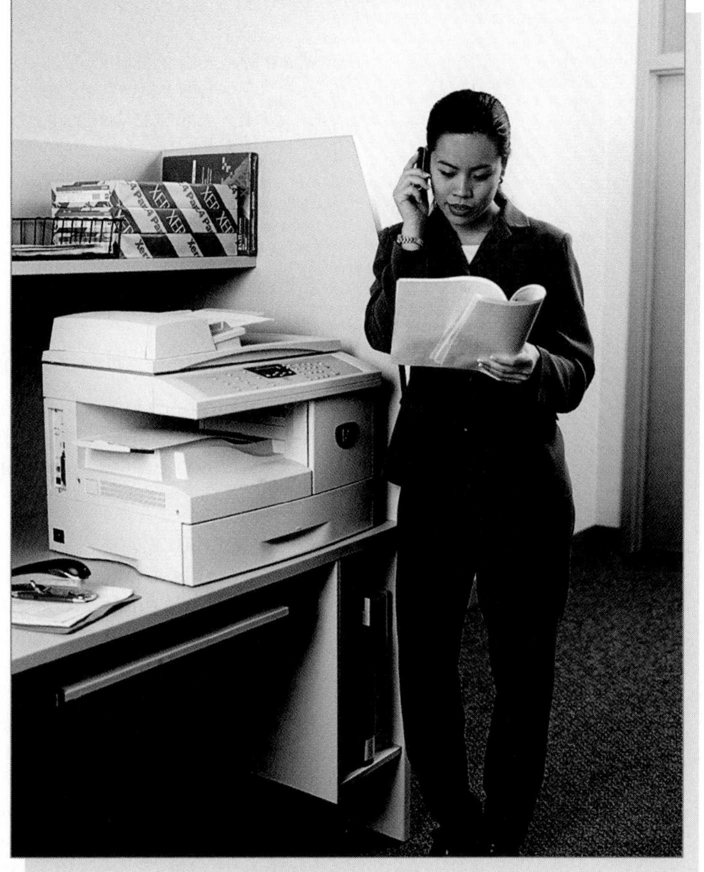

Xerox serviceperson checking with the home office on a repair call. Xerox's service standard is to put a disabled machine back in operation within three hours after receiving a call.

Market-Logistics Objectives

Many companies state their market-logistics objective as "getting the right goods to the right places at the right time for the least cost." Unfortunately, this objective provides little practical guidance. No system can simultaneously maximize customer service and minimize distribution cost. Maximum customer service implies large inventories, premium transportation, and multiple warehouses, all of which raise market-logistics costs.

A company cannot achieve market-logistics efficiency by asking each market-logistics manager to minimize his or her own logistics costs. Market-logistics costs interact and are often negatively related. For example:

- The traffic manager favors rail shipment over air shipment because rail costs less. However, because the railroads are slower, rail shipment ties up working capital longer, delays customer payment, and might cause customers to buy from competitors who offer faster service.
- The shipping department uses cheap containers to minimize shipping costs. Cheaper containers lead to a higher rate of damaged goods and customer ill will.
- The inventory manager favors low inventories. This increases stockouts, back orders, paperwork, special production runs, and high-cost, fast-freight shipments.

Given that market-logistics activities involve strong trade-offs, decisions must be made on a total system basis. The starting point is to study what customers require and what competitors are offering. Customers are interested in on-time delivery, supplier willingness to meet emergency needs, careful handling of merchandise, supplier willingness to take back defective goods and resupply them quickly.

The company must then research the relative importance of these service outputs. For example, service-repair time is very important to buyers of copying equipment. Xerox developed a service delivery standard that "can put a disabled machine anywhere in the continental United States back into operation within three hours after receiving the service request." It then designed a service division of personnel, parts, and locations to deliver on this promise.

The company must also consider competitors' service standards. It will normally want to match or exceed the competitors' service level, but the objective is to maximize profits, not sales. The company has to look at the costs of providing higher levels of service. Some companies offer less service and charge a lower price; other companies offer more service and charge a premium price.

The company ultimately has to establish some promise to the market. Coca-Cola wants to "put Coke within an arm's length of desire." Lands' End, the giant clothing retailer, aims to respond to every phone call within 20 seconds, and to ship out every order within 24 hours of its receipt. Some companies define standards for each service factor. One appliance manufacturer has established the following service standards: to deliver at least 95 percent of the dealer's orders within seven days of order receipt, to fill the dealer's orders with 99 percent accuracy, to answer dealer inquiries on order status within three hours, and to ensure that damage to merchandise in transit does not exceed 1 percent.

Given the market-logistics objectives, the company must design a system that will minimize the cost of achieving these objectives. Each possible market-logistics system will lead to the following cost:

$$M = T + FW + VW + S$$

where M = total market-logistics cost of proposed system
T = total freight cost of proposed system
FW = total fixed warehouse cost of proposed system
VW = total variable warehouse costs (including inventory) of proposed system
S = total cost of lost sales due to average delivery delay under proposed system

Choosing a market-logistics system calls for examining the total cost *(M)* associated with different proposed systems and selecting the system that minimizes it. If it is hard to measure *S*, the company should aim to minimize $T + FW + VW$ for a target level of customer service.

Market-Logistics Decisions

Four major decisions must be made with regard to market logistics: (1) How should orders be handled? (order processing); (2) Where should stocks be located? (warehousing); (3) How much stock should be held? (inventory); and (4) How should goods be shipped? (transportation).

ORDER PROCESSING Most companies today are trying to shorten the *order-to-payment cycle*—that is, the elapsed time between an order's receipt, delivery, and payment. This cycle involves many steps, including order transmission by the salesperson, order entry and customer credit check, inventory and production scheduling, order and invoice shipment, and receipt of payment. The longer this cycle takes, the lower the customer's satisfaction and the lower the company's profits. Salespeople may be slow in sending in orders and use inefficient communications; these orders may pile up on the desk of order processors while they wait for credit department approval and inventory availability information from the warehouse.

Companies need to prepare criteria for the Perfect Order. Suppose the customer expects on-time delivery, order completeness, picking accuracy, and billing accuracy. Suppose the supplier has a 70 percent chance of delivering all four of these perfectly on any order. Then the probability that the supplier will fulfill perfect orders five times in a row to that customer would be $.70^5 = .168$. The customer's series of disappointments is likely to lead him to drop this supplier. A 70 percent standard is not good enough.

Companies are making progress, however. For example, General Electric operates an information system that checks the customer's credit standing upon receipt of an order, and determines whether and where the items are in stock. The computer issues an order to ship, bills the customer, updates the inventory records, sends a production order for new stock, and relays the message back to the sales representative that the customer's order is on its way—all in less than 15 seconds.

WAREHOUSING Every company has to store finished goods until they are sold, because production and consumption cycles rarely match. The storage function helps to smooth discrepancies between production and quantities desired by the market. The company must decide on the number of inventory stocking locations. Consumer-packaged-goods companies have been reducing their number of stocking locations from 10–15 to about 5–7; and pharmaceutical and medical distributors have cut their stocking locations from 90 to about 45. On the one hand, more stocking locations means that goods can be delivered to customers more quickly, but it also means higher warehousing and inventory costs. To reduce warehousing and inventory duplication costs, the company might centralize its inventory in one place and use fast transportation to fulfill orders. After National Semiconductor shut down its six storage warehouses and set up a central distribution warehouse in Singapore, its standard delivery time decreased by 47 percent, its distribution costs fell 2.5 percent, and its sales increased 34 percent.[53]

Some inventory is kept at or near the plant, and the rest is located in warehouses in other locations. The company might own private warehouses and also rent space in public warehouses. *Storage warehouses* store goods for moderate to long periods of time. *Distribution warehouses* receive goods from various company plants and suppliers and move them out as soon as possible. *Automated warehouses* employ advanced materials-handling systems under the control of a central computer. When the Helene Curtis Company replaced its six antiquated warehouses with a new $32 million facility, it cut its distribution costs by 40 percent.[54]

Some warehouses are now taking on activities formerly done in the plant. These include assembly, packaging, and constructing promotional displays. "Postponing" finalization of the offering can achieve savings in costs and finer matching of offerings to demand.

INVENTORY Inventory levels represent a major cost. Salespeople would like their companies to carry enough stock to fill all customer orders immediately. However, this is not cost-effective. *Inventory cost increases at an accelerating rate as the customer service level approaches 100 percent.* Management needs to know how much sales and profits would increase as a result of carrying larger inventories and promising faster order fulfillment times, and then make a decision.

Inventory decision making involves knowing when to order and how much to order. As inventory draws down, management must know at what stock level to place a new order. This stock level is called the *order (reorder) point.* An order point of 20 means reordering when the stock falls to 20 units. The order point should balance the risks of stockout against the costs of overstock. The other decision is how much to order. The larger the quantity ordered, the less frequently an order has to be placed. The company needs to balance order-processing costs and inventory-carrying costs. *Order-processing costs* for a manufacturer consist of *setup costs* and *running costs* (operating costs when production is running) for the item. If setup costs are low, the manufacturer can produce the item often, and the average cost per item is stable and equal to the running costs. If setup costs are high, however, the manufacturer can reduce the average cost per unit by producing a long run and carrying more inventory.

Order-processing costs must be compared with *inventory-carrying costs.* The larger the average stock carried, the higher the inventory-carrying costs. These carrying costs include storage charges, cost of capital, taxes and insurance, and depreciation and obsolescence. Carrying costs might run as high as 30 percent of inventory value. This means that marketing managers who want their companies to carry larger inventories need to show that the larger inventories would produce incremental gross profits to exceed incremental carrying costs.

FIG. 16.2

Determining Optimal Order Quantity

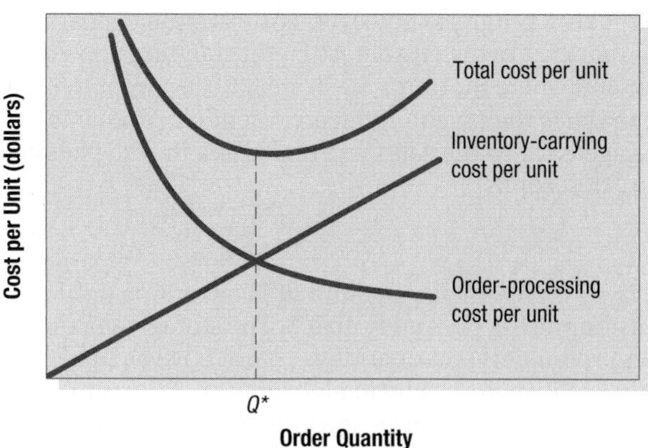

The optimal order quantity can be determined by observing how order-processing costs and inventory-carrying costs sum up at different order levels. Figure 16.2 shows that the order-processing cost per unit decreases with the number of units ordered because the order costs are spread over more units. Inventory-carrying charges per unit increase with the number of units ordered because each unit remains longer in inventory. The two cost curves are summed vertically into a total-cost curve. The lowest point on the total-cost curve is projected down on the horizontal axis to find the optimal order quantity Q^*.[55]

Companies are reducing their inventory costs by treating inventory items differently. They are positioning inventory items according to risk and opportunity. They distinguish between bottleneck items (high risk, low opportunity), critical items (high risk, high opportunity), commodities (low risk, high opportunity), and nuisance items (low risk, low opportunity).[56] They are also keeping slow-moving items in a central location while carrying fast-moving items in warehouses closer to customers.

The ultimate answer to carrying *near-zero inventory* is to build for order, not for stock. Sony calls it SOMA, "sell-one, make-one." Dell, for example, gets the customer to order a computer and pay for it in advance. Then Dell uses the customer's money to pay suppliers to ship the necessary components. As long as customers do not need the item immediately, everyone can save money.

Some retailers are using eBay to unload excess inventory. At least a half a dozen big chains have set up "eBay Stores," Web pages devoted to their merchandise. They use the pages to auction off an assortment of items ranging from overstock goods to returned, reconditioned, or slightly damaged products. By cutting out the traditional liquidator middleman, retailers can make 60 to 80 cents on the dollar as opposed to 10 cents on the dollar. Among those who have hung out their eBay shingles are Sharper Image, Sears, Ritz Camera, and Best Buy.[57]

TRANSPORTATION Marketers need to be concerned with transportation decisions. Transportation choices will affect product pricing, on-time delivery performance, and the condition of the goods when they arrive, all of which affects customer satisfaction.

In shipping goods to its warehouses, dealers, and customers, the company can choose among five transportation modes: rail, air, truck, waterway, and pipeline. Shippers consider such criteria as speed, frequency, dependability, capability, availability, traceability, and cost. For speed, air, rail, and truck are the prime contenders. If the goal is low cost, then it is water and pipeline.

Shippers are increasingly combining two or more transportation modes, thanks to containerization. **Containerization** consists of putting the goods in boxes or trailers that are easy to transfer between two transportation modes. *Piggyback* describes the use of rail and trucks; *fishyback,* water and trucks; *trainship,* water and rail; and *airtruck,* air and trucks. Each coordinated mode offers specific advantages. For example, piggyback is cheaper than trucking alone, yet provides flexibility and convenience.

In deciding on transportation modes, shippers can choose from private, contract, and common carriers. If the shipper owns its own truck or air fleet, the shipper becomes a *private carrier.* A *contract carrier* is an independent organization selling transportation services to others on a contract basis. A *common carrier* provides services between predetermined points on a scheduled basis and is available to all shippers at standard rates.

Today billions of dollars are being invested to develop "last-mile delivery systems" to bring products to homes within a short delivery period. Domino's Pizza organized its franchised stores to be in locations where it could promise to deliver hot pizzas to homes within one-half hour. Consumers may soon think twice about whether they should exert themselves to travel to stores to get their food, videos, or clothes or simply ask the stores to bring it to them in about the same amount of time.

Mexico City: Domino's deliveryperson speeds hot pizza to waiting customers.

Organizational Lessons

Experience with market logistics has taught executives three major lessons:

1. Companies should appoint a senior vice president of logistics to be the single point of contact for all logistical elements. This executive should be accountable for logistical performance on both cost and customer satisfaction criteria.
2. The senior vice president of logistics should hold periodic meetings (weekly, biweekly) with sales and operations people to review inventory, operating costs, and customer service and satisfaction, as well as to consider market conditions and whether changes should be made in production schedules.
3. New software and systems are the key to achieving competitively superior logistics performance in the future.

Market-logistics strategies must be derived from business strategies, rather than solely from cost considerations. The logistics system must be information-intensive and establish electronic links among all the significant parties. Finally, the company should set its logistics goals to match or exceed competitors' service standards and should involve members of all relevant teams in the planning process.

What happens if a firm's market logistics are not set up properly? Kodak launched a national advertising campaign for a new instant camera before it had delivered enough cameras to the stores. Customers found that it was not available and bought Polaroid cameras instead.

Today's stronger demands for logistical support from large customers will increase suppliers' costs. Customers want more frequent deliveries so that they do not have to carry as much inventory. They want shorter order-cycle times, which means that suppliers will have to carry high in-stock availability. Customers often want direct store delivery rather than shipments to distribution centers. They want mixed pallets rather than separate pallets. They want tighter promised delivery times. They may want custom packaging, price tagging, and display building.

Suppliers cannot say no to many of these requests, but at least they can set up different logistical programs with different service levels and customer charges. Smart companies will adjust their offerings to each major customer's requirements. The company's trade group will set up *differentiated distribution* by offering different bundled service programs for different customers.

SUMMARY :::

1. Retailing includes all the activities involved in selling goods or services directly to final consumers for personal, nonbusiness use. Retailers can be understood in terms of store retailing, nonstore retailing, and retail organizations.
2. Like products, retail-store types pass through stages of growth and decline. As existing stores offer more services to remain competitive, costs and prices go up, which opens the door to new retail forms that offer a mix of merchandise and services at lower prices. The major types of retail stores are specialty stores; department stores; supermarkets; convenience stores; discount stores; off-price retailers (factory outlets, independent off-price retailers, and warehouse clubs); superstores (combination stores and supermarkets); and catalog showrooms.
3. Although most goods and services are sold through stores, nonstore retailing has been growing. The major types of nonstore retailing are direct selling (one-to-one selling, one-to-many-party selling, and multilevel network marketing); direct marketing (which includes e-commerce and Internet retailing); automatic vending; and buying services.
4. Although many retail stores are independently owned, an increasing number are falling under some form of corporate retailing. Retail organizations achieve many economies of scale, such as greater purchasing power, wider brand recognition, and better-trained employees. The major types of corporate retailing are corporate chain stores, voluntary chains, retailer cooperatives, consumer cooperatives, franchise organizations, and merchandising conglomerates.
5. Like all marketers, retailers must prepare marketing plans that include decisions on target markets, product assortment and procurement, services and store atmosphere, price, promotion, and place. These decisions must take into account major trends, such as the growth of private labels, new retail forms and combinations, growth of intertype retail competition, competition between store-based and non-store-based retailing, growth of giant retailers, decline of middle-market retailers, growing investment in technology, and global presence of major retailers.
6. Wholesaling includes all the activities involved in selling goods or services to those who buy for resale or business use. Wholesalers can perform functions better and more cost-effectively than the manufacturer can. These functions include selling and promoting, buying and assortment building, bulk breaking, warehousing, transportation, financing, risk bearing, dissemination of market information, and provision of management services and consulting.
7. There are four types of wholesalers: merchant wholesalers; brokers and agents; manufacturers' and retailers' sales branches, sales offices, and purchasing offices; and miscellaneous wholesalers such as agricultural assemblers and auction companies.
8. Like retailers, wholesalers must decide on target markets, product assortment and services, price, promotion, and place. The most successful wholesalers are those who adapt their services to meet suppliers' and target customers' needs.
9. Producers of physical products and services must decide on market logistics—the best way to store and move goods and services to market destinations; to coordinate the activities of suppliers, purchasing agents, manufacturers, marketers, channel members, and customers. Major gains in logistical efficiency have come from advances in information technology.

APPLICATIONS :::

Marketing Debate Should National Brand Manufacturers also Supply Private Label Brands?

One controversial move by some marketers of major brands is to supply private label makers. For example, Ralston-Purina, Borden, ConAgra, and Heinz have all admitted to supplying products—sometimes lower in quality—to be used for private labels. Other marketers, however, criticize this "if you can't beat them, join them" strategy, maintaining that these actions, if revealed, may create confusion or even reinforce a perception by consumers that all brands in a category are essentially the same.

Take a position: Manufacturers should feel free to sell private labels as a source of revenue versus National manufacturers should never get involved with private labels.

Marketing Discussion

Think of your favorite stores. What do they do that encourages your loyalty? What do you like about the in-store experience?

PART

7

COMMUNICATING VALUE

LET'S MESS WITH PERFECTION. Let's Daniel Boone-flag it. Let's fla
paint it. Let's detail it. Let's whale tail it. Let's fuzzy dice it. Let's trick it c
Let's spoiler kit it. Let's mirror tint it. Let's whitewall it. Let's hot rod it. Le
lower it. Let's raise it. Let's do nothing. Let's do whatever. **LET'S MOTO**

11223344556677880

MINI

IN THIS CHAPTER, WE WILL ADDRESS THE FOLLOWING QUESTIONS:

1. What is the role of marketing communications?
2. How do marketing communications work?
3. What are the major steps in developing effective communications?
4. What is the communications mix and how should it be set?
5. What is an integrated marketing communications program?

CHAPTER 17 ::: DESIGNING AND MANAGING INTEGRATED MARKETING COMMUNICATIONS

seventeen

Modern marketing calls for more than developing a good product, pricing it attractively, and making it accessible. Companies must also communicate with present and potential stakeholders, and the general public. For most companies, the question is not whether to communicate but rather what to say, how to say it, to whom, and how often. But communications get harder and harder as more and more companies clamor to grab the consumer's increasingly divided attention. To reach target markets and build brand equity, holistic marketers are creatively employing multiple forms of communications.[1] In introducing the Mini, for example, BMW did not even use TV advertising.

The tiny Mini automobile was sold for only seven years in the United States, during the 1960s, before it was withdrawn due to stiff emission regulations. In March 2002, BMW decided to relaunch a new, modernized Mini Cooper in the United States, targeting hip city dwellers who wanted a cool, fun, small car for under $20,000. With only $20 million to spend on the introduction, the Mini marketers decided to launch a guerrilla communications campaign featuring nontraditional uses of billboards, posters, print ads, and grassroots efforts. No TV ads. The Mini was stacked on top of three Ford Excursion SUVs and driven around national auto shows and 21 major cities. The car showed up in other unusual places such as inside >>>

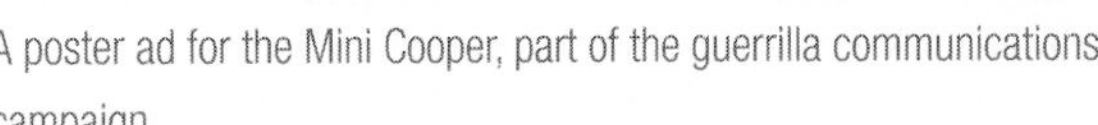

A poster ad for the Mini Cooper, part of the guerrilla communications campaign.

a sports stadium as seats and inside Playboy as a centerfold. Text-only billboards proclaimed: "THE SUV BACKLASH OFFICIALLY STARTS NOW," "GOLIATH LOST," and "XXL-XL-L-M-S-MINI." Many communications were linked to a cleverly designed Web site that provided necessary product information. The imaginative campaign resulted in a buyer waiting list that was six months long in spring 2002.[2]

Marketing communications can have a huge payoff. This chapter describes how communications work and what marketing communications can do for a company. It also addresses how holistic marketers combine and integrate marketing communications. Chapter 18 examines the different forms of mass (nonpersonal) communications (advertising, sales promotion, events and experiences, and public relations and publicity); Chapter 19 examines the different forms of personal communications (direct marketing, including e-commerce, and personal selling).

::: The Role of Marketing Communications

Marketing communications are the means by which firms attempt to inform, persuade, and remind consumers—directly or indirectly—about the products and brands that they sell. In a sense, marketing communications represent the "voice" of the brand and are a means by which it can establish a dialogue and build relationships with consumers.

Marketing communications perform many functions for consumers. Consumers can be told or shown how and why a product is used, by what kind of person, and where and when; consumers can learn about who makes the product and what the company and brand stand for; and consumers can be given an incentive or reward for trial or usage. Marketing communications allow companies to link their brands to other people, places, events, brands, experiences, feelings, and things. Marketing communications can contribute to brand equity by establishing the brand in memory and crafting a brand image.

Marketing Communications and Brand Equity

Although advertising is often a central element of a marketing communications program, it is usually not the only one—or even the most important one—in terms of building brand equity. The **marketing communications mix** consists of six major modes of communication:[3]

1. ***Advertising*** – Any paid form of nonpersonal presentation and promotion of ideas, goods, or services by an identified sponsor.
2. ***Sales promotion*** – A variety of short-term incentives to encourage trial or purchase of a product or service.
3. ***Events and experiences*** – Company-sponsored activities and programs designed to create daily or special brand-related interactions.
4. ***Public relations and publicity*** – A variety of programs designed to promote or protect a company's image or its individual products.
5. ***Direct marketing*** – Use of mail, telephone, fax, e-mail, or Internet to communicate directly with or solicit response or dialogue from specific customers and prospects.
6. ***Personal selling*** – Face-to-face interaction with one or more prospective purchasers for the purpose of making presentations, answering questions, and procuring orders.

Table 17.1 lists numerous communication platforms. Company communication goes beyond those specific platforms. The product's styling and price, the shape and color of the package, the salesperson's manner and dress, the store décor, the company's stationery—all

TABLE 17.1 | Common Communication Platforms

Advertising	Sales Promotion	Events/Experiences	Public Relations	Personal Selling	Direct Marketing
Print and broadcast ads	Contests, games, sweepstakes, lotteries	Sports	Press kits	Sales presentations	Catalogs
Packaging–outer	Premiums and gifts	Entertainment	Speeches	Sales meetings	Mailings
Packaging inserts	Sampling	Festivals	Seminars	Incentive programs	Telemarketing
Motion pictures	Fairs and trade shows	Arts	Annual reports	Samples	Electronic shopping
Brochures and booklets	Exhibits	Causes	Charitable donations	Fairs and trade shows	TV shopping
Posters and leaflets	Demonstrations	Factory tours	Publications		Fax mail
Directories	Coupons	Company museums	Community relations		E-mail
Reprints of ads	Rebates	Street activities	Lobbying		Voice mail
Billboards	Low-interest financing		Identity media		
Display signs	Entertainment		Company magazine		
Point-of-purchase displays	Trade-in allowances				
Audiovisual material	Continuity programs				
Symbols and logos	Tie-ins				
Videotapes					

communicate something to buyers. Every *brand contact* delivers an impression that can strengthen or weaken a customer's view of the company.

As Figure 17.1 shows, marketing communications activities contribute to brand equity in many ways: by creating awareness of the brand; linking the right associations to the brand image in consumers' memory; eliciting positive brand judgments or feelings; and/or facilitating a stronger consumer–brand connection.

One implication of the concept of brand equity is that the manner in which brand associations are formed does not matter. In other words, if a consumer has an equally strong, favorable, and unique brand association of Subaru with the concepts "outdoors," "active,"

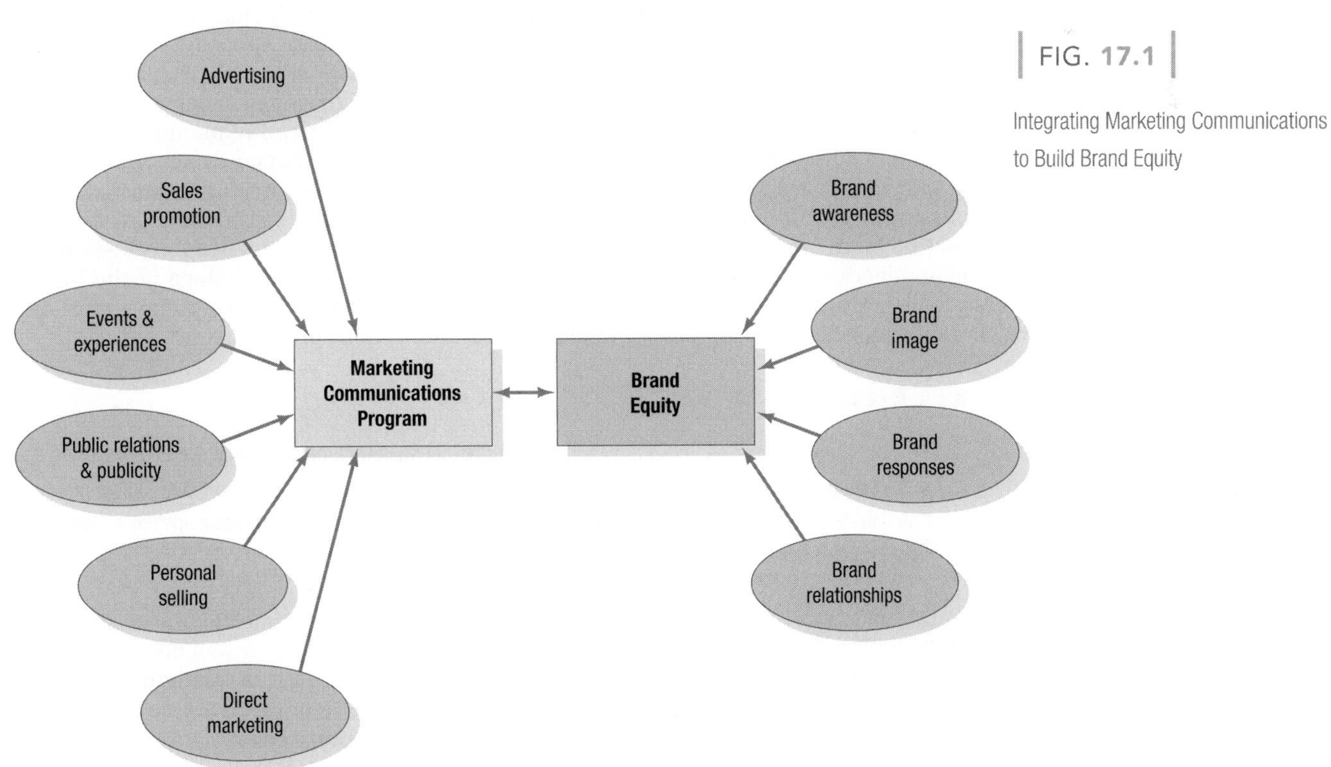

FIG. 17.1 | Integrating Marketing Communications to Build Brand Equity

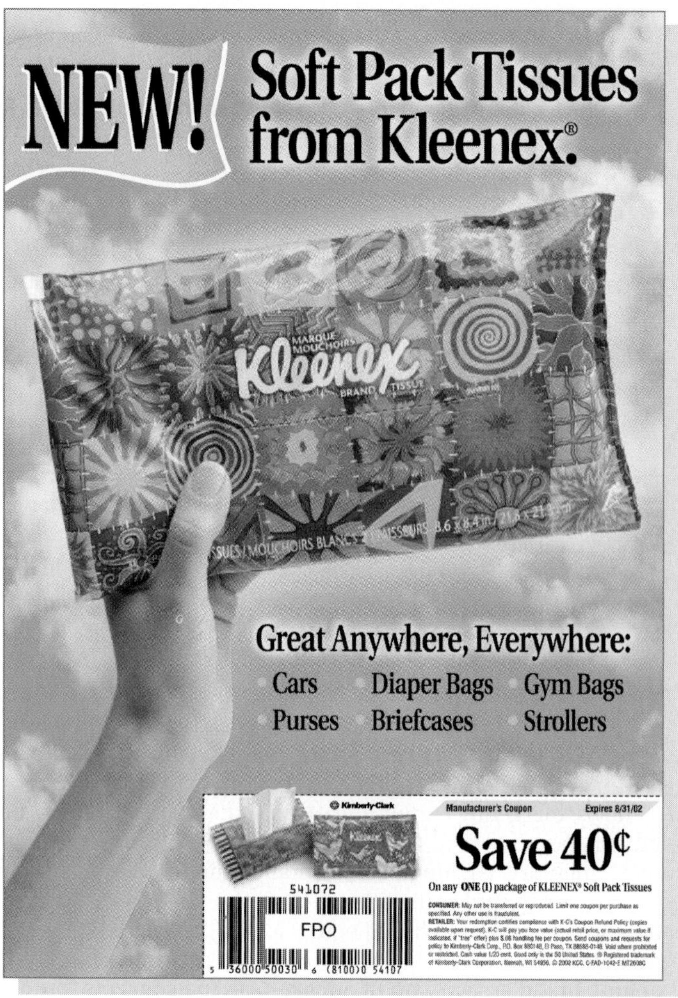

A magazine ad, with coupon, for Kleenex® Soft Pack Tissues.

and "rugged" because of exposure to a TV ad that shows the car driving over rugged terrain at different times of the year, or because of the fact that Subaru sponsors ski, kayak, and mountain bike events, the impact in terms of brand equity should be identical.

But these marketing communications activities must be integrated to deliver a consistent message and achieve the strategic positioning. The starting point in planning marketing communications is an audit of all the potential interactions that customers in the target market may have with the brand and the company. For example, someone interested in purchasing a new computer might talk to others, see television ads, read articles, look for information on the Internet, and look at computers in a store. Marketers need to assess which experiences and impressions will have the most influence at each stage of the buying process. This understanding will help them allocate communications dollars more efficiently and design and implement the right communications programs.

KLEENEX SOFT PACK

To launch its new Kleenex Soft Pack product, Kimberly-Clark budgeted 75 percent of its overall advertising dollars to television, 23 percent for print, and 2 percent online to build awareness and drive trial. Online ads were found to help reach an audience that TV might have overlooked, and online and magazine ads were found to be the most effective mix for brand awareness.[4]

Armed with these insights, marketers can judge marketing communications according to its ability to build brand equity and drive brand sales. For example, how well does a proposed ad campaign contribute to awareness or to creating, maintaining, or strengthening brand associations? Does a sponsorship cause consumers to have more favorable brand judgments and feelings? To what extent does a promotion encourage consumers to buy more of a product? At what price premium?

From the perspective of building brand equity, marketers should evaluate *all* the different possible communication options according to effectiveness criteria (how well does it work) as well as efficiency considerations (how much does it cost). This broad view of brand-building activities is especially relevant when marketers are considering strategies to improve brand awareness.

Brand awareness is a function of the number of brand-related exposures and experiences accumulated by the consumer.[5] *Anything* that causes the consumer to notice and pay attention to the brand can increase brand awareness, at least in terms of brand recognition. The visibility of the brand typically found with sponsorships suggests that these activities may be especially valuable for enhancing brand recognition. To enhance brand recall, however, more intense and elaborate processing may be necessary so that stronger brand links to the product category or consumer needs are established to improve memory performance.

Similarly, because brand associations, responses, and relationships can be created in many different ways, *all* possible marketing communication options should be considered to create the desired brand image and knowledge.

BOSTON SYMPHONY ORCHESTRA INC.

With classical music audiences dwindling to a small core of older and more affluent concertgoers, the Boston Symphony Orchestra (BSO) knew that it had to revamp its advertising to reach new audiences through a variety of communications channels. Prior to 1998, the BSO rarely relied on the Internet. But then, through a carefully coordinated series of market research efforts that included detailed surveys and focus groups, it discovered that while there was little difference between older and younger audiences when it came to product interest, there was a big gap in terms of media preferences. The older concertgoers were more avid readers of both books and magazines while younger people were more involved with the Internet and electronic media. The BSO developed an integrated campaign that combined direct mail, e-mail marketing, customized online infomercials, and taxi-top ads. As a result, it increased online revenues from tickets and other sales to $3.7 million in fiscal year 2002, up from $320,000 in fiscal year 1997. Total sales reached $19 million in 2002, up from $16.7 million in 1997.[6]

The Communications Process Models

Marketers should understand the fundamental elements of effective communications. Two models are useful: a macromodel and a micromodel.

MACROMODEL OF THE COMMUNICATIONS PROCESS Figure 17.2 shows a communications macromodel with nine elements. Two represent the major parties in a communication—*sender* and *receiver.* Two represent the major communication tools—*message* and *media.* Four represent major communication functions—*encoding, decoding, response,* and *feedback.* The last element in the system is *noise* (random and competing messages that may interfere with the intended communication).[7]

The model emphasizes the key factors in effective communication. Senders must know what audiences they want to reach and what responses they want to get. They must encode their messages so that the target audience can decode them. They must transmit the message through media that reach the target audience and develop feedback channels to monitor the responses. The more the sender's field of experience overlaps with that of the receiver, the more effective the message is likely to be.

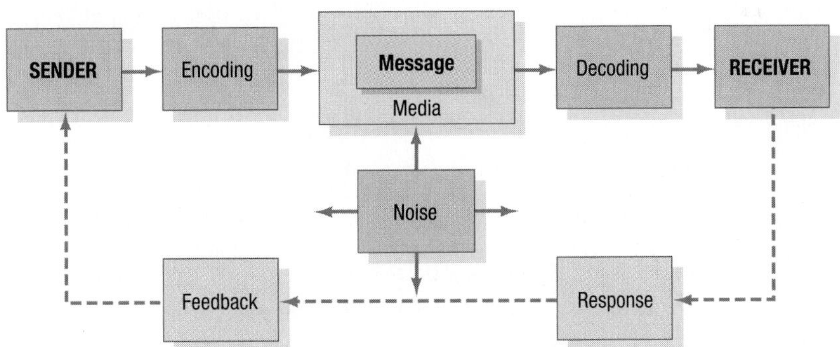

FIG. 17.2

Elements in the Communications Process

Note that selective attention, distortion, and retention processes—concepts first introduced in Chapter 6—may be operating during communication, as follows.

1. ***Selective attention*** – People are bombarded by about 1,500 commercial messages a day, which explains why advertisers sometimes go to great lengths to grab audience attention through fear, music, or sex appeals, or bold headlines promising something, such as "How to Make a Million." Ad clutter is also a major obstacle to gaining attention—noneditorial or programming content ranges from 25 to 33 percent for TV and radio to over 50 percent for magazines and newspapers.
2. ***Selective distortion*** – Receivers will hear what fits into their belief systems. As a result, receivers often add things to the message that are not there (amplification) and do not notice other things that are there (leveling). The task is to strive for simplicity, clarity, interest, and repetition to get the main points across.
3. ***Selective retention*** – People will retain in long-term memory only a small fraction of the messages that reach them. If the receiver's initial attitude toward the object is positive and he or she rehearses support arguments, the message is likely to be accepted and have high recall. If the initial attitude is negative and the person rehearses counterarguments, the message is likely to be rejected but to stay in long-term memory. Because persuasion requires the receiver's rehearsal of his or her own thoughts, much of what is called persuasion is actually self-persuasion.[8]

MICROMODEL OF CONSUMER RESPONSES Micromodels of marketing communications concentrate on consumers' specific responses to communications. Figure 17.3 summarizes four classic *response hierarchy models.*

All these models assume that the buyer passes through a cognitive, affective, and behavioral stage, in that order. This "learn-feel-do" sequence is appropriate when the audience has high involvement with a product category perceived to have high differentiation, as in purchasing an automobile or house. An alternative sequence, "do-feel-learn," is relevant when the audience has high involvement but perceives little or no differentiation within the product category, as in purchasing an airline ticket or personal computer. A third sequence, "learn-do-feel," is relevant when the audience has low involvement and perceives little differentiation within the product category, as in purchasing salt or batteries. By choosing the right sequence, the marketer can do a better job of planning communications.[9]

Here we will assume that the buyer has high involvement with the product category and perceives high differentiation within the category. We will illustrate the *hierarchy-of-effects model* (in the second column of Figure 17.3) in the context of a marketing communications campaign for a small Iowa college named Pottsville:

FIG. 17.3

Response Hierarchy Models

Sources: [a]E. K. Strong. *The Psychology of Selling* (New York: McGraw-Hill. 1925), p. 9;[b]Robert J. Lavidge and Gary A. Steiner, "A Model for Predictive Measurements of Advertising Effectiveness," *Journal of Marketing* (October 1961): 61; [c]Everett M. Rogers, *Diffusion of Innovation* (New York: The Free Press, 1962), pp. 79–86; [d]various sources.

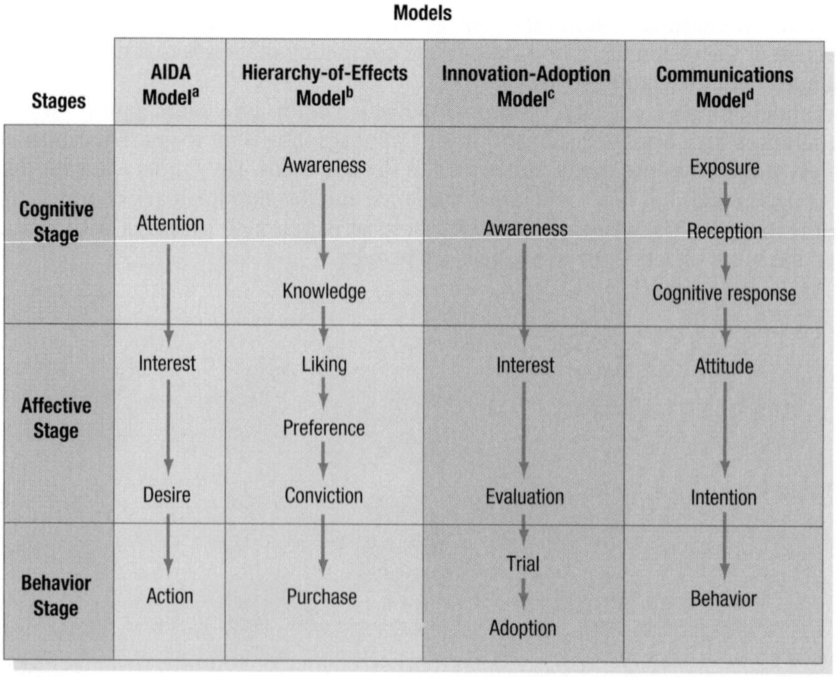

Models

Stages	AIDA Model[a]	Hierarchy-of-Effects Model[b]	Innovation-Adoption Model[c]	Communications Model[d]
Cognitive Stage	Attention	Awareness ↓ Knowledge	Awareness	Exposure ↓ Reception ↓ Cognitive response
Affective Stage	Interest ↓ Desire	Liking ↓ Preference ↓ Conviction	Interest ↓ Evaluation	Attitude ↓ Intention
Behavior Stage	Action	Purchase	Trial ↓ Adoption	Behavior

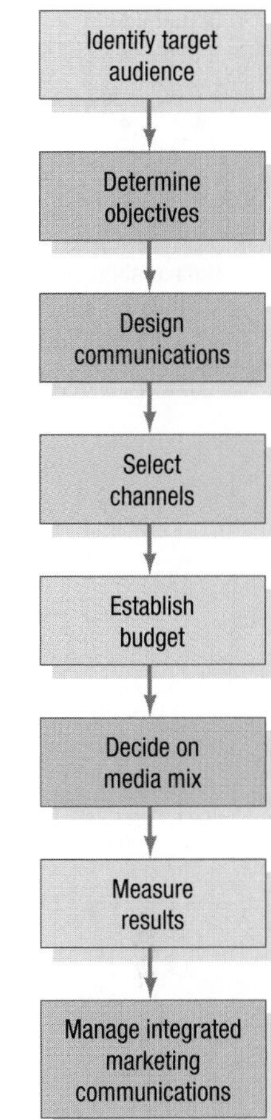

FIG. 17.4

Steps in Developing Effective Communications

- ***Awareness.*** If most of the target audience is unaware of the object, the communicator's task is to build awareness. Suppose Pottsville seeks applicants from Nebraska but has no name recognition there. Suppose there are 30,000 high school juniors and seniors in Nebraska who may potentially be interested in Pottsville College. The college might set the objective of making 70 percent of these students aware of Pottsville's name within one year.
- ***Knowledge.*** The target audience might have brand awareness but not know much more. Pottsville may want its target audience to know that it is a private four-year college with excellent programs in English, foreign languages, and history. It needs to learn how many people in the target audience have little, some, or much knowledge about Pottsville. If knowledge is weak, Pottsville may decide to select brand knowledge as its communications objective.
- ***Liking.*** If target members know the brand, how do they feel about it? If the audience looks unfavorably on Pottsville College, the communicator has to find out why. If the unfavorable view is based on real problems, Pottsville will have to fix its problems and then communicate its renewed quality. Good public relations calls for "good deeds followed by good words."
- ***Preference.*** The target audience might like the product but not prefer it to others. In this case, the communicator must try to build consumer preference by comparing quality, value, performance, and other features to likely competitors.
- ***Conviction.*** A target audience might prefer a particular product but not develop a conviction about buying it. The communicator's job is to build conviction and purchase intent among students interested in Pottsville College.
- ***Purchase.*** Finally, some members of the target audience might have conviction but may not quite get around to making the purchase. The communicator must lead these consumers to take the final step, perhaps by offering the product at a low price, offering a premium, or letting consumers try it out. Pottsville might invite selected high school students to visit the campus and attend some classes, or it might offer partial scholarships to deserving students.

To show how fragile the whole communications process is, assume that the probability of *each* of the six steps being successfully accomplished is 50 percent. The laws of probability suggest that the probability of *all* six steps occurring successfully, assuming they are independent events, would be $.5 \times .5 \times .5 \times .5 \times .5 \times .5$, which equals 1.5625 percent. If the probability of each step occurring, on average, was a more moderate 10 percent, then the joint probability of all six events occurring would be .0001; in other words, only 1 in 10,000!

To increase the odds for a successful marketing communications campaign, marketers must attempt to increase the likelihood that *each* step occurs. For example, from an advertising standpoint, the ideal ad campaign would ensure that:

1. The right consumer is exposed to the right message at the right place and at the right time.
2. The ad causes the consumer to pay attention to the ad but does not distract from the intended message.
3. The ad properly reflects the consumer's level of understanding about the product and the brand.
4. The ad correctly positions the brand in terms of desirable and deliverable points-of-difference and points-of-parity.
5. The ad motivates consumers to consider purchase of the brand.
6. The ad creates strong brand associations with all of these stored communications effects so that they can have an impact when consumers are considering making a purchase.

::: Developing Effective Communications

Figure 17.4 shows the eight steps in developing effective communications. We begin with the basics: identifying the target audience, determining the objectives, designing the communications, selecting the channels, and establishing the budget.

Identify the Target Audience

The process must start with a clear target audience in mind: potential buyers of the company's products, current users, deciders, or influencers; individuals, groups, particular publics, or the general public. The target audience is a critical influence on the communicator's decisions on what to say, how to say it, when to say it, where to say it, and to whom to say it.

The target audience can potentially be profiled in terms of any the market segments identified in Chapter 8. It is often useful to define target audience in terms of usage and loyalty.

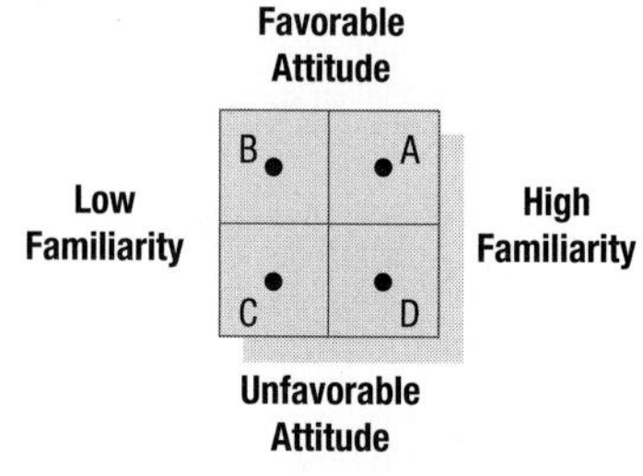

FIG. 17.5

Familiarity–Favorability Analysis

Is the target new to the category or a current user? Is the target loyal to the brand, loyal to a competitor, or someone who switches between brands? If the target is a brand user, is he or she a heavy or light user? Communication strategy will differ depending on the usage and loyalty involved. *Image analysis* can be conducted to profile the target audience in terms of brand knowledge to provide further insight.

A major part of audience analysis is assessing the current image of the company, its products, and its competitors. **Image** is the set of beliefs, ideas, and impressions a person holds regarding an object. People's attitudes and actions toward an object are highly conditioned by that object's image.

The first step is to measure the target audience's knowledge of the object, using the *familiarity scale:*

Never Heard of	Heard of Only	Know a Little Bit	Know a Fair Amount	Know Very Well

If most respondents circle only the first two categories, the challenge is to build greater awareness.

Respondents who are familiar with the product can be asked how they feel toward it, using the *favorability scale:*

Very Unfavorable	Somewhat Unfavorable	Indifferent	Somewhat Favorable	Very Favorable

If most respondents circle the first two categories, then the organization must overcome a negative image problem.

The two scales can be combined to develop insight into the nature of the communication challenge. Suppose area residents are asked about their familiarity with and attitudes toward four local hospitals, A, B, C, and D. Their responses are averaged and shown in Figure 17.5. Hospital A has the most positive image: Most people know it and like it. Hospital B is less familiar to most people, but those who know it like it. Hospital C is viewed negatively by those who know it, but (fortunately for the hospital) not too many people know it. Hospital D is seen as a poor hospital, and everyone knows it!

Each hospital faces a different communications task. Hospital A must work at maintaining its good reputation and high awareness. Hospital B must gain the attention of more people. Hospital C must find out why people dislike it and take steps to improve its quality while keeping a low profile. Hospital D should lower its profile, improve its quality, and then seek public attention.

Images are "sticky"; they persist long after the organization has changed. Image persistence is explained by the fact that once people have a certain image, they perceive what is consistent with that image. It will take highly disconfirming information to raise doubts and open their minds, especially when people do not have continuous or new firsthand experiences with the changed object.

HÄAGEN-DAZS

In recent years, the premium ice cream maker has battled an onslaught of new premium brands hampered by the image it acquired back in the 1980s. The brand hired ad agency Goodby, Silverstein and Partners to peel off Häagen-Dazs's sticky image with a new campaign. "The name brought up cheesy luxury and [people] thought of the snobby hedonism of the '80s, like the guy in the ascot leaning against the Bentley," said Goodby's associate creative director Albert Kelly. Goodby developed a campaign that focused on the product's high quality, especially the quality of its ingredients. Two spots, "Strawberry" and "Vanilla," show strawberry fields and vanilla plants with the tagline "Häagen-Dazs. Made Like No Other," in contrast to previous advertising that focused on luxury with lines such as "Pure Pleasure," or "Just Perfect."[10]

Determine the Communications Objectives

As we showed with Pottsville College, communications objectives can be set at any level of the hierarchy-of-effects model. Rossiter and Percy identify four possible objectives, as follows:[11]

1. ***Category Need*** – Establishing a product or service category as necessary to remove or satisfy a perceived discrepancy between a current motivational state and a desired emotional state. A new-to-the-world product such as electric cars would always begin with a communications objective of establishing category need.

Developing creative strategy: This ad for Tilex, a household product, focuses on problem-solution—Tilex is called The Mold Killer™.

2. ***Brand Awareness*** – Ability to identify (recognize or recall) the brand within the category, in sufficient detail to make a purchase. Recognition is easier to achieve than recall—consumers are more likely to recognize Stouffer's distinctive orange packages than recall the brand if asked to think of a brand of frozen entrees. Brand recall is important outside the store; brand recognition is important inside the store. Brand awareness provides a foundation for brand equity.
3. ***Brand Attitude*** – Evaluation of the brand with respect to its perceived ability to meet a currently relevant need. Relevant brand needs may be negatively oriented (problem removal, problem avoidance, incomplete satisfaction, normal depletion) or positively oriented (sensory gratification, intellectual stimulation, or social approval). Household cleaning products often use problem-solution; food products, on the other hand, often use sensory-oriented ads emphasizing appetite appeal.
4. ***Brand Purchase Intention*** – Self-instructions to purchase the brand or to take purchase-related action. Promotional offers in the form of coupons or two-for-one deals encourage consumers to make a mental commitment to buy a product. But many consumers do not have an expressed category need and may not be in the market when exposed to an ad, making intentions less likely to be formed. For example, in any given week, only about 20 percent of adults may be planning to buy detergent; only 2 percent may be planning to buy a carpet cleaner; and only 0.25 percent may be planning to buy a car.

The most effective communications often can achieve multiple objectives. For example, Geico advertises that a 15-minute phone call can result in a 15 percent reduction on auto insurance, combining both brand attitude and a call to action to build brand purchase intentions.

Design the Communications

Formulating the communications to achieve the desired response will require solving three problems: what to say (message strategy), how to say it (creative strategy), and who should say it (message source).

MESSAGE STRATEGY In determining message strategy, management searches for appeals, themes, or ideas that will tie into the brand positioning and help to establish points-of-parity or points-of-difference. Some of these may be related directly to product or service performance (the quality, economy, or value of the brand) whereas others may relate to more extrinsic considerations (the brand as being contemporary, popular, or traditional).

John Maloney saw buyers as expecting one of four types of reward from a product: rational, sensory, social, or ego satisfaction.[12] Buyers might visualize these rewards from results-of-use experience, product-in-use experience, or incidental-to-use experience. Crossing the four types of rewards with the three types of experience generates 12 types of messages. For example, the appeal "gets clothes cleaner" is a rational-reward promise following results-of-use experience. The phrase "real beer taste in a great light beer" is a sensory-reward promise connected with product-in-use experience.

It is widely believed that industrial buyers are most responsive to performance messages. They are knowledgeable about the product, trained to recognize value, and accountable to others for their choices. Consumers, when they buy certain big-ticket items, also tend to gather information and estimate benefits.

CREATIVE STRATEGY Communications effectiveness depends on how a message is being expressed as well as the content of the message itself. An ineffective communication may mean that the wrong message was used or the right message was just being expressed poorly. *Creative strategies* are how marketers translate their messages into a specific communication. Creative strategies can be broadly classified as involving either "informational" or "transformational" appeals.[13] These two general categories each encompass several different specific creative approaches.

Informational Appeals An *informational appeal* elaborates on product or service attributes or benefits. Examples in advertising are problem-solution ads (Excedrin stops headache pain quickly), product demonstration ads (Thompson Water Seal can withstand intense rain, snow, and heat), product comparison ads (Verizon offers better on-line Internet access than Comcast), and testimonials from unknown or celebrity endorsers (NBA phenomenon LeBron James pitching Coca-Cola and Nike). Informational appeals assume very rational processing of the communication on the part of the consumer. Logic and reason rule.

Hovland's research at Yale has shed much light on informational appeals and their relation to such issues as conclusion drawing, one-versus two-sided arguments, and order of argument presentation. Some early experiments supported stating conclusions for the audience. Subsequent research, however, indicates that the best ads ask questions and allow readers and viewers to form their own conclusions.[14] If Honda had hammered away that the Element was for young people, this strong definition might have blocked older age groups from buying it. Some stimulus ambiguity can lead to a broader market definition and more spontaneous purchases.

You would think that one-sided presentations that praise a product would be more effective than two-sided arguments that also mention shortcomings. Yet two-sided messages may be more appropriate, especially when negative associations must be overcome. Heinz ran the message "Heinz Ketchup is slow good" and Listerine ran the message "Listerine tastes bad twice a day."[15] Two-sided messages are more effective with more educated audiences and those who are initially opposed.[16]

Finally, the order in which arguments are presented is important.[17] In the case of a one-sided message, presenting the strongest argument first has the advantage of arousing attention and interest. This is important in media where the audience often does not attend to the whole message. With a captive audience, a climactic presentation might be more effective. In the case of a two-sided message, if the audience is initially opposed, the communicator might start with the other side's argument and conclude with his or her strongest argument.[18]

Transformational Appeals A *transformational appeal* elaborates on a non-product-related benefit or image. It might depict what kind of person uses a brand (VW advertises to active, youthful people with their "Drivers Wanted" campaign) or what kind of experience results from using the brand (Coast soap has been advertised as "The Eye

Opener!"). Transformational appeals often attempt to stir up emotions that will motivate purchase. This is the route Clairol took to revive a moribund brand from the 1970s.

CLAIROL HERBAL ESSENCES

"Yes, Yes, Yes," actresses exclaim as they simulate sexual ecstasy while washing their hair and enjoying what the tag line dubs, "A Truly Organic Experience." Some women find the ad's coy double entendre demeaning. The Advertising Women of New York Club even gave the ad "The Grand Ugly" Award. However, Proctor & Gamble, which acquired Clairol in 2002, credits the ad with bringing the near-dead brand back to life. Herbal Essences became one of the fastest-growing brands in the world, climbing in sales from zero to $700 million in seven years. In explaining its success, the agency creator, The Kaplan Thaler Group, maintains "emotion is the lightning rod, the trigger to making a purchase."[19]

Communicators use negative appeals such as fear, guilt, and shame to get people to do things (brush their teeth, have an annual health checkup) or stop doing things (smoking, alcohol abuse, overeating). Fear appeals work best when they are not too strong. Furthermore, fear appeals work better when source credibility is high and when the communication promises to relieve, in a believable and efficient way, the fear it arouses.[20] Messages are most persuasive when they are moderately discrepant with what the audience believes. Messages that state only what the audience already believes at best only reinforce beliefs, and if the messages are too discrepant, they will be counter-argued and disbelieved.

Communicators also use positive emotional appeals such as humor, love, pride, and joy. Motivational or "borrowed interest" devices—such as the presence of cute babies, frisky puppies, popular music, or provocative sex appeals—are often employed to attract consumer attention and raise their involvement with an ad.

Borrowed interest techniques are thought to be necessary in the tough new media environment characterized by low-involvement consumer processing and much competing ad and programming clutter. In 2003, British singer Sting, who in the 1980s had refused to allow the lyrics of "Don't Stand So Close to Me" to be used in a deodorant ad, made a lucrative deal with Ford Motor Company as part of the company's efforts to reach consumers aged 35 and over. In an ad for Jaguar, he was shown being driven around in the car while his latest single, "Desert Rose," played in the background.[21]

Although these borrowed interest approaches can attract attention and create more liking and belief in the sponsor, they may also detract from comprehension, wear out their welcome fast, and overshadow the product.[22] Attention-getting tactics are often *too* effective and distract from brand or product claims. Thus, one challenge in arriving at the best creative strategy is figuring out how to "break through the clutter" to attract the attention of consumers—but still be able to deliver the intended message.

The magic of advertising is to bring concepts on a piece of paper to life in the minds of the consumer target. In a print ad, the communicator has to decide on headline, copy, illustration, and color. For a radio message, the communicator has to choose words, voice qualities, and vocalizations. The "sound" of an announcer promoting a used automobile has to be different from one promoting a new Cadillac. If the message is to be carried on television or in person, all these elements plus body language (nonverbal clues) have to be planned. Presenters have to pay attention to facial expressions, gestures, dress, posture, and hairstyle. If the message is carried by the product or its packaging, the communicator has to pay attention to color, texture, scent, size, and shape.

Every detail matters. Think how the legendary ad taglines listed on the right were able to bring to life the brand themes listed on the left.

Brand Theme	**Ad Tagline**
Our hamburgers are bigger.	Where's the Beef? (Wendy's restaurants)
Our tissue is softer.	Please, Don't Squeeze the Charmin (Charmin bathroom tissue)
No hard sell, just a good car.	Drivers Wanted (Volkswagen automobiles)
We don't rent as many cars, so we have to do more for our customers.	We Try Harder (Avis auto rental)
We provide long-distance phone service.	Reach Out and Touch Someone (AT&T telecommunications)

MESSAGE SOURCE Many communications do not use a source beyond the company itself. Others use known or unknown people. Messages delivered by attractive or popular sources can potentially achieve higher attention and recall, which is why advertisers often use celebrities as spokespeople. Celebrities are likely to be effective when they personify a key product attribute. Catherine Deneuve's beauty did this for Chanel No. 5 perfume, and Paul Hogan's Aussie ruggedness did this for the Subaru Outback wagon. On the other hand, using James Garner and Cybill Shepherd to sell beef backfired: Garner subsequently had quintuple bypass surgery, and Shepherd proclaimed she was a vegetarian.

What is important is the spokesperson's credibility. What factors underlie source credibility? The three most often identified are expertise, trustworthiness, and likability.[23] *Expertise* is the specialized knowledge the communicator possesses to back the claim. *Trustworthiness* is related to how objective and honest the source is perceived to be. Friends are trusted more than strangers or salespeople, and people who are not paid to endorse a product are viewed as more trustworthy than people who are paid.[24] *Likability* describes the source's attractiveness. Qualities like candor, humor, and naturalness make a source more likable.

The most highly credible source would be a person who scores high on all three dimensions. Pharmaceutical companies want doctors to testify about product benefits because doctors have high credibility. Anti-drug crusaders will use ex-drug addicts because they have higher credibility. Before his death, Dave Thomas, who had folksy appeal and inherent credibility, did over 800 Wendy's commercials in his trademark red tie and short-sleeve shirt.

A well-chosen celebrity endorsement can catapult even the most unlikely product to stardom.

SALTON AND GEORGE FOREMAN

Salton was a little-known manufacturer of oddball appliances that gained temporary fame in the 1950s with its Salton Hot Tray, a must-have item for every bridal registry at the time. In the early 1990s, the company came up with an indoor grill that seemed destined for obscurity until two-time heavyweight champ George Foreman chose to not only endorse it, but partner with the company to sell it. Foreman and his Lean, Mean, Fat-Reducing Grilling Machine proved to be a match made in hamburger heaven. Foreman, now presented as a lovable lug, was renowned for his love of cheeseburgers. A year after the launch, he went on home shopping channel QVC to sell the grills. The camera caught him in an unscripted moment while presenters were chatting, leaving George with nothing to do except look at the sizzling burgers. He took a roll, grabbed one, started eating, and the phone lines began to buzz. Foreman has helped Salton sell more than 40 million grilling machines since the mid-1990s, and because he gets a share of the proceeds, he has earned more than he did as a boxer—over $150 million. While the overall housewares industry expands only 7 percent annually, Salton has grown more than 46 percent a year since 1995.[25]

"Marketing Insight: Celebrity Endorsements as a Strategy" focuses on the use of testimonials.

If a person has a positive attitude toward a source and a message, or a negative attitude toward both, a state of *congruity* is said to exist. What happens if the person holds one attitude toward the source and the opposite toward the message? Suppose a consumer hears a likable celebrity praise a brand that she dislikes? Osgood and Tannenbaum say that *attitude change will take place in the direction of increasing the amount of congruity between the two evaluations*.[26] The consumer will end up respecting the celebrity somewhat less or respecting the brand somewhat more. If a person encounters the same celebrity praising other disliked brands, he or she will eventually develop a negative view of the celebrity and maintain negative attitudes toward the brands. The **principle of congruity** implies that communicators can use their good image to reduce some negative feelings toward a brand but in the process might lose some esteem with the audience.

Multinational companies wrestle with a number of challenges in developing global communications programs: They must decide whether the product is appropriate for a country. They must make sure the market segment they address is both legal and customary. They must decide if the style of the ad is acceptable, and they must decide whether ads should be created at headquarters or locally.[27]

1. ***Product*** – Many products are restricted or forbidden in certain parts of the world. Beer, wine, and spirits cannot be advertised or sold in Muslim countries. Tobacco products are subject to strict regulation in many countries.

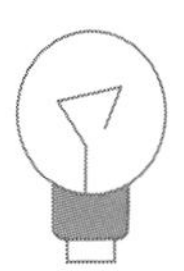

MARKETING INSIGHT | CELEBRITY ENDORSEMENTS AS A STRATEGY

A well-chosen celebrity can draw attention to a product or brand, as when Sarah, Duchess of York—better known as "Fergie"—showed how she slimmed down thanks to Weight Watchers; or, the celebrity's mystique can transfer to the brand—Bill Cosby entertains a group of kids while eating a bowl of Jell-O.

The choice of the celebrity is critical. The celebrity should have high recognition, high positive affect, and high appropriateness to the product. Britney Spears has high recognition but negative affect among many groups. Robin Williams has high recognition and high positive affect but might not be appropriate for advertising a World Peace Conference. Tom Hanks, Meryl Streep, and Oprah Winfrey could successfully advertise a large number of products because they have extremely high ratings for familiarity and likability (known as the Q factor in the entertainment industry).

Celebrities show up everywhere. In the hotly contested male-impotence drug category, pharmaceutical marketers have turned to celebrities to gain product attention and relevance. Initially advertised by retired politician Bob Dole, Pfizer turned to 40-year-old baseball slugger Rafael Palmeiro and 45-year-old NASCAR driver Mark Martin to give its market leader drug, Viagra, a younger appeal. Competitor Levitra turned to famed football coach Iron Mike Ditka to assure its audience of its speed and quality. Only number-three brand Cialis eschewed celebrity endorsers, spending $100 million to run ads showing couples in romantic settings.

Athletes are commonly employed to endorse athletic products, beverages, and apparel. One of the premier athletic endorsers is cyclist Lance Armstrong, who battled and beat testicular cancer on his way to winning six consecutive Tour de France championships. He endorses a number of bicycle and sports products companies, including Trek, PowerBar, and Nike. Armstrong's improbable "against all odds" success story enabled him to win endorsement contracts from companies not affiliated with sports, such as Bristol-Myers Squibb pharmaceuticals, Coca-Cola, Subaru, and the U.S. Postal Service. The total amount he earned from endorsements in 2003 topped $10 million.

Celebrities can play a more strategic role for their brands, not only endorsing a product but also helping design, position, and sell merchandise and services. Since signing Tiger Woods in 1996, Nike has seen its share of the golf ball market jump from 1 to 6 percent. Woods has played a key role in developing a series of golf products and apparel that Nike has periodically altered to reflect his changing personality and design tastes.

Using celebrities poses certain risks. The celebrity might hold out for a larger fee at contract renewal time or withdraw. Just as can happen with movies and records, celebrity campaigns can sometimes be an expensive flop. Even though Celine Dion was locked into a three-year, $14 million deal, Chrysler chose to discontinue her ads when they deemed them ineffective. Similarly, Pepsi chose to drop star endorsers Britney Spears and Beyoncé Knowles, whose personalities may have been too overpowering for the brand, to focus on promoting occasions that go well with drinking Pepsi.

The celebrity might lose popularity or, even worse, get caught in a scandal or embarrassing situation. After NBA legend Magic Johnson went public with his HIV diagnosis and his extramarital affairs in 1991, his ads were pulled from the air and his endorsement deals were not renewed. McDonald's chose not to renew a $12 million annual contract with basketball star Kobe Bryant after accusations of rape.

Sources: Irving Rein, Philip Kotler, and Martin Scoller, *The Making and Marketing of Professionals into Celebrities* (Chicago: NTC Business Books, 1997); Greg Johnson, "Woods Cautious Approach to the Green," *Los Angeles Times,* July 26, 2000, p. A1; Bruce Horovitz, "Armstrong Rolls to Market Gold," *USA Today,* May 4, 2000, p. 1B; Theresa Howard, "Pepsi Takes Some Fizz off Vanilla Rival," *USA Today,* November 16, 2003; Keith Naughton, "The Soft Sell," *Newsweek,* February 2, 2004, pp. 46–47; Betsy Cummings, "Star Power," *Sales & Marketing Management,* (April 2001): 52–59.

2. ***Market Segment*** – U.S. toy makers were surprised to learn that in many countries (Norway and Sweden, for example) no TV ads may be directed at children under 12. Sweden lobbied hard to extend that ban to all EU member countries in 2001 but failed. To play it safe, McDonald's advertises itself as a family restaurant in Sweden.
3. ***Style*** – Comparative ads, while acceptable and even common in the United States and Canada, are less commonly used in the United Kingdom, unacceptable in Japan, and illegal in India and Brazil. PepsiCo had a comparative taste test ad in Japan that was refused by many TV stations and eventually led to a lawsuit.
4. ***Local or Global*** – Today, more and more multinational companies are attempting to build a global brand image by using the same advertising in all markets. When Daimler AG and Chrysler merged to become the world's fifth-largest automaker, they ran a three-week ad campaign in more than 100 countries consisting of a 12-page magazine insert, 9 newspaper spreads, and a 24-page brochure that was sent to business, government, and union leaders and to the news media. The campaign's tagline was "Expect the extraordinary," and it featured people from both companies working together.

Companies that sell their products to different cultures or in different countries must be prepared to vary their messages. In advertising its hair care products in different countries, Helene Curtis adjusts its messages. Middle-class British women wash their hair frequently, whereas the opposite is true among Spanish women. Japanese women avoid overwashing their hair for fear of removing protective oils.

The California Milk Processor Board's famed ad campaign "Got Milk?" successfully appealed to every major demographic group—but one.

GOT MILK?

When the California Milk Processor Board set out to target Hispanics whose dominant language was Spanish, research uncovered an interesting finding: The "Got Milk?" tagline translated roughly to "Are You Lactating?" Moreover, Hispanics' reaction to the irreverent ads showing what a pain it was to be out of milk was decidedly different. Executive Director Jeff Manning observed, "We found out that not having milk or rice in Hispanic households is not funny; running out of milk means you failed your family." A totally different campaign, with the theme "Generations," was created to target Hispanic mothers, posing the question, "Have You Given Them Enough Milk Today?" Instead of deprivation, the ads showed milk as an almost sacred ingredient in cherished recipes, handed down from grandmother to mother to daughter in traditional Mexican families.[28]

Select the Communications Channels

Selecting efficient channels to carry the message becomes more difficult as channels of communication become more fragmented and cluttered. Think of the challenges in the pharmaceutical industry: Over 63,000 U.S. sales reps "detail" doctors every day, hoping to get five minutes of a busy doctor's time. Some 40 percent of calls do not even result in seeing the doctor, which makes sales calling extremely expensive. The industry has had to expand its battery of communications channels to include ads in medical journals, direct mail (including audio and videotapes), free samples, and even telemarketing. Pharmaceutical companies sponsor clinical conferences at which they pay physicians to spend a weekend listening to leading physicians extol certain drugs in the morning, followed by an afternoon of golf or tennis.

All of these channels are used in the hope of building physician preference for their branded therapeutic agent. Pharmaceutical companies are also using new technologies to reach doctors through handheld devices, online services, and videoconferencing equipment.[29]

Communications channels may be personal and nonpersonal. Within each are many subchannels.

PERSONAL COMMUNICATIONS CHANNELS **Personal communications channels** involve two or more persons communicating directly face-to-face, person-to-audience, over the telephone, or through e-mail. Instant messaging and independent sites to collect consumer reviews are another means of growing importance in recent years. Personal communication channels derive their effectiveness through individualized presentation and feedback.

A further distinction can be drawn among advocate, expert, and social communications channels. *Advocate channels* consist of company salespeople contacting buyers in the target market. *Expert channels* consist of independent experts making statements to target buyers. *Social channels* consist of neighbors, friends, family members, and associates talking to target buyers. In a study of 7,000 consumers in seven European countries, 60 percent said they were influenced to use a new brand by family and friends.[30]

A study by Burson-Marsteller and Roper Starch Worldwide found that one influential person's word of mouth tends to affect the buying attitudes of two other people, on average. That circle of influence, however, jumps to eight online. There is considerable consumer-to-consumer communication on the Web on a whole range of subjects. Online visitors increasingly create product information, not just consume it. They join Internet interest groups to share information, so that "word of Web" is joining "word of mouth" as an important buying influence. Words about good companies travel fast; words about bad companies travel even faster. As one marketer noted, "You don't need to reach 2 million people to let them know about a new product—you just need to reach the right 2,000 people in the right way and they will help you reach 2 million."[31]

Personal influence carries especially great weight in two situations. One is with products that are expensive, risky, or purchased infrequently. The other is where the product suggests something about the user's status or taste. People often ask others for a recommendation for a doctor, plumber, hotel, lawyer, accountant, architect, insurance agent, interior decorator, or financial consultant. If we have confidence in the recommendation, we normally act on the referral. In such cases, the recommender has potentially benefited the service provider

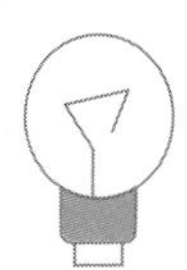

MARKETING INSIGHT | BUZZ MARKETING

Marketers' growing interest in word-of-mouth, buzz, and viral marketing have led to a number of new concepts and ideas. Here are three sets of such insights.

- ***Renée Dye, The 5 Myths of Buzz***

  Research conducted by Renée Dye, a strategy expert with McKinsey, suggests that buzz evolves according to basic principles. Dye contends that companies seeking to take advantage of buzz must first overcome five misconceptions about marketing contagion. Here are "The 5 Myths of Buzz":

  1. ***Only outrageous or edgy products are buzz-worthy.*** The most unlikely products, like prescription drugs, can generate tremendous buzz.
  2. ***Buzz just happens.*** Buzz is increasingly the result of shrewd marketing tactics in which companies seed a vanguard group, ration supplies, use celebrities to generate buzz, leverage the power of lists, and initiate grassroots marketing.
  3. ***The best buzz-starters are your best customers.*** Often, a counterculture has a greater ability to start buzz.
  4. ***To profit from buzz, you must act first and fast.*** Copycat companies can reap substantial profits if they know when to jump in—and when not to.
  5. ***The media and advertising are needed to create buzz.*** When used either too early or too much, the media and advertising can squelch buzz before it ignites.

- ***Michael Cafferky: Word-of-Mouth Marketing Tips***

  Marketing author Michael Cafferky's Word-of-Mouth Marketing Tips Web site offers many suggestions on how to build a network of referral sources. Here are five:

  1. ***Involve your customers in the process of making or delivering your product or service.***
  2. ***Solicit testimonials from your customers:*** Use a response form that asks for feedback—and permission to quote it.
  3. ***Tell true stories to your customers:*** Stories are the central vehicle for spreading reputations because they communicate on an emotional level.
  4. ***Educate your best customers:*** You can pick any topic that is relevant to your best customers and have them become the source of credible, up-to-date information on that topic.
  5. ***Offer fast complaint handling:*** A speedy response is vital to preventing negative word of mouth from starting, because negative feelings about a product or service may linger for years.

- ***Malcolm Gladwell, The Law of the Few, Stickiness, and the Power of Context***

  Malcolm Gladwell claims that three factors work to ignite public interest in an idea. He calls the first "The Law of the Few." Three types of people help spread an idea like an epidemic. First are *Mavens,* people who are knowledgeable about big and small things. Second are *Connectors,* people who know and communicate with a great number of other people. Third are *Salesmen,* those who possess great natural persuasive power.

  Any idea that catches the interest of Mavens, Connectors, and Salesmen is likely to be broadcast far and wide. A second factor is "stickiness." An idea must be expressed so that it motivates people to act. Otherwise "The Law of the Few" will not lead to a self-sustaining epidemic. A third factor, the Power of Context, will control whether those spreading an idea are able to organize groups and communities around it.

Sources: Renée Dye, "The Buzz on Buzz," *Harvard Business Review* (November–December 2000): 139; Scott R. Herriott, "Identifying and Developing Referral Channels," *Management Decision* 30, no. 1 (1992): 4–9; Peter H. Riengen and Jerome B. Kernan, "Analysis of Referral Networks in Marketing: Methods and Illustration," *Journal of Marketing Research* (November 1986): 37–78; Jerry R. Wilson, *Word of Mouth Marketing* (New York: John Wiley, 1991); Cafferky's Free Word-of-Mouth Marketing Tips, 1999, available at <www.geocities.com/wallstreet/6246>. Also see Emanuel Rosen, *The Anatomy of Buzz* (New York: Doubleday, 2000); Malcolm Gladwell, *The Tipping Point: How Little Things Can Make a Big Difference* (Boston: Little, Brown & Company, 2000).

as well as the service seeker. Service providers clearly have a strong interest in building referral sources.

Communication researchers are moving toward a social-structure view of interpersonal communication.[32] They see society as consisting of *cliques,* small groups whose members interact frequently. Clique members are similar, and their closeness facilitates effective communication but also insulates the clique from new ideas. The challenge is to create more openness so that cliques exchange information with others in the society. This openness is helped by people who function as liaisons and bridges. A *liaison* is a person who connects two or more cliques without belonging to either. A *bridge* is a person who belongs to one clique and is linked to a person in another clique.

Many companies are becoming acutely aware of the power of *word of mouth* or *buzz.* (See "Marketing Insight: Buzz Marketing.") Products and brands such as Converse sneakers, Hush Puppies shoes, JanSport knapsacks, Krispy Kreme doughnuts, and the blockbuster movie *The Passion of The Christ* were built through buzz.[33] Companies such as Body Shop, USAA, Starbucks, Palm Pilot, Red Bull, and Amazon were essentially built by word of mouth, with very little advertising. In some cases, positive word of mouth happens in a natural way.

KIEHL

Kiehl is a small, 153-year-old company that makes and sells hair and skin products, such as Kiehl's rosewater facial freshener-toner and pineapple papaya facial scrub. Its marketing practices defy normal wisdom. It does not advertise. Its packaging is bland and the text is difficult to read. It refuses to be carried by most stores, making exceptions only for high-priced stores such as Saks Fifth Avenue, Neiman Marcus, and Barney's. It gives away vast amounts of free samples to anyone coming into its own stores. It gets great coverage from the business press without ever soliciting attention. Kiehl has the gift of being carried by word of mouth.[34]

In most cases, "buzz" is managed.[35] Agencies have been created solely to help clients create buzz.

BZZAGENT

A two-year-old Boston, MA, company, BzzAgent has assembled a nationwide army of volunteers who will talk up any of the clients' products they deem worth promoting. Once a client signs on, the company searches a database for "agents" matching the demographic and psychographic profile of target customers. These agents are then offered the chance to sign up for the buzz campaign. For their efforts they get a sample product and a training manual on methods for creating buzz—from chatting up salespeople at retail outlets to how to bring the product up with friends and family. The company claims that the buzz is honest because the process requires just enough work that few agents enroll solely for freebies and agents don't talk up products they don't like.[36]

Companies can take several steps to stimulate personal influence channels to work on their behalf:

- ***Identify influential individuals and companies and devote extra effort to them.*** In technology, influencers might be large corporate customers, industry analysts and journalists, selected policy makers, and a sampling of early adopters.[37]
- ***Create opinion leaders by supplying certain people with the product on attractive terms.*** Pepsi liberally sampled its Mountain Dew spin-off, Code Red, and also encouraged its core 13-to-19-year-old target audience to stumble on the new flavor in such places as vending machines at malls. As one executive noted, "We allowed these teen influencers to be advocates for the brand. They launched it in their own little world."[38]
- ***Work through community influentials such as local disk jockeys, class presidents, and presidents of women's organizations.*** When Ford introduced the Focus, it handed out the cars to DJs and trendy people so they would be seen around town in them. Ford also identified 100 influential young consumers in five key marketing states and also gave them cars to drive around.[39]
- ***Use influential or believable people in testimonial advertising.*** Accenture, American Express, Nike, and Buick use golf megastar Tiger Woods as an endorser to talk up the virtues of their respective companies and products.
- ***Develop advertising that has high "conversation value,"*** or better yet, incorporate buzz-worthy features into your product design: Some ads have a slogan that becomes part of the cultural vernacular, such as Wendy's "Where's the beef?" Anheuser-Busch has crafted a number of catch phrases that have captured the public's imagination: "Yes I Am" and "I Love You, Man" for Bud Light in the 1990s, and more recently, "Whassup?!" for Budweiser.
- ***Develop word-of-mouth referral channels to build business.*** Professionals will often encourage clients to recommend their services. Weight Watchers found that word-of-mouth referrals from a relationship with someone in the program had a huge impact on its business.[40]
- ***Establish an electronic forum.*** Toyota owners who use an online service line such as America Online can hold online discussions to share experiences.
- ***Use viral marketing.*** Internet marketers are using **viral marketing** as form of word of mouth, or word of mouse, to draw attention to their sites.[41] Viral marketing involves passing on company-developed products, services, or information from user to user. As a classic

example, Hotmail, an Internet Service Provider (ISP), offered a free e-mail account to anyone who signed up. Each e-mail sent by a Hotmail subscriber included the simple tag at the bottom of each message: "Get your free private e-mail at http://www.hotmail.com." Users were in effect advertising Hotmail to others. Hotmail spent less than $500,000 on marketing and within 18 months attracted 12 million subscribers.

One team of viral marketing experts caution that while influencers or "alphas" start trends, they are often too introspective and socially alienated to spread them. They advise marketers to cultivate "bees," hyper-devoted customers who are not just satisfied knowing about the next trend but who live to spread the word.[42] Here's how one company cultivated bees and harvested "honey" in the form of millions of media impressions and huge sales:

INZONE BRANDS INC.

With a minuscule budget, InZone Brands relied at first on the power of licensing and packaging to create brand awareness for its BellyWashers, beverages for kids packaged in fun-looking bottles decorated with cartoon characters. They then set out to develop buzz by harnessing the most powerful force in kids' marketing: peer-to-peer influence. The company launched a Kids Board, a national panel that acts as a mini-business unit with the company. Every year, the company selects 15 extremely devoted customers and sponsors their community service projects. In turn, the kids help InZone come up with new product ideas and, more important, build grassroots fervor. In the past year alone, board members have organized 40 community service projects involving 60,000 kids, all under the BellyWashers banner. The program is estimated to have generated 4 million media impressions. The buzz generated by BellyWashers' fanatical customers and collectors has sent the products flying off the shelves at Kroger, Target, Toys "R" Us, and Wal-Mart. Word of mouth also created a vibrant aftermarket, with first-edition BellyWashers getting high bids on eBay.[43]

Marketers must be careful in reaching out to consumers. Consumers also can resent personal communications if unsolicited. A 2003 survey found that roughly 80 percent of the sample of consumers were very annoyed by pop-up ads, spam, and telemarketing.[44]

NONPERSONAL COMMUNICATIONS CHANNELS Nonpersonal channels are communications directed to more than one person and include media, sales promotions, events, and publicity.

- ***Media*** consist of print media (newspapers and magazines); broadcast media (radio and television); network media (telephone, cable, satellite, wireless); electronic media (audiotape, videotape, videodisk, CD-ROM, Web page); and display media (billboards, signs, posters). Most nonpersonal messages come through paid media.
- ***Sales promotions*** consist of consumer promotions (such as samples, coupons, and premiums); trade promotion (such as advertising and display allowances); and business and sales-force promotion (contests for sales reps).
- ***Events and experiences*** include sports, arts, entertainment, and cause events as well as less formal activities that create novel brand interactions with consumers.
- ***Public relations*** include communications directed internally to employees of the company or externally to consumers, other firms, the government, and media.

Much of the recent growth of nonpersonal channels has been with events and experiences. A company can build its brand image through creating or sponsoring events. Events marketers who once favored sports events are now using other venues such as art museums, zoos, or ice shows to entertain clients and employees. AT&T and IBM sponsor symphony performances and art exhibits; Visa is an active sponsor of the Olympics; Harley-Davidson sponsors annual motorcycle rallies; and Perrier sponsors sports and other events.

Companies are searching for better ways to quantify the benefits of sponsorship and are demanding greater accountability from event owners and organizers. Companies can also create events designed to surprise the public and create a buzz. Many amount to guerrilla marketing tactics. Here are some examples:

- Driver 2, a new car-chase video game, arranged for a convoy of 20 car wrecks with smoke pouring from their engines to crawl through Manhattan and Los Angeles to attract attention to the new game.

VISA ads at an ATM booth at the Athens Olympics, 2004.

- Ask Jeeves, the Internet search engine, sent 35 actors in British butlers' outfits to guide visitors to their seats and answer tennis trivia questions at the U.S. Open tennis tournament.
- Kibu.com pays hundreds of school girls to do "peer marketing" by hanging around with their peers, handing out free lip gloss, and talking up Kibu's cosmetic site.[45]

The increased use of attention-getting events is a response to the fragmentation of media: Consumers can turn to hundreds of cable channels, thousands of magazine titles, and millions of Internet pages. Events can create attention, although whether they have a lasting effect on brand awareness, knowledge, or preference will vary considerably, depending on the quality of the product, the event itself, and its execution.

INTEGRATION OF COMMUNICATIONS CHANNELS Although personal communication is often more effective than mass communication, mass media might be the major means of stimulating personal communication. Mass communications affect personal attitudes and behavior through a two-step process. Ideas often flow from radio, television, and print to opinion leaders and from these to the less media-involved population groups. This two-step flow has several implications. First, the influence of mass media on public opinion is not as direct, powerful, and automatic as supposed. It is mediated by opinion leaders, people whose opinions are sought or who carry their opinions to others. Second, the two-step flow challenges the notion that consumption styles are primarily influenced by a "trickle-down" or "trickle-up" effect from mass media. People interact primarily within their own social groups and acquire ideas from opinion leaders in their groups. Third, two-step communication suggests that mass communicators should direct messages specifically to opinion leaders and let them carry the message to others.

Finally, any discussion about the effectiveness of mass communication has to take into account the dramatic changes that have eroded the effectiveness of the mass media. For a look at the forces with which advertisers must contend today, see "Marketing Insight: Hitting the Bull's Eye in a Post-Mass-Market World."

Establish the Total Marketing Communications Budget

One of the most difficult marketing decisions is determining how much to spend on promotion. John Wanamaker, the department store magnate, once said, "I know that half of my advertising is wasted, but I don't know which half."

Industries and companies vary considerably in how much they spend on promotion. Expenditures might be 30 to 50 percent of sales in the cosmetics industry and 5 to 10 percent in the industrial-equipment industry. Within a given industry, there are low- and high-spending companies.

How do companies decide on the promotion budget? We will describe four common methods: the affordable method, percentage-of-sales method, competitive-parity method, and objective-and-task method.

AFFORDABLE METHOD Many companies set the promotion budget at what they think the company can afford. The affordable method completely ignores the role of promotion as an investment and the immediate impact of promotion on sales volume. It leads to an uncertain annual budget, which makes long-range planning difficult.

PERCENTAGE-OF-SALES METHOD Many companies set promotion expenditures at a specified percentage of sales (either current or anticipated) or of the sales price. Automobile companies typically budget a fixed percentage for promotion based on the planned car price. Oil companies set the appropriation at a fraction of a cent for each gallon of gasoline sold under their own label.

Supporters of the percentage-of-sales method see a number of advantages. First, promotion expenditures will vary with what the company can "afford." This satisfies financial managers, who believe that expenses should be closely related to the movement of corporate sales over the business cycle. Second, it encourages management to think of the relationship among promotion cost, selling price, and profit per unit. Third, it encourages stability when competing firms spend approximately the same percentage of their sales on promotion.

In spite of these advantages, the percentage-of-sales method has little to justify it. It views sales as the determiner of promotion rather than as the result. It leads to a budget set by the availability of funds rather than by market opportunities. It discourages experimentation with countercyclical promotion or aggressive spending. Dependence on year-to-year sales fluctuations interferes with long-range planning. There is no logical basis for choosing the specific percentage, except what has been done in the past or what competitors are doing.

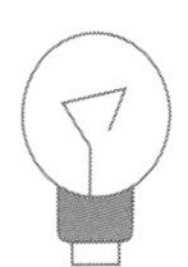

MARKETING **INSIGHT** | HITTING THE BULL'S EYE IN A POST-MASS-MARKET WORLD

In 1960, Procter & Gamble could reach 80 percent of American women with one 30-second Tide commercial aired simultaneously on only three TV networks: NBC, ABC, and CBS. Today, the same ad would have to run on 100 channels to achieve this marketing feat and even then, it would run an increasing risk of being "zapped" by consumers armed with Personal Video Recorders such as TiVo or Replay TV. In fact, a recent study by the Yankee Group, titled "The Death of the 30-Second Commercial," calculated that by 2007 some $5.5 billion spent on TV advertising will be wasted.

Two forces are to blame for the demise of what used to be the most powerful means of hitting the consumer marketing bull's eye. One is the fragmentation of American audiences and, with the advent of digital technology and the Internet, the media now used to reach them. Prime time ratings and circulations have been on the downslide since the 1970s. What's new is the proliferation of media and entertainment options—from hundreds of cable TV and radio stations and thousands of magazines and webzines to uncountable Web sites, blogs, video games, and cellphone screens. Consumers not only have more choice of which medium to use, they also have a choice as to whether and how they want to receive commercial content.

And that's part of the second force leaching oomph out of the 30-second spot. The new Personal Video Recorders (PVRs) allow consumers to eliminate commercials with the push of a fast forward button. The Yankee Group estimates that PVRs will be in almost 25 million homes or 20 percent of U.S. households by 2008 and of those who use them, between 65 and 70 percent will fast forward through commercials. The Internet is even more of a threat, with a U.S. penetration of 150 million users who can choose whether to view an ad by clicking on an icon.

So advertisers are adding a variety of new communication tools to their IMC kits, many of which are further blurring the line between advertising and entertainment. Participants on CBS's *Survivor* series subsisted on Frito-lay's Doritos, Pepsi-Cola's Mountain Dew, or Anheuser-Busch's Budweiser beer. Firms are also using exclusive TV sponsorships. Fox's series *24* premiered with a single sponsor, the Ford-150 truck. Instead of ads breaking up the show, a three-minute short film—very similar in style to the series and featuring the truck—ran both before and after the show. In addition, the main character drove a Ford Explorer. Other advertisers are just going beyond TV. Nike Europe has amassed a worldwide player base for the online soccer games it has launched in the past three years.

Sources: Noreen O'Leary, "The 30-second Spot Is Dead, Long Live the 30-second Spot," *Adweek,* November 17, 2003, pp. 12–21; Anthony Bianco, "The Vanishing Mass Market," *BusinessWeek,* July 12, 2004, pp. 60–68; Susan Thea Posnock, "It Can Control Madison Avenue," *American Demographics,* (February 2004): 28–33; Jennifer Pendleton, "Multi TASKERS," *Advertising Age,* March 29, 2004, pp. S1, S8; Hank Kim, "Madison Ave. Melds Pitches and Content," *Advertising Age,* October 7, 2002, pp. 1, 14; Christopher Reynolds, "Game Over," *American Demographics* (February 2004): 34–38.

Finally, it does not encourage building the promotion budget by determining what each product and territory deserves.

COMPETITIVE-PARITY METHOD Some companies set their promotion budget to achieve share-of-voice parity with competitors. Two arguments are made in support of the competitive-parity method. One is that competitors' expenditures represent the collective wisdom of the industry. The other is that maintaining competitive parity prevents promotion wars. Neither argument is valid. There are no grounds for believing that competitors know better. Company reputations, resources, opportunities, and objectives differ so much that promotion budgets are hardly a guide. Furthermore, there is no evidence that budgets based on competitive parity discourage promotional wars.

OBJECTIVE-AND-TASK METHOD The objective-and-task method calls upon marketers to develop promotion budgets by defining specific objectives, determining the tasks that must be performed to achieve these objectives, and estimating the costs of performing these tasks. The sum of these costs is the proposed promotion budget.

For example, suppose Cadbury Schweppes wants to introduce a new natural energy drink called Sunburst for the casual athlete.[46]

1. ***Establish the market share goal*** – The company estimates 50 million potential users and sets a target of attracting 8 percent of the market—that is, 4 million users.
2. ***Determine the percentage of the market that should be reached by advertising*** – The advertiser hopes to reach 80 percent (40 million prospects) with the advertising message.
3. ***Determine the percentage of aware prospects that should be persuaded to try the brand*** – The advertiser would be pleased if 25 percent of aware prospects (10 million) tried Sunburst. This is because it estimates that 40 percent of all triers, or 4 million people, would become loyal users. This is the market goal.
4. ***Determine the number of advertising impressions per 1 percent trial rate*** – The advertiser estimates that 40 advertising impressions (exposures) for every 1 percent of the population would bring about a 25 percent trial rate.
5. ***Determine the number of gross rating points that would have to be purchased*** – A gross rating point is one exposure to 1 percent of the target population. Because the company wants to achieve 40 exposures to 80 percent of the population, it will want to buy 3,200 gross rating points.
6. ***Determine the necessary advertising budget on the basis of the average cost of buying a gross rating point*** – To expose 1 percent of the target population to one impression costs an average of $3,277. Therefore, 3,200 gross rating points would cost $10,486,400 (= $3,277 × 3,200) in the introductory year.

The objective-and-task method has the advantage of requiring management to spell out its assumptions about the relationship among dollars spent, exposure levels, trial rates, and regular usage.

A major question is how much weight marketing communications should receive in relation to alternatives such as product improvement, lower prices, or better service. The answer depends on where the company's products are in their life cycles, whether they are commodities or highly differentiable products, whether they are routinely needed or have to be "sold," and other considerations. Marketing communications budgets tend to be higher when there is low channel support, much change in the marketing program over time, many hard-to-reach customers, more complex customer decision making, differentiated products and nonhomogeneous customer needs, and frequent product purchases in small quantities.[47]

In theory, the total communications budget should be established so that the marginal profit from the last communication dollar just equals the marginal profit from the last dollar in the best noncommunication use. Implementing this principle, however, is not easy.

::: Deciding on the Marketing Communications Mix

Companies must allocate the marketing communications budget over the six major modes of communication—advertising, sales promotion, public relations and publicity, events and experiences, sales force, and direct marketing. Here is how one company touches several bases.

SELECT COMFORT CORPORATION

A mattress is a mattress, or is it? We have heard of waterbeds. Now Select Comfort offers an "air bed." The mattress is air-inflated, and sleepers can adjust firmness by changing the air level. Two sleepers can even call for different degrees of firmness on their respective sides of the mattress. To market the mattresses, Select Comfort, headquartered in Minneapolis, has put together a strong combination of channels and promotion initiatives: 300 retail stores where prospects can take a "Test Rest on Air"; demonstration videos and collateral material discussing "Sleep Science"; a company Web site (www.selectcomfort.com) describing the products and offering advice on how to sleep better; a late-night infomercial; celebrity endorsements; and giving customers who recommend others who buy the mattress a merchandise certificate.

Within the same industry, companies can differ considerably in their media and channel choices. Avon concentrates its promotional funds on personal selling, whereas Revlon spends heavily on advertising. Electrolux spends heavily on a door-to-door sales force, whereas Hoover relies more on advertising.

Companies are always searching for ways to gain efficiency by replacing one communications tool with others. Many companies are replacing some field sales activity with ads, direct mail, and telemarketing. One auto dealer dismissed his five salespeople and cut his prices, and sales exploded. Companies are shifting advertising funds into sales promotion. The substitutability among communications tools explains why marketing functions need to be coordinated. For example, a new Web site and a coordinated TV ad campaign targeting the greater Los Angeles area sparked record sales for Hawaii's Aloha Airlines, selling over $1 million worth of tickets on one day. The TV ads were designed to create awareness for Aloha and drive traffic to the Web site, where the sale would be closed.[48]

Characteristics of the Marketing Communications Mix

Each communication tool has its own unique characteristics and costs.

ADVERTISING Advertising can be used to build up a long-term image for a product (Coca-Cola ads) or trigger quick sales (a Sears ad for a weekend sale). Advertising can efficiently reach geographically dispersed buyers. Certain forms of advertising (TV) can require a large budget, whereas other forms (newspaper) do not. Just the presence of advertising might have an effect on sales: Consumers might believe that a heavily advertised brand must offer "good value."[49] Because of the many forms and uses of advertising, it is difficult to make generalizations.[50] Yet the following qualities can be noted:

1. ***Pervasiveness*** – Advertising permits the seller to repeat a message many times. It also allows the buyer to receive and compare the messages of various competitors. Large-scale advertising says something positive about the seller's size, power, and success.
2. ***Amplified expressiveness*** – Advertising provides opportunities for dramatizing the company and its products through the artful use of print, sound, and color.
3. ***Impersonality*** – The audience does not feel obligated to pay attention or respond to advertising. Advertising is a monologue in front of, not a dialogue with, the audience.

SALES PROMOTION Companies use sales promotion tools—coupons, contests, premiums, and the like—to draw a stronger and quicker buyer response. Sales promotion can be used for short-run effects such as to highlight product offers and boost sagging sales. Sales promotion tools offer three distinctive benefits:

1. ***Communication*** – They gain attention and may lead the consumer to the product.
2. ***Incentive*** – They incorporate some concession, inducement, or contribution that gives value to the consumer.
3. ***Invitation*** – They include a distinct invitation to engage in the transaction now.

PUBLIC RELATIONS AND PUBLICITY Marketers tend to underuse public relations, yet a well-thought-out program coordinated with the other communications-mix elements can be extremely effective. The appeal of public relations and publicity is based on three distinctive qualities:

1. ***High credibility*** – News stories and features are more authentic and credible to readers than ads.

2. ***Ability to catch buyers off guard*** – Public relations can reach prospects who prefer to avoid salespeople and advertisements.
3. ***Dramatization*** – Public relations has the potential for dramatizing a company or product.

EVENTS AND EXPERIENCES There are many advantages to events and experiences:

1. ***Relevant*** – A well-chosen event or experience can be seen as highly relevant as the consumer gets personally involved.
2. ***Involving*** – Given their live, real-time quality, consumers can find events and experiences more actively engaging.
3. ***Implicit*** – Events are more of an indirect "soft-sell."

DIRECT MARKETING The many forms of direct marketing—direct mail, telemarketing, Internet marketing—share three distinctive characteristics. Direct marketing is:

1. ***Customized*** – The message can be prepared to appeal to the addressed individual.
2. ***Up-to-date*** – A message can be prepared very quickly.
3. ***Interactive*** – The message can be changed depending on the person's response.

PERSONAL SELLING Personal selling is the most effective tool at later stages of the buying process, particularly in building up buyer preference, conviction, and action. Personal selling has three distinctive qualities:

1. ***Personal interaction*** – Personal selling involves an immediate and interactive relationship between two or more persons. Each party is able to observe the other's reactions.
2. ***Cultivation*** – Personal selling permits all kinds of relationships to spring up, ranging from a matter-of-fact selling relationship to a deep personal friendship.
3. ***Response*** – Personal selling makes the buyer feel under some obligation for having listened to the sales talk.

Factors in Setting the Marketing Communications Mix

Companies must consider several factors in developing their communications mix: type of product market, consumer readiness to make a purchase, and stage in the product life cycle. Also important is the company's market rank.

TYPE OF PRODUCT MARKET Communications mix allocations vary between consumer and business markets. Consumer marketers tend to spend comparatively more on sales promotion and advertising; business marketers tend to spend comparatively more on personal selling. In general, personal selling is used more with complex, expensive, and risky goods and in markets with fewer and larger sellers (hence, business markets).

Although advertising is used less than sales calls in business markets, it still plays a significant role:

- Advertising can provide an introduction to the company and its products.
- If the product has new features, advertising can explain them.
- Reminder advertising is more economical than sales calls.
- Advertisements offering brochures and carrying the company's phone number are an effective way to generate leads for sales representatives.
- Sales representatives can use tear sheets of the company's ads to legitimize their company and products.
- Advertising can remind customers of how to use the product and reassure them about their purchase.

A number of studies have underscored advertising's role in business markets. Advertising combined with personal selling can increase sales over what would have resulted if there had been no advertising.[51] Corporate advertising can improve a company's reputation and improve the sales force's chances of getting a favorable first hearing and early adoption of the product.[52]

Personal selling can also make a strong contribution in consumer-goods marketing. Some consumer marketers use the sales force mainly to collect weekly orders from dealers

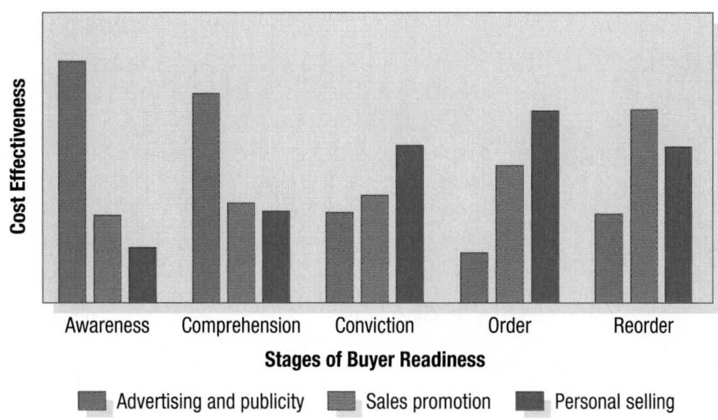

FIG. 17.6

Cost-Effectiveness of Three Different Communication Tools at Different Buyer-Readiness Stages

and to see that sufficient stock is on the shelf. Yet an effectively trained company sales force can make four important contributions:

1. ***Increased stock position*** – Sales reps can persuade dealers to take more stock and devote more shelf space to the company's brand.
2. ***Enthusiasm building*** – Sales reps can build dealer enthusiasm by dramatizing planned advertising and sales promotion backup.
3. ***Missionary selling*** – Sales reps can sign up more dealers.
4. ***Key account management*** – Sales reps can take responsibility for growing business with the most important accounts.

BUYER-READINESS STAGE Communication tools vary in cost-effectiveness at different stages of buyer readiness. Figure 17.6 shows the relative cost-effectiveness of three communication tools. Advertising and publicity play the most important roles in the awareness-building stage. Customer comprehension is primarily affected by advertising and personal selling. Customer conviction is influenced mostly by personal selling. Closing the sale is influenced mostly by personal selling and sales promotion. Reordering is also affected mostly by personal selling and sales promotion, and somewhat by reminder advertising.

PRODUCT LIFE-CYCLE STAGE Communication tools also vary in cost-effectiveness at different stages of the product life cycle. In the introduction stage, advertising, events and experiences, and publicity have the highest cost effectiveness, followed by personal selling to gain distribution coverage and sales promotion and direct marketing to induce trial. In the growth stage, demand has its own momentum through word of mouth. In the maturity stage, advertising, events and experiences, and personal selling all grow more important. In the decline stage, sales promotion continues strong, other communication tools are reduced, and salespeople give the product only minimal attention.

Measuring Communication Results

Senior managers want to know the *outcomes* and *revenues* resulting from their communications investments. Too often, however, their communications directors supply only *outputs* and *expenses:* press clipping counts, numbers of ads placed, media costs. In fairness, the communications directors try to translate outputs into intermediate outputs such as reach and frequency, recall and recognition scores, persuasion changes, and cost-per-thousand calculations. Ultimately, behavior-change measures capture the real payoff.

After implementing the communications plan, the communications director must measure its impact on the target audience. Members of the target audience are asked whether they recognize or recall the message, how many times they saw it, what points they recall, how they felt about the message, and their previous and current attitudes toward the product and the company. The communicator should also collect behavioral measures of audience response, such as how many people bought the product, liked it, and talked to others about it.

Figure 17.7 provides an example of good feedback measurement. We find that 80 percent of the consumers in the total market are aware of brand A, 60 percent have tried it, and only 20 percent who have tried it are satisfied. This indicates that the communications program is effective in creating awareness, but the product fails to meet consumer expectations. In

FIG. 17.7

Current Consumer States for Two Brands

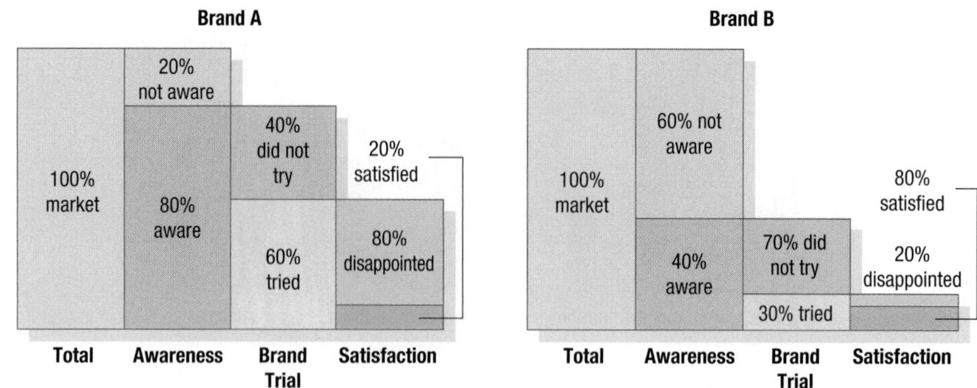

contrast, only 40 percent of the consumers in the total market are aware of brand B, and only 30 percent have tried it, but 80 percent of those who have tried it are satisfied. In this case, the communications program needs to be strengthened to take advantage of the brand's power.

::: Managing the Integrated Marketing Communications Process

As defined by the American Association of Advertising Agencies, **integrated marketing communications (IMC)** is a concept of marketing communications planning that recognizes the added value of a comprehensive plan. Such a plan evaluates the strategic roles of a variety of communications disciplines—for example, general advertising, direct response, sales promotion and public relations—and combines these disciplines to provide clarity, consistency, and maximum impact through the seamless integration of messages.

Unfortunately, many companies still rely on one or two communication tools. This practice persists in spite of the fragmenting of mass markets into a multitude of mini markets, each requiring its own approach; the proliferation of new types of media; and the growing sophistication of consumers. The wide range of communication tools, messages, and audiences makes it imperative that companies move toward integrated marketing communications. Companies must adopt a "360-degree view" of consumers to fully understand all the different ways that communications can affect consumer behavior in their daily lives.

Here is a successful example of an integrated marketing communications program.

ACCENTURE

Forced to change its company name from Andersen Consulting after an arbitrator's decision, Accenture developed a rebranding campaign that utilized a fully integrated communications program. By January 2001, television, print, Internet, and poster ads featuring the Accenture name appeared in each of 48 different countries where the company did business. Between January and March 2001, over 6,000 television commercial spots and 1,000 print ads were run in global markets. In Australia, the company placed a "cover wrap" on the magazine *Business Review Weekly* and advertising on bus stops and park benches in Sydney's business district. The company placed large-scale outdoor ads in Milan's Oberdan Square and coated 10 taxis in London with Accenture signage. The January 2001 Accenture World Match Play Championship allowed the company to run some 300 commercials in its international markets and 100 commercials in the United States, plus print advertisements in major newspapers, business periodicals, and golf magazines in the United States. Additional high-profile global advertising sponsorship opportunities included the Formula 1 Racing Series, several European skiing events, the Six Nations Rugby tournament, the Asian PGA tour, the World Soccer Dream Match in Japan, and the Italian Football Championship.

Coordinating Media

Media coordination can occur across and within media types. Personal and nonpersonal communications channels should be combined to achieve maximum impact. Imagine a marketer using a single tool in a "one-shot" effort to reach and sell a prospect. An example of

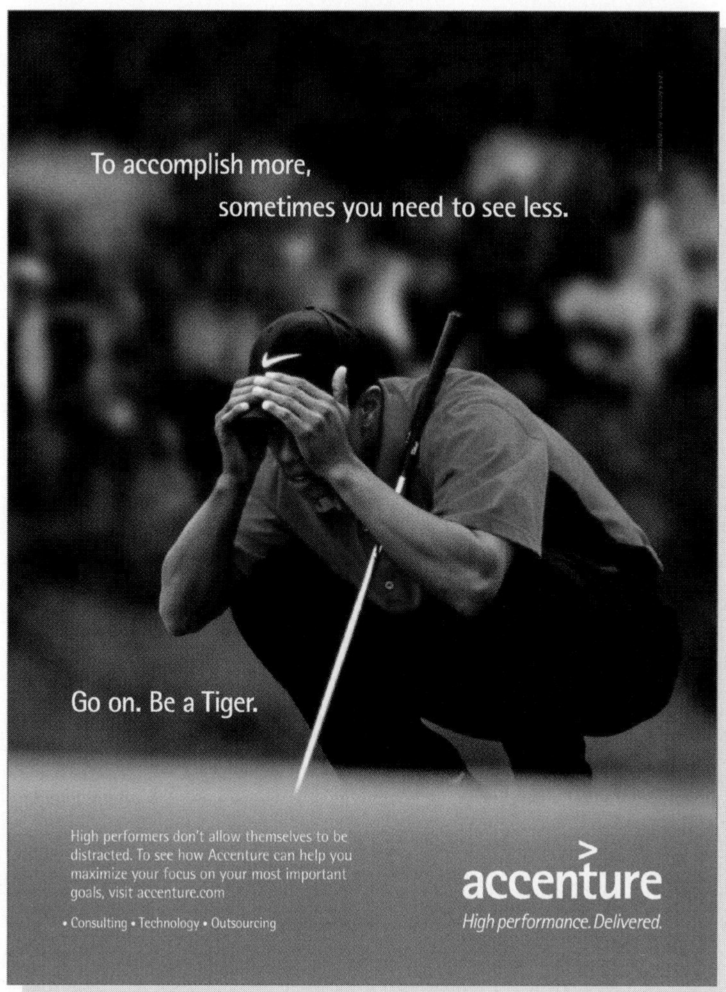

One of a series of Tiger Woods ads that are part of the Accenture rebranding campaign.

a *single-vehicle, single-stage campaign* is a one-time mailing offering a cookware item. A *single-vehicle, multiple-stage campaign* would involve successive mailings to the same prospect. Magazine publishers, for example, send about four renewal notices to a household before giving up. A more powerful approach is the *multiple-vehicle, multiple-stage campaign*. Consider the following sequence:

News campaign about a new product → Paid ad with a response mechanism → Direct mail → Outbound telemarketing → Face-to-face sales call → Ongoing communication.

Multiple media deployed within a tightly defined time frame can increase message reach and impact. For a Citibank campaign to market home equity loans, instead of using only "mail plus an 800 number," Citibank used "mail plus coupon plus 800 number plus outbound telemarketing plus print advertising." Although the second campaign was more expensive, it resulted in a 15 percent increase in the number of new accounts compared with direct mail alone.[53]

Research has also shown that promotions can be more effective when combined with advertising.[54] The awareness and attitudes created by advertising campaigns can improve the success of more direct sales pitches. "Marketing Insight: Coordinating Media to Build Brand Equity" describes how to leverage television advertising in other media.

Many companies are coordinating their online and offline communications activities. About a third of advertisers who bought television advertising for the 2002–2003 season bought ad space on the station's Web sites.[55] Listing URL Web addresses in ads (especially print) and on packages allows people to more fully explore a company's products, find store locations, and get more product or service info. Dannon makes it a priority to drive traffic to its Dannon Yogurt homepage so that the company can benefit from the twin paybacks of (1) forging direct relationships with customers and (2) building a database of its best customers whose loyalty can be strengthened with more targeted coupon and direct-mail promotional efforts.[56]

Pepsi has been highly successful in linking its online and offline efforts. In 2001, Pepsi and Yahoo! joined forces for an online promotion that increased sales 5 percent at a cost of about one-fifth of the previous mail-in promotion. During the promotion, Pepsi displayed the portal's logo on 1.5 billion cans while Yahoo! created a co-branded PepsiStuff.com e-commerce site where visitors could redeem points from bottle caps for prizes ranging from electronic goods to concert tickets.[57] When Dutch financial services firm ING Group launched its brand in the United States, TV and print ads were paired with online ads. In one campaign on financial news sites, all the "ings" in the news text turned orange—matching ING's corporate colors.[58]

Even if consumers do not order online, they can use Web sites in ways that drive them into stores to buy. Best Buy's Web site can be seen as a research tool for consumers, as surveys revealed that 40 percent of its customers looked online first before coming into the store.[59]

Implementing IMC

Integrated marketing communications has been slow to take hold for several reasons. Large companies often employ several communications specialists to work with their brand managers who may know comparatively little about the other communication tools. Further

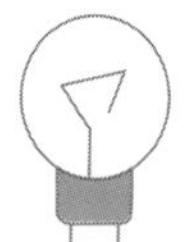

MARKETING **INSIGHT** | COORDINATING MEDIA TO BUILD BRAND EQUITY

To develop effective integrated marketing communications programs, marketers sometimes must explicitly tie marketing communications together to create or enhance brand equity.

Problem: Weak Brand Links

To build brand equity, communication effects created by advertising must be linked to the brand. Often, such links are difficult to create because of:

- ***Competitive Clutter.*** Competing ads in the product category can create "interference" and consumer confusion as to which ad goes with which brand.[61] When Eveready launched a clever ad campaign for Energizer batteries featuring a pink toy bunny that kept on "going . . . and going . . . and going," 40 percent mistakenly attributed it to Eveready's main competitor, Duracell.
- ***Ad Content and Structure.*** Although "borrowed interest" tactics may grab consumers' attention, the resulting processing may *not* create strong brand associations. When the popular actor James Garner was advertising for Polaroid, marketing research surveys routinely noted that interview respondents mistakenly attributed his promotion to Kodak, its chief competitor. Delaying brand identification or providing few brand mentions in an ad may raise processing intensity but result in attention directed away from thinking about the brand, contributing to weak brand links.[62]
- ***Consumer Involvement.*** Consumers may not have any inherent interest in the product or service category or may lack knowledge of the specific brand. The resulting decrease in consumer motivation and ability to process also translates to weaker brand links.[63]

Solution: Strengthening Communication Effects

Advertising may "work" in the sense that communication effects are stored in memory. Yet advertising may "fail" in the sense that these communication effects are *not* accessible when consumers make critical brand-related decisions. To address this problem, one common tactic is to make the brand name and package information prominent in the ad. Unfortunately, although consumers are better able to recall the advertised brand with this tactic, there is less other information about the brand to actually recall. Three potentially more effective strategies are brand signatures, ad retrieval cues, and media interactions.

- ***Brand Signatures.*** The *brand signature* is the manner by which the brand is identified at the conclusion of a TV or radio ad or displayed within a print ad. An effective brand signature provides a seamless connection to the ad as a whole. For example, the famous "Got milk?" campaign always displayed that tagline or slogan in a manner fitting the ad (e.g., in flames for the "yuppie in hell" ad or in primary school print for the "school lunchroom bully" ad).
- ***Ad Retrieval Cues.*** An *advertising retrieval cue* is a key visual, a catchy slogan, or any unique advertising element that serves as an effective reminder to consumers. Eveready featured a picture of the pink bunny character on the packages of Energizer batteries to reduce confusion with Duracell. Ad retrieval cues can be placed in the store (on the package or as part of a shelf-talker or some other point-of-purchase device), combined with a promotion (an FSI coupon), included as part of a yellow pages directory listing, or embedded in any marketing communication option where recall of communication effects can be advantageous.
- ***Media Interactions.*** Print and radio reinforcement of TV ads—where the video and audio components of a TV ad serve as the basis for other types of ads—can be an effective means to leverage existing communication effects from TV ad exposure and more strongly link them to the brand. A potentially useful, although rarely employed, media strategy is to run explicitly linked print or radio ads *prior* to the accompanying TV ad. The print and radio ads increase consumer motivation to process the more "complete" TV ad.

Source: Kevin Lane Keller, *Strategic Brand Management,* 2nd ed. (Upper Saddle River, NJ: Prentice Hall, 2002).

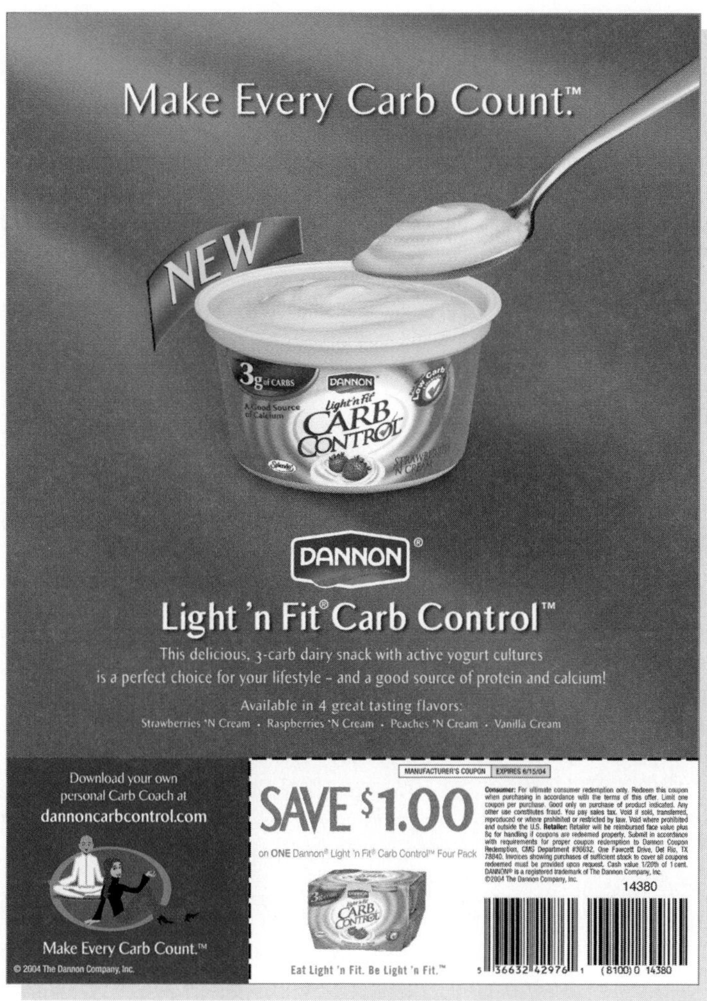

This Dannon print ad includes a Web address as well as a coupon, to drive readers and customers to the Dannon Web site as well as to buy the product.

complicating matters is that many global companies use a large number of ad agencies located in different countries and serving different divisions, resulting in uncoordinated communications and image diffusion.

Today, however, a few large agencies have substantially improved their integrated offerings. To facilitate one-stop shopping, major ad agencies have acquired promotion agencies, public relations firms, package-design consultancies, Web site developers, and direct-mail houses. Many international clients have opted to put a substantial portion of their communications work through one agency. An example is IBM turning all of its advertising over to Ogilvy to attain uniform branding. The result is integrated and more effective marketing communications and a much lower total communications cost.

Integrated marketing communications can produce stronger message consistency and greater sales impact. It forces management to think about every way the customer comes in contact with the company, how the company communicates its positioning, the relative importance of each vehicle, and timing issues. It gives someone the responsibility—where none existed before—to unify the company's brand images and messages as they come through thousands of company activities. IMC should improve the company's ability to reach the right customers with the right messages at the right time and in the right place.[60] "Marketing Memo: How Integrated Is Your IMC Program?" provides some guidelines.

IMC advocates describe it as a way of looking at the whole marketing process instead of focusing on individual parts of it. Companies such as Motorola, Xerox, and Hewlett-Packard are bringing together advertising, direct marketing, public relations, and employee communications experts into "supercouncils" that meet a few times each year for training and improved communications among them. Procter & Gamble recently revised its communications planning by requiring that each new program be formulated jointly, with its ad agency sitting together with P&G's public relations agencies, direct-marketing units, promotion-merchandising firms, and Internet operations.

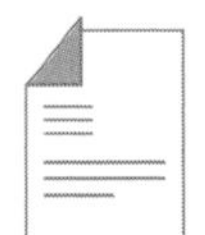

MARKETING MEMO | HOW INTEGRATED IS YOUR IMC PROGRAM?

In assessing the collective impact of an IMC program, the overriding goal is to create the most effective and efficient communications program possible. The following six criteria can be used to help determine whether communications are truly integrated.

- ***Coverage.*** Coverage is the proportion of the audience that is reached by each communication option employed, as well as how much overlap exists among communication options. In other words, to what extent do different communication options reach the designated target market and the same or different consumers making up that market?
- ***Contribution.*** Contribution is the inherent ability of a marketing communication to create the desired response and communication effects from consumers in the absence of exposure to any other communication option. How much does a communication affect consumer processing and build awareness, enhance image, elicit responses, and induce sales?
- ***Commonality.*** Commonality is the extent to which *common* associations are reinforced across communication options, that is, the extent to which information conveyed by different communication options share meaning. The consistency and cohesiveness of the brand image is important because it determines how easily existing associations and responses can be recalled and how easily additional associations and responses can become linked to the brand in memory.
- ***Complementarity.*** Communication options are often more effective when used in tandem. Complementarity relates to the extent to which *different* associations and linkages are emphasized across communication options. Different brand associations may be most effectively established by capitalizing on those marketing communication options best suited to eliciting a particular consumer response or establishing a particular type of brand association. As part of the highly successful "Drivers Wanted" campaign, VW has used television to introduce a story line that it continued and embellished on its Web site.
- ***Versatility.*** With any integrated communication program, when consumers are exposed to a particular marketing communication, some consumers will have already been exposed to other marketing communications for the brand, whereas other consumers will not have had any prior exposure. Versatility refers to the extent to which a marketing communication option is robust and "works" for different groups of consumers. The ability of a marketing communication to work at "two levels"—effectively communicating to consumers who have or have *not* seen other communications—is critically important.
- ***Cost.*** Evaluations of marketing communications on all of these criteria must be weighed against their cost to arrive at the most effective *and* efficient communications program.

Source: Kevin Lane Keller (2003), *Strategic Brand Management,* 2nd ed. (Upper Saddle River, NJ: Prentice Hall, 2002).

SUMMARY :::

1. Modern marketing calls for more than developing a good product, pricing it attractively, and making it accessible to target customers. Companies must also communicate with present and potential stakeholders, and with the general public.
2. The marketing communications mix consists of six major modes of communication: advertising, sales promotion, public relations and publicity, events and experiences, direct marketing, and personal selling.
3. The communications process consists of nine elements: sender, receiver, message, media, encoding, decoding, response, feedback, and noise. To get their messages through, marketers must encode their messages in a way that takes into account how the target audience usually decodes messages. They must also transmit the message through efficient media that reach the target audience and develop feedback channels to monitor response to the message. Consumer response to a communication can be often modeled in terms of a response hierarchy and "learn-feel-do" sequence.
4. Developing effective communications involves eight steps: (1) Identify the target audience, (2) determine the communications objectives, (3) design the communications, (4) select the communications channels, (5) establish the total communications budget, (6) decide on the communications mix, (7) measure the communications results, and (8) manage the integrated marketing communications process.
5. In identifying the target audience, the marketer needs to close any gap that exists between current public perception and the image sought. Communications objectives may involve category need, brand awareness, brand attitude, or brand purchase intention. Formulating the communication requires solving three problems: what to say (message strategy), how to say it (creative strategy), and who should say it (message source). Communications channels may be personal (advocate, expert, and social channels) or nonpersonal (media, atmospheres, and events). The objective-and-task method of setting the promotion budget, which calls upon marketers to develop their budgets by defining specific objectives, is the most desirable.

6. In deciding on the marketing communications mix, marketers must examine the distinct advantages and costs of each communication tool and the company's market rank. They must also consider the type of product market in which they are selling, how ready consumers are to make a purchase, and the product's stage in the product life cycle. Measuring the effectiveness of the marketing communications mix involves asking members of the target audience whether they recognize or recall the communication, how many times they saw it, what points they recall, how they felt about the communication, and their previous and current attitudes toward the product and the company.
7. Managing and coordinating the entire communications process calls for integrated marketing communications (IMC): marketing communications planning that recognizes the added value of a comprehensive plan that evaluates the strategic roles of a variety of communications disciplines and combines these disciplines to provide clarity, consistency, and maximum impact through the seamless integration of discrete messages.

APPLICATIONS :::

Marketing Debate What Is the Biggest Obstacle to Integrating Marketing Communications?

Although integrated marketing communications is a frequently espoused goal, truly integrated programs have been hard to come by. Some critics maintain the problem is an organizational one—the agencies have not done a good job of putting together all the different teams and organizations involved with a communications campaign. Others maintain that the biggest problem is the lack of managerial guidelines for evaluating IMC programs. How does a manager know when his or her IMC program is satisfactorily integrated?

Take a position: The biggest obstacle to effective IMC programs is a lack of agency coordination across communication units versus The biggest obstacle to effective IMC programs is a lack of understanding as to how to optimally design and evaluate such programs.

Marketing Discussion

Pick a brand and go to the Web site. Locate as many forms of communication as you can find. Conduct an informal communications audit. What do you notice? How consistent are the different communications?

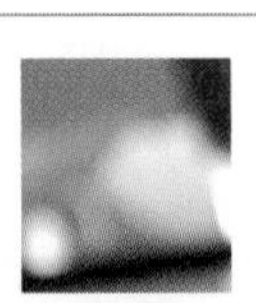

IN THIS CHAPTER, WE WILL ADDRESS THE FOLLOWING QUESTIONS:

1. What steps are involved in developing an advertising program?
2. How should sales promotion decisions be made?
3. What are the guidelines for effective brand-building events and experiences?
4. How can companies exploit the potential of public relations and publicity?

CHAPTER 18 ::: MANAGING MASS COMMUNICATIONS: ADVERTISING, SALES PROMOTIONS, EVENTS, AND PUBLIC RELATIONS

eighteen

At the American Association of Advertising Agencies' annual media conference in 1994, Procter & Gamble CEO Ed Atrzt shook up the advertising world by proclaiming that marketers needed to develop and embrace new media. Ten years later, at that same conference, P&G CMO Jim Stengel gave a status report on how well he felt marketers have fared.[1] Stengel pointed out that although new media were now abundant, marketers and agencies were not using or measuring them sufficiently. In 1994, 90 percent of P&G's global ad spending was on TV, but one of its most successful brand launches in history, for Prilosec OTC in 2003, allocated only about one-quarter of its spending to TV. Here is some of what he said:

There must be—and is—life beyond the 30-second spot. But our systems still revolve around that. Today's marketing world is broken. . . . We are still too dependent on marketing tactics that are not in touch with today's consumers. . . . All marketing should be permission marketing. All marketing should be so appealing that consumers want us in their lives. . . . The traditional marketing model is obsolete. Holistic marketing is driving our business."

>>>

Jim Stengel, Procter & Gamble CMO, in his office.

Procter & Gamble is not alone. Marketers of all kinds are trying to come to grips with how to best use mass media in the new communication environment. In this chapter, we examine the nature and use of four mass communication tools—advertising, sales promotion, events and experiences, and public relations and publicity.

::: Developing and Managing an Advertising Program

Advertising is any paid form of nonpersonal presentation and promotion of ideas, goods, or services by an identified sponsor. Ads can be a cost-effective way to disseminate messages, whether to build a brand preference or to educate people.

Organizations handle advertising in different ways. In small companies, advertising is handled by someone in the sales or marketing department, who works with an advertising agency. A large company will often set up its own department, whose manager reports to the vice president of marketing. The department's job is to propose a budget, develop strategy, approve ads and campaigns, and handle direct-mail advertising, dealer displays, and other forms of advertising.

Most companies use an outside agency to help create advertising campaigns and to select and purchase media. Today, advertising agencies are redefining themselves as *communications companies* that assist clients to improve their overall communications effectiveness by offering strategic and practical advice on many forms of communication.[2]

In developing an advertising program, marketing managers must always start by identifying the target market and buyer motives. Then they can make the five major decisions, known as "the five Ms": *Mission:* What are the advertising objectives? *Money:* How much can be spent? *Message:* What message should be sent? *Media:* What media should be used? *Measurement:* How should the results be evaluated? These decisions are summarized in Figure 18.1 and described in the following sections.

Setting the Objectives

The advertising objectives must flow from prior decisions on target market, brand positioning, and the marketing program.

FIG. 18.1

The Five Ms of Advertising

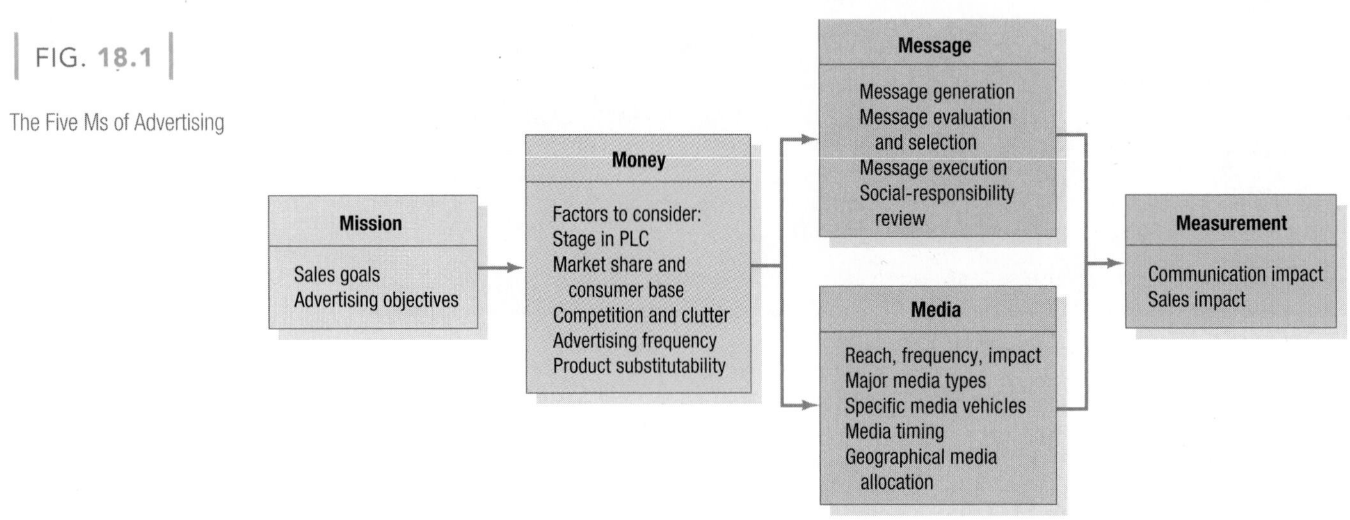

An **advertising goal** (or objective) is a specific communications task and achievement level to be accomplished with a specific audience in a specific period of time:[3]

> To increase among 30 million homemakers who own automatic washers the number who identify brand X as a low-sudsing detergent and who are persuaded that it gets clothes cleaner from 10 percent to 40 percent in one year.

Advertising objectives can be classified according to whether their aim is to inform, persuade, remind, or reinforce. They aim at different stages in the *hierarchy-of-effects* discussed in Chapter 17.

- ***Informative advertising*** aims to create brand awareness and knowledge of new products or new features of existing products. One of the all-time most memorable ads starred Australian rugby player Jacko for Energizer batteries. He was shown dressed as a battery, bursting into an early morning subway car, repeatedly shouting out the brand name to the commuters. Unfortunately, people remembered the name—but hated the ad! Brand awareness cannot come at the expense of brand attitudes.
- ***Persuasive advertising*** aims to create liking, preference, conviction, and purchase of a product or service. Chivas Regal attempts to persuade consumers that it delivers more taste and status than other brands of Scotch whiskey. Some persuasive advertising uses comparative advertising, which makes an explicit comparison of the attributes of two or more brands.[4] For years, VISA has run a successful ad campaign called "It's Everywhere You Want to Be," that showcases desirable locations and events that don't accept the American Express card. Comparative advertising works best when it elicits cognitive and affective motivations simultaneously.[5]
- ***Reminder advertising*** aims to stimulate repeat purchase of products and services. Expensive, four-color Coca-Cola ads in magazines are intended to remind people to purchase Coca-Cola.
- ***Reinforcement advertising*** aims to convince current purchasers that they made the right choice. Automobile ads often depict satisfied customers enjoying special features of their new car.

The advertising objective should emerge from a thorough analysis of the current marketing situation. If the product class is mature, the company is the market leader, and brand usage is low, the proper objective should be to stimulate more usage. If the product class is new, the company is not the market leader, but the brand is superior to the leader, then the proper objective is to convince the market of the brand's superiority.

Deciding on the Advertising Budget

How does a company know if it is spending the right amount? Some critics charge that large consumer-packaged-goods firms tend to overspend on advertising as a form of insurance against not spending enough, and that industrial companies underestimate the power of company and product image building and tend to underspend.[6]

Although advertising is treated as a current expense, part of it is really an investment in building brand equity. When $5 million is spent on capital equipment, the equipment may be treated as a five-year depreciable asset and only one-fifth of the cost is written off in the first year. When $5 million is spent on advertising to launch a new product, the entire cost must be written off in the first year. This reduces the company's reported profit and therefore limits the number of new-product launches a company can undertake in any one year.

In Chapter 17, we described some general methods to estimate communications budgets. Here are five specific factors to consider when setting the advertising budget:[7]

1. ***Stage in the product life cycle*** – New products typically receive large advertising budgets to build awareness and to gain consumer trial. Established brands usually are supported with lower advertising budgets as a ratio to sales.[8]
2. ***Market share and consumer base*** – High-market-share brands usually require less advertising expenditure as a percentage of sales to maintain share. To build share by increasing market size requires larger expenditures. On a cost-per-impression basis, it is less expensive to reach consumers of a widely used brand than to reach consumers of low-share brands.
3. ***Competition and clutter*** – In a market with a large number of competitors and high advertising spending, a brand must advertise more heavily to be heard. Even simple

clutter from advertisements not directly competitive to the brand creates a need for heavier advertising.

4. ***Advertising frequency*** – The number of repetitions needed to put across the brand's message to consumers has an important impact on the advertising budget.
5. ***Product substitutability*** – Brands in less-well-differentiated or commodity-like product classes (beer, soft drinks, banks, and airlines) require heavy advertising to establish a differential image. Advertising is also important when a brand can offer unique physical benefits or features.

In one study of budget allocation, Low and Mohr found that managers allocate less to advertising as brands move to the more mature phase of the product life cycle; when a brand is well-differentiated from the competition; when managers are rewarded on short-term results; as retailers gain more power; and when managers have less experience with the company.[9]

Developing the Advertising Campaign

In designing and evaluating an ad campaign, it is important to distinguish the *message strategy* or positioning of an ad (what the ad attempts to convey about the brand) from its *creative strategy* (how the ad expresses the brand claims). So designing effective advertising campaigns is both an art and a science. To develop a message strategy, advertisers go through three steps: message generation and evaluation, creative development and execution, and social-responsibility review.

MESSAGE GENERATION AND EVALUATION It is important to generate fresh insights and avoid using the same appeals and positions as others. Many of today's automobile ads have a sameness about them—a car driving at high speed on a curved mountain road or across a desert. The result is that only a weak link is established between the brand and the message.

A good ad normally focuses on one or two core selling propositions. As part of refining the brand positioning, the advertiser should conduct market research to determine which appeal works best with its target audience. Once they find an effective appeal, advertisers should prepare a *creative brief,* typically covering one or two pages. It is an elaboration of the *positioning statement* (see Chapter 10) and includes: key message, target audience, communications objectives (to do, to know, to believe), key brand benefits, supports for the brand promise, and media. All the team members working on the campaign need to agree on the creative brief before investing in costly ads.

How many alternative ad themes should the advertiser create before making a choice? The more ads created, the higher the probability of finding an excellent one. Under a commission system, an agency may not like to go to the expense of creating and pretesting many ads. Fortunately, the expense of creating rough ads is rapidly falling due to computers. An ad agency's creative department can compose many alternative ads in a short time by drawing from computer files containing still and video images.

CREATIVE DEVELOPMENT AND EXECUTION The ad's impact depends not only on what is said, but often more important, on how it is said. Message execution can be decisive. In preparing an ad campaign, the advertiser can prepare a *copy strategy statement* describing the objective, content, support, and tone of the desired ad. Here is the strategy statement for a Pillsbury product called 1869 Brand Biscuits.

PILLSBURY

The advertising *objective* is to convince biscuit users they can buy a canned biscuit that is as good as homemade—Pillsbury's 1869 Brand Biscuits. The *content* consists of emphasizing the following product characteristics: They look like, have the same texture as, and taste like homemade biscuits. *Support* for the "good as homemade" promise will be twofold: (1) 1869 Brand Biscuits are made from a special kind of flour used to make homemade biscuits but never before used in making canned biscuits, and (2) the use of traditional American biscuit recipes. The tone of the advertising will be a news announcement, tempered by a warm, reflective mood emanating from a look back at traditional American baking quality.

Every advertising medium has specific advantages and disadvantages. Here, we review television, radio, and print advertising media.

Television Ads Television is generally acknowledged as the most powerful advertising medium and reaches a broad spectrum of consumers. The wide reach translates to low cost per exposure. From a brand-building perspective, TV advertising has two particularly important strengths. First, it can be an effective means of vividly demonstrating product attributes and persuasively explaining their corresponding consumer benefits. Second, TV advertising can be a compelling means for dramatically portraying user and usage imagery, brand personality, and other brand intangibles.

Television advertising also has its drawbacks. Because of the fleeting nature of the message and the potentially distracting creative elements often found in a TV ad, product-related messages and the brand itself can be overlooked. Moreover, the large number of ads and nonprogramming material on television creates clutter that makes it easy for consumers to ignore or forget ads. Another important disadvantage is the high cost of production and placement. Even though the price of TV advertising has skyrocketed, the share of the prime time audience for the major networks has steadily declined. By any number of measures, the effectiveness of any one ad, on average, has diminished. For example, Video Storyboards reported that the number of viewers who said that they paid attention to TV ads dropped significantly in the last decade.

Nevertheless, properly designed and executed TV ads can improve brand equity and affect sales and profits. Over the years, one of the most consistently successful TV advertisers has been Apple. The "1984" ad for the introduction of the Macintosh personal computer—portraying a stark Orwellian future with a feature film look—ran only once on TV but is one of the best known ads ever. In the years that followed, Apple advertising successfully created awareness and image for a series of products, most recently with its acclaimed "Think Different" campaign. Even with the decline in audiences for the TV advertisement, a well-done TV commercial can still be a powerful marketing tool.

AFLAC INC.

Insurance companies have a particularly hard time creating brand awareness as well as differentiating themselves from competing insurers. Insurance company Aflac Inc., was relatively unknown until a highly creative ad campaign made it one of the most recognized brands in recent history. The lighthearted campaign features an irascible duck incessantly shouting the company's name, "Aflac!" while consumers or celebrities discuss its supplemental health insurance. The duck's frustrated bid for attention appealed to consumers, who are now paying the company a lot of attention. Sales were up 28 percent in the first year the duck aired, and name recognition went from 13 percent to 91 percent in that time.[10]

Print Ads Print media offer a stark contrast to broadcast media. Because of their self-paced nature, magazines and newspapers can provide much detailed product information and can also effectively communicate user and usage imagery. At the same time, the static nature of the visual images in print media makes it difficult to provide dynamic presentations or demonstrations. Another disadvantage is that print media can be fairly passive.

In general, the two main print media—magazines and newspapers—have many of the same advantages and disadvantages. Although newspapers are timely and pervasive, magazines are typically more effective at building user and usage imagery. Daily newspapers are read by roughly three-fourths of the population and tend to be used a lot for local—especially retailer—advertising. Although advertisers have some flexibility in designing and placing newspaper ads, poor reproduction quality and short shelf life can diminish their impact.

Format elements such as ad size, color, and illustration also affect a print ad's impact. A minor rearrangement of mechanical elements can improve attention-getting power. Larger ads gain more attention, though not necessarily by as much as their difference in cost. Four-color illustrations increase ad effectiveness and ad cost. New electronic eye movement studies show that consumers can be led through an ad by strategic placement of dominant elements.

Researchers studying print advertisements report that the *picture, headline,* and *copy* are important, in that order. The picture must be strong enough to draw attention. Then the headline must reinforce the picture and lead the person to read the copy. The copy itself must be engaging and the advertised brand's name must be sufficiently prominent. Even then, a really outstanding ad will be noted by less than 50 percent of the exposed audience. About 30 percent might recall the headline's main point; about 25 percent might remember the advertiser's name; and less than 10 percent will read most of the body copy. Ordinary ads do not achieve even these results.

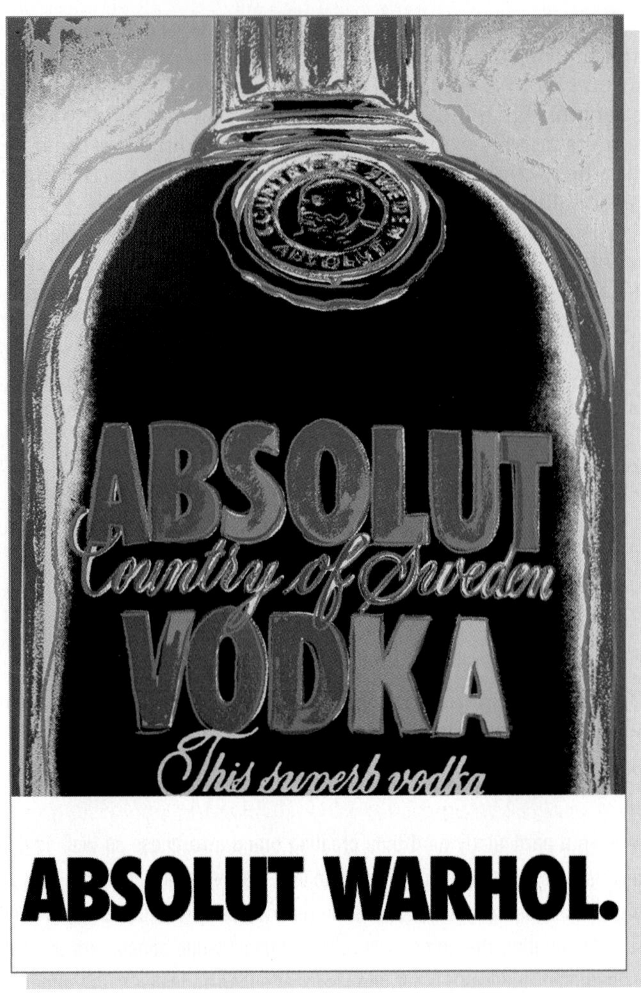

Building a unique brand image: Absolut Warhol, The Absolut print ad by Andy Warhol.

Given how consumers process print ads, some clear managerial implications emerge, as summarized in "Marketing Memo: Print Ad Evaluation Criteria." One print ad campaign that successfully carved out a brand image is Absolut vodka.

ABSOLUT VODKA

Vodka is generally viewed as a commodity product, yet the amount of brand preference and loyalty in the vodka market is astonishing. Most of this preference and loyalty is attributed to brand image. When the Swedish brand Absolut entered the U.S. market in 1979, the company sold a disappointing 7,000 cases. By 1991, sales had soared to over 2 million cases. Absolut became the largest-selling imported vodka in the United States, with 65 percent of the market, thanks in large part to its marketing strategy. In the U.S. market, Absolut has aimed for sophisticated, upwardly mobile, affluent drinkers. The vodka comes in a distinctive clear bottle that is used as the centerpiece of every ad. Well-known artists—including Warhol, Haring, and Scharf—have designed Absolut ads, and the bottle image always fits with the caption in a clever way.[11]

Radio Ads Radio is a pervasive medium: 96 percent of all Americans age 12 and older listen to the radio daily and, on average, for over 20 hours a week. Perhaps radio's main advantage is flexibility—stations are very targeted, ads are relatively inexpensive to produce and place, and short closings allow for quick response. Radio is a particularly effective medium in the morning; it can also let companies achieve a balance between broad and localized market coverage. AT&T uses radio to target African American consumers because African Americans spend an average of four hours every day listening to the radio, far more time than the national average of 2.8 hours.[12] As the centerpiece of its 2000 multimedia campaign, AT&T sponsored a live radio broadcast of a Destiny's Child concert that included a promotion where listeners could win a trip to New Orleans.

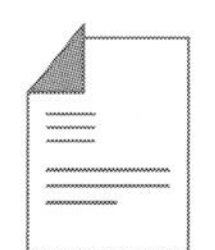

MARKETING MEMO | PRINT AD EVALUATION CRITERIA

In judging the effectiveness of a print ad, in addition to considering the communication strategy (target market, communications objectives, and message and creative strategy), the following questions should be answered affirmatively concerning the executional elements:

1. Is the message clear at a glance? Can you quickly tell what the advertisement is all about?
2. Is the benefit in the headline?
3. Does the illustration support the headline?
4. Does the first line of the copy support or explain the headline and illustration?
5. Is the ad easy to read and follow?
6. Is the product easily identified?
7. Is the brand or sponsor clearly identified?

Source: Philip Ward Burton and Scott C. Purvis, *Which Ad Pulled Best,* 9th ed. (Lincolnwood, IL: NTC Business Books, 2002).

The obvious disadvantages of radio are the lack of visual images and the relatively passive nature of the consumer processing that results.[13] Nevertheless, radio ads can be extremely creative. Some see the lack of visual images as a plus because they feel the clever use of music, sound, and other creative devices can tap into the listener's imagination to create powerfully relevant and liked images. Here is an example:

MOTEL 6

Motel 6, the nation's largest budget motel chain, was founded in 1962 when the "6" stood for $6 a night. After finding its business fortunes hitting bottom in 1986 with an occupancy rate of only 66.7 percent, Motel 6 made a number of marketing changes. It included the launch of a radio campaign of humorous 60-second ads featuring folksy contractor-turned-writer Tom Bodett with the clever tagline "We'll leave the light on for you." The ad campaign is credited with a rise in occupancy and a revitalization of the brand that continues to this day.

SOCIAL-RESPONSIBILITY REVIEW Advertisers and their agencies must be sure advertising does not overstep social and legal norms. Public policy makers have developed a substantial body of laws and regulations to govern advertising.

Under U.S. law, advertisers must not make false claims, such as stating that a product cures something when it does not. They must avoid false demonstrations, such as using sand-covered plexiglass instead of sandpaper to demonstrate that a razor blade can shave sandpaper. It is illegal in the United States to create ads that have the capacity to deceive, even though no one may actually be deceived. For example, a floor wax cannot be advertised as giving six months' protection unless it does so under typical conditions, and a diet bread cannot be advertised as having fewer calories simply because its slices are thinner. The problem is how to tell the difference between deception and "puffery"—simple exaggerations not intended to be believed which are permitted by law.

Sellers in the United States are legally obligated to avoid bait-and-switch advertising that attracts buyers under false pretenses. Suppose a seller advertises a sewing machine at $149. When consumers try to buy the advertised machine, the seller cannot then refuse to sell it, downplay its features, show a faulty one, or promise unreasonable delivery dates in order to switch the buyer to a more expensive machine.[14]

To be socially responsible, advertisers must be careful not to offend the general public as well as any ethnic groups, racial minorities, or special-interest groups.[15] Ads for Calvin Klein apparel have often been accused of crossing the lines of decency, with ads featuring the waifish model Kate Moss that came under attack from Boycott Anorexic Marketing, and ads featuring pubescent models—some reportedly as young as 15—in provocative poses, which resulted in a massive letter-writing campaign from the American Family Association.[16]

Every year, the nonprofit trade group Advertising Women of New York singles out TV and print ads that it feels portray particularly good or bad images of women. In 2004, Sirius Satellite Radio won the TV Grand Ugly award for its "Car Wash" ad, which featured Pam Anderson in a wet tank top using her entire body to clean a young man's car. Print Grand Ugly went to a Sony Playstation ad that featured a woman giving birth to the head of a grown man. The TV Grand Good ad went to a MasterCard commercial in which a woman opens a jar of pickles after her weakling husband fails the test.[17]

::: Deciding on Media and Measuring Effectiveness

After choosing the message, the advertiser's next task is to choose media to carry it. The steps here are deciding on desired reach, frequency, and impact; choosing among major media types; selecting specific media vehicles; deciding on media timing; and deciding on geographical media allocation. Then the results of these decisions need to be evaluated.

Deciding on Reach, Frequency, and Impact

Media selection is finding the most cost-effective media to deliver the desired number and type of exposures to the target audience. What do we mean by the desired number of exposures? Presumably, the advertiser is seeking a specified advertising objective and response from the target audience—for example, a target level of product trial. The rate of product trial will depend, among other things, on level of brand awareness. Suppose the rate of product trial increases at a diminishing rate with the level of audience awareness, as shown in Figure 18.2(a). If the advertiser seeks a product trial rate of (say) T^*, it will be necessary to achieve a brand awareness level of A^*.

The next task is to find out how many exposures, E^*, will produce a level of audience awareness of A^*. The effect of exposures on audience awareness depends on the exposures' reach, frequency, and impact:

- ***Reach (R).*** The number of different persons or households exposed to a particular media schedule at least once during a specified time period.
- ***Frequency (F).*** The number of times within the specified time period that an average person or household is exposed to the message.
- ***Impact (I).*** The qualitative value of an exposure through a given medium (thus a food ad in *Good Housekeeping* would have a higher impact than in *Fortune* magazine).

Figure 18.2(b) shows the relationship between audience awareness and reach. Audience awareness will be greater, the higher the exposures' reach, frequency, and impact. There are important trade-offs among reach, frequency, and impact. Suppose the planner has an advertising budget of $1,000,000 and the cost per thousand exposures of average quality is $5. This means the advertiser can buy 200,000,000 exposures ($1,000,000 ÷ [$5/1,000]). If the advertiser seeks an average exposure frequency of 10, then the advertiser can reach 20,000,000 people (200,000,000 ÷ 10) with the given budget. But if the advertiser wants higher-quality media costing $10 per thousand exposures, it will be able to reach only 10,000,000 people unless it is willing to lower the desired exposure frequency.

The relationship between reach, frequency, and impact is captured in the following concepts:

- ***Total number of exposures (E).*** This is the reach times the average frequency; that is, $E = R \times F$. This measure is referred to as the gross rating points (GRP). If a given media schedule reaches 80 percent of the homes with an average exposure frequency of 3, the

FIG. 18.2

Relationship Among Trial, Awareness, and the Exposure Function

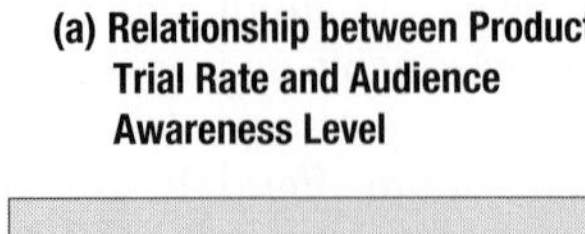

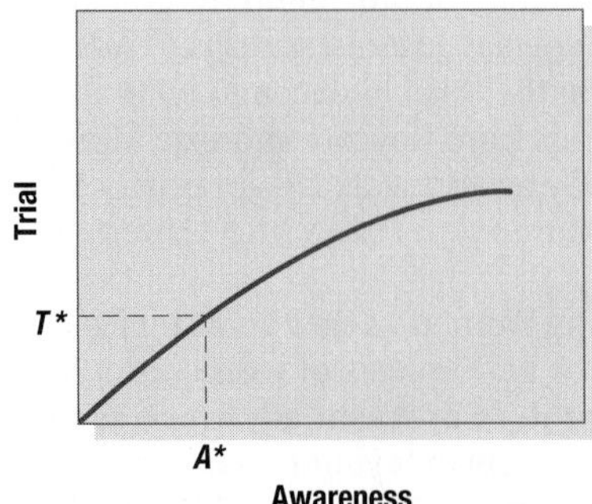

(b) Relationship between Audience Awareness Level and Exposure Reach and Frequency

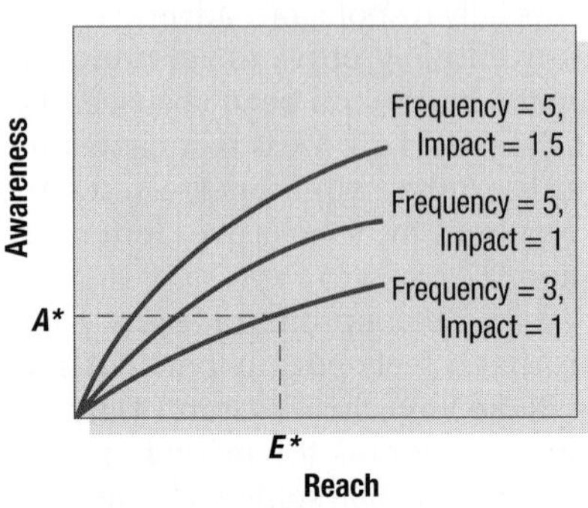

media schedule is said to have a GRP of 240 (80×3). If another media schedule has a GRP of 300, it is said to have more weight, but we cannot tell how this weight breaks down into reach and frequency.

- ***Weighted number of exposures (WE).*** This is the reach times average frequency times average impact, that is $WE = R \times F \times I$.

The media planner has to figure out the most cost-effective combination of reach, frequency, and impact. Reach is most important when launching new products, flanker brands, extensions of well-known brands, or infrequently purchased brands; or going after an undefined target market. Frequency is most important where there are strong competitors, a complex story to tell, high consumer resistance, or a frequent-purchase cycle.[18]

Many advertisers believe a target audience needs a large number of exposures for the advertising to work. Others doubt the value of high frequency. They believe that after people see the same ad a few times, they either act on it, get irritated by it, or stop noticing it.[19]

Another factor arguing for repetition is that of forgetting. The job of repetition is partly to put the message back into memory. The higher the forgetting rate associated with a brand, product category, or message, the higher the warranted level of repetition. However, repetition is not enough; ads wear out and viewers tune out. Advertisers should not coast on a tired ad but should insist on fresh executions by their advertising agency.

Choosing Among Major Media Types

The media planner has to know the capacity of the major advertising media types to deliver reach, frequency, and impact. The major advertising media along with their costs, advantages, and limitations are profiled in Table 18.1.

Media planners make their choices by considering the following variables:

- ***Target audience media habits.*** Radio and television are the most effective media for reaching teenagers.
- ***Product characteristics.*** Media types have different potential for demonstration, visualization, explanation, believability, and color. Women's dresses are best shown in color magazines, and Kodak cameras are best demonstrated on television.

TABLE 18.1 | Profiles of Major Media Types

Medium	Advantages	Limitations
Newspapers	Flexibility; timeliness; good local market coverage; broad acceptance; high believability	Short life; poor reproduction quality; small "pass-along" audience
Television	Combines sight, sound, and motion; appealing to the senses; high attention; high reach	High absolute cost; high clutter; fleeting exposure; less audience selectivity
Direct mail	Audience selectivity; flexibility; no ad competition within the same medium; personalization	Relatively high cost; "junk mail" image
Radio	Mass use; high geographic and demographic selectivity; low cost	Audio presentation only; lower attention than television; nonstandardized rate structures; fleeting exposure
Magazines	High geographic and demographic selectivity; credibility and prestige; high-quality reproduction; long life; good pass-along readership	Long ad purchase lead time; some waste circulation; no guarantee of position
Outdoor	Flexibility; high repeat exposure; low cost; low competition	Limited audience selectivity; creative limitations
Yellow Pages	Excellent local coverage; high believability; wide reach; low cost	High competition; long ad purchase lead time; creative limitations
Newsletters	Very high selectivity; full control; interactive opportunities; relative low costs	Costs could run away
Brochures	Flexibility; full control; can dramatize messages	Overproduction could lead to runaway costs
Telephone	Many users; opportunity to give a personal touch	Relative high cost unless volunteers are used
Internet	High selectivity; interactive possibilities; relatively low cost	Relatively new media with a low number of users in some countries

TABLE 18.2

Marketing Communication Expenditures (U.S., 2001, Billions of Dollars)

	$	% of Total
TV	52.7	22%
Radio	19.4	8%
Newspaper	49.4	21%
Magazines	12.3	5%
Yellow Pages	13.3	6%
Internet	3.4	1%
Direct Response	44.7	19%
Other	40.0	17%
Total	141.7	

Source: Tom Duncan, *IMC: Using Advertising and Promotion to Build Brands* (New York: McGraw-Hill, 2002).

- ***Message characteristics.*** Timeliness and information content will influence media choice. A message announcing a major sale tomorrow will require radio, TV, or newspaper. A message containing a great deal of technical data might require specialized magazines or mailings.
- ***Cost.*** Television is very expensive, whereas newspaper advertising is relatively inexpensive. What counts is the cost per thousand exposures.

Given the abundance of media, the planner must first decide how to allocate the budget to the major media types (see Table 18.2). In launching a new biscuit, Pillsbury might decide to allocate $3 million to daytime network television, $2 million to women's magazines, $1 million to daily newspapers in 20 major markets, $500,000 to various grassroots cooking events and competitions, and $50,000 to maintaining its homepage on the Internet.

The distribution must be planned with the awareness that people are increasingly time-starved. They are assaulted daily by ads and information from traditional media plus e-mail, voice mail, and instant messages. There is little time for thinking about experiences, let alone for hobbies and other diversions. Attention is becoming a scarce currency, and advertisers need strong devices to capture people's attention.[20] In deciding on the ad budget, marketers must also recognize that consumer response can be S-shaped: An ad threshold effect exists where some positive amount of advertising is necessary before any sales impact can be detected, but sales increases eventually flatten out.[21]

Alternative Advertising Options

For a long time, television was the dominant medium. In recent years, researchers have noticed reduced effectiveness due to increased commercial clutter (advertisers beaming shorter and more numerous commercials at the audience), increased "zipping and zapping" of commercials (aided by the arrival of new TV systems such as TiVo and Replay TV), and lower viewing owing to the growth in cable and satellite TV and DVD/VCRs.[22] Table 18.3 shows how the home media environment has changed dramatically in the last 25 years or so. Furthermore, television advertising costs have risen faster than other media costs. Many marketers are looking for alternative advertising media.[23] One brewer, Canada's Molson, is taking an even more innovative tack by putting catchy phrases right on the bottles.

MOLSON

Crispin, Porter, + Bogusky's campaign for Canadian brewer Molson won *Adweek*'s award for Media Plan of the Year spending less than $10 million. CP+B was hired to revitalize Molson's brand in the United States and renew its relevance among its core target of men ages 21 to 27 who are not necessarily sitting in front of the TV waiting for 30-second beer commercials. CP+B made a radical suggestion: Don't spend more ad money; dress up your beer bottles. The CP+B team came up with the idea of bottle label as badge, to let the product help men

TABLE 18.3

The Changing Video Environment

	1980	2003
TV Households	**80MM**	**108MM**
Own VCR	2%	92%
Have Cable TV	30%	70%
Have Satellite TV	—	13%
Have 2+ TV Sets	53%	75%
Remote Control TV	20%	98%
Own Home PC	—	69%
Home Internet Access	—	62%

say something about themselves—mostly to the opposite sex. They designed clever labels featuring icebreakers guaranteed to get barflies buzzing. Used only on bottles sold in bars, the labels included such catchy phrases as "100% Available," "Hottie Magnet," "On the Rebound," "Guess Where My Tattoo Is?" "Wealthy Industrialist" and, perhaps most to the point, "I'm Not Wearing Any Underwear."[24]

PLACE ADVERTISING **Place advertising,** also called out-of-home advertising, is a broadly defined category that captures many different alternative advertising forms. Marketers are using creative and unexpected ad placements to grab consumers' attention. The rationale often given is that marketers are better off reaching people in other environments, such as where they work, play, and, of course, shop. Some of the options available include billboards, public spaces, product placement, and point-of-purchase.

Billboards Billboards have been transformed over the years and now use colorful, digitally produced graphics, backlighting, sounds, movement, and unusual—even three-dimensional—images.[25] Some ads are even human. Adidas hoisted human billboards in Tokyo and Osaka, Japan. Two soccer players competed for shots during 15-minute matches scheduled 5 times a day while they and a ball dangled from ropes 12 stories above ground.[26] Billboards do not even necessarily have to stay in one place. Marketers can buy ad space on billboard-laden trucks that are driven continuously all day in selected areas. Oscar Mayer sends six "Wienermobiles" traveling across the United States each year to increase brand exposure and goodwill. Software company Oracle used a boat to tow a floating banner bearing the company's logo across San Francisco Bay.

Using place advertising to increase brand exposure and goodwill: The Oscar Mayer Wienermobile.

Public Spaces Advertisers are placing traditional TV and print ads in unconventional places such as movies, airlines, and lounges, as well as classrooms, sports arenas, office and hotel elevators, and other public places. Billboard-type poster ads are showing up everywhere. Transit ads on buses, subways, and commuter trains—around for years—have become a valuable way to reach working women. "Street furniture"—bus shelters, kiosks, and public areas—is another fast-growing option. Coca-Cola, for example, mounted illuminated rectangular displays called "light boxes" on New York subway tunnel walls to advertise its Dasani brand water.

Advertisers can buy space in stadiums and arenas and on garbage cans, bicycle racks, parking meters, airport luggage carousels, elevators, gasoline pumps, the bottom of golf cups, airline snack packages, and supermarket produce in the form of tiny labels on apples and bananas. Advertisers can even buy space in toilet stalls and above urinals which, according to research studies, office workers visit an average of three to four times a day for roughly four minutes per visit.[27]

PRODUCT PLACEMENT Product placement has expanded from movies to all types of TV shows. Marketers pay fees of $50,000 to $100,000 and even higher so that their products make cameo appearances in movies and on television. The exact sum depends on the amount and nature of the brand exposure. Sometimes placements are the result of a larger network advertising deal, but other times they are the work of small product placement shops that maintain close ties with prop masters, set designers, and production executives.[28]

Product placements can be combined with special promotions to publicize entertainment tie-ins. 7-UP, Aston Martin, Finlandia, VISA, and Omega all initiated major promotional pushes based on product placement tie-ins with the James Bond film "Die Another Day."[29] With over $100 million paid for product placement rights, some critics called the film "Buy Another Day."

Some firms get product placement at no cost by supplying their product to the movie company (Nike does not pay to be in movies but often supplies shoes, jackets, bags, etc.).[30] Firms sometime just get lucky and are included in shows for plot reasons. FedEx received lots of favorable exposure from the movie *Castaway.*[31] Some television shows revolve around a central product placement: Ford and the WB network created a commercial-free program in 2001 called *No Boundaries,* which features Ford SUVs.

Marketers are finding other inventive ways to advertise during actual television broadcasts. Sports fans are familiar with the virtual logos networks add digitally to the playing field. Invisible to spectators at the event, these ads look just like painted-on logos to home viewers. Ads also appear in best-selling paperback books and movie videotapes. Written material such as annual reports, data sheets, catalogs, and newsletters increasingly carry ads. **Advertorials** are print ads that offer editorial content that reflects favorably on the brand and is difficult to distinguish from newspaper or magazine content. Many companies include advertising inserts in monthly bills. Some companies mail audiotapes or videotapes to prospects.

Other firms are exploring **branded entertainment** such as online mini-films. For its American Express client, Ogilvy and Digitas are creating a series of three- to five-minute "Webisodes" starring its pitchman, Jerry Seinfeld, in "The Adventures of Seinfeld and Superman," and also using teaser TV spots.[32] Automakers are promoting cars with exciting online videos with special effects that pack more punch than the typical car ad.

Product placement: The Omega—James Bond tie-in ad for "Die Another Day."

BMWFILMS.COM

BMW was one of the first automakers to launch a successful video campaign. In 2001, the company hired some of Hollywood's top action movie directors such as John Woo, Guy Ritchie, and Ang Lee to create short films featuring the company's cars and starring actors such as Mickey Rourke and Madonna. To build traffic to the bmwfilms.com Web site, BMW used television spots that mirrored movie trailers. According to BMW's ad agency, 55.1 million people viewed "The Hire" series. Mazda has followed suit with its "Venus Flytrap" video promoting its RX-8, while Ford's "Evil Twin" video advertises the Sportka. As might be evident from their names, these online videos are designed to cater to 18- to 34-year-old men who are spending less and less time watching television and more and more time online.[33]

POINT-OF-PURCHASE There are so many ways to communicate with consumers at the ***point-of-purchase*** **(P-O-P).** In-store advertising includes ads on shopping carts, cart straps, aisles, and shelves, as well as promotion options such as in-store demonstrations, live sampling, and instant coupon machines. Some supermarkets are selling floor space for company logos and experimenting with talking shelves. P-O-P radio provides FM-style programming and commercial messages to thousands of food stores and drugstores nationwide. Programming includes a store-selected music format, consumer tips, and commercials. Ads on Wal-Mart TV run in 2,500 stores and appear three times an hour. Airtime costs between $50,000 and $300,000 for a four-week flight of ads, depending on frequency. The impact can be considerable: According to one research study, more than half of American shoppers visit a Wal-Mart at least once a month and one-third go once a week.[34]

The appeal of point-of-purchase advertising lies in the fact that numerous studies show that in many product categories consumers make the bulk of their final brand decisions in the store. One study suggested that 70 percent of all buying decisions are made in the store. In-store advertising is designed to increase the number of spontaneous buying decisions.

EVALUATING ALTERNATIVE MEDIA Alternative media present some interesting options for marketers. Ads now can appear virtually anywhere consumers have a few spare minutes or even seconds and thus enough time to notice them. The main advantage of nontraditional media is that a very precise and—because of the nature of the setting involved—captive audience often can be reached in a cost-effective manner. The message must be simple and direct. In fact, outdoor advertising is often called the "15-second sell." Strategically, out-of-home advertising is often more effective at enhancing brand awareness or reinforcing brand image than creating new brand associations.

The challenge with nontraditional media is demonstrating its reach and effectiveness through credible, independent research. These new marketing strategies and tactics must be ultimately judged on how they contribute, directly or indirectly, to brand equity. Unique ad placements designed to break through clutter may also be perceived as invasive and obtrusive. There has been some consumer backlash when people see ads in traditionally ad-free spaces, such as in schools, on police cruisers, and in doctors' waiting rooms. Consumer advocate Ralph Nader says, "What these people on Madison Avenue don't understand is consumers will reach a saturation point."

But not all Americans are turned off by the proliferation of advertising. One marketing consultant says, "Kids 18 and under aren't thinking twice about it. Branded merchandise is just the landscape of their lives." Perhaps because of the sheer pervasiveness of advertising, consumers seem to be less bothered by nontraditional media now than in the past.

Consumers must be favorably affected in some way to justify the marketing expenditures for nontraditional media. Some firms offering ad placement in supermarket checkout lines, fast-food restaurants, physicians' waiting rooms, health clubs, and truck stops have suspended business at least in part because of a lack of consumer interest. The bottom line, however, is that there will always be room for creative means of placing the brand in front of consumers. The possibilities are endless: "Marketing Insight: Playing Games with Brands" describes the emergence of yet another new media trend.

Selecting Specific Vehicles

The media planner must search for the most cost-effective vehicles within each chosen media type. The advertiser who decides to buy 30 seconds of advertising on network television can pay around $100,00 for a new show, over $400,000 for a popular prime time show

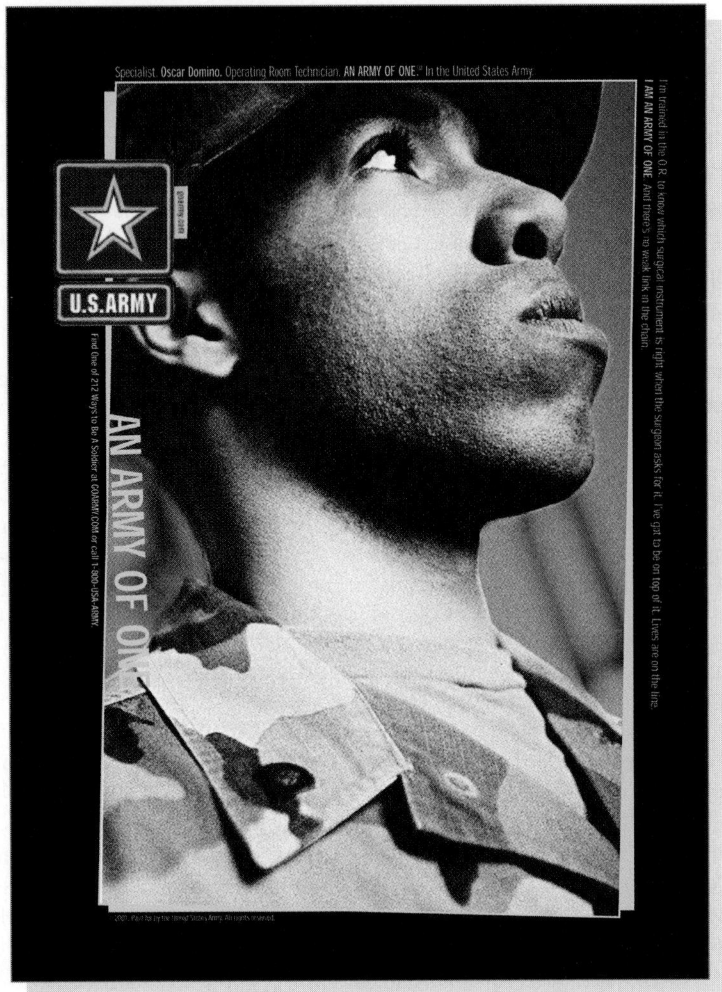

A print ad for the U.S. Army's "Army of One" campaign.

such as *Will & Grace, ER,* or *Survivor,* or over \$2 million for an event like the Super Bowl.[35] These choices are critical: The average cost to produce a national 30-second television commercial in 2001 was about \$350,000. It can cost as much to run an ad once on network TV as to make it to start with!

In making choices, the planner has to rely on measurement services that provide estimates of audience size, composition, and media cost. Audience size has several possible measures:

- ***Circulation.*** The number of physical units carrying the advertising.
- ***Audience.*** The number of people exposed to the vehicle. (If the vehicle has pass-on readership, then the audience is larger than circulation.)
- ***Effective audience.*** The number of people with target audience characteristics exposed to the vehicle.
- ***Effective ad-exposed audience.*** The number of people with target audience characteristics who actually saw the ad.

Media planners calculate the cost per thousand persons reached by a vehicle. If a full-page, four-color ad in *Newsweek* costs \$200,000 and *Newsweek*'s estimated readership is 3.1 million people, the cost of exposing the ad to 1,000 persons is approximately \$65. The same ad in *BusinessWeek* may cost \$70,000 but reach only 970,000 persons—at a cost-per-thousand of \$72. The media planner ranks each magazine by cost-per-thousand and favors magazines with the lowest cost-per-thousand for reaching target consumers. The magazines themselves often put together a "reader profile" for their advertisers, summarizing the characteristics of the magazine's readers with respect to age, income, residence, marital status, and leisure activities.

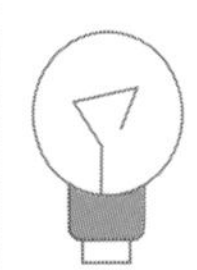

MARKETING **INSIGHT** | **PLAYING GAMES WITH BRANDS**

Given the explosive popularity of video games with younger consumers, many advertisers have adopted an "if you can't beat them, join them" attitude. Online games have wide appeal. Fifty-eight million people were thought to have played in 2002, and half are women with an average age of 28. Women seem to prefer puzzles and collaborative games, whereas men seem more attracted to competitive or simulation games. A top-notch "advergame" can cost between $100,000 and $500,000 to develop. The game can be played on the sponsor's corporate homepage, on gaming portals, or even at restauarants. The NTN iTV Network is an out-of-home interactive entertainment network that delivers entertainment and sports games in approximately 3,600 North American hospitality locations such as Applebee's, Bennigan's, TGIFriday's, and others.

7-Up, McDonald's, and Porsche have all been featured in games. Honda developed a game that allowed players to choose a Honda and zoom around city streets plastered with Honda logos. In the first three months, 78,000 people played for an average of eight minutes. The cost per thousand (CPM) of $7 compared favorably to a prime time TV commercial CPM of $11.65. Marketers collect valuable customer data upon registration and often seek permission to send e-mail. Of game players sponsored by Ford Escape SUV, 54 percent signed up to receive e-mail.

The U.S. Army has also employed games in its marketing arsenal. Recognizing that 90 percent of the target audience was online at least once a week, the U.S. Army decided to make its Web site the centerpiece of the new "Army of One" campaign. The sleekly designed site had fancy animation graphics and a chat room. The centerpiece was a game titled "America's Army: Operations" which half a million people play each weekend. The army also sponsored a NASCAR car and toured black colleges and high schools with an Army of One Hummer fitted with a basketball hoop and blaring hip-hop. A TV campaign shot by famed *Top Gun* movie director Tony Scott featured actual soldiers in real situations. Helped by a coordinated print ad campaign, over 201,000 leads were generated on the toll-free phone number. Overall, the campaign almost doubled the number of leads and produced higher-quality applicants in terms of aptitude tests and college experience.

Sources: Keith Ferrazzi, "Advertising Shouldn't Be Hard Work, but Lately the Game Has Changed," *Wall Street Journal,* April 30, 2002; Marc Weingarten, "It's an Ad! It's a Game! It's . . . Both!" *Business 2.0,* March 2002, p. 102; Thomas Mucha, "Operation Sign 'Em Up," *Business 2.0,* April 2003, pp. 43–45; Dorothy Pomerantz, "You Play, They Win," *Forbes,* October 14, 2002, pp. 201–202; Suzanne Vranica, "Y&R Bets on Videogame Industry," *Wall Street Journal,* May 11, 2004; Hassan Fattah and Pamela Paul, "Gaming Gets Serious," *American Demographics* (May 2002): 39–43.

Several adjustments have to be applied to the cost-per-thousand measure. First, the measure should be adjusted for *audience quality.* For a baby lotion ad, a magazine read by 1 million young mothers would have an exposure value of 1 million; if read by 1 million teenagers, it would have almost a zero exposure value. Second, the exposure value should be adjusted for the *audience-attention probability.* Readers of *Vogue* may pay more attention to ads than do readers of *Newsweek.* A "happy" commercial placed within an upbeat television show is more likely to be effective than a downbeat commercial in the same place.[36] Third, the exposure value should be adjusted for the magazine's *editorial quality* (prestige and believability). In addition, people are more likely to believe a TV or radio ad and to become more positively disposed toward the brand when the ad is placed within a program they like.[37] Fourth, the exposure value should be adjusted for the magazine's *ad placement policies and extra services* (such as regional or occupational editions and lead-time requirements).

Media planners are increasingly using more sophisticated measures of effectiveness and employing them in mathematical models to arrive at the best media mix. Many advertising agencies use a computer program to select the initial media and then make further improvements based on subjective factors.[38]

Deciding on Media Timing and Allocation

In choosing media, the advertiser faces both a macroscheduling and a microscheduling problem. The *macroscheduling problem* involves scheduling the advertising in relation to seasons and the business cycle. Suppose 70 percent of a product's sales occur between June and September. The firm can vary its advertising expenditures to follow the seasonal pattern, to oppose the seasonal pattern, or to be constant throughout the year.

The *microscheduling problem* calls for allocating advertising expenditures within a short period to obtain maximum impact. Suppose the firm decides to buy 30 radio spots in the month of September. Figure 18.3 shows several possible patterns. The left side shows that advertising messages for the month can be concentrated ("burst" advertising), dispersed continuously throughout the month, or dispersed intermittently. The top side shows that the advertising messages can be beamed with a level, rising, falling, or alternating frequency.

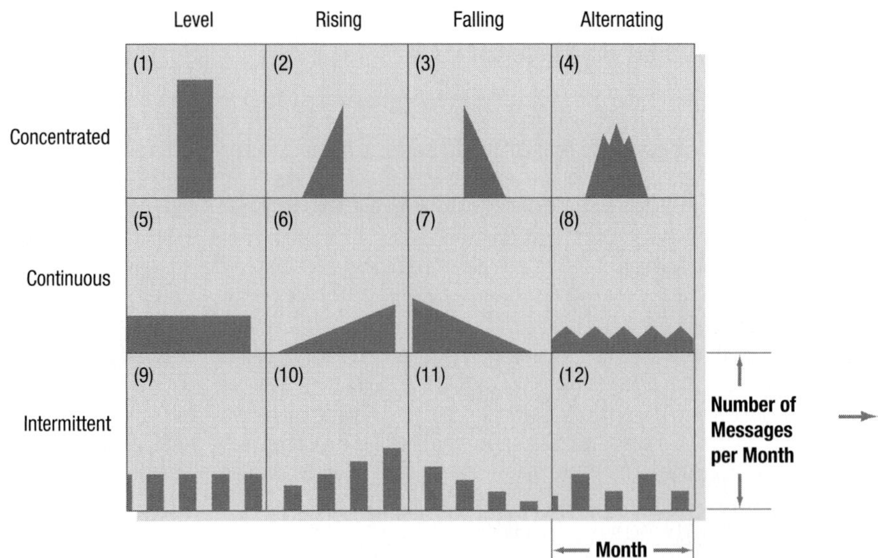

FIG. 18.3

Classification of Advertising Timing Patterns

The most effective pattern depends on the communications objectives in relation to the nature of the product, target customers, distribution channels, and other marketing factors. The timing pattern should consider three factors. *Buyer turnover* expresses the rate at which new buyers enter the market; the higher this rate, the more continuous the advertising should be. *Purchase frequency* is the number of times during the period that the average buyer buys the product; the higher the purchase frequency, the more continuous the advertising should be. The *forgetting rate* is the rate at which the buyer forgets the brand; the higher the forgetting rate, the more continuous the advertising should be.

In launching a new product, the advertiser has to choose among continuity, concentration, flighting, and pulsing.

- ***Continuity*** is achieved by scheduling exposures evenly throughout a given period. Generally, advertisers use continuous advertising in expanding market situations, with frequently purchased items, and in tightly defined buyer categories.
- ***Concentration*** calls for spending all the advertising dollars in a single period. This makes sense for products with one selling season or holiday.
- ***Flighting*** calls for advertising for a period, followed by a period with no advertising, followed by a second period of advertising activity. It is used when funding is limited, the purchase cycle is relatively infrequent, and with seasonal items.
- ***Pulsing*** is continuous advertising at low-weight levels reinforced periodically by waves of heavier activity. Pulsing draws on the strength of continuous advertising and flights to create a compromise scheduling strategy.[39] Those who favor pulsing believe that the audience will learn the message more thoroughly, and money can be saved.

A company has to decide how to allocate its advertising budget over space as well as over time. The company makes "national buys" when it places ads on national TV networks or in nationally circulated magazines. It makes "spot buys" when it buys TV time in just a few markets or in regional editions of magazines. These markets are called *areas of dominant influence* (ADIs) or *designated marketing areas* (DMAs). Ads reach a market 40 to 60 miles from a city center. The company makes "local buys" when it advertises in local newspapers, radio, or outdoor sites. Consider the following example.

PIZZA HUT

Pizza Hut levies a 4 percent advertising fee on its franchisees. It spends half of its budget on national media and half on regional and local media. Some national advertising is wasted because of low penetration in certain areas. Even though Pizza Hut may have a 30 percent share of the franchised pizza market nationally, this share may vary from

5 percent in some cities to 70 percent in others. The franchisees in the higher market share cities want much more advertising money spent in their areas, but Pizza Hut does not have enough money to cover the whole nation by region. National advertising offers efficiency but fails to address the different local situations effectively.

Evaluating Advertising Effectiveness

Good planning and control of advertising depend on measures of advertising effectiveness. Most advertisers try to measure the communication effect of an ad—that is, its potential effect on awareness, knowledge, or preference. They would also like to measure the ad's sales effect.

COMMUNICATION-EFFECT RESEARCH **Communication-effect research** seeks to determine whether an ad is communicating effectively. Called *copy testing,* it can be done before an ad is put into media and after it is printed or broadcast.

There are three major methods of pretesting. The *consumer feedback method* asks consumers for their reactions to a proposed ad. They respond to questions such as these:

1. What is the main message you get from this ad?
2. What do you think they want you to know, believe, or do?
3. How likely is it that this ad will influence you to undertake the action?
4. What works well in the ad and what works poorly?
5. How does the ad make you feel?
6. Where is the best place to reach you with this message? Where would you be most likely to notice it and pay attention to it? Where are you when you make decisions about this action?

Portfolio tests ask consumers to view or listen to a portfolio of advertisements. Consumers are then asked to recall all the ads and their content, aided or unaided by the interviewer. Recall level indicates an ad's ability to stand out and to have its message understood and remembered.

Laboratory tests use equipment to measure physiological reactions—heartbeat, blood pressure, pupil dilation, galvanic skin response, perspiration—to an ad; or consumers may be asked to turn a knob to indicate their moment-to-moment liking or interest while viewing sequenced material.[40] These tests measure attention-getting power but reveal nothing about impact on beliefs, attitudes, or intentions. Table 18.4 describes some specific advertising research techniques.

Pretest critics maintain that agencies can design ads that test well but may not necessarily perform well in the marketplace. Proponents of ad pretesting maintain that useful diagnostic information can emerge and that pretests should not be used as the sole decision criterion anyway. Widely acknowledged as being one of the best advertisers around, Nike is notorious for doing very little ad pretesting. "Marketing Memo: How to Sell in Hard Times" offers some communication insights from its ad agency, Weiden & Kennedy.

TABLE 18.4

Advertising Research Techniques

For Print Ads. Starch and Gallup & Robinson, Inc., are two widely used print pretesting services. Test ads are placed in magazines, which are then circulated to consumers. These consumers are contacted later and interviewed. Recall and recognition tests are used to determine advertising effectiveness.

For Broadcast Ads. ***In-home tests:*** A video tape is taken or downloaded into the homes of target consumers, who then view the commercials.

Trailer tests: In a trailer in a shopping center, shoppers are shown the products and given an opportunity to select a series of brands. They then view commercials and are given coupons to be used in the shopping center. Redemption rates indicate commercials' influence on purchase behavior.

Theater tests: Consumers are invited to a theater to view a potential new television series along with some commercials. Before the show begins, consumers indicate preferred brands in different categories; after the viewing, consumers again choose preferred brands. Preference changes measure the commercials' persuasive power.

On-air tests: Respondents are recruited to watch a program on a regular TV channel during the test commercial or are selected based on their having viewed the program. They are asked questions about commercial recall.

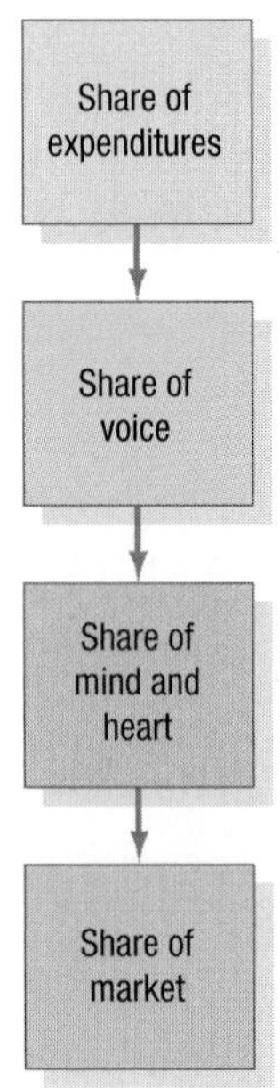

FIG. 18.4

Formula for Measuring Sales Impact of Advertising

Many advertisers use posttests to assess the overall impact of a completed campaign. If a company hoped to increase brand awareness from 20 percent to 50 percent and succeeded in increasing it to only 30 percent, then the company is not spending enough, its ads are poor, or some other factor has been ignored.

SALES-EFFECT RESEARCH What sales are generated by an ad that increases brand awareness by 20 percent and brand preference by 10 percent? Advertising's sales effect is generally harder to measure than its communication effect. Sales are influenced by many factors, such as features, price, and availability, as well as competitors' actions. The fewer or more controllable these other factors are, the easier it is to measure effect on sales. The sales impact is easiest to measure in direct-marketing situations and hardest to measure in brand or corporate image-building advertising.

Companies are generally interested in finding out whether they are overspending or underspending on advertising. One approach to answering this question is to work with the formulation shown in Figure 18.4.

A company's *share of advertising expenditures* produces a *share of voice* (i.e., proportion of company advertising of that product to all advertising of that product) that earns a *share of consumers' minds and hearts* and, ultimately, a *share of market.*

Researchers try to measure the sales impact through analyzing historical or experimental data. The *historical approach* involves correlating past sales to past advertising expenditures using advanced statistical techniques.[41] Other researchers use an *experimental design* to measure advertising's sales impact. Here is an example.

INFORMATION RESOURCES, INC.

Information Resources offers a service called BehaviorScan that provides marketers in the United States with data about advertising effectiveness by tracking consumer purchases tied to specific advertising. Consumers in test markets who sign up to be members of IRI's "Shoppers Hotline" panel agree to have microcomputers record when the TV set is on and to which station it is tuned, while electronic scanners record UPC codes of their household purchases at supermarkets. IRI has the capability to send different commercials to different homes. The company also conducts in-store tests in most chains and in most markets in the United States to study the effects of promotions, displays, coupons, store features, and packaging.[42]

"Marketing Insight: Understanding the Effects of Advertising and Promotion" provides a summary of a meta-analysis of IRI research studies.

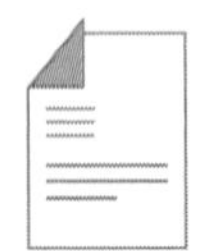

MARKETING MEMO — HOW TO SELL IN HARD TIMES

With one of the best ad campaigns of the last decade ("Just Do It"), Nike's ad agency Weiden & Kennedy (W&K) from Portland, Oregon, knows a lot about what works in good economic times as well as bad. Here are six tips.

1. ***Make noise.*** During boom times, no one can be heard above the din. In slower times, anyone with a creative message will stand out—and gain an advantage on competitors who have gone quiet.
2. ***Open up.*** Customers look for brands they can trust. You have to give people an insight into who you really are as a brand—what you believe and stand for.
3. ***Trust your gut.*** Nike and W&K never show their ads to focus groups because they often will reject original or unconventional ideas simply because they are different.
4. ***Look past the tube.*** Television is expensive and not always necessary. W&K trusts street-level guerilla advertising, such as ad messages on sandwich boards, custom-made magazines, and toys, to spread the word.
5. ***Target the tribes.*** To reach small, influential customer groups, or "tribes," W&K hits them where they live. Messages are projected on sidewalks and the sides of buildings, and CDs and DVDs that promote Nike shoes are handed out at parties and live events.
6. ***Lure them to the Web.*** W&K uses intrigue to draw customers to the brand's Web site—the most efficient marketing tool. The agency has used cliff-hanger commercials that started on TV but whose endings could be found only on the Nike Web site, as well as print ads, billboards, and even window displays as teasers.

Source: Warren Berger, "Just Do It Again," *Business 2.0,* September 2002, p. 81.

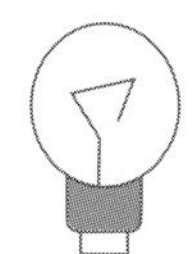

MARKETING **INSIGHT** | **UNDERSTANDING THE EFFECTS OF ADVERTISING AND PROMOTION**

Information Resources Institute (IRI) has provided a unique, in-depth examination into how advertising works. IRI reviewed the results of 389 research studies conducted over a seven-year period and offered the following general principles concerning advertising and promotion effectiveness:

1. ***TV advertising weight alone is not enough.*** Only roughly half of TV advertising heavy-up plans have a measurable effect on sales, although when they do have an effect it is often large. The success rate is higher on new products or line extensions than on established brands.
2. ***TV advertising is more likely to work when there are changes in copy or media strategy*** (a new copy strategy or an expanded target market).
3. ***When advertising is successful in increasing sales, its impact lasts beyond the period of peak spending.*** Recent evidence shows the long-term positive effects of advertising lasting up to two years after peak spending. Moreover, the long-term incremental sales generated are approximately double the incremental sales observed in the first year of an advertising spending increase.
4. ***About 20 percent of advertising plans payout in the short term.*** However, when the long-term effect of advertising is considered, it is likely that most advertising plans that show a significant effect in a split cable experiment would pay out.
5. ***Promotions almost always have a measurable impact on sales. However, the effect is usually purely short term.***
6. ***Payout statistics on promotions are dismal.*** Roughly 16 percent of trade promotions are profitable. Furthermore, promotions' effects are often purely short term, except for new products.
7. ***The above statistics on advertising and promotion payouts show that many brands are overspending on marketing support.*** Many classes of spending can be reduced at an increase in profits.
8. ***Allocating marketing funds involves a continuous search for marketing programs that offer the highest return on the marketing dollar.*** Trade-offs between advertising, trade, and consumer promotions can be highly profitable when based on reliable evaluation systems measuring this productivity at any point in time.
9. ***The current trend toward promotion spending is not sound from a marketing productivity standpoint.*** When the strategic disadvantages of promotions are included, that is, losing control to the trade and training consumers to buy only on deal, the case is compelling for a reevaluation of current practices and the incentive systems responsible for this trend.

A 2004 IRI study of 23 brands reinforced these assertions, finding that advertising often didn't increase sales for mature brands or categories in decline.

Sources: Leonard M. Lodish, Magid Abraham, Stuart Kalmenson, Jeanne Livelsberger, Beth Lubetkin, Bruce Richardson, and Mary Ellen Stevens, "How T.V. Advertising Works: A Meta Analysis of 389 Real World Split Cable T.V. Advertising Experiments," *Journal of Marketing Research* 32 (May 1995): 125–139; Jack Neff, "TV Doesn't Sell Package Goods," *Advertising Age,* May 24, 2004, pp. 1, 30.

A growing number of researchers are striving to measure the sales effect of advertising expenditures instead of settling for communication-effect measures.[43] Millward Brown International has conducted tracking studies in the United Kingdom for many years to provide information to help advertisers decide whether their advertising is benefiting their brand.[44]

::: Sales Promotion

Sales promotion, a key ingredient in marketing campaigns, consists of a collection of incentive tools, mostly short term, designed to stimulate quicker or greater purchase of particular products or services by consumers or the trade.[45]

Whereas advertising offers a *reason* to buy, sales promotion offers an *incentive* to buy. Sales promotion includes tools for *consumer promotion* (samples, coupons, cash refund offers, prices off, premiums, prizes, patronage rewards, free trials, warranties, tie-in promotions, cross-promotions, point-of-purchase displays, and demonstrations); *trade promotion* (prices off, advertising and display allowances, and free goods); and *business* and *sales-force promotion* (trade shows and conventions, contests for sales reps, and specialty advertising).

Objectives

Sales promotion tools vary in their specific objectives. A free sample stimulates consumer trial, whereas a free management-advisory service aims at cementing a long-term relationship with a retailer.

Sellers use incentive-type promotions to attract new triers, to reward loyal customers, and to increase the repurchase rates of occasional users. Sales promotions often attract brand switchers, who are primarily looking for low price, good value, or premiums. Sales promotions generally are unlikely to turn them into loyal users, although they may be induced to make some subsequent purchases.[46] Sales promotions used in markets of high brand similarity can produce a high sales response in the short run but little permanent gain in market share. In markets of high brand dissimilarity, sales promotions may be able to alter market shares permanently. In addition to brand switching, consumers may engage in stockpiling—purchasing earlier than usual (purchase acceleration) or purchasing extra quantities.[47] But sales may then hit a post-promotion dip.[48]

A number of sales promotion benefits flow to manufacturers and consumers.[49] Sales promotions enable manufacturers to adjust to short-term variations in supply and demand. They enable manufacturers to test how high a list price they can charge, because they can always discount it. They induce consumers to try new products instead of never straying from current ones. They lead to more varied retail formats, such as the everyday-low-price store and the promotional-pricing store. For retailers, promotions may increase sales of complementary categories (cake mix promotions may help to drive frosting sales) as well as induce some store-switching by consumers. They promote greater consumer awareness of prices. They permit manufacturers to sell more than they would normally sell at the list price. They help the manufacturer adapt programs to different consumer segments. Consumers themselves enjoy some satisfaction from being smart shoppers when they take advantage of price specials.

Service marketers also employ sales promotions to achieve marketing objectives. Some service firms use promotions to attract new customers and establish loyalty.

CITIBANK

In an increasingly competitive banking market, New York City banks are returning to the giveaways that had faded out of favor for over a decade. Rather than give them to all comers, however, banks are using prizes to help spur loyalty and retain customers. Citibank is offering $100 in cash to new account holders, but the hook is that customers have to at least start paying bills online through Citibank before they get the cash. The bank has found that customers who pay online end up being more loyal customers and using more of the bank's services, so this is one way to reward them.[50]

Advertising versus Promotion

A decade ago, the advertising-to-sales-promotion ratio was about 60:40. Today, in many consumer-packaged-goods companies, sales promotion accounts for 75 percent of the combined budget (roughly 50 percent is trade promotion and 25 percent is consumer promotion). Sales promotion expenditures have been increasing as a percentage of budget expenditure annually for the last two decades. Several factors contribute to this rapid growth, particularly in consumer markets.[51]

Promotion is now more accepted by top management as an effective sales tool; more product managers are qualified to use sales promotion tools; and product managers are under greater pressure to increase current sales. In addition, the number of brands has increased; competitors use promotions frequently; many brands are seen as similar; consumers are more price-oriented; the trade has demanded more deals from manufacturers; and advertising efficiency has declined because of rising costs, media clutter, and legal restraints.

There is a danger, however, in letting advertising take too much of a back seat to promotions, because advertising typically builds brand loyalty. The question of whether or not sales promotion weakens brand loyalty is subject to interpretation. Sales promotion, with its incessant prices off, coupons, deals, and premiums, may devalue the product offering in buyers' minds. However, before jumping to any conclusion, we need to distinguish between price promotions and added-value promotions. Certain types of sales promotions can actually enhance brand image. The rapid growth of sales promotion media has created clutter similar to advertising clutter. Manufacturers have to find ways to rise above the clutter—for instance, by offering larger coupon-redemption values or using more dramatic point-of-purchase displays or demonstrations.

Usually, when a brand is price promoted too often, the consumer begins to devalue it and buy it mainly when it goes on sale. So there is risk in putting a well-known brand on promotion over 30 percent of the time.[52] Automobile manufacturers turned to 0 percent financing and hefty cash rebates to ignite sales in the soft economy of 2000–2001, but have found it difficult to wean consumers from all the discounts since then: Two-thirds of Americans indicated that the timing of their next vehicle purchases will be affected by the level of sales incentives and one-third said they wouldn't buy without them.[53]

Dominant brands offer deals less frequently, because most deals subsidize only current users. Prior research has shown that sales promotions yield faster and more measurable responses in sales than advertising does but do not tend to yield new, long-term buyers in mature markets. Loyal brand buyers tend not to change their buying patterns as a result of competitive promotion. Advertising appears to be more effective at deepening brand loyalty.[54]

There is also evidence that price promotions do not build permanent total-category volume. One study of more than 1,000 promotions concluded that only 16 percent paid off.[55] Small-share competitors find it advantageous to use sales promotion, because they cannot afford to match the market leaders' large advertising budgets; nor can they obtain shelf space without offering trade allowances or stimulate consumer trial without offering incentives. Price competition is often used by a small brand seeking to enlarge its share, but it is less effective for a category leader whose growth lies in expanding the entire category.[56] The upshot is that many consumer-packaged-goods companies feel they are forced to use more sales promotion than they wish. They blame the heavy use of sales promotion for decreasing brand loyalty, increasing consumer price sensitivity, brand-quality-image dilution, and a focus on short-run marketing planning.

Major Decisions

In using sales promotion, a company must establish its objectives, select the tools, develop the program, pretest the program, implement and control it, and evaluate the results.

ESTABLISHING OBJECTIVES Sales promotion objectives are derived from broader promotion objectives, which are derived from more basic marketing objectives developed for the product. For consumers, objectives include encouraging purchase of larger-sized units, building trial among nonusers, and attracting switchers away from competitors' brands. Ideally, promotions with consumers would have short-run sales impact as well as long-run brand equity effects. For retailers, objectives include persuading retailers to carry new items and higher levels of inventory, encouraging off-season buying, encouraging stocking of related items, offsetting competitive promotions, building brand loyalty, and gaining entry into new retail outlets. For the sales force, objectives include encouraging support of a new product or model, encouraging more prospecting, and stimulating off-season sales.[57]

SELECTING CONSUMER PROMOTION TOOLS The promotion planner should take into account the type of market, sales promotion objectives, competitive conditions, and each tool's cost-effectiveness. The main consumer promotion tools are summarized in Table 18.5. We can distinguish between *manufacturer promotions* and *retailer promotions.* The former are illustrated by the auto industry's frequent use of rebates, gifts to motivate test-drives and purchases, and high-value trade-in credit. The latter include price cuts, feature advertising, retailer coupons, and retailer contests or premiums.

We can also distinguish between sales-promotion tools that are *consumer franchise-building* and those that are not. The former impart a selling message along with the deal, as in the case of free samples, frequency awards, coupons when they include a selling message, and premiums when they are related to the product. Sales promotion tools that typically are not brand-building include price-off packs, consumer premiums not related to a product, contests and sweepstakes, consumer refund offers, and trade allowances. Consumer franchise-building promotions offer the best of both worlds—they build brand equity while moving product. Here's an example of a highly effective consumer franchise-building promotion.

DIGIORNO

Kraft has advertised its DiGiorno frozen pizza with the tagline "It's Not Delivery. It's DiGiorno," since its national debut in 1996. The 2001 "Be a DiGiorno Delivery Guy" promotion contest was based on the fact that the pizza was not actually delivered but instead fresh baked at home. The sweepstakes winner was given "nothing to do" in terms of a $100,000 salary (to do nothing), a Chrysler PT Cruiser (which winners were not required to drive), $1,500 toward the purchase of a cell phone and service (for orders not taken), and a customized DiGiorno

TABLE 18.5

Major Consumer-Promotion Tools

Samples: Offer of a free amount of a product or service delivered door-to-door, sent in the mail, picked up in a store, attached to another product, or featured in an advertising offer.

Coupons: Certificates entitling the bearer to a stated saving on the purchase of a specific product: mailed, enclosed in other products or attached to them, or inserted in magazine and newspaper ads.

Cash Refund Offers (rebates): Provide a price reduction after purchase rather than at the retail shop: consumer sends a specified "proof of purchase" to the manufacturer who "refunds" part of the purchase price by mail.

Price Packs (cents-off deals): Offers to consumers of savings off the regular price of a product, flagged on the label or package. A *reduced-price pack* is a single package sold at a reduced price (such as two for the price of one). A *banded pack* is two related products banded together (such as a toothbrush and toothpaste).

Premiums (gifts): Merchandise offered at a relatively low cost or free as an incentive to purchase a particular product. A *with-pack premium* accompanies the product inside or on the package. A *free in-the-mail premium* is mailed to consumers who send in a proof of purchase, such as a box top or UPC code. A *self-liquidating premium* is sold below its normal retail price to consumers who request it.

Frequency Programs: Programs providing rewards related to the consumer's frequency and intensity in purchasing the company's products or services.

Prizes (contests, sweepstakes, games): *Prizes* are offers of the chance to win cash, trips, or merchandise as a result of purchasing something. A *contest* calls for consumers to submit an entry to be examined by a panel of judges who will select the best entries. A *sweepstakes* asks consumers to submit their names in a drawing. A *game* presents consumers with something every time they buy—bingo numbers, missing letters—which might help them win a prize.

Patronage Awards: Values in cash or in other forms that are proportional to patronage of a certain vendor or group of vendors.

Free Trials: Inviting prospective purchasers to try the product without cost in the hope that they will buy.

Product Warranties: Explicit or implicit promises by sellers that the product will perform as specified or that the seller will fix it or refund the customer's money during a specified period.

Tie-in Promotions: Two or more brands or companies team up on coupons, refunds, and contests to increase pulling power.

Cross-Promotions: Using one brand to advertise another noncompeting brand.

Point-of-Purchase (POP) Displays and Demonstrations: POP displays and demonstrations take place at the point-of-purchase or sale.

Delivery Guy uniform (for not delivering pizzas). The effort was backed with a national TV and print campaign, dedicated promotional packages, and entry via an 800 number. It led to a substantial hike in incremental sales volume and resulted in an 18.1 percent market share, the highest in DiGiorno's history.[58]

Sales promotion seems most effective when used together with advertising. In one study, a price promotion alone produced only a 15 percent increase in sales volume. When combined with feature advertising, sales volume increased 19 percent; when combined with feature advertising and a point-of-purchase display, sales volume increased 24 percent.[59]

Many large companies have a sales promotion manager whose job is to help brand managers choose the right promotional tools. Some marketers such as Colgate-Palmolive and Hershey Foods are also going online with their coupons, aided by various online coupon sites.

COOLSAVINGS.COM

Consumers can click on coolsavings.com, which has 20 million members, and select and print out coupons of their choice redeemable at local stores. The most popular categories are groceries, books, health, music, beauty, fast food, apparel, and toys. The fact that consumers are choosing the coupons is resulting in a 57 percent redemption rate, compared to the normal 1.2 percent redemption rate of Sunday paper coupons. Merchants are pleased because they can build a relationship with the customers that initially buy from them with coupons. E-couponing also covers cases where consumers see a code in a print ad that they can type into an online site such as CDNow and get a further discount.[60]

TABLE 18.6

Major Trade Promotion Tools

Price-Off (off-invoice or off-list): A straight discount off the list price on each case purchased during a stated time period.

Allowance: An amount offered in return for the retailer's agreeing to feature the manufacturer's products in some way. An *advertising allowance* compensates retailers for advertising the manufacturer's product. A *display allowance* compensates them for carrying a special product display.

Free Goods: Offers of extra cases of merchandise to intermediaries who buy a certain quantity or who feature a certain flavor or size.

Source: For more information, see Betsy Spethman, "Trade Promotion Redefined," *Brandweek,* March 13, 1995, pp. 25–32.

SELECTING TRADE PROMOTION TOOLS Manufacturers use a number of trade promotion tools (Table 18.6). Surprisingly, a higher proportion of the promotion pie is devoted to trade promotion tools (46.9 percent) than to consumer promotion (27.9 percent). Manufacturers award money to the trade (1) to persuade the retailer or wholesaler to carry the brand; (2) to persuade the retailer or wholesaler to carry more units than the normal amount; (3) to induce retailers to promote the brand by featuring, display, and price reductions; and (4) to stimulate retailers and their sales clerks to push the product.

The growing power of large retailers has increased their ability to demand trade promotion at the expense of consumer promotion and advertising.[61] These retailers depend on promotion money from the manufacturers. No manufacturer could unilaterally stop offering trade allowances without losing retailer support. The company's sales force and its brand managers are often at odds over trade promotion. The sales force says that the local retailers will not keep the company's products on the shelf unless they receive more trade promotion money, whereas the brand managers want to spend the limited funds on consumer promotion and advertising.

Manufacturers face several challenges in managing trade promotions. First, they often find it difficult to police retailers to make sure they are doing what they agreed to do. Manufacturers are increasingly insisting on proof of performance before paying any allowances. Second, more retailers are doing *forward buying*—that is, buying a greater quantity during the deal period than they can sell during the deal period. Retailers might respond to a 10-percent-off-case allowance by buying a 12-week or longer supply. The manufacturer has to schedule more production than planned and bear the costs of extra work shifts and overtime. Third, retailers are doing more diverting, buying more cases than needed in a region in which the manufacturer offered a deal, and shipping the surplus to their stores in nondeal regions. Manufacturers are trying to handle forward buying and diverting by limiting the amount they will sell at a discount, or producing and delivering less than the full order in an effort to smooth production.[62]

All said, manufacturers feel that trade promotion has become a nightmare. It contains layers of deals, is complex to administer, and often leads to lost revenues.

TABLE 18.7

Major Business and Sales Force Promotion Tools

Trade Shows and Conventions: Industry associations organize annual trade shows and conventions. Business marketers may spend as much as 35 percent of their annual promotion budget on trade shows. Over 5,600 trade shows take place every year, drawing approximately 80 million attendees. Trade show attendance can range from a few thousand people to over 70,000 for large shows held by the restaurant or hotel-motel industries. Participating vendors expect several benefits, including generating new sales leads, maintaining customer contacts, introducing new products, meeting new customers, selling more to present customers, and educating customers with publications, videos, and other audiovisual materials.

Sales Contests: A sales contest aims at inducing the sales force or dealers to increase their sales results over a stated period, with prizes (money, trips, gifts, or points) going to those who succeed.

Specialty Advertising: Specialty advertising consists of useful, low-cost items bearing the company's name and address, and sometimes an advertising message that salespeople give to prospects and customers. Common items are ballpoint pens, calendars, key chains, flashlights, tote bags, and memo pads.

SELECTING BUSINESS AND SALES FORCE PROMOTION TOOLS Companies spend billions of dollars on business and sales force promotion tools (Table 18.7). These tools are used to gather business leads, impress and reward customers, and motivate the sales force to greater effort. Companies typically develop budgets for each business promotion tool that remain fairly constant from year to year.

DEVELOPING THE PROGRAM In planning sales promotion programs, marketers are increasingly blending several media into a total campaign concept.

SAMSUNG AND *MATRIX RELOADED*

Eager to make a mark with 19- to 49-year-olds, Samsung leveraged its unique hand phone from the *Matrix Reloaded* movie sequel to launch a global, multimedia promotion. Designed to reinforce brand values of being advanced and fashionable, the promotion was seen as cool and relevant by the target market. A $100 million global budget was set for TV, print, outdoor, and online ads, customized for each global market (30 different languages were used). Among the unprecedented efforts: purchasing all the signage in the trains and train stations in Tokyo for two days; wrapping a 10-story building in Singapore with Samsung visuals; and a slew of billboards in 50+ markets from Paris to Paraguay. In-store merchandising featured gifts and posters with purchase at Best Buy and Radio Shack stores. An online sweepstakes helped to increase site visits by 65 percent. All this marketing effort resulted in a 25 percent jump in sales during the promotional period from April to June 2003.[63]

In deciding to use a particular incentive, marketers have several factors to consider. First, they must determine the *size* of the incentive. A certain minimum is necessary if the promotion is to succeed. Second, the marketing manager must establish *conditions* for participation. Incentives might be offered to everyone or to select groups. Third, the marketer has to decide on the *duration* of the promotion. According to one researcher, the optimal frequency is about three weeks per quarter, and optimal duration is the length of the average purchase cycle.[64] Fourth, the marketer must choose a *distribution vehicle.* A 15-cents-off coupon can be distributed in the package, in stores, by mail, or in advertising. Fifth, the marketing manager must establish the *timing* of promotion. Finally, the marketer must determine the *total sales promotion budget.* The cost of a particular promotion consists of the administrative cost (printing, mailing, and promoting the deal) and the incentive cost (cost of premium or cents-off, including redemption costs), multiplied by the expected number of units that will be sold on the deal. In the case of a coupon deal, the cost would take into account the fact that only a fraction of the consumers will redeem the coupons.

PRETESTING, IMPLEMENTING, CONTROLLING, AND EVALUATING THE PROGRAM Although most sales promotion programs are designed on the basis of experience, pretests can determine if the tools are appropriate, the incentive size optimal, and the presentation method efficient. Consumers can be asked to rate or rank different possible deals, or trial tests can be run in limited geographic areas.

Marketing managers must prepare implementation and control plans that cover lead time and sell-in time for each individual promotion. *Lead time* is the time necessary to prepare the program prior to launching it: initial planning, design, and approval of package modifications or material to be mailed or distributed; preparation of advertising and point-of-sale materials; notification of field sales personnel; establishment of allocations for individual distributors; purchasing and printing of special premiums or packaging materials; production of advance inventories in preparation for release at a specific date; and, finally, the distribution to the retailer.[65] *Sell-in time* begins with the promotional launch and ends when approximately 95 percent of the deal merchandise is in the hands of consumers.

Manufacturers can evaluate the program using three methods: sales data, consumer surveys, and experiments. The first method involves scanner sales data. Marketers can analyze the types of people who took advantage of the promotion, what they bought before the promotion, and how they behaved later toward the brand and other brands. Did the promotion attract new triers and also stimulate more purchasing by existing customers?

In general, sales promotions work best when they attract competitors' customers who then switch. If the company's product is not superior, the brand's share is likely to return to its pre-promotion level. *Consumer surveys* can be conducted to learn how many recall the promotion, what they thought of it, how many took advantage of it, and how the promotion affected subsequent brand-choice behavior.[66] Sales promotions can also be evaluated through *experiments* that vary such attributes as incentive value, duration, and distribution media. For example, coupons can be sent to half of the households in a consumer panel. Scanner data can be used to track whether the coupons led more people to buy the product and when.

There are additional costs beyond the cost of specific promotions. First, promotions might decrease long-run brand loyalty. Second, promotions can be more expensive than they appear. Some are inevitably distributed to the wrong consumers. Third, there are the costs of special production runs, extra sales force effort, and handling requirements. Finally, certain promotions irritate retailers, who may demand extra trade allowances or refuse to cooperate.[67]

::: Events and Experiences

According to the IEG Sponsorship Report, $11.14 billion will be spent on sponsorships in North America during 2004, with 69 percent of this going to sports; another 10 percent to entertainment tours and attractions; 7 percent to festivals, fairs, and annual events; 5 percent to the arts; and 9% to cause marketing. By becoming part of a special and more personally relevant moment in consumers' lives, involvement with events can broaden and deepen the relationship of a company with the target market.

At the same time, daily encounters with brands may also affect consumers' brand attitudes and beliefs. *Atmospheres* are "packaged environments" that create or reinforce leanings toward product purchase. Law offices decorated with Oriental rugs and oak furniture communicate "stability" and "success."[68] A five-star hotel will use elegant chandeliers, marble columns, and other tangible signs of luxury.

Recognizing that it can now reach only 15 percent of the population with a prime time ad as compared to 40 percent as recently as the mid-1980s, Coca-Cola has diverted money into new initiatives that allow it to embed itself into the favorite activities of its target audience. The company has created "teen lounges" in Chicago and Los Angeles where kids can hang out and buy Cokes from see-through vending machines; it has placed downloadable songs on its myCokeMusic.com Web site in Britain; and it has blended its brand into the content of TV shows from the United States to Venezuela.[69]

Coca-Cola is not alone. More firms are creating on-site and off-site product and brand experiences. There is Everything Coca-Cola in Las Vegas, M&M World in Times Square in New York, and General Mills Cereal Adventure in Mall of America in Minnesota.[70] Small brands, of necessity, are even more likely to take less obvious and less expensive paths in sponsorship and communications. With a limited budget, Yoo-hoo chose to target teens by sponsoring the Warped Tour, an alternative music festival, via free samples and off-the-wall contests. For example, concertgoers could get free products if they were willing to chug the chocolate drink out of a boot (dubbed a "shoe-hoo").[71]

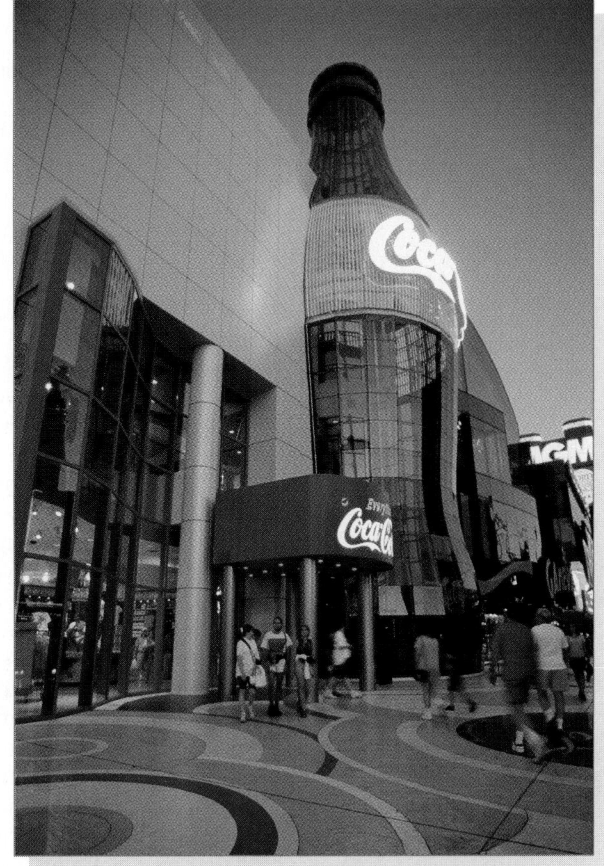
Creating a brand experience: Everything Coca-Cola in Las Vegas, with a 100-foot lighted Coke bottle as part of the front of the building.

HARLEY-DAVIDSON

To create a memorable brand experience, Harley-Davidson decided to "bring the party to the people" to celebrate its 100th-year anniversary in 2003. The Centennial Celebration was a gala of road tours, parades, music, test rides, exhibits, exclusive parties, and even a couple of weddings. A Ride Home Tour caravan motored along four different routes around the country before arriving at Harley's Milwaukee headquarters for a three-day grand finale bash attended by 150,000 people. Besides reinforcing customer loyalty, the celebration helped to reach out to a new audience as well as raise money for the Muscular Dystrophy Association.[72]

Events Objectives

Marketers report a number of reasons why they sponsor events:

1. ***To identify with a particular target market or life style.*** Customers can be targeted geographically, demographically, psychographically, or behaviorally according to events. Events can be chosen based on attendees' attitudes toward and usage of

certain products or brands. Advertisers such as Sony, Gillette, and Pepsi have advertised during ESPN's twice-yearly X Games to reach the elusive 12- to 19-year-old audience.[73]

2. ***To increase awareness of company or product name.*** Sponsorship often offers sustained exposure to a brand, a necessary condition to build brand recognition. By skillfully choosing sponsorship events or activities, identification with a product and thus brand recall can also be enhanced.
3. ***To create or reinforce consumer perceptions of key brand image associations.*** Events themselves have associations that help to create or reinforce brand associations. Anheuser-Busch chose to have Bud Light become a sponsor of the Ironman and other triathlons because it wanted a "healthy" image for the beer.
4. ***To enhance corporate image dimensions.*** Sponsorship is seen as a means to improve perceptions that the company is likable, prestigious, and so on, so that consumers will credit the company and favor it in later product choices.
5. ***To create experiences and evoke feelings.*** The feelings engendered by an exciting or rewarding event may also indirectly link to the brand. Marketers can use the Web to provide further event support and additional experiences.
6. ***To express commitment to the community or on social issues.*** Cause-related marketing consists of sponsorships that involve corporate tie-ins with nonprofit organizations and charities. Firms such as Timberland, Stoneyfield Farms, The Home Depot, Starbucks, American Express, and Tom's of Maine have made cause-related marketing an important cornerstone of their marketing programs.
7. ***To entertain key clients or reward key employees.*** Many events include lavish hospitality tents and other special services or activities which are only available for sponsors and their guests. Involving clients with the event in these and other ways can engender goodwill and establish valuable business contacts. From an employee perspective, events can build participation and morale or be used as an incentive.
8. ***To permit merchandising or promotional opportunities.*** Many marketers tie in contests or sweepstakes, in-store merchandising, direct response, or other marketing activities with an event. Ford, AT&T Wireless, and Nokia all used their sponsorship of the hit TV show *American Idol* in this way.

Despite these potential advantages, there are a number of potential disadvantages to sponsorship. The success of an event can be unpredictable and beyond the control of the sponsor. Although many consumers will credit sponsors for providing the financial assistance to make an event possible, some consumers may still resent the commercialization of events.

Major Decisions

Developing successful sponsored events involves choosing the appropriate events; designing the optimal sponsorship program for the event; and measuring the effects of sponsorship.[74]

CHOOSING EVENT OPPORTUNITIES. Because of the huge amount of money involved and the number of event opportunities that exist, many marketers are becoming much more strategic about the events with which they will get involved and the manner in which they will do so.

The marketing objectives and communication strategy that have been defined for the brand must be met by the event. The audience delivered by the event must match the target market of the brand. The event must have sufficient awareness, possess the desired image, and be capable of creating the desired effects with that target market. Consumers must make favorable attributions to the sponsor for its event involvement. An "ideal event" might be one (1) whose audience closely matches the desired target market, (2) that generates much favorable attention, (3) that is unique but not encumbered with many sponsors, (4) that lends itself to ancillary marketing activities, and (5) that reflects or enhances the brand or corporate image of the sponsor.

More and more firms are also using their names to sponsor the arenas, stadiums, and other venues that actually hold the events.[75] From 1999 to 2004, over $2 billion was spent for naming rights to major North America sports facilities. For example, Petco will pay $60 million over 22 years for the rights to have San Diego's new baseball stadium called Petco Park.

DESIGNING SPONSORSHIP PROGRAMS Many marketers believe that it is the marketing program accompanying an event sponsorship that ultimately determines its success. A sponsor can strategically identify itself at an event in a number of ways, including banners, signs, and programs. For more significant impact, sponsors typically supplement such activities with samples, prizes, advertising, retail promotions, and publicity. At least two to three times the amount of the sponsorship expenditure should be spent on related marketing activities. Jamba Juice augments its running-race sponsorships with bunches of runners in banana costumes. Any runner who finishes the race before a banana gets free smoothies for a year. Jamba Juice banners are displayed all around and smoothies are sampled by race finishers and onlookers.[76]

Event creation is a particularly important skill in publicizing fund-raising drives for nonprofit organizations. Fund-raisers have developed a large repertoire of special events, including anniversary celebrations, art exhibits, auctions, benefit evenings, bingo games, book sales, cake sales, contests, dances, dinners, fairs, fashion shows, parties in unusual places, phonathons, rummage sales, tours, and walkathons. No sooner is one type of event created, such as a walkathon, than competitors spawn new versions, such as readathons, bikeathons, and jogathons.[77]

MEASURING SPONSORSHIP ACTIVITIES As with public relations, measurement of events is difficult. There are two basic approaches to measuring the effects of sponsorship activities: The *supply-side* method focuses on potential exposure to the brand by assessing the extent of media coverage; and the *demand-side* method focuses on reported exposure from consumers. We examine each in turn.

Supply-side methods attempt to approximate the amount of time or space devoted to media coverage of an event. For example, the number of seconds that the brand is clearly visible on a television screen or column inches of press clippings covering an event that mention the brand can be estimated. This measure of potential "impressions" is then translated into an equivalent "value" in advertising dollars according to the fees associated in actually advertising in the particular media vehicle. Some industry consultants have estimated that 30 seconds of TV logo exposure during a televised event can be worth 6 to 10 or as much as 25 percent of a 30-second TV ad spot.

Although supply-side exposure methods provide quantifiable measures, their validity can be questioned. The difficulty lies in the fact that equating media coverage with advertising exposure ignores the content of the respective communications consumers receive. The advertiser uses media space and time to communicate a strategically designed message. Media coverage and telecasts only expose the brand and don't necessarily embellish its meaning in any direct way. Although some public relations professionals maintain that positive editorial coverage can be worth five to ten times the advertising equivalency value, it is rare that sponsorship provides such favorable treatment.[78]

The "demand-side" method attempts to identify the effects sponsorship has on consumers' brand knowledge. Tracking or customized surveys can explore the ability of the event sponsorship to affect awareness, attitudes, or even sales. Event spectators can be identified and surveyed to measure sponsor recall of the event as well as resulting attitudes and intentions toward the sponsor.

::: Public Relations

Not only must the company relate constructively to customers, suppliers, and dealers, it must also relate to a large number of interested publics. A **public** is any group that has an actual or potential interest in or impact on a company's ability to achieve its objectives. **Public relations (PR)** involves a variety of programs designed to promote or protect a company's image or its individual products.

The wise company takes concrete steps to manage successful relations with its key publics. Most companies have a public relations department that monitors the attitudes of the organization's publics and distributes information and communications to build goodwill. The best PR departments spend time counseling top management to adopt positive programs and to eliminate questionable practices so that negative publicity does not arise in the first place. They perform the following five functions:

1. ***Press relations*** – Presenting news and information about the organization in the most positive light.
2. ***Product publicity*** – Sponsoring efforts to publicize specific products.
3. ***Corporate communications*** – Promoting understanding of the organization through internal and external communications.

4. ***Lobbying*** – Dealing with legislators and government officials to promote or defeat legislation and regulation.
5. ***Counseling*** – Advising management about public issues and company positions and image during good times and bad.

Marketing Public Relations

Many companies are turning to **marketing public relations (MPR)** to support corporate or product promotion and image making. MPR, like financial PR and community PR, serves a special constituency, the marketing department.[79]

The old name for MPR was **publicity**, which was seen as the task of securing editorial space—as opposed to paid space—in print and broadcast media to promote or "hype" a product, service, idea, place, person, or organization. MPR goes beyond simple publicity and plays an important role in the following tasks:

- ***Assisting in the launch of new products.*** The amazing commercial success of toys such as Teenage Mutant Ninja Turtles, Mighty Morphin' Power Rangers, Beanie Babies, and Pokémon owes a great deal to clever publicity.
- ***Assisting in repositioning a mature product.*** New York City had extremely bad press in the 1970s until the "I Love New York" campaign.
- ***Building interest in a product category.*** Companies and trade associations have used MPR to rebuild interest in declining commodities such as eggs, milk, beef, and potatoes, and to expand consumption of such products as tea, pork, and orange juice.
- ***Influencing specific target groups.*** McDonald's sponsors special neighborhood events in Latino and African American communities to build goodwill.
- ***Defending products that have encountered public problems.*** PR professionals must be adept at managing crises, such as the Coca-Cola incident in Belgium over allegedly contaminated soda, and Firestone's crisis with regard to the tire tread separation problem.
- ***Building the corporate image in a way that reflects favorably on its products.*** Bill Gates's speeches and books have helped to create an innovative image for Microsoft Corporation.

As the power of mass advertising weakens, marketing managers are turning to MPR to build awareness and brand knowledge for both new and established products. MPR is also effective in blanketing local communities and reaching specific groups. In several cases, MPR proved more cost-effective than advertising. Nevertheless, it must be planned jointly with advertising.[80] In addition, marketing managers need to acquire more skill in using MPR resources. Gillette is a trendsetter here: Each brand manager is required to have a budget line for MPR and to justify not using it. Done right, the impact can be substantial.

MEOW MIX CO.

Meow Mix is showing what it calls "cattitude" by adding public relations to its media mix. After the company reprised its famous singing cats commercials from the 1970s, consumer research revealed that cat owners often leave the TV on for their pets. The company's advertising and PR agencies, working together, took off on the idea of creating a TV show for cats and their owners. Meow TV, featuring Cat Yoga and other fare for felines and owners, airs on the Oxygen Cable Network. The PR value of the show has been tremendous. Media interest in the TV show's production and the related talent search for cat lovers in major markets generated over 153 million impressions in local print and TV outlets—and all on a relatively modest budget of $400,000.[81]

Clearly, creative public relations can affect public awareness at a fraction of the cost of advertising. The company does not pay for the space or time obtained in the media. It pays only for a staff to develop and circulate the stories and manage certain events. If the company develops an interesting story, it could be picked up by the media and be worth millions of dollars in equivalent advertising. Some experts say that consumers are five times more likely to be influenced by editorial copy than by advertising. Here's an example of a powerful PR campaign.

CONAGRA

In its *PRWeek* Campaign of the Year in 2001, ConAgra found a way to unite 80,000 employees and 80 independent operating companies through a PR-fueled cause campaign, "Feeding Children Better." Research suggested that 12 million children went to bed hungry on a regular basis. A three-pronged strategy was developed: getting food to needy children through 100 Kids Cafes; repairing breakdowns in food distribution; and raising national awareness about child hunger through a three-year public service campaign with the Ad Council (and encouraging the company's brands to develop their own hunger promotions).[82]

Major Decisions in Marketing PR

In considering when and how to use MPR, management must establish the marketing objectives, choose the PR messages and vehicles, implement the plan carefully, and evaluate the results. The main tools of MPR are described in Table 18.8.[83]

ESTABLISHING OBJECTIVES MPR can build *awareness* by placing stories in the media to bring attention to a product, service, person, organization, or idea. It can build *credibility* by communicating the message in an editorial context. It can help boost sales force and dealer enthusiasm with stories about a new product before it is launched. It can hold down *promotion cost* because MPR costs less than direct-mail and media advertising.

Whereas PR practitioners reach their target publics through the mass media, MPR is increasingly borrowing the techniques and technology of direct-response marketing to reach target audience members one-on-one.

CHOOSING MESSAGES AND VEHICLES The MPR manager must identify or develop interesting stories about the product. Suppose a relatively unknown college wants more visibility. The MPR practitioner will search for stories. Do any faculty members have unusual backgrounds, or are any working on unusual projects? Are any new and unusual courses being taught? Are any interesting events taking place on campus? If there are no interesting stories, the MPR practitioner should propose newsworthy events the college could sponsor. Here the challenge is to create news. PR ideas include hosting major academic conventions, inviting expert or celebrity speakers, and developing news conferences. Each event is an opportunity to develop a multitude of stories directed at different audiences.

The best MPR practitioners are able to find or create stories even for mundane or out-of-fashion products. Here is a recent success story.

TABLE 18.8

Major Tools in Marketing PR

Publications: Companies rely extensively on published materials to reach and influence their target markets. These include annual reports, brochures, articles, company newsletters and magazines, and audiovisual materials.

Events: Companies can draw attention to new products or other company activities by arranging special events like news conferences, seminars, outings, trade shows, exhibits, contests and competitions, and anniversaries that will reach the target publics.

Sponsorships: Companies can promote their brands and corporate name by sponsoring sports and cultural events and highly regarded causes.

News: One of the major tasks of PR professionals is to find or create favorable news about the company, its products, and its people, and get the media to accept press releases and attend press conferences.

Speeches: Increasingly, company executives must field questions from the media or give talks at trade associations or sales meetings, and these appearances can build the company's image.

Public-Service Activities: Companies can build goodwill by contributing money and time to good causes.

Identity Media: Companies need a visual identity that the public immediately recognizes. The visual identity is carried by company logos, stationery, brochures, signs, business forms, business cards, buildings, uniforms, and dress codes.

PBS BLUES

With the goal of dispelling the common perception that the musical genre of the "blues" was dying, PBS launched the Blues Project to remind people of how influential the blues have been on other genres like rock and hip-hop and to spark a renewed interest. The comprehensive multimedia effort, spearheaded by famed movie director Martin Scorsese, first succeeded at having Congress declare 2003 the Year of the Blues. A series of events and activities were then lined up: a seven-film television series, a Web site, a 13-week radio program, a teachers' guide, a book by Scorsese, a traveling exhibit, and a concert at Radio City Music Hall. The campaign received almost a billion positive media impressions and over 1,000 hits in major media publications, and actually led to a surge in CD sales of blues music.[84]

IMPLEMENTING THE PLAN AND EVALUATING RESULTS MPR's contribution to the bottom line is difficult to measure, because it is used along with other promotional tools. The three most commonly used measures of MPR effectiveness are number of exposures; awareness, comprehension, or attitude change; and contribution to sales and profits.

The easiest measure of MPR effectiveness is the number of *exposures* carried by the media. Publicists supply the client with a clippings book showing all the media that carried news about the product and a summary statement such as the following:

> Media coverage included 3,500 column inches of news and photographs in 350 publications with a combined circulation of 79.4 million; 2,500 minutes of air time of 290 radio stations and an estimated audience of 65 million; and 660 minutes of air time on 160 television stations with an estimated audience of 91 million. If this time and space had been purchased at advertising rates, it would have amounted to $1,047,000.[85]

This measure is not very satisfying because it contains no indication of how many people actually read, heard, or recalled the message and what they thought afterward; nor does it contain information on the net audience reached, because publications overlap in readership. Because publicity's goal is reach, not frequency, it would be more useful to know the number of unduplicated exposures.

A better measure is the change in product awareness, comprehension, or attitude resulting from the MPR campaign (after allowing for the effect of other promotional tools). For example, how many people recall hearing the news item? How many told others about it (a measure of word of mouth)? How many changed their minds after hearing it?

Sales-and-profit impact is the most satisfactory measure. For example, 9-Lives cat food sales increased 43 percent by the end of the Morris the Cat PR campaign. However, advertising and sales promotion had also been stepped up. Suppose total sales have increased by $1.5 million, and management estimates that MPR contributed 15 percent of the total increase. Then the return on MPR investment is calculated as follows:

Total sales increase	$1,500,000
Estimated sales increase due to PR (15 percent)	225,000
Contribution margin on product sales (10 percent)	22,500
Total direct cost of MPR program	210,000
Contribution margin added by PR investment	12,500
Return on MPR investment ($12,500/$10,000)	125%

SUMMARY :::

1. Advertising is any paid form of nonpersonal presentation and promotion of ideas, goods, or services by an identified sponsor. Advertisers include not only business firms but also charitable, nonprofit, and government agencies.

2. Developing an advertising program is a five-step process: (1) Set advertising objectives; (2) establish a budget; (3) choose the advertising message and creative strategy; (4) decide on the media; and (5) evaluate communication and sales effects.

3. Sales promotion consists of a diverse collection of incentive tools, mostly short term, designed to stimulate quicker or greater purchase of particular products or services by consumers or the trade. Sales promotion includes tools for consumer promotion, trade promotion, and business and sales force promotion (trade shows and conventions, contests for sales reps, and specialty advertising). In using sales promotion, a company must establish its objectives, select the tools, develop the program, pretest the program, implement and control it, and evaluate the results.
4. Events and experiences are a means to become part of special and more personally relevant moments in consumers' lives. Involvement with events can broaden and deepen the relationship of the sponsor with its target market, but only if managed properly.
5. Public relations (PR) involves a variety of programs designed to promote or protect a company's image or its individual products. Many companies today use marketing public relations (MPR) to support the marketing department in corporate or product promotion and image making. MPR can affect public awareness at a fraction of the cost of advertising, and is often much more credible. The main tools of PR are publications, events, news, speeches, public service activities, and identity media.

APPLICATIONS :::

Marketing Debate Has TV Advertising Lost Power?

Long deemed the most successful medium, television advertising has received increased criticism as being too expensive and, even worse, no longer as effective as it once was. Critics maintain that consumers tune out too many ads by zipping and zapping and that it is difficult to make a strong impression. The future, claim some, is with online advertising. Supporters of TV advertising disagree, contending that the multisensory impact of TV is unsurpassed and that no other media option offers the same potential impact.

Take a position: TV advertising has faded in importance versus TV advertising is still the most powerful advertising medium.

Marketing Discussion

What are some of your favorite TV ads? Why? How effective are the message and creative strategies? How are they building brand equity?

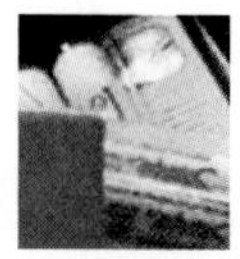

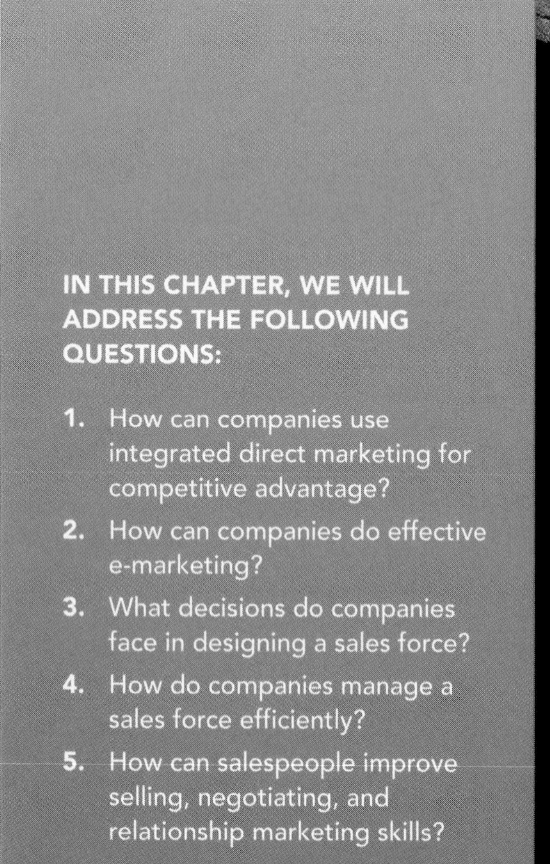

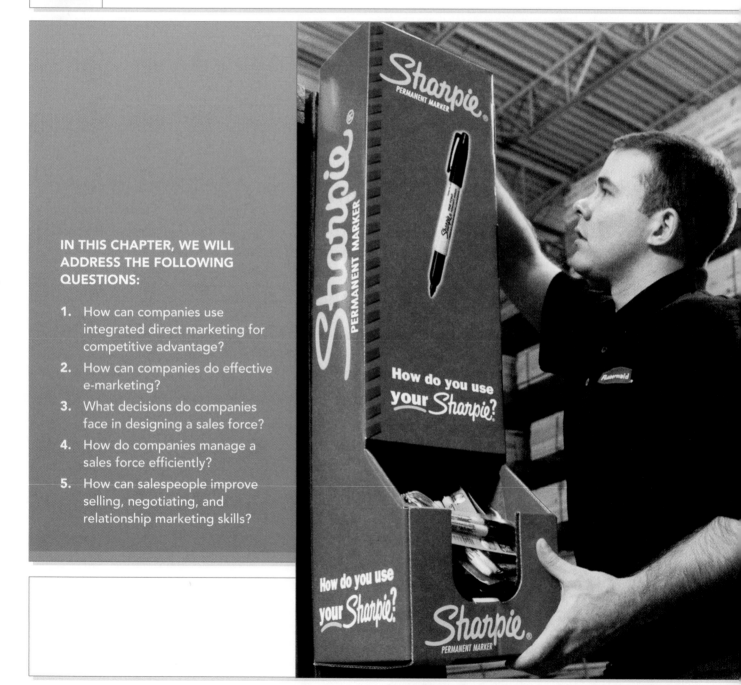

IN THIS CHAPTER, WE WILL ADDRESS THE FOLLOWING QUESTIONS:

1. How can companies use integrated direct marketing for competitive advantage?
2. How can companies do effective e-marketing?
3. What decisions do companies face in designing a sales force?
4. How do companies manage a sales force efficiently?
5. How can salespeople improve selling, negotiating, and relationship marketing skills?

CHAPTER 19 ::: MANAGING PERSONAL COMMUNICATIONS: DIRECT MARKETING AND PERSONAL SELLING

nineteen

Today, marketing communications are increasingly seen as an interactive dialogue between the company and its customers. To make the sale to customers, marketers must work hard and work smart. Companies must ask not only "How can we reach our customers?" but also, "How can our customers reach us?" Thanks to technological breakthroughs, people can now communicate through traditional media (newspapers, magazines, radio, telephone, television, billboards), as well as through computers, fax machines, cellular phones, pagers, and wireless appliances. By decreasing communications costs, the new technologies have encouraged more companies to move from mass communication to more targeted communications and one-to-one dialogue. But companies are also using their sales force to provide a human touch to their marketing.

Newell Rubbermaid's Phoenix program takes college graduates and assigns them to Wal-Mart, The Home Depot, Lowe's, and other retailers where they do everything from stocking shelves to demonstrating new stain-resistant plastic food containers to organizing in-store scavenger hunts. The 500+ college graduates selected for the program are chosen based on their accomplishments outside the classroom. Personable jocks or sorority presidents are favored on the basis of evidence of ambition, leadership, and teamwork. They then receive intensive training >>>

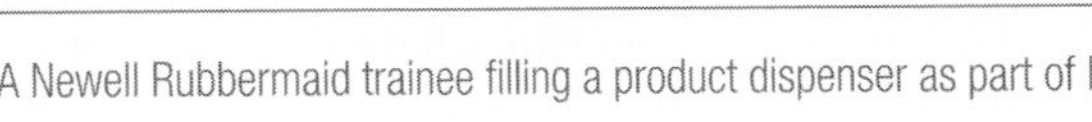

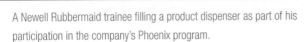

A Newell Rubbermaid trainee filling a product dispenser as part of his participation in the company's Phoenix program.

on effective retail marketing strategies to increase consumer demand in the seven to eight stores to which they are assigned. With their logo-emblazoned Chevy Trailblazers, the highly motivated and energetic sales force has generated, on average, double-digit, year-to-year sales increases.[1]

Personalizing communications—and saying and doing the right thing to the right person at the right time—is critical. In this chapter, we consider how companies personalize their marketing communications to have more of an impact. We begin by evaluating direct marketing; then we consider personal selling and the sales force.

::: Direct Marketing

Direct marketing is the use of consumer-direct (CD) channels to reach and deliver goods and services to customers without using marketing middlemen. These channels include direct mail, catalogs, telemarketing, interactive TV, kiosks, Web sites, and mobile devices.

Direct marketers seek a measurable response, typically a customer order. This is sometimes called **direct-order marketing**. Today, many direct marketers use direct marketing to build a long-term relationship with the customer.[2] They send birthday cards, information materials, or small premiums to certain customers. Airlines, hotels, and other businesses build strong customer relationships through frequency award programs and club programs.

Direct marketing is one of the fastest-growing avenues for serving customers. More and more business marketers have turned to direct mail and telemarketing in response to the high and increasing costs of reaching business markets through a sales force. In total, sales from direct marketing generate almost 9 percent of the U.S. economy.[3]

In addition to trying to increase sales force productivity, companies are seeking to substitute mail- and phone-based selling units to reduce field sales expenses. Sales produced through traditional direct-marketing channels (catalogs, direct mail, and telemarketing) have been growing rapidly. Whereas U.S. retail sales grow around 3 percent annually, catalog and direct-mail sales grow at about double that rate. Direct sales include sales to the consumer market (53 percent), B2B (27 percent), and fund-raising by charitable institutions (20 percent). Total media expenditures for direct marketing in 2000 (including direct mail, telephone, broadcast, Internet, newspaper, magazine, etc.) has been estimated at $236.3 billion.[4] Figure 19.1 provides a breakdown of the various types of direct marketing.

The Benefits of Direct Marketing

The extraordinary growth of direct marketing is the result of many factors. *Market demassification* has resulted in an ever-increasing number of market niches. Higher costs of driving, traffic congestion, parking headaches, lack of time, a shortage of retail sales help, and lines at checkout counters all encourage at-home shopping. Consumers appreciate toll-free phone numbers and Web sites available 24 hours a day, 7 days a week, and direct marketers' commitment to customer service. The growth of next-day delivery via FedEx, Airborne, and UPS has made ordering fast and easy. In addition, many chain stores have dropped slower-moving specialty items, creating an opportunity for direct marketers to promote these items to interested buyers. The growth of the Internet, e-mail, mobile phones, and fax machines has made product selection and ordering much simpler.

Direct marketing benefits customers in many ways. Home shopping can be fun, convenient, and hassle-free. It saves time and introduces consumers to a larger selection of merchandise. They can do comparative shopping by browsing through mail catalogs and online shopping

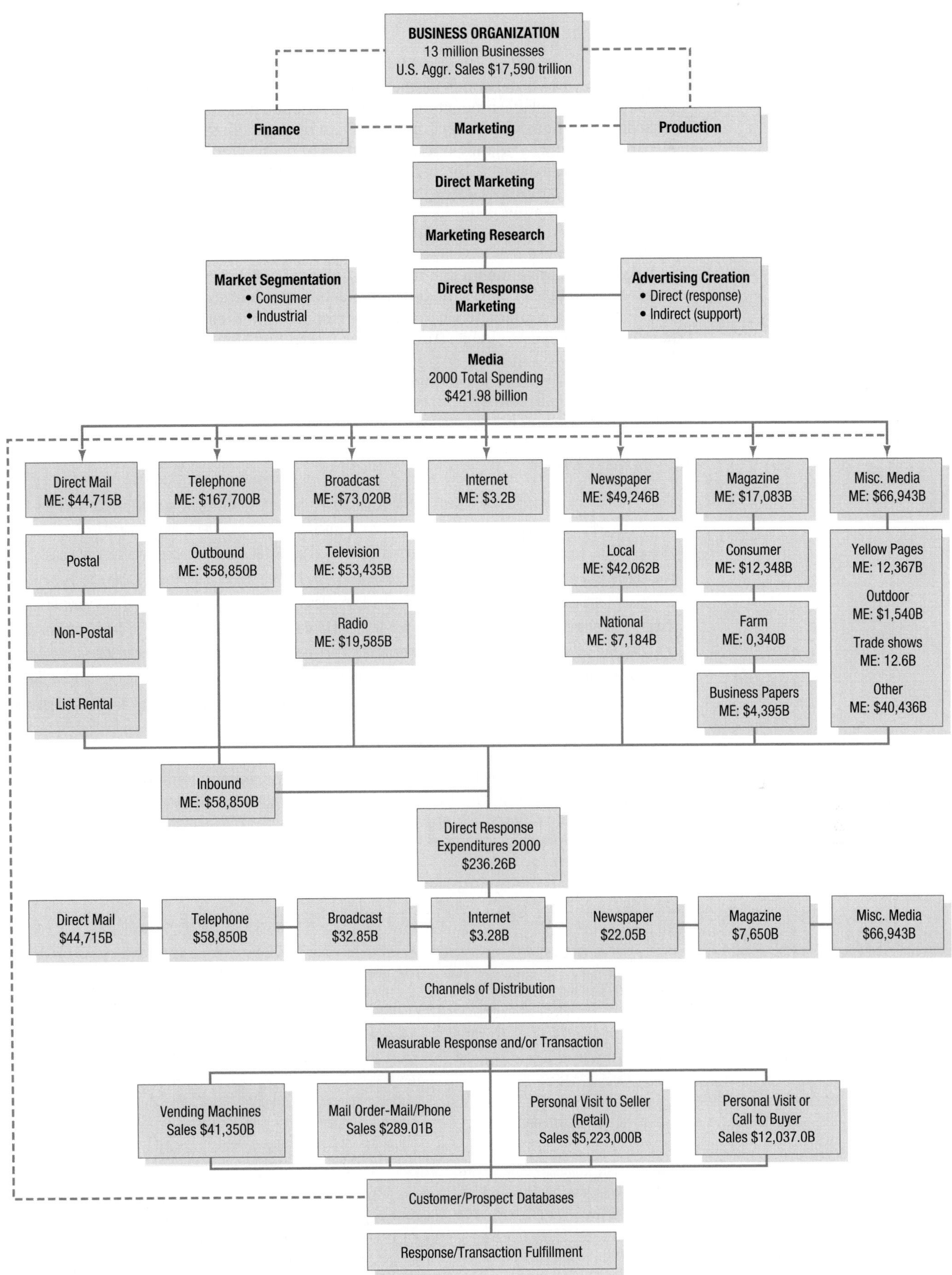

FIG. 19.1 Direct Marketing Flow Chart

Source: Reprinted with permission from *Direct Marketing* magazine, 224 Seventh Street, Garden City, New York, 11530-5771.

services. They can order goods for themselves or others. Business customers also benefit by learning about available products and services without tying up time in meeting salespeople.

Sellers benefit as well. Direct marketers can buy a mailing list containing the names of almost any group: left-handed people, overweight people, millionaires. They can customize and personalize messages. Direct marketers can build a continuous relationship with each customer. The parents of a newborn baby will receive periodic mailings describing new clothes, toys, and other goods as the child grows.

Direct marketing can be timed to reach prospects at the right moment and receive higher readership because it is sent to more interested prospects. Direct marketing permits the testing of alternative media and messages in search of the most cost-effective approach. Direct marketing also makes the direct marketer's offer and strategy less visible to competitors. Finally, direct marketers can measure responses to their campaigns to decide which have been the most profitable. (However, see "Marketing Memo: Public and Ethical Issues in Direct Marketing.")

Direct marketers can use a number of channels to reach individual prospects and customers: direct mail, catalog marketing, telemarketing, TV and other direct-response media, kiosk marketing, and e-marketing.

LANDS' END

A direct merchant of traditionally styled, upscale clothing for the family, soft luggage, and products for the home, Lands' End sells its offerings through catalogs, on the Internet, and in stores, after being acquired by Sears for $1.86 billion in 2002. The catalogs came out four times a year starting in 1964 and included detailed write-ups of products. Lands' End was an early adopter of the Internet, launching its Web site in 1995. The U.S. site offers every Lands' End product and is the world's largest apparel Web site in sales volume. A leader in developing new ways to enhance shopping experiences, customers can create a 3-D Virtual Model of themselves by providing critical measurements or a "personal wardrobe consultant" by answering questions about their clothing preferences. Weekly e-mails with quirky tales and discounts also drive sales. A story of how a customer wore his Lands' End mesh shirt to a preserve for orphaned chimpanzees in the Republic of Ghana led to an increase of 40 percent in sales of the shirt that week.[5]

Direct Mail

Direct-mail marketing involves sending an offer, announcement, reminder, or other item to a person. Using highly selective mailing lists, direct marketers send out millions of mail pieces each year—letters, flyers, foldouts, and other "salespeople with wings." Some direct marketers mail audiotapes, videotapes, CDs, and computer diskettes to prospects and customers.

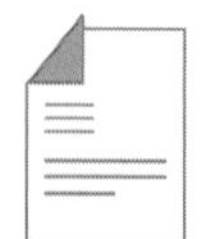

MARKETING MEMO | THE PUBLIC AND ETHICAL ISSUES IN DIRECT MARKETING

Direct marketers and their customers usually enjoy mutually rewarding relationships. Occasionally, however, a darker side emerges:

- ***Irritation:*** Many people do not like the increasing number of hard-sell, direct-marketing solicitations. Especially bothersome are dinnertime or late-night phone calls, poorly trained callers, and computerized calls placed by auto-dial recorded-message players.
- ***Unfairness:*** Some direct marketers take advantage of impulsive or less sophisticated buyers. TV shopping shows and infomercials may be the worst culprits with their smooth-talking hosts and claims of drastic price reductions.
- ***Deception and fraud:*** Some direct marketers design mailers and write copy intended to mislead buyers. They may exaggerate product size, performance claims, or the "retail price." The Federal Trade Commission receives thousands of complaints each year about fraudulent investment scams or phony charities.
- ***Invasion of privacy:*** It seems that almost every time consumers order products by mail or telephone, enter a sweepstakes, apply for a credit card, or take out a magazine subscription, their names, addresses, and purchasing behavior may be added to several company databases. Critics worry that marketers may know too much about consumers' lives, and that they may use this knowledge to take unfair advantage.

People in the direct-marketing industry are attempting to address these issues. They know that, left unattended, such problems will lead to increasingly negative consumer attitudes, lower response rates, and calls for greater state and federal regulation. In the final analysis, most direct marketers want the same thing that consumers want: honest and well-designed marketing offers targeted only to those consumers who appreciate hearing about the offer.

Direct mail is a popular medium because it permits target market selectivity, can be personalized, is flexible, and allows early testing and response measurement. Although the cost per thousand people reached is higher than with mass media, the people reached are much better prospects. Direct mail may be paper-based and handled by the U.S. Postal Service, telegraphic services, or for-profit mail carriers such as FedEx, DHL, or Airborne Express. Alternatively, marketers may employ fax mail, e-mail, or voice mail to sell direct.

Direct-mail marketing has passed through a number of stages:

- ***"Carpet bombing."*** Direct mailers gather or buy as many names as possible and send out a mass mailing. Usually the response rate is very low.
- ***Database marketing.*** Direct marketers mine the database to identify prospects who would have the most interest in an offer.
- ***Interactive marketing.*** Direct marketers include a telephone number and Web address, and offer to print coupons from the Web site. Recipients can contact the company with questions. The company uses the interaction as an opportunity to up-sell, cross-sell, and deepen the relationship.
- ***Real-time personalized marketing.*** Direct marketers know enough about each customer to customize and personalize the offer and message.
- ***Lifetime value marketing.*** Direct marketers develop a plan for lifetime marketing to each valuable customer, based on knowledge of life events and transitions.

One company long recognized for its strong, beneficial focus on customers is Maine's L.L. Bean, Inc., which sells outdoor/casual clothing and equipment through mail order, online catalogs, and retail stores and factory outlets. To maximize customer satisfaction, the company has an unequivocal, 100 percent guarantee for all purchases. Founder L.L. Bean placed a notice on the wall of the Freeport store in 1916, which proclaimed, "I do not consider a sale complete until goods are worn out and customer still satisfied." Bean even once refunded the money on a pair of two-year-old shoes because the customer said the pair did not wear as well as expected![6]

In constructing an effective direct-mail campaign, direct marketers must decide on their objectives, target markets, and prospects; offer elements, means of testing the campaign, and measures of campaign success.

ANZ BANK

Australia's ANZ Bank's "Change Your Home to Suit Your Life" campaign was chosen winner of the 2003 Direct Marketing Association award as top international direct and interactive marketing campaign. Direct-response agency M&C Saatchi used sophisticated data analysis to identify and tailor a campaign to raise interest in home loans. Database profiling was used to select customers from 16 distinct groups of targets. Direct mail then offered information specific to each target audience, reflecting the recipient's situation and specific needs. As a result of the campaign, ANZ received a record number of calls to its home buyers' line—an 83 percent year-on-year increase—a 3 percent rise in home loan applications, and a 47 percent increase in campaign recognition. The direct-mail campaign specifically resulted in 4,922 new accounts or mortgages with a conversion rate of 6 percent.[7]

OBJECTIVES Most direct marketers aim to receive an order from prospects. A campaign's success is judged by the response rate. An order-response rate of 2 percent is normally considered good, although this number varies with product category and price. Direct mail can achieve other communication objectives as well, such as producing prospect leads, strengthening customer relationships, informing and educating customers, reminding customers of offers, and reinforcing recent customer purchase decisions.

TARGET MARKETS AND PROSPECTS Direct marketers need to identify the characteristics of prospects and customers who are most able, willing, and ready to buy. Most direct marketers apply the R-F-M formula (*recency, frequency, monetary amount*) for rating and selecting customers. For any proposed offering, the company selects customers according to how much time has passed since their last purchase, how many times they have purchased, and how much they have spent since becoming a customer. Suppose the company is offering a leather jacket. It might make this offer to customers who made their last purchase between 30 and 60 days ago, who make three to six purchases a year, and who have spent at least $100

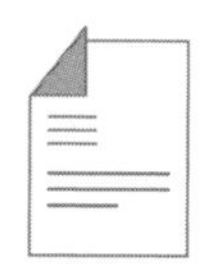

MARKETING MEMO | WHEN YOUR CUSTOMER IS A COMMITTEE

One of the many advantages of database marketing and direct mail is that they allow you to tailor format, offer, and sell messages to the target audience(s). Business marketers can create a series of interrelated and reinforced mailings to decision makers and decision influencers. Here are some tips for increasing success in selling to a customer-by-committee:

- When creating lead generation and follow-up mailings, remember that most business mailings are screened once, twice, or even more before reaching your targeted audience.
- Plan and budget for a series of mailings to each of your customer-by-committee members. Timing and multiple exposures are critical in reaching these audiences.
- Whenever possible, mail to individuals by name and title. Using the title helps the in-office mail screener reroute your mailing if the individual addressed has moved on to another job.
- Do not necessarily use the same format and size for reaching all your targeted audiences. A more expensive-looking envelope may reach the president or CEO, but it may be equally effective to use a less expensive, less personal format to reach other decision influencers.
- Tell your customer-by-committee that you are communicating with others in the organization.
- Make your decision influencers feel important. They can be your biggest advocates.
- When communicating with different audiences, make sure you anticipate—and address—their individual buying objectives and objections.
- When your database or mailing lists cannot help you reach all the key people, ask the individual you are addressing to pass along your information.
- When doing a lead-generation mailing, make sure to ask for the names and titles of those who might be interested and involved in the buying decision. Enter this information into your database.
- Even though it may seem like a lot of work (and expense) to write different versions of the same letter and create different offers, there is a big payoff. The final decision maker may be interested in having a payback calculated, but others may be interested in day-to-day benefits such as safety, convenience, and time savings. Tailor your offer to your targets.

Source: Adapted from Pat Friesen, "When Your Customer Is a Committee," *Target Marketing* (August 1998): 40.

since becoming customers. Points are established for varying R-F-M levels, and each customer is scored. The higher the score, the more attractive the customer. The mailing is sent only to the most attractive customers.[8]

Prospects can also be identified on the basis of such variables as age, sex, income, education, and previous mail-order purchases. Occasions provide a good departure point for segmentation. New parents will be in the market for baby clothes and baby toys; college freshmen will buy computers and small television sets; newlyweds will be looking for housing, furniture, appliances, and bank loans. Another useful segmentation variable is consumer lifestyle or "passion" groups, such as computer buffs, cooking buffs, and outdoor buffs. For business markets, Dun & Bradstreet operates an information service that provides a wealth of data.

In B2B direct marketing, the prospect is often not an individual but a group of people or a committee that includes both decision makers and multiple decision influencers. See "Marketing Memo: When Your Customer Is a Committee" for tips on crafting a direct-mail campaign aimed at business buyers.

Once the target market is defined, the direct marketer needs to obtain specific names. The company's best prospects are customers who have bought its products in the past. Additional names can be obtained by advertising some free offer. The direct marketer can also buy lists of names from list brokers, but these lists often have problems, including name duplication, incomplete data, and obsolete addresses. The better lists include overlays of demographic and psychographic information. Direct marketers typically buy and test a sample before buying more names from the same list.

OFFER ELEMENTS Nash sees the offer strategy as consisting of five elements—the *product,* the *offer,* the *medium,* the *distribution method,* and the *creative strategy.*[9] Fortunately, all of these elements can be tested.

In addition to these elements, the direct-mail marketer has to decide on five components of the mailing itself: the outside envelope, sales letter, circular, reply form, and reply envelope. Here are some findings:

1. The outside envelope will be more effective if it contains an illustration, preferably in color, or a catchy reason to open the envelope, such as the announcement of a contest,

premium, or benefit. Envelopes are more effective when they contain a colorful commemorative stamp, when the address is hand-typed or handwritten, and when the envelope differs in size or shape from standard envelopes.[10]

2. The sales letter should use a personal salutation and start with a headline in bold type. The letter should be printed on good-quality paper and be brief. A computer-typed letter usually outperforms a printed letter, and the presence of a pithy P.S. increases the response rate, as does the signature of someone whose title is important.
3. In most cases, a colorful circular accompanying the letter will increase the response rate by more than its cost.
4. Direct mailers should feature a toll-free number and also send recipients to their Web site. Coupons should be printed out at the Web site.
5. The inclusion of a postage-free reply envelope will dramatically increase the response rate.

Direct mail should be followed up by an e-mail, which is less expensive and less intrusive than a telemarketing call.

TESTING ELEMENTS One of the great advantages of direct marketing is the ability to test, under real marketplace conditions, different elements of an offer strategy, such as products, product features, copy platform, mailer type, envelope, prices, or mailing lists.

Direct marketers must remember that response rates typically understate a campaign's long-term impact. Suppose only 2 percent of the recipients who receive a direct-mail piece advertising Samsonite luggage place an order. A much larger percentage became aware of the product (direct mail has high readership), and some percentage may have formed an intention to buy at a later date (either by mail or at a retail outlet). Furthermore, some of them may mention Samsonite luggage to others as a result of the direct-mail piece. To derive a more comprehensive estimate of the promotion's impact, some companies are measuring the impact of direct marketing on awareness, intention to buy, and word of mouth.

MEASURING CAMPAIGN SUCCESS: LIFETIME VALUE By adding up the planned campaign costs, the direct marketer can figure out in advance the needed break-even response rate. This rate must be net of returned merchandise and bad debts. Returned merchandise can kill an otherwise effective campaign. The direct marketer needs to analyze the main causes of returned merchandise (late shipment, defective merchandise, damage in transit, not as advertised, incorrect order fulfillment).

By carefully analyzing past campaigns, direct marketers can steadily improve performance. Even when a specific campaign fails to break even in the short run, it can still be profitable in the long run if customer lifetime is factored in (see Chapter 5). A customer's ultimate value is not revealed by a purchase response to a particular mailing. Rather, it is the expected profit made on all future purchases net of customer acquisition and maintenance costs. For an average customer, one would calculate the average customer longevity, average customer annual expenditure, and average gross margin, minus the average cost of customer acquisition and maintenance (properly discounted for the opportunity cost of money).[11]

Catalog Marketing

In catalog marketing, companies may send full-line merchandise catalogs, specialty consumer catalogs, and business catalogs, usually in print form but also sometimes as CDs, videos, or online. JCPenney and Spiegel send general merchandise catalogs. Victoria's Secret and Saks Fifth Avenue send specialty clothing catalogs to the upper-middle-class market. Through their catalogs, Avon sells cosmetics, W. R. Grace sells cheese, and IKEA sells furniture. Many of these direct marketers have found that combining catalogs and Web sites can be an effective way to sell. Thousands of small businesses also issue specialty catalogs. Large businesses such as Grainger, Merck, and others send catalogs to business prospects and customers.

Catalogs are a huge business—about 71 percent of Americans shop from home using catalogs by phone, mail, and Internet. They spent an average of $149 per catalog order in 2002.[12] The success of a catalog business depends on the company's ability to manage its customer lists carefully so that there is little duplication or bad debts, to control its inventory carefully, to offer quality merchandise so that returns are low, and to project a distinctive image. Some companies distinguish their catalogs by adding literary or information features, sending swatches of materials, operating a special hot line to answer questions, sending gifts to their best customers, and donating a percentage of the profits to good causes.

PATAGONIA

"Stunning," "soaring," and "wonderful" were a few of the adjectives that *Catalog Age* judges used in awarding Patagonia's fall 2002 edition their Catalog of the Year prize. The judges cited the spectacular cover shot of South American mountains, the excellent selection of merchandise, and the superb presentation. Copy was lauded as being highly detailed without being technical, high-quality photographs were seen as providing strong visual images, and environmental essays and field reports were deemed to add relevant editorial substance. The judges also cited the catalog's strong customer service policies and ease of ordering.[13]

Global consumers in Asia and Europe are catching on to the catalog craze. In the 1990s, U.S. catalog companies such as L.L. Bean, Lands' End, Eddie Bauer, and Patagonia began setting up operations in Japan—and with great success. In just a few years foreign catalogs—mostly from the United States and a few from Europe—have won 5 percent of the $20 billion Japanese mail-order catalog market. A full 90 percent of L.L. Bean's international sales come from Japan. Consumer catalog companies such as Tiffany & Co., Patagonia, Eddie Bauer, and Lands' End are also entering Europe.

Business marketers are making inroads as well. Sales to foreign (mainly European) markets have driven earnings increases at Viking Office Products and computer and network equipment cataloger Black Box Corporation. Viking has had success in Europe because, unlike the United States, Europe has fewer superstores and is very receptive to mail order. Black Box owes much of its international growth to its customer service policies, which are unmatched in Europe.[14] By putting their entire catalogs online, catalog companies have better access to global consumers than ever before, and save considerable printing and mailing costs in the process.

The cover of the award-winning Patagonia catalog, Fall 2002 edition.

Telemarketing

Telemarketing is the use of the telephone and call centers to attract prospects, sell to existing customers, and provide service by taking orders and answering questions. Telemarketing helps companies increase revenue, reduce selling costs, and improve customer satisfaction. Companies use call centers for *inbound telemarketing* (receiving calls from customers) and *outbound telemarketing* (initiating calls to prospects and customers). In fact, companies carry out four types of telemarketing:

- ***Telesales.*** Taking orders from catalogs or ads and also doing outbound calling. They can cross-sell the company's other products, upgrade orders, introduce new products, open new accounts, and reactivate former accounts
- ***Telecoverage.*** Calling customers to maintain and nurture key account relationships and give more attention to neglected accounts.
- ***Teleprospecting.*** Generating and qualifying new leads for closure by another sales channel.
- ***Customer service and technical support.*** Answering service and technical questions.

Although telemarketing has become a major direct-marketing tool, its sometimes intrusive nature led to the establishment by the Federal Trade Commission of a National Do Not Call Registry in October 2003 so that consumers could indicate if they did not want telemarketers to call them at home. Only political organizations, charities, telephone surveyors, or companies with existing relationships with consumers were exempt.[15]

Telemarketing is increasingly used in business as well as consumer marketing. Raleigh Bicycles uses telemarketing to reduce the amount of personal selling needed for contacting its dealers. In the first year, sales force travel costs were reduced by 50 percent and sales in a single quarter went up 34 percent. Telemarketing, as it improves with the use of videophones, will increasingly replace, though never eliminate, more expensive field sales calls. An increasing number of salespeople have made five- and six-figure sales without ever meeting the customer face-to-face. Effective telemarketing depends on choosing the right telemarketers, training them well, and providing performance incentives. Here is an example of successful telemarketing.

USAA

USAA, located in San Antonio, Texas, proves that a company can successfully conduct its entire insurance business over the phone without ever meeting customers face-to-face. From its beginnings, USAA focused on selling auto insurance, and later other insurance products, to those with military service. It increased its share of each customer's business by launching a consumer bank, issuing credit cards, opening a discount brokerage, and offering a selection of no-load mutual funds. In spite of transactions taking place on the phone, USAA boasts one of the highest customer satisfaction ratings of any company in the United States. It received the Chairman's Award from J. D. Power & Associates in 2002.[16]

Other Media for Direct-Response Marketing

Direct marketers use all the major media to make offers to potential buyers. Newspapers and magazines carry abundant print ads offering books, articles of clothing, appliances, vacations, and other goods and services that individuals can order by dialing a toll-free number. Radio ads present offers to listeners 24 hours a day.

TELEVISION Television is used by direct marketers in several ways:

1. ***Direct-response advertising*** – Some companies prepare 30- and 60-minute infomercials that attempt to combine the sell of commercials with the draw of educational information and entertainment. *Infomercials* can be seen as a cross between a sales call and a television ad and cost roughly $250,000 to $500,000 to make. A number of people have become famous with late-night channel switchers (e.g., Tony Robbins, Victoria Principal, and Kathy Smith). Increasingly, companies selling products that are complicated, technologically advanced, or simply require a great deal of explanation are turning to infomercials (Callaway Golf, Carnival Cruises, Mercedes, Microsoft, Philips Electronics, Universal Studios, and even the online job search site, Monster.com).[17] They share the

product's story and benefits with millions of additional prospects at a cost-per-lead or cost-per-order that usually matches or beats direct mail or print ads.[18]

2. ***At-home shopping channels*** – Some television channels are dedicated to selling goods and services. On Home Shopping Network (HSN), which broadcasts 24 hours a day, the program's hosts offer bargain prices on such products as clothing, jewelry, lamps, collectible dolls, and power tools. Viewers call in orders on a toll-free number and receive delivery within 48 hours. Millions of adults watch home shopping programs, and close to half of them buy merchandise.
3. ***Videotext and interactive TV*** – The consumer's TV set is linked with a seller's catalog by cable or telephone lines. Consumers can place orders via a special keyboard device connected to the system. Much research is now going on to combine TV, telephones, and computers into interactive TV.

KIOSK MARKETING A kiosk is a small building or structure that might house a selling or information unit. The name describes newsstands, refreshment stands, and free-standing carts whose vendors sell watches, costume jewelry, and other items. The carts appear in bus and rail stations and along aisles in a mall. The term also covers computer-linked vending machines and "customer-order-placing machines" in stores, airports, and other locations. All of these are direct-selling tools. Some marketers have adapted the self-service feature of kiosks to their businesses. Continental Airlines found that 66 percent of its U.S. passengers checked themselves in via kiosks with a mean check-in time of only 66 seconds with bags and 30 seconds without bags. McDonald's found that customers who used its kiosks to order spent 30 percent more per order.[19]

::: Interactive Marketing

The newest channels for direct marketing are electronic.[20] The Internet provides marketers and consumers with opportunities for much greater *interaction* and *individualization.* Companies in the past would send standard media—magazines, newsletters, ads—to everyone. Today these companies can send individualized content and consumers themselves can further individualize the content. Today companies can interact and dialogue with much larger groups than ever in the past.

The exchange process in the age of information, however, has become increasingly customer-initiated and customer-controlled. Marketers and their representatives must wait until customers agree to participate in the exchange. Even after marketers enter the exchange process, customers define the rules of engagement, and insulate themselves with the help of agents and intermediaries if they so choose. Customers define what information they need, what offerings they are interested in, and what prices they are willing to pay.[21]

Electronic marketing is showing explosive growth: $2.2 billion was spent in online advertising during the fourth quarter of 2003; 43 percent of PC users, or 51 million U.S. households, could connect to the Internet via the broadband connection necessary for swift downloading of dense video and music digital files.[22] These new capabilities will spur the growth of rich media ads that combine animation, video, and sound with interactive features.

AXE DEODORANT

Winner of *Business 2.0*'s 2003 Sweet Spot Award for Most Innovative Campaign, Unilever's Axe Deodorant body spray was launched in 2002 targeting the 18- to 24-year-old male audience interested in improving their appeal to the opposite sex. The centerpiece of the effort, designed by ad agency Bartle Bogle Hegarty, was a set of commercials purporting to be home videos and playing only on Axe's Web site (www.theaxeeffect.com). In each, a pretty young woman is instantly attracted by a whiff of Axe deodorant. In one 25-second clip, a high school cheerleader sprints onto a football field to tackle an Axe-saturated ball carrier. The agency's assumption was that this demographic group—95 percent of whom spent at least four hours online—preferred to discover brands, not to be sold them. The campaign bypassed conventional TV ads in favor of banner ads on Web sites of men's magazines *Maxim* and *FHM* as well as on AtomFilms, a repository of quirky short movies. The banners clicked through to a flashy Web site where surfers could view the video clips. The campaign ROI exceeded all expectations. The site received seven times as many hits as expected. Four months into the campaign, 1.7 million people had visited the site and a third of them reported that they had been sent there by friends. By year end, Axe had captured almost 4 percent of the $2 billion U.S. male deodorant market.[23]

The Benefits of Interactive Marketing

Interactive marketing offers many unique benefits.[24] It is highly accountable and its effects can be easily traced. Eddie Bauer cut its marketing cost per sale by 74 percent by concentrating on higher-performing ads.[25] The Web offers the advantage of "contextual placements." Marketers can buy ads from sites that are related to their offerings, as well as place advertising based on contextual keywords from online search outfits like Google. In that way, the Web can reach people when they have actually started the buying process. Light consumers of other media, especially television, can be reached. The Web is especially effective at reaching people during the day. Young, high-income, high-education customers' total online media consumption exceeds that of TV.[26]

Designing an Attractive Web Site

Clearly, all companies need to consider and evaluate e-marketing and e-purchasing opportunities. A key challenge is designing a site that is attractive on first viewing and interesting enough to encourage repeat visits.

Rayport and Jaworski have proposed that effective Web sites feature seven design elements that they call the 7Cs:[27]

- ***Context.*** Layout and design.
- ***Content.*** Text, pictures, sound, and video the site contains.
- ***Community.*** How the site enables user-to-user communication.
- ***Customization.*** Site's ability to tailor itself to different users or to allow users to personalize the site.
- ***Communication.*** How the site enables site-to-user, user-to-site, or two-way communication.
- ***Connection.*** Degree that the site is linked to other sites.
- ***Commerce.*** Site's capabilities to enable commercial transactions.

To encourage repeat visits, companies need to pay special attention to context and content factors and also embrace another "C"—constant change.[28]

Visitors will judge a site's performance on its ease of use and its physical attractiveness. Ease-of-use breaks down into three attributes: (1) The Web site downloads quickly, (2) the first page is easy to understand, and (3) the visitor finds it easy to navigate to other pages that open quickly. Physical attractiveness is determined by the following factors: (1) The individual pages are clean looking and not overly crammed with content, (2) the typefaces and font sizes are very readable, and (3) the site makes good use of color (and sound).

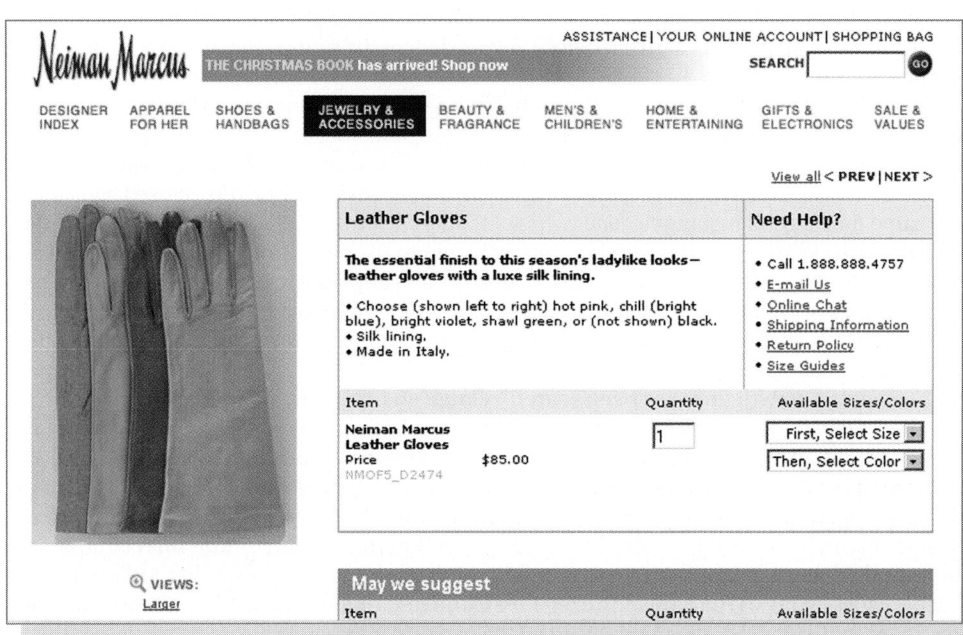

The Neiman Marcus Web site is both attractive and functional: It is easy to navigate and easy to shop from. If you want to buy these leather gloves, you can see a full description plus color choices, and follow instructions to order in a few clicks of the mouse.

MARKETING MEMO | JUST YOUR TYPE

Marketers have analyzed customers and markets in terms of gender, age, ethnicity, and other characteristics for decades. But demographics aren't the only tools for slicing up an online market. San Diego market research firm Miller-Williams Inc. splits online buyers into five categories:

Sensibles, at 37%, are the most numerous of all online shoppers, the easiest to satisfy, and probably the best customers. *Agonizers,* representing 10%, do lots of comparison shopping, but aren't as price-oriented as *Hagglers,* who make up 34 percent. *Loaners,* representing 15 percent, emphasize ease of use in their shopping experience. About 5 percent of online shoppers are Web-savvy but fickle *Techies.*

The takeaway of this segmentation is that you need to know who your customers are and make sure you aren't offering something they don't want or need. "If you know your buyers are hagglers," reasons Amy Ferraro, director of research for Miller-Williams Inc., "you know you need to target them with coupons."

Source: Adapted from Mark Henricks, "Net Meeting," *Entrepreneur,* February 2003, p. 55.

Context factors facilitate repeat visits, but they do not ensure that this happens. Returning to a site depends on content. The content must be interesting, useful, and continuously changing. Certain types of content function well to attract first-time visitors and to bring them back again: (1) deep information with links to related sites, (2) changing news of interest, (3) changing free offers to visitors, (4) contests and sweepstakes, (5) humor and jokes, and (6) games.

Companies are also paying attention to how people buy once they are shopping online. See "Marketing Memo: Just Your Type" for a look at five categories of online buyers.

Placing Ads and Promotion Online

A company has to decide which forms of Internet advertising will be most cost-effective in achieving advertising objectives. **Banner ads** are small, rectangular boxes containing text and perhaps a picture. Companies pay to place banner ads on relevant Web sites. The larger the audience reached, the more the placement will cost. Some banners on Web sites are not paid for, but instead are accepted on a barter basis. In the early days of the Internet, viewers clicked on roughly 2 to 3 percent of the banner ads they saw, but that percentage quickly plummeted and advertisers began to explore other forms of communication.

Many companies get their name on the Internet by sponsoring special content on Web sites that carry news, financial information, and so on. **Sponsorships** are best placed in well-targeted sites where they can offer relevant information or service. The sponsor pays for showing the content and in turn receives acknowledgment as the sponsor of that particular service on the Web site.

A **microsite** is a limited area on the Web managed and paid for by an external advertiser/company. Microsites are particularly relevant for companies selling low-interest products such as insurance. People rarely visit an insurance company's Web site. However, the insurance company can create a microsite on used-car sites that offers advice for buyers of used cars and at the same time a good insurance deal.

Interstitials are advertisements, often with video or animation, that pop up between changes on a Web site. Ads for Johnson & Johnson's Tylenol headache reliever pop up on brokers' Web sites whenever the stock market falls by 100 points or more. Because consumers found pop-up ads intrusive and distracting, many computer users such as AOL installed software to block these ads.[29]

The hottest growth area has been **search-related ads**.[30] Thirty-five percent of all searches are reportedly for products or services. Search terms are used as a proxy for the consumer's consumption interests and relevant links to product or service offerings are listed along side the search results from Google, MSN, and Yahoo!. Advertisers pay only if people click on the links. The cost per click depends on how high the link is ranked and the popularity of the keyword searched. Average click-through is about 2 percent, much more than comparable online ads.[31] At an average of 35 cents, paid search is a lot cheaper than the $1-per-lead for Yellow Pages listings. One Samsung executive estimated that it was 50 times cheaper to reach

1,000 people online than on TV. The company now spends 10 percent of its advertising budget online.[32] A newer trend, **content-target advertising**, links ads not to keywords but to the content of Web pages.

Companies can set up **alliances** and **affiliate programs**. When one Internet company works with another one, they end up advertising each other. AOL has created many successful alliances with other companies. Amazon has almost 1 million affiliates that post Amazon banners on their Web sites. Companies can also undertake guerrilla marketing actions to publicize the site and generate word of mouth. When Yahoo! started its Denmark site, it distributed apples at the busiest train station in Denmark with the message that in the next hours a trip to New York could be won on the Yahoo! site; it also managed to get this mentioned in Danish newspapers. Companies can offer to push content and ads to targeted audiences who agree to receive them and are presumably more interested in the product or product category.

Web advertising is showing double-digit growth. Costs are reasonable compared with those of other advertising media. For example, ESPN.com (www.espn.com), the number-one Internet sports site, attracts more than 5 million Web surfers a week. Based on current advertising rates, running advertising on the site for an entire year may range from $500,000 to $1,000,000 (depending on impression levels).[33] Yahoo! employs 100 salespeople who demonstrate how online ads can reach people with certain interests or who live in specific zip codes.

E-Marketing Guidelines

If a company does an e-mail campaign right, it can not only build customer relationships, but also reap additional profits. E-mail involves only a fraction of the cost of a "d-mail," or direct-mail, campaign. For example, Microsoft spent approximately $70 million a year on paper-driven campaigns. Now, it sends out 20 million pieces of e-mail every month at a significant savings over the cost of paper-based campaigns. Also, compared to other forms of online marketing, e-mail is a hands-down winner. Click-through rates for ad banners have dropped to less than 1 percent, whereas click-through rates for well-crafted e-mail are running around 80 percent.

Here are some important guidelines followed by pioneering e-mail marketers:[34]

- ***Give the customer a reason to respond.*** Companies should offer surfers powerful incentives for reading e-mail pitches and online ads, like e-mail trivia games, scavenger hunts, and instant-win sweepstakes.
- ***Personalize the content of your e-mails.*** IBM's iSource is distributed directly to customers' office e-mail each week, delivering only "the news they choose" in terms of Announcements and Weekly Updates. Customers who agree to receive the newsletter select from topics listed on an interest profile.
- ***Offer something the customer could not get via direct mail.*** Because e-mail campaigns can be carried out quickly, they can offer time-sensitive information. Travelocity sends frequent e-mails pitching last-minute cheap airfares. Club Med uses e-mail to pitch unsold, discounted vacation packages to prospects in its database.
- ***Make it easy for customers to "unsubscribe."*** It is important that online customers have a positive exit experience. According to a Burston-Marsteller and Roper Strach Worldwide study, the top 10 percent of Web users who communicate much more often online typically share their views by e-mail with 11 friends when satisfied, but contact 17 friends when they are dissatisfied.[35]

Online merchants face many challenges in expanding the public's use of e-commerce. Customers will have to feel that the information they supply is confidential and not to be sold to others. Customers will need to trust that online transactions are secure. Companies must encourage communication by inviting prospects and customers to send in questions, suggestions, and even complaints via e-mail. Some sites include a call-me button—the customer clicks on it and his or her phone rings with a customer representative ready to answer a question. Customer service representatives can in principle respond quickly to these messages. Smart online marketers will answer quickly, by sending out newsletters, special product or promotion offers based on purchase histories, reminders of service requirements or warranty renewals, or announcements of special events.

Direct marketing must be integrated with other communications and channel activities.[36] Citigroup, AT&T, IBM, Ford, and American Airlines have used integrated direct marketing to build profitable relationships with customers over the years. Retailers such as

Nordstrom, Nieman Marcus, Saks Fifth Avenue, and Bloomingdale's regularly send catalogs to supplement in-store sales. Direct-marketing companies such as L.L. Bean, Eddie Bauer, Franklin Mint, and The Sharper Image made fortunes in the direct-marketing mail-order and phone-order business, then opened retail stores after establishing strong brand names as direct marketers. They cross-promote their stores, catalogs, and Web sites, for example, by putting their Web addresses on their shopping bags.

VIRGIN MOBILE

In a campaign that received the top prize at the 2004 Cannes Lion awards, Virgin Mobile created a wireless phone service campaign in Australia to sell 5-cent text messaging that combined TV and outdoor ads and a Web page, all based on Warren, a fictitious, love-hungry character. Outdoor ads with Warren's text address and photo read "Be my text kitten" and "Tell me your favorite text position." During the 10-week campaign, Warren got 600,000 text responses, and the Web site got 3 million hits. Sales increased by over 35 percent month-on-month with existing users making 15 percent more calls and sending 20 percent more text messages.[37]

::: Designing the Sales Force

The original and oldest form of direct marketing is the field sales call. Today most industrial companies rely heavily on a professional sales force to locate prospects, develop them into customers, and grow the business; or they hire manufacturers' representatives and agents to carry out the direct-selling task. In addition, many consumer companies use a direct-selling force: insurance agents, stockbrokers, and distributors work for direct-sales organizations such as Avon, Amway, Mary Kay, and Tupperware.

U.S. firms spend over a trillion dollars annually on sales forces and sales force materials—more than they spend on any other promotional method. Nearly 12 percent of the total workforce work full-time in sales occupations. Sales forces are found in nonprofit as well as for-profit organizations. Hospitals and museums, for example, use fund-raisers to contact donors and solicit donations.

No one debates the importance of the sales force in marketing programs. However, companies are sensitive to the high and rising costs (salaries, commissions, bonuses, travel expenses, and benefits) of maintaining a sales force. Because the average cost of a personal sales call ranges from $200 to $300, and closing a sale typically requires four calls, the total cost can range from $800 to $1,200.[38] Not surprisingly, companies are trying to increase the productivity of the sales force through better selection, training, supervision, motivation, and compensation.

The term *sales representative* covers a broad range of positions. Six can be distinguished, ranging from the least to the most creative types of selling:[39]

1. ***Deliverer*** – A salesperson whose major task is the delivery of a product (water, fuel, oil).
2. ***Order taker*** – A salesperson who acts predominantly as an inside order taker (the salesperson standing behind the counter) or outside order taker (the soap salesperson calling on the supermarket manager).
3. ***Missionary*** – A salesperson who is not expected or permitted to take an order but whose major task is to build goodwill or to educate the actual or potential user (the medical "detailer" representing an ethical pharmaceutical house).
4. ***Technician*** – A salesperson with a high level of technical knowledge (the engineering salesperson who is primarily a consultant to the client companies).
5. ***Demand creator*** – A salesperson who relies on creative methods for selling tangible products (vacuum cleaners, cleaning brushes, household products) or intangibles (insurance, advertising services, or education).
6. ***Solution vendor*** – A salesperson whose expertise is in the solving of a customer's problem, often with a system of the company's products and services (for example, computer and communications systems).

Sales personnel serve as the company's personal link to the customers. The sales representative is the company to many of its customers. It is the sales rep who brings back much-needed information about the customer. Therefore, the company needs to carefully consider issues in sales force design—namely, the development of sales force objectives, strategy, structure, size, and compensation. (See Figure 19.2.)

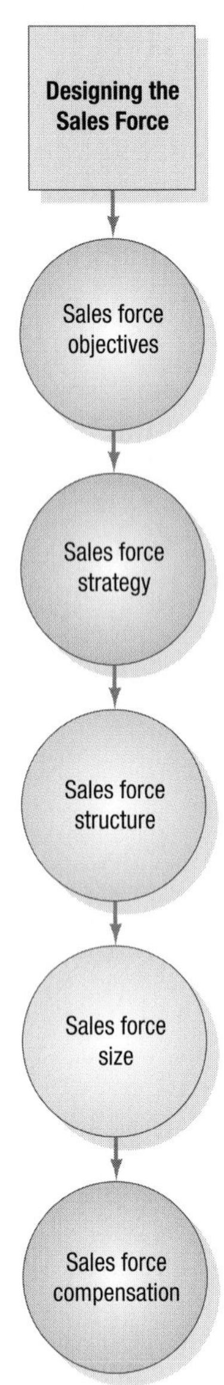

FIG. 19.2

Designing a Sales Force

SOBE

John Bello, founder of SoBe nutritionally enhanced teas and juices, gives much credit to his sales force for the brand's success. Bello claims that the superior quality and consistent sales effort it got from the 150 salespeople the company had at its peak was directed toward one simple goal: "SoBe won in the street because our sales people were there more often and in greater numbers than the competition, and they were more motivated by far." SoBe's sales force operated at every level of the distribution chain: At the distributor level, steady communication gave SoBe disproportionate focus relative to the other brands; at the trade level, with companies such as 7-Eleven, Costco, and Safeway, most of the senior salespeople had strong personal relationships; and at the individual store level, the SoBe team was always at work setting shelves, cutting in product, restocking shelves, and putting up point-of-sale and displays.[40] According to Bello, bottom-line success in any entrepreneurial endeavor depends on sales execution.

Sales Force Objectives and Strategy

The days when all the sales force did was "sell, sell, and sell" are long gone. Sales reps need to know how to diagnose a customer's problem and propose a solution. Salespeople show a customer-prospect how their company can help a customer improve profitability.

Companies need to define the specific objectives they want their sales force to achieve. For example, a company might want its sales representatives to spend 80 percent of their time with current customers and 20 percent with prospects, and 85 percent of their time on established products and 15 percent on new products. The specific allocation scheme depends on the kind of products and customers, but regardless of the selling context, salespeople will have one or more of the following specific tasks to perform:

- ***Prospecting.*** Searching for prospects, or leads.
- ***Targeting.*** Deciding how to allocate their time among prospects and customers.
- ***Communicating.*** Communicating information about the company's products and services.
- ***Selling.*** Approaching, presenting, answering questions, overcoming objections, and closing sales.
- ***Servicing.*** Providing various services to the customers—consulting on problems, rendering technical assistance, arranging financing, expediting delivery.
- ***Information gathering.*** Conducting market research and doing intelligence work.
- ***Allocating.*** Deciding which customers will get scarce products during product shortages.

Because of the expense, most companies are moving to the concept of a *leveraged sales force.* A sales force focuses on selling the company's more complex and customized products to large accounts, while low-end selling is done by inside salespeople and through Web ordering. Tasks such as lead generation, proposal writing, order fulfillment, and postsale support are turned over to others. Salespeople handle fewer accounts, and are rewarded for key account growth. This is far different from expecting salespeople to sell to every possible account, which is usually the weakness of geographically based sales forces.[41]

Companies must deploy sales forces strategically so that they call on the right customers at the right time and in the right way. Today's sales representatives act as "account managers" who arrange fruitful contact between various people in the buying and selling organizations. Selling increasingly calls for teamwork requiring the support of other personnel, such as *top management,* especially when national accounts or major sales are at stake; *technical people,* who supply technical information and service to the customer before, during, or after product purchase; *customer service representatives,* who provide installation, maintenance, and other services; and an *office staff,* consisting of sales analysts, order expediters, and assistants.

To maintain a market focus, salespeople should know how to analyze sales data, measure market potential, gather market intelligence, and develop marketing strategies and plans. Sales representatives need analytical marketing skills, and these skills become especially important at the higher levels of sales management. Marketers believe that sales forces will be more effective in the long run if they understand marketing as well as selling.

Once the company decides on an approach, it can use a direct or a contractual sales force. A **direct (company) sales force** consists of full- or part-time paid employees who work exclusively for the company. This sales force includes inside sales personnel who conduct business from the office using the telephone and receive visits from prospective buyers, and

A service representative provides personalized, customized service to a customer purchasing a Navistar truck.

field sales personnel who travel and visit customers. A **contractual sales force** consists of manufacturers' reps, sales agents, and brokers, who are paid a commission based on sales.

Sales Force Structure

The sales force strategy has implications for the sales force structure. A company that sells one product line to one end-using industry with customers in many locations would use a territorial structure. A company that sells many products to many types of customers might need a product or market structure. Some companies need a more complex structure. Motorola, for example, manages four types of sales forces: (1) a strategic market sales force composed of technical, applications, and quality engineers and service personnel assigned to major accounts; (2) a geographic sales force calling on thousands of customers in different territories; (3) a distributor sales force calling on and coaching Motorola distributors; and (4) an inside sales force doing telemarketing and taking orders via phone and fax.

Established companies need to revise their sales force structures as market and economic conditions change. SAS, seller of business intelligence software, reorganized its sales force into industry-specific groups such as banks, brokerages, and insurers and saw revenue soar by 14 percent.[42] "Marketing Insight: Major Account Management" discusses major account management, a specialized form of sales force structure.

Sales Force Size

Once the company clarifies its strategy and structure, it is ready to consider sales force size. Sales representatives are one of the company's most productive and expensive assets. Increasing their number will increase both sales and costs.

Once the company establishes the number of customers it wants to reach, it can use a *workload approach* to establish sales force size. This method consists of the following five steps:

1. Customers are grouped into size classes according to annual sales volume.
2. Desirable call frequencies (number of calls on an account per year) are established for each class.
3. The number of accounts in each size class is multiplied by the corresponding call frequency to arrive at the total workload for the country, in sales calls per year.
4. The average number of calls a sales representative can make per year is determined.
5. The number of sales representatives needed is determined by dividing the total annual calls required by the average annual calls made by a sales representative.

Suppose the company estimates that there are 1,000 A accounts and 2,000 B accounts in the nation. A accounts require 36 calls a year, and B accounts require 12 calls a year. The

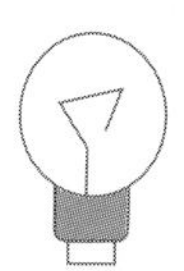

MARKETING INSIGHT | MAJOR ACCOUNT MANAGEMENT

Major accounts (also called key accounts, national accounts, global accounts, or house accounts) are typically singled out for special attention. Important customers who have multiple divisions in many locations are offered major account contracts, which provide uniform pricing and coordinated service for all customer divisions. A major account manager (MAM) supervises field reps calling on customer plants within their territories. Large accounts are often handled by a strategic account management team with cross-functional personnel who handle all aspects of the relationship. For example, in 1992, Procter & Gamble stationed a strategic account management team to work with Wal-Mart in its Bentonville, Arkansas, headquarters. By 1998, P&G and Wal-Mart had already jointly saved $30 billion through supply-chain improvements. Today, the P&G team in Bentonville consists of approximately 100 staffers dedicated to serving Wal-Mart.

The average company manages about 75 key accounts. If a company has several such accounts, it is likely to organize a major account management division, in which the average MAM handles nine accounts. MAMs typically report to the national sales manager who reports to the vice president of marketing and sales, who in turn reports to the CEO.

Major account management is growing. As buyer concentration increases through mergers and acquisitions, fewer buyers account for a larger share of a company's sales. Many buyers are centralizing their purchases for certain items, which gives them more bargaining power. Sellers in turn need to devote more attention to these major buyers. Still another factor is that as products become more complex, more groups in the buyer's organization become involved in the purchase process. The typical salesperson might not have the skill, authority, or coverage to be effective in selling to the large buyer.

In selecting major accounts, companies look for accounts that purchase a high volume (especially of more profitable products), purchase centrally, require a high level of service in several geographic locations, may be price sensitive, and may want a long-term partnering relationship. Major account managers have a number of duties: acting as the single point of contact; developing and growing customer business; understanding customer decision processes; identifying added-value opportunities; providing competitive intelligence; negotiating sales; and orchestrating customer service. MAMs are typically evaluated on their effectiveness in growing their share of the account's business and on their achievement of annual profit-and-sales volume goals. One MAM said, "My position must not be as a salesman, but as a 'marketing consultant' to our customers and a salesman of my company's capabilities as opposed to my company's products."

Major accounts normally receive more favorable pricing based on their purchase volume, but marketers cannot rely exclusively on this incentive to retain customer loyalty. There is always a risk that competitors can match or beat a price or that increased costs may necessitate raising prices. Many major accounts look for added value more than for a price advantage. They appreciate having a single point of dedicated contact; single billing; special warranties; EDI links; priority shipping; early information releases; customized products; and efficient maintenance, repair, and upgraded service. In addition to these practical considerations, there is the value of goodwill. Personal relationships with personnel who value the major account's business and who have a vested interest in the success of that business are compelling reasons for being a loyal customer.

Sources: S. Tubridy, "Major Account Management," in *AMA Management Handbook* (3rd ed.), edited by John J. Hampton (New York: Amacom, 1994), pp. 3–25, 3–27; Sanjit Sengupta, Robert E. Krapfel, and Michael A. Pusateri, "The Strategic Sales Force," *Marketing Management* (Summer 1997): 29–34; Robert S. Duboff and Lori Underhill Sherer, "Customized Customer Loyalty," *Marketing Management* (Summer 1997): 21–27; Tricia Campbell, "Getting Top Executives to Sell," *Sales & Marketing Management* (October 1998): 39; "Promotion Marketer of the Decade: Wal-Mart," *Promo,* December 1, 1999; Noel Capon, *Key Account Management and Planning: The Comprehensive Handbook for Managing Your Company's Most Important Strategic Asset* (New York: Free Press, 2001); Sallie Sherman, Joseph Sperry, and Samuel Reese, *The Seven Keys to Managing Strategic Accounts* (New York: McGraw-Hill Trade, 2003). More information can be obtained from NAMA (National Account Management Association), <www.nasm.com>.

company needs a sales force that can make 60,000 sales calls a year. Suppose the average rep can make 1,000 calls a year. The company would need 60 full-time sales representatives.

Sales Force Compensation

To attract top-quality sales reps, the company has to develop an attractive compensation package. Sales reps want income regularity, extra reward for above-average performance, and fair payment for experience and longevity. Management wants control, economy, and simplicity. Some of these objectives will conflict. No wonder compensation plans exhibit a tremendous variety from industry to industry and even within the same industry.

The company must determine the four components of sales force compensation—a fixed amount, a variable amount, expense allowances, and benefits. The *fixed amount,* a salary, is intended to satisfy the need for income stability. The *variable amount,* which might be commissions, bonus, or profit sharing, is intended to stimulate and reward effort. *Expense allowances* enable sales reps to meet the expenses involved in travel and entertaining. *Benefits,* such as paid vacations, sickness or accident benefits, pensions, and life insurance, are intended to provide security and job satisfaction.

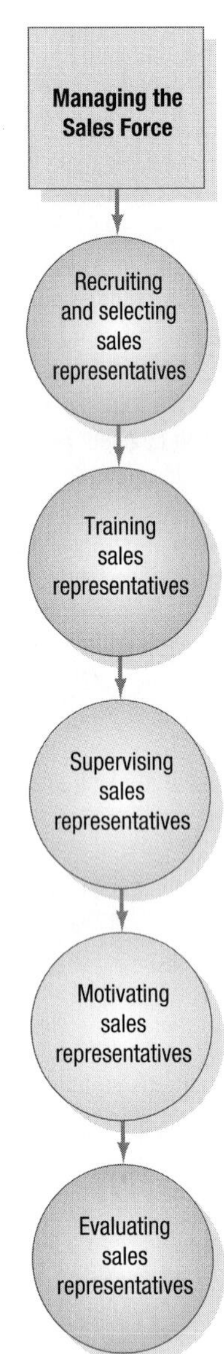

FIG. 19.3

Managing the Sales Force

Fixed compensation receives more emphasis in jobs with a high ratio of nonselling to selling duties and in jobs where the selling task is technically complex and involves teamwork. Variable compensation receives more emphasis in jobs where sales are cyclical or depend on individual initiative. Fixed and variable compensation give rise to three basic types of compensation plans—straight salary, straight commission, and combination salary and commission. Three-quarters of firms use a combination of salary and commission, though the relative proportion varies widely.[43]

Straight-salary plans provide sales reps with a secure income, make them more willing to perform nonselling activities, and give them less incentive to overstock customers. From the company's perspective, they provide administrative simplicity and lower turnover. Straight-commission plans attract higher performers, provide more motivation, require less supervision, and control selling costs. On the negative side, commission plans overemphasize getting the sale rather than building the relationship. Combination plans feature the benefits of both plans while reducing their disadvantages.

With compensation plans that combine fixed and variable pay, companies may link the variable portion of a salesperson's pay to a wide variety of strategic goals. Some see a new trend toward deemphasizing volume measures in favor of factors such as gross profitability, customer satisfaction, and customer retention. For example, IBM now partly rewards salespeople on the basis of customer satisfaction as measured by customer surveys.[44] Other companies are basing the rep's reward partly on a sales team's performance or even company-wide performance. This should get reps to work more closely together for the common good.

::: Managing the Sales Force

Once the company has established objectives, strategy, structure, size, and compensation, it has to recruit, select, train, supervise, motivate, and evaluate sales representatives. Various policies and procedures guide these decisions (see Figure 19.3).

Recruiting and Selecting Representatives

At the heart of a successful sales force is the selection of effective representatives. One survey revealed that the top 27 percent of the sales force brought in over 52 percent of the sales. Beyond differences in productivity is the great waste in hiring the wrong people. The average annual turnover rate for all industries is almost 20 percent. Sales force turnover leads to lost sales, costs of finding and training replacements, and often a strain on existing salespeople to pick up the slack.

Selecting sales reps would be simple if one knew what traits to look for. One good starting point is to ask customers what traits they prefer. Most customers say they want the rep to be honest, reliable, knowledgeable, and helpful. Determining what traits will actually lead to sales success, however, is a challenge. Numerous studies have shown little relationship between sales performance on one hand, and background and experience variables, current status, lifestyle, attitude, personality, and skills on the other. More effective predictors have been composite tests and assessment centers where the working environment is simulated and applicants are assessed in an environment similar to the one in which they would work.[45]

After management develops its selection criteria, it must recruit. The human resources department seeks applicants by soliciting names from current sales representatives, using employment agencies, placing job ads, and contacting college students. Selection procedures can vary from a single informal interview to prolonged testing and interviewing. Many companies give sales applicants formal tests. Although test scores are only one information element in a set that includes personal characteristics, references, past employment history, and interviewer reactions, they are weighted quite heavily by such companies as IBM, Prudential, and Procter & Gamble. Gillette claims that tests have reduced turnover and correlated well with the subsequent progress of new reps in the sales organization.

Training and Supervising Sales Representatives

Today's customers expect salespeople to have deep product knowledge, to add ideas to improve the customer's operations, and to be efficient and reliable. These demands have required companies to make a much higher investment in sales training.

New reps may spend a few weeks to several months in training. The median training period is 28 weeks in industrial-products companies, 12 in service companies, and 4 in consumer-products companies. Training time varies with the complexity of the selling task and the type of person recruited into the sales organization.

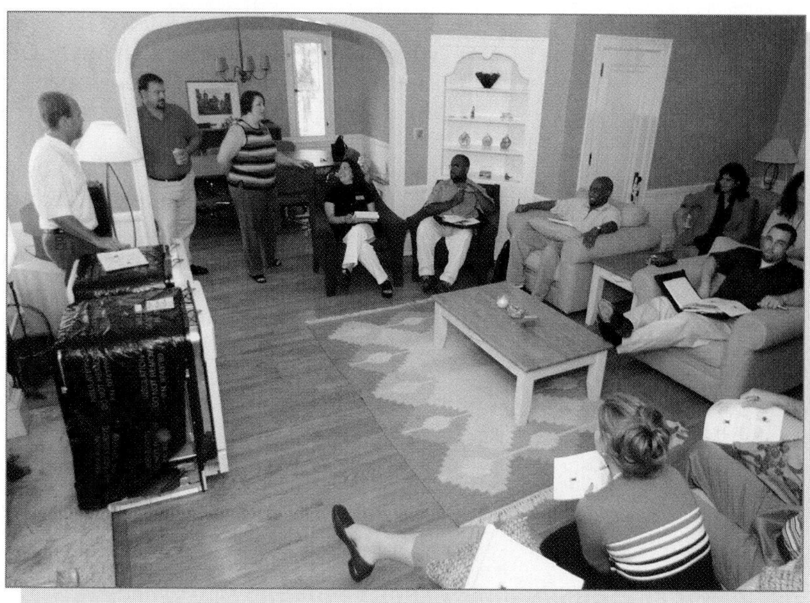

Whirlpool uses local households to train salespeople and to help its researchers develop intelligent major appliances.

IBM

At IBM, new reps receive extensive initial training and may spend 15 percent of their time each year in additional training. IBM has now switched 25 percent of the training from classroom to e-learning, saving a great deal of money in the process. It uses a self-study system called Info-Window that combines a personal computer and a laser videodisc. A trainee can practice sales calls with an on-screen actor who portrays a buying executive in a particular industry. The actor-buyer responds differently depending on what the trainee says.

New methods of training are continually emerging, such as role playing and sensitivity training; the use of cassette tapes, videotapes, and CD-ROMs; and programmed learning, distance learning, and films on selling.

WHIRLPOOL

In order to increase its sales reps' understanding of its appliances, Whirlpool rented an eight-bedroom farmhouse near its headquarters in Benton Harbor, Michigan, and outfitted it with Whirlpool dishwashers, microwaves, washers, dryers, and refrigerators. It sent eight new salespeople to live in the house, to cook and do laundry and household chores. When they emerged, they knew a great deal about Whirlpool appliances and gained more confidence than if they had taken the traditional two-week classroom training course.[46]

Companies vary in how closely they supervise sales reps. Reps paid mostly on commission generally receive less supervision. Those who are salaried and must cover definite accounts are likely to receive substantial supervision. With multilevel selling, used by Avon, Sara Lee, Virgin, AOL Time Warner, and others, independent distributors are also in charge of their own sales force selling company products. These independent contractors or reps are paid a commission not only on their own sales but also on the sales of people they recruit and train.[47]

Sales Rep Productivity

How many calls should a company make on a particular account each year? Some research has suggested that today's sales reps are spending too much time selling to smaller, less profitable accounts when they should be focusing more of their efforts on selling to larger, more profitable accounts.[48]

NORMS FOR PROSPECT CALLS Companies often specify how much time reps should spend prospecting for new accounts. Spector Freight wants its sales representatives to spend 25 percent of their time prospecting and to stop calling on a prospect after three unsuccessful calls.

Companies set up prospecting standards for a number of reasons. Left to their own devices, many reps will spend most of their time with current customers, who are known quantities. Reps can depend on them for some business, whereas a prospect might never deliver any business. Some companies rely on a missionary sales force to open new accounts.

USING SALES TIME EFFICIENTLY Studies have shown that the best sales reps are those who manage their time efficiently.[49] One planning tool is *time-and-duty analysis,* which helps reps understand how they spend their time and how they might increase their productivity. In the course of a day, sales reps spend time planning, traveling, waiting, selling, and in administrative tasks (report writing and billing, attending sales meetings, and talking to others in the company about production, delivery, billing, sales performance, and other matters). With so many duties, it is no wonder that actual face-to-face selling time amounts to as little as 29 percent of total working time![50]

Companies are constantly seeking ways to improve sales force productivity. Their methods take the form of training sales representatives in the use of "phone power," simplifying record keeping and administrative time, and using the computer and the Internet to develop call and routing plans, supply customer and competitive information, and automate the order preparation process.

OWENS-CORNING

Owens-Corning put its sales force online with FAST—its Field Automation Sales Team system. FAST empowers salespeople to make more of their own decisions by giving them a constant supply of information about the company and the people they are dealing with. Using laptop computers, each salesperson can access valuable product and customer information. With a few keystrokes, salespeople can prime themselves on backgrounds of clients; call up prewritten sales letters; transmit orders and resolve customer service issues on the spot during customer calls; and have samples, pamphlets, brochures, and other materials sent to clients.

To cut costs, reduce time demands on their outside sales force, and take advantage of computer and telecommunications innovations, many companies have increased the size and responsibilities of their inside sales force.[51]

Inside salespeople are of three types. There are *technical support people,* who provide technical information and answers to customers' questions. There are *sales assistants,* who provide clerical backup for the outside salespersons. They call ahead and confirm appointments, carry out credit checks, follow up on deliveries, and answer customers' questions. *Telemarketers* use the phone to find new leads, qualify them, and sell to them. Telemarketers can call up to 50 customers a day, compared to the four an outside salesperson can contact.

The inside sales force frees the outside reps to spend more time selling to major accounts, identifying and converting new major prospects, placing electronic ordering systems in customers' facilities, and obtaining more blanket orders and systems contracts. The inside salespeople spend more time checking inventory, following up orders, and phoning smaller accounts. The outside sales reps are paid largely on an incentive-compensation basis, and the inside reps on a salary or salary-plus-bonus pay.

Another dramatic breakthrough is the new high-tech equipment—desktop and laptop PCs, PDAs, videocassette recorders, videodiscs, automatic dialers, e-mail, fax machines, and teleconferencing and videophones. The salesperson has truly gone "electronic." Not only is sales and inventory information transferred much faster, but specific computer-based decision support systems on CDs have been created for sales managers and sales representatives.

One of the most valuable electronic tools for the sales rep is the company Web site, and one of its most useful applications is as a prospecting tool. Company Web sites can help define the firm's relationships with individual accounts and identify those whose business warrants a personal sales call. The Web site provides an introduction to self-identified potential customers. Depending on the nature of the business, the initial order may even take place online. For more complex transactions, the site provides a way for the buyer to contact the seller. Pall Corporation, a manufacturer of fluid filtration and purification technologies, has all e-mail directed to company headquarters, with leads going directly to the appropriate sales rep.[52]

Selling over the Internet supports relationship marketing by solving problems that do not require live intervention and thus allows more time to be spent on issues that are best addressed face-to-face.

Motivating Sales Representatives

The majority of sales representatives require encouragement and special incentives. This is especially true of field selling: Reps usually work alone, their hours are irregular, and they are often away from home. They confront aggressive, competing sales reps; they have an inferior status relative to the buyer; they often do not have the authority to do what is necessary to win an account; and they sometimes lose large orders they have worked hard to obtain.[53]

Most marketers believe that the higher the salesperson's motivation, the greater the effort and the resulting performance, rewards, and satisfaction—and thus further motivation. Such thinking is based on several assumptions.

- ***Sales managers must be able to convince salespeople that they can sell more by working harder or by being trained to work smarter.*** But if sales are determined largely by economic conditions or competitive actions, this link is undermined.
- ***Sales managers must be able to convince salespeople that the rewards for better performance are worth the extra effort.*** But if the rewards seem to be set arbitrarily or are too small or of the wrong kind, this link is undermined.

To increase motivation, marketers reinforce intrinsic and extrinsic rewards of all types. One research study that measured the importance of different rewards found that the reward with the highest value was pay, followed by promotion, personal growth, and sense of accomplishment.[54] The least-valued rewards were liking and respect, security, and recognition. In other words, salespeople are highly motivated by pay and the chance to get ahead and satisfy their intrinsic needs, and less motivated by compliments and security. However, the researchers also found that the importance of motivators varied with demographic characteristics: Financial rewards were mostly valued by older, longer-tenured people and those who had large families. Higher-order rewards (recognition, liking and respect, sense of accomplishment) were more valued by young salespeople who were unmarried or had small families and usually more formal education.

Many companies set annual sales quotas. Quotas can be set on dollar sales, unit volume, margin, selling effort or activity, and product type. Compensation is often tied to degree of quota fulfillment. Sales quotas are developed from the annual marketing plan. The company first prepares a sales forecast that becomes the basis for planning production, workforce size, and financial requirements. Management then establishes quotas for regions and territories, which typically add up to more than the sales forecast to encourage managers and salespeople to perform at their best levels. Even if they fail to make their quotas, the company nevertheless may reach its sales forecast.

Each area sales manager divides the area's quota among the area's reps. Sometimes a rep's quotas are set high, to spur extra effort, or more modestly, to build confidence. One general view is that a salesperson's quota should be at least equal to the person's last year's sales plus some fraction of the difference between territory sales potential and last year's sales. The more favorably the salesperson reacts to pressure, the higher the fraction should be.

Conventional wisdom is that profits are maximized by sales reps focusing on the more important products and more profitable products. Reps are not likely to achieve their quotas for established products when the company is launching several new products at the same time. The company will need to expand its sales force for new-product launches.

Setting sales quotas creates problems. If the company underestimates and the sales reps easily achieve their quotas, the company has overpaid its reps. If the company overestimates sales potential, the sales people will find it very hard to reach their quotas and be frustrated or quit. Another downside is that quotas can drive reps to get as much business as possible—often resulting in their ignoring the service side of the business. The company gains short-term results at the cost of long-term customer satisfaction.

Some companies are dropping quotas.[55] Siebel, the leading supplier of sales automation software, judges its sales reps using a number of metrics, such as customer satisfaction, repeat business, and profitable revenues. Almost 40 percent of incentive compensation is based on customers' reported satisfaction with service and product. The company's close scrutiny of the sales process leads to satisfied customers: Over 50 percent of Siebel's revenue comes from repeat business.[56] Nortel and AT&T Worldnet also prefer to use a larger set of measures for motivating and rewarding sales reps. Even hard-driving Oracle has changed its approach to sales compensation.

ORACLE

Finding sales flagging and customers griping, Oracle, the second-largest software company in the world, overhauled its sales department in 2002. Oracle's rapidly expanding capabilities, with diverse applications such as human resources, supply chain, and CRM, made its account management system difficult. One rep could no longer be responsible for selling all Oracle products to certain customers. Reorganization resulted in reps' specializing in a few particular products. To try to tone down the sales force's reputation as overly aggressive, the commission structure was changed to a flat 4 to 6 percent, as compared to a wider range of 2 to 12 percent depending on how close to the end of the quarter the sale was made.[57]

Evaluating Sales Representatives

We have been describing the *feed-forward* aspects of sales supervision—how management communicates what the sales reps should be doing and motivates them to do it. But good feed-forward requires good *feedback,* which means getting regular information from reps to evaluate performance.

SOURCES OF INFORMATION The most important source of information about reps is sales reports. Additional information comes through personal observation, salesperson self-reports, customer letters and complaints, customer surveys, and conversations with other sales representatives.

Sales reports are divided between *activity plans* and *write-ups of activity results.* The best example of the former is the salesperson's work plan, which reps submit a week or month in advance. The plan describes intended calls and routing. This report forces sales reps to plan and schedule their activities and inform management of their whereabouts. It provides a basis for comparing their plans and accomplishments. Sales reps can be evaluated on their ability to "plan their work and work their plan."

Many companies require representatives to develop an annual territory-marketing plan in which they outline their program for developing new accounts and increasing business from existing accounts. This type of report casts sales reps into the role of market managers and profit centers. Sales managers study these plans, make suggestions, and use them to develop sales quotas. Sales reps write up completed activities on *call reports.* Sales representatives also submit expense reports, new-business reports, lost-business reports, and reports on local business and economic conditions.

These reports provide raw data from which sales managers can extract key indicators of sales performance: (1) average number of sales calls per salesperson per day, (2) average sales call time per contact, (3) average revenue per sales call, (4) average cost per sales call, (5) entertainment cost per sales call, (6) percentage of orders per hundred sales calls, (7) number of new customers per period, (8) number of lost customers per period, and (9) sales force cost as a percentage of total sales.

FORMAL EVALUATION The sales force's reports along with other observations supply the raw materials for evaluation. There are several approaches to conducting evaluations. One type of evaluation compares current performance to past performance. An example is shown in Table 19.1.

The sales manager can learn many things about a rep from this table. Total sales increased every year (line 3). This does not necessarily mean that the person is doing a better job. The product breakdown shows that he has been able to push the sales of product B further than the sales of product A (lines 1 and 2). According to his quotas for the two products (lines 4 and 5), his success in increasing product B sales could be at the expense of product A sales. According to gross profits (lines 6 and 7), the company earns more selling A than B. The rep might be pushing the higher-volume, lower-margin product at the expense of the more profitable product. Although he increased total sales by $1,100 between 2003 and 2004 (line 3), the gross profits on total sales actually decreased by $580 (line 8).

Sales expense (line 9) shows a steady increase, although total expense as a percentage of total sales seems to be under control (line 10). The upward trend in total dollar expense does not seem to be explained by any increase in the number of calls (line 11), although it might be related to success in acquiring new customers (line 14). There is a possibility that in

TABLE 19.1

Form for Evaluating Sales Representative's Performance

Territory: Midland Sales Representative: John Smith	2001	2002	2003	2004
1. Net sales product A	$251,300	$253,200	$270,000	$263,100
2. Net sales product B	423,200	439,200	553,900	561,900
3. Net sales total	674,500	692,400	823,900	825,000
4. Percent of quota product A	95.6	92.0	88.0	84.7
5. Percent of quota product B	120.4	122.3	134.9	130.8
6. Gross profits product A	$50,260	$50,640	$54,000	$52,620
7. Gross profits product B	42,320	43,920	55,390	56,190
8. Gross profits total	92,580	94,560	109,390	108,810
9. Sales expense	$10,200	$11,100	$11,600	$13,200
10. Sales expense to total sales (%)	1.5	1.6	1.4	1.6
11. Number of calls	1,675	1,700	1,680	1,660
12. Cost per call	$6.09	$6.53	$6.90	$7.95
13. Average number of customers	320	24	328	334
14. Number of new customers	13	14	15	20
15. Number of lost customers	8	10	11	14
16. Average sales per customer	$2,108	$2,137	$2,512	$2,470
17. Average gross profit per customer	$289	$292	$334	$326

prospecting for new customers, this rep is neglecting present customers, as indicated by an upward trend in the annual number of lost customers (line 15).

The last two lines show the level and trend in sales and gross profits per customer. These figures become more meaningful when they are compared with overall company averages. If this rep's average gross profit per customer is lower than the company's average, he could be concentrating on the wrong customers or not spending enough time with each customer. A review of annual number of calls (line 11) shows that he might be making fewer annual calls than the average salesperson. If distances in the territory are similar to other territories, this could mean that he is not putting in a full workday, he is poor at sales planning and routing, or he spends too much time with certain accounts.

The rep might be quite effective in producing sales but not rate high with customers. Perhaps he is slightly better than the competitors' salespeople, or his product is better, or he keeps finding new customers to replace others who do not like to deal with him. The customers' opinion of the salesperson, product, and service can be measured by mail questionnaires or telephone calls.

Evaluations can also assess the salesperson's knowledge of the company, products, customers, competitors, territory, and responsibilities. Personality characteristics can be rated, such as general manner, appearance, speech, and temperament. The sales manager can review any problems in motivation or compliance.[58] Sales reps can provide attributions as to the success or failure of a sales call and how they would propose to improve the odds on subsequent calls. Possible explanations for their performance could be related to internal (effort, ability, and strategy) and external (task and luck) factors.[59]

::: Principles of Personal Selling

Personal selling is an ancient art. It has spawned a large literature and many principles. Effective salespeople have more than instinct; they are trained in methods of analysis and customer management. Today's companies spend hundreds of millions of dollars each year to train salespeople in the art of selling. Sales training approaches try to transform a salesperson from a passive order taker into an active order getter who engages in customer problem solving. An active order getter learns how to listen and question in order to identify customer

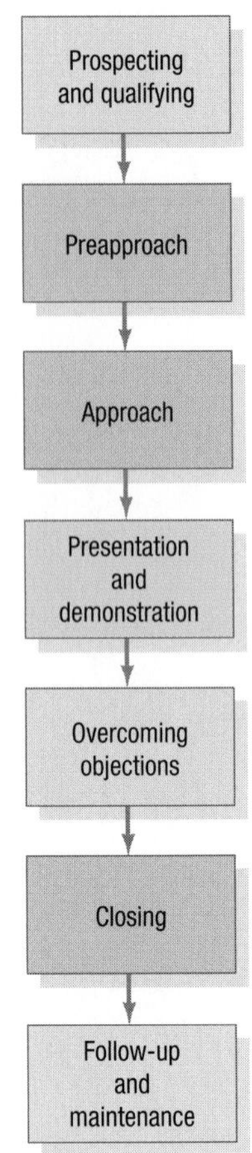

FIG. 19.4

Major Steps in Effective Selling

needs and come up with sound product solutions. This approach assumes that customers have latent needs that constitute opportunities and that they will be loyal to sales reps who can analyze their needs and who have their long-term interests at heart. "Marketing Insight: Principles of Customer-Oriented Selling" offers some guidelines.

Most sales training programs agree on the major steps involved in any effective sales process. We show these steps in Figure 19.4, and discuss their application to industrial selling next.[60]

The Six Steps

PROSPECTING AND QUALIFYING The first step in selling is to identify and qualify prospects. More companies are taking responsibility for finding and qualifying leads so that the salespeople can use their expensive time doing what they can do best: selling. Companies can qualify the leads by contacting them by mail or phone to assess their level of interest and financial capacity. The leads can be categorized, with "hot" prospects turned over to the field sales force and "warm" prospects turned over to the telemarketing unit for follow-up. Even then, it usually takes about four calls on a prospect to consummate a business transaction.

PREAPPROACH The salesperson needs to learn as much as possible about the prospect company (what it needs, who is involved in the purchase decision) and its buyers (personal characteristics and buying styles). The salesperson should set call objectives: to qualify the prospect, gather information, make an immediate sale. Another task is to decide on the best contact approach, which might be a personal visit, a phone call, or a letter. Finally, the salesperson should plan an overall sales strategy for the account.

PRESENTATION AND DEMONSTRATION The salesperson now tells the product "story" to the buyer, following the AIDA formula of gaining *attention,* holding *interest,* arousing *desire,* and obtaining *action.* The salesperson uses a *features, advantages, benefits,* and *value* approach (FABV). Features describe physical characteristics of a market offering, such as chip processing speeds or memory capacity. Advantages describe why the features provide an advantage to the customer. Benefits describe the economic, technical, service, and social benefits delivered by the offering. Value describes the worth (often in monetary terms) of the offering. Too often, salespeople spend too much time dwelling on product features (a product orientation) and not enough stressing the offering's benefits and value (a customer orientation).

OVERCOMING OBJECTIONS Customers typically pose objections during the presentation or when asked for the order. *Psychological resistance* includes resistance to interference, preference for established supply sources or brands, apathy, reluctance to giving up something, unpleasant associations created by the sales rep, predetermined ideas, dislike of making decisions, and neurotic attitude toward money. *Logical resistance* might consist of objections to the price, delivery schedule, or certain product or company characteristics.

To handle these objections, the salesperson maintains a positive approach, asks the buyer to clarify the objection, questions the buyer in a way that the buyer has to answer his or her own objection, denies the validity of the objection, or turns the objection into a reason for buying. Handling and overcoming objections is a part of the broader skills of negotiation.

One potential problem is for salespeople to give in too often when customers demand a discount. One company recognized this as a problem when its sales revenues went up by 25 percent but its profit had remained flat. The company decided to retrain its salespeople to "sell the price," rather than "sell through price." Salespeople were given richer information about each customer's sales history and behavior. They received training to recognize value-adding opportunities rather than price-cutting opportunities. As a result, the company's sales revenues climbed and so did its margins.[61]

CLOSING Now the salesperson attempts to close the sale. Salespeople need to know how to recognize closing signs from the buyer, including physical actions, statements or comments, and questions. There are several closing techniques. They can ask for the order, recapitulate the points of agreement, offer to help the secretary write up the order, ask

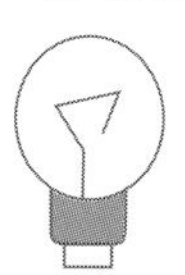

MARKETING INSIGHT | PRINCIPLES OF CUSTOMER-ORIENTED SELLING

Two vocal exponents of a customer-oriented approach to selling are Neil Rackham and Sharon Drew Morgen. Neil Rackham has developed a method that he calls *SPIN selling* (Situation, Problem, Implication, Need-Payoff). Gone is the script of the slick salesperson, and in its place is the salesperson who knows how to raise good questions and listen and learn. Neil Rackham trains salespeople to raise four types of questions with the prospect:

1. ***Situation questions:*** These ask about facts or explore the buyer's present situation. For example, "What system are you using to invoice your customers?"
2. ***Problem questions:*** These deal with problems, difficulties, and dissatisfactions the buyer is experiencing. For example, "What parts of the system create errors?"
3. ***Implication questions:*** These ask about the consequences or effects of a buyer's problems, difficulties, or dissatisfactions. For example, "How does this problem affect your people's productivity?"
4. ***Need-payoff questions:*** These ask about the value or usefulness of a proposed solution. For example, "How much would you save if our company could help reduce the errors by 80 percent?"

Rackham suggests that companies, especially those selling complex products or services, should have their salespeople move from *preliminaries,* to *investigating* the prospect's problems and needs, to *demonstrating* the supplier's superior capabilities, and then *obtaining* a long-term commitment. This approach reflects the growing interest of many companies in moving from pursuing an immediate sale to developing a long-term customer relationship.

Sharon Drew Morgen takes Rackham's approach a step further with what she calls the Buying Facilitation Method. She holds that the job of a salesperson is to help prospects go through a process to decide first whether their company's performance can be improved, and second whether the seller's offering would provide a solution. Prospects only buy when they realize they have a problem, that they lack resources to solve their problem, and that the seller's offering can add value.

Sales guru Tom Hopkins offers some additional tips to help close a deal:

1. ***Ask questions that don't leave room for no.*** "I could visit you today at 3, or would tomorrow at 9 be better?"
2. ***Never use the word "price" or "cost."*** Say investment.
3. ***Never ask for "an appointment."*** It suggests a serious time commitment. Say "I'll be in the area, and I was hoping I could just pop by and visit."
4. ***Don't ask, "May I help you?"*** They'll reply, "We're just looking." Ask instead what brought them into the store today.
5. ***Isolate areas of agreement.*** You need a lot of "little yeses" on the way to getting a "big yes."

Sources: Neil Rackham, *SPIN Selling* (New York: McGraw-Hill, 1988). Also see his *The SPIN Selling Fieldbook* (New York: McGraw-Hill, 1996); Neil Rackham and John De Vincentis, *Rethinking the Sales Force* (New York: McGraw-Hill, 1996); Sharon Drew Morgen, *Selling with Integrity: Reinventing Sales Through Collaboration, Respect, and Serving* (New York: Berkeley Books, 1999); James Lardner, "Selling Salesmenship," *Business 2.0,* December 2002/January 2003, p. 66.

whether the buyer wants A or B, get the buyer to make minor choices such as the color or size, or indicate what the buyer will lose if the order is not placed now. The salesperson might offer the buyer specific inducements to close, such as a special price, an extra quantity, or a token gift.

FOLLOW-UP AND MAINTENANCE Follow-up and maintenance are necessary if the salesperson wants to ensure customer satisfaction and repeat business. Immediately after closing, the salesperson should cement any necessary details on delivery time, purchase terms, and other matters that are important to the customer. The salesperson should schedule a follow-up call when the initial order is received to make sure there is proper installation, instruction, and servicing. This visit or call will detect any problems, assure the buyer of the salesperson's interest, and reduce any cognitive dissonance that might have arisen. The salesperson should also develop a maintenance and growth plan for the account.

Negotiation

Marketing is concerned with exchange activities and the manner in which the terms of exchange are established. In *routinized exchange,* the terms are established by administered programs of pricing and distribution. In *negotiated exchange,* price and other terms are set via bargaining behavior, in which two or more parties negotiate long-term binding agreements. Although price is the most frequently negotiated issue, other issues include contract completion time; quality of goods and services offered; purchase volume; responsibility for financing, risk taking, promotion, and title; and product safety.

Marketers who find themselves in bargaining situations need certain traits and skills to be effective. The most important are preparation and planning skill, knowledge of subject matter being negotiated, ability to think clearly and rapidly under pressure and uncertainty, ability to express thoughts verbally, listening skill, judgment and general intelligence, integrity, ability to persuade others, and patience.[62]

Relationship Marketing

The principles of personal selling and negotiation we have described are largely transaction-oriented because their purpose is to close a specific sale. But in many cases the company is not seeking an immediate sale, but rather to build a long-term supplier–customer relationship. The company wants to demonstrate that it has the capabilities to serve the account's needs in a superior way. Today's customers are large and often global. They prefer suppliers who can sell and deliver a coordinated set of products and services to many locations; who can quickly solve problems that arise in different locations; and who can work closely with customer teams to improve products and processes.

Salespeople working with key customers must do more than call when they think customers might be ready to place orders. They should call or visit at other times, take customers to dinner, and make useful suggestions about the business. They should monitor key accounts, know customers' problems, and be ready to serve them in a number of ways.

When a relationship management program is properly implemented, the organization will begin to focus as much on managing its customers as on managing its products. At the same time, companies should realize that while there is a strong and warranted move toward relationship marketing, it is not effective in all situations. Ultimately, companies must judge which segments and which specific customers will respond profitably to relationship management.

SUMMARY :::

1. Direct marketing is an interactive marketing system that uses one or more media to effect a measurable response or transaction at any location. Direct marketing, especially electronic marketing, is showing explosive growth.
2. Direct marketers plan campaigns by deciding on objectives, target markets and prospects, offers, and prices. This is followed by testing and establishing measures to determine the campaign's success.
3. Major channels for direct marketing include face-to-face selling, direct mail, catalog marketing, telemarketing, interactive TV, kiosks, Web sites, and mobile devices.
4. Interactive marketing provides marketers with opportunities for much greater interaction and individualization through well-designed Web sites as well as online ads and promotions.
5. Sales personnel serve as a company's link to its customers. The sales rep *is* the company to many of its customers, and it is the rep who brings back to the company much-needed information about the customer.
6. Designing the sales force requires decisions regarding objectives, strategy, structure, size, and compensation. Objectives may include prospecting, targeting, communicating, selling, servicing, information gathering, and allocating. Determining strategy requires choosing the most effective mix of selling approaches. Choosing the sales force structure entails dividing territories by geography, product, or market (or some combination of these). Estimating how large the sales force needs to be involves estimating the total workload and how many sales hours (and hence salespeople) will be needed. Compensating the sales force entails determining what types of salaries, commissions, bonuses, expense accounts, and benefits to give, and how much weight customer satisfaction should have in determining total compensation.
7. There are five steps involved in managing the sales force: (1) recruiting and selecting sales representatives; (2) training the representatives in sales techniques and in the company's products, policies, and customer-satisfaction orientation; (3) supervising the sales force and helping reps to use their time efficiently; (4) motivating the sales force and balancing quotas, monetary rewards, and supplementary motivators; (5) evaluating individual and group sales performance.
8. Effective salespeople are trained in the methods of analysis and customer management, as well as the art of sales professionalism. No approach works best in all circumstances, but most trainers agree that selling is a seven-step process: prospecting and qualifying customers, preapproach, approach, presentation and demonstration, overcoming objections, closing, and follow-up and maintenance.

APPLICATIONS :::

Marketing Debate Are Great Salespeople Born or Made?

One difference of opinion with respect to sales concerns the potential impact of training versus selection in developing an effective sales force. Some observers maintain that the best salespeople are "born" that way and are effective due to their personalities and all the interpersonal skills they have developed over a lifetime. Others contend that application of leading-edge sales techniques can make virtually anyone a sales star.

Take a position: The key to developing an effective sales force is selection versus The key to developing an effective sales force is training.

Marketing Discussion

Pick a company and go to the Web site. How would you evaluate the Web site? How well does it score on the 7Cs design elements: context, content, community, customization, communication, connection, and commerce?

PART 8

CREATING SUCCESSFUL LONG-TERM GROWTH

IN THIS CHAPTER, WE WILL ADDRESS THE FOLLOWING QUESTIONS:

1. What challenges does a company face in developing new products?
2. What organizational structures are used to manage new-product development?
3. What are the main stages in developing new products?
4. What is the best way to set up the new-product development process?
5. What factors affect the rate of diffusion and consumer adoption of newly launched products?

CHAPTER 20 ::: INTRODUCING NEW MARKET OFFERINGS

twenty

Companies need to grow their revenue over time by developing new products and expanding into new markets. New-product development shapes the company's future; improved or replacement products will maintain or build sales. Some companies put product innovation at the forefront of all they do. 3M Company, one of the most innovative U.S. companies, puts tremendous emphasis on new products.[1]

3M makes more than 50,000 products, including sandpaper, adhesives, optical films, and fiber-optic connectors. It invests more than \$1 billion annually in research and development, with a staff of more than 6,000 scientists worldwide, and launches scores of new products every year. In 2003, 3M generated \$18 billion in sales. The company's policy of allowing all employees to spend up to 15 percent of their time working on projects of personal interest helped to produce Post-it® notes, masking tape, and 3M's microreplication technology. At the same, 3M carefully monitors the commercialization potential for new-product candidates, making sure scientists and marketers collaborate early in the process and putting more resources behind the likely winners. 3M's Golden Step Award program honors 3M employees and team members who have developed significant new products, product lines, or markets, and successfully generated at least \$10 million in annual global sales within three years of product introduction. >>>

A new, innovative 3M product: The 3M™ Paint Preparation System allows painters to paint at any angle, helping to ensure high-quality work even in hard-to-reach places. It has won strong acceptance in auto body repair, aerospace, marine, and other markets worldwide.

Marketers play a key role in the new-product process by identifying and evaluating new-product ideas and working with R&D and others in every stage of development. This chapter provides a detailed analysis of the new-product development process. Chapter 21 considers how marketers can tap into global markets as another source of long-term growth.

::: Challenges in New-Product Development

A company can add new products through acquisition or development. The acquisition route can take three forms. The company can buy other companies, it can acquire patents from other companies, or it can buy a license or franchise from another company. Swiss food giant Nestlé increased its presence in North America via its acquisition of such diverse brands as Carnation, Hills Brothers, Stouffer's, Ralston Purina, Dreyer's Ice Cream, and Chef America.[2]

The development route can take two forms. The company can develop new products in its own laboratories, or it can contract with independent researchers or new-product development firms to develop specific new products. We can identify six categories of new products:[3]

1. ***New-to-the-world products*** – New products that create an entirely new market.
2. ***New product lines*** – New products that allow a company to enter an established market for the first time.
3. ***Additions to existing product lines*** – New products that supplement established product lines (package sizes, flavors, and so on).
4. ***Improvements and revisions of existing products*** – New products that provide improved performance or greater perceived value and replace existing products.
5. ***Repositionings*** – Existing products that are targeted to new markets or market segments.
6. ***Cost reductions*** – New products that provide similar performance at lower cost.

Less than 10 percent of all new products are truly innovative and new to the world. These products involve the greatest cost and risk because they are new to both the company and the marketplace. W.L. Gore, best known for its durable Gore-Tex outdoor fabric, has innovated breakthrough new products in a number of diverse areas—guitar strings, dental floss, medical devices, and fuel cells. It has adopted several principles to guide its new-product development:[4]

1. ***Work with potential customers.*** Its thoracic graft, designed to combat heart disease, was developed in close collaboration with physicians.
2. ***Let employees choose projects.*** Few actual product leaders and teams are appointed. Gore likes to nurture "passionate champions" who convince others a project is worth their time and commitment. The development of the fuel cell rallied over 100 of the company's 6,000 research associates.
3. ***Give employees "dabble" time.*** All research associates spend 10 percent of their work hours developing their own ideas. Promising ideas are pushed forward and judged according to a "Real, Win, Worth" exercise. Is the opportunity real? Can we win? Can we make money?
4. ***Know when to let go.*** Sometimes dead ends in one area can spark an innovation in another. Elixir acoustic guitar strings were a result of a failed venture into bike cables. Even successful ventures may have to move on. Glide shred-resistant dental floss was sold to Procter & Gamble because Gore-Tex knew that retailers would want to deal with a company selling a whole family of health care products.

Most new-product activity is devoted to improving existing products. At Sony, over 80 percent of new-product activity is actually devoted to modifying and improving existing prod-

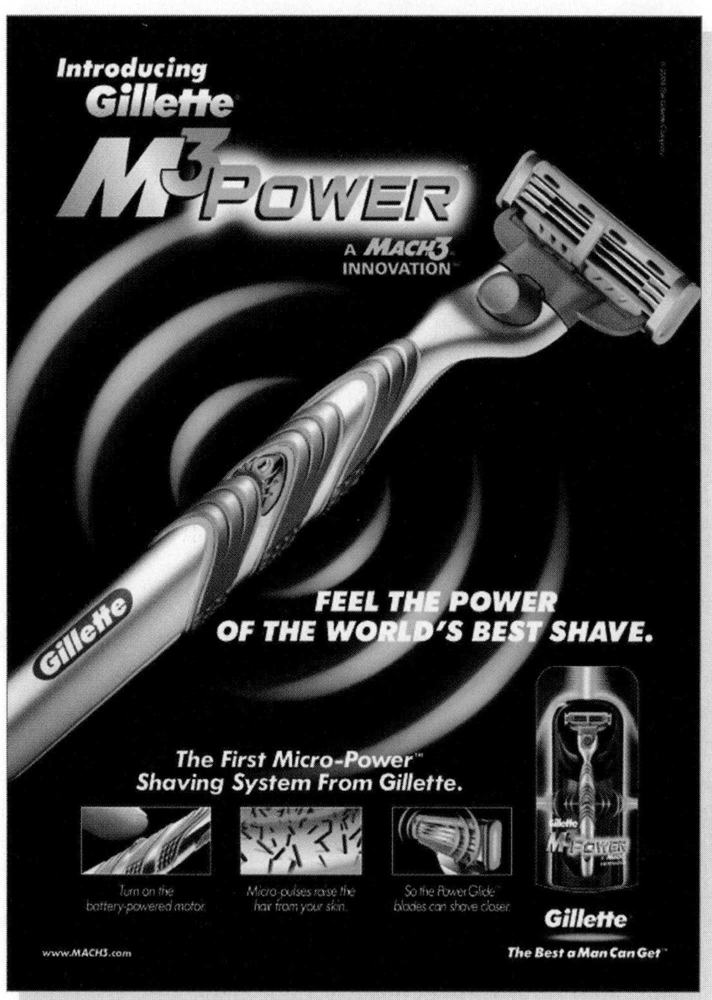

Improving existing products: Print ad for the new Gillette M3Power shaver for men.

ucts. Gillette frequently updates its razor systems: It launched the new M3Power wet shaver for men and Venus Divine for women in 2004.[5] In many categories, it is becoming increasingly difficult to identify blockbuster products that will transform a market; but continuous innovation to better satisfy consumer needs can force competitors to play catch-up.[6]

BLACKBERRY

Indispensable to subscribers including Jeb Bush, Sarah Jessica Parker, and Jack Welch, Research in Motion's (RIM) Blackberry, introduced in 1999, has become almost synonymous with wireless e-mail. E-mail is automatically directed to Blackberry as it is going to the desktop and can be answered with an intuitive thumb-operated keyboard. The corporate goal is to "enable wireless e-mail whenever and on whatever device people want." Adding new features such as voice and speakerphones, brighter-color screens, backlit keyboards, and international roaming have fueled explosive growth. Its fanatical appeal has led some to dub the product "CrackBerries." With a subscriber base reaching 2 million in 2004, it's no surprise that the stock price increased tenfold during the previous year.[7]

Launching new products as brand extensions into related product categories is one means of broadening the brand meaning. Nike started as a running-shoe manufacturer but now competes in the sports market with all types of athletic shoes, clothing, and equipment. Armstrong World Industries moved from selling floor coverings to ceilings to total interior surface decoration. Product innovation and effective marketing programs have allowed these firms to expand their "market footprint."

In an economy of rapid change, continuous innovation is necessary. Most companies rarely innovate, some innovate occasionally, and a few innovate continuously. In the last category, Sony, 3M, Charles Schwab, Dell Computer, Sun Microsystems, Oracle, Southwest Airlines, Maytag, Costco, and Microsoft have been stock-price gain leaders in their respective industries.[8] These companies have created a positive attitude toward innovation and risk taking; they have routinized the innovation process; they practice teamwork; and they allow their people to experiment and even fail.

Companies that fail to develop new products are putting themselves at risk. Their existing products are vulnerable to changing customer needs and tastes, new technologies, shortened product life cycles, and increased domestic and foreign competition. New technologies are especially threatening.

Most established companies focus on *incremental innovation.* Newer companies create *disruptive technologies* that are cheaper and more likely to alter the competitive space. Established companies can be slow to react or invest in these disruptive technologies because they threaten their investment. Then they suddenly find themselves facing formidable new competitors, and many fail.[9] To ensure that they don't fall into this trap, incumbent firms must carefully monitor the preferences of both customers and noncustomers over time and uncover evolving, difficult-to-articulate customer needs.[10]

PEPSICO

Determined to develop new products to reflect changing consumer tastes and demographics, food and beverage giant PepsiCo adds more than 200 product variations to its global portfolio each year, ranging from Quaker Soy Crisps to Gatorade Xtremo Thirst Quencher. Chairman and CEO Steven Reinmund believes that innovation is the key to consistent double-digit earnings growth: "Innovation is what consumers are looking for, particularly in the small, routine things of life." PepsiCo emphasizes new flavors and healthier ingredients with existing brands. It has also successfully launched new product lines in the United States such as Sabritas chips, a $100 million success brought over from its Mexican subsidiary, and Propel fitness water, which achieved similar sales success only a year after its launch.[11]

At the same time, new-product development can be quite risky. Texas Instruments lost $660 million before withdrawing from the home computer business; RCA lost $500 million on its videodisc players; FedEx lost $340 million on its Zap mail; DuPont lost an estimated $100 million on a synthetic leather called Corfam; and the British-French Concorde aircraft never recovered its investment.[12] Even these amounts are paltry compared to the $5 billion Iridium fiasco (see "Marketing Insight: Iridium Disconnects with Global Customers").

New products continue to fail at a disturbing rate. Recent studies put the rate at 95 percent in the United States and 90 percent in Europe.[13] New products can fail for many reasons: ignoring or misinterpreting market research; overestimating market size; high development costs; poor design; incorrect positioning, ineffective advertising, or wrong price; insufficient distribution support; and competitors who fight back hard.

Several factors also tend to hinder new-product development:

- ***Shortage of important ideas in certain areas.*** There may be few ways left to improve some basic products (such as steel or detergents).
- ***Fragmented markets.*** Companies have to aim their new products at smaller market segments, and this can mean lower sales and profits for each product.
- ***Social and governmental constraints.*** New products have to satisfy consumer safety and environmental concerns.
- ***Cost of development.*** A company typically has to generate many ideas to find just one worthy of development, and often faces high R&D, manufacturing, and marketing costs.
- ***Capital shortages.*** Some companies with good ideas cannot raise the funds needed to research and launch them.
- ***Faster required development time.*** Companies must learn how to compress development time by using new techniques, strategic partners, early concept tests, and advanced marketing planning.
- ***Shorter product life cycles.*** When a new product is successful, rivals are quick to copy it. Sony used to enjoy a three-year lead on its new products. Now Matsushita will copy the product within six months, leaving hardly enough time for Sony to recoup its investment.

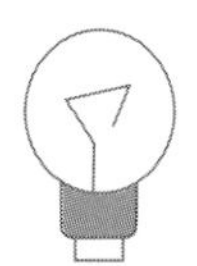

MARKETING INSIGHT | IRIDIUM DISCONNECTS WITH GLOBAL CUSTOMERS

In the late 1990s, Motorola and several partners launched Iridium, a $5 billion global satellite-based wireless telephone system. Motorola's engineers envisioned 66 telecommunications satellites that would circle the earth and make it possible for consumers to place and receive calls with one phone anywhere in the world. Motorola's aim was to establish a universal standard for wireless telephony.

Yet in August 1999, Iridium had to file for bankruptcy because it was unable to meet a $90 million bond payment, and in March 2000, a judge ordered that the bankrupt system be shut down. Motorola was forced to pull the plug on the project. Now, it's clear that the project's sponsors did a poor job of thinking through the marketing issues.

1. The Iridium handset weighed about one pound; most cell phones weigh a couple of ounces. The handset was shaped like a brick and was awkward to carry or pack in a briefcase. The user had to carry a bag of attachments to achieve full functionality. Transmission problems included frequent incomplete calls and lost calls, and the voice quality was poorer than callers were used to on their cellular phones.
2. Iridium was originally launched at $3,000 and eventually came down to $1,500. Worse, airtime charges ranged from $4 to $9 a minute, whether the caller was phoning in his own city or calling from a Borneo jungle.
3. Although the phone was touted to be workable anywhere, it could not be used inside buildings or in moving cars. Users had to have a clear path between the handset and the orbiting satellites. Furthermore, large areas in Europe, Asia, and Africa lacked service.
4. Iridium budgeted $180 million for promotion. Its advertising campaign showed a man in a heavy parka pulling a sled in a desolate, snowbound place. His phone suddenly rings: He has contact with the outside world. This ad campaign was supplemented with a direct-mail campaign and a strong public relations program, but all this promotion needed to be followed up by competent personal selling. This was the hardest challenge, because prospects would raise questions about price, service breakdowns, and the bulky handset, and often conclude that the benefits were not worth the price.
5. Motorola chose selling partners in other parts of the world who often lacked marketing skills. Although the promotion campaign generated about 1.5 million inquiries, most were not answered or not answered quickly enough.

Senior management set a drop-dead launch date of September 23, 1998, but had to delay this until November 1. Even then, the company still had problems with the product, service, distribution, support, and finances. With all these complications, no wonder the project never attracted more than 50,000 buyers. The lesson: No amount of promotion can make a success out of a poorly designed product plagued with poor quality and poor service.

Sources: Jonathan Sidener, "Iridium's Adventure Over Satellite Phone System Ordered Shut Down," *Arizona Republic,* March 18, 2000; Kevin Maney, "$3,000 Gadget Might Be Globe-Trotters Best Friend," *USA Today,* September 17, 1998; Leslie Cauley, "Iridium's Downfall," *Wall Street Journal,* August 18, 1999; Eric M. Olson, Stanley F. Slater, and Andrew J. Czaplewski, "The Iridium Story: A Marketing Disconnect?" *Marketing Management* (Summer 2000): 54–57.

What can a company do to develop successful new products? Cooper and Kleinschmidt found that the number-one success factor is a unique, superior product. Such products succeed 98 percent of the time, compared to products with a moderate advantage (58 percent success) or minimal advantage (18 percent success). Another key factor is a well-defined product concept. The company carefully defines and assesses the target market, product requirements, and benefits before proceeding. Other success factors are technological and marketing synergy, quality of execution in all stages, and market attractiveness.[14] (See "Marketing Memo: Lessons for New Product Success.")

::: Organizational Arrangements

Once a company has carefully segmented the market, chosen its target customers, identified their needs, and determined its market positioning, it is better able to develop new products. Many companies today use *customer-driven engineering* to design new products. Customer-driven engineering attaches high importance to incorporating customer preferences in the final design.

New-product development requires senior management to define business domains, product categories, and specific criteria. General Motors has a hefty $400 million benchmark it must apply to new car models—this is what it costs to get a new vehicle into production.[15] One company established the following acceptance criteria:

- The product can be introduced within five years.
- The product has a market potential of at least $50 million and a 15 percent growth rate.

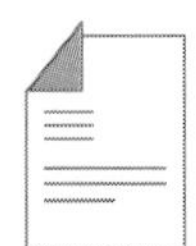

MARKETING MEMO | LESSONS FOR NEW-PRODUCT SUCCESS

Strolling the aisles at Robert McMath's New Product Showcase and Learning Center is like being in some nightmare version of a supermarket. There is Gerber food for adults—pureed sweet-and-sour pork and chicken Madeira—microwaveable ice cream sundaes, parsnip chips, aerosol mustard, Ben-Gay aspirin, and Miller Clear Beer. How about Richard Simmons Dijon Viniagrette Salad Spray, garlic cake in a jar, and Farrah shampoo?

McMath's unusual showcase represents $4 billion in product investment. Behind each of the 80,000 products on display are squandered dollars and hopes. From them he has distilled dozens of lessons for an industry that, by its own admission, has a very short memory. McMath, a former marketer for Colgate-Palmolive, has now put his unique insights into a book called *What Were They Thinking?* Here are a few of the marketing lessons McMath espouses:

- ***The value of a brand is its good name, which it earns over time.*** People trust it to deliver a consistent set of attributes. Do not squander this trust by attaching your good name to something totally out of character. Louis Sherry No Sugar Added Gorgonzola Cheese dressing was everything that Louis Sherry, known for its rich candies and ice cream, should not be: sugarless, cheese, and salad dressing.
- ***Me-too marketing is the number-one killer of new products.*** Pepsi is one of the few survivors among dozens of other brands that have challenged Coke for more than a century. Ever hear of Toca-Cola? Coco-Cola? Yum-Yum Cola? French Wine of Cola? How about King-Cola, "the royal drink"?
- ***People usually do not buy products that remind them of their shortcomings.*** Gillette's For Oily Hair Only shampoo flopped because people did not want to confess that they had oily hair; nor do they wish to advertise their faults and foibles to other people by carrying such products in their grocery carts.
- ***Some products are too different from the products, services, or experiences consumers normally purchase.*** You can tell that some innovative products are doomed as soon as you hear their names: Toaster Eggs, Cucumber Antiperspirant Spray, Health-Sea Sea Sausage.

Sources: Paul Lukas, "The Ghastliest Product Launches," *Fortune,* March 16, 1996, p. 44; Jan Alexander, "Failure Inc.," *Worldbusiness* (May–June 1996): 46; Ted Anthony, "Where's Farrah Shampoo? Next to the Salsa Ketchup," *Marketing News,* May 6, 1996, p. 13. Bulleted points are adapted from Robert M. McMath and Thom Forbes, *What Were They Thinking? Marketing Lessons I've Learned from Over 80,000 New-Product Innovations and Idiocies* (New York: Times Business, 1998), pp. 22–24, 28, 30–31, and 129–130.

- The product would provide at least 30 percent return on sales and 40 percent on investment.
- The product would achieve technical or market leadership.

Budgeting for New-Product Development

Senior management must decide how much to budget for new-product development. R&D outcomes are so uncertain that it is difficult to use normal investment criteria. Some companies solve this problem by financing as many projects as possible, hoping to achieve a few winners. Other companies apply a conventional percentage of sales figures or spend what the competition spends. Still other companies decide how many successful new products they need and work backward to estimate the required investment.

Table 20.1 shows how a company might calculate the cost of new-product development. The new-products manager at a large consumer-packaged-goods company reviewed the

TABLE 20.1

Finding One Successful New Product (Starting with 64 new Ideas)

Stage	Number of Ideas	Pass Ratio	Cost per Product Idea	Total Cost
1. Idea screening	64	1:4	$ 1,000	$ 64,000
2. Concept testing	16	1:2	20,000	320,000
3. Product development	8	1:2	200,000	1,600,000
4. Test marketing	4	1:2	500,000	2,000,000
5. National launch	2	1:2	5,000,000	10,000,000
			$5,721,000	$13,984,000

results of 64 ideas. Only one in four, or 16, passed the screening stage. It cost $1,000 to review each idea at this stage. Half of these ideas, or eight, survived the concept-testing stage, at a cost of $20,000 each. Half of these, or four, survived the product-development stage, at a cost of $200,000 each. Half of these, or two, did well in the test market, at a cost of $500,000 each. When these two ideas were launched, at a cost of $5 million each, only one was highly successful. Thus the one successful idea cost the company $5,721,000 to develop.

In the process, 63 other ideas fell by the wayside. The total cost for developing one successful new product was $13,984,000. Unless the company can improve the pass ratios and reduce the costs at each stage, it will have to budget nearly $14 million for each successful new idea it hopes to find. If top management wants four successful new products in the next few years, it will have to budget at least $56 million (4 × $14 million) for new-product development.

Organizing New-Product Development

Companies handle the organizational aspect of new-product development in several ways.[16] Many companies assign responsibility for new-product ideas to *product managers.* But product managers are often so busy managing existing lines that they give little thought to new products other than line extensions. They also lack the specific skills and knowledge needed to develop and critique new products. Kraft and Johnson & Johnson have *new-product managers* who report to category managers. Some companies have a *high-level management committee* charged with reviewing and approving proposals. Large companies often establish a *new-product department* headed by a manager who has substantial authority and access to top management. The department's major responsibilities include generating and screening new ideas, working with the R&D department, and carrying out field testing and commercialization.

3M, Dow, and General Mills often assign new-product development work to *venture teams.* A **venture team** is a cross-functional group charged with developing a specific product or business. These "intrapreneurs" are relieved of their other duties and given a budget, a time frame, and a "skunkworks" setting. *Skunkworks* are informal workplaces, sometimes garages, where intrapreneurial teams attempt to develop new products.

Cross-functional teams can collaborate and use concurrent new-product development to push new products to market.[17] Concurrent product development resembles a rugby match, with team members passing the new product back and forth as they head toward the goal. Using this system, the Allen-Bradley Corporation (a maker of industrial controls) was able to develop a new electrical control device in just two years, as opposed to six years under its old system.

Cross-functional teams help to ensure that engineers are not just driven to create a "better mousetrap" when potential customers do not really need or want one. Some possible criteria for staffing cross-functional new-product venture teams include:[18]

- ***Desired team leadership style and level of expertise.*** The more complex the new-product concept, the greater the desired expertise.
- ***Team member skills and expertise.*** New-venture teams for Aventis, part of a pharmaceutical, agricultural, and chemical conglomerate, contain people with expertise in chemistry, engineering, market research, financial analysis, and manufacturing.
- ***Level of interest in the particular new-product concept.*** Is there interest or, even better, a high level of ownership and commitment (a "concept champion")?
- ***Potential for personal reward.*** What motivates individuals to want to participate in this effort?
- ***Diversity of team members.*** This includes race, gender, nationality, breadth of experience, depth of experience, and personality. The greater the diversity, the greater the range of viewpoints and decision-making potential.

3M, Hewlett-Packard, Lego, and many other companies use the *stage-gate system* to manage the innovation process.[19] The process is divided into stages, and at the end of each stage is a gate or checkpoint. The project leader, working with a cross-functional team, must bring a set of known deliverables to each gate before the project can pass to the next stage. To move from the business plan stage into product development requires a convincing market research study of consumer needs and interest, a competitive analysis, and a technical appraisal. Senior managers review the criteria at each gate to judge whether the project deserves to move to the next stage. The gatekeepers make one of four decisions: *go, kill,*

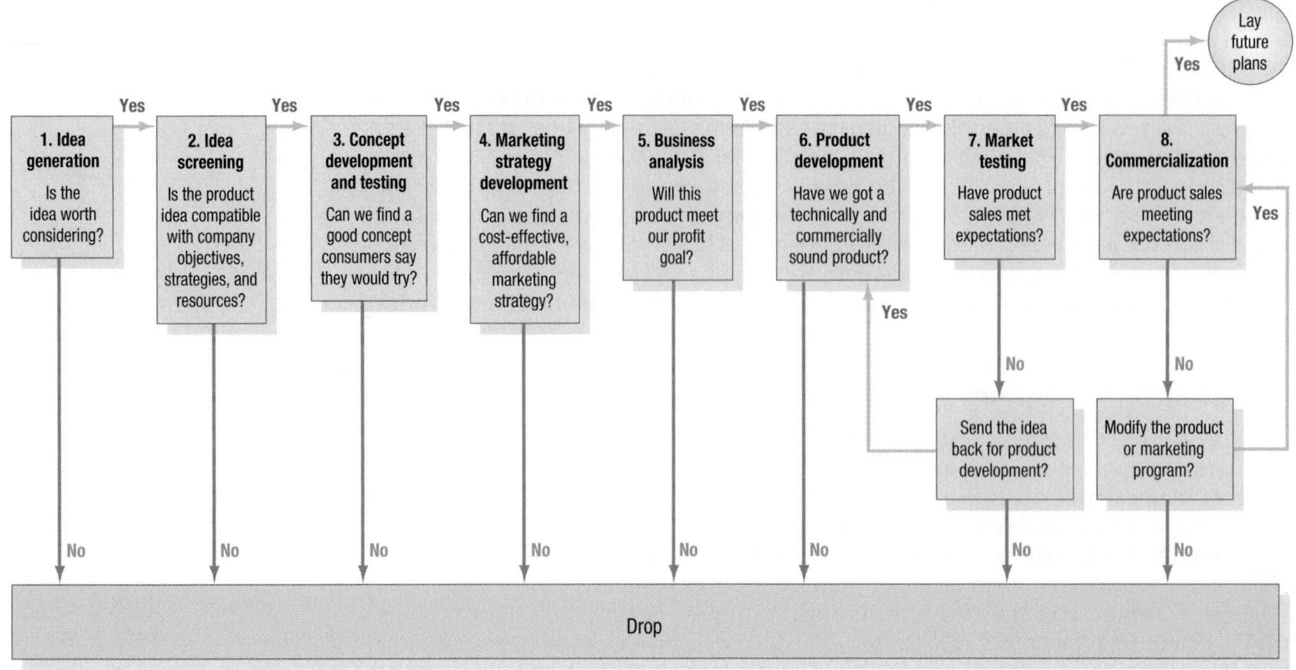

FIG. 20.1 | The New-Product Development Decision Process

hold, or *recycle.* Stage-gate systems make the innovation process visible to all involved and clarify the project leader's and team's responsibilities at each stage.[20]

The stages in the new-product development process are shown in Figure 20.1. Many firms have multiple, parallel sets of projects working through the process, each at a different stage.[21] The process can be depicted as a *funnel:* A large number of initial new product ideas and concepts are winnowed down to a few high-potential products that are ultimately launched. But the process is not always linear. Many firms use a *spiral development process* that recognizes the value of returning to an earlier stage to make improvements before moving forward.

ELI LILLY

Recognizing that 90 percent of experimental drugs fail, Eli Lilly has established a corporate culture that looks at failure as an inevitable part of discovery. If a drug fails at its intended use, Lilly scientists are taught to look for new uses. Lilly often assigns a team of doctors and scientists to analyze every compound that fails at any stage in a human clinical trial. Many of Lilly's drug successes actually started out as failures. Evista was a failed contraceptive that became a $1 billion-a-year drug for osteoporosis. Stattera was unsuccessful as an antidepressant, but became a top seller for attention deficit/hyperactivity disorder. One promising cardiovascular drug in development started as an asthma project.[22]

We now look at the marketing challenges arising at each of the eight stages.

::: Managing the Development Process: Ideas

Idea Generation

The new-product development process starts with the search for ideas. Some marketing experts believe that the greatest opportunities and highest leverage with new products are found by uncovering the best possible set of unmet customer needs or technological innovation.[23] New-product ideas can come from interacting with various groups and from using creativity-generating techniques. (See "Marketing Memo: Ten Ways to Great New-Product Ideas.")

INTERACTING WITH OTHERS Ideas for new products can come from many sources, such as customers, scientists, competitors, employees, channel members, and top management.

Customer needs and wants are the logical place to start the search. One-on-one interviews and focus group discussions can explore product needs and reactions. Griffin and Hauser suggest that conducting 10 to 20 in-depth experiential interviews per market segment often uncovers the vast majority of customer needs.[24]

Procter & Gamble emphasizes observational techniques with its customers. Brand marketers there spend at least 12 hours a month with consumers in their homes, watching how they wash dishes, clean floors, and brush teeth and asking them about their habits and sources of frustration. They also have on-site labs such as a diaper-testing center where dozens of mothers bring their babies to be studied. This close scrutiny has led to several new-product successes.

PROCTER & GAMBLE

To develop its Cover Girl Outlast all-day lip color, P&G tested the product on nearly 30,000 women: It invited 500 of them to come to its labs each morning to apply the lipstick, record their activities, and return eight hours later so it could measure remaining lip color. The activities, dubbed "torture tests" by P&G, ranged from eating spaghetti to kickboxing to showering. The product comes with a tube of glossy moisturizer that women can reapply on top of their color—without having to look at a mirror. The blockbuster product quickly became the market leader.[25]

Technical companies can learn a great deal by studying customers who make the most advanced use of the company's products and who recognize the need for improvements before other customers do.[26] Microsoft studied 13- to 24-year-olds—the NetGen—and developed its threedegrees software product to satisfy their instant messaging needs.[27] (For the special case of high-tech products, see "Marketing Insight: Developing Successful High-Tech Products.")

Employees throughout the company can be a source of ideas for improving production, products, and services. Toyota claims its employees submit 2 million ideas annually (about 35 suggestions per employee), over 85 percent of which are implemented. Kodak, Milliken, and other firms give monetary, holiday, or recognition awards to employees who submit the best ideas.

Companies can also find good ideas by researching competitors' products and services. They can find out what customers like and dislike about competitors' products. They can buy their competitors' products, take them apart, and build better ones. Company sales representatives and intermediaries are a particularly good source of ideas. These groups have firsthand exposure to customers and are often the first to learn about competitive developments.

Top management can be another major source of ideas. Some company leaders, such as the late Edwin H. Land, former CEO of Polaroid, or Andy Grove of Intel, took personal responsibility for technological innovation in their companies. New-product ideas can also come from inventors, patent attorneys, university and commercial laboratories, industrial consultants, advertising agencies, marketing research firms, and industrial publications. However, although ideas can flow from many sources, their chances of receiving serious attention often depend on someone in the organization taking the role of product champion.

A blockbuster product: Cover Girl Outlast all-day lip color. The product comes with a tube of moisturizer to be applied on top of the color.

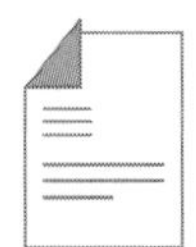

MARKETING MEMO — TEN WAYS TO GREAT NEW-PRODUCT IDEAS

1. Run informal sessions where groups of customers meet with company engineers and designers to discuss problems and needs and brainstorm potential solutions.
2. Allow time off—scouting time—for technical people to putter on their own pet projects. 3M allows 15 percent time off; Rohm & Haas allows 10 percent.
3. Make a customer-brainstorming session a standard feature of plant tours.
4. Survey your customers: Find out what they like and dislike in your and competitors' products.
5. Undertake "fly-on-the-wall" or "camping out" research with customers, as do Fluke and Hewlett-Packard.
6. Use iterative rounds: a group of customers in one room, focusing on identifying problems, and a group of your technical people in the next room, listening and brainstorming solutions. The proposed solutions are then tested immediately on the group of customers.
7. Set up a keyword search that routinely scans trade publications in multiple countries for new-product announcements.
8. Treat trade shows as intelligence missions, where you view all that is new in your industry under one roof.
9. Have your technical and marketing people visit your suppliers' labs and spend time with their technical people—find out what is new.
10. Set up an idea vault, and make it open and easily accessed. Allow employees to review the ideas and add constructively to them.

Source: Adapted from Robert Cooper, *Product Leadership: Creating and Launching Superior New Products* (New York: Perseus Books, 1998).

CREATIVITY TECHNIQUES Here is a sampling of techniques for stimulating creativity in individuals and groups.[28]

- ***Attribute listing.*** List the attributes of an object, such as a screwdriver. Then modify each attribute, such as replacing the wooden handle with plastic, providing torque power, adding different screw heads, and so on.
- ***Forced relationships.*** List several ideas and consider each one in relation to each other one. In designing new office furniture, for example, consider a desk, bookcase, and filing cabinet as separate ideas. One can then imagine a desk with a built-in bookcase or a desk with built-in files or a bookcase with built-in files.
- ***Morphological analysis.*** Start with a problem, such as "getting something from one place to another via a powered vehicle." Now think of dimensions, such as the type of platform (cart, chair, sling, bed), the medium (air, water, oil, rails), and the power source (compressed air, electric motor, magnetic fields). By listing every possible combination, one can generate many new solutions.

A cyber café: cafeteria + Internet.

- ***Reverse assumption analysis.*** List all the normal assumptions about an entity and then reverse them. Instead of assuming that a restaurant has menus, charges for food, and serves food, reverse each assumption. The new restaurant may decide to serve only what the chef bought that morning and cooked; may provide some food and charge only for how long the person sits at the table; and may design an exotic atmosphere and rent out the space to people who bring their own food and beverages.
- ***New contexts.*** Take familiar processes, such as people-helping services, and put them into a new context. Imagine helping dogs and cats instead of people with day care service, stress reduction, psychotherapy, animal funerals, and so on. As another example, instead of hotel guests going to the front desk to check in, greet them at curbside and use a wireless device to register them.

- ***Mind-mapping.*** Start with a thought, such as a car, write it on a piece of paper, then think of the next thought that comes up (say Mercedes), link it to car, then think of the next association (Germany), and do this with all associations that come up with each new word. Perhaps a whole new idea will materialize.

Increasingly, new-product ideas arise from *lateral marketing* that combines two product concepts or ideas to create a new offering. Here are some successful examples:

- Gas station stores = gas stations + food
- Cyber cafés = cafeteria + Internet
- Cereal bars = cereal + snacking
- Kinder Surprise = candy + toy
- Sony Walkman = audio + portable

Idea Screening

A company should motivate its employees to submit new ideas to an *idea manager* whose name and phone number are widely circulated. Ideas should be written down and reviewed each week by an *idea committee.* The company then sorts the proposed ideas into three groups: promising ideas, marginal ideas, and rejects. Each promising idea is researched by a committee member, who reports back to the committee. The surviving ideas then move into a full-scale screening process. In screening ideas, the company must avoid two types of errors.

A *DROP-error* occurs when the company dismisses an otherwise good idea. It is extremely easy to find fault with other people's ideas (Figure 20.2). Some companies shudder when they look back at ideas they dismissed or breathe sighs of relief when they realize how close they came to dropping what eventually became a huge success. This was the case with the television show *Friends.*

FRIENDS

The NBC situation comedy *Friends* enjoyed a 10-year run from 1994 to 2004 as a perennial ratings powerhouse. But the show almost didn't see the light of the day. According to an internal NBC research report, the pilot episode was described as "not very entertaining, clever, or original" and was given a failing grade, scoring 41 out of 100. Ironically, the pilot for an earlier hit sit-com, *Seinfeld,* also was rated as "weak," although the pilot for the medical drama *ER* scored a healthy 91. Courtney Cox's Monica was the *Friends* character that scored best with test audiences, but characters portrayed by Lisa Kudrow and Matthew Perry were deemed to have marginal appeal, and the Rachel, Ross, and Joey characters scored even lower. Adults 35 and over in the sample found the characters as a whole, "smug, superficial, and self-absorbed."[29]

A *GO-error* occurs when the company permits a poor idea to move into development and commercialization. An *absolute product failure* loses money; its sales do not cover variable costs. A *partial product failure* loses money, but its sales cover all its variable costs and some of its fixed costs. A *relative product failure* yields a profit that is less than the company's target rate of return.

The purpose of screening is to drop poor ideas as early as possible. The rationale is that product-development costs rise substantially with each successive development stage. Most companies require new-product ideas to be described on a standard form that can be reviewed by a new-product committee. The description states the product idea, the target market, and the competition, and roughly estimates market size, product price, development time and costs, manufacturing costs, and rate of return.

The executive committee then reviews each idea against a set of criteria. Does the product meet a need? Would it offer superior value? Can it be distinctively advertised? Does the company have the necessary know-how and capital? Will the new product deliver the expected sales volume, sales growth, and profit?

The surviving ideas can be rated using a weighted-index method like that in Table 20.2. The first column lists factors required for successful product launches, and the second column assigns importance weights. The third column scores the product idea on a scale from 0 to 1.0, with 1.0 the highest score. The final step multiplies each factor's importance by the

"I've got a great idea!"

"It won't work here."

"We've tried it before."

"This isn't the right time."

"It can't be done."

"It's not the way
we do things."

"We've done all
right without it."

"It will cost too much."

"Let's discuss it at
our next meeting."

FIG. 20.2

Forces Fighting New Ideas

Source: With permission of Jerold Panas, Young & Partners, Inc.

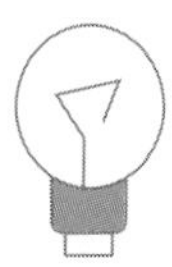

MARKETING INSIGHT | DEVELOPING SUCCESSFUL HIGH-TECH PRODUCTS

High tech covers a wide range of industries—telecommunications, computers, consumer electronics, biotech, software. Radical innovations carry a high level of risk and typically hurt the company's bottom line, at least in the short run. The good news is that success can create a greater sustainable competitive advantage than that which might come from more ordinary products.

One way to define the scope of high tech is by its common characteristics:

- ***High technological uncertainty:*** Scientists working on high-tech products are never sure they will function as promised and be delivered on time.
- ***High market uncertainty:*** Marketers are not sure what needs the new technology will meet. How will buyers use Interactive TV? Which DVD format will prevail after Toshiba's introduction of HD (high definition) DVD in 2005?
- ***High competitive volatility:*** Will the strongest competition come from within the industry or from outside? Will competitors rewrite the rules? What products will this new technology replace?
- ***High investment cost, low variable cost:*** Many high-tech products require a large up-front investment to develop the first unit, but the costs fall rapidly on additional units. The cost of developing a new piece of software is very high, but the cost of distributing it in a CD-ROM is relatively low.
- ***Short life:*** Most high-tech products must be constantly upgraded. Competitors will often force the innovator to produce a second generation before recouping its investment on the first generation.
- ***Finding funding sources for such risky projects is not easy:*** Companies must create a strong R&D/marketing partnership to pull it off. Few reliable techniques exist for estimating demand for radical innovations. Focus groups will provide some perspectives on customer interest and need, but high-tech marketers will have to use a probe-and-learn approach based on observation of early users and collection of feedback on their experiences.

High-tech marketers also face difficult questions related to the marketing mix:

- ***Product:*** What features and functions should they build into the new product? Should manufacturing be done in-house or be outsourced?
- ***Price:*** Should the price be set high? Would a low price be better in order to sell more quickly and go down the experience curve faster? Should the product be almost given away to accelerate adoption?
- ***Distribution:*** Is the product best sold through the company's own sales force or should it be put in the hands of agents, distributors, and dealers? Should the company start with one channel or build multiple sales channels early?
- ***Communication:*** What are the best messages to convey the basic benefits and features of the new product? What are the best media for communicating these messages? What sales promotion incentives would drive early interest and purchase?

Source: For further ideas, see Jakki Mohr, *Marketing of High-Technology Products and Innovations,* 2nd ed. (Upper Saddle River, NJ: Prentice Hall, 2005).

product score to obtain an overall rating. In this example, the product idea scores .69, which places it in the "good idea" level. The purpose of this basic rating device is to promote systematic evaluation and discussion. It is not supposed to make the decision for management.

As the idea moves through development, the company will constantly need to revise its estimate of the product's overall probability of success, using the following formula:

TABLE 20.2

Product–Idea Rating Device

Product Success Requirements	Relative Weight (a)	Product Score (b)	Product Rating (c = a × b)
Unique or superior product	.40	.8	.32
High performance-to-cost ratio	.30	.6	.18
High marketing dollar support	.20	.7	.14
Lack of strong competition	.10	.5	.05
Total	1.00		.69[a]

[a]Rating scale: .00–.30 poor; .31–.60 fair; .61–.80 good. Minimum acceptance rate: .61

Overall	**Probability**	**Probability of**	**Probability of**
probability of =	of technical ×	commercialization ×	economic
success	completion	given technical	success given
	completion	commercialization	

For example, if the three probabilities are estimated as .50, .65, and .74, respectively, the overall probability of success is .24. The company then has to judge whether this probability is high enough to warrant continued development.

::: Managing the Development Process: Concept to Strategy

Attractive ideas must be refined into testable product concepts. A *product idea* is a possible product the company might offer to the market. A *product concept* is an elaborated version of the idea expressed in consumer terms.

Concept Development and Testing

CONCEPT DEVELOPMENT Let us illustrate concept development with the following situation: A large food-processing company gets the idea of producing a powder to add to milk to increase its nutritional value and taste. This is a product idea, but consumers do not buy product ideas; they buy product concepts.

A product idea can be turned into several concepts. The first question is: Who will use this product? The powder can be aimed at infants, children, teenagers, young or middle-aged adults, or older adults. Second, what primary benefit should this product provide? Taste, nutrition, refreshment, energy? Third, when will people consume this drink? Breakfast, mid-morning, lunch, mid-afternoon, dinner, late evening? By answering these questions, a company can form several concepts:

- ***Concept 1.*** An instant breakfast drink for adults who want a quick nutritious breakfast without preparation.
- ***Concept 2.*** A tasty snack drink for children to drink as a midday refreshment.
- ***Concept 3.*** A health supplement for older adults to drink in the late evening before they go to bed.

Each concept represents a *category concept* that defines the product's competition. An instant breakfast drink would compete against bacon and eggs, breakfast cereals, coffee and pastry, and other breakfast alternatives. A tasty snack drink would compete against soft drinks, fruit juices, and other thirst quenchers.

Suppose the instant-breakfast-drink concept looks best. The next task is to show where this powdered product would stand in relation to other breakfast products. Figure 20.3(a) uses the two dimensions of cost and preparation time to create a *product-positioning map* for the breakfast drink. An instant breakfast drink offers low cost and quick preparation. Its nearest competitor is cold cereal or breakfast bars; its most distant competitor is bacon and eggs. These contrasts can be utilized in communicating and promoting the concept to the market.

Next, the product concept has to be turned into a *brand concept.* Figure 20.3(b) is a brand-positioning map showing the current positions of three existing brands of instant breakfast drinks. The company needs to decide how much to charge and how calorific to make its drink. The new brand would be distinctive in the medium-price, medium-calorie market or in the high-price, high-calorie market. The company would not want to position it next to an existing brand, unless that brand is weak or inferior.

CONCEPT TESTING Concept testing involves presenting the product concept to target consumers and getting their reactions. The concepts can be presented symbolically or physically. The more the tested concepts resemble the final product or experience, the more dependable concept testing is.

(a) Product-positioning Map (Breakfast Market)

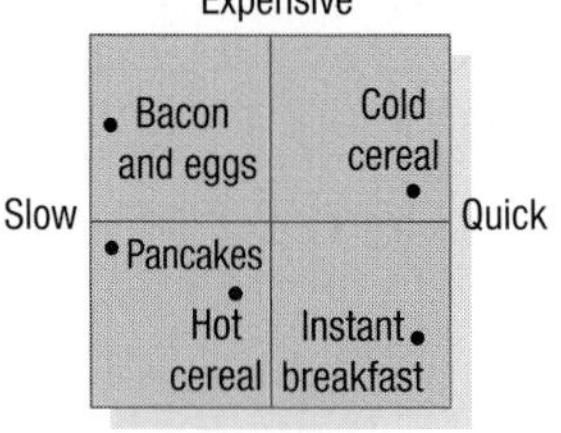

(b) Brand-positioning Map (Instant Breakfast Market)

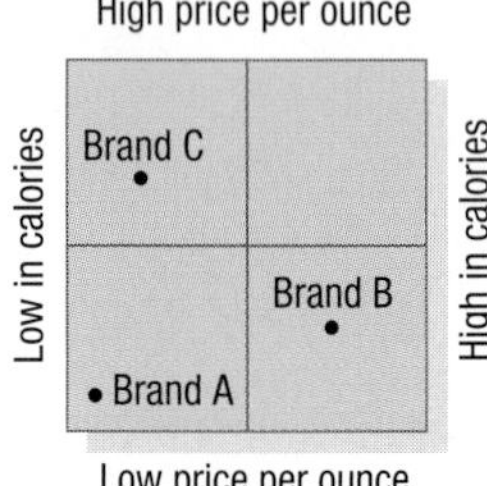

FIG. 20.3

Product and Brand Positioning

In the past, creating physical prototypes was costly and time-consuming, but computer-aided design and manufacturing programs have changed that. Today firms can use *rapid prototyping* to design products (for example, small appliances or toys) on a computer, and then produce plastic models of each. Potential consumers can view the plastic models and give their reactions.[30] Companies are also using *virtual reality* to test product concepts. Virtual reality programs use computers and sensory devices (such as gloves or goggles) to simulate reality.

Concept testing entails presenting consumers with an elaborated version of the concept. Here is the elaboration of concept 1 in our milk example:

> Our product is a powdered mixture that is added to milk to make an instant breakfast that gives the person all the needed nutrition along with good taste and high convenience. The product would be offered in three flavors (chocolate, vanilla, and strawberry) and would come in individual packets, six to a box, at $2.49 a box.

After receiving this information, researchers measure product dimensions by having consumers respond to the following questions:

1. ***Communicability and believability*** – Are the benefits clear to you and believable? If the scores are low, the concept must be refined or revised.
2. ***Need level*** – Do you see this product solving a problem or filling a need for you? The stronger the need, the higher the expected consumer interest.
3. ***Gap level*** – Do other products currently meet this need and satisfy you? The greater the gap, the higher the expected consumer interest. The need level can be multiplied by the gap level to produce a *need-gap score*. A high need-gap score means that the consumer sees the product as filling a strong need that is not satisfied by available alternatives.
4. ***Perceived value*** – Is the price reasonable in relation to the value? The higher the perceived value, the higher the expected consumer interest.
5. ***Purchase intention*** – Would you (definitely, probably, probably not, definitely not) buy the product? This would be high for consumers who answered the previous three questions positively.
6. ***User targets, purchase occasions, purchasing frequency*** – Who would use this product, and when and how often will the product be used?

Respondents' answers indicate whether the concept has a broad and strong consumer appeal, what products this new product competes against, and which consumers are the best targets. The need-gap levels and purchase-intention levels can be checked against norms for the product category to see whether the concept appears to be a winner, a long shot, or a loser. One food manufacturer rejects any concept that draws a definitely-would-buy score of less than 40 percent.

CONJOINT ANALYSIS Consumer preferences for alternative product concepts can be measured through **conjoint analysis**, a method for deriving the utility values that consumers attach to varying levels of a product's attributes.[31] Respondents are shown different hypothetical offers formed by combining varying levels of the attributes, then asked to rank the various offers. Management can identify the most appealing offer and the estimated market share and profit the company might realize.

Green and Wind have illustrated this approach in connection with developing a new spot-removing, carpet-cleaning agent for home use.[32] Suppose the new-product marketer is considering five design elements:

- Three package designs (A, B, C—see Figure 20.4)
- Three brand names (K2R, Glory, Bissell)
- Three prices ($1.19, $1.39, $1.59)
- A possible *Good Housekeeping* seal (yes, no)
- A possible money-back guarantee (yes, no)

Although the researcher can form 108 possible product concepts ($3 \times 3 \times 3 \times 2 \times 2$), it would be too much to ask consumers to rank 108 concepts. A sample of, say, 18 contrasting product concepts can be chosen, and consumers would rank them from the most to the least preferred.

The marketer now uses a statistical program to derive the consumer's utility functions for each of the five attributes (see Figure 20.5). Utility ranges between zero and one; the higher the utility, the stronger the consumer's preference for that level of the attribute. Looking at packaging, we see that package B is the most favored, followed by C and then A (A hardly has any utility). The preferred names are Bissell, K2R, and Glory, in that order. The consumer's utility varies inversely with price. A *Good Housekeeping* seal is preferred, but it does not add that much utility and may not be worth the effort to obtain it. A money-back guarantee is strongly preferred.

The consumer's most desired offer would be package design B, with the brand name Bissell, selling at the price of $1.19, with a *Good Housekeeping* seal and a money-back guarantee. We can also determine the relative importance of each attribute to this consumer—the difference between the highest and lowest utility level for that attribute. The greater the difference, the more important the attribute. Clearly, this consumer sees price and package design as the most important attributes, followed by money-back guarantee, brand name and, a *Good Housekeeping* seal.

When preference data are collected from a sufficient sample of target consumers, the data can be used to estimate the market share any specific offer is likely to achieve, given any assumptions about competitive response. The company, however, may not launch the market offer that promises to gain the greatest market share because of cost considerations. The most customer-appealing offer is not always the most profitable offer to make.

Under some conditions, researchers will collect the data not with a full-profile description of each offer, but by presenting two factors at a time. For example, respondents may be shown a table with three price levels and three package types and asked which of the nine combinations they would like most, followed by which one they would prefer next, and so on. They would then be shown a further table consisting of trade-offs between two other variables. The trade-off approach may be easier to use when there are many variables and possible offers. However, it is less realistic in that respondents are focusing on only two variables at a time.

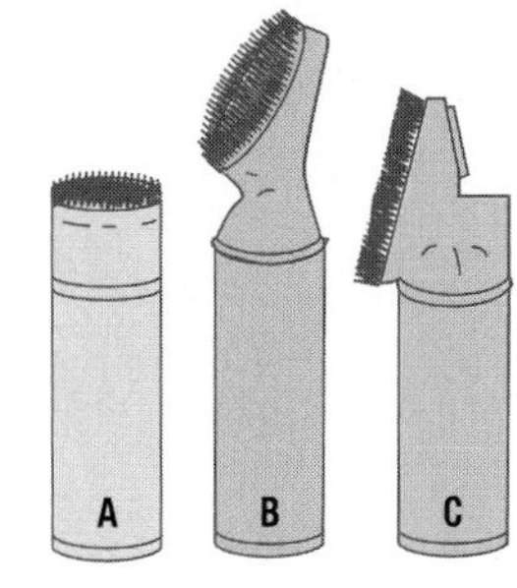

FIG. 20.4

Samples for Conjoint Analysis

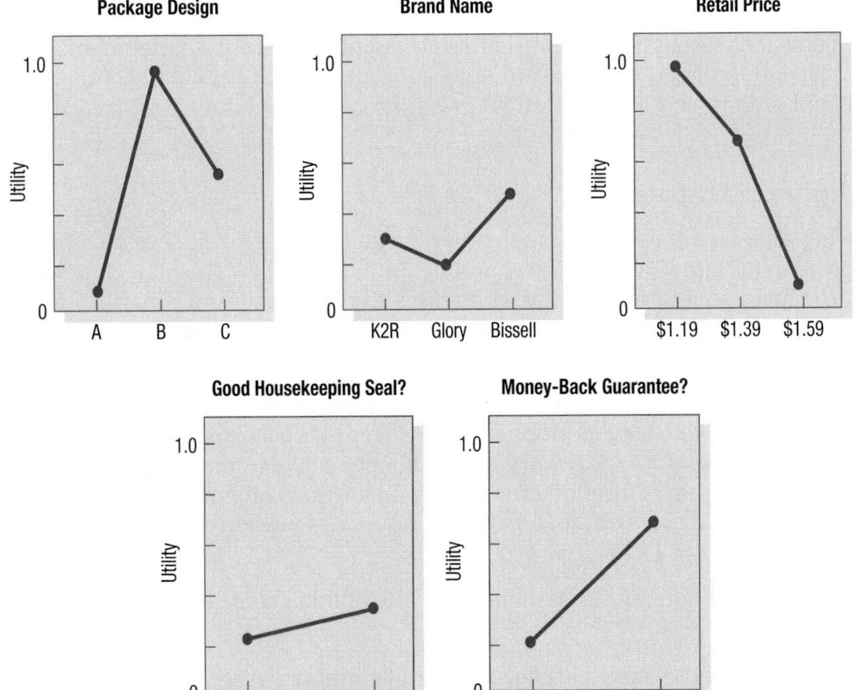

FIG. 20.5

Utility Functions Based on Conjoint Analysis

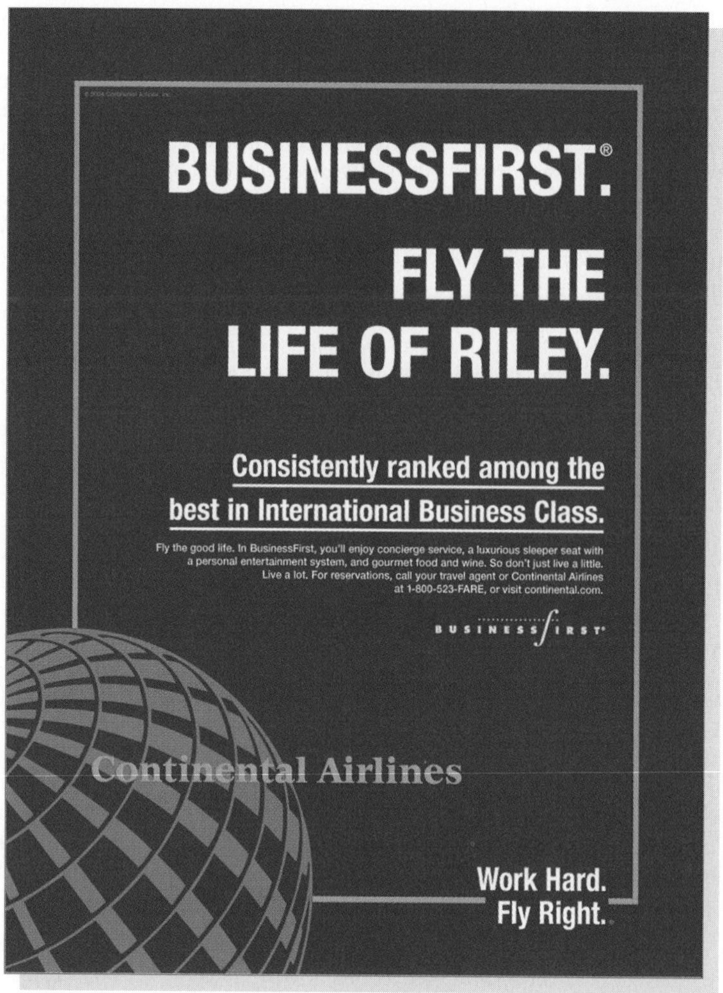

An ad for Continental Airlines Business First service, the kind of travel service for which airlines often do conjoint analysis.

Conjoint analysis has become one of the most popular concept-development and testing tools. Marriott designed its Courtyard hotel concept with the benefit of conjoint analysis. Other applications have included airline travel services, ethical drug design, and credit card features.

Marketing Strategy

Following a successful concept test, the new-product manager will develop a preliminary strategy plan for introducing the new product into the market. The plan consists of three parts. The first part describes the target market's size, structure, and behavior; the planned product positioning; and the sales, market share, and profit goals sought in the first few years:

> The target market for the instant breakfast drink is families with children who are receptive to a new, convenient, nutritious, and inexpensive form of breakfast. The company's brand will be positioned at the higher-price, higher-quality end of the instant-breakfast-drink category. The company will aim initially to sell 500,000 cases or 10 percent of the market, with a loss in the first year not exceeding $1.3 million. The second year will aim for 700,000 cases or 14 percent of the market, with a planned profit of $2.2 million.

The second part outlines the planned price, distribution strategy, and marketing budget for the first year:

> The product will be offered in chocolate, vanilla, and strawberry, in individual packets of six to a box, at a retail price of $2.49 a box. There will be 48 boxes per case, and

the case price to distributors will be $24. For the first two months, dealers will be offered one case free for every four cases bought, plus cooperative-advertising allowances. Free samples will be distributed door-to-door. Coupons for 20 cents off will appear in newspapers. The total sales promotional budget will be $2.9 million. An advertising budget of $6 million will be split 50:50 between national and local. Two-thirds will go into television and one-third into newspapers. Advertising copy will emphasize the benefit concepts of nutrition and convenience. The advertising-execution concept will revolve around a small boy who drinks instant breakfast and grows strong. During the first year, $100,000 will be spent on marketing research to buy store audits and consumer-panel information to monitor market reaction and buying rates.

The third part of the marketing-strategy plan describes the long-run sales and profit goals and marketing-mix strategy over time:

The company intends to win a 25 percent market share and realize an after-tax return on investment of 12 percent. To achieve this return, product quality will start high and be improved over time through technical research. Price will initially be set at a high level and lowered gradually to expand the market and meet competition. The total promotion budget will be boosted each year about 20 percent, with the initial advertising–sales promotion split of 65:35 evolving eventually to 50:50. Marketing research will be reduced to $60,000 per year after the first year.

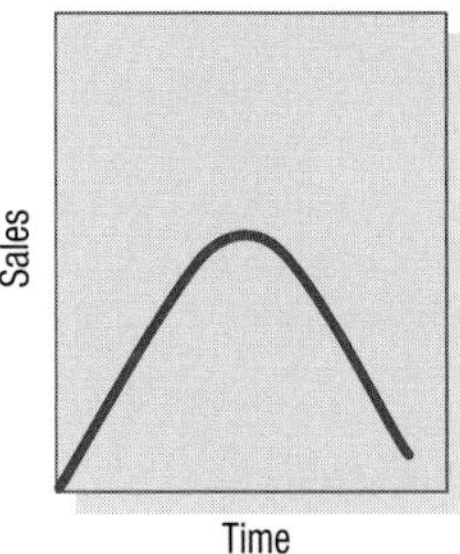

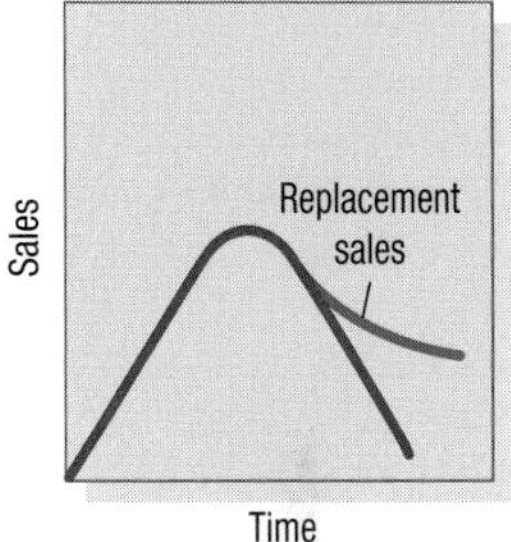

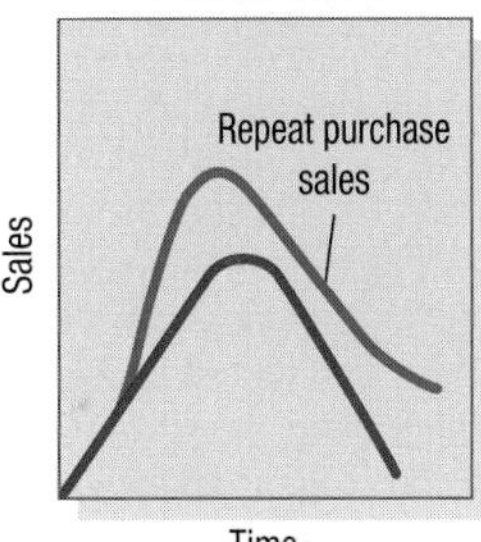

FIG. 20.6

Product Life-Cycle Sales for Three Types of Products

Business Analysis

After management develops the product concept and marketing strategy, it can evaluate the proposal's business attractiveness. Management needs to prepare sales, cost, and profit projections to determine whether they satisfy company objectives. If they do, the concept can move to the development stage. As new information comes in, the business analysis will undergo revision and expansion.

ESTIMATING TOTAL SALES Total estimated sales are the sum of estimated first-time sales, replacement sales, and repeat sales. Sales-estimation methods depend on whether the product is a one-time purchase (such as an engagement ring or retirement home), an infrequently purchased product, or a frequently purchased product. For one-time purchased products, sales rise at the beginning, peak, and later approach zero as the number of potential buyers is exhausted (see Figure 20.6 [a]). If new buyers keep entering the market, the curve will not go down to zero.

Infrequently purchased products—such as automobiles, toasters, and industrial equipment—exhibit replacement cycles dictated by physical wearing out or by obsolescence associated with changing styles, features, and performance. Sales forecasting for this product category calls for estimating first-time sales and replacement sales separately (see Figure 20.6[b]).

Frequently purchased products, such as consumer and industrial nondurables, have product life-cycle sales resembling Figure 20.6[c]. The number of first-time buyers initially increases and then decreases as fewer buyers are left (assuming a fixed population). Repeat purchases occur soon, providing that the product satisfies some buyers. The sales curve eventually falls to a plateau representing a level of steady repeat-purchase volume; by this time, the product is no longer a new product.

In estimating sales, the manager's first task is to estimate first-time purchases of the new product in each period. To estimate replacement sales, management has to research the product's *survival-age distribution*—that is, the number of units that fail in year one, two, three, and so on. The low end of the distribution indicates when the first replacement sales will take place. The actual timing will be influenced by a variety of factors. Because replacement sales are difficult to estimate before the product is in use, some manufacturers base the decision to launch a new product solely on the estimate of first-time sales.

For a frequently purchased new product, the seller has to estimate repeat sales as well as first-time sales. A high rate of repeat purchasing means that customers are satisfied; sales are likely to stay high even after all first-time purchases take place. The seller should note the percentage of repeat purchases that take place in each repeat-purchase class: those who rebuy once, twice, three times, and so on. Some products and brands are bought a few times and dropped.[33]

ESTIMATING COSTS AND PROFITS Costs are estimated by the R&D, manufacturing, marketing, and finance departments. Table 20.3 illustrates a five-year projection of sales, costs, and profits for the instant breakfast drink.

Row 1 shows the projected sales revenue over the five-year period. The company expects to sell $11,889,000 (approximately 500,000 cases at $24 per case) in the first year. Behind this sales projection is a set of assumptions about the rate of market growth, the company's market share, and the factory-realized price. *Row 2* shows the cost of goods sold, which hovers around 33 percent of sales revenue. This cost is found by estimating the average cost of labor, ingredients, and packaging per case. *Row 3* shows the expected gross margin, which is the difference between sales revenue and cost of goods sold.

Row 4 shows anticipated development costs of $3.5 million, including product-development cost, marketing-research costs, and manufacturing-development costs. *Row 5* shows the estimated marketing costs over the five-year period to cover advertising, sales promotion, and marketing research and an amount allocated for sales force coverage and marketing administration. *Row 6* shows the allocated overhead to this new product to cover its share of the cost of executive salaries, heat, light, and so on.

Row 7, the gross contribution, is found by subtracting the preceding three costs from the gross margin. *Row 8,* supplementary contribution, lists any change in income from other company products caused by the introduction of the new product. It has two components. *Dragalong income* is additional income on other company products resulting from adding this product to the line. *Cannibalized income* is the reduced income on other company products resulting from adding this product to the line.[34] Table 20.3 assumes no supplementary contributions. *Row 9* shows the net contribution, which in this case is the same as the gross contribution. *Row 10* shows the discounted contribution—that is, the present value of each future contribution discounted at 15 percent per annum. For example, the company will not receive $4,716,000 until the fifth year. This amount is worth only $2,346,000 today if the company can earn 15 percent on its money through other investments.[35]

Finally, *row 11* shows the cumulative discounted cash flow, which is the cumulation of the annual contributions in row 10. Two things are of central interest. The first is the maximum investment exposure, which is the highest loss that the project can create. We see that the

TABLE 20.3 Projected Five-Year Cash-Flow Statement (in thousands of dollars)

	Year 0	Year 1	Year 2	Year 3	Year 4	Year 5
1. Sales revenue	$ 0	$11,889	$15,381	$19,654	$28,253	$32,491
2. Cost of goods sold	0	3,981	5,150	6,581	9,461	10,880
3. Gross margin	0	7,908	10,231	13,073	18,792	21,611
4. Development costs	−3,500	0	0	0	0	0
5. Marketing costs	0	8,000	6,460	8,255	11,866	13,646
6. Allocated overhead	0	1,189	1,538	1,965	2,825	3,249
7. Gross contribution	−3,500	−1,281	2,233	2,853	4,101	4,716
8. Supplementary contribution	0	0	0	0	0	0
9. Net contribution	−3,500	−1,281	2,233	2,853	4,101	4,716
10. Discounted contribution (15%)	−3,500	−1,113	1,691	1,877	2,343	2,346
11. Cumulative discounted cash flow	−3,500	−4,613	−2,922	−1,045	1,298	3,644

company will be in a maximum loss position of $4,613,000 in year 1. The second is the payback period, which is the time when the company recovers all of its investment, including the built-in return of 15 percent. The payback period here is approximately three and a half years. Management therefore has to decide whether to risk a maximum investment loss of $4.6 million and a possible payback period of three and a half years.

Companies use other financial measures to evaluate the merit of a new-product proposal. The simplest is **breakeven analysis**, in which management estimates how many units of the product the company would have to sell to break even with the given price and cost structure. Or the estimate may be in terms of how many years it will take to break even. If management believes sales could easily reach the break-even number, it is likely to move the project into product development.

The most complex method of estimating profit is **risk analysis**. Here three estimates (optimistic, pessimistic, and most likely) are obtained for each uncertain variable affecting profitability under an assumed marketing environment and marketing strategy for the planning period. The computer simulates possible outcomes and computes a rate-of-return probability distribution showing the range of possible rates of returns and their probabilities.[36]

::: Managing the Development Process: Development to Commercialization

Up to now, the product has existed only as a word description, a drawing, or a prototype. This next step involves a jump in investment that dwarfs the costs incurred in the earlier stages. At this stage the company will determine whether the product idea can be translated into a technically and commercially feasible product. If it cannot, the accumulated project cost will be lost except for any useful information gained in the process.

Product Development

The job of translating target customer requirements into a working prototype is helped by a set of methods known as *quality function deployment* (QFD). The methodology takes the list of desired *customer attributes* (CAs) generated by market research and turns them into a list of *engineering attributes* (EAs) that the engineers can use. For example, customers of a proposed truck may want a certain acceleration rate (CA). Engineers can turn this into the required horsepower and other engineering equivalents (EAs). The methodology permits the measuring of the trade-offs and costs of providing the customer requirements. A major contribution of QFD is that it improves communication between marketers, engineers, and the manufacturing people.[37]

PHYSICAL PROTOTYPES The R&D department will develop one or more physical versions of the product concept. Its goal is to find a prototype that embodies the key attributes described in the product-concept statement, that performs safely under normal use and conditions, and that can be produced within the budgeted manufacturing costs. Developing and manufacturing a successful prototype can take days, weeks, months, or even years. Sophisticated virtual-reality technology is now speeding the process. By designing and testing product designs through simulation, for example, companies achieve the flexibility to respond to new information and to resolve uncertainties by quickly exploring alternatives.

BOEING

Boeing designed its 777 aircraft on a totally digital basis. Engineers, designers, and more than 500 suppliers designed the aircraft on a special computer network without ever making a blueprint on paper. Its partners were connected by an extranet enabling them to communicate, share ideas, and work on the design at a distance. A computer-generated "human" could climb inside the three-dimensional design on-screen to show how difficult maintenance access would be for a live mechanic. Such computer modeling allowed engineers to spot design errors that otherwise would have remained undiscovered until a person began to work on a physical prototype. Avoiding the time and cost associated with building physical prototypes reduced development time and scrappage and rework by 60 to 90 percent.[38]

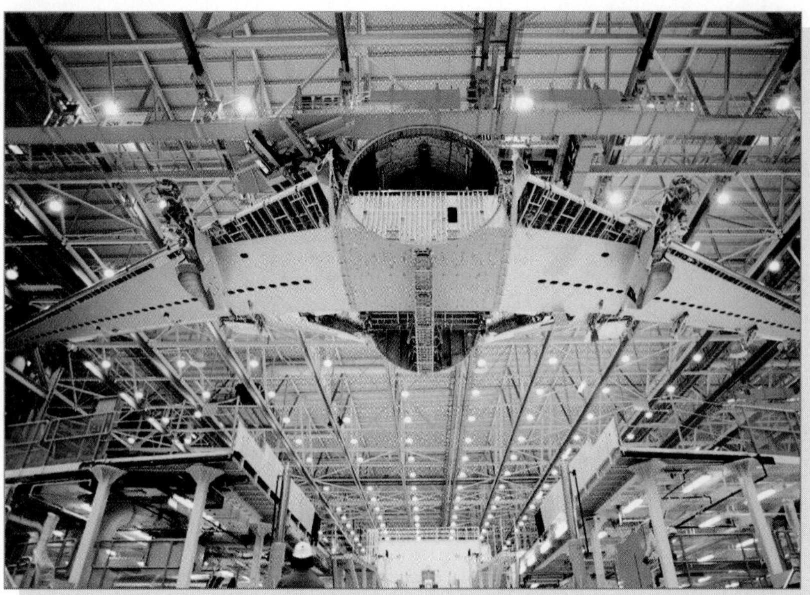

Boeing's 777, designed digitally without a physical prototype, takes its first "flight" across the world's largest building, the Boeing assembly plant in Everett, WA.

With the emergence of the Web, there is a need for more rapid prototyping and more flexible development processes. Michael Schrage, research associate at MIT's media lab, has correctly predicted: "Effective prototyping may be the most valuable 'core competence' an innovative organization can hope to have."[39] This has certainly been true for software companies such as Microsoft, Netscape, and the hundreds of Silicon Valley start-ups. Although Schrage says that specification-driven companies require that every "i" be dotted and "t" be crossed before anything can be shown to the next level of management, prototype-driven companies—such as Yahoo!, Microsoft, and Netscape—cherish quick-and-dirty tests and experiments.

Lab scientists must not only design the product's functional characteristics, but also communicate its psychological aspects through physical cues. How will consumers react to different colors, sizes, and weights? In the case of a mouthwash, a yellow color supports an "antiseptic" claim (Listerine), a red color supports a "refreshing" claim (Lavoris), and a green or blue color supports a "cool" claim (Scope). Marketers need to supply lab people with information on what attributes consumers seek and how consumers judge whether these attributes are present.

CUSTOMER TESTS When the prototypes are ready, they must be put through rigorous functional tests and *customer tests. Alpha testing* is the name given to testing the product within the firm to see how it performs in different applications. After refining the prototype further, the company moves to *beta testing* with customers.[40] It enlists a set of customers to use the prototype and give feedback. Table 20.4 shows some of the functional tests products go through before they enter the marketplace.

Consumer testing can take several forms, from bringing consumers into a laboratory to giving them samples to use in their homes. In-home placement tests are common with products ranging from ice cream flavors to new appliances. When DuPont developed its new synthetic carpeting, it installed free carpeting in several homes in exchange for the homeowners' willingness to report their likes and dislikes about the product.

Consumer preferences can be measured in several ways. Suppose a consumer is shown three items—A, B, and C, such as three cameras, three insurance plans, or three advertisements.

- ***The rank-order*** method asks the consumer to rank the three items in order of preference. The consumer might respond with A>B>C. Although this method has the advantage of simplicity, it does not reveal how intensely the consumer feels about each item nor whether the consumer likes any item very much. It is also difficult to use this method when there are many objects to be ranked.
- ***The paired-comparison*** method calls for presenting pairs of items and asking the consumer which one is preferred in each pair. Thus the consumer could be presented with the pairs AB, AC, and BC and say that she prefers A to B, A to C, and B to C. Then we could conclude that A>B>C. People find it easy to state their preference between two items, and this method allows the consumer to focus on the two items, noting their differences and similarities.
- ***The monadic-rating*** method asks the consumer to rate liking of each product on a scale. Suppose a seven-point scale is used, where 1 signifies intense dislike, 4 indiffer-

TABLE 20.4

Examples of Customer Product Tests

Shaw Industries

At Shaw Industries, temps are paid $5 an hour to pace up and down five long rows of sample carpets for up to 8 hours a day, logging an average of 14 miles each. One regular reads three mysteries a week while pacing and shed 40 pounds in two years. Shaw Industries counts walkers' steps and figures that 20,000 steps equal several years of average wear.

Apple Computer

Apple Computer assumes the worst for its PowerBook customers and submits the computers to a battery of indignities: It drenches the computers in Pepsi and other sodas, smears them with mayonnaise, and bakes them in ovens at temperatures of 140 degrees or more to simulate conditions in a car trunk.

Gillette

At Gillette, 200 volunteers from various departments come to work unshaven each day, troop to the second floor of the company's South Boston manufacturing and research plant, and enter small booths with a sink and mirror. There they take instructions from technicians on the other side of a small window as to which razor, shaving cream, or aftershave to use, and then they fill out questionnaires. "We bleed so you'll get a good shave at home," says one Gillette employee.

Sources: Faye Rice, "Secrets of Product Testing," *Fortune,* November 28, 1994, pp. 172–174; Lawrence Ingrassia, "Taming the Monster: How Big Companies Can Change: Keeping Sharp: Gillette Holds Its Edge by Endlessly Searching for a Better Shave," *Wall Street Journal,* December 10, 1992, p. A1.

ence, and 7 intense like. Suppose the consumer returns the following ratings: A=6, B=5, C=3. We can derive the individual's preference order (i.e., A>B>C), and even know the qualitative levels of the person's preference for each and the rough distance between preferences.

Market Testing

After management is satisfied with functional and psychological performance, the product is ready to be dressed up with a brand name and packaging, and put into a market test. The new product is introduced into an authentic setting to learn how large the market is and how consumers and dealers react to handling, using, and repurchasing the product.

Not all companies undertake market testing. A company officer at Revlon, Inc., stated: "In our field—primarily higher-priced cosmetics not geared for mass distribution—it would be unnecessary for us to market test. When we develop a new product, say an improved liquid makeup, we know it's going to sell because we're familiar with the field. And we've got 1,500 demonstrators in department stores to promote it." Many companies, however, believe that market testing can yield valuable information about buyers, dealers, marketing program effectiveness, and market potential. The main issues are: How much market testing should be done, and what kind(s)?

The amount of market testing is influenced by the investment cost and risk on the one hand, and the time pressure and research cost on the other. High investment–high risk products, where the chance of failure is high, must be market tested; the cost of the market tests will be an insignificant percentage of the total project cost. High-risk products—those that create new-product categories (first instant breakfast drink) or have novel features (first gum-strengthening toothpaste)—warrant more market testing than modified products (another toothpaste brand).

The amount of market testing may be severely reduced if the company is under great time pressure because the season is just starting or because competitors are about to launch their brands. The company may therefore prefer the risk of a product failure to the risk of losing distribution or market penetration on a highly successful product.

CONSUMER-GOODS MARKET TESTING In testing consumer products, the company seeks to estimate four variables: *trial, first repeat, adoption,* and *purchase frequency.* The company hopes to find all these variables at high levels. In some cases, it will find many consumers trying the product but few rebuying it; or it might find high permanent adoption but low purchase frequency (as with gourmet frozen foods).

Here are four major methods of consumer-goods market testing, from the least to the most costly.

Sales-Wave Research In *sales-wave research,* consumers who initially try the product at no cost are reoffered the product, or a competitor's product, at slightly reduced prices. They might be reoffered the product as many as three to five times (sales waves), with the company noting how many customers selected that product again and their reported level of satisfaction. Sales-wave research can also expose consumers to one or more advertising concepts to see the impact of that advertising on repeat purchase.

Sales-wave research can be implemented quickly, conducted with a fair amount of security, and carried out without final packaging and advertising. However, it does not indicate the trial rates that would be achieved with different sales promotion incentives, because the consumers are preselected to try the product; nor does it indicate the brand's power to gain distribution and favorable shelf position.

Simulated Test Marketing Simulated test marketing calls for finding 30 to 40 qualified shoppers and questioning them about brand familiarity and preferences in a specific product category. These people are then invited to a brief screening of both well-known and new commercials or print ads. One ad advertises the new product, but it is not singled out for attention. Consumers receive a small amount of money and are invited into a store where they may buy any items. The company notes how many consumers buy the new brand and competing brands. This provides a measure of the ad's relative effectiveness against competing ads in stimulating trial. Consumers are asked the reasons for their purchases or nonpurchases. Those who did not buy the new brand are given a free sample. Some weeks later, they are reinterviewed by phone to determine product attitudes, usage, satisfaction, and repurchase intention and are offered an opportunity to repurchase any products.

This method gives fairly accurate results on advertising effectiveness and trial rates (and repeat rates if extended) in a much shorter time and at a fraction of the cost of using real test markets. Pretests often take only three months and may cost $250,000.[41] The results are incorporated into new-product forecasting models to project ultimate sales levels. Marketing research firms report surprisingly accurate predictions of sales levels of products that are subsequently launched in the market.[42]

Controlled Test Marketing In this method, a research firm manages a panel of stores that will carry new products for a fee. The company with the new product specifies the number of stores and geographic locations it wants to test. The research firm delivers the product to the participating stores and controls shelf position; number of facings, displays, and point-of-purchase promotions; and pricing. Sales results can be measured through electronic scanners at the checkout. The company can also evaluate the impact of local advertising and promotions.

Controlled test marketing allows the company to test the impact of in-store factors and limited advertising on buying behavior. A sample of consumers can be interviewed later to give their impressions of the product. The company does not have to use its own sales force, give trade allowances, or "buy" distribution. However, controlled test marketing provides no information on how to sell the trade on carrying the new product. This technique also exposes the product and its features to competitors' scrutiny.

Test Markets The ultimate way to test a new consumer product is to put it into full-blown test markets. The company chooses a few representative cities, and the sales force tries to sell the trade on carrying the product and giving it good shelf exposure. The company puts on a full advertising and promotion campaign similar to the one it would use in national marketing. Test marketing also permits testing the impact of alternative marketing plans by varying the marketing program in different cities: A full-scale test can cost over $1 million, depending on the number of test cities, the test duration, and the amount of data the company wants to collect.

Management faces several decisions:

1. ***How many test cities?*** Most tests use between two and six cities. The greater the maximum possible loss, the greater the number of contending marketing strategies, the greater the regional differences, and the greater the chance of test-market interference by competitors, the greater the number of cities that should be used.
2. ***Which cities?*** Each company must develop selection criteria such as having good media coverage, cooperative chain stores, and average competitive activity.
3. ***Length of test?*** Market tests last anywhere from a few months to a year. The longer the average repurchase period, the longer the test period.
4. ***What information?*** Warehouse shipment data will show gross inventory buying but will not indicate weekly sales at the retail level. Store audits will show retail sales and competitors' market shares but will not reveal buyer characteristics. Consumer panels will indicate which people are buying which brands and their loyalty and switching rates. Buyer surveys will yield in-depth information about consumer attitudes, usage, and satisfaction.
5. ***What action to take?*** If the test markets show high trial and repurchase rates, the product should be launched nationally; if they show a high trial rate and a low repurchase rate, the product should be redesigned or dropped; if they show a low trial rate and a high repurchase rate, the product is satisfying but more people have to try it. This means increasing advertising and sales promotion. If trial and repurchase rates are both low, the product should be abandoned.

In spite of its benefits, many companies today skip test marketing and rely on faster and more economical testing methods. General Mills prefers to launch new products in perhaps 25 percent of the country, an area too large for rivals to disrupt. Managers review retail scanner data, which tell them within days how the product is doing and what corrective fine-tuning to do. Colgate-Palmolive often launches a new product in a set of small "lead countries" and keeps rolling it out if it proves successful.

BUSINESS-GOODS MARKET TESTING Business goods can also benefit from market testing. Expensive industrial goods and new technologies will normally undergo alpha testing (within the company) and beta testing (with outside customers). During beta testing, the vendor's technical people observe how test customers use the product, a practice that often exposes unanticipated problems of safety and servicing and alerts the vendor to customer training and servicing requirements. The vendor can also observe how much value the equipment adds to the customer's operation as a clue to subsequent pricing.

The vendor will ask the test customers to express their purchase intention and other reactions after the test. Vendors must carefully interpret the beta test results because only a small number of test customers are used, they are not randomly drawn, and the tests are somewhat customized to each site. Another risk is that test customers who are unimpressed with the product may leak unfavorable reports about it.

A second common test method for business goods is to introduce the new product at trade shows. The vendor can observe how much interest buyers show in the new product, how they react to various features and terms, and how many express purchase intentions or place orders.

New industrial products can be tested in distributor and dealer display rooms, where they may stand next to the manufacturer's other products and possibly competitors' products. This method yields preference and pricing information in the product's normal selling atmosphere. The disadvantages are that the customers might want to place early orders that cannot be filled, and those customers who come in might not represent the target market.

Industrial manufacturers come close to using full test marketing when they give a limited supply of the product to the sales force to sell in a limited number of areas that receive promotion support and printed catalog sheets.

Commercialization

If the company goes ahead with commercialization, it will face its largest costs to date. The company will have to contract for manufacture or build or rent a full-scale manufacturing facility. Plant size will be a critical decision. When Quaker Oats launched its 100 Percent Natural breakfast cereal, it built a smaller plant than called for by the sales forecast. The demand so exceeded the forecast that for about a year it could not supply enough product to stores. Although Quaker Oats was gratified with the response, the low forecast cost it a considerable amount of profit.

Another major cost is marketing. To introduce a major new consumer packaged good into the national market, the company may have to spend from $25 million to as much as $100 million in advertising, promotion, and other communications in the first year. In the introduction of new food products, marketing expenditures typically represent 57 percent of sales during the first year. Most new-product campaigns rely on a sequenced mix of market communication tools.

WHEN (TIMING) In commercializing a new product, market-entry timing is critical. Suppose a company has almost completed the development work on its new product and learns that a competitor is nearing the end of its development work. The company faces three choices:

1. ***First entry*** – The first firm entering a market usually enjoys the "first mover advantages" of locking up key distributors and customers and gaining leadership. But if the product is rushed to market before it is thoroughly debugged, the first entry can backfire.
2. ***Parallel entry*** – The firm might time its entry to coincide with the competitor's entry. The market may pay more attention when two companies are advertising the new product.
3. ***Late entry*** – The firm might delay its launch until after the competitor has entered. The competitor will have borne the cost of educating the market, and its product may reveal faults the late entrant can avoid. The late entrant can also learn the size of the market.

The timing decision involves additional considerations. If a new product replaces an older product, the company might delay the introduction until the old product's stock is drawn down. If the product is seasonal, it might be delayed until the right season arrives;[43] often a product waits for a "killer application" to occur. Complicating new-product launches, many companies are encountering competitive "design-arounds"—rivals are imitating inventions but making their own versions just different enough to avoid patent infringement and the need to pay royalties.

RADIORAY

Nebraska rancher Gerald Gohl's innovation was to create a remote- controlled spotlight so he wouldn't have to roll down the window of his pickup truck and stick out a handheld beacon to search for cattle on frigid nights. By 1997, he held a patent on the RadioRay, a wireless version of his spotlight that was mounted on suctions cups or brackets and could rotate 360 degrees. Selling for $200, RadioRay attracted attention from ranchers, boaters, hunters, and police—even Wal-Mart's Sam's Club chain. Gohl rejected the retailers' overtures, however, fearing that it might seek lower prices that would anger his distributors. Shortly thereafter, Sam's Club began to sell its own wireless, remote-controlled spotlight that was nearly identical to the RadioRay except for a small plastic part restricting the light's rotation to slightly less than 360 degrees and its price—$60. Gohl successfully sued for patent infringement in 2000, but still could face an appeal.[44]

WHERE (GEOGRAPHIC STRATEGY) The company must decide whether to launch the new product in a single locality, a region, several regions, the national market, or the international market. Most will develop a planned market rollout over time. Coca-Cola launched its new soda, Citra, a caffeine-free, grapefruit-flavored drink, in about half the United States. The multistaged rollout, following test marketing in Phoenix, southern Texas, and southern Florida, began in January 1998 in Dallas, Denver, and Cincinnati.[45]

Company size is an important factor here. Small companies will select an attractive city and put on a blitz campaign. They will enter other cities one at a time. Large companies will introduce their product into a whole region and then move to the next region. Companies with national distribution networks, such as auto companies, will launch their new models in the national market.

Most companies design new products to sell primarily in the domestic market. If the product does well, the company considers exporting to neighboring countries or the world

A Web ad from the Phillips Pronto site for the TSU7000 model Pronto Pro.

market, redesigning if necessary. Cooper and Kleinschmidt, in their study of industrial products, found that domestic products designed solely for the domestic market tend to show a high failure rate, low market share, and low growth. In contrast, products designed for the world market—or at least to include neighboring countries—achieve significantly more profits, both at home and abroad. Yet only 17 percent of the products in Cooper and Kleinschmidt's study were designed with an international orientation.[46] The implication is that companies should adopt an international focus in designing and developing new products.

In choosing rollout markets, the major criteria are market potential, the company's local reputation, the cost of filling the pipeline, the cost of communication media, the influence of the area on other areas, and competitive penetration. The presence of strong competitors will influence rollout strategy. Suppose McDonald's wants to launch a new chain of fast-food pizza parlors. Pizza Hut, a formidable competitor, is strongly entrenched on the East Coast. Another pizza chain is entrenched on the West Coast but is weak. The Midwest is the battleground between two other chains. The South is open, but Shakey's is planning to move in. McDonald's faces a complex decision in choosing a geographic rollout strategy.

With the Web connecting far-flung parts of the globe, competition is more likely to cross national borders. Companies are increasingly rolling out new products simultaneously across the globe, rather than nationally or even regionally. However, masterminding a global launch poses challenges.

Companies will increasingly add the Web as another advertising medium to launch and describe each important new product:

PHILIPS

Philips, the Dutch electronics company, recently launched Pronto, an "Intelligent Remote Control" to replace all other devices that receive infrared signals. Its Web address, www.pronto.philips.com, contains several features: About Pronto, A Virtual Tour, Where to Buy, Pronto News, Pronto Communities, and FAQs and Contacts. This is much richer information than any ad could offer.

TO WHOM (TARGET-MARKET PROSPECTS) Within the rollout markets, the company must target its initial distribution and promotion to the best prospect groups. Presumably, the company has already profiled the prime prospects, who would ideally have the following characteristics: They would be early adopters, heavy users, and opinion leaders, and they could be reached at a low cost.[47] Few groups have all these characteristics. The company should rate the various prospect groups on these characteristics and target the best group. The aim is to generate strong sales as soon as possible to attract further prospects.

HOW (INTRODUCTORY MARKET STRATEGY) The company must develop an action plan for introducing the new product into the rollout markets. In 1998, Apple Computer staged a massive marketing blitz to launch the iMac, its reentry into the computer PC business after a hiatus of 14 years. Five years later, Apple struck gold again with the launch of the iPod.

APPLE IPOD

As with virtually all its products, Apple's design for its iPod MP3 player is striking. Sleek and cool, the product also offers much functionality. Apple paired iPod with the legitimate download song service iTunes through catchy TV commercials featuring black silhouettes of people listening to music with N.E.R.D.'s remix of "Rock Star" in the background. To target Gen Y, Apple created the Web site, www.ipodrocks.com, in November 2003. It touts the iPod as a gift for the holidays and offers suggestions to convince parents to buy one ("Ask nicely," "Stake your grades on it," "Do a good deed," and "Subliminal advertising"). Apple also initiated marketing collaborations with corporate icons America Online and Volkswagen. Apple sold more than 2 million iPods and its iTunes support in less than a year and captured more than 50 percent of the new market. It then broadened the market further by pushing the iPod mini—a 3.6-ounce player capable of holding 1,000 CD-quality songs.[48]

To coordinate the many activities involved in launching a new product, management can use network-planning techniques such as critical path scheduling. **Critical path scheduling (CPS)** calls for developing a master chart showing the simultaneous and sequential activities that must take place to launch the product. By estimating how much time each activity takes, the planners estimate completion time for the entire project. Any delay in any activity on the critical path will cause the project to be delayed. If the launch must be completed earlier, the planner searches for ways to reduce time along the critical path.[49]

::: The Consumer-Adoption Process

Adoption is an individual's decision to become a regular user of a product. How do potential customers learn about new products, try them, and adopt or reject them? The *consumer-adoption process* is later followed by the *consumer-loyalty process,* which is the concern of the established producer. Years ago, new-product marketers used a *mass-market approach* to launch products. This approach had two main drawbacks: It called for heavy marketing expenditures, and it involved many wasted exposures. These drawbacks led to a second approach, *heavy-user target marketing.* This approach makes sense, provided that heavy users are identifiable and are early adopters. However, even within the heavy-user group, many heavy users are loyal to existing brands. New-product marketers now aim at consumers who are early adopters.

The theory of innovation diffusion and consumer adoption helps marketers identify early adopters.

Stages in the Adoption Process

An **innovation** is any good, service, or idea that is *perceived* by someone as new. The idea may have a long history, but it is an innovation to the person who sees it as new. Innovations take time to spread through the social system. Rogers defines the **innovation diffusion process** as "the spread of a new idea from its source of invention or creation to its ultimate users or adopters."[50] The consumer-adoption process focuses on the mental process through which an individual passes from first hearing about an innovation to final adoption.[51]

Adopters of new products have been observed to move through five stages:

1. ***Awareness*** – The consumer becomes aware of the innovation but lacks information about it.
2. ***Interest*** – The consumer is stimulated to seek information about the innovation.
3. ***Evaluation*** – The consumer considers whether to try the innovation.
4. ***Trial*** – The consumer tries the innovation to improve his or her estimate of its value.
5. ***Adoption*** – The consumer decides to make full and regular use of the innovation.

The new-product marketer should facilitate movement through these stages. A portable electric-dishwasher manufacturer might discover that many consumers are stuck in the interest stage; they do not buy because of their uncertainty and the large investment cost. But these same consumers would be willing to use an electric dishwasher on a trial basis for a small monthly fee. The manufacturer should consider offering a trial-use plan with option to buy.

Factors Influencing the Adoption Process

Marketers recognize the following characteristics of the adoption process: differences in individual readiness to try new products; the effect of personal influence; differing rates of adoption; and differences in organizations' readiness to try new products.

READINESS TO TRY NEW PRODUCTS AND PERSONAL INFLUENCE Everett Rogers defines a person's level of innovativeness as "the degree to which an individual is relatively earlier in adopting new ideas than the other members of his social system." In each product area, there are pioneers and early adopters. Some people are the first to adopt new clothing fashions or new appliances; some doctors are the first to prescribe new medicines; and some farmers are the first to adopt new farming methods.[52] People can be classified into the adopter categories shown in Figure 20.7. After a slow start, an increasing number of people adopt the innovation, the number reaches a peak, and then it diminishes as fewer non-adopters remain. The five adopter groups differ in their value orientations and their motives for adopting or resisting the new product.[53]

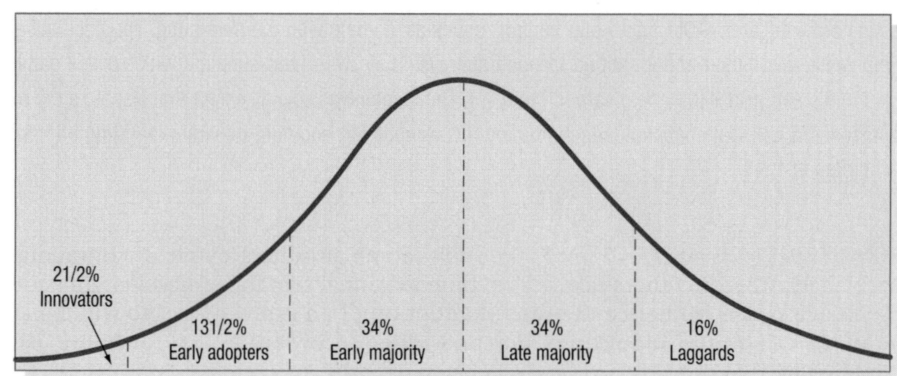

FIG. 20.7

Adopter Categorization on the Basis of Relative Time of Adoption of Innovations

Source: Redrawn from Everett M. Rogers, *Diffusion of Innovations* (New York: The Free Press, 1983).

Gwyneth Paltrow with her Vespa. *In Style* magazine ran this photo in its October 2003 issue with the caption, "**Downsizing** Gas-guzzling, out. Fuel-efficient modes of transport, in. Gwyneth Paltrow (here), Matthew Broderick, and Sandra Bullock ride Vespas, which get up to 65 mpg (from $3,000; vespa.usa.com)."

- ***Innovators*** are technology enthusiasts; they are venturesome and enjoy tinkering with new products and mastering their intricacies. In return for low prices, they are happy to conduct alpha and beta testing and report on early weaknesses.
- ***Early adopters*** are opinion leaders who carefully search for new technologies that might give them a dramatic competitive advantage. They are less price sensitive and willing to adopt the product if given personalized solutions and good service support.
- ***Early majority*** are deliberate pragmatists who adopt the new technology when its benefits are proven and a lot of adoption has already taken place. They make up the mainstream market.
- ***Late majority*** are skeptical conservatives who are risk averse, technology shy, and price sensitive.
- ***Laggards*** are tradition-bound and resist the innovation until they find that the status quo is no longer defensible.

Each of the five groups must be approached with a different type of marketing if the firm wants to move its innovation through the full product life cycle.[54]

Personal influence is the effect one person has on another's attitude or purchase probability. Although personal influence is an important factor, its significance is greater in some situations and for some individuals than for others. Personal influence is more important in the evaluation stage of the adoption process than in the other stages. It has more influence on late adopters than early adopters. It also is more important in risky situations.

Companies often target innovators and early adopters with product rollouts. For Vespa scooters, Piaggio hired models to go around cafés and clubs in trendy Los Angeles areas to talk up the brand.[55] When Nike decided to enter the skateboarding market, it recognized that an anti-establishment, big company bias from the teen target skater market could present a sizable challenge. To gain some "street cred," it sold exclusively to independent shops, advertised nowhere but skate magazines, and gained sponsorships from well-admired pro riders by incorporating them into product design.[56]

HASBRO POX

Pox is a warrior-fighting game played roughly like a Gameboy, except that the device has a radio transmitter and receiver built into it. One Pox player can play the game against another person or multiple people, including unknown people who just happen to be within radio range. Hasbro launched the game by choosing a high potential area—Chicago—and finding "cool kids" to help with the marketing. The cool kids were geographically distributed and identified through surveys. They were then supplied with 10 Pox games to give to friends and paid $30 to help spread the word. The launch was so successful that Hasbro's toy retailers demanded a full-scale national launch, forcing the company to augment its viral marketing efforts with mass marketing.[57]

CHARACTERISTICS OF THE INNOVATION Some products catch on immediately (rollerblades), whereas others take a long time to gain acceptance (diesel engine autos). Five characteristics influence the rate of adoption of an innovation. We will consider them in relation to the adoption of personal video recorders (PVRs) for home use, as exemplified by TiVo.[58]

The first is *relative advantage*—the degree to which the innovation appears superior to existing products. The greater the perceived relative advantage of using a PVR, say, for easily recording favorite shows, pausing live TV or skipping commercials, the more quickly it will be adopted. The second is *compatibility*—the degree to which the innovation matches the values and experiences of the individuals. PVRs, for example, are highly compatible with avid television watchers. Third is *complexity*—the degree to which the innovation is relatively difficult to understand or use. PVRs are somewhat complex and will therefore take a slightly longer time to penetrate into home use. Fourth is *divisibility*—the degree to which the innovation can be tried on a limited basis. This provides a sizable challenge for PVRs—sampling can only occur in a retail store or perhaps a friend's house. Fifth is *communicability*—the degree to which the beneficial results of use are observable or describable to others. The fact that PVRs have some clear advantages can help create interest and curiosity.

Other characteristics that influence the rate of adoption are cost, risk and uncertainty, scientific credibility, and social approval. The new-product marketer has to research all these factors and give the key ones maximum attention in designing the new-product and marketing program.[59]

ORGANIZATIONS' READINESS TO ADOPT INNOVATIONS The creator of a new teaching method would want to identify innovative schools. The producer of a new piece of medical equipment would want to identify innovative hospitals. Adoption is associated with variables in the organization's environment (community progressiveness, community income), the organization itself (size, profits, pressure to change), and the administrators (education level, age, sophistication). Other forces come into play in trying to get a product adopted into organizations that receive the bulk of their funding from the government, such as public schools. A controversial or innovative product can be squelched by negative public opinion.

SUMMARY :::

1. Once a company has segmented the market, chosen its target customer groups and identified their needs, and determined its desired market positioning, it is ready to develop and launch appropriate new products. Marketing should participate with other departments in every stage of new-product development.
2. Successful new-product development requires the company to establish an effective organization for managing the development process. Companies can choose to use product managers, new-product managers, new-product committees, new-product departments, or new-product venture teams. Increasingly, companies are adopting cross-functional teams and developing multiple product concepts.
3. Eight stages are involved in the new-product development process: idea generation, screening, concept development and testing, marketing-strategy development, business analysis, product development, market testing, and commercialization. At each stage, the company must determine whether the idea should be dropped or moved to the next stage.
4. The consumer-adoption process is the process by which customers learn about new products, try them, and adopt or reject them. Today many marketers are targeting heavy users and early adopters of new products, because both groups can be reached by specific media and tend to be opinion leaders. The consumer-adoption process is influenced by many factors beyond the marketer's control, including consumers' and organizations' willingness to try new products, personal influences, and the characteristics of the new product or innovation.

APPLICATIONS :::

Marketing Debate Who Should You Target with New Products?

Many firms target lead users or innovators with their new products, with the assumption that their adoption will trickle down to influence the broader market. Others disagree with this approach and contend that the most efficient and quickest route is to target the broader or even mass market directly.

Take a position: New products should always target new adopters versus New products should target the broadest market possible.

Marketing Discussion

Think about the last new product you bought. How do you think its success will be affected by the five characteristics of an innovation: relative advantage, compatibility, complexity, divisibility, and communicability?

IN THIS CHAPTER, WE WILL ADDRESS THE FOLLOWING QUESTIONS:

1. What factors should a company review before deciding to go abroad?
2. How can companies evaluate and select specific foreign markets to enter?
3. What are the major ways of entering a foreign market?
4. To what extent must the company adapt its products and marketing program to each foreign country?
5. How should the company manage and organize its international activities?

CHAPTER 21 ::: TAPPING INTO GLOBAL MARKETS

twenty one

With faster communication, transportation, and financial flows, the world is rapidly shrinking. Products developed in one country—Gucci purses, Mont Blanc pens, McDonald's hamburgers, Japanese sushi, Chanel suits, German BMWs—are finding enthusiastic acceptance in others. A German businessman may wear an Armani suit to meet an English friend at a Japanese restaurant, who later returns home to drink Russian vodka and watch an American soap on TV. Consider the international success of Red Bull.

A billion-dollar brand in less than 15 years, Red Bull has gained 70 percent of the worldwide energy drink market by skillfully connecting with global youth. Founded in Austria by Dietrich Mateschitz, Red Bull was introduced into its first foreign market, Hungary, in 1992, and is now sold in over 100 countries. Red Bull consists of amino acid taurine, B-complex vitamins, caffeine, and carbohydrates. The drink was sold originally in only one size—the silver 250 ml (8.3 oz.) can—and received little traditional advertising support beyond animated television commercials with the tagline "Red Bull Gives You Wiiings." Red Bull built buzz about the product through its "seeding program": the company microtargets "in" shops, clubs, bars, and stores, gradually moves from bars and clubs to convenience stores and restaurants, and finally enters supermarkets. It targets "opinion leaders" by making Red Bull available at sports competitions, in limos before >>>

Red Bull X-Fighters event, 2004.

award shows, and at exclusive after-parties. Red Bull also built its cool image through sponsorship of extreme sports like its X-Fighters events, and unique grass-roots efforts. In cities throughout the world, for example, the company sponsors an annual Flugtag where contestants build flying machines that they launch off ramps into water, true to the brand's slogan![1]

Although the opportunities for companies to enter and compete in foreign markets are significant, the risks can also be high. Companies selling in global industries, however, really have no choice but to internationalize their operations. In this chapter, we review the major decisions in expanding into global markets.

::: Competing on a Global Basis

Two hundred giant corporations, most of them larger than many national economies, have sales that in total exceed a quarter of the world's economic activity. On that basis, Philip Morris is larger than New Zealand and operates in 170 countries. International trade in 2003 accounted for over one-quarter of U.S. GDP, up from 11 percent in 1970.[2]

Many companies have conducted international marketing for decades—Nestlé, Shell, Bayer, and Toshiba are familiar to consumers around the world. But global competition is intensifying. Domestic companies that never thought about foreign competitors suddenly find them in their backyards. Newspapers report on the gains of Japanese, German, Swedish, and Korean car imports in the U.S. market, and the loss of textile and shoe markets to imports from developing countries in Latin America, Eastern Europe, and Asia. Many companies that are thought to be American firms are really foreign firms. Dannon, Red Roof Inn, Wild Turkey, Interscope, and L'Oréal, for example, are all French-owned.[3]

Although some U.S. businesses may want to eliminate foreign competition through protective legislation, the better way to compete is to continuously improve products at home and expand into foreign markets. A **global industry** is an industry in which the strategic positions of competitors in major geographic or national markets are fundamentally affected by their overall global positions.[4] A **global firm** is a firm that operates in more than one country and captures R&D, production, logistical, marketing, and financial advantages in its costs and reputation that are not available to purely domestic competitors.

Global firms plan, operate, and coordinate their activities on a worldwide basis. Ford's "world truck" has a European-made cab and a North American–built chassis, is assembled in Brazil, and is imported into the United States for sale. Otis Elevator gets its door systems from France, small geared parts from Spain, electronics from Germany, and special motor drives from Japan; it uses the United States for systems integration. One of the most successful global companies is ABB, formed by a merger between the Swedish company ASEA and the Swiss company Brown Boveri.[5]

ABB

ABB's products include power transformers, electrical installations, instrumentation, auto components, air-conditioning equipment, and railroad equipment. The company has annual revenues of $32 billion and 200,000 employees. Its motto: "ABB is a global company local everywhere." English is its official language (all ABB managers must be conversant in English), and all financial results must be reported in dollars. ABB aims to reconcile three contradictions: to be global and local; to be big and small; and to be radically decentralized with centralized reporting and control. It has fewer than 200 staff at company headquarters in Switzerland, compared to the 3,000 people who populate the Siemens headquarters. The company's many product lines are organized into 8 business segments, 65 business areas, 1,300 companies, and 5,000 profit centers, with the average employee belonging to a profit center of around 50 employees. Managers are regularly rotated among countries and mixed-nationality teams are encouraged. Depending on the type of business, some units are treated as super-local businesses with lots of autonomy, while others are governed with major central control and are considered global businesses.[6]

A company need not be large, however, to sell globally. Small and medium-sized firms can practice global nichemanship. The Poilane Bakery sells 15,000 loaves of old-style bread each day in Paris—2.5 percent of all bread sold in that city—via company-owned delivery trucks. But each day, Poilane-branded bread is also shipped via FedEx to loyal customers in roughly 20 countries around the world.[7]

For a company of any size to go global, it must make a series of decisions (see Figure 21.1). We'll examine each of these decisions here.

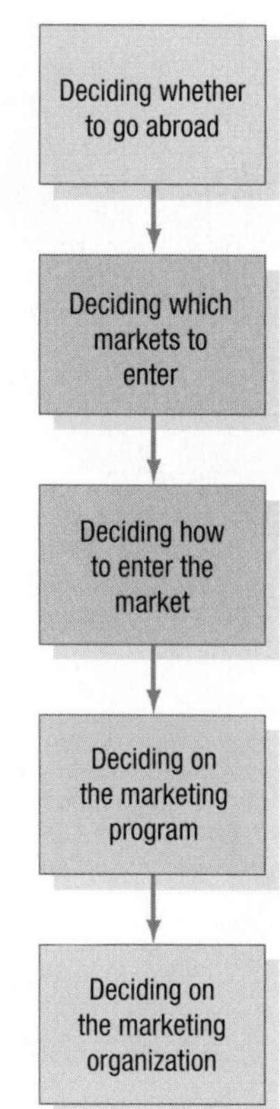

FIG. 21.1

Major Decisions in International Marketing

::: Deciding Whether to Go Abroad

Most companies would prefer to remain domestic if their domestic market were large enough. Managers would not need to learn other languages and laws, deal with volatile currencies, face political and legal uncertainties, or redesign their products to suit different customer needs and expectations. Business would be easier and safer. Yet several factors are drawing more and more companies into the international arena:

- The company discovers that some foreign markets present higher profit opportunities than the domestic market.
- The company needs a larger customer base to achieve economies of scale.
- The company wants to reduce its dependence on any one market.
- Global firms offering better products or lower prices can attack the company's domestic market. The company might want to counterattack these competitors in their home markets.
- The company's customers are going abroad and require international servicing.

Before making a decision to go abroad, the company must weigh several risks:

- The company might not understand foreign customer preferences and fail to offer a competitively attractive product.
- The company might not understand the foreign country's business culture or know how to deal effectively with foreign nationals.
- The company might underestimate foreign regulations and incur unexpected costs.
- The company might realize that it lacks managers with international experience.
- The foreign country might change its commercial laws, devalue its currency, or undergo a political revolution and expropriate foreign property.

Because of the conflicting advantages and risks, companies often do not act until some event thrusts them into the international arena. Someone—a domestic exporter, an international importer, a foreign government—solicits the company to sell abroad, or the company is saddled with overcapacity and must find additional markets for its goods.

Most countries lament that too few of their companies participate in international trade. This keeps the country from earning foreign exchange to pay for needed imports. It also raises the specter of domestic companies eventually being hurt or taken over by foreign multinationals. These countries are trying to encourage their domestic companies to grow domestically and expand globally. Many countries sponsor aggressive export-promotion programs to get their companies to export. These programs require a deep understanding of how companies become internationalized.

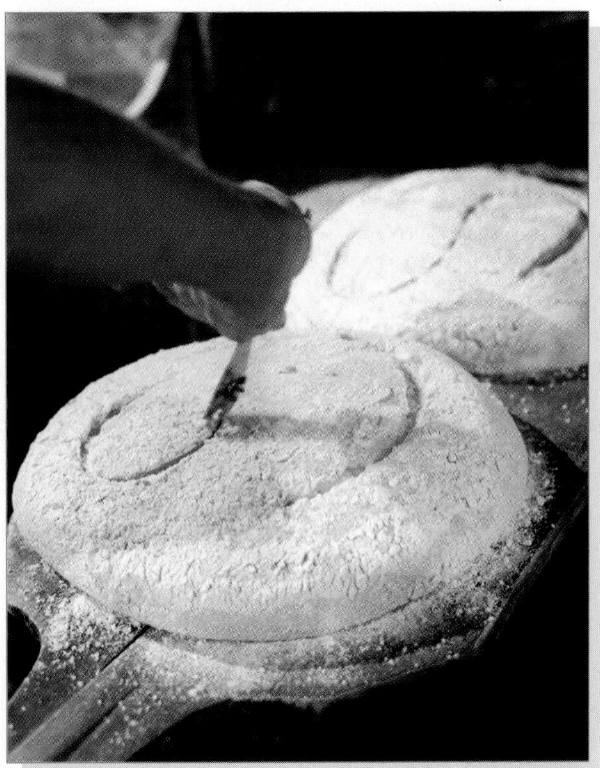

The company logo being carved into a loaf of Poilane bread, which is shipped daily via FedEx to loyal customers in countries around the world.

The *internationalization process* has four stages:[8]

1. No regular export activities.
2. Export via independent representatives (agents).
3. Establishment of one or more sales subsidiaries.
4. Establishment of production facilities abroad.

The first task is to get companies to move from stage 1 to stage 2. This move is helped by studying how firms make their first export decisions.[9] Most firms work with an independent agent and enter a nearby or similar country. A company then engages further agents to enter additional countries. Later, it establishes an export department to manage its agent relationships. Still later, the company replaces its agents with its own sales subsidiaries in its larger export markets. This increases the company's investment and risk, but also its earning potential.

To manage these subsidiaries, the company replaces the export department with an international department. If certain markets continue to be large and stable, or if the host country insists on local production, the company takes the next step of locating production facilities in those markets. This means a still larger commitment and still larger potential earnings. By this time, the company is operating as a multinational and is engaged in optimizing its global sourcing, financing, manufacturing, and marketing. According to some researchers, top management begins to pay more attention to global opportunities when they find that over 15 percent of revenues comes from foreign markets.[10]

::: Deciding Which Markets to Enter

In deciding to go abroad, the company needs to define its marketing objectives and policies. What proportion of foreign to total sales will it seek? Most companies start small when they venture abroad. Some plan to stay small; others have bigger plans. Ayal and Zif have argued that a company should enter fewer countries when:

- Market entry and market control costs are high.
- Product and communication adaptation costs are high.
- Population and income size and growth are high in the initial countries chosen.
- Dominant foreign firms can establish high barriers to entry.[11]

How Many Markets to Enter

The company must decide how many countries to enter and how fast to expand. Consider Amway's experience:

AMWAY

Amway Corp., one of the world's largest direct-selling companies, markets its products and services through independent business owners worldwide. Amway expanded into Australia in 1971. In the 1980s, it moved into 10 more countries. By 2004, Amway had evolved into a multinational juggernaut with a sales force of more than 3.6 million independent distributors hauling in $4.5 billion in sales. Established in 1998, Amway India quickly grew to 200,000 active Amway distributors by 2004. Amway currently sells products in 80 countries and territories worldwide. The corporate goal is to have overseas markets account for 80 percent of its sales. This is not unrealistic or overly ambitious considering that Amway already gains 70 percent of its sales from markets outside North America.[12]

A company's entry strategy typically follows one of two possible approaches: a *waterfall* approach, in which countries are gradually entered sequentially; or a *sprinkler* approach, in which many countries are entered simultaneously within a limited period of time. Increasingly, especially with technology-intensive firms, they are *born global* and market to the entire world right from the outset.[13]

Generally speaking, companies such as Matsushita, BMW, and General Electric, or even newer companies such as Dell, Benetton, and The Body Shop, follow the waterfall approach. Expansion can be carefully planned and is less likely to strain human and financial resources. When first-mover advantage is crucial and a high degree of competitive intensity prevails, the sprinkler approach is preferred, as when Microsoft introduces a new form of Windows software. The main risk is the substantial resources involved and the difficulty of planning entry strategies in so many potentially diverse markets.

The company must also decide on the types of countries to consider. Attractiveness is influenced by the product, geography, income and population, political climate, and other factors. Kenichi Ohmae recommends that companies concentrate on selling in the "triad markets"—the United States, Western Europe, and the Far East—because these markets account for a large percentage of all international trade.[14]

Developed versus Developing Markets

Although Ohmae's position makes short-run sense, it can spell disaster for the world economy in the long run. The unmet needs of the emerging or developing world represent huge potential markets for food, clothing, shelter, consumer electronics, appliances, and other goods. Many market leaders are rushing into Eastern Europe, China, and India. Colgate now draws more personal and household products business from Latin America than North America.[15]

The developed nations and the prosperous parts of developing nations account for less than 15 percent of the world's population. Is there a way for marketers to serve the other 85 percent, which has much less purchasing power? Successfully entering developing markets requires a special set of skills and plans. Consider how the following companies are pioneering ways to serve these invisible consumers:[16]

- Grameen-Phone markets cell phones to 35,000 villages in Bangladesh by hiring village women as agents who lease phone time to other villagers, one call at a time.
- Colgate-Palmolive rolls into Indian villages with video vans that show the benefits of toothbrushing; it expects to earn over half of its Indian revenue from rural areas by 2003.
- An Indian-Australian car manufacturer created an affordable rural transport vehicle to compete with bullock carts rather than cars. The vehicle functions well at low speeds and carries up to two tons.
- Fiat developed a "third-world car," the Palio, that far outsells the Ford Fiesta in Brazil and that will be launched in other developing nations.
- Corporacion GEO builds low-income housing in Mexico. The two-bedroom homes are modular and can be expanded. The company is now moving into Chile and southern U.S. communities.
- A Latin American building-supply retailer offers bags of cement in smaller sizes to customers building their own homes.

These marketers are able to capitalize on the potential of developing markets by changing their conventional marketing practices to sell their products and services more effectively.[17] It cannot be business as usual when selling in developing markets. Economic and cultural differences abound; a marketing infrastructure may barely exist; and local competition can be surprisingly stiff. In China, PC maker Legend and mobile-phone provider TCL have thrived despite strong foreign competition. Besides their close grasp on Chinese tastes, they also have their vast distribution networks, especially in rural areas.[18]

Smaller packaging and lower sales prices are often critical in markets where incomes are limited. Unilever's 4-cent sachets of detergent and shampoo have been a big hit in rural India, where 70 percent of the country's population still lives. When Coke moved to a smaller, 200 ml bottle in India, selling for 10 to 12 cents in small shops, bus-stop stalls, and roadside

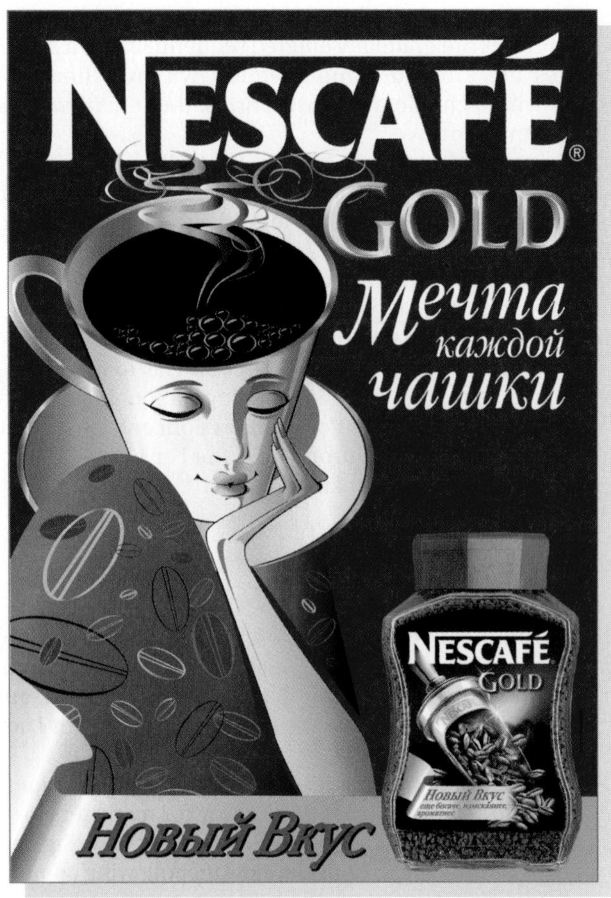

A Russian ad for Nestlé's Nescafé. As consumer spending has risen in Russia, the market for products of major multinationals like Nestlé has boomed.

eateries, sales jumped.[19] A Western image can also be helpful, as Coke discovered in China. Part of its success against local cola brand Jianlibao was due to its symbolic values of modernity and affluence.[20]

Recognizing that its cost structure made it difficult to compete effectively in developing markets, Procter & Gamble devised cheaper, clever ways to make the right kinds of products to suit consumer demand. It now uses contract manufacturers in certain markets and gained eight share points in Russia for Always feminine protection pads by responding to consumer wishes for a thicker pad.[21] Due to a boom in consumer spending, Russia has been the fastest-growing market for many major multinationals, including Nestlé, L'Oréal, and IKEA.[22]

The challenge is to think creatively about how marketing can fulfill the dreams of most of the world's population for a better standard of living. Many companies are betting that they can do that.

GENERAL MOTORS

After launching Buick in China in 1999, GM poured more than $2 billion into the region over the next five years, expanding the lineup to 14 models, ranging from the $8,000 Chevrolet Spark mini-car to high-end Cadillacs. Although competition in the third-largest car market is fierce, GM was able to secure 11 percent market share in 2004 and reap sizable profits. But initial gains in the Chinese market do not necessarily spell long-term success. After investing to establish the markets, foreign pioneers in television sets and motorcycles saw domestic Chinese firms emerge as rivals. In 1995, virtually all mobile phones in China were made by global giants Nokia, Motorola, and Ericsson. Within 10 years, their market share had dropped to 60 percent. To secure and build on its gains, General Motors pledged to invest another $3 billion in the region to boost capacity and build its reputation.[23]

Regional Free Trade Zones

Regional economic integration—trading agreements between blocs of countries—has intensified in recent years. This development means that companies are more likely to enter entire regions at the same time. Certain countries have formed free trade zones or economic communities—groups of nations organized to work toward common goals in the regulation of international trade. One such community is the European Union (EU).

THE EUROPEAN UNION Formed in 1957, the European Union set out to create a single European market by reducing barriers to the free flow of products, services, finances, and labor among member countries, and by developing trade policies with nonmember nations. Today, the European Union is one of the world's largest single markets. The 15 member countries making up the EU increased by 10 in May 2004 with the addition of Cyprus, the Czech Republic, Estonia, Hungary, Latvia, Lithuania, Malta, Poland, Slovakia, and Slovenia. The EU now contains more than 454 million consumers and accounts for 23 percent of the world's exports. It has a common currency, the euro monetary system.

European unification offers tremendous trade opportunities for non-European firms. However, it also poses threats. European companies will grow bigger and more competitive. Witness the competition in the aircraft industry between Europe's Airbus consortium and Boeing in the United States. Perhaps an even bigger concern, however, is that lower barriers inside Europe will only create thicker outside walls. Some observers envision a "fortress Europe" that heaps favors on firms from EU countries but hinders outsiders by imposing obstacles such as stiffer import quotas, local content requirements, and other nontariff (nontax) barriers.

Also, companies that plan to create "pan-European" marketing campaigns directed to a unified Europe should proceed with caution. Even as the EU standardizes its general trade regulations and currency, creating an economic community will not create a homogeneous market. Companies marketing in Europe face 14 different languages, 2,000 years of historical and cultural differences, and a daunting mass of local rules.

NAFTA Closer to home, in North America, the United States and Canada phased out trade barriers in 1989. In January 1994, the North American Free Trade Agreement (NAFTA) established a free trade zone among the United States, Mexico, and Canada. The agreement created a single market of 360 million people who produce and consume $6.7 trillion worth of goods and services annually. As it is implemented over a 15-year period, NAFTA will eliminate all trade barriers and investment restrictions among the three countries. Prior to NAFTA, tariffs on American products entering Mexico averaged 13 percent, whereas U.S. tariffs on Mexican goods averaged 6 percent.

MERCOSUL Other free trade areas are forming in Latin America. For example, MERCOSUL now links Brazil, Argentina, Paraguay, and Uruguay. Chile and Mexico have formed a successful free trade zone. It is likely that NAFTA will eventually merge with this and other arrangements to form an all-Americas free trade zone.

It is the European nations that have tapped Latin America's enormous potential. As Washington's efforts to extend NAFTA to Latin America have stalled, European countries have moved in with a vengeance. When Latin American countries instituted market reforms and privatized public utilities, European companies rushed in to grab up lucrative contracts for rebuilding Latin America's infrastructure. Spain's Telefonica de Espana spent $5 billion buying phone companies in Brazil, Chile, Peru, and Argentina. In Brazil, seven of the ten largest private companies are European owned, compared to two controlled by Americans. Among the notable European companies operating in Latin America are automotive giants Volkswagen and Fiat, the French supermarket chain Carrefours, and the Anglo-Dutch personal-care products group Gessy-Lever.

APEC Twenty-one Pacific Rim countries, including the NAFTA member states, Japan, and China, are working to create a pan-Pacific free trade area under the auspices of the Asian Pacific Economic Cooperation forum (APEC). There are also active attempts at regional economic integration in the Caribbean, Southeast Asia, and parts of Africa.

Evaluating Potential Markets

Yet, however much nations and regions integrate their trading policies and standards, each nation still has unique features that must be understood. A nation's readiness for different

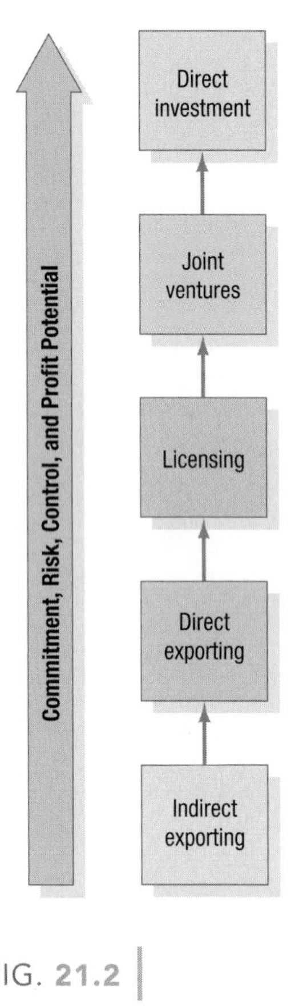

FIG. 21.2

Five Modes of Entry into Foreign Markets

products and services and its attractiveness as a market to foreign firms depend on its economic, political-legal, and cultural environments.

Suppose a company has assembled a list of potential markets to enter. How does it choose among them? Many companies prefer to sell to neighboring countries because they understand these countries better and can control their costs more effectively. It is not surprising that the two largest U.S. export markets are Canada and Mexico, or that Swedish companies first sold to their Scandinavian neighbors. As growing numbers of U.S. companies expand abroad, many are deciding the best place to start is next door.

At other times, *psychic proximity* determines choices. Many U.S. firms prefer to sell in Canada, England, and Australia—rather than in larger markets such as Germany and France—because they feel more comfortable with the language, laws, and culture. Companies should be careful, however, in choosing markets according to cultural distance. Besides the fact that potentially better markets may be overlooked, it also may result in a superficial analysis of some very real differences among the countries. It may also lead to predictable marketing actions that would be a disadvantage from a competitive standpoint.[24]

Regardless of how chosen, it often makes sense to operate in fewer countries with a deeper commitment and penetration in each. In general, a company prefers to enter countries (1) that rank high on market attractiveness, (2) that are low in market risk, and (3) in which it possesses a competitive advantage. Here is how Bechtel Corporation, the construction giant, goes about evaluating overseas markets.

BECHTEL CORPORATION

Bechtel provides premier technical, management, and directly related services to develop, manage, engineer, build, and operate installations for customers in nearly 60 countries worldwide. Before Bechtel ventures into new markets, the company starts with a detailed strategic market analysis. It looks at its markets and tries to determine where it should be in four or five years' time. A management team does a cost-benefit analysis that factors in the position of competitors, infrastructure, regulatory and trade barriers, and the tax situation (both corporate and individual). Ideally, the new market should be a country with an untapped need for its products or services; a quality, skilled labor pool capable of manufacturing the product; and a welcoming environment (governmental and physical).

Are there countries that meet Bechtel's requirements? Although Singapore has an educated, English-speaking labor force, basks in political stability, and encourages foreign investment, it has a small population. Although many countries in central Europe possess an eager, hungry-to-learn labor pool, their infrastructures create difficulties. The team evaluating a new market must determine whether the company could earn enough on its investment to cover the risk factors or other negatives.[25]

::: Deciding How to Enter the Market

Once a company decides to target a particular country, it has to determine the best mode of entry. Its broad choices are *indirect exporting, direct exporting, licensing, joint ventures,* and *direct investment.* These five market-entry strategies are shown in Figure 21.2. Each succeeding strategy involves more commitment, risk, control, and profit potential.

Indirect and Direct Export

The normal way to get involved in an international market is through export. *Occasional exporting* is a passive level of involvement in which the company exports from time to time, either on its own initiative or in response to unsolicited orders from abroad. *Active exporting* takes place when the company makes a commitment to expand into a particular market. In either case, the company produces its goods in the home country and might or might not adapt them to the international market.

Companies typically start with *indirect exporting*—that is, they work through independent intermediaries. *Domestic-based export merchants* buy the manufacturer's products and then sell them abroad. *Domestic-based export agents* seek and negotiate foreign purchases and are paid a commission. Included in this group are trading companies. *Cooperative organizations* carry on exporting activities on behalf of several producers and are partly under their administrative control. They are often used by producers of primary products such as fruits or nuts. *Export-management companies* agree to manage a company's export activities for a fee.

Indirect export has two advantages. First, it involves less investment: The firm does not have to develop an export department, an overseas sales force, or a set of international contacts. Second, it involves less risk: Because international-marketing intermediaries bring know-how and services to the relationship, the seller will normally make fewer mistakes.

Companies eventually may decide to handle their own exports.[26] The investment and risk are somewhat greater, but so is the potential return. A company can carry on direct exporting in several ways:

- ***Domestic-based export department or division.*** Might evolve into a self-contained export department operating as a profit center.
- ***Overseas sales branch or subsidiary.*** The sales branch handles sales and distribution and might handle warehousing and promotion as well. It often serves as a display and customer service center.
- ***Traveling export sales representatives.*** Home-based sales representatives are sent abroad to find business.
- ***Foreign-based distributors or agents.*** These distributors and agents might be given exclusive rights to represent the company in that country, or only limited rights.

Whether companies decide to export indirectly or directly, many companies use exporting as a way to "test the waters" before building a plant and manufacturing a product overseas. University Games of Burlingame, California, maker of education games that encourage social interaction and imagination, has blossomed into a $50 million-per-year international company through careful entry into overseas ventures.

UNIVERSITY GAMES

Bob Moog, president and founder of University Games, says his company's international sales strategy relies heavily on third-party distributors and has a fair degree of flexibility. "We identify the international markets we want to penetrate," says Moog, "and then form a business venture with a local distributor that will give us a large degree of control. In Australia, we expect to run a print of 5,000 board games. These we will manufacture in the United States. If we reach a run of 25,000 games, however, we would then establish a sub-contracting venture with a local manufacturer in Australia or New Zealand to print the games." The company now sells in 28 countries.[27]

Using a Global Web Strategy

One of the best ways to initiate or extend export activities used to be to exhibit at an overseas trade show. With the Web, it is not even necessary to attend trade shows to show one's wares: Electronic communication via the Internet is extending the reach of companies large and small to worldwide markets.

Major marketers doing global e-commerce range from automakers (GM) to direct-mail companies (L.L. Bean and Lands' End) to running-shoe giants (Nike and Reebok) to Amazon.com. Marketers like these are using the Web to reach new customers outside their home countries, to support existing customers who live abroad, to source from international suppliers, and to build global brand awareness.

These companies adapt their Web sites to provide country-specific content and services to their best potential international markets, ideally in the local language. The number of Internet users is rising quickly as access costs decline, local-language content increases, and infrastructure improves. Upscale retailer and cataloger The Sharper Image now gets more than 25 percent of its online business from overseas customers.[28]

The Internet has become an effective means of everything from gaining free exporting information and guidelines to conducting market research and offering customers several time zones away a secure process for ordering and paying for products. "Going abroad" on the Internet does pose special challenges. The global marketer may run up against governmental or cultural restrictions. In Germany, a vendor cannot accept payment via credit card until two weeks after an order has been sent. German law also prevents companies from using certain marketing techniques like unconditional lifetime guarantees. On a wider scale, the issue of who pays sales taxes and duties on global e-commerce is murkier still.

Finding free information about trade and exporting has never been easier. Here are some places to start a search:

www.ita.doc.gov	U.S. Department of Commerce's International Trade Administration
www.exim.gov	Export-Import Bank of the United States
www.sba.gov	U.S. Small Business Administration
www.bxa.doc.gov	Bureau of Industry and Security, a branch of the Commerce Department

Also, many states' export-promotion offices have online resources and allow businesses to link to their sites.

Licensing

Licensing is a simple way to become involved in international marketing. The licensor issues a license to a foreign company to use a manufacturing process, trademark, patent, trade secret, or other item of value for a fee or royalty. The licensor gains entry at little risk; the licensee gains production expertise or a well-known product or brand name.

Licensing has potential disadvantages. The licensor has less control over the licensee than it does over its own production and sales facilities. Furthermore, if the licensee is very successful, the firm has given up profits; and if and when the contract ends, the company might find that it has created a competitor. To avoid this, the licensor usually supplies some proprietary ingredients or components needed in the product (as Coca-Cola does). But the best strategy is for the licensor to lead in innovation so that the licensee will continue to depend on the licensor.

There are several variations on a licensing arrangement. Companies such as Hyatt and Marriott sell *management contracts* to owners of foreign hotels to manage these businesses for a fee. The management firm may even be given the option to purchase some share in the managed company within a stated period.

In *contract manufacturing,* the firm hires local manufacturers to produce the product. When Sears opened department stores in Mexico and Spain, it found qualified local manufacturers to produce many of its products. Contract manufacturing gives the company less control over the manufacturing process and the loss of potential profits on manufacturing. However, it offers a chance to start faster, with less risk and with the opportunity to form a partnership or buy out the local manufacturer later.

Finally, a company can enter a foreign market through *franchising,* which is a more complete form of licensing. The franchiser offers a complete brand concept and operating system. In return, the franchisee invests in and pays certain fees to the franchiser. McDonald's, KFC, and Avis have entered scores of countries by franchising their retail concepts and making sure their marketing is culturally relevant.

KFC CORPORATION

KFC is the world's largest fast-food chicken chain, owning or franchising 12,800 outlets in about 90 countries—60 percent of them outside the United States. KFC had a number of obstacles to overcome when it entered the Japanese market. The Japanese saw fast food as artificial, made by mechanical means, and unhealthy. To build trust in the KFC brand, advertising showed scenes depicting Colonel Sanders' beginnings in Kentucky that conveyed southern hospitality, old American tradition, and authentic home cooking. The campaign was hugely successful, and in less than eight years KFC expanded its presence from 400 locations to more than 1,000. KFC is China's largest, oldest, and most popular quick-service restaurant chain, also with over 1,000 locations. KFC is the most popular international brand throughout China, ranking higher than all others, according to a consumer survey conducted by A.C. Nielsen. China operations offer such fare as an "Old Beijing Twister"—a wrap modeled after the way Peking duck is served, but with fried chicken inside.[29]

Joint Ventures

Foreign investors may join with local investors to create a **joint venture** company in which they share ownership and control. For instance:[30]

- Coca-Cola and Nestlé joined forces to develop the international market for "ready-to-drink" tea and coffee, which currently they sell in significant amounts in Japan.

- Procter & Gamble formed a joint venture with its Italian archrival Fater to cover babies' bottoms in the United Kingdom and Italy.
- Whirlpool took a 53 percent stake in the Dutch electronics group Philips's white-goods business to leapfrog into the European market.

A joint venture may be necessary or desirable for economic or political reasons. The foreign firm might lack the financial, physical, or managerial resources to undertake the venture alone; or the foreign government might require joint ownership as a condition for entry. Even corporate giants need joint ventures to crack the toughest markets. When it wanted to enter China's ice cream market, Unilever joined forces with Sumstar, a state-owned Chinese investment company. The venture's general manager says Sumstar's help with the formidable Chinese bureaucracy was crucial in getting a high-tech ice cream plant up and running in just 12 months.[31]

Joint ownership has certain drawbacks. The partners might disagree over investment, marketing, or other policies. One partner might want to reinvest earnings for growth, and the other partner might want to declare more dividends. Joint ownership can also prevent a multinational company from carrying out specific manufacturing and marketing policies on a worldwide basis.

Direct Investment

The ultimate form of foreign involvement is direct ownership of foreign-based assembly or manufacturing facilities. The foreign company can buy part or full interest in a local company or build its own facilities. General Motors has invested billions of dollars in auto manufacturers around the world, such as Shangai GM, Fiat Auto Holdings, Isuzu, Daewoo, Suzuki, Saab, Fuji Heavy Industries, Jinbei GM Automotive Co., and AvtoVAZ.[32]

If the market appears large enough, foreign production facilities offer distinct advantages. First, the firm secures cost economies in the form of cheaper labor or raw materials, foreign-government investment incentives, and freight savings. Second, the firm strengthens its image in the host country because it creates jobs. Third, the firm develops a deeper relationship with government, customers, local suppliers, and distributors, enabling it to adapt its products better to the local environment. Fourth, the firm retains full control over its investment and therefore can develop manufacturing and marketing policies that serve its long-term international objectives. Fifth, the firm assures itself access to the market in case the host country starts insisting that locally purchased goods have domestic content.

The main disadvantage of direct investment is that the firm exposes a large investment to risks such as blocked or devalued currencies, worsening markets, or expropriation. The firm will find it expensive to reduce or close down its operations, because the host country might require substantial severance pay to the employees.

::: Deciding on the Marketing Program

International companies must decide how much to adapt their marketing strategy to local conditions.[33] At one extreme are companies that use a globally *standardized marketing mix* worldwide. Standardization of the product, communication, and distribution channels promises the lowest costs. Table 21.1 summarizes some of the pros and cons of standardizing the marketing program. At the other extreme is an *adapted marketing mix,* where the producer adjusts the marketing program to each target market. For a discussion of the main issues, see "Marketing Insight: Global Standardization or Adaptation?"

Between the two extremes, many possibilities exist. Most brands are adapted to some extent to reflect significant differences in consumer behavior, brand development, competitive forces, and the legal or political environment. Satisfying different consumer needs and wants can require different marketing programs. Cultural differences can often be pronounced across countries. Hofstede identifies four cultural dimensions that can differentiate countries:[34]

1. ***Individualism vs. collectivism.*** In collectivist societies, such as Japan, the self-worth of an individual is rooted more in the social system than in individual achievement.
2. ***High vs. low power distance.*** High power distance cultures tend to be less egalitarian.
3. ***Masculine vs. feminine.*** How much the culture is dominated by assertive males versus nurturing females.
4. ***Weak vs. strong uncertainty avoidance.*** How risk tolerant or aversive people are.

TABLE 21.1

Global Marketing Pros and Cons

Advantages
Economies of scale in production and distribution
Lower marketing costs
Power and scope
Consistency in brand image
Ability to leverage good ideas quickly and efficiently
Uniformity of marketing practices
Disadvantages
Differences in consumer needs, wants, and usage patterns for products
Differences in consumer response to marketing-mix elements
Differences in brand and product development and the competitive environment
Differences in the legal environment
Differences in marketing institutions
Differences in administrative procedures

Even global brands, such as Pringles, Always, and Toyota, will undergo some changes in product features, packaging, channels, pricing, or communications in different global markets. (See "Marketing Memo: The Ten Commandments of Global Branding.") Marketers must make sure that their marketing is relevant to consumers in every market.

WALT DISNEY CO.

When Walt Disney launched the Euro Disney theme park outside Paris in 1992, it was harshly criticized as being an example of American cultural imperialism. A number of local French customs and values, such as serving wine with meals, were ignored. As one Euro Disney executive noted, "When we first launched, there was the belief that it was enough to be Disney. Now we realize our guests need to be welcomed on the basis of their own culture and travel habits." Renamed Disneyland Paris, the theme park eventually became Europe's biggest tourist attraction—even more popular than the Eiffel Tower—by making a number of changes and adding more local touches.[35]

Disneyland Paris, Europe's biggest tourist attraction.

Product

Some types of products travel better across borders than others—food and beverage marketers have to contend with widely varying tastes.[36] "Marketing Insight: Establishing Global Service Brands" describes some of the special concerns for marketing services globally. Warren Keegan has distinguished five adaptation strategies of product and communications to a foreign market (see Figure 21.3).[37]

Straight extension means introducing the product in the foreign market without any change. Straight extension has been successful with cameras, consumer electronics, and many machine tools. In other cases, it has been a disaster. General Foods introduced its standard powdered Jell-O in the British market only to find that British consumers prefer the solid wafer or cake form. Campbell Soup Company lost an estimated $30 million in introducing its condensed soups in England;

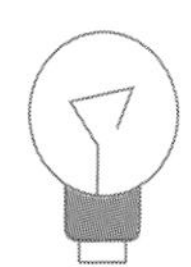

MARKETING INSIGHT | GLOBAL STANDARDIZATION OR ADAPTATION?

The marketing concept holds that consumer needs vary and that marketing programs will be more effective when they are tailored to each target group. This also applies to foreign markets. Yet in 1983, in a groundbreaking article in the *Harvard Business Review,* Harvard Professor Theodore Levitt challenged this view and supplied the intellectual rationale for global standardization: "The world is becoming a common marketplace in which people—no matter where they live—desire the same products and lifestyles."

The development of the Web, the rapid spread of cable and satellite TV around the world, and the global linking of telecommunications networks have led to a convergence of lifestyles. The convergence of needs and wants has created global markets for standardized products, particularly among the young middle class.

Levitt favors global corporations that try to sell the same product the same way to all consumers. They focus on similarities across world markets and "sensibly force suitably standardized products and services on the entire globe." These global marketers achieve economies through standardization of production, distribution, marketing, and management. They translate their efficiency into greater value for consumers by offering high-quality and more reliable products at lower prices.

Coca-Cola, McDonald's, Marlboro, Nike, the NBA, and Gillette are among the companies that have successfully marketed global products. Consider Gillette: Some 1.2 billion people use at least one Gillette product daily, according to the company's estimates. Gillette enjoys huge economies of scale by selling a few types of razor blades in every single market.

Many companies have tried to launch their version of a world product. Yet, most products require some adaptation. Toyota's Corolla will exhibit some differences in styling. McDonald's offers a ham and cheese "Croque McDo" in France, a variation of the French favorite croque monsieur. Coca-Cola is sweeter or less carbonated in certain countries. Rather than assuming that its domestic product can be introduced "as is" in another country, the company should review the following elements and determine which would add more revenue than cost:

- Product features
- Brand name
- Labeling
- Packaging
- Colors
- Advertising execution
- Materials
- Prices
- Sales promotion
- Advertising themes
- Advertising media

Consumer behavior can dramatically differ across markets. Take annual beverage consumption. One of the highest per capita consumers of carbonated soft drinks is the United States, with 203.9 liters per capita consumption; Italy is among the lowest. But Italy is one of the highest per capita drinkers of bottled water with 164.4 liters, whereas the United Kingdom is only 20 liters. When it comes to beer, Ireland and the Czech Republic lead the pack, with over 150 liters per capita, with France among the lowest at 35.9 liters.

Besides demand-side differences, other types of supply-side differences can also prevail. Levitt's critics pointed out that flexible manufacturing techniques made it easier to produce many different product versions, tailored to particular countries. One study showed that companies made one or more marketing-mix adaptations in 80 percent of their foreign products and that the average number of adapted elements was four. So perhaps Levitt's globalization dictum should be rephrased. Global marketing, yes; global standardization, not necessarily.

Sources: Theodore Levitt, "The Globalization of Markets," *Harvard Business Review* (May–June 1983): 92–102; Bernard Wysocki Jr., "The Global Mall: In Developing Nations, Many Youths Splurge, Mainly on U.S. Goods," *Wall Street Journal,* June 26, 1997, p. A1; "What Makes a Company Great?" *Fortune,* October 26, 1998, pp. 218–226; David M. Szymanski, Sundar G. Bharadwaj, and P. Rajan Varadarajan, "Standardization versus Adaptation of International Marketing Strategy: An Empirical Investigation," *Journal of Marketing* (October 1993): 1–17; "Burgers and Fries a la Francaise," *The Economist,* April 17, 2004, pp. 60–61; Johny K. Johansson, "Global Marketing: Research on Foreign Entry, Local Marketing, Global Management," in *Handbook of Marketing,* edited by Bart Weitz and Robin Wensley (London: Sage Publications, 2002), pp. 457–483.

consumers saw expensive small-sized cans and did not realize that water needed to be added. Straight extension is tempting because it involves no additional R&D expense, manufacturing retooling, or promotional modification; but it can be costly in the long run.

Product adaptation involves altering the product to meet local conditions or preferences. There are several levels of adaptation.

- A company can produce a *regional version* of its product, such as a Western European version. Finnish cellular phone superstar Nokia customized its 6100 series phone for every major market. Developers built in rudimentary voice recognition for Asia, where keyboards are a problem, and raised the ring volume so the phone could be heard on crowded Asian streets.

FIG. 21.3

Five International Product and Communication Strategies

Communications	Do Not Change Product	Adapt Product	Develop New Product
Do Not Change Communications	Straight extension	Product adaptation	Product invention
Adapt Communications	Communication adaptation	Dual adaptation	Product invention

- A company can produce a *country version* of its product. In Japan, Mister Donut's coffee cup is smaller and lighter to fit the hand of the average Japanese consumer; even the doughnuts are a little smaller. Kraft blends different coffees for the British (who drink their coffee with milk), the French (who drink their coffee black), and Latin Americans (who want a chicory taste).
- A company can produce a *city version* of its product—for instance, a beer to meet Munich tastes or Tokyo tastes.
- A company can produce different *retailer versions* of its product, such as one coffee brew for the Migros chain store and another for the Cooperative chain store, both in Switzerland.

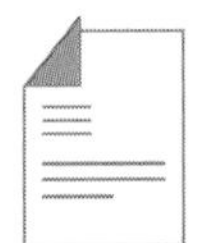

MARKETING MEMO | THE TEN COMMANDMENTS OF GLOBAL BRANDING

For many companies, global branding has been both a blessing and a curse. A global branding program can lower marketing costs, realize greater economies of scale in production, and provide a long-term source of growth. If not designed and implemented properly, it may ignore important differences in consumer behavior and/or the competitive environment in the individual countries. These suggestions can help a company retain many of the advantages of global branding while minimizing the potential disadvantages:

1. ***Understand similarities and differences in the global branding landscape.*** International markets can vary in terms of brand development, consumer behavior, competitive activity, legal restrictions, and so on.
2. ***Do not take shortcuts in brand-building.*** Building a brand in new markets should be done from the "bottom-up," both strategically (building awareness before brand image) and tactically (creating sources of brand equity in new markets).
3. ***Establish a marketing infrastructure.*** A company must either build marketing infrastructure "from scratch" or adapt to existing infrastructure in other countries.
4. ***Embrace integrated marketing communications.*** A company must often use many forms of communication in overseas markets, not just advertising.
5. ***Establish brand partnerships.*** Most global brands have marketing partners in their international markets that help companies achieve advantages in distribution, profitability, and added value.
6. ***Balance standardization and customization.*** Some elements of a marketing program can be standardized (packaging, brand name); others typically require greater customization (distribution channels).
7. ***Balance global and local control.*** Companies must balance global and local control within the organization and distribute decision making between global and local managers.
8. ***Establish operable guidelines.*** Brand definition and guidelines must be established, communicated, and properly enforced so that marketers everywhere know what they are expected to do and not do. The goal is to set rules for how the brand should be positioned and marketed.
9. ***Implement a global brand equity measurement system.*** A global brand equity system is a set of research procedures designed to provide timely, accurate, and actionable information for marketers so they can make the best possible short-run tactical decisions and long-run strategic decisions.
10. ***Leverage brand elements.*** Proper design and implementation of brand elements (brand name and trademarked brand identifiers) can be an invaluable source of brand equity worldwide.

Source: Adapted from Kevin Lane Keller and Sanjay Sood, "The Ten Commandments of Global Branding," *Asian Journal of Marketing* 8, no. 2 (2001): 97–108.

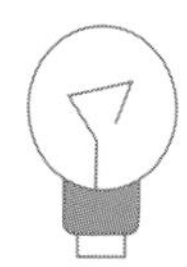

MARKETING INSIGHT | ESTABLISHING GLOBAL SERVICE BRANDS

The world market for services is growing at double the rate of world merchandise trade. Large firms in accounting, advertising, banking, communications, construction, insurance, law, management consulting, and retailing are pursuing global expansion. Pricewaterhouse, American Express, Citigroup, Club Med, Hilton, and Thomas Cook are known worldwide. U.S. credit card companies have streamed across the Atlantic to convince Europeans of the joys of charge cards. In Britain, industry heavyweights Citibank and American Express have wrested a lot of business from big British banks like Barclay's.

Many countries, however, have erected entry barriers or regulations. Brazil requires all accountants to possess a professional degree from a Brazilian university. Many Western European countries want to limit the number of U.S. television programs and films shown in their countries. Many U.S. states bar foreign bank branches. At the same time, the United States is pressuring South Korea to open its markets to U.S. banks. The World Trade Organization, consisting of 147 countries, and the General Agreement on Tariffs and Trade (GATT), consisting of 110 countries, continue to press for more free trade in international services and other areas.

Retailers who sell books, videos, and CD-ROMs, and entertainment companies have also had to contend with a culture of censorship in countries such as China and Singapore. In Singapore, for example, book retailers must submit potentially "hot" materials to the Committee on Undesirable Publications.

Sources: Charles P. Wallace, "Charge!" *Fortune,* September 28, 1998, pp. 189–196; <www.wto.org>; Ben Dolven, "Find the Niche," *Far Eastern Economic Review,* March 26, 1998, pp. 58–59.

Product invention consists of creating something new. It can take two forms. **Backward invention** is reintroducing earlier product forms that are well adapted to a foreign country's needs. The National Cash Register Company reintroduced its crank-operated cash register at half the price of a modern cash register and sold substantial numbers in Latin America and Africa.

Forward invention is creating a new product to meet a need in another country. There is an enormous need in less developed countries for low-cost, high-protein foods. Companies such as Quaker Oats, Swift, and Monsanto are researching these countries' nutrition needs, formulating new foods, and developing advertising campaigns to gain product trial and acceptance. Toyota produces vehicles specifically designed, with the help of local employees, to suit the tastes of these markets.[38]

Product invention is a costly strategy, but the payoffs can be great, particularly if a company can parlay a product innovation into other countries. In globalization's latest twist, American companies are not only inventing new products for overseas markets, but also lifting products and ideas from their international operations and bringing them home.

HÄAGEN-DAZS

Häagen-Dazs had developed a flavor for sale solely in Argentina, called "dulce de leche." Translated as "sweet of milk," it was named for the caramelized milk that is one of the most popular flavors in Argentina. Just one year later, the company rolled out dulce de leche in supermarkets from Boston to Los Angeles to Paris. The co-opted flavor soon did $1 million a month in the United States, becoming one of the top 10 flavors. It was particularly popular in Miami, where it sold twice as fast as any other flavor.[39]

In launching products and services globally, certain brand elements may have to be changed. When Clairol introduced the "Mist Stick," a curling iron, into Germany, it found that *mist* is slang for manure. Few Germans wanted to purchase a "manure stick." Brand slogans or ad taglines sometimes have to be changed too:[40]

- When Coors put its brand slogan "Turn it loose" into Spanish, it was read by some as "suffer from diarrhea."
- A laundry soap ad claiming to wash "really dirty parts" was translated in French-speaking Quebec to read "a soap for washing private parts."
- Perdue's slogan—"It takes a tough man to make a tender chicken"—was rendered into Spanish as "It takes a sexually excited man to make a chick affectionate."

TABLE 21.2

Blunders in International Marketing

- Hallmark cards failed when they were introduced in France. The French dislike syrupy sentiment and prefer writing their own cards.
- Philips began to earn a profit in Japan only after it had reduced the size of its coffeemakers to fit into smaller Japanese kitchens and its shavers to fit smaller Japanese hands.
- Coca-Cola had to withdraw its two-liter bottle in Spain after discovering that few Spaniards owned refrigerators with large enough compartments to accommodate it.
- General Foods' Tang initially failed in France because it was positioned as a substitute for orange juice at breakfast. The French drink little orange juice and almost none at breakfast.
- Kellogg's Pop-Tarts failed in Britain because the percentage of British homes with toasters was significantly lower than in the United States, and the product was too sweet for British tastes.
- Procter & Gamble's Crest toothpaste initially failed in Mexico when it used the U.S. campaign. Mexicans did not care as much for the decay-prevention benefit, nor did scientifically oriented advertising appeal to them.
- General Foods squandered millions trying to introduce packaged cake mixes to Japanese consumers. The company failed to note that only 3 percent of Japanese homes were equipped with ovens.
- S. C. Johnson's wax floor polish initially failed in Japan. The wax made the floors too slippery, and Johnson had overlooked the fact that Japanese do not wear shoes in their homes.

- Electrolux's British ad line for its vacuum cleaners—"Nothing sucks like an Electrolux"—would certainly not lure customers in the United States!

Table 21.2 lists some other famous blunders in this arena.

Communications

Companies can run the same marketing communications programs as used in the home market or change them for each local market, a process called **communication adaptation.** If it adapts both the product and the communications, the company engages in **dual adaptation.**

Consider the message. The company can use one message everywhere, varying only the language, name, and colors.[41] Exxon used "Put a tiger in your tank" with minor variations and gained international recognition. Colors can be changed to avoid taboos in some countries. Purple is associated with death in Burma and some Latin American nations; white is a mourning color in India; and green is associated with disease in Malaysia.[42]

The second possibility is to use the same theme globally but adapt the copy to each local market. For example, a Camay soap commercial showed a beautiful woman bathing. In Venezuela, a man was seen in the bathroom; in Italy and France, only a man's hand was seen; and in Japan, the man waited outside. The positioning stays the same, but the creative execution reflects local sensibilities, as with Unilever.

UNILEVER

Global marketing powerhouse Unilever decided to base the positioning of its detergent brands around the world on the consumer insight that parents universally saw dirty clothes and stains as a favorable sign of their children's experiences. The pitch in Europe for Omo detergent was a sentimental 60-second spot themed "Dirt is Good" that exhorted viewers to love their dirt. In North America, a different pitch was used. The ad slogan for Wisk detergent was "Go Ahead. Get Dirty," and communications featured a sponsorship with baseball legend Cal Ripken.[43]

The third approach consists of developing a global pool of ads, from which each country selects the most appropriate one. Coca-Cola and Goodyear have used this approach. Finally,

A Lands' End ad for Germany. Because Germany has a number of laws preventing or limiting the use of sales promotion tools, Land's End cannot advertise its money-back guarantee, though it can accept merchandise returns.

some companies allow their country managers to create country-specific ads—within guidelines, of course. Kraft uses different ads for Cheez Whiz in different countries, given that household penetration is 95 percent in Puerto Rico, where the cheese is put on everything, and 65 percent in Canada, where it is spread on morning breakfast toast. In the United States, it is considered a junk food.

The use of media also requires international adaptation because media availability varies from country to country. Norway, Belgium, and France (and now the United States) do not allow cigarettes and alcohol (except for beer in the United States) to be advertised on TV. Austria and Italy regulate TV advertising to children. Saudi Arabia does not want advertisers to use women in ads. India taxes advertising. Magazines vary in availability and effectiveness; they play a major role in Italy and a minor one in Austria.

Marketers must also adapt sales promotion techniques to different markets. Several European countries have laws preventing or limiting sales promotion tools such as discounts, rebates, coupons, games of chance, and premiums. In Germany, Lands' End could not advertise its money-back guarantee, although it does accept returned merchandise. American Express could not award points based on charges to its card for redeeming merchandise. A German store could not advertise that it would contribute a small sum to the fight against AIDS for each transaction; a German law limits discounts to 3 percent of list price. However, these restrictions are under attack and are beginning to crumble.

Personal selling tactics may have to change too. The direct, no-nonsense approach favored by Americans (characterized by more of a "let's get down to business" and "what's in it for me" stance) may not work as well in Europe, Asia, and other places where a more indirect, subtle approach can be more effective.[44] With younger, more worldly employees, however, such cultural differences may be less pronounced.

Price

Multinationals face several pricing problems when selling abroad. They must deal with price escalation, transfer prices, dumping charges, and gray markets.

When companies sell their goods abroad, they face a **price escalation** problem. A Gucci handbag may sell for $120 in Italy and $240 in the United States. Why? Gucci has to add the cost of transportation, tariffs, importer margin, wholesaler margin, and retailer margin to its factory price. Depending on these added costs, as well as the currency-fluctuation risk, the product might have to sell for two to five times as much in another country to make the same profit for the manufacturer. Because the cost escalation varies from country to country, the question is how to set the prices in different countries. Companies have three choices:

1. ***Set a uniform price everywhere*** – Coca-Cola might want to charge 75 cents for Coke everywhere in the world, but then Coca-Cola would earn quite different profit rates in different countries. Also, this strategy would result in the price being too high in poor countries and not high enough in rich countries.
2. ***Set a market-based price in each country*** – Here Coca-Cola would charge what each country could afford, but this strategy ignores differences in the actual cost from country to country. Also, it could lead to a situation in which intermediaries in low-price countries reship their Coca-Cola to high-price countries.
3. ***Set a cost-based price in each country*** – Here Coca-Cola would use a standard markup of its costs everywhere, but this strategy might price Coca-Cola out of the market in countries where its costs are high.

Another problem arises when a company sets a **transfer price** (the price it charges another unit in the company) for goods that it ships to its foreign subsidiaries. If the company charges too high a price to a subsidiary, it may end up paying higher tariff duties, although it may pay lower income taxes in the foreign country. If the company charges too low a price to its subsidiary, it can be charged with dumping. **Dumping** occurs when a company charges either less than its costs or less than it charges in its home market, in order to enter or win a market. In 2000, Stelco, a Canadian steelmaker, successfully fought dumping of steel products by steelmakers in Brazil, Finland, India, Indonesia, Thailand, and Ukraine. A Canadian tribunal found that cut-price steel imports from these countries caused "material injury to Canadian producers, including Stelco."[45]

When the U.S. Customs Bureau finds evidence of dumping, it can levy a dumping tariff on the guilty company. Various governments are watching for abuses and often force companies to charge the **arm's-length price**—that is, the price charged by other competitors for the same or a similar product.

Many multinationals are plagued by the gray market problem. The **gray market** consists of branded products diverted from normal or authorized distributions channels in the country of product origin or across international borders. Dealers in the low-price country find ways to sell some of their products in higher-price countries, thus earning more. Industry research suggests that gray market activity accounts for over $40 billion in revenue each year. In 2004, 3Com successfully sued several companies in Canada (for a total of $10 million) who provided written and oral misrepresentations to get deep discounts on 3Com networking equipment. The equipment, worth millions of dollars, was to be sold to a U.S. education software company and sent to China and Australia, but instead ended up back in the United States.[46]

Very often a company finds some enterprising distributors buying more than they can sell in their own country and reshipping the goods to another country to take advantage of price differences. Multinationals try to prevent gray markets by policing the distributors, by raising their prices to lower-cost distributors, or by altering the product characteristics or service warranties for different countries. In the European Union, the gray market may disappear altogether with the transition to a single currency unit. Once consumers recognize price differentiation by country, companies will be forced to harmonize prices throughout the countries that have adopted the single currency. Companies and marketers that offer the most innovative, specialized, or necessary products or services will be least affected by price transparency.[47]

The Internet will also reduce price differentiation between countries. When companies sell their wares over the Internet, price will become transparent: Customers can easily find out how much products sell for in different countries. Take an online training course, for instance. Whereas the price of a classroom-delivered day of training can vary significantly from the United States to France to Thailand, the price of an online-delivered day of training would have to be similar.[48]

Another global pricing challenge that has arisen in recent years is that countries with overcapacity, cheap currencies, and the need to export aggressively have pushed prices down and devalued their currencies. For multinational firms this poses challenges: Sluggish demand and reluctance to pay higher prices make selling in these emerging markets difficult. Instead of lowering prices, and taking a loss, some multinationals have found more lucrative and creative means of coping.[49]

GENERAL ELECTRIC COMPANY

Rather than striving for larger market share, GE's power systems unit focused on winning a larger percentage of each customer's expenditures. The unit asked its top 100 customers what services were most critical to them and how GE could provide or improve them. The answers prompted the company to cut its response time for replacing old or damaged parts from 12 weeks to 6. It began advising customers on the nuances of doing business in the diverse environments of Europe and Asia and providing the maintenance staff for occasional equipment upgrades. By adding value and helping customers reduce their costs and become more efficient, GE was able to avoid a move to commodity pricing and was actually able to generate bigger margins. These margins led to record revenues of $15 billion in 2000, a 50 percent rise from the previous year.[50]

Distribution Channels

Too many U.S. manufacturers think their job is done once the product leaves the factory. They should pay attention to how the product moves within the foreign country. They should take a whole-channel view of the problem of distributing products to final users. Figure 21.4 shows the three major links between seller and ultimate buyer. In the first link, *seller's international marketing headquarters,* the export department or international division makes decisions on channels and other marketing-mix elements. The second link, *channels between nations,* gets the products to the borders of the foreign nation. The decisions made in this link include the types of intermediaries (agents, trading companies) that will be used, the type of transportation (air, sea), and the financing and risk arrangements. The third link, *channels within foreign nations,* gets the products from their entry point to final buyers and users.

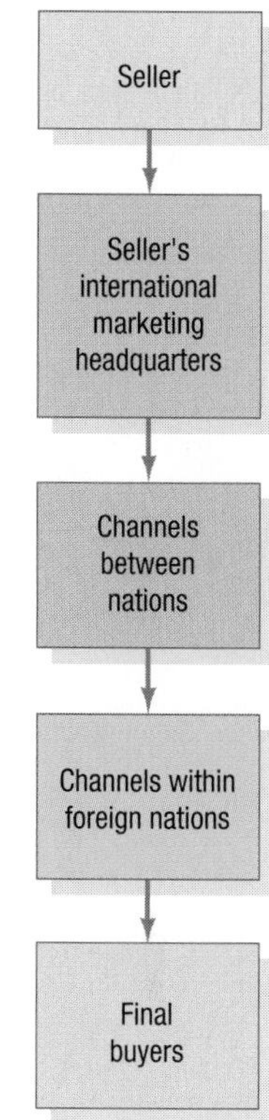

FIG. 21.4

Whole-Channel Concept for International Marketing

Distribution channels within countries vary considerably. To sell soap in Japan, Procter & Gamble has to work through one of the most complicated distribution systems in the world. It must sell to a general wholesaler, who sells to a product wholesaler, who sells to a product-specialty wholesaler, who sells to a regional wholesaler, who sells to a local wholesaler, who finally sells to retailers. All these distribution levels can mean that the consumer's price ends up double or triple the importer's price. If P&G takes the soap to tropical Africa, the company might sell to an import wholesaler, who sells to several jobbers, who sell to petty traders (mostly women) working in local markets.

Another difference lies in the size and character of retail units abroad. Large-scale retail chains dominate the U.S. scene, but much foreign retailing is in the hands of small, independent retailers. In India, millions of retailers operate tiny shops or sell in open markets. Their markups are high, but the real price is brought down through haggling. Incomes are low, and people must shop daily for small amounts; they are limited to whatever quantity can be carried home on foot or on a bicycle. Most homes lack storage space and refrigeration. Packaging costs are kept low in order to keep prices low. In India, cigarettes are often bought singly. Breaking bulk remains an important function of intermediaries and helps perpetuate the long channels of distribution, which are a major obstacle to the expansion of large-scale retailing in developing countries.

When multinationals first enter a country, they prefer to work with local distributors who have good local knowledge, but friction often arises later.[51] The multinational complains that the local distributor does not invest in business growth, does not follow company policy, does not share enough information. The local distributor complains of insufficient corporate support, impossible goals, and confusing policies. The multinational must choose the right distributors, invest in them, and set up performance goals to which they can agree.[52]

Some companies choose to invest in infrastructure to ensure that they benefit from the right channels. Peruvian cola company Kola Real has been able to survive despite competing with Coca-Cola and Pepsi-Cola in Mexico by setting up its own distribution network of 600 leased lorries, 24 distribution centers, and 800 salespeople.[53]

Many retailers are trying to make inroads into global markets. France's Carrefour, Germany's Metro, and United Kingdom's Tesco have all established global positions.

Germany's Aldi follows a simple formula globally. It stocks only about 700 products, compared with more than 20,000 at a traditional grocer such as Royal Ahold's Albert Heijin, almost all on their own exclusive label. Because it sells so few products, Aldi can exert strong control over quality and price and can simplify shipping and handling, leading to large margins. Retail experts expect Aldi to have 1,000 stores in the United States by 2010, with as much as 2 percent of the U.S. grocery market. American retail giant Wal-Mart is also expanding overseas, although sometimes with mixed results.[54]

WAL-MART

Wal-Mart has more than 1,000 stores in Mexico, Canada, Germany, Argentina, China, Britain, South Korea, Brazil, and Puerto Rico. By 2003, Wal-Mart was receiving 20 percent of its revenue from overseas, up from 12 percent in 2000. The company has learned along the way. German operations have encountered a number of obstacles. When Wal-Mart opened its stores in Latin America, sales were disappointing. Wal-Mart designed its Latin American stores like those in the United States: narrow aisles crowded with merchandise, huge parking lots, many products with red, white, and blue banners, and so on. However, Latin American shoppers expect wider aisles since they come with larger families; many do not have a car and need door-to-door bus transportation, and the red, white, and blue banners seem like Yankee imperialism.[55]

::: Country-of-Origin Effects

In an increasingly connected, highly competitive global marketplace, government officials and marketers are concerned with how attitudes and beliefs about their country affect consumer and business decision making. *Country-of-origin perceptions* are the mental associations and beliefs triggered by a country. Government officials want to strengthen their country's image to help domestic marketers who export and to attract foreign firms and investors. Marketers want to use country-of-origin perceptions in the most advantageous way possible to sell their products and services.

Building Country Images

Governments now recognize that the images of their cities and countries affect more than tourism and have important value in commerce. Attracting foreign business can improve the local economy, provide jobs, and improve infrastructure. City officials in Kobe, Japan, were able to entice multinationals Procter & Gamble, Nestlé, and Eli Lilly to locate their Japanese headquarters in the city through traditional marketing techniques, with careful targeting and positioning.[56] Across the globe, after seeing its name being used to help sell everything from pizza to perfume to blinds, the city of Venice made it a priority to capitalize on its image. City officials developed a trademark that could be licensed to product marketers.[57] Hong Kong officials also developed a symbol—a stylized dragon—to represent their city's core brand values.[58]

Countries all over the world are being marketed like any other brand. In some cases, negative perceptions must be overcome. Research by the British Council in 2000 revealed that young opinion leaders in 28 countries saw Britons as weak on creativity and innovation, class-ridden, racist, and cold. Emphasizing the country's traditional values and heritage, as has typically been done, might only exacerbate the situation. One commentator's recommendation was to concentrate on the 1,700 foreign media correspondents in London who play a critical role in conveying the British image to their respective countries.[59]

Attitudes toward country of origin can change over time. Before World War II, Japan had a poor quality image. The success of Sony and its Trinitron TV sets and Japanese automakers Honda and Toyota helped to change people's opinions. Relying partly on the global success of Nokia, Finland launched a campaign to enhance its image as a center of high-tech innovation.[60] "Marketing Insight: The Ups and Downs of Brand America" describes some of the issues that arose due to the anti-American sentiment after the commencement of the Iraq war in 2003.

Consumer Perceptions of Country of Origin

Global marketers know that buyers hold distinct attitudes and beliefs about brands or products from different countries.[61] These country-of-origin perceptions can affect consumer decision making directly and indirectly. The perceptions may be included as an attribute in

Hong Kong's trademark, a stylized dragon with the tagline "Asia's world city."

decision making or influence other attributes in the process ("if it is French, it must be stylish"). The mere fact that a brand is perceived as being successful on a global stage may lend credibility and respect.[62] Several studies have found the following:[63]

- People are often ethnocentric and favorably predisposed to their own country's products, unless they come from a less developed country.
- The more favorable a country's image, the more prominently the "Made in . . ." label should be displayed.
- The impact of country of origin varies with the type of product. Consumers want to know where a car was made but not the lubricating oil.
- Certain countries enjoy a reputation for certain goods: Japan for automobiles and consumer electronics; the United States for high-tech innovations, soft drinks, toys, cigarettes, and jeans; France for wine, perfume, and luxury goods.
- Sometimes country-of-origin perception can encompass an entire country's products. In one study, Chinese consumers in Hong Kong perceived American products as prestigious, Japanese products as innovative, and Chinese products as cheap.

The favorability of country-of-origin perceptions must be considered both from a domestic and foreign perspective. In the domestic market, country-of-origin perceptions may stir consumers' patriotic notions or remind them of their past. As international trade grows, consumers may view certain brands as symbolically important in their own cultural heritage and identity. Patriotic appeals have been the basis of marketing strategies all over the world. Patriotic appeals, however, can lack uniqueness and even be overused. For example, during the Reagan administration in the 1980s, a number of different U.S. brands in a diverse range of product categories (e.g., cars, beer, clothing, etc.) used pro-American themes in their advertising, perhaps diluting the efforts of all as a result.

A company has several options when its products are competitively priced but their place of origin turns consumers off. The company can consider co-production with a foreign company that has a better name: South Korea could make a fine leather jacket that it sends to Italy for finishing; or the company can adopt a strategy to achieve world-class quality in the local industry, as is the case with Belgian chocolates, Polish ham, and Colombian coffee.

Companies can target niches to establish a footing in new markets. China's leading maker of refrigerators, washing machines, and air conditioners, Haier, is building a beachhead in the United States with American college students who loyally buy its

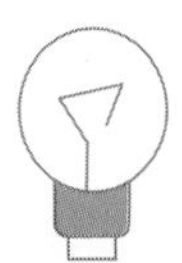

MARKETING INSIGHT | THE UPS AND DOWNS OF BRAND AMERICA

One concern for global marketers is how political issues about their domestic country can spill over to influence consumers' perceptions of their products and services in overseas markets. As the United States found itself at odds with other countries in recent years over various issues, including the war in Iraq, marketers wondered how it might influence the effectiveness of their marketing programs.

Initially, the answer appeared to be little. As one protester against the U.S. policy on North Korea observed, "Calling for political independence is one thing, and liking American brands is another. I like IBM, Dell, Microsoft, Starbucks, and Coke." Many consumers seemed willing to separate politics and products. American technology was widely admired and young people all over the world continued to embrace American youth culture. Perhaps the most compelling example of the power of American brands overseas is the fact that McDonald's most successful market in Europe has been France, a country often dismissive of American politics and culture.

Part of the explanation for this mental compartmentalization may be the way these global American brands had been built and marketed over the years. Many of them successfully tapped into universal consumer values and needs—such as Nike with athletic performance, Levi's with rugged individualism, and Coca-Cola with youthful optimism. Further, these firms hire thousands of employees and make sure their products and marketing activities are consistent with local sensibilities.

Many of these same brands also had gone to great lengths through the years to weave themselves into the cultural fabric of their foreign markets. One story told by a Coca-Cola executive is about a young child visiting America from Japan who commented to her parents on seeing a Coca-Cola vending machine—"Look, they have Coca-Cola too!" As far as she was concerned, Coca-Cola was a Japanese brand.

In some cases, consumers actually don't know where brands come from, either because the brand has become so intertwined with multiple countries or the country of origin is just not that well known. In surveys, consumers routinely guess that Heineken is German and that Nokia is Japanese (Dutch and Finnish, respectively). Few consumers know that Häagen-Dazs and Estée Lauder originated in the United States.

Concerned about a potentially tarnished American image, Charlotte Beers, former chief executive of the Ogilvy & Mather ad agency, was sworn in as President Bush's Under Secretary for Public Diplomacy and Public Affairs on October 2, 2001, and charged with helping to improve the national reputation in the Middle East, where public perceptions were especially negative. Despite these efforts, as time wore on after the commencement of the Iraq war, some U.S. brands such as McDonald's, Coca-Cola, Microsoft, and Yahoo! did appear to sustain some tarnishing of their images.

Sources: Janet Guyon, "Brand America," *Fortune,* October 27, 2003, pp. 179–182; Richard Tompkins, "As Hostility Towards America Grows, Will the World Lose Its Appetite for Coca-Cola, McDonald's and Nike," *Financial Times,* March 27, 2003, p. 13; Gerry Kermouch and Diane Brady, "Brands in an Age of Anti-Americanism, *BusinessWeek,* August 4, 2003, pp. 69–78; Parija Bhatnagar, "U.S. Brands Losing Luster," *CNN/Money,* May 21, 2004; "Burgers and Fries a la Francaise," *The Economist,* April 17, 2004, pp. 60–61.

mini-fridges, which are sold at Wal-Mart and elsewhere.[64] Haier's long-term plans are to introduce innovative products in other areas, such as flat-screen TV sets and wine-cooling cabinets.

As progress is made, companies can start to build local roots to increase relevance, as exemplified by Toyota.

TOYOTA

Toyota has made sales in North America a top priority. As one executive bluntly stated, "We must Americanize." As proof of their conviction, consider the following. Toyota has become the number-three player in the U.S. car market. In 2001, it sold more vehicles in the United States than in Japan, and over two-thirds of these sales were manufactured locally. An estimated two-thirds of its corporate operating profit comes from the United States. Toyota's U.S. factories and dealerships employ 123,000 Americans—more than Coca-Cola, Microsoft, and Oracle combined.[65]

Toyota is not alone in emphasizing the American market. BMW sold more cars in the United States in 2003 than it did in Germany.[66]

::: Deciding on the Marketing Organization

Companies manage their international marketing activities in three ways: through export departments, international divisions, or a global organization.

Export Department

A firm normally gets into international marketing by simply shipping out its goods. If its international sales expand, the company organizes an export department consisting of a sales manager and a few assistants. As sales increase, the export department is expanded to include various marketing services so that the company can go after business more aggressively. If the firm moves into joint ventures or direct investment, the export department will no longer be adequate to manage international operations.

International Division

Many companies become involved in several international markets and ventures. Sooner or later they will create international divisions to handle all their international activity. The international division is headed by a division president, who sets goals and budgets and is responsible for the company's international growth.

The international division's corporate staff consists of functional specialists who provide services to various operating units. Operating units can be organized in several ways. First, they can be *geographical organizations*. Reporting to the international-division president might be regional vice presidents for North America, Latin America, Europe, Africa, the Middle East, and the Far East. Reporting to the regional vice presidents are country managers who are responsible for a sales force, sales branches, distributors, and licensees in the respective countries. The operating units may be *world product groups*, each with an international vice president responsible for worldwide sales of each product group. The vice presidents may draw on corporate-staff area specialists for expertise on different geographical areas. Finally, operating units may be *international subsidiaries*, each headed by a president. The various subsidiary presidents report to the president of the international division.

Many multinationals shift between types of organization.

IBM

Part of IBM's massive reorganization strategy has been to put 235,000 employees into 14 customer-focused groups such as oil and gas, entertainment, and financial services. This way a big customer will be able to cut one deal with a central sales office to have IBM computers installed worldwide. Under the old system, a corporate customer with operations in 20 countries had to contract with 20 little Big Blues, each with its own pricing structure and service standards.[67]

Global Organization

Several firms have become truly global organizations. Their top corporate management and staff plan worldwide manufacturing facilities, marketing policies, financial flows, and logistical systems. The global operating units report directly to the chief executive or executive committee, not to the head of an international division. Executives are trained in worldwide operations. Management is recruited from many countries; components and supplies are purchased where they can be obtained at the least cost; and investments are made where the anticipated returns are greatest.

These companies face several organizational complexities. For example, when pricing a company's mainframe computers to a large banking system in Germany, how much influence should the headquarters product manager have? And the company's market manager for the banking sector? And the company's German country manager?

Bartlett and Ghoshal have proposed circumstances under which different approaches work best. In *Managing Across Borders,* they describe forces that favor "global integration" (capital-intensive production, homogeneous demand) versus "national responsiveness" (local standards and barriers, strong local preferences). They distinguish three organizational strategies:[68]

1. ***A global strategy treats the world as a single market*** – This strategy is warranted when the forces for global integration are strong and the forces for national responsiveness are weak. This is true of the consumer electronics market, for example, where most buyers will accept a fairly standardized pocket radio, CD player, or TV. Matsushita has performed better than GE and Philips in the consumer-electronics market because Matsushita operates in a more globally coordinated and standardized way.

2. ***A multinational strategy treats the world as a portfolio of national opportunities*** – This strategy is warranted when the forces favoring national responsiveness are strong and the forces favoring global integration are weak. This is the situation in the branded packaged-goods business (food products, cleaning products). Bartlett and Ghoshal cite Unilever as a better performer than Kao and P&G because Unilever grants more decision-making autonomy to its local branches.
3. ***A "glocal" strategy standardizes certain core elements and localizes other elements*** – This strategy makes sense for an industry (such as telecommunications) where each nation requires some adaptation of its equipment, but the providing company can also standardize some of the core components. Bartlett and Ghoshal cite Ericsson as balancing these considerations better than NEC (too globally oriented) and ITT (too locally oriented).

Many firms seek a blend of centralized global control from corporate headquarters with input from local and regional marketers. Finding that balance can be tricky. Coca-Cola's "think local, act local" philosophy, which decentralized much of the power and responsibility to design marketing programs and activities, fell apart when many local managers lacked the necessary skills or discipline. Decidedly un-Coke-like ads appeared—such as skinny-dippers streaking down a beach in Italy—and sales stalled. The pendulum swung back, and Coke executives in Atlanta began to play a stronger strategic role again.[69]

SUMMARY :::

1. Despite the many challenges in the international arena (shifting borders, unstable governments, foreign-exchange problems, corruption, and technological pirating), companies selling in global industries need to internationalize their operations. Companies cannot simply stay domestic and expect to maintain their markets.
2. In deciding to go abroad, a company needs to define its international marketing objectives and policies. The company must determine whether to market in a few countries or many countries. It must decide which countries to consider. In general, the candidate countries should be rated on three criteria: market attractiveness, risk, and competitive advantage. Developing countries offer a unique set of opportunities and risks.
3. Once a company decides on a particular country, it must determine the best mode of entry. Its broad choices are indirect exporting, direct exporting, licensing, joint ventures, and direct investment. Each succeeding strategy involves more commitment, risk, control, and profit potential.
4. In deciding on the marketing program, a company must decide how much to adapt its marketing program—product, communications, distribution, and price—to local conditions. At the product level, firms can pursue a strategy of straight extension, product adaptation, or product invention. At the communication level, firms may choose communication adaptation or dual adaptation. At the price level, firms may encounter price escalation and gray markets. At the distribution level, firms need to take a whole-channel view of the challenge of distributing products to the final users. In creating all elements of the marketing program, firms must be aware of the cultural, social, political, technological, environmental, and legal limitations they face in other countries.
5. Country-of-origin perceptions can affect consumers and businesses alike. Managing those perceptions in the most advantageous way possible is an important marketing priority.
6. Depending on the level of international involvement, companies manage their international marketing activity in three ways: through export departments, international divisions, or a global organization.

APPLICATIONS :::

Marketing Debate Is the World Coming Closer Together?

Many social commentators maintain that youth and teens are becoming more and more alike across countries as time goes on. Others, while not disputing that fact, point out that the differences between cultures at even younger ages by far exceed the similarities.

Take a position: People are becoming more and more similar versus The differences between people of different cultures far outweigh their similarities.

Marketing Discussion

Think of some of your favorite brands. Do you know where they come from? Where and how they are made or provided? Do you think it would affect your perceptions of quality or satisfaction?

IN THIS CHAPTER, WE WILL ADDRESS THE FOLLOWING QUESTIONS:

1. What are important trends in marketing practices?
2. What are the keys to effective internal marketing?
3. How can companies be responsible social marketers?
4. How can a company improve its marketing implementation skills?
5. What tools are available to help companies monitor and improve their marketing activities?

CHAPTER 22 ::: MANAGING A HOLISTIC MARKETING ORGANIZATION

twenty two

Healthy long-term growth for a brand requires that the marketing organization be managed properly. Holistic marketers must embrace the complexity of marketing by engaging in a host of carefully planned, interconnected marketing activities.[1] Consider L'Oréal.

L'Oréal, the world's most successful cosmetic company, has experienced almost two decades of double-digit profit growth. The century-old $15.3 billion company has leveraged its cultural heritage and Parisian origins to sell products that make its customers feel special. Higher-than-average R&D expenditures have led to numerous breakthroughs and a strong technological reputation. Innovative products and sexy endorsers such as supermodel Claudia Schiffer, singer Beyoncé Knowles, and actress Heather Locklear have enabled L'Oréal to sustain a premium pricing strategy and justify the enticing slogan, "Because You're Worth It." Although French actress Catherine Deneuve is one of the official company faces, L'Oréal does not offer just one type of beauty in its marketing. The company has skillfully acquired local cosmetics brands, such as Maybelline and Soft Sheen-Carson, and given them a facelift before exporting them around the world. CEO Lindsay Owen-Jones notes: "It's a very carefully crafted portfolio . . . each brand is positioned on a very precise market segment which overlaps as little as possible with others."[2]

>>>

An ad for L'Oréal Paris.

Successful holistic marketing requires effective relationship marketing, integrated marketing, internal marketing, and socially responsible marketing. Previous chapters addressed the first two topics and the strategy and tactics of marketing.[3] In this chapter, we consider internal and socially responsible marketing and how marketing should be administered and conducted responsibly. In our discussion, we look at how firms organize, implement, evaluate, and control marketing activities. We also discuss the increased importance of social responsibility. We begin by examining changes in how companies conduct marketing today.

::: Trends in Marketing Practices

Chapters 1 and 3 describe some important changes in the marketing macroenvironment, such as globalization, deregulation, technological advances, customer empowerment, and market fragmentation. In response to this rapidly changing environment, companies have restructured their business and marketing practices in some of the following ways:

- ***Reengineering.*** Appointing teams to manage customer-value-building processes and break down walls between departments.
- ***Outsourcing.*** Greater willingness to buy more goods and services from outside domestic or foreign vendors.
- ***Benchmarking.*** Studying "best practice companies" to improve performance.
- ***Supplier partnering.*** Increased partnering with fewer but better value-adding suppliers.
- ***Customer partnering.*** Working more closely with customers to add value to their operations.
- ***Merging.*** Acquiring or merging with firms in the same or complementary industries to gain economies of scale and scope.
- ***Globalizing.*** Increased effort to "think global" and "act local."
- ***Flattening.*** Reducing the number of organizational levels to get closer to the customer.
- ***Focusing.*** Determining the most profitable businesses and customers and focusing on them.
- ***Accelerating.*** Designing the organization and setting up processes to respond more quickly to changes in the environment.
- ***Empowering.*** Encouraging and empowering personnel to produce more ideas and take more initiative.

The role of marketing in the organization is also changing.[4] Traditionally, marketers have played the roles of middlemen, charged with understanding customer needs and transmitting the voice of the customer to various functional areas in the organization. In a networked enterprise, every functional area can interact directly with customers. Marketing no longer has sole ownership of customer interactions; rather, marketing needs to integrate all the customer-facing processes so that customers see a single face and hear a single voice when they interact with the firm.

CISCO

Founded in 1984 by two Stanford University computer scientists, Cisco initially built its business on routers and switches to provide end-to-end network solutions. Throughout the 1990s, Cisco fully embraced the Web in its business strategy, going so far as to include the company vision on all employee badges: "The Internet changes the way we work, live, play, and learn." By the end of the decade, however, the company found that placing all its internal and external business operations online was unwieldy and counterproductive. To ensure harmony in its sprawling Web-based strategy, Cisco applied newly introduced Web technology to ensure a unified Internet, intranet, and extranet. The company's goals: "One site . . . many views into the company"[5]

::: Internal Marketing

Internal marketing requires that everyone in the organization buy into the concepts and goals of marketing and engage in choosing, providing, and communicating customer value. Over the years, marketing has evolved as it has grown from work done by the sales department into a complex group of activities spread through the organization.[6] Because simple sales departments were unable to conduct important functions such as marketing research, new-product development, advertising, sales promotion, and customer service, firms began to create marketing departments. When conflict arose between marketing and sales departments, many firms merged the two.

A company can have an excellent marketing department, however, and yet fail at marketing. Much depends on how other company departments view customers. If they point to the marketing department and say, "They do the marketing," the company has not implemented effective marketing. Only when all employees realize that their jobs are to create, serve, and satisfy customers does the company become an effective marketer.[7] "Marketing Memo: Characteristics of Company Departments That Are Truly Customer-Driven" presents a measurement tool that can be used to evaluate which company departments have fully embraced the importance of being customer-driven.[8]

Many companies are now focusing on key processes rather than departments because departmental organization is viewed as a barrier to the smooth performance of fundamental business processes. To achieve customer-related outcomes, companies appoint process leaders who manage cross-disciplinary teams. Marketing and sales people spend an increasing percentage of their time as process team members. As a result, marketing personnel may have a solid-line responsibility to their teams and a dotted-line responsibility to the marketing department. The marketing department is also responsible for training marketing personnel, assigning them to new teams, and evaluating their overall performance.

Let's look at how marketing departments are being organized, how they can work effectively with other departments, and how firms can foster a creative marketing culture within the entire organization.

Organizing the Marketing Department

Modern marketing departments may be organized in a number of different, sometimes overlapping ways:[9] functionally, geographically, by product or brand, by market, in a matrix, by corporate/division.

FUNCTIONAL ORGANIZATION The most common form of marketing organization consists of functional specialists reporting to a marketing vice president, who coordinates their activities. Figure 22.1 shows five specialists. Additional specialists might include a customer service manager, a marketing planning manager, a market logistics manager, a direct marketing manager, and an Internet marketing manager.

The main advantage of a functional marketing organization is its administrative simplicity. It can be quite a challenge to develop smooth working relations, however, within the marketing department.[10] This form also can lose its effectiveness as products and markets increase. A functional organization often leads to inadequate planning for specific products

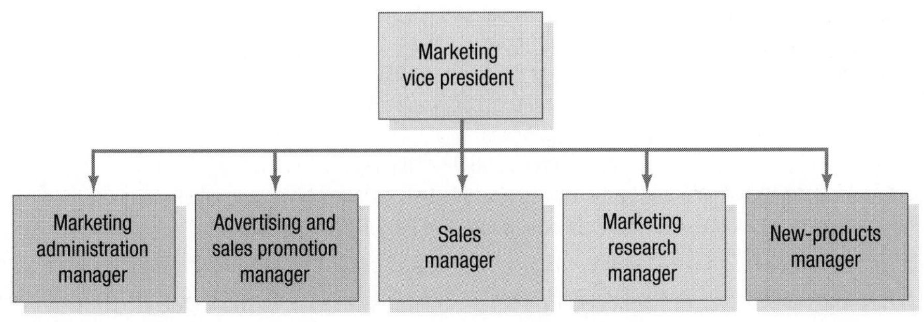

FIG. 22.1

Functional Organization

and markets. Products that are not favored by anyone are neglected. Then, each functional group competes with others for budget and status. The marketing vice president constantly has to weigh the claims of competing functional specialists and faces a difficult coordination problem.

GEOGRAPHIC ORGANIZATION A company selling in a national market often organizes its sales force (and sometimes other functions, including marketing) along geographic lines. The national sales manager may supervise four regional sales managers, who each supervise six zone managers, who in turn supervise eight district sales managers, who supervise ten salespeople.

Several companies are now adding *area market specialists* (regional or local marketing managers) to support the sales efforts in high-volume markets. One such market might be

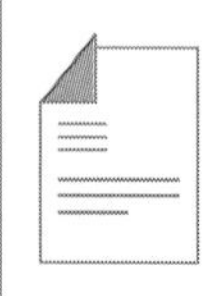

MARKETING MEMO | CHARACTERISTICS OF COMPANY DEPARTMENTS THAT ARE TRULY CUSTOMER-DRIVEN

R&D	___	They spend time meeting customers and listening to their problems.
	___	They welcome the involvement of marketing, manufacturing, and other departments on each new project.
	___	They benchmark competitors' products and seek "best of class" solutions.
	___	They solicit customer reactions and suggestions as the project progresses.
	___	They continuously improve and refine the product on the basis of market feedback.
Purchasing	___	They proactively search for the best suppliers rather than choose only from those who solicit their business.
	___	They build long-term relations with fewer but more reliable high-quality suppliers.
	___	They do not compromise quality for price savings.
Manufacturing	___	They invite customers to visit and tour their plants.
	___	They visit customer factories to see how customers use the company's products.
	___	They willingly work overtime when it is important to meet promised delivery schedules.
	___	They continuously search for ways to produce goods faster and/or at lower costs.
	___	They continuously improve product quality, aiming for zero defects.
	___	They meet customer requirements for "customization" where this can be done profitably.
Marketing	___	They study customer needs and wants in well-defined market segments.
	___	They allocate marketing effort in relation to the long-run profit potential of the targeted segments.
	___	They develop winning offerings for each target segment.
	___	They measure company image and customer satisfaction on a continuous basis.
	___	They continuously gather and evaluate ideas for new products, product improvements, and services to meet customers' needs.
	___	They influence all company departments and employees to be customer-centered in their thinking and practice.
Sales	___	They have specialized knowledge of the customer's industry.
	___	They strive to give the customer "the best solution."
	___	They make only promises that they can keep.
	___	They feed back customers' needs and ideas to those in charge of product development.
	___	They serve the same customers for a long period of time.
Logistics	___	They set a high standard for service delivery time and they meet this standard consistently.
	___	They operate a knowledgeable and friendly customer service department that can answer questions, handle complaints, and resolve problems in a satisfactory and timely manner.
Accounting	___	They prepare periodic "profitability" reports by product, market segment, geographic areas (regions, sales territories), order sizes, and individual customers.
	___	They prepare invoices tailored to customer needs and answer customer queries courteously and quickly.
Finance	___	They understand and support marketing expenditures (e.g., image advertising) that represent marketing investments that produce long-term customer preference and loyalty.
	___	They tailor the financial package to the customers' financial requirements.
	___	They make quick decisions on customer creditworthiness.
Public Relations	___	They disseminate favorable news about the company and they "damage control" unfavorable news.
	___	They act as an internal customer and public advocate for better company policies and practices.
Other Customer Contact Personnel	___	They are competent, courteous, cheerful, credible, reliable, and responsive.

Miami, Florida, where 46 percent of the households are Latino. The Miami specialist would know Miami's customer and trade makeup, help marketing managers at headquarters adjust their marketing mix for Miami, and prepare local annual and long-range plans for selling all the company's products in Miami.

Improved information and marketing research technologies have spurred regionalization. Data from retail-store scanners allow instant tracking of product sales, helping companies pinpoint local problems and opportunities. Retailers themselves strongly prefer local programs aimed at consumers in their cities and neighborhoods. To keep retailers happy, manufacturers now create more local marketing plans.

Companies that have shifted to a greater regional marketing emphasis are McDonald's, which now spends about 50 percent of its total advertising budget regionally; American Airlines, which realized that the travel needs of Chicagoans and Southwesterners are very different in the winter months; and Anheuser-Busch, which has subdivided its regional markets into ethnic and demographic segments, with different ad campaigns for each. Some companies have to develop different marketing programs in different parts of the country out of necessity because their brand development varies so much.

PACE

In 1947, a young Texan named David Pace had a passion for producing the freshest-tasting picante sauce. Experimenting with ingredients and bottling techniques, the final product he produced—a special blend of tomatoes, onions, and jalapeños and a unique production process—became Pace Picante Sauce. Over time, the company launched Pace salsa before being acquired by the Campbell Soup Company in 1994. Pace's historical strength, however, is west of the Mississippi. The brand registers only single digits in market share in the Northeast. The vast disparity in regional strengths has led to tailored marketing programs in different parts of the country. Pace's trailgating tour, blending cowboy-style chuckwagon cooking and tailgate barbecuing, coincides with its rodeo event sponsorship and appeals to the core customer base; New England promotions are designed for trial and market penetration.[11]

PRODUCT- OR BRAND-MANAGEMENT ORGANIZATION Companies producing a variety of products and brands often establish a product- (or brand-) management organization. The product-management organization does not replace the functional organization, but serves as another layer of management. A product manager supervises product category managers, who in turn supervise specific product and brand managers.

A product-management organization makes sense if the company's products are quite different, or if the sheer number of products is beyond the ability of a functional organization to handle. Kraft has used a product-management organization in its Post division, with separate product category managers in charge of cereals, pet food, and beverages. Within the cereal-product group, Kraft has had separate subcategory managers for nutritional cereals, children's presweetened cereals, family cereals, and miscellaneous cereals.

Product and brand management is sometimes characterized as a **hub-and-spoke** system. The brand or product manager is figuratively at the center with spokes emanating out to various departments (see Figure 22.2). Some of the tasks that product or brand managers may perform include:

- Developing a long-range and competitive strategy for the product.
- Preparing an annual marketing plan and sales forecast.
- Working with advertising and merchandising agencies to develop copy, programs, and campaigns.
- Increasing support of the product among the sales force and distributors.
- Gathering continuous intelligence on the product's performance, customer and dealer attitudes, and new problems and opportunities.
- Initiating product improvements to meet changing market needs.

The product-management organization has several advantages. The product manager can concentrate on developing a cost-effective marketing mix for the product; he or she can react more quickly to new products in the marketplace; the company's smaller brands have a product advocate. However, this organization has some disadvantages too:

FIG. 22.2

The Product Manager's Interactions

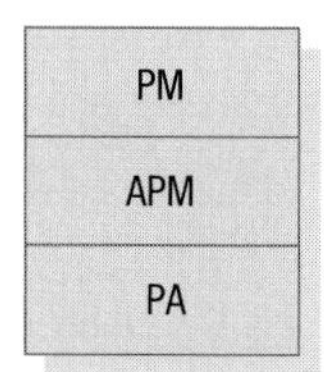

(a) Vertical Product Team

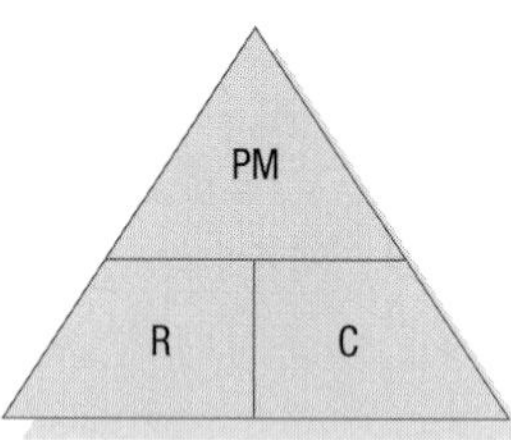

(b) Triangular Product Team

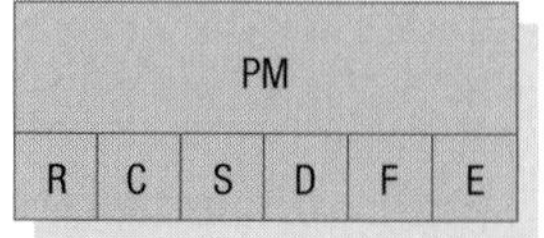

(c) Horizontal Product Team

PM = product manager
AP = associate product manager
PA = product assistant
R = market researcher
C = communication specialist
S = sales manager
D = distribution specialist
F = finance/accounting specialist
E = engineer

FIG. 22.3

Three Types of Product Teams

- Product managers and specifically brand managers are not given enough authority to carry out their responsibilities. They have to rely on persuasion to get the cooperation of other departments.
- Product and brand managers become experts in their product area but rarely achieve functional expertise. They vacillate between acting as experts and having to defer to real experts.
- The product management system often turns out to be costly. One person is appointed to manage each major product or brand and soon managers are appointed to manage even minor products and brands.
- Brand managers normally manage a brand for only a short time. Short-term involvement leads to short-term planning and plays havoc with building long-term strengths.
- The fragmentation of markets makes it harder to develop a national strategy from headquarters. Brand managers must increasingly please regional and local sales groups, resulting in a transfer of power from marketing to sales.
- Product and brand managers cause the company to focus on building market share rather than building the customer relationship. Yet the customer relationship, not the brand, may be the primary lever for value creation.

A second alternative with a product-management organization is to switch from product managers to *product teams.* There are three types of potential product-team structures: vertical product team, triangular product team, and the horizontal product team (see Figure 22.3).

The triangular and horizontal product-team approaches are favored by those who advocate brand-asset management. They believe that each major brand should be run by a ***brand-asset management team (BAMT)*** consisting of key representatives from major functions affecting the brand's performance. The company is comprised of several BAMTs which periodically report to a BAMT Directors Committee, which itself reports to a Chief Branding Officer. This is quite different from the way brands have traditionally been handled.

A third alternative for product-management organization is to eliminate product manager positions for minor products and assign two or more products to each remaining manager. This is feasible where two or more products appeal to a similar set of needs. A cosmetics company does not need separate product managers for each product because cosmetics serve one major need—beauty. A toiletries company needs different managers for headache remedies, toothpaste, soap, and shampoo, because these products differ in use and appeal.

A fourth alternative for product-management organization is to introduce *category management,* in which a company focuses on product categories to manage its brands. Procter & Gamble, pioneers of the brand-management system, and several other top firms have made a significant shift in recent years to category management.[12,13,14]

manufacturing consultants
maintenance specialists
nanotechnologists
service providers
global expanders
silicone suppliers
imagination stimulators
technology innovators
plant converters
wish fulfillers
photonics pioneers
profitability maximizers
product enhancers
cost reducers
contract manufacturers
dream realizers
tech support providers
efficiency experts
automation engineers
product developers
troubleshooters
design enablers
productivity increasers
future inventors
Which Dow Corning do you need today?
Even if you don't need silicones, you may still need us. Like the U.S. company that was looking to expand to Brazil. We listened and learned and provided exactly what they needed — not silicones, but contract manufacturing to facilitate their expansion. To find out how Dow Corning can help you in unexpected ways, visit us at www.dowcorningnow.com.
We help you invent the future.™
DOW CORNING

A print ad spells out the services Dow Corning can provide for customers. Dow Corning uses a horizontal product team organization. Teams consist of from five to eight people, and each team manages a specific product, market, and process.

P&G cites a number of advantages to a category-management structure. By fostering internal competition among brand managers, the traditional brand-management system created strong incentives to excel, but also much internal competition for resources and a lack of coordination. Whereas a smaller share category might have become relatively neglected before (e.g., in product categories such as "hard surface cleaners"), the new scheme was designed to ensure that all categories would be able to receive adequate resources.

Another rationale for category management is the increasing power of the trade. Because the retail trade has tended to think in terms of product categories and the profitability derived from different departments and sections of their stores, P&G felt it only made sense for it to deal with the trade along similar lines. Retailers such as Wal-Mart and regional grocery chains such as Dominick's have embraced category management themselves as a means to define a particular product category's strategic role within the store and to address such operating issues as logistics, the role of private-label products, and the trade-offs between offering product variety and avoiding inefficient duplication.

Category management is not a panacea. It is still a product-driven system. Colgate has moved from brand management (Colgate toothpaste) to category management (toothpaste category) to a new stage called "customer-need management" (mouth care). This last step finally focuses the organization on a basic customer need.[15]

MARKET-MANAGEMENT ORGANIZATION Many companies sell their products to different markets. Canon sells its fax machines to consumer, business, and government markets. U.S. Steel sells its steel to the railroad, construction, and public utility industries. When customers fall into different user groups with distinct buying preferences and practices, a ***market-management organization*** is desirable. A market manager supervises several market managers (also called market-development managers, market specialists, or industry specialists). The market managers draw on functional services as needed. Market managers of important markets might even have functional specialists reporting to them.

FIG. 22.4

Product- /Market-Management Matrix System

Product Managers	Menswear	Women's wear	Home furnishings	Industrial markets
Rayon				
Acetate				
Nylon				
Orlon				
Dacron				

(Column heading: Market Managers)

Market managers are staff (not line) people, with duties similar to those of product managers. Market managers develop long-range and annual plans for their markets. Their performance is judged by their market's growth and profitability. This system carries many of the same advantages and disadvantages of product-management systems. Its strongest advantage is that the marketing activity is organized to meet the needs of distinct customer groups rather than being focused on marketing functions, regions, or products. Many companies are reorganizing along market lines and becoming ***market-centered organizations***. Xerox has converted from geographic selling to selling by industry, as have IBM and Hewlett-Packard.

In a ***customer-management organization***, companies can organize themselves to understand and deal with individual customers rather than with the mass market or even market segments.

MATRIX-MANAGEMENT ORGANIZATION Companies that produce many products flowing into many markets may adopt a matrix organization. DuPont was a pioneer in developing the matrix structure (see Figure 22.4).

DUPONT

Before being spun off, DuPont's textile fibers department consisted of separate product managers for rayon, acetate, nylon, orlon, and dacron; and separate market managers for menswear, women's wear, home furnishings, and industrial markets. The product managers planned the sales and profits for their respective fibers. They asked market managers to estimate how much of their fiber they could sell in each market at a proposed price. Market managers, however, were generally more interested in meeting their market's needs than pushing a particular fiber. In preparing their market plans, they asked each product manager about the fiber's planned prices and availabilities. The final sales forecast of the market managers and the product managers should have added up to the same grand total.

Companies like DuPont can go one step further and view the market managers as the main marketers, and their product managers as suppliers. The menswear market manager, for example, would be empowered to buy textile fibers from DuPont's product managers or, if DuPont's price is too high, from outside suppliers. This system would force Dupont product managers to become more efficient. If a DuPont product manager could not match the "arm's-length pricing" levels of competitive suppliers, then perhaps Dupont should not continue to produce that fiber.

A matrix organization would seem desirable in a multiproduct, multimarket company. The rub is that this system is costly and often creates conflicts. There is the cost of supporting all the managers. There are also questions about where authority and responsibility should reside.

Matrix management gained advocates because companies provide the context in which a matrix can thrive—flat, lean team organizations focused around business processes that cut horizontally across functions.[16]

CORPORATE-DIVISIONAL ORGANIZATION As multiproduct, multimarket companies grow, they often convert their larger product or market groups into separate divisions. The divisions set up their own departments and services. This raises the question of what marketing services and activities should be retained at company headquarters. Divisionalized companies have reached different answers to this question:

- ***No Corporate Marketing.*** Some companies lack a corporate marketing staff. They do not see any useful function for marketing at the corporate level. Each division has its own marketing department.
- ***Moderate Corporate Marketing.*** Some companies have a small corporate marketing staff that performs a few functions, primarily (1) assisting top management with overall opportunity evaluation, (2) providing divisions with consulting assistance on request, (3) helping divisions that have little or no marketing, and (4) promoting the marketing concept throughout the company.
- ***Strong Corporate Marketing.*** Some companies have a corporate marketing staff that, in addition to the preceding activities, also provides various marketing services to the divisions, such as specialized advertising services, sales promotion services, marketing research services, and sales administration services.

Regardless of how formalized corporate marketing is, certain activities must occur within the organization in a "top-down" fashion. Webster sees the role of marketing at the corporate level as:[17]

1. To promote a culture of customer orientation and to be an advocate for the customer in the deliberations of top-management strategy formulators.
2. To assess market attractiveness by analyzing customer needs and wants and competitive offerings.
3. To develop the firm's overall value proposition, the vision and articulation of how it proposes to deliver superior value to customers.

Relations with Other Departments

In principle, all business functions should interact harmoniously to pursue the firm's overall objectives. In practice, however, interdepartmental relations are often characterized by deep rivalries and distrust. Some conflict stems from differences of opinion as to what is in the company's best interests, some from real trade-offs between departmental well-being and company well-being, and some from unfortunate stereotypes and prejudices.

In the typical organization, each business function has a potential impact on customer satisfaction. Under the marketing concept, all departments need to "think customer" and work together to satisfy customer needs and expectations. The marketing department must drive this point home. The marketing vice president, or CMO, has two tasks: (1) to coordinate the company's internal marketing activities and (2) to coordinate marketing with finance, operations, and other company functions to serve the customer.

Yet, there is little agreement on how much influence and authority marketing should have over other departments. Typically, the marketing vice president must work through persuasion rather than authority. Other departments often resist changing their ways of working to fulfill the customer's interests. Inevitably, departments define company problems and goals from their viewpoint, so conflicts of interest are unavoidable. Breakdowns in communication further exacerbate the problem. Consider the following potential negative reactions that marketing can receive from different functional groups.

- ***Engineering*** comes into conflict with marketing executives when the latter want several models produced, often with product features requiring custom components. Engineers often think of marketing people as inept technically, as continually changing priorities, and as not fully credible or trustworthy.
- ***Purchasing Executives*** see marketing executives pushing for several models in a product line, which requires purchasing small quantities of many items rather than large quantities of few items. They think that marketing insists on too high a quality for materials and components. They also dislike marketing's forecasting inaccuracy, which causes them to place rush orders at unfavorable prices or to carry excessive inventories.
- ***Financial Executives*** suspect that marketing forecasts are self-serving. They think marketers are too quick to slash prices to win orders, instead of pricing to make a profit. They claim that marketers "know the value of everything and cost of nothing."
- ***Accountants*** see marketing people as lax in providing sales reports on time. They dislike the special deals salespeople make with customers because these require special accounting

procedures. Credit officers evaluate potential customers' credit standing and deny or limit credit to the more doubtful ones. They think marketers will sell to anyone, including those from whom payment is doubtful.

Companies need to develop a balanced orientation in which marketing and other functions jointly determine what is in the company's best interests. Solutions include joint seminars to understand each others' viewpoints, joint committees and liaison personnel, personnel exchange programs, and analytical methods to determine the most profitable course of action.[18]

Perhaps the best solution is for marketing to periodically propose a *function-to-function* meeting with departments where greater understanding and collaboration is warranted. Even if each function indulges in stereotypical charges and complaints about the other, such a meeting can lead to a clearing of the air and a basis for a more constructive collaboration. Each department needs to understand the operating logic of the other departments. When departments work together toward common goals, marketing is more effective.

PROCTER & GAMBLE

With 19 of their 20 largest brands gaining share and a stock price that doubled, Procter & Gamble was clearly on a roll during 2002–2004. Organic growth in core businesses provided much of the impetus. P&G's new product hit rate, defined in terms of when returns exceeded the cost of capital, was 70 percent to 90 percent. Although this extraordinary performance was due to many factors, close interactions between marketing and 7,500 R&D personnel worldwide was critical. To facilitate interaction, problems and solutions are posted on an internal Web site and "communities of practice" dedicated to particular expertise (e.g., "whiteners") meet frequently. Joint collaboration between different units of P&G has produced such diverse products as Crest Whitestrips teeth whiteners, Iams Dental Defense tartar-fighting pet food, and Olay Daily facials cleansing cloths. Mr. Clean AutoDry carwash system was designed with input from R&D experts who worked on the Pur water purification and Cascade automatic dishwasher powder brands.[19]

Building a Creative Marketing Organization

Many companies are beginning to realize that they are not really market- and customer-driven—they are product-and-sales driven. Companies such as Baxter, General Motors, Shell, and J.P. Morgan are attempting to transform themselves into true market-driven companies. This will require:

1. Developing a company-wide passion for customers.
2. Organizing around customer segments instead of around products.
3. Developing a deep understanding of customers through qualitative and quantitative research.

The payoffs are considerable. Two researchers recently concluded: "We found that the more aggressive a company's customer-focused strategy, the higher its productivity. Those with a customer focus were almost 7 percent more productive than their competitors."[20]

The task is not easy. It will not happen as a result of the CEO making speeches and urging every employee to "think customer." The change will require a change in job and department definitions, responsibilities, incentives, and relationships. See "Marketing Insight: The Marketing CEO" for actions a CEO can take to improve marketing capabilities.

Although it is necessary in a hypercompetitive economy that an organization be customer-oriented, it is not enough. The organization must also be creative. Companies today copy each others' advantages and strategies with increasing speed. Differentiation gets harder to achieve, let alone maintain. Margins fall when firms become more alike. The only answer is for the firm to build a capability in strategic innovation and imagination (see "Marketing Insight: Fueling Strategic Innovation"). This capability comes from assembling tools, processes, skills, and measures that will enable the firm to generate more and better new ideas than its competitors.[21]

Companies must watch trends and be ready to capitalize on them. Motorola was 18 months late in moving from analog to digital cellular phones, giving Nokia and Ericsson a big lead. Barnes & Noble was late in recognizing online ordering of books and music, giving Amazon the lead. Nestlé was late in recognizing the trend toward coffeehouses such as Starbucks. Coca-Cola was slow in recognizing beverage trends toward fruit-flavored drinks such as Snapple, energy drinks such as Gatorade, and designer water

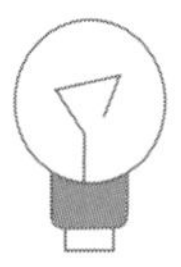

MARKETING INSIGHT | THE MARKETING CEO

What steps can a CEO take to create a market- and customer-focused company?

1. ***Convince Senior Management of the Need to Become Customer-Focused:*** The CEO personally exemplifies strong customer commitment and rewards those in the organization who do likewise. For example, former CEOs Jack Welch of GE and Lou Gerstner of IBM are said to have spent 100 days a year visiting with customers, in spite of their many strategic, financial, and administrative burdens; and IBM's top 470 executives are personally responsible for more than 1,300 customer accounts.
2. ***Appoint a Senior Marketing Officer and Marketing Task Force:*** The marketing task force should include the CEO; the vice presidents of sales, R&D, purchasing, manufacturing, finance, and human resources; and other key individuals.
3. ***Get Outside Help and Guidance:*** Consulting firms have considerable experience in helping companies move toward a marketing orientation.
4. ***Change the Company's Reward Measurement and System:*** As long as purchasing and manufacturing are rewarded for keeping costs low, they will resist accepting some costs required to serve customers better. As long as finance focuses on short-term profit, it will oppose major investments designed to build satisfied, loyal customers.
5. ***Hire Strong Marketing Talent:*** The company needs a strong marketing vice president who not only manages the marketing department but also gains respect from and influence with the other vice presidents. A multidivisional company would benefit from establishing a strong corporate marketing department.
6. ***Develop Strong In-house Marketing Training Programs:*** The company should design well-crafted marketing training programs for corporate management, divisional general managers, marketing and sales personnel, manufacturing personnel, R&D personnel, and others. GE, Motorola, and Accenture run these programs.
7. ***Install a Modern Marketing Planning System:*** The planning format will require managers to think about the marketing environment, opportunities, competitive trends, and other forces. These managers then prepare strategies and sales-and-profit forecasts for specific products and segments and are accountable for performance.
8. ***Establish an Annual Marketing Excellence Recognition Program:*** Business units that believe they have developed exemplary marketing plans should submit a description of their plans and results. The winning teams would be rewarded at a special ceremony. The plans would be disseminated to the other business units as "models of marketing thinking." Such programs are carried on by Accenture, Becton-Dickenson, and DuPont.
9. ***Shift from a Department Focus to a Process-Outcome Focus:*** After defining the fundamental business processes that determine its success, the company should appoint process leaders and cross-disciplinary teams to reengineer and implement these processes.
10. ***Empower the Employees:*** Progressive companies encourage and reward their employees for coming up with new ideas. They also empower them to settle customer complaints in order to save the customer's business. IBM, for example, lets its frontline employees spend up to $5,000 to solve a customer problem on the spot.

brands. The company is now fiercely playing catch-up, using innovation to challenge these category leaders with Fruitopia noncarbonated fruit beverage, POWERade energy drink, and Dasani water.

POWERADE

Challenging leader Gatorade in the energy drink market has been a tough task. After introducing several innovations subsequent to its launch in 1990, such as sports cap packaging and offbeat flavors, Coca-Cola found its POWERade brand was stagnating by the end of the decade. Relaunched in 2001, the brand was positioned on the basis of active consumer lifestyles as "Fuel for Life" to distinguish it from sports-focused Gatorade. The logo was completely revamped to feature a snake-like "P," and the product was reformulated with B vitamins. Ads themed "Very Real Power" showed athletes doing seemingly impossible feats by virtue of realistic special effects. Innovation has continued to drive a turnaround in sales. In the summer of 2003, the company introduced special edition Martix Reloaded POWERade with a custom-shaped package and new flavor to create a tie-in with the blockbuster movie franchise. Other special editions tied to the Olympics, NASCAR, and NHRA followed. September 2004 saw the launch of sourberry-flavored POWERade FLAVA23, backed by an integrated marketing program that featured a DC Comics depiction of NBA star and POWERade spokesman LeBron James.[22]

Market leaders tend to miss trends when they are risk-averse, obsessed about protecting their existing markets and physical resources, and more interested in efficiency than innovation.

::: Socially Responsible Marketing

Effective internal marketing must be matched by a strong sense of social responsibility.[23] Companies need to evaluate whether they are truly practicing ethical and socially responsible marketing. Several forces are driving companies to practice a higher level of corporate social responsibility: rising customer expectations, changing employee expectations, government legislation and pressure, investor interest in social criteria, and changing business procurement practices.[24]

Business success and continually satisfying the customer and other stakeholders are closely tied to adoption and implementation of high standards of business and marketing conduct. The most admired companies in the world abide by a code of serving people's interests, not only their own.

Business practices are often under attack because business situations routinely pose tough ethical dilemmas. The issues are complicated: It is not easy to draw a clear line between normal marketing practice and unethical behavior. At the same time, certain business practices are clearly unethical or illegal. These include bribery or stealing trade secrets; false and deceptive advertising; exclusive dealing and tying agreements; quality or safety defects; false warranties; inaccurate labeling; price-fixing or undue discrimination; and barriers to entry and predatory competition.

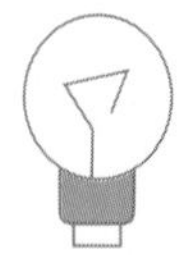

MARKETING **INSIGHT** | FUELING STRATEGIC INNOVATION

Professor Stephen Brown of Ulster University has challenged a number of fundamental assumptions underlying the marketing concept. He thinks that marketers make too much of researching and satisfying consumers, and as a result, risk losing marketing imagination and significant consumer impact. Here are his criticisms:

1. If marketers pay too much attention to what consumers say they need or want, marketers will simply make products similar to those that already exist. Consumers normally start from what they know, not from what might be possible. For example, they might say they want a smaller cellular phone but would not ask for one that includes a Palm Pilot or voice recognition. It is the marketer's job to go beyond what customers say they want.
2. The marketing concept assumes that consumers have clear goals and pursue them rationally. But consumers are buffeted by all kinds of forces. Many respond to hyped products and stories. Therefore marketers need skills beyond APIC—analysis, planning, implementation, and control. Marketers need to be able to create dramas, new realities, artificial scarcities, celebrations, and the like.
3. The marketing concept implies that marketers must be submissive to customers, and go all out to please them. Any suggestion that marketers might "play" with the customer, even manipulate the public, is taboo. Yet some of the greatest marketers of the past, such as P.T. Barnum, teased the public, overdramatized offerings, and yet the public loved it. Why should the customer be dominant and the marketer always be submissive?

How can companies build a capability for strategic innovation? Here are some approaches:

- Hire some marketers who are unusually creative to counterbalance the majority who do marketing by the textbook. These people may be more unconventional, more rule-breaking, more risk-taking, and even more argumentative, but their ideas will at least present a challenge.
- Train your employees in the use of creativity techniques, including group techniques (brainstorming, synectics) and individual techniques (visualization, attribute listing, forced relationships, morphological analysis, mind-mapping).
- List observable trends such as longer working hours, single parents, and new life styles, and tease out their implications for your firm.
- List unmet needs and imagine new offerings or solutions: how to help people lose weight, stop smoking, relieve stress, meet others, and so on.
- Set up rewards and prizes for new ideas. Run a "best idea" competition once a month. Give a cash reward, extra vacation time, or travel awards to those who come up with the best ideas.
- Senior managers should take small sets of employees out to lunch or dinner once a week to discuss ideas they might have on improving the business. Sometimes take them into new settings, such as a wrestling match, a drug rehabilitation center, a poor neighborhood.
- Set up groups of employees to critique the company's and competitors' products and services. Also have them critique the company's cherished beliefs and consider turning them upside down.
- Occasionally hire creative resources from outside the firm. Many large advertising agencies, such as Leo Burnett, run a creativity service for clients.

Sources: For more on Brown's views, see Stephen Brown, *Marketing—The Retro Revolution* (Thousand Oaks, CA: Sage Publications, 2001). For more on creativity, see Michael Michalko, *Cracking Creativity: The Secrets of Creative Genius* (Berkeley, CA: Ten Speed Press, 1998); James M. Higgins, *101 Creative Problem Solving Techniques* (New York: New Management Publishing Company, 1994); and all of the books by Edward DeBono.

Today companies that do not perform ethically or well are at greater risk of being exposed, thanks to the Internet. In the past, a disgruntled customer might bad-mouth a manufacturer or merchant to 12 other people; today he or she can reach thousands of people on the Internet. Microsoft, for example, has attracted scores of anti-Microsoft sites, including Hate Microsoft and Boycott Microsoft. Well-managed PR campaigns can also have an effect. The Rainforest Action Network launched a punishing PR campaign in 1997 to stop The Home Depot from selling old-growth lumber. After two years of bad publicity and resistance to new store locations, The Home Depot agreed to have its suppliers work with environmental and forestry groups to certify that its wood products are not from endangered areas.[25]

Corporate Social Responsibility

Raising the level of socially responsible marketing calls for a three-pronged attack that relies on proper legal, ethical, and social responsibility behavior.

LEGAL BEHAVIOR Society must use the law to define, as clearly as possible, those practices that are illegal, antisocial, or anticompetitive. Organizations must ensure that every employee knows and observes any relevant laws. For example, sales managers can check that sales representatives know and observe the law, such as the fact that it is illegal for salespeople to lie to consumers or mislead them about the advantages of buying a product. Under U.S. law, salespeople's statements must match advertising claims. In selling to businesses, salespeople may not offer bribes to purchasing agents or others influencing a sale. They may not obtain or use competitors' technical or trade secrets through bribery or industrial espionage. Finally, salespeople must not disparage competitors or competing products by suggesting things that are not true. Every sales representative must understand these laws and act accordingly.[26]

ETHICAL BEHAVIOR Companies must adopt and disseminate a written code of ethics, build a company tradition of ethical behavior, and hold its people fully responsible for observing ethical and legal guidelines.[27] A 1999 poll by Environics International, a public opinion research firm, found that 67 percent of North Americans are willing to buy or boycott products on ethical grounds. In response to heightened consumer sensitivity on the topic, KPMG's 1999 survey of 1,100 global companies found that 24 percent produce annual "sustainability" reports.[28]

SOCIAL RESPONSIBILITY BEHAVIOR Individual marketers must practice a "social conscience" in specific dealings with customers and stakeholders.[29] Increasingly, people say that they want information about a company's record on social and environmental responsibility to help decide which companies to buy from, invest in, and work for.[30] Table 22.1 lists

TABLE 22.1

Top-Rated Companies for Social Responsibility

1.	Johnson & Johnson
2.	Coca-Cola
3.	Wal-Mart
4.	Anheuser-Busch
5.	Hewlett-Packard
6.	Walt Disney
7.	Microsoft
8.	IBM
9.	McDonald's
10.	3M
11.	UPS
12.	FedEx
13.	Target
14.	The Home Depot
15.	General Electric

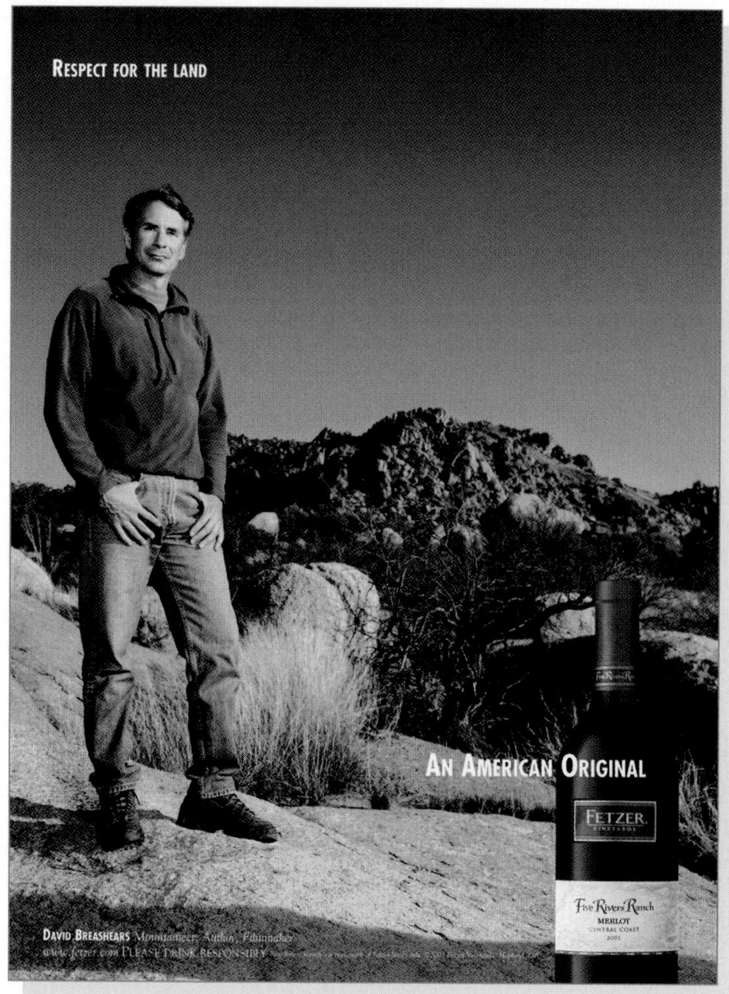

This Fetzer ad reinforces the company's commitment to social responsibility. David Breashears is an author, filmmaker, and world-renowned climber who has ascended Everest several times.

companies who receive high marks for social responsibility. Fetzer Vineyards is one company that has fully embraced social responsibility.

FETZER VINEYARDS

The sixth-largest winery in the United States and winner of many product-quality awards, Fetzer has transformed its business according to the triple bottom line—measuring corporate success by social and environmental impact as well as profit and loss. Every one of the 2,000 acres owned by Fetzer is certified as organic and the vineyards are designated a "zero waste" business by the state of California. Its philosophy even extends to product packaging. To spare trees, labels are made from a plant fiber known as kenaf and printed with soy-based inks; the corks aren't sanitized with chlorine; and the cases are made from recycled cardboard. The winery uses alternative solar and biodiesel energy sources, and broke with convention by providing extensive programs and benefits for part-time workers as well as full-time employees. Even though it belongs to the highly competitive wine industry, Fetzer believes that business and social progress should go hand-in-hand. Its financial and marketing success has led the Wine Institute, a trade group for the California wine industry, to introduce the first statewide sustainable wine-growing practices.[31]

Deciding how to communicate corporate attitudes and behaviors toward social responsibility can be difficult. Corporate philanthropy, for example, poses problems.[32] Merck, DuPont, Wal-Mart, and Bank of America are examples of firms that have donated $100 million or more to charities in a year. Although companies can be credited for good deeds, the deeds can be easily overlooked if not publicized and easily resented if the company is seen as being exploitative or fails to live up to a "good guys" image.[33] Philip Morris Company's $250 million ad campaign touting its charitable activities was met with skepticism because of its negative corporate image.

Socially Responsible Business Models

The future holds a wealth of opportunities for companies.[34] Technological advances in solar energy, online networks, cable and satellite television, biotechnology, and telecommunications promise to change the world as we know it. At the same time, forces in the socioeconomic, cultural, and natural environments will impose new limits on marketing and business practices. Companies that are able to innovate new solutions and values in a socially responsible way are the most likely to succeed.[35]

Many companies such as The Body Shop, Stonyfield Farms, and Smith and Hawken are giving social responsibility a more prominent role. Actor Paul Newman's homemade salad dressing has grown to a huge business.[36] The Newman's Own brand is on additional products such as pasta sauce, salsa, popcorn, and lemonade, and is sold in eight countries. The company has given away all its profits—$150 million—to educational and charitable programs such as the Hole in the Wall Gang camps Newman created for children with serious illnesses. Another example of a company with social responsibility at the core of its business model is Working Assets.

WORKING ASSETS

Working Assets was established in 1985 to help people support causes through everyday activities like talking on the phone. Every time a customer uses one of Working Assets' donation-linked services (Long Distance, Local, Wireless, Credit Card, or Online), the company donates a portion of the customer's bill to nonprofit groups. Working Assets donates at least 1 percent of annual revenues to charity and lets customers vote on which nonprofit groups receive money. To date, $40 million has been raised by the company for causes including Greenpeace, Oxfam America, Rainforest Action Network, Human Rights Watch, Planned Parenthood, Stand for Children, and Doctors Without Borders, among many others. The customers addressed in the company's clever tagline "We make your voice heard" are people who identify themselves as supporters of progressive causes. Working Assets' corporate idealism has had a favorable effect on the bottom line. Revenue shot up from $2 million in 1991 to roughly $300 million in 2003.[37]

Cause-Related Marketing

Many firms are blending their corporate social responsibility initiatives with their marketing activities.[38] **Cause-related marketing** is marketing that links the firm's contributions to a designated cause to customers' engaging directly or indirectly in revenue-producing transactions with the firm.[39] Cause marketing has also been called a part of *corporate societal marketing (CSM)* which Drumwright and Murphy define as marketing efforts "that have at least one non-economic objective related to social welfare and use the resources of the company and/or of its partners."[40] They also include other activities such as traditional and strategic philanthropy and volunteerism as part of CSM.

Cause-related marketing began in earnest in the 1980s. Many observers credit American Express with raising awareness of the mutual benefits of cause-related marketing through its 1983 campaign to help restore the Statue of Liberty. By donating a penny for every credit card transaction and a dollar for each new card issued, American Express gave $1.7 million to the Statue of Liberty—Ellis Island Foundation. In the process, transactions for American Express rose 30 percent, and new cards issued increased by 15 percent during this period.

Cause-related marketing comes in many forms. Tesco, a leading U.K. retailer, has created a "Computers for Schools" program: Customers receive vouchers for every 10 pounds spent, which can be donated to the school of their choice; the school can then exchange the vouchers for new computer equipment. Dawn, the top dishwashing liquid in the United States, launched a campaign highlighting the fact that the product's grease-cleaning power had an unusual side benefit—it could be used to clean birds caught in oil spills. A Web site, www.saveaduck.com, outlines its financial donations and educational program. Nike is the title sponsor of the Nike 26.2 Women's Marathon in San Francisco, whose proceeds go to the Leukemia and Lymphoma Society. In addition, Nike works with more than 60 Indian tribes to help combat Type 2 diabetes by giving sneakers to patients who have their blood tested for diabetes. British Airways has a particularly successful and highly visible program.

BRITISH AIRWAYS

British Airways partnered with UNICEF and developed a cause-marketing campaign called Change for Good. Passengers on British Airways flights are encouraged to donate leftover foreign currency from their travels. The scheme is simple: Passengers deposit their surplus currency in envelopes provided by British Airways, which collects the deposits and donates them directly to UNICEF. British Airways advertises its program during an in-flight video, on the backs of seat cards, and with in-flight announcements. The company also developed a television ad that featured a child thanking British Airways for its contribution to UNICEF. Because Change for Good can be directly targeted to passengers and can produce immediate results, it does not require extensive advertising or promotion and is highly cost-efficient. Since 1994, almost $40 million has been raised and distributed around the world.[41]

CAUSE MARKETING BENEFITS AND COSTS A successful cause marketing program can produce a number of benefits: improving social welfare; creating differentiated brand positioning; building strong consumer bonds; enhancing the company's public image with government officials and other decision makers; creating a reservoir of goodwill; boosting internal morale and galvanizing employees; and driving sales.[42]

By humanizing the firm, consumers may develop a strong, unique bond with the firm that transcends normal marketplace transactions.[43] Some of the specific means by which cause marketing programs can build brand equity with consumers include: (1) building brand awareness, (2) enhancing brand image, (3) establishing brand credibility, (4) evoking brand feelings, (5) creating a sense of brand community, and (6) eliciting brand engagement.[44] Liz Claiborne has exhibited strong commitment to its cause.

LIZ CLAIBORNE

In 1991, at a time when domestic violence was often a taboo or "hot potato" issue, Liz Claiborne developed its Women's Work program against domestic violence, now dubbed, "Love Is Not Abuse." Prior to starting the campaign, the company had conducted research which revealed that 96 percent of its customers believed domestic violence was a problem and 91 percent of those same customers would have a positive opinion of a company that started an awareness campaign about the issue. The major fund-raising event is an annual charity shopping day every October at Liz Claiborne stores across the United States. The company donates 10 percent of sales to local domestic violence organizations. Liz Claiborne also contributes proceeds from the sale of T-shirts, jewelry, and other products related to the campaign. Additionally, the company pays for public service campaigns that appear on television, radio, billboards, and bus shelters and distributes awareness posters, brochures, and mailings. Over the years, Liz Claiborne has also sponsored workshops, surveys, celebrity-endorsed awareness campaigns, and other events.[45]

The danger, however, is that the promotional efforts behind a cause-related marketing program could backfire if cynical consumers question the link between the product and the cause and see the firm as being self-serving and exploitative.[46] For example, Bristol-Meyers Squibb (BMS) supports the Tour de Cure, which funds diabetes research and prevention. On the official Web page of the tour, the BMS logo includes the statement that BMS is "A leader in Type 2 Diabetes Care." This potentially profitable connection between the sponsor and the event may lead some consumers to view BMS's support for the Tour de Cure as opportunistic.[47]

A number of decisions must be made in designing and implementing a cause marketing program, such as how many and which cause(s) to choose and how to brand the cause program.

CHOOSING A CAUSE Some experts believe that the positive impact on a brand from cause-related marketing may be lessened by sporadic involvement with numerous causes. For example, Cathy Chizauskas, Gillette's director of civic affairs, states: "When you're spreading out your giving in fifty-dollar to one-thousand-dollar increments, no one knows what you are doing. . . It doesn't make much of a splash."[48]

Many companies choose to focus on one or a few main causes to simplify execution and maximize impact. One of the more focused cause marketers is McDonald's. Ronald McDonald Houses in more than 20 countries offer more than 5,000 rooms each night to families needing support while their child is in the hospital. Ronald McDonald House program has provided a "home away from home" for nearly 4 million family members since its beginning in 1974.

Limiting support to a single cause, however, may limit the pool of consumers or other stakeholders who could transfer positive feelings from the cause to the firm. In addition, many popular causes already have numerous corporate sponsors. Reportedly, over 300 companies, including Avon, Ford, Estée Lauder, Revlon, Lee Jeans, Polo Ralph Lauren, Yoplait, Saks, BMW, and American Express, currently associate themselves with breast cancer as a cause in some way.[49] As a consequence, the brand may find itself "lost in the shuffle," overlooked in a sea of symbolic pink ribbons.

Opportunities can potentially be greater with "orphan causes"—causes such as diseases that afflict less than 200,000 people.[50] Another option is overlooked diseases, such as pancreatic cancer, which is the fourth-deadliest form of cancer behind skin, lung, and breast and yet has received little or no corporate support.

The LensCrafters Give the Gift of Sight program in action.

Most firms tend to choose causes that fit their corporate or brand image and matter to their employees and shareholders. LensCrafters' Give the Gift of Sight program is a family of charitable vision care programs that has provided free vision screenings, eye exams, and glasses to more than 3 million needy people throughout North America and in developing countries around the world. All stores are empowered to deliver free glasses in their communities. In addition, Give the Gift of Sight sponsors two traveling Vision Vans targeting children in North America as well as monthly two-week optical missions overseas.

BRANDING THE CAUSE MARKETING PROGRAM There are three potential options for branding a cause marketing program:

1. ***Self-branded: Create Own Cause Program.*** The firm takes ownership of a cause and develops an entirely new organization to deliver benefits associated with the cause. The newly created self-branded cause could be branded with the parent brand or an individual product brand. The Ronald McDonald House Charities and the Avon Breast Cancer Crusade are classic examples of self-branded cause entities.
2. ***Co-branded: Link to Existing Cause Program.*** The firm partners with an existing cause. Typically, the identification of the brand affiliation with the cause is only in the form of its designation as a sponsor or supporter—the actual involvement is not branded as a program in any way. Currently, co-branding relationships with causes are the most popular type of activity. An example is Sealy's sponsorship of NASCAR's Victory Junction Gang Camp, which involves the donation of beds to an auto-racing-themed camp for children with life-threatening illnesses.
3. ***Jointly Branded: Link to Existing Cause Program.*** In this hybrid approach, firms partner with an existing cause but explicitly brand the program that links to the cause. An example of this is The Rocky Mountain Challenge, an organized three-day benefit bike ride, which is sponsored by the bike retailer Colorado Cyclist to provide funds for the Tyler Hamilton Foundation for MS, a charity established by the Tour de France cyclist (and University of Colorado graduate).

Co-branding with an existing cause is a means for firms to complement their existing brand image with specific associations that are "borrowed" or "transferred" from a cause. Self-branding can be useful when a firm is trying to augment existing consumer associations via emotional and imagery appeals. Joint branding may permit the best of both worlds by establishing a strong connection with an existing cause but maintaining a distinct identity at the same time.

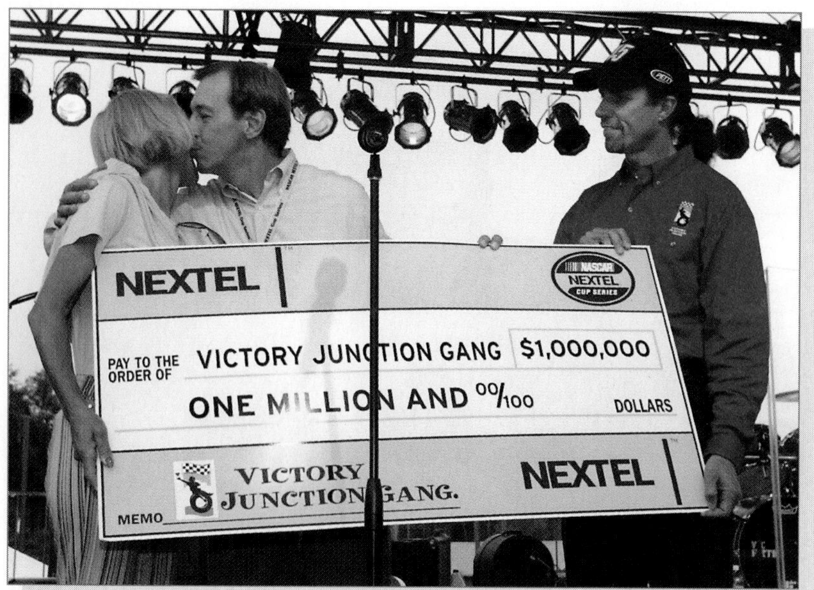

Co-branding: NASCAR racer Kyle Petty and his wife Pattie created the Victory Junction Gang Camp in Randelman NC for special kids. Here they receive a check from Nextel for $1 million.

"Marketing Memo: Making A Difference" provides some tips from a top cause marketing firm.

Social Marketing

Some marketing is conducted to directly address a social problem or cause. Cause-related marketing is done by a company to support a cause. **Social marketing** is done by a nonprofit or government organization to further a cause, such as "say no to drugs" or "exercise more and eat better."[51] The need for social marketing is evident: Consider the following recent facts and figures from 2002.

- An estimated 1 million teens became pregnant.
- 5–10 million adolescent girls and women struggled with eating disorders.
- More than 16,000 people were killed in alcohol-related crashes.
- More than 3,000 children and teens died from gunshot wounds.
- More than 5,000 people on waiting lists for organ transplants died.

Social marketing is a global phenomenon that goes back for years. In the 1950s, India started family planning campaigns. In the 1970s, Sweden started social marketing campaigns to turn the country into a nation of nonsmokers and nondrinkers. In the 1970s, the Australian government ran "Wear Your Seat Belt Campaigns." In the late 1970s, the Canadian government launched campaigns to "Say No to Drugs," "Stop Smoking," and "Exercise for Health." In the 1980s, the World Bank, World Health Organization, and Centers for Disease Control and Prevention started to use the term and promote interest in social marketing. Some notable global social marketing successes include these:

- Oral rehydration therapy in Honduras significantly decreased deaths from diarrhea in small children under the age of 5.
- Social marketers created booths in marketplaces where Ugandan midwives sold contraceptives at affordable prices.
- Population Communication Services created and promoted two extremely popular songs in Latin America, "Stop" and "When We Are Together," to help young women "say no."
- The National Heart, Lung, and Blood Institute successfully raised awareness about cholesterol and high blood pressure, which helped to significantly reduce deaths.

A number of different types of organizations conduct social marketing in the United States. Government agencies include the Centers for Disease Control and Prevention, Departments of Health, Social and Human Services, Department of Transportation, and the U.S. Environmental Protection Agency. Literally hundreds of nonprofit organizations are involved with social marketing, including the American Red Cross, the World Wildlife Fund, and the American Cancer Society.

BOYS & GIRLS CLUB OF AMERICA

Known as "the positive after-school place for kids," the Boys & Girls Club of America serves more than 6 million youngsters annually in 3,400 club locations. The children's time in the program is spent on such activities as sports, recreation, and fitness, as well as on schoolwork, and even on programs centered on character development, leadership, and life skills. Distinguished alumni of the Boys & Girls Club include Bill Cosby, Brad Pitt, and Denzel Washington. In a little over a decade, the organization built a roster of corporate partners to help provide programs and services for its members. The Crest Cavity Free Zone improves dental health of underserved children; Club Tech uses a $100 million cash and in-kind grant from Microsoft to place computers and software in clubs; and Blockbuster's support of the Boys & Girls Clubs' National Kids Day promotion has generated millions in funding.[52]

Choosing the right goal or objective for a social marketing program is critical. Should a family planning campaign focus on abstinence or birth control? Should a campaign to fight air pollution focus on ride-sharing or mass transit? Social marketing campaigns may have objectives related to changing people's cognitions, values, actions, or behaviors. The following examples illustrate the range of possible objectives.

Cognitive campaigns

- Explain the nutritional value of different foods.
- Explain the importance of conservation.

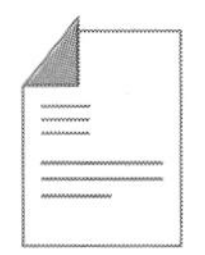

MARKETING MEMO | MAKING A DIFFERENCE

One of the most accomplished cause marketing consulting firms is Boston's Cone, Inc. It offers the following perspectives on the current state of cause marketing and how it should best be practiced:

> With new vigor, consumers, customers, employees, investors and communities are closely watching how companies behave in relation to them and to society. Influential groups such as Business for Social Responsibility, Dow Jones Sustainability Index, *Fortune* magazine and others are judging companies based on a complex series of global standards. Business practices such as governance, philanthropy, sourcing, the environment, employee relations and community relations have moved from behind the scenes to center stage. For executives today, appropriately defining, executing and communicating corporate social responsibility (CSR) has never been more important.

To help execute and communicate CSR more effectively, Cone offers the following considerations:

- ***Define CSR for your company.*** Make sure that your senior executives are all talking about the same thing. CSR includes a broad range of complex internal and external business practices. Although they are vital components of the CSR mix, corporate philanthropy and community relations don't define CSR alone.
- ***Build a diverse team.*** The development and execution of CSR strategies require a collaborative, concerted team effort. Create a decision-making task force that integrates and brings together a range of expertise and resources, including marketing, public affairs, community relations, legal, human resources, manufacturing and others. Put a formal process in place to approach CSR strategy development, ongoing implementation and continuous improvement.
- ***Analyze your current CSR-related activities and revamp them if necessary.*** Do your due diligence at the outset to understand CSR gaps and risks specific to your company. Research industry examples and cull best practices from leading case studies. Make sure to consider global trends, as Europe is far advanced of the U.S.
- ***Forge and strengthen NGO relationships.*** The more than 300,000 non-governmental organizations (NGO) around the world are a powerful force on corporate policies and behavior, serving as both advocates and loud critics. Forge sincere partnerships with organizations that can offer you independent, unbiased insight into and evaluation of your CSR activities; provide expertise on social issues and developing global markets; and offer access to key influentials.
- ***Develop a cause branding initiative.*** Create a public face for your citizenship activities through a signature Cause Branding initiative that integrates philanthropy, community relations, marketing and human resources assets. ConAgra Foods, Feeding Children Better program, for example, is a multi-year initiative created to feed millions of hungry children through innovative partnerships, grant-making, employee volunteerism and education and awareness. This program recently earned ConAgra Foods the U.S. Chamber of Commerce's Corporate Citizenship Award.
- ***Walk your talk.*** Critics often assert that companies exploit CSR as a PR smokescreen to conceal or divert attention from corporate misdeeds and blemishes. Before introducing any new CSR initiative or drawing attention to good corporate behavior, make sure that your company is addressing stakeholder expectations of CSR at the most basic level.
- ***Don't be silent.*** Not only do Americans expect businesses to behave socially, the majority want companies to tell them how they are doing so. An overwhelming majority also say they prefer to find out about CSR activities from a third-party source, particularly the media.
- ***Beware.*** Greater public awareness for your corporate citizenship record can be double-edged. Claims of socially responsible behavior, even sincere ones, often invite public scrutiny. Be prepared. Even if your company is not ready to proactively communicate about your CSR activities, be ready to respond to public inquiries immediately. Don't let the threat of public scrutiny keep you mute, though. More often than not, silence regarding CSR issues is translated as indifference, or worse, inaction.

Sources: Cone Buzz, April 2004. See also, Carol L. Cone, Mark A. Feldman, and Alison T. DaSilva, "Cause and Effects," *Harvard Business Review* (July 2003): 95–101.

Action campaigns

- Attract people for mass immunization.
- Motivate people to vote "yes" on a certain issue.
- Motivate people to donate blood.
- Motivate women to take a pap test.

Behavioral campaigns

- Demotivate cigarette smoking.
- Demotivate hard-drug usage.
- Demotivate excessive consumption of alcohol.

Value campaigns

- Alter ideas about abortion.
- Change attitudes of bigoted people.

Social marketing may employ a number of different tactics to achieve its goals.[53] The social marketing planning process follows many of the same steps as the process for traditional products and services (see Table 22.2). Some key success factors in developing and implementing a social marketing program include:

- Study the literature and previous campaigns.
- Choose target markets that are most ready to respond.
- Promote a single, doable behavior in clear, simple terms.
- Explain the benefits in compelling terms.
- Make it easy to adopt the behavior.
- Develop attention-grabbing messages and media.
- Consider an education-entertainment approach

Given the complexity and challenges of the issues involved with social marketing, it is important to take a long-run view. Social marketing programs take time and may involve a

TABLE 22.2

Social Marketing Planning Process

Where Are We?

- Determine program focus.
- Identify campaign purpose.
- Conduct an analysis of Strengths, Weaknesses, Opportunities, and Threats (SWOT).
- Review past and similar efforts.

Where Do We Want to Go?

- Select target audiences.
- Set objectives and goals.
- Analyze target audiences and the competition.

How Will We Get There?

- Product: Design the market offering.
- Price: Manage costs of behavior change.
- Distribution: Make the product available.
- Communications: Create messages and choose media.

How Will We Stay on Course?

- Develop a plan for evaluation and monitoring.
- Establish budgets and find funding sources.
- Complete an implementation plan.

series of phased programs or actions. For example, take the sequence of actions that have been involved in discouraging smoking: cancer reports, labeling of cigarettes, banning cigarette advertising, education about secondary smoke effects, no smoking in homes, no smoking in restaurants, no smoking on planes, raising taxes on cigarettes to pay for antismoking campaigns, states suing cigarette companies.

The actual success of the social marketing program must be evaluated in terms of the program objectives. Criteria might include the following: high incidence of adoption, high speed of adoption, high continuance of adoption, low cost per unit of adoption, and no major counterproductive consequences.

::: Marketing Implementation

Table 22.3 summarizes the characteristics of a great marketing company. A marketing company is great not by "what it is," but by "what it does."[54] **Marketing implementation** is the process that turns marketing plans into action assignments and ensures that such assignments are executed in a manner that accomplishes the plan's stated objectives.[55]

A brilliant strategic marketing plan counts for little if it is not implemented properly. Consider the following example:

> A chemical company learned that the customers were not getting good service from any of the competitors. The company decided to make customer service its strategic thrust. When this strategy failed, a postmortem revealed a number of implementation failures. The customer service department continued to be held in low regard by top management; it was understaffed; and it was used as a dumping ground for weak managers. Furthermore, the company's reward system continued to focus on cost containment and current profitability. The company had failed to make the changes required to carry out its strategy.

Strategy addresses the *what* and *why* of marketing activities; implementation addresses the *who, where, when,* and *how.* Strategy and implementation are closely related: One layer of strategy implies certain tactical implementation assignments at a lower level. For example, top management's strategic decision to "harvest" a product must be translated into specific actions and assignments.

Thomas Bonoma identified four sets of skills for implementing marketing programs:

1. ***Diagnostic skills*** – When marketing programs do not fulfill expectations, was it the result of poor strategy or poor implementation? If implementation, what went wrong?
2. ***Identification of company level*** – Implementation problems can occur in three levels: the marketing function, the marketing program, and the marketing policy level.
3. ***Implementation skills*** – To implement programs successfully, marketers need other skills: *allocating skills* for budgeting resources, *organizing skills* to develop an effective organization, and *interaction skills* to motivate others to get things done.
4. ***Evaluation skills*** – Marketers also need monitoring skills to track and evaluate marketing actions.[56]

TABLE 22.3

Characteristics of a Great Marketing Company

- The company selects target markets in which it enjoys superior advantages, and exits or avoids markets where it is intrinsically weak.
- Virtually all the company's employees and departments are customer- and market-minded.
- There is a good working relationship between marketing, R&D, and manufacturing.
- There is a good working relationship between marketing, sales, and customer service.
- The company has installed incentives designed to lead to the right behaviors.
- The company continuously builds and tracks customer satisfaction and loyalty.
- The company manages a value-delivery system in partnership with strong suppliers and distributors.
- The company is skilled in building its brand name(s) and image.
- The company is flexible in meeting customers' varying requirements.

Companies today are striving to make their marketing operations more efficient and their return on marketing investment more measurable (see Chapter 4). Marketing costs can amount to 20 to 40 percent of a company's total operating budget. Companies recognize the high amount of waste in many practices: too many meetings lasting too long, undue time spent in looking for documents, delays in receiving approvals, and difficulties in coordinating vendor partners.

Most marketing departments use a limited number of unconnected technology tools such as e-mail, spreadsheets, project management software, and customer databases. But unconnected tools cannot deal with the increasingly complex nature of business, the increased number of collaborators, and the global scope of operations. Companies use information technology to improve the management of their marketing resources. They need better templates for marketing processes, better management of marketing assets, and better allocation of marketing resources. Certain repetitive processes can be automated. This drive is going under such names as *marketing resource management (MRM), enterprise marketing management (EMM),* and *marketing automation systems (MAS).*[57]

Several software companies now offer software packages to help companies better manage their marketing processes, assets, and resources. The packages are customized so different marketing managers—vice president of marketing, product and brand managers, field sales managers, marketing communications managers—can do their planning, implementation, and control.

Marketing resource management (MRM) software provides a set of Web-based applications that automate and integrate such activities as project management, campaign management, budget management, asset management, brand management, customer relationship management, and knowledge management. The knowledge management component consists of process templates, how-to wizards, and best practices.

The software packages are Web-hosted and available to users with passwords. They add up to what some have called *desktop marketing* in that marketers can find whatever information and decision structures they need on their computers. The computer will host a dashboard on which marketers can manage their activities. In the next few years, MRM software will enable marketers to greatly improve spending and investment decisions, bring new products to market more quickly, and reduce decision time and costs.

::: Evaluation and Control

In spite of the need to monitor and control marketing activities, many companies have inadequate control procedures. A study of 75 companies turned up these findings:

- Smaller companies do a poorer job of setting clear objectives and establishing systems to measure performance.
- Less than half the companies studied knew their individual products' profitability. About one-third had no regular review procedures for spotting and deleting weak products.
- Almost half of the companies failed to compare their prices with those of the competition, to analyze their warehousing and distribution costs, to analyze the causes of returned merchandise, to conduct formal evaluations of advertising effectiveness, and to review their sales forces' call reports.
- Many companies take four to eight weeks to develop control reports, which are occasionally inaccurate.

Table 22.4 lists four types of marketing control needed by companies: annual-plan control, profitability control, efficiency control, and strategic control. Chapter 4 described how companies can use marketing metrics to analyze marketing plans and their profitability. Annual-plan control aims to ensure that the company achieves the sales, profits, and other goals established in its annual plan. The heart of annual-plan control is management by objectives. Four steps are involved (see Figure 22.5). First, management sets monthly or quarterly goals. Second, management monitors its performance in the marketplace. Third, management determines the causes of serious performance deviations. Fourth, management takes corrective action to close the gaps between goals and performance.

This control model applies to all levels of the organization. Top management sets annual sales and profit goals that become specific goals for lower levels of management. Each prod-

TABLE 22.4 Types of Marketing Control

Type of Control	Prime Responsibility	Purpose of Control	Approaches
I. Annual-plan control	Top management Middle management	To examine whether the planned results are being achieved	■ Sales analysis ■ Market share analysis ■ Sales-to-expense ratios ■ Financial analysis ■ Market-based scorecard analysis
II. Profitability control	Marketing controller	To examine where the company is making and losing money	Profitability by: ■ product ■ territory ■ customer ■ segment ■ trade channel ■ order size
III. Efficiency control	Line and staff management Marketing controller	To evaluate and improve the spending efficiency and impact of marketing expenditures	Efficiency of: ■ sales force ■ advertising ■ sales promotion ■ distribution
IV. Strategic control	Top management Marketing auditor	To examine whether the company is pursuing its best opportunities with respect to markets, products, and channels	■ Marketing-effectiveness rating instrument ■ Marketing audit ■ Marketing excellence review ■ Company ethical and social responsibility review

uct manager is committed to attaining specified levels of sales and costs; each regional district and sales manager and each sales representative is also committed to specific goals. Each period, top management reviews and interprets the results.

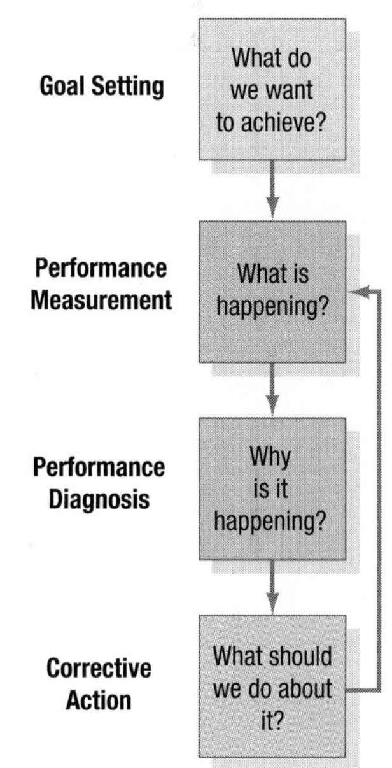

FIG. 22.5

The Control Process

Efficiency Control

Suppose a profitability analysis reveals that the company is earning poor profits in certain products, territories, or markets. Are there more efficient ways to manage the sales force, advertising, sales promotion, and distribution in connection with these marketing entities?

Some companies have established a *marketing controller* position to improve marketing efficiency. Marketing controllers work out of the controller's office but specialize in the marketing side of the business. At companies such as General Foods, DuPont, and Johnson & Johnson, they perform a sophisticated financial analysis of marketing expenditures and results. They examine adherence to profit plans, help prepare brand managers' budgets, measure the efficiency of promotions, analyze media production costs, evaluate customer and geographic profitability, and educate marketing personnel on the financial implications of marketing decisions.[58]

SALES FORCE EFFICIENCY Sales managers need to monitor the following key indicators of efficiency in their territories:

- Average number of calls per salesperson per day.
- Average sales call time per contact.
- Average revenue per sales call.
- Average cost per sales call.
- Entertainment cost per sales call.

- Percentage of orders per 100 sales calls.
- Number of new customers per period.
- Number of lost customers per period.
- Sales force cost as a percentage of total sales.

When a company starts investigating sales force efficiency, it often finds areas for improvement. General Electric reduced the size of one of its divisional sales forces after discovering that its salespeople were calling on customers too often. When a large airline found that its salespeople were both selling and servicing, they transferred the servicing function to lower-paid clerks. Another company conducted time-and-duty studies and found ways to reduce the ratio of idle-to-productive time.

ADVERTISING EFFICIENCY Many managers believe it is almost impossible to measure what they are getting for their advertising dollars; but they should try to keep track of at least the following statistics:

- Advertising cost per thousand target buyers reached by media vehicle.
- Percentage of audience who noted, saw, or associated and read most of each print ad.
- Consumer opinions on the ad's content and effectiveness.
- Before and after measures of attitude toward the product.
- Number of inquiries stimulated by the ad.
- Cost per inquiry.

Management can take a number of steps to improve advertising efficiency, including doing a better job of positioning the product, defining objectives, pretesting messages, using computer technology to guide the selection of media, looking for better media buys, and doing posttesting.

SALES PROMOTION EFFICIENCY Sales promotion includes dozens of devices for stimulating buyer interest and product trial. To improve sales promotion efficiency, management should record the costs and sales impact of each promotion. Management should watch the following statistics:

- Percentage of sales sold on deal.
- Display costs per sales dollar.
- Percentage of coupons redeemed.
- Number of inquiries resulting from a demonstration.

A sales promotion manager can analyze the results of different promotions and advise product managers on the most cost-effective promotions to use.

DISTRIBUTION EFFICIENCY Management needs to search for distribution economies in inventory control, warehouse locations, and transportation modes. It should track such measures as:

- Logistics costs as a percentage of sales.
- Percentage of orders filled correctly.
- Percentage of on-time deliveries.
- Number of billing errors.

Management should strive to reduce inventory while at the same time speeding up the order-to-delivery cycle. That both can be done simultaneously is shown by Dell Computer.

DELL

A customer-customized computer that is ordered from Dell's Web site at 9:00 A.M. on Wednesday can be on the delivery truck by 9:00 P.M. Thursday. In that short period, Dell electronically orders the computer components from its suppliers' warehouses. Equally impressive, Dell gets paid electronically within 24 hours while Compaq, supplying its computers to retailers, receives payment days later.

One problem is that distribution efficiency declines when the company experiences strong sales increases. Peter Senge describes a situation in which a strong sales surge causes the company to fall behind in meeting delivery dates (see Figure 22.6).[59] This causes customers to bad-mouth the company and eventually sales fall. Management responds by increasing sales force incentives to secure more orders. The sales force succeeds, but once again the company slips in meeting delivery dates. Management needs to identify the real bottleneck and invest in more production and distribution capacity.

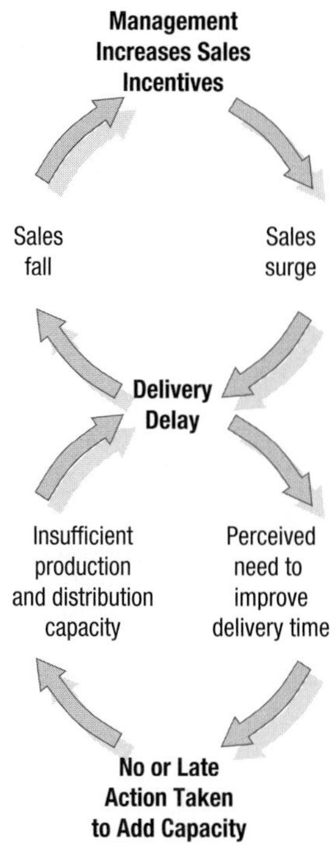

FIG. 22.6

Dynamic Interactions Between Sales Orders and Distribution Efficiency

Source: Adapted from Peter M. Senge, *The Fifth Discipline.* ©1990 by Peter M. Senge. Used by permission of Doubleday, a division of Bantam Doubleday Dell Publishing Group, Inc.

Strategic Control

From time to time, companies need to undertake a critical review of overall marketing goals and effectiveness. Each company should periodically reassess its strategic approach to the marketplace with marketing effectiveness reviews and marketing audits. Companies can also perform marketing excellence reviews and ethical/social responsibility reviews.

THE MARKETING EFFECTIVENESS REVIEW A company's or division's marketing effectiveness is reflected in the degree to which it exhibits the five major attributes of a marketing orientation: *customer philosophy, integrated marketing organization, adequate marketing information, strategic orientation,* and *operational efficiency* (see "Marketing Memo: Marketing Effectiveness Review Instrument"). Most companies and divisions receive scores in the fair-to-good range.[60]

THE MARKETING AUDIT The average U.S. corporation loses half of its customers in five years, half of its employees in four years, and half of its investors in less than one year. Clearly, this points to some weaknesses. Companies that discover weaknesses should undertake a thorough study known as a marketing audit.[61] A **marketing audit** is a comprehensive, systematic, independent, and periodic examination of a company's or business unit's marketing environment, objectives, strategies, and activities with a view to determining problem areas and opportunities and recommending a plan of action to improve the company's marketing performance.

Let us examine the marketing audit's four characteristics:

1. ***Comprehensive*** – The marketing audit covers all the major marketing activities of a business, not just a few trouble spots. It would be called a functional audit if it covered only the sales force, pricing, or some other marketing activity. Although functional audits are useful, they sometimes mislead management. Excessive sales force turnover, for example, could be a symptom not of poor sales force training or compensation but of weak company products and promotion. A comprehensive marketing audit usually is more effective in locating the real source of problems.
2. ***Systematic*** – The marketing audit is an orderly examination of the organization's macro- and micromarketing environments, marketing objectives and strategies, marketing systems, and specific activities. The audit indicates the most-needed improvements, which are then incorporated into a corrective action plan involving both short-run and long-run steps to improve overall effectiveness.
3. ***Independent*** – A marketing audit can be conducted in six ways: self-audit, audit from across, audit from above, company auditing office, company task force audit, and outsider audit. Self-audits, in which managers use a checklist to rate their own operations, lack objectivity and independence.[62] The 3M Company has made good use of a corporate auditing office, which provides marketing audit services to divisions on request.[63] Generally speaking, however, the best audits come from outside consultants who have the necessary objectivity, broad experience in a number of industries, some familiarity with the industry being audited, and the undivided time and attention to give to the audit.
4. ***Periodic*** – Typically, marketing audits are initiated only after sales have turned down, sales force morale has fallen, and other problems have occurred. Companies are thrown into a crisis partly because they failed to review their marketing operations during good times. A periodic marketing audit can benefit companies in good health as well as those in trouble.

A marketing audit starts with a meeting between the company officer(s) and the marketing auditor(s) to work out an agreement on the audit's objectives, coverage, depth, data

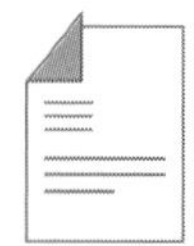

MARKETING MEMO | MARKETING EFFECTIVENESS REVIEW INSTRUMENT

(Check One Answer to Each Question)

Customer Philosophy

A. *Does management recognize the importance of designing the company to serve the needs and wants of chosen markets?*
  0 __ Management primarily thinks in terms of selling current and new products to whomever will buy them.
  1 __ Management thinks in terms of serving a wide range of markets and needs with equal effectiveness.
  2 __ Management thinks in terms of serving the needs and wants of well-defined markets and market segments chosen for their long-run growth and profit potential for the company.

B. *Does management develop different offerings and marketing plans for different segments of the market?*
  0 __ No. 1 __ Somewhat. 2 __ To a large extent.

C. *Does management take a whole marketing-system view (suppliers, channels, competitors, customers, environment) in planning its business?*
  0 __ No. Management concentrates on selling and servicing its immediate customers.
  1 __ Somewhat. Management takes a long view of its channels, although the bulk of its effort goes to selling and servicing the immediate customers.
  2 __ Yes. Management takes a whole marketing-systems view, recognizing the threats and opportunities created for the company by changes in any part of the system.

Integrated Marketing Organization

D. *Is there high-level marketing integration and control of the major marketing functions?*
  0 __ No. Sales and other marketing functions are not integrated at the top and there is some unproductive conflict.
  1 __ Somewhat. There is formal integration and control of the major marketing functions but less than satisfactory coordination and cooperation.
  2 __ Yes. The major marketing functions are effectively integrated.

E. *Does marketing management work well with management in research, manufacturing, purchasing, logistics, and finance?*
  0 __ No. There are complaints that marketing is unreasonable in the demands and costs it places on other departments.
  1 __ Somewhat. The relations are amicable, although each department pretty much acts to serve its own interests.
  2 __ Yes. The departments cooperate effectively and resolve issues in the best interest of the company as a whole.

F. *How well organized is the new-product development process?*
  0 __ The system is ill-defined and poorly handled.
  1 __ The system formally exists but lacks sophistication.
  2 __ The system is well structured and operates on teamwork principles.

Adequate Marketing Information

G. *When were the latest marketing research studies of customers, buying influences, channels, and competitors conducted?*
  0 __ Several years ago. 1 __ A few years ago. 2 __ Recently.

H. *How well does management know the sales potential and profitability of different market segments, customers, territories, products, channels, and order sizes?*
  0 __ Not at all. 1 __ Somewhat. 2 __ Very well.

I. *What effort is expended to measure and improve the cost-effectiveness of different marketing expenditures?*
  0 __ Little or no effort. 1 __ Some effort. 2 __ Substantial effort.

Strategic Orientation

J. *What is the extent of formal marketing planning?*
  0 __ Management conducts little or no formal marketing planning.
  1 __ Management develops an annual marketing plan.
  2 __ Management develops a detailed annual marketing plan and a strategic long-range plan that is updated annually.

K. *How impressive is the current marketing strategy?*
  0 __ The current strategy is not clear.
  1 __ The current strategy is clear and represents a continuation of traditional strategy.
  2 __ The current strategy is clear, innovative, data-based, and well reasoned.

L. *What is the extent of contingency thinking and planning?*
  0 __ Management does little or no contingency thinking.
  1 __ Management does some contingency thinking but little formal contingency planning.
  2 __ Management formally identifies the most important contingencies and develops contingency plans.

Operational Efficiency

M. *How well is the marketing strategy communicated and implemented?*
 0 __ Poorly. 1 __ Fairly. 2 __ Successfully.

N. *Is management doing an effective job with its marketing resources?*
 0 __ No. The marketing resources are inadequate for the job to be done.
 1 __ Somewhat. The marketing resources are adequate but they are not employed optimally.
 2 __ Yes. The marketing resources are adequate and are employed efficiently.

O. *Does management show a good capacity to react quickly and effectively to on-the-spot developments?*
 0 __ No. Sales and market information is not very current and management reaction time is slow.
 1 __ Somewhat. Management receives fairly up-to-date sales and market information; management reaction time varies.
 2 __ Yes. Management has installed systems yielding highly current information and fast reaction time.

Total Score

The instrument is used in the following way. The appropriate answer is checked for each question. The scores are added—the total will be somewhere between 0 and 30. The following scale shows the level of marketing effectiveness:

0–5 = None	11–15 = Fair	21–25 = Very good
6–10 = Poor	16–20 = Good	26–30 = Superior

Source: Philip Kotler, "From Sales Obsession to Marketing Effectiveness," *Harvard Business Review* (November–December 1977): 67–75.

sources, report format, and time frame. A detailed plan regarding who is to be interviewed, the questions to be asked, the time and place of contact, and so on is prepared so that auditing time and cost are kept to a minimum. The cardinal rule in marketing auditing is: Do not rely solely on company managers for data and opinions. Customers, dealers, and other outside groups must also be interviewed. Many companies do not really know how their customers and dealers see them, nor do they fully understand customer needs.

The marketing audit examines six major components of the company's marketing situation. The major questions are listed in Table 22.5.

THE MARKETING EXCELLENCE REVIEW Companies can use another instrument to rate their performance in relation to the best practices of high-performing businesses. The three columns in Table 22.6 distinguish among poor, good, and excellent business and marketing practices. Management can place a checkmark to indicate its perception of where the business stands. The resulting profile exposes weaknesses and strengths, highlighting where the company might make changes to become a truly outstanding player in the marketplace.

::: The Future of Marketing

Top management has recognized that past marketing has been highly wasteful and is demanding more accountability from marketing. "Marketing Memo: The Major Marketing Weaknesses" summarizes the major deficiencies that companies have in marketing, how to spot these deficiencies, and what to do about them.

Going forward, there are a number of imperatives to achieve marketing excellence. Marketing must be "holistic" and less departmental. Marketers must achieve larger influence in the company if they are to be the main architects of business strategy. Marketers must continuously create new ideas if the company is to prosper in a hypercompetitive economy. Marketers must strive for customer insight and treat customers differently but appropriately. Marketers must build their brands through performance, more than through promotion. Marketers must go electronic and win through building superior information and communication systems.

In these ways, modern marketing will continue to evolve and confront new challenges and opportunities. As a result, the coming years will see:

- The demise of the marketing department and the rise of holistic marketing.
- The demise of free-spending marketing and the rise of ROI marketing.

TABLE 22.5 Components of a Marketing Audit

Part I. Marketing Environment Audit	
Macroenvironment	
A. Demographic	What major demographic developments and trends pose opportunities or threats to this company? What actions has the company taken in response to these developments and trends?
B. Economic	What major developments in income, prices, savings, and credit will affect the company? What actions has the company been taking in response to these developments and trends?
C. Environmental	What is the outlook for the cost and availability of natural resources and energy needed by the company? What concerns have been expressed about the company's role in pollution and conservation, and what steps has the company taken?
D. Technological	What major changes are occurring in product and process technology? What is the company's position in these technologies? What major generic substitutes might replace this product?
E. Political	What changes in laws and regulations might affect marketing strategy and tactics? What is happening in the areas of pollution control, equal employment opportunity, product safety, advertising, price control, and so forth, that affects marketing strategy?
F. Cultural	What is the public's attitude toward business and toward the company's products? What changes in customer lifestyles and values might affect the company?
Task Environment	
A. Markets	What is happening to market size, growth, geographical distribution, and profits? What are the major market segments?
B. Customers	What are the customers' needs and buying processes? How do customers and prospects rate the company and its competitors on reputation, product quality, service, sales force, and price? How do different customer segments make their buying decisions?
C. Competitors	Who are the major competitors? What are their objectives, strategies, strengths, weaknesses, sizes, and market shares? What trends will affect future competition and substitutes for the company's products?
D. Distribution and Dealers	What are the main trade channels for bringing products to customers? What are the efficiency levels and growth potentials of the different trade channels?
E. Suppliers	What is the outlook for the availability of key resources used in production? What trends are occurring among suppliers?
F. Facilitators and Marketing Firms	What is the cost and availability outlook for transportation services, warehousing facilities, and financial resources? How effective are the company's advertising agencies and marketing research firms?
G. Publics	Which publics represent particular opportunities or problems for the company? What steps has the company taken to deal effectively with each public?
Part II. Marketing Strategy Audit	
A. Business Mission	Is the business mission clearly stated in market-oriented terms? Is it feasible?
B. Marketing Objectives and Goals	Are the company and marketing objectives and goals stated clearly enough to guide marketing planning and performance measurement? Are the marketing objectives appropriate, given the company's competitive position, resources, and opportunities?
C. Strategy	Has the management articulated a clear marketing strategy for achieving its marketing objectives? Is the strategy convincing? Is the strategy appropriate to the stage of the product life cycle, competitors' strategies, and the state of the economy? Is the company using the best basis for market segmentation? Does it have clear criteria for rating the segments and choosing the best ones? Has it developed accurate profiles of each target segment? Has the company developed an effective positioning and marketing mix for each target segment? Are marketing resources allocated optimally to the major elements of the marketing mix? Are enough resources or too many resources budgeted to accomplish the marketing objectives?
Part III. Marketing Organization Audit	
A. Formal structure	Does the marketing vice president have adequate authority and responsibility for company activities that affect customers' satisfaction? Are the marketing activities optimally structured along functional, product, segment, end-user, and geographical lines?

TABLE 22.5 Continued

B. Functional Efficiency	Are there good communication and working relations between marketing and sales? Is the product-management system working effectively? Are product managers able to plan profits or only sales volume? Are there any groups in marketing that need more training, motivation, supervision, or evaluation?
C. Interface Efficiency	Are there any problems between marketing and manufacturing, R&D, purchasing, finance, accounting, and/or legal that need attention?
Part IV. Marketing Systems Audit	
A. Marketing Information System	Is the marketing intelligence system producing accurate, sufficient, and timely information about marketplace developments with respect to customers, prospects, distributors and dealers, competitors, suppliers, and various publics? Are company decision makers asking for enough marketing research, and are they using the results? Is the company employing the best methods for market measurement and sales forecasting?
B. Marketing Planning Systems	Is the marketing planning system well conceived and effectively used? Do marketers have decision support systems available? Does the planning system result in acceptable sales targets and quotas?
C. Marketing Control System	Are the control procedures adequate to ensure that the annual plan objectives are being achieved? Does management periodically analyze the profitability of products, markets, territories, and channels of distribution? Are marketing costs and productivity periodically examined?
D. New-Product Development System	Is the company well organized to gather, generate, and screen new-product ideas? Does the company do adequate concept research and business analysis before investing in new ideas? Does the company carry out adequate product and market testing before launching new products?
PART V. Marketing Productivity Audit	
A. Profitability Analysis	What is the profitability of the company's different products, markets, territories, and channels of distribution? Should the company enter, expand, contract, or withdraw from any business segments?
B. Cost-Effectiveness Analysis	Do any marketing activities seem to have excessive costs? Can cost-reducing steps be taken?
Part VI. Marketing Function Audits	
A. Products	What are the company's product-line objectives? Are they sound? Is the current product line meeting the objectives? Should the product line be stretched or contracted upward, downward, or both ways? Which products should be phased out? Which products should be added? What are the buyers' knowledge and attitudes toward the company's and competitors' product quality, features, styling, brand names, and so on? What areas of product and brand strategy need improvement?
B. Price	What are the company's pricing objectives, policies, strategies, and procedures? To what extent are prices set on cost, demand, and competitive criteria? Do the customers see the company's prices as being in line with the value of its offer? What does management know about the price elasticity of demand, experience-curve effects, and competitors' prices and pricing policies? To what extent are price policies compatible with the needs of distributors and dealers, suppliers, and government regulation?
C. Distribution	What are the company's distribution objectives and strategies? Is there adequate market coverage and service? How effective are distributors, dealers, manufacturers' representatives, brokers, agents, and others? Should the company consider changing its distribution channels?
D. Advertising, Sales Promotion, Publicity, and Direct Marketing	What are the organization's advertising objectives? Are they sound? Is the right amount being spent on advertising? Are the ad themes and copy effective? What do customers and the public think about the advertising? Are the advertising media well chosen? Is the internal advertising staff adequate? Is the sales-promotion budget adequate? Is there effective and sufficient use of sales-promotion tools such as samples, coupons, displays, and sales contests? Is the public relations staff competent and creative? Is the company making enough use of direct, online, and database marketing?
E. Sales Force	What are the sales force's objectives? Is the sales force large enough to accomplish the company's objectives? Is the sales force organized along the proper principles of specialization (territory, market, product)? Are there enough (or too many) sales managers to guide the field sales representatives? Do the sales-compensation level and structure provide adequate incentive and reward? Does the sales force show high morale, ability, and effort? Are the procedures adequate for setting quotas and evaluating performance? How does the company's sales force compare to competitors' sales forces?

TABLE 22.6

The Marketing Excellence Review: Best Practices

Poor	Good	Excellent
Product-Driven	Market-Driven	Market-Driving
Mass-Market Oriented	Segment Oriented	Niche Oriented and Customer Oriented
Product Offer	Augmented Product Offer	Customer Solutions Offer
Average Product Quality	Better Than Average	Legendary
Average Service Quality	Better Than Average	Legendary
End-Product Oriented	Core-Product Oriented	Core-Competency Oriented
Function Oriented	Process Oriented	Outcome Oriented
Reacting to Competitors	Benchmarking Competitors	Leapfrogging Competitors
Supplier Exploitation	Supplier Preference	Supplier Partnership
Dealer Exploitation	Dealer Support	Dealer Partnership
Price-Driven	Quality-Driven	Value-Driven
Average Speed	Better Than Average	Legendary
Hierarchy	Network	Teamwork
Vertically Integrated	Flattened Organization	Strategic Alliances
Stockholder-Driven	Stakeholder-Driven	Societally-Driven

- The demise of marketing intuition and the rise of marketing science.
- The demise of manual marketing and the rise of automated marketing.
- The demise of mass marketing and the rise of precision marketing.

To accomplish these changes and become truly holistic with marketing, a new set of skills and competencies is needed. Proficiency will be demanded in areas such as:

- Customer relationship management (CRM).
- Partner relationship management (PRM).
- Database marketing and data-mining.
- Contact center management and telemarketing.
- Public relations marketing (including event and sponsorship marketing).
- Brand-building and brand-asset management.
- Experiential marketing.
- Integrated marketing communications.
- Profitability analysis by segment, customer, channel.

It is an exciting time for marketing. In the relentless pursuit of marketing superiority and dominance, new rules and practices are emerging. The benefits of successful twenty-first-century marketing are many, but will only come with hard work, insight, and inspiration. The words of nineteenth-century American author Ralph Waldo Emerson may never have been more true: "This time like all times is a good one, if we but know what to do with it."

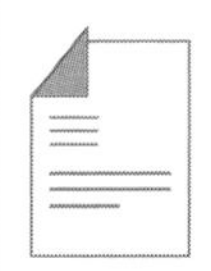

MARKETING MEMO | MAJOR MARKETING WEAKNESSES

A number of "deadly sins" signal that the marketing program is in trouble. Here are ten deadly sins, the signs, and some solutions.

Deadly Sin: The company is not sufficiently market-focused and customer-driven.

Signs: Poor identification of market segments, poor prioritization of market segments, no market segment managers, employees who think it is the job of marketing and sales to serve customers, no training program to create a customer culture, no incentives to treat the customer especially well.
Solutions:
Use more advanced segmentation techniques, prioritize segments, specialize the sales force, develop a clear hierarchy of company values, foster more "customer consciousness" in employees and company agents, make it easy for customers to reach the company and respond quickly to any communication.

Deadly Sin: The company does not fully understand its target customers.

Signs: Latest study of customers is three years old, customers are not buying your product like they once did, competitors' products are selling better, high level of customer returns and complaints.
Solutions: Do more sophisticated consumer research, use more analytical techniques, establish customer and dealer panels, use customer relationship software, do data mining.

Deadly Sin: The company needs to better define and monitor its competitors.

Signs: The company focuses on near competitors, misses distant competitors and disruptive technologies, no system for gathering and distributing competitive intelligence.
Solutions: Establish an office for competitive intelligence, hire competitors' people, watch for technology that might affect the company, prepare offerings like competitors'.

Deadly Sin: The company does not properly manage relationships with stakeholders.

Signs: Employees, dealers, and investors are not happy; good suppliers do not come.
Solutions: Move from zero-sum thinking to positive-sum thinking; do a better job of managing employees, supplier relations, distributors, dealers, and investors.

Deadly Sin: The company is not good at finding new opportunities.

Signs:
The company has not identified any exciting new opportunities for years, the new ideas the company has launched have largely failed.
Solutions:
Set up a system for stimulating the flow of new ideas.

Deadly Sin: The company's marketing planning process is deficient.

Signs:
The marketing plan format does not have the right components, there is no way to estimate the financial implications of different strategies, there is no contingency planning.
Solutions:
Establish a standard format including situational analysis, SWOT, major issues, objectives, strategy, tactics, budgets, and controls; ask marketers what changes they would make if they were given 20 percent more or less budget; run an annual marketing awards program with prizes for best plans and performance.

Deadly Sin: Product and service policies need tightening.

Signs: Too many products and many are losing money, the company is giving away too many services, the company is poor at cross-selling products and services.
Solutions: Establish a system to track weak products and fix or drop them, offer and price services at different levels, improve processes for cross-selling and upselling.

Deadly Sin: The company's brand-building and communications skills are weak.

Signs: The target market does not know much about the company, the brand is not seen as distinctive, the company allocates its budget to the same marketing tools in about the same proportion each year, there is little evaluation of the ROI impact of promotions.
Solutions:
Improve brand-building strategies and measurement of results, shift money into effective marketing instruments, require marketers to estimate the ROI impact in advance of funding requests.

Deadly Sin: The company is not organized for effective and efficient marketing.

Signs: Staff lacks twenty-first-century marketing skills, bad vibes between marketing/sales and other departments.
Solutions: Appoint a strong leader and build new skills in the marketing department, improve relationships between marketing and other departments.

Deadly Sin: The company has not made maximum use of technology.

Signs: Minimal use of the Internet, outdated sales automation system, no market automation, no decision-support models, no marketing dashboards.
Solutions: Use the Internet more, improve the sales automation system, apply market automation to routine decisions, develop formal marketing decision models and marketing dashboards.

Source: Philip Kotler, *Ten Deadly Marketing Sins: Signs and Solutions* (Hoboken, NJ: John Wiley & Sons, 2004).

SUMMARY :::

1. The modern marketing department has evolved through the years from a simple sales department to an organizational structure where marketing personnel work mainly on cross-disciplinary teams.
2. Modern marketing departments can be organized in a number of ways. Some companies are organized by functional specialization, while others focus on geography and regionalization. Still others emphasize product and brand management or market-segment management. Some companies establish a matrix organization consisting of both product and market managers. Finally, some companies have strong corporate marketing, others have limited corporate marketing, and still others place marketing only in the divisions.
3. Effective modern marketing organizations are marked by a strong cooperation and customer focus among the company's departments: marketing, R&D, engineering, purchasing, manufacturing, operations, finance, accounting, and credit.
4. Companies must practice social responsibility through their legal, ethical, and social words and actions. Cause marketing can be a means for companies to productively link social responsibility to consumer marketing programs. Social marketing is done by a nonprofit or government organization to directly address a social problem or cause.
5. A brilliant strategic marketing plan counts for little if it is not implemented properly. Implementing marketing plans calls for skills in recognizing and diagnosing a problem, assessing the company level where the problem exists, implementation skills, and skills in evaluating the results.
6. The marketing department has to monitor and control marketing activities continuously. Efficiency control focuses on finding ways to increase the efficiency of the sales force, advertising, sales promotion, and distribution. Strategic control entails a periodic reassessment of the company and its strategic approach to the marketplace using the tools of the marketing effectiveness and marketing excellence reviews, as well as the marketing audit.

APPLICATIONS :::

Marketing Debate Is Marketing Management an Art or a Science?

Some marketing observers maintain that good marketing is something that is more than anything an art and does not lend itself to rigorous analysis and deliberation. Others strongly disagree and contend that marketing management is a highly disciplined enterprise that shares much in common with other business disciplines.

Take a position: Marketing management is largely an artistic exercise and therefore highly subjective versus Marketing management is largely a scientific exercise with well-established guidelines and criteria.

Marketing Discussion

How does cause or corporate societal marketing affect your personal consumer behavior? Do you ever buy or not buy any products or services from a company because of its environmental policies or programs? Why or why not?

APPENDIX

::: SONIC MARKETING PLAN EXERCISES

The Marketing Plan: An Introduction

As a marketer, you'll need a good marketing plan to provide direction and focus for your brand, product, or company. With a detailed plan, any business will be better prepared to launch a new product or build sales for existing products. Nonprofit organizations also use marketing plans to guide their fundraising and outreach efforts. Even government agencies put together marketing plans for initiatives such as building public awareness of proper nutrition and stimulating area tourism.

The Purpose and Content of a Marketing Plan

Unlike a business plan, which offers a broad overview of the entire organization's mission, objectives, strategy, and resource allocation, a marketing plan has a more limited scope. It spells out how the organization's strategic objectives will be achieved through specific marketing strategies and tactics, with the customer as the starting point. It is also linked to the plans of other departments within the organization. Suppose a marketing plan calls for selling 200,000 units annually. The production department must gear up to make that many units, the finance department must have funding available to cover the expenses, the human resources department must be ready to hire and train staff, and so on. Without the appropriate level of organizational support and resources, no marketing plan can succeed. Although the exact length and layout will vary from company to company, a marketing plan usually contains the sections described in Chapter 2. Smaller businesses may create shorter or less formal marketing plans, whereas corporations frequently require highly structured marketing plans. But to ensure correct implementation, every part of the plan must be described in considerable detail. Sometimes a company will post its marketing plan on an internal Web site, which allows managers and employees in different locations to consult specific sections and collaborate on additions or changes.

The Role of Research

To develop successful strategies and action programs, marketers need up-to-date information about the environment, the competition, and the market segments to be served. Often, analysis of internal data is the starting point for assessing the current marketing situation, supplemented by marketing intelligence and research investigating the overall market, the competition, key issues, and threats and opportunities. As the plan is put into effect, marketers use advertising and other forms of research to measure progress toward objectives and identify areas for improvement if results fall short of projections. Finally, marketers use marketing research to learn more about their customers' requirements, expectations, perceptions, and satisfaction levels. This deeper understanding provides a foundation for building competitive advantage through well-informed segmenting, targeting, and positioning decisions. Thus, the marketing plan should outline what marketing research will be conducted and how the findings will be applied.

The Role of Relationships

The marketing plan shows how the company will establish and maintain profitable customer relationships. In the process, however, it also shapes a number of internal and external relationships.

First, it affects how marketing personnel work with one another and with other departments to deliver value and satisfy customers. Second, it affects how the company works with suppliers, distributors, and strategic alliance partners to achieve the objectives listed in the plan. Third, it influences the company's dealings with other stakeholders, including government regulators, the media, and the community at large. All these relationships are important to the organization's success.

From Marketing Plan to Marketing Action

Companies generally create yearly marketing plans, although some plans cover a longer period. Marketers start planning well in advance of the implementation date to allow time for marketing research, thorough analysis, management review, and coordination between departments. Then, after each action program begins, marketers monitor ongoing results, compare them with projections, analyze any differences, and take corrective steps. Because of inevitable and sometimes unpredictable environmental changes, marketers must be ready to update and adapt marketing plans at any time. Some marketers also design contingency plans.

For effective implementation and control, the marketing plan should define how progress toward objectives will be measured. Managers typically use budgets, schedules, and performance standards for monitoring and evaluating results. With budgets, they can compare planned expenditures with actual expenditures for a given week, month, or other period. Schedules allow management to see when tasks were supposed to be completed—and when they were actually completed. Performance standards track the outcomes of marketing programs to see whether the company is moving toward its objectives. Some examples of performance standards are: market share, sales volume, product profitability, and customer satisfaction.

Sample Marketing Plan for Sonic

This section takes you inside the sample marketing plan for Sonic, a hypothetical start-up company. The company's first product is the Sonic 1000, a multifunction personal digital assistant (PDA), also known as a handheld computer. Sonic will be competing with palmOne, Hewlett-Packard, and other well-established rivals. The annotations explain more about what each section of the plan should contain.

The Executive Summary is for senior managers who must review and approve the marketing plan.

The Executive Summary is an overview of the market opportunity and strategy for meeting needs of targeted market segments.

The Executive Summary includes marketing and financial objectives and expected results.

1.0 Executive Summary

Sonic is preparing to launch a PDA product, the Sonic 1000, in a maturing market. Despite the dominance of PDA leader palmOne, we can compete because our offering combines exclusive features at a value-added price. We are targeting specific segments in consumer and business markets, taking advantage of opportunities indicated by demand for easy-to-use, wireless-enabled PDAs with expanded communications functionality.

The primary marketing objectives of this plan are to achieve first-year U.S. market share of 3 percent and unit sales of 240,000. The primary financial objectives are to achieve first-year sales revenues of $60 million, keep first-year losses to less than $10 million, and break even early in the second year.

The Situation Analysis focuses on market definition and the current capability of the company to serve the market.

2.0 Situation Analysis

Sonic, founded 18 months ago by two entrepreneurs with experience in the PC market, is about to enter the PDA market dominated by palmOne. Overall PDA sales have slowed and profitability has suffered. The emergence of multifunction PDAs and advanced cell phones has increased competitive pressures. Estimated market size for multifunction PDAs and cell phones is $63.7 billion, with 50% growth expected within 4 years. To gain market share in this environment, Sonic must carefully target specific market segments.

Market Summary includes size, needs, growth, and trends.

Description of targeted segments provides context for the marketing strategies and action programs discussed later in the plan.

2.1 MARKET SUMMARY Sonic's market consists of consumers and business users who need to conveniently store, communicate, and exchange information on the go. Segments being targeted during the first year include professionals, students, corporations, entrepreneurs, and medical users. Exhibit 1 shows how the Sonic 1000 addresses the needs of targeted consumer and business segments.

PDA purchasers can choose between models based on two different operating systems created by Palm and Microsoft. Sonic licenses the market-dominant Palm system because thousands of software applications and hardware peripherals are compatible with this sys-

| EXHIBIT 1 | Needs and Corresponding Features/Benefits of Sonic PDA

Targeted Segment	Customer Need	Corresponding Feature/Benefit
Professionals (consumer market)	■ Stay in touch while on the go	■ Wireless e-mail to conveniently send and receive messages from anywhere; cell phone capability for voice communication from anywhere
	■ Record information while on the go	■ Voice recognition for no-hands recording
Students (consumer market)	■ Perform many functions without carrying multiple gadgets	■ Compatible with numerous applications and peripherals for convenient, cost-effective functionality
	■ Express style and individuality	■ Case wardrobe of different colors and patterns allows users to make a fashion statement
Corporate users (business market)	■ Input and access critical data on the go	■ Compatible with widely available software
	■ Use for proprietary tasks	■ Customizable to fit diverse corporate tasks and networks
Entrepreneurs (business market)	■ Organize and access contacts, schedule details	■ No-hands, wireless access to calendar and address book to easily check appointments and connect with contacts
Medical users (business market)	■ Update, access, and exchange medical records	■ No-hands, wireless recording and exchange of information to reduce paperwork and increase productivity

tem. Product proliferation and increased competition have resulted in lower prices and lower profit margins. Lower prices are helping sales of PDAs in the lower end of the consumer market, but at the expense of gross margins. Customers with first-generation PDAs are reentering the market by buying newer, high-end multifunction units.

2.2 STRENGTHS, WEAKNESSES, OPPORTUNITIES, AND THREAT (SWOT) ANALYSIS

Sonic has several powerful strengths on which to build, but our major weakness is lack of brand awareness and image. The major opportunity is growing demand for multifunction PDAs that deliver communication-specific benefits. We also face the threat of ever-greater competition and downward pressure on pricing.

Market trends must be considered as the company develops its marketing strategies.

Strengths Sonic can build on three important strengths:

Strengths are internal capabilities that can help the company reach its objectives.

1. ***Innovative product.*** Sonic 1000 includes a voice recognition system that simplifies usage and allows hands-free operation. It also offers features such as built-in cell phone functionality, wireless communication, and MP3 capabilities.
2. ***Compatibility.*** Our PDA can work with the hundreds of Palm-compatible peripherals and applications currently available.
3. ***Pricing.*** Our product is priced lower than competing multifunction models—all of which lack voice recognition—which gives us an edge with price-conscious customers.

Weaknesses By waiting to enter the PDA market until the initial shakeout and consolidation of competitors has occurred, Sonic has learned from the successes and mistakes of others. Nonetheless, we have two main weaknesses:

Weaknesses are internal elements that may interfere with the company's ability to achieve its objectives.

1. ***Lack of brand awareness.*** Sonic has not yet established a brand or image in the marketplace, whereas palmOne and other rivals have strong brand recognition. This is an area we will address with promotion.
2. ***Heavier weight.*** To accommodate the multifunction features, the Sonic 1000 is slightly heavier than most competing models. To counteract this, we will emphasize our multifunction features and value-added pricing, two important competitive strengths.

Opportunities Sonic can take advantage of three major market opportunities:

Opportunities are areas of buyer need or potential interest in which the company might perform profitably.

1. ***Increasing demand for multiple communication methods.*** The market for wireless Web-enabled PDAs with cell phone functionality is projected to grow faster than the market for nonwireless models. There are more users with PDAs in work and educational settings, which is boosting primary demand. Also, customers who bought entry-level models are now trading up.
2. ***Add-on peripherals.*** More peripherals, such as digital cameras and global positioning systems, are available for the Palm operating system. Consumers and business users who are interested in any of these peripherals will see the Sonic 1000 as a value-priced device able to be conveniently and quickly expanded for multiple functions.
3. ***Diverse applications.*** The wide range of Palm-compatible software applications available for home and business use allows the Sonic PDA to satisfy communication and information needs.

Threats We face three main threats at the introduction of the Sonic 1000:

Threats are challenges posed by an unfavorable trend or development that could lead to lower sales and profits.

1. ***Increased competition.*** More companies are entering the U.S. PDA market with models that offer some but not all of the features and benefits provided by Sonic's PDA. Therefore, Sonic's marketing communications must stress our clear differentiation and value-added pricing.
2. ***Downward pressure on pricing.*** Increased competition and market-share strategies are pushing PDA prices down. Still, our objective of seeking a 10% profit on second-year sales of the original model is realistic, given the lower margins in the PDA market.
3. ***Compressed product life cycle.*** PDAs seem to be reaching the maturity stage of their life cycle more quickly than earlier technology products. We have contingency plans to keep sales growing by adding new features, targeting additional segments, and adjusting prices.

Competition identifies key competitors, describes their market positions, and provides an overview of their strategies.

2.3 COMPETITION Increased entry of established computer and cell phone companies has pressured industry participants to continually add features and cut prices. Competition from specialized devices for text and e-mail messaging, such as Blackberry devices, is also a factor. Key competitors:

- ***palmOne*** has had financial struggles because of the need to reduce prices for competitive reasons. Its acquisition of Handspring boosted its product development strength and expanded its product mix. As the best-known maker of PDAs, palmOne has achieved distribution in nearly every channel, including distribution by U.S. cell phone service carriers. At present, palmOne products lack some of the voice recognition software standard in the Sonic 1000.
- ***Hewlett-Packard*** targets business markets with its iPAQ Pocket PC devices, many with wireless capabilities to accommodate corporate users. For extra security, one model allows access by fingerprint match as well as by password. HP enjoys excellent distribution, and its products are priced from below $300 to more than $600.
- ***Garmin's*** iQue 3600 was the first PDA with built-in global position system (GPS) capability. Priced at $589, its mapping software and verbal commands eliminate the need for an automotive device. Garmin's PDA uses the Palm operating system and has other unique functions, such as a digital voice recorder for brief memos.
- ***Dell's*** PDA model is priced starting at $199. However, this product is larger than competing palmOne products, and it lacks wireless functionality as a standard feature. New, slimmer models are expected at regular intervals from this low-cost competitor, which markets directly to customers.
- ***Samsung*** is one of several manufacturers that have married cell phone capabilities with multifunction PDA features. Its i500 uses the Palm operating system, provides speedy e-mail and MP3 downloads, plays video clips, and offers PDA functions such as address book, calendar, and speed dial.

Despite strong competition, Sonic can carve out a definite image and gain recognition among targeted segments. Our licensing arrangement with Cellport Systems allows us to provide the exclusive feature of voice recognition for hands-off operation, a critical point of differentiation for competitive advantage. Exhibit 2 shows a selection of competitive PDA products and prices.

Product Offering summarizes main features of the company's products.

2.4 PRODUCT OFFERING The Sonic PDA 1000 offers the following standard features:

- Voice recognition for hands-free commands and communication
- Built-in cell phone functionality
- Wireless Web access and e-mail capabilities
- MP3 music downloading and player capabilities
- Full organization and communication functions, including calendar, address book, memo pad, Internet browser, e-mail program, and text and instant messaging programs
- Connectors to accommodate all palmOne-compatible peripherals

EXHIBIT 2 | Selected PDA Products and Pricing

Competitor	Model	Features	Price
PalmOne	Tungsten C	PDA functions, wireless capabilities, color screen, tiny keyboard, wireless capabilities	$499
palmOne	M130	PDA functions, color screen, expandable functionality	$199
Handspring	Treo 270	PDA and cell phone functions, color screen, tiny keyboard, speakerphone capabilities; no expansion slot	$499
Samsung	i500	PDA functions, cell phone functions, MP3 player, color screen, video capabilities	$599
Garmin	iQue 3600	PDA functions, global positioning system technology, voice recorder, expansion slot, MP3 player	$589
Dell	Axim X5	PDA functions, color screen, e-mail capable, voice recorder, speaker, expandable	$199
Sony	Clie PEG-NX73V	PDA functions, digital camera, tiny keyboard, games, presentation software, MP3 player, voice recorder	$499

- Ability to run any palmOne-compatible application
- Large color display
- Keyboard for input
- Cradle for synchronizing data with PC
- Interchangeable case wardrobe of different colors and patterns

First-year sales revenues are projected at $60 million, based on sales of 240,000 Sonic 1000 units at a wholesale price of $250 each. During the second year, we plan to introduce the Sonic 2000 as a higher-end product with the following standard features:

- Global positioning system (GPS) for identifying locations, obtaining directions
- Built-in digital camera
- Translation capabilities to send English text as Spanish text (other languages to be offered as add-on options)

2.5 DISTRIBUTION Sonic-branded products will be distributed through a network of select store and nonstore retailers in the top 50 U.S. markets. Among the most important channel partners being contacted are:

Distribution describes each channel used by the company for this product and mentions new developments and trends.

- ***Office supply superstores.*** Office Depot and Staples will both carry Sonic products in stores, in catalogs, and on Web sites.
- ***Computer stores.*** Gateway stores will carry Sonic products.
- ***Electronic specialty stores.*** Circuit City and Best Buy will carry Sonic PDAs.
- ***Online retailers.*** Amazon.com will carry Sonic PDAs and, for a promotional fee, will give Sonic prominent placement on its home page during the introduction.

Distribution will initially be restricted to the United States. We plan to expand into Canada and beyond.

We will emphasize trade sales promotion in the first year.

3.0 Marketing Strategy

3.1 OBJECTIVES We have set aggressive but achievable objectives for the first and second years of market entry.

The marketing and financial objectives should be defined in specific terms so management can measure progress and take corrective action to stay on track.

- ***First-year Objectives*** We are aiming for a 3 percent share of the U.S. PDA market through unit sales volume of 240,000.
- ***Second-year Objectives*** Our second-year objectives are to achieve a 6 percent share based on sales of two models and to achieve break-even early in this period.

An important objective will be to establish a well-regarded brand name linked to a meaningful positioning. We will have to invest heavily in marketing to create a memorable and distinctive brand image projecting innovation, quality, and value. We also must measure awareness and response so we can adjust our marketing efforts if necessary.

This section describes issues that might affect the company's marketing strategy and implementation.

3.2 TARGET MARKETS Sonic's marketing strategy is based on a positioning of product differentiation. Our primary consumer target is middle- to upper-income professionals who need one portable device to coordinate their busy schedules and communicate with family and colleagues. Our secondary consumer target is high school, college, and graduate students who need a multifunction device. This segment can be described by age (16–30) and education.

All marketing strategies start with Segmentation, Targeting and Positioning.

Our primary business target is mid- to large-sized corporations that want to help their managers and employees stay in touch and input or access critical data on the go. This segment consists of companies with more than $25 million in annual sales and more than 100 employees. A secondary business target is entrepreneurs and small-business owners. We are also targeting medical users who want to reduce paperwork and update or access patients' medical records.

Target segments must be defined before positioning can be done, since positioning requires identification of competitive positions available to the company as potential points of difference.

Positioning identifies the brand, customer benefits, and point(s) of difference and parity for this product or product line.

Product Strategy calls for coordinated decisions on product mixes, product lines, brands, packaging and labeling, and warranties.

Pricing strategy includes policy, objectives, and action programs to set initial prices and for adapting prices in response to opportunities and challenges from competitors.

Distribution strategy includes selection and management of channel relationships required to deliver value to customers.

Marketing Communications strategy includes management of all efforts to communicate value to customers, potential customers, and channel members.

Each of the four marketing-mix strategies conveys Sonic's differentiation to the target market segments identified above.

3.3 POSITIONING Using product differentiation, we are positioning the Sonic PDA as the most versatile, convenient, value-added model for personal and professional use. The marketing strategy will focus on the voice-recognition system as the main feature differentiating the Sonic 1000.

3.4 STRATEGIES Marketing strategies need to be broken down into strategies in specific areas such as product, pricing, distribution, and marketing communications.

Product The Sonic 1000, including all the features described in the Product Review section, will be sold with a one-year warranty. We will introduce a more compact, more powerful high-end model (the Sonic 2000) during the following year, with GPS functionality and other features. Building the Sonic brand is an integral part of our product strategy. The brand and logo (Sonic's distinctive yellow thunderbolt) will be displayed on the product and packaging, and reinforced by its prominence in the introductory marketing campaign.

Pricing The Sonic 1000 will be introduced at $250 wholesale, $350 estimated retail price per unit. We expect to lower the price of this first model when we expand the product line by launching the Sonic 2000, to be priced at $350 wholesale per unit. These prices reflect a strategy of (1) attracting desirable channel partners and (2) taking market share from palmOne.

Distribution Our channel strategy is to use selective distribution to have Sonic PDAs sold through well-known stores and online retailers. During the first year, we will add channel partners until we have coverage in all major U.S. markets and the product is included in the major electronics catalogs and Web sites. We will also investigate distribution through cellphone outlets maintained by major carriers such as Cingular Wireless. In support of our channel partners, Sonic will provide demonstration products, detailed specification handouts, and full-color photos and displays featuring the product. We will also arrange special trade terms for retailers that place volume orders.

Marketing Communications By integrating all messages in all media, we will reinforce the brand name and the main points of product differentiation, especially our exclusive voice-recognition feature. Research about media consumption patterns will help our advertising agency choose appropriate media and timing to reach prospects before and during product introduction. Thereafter, advertising will appear on a pulsing basis to maintain brand awareness and communicate various differentiation messages. The agency will also coordinate public relations efforts to build the Sonic brand and support the differentiation message. To attract market attention and encourage purchasing, we will offer as a limited-time premium a leather carry-case. To attract, retain, and motivate channel partners for a push strategy, we will use trade sales promotions and personal selling to channel partners. Until the Sonic brand has been established, our communications will encourage purchases through channel partners rather than from our Web site.

The marketing mix includes the tactics and programs that support each marketing strategy. These programs should be specific and measurable, with a name, a responsible person, milestone dates, and a budget.

Programs should be coordinated with the resources and activities of other departments that contribute to the creation, delivery, or communication of customer value for this product.

3.5 MARKETING MIX The Sonic 1000 will be introduced in February. Here are summaries of action programs we will use during the first six months to achieve our stated objectives.

- ***January*** We will initiate a $200,000 trade sales promotion campaign to educate dealers and generate excitement for the product launch in February. We will exhibit at the major consumer electronics trade shows and provide samples to selected product reviewers, opinion leaders, and celebrities as part of our public relations strategy. Our training staff will work with sales personnel at major retail chains to explain the Sonic 1000's features, benefits, and competitive advantages.
- ***February*** We will start an integrated print/radio/Internet campaign targeting professionals and consumers. The campaign will show how quickly Sonic PDA users can accomplish tasks using voice recognition. This multimedia campaign will be supported by point-of-sale signage as well as online-only specials.
- ***March*** As the multimedia advertising campaign continues, we will add consumer sales promotion tactics such as giving away leather carry-cases as a premium. We will also distribute new point-of-purchase displays to support our retailers.

- ***April*** We will hold a trade sales contest offering prizes for the salesperson and retail organization that sells the most Sonic PDAs during the 4-week period.
- ***May*** We plan to roll out a new national advertising campaign this month. The radio ads will feature celebrity voices using the voice-recognition system to operate their Sonic PDAs. The print ads will show these celebrities holding their Sonic PDAs.
- ***June*** Our radio campaign will add a new voice-over tag line promoting the Sonic 1000 as a graduation gift. We will also exhibit at the semiannual electronics trade show and provide channel partners with new competitive comparison handouts as a sales aid. In addition, we will tally and analyze results of customer satisfaction surveys for future promotions and to provide feedback for product and marketing activities.

3.6 MARKETING RESEARCH Using research, we will identify specific features and benefits our target market segments value. Feedback from market tests, surveys, and focus groups will help us develop the Sonic 2000. We are also measuring and analyzing customers' attitudes toward competing brands and products. Brand awareness research will help us determine the effectiveness and efficiency of our messages and media. Finally, we will use customer satisfaction studies to gauge market reaction.

Marketing Research is used to support development, implementation, and evaluation of strategies and action programs.

4.0 Financials

Total first-year sales revenue for the Sonic 1000 is projected at $60 million, with an average wholesale price of $250 per unit and variable cost per unit of $150 for unit sales volume of 240,000. We anticipate a first-year loss of up to $10 million. Break-even calculations indicate that Sonic 1000 will become profitable after the sales volume exceeds 267,500, early in the product's second year. Our breakeven analysis assumes per-unit wholesale revenue of $250 per unit, variable cost of $150 per unit, and estimated first-year fixed costs of $26,750,000. Based on these assumptions, the breakeven calculation is:

$$\frac{26{,}750{,}000}{\$250 - \$150} = 267{,}500 \text{ units}$$

Financials include marketing budgets and sales forecasts to plan for expenditures, scheduling, and operations related to each action program.

Breakeven Analysis includes estimated revenues, relevant fixed costs, and variable costs for the product for the time period covered by the marketing plan.

5.0 Controls

Controls help management measure results and identify problems or performance variations that need correction.

5.1 IMPLEMENTATION We are planning tight control measures to closely monitor quality and customer service satisfaction. This will enable us to react very quickly in correcting any problems that may occur. Other early warning signals that will be monitored for signs of deviation from the plan include monthly sales (by segment and channel) and monthly expenses.

5.2 MARKETING ORGANIZATION Sonic's chief marketing officer, Jane Melody, holds overall responsibility for marketing strategy and direction. Exhibit 3 shows the structure of the eight-person marketing organization. Sonic has hired Worldwide Marketing to handle national sales campaigns, trade and consumer sales promotions, and public relations efforts.

The Marketing Organization may be organized by function, as in this example, or by product, customer, or some combination of these.

| EXHIBIT 3 | Sonic's Marketing Organization

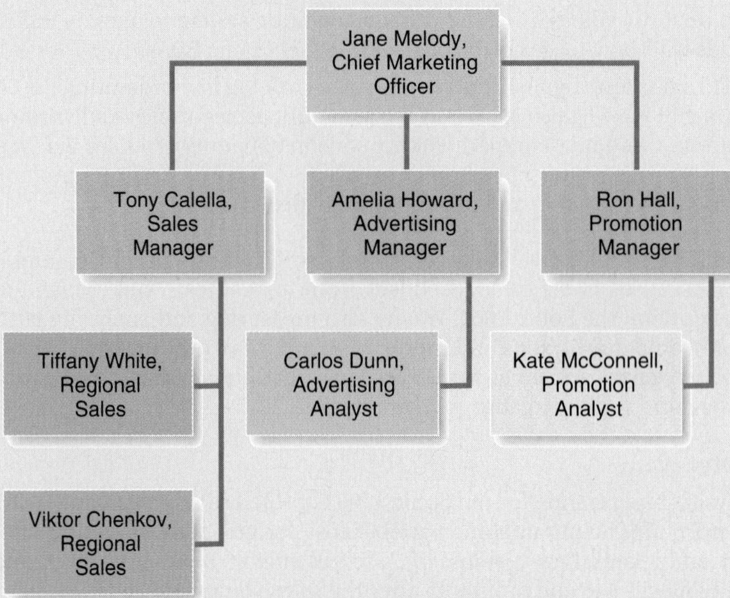

Sources: Background information and market data adapted from: Pui-Wing Tam, "Palm Unveils palmOne Name, after Breakup," *Wall Street Journal*, August 18, 2003, p. B4; Elaine C.Y. Chen, "Lean, Mean Multimedia Machine," *Laptop*, August 2003, p. 20; Michael V. Copeland, Om Malik, and Rafe Needleman, "The Next Big Thing," *Business 2.0*, July 2003, pp. 62–69; Steve Hamm, "Tech Comes Out Swinging," *Business Week*,June 23, 2003, pp. 62–66; "Dell Rides Wireless Wave," *eWeek*, July 7, 2003, http://www.eweek.com; Stephen H. Wildstrom, "Wi-Fi Handhelds? Not for the Footloose," *Business Week*, June 16, 2003, p. 24; Bob Brewin, "Palm to Buy Handspring to Bolster Hardware Unit," *Computerworld*, June 9, 2003, p. 12; "PDAs with Phones," *PC Magazine*, May 6, 2003, p. 108; "Handheld Market Declines in 2002," *Health Management Technology*,March 2003, p. 6; Bob Brewin, "Palm Slashes Pricing to Match the Competition," *Computerworld*, February 10, 2003, p. 36.

Sonic PDA Marketing Plan Chapter Assignments

Chapter 2 Developing Marketing Strategies and Plans

Every marketing plan must include the company mission, analysis of strengths, weaknesses, opportunities and threats and state the marketing and financial objectives for the plan period. As shown in the sample marketing plan on pages A1–A7, Sonic is a start-up company that will soon introduce a new multi-function personal digital assistant (PDA) to compete with established products made by Palm, Hewlett Packard, Sony and others. As an assistant to Jane Melody, Sonic's chief marketing officer, you have been assigned to:

- Draft a mission statement for Sonic's senior management to review.
- Prepare a summary of strengths, weaknesses, opportunities and threats (SWOTs).
- List the marketing and financial objectives the company has for the new PDA being developed by Sonic.

As your instructor directs, enter Sonic's mission statement, SWOTs, and financial and marketing objectives in a written marketing plan, or type them into the Mission, SWOT, and Objectives sections of Marketing Plan Pro.

Chapter 3 Gathering Information and Scanning the Environment

Marketing information systems, marketing intelligence systems, and marketing research systems are used to gather and analyze data for various parts of the marketing plan. These systems help marketers examine changes and trends in markets, competition, customer needs, product usage, and distribution channels. Some changes and trends may turn up evidence of opportunities or threats.

Sonic has developed information about the competition and competitive situation, but Jane Melody believes more information is needed in preparation for launching the first PDA. Based on the marketing plan contents discussed in Chapter 2, how can you use MIS and marketing research to support the marketing planning for the new PDA:

- For which sections of the plan will you need secondary data? Primary data? Why do you need information for each section?
- Where can you find secondary data that will be useful? Identify two Internet sources and two non-Internet sources. Describe what you plan to draw from each source, and indicate how you will use the data in your marketing plan.
- What primary research will Sonic need to support its marketing strategy, including product management, pricing, distribution, and marketing communication? What questions or issues should Sonic seek to resolve using primary data?
- What technological, demographic and/or economic changes can potentially affect PDA development, buyer acceptance of PDAs, and development of substitute or enhanced products?

Enter your answers about Sonic's use of marketing research in a written marketing plan or in the Marketing Research, Market Analysis, and Market Trends sections of Marketing Plan Pro.

Chapter 4 Conducting Marketing Research and Forecasting Demand

Sonic has developed a sales forecast for its new PDA for the next two years. Jane Melody wants to review estimates of industry demand for PDAs. She also wants to develop an approach for measuring the effectiveness of Sonic's marketing efforts. She has asked you to:

- Determine, from available secondary data, estimates of total demand for PDAs for the next two years. She understands you will have to do Internet searches and determine industry trade association sources for such data.
- Look at the various ways to evaluate marketing effectiveness and recommend to her the best way that Sonic can determine the effectiveness of its marketing efforts.

Enter the answers to these questions in a written marketing plan or into the Sales Forecasting and Controls sections of Marketing Plan Pro.

Chapter 5 Creating Customer Value, Satisfaction and Loyalty

Sonic has decided to focus on total customer satisfaction, since studies have shown that customers who are "completely satisfied" with the product or service are much more likely to buy more from the company than customers who report they are "satisfied." You have been asked by Jane Melody to:

- Recommend how Sonic should measure total customer satisfaction.

Review the possible ways to gain customer satisfaction information and write the recommended approach in a marketing plan or into the Positioning section of Marketing Plan Pro.

Chapter 6 Analyzing Consumer Markets

Every company has to study customer markets and behavior prior to developing a marketing plan. Marketers need to understand who constitutes the market, what and why they buy, who participates in and influences the buying process, and how, when and where they buy.

You are responsible for researching and analyzing the consumer market for Sonic's PDA. These are the questions Sonic needs to answer:

- What cultural, social, personal, and psychological factors have the most influence on consumers buying PDAs?
- What research tools will help you better understand the effect of these factors on buyer attitudes and behavior?
- What consumer buying roles and buying behaviors are particularly relevant for PDA products?

- What kind of marketing activities should Sonic plan to coincide with each stage of the consumer buying process?

Document your findings and conclusions in a written marketing plan or type them into the Market Demographics and Target Markets sections of Marketing Plan Pro.

Chapter 7 Analyzing Business Markets

Business-to-business marketers have to understand their markets and the behavior of members of the buying center in order to develop appropriate marketing plans. Jane Melody has defined the business market at Sonic as mid- to large-sized corporations that need to help their workforces stay in touch and input or access important data from any location. She has asked you to find out:

- What specific types of businesses appear to fit the business market definition used at Sonic?
- What needs could Sonic's PDA address for these businesses?
- Who would participate in and influence the purchase of PDAs for use in these businesses?
- Which environmental, interpersonal, and individual influences are likely to be most important to business buyers of PDA products—and why?

Report your findings and conclusions in a written marketing plan or type them into the Market Demographics and Target Markets sections of Marketing Plan Pro.

Chapter 8 Identifying Market Segments and Targets

Market segmentation is an important part of any marketing plan. It is the first step in the STP process that precedes any marketing strategy: Segmentation, Targeting, and Positioning. The purpose of STP is to identify and describe distinct market segments, target-specific segments, and then pinpoint the differentiating benefits to be stressed in marketing.

In your role as Jane Melody's assistant, you are responsible for market segmentation and targeting for Sonic's PDA product. Look at the SWOT analysis, Market Description, and Competitive Review sections and then answer:

- Which variables should Sonic use to segment its consumer markets?
- Which variables should Sonic use to segment its business markets?
- How can Sonic evaluate the attractiveness of each identified segment?
- Should Sonic pursue full market coverage, market specialization, product specialization, selective specialization, or single-segment concentration? Why?

Summarize your conclusions in a written marketing plan or enter them in the market Demographics and Target Markets sections of Marketing Plan Pro. Note any additional research you may need in the Marketing Research Section of Marketing Plan Pro.

Chapter 9 Creating Brand Equity

Decisions about branding are critical for any marketing plan. During the planning process, marketers must consider issues related to brand strategies and brand equity. Sonic's PDA is a new brand name entering the market. Sonic begins with zero brand equity. Brand equity is built via choices with brand elements and marketing activities and programs. A strong brand has awareness and a positive brand image. Sonic begins with no meaning. Jane Melody has asked you to:

- Suggest what Sonic 1000 with its distinctive yellow thunderbolt might mean for attributes and benefits levels of meaning.
- Determine what strategies and action programs should be used to build brand equity for Sonic 1000.

Summarize your ideas in a written marketing plan or type them into the Marketing Mix section of Marketing Plan Pro. Also indicate in the Marketing Research section what studies you will need to support decisions about managing the brand equity for Sonic 1000.

Chapter 10 Crafting the Brand Positioning

The third part of STP is to select and communicate an effective positioning to differentiate your offering from competitors' offerings. The marketer must also plan for appropriate marketing strategies for each stage of the product life cycle. As you continue your work to develop Sonic's marketing plan for launching Sonic 1000, consider these questions about positioning and life-cycle strategies:

- Which of the differentiation variables related to product, services, personnel, channels, and image are best suited for Sonic's situation, strategy, and marketing objectives? Why?
- Write the positioning statement for Sonic 1000.
- Knowing the stage of the product life cycle for Sonic 1000, what are the implications for the marketing mix, product management strategy, service strategy, and R&D strategy?

Record your answers in a written marketing plan or type them in the Positioning section of Marketing Plan Pro. Note any additional research you may need in the Marketing Research section of Marketing Plan Pro.

Chapter 11 Dealing with Competition

Competitive strategy analysis is an important part of two areas within the marketing plan. First, in assessing the Current Situation, businesses need to identify key competitors and learn about each rival's strengths and weaknesses. Second, competitive intelligence and analysis shapes the competitive strategy, which is supported by the marketing mix.

Sonic is a new entrant in an established industry which has competitors with relatively high brand identity and strong market positions. As you assist Jane Melody in development of the Sonic marketing plan, consider the following key issues that will affect Sonic's ability to introduce a new PDA successfully:

- What is the strategic group for Sonic?
- Which firm is the market leader, and what are its objectives, strengths, weaknesses?
- What additional competitive intelligence is needed to answer the question about the market leader more completely, and how should Sonic go about getting the information?
- Which competitive strategy should be most effective for Sonic?

Enter your answers in a written marketing plan or enter them into the Competition, SWOT Analysis, and Critical Issues sections of Marketing Plan Pro.

Chapter 12 Setting Product Strategy

Decisions about products are critical elements of any marketing plan. During the planning process, marketers must consider issues related to product mix and product lines. Product marketers distinguish five levels of product, each adding more customer value: core benefit, basic, expected, augmented, and potential. In assessing product strategy:

- How would you define the core benefit for Sonic 1000?
- How would you define the augmented product for Sonic 2000, the second product to be launched by Sonic next year?

Write your answer to the questions in a written marketing plan or enter it in the Product Offering and Marketing Mix sections of Marketing Plan Pro.

Chapter 13 Designing and Managing Services

All marketers need to develop a service strategy when preparing their marketing plans. Marketers of intangible products must consider how to manage customer expectations and satisfaction. Marketers of tangible products must create suitable support services. You are planning product support services for Sonic's PDA. The following questions will help you map your service strategy:

- What support services do buyers of PDA products want and need? Consider what Sonic's competitors are doing in this area.

- How can Sonic identify and manage gaps between expected and perceived service to satisfy customers?
- What post-sale services must Sonic make available to customers who buy the Sonic PDA?
- What internal marketing does Sonic need to do to implement its service strategy?

Summarize your recommendations in a written marketing plan or enter the information in the Marketing Mix section of Marketing Plan Pro.

Chapter 14 Developing Pricing Strategies and Programs

Pricing is a critical element in any company's marketing plan, because it directly affects revenue and profit goals. Effective pricing strategies must consider costs as well as customer perceptions and competitor reactions, especially in highly competitive markets.

You are in charge of pricing Sonic's first PDA. Review your SWOT Analysis and Competition Analysis. Also think about the markets you are targeting and the positioning you want to achieve. Then, answer the following questions about pricing:

- What should Sonic's primary pricing objective be? Why?
- Are PDA customers likely to be price-sensitive? Is demand elastic or inelastic? What are the implications of the answers for pricing decisions?
- What price adaptations such as discounts, allowances, and promotional pricing should Sonic include in its marketing plan?

Document your pricing strategies and programs in a written marketing plan or type them into the Marketing Mix section of Marketing Plan Pro.

Chapter 15 Designing and Managing Value Networks and Channels

Manufacturers need to pay close attention to their marketing channels. By planning the design, management, evaluation, and modification of their marketing channels, manufacturers can ensure their products are available when and where customers want to buy.

At Sonic, you have been asked to develop a channel strategy for Sonic 1000. Based on the information you previously gathered and the decisions you have already made about the target market, product, and pricing, answer the following:

- What decisions must Sonic make to develop the five marketing flows (physical product, title, payment, information, and promotion) for Sonic 1000?
- How many levels would be appropriate for the consumer and business markets you are targeting for Sonic 1000?
- Should you plan for exclusive, selective, or intensive distribution?
- What decisions must Sonic make to develop the five service outputs (lot size, waiting time, spatial convenience, product variety, and service back up) for Sonic 1000?

Document your recommendations about marketing channels and strategy in a written marketing plan or type the recommendations into the Marketing Mix section of Marketing Plan Pro.

Chapter 16 Managing Retailing, Wholesaling, and Logistics

Retailers and wholesalers play a critical role in marketing strategy because of their relationships with the final consumer. Manufacturers need to manage their connections with these channel intermediaries.

You are responsible for channel management for Sonic's PDA. Based on your previous strategic choices, respond to the following questions about wholesaling and retailing strategy:

- What types of retailers will be most appropriate for distributing Sonic 1000? What are advantages and disadvantages of selling through these types of retailers?
- What role should wholesalers play in Sonic's distribution strategy? Why?
- What market logistics issues must Sonic consider for the launch of its first PDA?

Summarize your answers in a written marketing plan or type them into the Marketing Mix section of Marketing Plan Pro.

Chapter 17 Designing and Managing Integrated Marketing Communications

Every marketing plan must include a section showing how the company will use marketing communications. The question is not whether to communicate, but rather what to say, to whom, how to say it, how often, and which promotional tools to use.

You are responsible for planning integrated marketing communications for Sonic's new PDA. Review the strategies you previously documented in the marketing plan for the targeting, positioning, branding, product management, pricing, and distribution of the Sonic 1000. Now use your knowledge of communications to answer these questions:

- What audience(s) should Sonic target in its integrated marketing communications plan?
- What image should Sonic seek to create for its first PDA product?
- What objectives are appropriate for Sonic's initial communications campaign?
- What message design and communication channels are likely to be most effective for the target audience?
- Which promotional tools would be most effective in Sonic's promotional mix? Why?
- How should Sonic decide the amount to allocate to its marketing communications budget?

Summarize your answers in a written marketing plan or type them into the Marketing Mix section of Marketing Plan Pro.

Chapter 18 Managing Mass Communications: Advertising, Promotion, Events, and Public Relations

Advertising, sales promotion, and public relations are among the most visible outcomes of any marketing plan. These mass communications tools provide support for branding, product, pricing, and distribution strategies.

At Sonic, you are starting to plan promotional support for launching the new PDA. After reviewing your earlier marketing mix decisions and your current situation as a new player in the PDA market, respond to the following questions about your promotion strategy:

- Should Sonic use advertising to support the PDA introduction? If so, what advertising goals will you set, and how will you measure your results?
- What message(s) do you want to communicate to your target audience? What media are most appropriate, and why?
- Should you use consumer or trade promotion or both?
- Should you use public relations to promote Sonic and its products? If so, what objectives will you set for your public relations program(s)?

Summarize your answers in a written marketing plan or type them into the Marketing Mix section of Marketing Plan Pro.

Chapter 19 Managing Personal Communications: Direct Marketing and the Sales Force

Many marketers have to consider sales force management in their marketing plans. The high cost of maintaining a direct sales force and the need to establish multiple channels of distribution have led some companies to include online, mail, and telephone sales for some of their personal selling efforts.

In your marketing role at Sonic, you are planning a sales strategy for the new PDA. After reviewing your decisions about other marketing mix activities, answer these questions about personal selling:

- Does Sonic need a direct sales force, or can it sell through agents and outside representatives?
- Toward whom should Sonic's selling activities be focused?
- What kinds of sales objectives should Sonic set for its sales personnel?

- What role should e-marketing play in the new PDA launch?
- What training will sales representatives need to sell the Sonic 1000?

Summarize your answers in a written marketing plan or type them into the Marketing Mix, Marketing Organization, and Sales Forecast sections of Marketing Plan Pro.

Chapter 20 Introducing New Market Offerings

Product strategy is based on the choices companies make as they select target segments and create a distinctive positioning for their brand and products. With this foundation, a marketer is ready to plan for new product development and management.

Now that you have developed the marketing plan for Sonic 1000, you are considering new product options for the Sonic 2000. Answers to the following questions will help you narrow the options for the second Sonic PDA product:

- What specific needs of the targeted customer segments should Sonic seek to satisfy with a second PDA product?
- Working alone or with other students, generate at least four new ideas for new PDA products, and indicate the criteria Sonic should use to screen these ideas.
- Develop the most promising idea into a product concept and explain how Sonic can test this concept.
- Assuming the most promising idea tested well, develop a marketing strategy for introducing the new product, including: 1. description of the target market(s), 2. product positioning, 3. objectives for sales, profit, and market share for first year, 4. channel strategy, and 5. marketing budget for first year.
- Into which of the six categories of new products identified by Booz, Allen, and Hamilton does Sonic's first PDA product fit? Into which of these categories does the suggested second PDA product fit? What are the implications of the answers to this question for Sonic's marketing plan for the second PDA?

Summarize your answers to these questions in a written marketing plan or enter the answers into the Marketing Mix, Marketing Research, Breakeven Analysis, Sales Forecast, and Milestone sections of Marketing Plan Pro.

Chapter 21 Tapping into Global Markets

Global marketing offers a way for companies to grow by expanding the customer base beyond the domestic market. However, the complexities of global marketing demand careful planning and implementation.

As Jane Melody's assistant, you are researching markets outside the United States for Sonic's first PDA product. Review the recommendations you have made for Sonic's marketing plan. Then answer these questions about how Sonic can approach global marketing:

- Should Sonic use licensing, joint ventures, direct investment, or exporting to enter the Canadian market? To enter other markets?
- If Sonic wants to start marketing a PDA in other countries, which of the five international product strategies (straight extension, communication adaptation, product adaptation, dual adaptation, product/forward invention) is most appropriate? Why?
- Identify one international market that seems most promising for Sonic. Why did you select this international market as most promising?

Summarize your answers in a written marketing plan or enter the answers in the SWOT, Critical Issues, Marketing Strategy, and Marketing Research sections of Marketing Plan Pro.

Chapter 22 Managing a Holistic Marketing Organization

The last step in completing a marketing plan is to provide for organizing, implementing, evaluating, and controlling the total marketing effort. In addition to measuring progress toward financial targets and other objectives, marketers need to plan how to audit and improve their marketing activities.

Sonic has asked you to plan the management of the marketing effort for the PDA product. Look back at the objectives, strategies, and programs you have developed. Then answer these questions:

- What is the most appropriate organization for Sonic's marketing and sales departments?
- What control measures should Sonic incorporate into its marketing plan?
- What can Sonic do to evaluate its marketing?
- How can Sonic evaluate its level of ethically and socially responsible marketing?

Summarize your answers in a written marketing plan or enter the answers in the Marketing Organization and Implementation sections of Marketing Plan Pro.

GLOSSARY

A

activity-based cost (ABC) accounting procedures that can quantify the true profitability of different activities by identifying their actual costs.

advertising any paid form of nonpersonal presentation and promotion of ideas, goods, or services by an identified sponsor.

advertorials print ads that offer editorial content that reflects favorably on the brand and are resemble newspaper or magazine content.

anchoring and adjustment heuristic when consumers arrive at an initial judgment and then make adjustments of their first impressions based on additional information.

arm's-length price the price charged by other competitors for the same or a similar product.

aspirational groups groups a person hopes or would like to join.

associative network memory model a conceptual representation that views memory as consisting of a set of nodes and interconnecting links where nodes represent stored information or concepts and links represent the strength of association between this information or concepts.

attitude a person's enduring favorable or unfavorable evaluation, emotional feeling, and action tendencies toward some object or idea.

augmented product a product that includes features that go beyond consumer expectations and differentiate the product from competitors.

available market the set of consumers who have interest, income, and access to a particular offer.

availability heuristic when consumers base their predictions on the quickness and ease with which a particular example of an outcome comes to mind.

average cost the cost per unit at a given level of production; it is equal to total costs divided by production.

B

backward invention reintroducing earlier product forms that can be well adapted to a foreign country's needs.

banner ads (Internet) small, rectangular boxes containing text and perhaps a picture to support a brand.

basic product what specifically the actual product is.

belief a descriptive thought that a person holds about something.

brand a name, term, sign, symbol, or design, or a combination of them, intended to identify the goods or services of one seller or group of sellers and to differentiate them from those of competitors.

brand associations all brand-related thoughts, feelings, perceptions, images, experiences, beliefs, attitudes, and so on that become linked to the brand node.

brand audit a consumer-focused exercise that involves a series of procedures to assess the health of the brand, uncover its sources of brand equity, and suggest ways to improve and leverage its equity.

brand awareness consumers' ability to identify the brand under different conditions, as reflected by their brand recognition or recall performance.

brand contact any information-bearing experience a customer or prospect has with the brand, the product category, or the market that relates to the marketer's product or service.

brand development index (BDI) the index of brand sales to category sales.

brand dilution when consumers no longer associate a brand with a specific product or highly similar products or start thinking less favorably about the brand.

brand elements those trademarkable devices that serve to identify and differentiate the brand such as a brand name, logo, or character.

brand equity the added value endowed to products and services.

brand extension a company's use of an established brand to introduce a new product.

brand image the perceptions and beliefs held by consumers, as reflected in the associations held in consumer memory.

brand knowledge all the thoughts, feelings, images, experiences, beliefs, and so on that become associated with the brand.

brand line all products, original as well as line and category extensions, sold under a particular brand name.

brand mix the set of all brand lines that a particular seller makes available to buyers.

brand personality the specific mix of human traits that may be attributed to a particular brand.

brand portfolio the set of all brands and brand lines a particular firm offers for sale to buyers in a particular category.

brand promise the marketer's vision of what the brand must be and do for consumers.

brand valuation an estimate of the total financial value of the brand.

brand value chain a structured approach to assessing the sources and outcomes of brand equity and the manner in which marketing activities create brand value.

branded entertainment using sports, music, arts, or other entertainment activities to build brand equity.

branded variants specific brand lines uniquely supplied to different retailers or distribution channels.

branding endowing products and services with the power of a brand.

branding strategy the number and nature of common and distinctive brand elements applied to the different products sold by the firm.

breakeven analysis a means by which management estimates how many units of the product the company would have to sell to break even with the given price and cost structure.

brick-and-click existing companies that have added an online site for information and/or e-commerce.

business database complete information about business customers' past purchases; past volumes, prices, and profits.

business market all the organizations that acquire goods and services used in the production of other products or services that are sold, rented, or supplied to others.

C

capital items long-lasting goods that facilitate developing or managing the finished product.

captive products products that are necessary to the use of other products, such as razor blades or film.

category extension Using the parent brand to brand a new product outside the product category currently served by the parent brand.

category membership the products or sets of products with which a brand competes and which function as close substitutes.

cause-related marketing marketing that links a firm's contributions to a designated cause to customers' engaging directly or indirectly in revenue-producing transactions with the firm.

channel advantage when a company successfully switches its customers to lower-cost channels, while assuming no loss of sales or deterioration in service quality.

channel conflict when one channel member's actions prevent the channel from achieving its goal.

channel coordination when channel members are brought together to advance the goals of the channel, as opposed to their own potentially incompatible goals.

channel power the ability to alter channel members' behavior so that they take actions they would not have taken otherwise.

communication adaptation changing marketing communications programs for each local market.

communication-effect research determining whether an ad is communicating effectively.

company demand the company's estimated share of market demand at alternative levels of company marketing effort in a given time period.

company sales forecast the expected level of company sales based on a chosen marketing plan and an assumed marketing environment.

competitive advantage a company's ability to perform in one or more ways that competitors cannot or will not match.

conformance quality the degree to which all the produced units are identical and meet the promised specifications.

conjoint analysis a method for deriving the utility values that consumers attach to varying levels of a product's attributes.

conjunctive heuristic the consumer sets a minimum acceptable cutoff level for each attribute and chooses the first alternative that meets the minimum standard for all attributes.

consumer involvement the level of engagement and active processing undertaken by the consumer in responding to a marketing stimulus.

consumerist movement an organized movement of citizens and government to strengthen the rights and powers of buyers in relation to sellers.

consumption system the way the user performs the tasks of getting and using products and related services.

containerization putting the goods in boxes or trailers that are easy to transfer between two transportation modes.

content-target advertising links ads not to keywords but to the contents of Web pages.

contractual sales force manufacturers' reps, sales agents, and brokers, who are paid a commission based on sales.

convenience goods goods the consumer purchases frequently, immediately, and with a minimum of effort.

conventional marketing channel an independent producer, wholesaler(s), and retailer(s).

core benefit the service or benefit the customer is really buying.

core competency attribute that (1) is a source of competitive advantage in that it makes a significant contribution to perceived customer benefits, (2) has applications in a wide variety of markets, (3) is difficult for competitors to imitate.

core values the belief systems that underlie consumer attitudes and behavior, and that determine people's choices and desires over the long term.

corporate culture the shared experiences, stories, beliefs, and norms that characterize an organization.

corporate retailing corporately owned retailing outlets that achieve economies of scale, greater purchasing power, wider brand recognition, and better-trained employees.

cues stimuli that determine when, where, and how a person responds.

culture the fundamental determinant of a person's wants and behavior.

customer-based brand equity the differential effect that brand knowledge has on a consumer response to the marketing of that brand.

customer churn high customer defection.

customer consulting data, information systems, and advice services that the seller offers to buyers.

customer database an organized collection of comprehensive information about individual customers or prospects that is current, accessible, and actionable for marketing purposes.

customer lifetime value (CLV) the net present value of the stream of future profits expected over the customer's lifetime purchases.

customer mailing list a set of names, addresses, and telephone numbers.

customer perceived value(CPV) the difference between the prospective customer's evaluation of all the benefits and all the costs of an offering and the perceived alternatives.

customer-performance scorecard how well the company is doing year after year on particular customer-based measures.

customer profitability analysis (CPA) a means of assessing and ranking customer profitability through accounting techniques such as Activity-Based Costing (ABC).

customer training training the customer's employees to use the vendor's equipment properly and efficiently.

customer value analysis report of the company's strengths and weaknesses relative to various competitors.

customer value hierarchy five product levels that must be addressed by marketers in planning a market offering.

customerization combination of operationally driven mass customization with customized marketing in a way that empowers consumers to design the product and service offering of their choice.

D

data warehouse a collection of current data captured, organized, and stored in a company's contact center.

database marketing the process of building, maintaining, and using customer databases and other databases for the purpose of contacting, transacting, and building customer relationships.

datamining the extracting of useful information about individuals, trends, and segments from the mass of data.

delivery how well the product or service is delivered to the customer.

demand chain planning the process of designing the supply chain based on adopting a target market perspective and working backward.

direct marketing the use of consumer-direct (CD) channels to reach and deliver goods and services to customers without using marketing middlemen.

direct-order marketing marketing in which direct marketers seek a measurable response, typically a customer order.

direct product profitability (DDP) a way of measuring a product's handling costs from the time it reaches the warehouse until a customer buys it in the retail store.

direct (company) sales force full-or part-time paid employees who work exclusively for the company.

discrimination the process of recognizing differences in sets of similar stimuli and adjusting responses accordingly.

dissociative groups those groups whose values or behavior an individual rejects.

distribution programming building a planned, professionally managed, vertical marketing system that meets the needs of both manufacturer and distributors.

drive a strong internal stimulus impelling action.

dual adaptation adapting both the product and the communications to the local market.

dumping situation in which a company charges either less than its costs or less than it charges in its home market, in order to enter or win a market.

durability a measure of a product's expected operating life under natural or stressful conditions.

E

e-business the use of electronic means and platforms to conduct a company's business.

e-commerce a company or site offers to transact or facilitate the selling of products and services online.

e-marketing company efforts to inform buyers, communicate, promote, and sell its products and services over the Internet.

e-purchasing purchase of goods, services, and information from various online suppliers.

elimination-by-aspects heuristic situation in which the consumer compares brands on an attribute selected probabilistically, and brands are eliminated if they do not meet minimum acceptable cutoff levels.

environmental threat a challenge posed by an unfavorable trend or development that would lead to lower sales or profit.

everyday low pricing (EDLP) in retailing, a constant low price with few or no price promotions and special sales.

exchange the process of obtaining a desired product from someone by offering something in return.

exclusive distribution severely limiting the number of intermediaries, in order to maintain control over the service level and outputs offered by resellers.

expectancy-value model consumers evaluate products and services by combining their brand beliefs—positive and negative—according to their weighted importance.

expected product a set of attributes and conditions buyers normally expect when they purchase this product.

experience curve (learning curve) a decline in the average cost with accumulated production experience.

F

fad a craze that is unpredictable, short-lived, and without social, economic and political significance.

family brand situation in which the parent brand is already associated with multiple products through brand extensions.

family of orientation parents and siblings.

family of procreation spouse and children.

features things that enhance the basic function of a product.

fixed costs (overhead) costs that do not vary with production or sales revenue.

flexible market offering (1) a naked solution containing the product and service elements that all segment members value, and (2) discretionary options that some segment members value.

focus group a gathering of six to ten people who are carefully selected based on certain demographic, psychographic, or other considerations and brought together to discuss various topics of interest.

forecasting the art of anticipating what buyers are likely to do under a given set of conditions.

form the size, shape, or physical structure of a product.

forward invention creating a new product to meet a need in another country.

frequency programs (FPs) designed to provide rewards to customers who buy frequently and in substantial amounts.

G

global firm a firm that operates in more than one country and captures R&D, production, logistical, marketing, and financial advantages in its costs and reputation that are not available to purely domestic competitors.

global industry an industry in which the strategic positions of competitors in major geographic or national markets are fundamentally affected by their overall global positions.

goal formulation the process of developing specific goals for the planning period.

going-rate pricing price based largely on competitors' prices.

gray market branded products diverted from normal or authorized distributions channels in the country of product origin or across international borders.

H

heuristics rules of thumb or mental shortcuts in the decision process.

high-low pricing charging higher prices on an everyday basis but then running frequent promotions and special sales.

holistic marketing a concept based on the development, design, and implementation of marketing programs, processes, and activities that recognizes their breadth and interdependencies.

horizontal marketing system two or more unrelated companies put together resources or programs to exploit an emerging market opportunity.

hybrid channels use of multiple channels of distribution to reach customers in a defined market.

I

image the set of beliefs, ideas, and impressions a person holds regarding an object.

industry a group of firms that offer a product or class of products that are close substitutes for one another.

ingredient branding a special case of co-branding that involves creating brand equity for materials, components, or parts that are necessarily contained within other branded products.

innovation any good, service, or idea that is perceived by someone as new.

innovation diffusion process the spread of a new idea from its source of invention or creation to its ultimate users or adopters.

installation the work done to make a product operational in its planned location.

institutional market schools, hospitals, nursing homes, prisons, and other institutions that must provide goods and services to people in their care.

integrated logistics systems (ILS) materials management, material flow systems, and physical distribution, abetted by information technology (IT).

integrated marketing mixing and matching marketing activities to maximize their individual and collective efforts.

integrated marketing communications (IMC) a concept of marketing communications planning that recognizes the added value of a comprehensive plan.

intensive distribution the manufacturer placing the goods or services in as many outlets as possible.

internal branding activities and processes that help to inform and inspire employees.

interstitials advertisements, often with video or animation, that pop up between changes on a Web site.

J

joint venture a company in which multiple investors share ownership and control.

L

learning changes in an individual's behavior arising from experience.

lexicographic heuristic consumer choosing the best brand on the basis of its perceived most important attribute.

licensed product one whose brand name has been licensed to other manufacturers who actually make the product.

life-cycle cost the product's purchase cost plus the discounted cost of maintenance and repair less the discounted salvage value.

lifestyle a person's pattern of living in the world as expressed in activities, interests, and opinions.

line extension the parent brand is used to brand a new product that targets a new market segment within a product category currently served by the parent brand.

line stretching a company lengthens its product line beyond its current range.

long-term memory (LTM) a permanent repository of information.

loyalty a commitment to re-buy or re-patronize a preferred product or service.

M

maintenance and repair the service program for helping customers keep purchased products in good working order.

market-buildup method identifying all the potential buyers in each market and estimating their potential purchases.

market demand the total volume of a product that would be bought by a defined customer group in a defined geographical area in a defined time period in a defined marketing environment under a defined marketing program.

market forecast the market demand corresponding to the level of industry marketing expenditure.

market logistics planning the infrastructure to meet demand, then implementing and controlling the physical flows or materials and final goods from points of origin to points of use, to meet customer requirements at a profit.

market opportunity analysis (MOA) system used to determine the attractiveness and probability of success.

market partitioning the process of investigating the hierarchy of attributes consumers examine in choosing a brand if they use phased decision strategies.

market penetration index a comparison of the current level of market demand to the potential demand level.

market-penetration pricing pricing strategy where prices start low to drive higher sales volume from price-sensitive customers and produce productivity gains.

market potential the upper limit to market demand whereby increased marketing expenditures would not be expected to stimulate further demand.

market-skimming pricing pricing strategy where prices start high and are slowly lowered over time to maximize profits from less price-sensitive customers.

marketer someone who seeks a response (attention, a purchase, a vote, a donation) from another party, called the prospect.

marketing process of planning and executing the conception, pricing, promotion, and distribution of ideas, goods, and services to create exchanges that satisfy individual and organizational goals.

marketing audit a comprehensive, systematic, independent, and periodic examination of a company's or business unit's marketing environment, objectives, strategies, and activities.

marketing channel system the particular set of marketing channels employed by a firm.

marketing channels sets of interdependent organizations involved in the process of making a product or service available for use or consumption.

marketing communications the means by which firms attempt to inform, persuade, and remind consumers—directly or indirectly—about products and brands that they sell.

marketing communications mix advertising, sales promotion, events and experiences, public relations and publicity, direct marketing, and personal selling.

marketing decision support system (MDSS) a coordinated collection of data, systems, tools, and techniques with supporting software and hardware by which an organization gathers and interprets relevant information from business and the environment and turns it into a basis for marketing action.

marketing implementation the process that turns marketing plans into action assignments and ensures that such assignments are executed in a manner that accomplishes the plan's stated objectives.

marketing information system (MIS) people, equipment, and procedures to gather, sort, analyze, evaluate, and distribute information to marketing decision makers.

marketing intelligence system a set of procedures and sources managers use to obtain everyday information about developments in the marketing environment.

marketing management the art and science of choosing target markets and getting, keeping, and growing customers through creating, delivering, and communicating superior customer value.

marketing metrics the set of measures that helps firms to quantify, compare, and interpret their marketing performance.

marketing network the company and its supporting stakeholders, with whom it has built mutually profitable business relationships.

marketing opportunity an area of buyer need and interest in which there is a high probability that a company can profitably satisfy that need.

marketing plan written document that summarizes what the marketer has learned about the marketplace, indicates how the firm plans to reach its marketing objectives, and helps direct and coordinate the marketing effort.

marketing public relations (MPR) publicity and other activities that build corporate or product image to facilitate marketing goals.

marketing research the systematic design, collection, analysis, and reporting of data and findings relevant to a specific marketing situation facing the company.

markup pricing an item by adding a standard increase to the product's cost.

materials and parts goods that enter the manufacturer's product completely.

media selection finding the most cost-effective media to deliver the desired number and type of exposures to the target audience.

megamarketing the strategic coordination of economic, psychological, political, and public relations skills, to gain the cooperation of a number of parties in order to enter or operate in a given market.

megatrends large social, economic, political, and technological changes that are slow to form, and once in place, have an influence for seven to ten years or longer.

membership groups groups having a direct influence on a person.

memory encoding how and where information gets into memory.

memory retrieval how and from where information gets out of memory.

mental accounting the manner by which consumers code, categorize, and evaluate financial outcomes of choices.

microsales analysis examination of specific products and territories that fail to produce expected sales.

microsite a limited area on the Web managed and paid for by an external advertiser/company.

mission statements statements that organizations develop to share with managers, employees, and (in many cases) customers.

mixed bundling the seller offers goods both individually and in bundles.

multichannel marketing a single firm uses two or more marketing channels to reach one or more customer segments.

multitasking doing two or more things at the same time.

N

net price analysis analysis that encompasses company list price, average discount, promotional spending, and co-op advertising to arrive at net price.

noncompensatory models in consumer choice, when consumers do not simultaneously consider all positive and negative attribute considerations in making a decision.

O

Online alliances and affiliate programs when one Internet company works with another one and they advertise each other.

opinion leader the person in informal, product-related communications who offers advice or information about a specific product or product category.

ordering ease how easy it is for the customer to place an order with the company.

organization a company's structures, policies, and corporate culture.

organizational buying the decision-making process by which formal organizations establish the need for purchased products and services and identify, evaluate, and choose among alternative brands and suppliers.

overall market share the company's sales expressed as a percentage of total market sales.

P

parent brand an existing brand that gives birth to a brand extension.

partner relationship management (PRM) activities the firm undertakes to build mutually satisfying long-term relations with key partners such as suppliers, distributors, ad agencies, and marketing research suppliers.

penetrated market the set of consumers who are buying a company's product.

perceived value the value promised by the company's value proposition and perceived by the customer.

perception the process by which an individual selects, organizes, and interprets information inputs to create a meaningful picture of the world.

performance quality the level at which the product's primary characteristics operate.

personal communications channels two or more persons communicating directly face-to-face, person-to-audience, over the telephone, or through e-mail.

personal influence the effect one person has on another's attitude or purchase probability.

personality a set of distinguishing human psychological traits that lead to relatively consistent responses to environmental stimuli.

place advertising (also out-of-home advertising) ads that appear outside of home and where consumers work and play.

point-or-purchase (P-O-P) the location where a purchase is made, typically thought of in terms of a retail setting.

potential market the set of consumers who profess a sufficient level of interest in a market offer.

potential product all the possible augmentations and transformations the product or offering might undergo in the future.

price discrimination a company sells a product or service at two or more prices that do not reflect a proportional difference in costs.

price escalation an increase in the price of a product due to added costs of selling it in different countries.

primary groups groups with which a person interacts continuously and informally, such as family, friends, neighbors, and co-workers.

principle of congruity psychological mechanism that states that consumers like to see seemingly related objects as being as similar as possible in their favorability.

private label brand brands that retailers and wholesalers develop and market.

product adaptation altering the product to meet local conditions or preferences.

product assortment the set of all products and items a particular seller offers for sale.

product invention creating something new via product development or other means.

product mix see product assortment.

product penetration percentage the percentage of ownership or use of a product or service in a population.

product system a group of diverse but related items that function in a compatible manner.

profitable customer a person, household, or company that over time yields a revenue stream that exceeds by an acceptable amount the company's cost stream of attracting, selling, and servicing that customer.

prospect theory when consumers frame decision alternatives in terms of gains and losses according to a value function.

public any group that has an actual or potential interest in or impact on a company's ability to achieve its objectives.

public relations (PR) a variety of programs designed to promote or protect a company's image or its individual products.

publicity the task of securing editorial space—as opposed to paid space—in print and broadcast media to promote something.

pull strategy when the manufacturer uses advertising and promotion to persuade consumers to ask intermediaries for the product, thus inducing the intermediaries to order it.

purchase probability scale a scale to measure the probability of a buyer making a particular purchase.

pure bundling a firm only offers its products as a bundle.

pure-click companies that have launched a Web site without any previous existence as a firm.

push strategy when the manufacturer uses its sales force and trade promotion money to induce intermediaries to carry, promote, and sell the product to end users.

R

reference groups all the groups that have a direct or indirect influence on a person's attitudes or behavior.

reference prices pricing information a consumer retains in memory which is used to interpret and evaluate a new price.

relational equity the cumulative value of the firm's network of relationships with its customers, partners, suppliers, employees, and investors.

relationship marketing building mutually satisfying long-term relationships with key parties, in order to earn and retain their business.

relative market share market share in relation to a company's largest competitor.

reliability a measure of the probability that a product will not malfunction or fail within a specified time period.

repairability a measure of the ease of fixing a product when it malfunctions or fails.

representativeness heuristic when consumers base their predictions on how representative or similar an outcome is to other examples.

risk analysis a method by which possible rates of returns and their probabilities are calculated by obtaining estimates for uncertain variables affecting profitability.

role the activities a person is expected to perform.

S

sales analysis measuring and evaluating actual sales in relation to goals.

sales budget a conservative estimate of the expected volume of sales, used for making current purchasing, production, and cash flow decisions.

sales promotion a collection of incentive tools, mostly short term, designed to stimulate quicker or greater purchase of particular products or services by consumers or the trade.

sales quota the sales goal set for a product line, company division, or sales representative.

sales-variance analysis a measure of the relative contribution of different factors to a gap in sales performance.

satisfaction a person's feelings of pleasure or disappointment resulting from comparing a product's perceived performance or outcome in relation to his or her expectations.

scenario analysis developing plausible representations of a firm's possible future that make different assumptions about forces driving the market and include different uncertainties.

search-related ads ads in which search terms are used as a proxy for the consumer's consumption interests and relevant links to product or service offerings are listed along side the search results.

secondary groups groups which tend to be more formal and require less interaction than primary groups, such as religious, professional, and trade-union groups.

selective attention the mental process of screening out certain stimuli while noticing others.

selective distortion the tendency to interpret product information in a way that fit consumer perceptions.

selective distribution the use of more than a few but less than all of the intermediaries who are willing to carry a particular product.

selective retention good points about a product that consumers like are remembered and good points about competing products are forgotten.

served market all the buyers who are able and willing to buy a company's product.

served market share a company's sales expressed as a percentage of the total sales to its served market.

service any act or performance that one party can offer to another that is essentially intangible and does not result in the ownership of anything.

share penetration index a comparison of a company's current market share to its potential market share.

shopping goods goods that the consumer, in the process of selection and purchase, characteristically compares on such bases as suitability, quality, price, and style.

short-term memory (STM) a temporary repository of information.

social classes homogeneous and enduring divisions in a society, which are hierarchically ordered and whose members share similar values, interests, and behavior.

social marketing marketing done by a nonprofit or government organization to further a cause, such as "say no to drugs."

specialty goods goods that have unique characteristics or brand identification for which a sufficient number of buyers are willing to make a special purchasing effort.

sponsorship financial support of an event or activity in return for recognition and acknowledgment as the sponsor.

stakeholder-performance scorecard a measure to track the satisfaction of various constituencies who have a critical interest in and impact on the company' s performance.

status one's position within his or her own hierarchy or culture.

straight extension introducing a product in a foreign market without any change in the product.

strategic brand management the design and implementation of marketing activities and programs to build, measure, and manage brands to maximize their value.

strategic business units (SBUs) a single business or collection of related businesses that can be planned separately from the rest of the company, with its own set of competitors and a manager who is responsible for strategic planning and profit performance.

strategic group firms pursuing the same strategy directed to the same target market.

strategic marketing plan laying out the target markets and the value proposition that will be offered, based on analysis of the best market opportunities.

strategy a company's game plan for achieving its goals.

style a product's look and feel to the buyer.

sub-brand a new brand combined with an existing brand.

subculture subdivisions of a culture that provide more specific identification and socialization, such as nationalities, religions, racial groups, and geographical regions.

subliminal perception receiving and processing subconscious messages that affect behavior.

supersegment a set of segments sharing some exploitable similarity.

supplies and business services short-term goods and services that facilitate developing or managing the finished product.

supply chain management (SCM) procuring the right inputs (raw materials, components, and capital equipment); converting them efficiently into finished products; and dispatching them to the final destinations.

T

tactical marketing plan marketing tactics, including product features, promotion, merchandising, pricing, sales channels, and service.

target costing deducting the desired profit margin from the price at which a product will sell, given its appeal and competitors' prices.

target market the part of the qualified available market the company decides to pursue.

target-return pricing determining the price that would yield the firm's target rate of return on investment (ROI).

telemarketing the use of telephone and call centers to attract prospects, sell to existing, customers, and provide service by taking orders and answering questions.

total costs the sum of the fixed and variable costs for any given level of production.

total customer cost the bundle of costs customers expect to incur in evaluating, obtaining, using, and disposing of the given market offering, including monetary, time, energy, and psychic costs.

total customer value the perceived monetary value of the bundle of economic, functional, and psychological benefits customers expect from a given market offering.

total quality management (TQM) an organizationwide approach to continuously improving the quality of all the organization's processes, products, and services.

tracking studies collecting information from consumers on a routine basis over time.

transaction a trade of values between two or more parties: A gives X to B and receives Y in return.

transfer in the case of gifts, subsidies, and charitable contributions: A gives X to B but does not receive anything tangible in return.

transfer price the price a company charges another unit in the company for goods it ships to foreign subsidiaries.

trend a direction or sequence of events that has some momentum and durability.

two-part pricing a fixed fee plus a variable usage fee.

tying agreements agreement in which producers of strong brands sell their products to dealers only if dealers purchase related products or services, such as other products in the brand line.

U

unsought goods those the consumer does not know about or does not normally think of buying, like smoke detectors.

V

value-delivery network a company's supply chain and how it partners with specific suppliers and distributors to make products and bring them to markets.

value-delivery system all the expectancies the customer will have on the way to obtaining and using the offering.

value network a system of partnerships and alliances that a firm creates to source, augment, and deliver its offerings.

value pricing winning loyal customers by charging a fairly low price for a high-quality offering.

value proposition the whole cluster of benefits the company promises to deliver.

variable costs costs that vary directly with the level of production.

venture team a cross-functional group charged with developing a specific product or business.

vertical integration situation in which manufacturers try to control or own their suppliers, distributors, or other intermediaries

vertical marketing system (VMS) producer, wholesaler(s), and retailer(s) acting as a unified system.

viral marketing using the Internet to create word of mouth effects to support marketing efforts and goals.

Y

yield pricing situation in which companies offer (1) discounted but limited early purchases, (2) higher-priced late purchases, and (3) the lowest rates on unsold inventory just before it expires.

Z

zero-level channel (direct-marketing channel) a manufacturer selling directly to the final customer.

IMAGE CREDITS

Chapter 1
2 Courtesy of The Image Works; 5 Courtesy of the Boston Beer Company. Samuel Adams Utopias is a registered trademark of BBC Brands LLC.; 7 Courtesy of Rainer Stratmann for Lexus.; 9 Courtesy U.S. Department of Transportation. This ad was created pro bono on behalf of the Ad Council's Drunk Driving campaign.; 12 Courtesy of Corbis/Bettmann; 14 Courtesy of Shiseido Co., Ltd. Tokyo, Japan.; 23 Courtesy of the Avon Foundation.; 25 Courtesy of Volvo Cars of North America, LLC.

Chapter 2
32 Courtesy of H&M, Hennes & Mauritz L.P.; 35 Courtesy of Nike.; 44 Reprinted courtesy of Caterpillar, Inc.; 46 Courtesy of AP Wide World Photos; 51 Courtesy of Ken Cedeno Photography; 55 Photo courtesy of Star Alliance™.

Chapter 3
66 Courtesy of Atkins Nutritionals, Inc.; 76 HOT WHEELS is a trademark owned by and used with permission from Mattel, Inc. © 2005 Mattel, Inc. All Rights Reserved.; 78 Courtesy of Charles Schwab & Co., Inc.; 83 Courtesy of Getty Images, Inc–Liaison.; 90 Courtesy of Getty Images/Time Life Pictures; Courtesy of PhotoEdit; Courtesy of Bruce Coleman Inc.; 91 Courtesy of The Image Works.

Chapter 4
94 Courtesy of Build-A-Bear Workshop®.; 99 Courtesy of PhotoEdit.; 105 Courtesy of PhotoEdit.; 120 GLADWARE® is a registered trademark of The Glad Products Company. Used with permission. © 2004 The Glad Products Company. Reprinted with permission.; 123 Courtesy of PhotoEdit.

Chapter 5
130 Courtesy of Washington Mutual.; 134 Courtesy of The Image Works.; 137 Courtesy of Saturn.; 139 Courtesy of Countrywide Finance Corporation.; 142 Courtesy of Getty Images, Inc–Liaison.; 146 Courtesy of AP Wide World Photos.; 152 Courtesy of Pathmark Corporation.; 153 Courtesy of Corbis/Bettmann.; 158 Courtesy of Enterprise Rent-a-Car Company.

Chapter 6
162 Courtesy of Corbis/Bettmann.; 170 Courtesy of the Sherwin-Williams Co.; 172 Courtesy of Levi Strauss & Co.; 177 Courtesy of PepsiCo International.; 179 Courtesy GM Corporation/GM Media Archive. © 2004.; 182 Courtesy of Corbis/Bettmann.; 185 Courtesy of the National Fluid Milk Processor Promotion Board.; 191 KELLOGG'S®, ALL-BRAN®, and SMART START® are registered trademarks of Kellogg company. © 2004 Kellogg NA Co. KASHI® and HEART TO HEART™ are trademarks of Kashi Company. Used with permission.

Chapter 7
194 Courtesy of SAP America, Inc./© Dean Kaufman.; 201 Courtesy of Corbis/Bettmann.; 204 Courtesy of Eastman Kodak Company.; 207 Courtesy of HP.; 208 Courtesy of Covisint.; 218 Courtesy of Cardinal Health.

Chapter 8
222 Courtesy of Corbis/Bettmann.; 225 Courtesy of Henry Ford Museum and Greenfield Village.; 227 Courtesy of Tom's of Maine, and Josh Royte, Maine Chapter of The Nature Conservancy.; 230 Courtesy of VANS, Inc.; 239 Courtesy of Ocean Spray Cranberries, Inc.; 244 Courtesy of BB&T Bank.; 248 Courtesy of 98.7 KISS-FM and Emmis Communications.; 250 Courtesy of PepsiCo International.; 251 Courtesy of Colgate-Palmolive Company.

Chapter 9
254 Courtesy of Corbis/Bettmann.; 258 Courtesy of The Australian Tourist Commission.; 265 Courtesy of Allstate.; 268 Courtesy of Olive Garden® Italian Restaurants and Darden Corporation.; 275 Courtesy of Campbell Soup Company.; 281 Courtesy of Société des Produits Nestlé S.A., Vevey Switzerland.; 282 © The Procter & Gamble Company. Used by permission.

Chapter 10
286 Courtesy Thirteen/WNET New York.; 290 DiGiorno® Rising Crust Pizza print ad: Kraft trademarks are used with the permission of Kraft Foods.; 297 Courtesy of Getty Images, Inc.–Agence France Presse. Roslan Rahman/Agence France Presse/Getty Images.; 299 Courtesy of Corbis/Bettmann.; 304 Courtesy of Getty Images Inc.–Hulton Archive Photos. Mario Tama/Hulton Archive/Getty Images.; 306 Courtesy of Pinnacle Foods Corporation. © Bill Truran Productions.; 311 LEGO, the LEGO logo, and PLAY ON are trademarks of the LEGO Group, which does not sponsor or endorse this publication. © 2004 The LEGO Group and used here with permission.

Chapter 11
314 Courtesy of Corbis/Bettmann.; 319 Courtesy of Shell Oil Company.; 327 Courtesy of AP Wide World Photos.; 332 Courtesy of the Quaker Oats Company.; 335 Courtesy of S&S Cycle, Inc.; 337 Courtesy of A.T. Cross Company.

Chapter 12
342 Courtesy of Corbis/Bettmann.; 347 Courtesy of the Cattlemen's Beef Board.; 350 Courtesy of Woodfin Camp & Associates.; 353 Courtesy of palmOne, Inc.; 357 Courtesy of Gallo of Sonoma, Healdsburg, Sonoma County, CA. © 2003.; 360 Reprinted by permission of Intel Corporation, Copyright Intel Corporation 2003.; 362 Courtesy of General Mills, Inc.; 364 Courtesy of E. I. DuPont de Nemours and Company. Corian® is a registered trademark of DuPont or its affiliates.; 367 © The Procter & Gamble Company. Used by permission.

Chapter 13
370 Courtesy of IBM.; 373 Courtesy of eDiets.com, Inc., Copyright © 1996-2004 eDiets.com, Inc. All rights reserved.; 376 Courtesy of Getty Images, Inc.–Agence France Presse. Stringer/Agence France Presse/Getty Images.; 378 Courtesy of PhotoEdit.; 391 Courtesy of RE/MAX®.; 394 Courtesy of, Copyright, State Farm Mutual Automobile Insurance Company, 2003. Used by permission.

Chapter 14
398 Courtesy of Whirlpool Corporation.; 411 Courtesy of Pearson Learning Photo Studio.; 414 Courtesy of PhotoEdit.; 422 2004 © Lands' End, Inc. Used with permission.; 427 Courtesy of GlaxoSmithKline.

Chapter 15
430 Courtesy of Kmart Corporation.; 435 Courtesy of Nautilus.; 440 Courtesy of PhotoEdit.; 442 Courtesy of Calyx & Corolla.; 448 Courtesy of Corbis/Bettmann.; 449 Courtesy of Navistar/International Truck Intellectual Property Company, LLC.; 453 Courtesy of Parker-Hannifin.; 461 Courtesy of Stihl Incorporated.

Chapter 16
464 Courtesy of Getty Images, Inc–Liaison; David McNew/Getty Images, Inc.; 469 Courtesy of AP Wide World Photos.; 473 Courtesy of Hot Topic and Converse.; 481 Courtesy of Getty Images, Inc–Liaison; Courtesy of Heinz/Getty Images, Inc.; 487 Courtesy of Xerox.; 491 Courtesy of Corbis/SABA Press Photos, Inc.

Chapter 17
494 Courtesy of BMW.; 498 © Kimberly-Clark Worldwide, Inc. Reprinted with permission.; 503 TILEX® is a registered trademark of The Clorox Company. Used with Permission. © 2004 The Clorox

Company. Reprinted with permission.; 512 Courtesy of Getty Images, Inc–Liaison; Gareth Cattermole/Getty Images, Inc.; 519 © 2004 Accenture. All rights reserved. Reprinted with permission.; 521 © 2004 The Dannon Company, Inc. All rights reserved. Reprinted with permission.

Chapter 18

524 Courtesy of The Procter & Gamble Company, © Ross Van Pelt.; 530 Under permission by V&S Vin & Sprit AB (publ). ABSOLUT COUNTRY OF; SWEDEN VODKA,& LOGO, ABSOLUT, ABSOLUT BOTTLE DESIGN AND ABSOLUT CALLIGRAPHY ARE TRADEMARKS OWNED BY V&S VIN & SPRIT AB (publ). © 2004 V&S VIN & SPRIT AB (publ). Copyright © The Andy Warhol Foundation for the Visual Arts by V&S Vin & Sprit Aktiebolag under exclusive license.; 535 Courtesy of Corbis/Bettmann.; 536 Courtesy of Omega.; 538 Courtesy of the U.S. Army.; 549 Courtesy of Corbis/Bettmann.

Chapter 19

556 Courtesy of Newell Rubbermaid.; 564 David Anderson/Courtesy of Patagonia, Inc.; 567 Courtesy of Neiman Marcus Direct.; 572 Courtesy of Navistar/International Truck Intellectual Property Company, LLC.

Chapter 20

584 Courtesy of 3M.; 587 Courtesy of Gillette Blades & Razors.; 593 Courtesy of Procter & Gamble Cosmetics/Noxell Corporation.; 594 Courtesy of Corbis Digital Stock.; 600 Courtesy of Continental Airlines.; 604 Courtesy of The Boeing Company.; 609 © Koninklijke Philips Electronics N.V. All rights reserved.; 612 Courtesy of Retna Ltd.

Chapter 21

614 Courtesy of Red Bull. © Flo Hagena/Red Bull 2004.; 618 © Ethan Hill.; 620 Courtesy of Societé des Produits Nestle S.A., Vevey, Switzerland.; 626 Courtesy of Corbis/Sygma.; 631 © Lands' End, Inc. Used with permission.; 635 Logo: © Copyright Brand Hong Kong Management Office. a) Courtesy of Corbis Digital Stock b) Courtesy of Corbis Digital Stock c) Courtesy of Corbis/Bettmann.

Chapter 22

640 Courtesy of The Image Works.; 647 Courtesy of Dow Corning.; 654 Courtesy of Bown-Forman Wines/Fetzer Vineyards. Photo used by permission of Albert Watson and David Breashears.; 657 Courtesy of LensCrafters' Give the Gift of Sight/© Lyons Photography.; 658 AP Wide World Photos.

INDEX

Note: Italicized page numbers indicate illustrations or boxed text.

Name Index

Company, Brand, and Organization Index

Subject Index